James B. Conant

James B. Conant

HARVARD TO HIROSHIMA AND THE MAKING OF THE NUCLEAR AGE

James G. Hershberg

ALFRED A. KNOPF

New York

1993

ORZOI BOOK

RED A. KNOPF, INC.

Library of Congress Cataloging-in-Publication Data

Hershberg, James G., [date]
James B. Conant: Harvard to Hiroshima and the making of the nuclear age/James G. Hershberg.—1st ed.
p.   cm.
Includes bibliographical references and index.
ISBN 0-394-57966-6
1. Conant, James Bryant, 1893–1978. 2. Educators—United States—Biography. 3. College presidents—United States—Biography. 4. Chemists—United States—Biography. 5. Harvard University—Presidents—Biography. 6. Atomic Bomb—United States—History. 7. Science and state—United States—History. 8. Technology and state—United States—History. 9. United States—Foreign relations—20th century. I. Title.
CT275.C757H46   1993
370'.92—dc20
[B]
93-2828
CIP

Manufactured in the United States of America
First Edition

Composed by Superior Type,
Champaign, Illinois

Printed and bound by Arcata Graphics/Martinsburg,
Martinsburg, West Virginia

Designed by Cassandra J. Pappas

To my parents,
David and Arline Hershberg,
and to my wife, Annie

Contents

Introduction: "One of the Outstanding Kibitzers of the Age" 3

1. "Bound to Be Heard from Later as a Scholar and a Man":
   A Prodigy's Progress, 1893–1910 11

2. "Something of a Specialist": Harvard College, 1910–1913 20

3. "A Chemist's War": Conant and World War I, 1914–1918 35

4. "A Restless Soul": Professor of Chemistry, 1919–1933 49

5. "The Challenge Was Simply Not to Be Denied":
   Professor to President, 1933 65

6. "Tyranny Tempered by Assassination":
   Harvard President from Depression to War, 1933–1939 76

7. "I Believe That Actions Speak Louder Than Words":
   President Conant Goes to War, 1939–1940 111

8. "A Major Push Along the Lines Outlined":
   Commitments to Belligerency and the Bomb, 1941 135

9. "This Scientific Delirium Tremens":
   The Horse Race to the Bomb, 1942–1943 155

10. "The International Complications of S-1":
    Anglo-American Atomic Angst, 1943 172

11. "Another Experimental Arrangement": Conant, Bohr, and
    Fears of a Postwar Nuclear Arms Race, 1944 194

12. "The Animate Scheme":
    The Quest for Postwar Planning, October 1944–May 1945 208

13. " . . . Like the End of the World":
    Hiroshima and Alamogordo, Summer 1945 225

14. "My Fingers Are Still Crossed on the Bomb":
    Ominous Fallout, 1945 235

15. "The Only Possible Solution of a Desperate Problem":
    Trying to Control the Bomb, 1945–1946 258

16. Making History: Shaping Hiroshima's Legacy, 1945–1947   279

17. "Back in the Atomic Harness": Building Bombs, Again, 1947   305

18. "The Conant Alternative":
    A Secret Plan to Stop the Arms Race, 1947   322

 ⚹ 19. Secrecy and Security:
    Conant, Atomic Energy, and the Public, 1948–1949   349

20. The "Fishing Party":
    The Conant Committee on Nuclear Information Policy, 1949   374

21. Cold War Educator, Part I:
    "A Dark Shadow Has Been Cast," 1946–1948   391

22. Cold War Educator, Part II:
    "Nobody Is Safe," August 1948–May 1949   424

23. Cold War Educator, Part III:
    Commencement, June 1949   450

24. "Over My Dead Body":
    The Battle over the H-Bomb, 1949–1950   463

25. "Paul Reveres of the Atomic Age":
    The Committee on the Present Danger, 1950   491

26. "The Great Debate," 1951   515

27. "Doublecross" and Defeat:
    Campaigning for Military Conscription, 1950–1952   537

28. "I Told You So":
    Conant and the Militarization of American Science, 1950–1952   554

29. God and Man at Harvard   578

30. "A Bad Business Now Threatening to Become Really Bad!!":
    Conant and Nuclear Weapons, 1950–1952   590

31. Cold War Educator, Part IV:
    McCarthyism and the Crisis of the Liberal Educator,
    1950–1953   606

32. "Tired of Flexing Old Muscles":
    Educator to Diplomat, 1950–1953   638

33. "Explosion in the Offing":
    Intrigues in Bonn, Berlin, and Washington, 1953–1955   650

34. "I Want to Accentuate the Positive":
    Ambassador to West Germany, 1955–1957   687

35. "The Inspector General": Educational Statesman, 1957–1965   706

Contents

Epilogue: "Winter for the Conant Family!"   739

Appendixes   757

Acknowledgments   765

Abbreviations List   769

Principal Sources   773

Notes   783

Index   931

James B. Conant

INTRODUCTION

"One of the Outstanding Kibitzers of the Age"

It is one of the many ironies of James Bryant Conant's life that a man who devoted his career to scholarship and who participated in some of the twentieth century's most tumultuous events should write an autobiography so singularly disappointing to historians. Conant, a towering figure to his contemporaries, had presided over Harvard University for a turbulent two decades that stretched from the Depression to the era of McCarthyism; worked on poison gas in World War I and the atomic bomb in World War II, and fought against the hydrogen bomb; exhorted Americans to wage a hot war against Hitler and a cold one against Stalin; served as Eisenhower's man in Germany at the height of the Cold War; become the country's leading commentator, in the post-*Sputnik* era, on U.S. public schools; authored tomes on education, science, philosophy; worked and moved among the titans of his time: Roosevelt, Churchill, Truman, Eisenhower, Oppenheimer, Acheson, Marshall, Stimson, Rabi, Bush, Lippmann, Niebuhr, Forrestal, Marshall, McCloy, Adenauer, Dulles.

Yet, when Conant's *My Several Lives* was published in 1970, it landed with a thud—and not merely because of its 701-page bulk. Rarely in the annals of autobiography (excepting presidential memoirs) had so many pages been devoted to such important events while revealing so little about the author; the skeleton was there, but the marrow had been sucked out. "Good man, dull book," concluded John Leonard in the *New York Times,* complaining that "this swamp of an autobiography" seemed to have been written "in an airless room on some other planet. . . . Mr. Conant doesn't examine his life; he reports it as might an obituary writer." *Time* pronounced a similarly exasperated verdict: "It should be a great deal more interesting than it is. Part of the trouble is Conant's lack of total candor, perhaps the natural result of Yankee reticence . . . Conant tantalizes more than he satisfies."[1]

A reviewer who suspected that Conant had "commissioned and read too many committee reports for the good of his own prose" was right on the mark: the book itself been a committee project, extracted from its distinguished author like a tooth from a grouchy patient. Approaching his seventieth birthday, Conant had first been urged to write his life story by a friend at the

Carnegie Corporation, which was financing his studies of U.S. public education. "I reacted with no enthusiasm," he later recalled privately. "I had a strong prejudice against people who wrote autobiographies."[2] Ultimately friends talked him into going ahead, and arranged for two doctoral candidates to sift through the 527 boxes of correspondence he had accumulated during twenty years as Harvard president, as well as the file cabinets and crates of materials in his Manhattan apartment and New Hampshire summer cottage. In struggling to prod Conant into productive introspection, the two aspirant Ph.D.s, as well as his editors at Harper & Row, had to pierce a Maginot line of caution, propriety, and reticence that had been evident as early as his Yankee childhood and firmly reinforced over decades of life in positions of power.

Perhaps they wouldn't have even bothered to try had they read the terse message of farewell that Conant printed in the Harvard student newspaper after the bombshell announcement in January 1953 that he had resigned to become Eisenhower's high commissioner to Germany. Passing up a chance to disclose his motives for embarking on a diplomatic career and leaving the institution where he had spent almost his entire adult life — as college student, doctoral candidate, chemistry professor, and president — he wrote: "Never explain; your friends don't require it; your enemies won't believe you anyway."[3]

These cryptic, pessimistic words aptly expressed Conant's personal credo, but they were ominous for history. Even before he had left Harvard, journalists who trooped to Cambridge to call on the tall, lanky, dapper educator with steel-rimmed glasses and a broad smile were frustrated in trying to penetrate his cheerful, calm exterior. One wrote in 1947,

> Conant's kindly and inquisitive facial expression and his stooped, scholarly stance may conceal unimaginable inner bubblings of pride, ambition, rebellion, and the lust for power; or on the other hand they may not. Conant is a statesman. Before he was a statesman, he was a university president. Before he was a university president, he was a professional scientist, and of course, long before he was any of these things he was a New Englander. Confronted with this reinforced façade, the biographer must get what comfort he can from the obvious fact that Conant never speaks from impulse and always means just what he says.[4]

Even that comfort would prove fairly cold, for if Conant always *meant* what he said, that didn't mean he actually *believed* it, or that the reader could trust it as the candid and complete story. Like the hundreds of top-secret memos he wrote during the Manhattan Project, Conant's memoirs were carefully sanitized before release, with passages liable to inflict offense, reopen wounds, break security, or rattle old skeletons carefully scissored out. More precisely, he simply avoided some difficult subjects altogether. "Anything that he wrote or he said he always weighed the political consequences," relates his son Theodore, who spent many hours trying with limited success to convince his father to comment on sensitive topics, such as military research on campuses and other Harvard controversies, which he preferred to leave unmentioned.[5]

Conant's secretiveness kept even his marriage out of the first draft until an astonished editor forced him to include it. But on no terrain did this discreet man tread more warily than on his intimate involvement with the birth and early evolution of America's nuclear weapons program—the subject that first drew me to his story. From 1941 to 1945, while the rest of the world remained ignorant of the terrible force about to be unleashed, Harvard's president had been at the heart of the clandestine American enterprise that produced the atomic bomb. As a science administrator in Roosevelt's wartime administration, Conant in mid-1941 drew the assignment of assessing the feasibility of building a weapon employing the newly discovered principles of nuclear fission. After making the key recommendations, as deputy to Vannevar Bush, chief of the U.S. government's World War II science mobilization effort, that led to a crash program to build the bomb, Conant retained responsibility for considering the new weapon's long-range scientific, political, diplomatic, and military implications, and acted as intermediary between the White House on the one hand, and on the other the scientists, industrialists, and military men involved in the vast covert undertaking. In the summer of 1945, sitting on the elite, top-secret Interim Committee appointed by Truman that debated the use of the atomic bomb, he suggested dropping it on "a vital war plant employing a large number of workers and closely surrounded by workers' houses"—a formulation applied to Hiroshima. With Gen. Leslie R. Groves, J. Robert Oppenheimer, and the rest, he witnessed the blinding fireball that lit the predawn desert sky over Alamogordo, New Mexico, on July 16, 1945. After the Pacific war ended, he helped to craft the State Department's blueprint for the international control of atomic weapons, an idea briefly hailed as the globe's best hope for salvation but soon doomed by U.S.-Soviet distrust. When the Cold War set in, Conant remained in the inner sanctum. As an adviser to the U.S. Atomic Energy Commission (the chairmanship of which he had turned down) until 1952, he considered every question of importance that arose during the early years of the American nuclear arsenal, and in 1949-50 he led the secret, futile effort to sway Truman against developing the hydrogen bomb. And, in a bitter sequel to the dispute, he testified in defense of Oppenheimer during the government inquest that ultimately stripped the famous physicist of his security clearance, in part because of the lack of "enthusiasm" which he, like Conant, had shown for thermonuclear weaponry.

All in all, quite a significant record. Yet *My Several Lives* offered only a relatively short, unilluminating section on Conant's atomic career, derived mostly from previously published works. While tossing readers a few titillating tidbits, it shed little light on the historical record or the private emotions and calculations of the first U.S. government official in charge of figuring out what a nuclear world would look like. And even that cursory once-over had required the nagging of a persistent editor who pestered Conant to draft a couple of chapters "on the subject which I had said I would never touch," then died before she could coerce a more revealing redraft.[6]

It was, I later discovered, neither writer's block nor security restrictions but something much deeper that had constrained Conant. Nor, for that matter, was it a myopic scientist's lack of interest in human affairs. Conant had been an avid student of history for his entire life, and during the war he had scribbled a detailed, private report on the birth of the Manhattan Project. For some years after the war, he even toyed with writing an account of his atomic experiences based on a sheaf of highly classified documents that he and Bush had secreted in a locked safe in the bowels of a Washington office building.

When public criticism arose in 1946 over the destruction of Hiroshima, the issue of historical interpretation acquired further importance for Conant, who was anxious to ensure that the American public, especially what he called the "verbal-minded" and "sentimental" sort who would become the next generation's historians and teachers, steadfastly supported Truman's decision. Maneuvering stealthily, he convinced Henry L. Stimson, the venerated retired war secretary, to write a magazine article justifying the bomb's use—and thereby decisively sway both the public and the historical debate.

But as the Cold War set in and the prospect of World War III loomed, Conant's appetite for retelling the story of how he had helped usher in the atomic age waned. His failure to forestall the development of thermonuclear weapons only intensified his gloomy private premonition that humanity was headed toward catastrophe—a foreboding that once impelled him to check quietly into the possibility of Harvard's microfilming and burying the written record of civilization so that it might be preserved for the survivors of a nuclear holocaust. By 1954, when a McCarthy-era controversy mushroomed over the secret H-bomb dispute four years earlier, Conant's desire to dredge up the past had vanished entirely. Then serving in Germany, he was appalled to hear rumors that "the patriotism of some or all of us involved in this recommendation [against the H-bomb] has been impugned." It was "a pity," he lamented to Bush, that "the highly technical and highly classified nature of this whole atomic bomb business prevents a scholarly analysis of the goings on of the last 14 years in which you and I have been so much involved. But," he added, "the more I think of the past the more certain I am that it would be worse than useless to attempt to write the history of many of the dramatic events regarding the atomic bomb. Subsequent generations may damn all of us who had anything to do with the project for having started down the road which has led to the 'atomic age' but unless one goes in for such wholesale emotional condemnation, inquiries into the past would seem to me perhaps worse than fruitless."[7]

✳   ✳   ✳   ✳

This book constitutes part of an effort to explore, assess, and understand that history about which Conant showed such ambivalence and reticence. It is in part a story of one man's intersection with great events and issues, in part a story of those events and issues viewed through the prism of one central figure. It is also not intended to be, nor can it be, a definitive account. Aside from the inherent subjectivity and personal, temporal, and cultural limitations of any historical perspective,[8] researching the Conant story required lengthy efforts to pry access to sources from two large, secrecy-conscious bureaucratic institutions: the United States Government and Harvard University, which graciously allowed me considerable access to Conant's presidential papers yet still maintains a draconian fifty-year secrecy rule for official records, longer than the period most of the sensitive documents on the atomic bomb were kept under wraps. In addition, I brought to bear my own opinions and interests, largely directed at the issues surrounding the Cold War and the nuclear arms race, and with special attention to the attendant moral and intellectual dilemmas faced by policymakers and others during the war and early postwar periods. I have not attempted a full biography, which would deal extensively with Conant's careers as organic chemist and educational administrator and commentator, but have instead concentrated on those aspects of his life that most intrigued me — atomic bomb administrator, nuclear and scientific adviser to the government, Harvard president during the "Red scare," Cold War public figure, and envoy to Germany. That has proved both a sufficiently daunting challenge and a richly rewarding avenue to explore the roots and early evolution of post–World War II American politics, science, society, and foreign policy.

Oblivious to the magnitude of the task involved, I first undertook to study Conant's career in September 1981, the start of my senior year in college. I intended neither a "wholesale emotional condemnation" nor a "worse than fruitless" inquiry — merely a topic for my undergraduate history thesis. The idea arose after I encountered Martin J. Sherwin's study of atomic diplomacy during World War II, *A World Destroyed: The Atomic Bomb and the Grand Alliance.* I had until then never heard of Conant, who had died three years earlier. But reading Sherwin's account, I was struck by Conant's presence at the heart of the atomic project — why was the president of Harvard University so involved in the decisions to build and use the atomic bomb? The issue of nuclear weapons was in the air that fall: Ronald Reagan had just entered the White House, there was renewed bustle over the danger of nuclear war, protesters had taken to the streets of Western Europe (and occasionally, in smaller numbers, Cambridge) over the planned deployments of American Pershing and cruise missiles in West Germany, and the first glimmerings of the "freeze" movement were visible. Learning of the private warnings of a postwar nuclear arms race issued by Conant, Bush, and Niels Bohr well before Hiroshima, I could not help noticing parallels between their ideas, arguments, and fears and the issues dominating the newspaper headlines more than a generation later. Each day, it seemed, I heard echoes of long-forgotten discussions, saw more wheels being reinvented.

The Conant story beckoned for another reason. It promised a chance to explore questions that had bothered me ever since, as a kid born in 1960, I had watched the brutal, televised images of the Vietnam War: How did governments and the persons who ran them justify the infliction of violence, suffering, and death on a massive scale? Can power and morality be reconciled? What should America's role in the world be? Where had the conflict with Communism come from, and did it, or any other foreign policy goal, justify such grim actions? The decision to use the atomic bomb, it seemed, drama-tized the ends versus means dilemma in the starkest sense. And Conant, not a soldier following orders but the head of America's most exalted university, an institution established "to advance Learning and perpetuate it to Posterity," seemed an ideal figure through which to explore the ethical questions sur-rounding the use of science and knowledge in the service of the state to devise the most lethal implements of destruction imaginable—and in this case, the tools potentially to extinguish the civilization and Posterity to whose success Harvard was dedicated.

Frantically visiting archives in Washington, New Haven, Princeton, New York, and elsewhere in my effort to satisfy the Harvard history department's ironclad thesis deadline, I realized almost immediately that a far broader Conant story awaited discovery. His life was obviously far more interesting than his memoirs, and it offered a window on many of the revolutionary transformations in recent American history caused by World War II and the Cold War—the quantum jumps in the relationships tying U.S. science, universities, government, and the military; the shift in U.S. foreign policy from isolationism to global interventionism; the stresses on American educa-tion, society, and politics, exacerbated by McCarthyism and the bomb; the dizzying role-changes, from demonized enemy to trustworthy ally (or the reverse), that the Soviet Union and Germany underwent in American eyes and policy; the philosophical and existential alterations in humanity's relation-ship to the universe after Alamogordo.

Conant had been uniquely positioned both to affect and to observe these developments. Over highballs at the Cosmos and Century clubs, in long conversations on the Pullman trains chugging along the Boston–New York–Washington corridor, around oaken conference tables in confidential commit-tee meetings, in the tightly guarded, highly classified atmosphere of the atomic priesthood, Conant operated at the crossroads of America's power elite—gliding easily among educational, scientific, political, corporate, military, media, diplomatic, nuclear, and intellectual realms. A synecdoche for his era, he personified the East Coast establishment and "Wise Men" generation that guided America from Pearl Harbor to the Grand Alliance to the Cold War consensus to the disillusionment and fragmentation of Vietnam. Moreover, as a spokesman for Harvard and science (its "mouthpiece," claimed poet Robert

Frost), Conant embodied the Zeitgeist of his America—a turning toward the secular, technocratic, scientific expert to impose rationality and order on a chaotic century.

But for all his prominence, the *Time* and *Newsweek* covers, and the serious speculation that he might run for president, Conant remained in many respects a mystery—as enigmatic as the day in May 1933, a few months after Hitler and Roosevelt took their respective posts, that the previously obscure chemist first entered the public spotlight as the surprise choice to become the twenty-fourth president of Harvard University. To some, he would be classed as a liberal, a daring intellect who took unpopular stands in favor of the New Deal and FDR's support of the Allies before Pearl Harbor, a stalwart defender of Harvard and academic freedom against the McCarthyite onslaught (or even, as the Wisconsin senator charged, a Communist coddler himself), an opponent of the H-bomb and skeptic of nuclear power, a Jeffersonian proponent of educational egalitarianism, an outsider to Boston's Brahmin aristocracy, the man who barred classified military research at Harvard, a debunker of the notion of preventive war, a brave, calm, cool, rational, far-sighted voice in an age of anxiety and hysteria. Simultaneously, however, an image of another Conant arose—the scientist who perverted his talents to manufacture poison gas and the bomb, the cozy collaborator of General Groves and the army during the Manhattan Project, the quintessential Cold Warrior and reactionary propagandist for Pentagon budgets and a comprehensive peacetime draft, the establishment pillar who never rocked the boat, the loyal defender of the status quo and servant to conventional wisdom.

On a personal level, too, radically different Conants coexisted and persist in memory. Critics, including some associates, depicted a dour, priggish, brusque, unimaginative bureaucrat, of whom it was said that "red tape ran in his veins," with a stern, gray presence and a dour expression likened by Isaiah Berlin to that of "a gnostic priest about to cut out the heart of a sacrificial victim." Conant called himself a "cold reserved New Englander" and a "cranky New Englander," and even a sometimes admirer, Supreme Court Justice Felix Frankfurter, found him not only dogmatic and unimaginative but "incurably cold, without radiations."[9]

Yet, friends sketched a warm, brilliantly innovative man with a wry sense of humor, a broad smile, informal, considerate, unpretentious, as apt to engage in spirited talk, elbow propped against a bookcase, with a college sophomore as with a Nobel laureate or a rich alumnus; "kindliness, good humor, and dignity," were the words that Conant evoked for the historian Robert Tucker, who as a young translator at the U.S. embassy in Moscow accompanied Conant to meetings with commissars and sightseeing in Red Square during a 1945 foreign ministers' conference.[10] To the charge of aloofness, Conant once replied indirectly by citing the sad case of a fellow chemist who, disdained by peers for avoiding scientific meetings, had "suffered thereby the fate of more than one shy person whose aloofness is attributed to pride."[11]

Contrary to those who found him cold or humorless, one friend insisted that
Conant was "constantly at play; that is, acting with spontaneity, joy, humor
and becoming mischievously intrigued with the game for itself. But, significantly,
the 'play' is *always* a by-product of, and is sanctioned by, the conviction that
he is engaged simultaneously in socially significant work."[12]

Work he did—and one cannot but be astonished by the scope, variety,
and prolificity of Conant's protean life. In trying to ascertain a fuller picture
of a man who reckoned himself "one of the outstanding kibitzers of the
age,"[13] I encountered, at different times, all of the Conants described above,
and more. Predictably enough for someone engaged in a biographical study,
the question my friends most often asked (besides, "Are you *still* working on
that book?") was whether I "liked" Conant. The truth is, I'm still not sure. At
various times he provoked anger, admiration, and ambivalence. He was, and
is, a frustrating subject. At times, in the spirit of E. H. Carr's definition of
history as an "unending dialogue between the present and the past," I felt a
biographer's communion with an engaging subject—and not only the adver-
sarial relationship implicit in Conant's fear that one day a "verbal-minded"
and "sentimental" historian might cast a critical eye on the decision to bomb
Hiroshima. But there was always an element of suspense, as I tried to peel
away layer after layer of his carefully shrouded and sometimes contradictory
persona, when discovering how Conant had acted when faced with a difficult
moral or political choice.[14]

In some respects, from the perspective of a generation later, Conant
emerges as a far-sighted and lucid voice—a lucidity underlined by the anti-
Communist convulsions of 1989-91 that reshaped the international landscape
in ways that posthumously vindicated predictions he had made four decades
before. But Conant also displayed the limitations and failings of the American
establishment in a period of global conflict, technological change, and domestic tensions. Ultimately, any judgment on Conant must be mixed—and no
more or less complicated than coming to grips with the dangerous, fast-
changing world he lived in, influenced, and left behind.

CHAPTER I

"Bound to Be Heard from Later
as a Scholar and a Man"

A Prodigy's Progress
1893–1910

Born a quarter century earlier, I feel certain I should have had a quiet life in some academic chemical laboratory with little or no interest in the relatively meaningless world which lies beyond the test tube.
— JBC to college classmates at their twenty-fifth reunion in 1939[1]

This year he has practically lived in the laboratory, concocting every kind of condition of smell. We sincerely hope he will not blow up the laboratory at Harvard.
— High school yearbook assessment of JBC, 1910

An augury of the baby's ingenuity was present right at the start. The night before James Bryant Conant entered the world, six-year-old Marjorie Conant, breathless to find out if her mother had given birth, had agreed to go to sleep only after wresting a promise from her aunt that a certain book would be left open on a table in the morning as a signal that she had a new brother or sister. The book was *Through the Looking-Glass*, whose White Knight, Conant would point out in *My Several Lives*, is the model for the egotistical inventor. "If I was, in fact, born under the sign of the great inventor — the White Knight — much of my adult behavior could be readily explained," he observed dryly. "It would require only an extension of the present trend in psychology which explains all character in terms of experience in early childhood."[2]

In fact, by the end of his life, Conant settled on a more serious hypothesis to explain the long-term effect of a person's birth and childhood. Dismissing a friend's argument that IQ tests unfairly penalized late bloomers, Conant firmly held that a potential for brilliance either existed from the start or was unlikely to surface — "the percentage of those who have a delayed intellectual awakening was, he thought, too small to bother with."[3] Theodore Conant distinctly recalls his father's private position on the nature-nurture conundrum.

Discounting the chances that psychiatry or religion, "a conversion of Freud or the Church," or even education, could alter a person's fundamental nature, Conant believed that genetic imprint largely determined a human being's capabilities and potential, even if some luck along the way certainly helped: "He basically felt you were pretty well formed by heredity more than environment, and you were going to pretty well act out in sort of a Greek tragedy."[4] Though he would have scorned the notion that predestination in a religious sense pointed him toward chemistry, the Harvard presidency, or the atomic bomb, even a cursory glance at Conant's youth irresistibly foreshadows the life that lay ahead.

"Science and Puritanism merged in Jim Conant," two friends recalled after his death in 1978. "His scientific rigor replaced the Puritan vision of an austere God; his human straightness kept the colonists' sense of equality."[5] Perhaps, Conant might have attributed his sharp intellect, aptitude for science, and most of all his energetic, disciplined self-propulsion to the DNA inherited from generations of Puritan tanners, farmers, shoemakers who were his ancestors. Certainly one finds references enough to "hardy Puritan stock" and "sound Yankee ancestors" in the literature of New Englanders, hailing the gritty souls who escaped the religious and political persecutions of seventeenth-century Britain, made the rough ocean passage, and established the early settlements at Plymouth Rock and environs. Of those "eager but steadfast men," Conant once said: "There is no softness in that strain, no yielding to the wave of the future, no defeatism in that character."[6] Sure enough, Conant could trace his mother's family back to a passenger aboard the ship after the *Mayflower* — waiting to see how the first vessel fared was a typically prudent gesture for a Conant — and his father's line to Roger Conant, who founded Salem in 1626. Conant never tired of pointing out that despite this lineage, he was not a "proper Bostonian," one of the aristocratic Back Bay and Beacon Hill Brahmins that were so pungently evoked by Cleveland Amory and John P. Marquand, but the offspring of hardworking, middle-income parents, James Scott Conant and Jennett Orr Bryant, who came from small villages in Plymouth country to raise their son and two daughters in the working-class Boston suburb of Dorchester.

But even if one grants the hereditary theory attributed to him — which implied a belief not in a nobility of birth but an "aristocracy of talent" that could pop up anywhere and needed to be nurtured — nucleic acids alone could not account for the social, political, religious, and personal values and ideals that Conant began to develop in the years between his birth, on March 26, 1893, and his five-mile trek to Cambridge to enter Harvard College in the autumn of 1910. In the personalities inhabiting the two-story antebellum wood frame house near Peabody Square that Conant's father had purchased in 1880, in the high school where he met his first scientific mentor, and in the quickly modernizing face of turn-of-the-century Boston, one finds clues to the sometimes conflicting traits that characterized Conant's adult life: avid curiosity and breadth of interest, skepticism toward religious or political dogma, obedience to authority, fascination for military affairs, admiration for intellectual excellence, rigorous self-discipline and devotion to duty, awareness of and a desire to participate in an epoch of accelerating technological change.

At home, Conant was exposed to a clash of political and religious views that strayed from the de rigueur Boston combination of Republicanism and Protestantism (Unitarian, Episcopalian, or Congregational). The boy known to his family as "Bryant" and his schoolmates as "Jim" was thereby encouraged to take a relatively open-minded approach to issues. His parents were Swedenborgians, members of a sect that blended scientific inquiry and mysticism in a manner developed by the eighteenth-century Stockholm scientist Emanuel Swedenborg. An admiring Ralph Waldo Emerson had once described the prolific polymath as "a visionary and elixir of moonbeams" and sympathetically depicted his strenuous labors "to put science and the soul, long estranged from each other, at one again."[7] A notable tenet of the sect, which flourished in the Plymouth valley region where Conant's grandparents lived, encouraged the idea that systematic measurement and investigation of nature could lead one to the miraculous and the divine. Yet where Swedenborg turned from math, physics, anatomy, astronomy, and chemistry to theological illumination and a firm belief in immortality, Conant's inquisition into the nature of things appears to have led only to more profound puzzlement and curiosity.

Conant's parents, too, although they dutifully dragged their preschool son aboard the trolley to Swedenborgian services in Roxbury, gave evidence of doubt. His maternal grandmother, Jane Breed Bryant, a close childhood confidante who lived with Grandfather Seth Bryant on the second floor of the two-family home at 1937 Dorchester Avenue, remained an "unquestioning Swedenborgian" to her death. But his parents maintained only a "lukewarm interest" in the sect, and by the time he started kindergarten they had discontinued the weekly pilgrimages to church, and they never sent him to Sunday school as they had his two older sisters, Esther and Marjorie. The boy noticed further evidence of his parents' diminishing fealty to Swedenborgian doctrine when his mother began openly and "rather forcefully" dissenting from churchgoers who favored a rival interpretation of the founder's writings.

"Far more important," Conant would recall, "was my mother's final and complete condemnation of all Trinitarian doctrines. She never attempted to make me a Swedenborgian, perhaps because she had become less convinced as she grew older. She certainly succeeded, however, in making me at an early age more than suspicious of all the standard arguments in favor of Christianity." Later, Conant vaguely classified himself as a Unitarian "deist" who believed in a "cautious but optimistic theism," but outsiders had the impression that he genuflected more often to the gods of science, rationality, and pragmatism, and to Swedenborg's dictum that "The perfection of man is the love of use," than to any heavenly deity.[8]

The willingness of Jennett Conant to express strong opinions contrasted strikingly with the stolidity of her husband, James Scott Conant, a taciturn, distinguished-looking man with a white beard and mustache beneath wire-rimmed spectacles. In evocations of Conant's youth his "massively silent" father tends to recede to the fringes of a home life dominated by his mother, two sisters, grandmother, three or four aunts, and a female cousin—what he would describe as "the 'regiment of women' who watched over my growing up."[9]

From this matriarchal universe the pampered only son also learned political heresy, for his mother had strong views on contemporary as well as ecclesiastical controversies. In turn-of-the-century America, party affiliations still largely dated from loyalties at the time of the Civil War, in which Conant's father had served, and Conant recalls that "for vast numbers of New Englanders the words 'Republican' and 'patriotic' were still synonymous." Yet, scandalously, Grandfather Bryant had turned into a dyed-in-the-wool Democrat, ardently arguing the cause of William Jennings Bryan, and pugnaciously quarreling with his Republican son-in-law. Conant's mother had strongly opposed slavery and supported the North, yet by the early 1900s, the time of Teddy Roosevelt and the rough riders racing up San Juan Hill to fight their "splendid little war," she and one of her sisters had been disgusted by the Republican administration's jingoism and did not hesitate to express their views loudly. From such arguments Conant says he gathered, first, "that ladies could be emotionally involved as onlookers of the political scene" —evidently they did not thereby gain credentials as participants—and second, "that dissent was not only respectable but usually morally correct."[10]

Initially, however, Jennett Conant's anti-imperialism inspired an opposite reaction from her son, who like his childhood friends could not resist the glorious spectacle of the Spanish-American War, and cheered the troops marching off to battle in Cuba. Though it would, of course, be absurd to infer much about Conant's later views or actions from his boyhood ardor for playing soldier, he admits in *My Several Lives* to having enjoyed the martial simulations, the toy rifles and marching drills, that characterized "the play world of male children." A surviving photo shows a rather stern-faced, pudgy-cheeked eight-year-old in full Union Army regalia, complete with rifle, cap, uniform, boots, bedroll, and sword tucked in his belt, next to two similarly attired comrades. More tellingly, Conant admits to feeling a keen sense of disappointment that his father, an underage drummer boy for the Union army and then deckhand for the navy, did not witness or take part in the "man-to-man combat" that might have given the boy some gory, exciting tales to tell his mates.[11]

Conant did pay wide-eyed attention to one of his father's firsthand wartime reminiscences, the maritime battle between the *Monitor* and *Merrimack* that opened a new era in naval warfare. It was only one of a multitude of examples of the boy's fascination with technology during a childhood that, in the words of a contemporary, "opened with the horsecar and the herdic, and closed with the Cadillac and the airplane."[12] Observing the transition from the "horse-and-buggy age" to the era of subway, electric trolley car, and internal-combustion engine, Conant could watch the new century's theme of faster, bigger, more powerful vehicles and machines take shape right outside his front door, where the Ashmont train station now linked his neighborhood to an expanded transportation network that fostered new connections between Boston and its rapidly burgeoning outlying suburbs. Dorchester was one such suburb, its population soaring from 60,000 in 1870 to 227,000 by 1900, a growth that fueled a construction boom from which Conant's father, who speculated in real estate while moonlighting from the engraving business, profited.[13] Like many builders, the elder Conant catered to middle-class families by putting up two-story two-family houses, and he encouraged his son to tag along on inspection tours to the bustling construction sites. The experience gave the boy a palpable sense of the age's rough-hewn spirit of growth and expansion, as did an early beguilement with trains that led him at age seven to plot the conversion of his front yard into a vast railway network. Viewing the future "in terms of ever-expanding electric trolley car systems," he confidently imagined the imminent construction of a train line that would chauffeur him directly to the doorstep of the family's summer cottage in New Hampshire, a trip which then required an hour-long journey from the nearest station by horse-drawn carriage. But the days of horses clopping on Boston's cobblestones and suffusing its air with a "rich equine flavor" were fading. Gaslights were giving way to the newly voguish electricity, and Conant heard grown-ups speaking of "progress" that would shortly come to the roads that now in wintertime were given over to sledding. "The twentieth century, they said, would certainly bring new streets and more electric cars — possibly things called automobiles as well, though I had never seen one."[14]

Conant's lively inquisitiveness, already aroused by these newfangled spectacles, discovered further nourishment in his father's aptitude for technological innovation, reflected in his modest but constantly modernizing photo-engraving business. James Scott Conant's penchant for trying new methods and techniques to advance his business rubbed off on his son, who even as a ten-year-old developed an avid interest in investigating and manipulating nature — delighting in the discovery, for instance, that rubbing a hot-water bottle on the family cat could yield static electricity. At work, the elder Conant fascinated his son by demonstrating the intricate process used to etch copper plates, and in a side-door vestibule at home built him a makeshift laboratory complete with a Bunsen burner suitable for melting glass, distilling water, or oxidizing mercury. With the help of his allowance of five dollars a month for supplies, the young Conant dabbled in both pure and applied research, and even a small-scale business venture — supplementing his income by charging neighborhood kids a nickel each to witness his magic tricks. "You must be the Bryant I used to know in years gone by, maker of stinks in the little side room in your house ... of whom the gang stood in silent and nose-holding awe," wrote one childhood acquaintance in 1931 after noticing that a Harvard professor named Conant had won renown for his chemistry exploits.[15]

James Scott Conant encouraged his son's precocity, but the boy received an even more important boost at the Roxbury Latin School, which offered a six-year college preparatory program with a strong reputation in science and the classics. His enrollment in the prestigious school was a near thing; of the ninety boys who took the highly competitive examinations for 1904, only thirty-five were admitted. Conant rated high in reading, geography, and grammar, mediocre in arithmetic and writing, and came home crying after finding out that he had flunked the spelling section. Not to be denied, Mrs. Conant implored school authorities to admit her boy on the grounds that his ability in science compensated for this shortcoming.[16]

They relented—and shortly thereafter Conant met Newton Henry Black, a science instructor he later described as the "teacher who had the greatest influence on my life." Encountering the "towhead with a Dutch cut and a broad collar" in his second-year elementary science course, Black quickly sensed that the curious eleven-year-old possessed unusual devotion, energy, and talent. A man who gave generously of his time and enthusiasm, Black took Conant under his wing, mentored his interest in science, and shepherded him toward a career in chemistry and a first-class advanced-standing ticket to Harvard. For his remaining six years at Roxbury Latin, until his graduation in 1910, Conant marveled at Black's tabletop demonstrations of chemical reactions and such newfangled gizmos as the wireless radio and jumped at his offer to join fellow science hounds for lunch, after-school gossip, and experimental sessions in his lab. Black was happy to fan any spark of genuine interest, Conant later recalled, maintained "high standards and was impatient with any who were either lazy or extremely stupid."[17] At Black's side Conant absorbed physics and chemistry lore, fingered advanced texts, honed experimental techniques, and adopted his mentor's instinctual quest for empirical data rather than argument to attack difficult questions. Gradually but firmly, Black nurtured the innate curiosity, skepticism, and self-discipline that permanently colored Conant's outlook on scientific and human affairs. From Black, too, Conant enhanced his appreciation for Europe, and particularly Germany, as the Mecca of scientific scholarship—a realization that prompted Conant to choose the tongue of Göttingen and Berlin as his main Roxbury language for study. The young scientist soon grasped that a prerequisite to real accomplishment entailed a pilgrimage to the great German universities. Even at the age of fifteen, signs of his preoccupation abounded: an ideal gift to bring home, he wrote his sister Marjorie who was studying art in Paris, would be a copy of Ostwald's two-volume *Schule der Chemie*.[18]

Black's prodding soon transformed the boy's buoyant love affair with science into a firm engagement. Curious about his prodigy's progress, the teacher handed Conant a copy of the college entrance exam in chemistry two years before he was scheduled to take the test. "Why don't you take this and see what you can do?" he said offhandedly. Seizing the challenge, Conant filled out the bluebook—and even as an old man he could still savor the "trace of surprise" on Black's face when the teacher quickly glanced through and pronounced: "The grade is A."

"My career was now clearly set," Conant recalled. "I was to be a chemist."[19]

There was still, however, the minor technicality of getting the unknown teenager into Harvard. Though none of Conant's family had gone to Harvard, Black had taken his master's in chemistry there a few years before. And after his star student passed the college entrance exams at the end of his junior year, Black took it upon himself to design a private accelerated curriculum for Conant and trenchantly to lobby the Harvard chemistry department and its chairman, Theodore William Richards, not only to admit the high schooler but to allow him to skip first-year chemistry and immediately take classes usually reserved for upperclassmen. Impressed, Richards informed Black on October 29, 1909, that the department had decided that Conant, "considering his extraordinary ability," could anticipate Chemistry 1, but that motions to secure advanced standing in other classes had been lost. Undeterred, Black replied with a further plea to also allow Conant to bypass Chem 3, especially as Black sternly vowed to "put him through a good stiff course of salts and solutions" his senior year. Ominously he added that the boy was "very much in earnest about the matter, and asked me if there was not some other college where he could go and get what he wanted." Of course Black had discouraged such a heretical notion, but he pressed Richards to accept his assurance that Conant's exceptional work merited special consideration. The proud teacher declared victory when Richards responded tentatively accepting the condition, adding that formal approval might require correspondence with the dean "but we shall back you up in the negotiations."[20]

But as Jeanne Amster has pointed out, even more than his teacher's persistence or the advantages of his father's profession Conant's "inner drive" opened the door to a distinguished scientific career and the opportunities of a Harvard education. He carefully monitored his standing relative to other students, and before taking a college entrance exam wrote out the following somber pledge on the back of his grade card: "I, James Bryant Conant, on the eve of my Preliminary exams, testify that, I have in my opinion, done as well as could be under conditions and having nothing to regret during last year's work and I will not blame myself or anyone if I fail to pass."[21]

His hard work and Puritan self-discipline paid off. From mediocre grades at first (mostly Bs and Cs) in subjects outside of science—he ranked sixteenth out of a Roxbury class of thirty-two in 1906—by 1909 Conant not only had bested his peers in chemistry but was second in his class in Latin and third in German and History.[22] And by his graduation in June 1910, the lanky, purposeful, increasingly self-assured adolescent had climbed to the top of an intensely competitive heap: winner of a Harvard Club scholarship, and leading science student in a twenty-one-member class of which twelve graduates went to Harvard, and one each to Dartmouth, MIT, Amherst, and Yale. At closing exercises, he confidently displayed his pyrotechnic wizardry in front of a large crowd, performing and lucidly explaining several complicated chemistry experiments. After Greek and German recitations, an English essay, and a homily on patriotism from an ex-governor, the Roxbury Latin school journal, *The Tripod*, recorded, "James Bryant Conant then tried to blow up the building with some examples of combustion."[23]

But Conant had also blossomed in nonscientific pursuits; editor-in-chief of *The Tripod*, a monthly mishmash of class notes, school spirit, and apologies for the losing baseball team; class treasurer; a spirited member of the football and crew teams; and even a showstopper in the senior drama production, *Maître Corbeau*, a romance set in the home of a wealthy French family. Daintily attired in "petticoats and a blonde wig with long, dangling curls," Conant played the heroine, Lucille, who spurns the man who wishes to marry her in favor of a handsome young lawyer who appears at the door one day to seek refuge from the rain. Succumbing to the stranger's flattery, Conant won hoots and applause for his romantic embrace of the hero, played by friend and later college roommate Charlie Crombie. "Lucille certainly made a corking good fiancée," raved *The Tripod*'s admittedly partial critic.[24]

Even allowing for the boosterism that can infect a proud teacher, the letters that Roxbury Latin teachers wrote to Harvard authorities to plead for a freshman scholarship for their pupil testify to Conant's achievements. (The lad, whose parents were described by one teacher as "in moderate circumstances," listed his family's annual income for 1910–11 at $4,500.)[25] "He is manly, reliable, and in Physics & Chemistry perhaps the most-brilliant-fellow we ever had," averred one instructor, who predicted that any financial award would be "well deserved and well bestowed."[26] From Henry Black's quill came an effusive and more nuanced tribute suggestive of an affectionate mentor-protégé bond and of the qualities that already distinguished Conant from the crowd:

> In regard to Mr. James Bryant Conant, I may say that I have known him very well for the past five years. He is the best boy all around in his class, and in Chemistry and Physics is the best student I have had in the past ten years. He shows not only unusual mental power but real scientific enthusiasm and ini[ti]ative. Personally he is rather quiet, modest, and unassuming. He has shown real ability to get on with other boys, as is seen from the fact that he is editor-in-chief of the school-paper, played foot-ball, was in the school-play and is rowing on the school-crew. At the same time he is doing extra work in Science, so that he will anticipate Chem 1 & skip Chem. 3 & Physics C, and be ready to take Calculus next year. He really has a great capacity for [tearing?] off work and is very conscientious. He is looking forward to university teaching as a career. While his family could provide for his

expenses at college for a year or two, yet when one considers the long course of study yet ahead of him, I feel certain that he is decidedly the kind of boy to be helped by a scholarship.

Taking all things into consideration I consider him the most promising boy I have had in science during my ten years here in this school. He is bound to be heard from later as a scholar and a man.[27]

Conant's spirited emergence from science prodigy to veritable Renaissance teenager inspired a wry sendoff from his fellows. One class wag predicted at graduation that the boy wonder would end up as a druggist "serving, as a premium on all sales over three cents, a guaranteed chemically pure prussic acid ferrocyanide milkshake." His impressed fellow editors at *The Tripod* wrote: " 'Jim' has been with us from the sixth, but up to last year no one suspected him of owning more than his fair share of gray matter. When last June, he walked off with 18 points in his 'prelims,' we sat up and took notice. This year he has practically lived in the laboratory, concocting every kind of condition of a smell. We sincerely hope he will not blow up the laboratory at Harvard." But more profoundly than his peers' affectionate wisecrack, the quotation Conant chose to have printed beside his photograph in *The Tripod*'s farewell edition hinted at a future involvement with explosions far deadlier than those he had detonated at Roxbury Latin's graduation rituals.[28] A frank statement of ambivalence at the exercise of power taken from Shakespeare's *Measure for Measure*, it was a stunning choice for a teenager who would play a decisive role in the affairs of men and the use of weapons:

> "Tis great to have a giant's strength,
> but tyrannus to use it."[29]

CHAPTER 2

"Something of a Specialist"

Harvard College

1910–1913

those spring nights the streetcar wheels screech grinding in a rattle of loose trucks round the curved tracks of Harvard Square dust hangs in the powdery arclight glare allnight till dawn can't sleep

haven't got the nerve to break out of the bellglass

four years under the ethercone breathe deep gently now that's the way be a good boy one two three four five six get A's in some courses but don't be a grind be interested in literature but remain a gentleman don't be seen with Jews or Socialists

and all the pleasant contacts will be useful in Later Life say hello pleasantly to everybody crossing the yard

sit looking out into the twilight of the pleasantest four years of your life . . .

—From "Camera Eye 25," *The 42nd Parallel*
John Dos Passos, Harvard Class of 1916

Smile, damn it, *smile!!*

—Note in JBC's freshman diary, 1910–11

Education is what is left after all that has been learnt is forgotten.
—Inscription in JBC's freshman diary

In the autumn of 1910, when Conant—"a thin boy of seventeen whose outer gravity was lightened by a shy amiability and a capacity for friendship"[1]— hauled his books and clothes up to the third floor of the spartan Harvard Square boardinghouse where he would sleep for the next two years, the onrush of modernity he had scented in childhood was even more palpable in the air, the streets, the campus, and most of all in the minds of many fellow students at Harvard College.

America's foremost educational institution, and the locus of Conant's professional life for the next forty-three years, was smack in the midst of a transition. Outwardly, the most dramatic change was on top, where a new face, and a walrus-mustached one at that, peered out from behind the president's desk for the first time since Reconstruction. An era had ended the previous fall when Abbot Lawrence Lowell succeeded Charles William Eliot. During his four-decade reign, the stern, magisterial Eliot had been the prime mover in Harvard's rise from a sleepy, provincial New England college with loosely attached divinity, law, "scientific," and medical schools, into a far larger, more diverse university along the German model he admired, boasting nine professional schools, a new graduate school, museums, libraries, an observatory, and an illustrious international reputation. Between 1869 and 1909, Harvard's student body had doubled to twenty-two hundred and had broadened to include small but more visible minorities of Italian and Irish Catholics, Jews, and other recent immigrant groups alongside the dominant New England WASPs; its faculty ballooned almost sixfold to 169 professors; and its catalogue of course offerings grew larger and richer. Most of all, Eliot secured scholars whose intellectual brilliance brought Harvard renown: the philosophers George Santayana and William James, the economist Frank Taussig, the literary experts Charles Eliot Norton, Barrett Wendell, Bliss Perry, and George Lyman Kittredge, the jurist Oliver Wendell Holmes.

Eliot himself, acclaimed by Theodore Roosevelt as the "First Citizen of the Republic," was utilized for such exalted tasks as supplying the aphorisms with which to adorn the Library of Congress. His prominence (and Harvard's sense of self-importance) reached the point that, so the story went, a visitor at the doorstep of the great man's residence who inquired whether Eliot was home, heard the answer, "No, the president is in Washington, seeing Mr. Taft." By the time Eliot stepped down, Harvard had become, at once, "a national center of strenuous educational reform, a world center of research, the parochial pleasure ground of the clubmen (through which passed both Roosevelts), the teaching institution, and already the mecca of the disaffected young men who wanted to write."[2]

To most students, the jewel in Eliot's crown had been the unparalleled personal and scholastic freedom permitted undergraduates in the Harvard of his day—which persisted into the early Lowell years. Starting with symbolic gestures like eliminating the study of Greek as an entrance requirement and mandatory chapel attendance (a solemn obligation maintained by Yale until well into the twentieth century), Eliot's principal reform had been the elective system, which unshackled Harvard collegiates to custom design (or ignore) their studies. Free to concentrate on classes, to devote themselves to extracurricular activities, or to decipher and ascend the elaborate social progression of finals clubs, students indulged their intellectual, romantic, or preprofessional hankerings. A straight gentleman's C was good enough to graduate. The Harvard undergraduate, declared George Santayana, "does, except when the pressure or fear constrains him, only what he finds worth doing for its own sake."[3] Santayana thought Harvard, in Eliot's waning years, was "getting out of hand."[4] But John Reed, class of 1910, who blasted his

alma mater's foibles with the same intensity that he later chronicled the
Russian Revolution, found the anarchy liberating:

> All sorts of strange characters, of every race and mind, poets, philosophers,
> cranks of every twist, were in our Class. The very hugeness of it prevented
> any one man from knowing more than a few of his classmates. . . . What is
> known as "college spirit" was not very powerful; no odium attached to those
> who didn't go to football games and cheer. There was talk of the world, and
> daring thought, and intellectual insurgency; heresy has always been a Harvard
> and New England tradition. Students themselves criticized the faculty for
> not educating them, attacked the sacred institution of intercollegiate athletics,
> sneered at undergraduate clubs so holy that no one dared mention their
> names. No matter who you were or what you did — at Harvard you could find
> your kind.[5]

In classmates like Walter Lippmann, president of the newly formed Socialist
Club, and others who "had been reading and thinking and talking about
politics and economics, not as dry theoretical studies, but as live forces acting
on the world, on the University even," Reed discerned what he called "the
manifestation of the modern spirit." In sync with the progressive tide sweeping the country, a wave of youthful idealism and insurgency crested, inspiring
students to lobby for women's suffrage, workers' rights; to form a volunteer
brigade to help homeless victims of a fire in a poor neighborhood; to blast
cobwebbed Harvard institutions and seek new frontiers in undergraduate art,
music, journalism; to pepper the Massachusetts legislature with proposed
reform bills; even unabashedly to promote anarchism and invite speakers of
disreputably leftist taint. While undergraduates disputed ideological points in
all-night bull sessions, literary talents also flowered in the hothouse environment.
Although Lippmann, Reed, and T. S. Eliot, graduates of the Class of 1910,
had, as Dos Passos put it, "moved out into the great world of hellroaring and
confusion" a few months before Conant unpacked his valise, a stunning array
of upstart poets, novelists, and playwrights would populate Harvard during
his student days: between 1910 and 1916, the year Conant pocketed his
doctorate, the graduate student Eliot composed "The Love Song of J. Alfred
Prufrock"; collegiates Robert Hillyer, e. e. cummings, Malcolm Cowley, John
Dos Passos, and Robert Nathan wrote stories and poems for student monthlies;
Robert E. Sherwood wrote a play for the Hasty Pudding Club and songs for
Ziegfeld before flunking out; and Eugene O'Neill (whose tragic dramas would
appeal to Conant's pessimistic view of human nature) passed a year as a
special student.[6]

Not all Harvard undergraduates concerned themselves with such avant-
garde notions as Reed, who called for an assault on all bastions of student
elitism, or cummings, who nonplussed a 1915 graduation ceremony by
declaiming on "New Art" — cubism, futurism, and other mysterious currents
coming from across the Atlantic.[7] The burst of radicalism had shattered "the

Oscar Wildean dilettantism that had possessed undergraduate litterateurs for generations," but Reed readily conceded that it "made no ostensible difference in the look of Harvard society, and probably the clubmen and the athletes, who represented us to the world, never even heard of it."[8]

For that large chunk of entering freshmen, drawn from the progeny of wealthy New England business families whose menfolk had attended Harvard for generations, for Brahmins or Brahmin "wannabes," quick acceptance in society, not good grades or intellectual passion, held first priority during their freshman year. The arbiters of social taste quickly weeded out students deemed lacking the right stuff — too eccentric, too studious, too brash, too ethnic, too leftist, too Jewish, too individualistic. Far to be preferred were the safe, "socially presentable," well-bred graduates of the right prep schools, Groton, St. Paul's, Exeter, Andover, with pockets deep enough to rent rooms in the princely private dormitories on the "Gold Coast," Mt. Auburn Street, rather than among the "commoners" in the quotidian boardinghouses around Harvard Square. Above all, records Samuel Eliot Morison in *Three Centuries of Harvard,* conformity and credentials marked a prime recruit for social advancement:

> Family and race did not matter: an Irish-American, Jew, Italian, or Cuban was not regarded as such if he went to the right school and adopted the mores of his fellows; conversely, a lad of Mayflower and Porcellian ancestry who entered from a [public] high school was as much "out of it" as a ghetto Jew. Nor did wealth matter: men who worked their way through College were respected and eligible; but too much spending damned a freshman — a now prominent multimillionaire who came to Cambridge with a retinue of cars and servants, and hired a whole apartment, had no notice taken of him, and soon departed.
>
> These factors of school, site, and the Boston hall-mark determined the socially eligible class, which was always from 25 to 50 per cent greater than the number of places in the clubs. Consequently ambitious freshmen had to watch their steps very carefully. No "Harvard individualism" for them! You must say, do, wear, the "right thing," and, above all, eschew originality. Athletic success, except possibly a place on the freshman crew, was not much help. Intellect was no handicap, provided it was tactfully concealed, and all the social taboos observed. Once having "made" a club, you could reassert your individuality; often by that time you had none.[9]

Those freshmen who stayed "on the right side of the social chasm," about a fifth of each class, might be tapped for entry into the "Institute of 1770," and thence considered after further vetting for admission to one of the final clubs. Once welcomed into this select hierarchy, at whose pinnacle rested the Porcellian and the A.D. clubs, initiates might find intimate lifetime friends, future business contacts, and tickets to exclusive parties on Cape Cod and dinner engagements with the upper crust of Boston society. One witness who

grew up in Back Bay, where mothers assiduously lured these eligible bache-
lors to the company of their daughters, has recalled their distinctive mating
rituals: "Sunday afternoon was the time for Harvard upperclassmen to make
their party calls. One could see them, resplendent in frock coat, fancy
waistcoat and high hat, carrying a cane, walking up and down Commonwealth Avenue to call on the mammas who had invited them to dine or dance.
And woe betide them if they failed to turn up within a week or two—they
were struck off 'the list.' "[10]

Proper conduct for a Proper Harvardian who desired to become a Proper
Bostonian included tact and good taste in selecting friends and acquaintances.
Subtle and not-so-subtle racism, classism, and anti-Semitism persisted; one
classicist carped to e. e. cummings of the difficulty of teaching poetry to "such
a heterogeneous agglomeration" when he "had men like yourself sitting next
to some little rough-neck Irish Catholic or Polish Jew."[11] No less a struggler
for a classless society than John Reed was so desperate for elite approval that
he canceled plans to room with a Jewish friend his sophomore year in a futile
attempt to impress the aristocratic clublords—as an outsider from Portland,
Oregon, whose prep school was below the salt, he was already beyond the
pale.[12]

One may get a taste of the snobbery and snubbery pervading the man-
nered aristocracy that dominated Harvard's student social scene and entrenched
power structure, and the sense of threat it perceived from changing times and
eventually from Conant, in the wickedly sardonic novels of one of his classmates,
John P. Marquand, who long nursed his failure to gain acceptance in clubdom's
exclusive inner realms. In *The Late George Apley,* the protagonist's father is
alarmed to learn that George, a freshman in the Class of 1887, has befriended
a boy from an unfamiliar family. "What worries me," Thomas Apley writes
his son,

> . . . is a fear that you are not meeting the right people . . . nothing is more
> important than social consideration. You must bear in mind that the friend-
> ships and associations which you are now making at Harvard will be with
> you for the rest of your life. In my experience there is no truer axiom than
> that "a man is known by the company he keeps." Besides this, the connec-
> tions you are now forming are of definite importance to your subsequent
> career, both in college and in business.
>
> It is the fondest hope of your mother and me that you will be taken into
> the Club which has had an Apley for a member for many generations. But,
> your worthiness to be one of its members depends to a certain extent upon
> yourself. You must be sure to see the right people, which should not be
> difficult for you, as you have been born among them. Your mother and I have
> been greatly worried by your mention of this fellow student named Alger. It
> is all very well to be democratic and pleasant to an acquaintance who sits
> beside you in the class room by an alphabetical accident. I have no wish to
> limit your circle of acquaintance, as acquaintances are valuable and instructive,

but you must learn as soon as possible that friendship is another matter. Friends must be drawn from your own sort of people, or difficulty and embarrassment are very apt to be the result.[13]

Having fully digested these lessons, a generation later George Apley watches uneasily as his own son, John, a fictional classmate of Conant's, enters Harvard in the autumn of 1910:

Cambridge, like the world at large, was changing. Though many of the landmarks still remained, the Cambridge which John Apley faced was more of a city than a town. There were available for the students many luxurious accommodations. The vicinity of Mt. Auburn Street was called facetiously in the press the "Gold Coast," and it was not difficult to understand the connotation, when one considers the huge new student dormitories which had been built up in that neighborhood—Dunster, Claverly, Randolph, and Westmorly Halls. In addition to these a subway, connecting Cambridge and Boston, was nearing completion and eventually Boston would be twelve minutes, instead of an hour's distance, from Cambridge. These changes deeply bothered Apley, and he could not view them all as improvements for the better. In his opinion matters were moving too fast, far too fast.

Dear John:—

... A large part of your future life will be influenced by what you do this year. The habits and ties you form will be with you always. At least, they have been with me, and I want you to do the right thing. There is a great deal of talk about democracy. I thought there was something in it once but now I am not so sure. You cannot be too careful to select friends who have the same bringing-up as your own, and I want your friends to be my friends....

... your first object must be to "make" the Club. I believe that everything else, even including your studies, should be secondary to this. You may call this a piece of worldly counsel but it is worthwhile. I don't know what I should have done in life without the Club. When I leave Boston it is my shield. When I am in Boston it is one of my great diversions. The best people are always in it, the sort that you will understand and like. I once tried to understand a number of other people, but I am not so sure now that it was not a waste of time. Your own sort are the best friends and you will do well not to forget it.

I hope very much that you will do nothing to give you the reputation of being peculiar. I know well that it is hard always to be conventional, for one rather struggles against convention at your age. On the whole you find that this struggle is a mistake and really a great waste of time. Do not try to be different from what you are because in the end you will find that you cannot be different... Don't try to be different, John.[14]

Unlike the Brahmin protagonists of Marquand's novels, which he greatly enjoyed, Conant never had occasion to distill his wisdom to a son about to enter august Harvard.[15] But he came close in September 1933, when for the first time after becoming its president he addressed a crowd of incoming freshmen. Imploring the new arrivals to seek out "a real intellectual passion," which was the "best" experience a university could offer, Conant advised them to make the most of their opportunity to transcend a single social or intellectual realm: "You will never again in your life have a greater chance of liberalizing your point of view and broadening your outlook." Over the next few years, he told them, they had a chance to savor "living in a free and vigorous intellectual atmosphere" where "dogmas are courageously examined, compared, attacked, defended." Shun "intellectual snobbishness, school clannishness, and narrowness of outlook," he urged, and cultivate a "tolerant, skeptical spirit" that included friends and acquaintances with interests that span "almost the whole range of human activities." Understanding their hobbies "will lay the basis for your liberal education," even more than the knowledge derived in the classroom. "One can afford to be something of a specialist, even in one's undergraduate days," he concluded, "provided one has, as friends and companions, those who are interested in entirely different things. . . . A dinner table may be often as good an instrument of liberal education as a conference room or a lecture hall, and in my experience it is a great deal pleasanter than either."[16]

Conant's emphasis on friendships over classroom learning stemmed, at least in part, from his own experience. On taking office, Lowell had launched reforms to tighten Eliot's freewheeling elective system, imposing new requirements, inaugurated with Conant's class of 1914, for undergraduates to select major and minor fields of study.[17] But the "concentration and distribution" policy hardly proved an onus for a student like Conant, who was already intent on roaming beyond his primary specialty. In the spirit of the aphorism he jotted down in his freshman diary—"Education is what is left after all that has been learnt is forgotten"—Conant entered Harvard determined both to redeem Henry Black's confidence in his scientific promise, and to assuage the fears of the Conant female protectorate—his mother, sisters, aunts, and cousins—that he was fated to be "nothing but a narrow-minded chemist."[18] And, even more important than classes, once he had established himself in the lab Conant would enthusiastically sample the college's smorgasbord of extracurricular activities, broadening his social and intellectual sweep, and avoiding the label of grind. A year younger than most other freshmen, he also applied himself to overcoming the loneliness and social gaffes that can afflict any newcomer to college life, and to highfalutin Harvard in particular.

"*Smile,* damn it, *smile*!!" he scrawled one day on the inside cover of his pocket diary (Ward's *A Line a Day*), apparently in some agitation, for he underscored the first "smile" four times and the second one ten times—one can only imagine what awkward undergraduate encounter or needling snub could inspire such a burst of self-admonition. A few weeks after his eighteenth birthday, on April 15, 1911, Conant inscribed on the same prefatory page of his freshman diary a verse from *The Rubáiyát of Omar Khayyám* accompanied by a message to himself suggestive of an emerging dry-eyed distaste for self-pity, regret, or other traces of soft-headedness or "sentimentalism":

> The moving finger writes; and, having writ,
> Moves on; nor all your piety nor wit
> Shall lure it back to cancel half a line,
> Nor all your tears wash out a word of it.

Conant's moral: "HENCE: Don't act like a damn fool."[19] As Jeanne Amster perceptively observes: "From an early age Conant had an acute sense of his public personality and, like the scientific experiments in the laboratory, carefully constructed it so as to have a proper outcome."[20]

"Worked" is the word that recurs most frequently in his undergraduate diary, written in the same terse, laconic style as his father's Civil War journal. Half his courses were in chemistry, as Conant speedily vindicated his Roxbury Latin promise and demonstrated his mettle and abilities to a new mentor, Theodore William Richards. More than merely the chairman of the Harvard chemistry department, the professor to whom Newton Henry Black had entrusted his prize student was, in 1910, the most famous chemist in America. A painstaking experimentalist who "displayed the cool rationality and reserve that Americans often associate with the English gentry,"[21] Richards was to have a profound influence on Conant's life, first as a mentor who gave another dynamic push to a career that had already received such a helpful start from Black, and later as father-in-law. Born exactly a quarter-century before Conant, Richards was the scion of wealthy Philadelphia parents, the landscape painter William Trost Richards and Anna Matlock Richards, a pianist and poet who tutored the budding chemist at home, adding Greek, music, and drawing to the usual curriculum, and sent him off to college with a sonnet in his pocket enjoining him to

> Fear not to go where fearless Science leads,
> Who holds the keys of God. What reigning light
> Thine eyes discern in that surrounding night
> Whence we have come, what law that supersedes
> The fiat of all oracles and creeds,
> Thy soul will never find that Wrong is Right

When the heralded freshman from Roxbury Latin took his course on the history of chemistry, T. W. Richards was at the apex of his career and had achieved an international prominence of the sort normally reserved for Europeans; in 1915, already awash in honors from colleagues in the United States, Britain, and Germany, he became the first American to be awarded the Nobel Prize in chemistry. Firmly devoted to pure rather than applied science, Richards believed the mysteries of atomic theory could be unmasked through the precise measurement of each element's atomic weight, a task that required a steady hand, advanced technique and equipment, endless hours in the lab, and the patience to parse infinitesimal increments of matter. In 1901, after sabbaticals in Germany that gave him a chance to conduct research alongside such icons as Walther Nernst in Göttingen and Wilhelm Ostwald in Leipzig, Richards had received the honor, unheard-of for an American, of being invited to take a year's professorship in physical chemistry at Göttingen. That breakthrough, which thrust him to the top of his profession and won him a well-funded, tenured position at Harvard, embodied the fantasies of the boy in Dorchester, who was just beginning to learn the great names in German chemistry and was dreaming of writing his doctoral thesis under Richards's supervision.[22]

Richards's judiciousness, prudence, skepticism, and thoroughness appealed to Conant, as did his enshrinement of "the scientific independent, the chemical 'mugwump,'" as the fearless investigator of scientific truth. Indeed, the Keats verse that Conant scribbled on the leaf of his freshman diary bore more than passing resemblance to the homily Mrs. Richards had given her son, and embodied a comparably elevated devotion to physical data over dogma:

> . . . a friend to man, to whom thou say'st,
> "Beauty is truth, truth beauty,"—that is all
> Ye know on earth, and all ye need to know.

But other Harvard professors also caught Conant's eye. If Richards's rigorousness as an experimenter and dogged focus on "the grand strategy of the advance of science" impressed him, he sensed limitations in the older man's conservatism, aversion to critical argument or imaginative departures, and fixation on the quantitative analysis and meticulous measurements of heat and weight that Richards hoped would underpin his pet hypothesis of compressible atoms—a theory that "proved a *cul-de-sac,*" diverged from the cutting-edge ideas of Bohr, Rutherford, and Einstein, and contributed to an atmosphere some young chemists found stifling.[23]

In Elmer P. Kohler, a newly arrived professor of organic chemistry who in many respects was Richards's intellectual and temperamental opposite, Conant found an alternative source of inspiration. Indifferent to the scientific politics on which Richards thrived, Kohler derived pleasure from the lustful pursuit of whatever chemistry puzzles happened to distract him regardless of their intrinsic significance to the field, and from the injection of students and apprentices with his own infectious enthusiasm. Conant, who jumped at Kohler's invitation in 1912–13 to supervise students' lab work in the basic organic chemistry course, was rapidly ensnared by his pedagogical zest and tactical inventiveness, and found him more approachable than Richards as a personal and professional counselor. In a memoir of Kohler, Conant later affectionately depicted a man prone to "bivouac" in the laboratory, where he was "the happiest person in the entire world." One can sense Conant's own youthful delight in chemistry from his evocation of Kohler: "Only those who have seen him in his shirt sleeves, crystallizing and recrystallizing his precious materials on his own laboratory bench, have known the man; and only visitors to whom he explained the intricacies of the problem under study with the aid of pen and scratch paper have heard a great teacher at his best."[24]

By the end of his first semester, Conant felt confident enough that he had proven his chemistry proficiency to begin testing his mettle outside the lab, although he found only sporadic captivation in lecture halls once he had obtained the grades needed for a $300 sophomore scholarship. On the road to graduating with a Phi Beta Kappa in three years, Conant garnered respectable Bs while dabbling in Taussig's economics, French, the art and culture of the Italian Renaissance, and, especially, philosophy, the subject his mother had urged him to explore. Imbibing the spirit of William James's *Pragmatism*, published the year before he arrived, Conant took advantage of the opportunity to sign up for classes with two of the Philosophy Department's legends, George Santayana and George Herbert Palmer, and also seems to have caught a whiff of the ideas of Frederick Jackson Turner, the apostle of the frontier theory who came to Cambridge in 1912 to preach the virtues of the Midwest in American History.[25] Conant also received a pivotal boost toward a more historical approach to science in Chemistry 8, taught by Theodore Richards—a course Conant later described as a "highly exciting" year-long tour of physical chemistry's journey from alchemy to the latest advances in atomic theory.[26]

But what Conant recalled as his true liberal education came outside the lecture halls, beginning with his epic quest to join the *Harvard Crimson*, the daily student newspaper that requires would-be editors to undergo a demanding and occasionally demeaning initiation ritual known as the "comp"—short for "competence," but also for "competition"—prior to election. Several times a week during a two-month process, aspiring "compers" must write articles and submit them to the corrections, compliments, and criticisms (read: ridicule) of editors, write up nightly reports on their activities, and periodically perform menial tasks for the already anointed. At the four-week mark, the paper's staff votes whether to "cut or keep" compers, and a month later solemnly decides whether the survivors should be granted membership on the editorial board.

Neither talent nor class guaranteed success; the young FDR, though elected president of the *Crimson* his senior year, was cut the first time he comped, and Walter Lippmann and John Reed fled in disgust after being passed over, the latter complaining that "the aristocrats blackballed me."[27] A sampling of Conant's reports to senior editors conveys the flavor of his encounter with this competitive, socially charged enterprise:

At 11 o'clock I met an editor in the hall of Brooks House and received further directions. A. Beare '11 just then entered the hall and I read him the note with as much "friskiness" as I could. He seemed at first amused, then surprised and finally "peeved." He didn't say anything. I backed *out* with my thumb to my nose.

Sent to cover a Sunday sermon, Conant returned with a synopsis of a talk that reflected the influence of the late William James, whose *The Varieties of Religious Experience* was to strike a sympathetic chord with Conant's own nondogmatic religious inclinations:

Lord Melbourne early in the last century was indignant that religion should try to pervade personal affairs. Religion may be conceived as being either wholly an outward show or entirely a matter hidden in the brain. Both these suppositions are false because they are partial. Real religion is a deep inward feeling that is so forceful that it finds outward expression in words and deeds.[28]

Comping for "the Crime" gnaws at any undergraduate's class schedule, but it was an especially heavy burden for a chemistry major who actually *needed* to attend classes and labs, as opposed to, say, history or literature majors who could safely skip lectures and secure passing grades on the power of last-minute cramming. Trying out for the paper, Conant relates candidly in his memoirs, "nearly wrecked a half-year of work." In the spring of 1911, a month of "chasing *Crimson* hard," as he put in his diary, caused him to sleep through an English exam; nevertheless, he came tantalizingly close but failed to make the paper. Undaunted, he returned to the newspaper's offices in the basement of the Union the following fall to try again. His determination to comp twice, despite a heavy academic schedule and a tough defeat, testified to character traits, especially persistence and an ability to rebound from adversity, that served Conant well in later endeavors.[29]

The second time around, Conant also had some rough moments, as this sadistic, taunting note from an assignment editor (James Roosevelt) suggests:

Conant: You were badly scooped by the Yale News & all the city papers on Harvard entries in N.Y. meet. This makes it pretty glum for you, unless you can cover the five assignments Today in faultless style. You must also have 2 scoops in tonight's paper. There is plenty of space, so it is up to you.[30]

His labors finally found reward on Wednesday, January 17, 1912 — literally, a red-letter day. Customarily (and fastidiously) he noted in his diary weather, grades, and classes in gray pencil or black ink, but in fiery scarlet he wrote and circled these celebratory words: "Big Punch! AN EDITOR AT LAST."[31] For Conant, election to the paper meant more than the editor's privilege of being able to sign his initials — "JBC" — rather than full name in staff messages, or even the distinction of advancing to the executive board as assistant managing editor. It made him respectable in the Harvard universe outside the chemistry department.[32]

"What made all the effort worthwhile was the fact that success opened the doors to my election to a highly selective literary club, the Signet," Conant later wrote. "Here I found my general education."[33]

Here, too, Conant discovered an accessible pathway to respectability and acceptance in Harvard's caste-conscious environment. At the Signet, an invitation-only watering hole for faculty, students, and alumni to hobnob on an equal footing amid clinking glasses of sherry, stern oil portraits of the masters, and bookshelves groaning with classics, the affable, quick-witted, relaxed (at least outwardly) undergrad honed social skills, collected friends and acquaintances, and began to build a reputation as a chemist who felt equally at ease discussing politics, philosophy, literature, and other topics far removed from formulae and test tubes.

Though he was ignored by the "Institute of 1770," Conant widened his social cosmos again during sophomore year when he was tapped by the Delta Upsilon club, less pretentious than the Porcellian or the A.D. and a haven for less-well-off students. In the D.U.'s dingy, gloomy headquarters, Conant met future authors, lawyers, and businessmen he would turn to for advice, favors, and information for the rest of his life. The upperclassman who initiated Conant and recruited him to sell tickets to the club's all-male productions of Elizabethan dramas has described the club's upwardly mobile crowd of scholarship boys. "What a motley crew we seniors of 1912 were that year," recalled Clarence B. Randall, later a prominent businessman. "Not one of us was genuinely solvent, and most of us were on the Harvard dole together. There was Joe Kennedy, father of President Kennedy; Bob Benchley, who became America's favorite humorist; J. Gordon Gilkey, who went on to become one of the great Protestant preachers and religious leaders of our country; Bob Duncan, fund raiser extraordinary for educational institutions; and Oscar Haussermann, top-flight lawyer, civic leader, and humorous poet of Boston."[34]

It is pleasing to report, considering the somber and momentous events that lay ahead, that in between sweating chemistry courses and climbing the extracurricular social ladder, Conant also extracted some fun from college life. Preferring the company of *Crimson* or chemistry buddies to the gilded collegians who flouted their wealth and slept in the splendid comfort of Mt. Auburn Street digs, Conant gravitated toward ambitious, studious, non-Brahmin peers who specialized in science or literature. For two of his three college years, he lived in a ramshackle private boarding home at 5–7 Linden Street, off Harvard Square. Hooked up to electricity halfway through Conant's freshman year, the building was known wryly as "Mrs. Mooney's Pleasure Palace" in honor of the stark amenities Mrs. Mary E. Mooney supplied her tenants for their $160 a year. There Conant studied, let off steam, roomed with his erstwhile Roxbury Latin drama costar Charlie Crombie and made new friends such as the future novelist Marquand, a gangly small-town boy who attended Harvard on a chemistry scholarship and kept a green parrot who squawked personalized greetings to visitors ("Hello, boys!").

Despite comparatively shabby conditions, Marquand's biographer relates, the young men relished "the raffish Latin Quarter life of the rooming house and the first experience, always intoxicating, of personal freedom." At Friday night parties in Brattle Hall, Conant danced with "sub-debs" as part of a gang known as the "Baby Brats," and as an upperclassman "pursued the company of debutantes proper" in Boston. Putting his flair for experimentation to gratifying use, Conant served as the boardinghouse's chief prankster. His gags included jury-rigging a rubber tube, plucked from chem lab, from a punch bowl to the mouth of his sleeping roommate; organizing water-bag fights on the stairwells and duels with broomsticks and pillows; startling students who returned to the darkened building late at night by setting up a knight in armor on the third-floor landing; and devising with Marquand a game known as the "Two-Beer Dash," which put a competitive twist on the perennial undergraduate quest to circumvent Cambridge's puritanical drinking statutes. Taking advantage of the newly constructed subway line to downtown Boston, which replaced the above-ground electric trolley, contestants would sprint from dry Linden Street to wet Essex Street, gulp down two belts at the counter of an institution called the Holland Wine Company, and return. Besides strong legs and a sturdy stomach, the winner of Conant's evening track-and-field event required mastery of the fine arts of wheedling drinks from bartenders leery of serving underage students and selecting the best of several plausible alternative routes to complete the roundtrip in the shortest time.[35]

Marquand and Conant also ran another, less frivolous race — to transcend shyness and unfamiliarity with upper-crust social mores to earn with brains, initiative, and ingratiation the pedigree received as a birthright by more privileged Harvardians, such as the well-bred protagonist of Marquand's 1940 fictionalized portrait of the class of 1915, *H. M. Pulham, Esquire,* who instinctively recoiled if someone who was not born to society tried too hard to please. "There was nothing more undesirable back at Harvard than to be someone who 'sucked up,' " Pulham recalls. "You did not have to do it if you were the right sort of person."[36]

As a commoner at Mrs. Mooney's, Conant was hardly "the right sort." Yet Marquand soon came to feel a mixture of admiration and envy at his friend's ability to excel academically and socially while sacrificing neither grades nor self-respect, to be "brilliant without being grubby" and to "learn everything without the slightest damage to his poise and popularity." Not only could Conant come to the sartorial rescue by helping Marquand tie a white bow tie for a formal dance, but he made the *Crimson* while the fledgling author fell under the editors' axe, and then in the Signet Society charmed the literary and social elites whose shoulders Marquand so desperately sought to rub—all that, while steadily gaining a reputation as a chemistry *Wunderkind* as Marquand struggled for a B in Richards's physical chemistry course.[37]

By the time he was graduated from Harvard College in June 1913 and sped directly into a doctoral program in chemistry, Conant had laid a foundation for a solid future. As he was Richards's prodigy and Kohler's teaching assistant, heading for a double-barreled Ph.D., his scientific career appeared well headed. With more effort than he let on, he had methodically improved his writing, administrative, and social skills, cultivating an impressive roster of friends, ranging from ambitious chemistry grad students to an eclectic mix of nonscientists encountered at Mrs. Mooney's, the *Crimson,* Signet, and D.U. His spiraling personal trajectory, propelled by ambition and talent and boosted by receptive and interested teachers, also helped him to adopt broader philosophical attitudes, most importantly a deep belief in meritocratic ideals. In his college days, Conant already inclined toward the conviction that America should foster an equality of opportunity and social fluidity that would permit the talented to rise from modest roots as naturally as he had. By his sophomore year, the nineteen-year-old was already articulating some of the fundamental ideals of a "classless society," in the tradition of Jefferson and Tocqueville, that were to mark his future educational and political philosophy. His traits of open-mindedness and a willingness, nurtured in the lab, constantly to modify hypotheses from new data shine through a diary entry of a formative encounter in the summer of 1912. After attending a fraternity convention in Wisconsin, his first trip outside New England, he returned impressed by the midwestern students' "utilitarian broadness . . . and their ability to find solutions for problems rather than their exclusive scholastic knowledge of chemistry."

> We certainly have much to learn from their openness and general broadness of personality as well as their proper degree of earnestness, while they could well imbibe some of our academic and scientific spirit and possibly some of our appreciation of *culture,* i.e., the desire for an enjoying of things which are not in themselves materially fruitful or clearly useful.[38]

What he came to believe about the country applied no less to his school. A circle of student friends distinguished by sharp wits rather than refined manners or bottomless family allowances encouraged his instinctive view that Harvard needed to shed its self-imposed class and economic barriers and embrace instead a national mission and a more diverse student body.

In sum, the young century's prospect of accelerating changes in science, technology, and society gleamed with opportunity for the young man who entered Harvard College bursting with energy, ambitions, and talent, and who left it having added credentials, connections, and intellectual range. Conant had also changed personally—he had overcome shyness, grown more self-assured, started to learn his way around personages and institutions of power, whether the high-voltage *Crimson* or the chemistry department or the Signet. In later years, Conant occasionally took a rather cynical tone toward the value of an undergraduate education. Aboard a steamship heading toward Europe in 1941, he was pressed by an inquisitive Austrian baroness to explain, in simple English that she could understand, what people learned at college in the United States.

"It is," Conant declared, "a process of growing old for four years under the influence of so-called intellect."[39]

Life at blithe fin-de-siècle Harvard, however, had not yet forced Conant to face the graver life-and-death issues that would force him and his contemporaries to age even faster. "Never was College so exciting, or drunks so drunken, or the generous feelings of ardent youth so exalted," wrote Samuel Eliot Morison, "as in these last golden years before World War I."[40]

CHAPTER 3

"A Chemist's War"

Conant and World War I

1914–1918

Tell Bellamy that, as a true pacifist, I heartily approve of waging a vigorous war at this time.

— Letter to George L. Kelley, March 26, 1917

To me, the development of new and more effective gases seemed no more immoral than the manufacture of explosives and guns . . . I did not see in 1917, and do not see in 1968, why tearing a man's guts out by a high-explosive shell is to be preferred to maiming him by attacking his lungs or skin.

— My Several Lives

To the end of his days, whenever he "ticked off the dates of modern history" in his mind, Conant "almost always found myself starting off with a picture of that placid world which started to go to bits just when I graduated from college. . . . " A young man in a hurry, he had already completed a year's work toward his Ph.D. and was attending a graduate program at the Harvard Summer School in August 1914 when a young Bosnian nationalist named Gavrilo Princip aimed his pistol from a Sarajevo sidewalk and fired the shots that killed Archduke Franz Ferdinand of Austria and tipped the continent toward disaster. Conant's initial reaction to the war that soon raged across Europe was something close to smugness; the "poor European nations," he and his friends believed, "had fought each other for generations largely because the ambitions of their crowned heads required it. Americans knew better, so we thought. The war between France and England on one side and Germany and Austria on the other had nothing to do with us."[1]

Though he closely monitored news of the war, impressing visitors to the lab by chatting easily about the latest political, diplomatic, and military developments while performing experiments,[2] the doctoral candidate concentrated on his research. Under Kohler's influence, to which he later attributed many of his own methods as a teacher, tactical investigator, and problem-solver, Conant had by the time he finished his graduate studies in 1916 turned firmly from the physical chemistry of Richards to organic chemistry, although in a characteristic burst of energy he wrote a double Ph.D. dissertation that combined investigations in both branches, written under the supervision of both Kohler and Richards. And, even though both mentors shared a lofty disdain for applied, industrial chemistry, Conant glimpsed the future direction of his field. His grasp of a scientist's opportunities was widened after college graduation by a summer job with the Midvale Steel Company in Pennsylvania (he was invited there by a Harvard chemistry teacher who had become the firm's top chemist), and by a lecture he had heard given by a General Electric executive about the potential rewards of research in an industrial lab, which hinted at the opportunities for synthesizing cash from chemistry; this lure would lead Conant to a brief, sorrowful fling with entrepreneurship soon after obtaining his doctorate.[3]

But even while riveted to the lab he could not remain aloof from the furious debate that engulfed Cambridge over the conflagration overseas. As the first reports of German atrocities in Belgium and France aroused angry passions, Conant sided with a scientific minority who refused to join Harvard's overwhelming Anglophiliac majority. Motivated by admiration for the land that symbolized intellectual and academic achievement, and plain old "New England contrariness," the brash doctoral candidate became a "pro-German apologist . . . We were not pro-German, but we were highly critical of the emotional anti-German remarks of our professors."[4] As polite discourse dissolved and scholars "who had been bosom friends became vituperative enemies," Conant felt alienated, even despairing, as the emotional anti-German atmosphere enveloped even prewar champions of U.S.-German academic links such as Richards. He was appalled when Allied supporters at Harvard "snubbed and ostracized" professors of German descent and in some cases demanded their removal. "Separate worlds formed," Conant recalled later, and "soon ceased to communicate with each other by rational speech." Moreover, to take a position that failed to fall neatly into one camp or the other—as did the ambivalent Conant—risked incurring "a potent blast of hostile criticism from every side."[5]

The Germans' use of poison gas in April 1915 and sinking of the *Lusitania* the following month only sharpened the tense atmosphere in Cambridge. Until the United States' entry into the war two years later, an overwhelmingly pro-Allied Harvard "seethed with the stir-craziness of potential soldiers." Returning in 1915 from a teaching post at a western university where the fighting in Europe "seemed to the average student as unreal as the Wars of the Roses," Samuel Eliot Morison felt at Harvard as if "on the outskirts of battle." The Medical and Dental schools formed volunteer medical brigades whose members dispatched graphic accounts from the front, freshman dormitories became ROTC barracks, visiting French officers received a heroes' welcome, and hundreds of undergraduate and graduate students flocked to courses like "Military Science 1" and to a War Department officers summer training camp at Plattsburgh in upstate New York, an option personally commended to Harvard men by President Lowell and former President Roosevelt. Uniformed students toted rifles behind horse-drawn cavalry through Harvard Square, and the "sound of marching feet came dimly through the walls of the sanctum upstairs in the Harvard Union where we edited the Monthly," recalled John Dos Passos a half-century later. "When I graduated from college in 1916 the European War was the great national preoccupation. Teddy Roosevelt's boys were whooping it up for preparedness. Franco-British propaganda was beating the drums for American intervention. The professors were losing their minds; hating the Huns became a mania."[6]

Hundreds of youths, impatient to fight Germany or to witness the epic events of their generation, enlisted in the British or Canadian forces or as noncombatants in the volunteer medical and ambulance corps—an idealistic option that drew budding writers like cummings, Dos Passos, and Malcolm Cowley, as well as several of Conant's chemist friends. Even as late as 1916, however, Conant remained skeptical of the Allied cause and contemptuous of the martial fervor sweeping the country and campus. In that year's stormy presidential campaign, a *Crimson* straw poll found Harvard students 2-to-1 in favor of the more belligerent Charles Evans Hughes, but Conant abhorred the Hughes supporters' vilifying of President Wilson and favored the incumbent because he "kept us out of the war."[7]

The pull of events began to have some effect on Conant, however, as did the sight of friends and colleagues heading off to the front. He considered signing up for the ambulance corps, perhaps in combination with a postdoctoral fellowship in Zurich, but allowed himself to be talked out of the idea by horrified parents and teachers and was unwilling, in any case, to commit himself for the required year. Looking back a half-century later, he observed a bit testily if perhaps accurately, that for some students, volunteering for the medical services seemed less a sign of devotion to the Allied cause than "a manifestation of a desire to come dangerously close to a dangerous adventure without running much risk of becoming a casualty oneself."[8]

Largely immune to or inoculated against these fevers of patriotism, idealism, or *Wanderlust,* Conant sought a different role in the global drama: profiteer. After he finished his chemistry doctorate in the spring of 1916, his first impulse had been to fulfill the boyhood dream of studying with the masters in Germany—the "standard procedure" for an aspiring American chemist, he later recalled. "Most students went either to Berlin or to Munich, where the big scientists were. The University of Berlin was at its height then, and there were workshops and institutes galore. Berlin was a real intellectual center." With America not yet in the war, studying in Germany was still possible—and Conant received from Harvard in the spring of 1915 a John T. Kirkland Traveling Fellowship that gave him the means to do so—but the bloodbath made the prospect of a scientific apprenticeship in one of the major belligerents look, in Conant's dry understatement, "rather unpleasant."[9]

Instead, the scientist thought to study in neutral Switzerland, but then two friends and chemistry majors from the class of 1915, Chauncey C. Loomis and Stanley B. Pennock, an all-American guard on the champion 1914 Harvard football team, inveigled him to join a business venture designed to exploit war-induced shortages of certain chemicals traditionally procured from Europe. With the Allied blockade and U-boat warfare forcing industry to pay "fabulous prices," lucrative opportunities for chemists abounded. Loomis, Pennock, and Conant calculated, "in our ignorance," that "L.P.C. Laboratories" could with a relatively modest operation fabricate simple but scarce organic chemicals "in small batches and sell them without difficulty."[10]

Here was a pioneering enterprise, in Conant's words, "that appealed both to the scientific and the acquisitive instinct," as well as the challenge to "beat 'the Dutch' at their own game of manufacturing drugs and selling them at a fancy price."[11] A bit adrift after the rigorous dash to the doctorate, Conant (LPC's "director of research") intended to stay in business as long as the war lasted and build up a nest egg to shore up his finances for when he returned to academia—though not expected to "marry money" like their German counterparts, a young American chemist commencing a university career traditionally could count on little more than subsistence wages in the early stages. At Harvard, moreover, Conant had caught a tantalizing scent of the budding romance between U.S. chemistry and industry, as the number of industrial research labs multiplied and companies such as General Electric and Du Pont wooed academic scientists with promises of modern facilities, high salaries, and increased freedom to pursue research topics of intellectual as well as commercial interest. Plus, his summer job at Midvale Steel had yielded insight both into "the inner politics of a manufacturing plant" and the use of chemical reactions to catalyze profits.[12]

But LPC Labs' hopes of cashing in literally went up in flames. In the summer of 1916, Conant and his friends went to New York City, "bought a shack somewhere in Queens," and set up a pilot plant to produce benzoic acid, used as a preservative. Inexperienced in large-scale manufacturing, Conant and Loomis accidentally started a fire on a hot August morning that destroyed the small building. Unfazed, Pennock collected the insurance and rented a new headquarters in Newark, New Jersey; in an abandoned slaughterhouse. At this juncture, Conant received word from Harvard that, as a result of the sudden departure of Professor Roger Adams to the University of Illinois, a vacancy had unexpectedly opened up that fall to teach Chemistry 2, the basic organic chemistry course. His heart set on a Harvard career, Conant kept an interest in the fledgling company (rechristened Aromatic Chemical) but rushed back to Cambridge while his friends, armed with a revised blueprint, crossed the Hudson River to begin work on the new plant.

By mid-October the building at 344 Thomas Street was emanating foul odors from the copper mixing tanks of sulphur, chloride, bleaching powder, and other ingredients being combined and recombined in the search for the most efficient formula for benzoic acid. Then, on the day full production was to begin, disaster struck. On Monday afternoon, November 27, 1916, an explosion tore through the building, killing Pennock and two local hired hands, a mechanic, Samuel Welte, and a plumber, Max Stein, who were overcome by blast, fumes, and fire, their bodies charred almost beyond recognition as the conflagration set off new blasts that deterred firefighters from entering. Loomis, who had desperately tried to stop the fatal reaction when he noticed steam rushing from a gasket, was blown off a ladder, through a door and into a muddy ditch, his face and eyes scorched by corrosive acid and his clothes ablaze. Though temporarily blinded, he managed to save himself by rolling in the water and was soon released from the hospital. The factory, pulverized by concussions that shook buildings for several blocks around, lay in ruins.

Learning the news while lecturing in Boylston Hall at Harvard, Conant felt not only shock but guilt, stricken by the sense that, by not being present at the pilot plant's start-up, he had "deserted a post of danger." Loomis, in lengthy hospital-bed interviews reviewing the company's sad history, "his eyes still blood shot and half closed from the effects of the acid fumes," had politely kept his absent partner's name out of the newspapers. But Conant's sense of culpability in Pennock's death—not to mention the loss of profits— deepened when Loomis explained to his friend what had happened. The postmortem revealed flaws in the testing procedure that were, Conant wrote in his memoirs, "no one's fault except my own."[13]

Only a few scattered hints of the twenty-three-year-old's reaction to this traumatic event survive, and those that do testify to Conant's already considerable capacity to suppress emotional responses in favor of a pragmatic analysis of experiences, however disturbing, and to summon a stoic determination to press forward. "This tragic experience with applied chemistry should have discouraged me for a lifetime," he wrote in a rare burst of introspection in *My Several Lives*. "In fact it did not; within eighteen months I was to become involved again (as a chemist in military uniform) in developing a new manufacturing process for a certain chemical—this time a poison gas."[14]

By the rainy night of April 2, 1917, when President Wilson asked a thunderously cheering joint session of Congress for a declaration of war so that America could "make the world safe for democracy," Conant had finally fallen in step with public opinion after more than two years of wavering. Both the reluctant president and reluctant chemist had grudgingly yet, in the end, fully gone over the brink. The previous fall, his ill-fated "venture in free enterprise" behind him, Conant, busy with teaching, had kept a watchful eye on the fast-changing world situation. On Election Day in November 1916, he had gone to sleep gloomily expecting a Hughes victory but was thrilled the next morning when he walked to the new *Crimson* building on Plympton Street to read the late returns posted outside and discovered that California had given Wilson a narrow victory. During the next five months, however, such provocative events as Germany's announcement of unrestricted submarine warfare, the severing of U.S.–German diplomatic ties, the revelation of the Zimmerman telegram, and the U-boat sinkings of several American ships without warning and with heavy loss of life precipitated frenzied demands for belligerence. In late March 1917, with American entry all but inevitable, Conant canvassed his colleagues now working for the government for advice on how best to lend his services to the U.S. military effort and jocularly requested one contact to tell a mutual friend "that, as a true pacifist, I heartily approve of waging a vigorous war at this time."[15]

In *My Several Lives,* Conant renders his conversion from skeptic to hawk with more than a tinge of acerbity. "A whole series of incidents," he explains, "exploited by British and French propagandists, had swung the sympathy of the young as well as the old in Cambridge to the side of the Allies." With rather disarming frankness—indicative of the unusual candor present in the World War I chapter but nearly absent elsewhere[16]—he describes the night he learned of Wilson's speech to Congress. Reading the ticker tape at the Harvard Club, Conant felt "distress," not so much at the grim prospect of American boys going into combat or even at Wilson's betrayal of campaign promises to avoid involvement, but "because of the effect on my own personal plans." Having miraculously "gotten my foot on the bottom rung of the Harvard academic ladder," Conant was loath to see his prospects for quick advancement endangered. Yet, he realized, "Teaching chemistry was no place for a young man in wartime," and he would have to find some useful way to do his share when the academic year ended, though preferably without getting killed or jeopardizing his chances for tenure (it is hard to say which possibility disturbed him more). "It was going to be a period of painful choice," he remembers. "These highly personal considerations reinforced my lack of sympathy with the interventionist, pro-French, pro-British sentiment which had been building up in Cambridge. The spectacle of older men urging younger ones to fight seemed to me far from edifying."[17]

Edifying or not, emotions ran high at Harvard in the spring of 1917 after Congress voted the declaration of war. Exhilarated by the aroma of blood and the president's vaulting idealism, even the normally sardonic Harvard *Lampoon* radiated jingo and earnestness: "The United States has at last passed that brink upon which she has been hovering since the *Lusitania* disaster, and whatever she does now is done not as a cringing neutral but as an honorable co-worker in the cause of civilization. . . . She has regained her place among the nations of the world . . . waging glorious battle against an autocracy whose only doctrines are the doctrines of war and whose survival means unmitigated Hell on earth."[18] After the university held early exams and conferred special "war degrees," most students headed off to boot camp and, in many cases, then battle—375 were to be killed in the conflict.[19] Even normally aloof scientists who previously stood aside now heeded the call to duty.

Surrounded by such displays of valor—and friends, like John Marquand, catching trains to Plattsburgh—Conant felt that to await the draft's "long arm" would be "ignominious."[20] In one respect, Conant had an edge on most of his friends: of all the talents of wartime value to the government, expertise in chemistry was the most in demand.

World War I would go down in history as the "chemist's war," for reasons that became obvious to the world on April 22, 1915.[21] On that afternoon, after months of bloody trench warfare, French and Canadian soldiers at Ypres noticed a strange greenish yellow cloud heading in their direction across the no-man's-land from the German lines. What happened next shocked even hardened military observers:

> Following a heavy bombardment, the enemy attacked the French Division at about 5 p.m., using asphyxiating gases for the first time. Aircraft reported that at about 5 p.m. thick yellow smoke had been seen issuing from the German trenches between Langemarck and Bixschoote. What follows almost defied description. The effect of these poisonous gases was so virulent as to render the whole of the line held by the French Division mentioned above practically incapable of any action at all. It was at first impossible for anyone to realize what had actually happened. The smoke and fumes hid everything from sight, and hundreds of men were thrown into a comatose or dying condition, and within an hour the whole position had to be abandoned.[22]

The Germans' fifteen-minute attack, which shattered the Hague Conventions against poison gas warfare, stunned the Allies, who suffered more than 7,000 gas casualties of whom more than 5,000 died. Accustomed to dodging and returning the rat-tat-tat of machine guns, young men suddenly found their throats clogged by a gentle, silent breeze. A British officer recounted: "It is a hateful and terrible sensation to be *choked* and suffocated and unable to get breath: a casualty from gun fire may be dying from his wounds, but they don't give him the sensation that his life is being strangled out of him." To many, the horror of this eerie, terrifying spectacle aroused a revulsion eclipsing by its novelty even the meat grinder already well on its way to butchering a generation. Soon, despite claims by supporters that it caused lower mortality rates than other weapons and was thus more humane,[23] gas warfare would come to symbolize the depths to which science and technology had dragged humanity, an image captured in George Grosz's 1920s painting of Christ on the cross wearing a gas mask. The addition of a dystopic whiff of H. G. Wells to an already corpse-littered landscape out of Hieronymus Bosch reminded some of a passage from Lord Byron's "The Destruction of Sennacherib":

For the Angel of Death spread his winds on the blast,
And breathed in the face of the foe as he pass'd.

It quickly became known that among those responsible for the introduction of gas warfare by Germany were some of the legendary figures of German chemistry whom Conant so admired. With few exceptions, they, too, had joined August 1914's paroxysm of nationalism, hatred, bloodlust, and militarism. Even in cosmopolitan Berlin, home of the prestigious new Kaiser Wilhelm Society for the Advancement of Science, the vast majority of scientists (Albert Einstein notably not among them) loyally, often fanatically, raced to the front of the "war of intellectuals," the *Krieg der Geister,* even as much of the rest of the world recoiled from Germany's raids into Belgium and France. In a gesture that alienated foreign colleagues in the United States as well as in Britain and France, ninety-three leading German intellectuals issued a shrill manifesto "to protest before the whole civilized world against the calumnies and lies with which our enemies are striving to besmirch Germany's undefiled cause." In Berlin's elegant suburb of Dahlem, gas research found a warm welcome at the Kaiser Wilhelm Institute for Physical Chemistry and Electrochemistry, which bulged with present and future Nobel laureates— Fritz Haber, Walther Nernst, Otto Hahn, James Franck, and Richard Willstätter all donned uniforms and participated in war work. Their leader was the institute's director, Haber, who choreographed the chlorine attack at Ypres and administered its poison-gas research program for the *Oberste Heeresleitung,* the German military supreme high command.[24] Fritz Stern has described the motives of this talented, ambitious, zealously patriotic, converted Jew whose devotion to the German state would later be repaid by the Nazis with harassment that forced him into exile:

> Like others later, he was a scientist who under the pressures of war developed a new weapon, untroubled by its consequences, anticipatable and unanticipatable. Haber was above all concerned with the effectiveness of the new weapon; science, he once said, belonged to humanity in peacetime and to the fatherland in war. He looked for a weapon that would break the decimating stalemate, that would bring an early, victorious end.[25]

But chemical warfare failed to grant Germany a fast victory. After the initial shock, the British and French urgently fashioned "respirators" capable of blocking out the toxic vapors. Inevitably, the Germans pressed to design more potent gases that would penetrate their enemies' masks, and so the race was on. The British and French also fully mobilized their chemists to develop more advanced equipment: masks for defense, new gases and delivery systems for attack. From the basic building blocks of chlorine and the more toxic phosgene, initially the most effective agents, German and Allied scientists (usually afterwards) frantically concocted a panoply of molecular compounds whose sinister categories testified to their inventors' creativity: as well as mutilating the lungs and bloodstream through inhalation, lachrimators stung the eyes, vesicants produced blisters, sternutatories induced sneezing, "vomiting gas" caused nausea. Between mid-1915 and mid-1917, both sides desperately tried to overcome defenses through tactical surprise and technical innovation; but after the stunning success at Ypres, the Germans achieved diminishing results from cloud gas attacks, cylinders and howitzer shells, and by the end of 1916 improvements in British gas masks such as the Black Veil Respirator seemed to put a ceiling on gas's military effectiveness, even in support of conventional weapons. Rather than give up, however, Haber and the Kaiser Wilhelm Gesellschaft chemists redoubled their efforts, and in early 1917 battle-tested several new compounds, refined delivery methods using lethal shells, and expectantly looked forward to introducing a new gas thought to be the most murderous yet.[26]

Despite the wide publicity accorded poison gas warfare, the U.S. government in its long period of official neutrality had responded only fitfully to what appeared to many to be a revolutionary development in warfare. Recalling this period decades later, Conant liked to tell the story, possibly apocryphal, of a senior American chemist who in 1916 approached Wilson's secretary of war, Newton D. Baker, to offer his colleagues' aid for the national defense. A day later, Baker supposedly called back to say thank you very much, but the help "would be unnecessary because on looking into the matter he found the War Department already had *a* chemist."[27] Conant's anecdote overstated the case at least slightly; in 1915–16 the Wilson administration did move quietly to draw American scientists closer to their government in the interests of military preparedness, collaborating with the National Academy of Sciences and its activist foreign secretary, the astronomer George Ellery Hale, to create the quasi-governmental National Research Council for the express purpose of spurring pure and applied research to promote "the national security and welfare."[28]

Yet these tentative steps led to few practical results, and the rapid sequence of events leading to U.S. belligerence left Washington scrambling to catch up with an adversary that had been operating at full throttle for well over two years. Between the first German gas attack at Ypres and America's entry into the war, reports the most thorough student of this story, "there was practically no preparation for chemical warfare by the War Department." As of April 1917 the army had "no gas masks, no supply of offensive chemicals, and its troops had received no gas training." Suddenly faced with the need for crash development of chemical warfare before it had conducted even rudimentary studies of the problem, the government and military sent out an SOS to the nation's chemists.[29]

Restlessly observing these events from Harvard, Conant determined that he could not indefinitely stand aside. As early as February 1917, his profes-

sional organization, the American Chemical Society, motivated by both patriotic devotion and an awareness that the federal government's support for
science was about to take a significant leap, had enthusiastically offered its
services for the coming conflict.[30] Eager to participate in the chemists' mobilization but uncertain how, a week before Wilson's April 2 address Conant
sought advice from a senior colleague: "I have been wondering personally
whether if war comes (it seems inevitable now) I should enlist myself in the
army or navy," he wrote, correctly anticipating that "the trained chemists will
be more useful in connection with industrial military training than by fighting
themselves."[31] In putting his prodigious abilities at the state's disposal, Conant
merely followed the example of his colleagues, many of whom were already
working on war-related projects for the government, the armed forces, or
private industry. "The Chemistry Department," Harvard's quasi-official historian records, "notably Professor James B. Conant, became practically a
section of the War Department, producing masks for our troops and poison
gas for those of the enemy."[32]

For several months, however, Conant vacillated over which route to take
to the conflict. Deciding at the end of the spring term that the Bureau of
Chemistry was "the best place for me during the war," he went to Washington
in June and spent a few months working on matters "only remotely related to
the war" such as fabricating a drug formerly imported from Germany.[33] But
his attention, and that of the world, was soon forcefully redirected toward
chemical warfare on July 12, 1917, when Germany shocked the Allies by
effectively unleashing mustard gas against the French at Ypres. Upward of
50,000 artillery shells rained through the warm night, making a "plop-like
sound" when they burst and spreading vapors that caused thousands of
casualties — suppurating blisters, blindness, and bronchitis, among many other
ailments. Over the next few weeks of mustard-gas shelling, the British alone
suffered more than 14,000 casualties.[34]

The last and most acute phase of the chemical war had begun. Mustard
gas, a viscous liquid five times as toxic as phosgene and "an almost perfect
battle gas," for the first time promised to deliver concrete military benefits.
Quickly recognized as "the most powerful casualty producing agent yet
devised," even minute traces of mustard gas could insinuate clothing, including rubber boots and gloves, to incapacitate victims. Though a smaller proportion of soldiers were killed by them than by previously used chemicals,
mustard gas and a series of arsenic-based compounds introduced by Germany
in the war's final sixteen months sent Allied casualty totals soaring, damaged
morale, and imposed a heavy burden on medical resources: Britain sustained
160,970 gas casualties between July 1917 and November 1918, including
4,167 killed, compared to 20,013 wounded and 1,895 dead from gas in the
prior two and a half years; American infantry, arriving as the chemical
fighting hit its most intense stage, also incurred disproportionately high gas
casualties. By rendering the battlefield uninhabitable for six to twenty-four

hours, moreover, the Germans were able to employ the new vapors defensively to stall Allied advances.[35]

With winning the poison gas competition now an unsurpassed national priority, Conant thought of enlisting as an army NCO in a unit near the front in order to help make gas masks, the shortage of which was generating criticism. But elder colleagues quickly steered him away from this potentially risky notion. "You're crazy!" exclaimed James F. Norris, an MIT professor of organic chemistry, arguing that Conant could do more for his country (and himself) by synthesizing offensive poisons at home.[36]

The encounter with Norris, an old acquaintance from Cambridge, had important consequences. In June 1917, Norris had left MIT to become director of chemical research for the federal Bureau of Mines, to which had fallen chief responsibility for poison gas work by virtue of prior experience dealing with hazardous respiratory conditions, and he was actively recruiting for start-up operations in the fall. Spotting a likely prospect, "on the spot" he offered Conant a job as the leader of a research team that was soon to be installed at American University.[37] Conant accepted, attracted by the challenge and by the nearby presence of numerous close associates; a leading organizer of the U.S. chemical warfare effort in Washington was his friend and adviser E. P. Kohler.

It is not known whether Conant hesitated before jumping at Norris's offer, but once he did he never looked back. For the duration of the war he threw himself into the task of producing poison gases, confronting for the first time the moral quandaries involved in a scientist's participation in constructing deadly weapons rather than advancing knowledge. Contemporary documents contain few clues to Conant's inner feelings, but his actions suggest that he resolved any qualms with as little equivocation as did Haber in Germany; the morality of poison gas, he recalled later, was "rarely" addressed — after all, the Germans had used it first — and once he had thrown in his lot with the Allied cause he displayed little evident concern about the means employed to achieve victory.[38]

Conant's first stop was on the northwestern outskirts of Washington, where American University classrooms were being hurriedly retooled into the U.S. government's central gas warfare research laboratories. Employing more than 1,700 chemists, the project there was not only the highest priority research effort of the war but the largest federal scientific research project yet undertaken. Operating first under the civilian authority of the Bureau of Mines, then as a branch of the War Department's newly created Chemical Warfare Service after June 1918, the American University staff assembled hundreds of top-flight academic chemists from around the nation, including many of Conant's Cambridge colleagues — not only did Norris and Kohler have key positions overseeing offensive poison gas research, but another Harvard chemist, Arthur B. Lamb, headed the defensive section. By the war's end the scientists had occupied sixty buildings on the campus and tested the debilitating effects of more than 1,600 compounds on a kennel of unfortunate mice, dogs, and other animals, leading to the production of several lethal gases for use on humans. On the social level, they created a close-knit community that boasted "dances, a glee club, and basketball and baseball leagues," and forged professional contacts and friendships that endured long beyond the war.[39]

On September 22, 1917, Conant set to work on mustard gas research; commissioned a lieutenant in the Sanitary Corps, he was put in charge of an organic chemistry group that would become known as Organic Research Unit No. 1 of American University's Offense Research Section. He labored in a partially converted classroom building called Ohio Hall under working conditions distinctly inferior to those he had left behind at Harvard. "None of the windows were glazed, no ring-stands were available and condensers had to be hung by strings to shelves," an official report relates. "There was no heat in the Ohio building and the drafts in the hoods were uncontrollable." Nevertheless Conant and his men dove into their work "with enthusiasm," according to one account, and with strong motivation: German use of mustard gas was exponentially raising casualties, and had been the prime topic at the just-concluded Inter-Allied Gas Conference, meeting in Paris on September 17–19, which concluded that a crash program was needed to match and if possible overtake the enemy's new advance.[40]

Getting the United States into the mustard gas business was, in fact, Conant's first priority. And after collating reports from the front and from researchers at U.S. and British universities and comparing various chemical combinations, by mid-March 1918 his team had come up with a usable formula for high-yield mustard gas synthesis suitable for large-scale plant production. Construction of a plant at Edgewood Arsenal along the Chesapeake River soon began, and in June the Allies first employed mustard gas against the Germans; thirty tons a day were being pumped out when the armistice stopped the fighting.[41]

Long before then, however, Conant had moved on to new and more deadly assignments. Hoping to trump the Germans' vapor, the army desperately tried to develop a noxious fume with far more toxicity and military utility. Soon a likely candidate emerged: lewisite, dichloro (2-chlorovinyl) arsine, an oily, amber gas with "the fragrance of geranium blossoms" or putrid fruit but with an arsenic base designed to burn skin on contact. Unlike mustard gas, which took several hours to incapacitate victims and rendered battlefields uninhabitable for as long as a day, lewisite was more lethal and yet dissipated more quickly. It would serve, military commanders hoped, more effectively for offensive, advancing thrusts. In May 1918, Conant drew the assignment of investigating the feasibility of manufacturing the substance, named after its discoverer, Winford Lee Lewis, a Northwestern University chemist working for the army at Catholic University. By July 12, Conant's unit had successfully tested a small-scale plant, working under intense pressure to produce fast results despite dangerous conditions: "Pipes would frequently leak or vats would boil over. A vast tub of soapsuds awaited the frenzied plunges of men on whom the horrid stuff had settled."[42] A "serious explosion of the still" caused no serious casualties but aroused concern about safety, and once Conant's experiments seemed to support lewisite's adaptability for battlefield use, the research station's authorities quickly transferred the project from Washington to a more secure location for large-scale manufacture.

On July 20, the Chemical Warfare Service promoted Conant to major and immediately ordered the blue-eyed, mild-mannered twenty-five-year-old officer to board a train to Cleveland to supervise a top-secret project to mass-produce lewisite, also known by the code name of G-34. Of the hundreds of personnel to be involved, Conant was one of a handful of chemists who actually knew the details of the plant's mission. Before he left, senior chemists had coached him on the art of leadership, urging him to remember to keep a firm voice and to conceal doubts in order to project confidence and keep from undermining morale. It would have been natural for Conant to feel a sense of pride and self-importance in the mission he had been asked to undertake; now in uniform, having shot quickly from first lieutenant to captain to major, he imagined turning lewisite into "the great American gas which would win the war."[43]

Arriving in Cleveland, he hurried to a suburb where the army had hastily commandeered an auto factory (the Ben Hur Motor Company) that he would soon know as the "mouse trap"—because under the tight regime of secrecy those who entered did so with the knowledge that they would not emerge until the war had ended. Conant worked with a score of officers and five hundred soldier-scientists in a barracks-like stockade, guarded by a high wire fence, armed soldiers, and a Klaxon horn alarm system, their correspondence so strictly censored that the name of the plant's town, Willoughby, could not be mentioned. His address was a post office box—Lock Drawer 426, Cleveland. With gas masks, a squadron of firemen, and decontamination equipment ready to respond to an accident, by war's end the eleven-acre plant was churning out more than ten tons a day of the poison, the tiniest exposure to which was said to cause "intolerable agony and death after a few hours." For shipment to the European front, the gas was packed into 155-mm artillery shells and 350–400 aerial bombs. "Perhaps as much as any other person except the discoverer of the gas himself," concludes one historian, "Conant was responsible for the transition from the minuscule production of a few drops of Lewisite in the laboratory to quantities that could annihilate many people."[44]

Although the fighting ended in November 1918 before lewisite could be tested against the enemy—"A shipment was en route to Europe when the Armistice was signed," it was reported, "and the dangerous cargo was dumped into the sea"[45]—Conant's work as both scientist and administrator earned accolades from his military superiors. For accelerating "G-34" output two months ahead of schedule, Major Conant received a "Commendation for Unusual Service" from the director of the Chemical Warfare Service, who praised him for completing his "most exacting and hazardous" duties in a manner that was "all that could be desired."[46] Best of all, after the disaster that killed Pennock, Conant ended the project without a single fatal mishap.

Conant's wartime experience in Washington and Willoughby burnished new skills, prospects, and ambitions that would follow him as chemist, Harvard president, and World War II weapons administrator. It put him in touch with movers and shakers in science, business, the armed forces, and politics all over the country, exposed him to the possibilities of applied research and to the methods and tactics of secret wartime scientific adminis-tration and research. As the person responsible for a vital project, he experi-enced "both the frustrations and the satisfactions of a leader and the excitement which goes with the making of decisions," as he put it. Working at breakneck speed with fellow scientists and military officers to devise weapons of mass destruction under conditions of the tightest possible secrecy, Conant in effect lived through a low-tech preview of Los Alamos.[47]

"We were not soldiers," he said subsequently. "We were chemists dressed up as officers."[48] But, though relieved when the armistice freed him to return to civilian life, Conant had fully dedicated himself to the "highly unattractive task of producing poisons" for as long as it was deemed necessary. He is reported to have considered his job as primarily a "chemical challenge," but exhorted his charges with the words, "the fields of France look greener every day."[49] In *My Several Lives* he employed cold logic to defend the philosophy behind his willingness to devote his talents to a form of warfare subsequently outlawed by international convention. "To me, the development of new and more gases seemed no more immoral than the manufacture of explosives and guns," he wrote. "I did not see in 1917, and do not see in 1968, why tearing a man's guts out by a high-explosive shell is to be preferred to maiming him by attacking his lungs or skin."[50] Grudgingly, he conceded the immorality of using poison gas against soldiers in locales where breezes might waft it to adjacent civilian areas, but this argument struck him as "old-fashioned," for it assumed that those employing the weapon did not *want* to kill civilians. Conant's World War I actions presaged a far more significant role in a conflict during which that assumption no longer applied.

CHAPTER 4

"A Restless Soul"

Professor of Chemistry

1919–1933

My wife has more than once reminded me of a conversation shortly after we had become engaged. Looking into the distant future, I said that I had three ambitions. The first was to become the leading organic chemist in the United States; after that I would like to be president of Harvard; and after that, a Cabinet member, perhaps Secretary of the Interior. . . . I did not contemplate staying with chemistry for a lifetime. Even my administrative targets were those not of a committed man but a restless soul.   —*My Several Lives*

Looking back, these seem to have been the best years of my life.
                                                                —*My Several Lives*

World War I gave Conant, like many other American chemists, a taste of power, and he liked it. "Like the proverbial doughboys who found it hard to go back to the farm, so some scientists found it hard to return to the routine of classes and the narrow horizons of small-scale academic research after the excitement of wartime Washington," John W. Servos has written. "Their understanding of the scientists' role in American society had changed, as had the scope of their ambitions."[1]

While the war had in a general sense "greatly multiplied and strengthened the filaments connecting American science to American society," in Servos's words, more than any other field chemistry had been the prime mover and heir of this transformation. In contrast to World War II, when the most dramatic advances (radar, the atom bomb) were made by physicists, World War I spotlighted chemistry's importance to American society, security, and industry. "During the 1920s, a period of boom and prosperity for the most part, all branches of the natural sciences flourished," Conant later recounted. "But I think it was perhaps the chemists who led the way because of the impact of World War I on the industry of the country and on the actual carrying out of combat operations." While individual activities such as producing poison gas drew scorn as well as praise, from the standpoint of professional status the important thing was that chemistry's importance to society as a whole had been spectacularly demonstrated. When the war ended, the young chemists who had taken leading positions in the Chemical Warfare Service "were more ambitious in regard to research than had been their immediate predecessors"—and soon began courting, and found themselves courted by, a booming chemical industry that scoured universities for full- or part-time help from chemists to consolidate new inroads into markets for products, such as dyes and drugs, that been prewar German monopolies. Already prospering on the eve of battle, industrial chemistry mushroomed in its aftermath, yielding new opportunities for research, moneymaking, and career advancement in and out of the ivory tower.[2]

A full-fledged participant in this transformation, Conant returned to Harvard after demobilization—his appointment as an assistant professor of chemistry began on September 1, 1919—with inflated long-range goals that not only reflected but exceeded his field's new sense of ascendancy. His fatal brush with the hazards of free enterprise had soured him from serious consideration of a job with industry. Yet, for the first time, he imagined a life beyond the lab, and "cherished a carefully hidden ambition to try my wings someday in other fields than the scientific."[3] And in 1920, the twenty-seven-year-old bachelor also received inspiration to reach for a new dimension in his personal life.

A few years earlier, while finishing his doctorate, Conant had from time to time dined at the dignified Follen Street house of his mentor, Theodore Richards, absorbing the gossip and *haute* manners and conversation, and helping with the dishes like many a graduate student before and since. At one such Sunday evening meal in 1916 he had met the great man's eighteen-year-old daughter, Grace ("Patty") Thayer Richards, a shy, bookish young woman enamored of art, literature, and poetry. Patty Richards as a child had enjoyed the advantages and disadvantages of a famous faculty father and a cultured but inhibited Victorian household. Her mother, Miriam Thayer Richards, the daughter of a Harvard Divinity School professor, suffered from "nervous prostration" all her life, symptomatic of the neurasthenia found among so many upper-class intellectuals and litterateurs of the turn-of-the-century.[4] In the "refined," taut, pressure-cooker atmosphere of the Richards household, Patty inherited some of that psychic instability, along with a passion for art and finery that had her filling journals with flowery poetry, essays, and literary quotations before she was ten. For Patty, growing up in a family of social, artistic, and scientific overachievers—a famous landscape painter and a renowned biblical scholar for grandfathers, a Nobel Prize–winning father, two talented, ambitious brothers—seems to have created a sense of privilege and a suffocating presumption that stratospheric accomplishment must be achieved, along with an insecurity that was exacerbated by concerns about her appearance, health, and ungainliness (she hated the name "Grace" for this reason, according to relatives).[5] Though she never completed high school, after graduating from the exclusive Misses May's finishing school (with its optimistic motto of *De Mieux en Mieux* —"better and better"), the dark-haired Richards daughter joined a "sewing circle" and studied art history at the Boston Museum of Fine Arts, supplementing her knowledge of French and German—the latter enhanced by a childhood tour with her father of German universities, the trip Jim Conant had dreamed of since childhood. Though no scientist herself, Patty Richards's easy familiarity with the mystique radiating from chemistry and Germany gave her the surest conceivable entrée to her suitor's heart and mind.[6]

During the summer of 1920, Conant was reminded of this constellation of qualities during a visit to the Richardses' summer home at Seal Harbor, on Mount Desert Island off the Maine coast. Details of the months of determined courtship that ensued are skimpy—in part because Patty later ripped out the relevant pages of her diary—but the evidence that survives hints at both strong feelings and last-minute doubts. Theodore Richards learned of his daughter's intention to marry his junior colleague on September 20, less than a month after Conant's stay at Seal Harbor, and the couple made the engagement official on October 22; family lore recalls the suitor purchasing an engagement ring that took years to pay off at ten dollars a month. One finds a playful letter from Patty, sprinkled with French idioms as an "anticipatory hint" of their planned European honeymoon ("Very educational, and très chic!"):

> Much love, dear, accompanies and weighs down this letter. Much love plays about your room all the time, and keeps undulating in wireless waves to you from me. Oh, darling Jim, metaphors won't tell you anything of how much you mean to me. You must read between every line all the tender affection you can imagine, dearest,—it's yours, from
>
> Your
> Patty[7]

"B.'s tenderness never-to-be-forgotten," Patty confided to her diary after a "heavenly hour together" with her "Bryant" at a weekend rendezvous in New York City. Yet, at the same time, only a few weeks before their wedding, the bride-to-be wrote in her journal that she remained in a "half convinced state," haunted by unspecified "complexes" about her prospective husband.[8] But whatever doubts were soon overcome, and she and Conant exchanged vows in a small, hastily arranged ceremony in Harvard's Appleton Chapel on Sunday afternoon, April 17, 1921, a month after the groom's twenty-eighth birthday. Owing to the illness of Patty's mother, who needed exploratory surgery for a tumor that turned out to be benign, the wedding took place several weeks earlier than planned, in the presence of only the immediate families and wedding party. "Two people were never more fitly joined," one friend later rhapsodized. "Her grace and gifts of heart and mind, though uniquely her own, equalled his; their natures interwove."[9]

Nevertheless, Conant's leaden account of the romance in *My Several Lives,* included only grudgingly after an editor insisted that he account for the sudden presence of his wife in the narrative ("But, Dr. Conant, you never got *married!*"), emits the scent of a lawyer making a case to a dubious jury rather than the heady bouquet of a youthful couple dizzy with passion. "In the fall of 1920, I persuaded Grace Thayer Richards to agree to marry me," he writes, noting that to his prospective (and apparently hard-bargaining) wife the inducement of a European honeymoon was "the best of my arguments."[10]

It would be unkind to suggest that Conant courted and then married his boss's daughter to advance his career. Yet such a union was exceedingly astute in terms of academic politics — Conant's "matrimonial model" as well as scientific idol, Theodore Richards, had himself married the daughter of an eminent Harvard professor — as a junior faculty member and in line with the German tradition of fledgling academic scientists marrying for money and stature. It is, moreover, hard to conceive of his falling madly in love with a woman who his calculating mind might suspect would one day prove a social or emotional burden — the favored motif of many a novel of the Harvard or Boston elite in which a protagonist must choose between a "safe" spouse or an enticing outsider. In fact, however, vague family memories do recall a prior sweetheart, encountered in Cambridge during college or graduate school, whom Conant asked to marry. She reportedly said no, after which the rising scientist married Patty Richards "on the rebound" as a sensible alternative.[11]

Undoubtedly enhancing her appeal as a companion and spouse, as Conant surely recognized, Patty Richards possessed intellectual and social skills that figured to benefit the soaring private ambitions he divulged to her soon after they were engaged. Confessing the dreams of a "restless soul," he told his fiancée that he aimed to be, first, the country's leading organic chemist; second, president of Harvard; and third, "a Cabinet member."[12] The interesting thing about these vaulting aspirations, as Conant writes in his memoirs after his wife reminded him of the conversation, was that in 1920 he was already envisioning quitting chemistry, rather than emulating his father-in-law's lifetime quest for a Nobel Prize. They may also have been part of his campaign to convince the somewhat dubious Richards clan, accustomed to the genteel, moneyed pursuit of higher arts, that they were not making a mistake by allowing Patty to marry someone from the other side of the tracks, whose father was engaged in such grubby, moneymaking occupations as engraving and real estate.[13] Conant's early ambitions are also notable because, ultimately, he nearly achieved and in some ways surpassed them.

Before tackling this grandiose tripartite agenda Conant had some immediate priorities to take care of, namely, starting a family and establishing his stature as a top-flight chemist. First came the promised honeymoon, a trip that like many to come mingled sightseeing with professional activities and political reconnaissance. In June 1921, the newlyweds sailed for England, and a "young man's enthusiasm for Europe" suffuses the bubbly letters Conant mailed home to his family. Dropping in on chemistry departments at Oxford and other English universities, sightseeing along the craggy Scottish coast, along the Seine in Paris, in the Swiss Alps and the Italian lake country, the young couple clearly had a charming time, as Patty Conant escorted her husband to museums and churches in Florence and tested out her schoolgirl French in Paris and Belgium. Only one disappointment marred their excursion to post-Versailles Europe — the cloud of suspicion still hovering over Germany. Dissuaded by the chaotic political situation from visiting the land of scientific icons, Conant sampled the bitter residue of the "Great War" on the littered battlefields and wrecked buildings of France, driving along "Hill 108" near Rheims and finding (Patty recorded in her diary) "a blinding white chaos, lumps of clay and pits made by huge mine-explosions . . . incredibly devastated wild jungles which were once fields — barbed wire trenches now overgrown, gun-emplacements concealed, dead trees, — desolating when one thinks of the exquisite neatness & beauty of French farms." He also felt the lingering hostility at an international chemistry conference in Brussels, which was dominated by the victorious Allies, principally the French, who excluded German and Austrian participants, since (as Conant recalled) "all their scientists were considered to be tainted with war guilt and not fit to attend international meetings." This breach of science's fraternal traditions, symptomatic of the political divisions that emerged even more forcefully later in the century, appalled Conant but hardly prevented him from enjoying the sessions and merchandising his new brainchild — a series of reports known as *Organic Syntheses* that emerged from the "informal elite" of chemists who had worked together during the war — with the help of his wife's French.[14]

On his return to Cambridge, Conant and his wife moved into a modest house in the Shady Hill section of Cambridge, produced two sons — in May 1923 James Richards Conant was born, followed in July 1926 by Theodore Richards Conant — and settled into the routines of academic life. Gushing to her mother about "dear old Jim . . . the perfect husband, who is so devoted to me that it almost frightens me sometimes when I think what I have to live up to," Patty raised the boys (and endured the traumas and disappointments of several miscarriages), fussed over the always daunting travails of dealing with maids and running a household, and leapt into the high-intensity social obstacle course set for Harvard faculty wives. Joining the "Newcomers' Club," she was not above a bit of snobbery: gritting her teeth one day, she resolved to befriend the wife of a young English Ph.D. student from Indiana. "I in my virtue asked to come and see her in order to do my bit as a Harvard lady," Patty told her mother. "She lives right round the corner from us, I discovered — conveniently near for me. I hope, however, not so near that we'll see too much of her!"[15]

Her husband, meanwhile, embarked on a high-speed highway to tenure; letters from Patty describe a driven young scientist devoted to his work despite his wife's "schemes" to distract him with literature. While relishing "short draughts" of Shakespeare before and after meals, Patty reported to her mother, Conant also brought his work home — "we're all thriving. Jim seems very well indeed. . . . Jim and I are reading proofs together in the evenings. It's spicey matter—'520 gr. at 230°, yielding 2½ centimeters'—that sort of thing! We're living well on apples we collected at Duxbury."[16]

And nothing less than tenure at Harvard would do. At the end of the war, Conant had been wined and dined by the University of Chicago, but turned down a handsome offer in favor of a humble assistant professorship in Cambridge. "It is a severe blow to me, . . . to the University of Chicago, and to the West at large," a disappointed suitor chided, "that you are so rockbound in your provinciality as to insist on Boston in spite of anything and everything."[17]

Taking his place in Boylston Hall, he soon won a reputation as a popular enough teacher, employing the eye-catching techniques gleaned from Black and Kohler to set off the occasional classroom explosion or to startle students by flinging a raw egg dipped in solution against the wall to show the solidification of albumen.

But Conant's heart and soul went into his research, a sense of priorities which foreshadowed the emphasis he would place as Harvard president on scholarship over undergraduate tutoring. "I'm a slave driver," he told a prospective doctoral candidate, who insisted that in fact Conant disdained a "boss-servant relationship" with his research assistants and relied principally on inspiring maximum results by "impressing co-workers with his own work, not by raising the axe over them." Even when he was a chemistry professor, this former student recalled, Conant's impersonal, unsentimental, "cold logical approach" enabled him to take difficult decisions crisply and to focus his energies on the basis of a set of clearly laid out criteria.[18] That sort of single-minded dedication to the task at hand is evident in an anecdote from the early twenties. Like all faculty members in the Lowell era, Conant was required to advise undergraduates and review and approve their programs of study. One night, so the story goes, the chemist was hunched over his test tubes when an advisee walked into the lab. Years later, the young man recalled "how Conant, without ever removing his eye from the test tube, groped with one hand for a pencil, felt for the card, signed it and pushed it away, never once looking at it or the student."[19]

Such interruptions did not slow Conant much, and he racked up a lustrous *curriculum vitae* that won him international respect in physical and organic chemistry and nearly every possible award short of a Nobel prize. Aided by what some colleagues admiringly termed "scientific imagination," a gift for "intuitive guessing" and peering "into those shadowy regions where facts are missing and progress is made by groping," Conant conducted pathbreaking researches on a broad front, winning special acclaim for his analyses of chlorophyll and hemoglobin. In the years 1916 to 1933 he wrote or coauthored five chemistry textbooks (including the widely used *Practical Chemistry,* written with his Roxbury Latin mentor N. Henry Black), as well as scores (117 by one count) of journal articles.[20] A technical summary of his accomplishments by two colleagues gives the lay reader some sense of the breadth of his studies:

> Conant achieved an international reputation in both natural products chemistry and in physical-organic chemistry. In his research, he maintained a double-pronged approach that reflected his training with both Kohler and Richards. Although he took greatest pride in his research on natural products, his physical organic chemistry showed the most originality. He spanned the whole spectrum of the field, participating in all the areas of importance and anticipating many discoveries to come. He developed the ideas of superacidity, of measurements of the acid strengths of extremely weak acids, of acid and base catalysis in non-aqueous solvents, and of structure-reactivity series; he contributed to the chemistry of free radicals and steric effects, discovered the effects of pressure on reaction rates, and pioneered the use of radiocarbon to follow biochemical processes. In his studies on natural products he contributed to the determination of the structure of chlorophyll, to the understanding of the oxidation of haemoglobin to methaemoglobin and to the elucidation of the prosthetic group of haemocyanin.[21]

Rewards for Conant's chemistry prowess arrived with increasing frequency. He sped smoothly through the academic obstacle course, rising in 1924 to associate professor, to full professor three years later, with a sharply increased salary and research budget and reduced teaching obligations.[22] In 1931, three years after Theodore Richards's death, the new Sheldon Emery Professor of Organic Chemistry took another step in his father-in-law's footsteps, becoming department chairman, though he did not relish the administrative burden. Before ending his scientific career in 1933, Conant had solidified his reputation as one of America's best organic chemists by winning a raft of prestigious peer awards—the American Chemical Society's Nichols Medal, Columbia University's Chandler Medal, and others—and by winning speedy election to the American Academy of Arts and Sciences and the National Academy of Sciences.

Conant's exploits reflected and aided the maturation of American chemistry— still perceived (especially its organic branch) as lagging behind Europe's, but growing in scope, prestige, and recognized social and industrial applications. Building on a network featuring prominent chemists he had befriended during the war, conscientiously keeping up with research and contacts at home and abroad, Conant took on a myriad of professional activities. In a voluminous correspondence with colleagues he traded data and gossip; went to regional and national conferences; pored over and contributed to scores of journals; and while resisting temptations to stray from Harvard permanently, cheerfully boarded trains and boats to reconnoiter other lands and academic centers. He took semester-long research and teaching sabbaticals at the University of California at Berkeley in 1924 and the California Institute of Technology in 1927, cultivating contacts with such

rising West Coast leaders of American science as Gilbert N. Lewis, A. A.
Noyes, and Robert A. Millikan at Caltech, and made three trips to Europe (in
1921, 1925, and 1930), during which he became acquainted with the continent's
scientific avant-garde and learned something of the ominous political scene.
Greedily seeking out productive research assistants, he trained hordes of
graduate students, many of whom went on to successful careers in academia
and industry, and developed an aptitude for quickly sizing up colleagues and
students—his correspondence files for those years bulge with communications
with colleagues in which Conant rated in blunt, sometimes brutally frank
terms the prospects for scientific achievement of students under his direction.

    As his reputation in the field grew, powerful people took note. The
director of the U.S. government's bureau of chemistry consulted him on hiring
practices, and in 1930 the Rockefeller Institute for Medical Research invited
him to be a scientific adviser to its board of trustees, offering a new window
on the changing world of science and education as well as a chance to
broaden his familiarity with the New York financial and social establishment;
extended conversations with the institute's founder and president, Simon
Flexner, offered insight into administering a vast scientific enterprise.[23]
Conant's prominence also led to material benefits, and just in time. Supplementing a trust fund of more than $100,000 bequeathed to him by his father,
who had built up the sum by selling his business before his death in 1922, and
an assured and rising salary, Conant generated enough regular outside income
to safeguard his family from the Depression; his chemistry texts sold well,
and he overcame his "dim and often condescending view of industrial research"
enough to conclude consulting arrangements with the American Petroleum
Institute and the Du Pont Chemical Company. In the latter case, Conant had
to be persuaded by a friend and fellow Chemical Warfare Service section
leader, Roger Adams, that he would not be "signing away his soul to the
devil" by ceding research results to the company; Adams assured him that Du
Pont treated its employees equitably.[24] Ultimately, Conant agreed to consult
for Du Pont for $300 a month only three months before the October 1929
stock market crash. Though he rues in his memoirs that he let a big fish get
away by barely failing to discover a moneymaking technique for synthesizing
rubber, his moonlighting was apparently successful enough to convince Conant
that "any professor who could not double his salary, was not worth his salt."[25]
These varied sources of income, a prudent avoidance of the temptation to
"play the market," and the princely value of a steady salary in a deflationary
period, permitted Conant to read grim accounts of the Depression "with
considerable detachment," aside from his duties as a Rockefeller adviser.[26]

    The Depression's national and global dislocations forced Conant to exam-
ine more sharply his fluid and at times contradictory attitudes toward
nonscientific affairs. During the 1920s, a time of rampant social and political
conservatism both in the United States and at Harvard, he had quietly
evolved an idiosyncratic outlook that blended scientific skepticism, Jamesian

pragmatism, Wilsonian liberalism, and Jeffersonian idealism. His political and social philosophy tended to be cautiously liberal, but he was no boat-rocker. Broadminded enough to march for women's suffrage and subscribe to the leftist *New Republic,* in presidential elections he frequently dissented from the decade's pro-business tenor and his Republican affiliation, voting for Democrat James Cox in 1920, the Progressive candidate Robert M. La Follette in 1924, the Democrat Al Smith in 1928, and even for that Brahmin bête noir, FDR, in 1932.[27] As a member of a special faculty committee to examine entrance policies, Conant favored opening up Harvard's admissions standards to permit a more national, and geographically and economically diverse, student body with enhanced opportunities for talented poorer applicants, especially from smaller towns in areas of the country with little representation in Cambridge, such as the South and West. Foreshadowing his policies as university president, he lobbied vainly for a bolstered scholarship program, which was huffily rejected by President Lowell, who saw nothing wrong with the practice of making boys from low-income backgrounds earn their way through school.[28]

But Conant's liberalism had its limits, in tune with the stifling social conservatism of Harvard's leader during the 1920s. Carefully attuned to his times and his class, Lowell was bigoted, racist, and priggish, though he denied all but the most rarefied cogitations and motives to explain his views. Unalterably opposed to the idea of women attending Harvard—he denied an honorary degree to Madame Curie on the basis of her gender—Lowell tolerated students and faculty from outside the Brahmin norm so long as they kept their religious, ethnic, political, and even sexual proclivities carefully masked. Lowell's microscopic supervision of faculty behavior to assure that it conformed to his morals reached extremes. When an aged professor's homosexuality was disclosed, Lowell not only summarily demanded his resignation but suggested that he get a gun and "destroy" himself.[29] When a young tutor residing at an undergraduate dormitory desired to marry, he had to receive the president's approval, which was granted only on the condition that the prospective wife agree to entertain students.[30] Though he bravely rejected calls for the dismissal of liberal professors like Harold Laski and Zechariah Chafee, Lowell cemented his historical reputation for ingrained conservatism and defense of the status quo by heading the three-man commission that, in 1927, sanctioned the execution of Sacco and Vanzetti, two Boston anarchist immigrants who had been convicted of murder. For Harvard to put its seal of approval on a verdict and a sentence that had been sharply questioned evoked an anguished outcry from liberals around the country, led by Harvard's own professor of law, Felix Frankfurter, who prepared a point-by-point rebuttal of the judge's handling of the case and then frantically labored to reverse the death sentence ratified by Lowell until the hour the two men went to the electric chair.[31]

But unlike Frankfurter and Chafee, who had teamed up to denounce legal abuses committed by Boston and Justice Department Red hunters, Conant the hardworking chemist and nominal liberal eschewed active participation in these swirling local and national political controversies. And in a departure from the meritocratic ideals he touted so consistently, Conant went along with Lowell's attempt to impose quotas on Jewish undergraduates, the percentage of which had risen from 7.0 percent to 21.5 percent between 1900 and 1922.[32] Unfortunately for the children of emigrants from Russia and Poland, as well as other non-WASP minorities, Harvard and other Ivy League universities did not remain immune to the strains of racism, xenophobia, and "Red scare" phobias that flourished in America after World War I. Nor did Lowell. While deaf to demands from conservative alumni that he dismiss leftist teachers, he sympathized with their plea that he erect new ramparts to prevent their dear college from being overtaken by a Jewish Bolshevik rabble that somehow had gotten the notion that good grades gave them the right to attend Harvard. To Lowell, who also barred black students from living in the Yard, the only good Jews at Harvard were invisible ones—those "overcome with an oblivion of the fact that they were Jews"[33]—and the fewer the better. Perceiving his university's WASP domination and atmosphere as being under siege by battalions of science whizzes and radical troublemakers from New York City, the crusty Lowell in 1922 introduced measures to exclude "all but the clearly desirable Jews," aiming to reduce their number to 15 percent through restrictions on freshman admissions and transfers.[34]

But at a specially convened meeting on Friday evening, June 2, 1922, the faculty rejected, by a vote of 64–41, the resolution to "keep the proportion of Jews in Harvard college what it is at present," and rejected Lowell's idea of an explicit quota. Conant had voted for the quota, however, casting his aye with a conservative minority supporting the resolution, which had been introduced by his wife's uncle, L. J. Henderson, a biochemistry professor who disdained what he considered the "very objectionable and morally inferior" behavior and conduct of "the new Russian or Polish Jewish element."[35] Stymied from achieving a formal quota, over the next few years Lowell's administration accomplished the same objective by a subterfuge whose democratic veneer won Conant's support—by stressing recruitment from high schools in small towns and cities outside the Northeast.

Not surprisingly, in *My Several Lives* Conant highlights the plan's egalitarian results while delicately gliding over its anti-Jewish origins.[36] To be fair, one should state that Conant's 1922 vote did not presage a life of anti-Semitism. Too much the open-minded scientist and believer in America as a melting pot to express outright religious, ethnic, or racial biases—although his son Theodore recalls the occasional anti-Irish wisecrack,[37] and several relatives noted traces of anti-Semitism in his wife and her family[38]—he in fact presided over the demise of Harvard's quota system after succeeding Lowell. Perhaps Conant's 1922 vote stemmed from cowardice at offending those who would decide his academic future, or a desire to avoid alienating his in-laws, or a genuine belief that Jews were exceeding the delicate "balance" Lowell desired at the college. Whatever the explanation, his stand showed that he, too, could sway with prevailing political and social winds and take a position justifiably abhorred by later sensibilities.

Even in the midst of his chemistry career, Conant worked consistently to dilate his acumen in nonscientific affairs. He scanned newspapers and indulged in his inability to walk past bookstores without stopping to peek inside; his roaming curiosity was whetted by travel in the United States and in Europe, and he read widely in philosophy, literature, and history. Tackling thick tomes on German, American, and British history, he launched studies of the German university system and, especially, the Puritan rebellion against British oppression. In the interplay of "saints and sinners, rascals, fools, and heroes" crowding the canvas of seventeenth-century English history, he derived some deeply pessimistic notions about the behavior of people and societies in times of stress, shaping a lens through which he would view political upheavals in his own century; he admired Oliver Cromwell, who had been willing to rule with an iron first and commit massacres in the name of liberalism and tolerance, a relationship between ends and means compatible with Conant's own.[39]

In one effort to extend his intellectual and social reach, Conant sought to enliven discourse between diverse, rarely intersecting regions of the Harvard faculty, once likened by Santayana to "an anonymous concourse of coral insects, each secreting one cell, and leaving that fossil legacy to enlarge the earth."[40] Tossing together human beings much as he experimented with intriguing chemical mixtures in test tubes, Conant in 1922 helped to found the Shop Club, which each month gathered a few dozen professors — scientists, economists, historians, classicists, literary scholars, and so on — for dinner and an informal presentation of a current research passion.[41] The historian Arthur Schlesinger, Sr., praised these convivial evenings for introducing him "to areas of knowledge, especially in the scientific field, which had before been a closed book."[42] Of course, the same cross-fertilization in reverse applied to Conant; and in fact these wide-ranging sessions foreshadowed the ad hoc committees he would chair to consider appointments in every department of the university, as well as his lifelong quest to bridge the gulf between scientific and lay universes of discourse. With his disarming informality, easy smile, earnest curiosity, and impressive range of knowledge, Conant won new friends and admirers within a small but influential circle and enhanced his growing reputation as more than a narrow-gauge chemist — and he may have had just such results in mind, hoping to further his still-secret goal of one day winning the university's top job.

In his relations with the man who ran Harvard, Conant also showed mounting confidence and assertiveness. Lured by an exceptionally attractive offer from the California Institute of Technology in 1927 that would have made him the German-style doyen of organic chemistry, with a vastly increased salary and research budget, Conant and his wife had had their "trunks all packed, so to speak," after two months of sun-drenched hospitality in Pasadena. Playing academic hardball, Conant gave Harvard officials one last chance to keep him in Cambridge. "In dealing with the dean of the faculty I had turned down his first offer; then he very cagily came back with another one and said 'I understand that you would stay for this sum,' and I had to say at once I would. I learned something about the bargaining between administration and professors from the side of the professors during these last years of the gay 1920s." Lowell evidently had seen enough of Conant's adroitness to be impressed, warning prophetically that if he went to California "they will end by making you president."[43] The satisfying resolution of this negotiating experience bolstered Conant's confidence — perhaps overly so — in his deftness in handling disputes between administrators and professors.

So, in all likelihood, did his success in convincing Lowell to extend Harvard's construction bonanza to the popular but increasingly claustrophobic chemistry department. As chemistry's national standing rose and student enrollment in the field doubled to more than 3,300 in the 1920s, Lowell came to agree with Conant that Harvard's "most pressing need" and "dire necessity" was to build new chemistry labs "to include in our teaching the science of the greatest practicality to mankind." Conant's pestering and savvy horse-trading helped to produce dividends when the university coughed up resources for modernized equipment, a larger research staff, and two new laboratories — one of which, Mallinckrodt, became Conant's headquarters in 1928. Upon discovering that the house next door was available, the chemist immediately vacated his Shady Hill home and rushed his family to a two-and-a-half-story wood-frame house at 20 Oxford Street.

The purchase of the new home put the finishing touches on an idyllic lifestyle: raising a family a few steps away from the place where he exercised his creative powers, an estimable relationship with his Harvard and chemistry colleagues, summer vacations in the New Hampshire mountains hiking, fishing, painting, and skiing to revitalize his energies. In those rented cottages on isolated dirt roads in the White Mountains, without telephone, electricity, and the distractions of colleagues and students, Conant also found more time for his two young boys, taking them on climbing and fishing expeditions, nurturing their interests in science and nature, teaching them the uses of microscopes and other experimental gear just as his own father had. Though lacking the national and global prominence of his later endeavors, as Conant's term as a professor of chemistry receded into his past it acquired for him a luminous, nostalgic glow. "Since proximity to his laboratory is an important ingredient in the satisfaction of a chemist, I should have been completely happy with the new house and I was," Conant wrote in *My Several Lives*. "Looking back, these seem to have been the best years of my life."[44]

✻   ✻   ✻

More portentous than any of his professional exploits during the 1920s was Conant's fulfillment of his lifelong dream to visit Germany and pay homage to the great universities where great men did great science. Long curious as to how that tremendous reputation had been acquired, he later recalled, "I decided to see for myself how the Germans had done it." In the first few years after World War I, the trip seemed imprudent owing to the political tempests and inflationary spirals that gripped the unstable Weimar Republic. Many American scientists, including Conant's father-in-law, frowned at the idea of fraternizing with colleagues who had so ardently collaborated with an enemy army. But in February 1925, with their two-year-old son in tow, Conant and his wife sailed across the Atlantic, rented a cozy two-room Munich pension that catered to Harvard professors and students, and over the next nine months "fell in love" with Germany — "its historic past, its music, its advances in the arts and sciences, and with many of the academic people we met. We were a young married couple, and we had a great time touring the country."[45]

Dependent on Patty to tend the infant in Munich, on his poor but fast improving German (which he honed in letters to his wife), and on an introduction from his Nobel laureate father-in-law to a former student and a "first-rate analytical chemist," Professor Otto Hönigschmid, "who shepherded me around," Conant finally trod the fabled grounds of universities and institutes he had so long imagined. He visited Leipzig, where the now-retired Wilhelm Ostwald had evolved his school of *allgemeine Chemie;* Göttingen, pulsing with the excitement of physicists, led by Niels Bohr, exploring the atom's inner structure; Frankfurt, Hamburg, Würzburg, Tübingen, and most of all Berlin, the 1920s "empyrean of science." Talking shop, inspecting labs, attending professional meetings, downing *Bier* and *Wurst* and singing along in many a smoke-filled *Hofbrauhaus,* Conant relished the opportunity to see his German counterparts in their natural setting. By the end of his visit, he had compiled a scientific notebook full of names, addresses, sketches, and diagrams of experimental setups, and formulas studded with exclamation points.[46]

Even more than the data he collected, the intensely competitive, no-holds-barred atmosphere he discovered in German chemistry made a deep impression on Conant. Posing the key question — What had made German science, particularly organic chemistry, so fruitful? — he discerned the answer in the cutthroat competition among the country's universities. "The rivalry among universities as well as among individuals," he writes in his memoirs, "had resulted in a ruthless intolerance of mediocrity and showmanship." Foreshadowing the policies he advocated as Harvard president, he noted with approval the practice of young instructors at top institutions leaving after a few years for smaller schools and then clawing their way back by proving their mettle in published work; a premium on excellence justified "what foreigners considered an inhuman academic world."[47] Returning to the United States, Conant fairly bristled with contempt for what more than ever seemed like a provincial, second-rate field in his native country. "If you want to know how organic chemistry is really discussed by those who do it and hot from the stove, attend a meeting of an organic section of the German Chemical Society," he wrote to a colleague at Northwestern University in 1927. "You will blush for your country and its organic chemists from then on!"[48]

The highlight of Conant's first *in situ* exposure to *deutschen Wissenschaft* occurred one Tuesday in June in the verdant Berlin suburb of Dahlem, where he visited an internationally famous but highly controversial figure whose life and work, in retrospect, curiously paralleled his own. Winner of the Nobel Prize in chemistry in 1921, Fritz Haber cordially received the respectful young American who appeared at the Kaiser-Wilhelm-Institut für Physikalische Chemie to pay his respects and discuss common research interests.[49] It is worth a moment to reflect on this encounter, little noticed by historians, between the sixty-year-old titan of German science, reviled throughout the world for fathering chemical warfare, whose wife had committed suicide out of depression over her husband's poison gas work, and the Harvard chemist one quarter-century his junior, who later played a comparably seminal part in the creation of the atomic bomb. Unlike Theodore Richards, to whom Haber's name was "anathema," Conant was hardly one to shun German scientists who had loyally supported their government. Nor, for obvious reasons, did Conant share what he later described as the "strong moral feeling among some chemists and many non-chemists that those who had been engaged in producing poisonous gases were outside the pale of respectable people."[50] If anything, the two chemists, despite having done their best to massacre each other's countrymen with maximum efficiency, belonged to the same twentieth-century fraternity of scientists who had forged a new, mutually profitable relationship with the state, obtaining new status and material and professional gain, as well as patriotic luster, in exchange for active support and few if any questions asked of official wartime policies and practices.

Not that Conant and Haber spent their conversation chummily comparing recipes for lewisite and mustard gas, or commiserating on the misfortunes of chemists accused of war crimes for such activities. That seems unlikely, though Conant recorded in his journal that the two did discuss politics during their "cordial" conversation.[51] The American hardly wanted to reopen fresh wounds — and besides, they had other things to talk about. "I was particularly curious to meet Haber," Conant explained in *My Several Lives*, "because of his pioneer work on the electrochemical method of studying certain oxidation reactions in organic chemistry." Haber's oxidation advances, in fact, probably had riled Conant, if inadvertently, far more than his poison gas work. As an untenured Harvard chemistry professor in 1919, Conant had spent months studying oxidation reactions in pursuit of a new electrochemical battery. Finally, he had been thrilled to achieve "a great discovery" that he hoped might win him quick fame and tenure. "But, alas," after hearing an excited description of the breakthrough, an elder colleague informed a crestfallen

Conant that Haber had performed the same experiment a decade or more earlier, before the war.[52]

That sounds like the kind of anecdote Conant is likely to have related— mildly amusing, gently flattering, professionally interesting. Haber, for his part, like other senior German chemists, deeply resented their international ostracism, and must have enjoyed meeting this bright, deferential colleague from his erstwhile enemy's most prestigious university. Conant came away with fond memories—Haber betrayed no sign of the prevailing bitterness toward Allied scientists, and "paid me the greatest compliment an older man can pay a younger; he listened with interest as I spoke."

For all the scintillating scientific expertise Conant absorbed on his visit, the German sojourn was more educational for its revelations of sinister political undercurrents.[53] At the supposed zenith of the democratic, tolerant Weimar Republic, the Conants found instead a seething "republic without republicans." Over and over, they encountered dismal evidence of anti-Semitic, anti-democratic, reactionary views, and a defiant, sulky resentment (*Trotzigkeit*) about the war's outcome. Thanks to the "cordial and extremely helpful" Professor Hönigschmid, Conant had skimmed the top of the academic world and thus gained some ominous glimpses into the elite's political attitudes. "Almost everyone I talked to was anti-French, anti-British, and anti-American," he recalled in an interview on returning to Germany after World War II. "I argued for hours over the Treaty of Versailles and who started the war. The Germans were bitter about everything, and no wonder—so many of them were on their uppers. I had the impression you could count the supporters of the Weimar Republic on the fingers of your two hands. I saw the beginnings of anti-Semitism, too. There was a lot of talk about the recent Communist uprisings and Hitler's beer-hall Putsch."[54]

The Conants' disquieting memories loomed large in later years, especially that of the Germans' pervasive belief that their country had lost the war due to a "stab in the back" from traitors. In Munich, putting her German to good use while she cared for the infant, Patty Conant closely followed newspaper accounts of the hard-fought electoral campaigns that led to Field Marshal Paul von Hindenburg's ascension to the presidency, and recorded in her diary a sequence of conversations with fellow boarders and neighbors, including many battle-scarred veterans. She did not encounter Hitler himself, who spent the winter months of 1925 licking his wounds from a short prison sentence after the failed Beer Hall putsch in a small two-room apartment on the top floor of 41 Thierschstrasse. But Mrs. Conant's acquaintances were extreme enough: they spewed venom at the clause in the Treaty of Versailles indicting Germany for war guilt, indignantly condemning the "dastardly allies" and what they had done to the "noble, simple, innocent Germans." Asked at a restaurant whether she believed charges that German soldiers had committed atrocities, Mrs. Conant's mild response that "all armies did brutal things" and that she "didn't blame Germans especially" outraged her questioner.

"He said he'd put his right hand in the fire if any German soldier stabbed a child. 'Our system was too perfect to permit of it.' "[55]

Her itinerant husband, meanwhile, had his blood curdled by a conversation among an eminent group of senior academic and industrial chemists. As they applauded the improvement in Germany's situation since 1923 — a lowering of inflation, France's withdrawal from the Ruhr, Hindenburg's election — one chemist interjected: "That's all very well, but let us not forget the debt we owe to those men who went out, revolver in hand, and assassinated those who were leading the Fatherland astray!" Oblivious to the impact his words were making on the astonished American visitor, the Germans enthusiastically seconded this clear allusion to the murder in 1922, by a right-wing extremist, of Foreign Minister Walther Rathenau, a liberal Jew. Never having heard assassination justified before, Conant felt greater doubts about Weimar's future stability even as his admiration for Germany's scientists rose.[56]

When he returned for a brief visit five years later to attend a scientific conference, the situation had, as he feared, grown even worse. The world had spun into economic collapse, and the spiraling unemployment and misery provided grist for the demagoguery of the up-and-coming National Socialists. On their previous trip the Conants had heard only fleeting references to the party to whom more and more Germans were turning for salvation. But on the night of September 14, 1930, staying in a hotel near Freiburg, in the Black Forest, they could not avoid intimations of the disaster to come. "The Nazis were making their first big electoral gains, and there was not only bitterness in the air but a real spirit of revenge, too," Conant was to recall. "I remember asking a German scientist at the dinner table one night what the election news was. 'You foreigners!' he snapped. 'You're more interested in our voting than we are. But you don't understand German politics. Our foreign policy will remain the same no matter what happens.'

"I'm afraid I was an accurate prophet when we got home that fall. I predicted nothing but trouble ahead. After Hitler took over, I never expected to see Germany again. I tell my friends that 1933 was quite a year for Germany, America, and me — Hitler rose to power, Franklin Roosevelt took office, and I became president of Harvard."[57]

CHAPTER 5

"The Challenge Was Simply Not to Be Denied"

Professor to President

1933

There is altogether too much sentiment here lately for getting outsiders and so-called "new blood" into Harvard. The traditions of the place must not be spoiled. There is actually some talk about a new president, about whom no one seems to have heard.
— George Apley to his son, 1933, in *The Late George Apley*

It is the most thankless job in the U.S.A., — roughly speaking if the President does the right thing he can count on an almost unanimous howl of disapproval from alumni and others. After all how many people are there who really understand what a university is for and are interested in seeing such things furthered? . . . I have few illusions about the position. It will be interesting and I hope satisfying but on the whole unpleasant and trying, — a very, very lonely job. . . .

I have wept several times at leaving such a pleasant scientific life but the challenge was simply not to be denied. . . . Pray for me, I shall need it!
— JBC to his sister after becoming president of Harvard

On May 17, 1933, nine days after the Harvard Corporation had elected him president, James Bryant Conant sailed to Europe for a summer holiday that would afford a few calm months during which he might soberly assess the implications of the decision that had irrevocably changed his life. His mood was pensive, even pessimistic, but excited. For the chance to satisfy his ambition of leading Harvard, he had sacrificed a promising scientific career that had brought him prestige among his peers, a comfortable life, a chance to gratify his intellectual yearnings, and at least a reasonable shot at a Nobel Prize — a more than respectable set of achievements for a forty-year-old engraver's son from modest Dorchester.

But this was a year in which history was visibly accelerating toward a decisive moment, and Conant could not resist the chance, even the obligation, to play his part. His university, his country, and the world had all reached turning points. For Harvard, a new king had been crowned after the twenty-three-year reign of Abbot Lawrence Lowell, who left an expanse of impressive new buildings but an uncertain intellectual and financial legacy. In Washington, Franklin D. Roosevelt struggled to lift the nation out of the Depression, declaring a bank holiday, importing a "brains trust" to devise new programs, assuring his countrymen that they had "nothing to fear but fear itself." But the world had more to fear than fear itself. Hitler's National Socialists had brutally seized power in Germany, savagely repressing political opponents, Jews, intellectuals, burning "non-Aryan" books and arrogantly promising a thousand-year Reich. In Europe and in Asia, fascism, militarism, and anti-intellectualism were rising, and the ambitious, broad-minded chemist knew that he could not stay aloof from a battle that, unlike World War I, he deeply believed in.

To one person who inquired why he had traded a congenial academic existence for a burdensome administrative post, Conant replied simply and jauntily: "I guess it was my sense of adventure."[1] In a talk before the Harvard Club of New York not long after taking office, he compared the dilemma he had faced to that of an explorer tramping through the muddy Canadian wilderness who came before a sign advising: "Choose your rut carefully: You will be in it for the next 35 miles."[2]

Conant had chosen his rut only after careful consideration. Still, the decision to begin what he called "a second life" had been excruciatingly painful. Normally in tight control of his emotions, he had been unable to stop the tears from flowing—once he walked home and closed the front door behind him—after delivering his last lecture in Chemistry 5.[3] Cutting his beloved chemistry journals out of his life he later likened to amputating a leg—a missing limb that continued to ache. Still pining for "the love from which he has been divorced," he would, for several years, snatch a few free hours on Saturday afternoons to stroll over to Mallinckrodt and toss pebbles at the window until someone unlocked the front door, sneaking enough lab time to coauthor a few journal articles.[4] When he accepted an invitation to tea at a freshman's room during his first year in office, an undergraduate asked him point-blank why a man "at the height of his powers of creativity" would give up science to become a university administrator. Conant replied, the student later remembered, "that he would not have given up his scientific career for any other post than the presidency of Harvard; there could have been no other temptation that would have lured him away from his laboratory and his students. His strong love of Harvard and his devotion to his college and university provided a focus for his creative energy and he gladly accepted the challenge to make Harvard truly great: to make the College more representative of the whole nation and of every class of society and to transform the University into a center of science and learning for the whole world."[5]

Beyond grief at abdicating a chemistry career, doubts about the wisdom of taking the job arose from Conant's acute awareness of the fierce resistance he would encounter as president. Convinced that Lowell's policies had been leading Harvard downhill, he envisioned a bold reform agenda likely to rattle both the faculty and the Brahmin power structure. In line with his own meritocratic beliefs and vision of Harvard's national and global rather than provincial mission, he was determined to diversify the college, opening more positions for poorer but talented youths from around the country, and consequently cutting into the spaces traditionally reserved for the upper-class offspring of New England alumni. If Conant's search for "new blood" over "blue blood" was bound to alarm the aristocrats, segments of the faculty seemed likely to balk at his narrowly scientific background, his austere belt-tightening, and—most of all—any presidential intrusions into their prerogatives for hiring and firing. Yet, intent on stemming what he regarded as a slide in Harvard's reputation for academic excellence and on holding the university's budget in check, Conant planned to raise standards for tenure, weed out insufficiently productive scholars, and slap a ceiling on the number of years a lecturer could stay on before he either received a permanent appointment or, more likely, was forced to leave. That Conant had never administered an educational office outside the chemistry department, that he lacked a membership card or power base in the wealthy, elite social circle that had guided the university for generations and remained firmly entrenched in many of its governing institutions, and that the Depression darkened the outlook for any private institution reliant on private funds, only made matters worse.

Conant's forebodings, exacerbated by his propensity to "expect the worst when dealing with other people," coalesced as the ocean liner, the Norddeutscher Lloyd Bremen D. *Europa,* steamed toward England. Contemplating the storm before him, he spent the Atlantic crossing in relative solitude, for his wife had stayed behind to tend their younger son, Ted, who had suddenly contracted a serious ear infection requiring surgery. "I probably should not have gone," Conant later admitted, but he did anyway, eager to escape the press and assured by his wife that she would join him later.[6] Isolated from his usual confidant, Conant spilled his innermost apprehensions about the turn his life had taken in an exceptionally introspective letter to his sister:

May 17, 1933

Dear Marjorie,

I was so pleased to get your letter before I sailed and I'm glad you're pleased on the whole with the way things have turned out and you had best enjoy the reflected light while it shines pleasantly.—You'll have plenty of years of hearing and reading many nasty things about me if I'm not mistaken. It is the most thankless job in the U.S.A.,—roughly speaking if the President does the right thing he can count on an almost unanimous howl of disapproval from alumni and others. After all how many people are there who really understand what a university is for and are interested in seeing such things furthered? But that's all part of the contract and I'm prepared for it, I hope. Needless to say don't quote these pessimistic remarks, I don't intend to make

any more enemies than necessary and I shall try to make as many friends as
possible. Even in the most collegiate and football-mad of our alumni there is
a spark of intellectual interest and I shall try my best to fan and not water
this spark! You notice, I begin to preach already.

From the above and my previous letters you will notice that I have few
illusions about the position. It will be interesting and I hope satisfying but on
the whole unpleasant and trying,—a very, very lonely job. From May 8th till
I retire, it will be very hard to find anyone who will speak absolutely frankly
and fully to me about any Harvard matter. But all this is the price of "tyranny
tempered by assassination," as Mr. Lowell once described the Harvard
system of administration.

I have wept several times at leaving such a pleasant scientific life but
the challenge was simply not to be denied. I have no regrets and I'm sure I
shall have none in the future as to the correctness of the decision . . . Pray for
me, I shall need it!

As you already know, Teddy's ears have rather upset an already very
upset few months. I'm [heading] for Oxford and Cambridge, I hope Patty
will join me before long. After the few months in England we shall have a
real and complete vacation in preparation for the long pull. I'm looking
forward to this with the greatest delight. I hope we shall tour around in
France and sketch to our hearts' desire.—one last grand fling of freedom,
perhaps. . . .

> Much love,
> Bryant[7]

The five-and-a-half-month search that ended in the surprise selection of
the obscure organic chemist from Dorchester had begun on November 21,
1932, a few weeks after America elected Franklin Delano Roosevelt. As
Herbert Hoover left the White House, another incumbent withdrew voluntarily from a comparably august residence: Lowell, the seventy-year-old leader
of Harvard since 1909, announced his retirement, inaugurating a clamorous
succession struggle and a delicious festival of speculation that touched the
smoke-filled parlors and posh dining rooms of gentleman's clubs from Harvard
Yard to Wall Street to Capitol Hill.

The power to determine Lowell's replacement rested largely in the
six-man Harvard Corporation, a bastion of patrician Brahmin families who
had run the university for generations and a secretive body whose activities
were traditionally enshrouded by a thick fog of mystery, stealth, and wealth.
Under the eclectic governing structure laid down by the Puritans who had
founded America's oldest institution of higher education in 1636, the Corporation's decisions were theoretically subject to ratification by a thirty-member
Board of Overseers elected by the alumni, but in practice the elite body was
almost never challenged or overruled.

So the question of who would become Harvard's twenty-third president
was answered by six members of the New England elite—Thomas N. Perkins,

Dr. Roger I. Lee, Charles P. Curtis, Jr., Robert Homans, Grenville Clark, and the treasurer, Henry L. Shattuck. Once described by the *Crimson* as a "self-perpetuating body of a deeply conservative nature,"[8] the Corporation was normally risk-averse, and most participants in the farrago of rumor and speculation that instantly arose took it for granted that the ultimate choice would, like Lowell and Eliot, be drawn from New England's rarefied firmament of bankers, lawyers, and scholars of breeding and refinement.

Yet the man they chose was unknown on Beacon Hill and State Street, so uncelebrated outside the world of organic chemistry that the trustees of the Roxbury Latin School had recently eliminated him from contention to become the new headmaster on the grounds that he lacked the "seasoning" for such an important post.[9] Only once had Conant gotten his name in the Boston papers for an accomplishment outside chemistry. In 1923, the assistant professor had leapt a railing along the Charles River and paddled to the rescue of a drowning girl.[10] For the next decade, he had happily absented himself from public inspection behind the curtain of scientific anonymity. How, then, had the Corporation's deliberations yielded such a bold outcome? To *The New Yorker*, it flowed from evenings of genteel discourse:

> The selection of Conant took place at a series of dinners. They were informal stag affairs at which each Fellow acted as host in rotation. Cocktails were served. Considerable attention was devoted to the wines. After dinner, over coffee and liqueurs and cigars, the various candidates were discussed pro and con in an atmosphere of warmth and good-fellowship. Meanwhile, on one pretext or another, all the Fellows had called on Conant. They feigned interest, when they saw him, in his researches or asked for his frank opinion of some other candidate. Each returned, an enthusiastic Conantite, to the next dinner. So a decision was reached by April. President Lowell was delegated to ask Conant whether he would accept. Conant hesitated for a few days and then said he would. The formal nomination by the Corporation was made on May 8, 1933, and confirmed by Board of Overseers on June 22nd.[11]

In the correspondence and memories of several of the participants, however, Conant's ascension culminated months of backstage intrigue and maneuvering.[12] Corporation members fanned out to examine favored candidates, trade scuttlebutt, and, it was widely believed, so impress peers with their own qualities of foresight and judgment that they, too, would be in the running. The Fellows' clashing personal and philosophical ambitions coexisted uneasily with their sincere desire to find a leader capable of brushing away the Lowell era's cobwebs and propelling Harvard forward on a fresh course, of imparting freshness and energy on a par with the electricity that the new president in Washington was to emanate when he took command of his slumping nation, yet a candidate who was also level-headed enough to generate the confidence and contributions that would keep Harvard fiscally sound.

As the overlords compared their initial lists of potential candidates in late December, after allowing a decent interval of a few weeks to pass after Lowell's resignation, no obvious savior emerged. That didn't stop the rumor mill and gossip columnists from tallying their own lists of contenders, mostly professors and Corporation members, topped by the putative front-runner: Kenneth B. Murdock, a professor of literature then acting as faculty dean, who as master of Leverett House had cultivated close ties to students and to a stable of rising young humanities scholars like F. O. Matthiessen, John K. Fairbank, and Perry Miller. Murdock also happened to be Conant's friend since childhood, best man at his wedding, and a fellow member of the Shop Club.

Though miffed at his name's absence from the early lists being bandied about, Conant loyally proclaimed himself for Murdock when Corporation members solicited his ratings of possible candidates. But while naming his old friend as his choice, Conant had no qualms about fervently and articulately expressing his *own* vision about what was wrong with Harvard and where it ought to go. Still imbued with the vision of the unbridled pursuit of truth he had seen at the great German universities on his visits to Europe, Conant felt extra incentive to raise American standards for scholarship. "For a young man—I was forty then—I had acquired some pretty firm ideas about what education ought and ought not to be, and I was pretty brash; in fact, I'm afraid I was quite critical."13

To Corporation members who came calling at the modest house on Oxford Street, Conant firmly declared that Harvard needed to be turned around. Sympathizing far more with Eliot's priorities than with Lowell's, he argued that it was time for Harvard to concentrate on building strong departments filled with first-rate scholars rather than roomy new dormitories for undergraduates. Most of all, he condemned Lowell's emphasis on hiring numerous young tutors, and used harsh language to condemn the practice of keeping second-rate scholars merely because they were devoted to Harvard, personal friends, or good fellows. By doing so, he said heatedly, Harvard was "betraying its trust" and "guilty of almost criminal negligence." If the university truly wished to recoup its declining image as a beacon of scholarship and excellence, it needed to focus on permanent appointments of the highest quality—not only in the natural sciences, where Conant's colleagues complained of neglect, but in the humanities and social sciences as well.

Never did Conant communicate his views with more passion ("for a New Englander," he hastens to add) than he did to a visiting Corporation member on the wintry afternoon of January 24, 1933, a few days before a considerably nastier succession drama climaxed in Germany with Hitler's seizure of the chancellorship from a senile President von Hindenburg. Making himself comfortable in the Conants' living room, Robert Homans sipped tea and munched toasted muffins smilingly delivered by Mrs. Conant as her husband spilled his convictions and frustrations.

"Go on," Homans prompted him, restraining his building sense of excitement.

When his guest stepped out into the brittle Cambridge winter, Conant was left with the "peculiarly subtle feeling" that he had met a kindred spirit who was impressed enough to make him a possible candidate. He surmised correctly.[14]

"I think we've got the man," Homans enthused to his son that night. The next day he used more understated language to his fellow Corporation member Grenville Clark, himself rumored for the job, asserting that Conant seemed "as sensible and to have as good judgment of the man needed as anyone with whom I have conversed."[15]

By late February Conant learned that Murdock was out of the running — bounced by reports that he lacked "class," had fawned over Lowell, and, most damagingly, had been "seen crossing the Atlantic in the company of a woman not his wife"[16] — and began seriously to consider himself a viable contender. With the race wide open, the Corporation opened an intensive if still discreet probe to find out if the surging dark horse also had any skeletons in his closet. Their snooping revealed a moderate, engaging personality who "smoked cigars after dinner and cigarettes at receptions where women were present" but was not a chain smoker, who liked beer and the occasional cocktail but disdained strong drinks, who had a lively and sardonic sense of humor, read widely, expressed himself clearly and straightforwardly, enjoyed rigorous sports like skiing, tennis, and hiking, and "dabbled in painting but was a little ashamed of it." Above all, according to *The New Yorker,* Conant was said to have "a passion for first-rate mentalities and had proved himself more than a little intolerant in dealing with mediocrities."[17]

Some senior professors and Corporation fellows raised doubts about the wisdom of appointing, to a position that required visionary intellectual and administrative talents covering the broad spectrum of scholarly endeavors, a young scientist who might have a narrow outlook. And not only a scientist — a *chemist.* In contrast to dreamers, poets, philosophers, critics, even theoretical physicists and astronomers, who all laid claim to status as intellectuals, the stereotypical chemist, stooped over his test tubes, "cultivated an image of worldliness and matter-of-fact simplicity," as one historian of the field has acknowledged, not to say a lack of imagination. "In chemistry, so the image suggests, only facts matter, not interpretations or opinions; knowledge is good because it yields power; intense specialization breeds success."[18]

To some, it was precisely this intense specialization that made the prospect of a Conant presidency disturbing. In his 1925 treatise *Science and the Modern World,* Harvard's preeminent philosopher Alfred North Whitehead had decried the disastrous consequences suffered by Western civilization over the past few centuries by tilting toward a scientific cosmology at the expense of philosophy and religion, by adopting a materialistic mentality that worshipped "irreducible stubborn facts" but failed to harmonize radical changes in science and technology with ethical and moral precepts.[19] One important symptom of this development, Whitehead argued, was a rush toward the "professionalizing of knowledge." The same methods that produced trained professionals and advancements in one field, he warned, yielded myopic specialists who were unequipped to fruitfully coordinate ideas and information from various intellectual spheres—precisely the qualities desired in a university president. While cautioning that he was speaking generally and could have referred to various professions, the example he chose to illustrate this contention reflected a widely held impression of Conant's line of work. "The modern chemist," Whitehead judged, "is likely to be weak in zoology, weaker still in his general knowledge of Elizabethan drama, and completely ignorant of the principles of rhythm in English versification. It is probably safe to ignore his knowledge of ancient history. . . . Effective knowledge is professionalized knowledge, supported by a restricted acquaintance with useful subjects subservient to it."

> This situation has dangers. It produces minds in a groove. Each profession makes progress, but it is progress in a groove. Now to be mentally in a groove is to live in contemplating a given set of abstractions. The groove prevents straying across country, and the abstraction abstracts from something to which no further attention is paid. But there is no groove of abstractions which is adequate for the comprehension of human life. Thus in the modern world, the celibacy of the medieval learned class has been replaced by a celibacy of the intellect which is divorced from the concrete contemplation of the complete facts. Of course, no one is merely a mathematician, or merely a lawyer. People have lives outside their professions or their businesses. But the point is the restraint of serious thought within a groove. The remainder of life is treated superficially, with the imperfect categories of thought derived from one profession.[20]

One burning source of apprehensions that Conant might fulfill Whitehead's fears was Felix Frankfurter, the eminent law professor, controversial civil-liberties advocate, and future Supreme Court justice, who was fast emerging as Franklin Roosevelt's chief New Deal talent scout, political consultant, and intelligence collector at Harvard. Frankfurter and Roosevelt, graduates, respectively, of the Harvard Law School and Harvard College, had first met over lunch in 1906—and the man who had first introduced the two men who formed one of the key political collaborations in modern American politics was none other than Grenville Clark, Frankfurter's law school classmate and now, in 1933, a member of the Harvard Corporation. In counterpoise to Lowell's conservative suspicions about Conant, a non-aristocrat who made noises about shaking up old traditions, Clark and Frankfurter exemplified a liberal strain of wariness about the cautious, close-to-the-vest scientist whose philosophy remained unknown. In early March, while passing kind words about Harlow Shapley, a liberal astronomer rumored to be seeking the presidency, Frankfurter warned Clark that putting a parochial chemist like Conant in power at Harvard could spell disaster.

> The more I think about it the more distressed I am by the possibility of Conant. Concentration on him seems to me the counsel of despair. If you have read Whitehead's *Science and the Modern World* you will know how much science is responsible for the mess in which the world now finds itself. From all I have seen of Conant and all I have been able to learn about him from cross-examining others, he seems to me an essentially unperceptive mind, however distinguished in its own specialty. The testimony of a man like Kohler as to Conant's range does not seem to me very important, because fine as Kohler is, his own limited range hardly gives him the means of judging the range appropriate for the guidance of America's greatest university. We need a man and a mind of distinction. A distinguished chemist is not enough.[21]

As this and other warnings filtered into the Corporation's distended deliberations, Clark also seemed wary of choosing a narrow specialist to captain Harvard's $137-million annual budget, $125-million endowment, 4,200-employee payroll, and educational direction. Though impressed by Conant's "attractive personality and undoubted ability in his field," Clark confessed to fellow Corporation members that he would "feel safer and surer and would think I had exercised better judgment if I preferred a more mature and more experienced man of greater *demonstrated* ability to undertake so many-sided a job."[22]

Clark's own nominal favorite was a fellow founding partner at the Wall Street firm of Root, Clark, Buckner & Ballantine (originally Root, Clark & Bird) — Elihu "Sec" Root, Jr., son of the secretary of state and war, Clark's classmate at Harvard Law School and his partner in organizing the "Platts-burgh" military preparedness movement in 1915 to train officers in advance of American entry into the European war, a man of unquestioned distinction who would appeal to Harvard financiers.[23] Also very much in the running were Clark himself and Henry James, another member of the inner sanctum whose credentials were gilded by family ties to the famous novelist and philosopher.

But as Corporation members collected glowing testimonials to Conant's expertise and judgment, their doubts began to fade. Homans circulated an account of a conversation with the diplomatic historian James P. Baxter III who proclaimed Conant "almost a genius," so familiar with topics of general note that he could match his own knowledge of the intricacies of Woodrow Wilson's state of mind on the eve of the Great War.[24] And James reported that Simon Flexner, director of the Rockefeller Institute for Medical Research, had instantly perked up upon hearing that Conant was being considered. Conant hadn't spoken up much at board meetings, Flexner reported, but when he did he invariably had something noteworthy to say. While not corroborating reports that Conant "did not suffer fools gladly, and sometimes betrayed the fact with his elders," Flexner praised him as a sharp judge of colleagues. "Conant is exacting in his appraisals of men," concluded James after hearing several similar tales. "Probably a good fault."[25]

As the secret deliberations reached a climax in the spring of 1933, Conant edged steadily to the front of a thinning field. On April 12, Clark reported to a fellow Corporation member that the choice had narrowed to Conant and Root, with James a fading third.[26] As for Murdock, Conant told his sister, he had "been out of the running many months (although he doesn't know it and the absurd newspaper stories have rather deluded him, I'm afraid)."[27] Conant's own chief informant, his uncle-in-law the biochemist L. J. Henderson, claimed that Clark was the prime rival. Conant, initially incredulous at the prospect that he might actually be chosen, had argued the pros and cons back and forth with his wife several times and ultimately decided to say yes if asked. Several early conversations with Patty had dissolved in laughter at the seemingly outlandish notion of his becoming president, but by late March the danger was too real to brush off. "Assuming the worst," he began to rush the completion of research already in progress, and to seek the counsel of a few close colleagues, who advised him to take the job if offered.[28] Hearing that the final decision pitted himself against a prominent New York lawyer only stiffened Conant's vacillating will to be chosen, for he felt it to be "of the utmost importance that a scholar and not a non-scholar be in such a very important position at this trying time."[29]

Choosing Conant, as even his supporters on the Corporation realized, would be a big risk. Thomas N. Perkins judged him "intellectually first-class, a first-class fellow, for his age a great scientist; and of course he might become just the man, but I suspect he has got to become it."[30] One by one, the remaining Corporation members trooped up to Conant to feel him out, dropping all pretense of any purpose other than to determine if he was the right person to become Harvard's next president. Henderson paid an absurd official visit to collect personal data on his relatives. Clark still had his doubts, but after spending a morning with Conant in New York, he came away impressed enough to lend his blessing; when the head of the Overseers grouchily threatened to keep Conant from abandoning his scientific career, Clark soothingly wrote him to express satisfaction with this "fine fellow, not only as to ability, force and decision, but what is more important, as to his basic character."[31]

On April 24, with fingers crossed, the Corporation members voted—and with a huge gulp, a deep pang of regret about leaving chemistry, and a flutter of worries about his finances, Conant accepted their choice in a brief, awkward meeting with Lowell. "Well," was the younger man's resigned reaction after the president almost twice his age "rather coldly" told him the news.[32]

A few days later Conant sent Clark a warm, humble, handwritten note. "I hope events will prove that you and the Corporation have not made a mistake," he wrote. "Whatever people may say about the wisdom of your action they can not question your courage nor perhaps mine."[33] Seeking solace, privacy, and a few months to gather his wits and his strength, Conant hastily made preparations to sail for Europe.

Reaction to the May 8 announcement of his appointment was generally positive if a bit puzzled—blank stares from Boston and Harvard society cream ("Oh, but, my dear, it does seem strange that we should have to go way out to Dorchester for a president"); the observation that Harvard had chosen an "educational enigma," from the *New York Times;* and a mixture of applause and wait-and-sees from the faculty. Frankfurter, commiserating with Clark over the outcome as the two walked through Harvard Square on the day the Corporation announced its choice, felt so depressed that he wished he had bowed to FDR's wish that he leave academia to become solicitor general.[34] And Professor Whitehead delivered a memorable grumble.

"The Corporation should not have elected a chemist to the Presidency," Harvard's leading philosopher opined.

"But Eliot was a chemist," his colleague replied, "and our best president, too."

"I know," replied Whitehead, "but Eliot was a *bad* chemist!"[35]

CHAPTER 6

"Tyranny Tempered by Assassination"

Harvard President from
Depression to War

1933–1939

He won't get excited. Everything works out by formula; he'll compound his formula for running the university, and then stand over while it develops into substance.

—Jennett Bryant Conant, on her son's selection as Harvard's president

Our colleges and universities must not only guarantee the right of free inquiry, they must also see that the various points of view are represented so that a conflict of opinion really takes place ... We must have our share of thoughtful rebels on our faculties.

—JBC, "Free Inquiry or Dogma?" *The Atlantic,* April 1935

Unless you are vigorously on guard, there is great danger that the very evils of authoritarian rule in government which you so much deprecate, and rightly, may become operative where they are most mischievous, namely, in the government of a great university.

—Felix Frankfurter to Grenville Clark, June 14, 1938

The magician was late, and mood at the children's party began to droop. The two little Conant boys, Jim, ten, and Ted, almost seven, and their friends waited expectantly, but a search party failed to turn up the derelict performer. But all was not lost! The show must go on! Suddenly the lights dimmed, the excited chatter ceased, and a funny old man in a strange costume appeared. Eliciting oohs-and-aahs from his spellbound audience, the last-minute stand-in cajoled a glass of plain water to change color mysteriously, and was in the midst of an impressive repertoire of other tricks when the doorbell rang—and moments later, reporters and cameramen at the doorstep of 20 Oxford Street were startled to discover the newly enshrined president of Harvard University "dressed in a busted derby and wearing a false nose."[1]

It would be difficult to envision Abbot Lawrence Lowell in such a pose—and that was precisely the point. This and many other piquant anecdotes, some genuine, some embellished, some fanciful, were printed by reporters looking to "humanize" the new occupant of the second-floor office (no. 5) in University Hall in the center of Harvard Yard, and of the imposing official residence at 17 Quincy Street. Simple, direct, modest, down-to-earth, unassuming, straightforward—these adjectives soon began attaching themselves to Conant's name as he began his presidency in the autumn of 1933, and the impression was enhanced by his brief but dignified installation ceremony on October 9, a far cry from Lowell's regal three-day enthronement, which had featured a massive outdoor convocation. In tune with the country's austerity footing and his own disdain for pomp, Conant's inauguration heralded a series of gestures that communicated the opening of a new era. "Harvard has crowned a commoner," it was proclaimed.

Like Roosevelt's "Hundred Days" earlier in 1933, and Kennedy's succession to the golfing Eisenhower a generation later, Conant blew into office with a gust of youthful freshness and energy, in line with Lowell's private advice to "strike out a new path unlike that of your predecessors."[2] Observers quickly discerned that the new president put little stock in ancient rituals and traditions that might have outlived their usefulness. In a ceremony that consumed all of fourteen minutes, he accepted the same charter and 1650 seal presented to John Leverett in 1707 by Harvard's Puritan elders and Governor Dudley, but dispensed with the Latin oration, singing of *Gloria Patri,* and sumptuous feast of fowls, mutton, apple and mince pies, and wine that in Leverett's time had seemed de rigueur.[3] Students were soon pleased to find that they were no longer awakened by the bell that had tolled since 1760 at seven each morning (six after the first Sunday in April) to herald the morning chapel service. They also received a jolt when they stepped past the ersatz Greek columns at the entrance of 17 Quincy Street for Sunday tea. Formerly, undergraduates were demurely seated in gilded Louis XIV furniture and balanced china on their knees as members of the Lowell family engaged them in polite conversation. Conant's affairs offered less tea and less formality—a breezy, buzzing hubbub of animated chatter and chaos, with maids hurrying to and fro, the two frolicking Conant boys rounding out the picture of a typical young academic's household.[4]

Unsentimentally pruning away Harvard customs and fripperies that interfered with intellectual and scholarly pursuits, Conant soon banished spring football practice, class rankings, and the Latin requirement—in the last case venting a grudge against the force-feeding of what he termed the "old fashioned classical tradition" that he had nursed since Roxbury Latin, and that would later cause him to sever relations to his once-loved school.[5] But he pleasantly surprised those who doubted his erudition outside science, when he vanquished a classicist's implicit rebuke for his dropping of Latin with the impromptu reply, during a visit to his old literary salon, that he had "come to praise the Signet, not to bury Caesar."[6]

More important than these atmospheric refinements, Conant's celerity in privately and publicly articulating his goals for Harvard, and his patent eagerness to learn on the job, won favorable initial reviews—even from skeptics like Clark and Frankfurter. "I am perfectly satisfied we have a splendid man," gushed Clark, relieved to find Conant a "good fellow—tolerant and kindly" rather than a "regular" fellow, and ready to embark on a friendship that would last almost until the end of Conant's presidency. Clark's assessment pleased but did not surprise Frankfurter, who had deduced from his friendship with Conant's older sister that, as he put it to Clark, "all his environment and traditions are those of simplicity and tolerance and good sense." What impressed him more were Conant's educational priorities. Even before being formally inaugurated, Conant had alleviated Frankfurter's concerns by vigorously seconding the latter's assertion that a university above all "means men"—i.e., the quality of its faculty. "You're telling me!" Conant shot back, adding that this would be "the chief theme of all his academic song." After being solicited confidentially for advice on top-flight recruitment prospects not only in political science but in any field where he knew of a worthwhile scholar, Frankfurter had the sense that Harvard's leader "does care for quality and will go after it," although he implored Clark to make sure Conant got good advice outside the sciences, since he had much to learn and was likely to "form his judgments rather quickly and with a good deal of self-confidence."[7] "I hope that experience will stretch his mind," Frankfurter concluded, for Conant had been preoccupied with scientific problems to which there were often complicated but nevertheless "very definite answers"— but now his subject matter would be "the perversities and obscurities of human nature."[8]

When an enterprising reporter contacted Jennett Bryant Conant for a comment on her son's prospects, the elderly women uttered words that undoubtedly sent a chill through those who feared that her son might attempt too literally to apply his lab techniques in his new post. "He won't get excited," Mrs. Conant was quoted as saying. "Everything works out by formula; he'll compound his formula for running the university, and then stand over while it develops into substance."[9] Conant may have cringed at his mother's words, yet she was not far off the mark. He had sought high office not for the status or for the perquisites of power, but as a means to achieve larger ends. Eliot had converted Harvard from a parochial school for the betterment of the region to a regional university in the service of the nation; aiming still higher, Conant believed in a national university for the betterment of country, world, and species—and most of all, to advance *knowledge.*[10]

He aimed, he wrote in his first annual presidential report, to inculcate a "zest for intellectual adventure" and a "true reverence for learning in the community. It is not sufficient to train investigators and scholars, no matter how brilliant they may be; a large body of influential citizens must have a passionate interest in the growth of human knowledge."[11] To convert Harvard from a fast-ossifying gentleman's club to a meritocratic, high-intensity, Germanic free-for-all, Conant carefully laid the groundwork for an assault on the Brahmin power structure both on the student body and, ultimately, on the Corporation, and for a streamlining of the faculty into a leaner "collection of eminent scholars," a strategy that would simultaneously contain expenditures and raise Harvard's prestige.

Conant let it be known immediately that he would be a much tougher, "hands-on" president than Lowell when it came to monitoring faculty actions and composition. Taking advantage of a rarely exercised privilege, he undertook to preside over every faculty meeting in the university—at least sixteen regular sessions every month—which was unheard of. Accustomed to debating matters of the medical school or law school or business school in relative privacy, some deans and professors appreciated the interest, but others resented being watched over so closely. At the law school, faculty members sometimes circumvented Conant's intrusion by holding rump sessions before the formal meetings, then displaying a cheerful consensus on all issues.[12]

"To what do we owe this honor?" the surprised dean of the medical school is supposed to have asked his uninvited guest.

"To the fact that you have a new president."[13]

Conant in his first few years initiated many innovations including graduate degrees in education, public policy, and the history of science; the Nieman fellowships program, which allowed professional journalists to come to Harvard for unstructured year-long sabbaticals of study and scholarship; and, in an effort to enhance interdisciplinary cogitation, new roving university professorships unattached to any specific department.[14]

More controversial was Conant's firm intention, quickly stated but only gradually implemented, to scrutinize faculty appointments rigorously. Within a few months, he had passed the word, publicly and privately, that only the most "brilliant young men" among junior faculty would receive permanent posts. It was, he said, "mistaken philosophy to keep a mediocre man in a university during a time of depression"—a university was only obliged to give a young scholar a fair chance to show his promise. As early as in his first presidential report he warned: "Excellent tutoring, like excellent lecturing, should be given great weight in considering a young man for promotion, but by itself it should not be sufficient to insure a permanent career at Harvard." As at Berlin, Göttingen, or Leipzig, only rarely might young scholars stay at the same university for an entire career; more often, they should head off to another school, there to seek a reputation for scholarly merit and a call to return to the nest. Countering Harvard's incestuous hiring practices, Conant's envisioned tenure process required searching for the best person available in the world to fill each new vacancy. By the end of 1933, he was pressing Murdock to weed out young scholars unlikely to rise to the top. Presaging the "up or out" rule that later became the norm, he warned that after four years of temporary appointments any extra contracts would "be subject to the severest scrutiny and, except in extraordinary cases, will probably be denied."[15]

True to his mother's prediction, Bryant had prepared his formula—and begun waiting for the reaction to compound.

Democratizing the student body went more smoothly than reforming faculty tenure procedures—and within months of his taking office, with the freshman scholarships he instituted for gifted students of limited means from the Middle West, Conant's social philosophy started to transform Harvard. From a college dedicated to educating the privileged sons of the Anglo-Saxon establishment so that they might man the stations already awarded them by birth, Harvard under Conant's stewardship shifted its orientation to "training an ambitious elite to accept the responsibilities which will go with the privileges and power they will eventually acquire."[16] Henry Adams had described in his *Education* the kind of indolent gentlemen Conant felt Harvard would do better without, yet whose exclusion might raise the ire of socially and financially powerful alumni:

> For generation after generation, Adamses and Brookses and Boylstons and Gorhams had gone to Harvard College, and although none of them, as far as known, had ever done any good there, or thought himself the better for it, custom, social ties, convenience, and, above all, economy, kept each generation on the track. Any other education would have required a serious effort, but no one took Harvard College seriously. All went there because their friends went, and the College was their ideal of social self-respect.[17]

Impatient with privileged sloth, Conant sympathized with the "meatballs"—the ambitious, lower-middle-class local students, the first- and second-generation ethnic immigrants who worked overtime to overcome prejudice (and quotas) so as to enter the establishment at Harvard and then, with their degrees, in the outside world. Soon Dudley House opened, a headquarters in the Yard for commuters, transients, foreign students, and others previously consigned to the margins of campus existence. "Conant was the first president to recognize that meatballs were Harvard men, too," recalled Theodore H. White, a hungry, ambitious Jewish meatball from Boston who, after devouring John K. Fairbank's Chinese history lessons, was to graduate in 1938 with a letter of introduction from Conant to go off to cover the Chinese civil war. White fondly recalled the liberating welcome Conant gave to newcomers. "We all squatted on the floor of the Freshmen Union, and he told us what a university was: a place for free minds. 'If you call everyone to the right of you a Bourbon and everyone to the left of you a Communist, you'll get nothing out of Harvard,' he said to us. And went on to explain that what we would get out of Harvard was what we could take from it ourselves: Harvard was open, so—go seek."[18]

Finding and selecting the exceptional youths around the country deserving of Harvard's new fellowships presented a new challenge, and to meet it Conant acted to advance the trend toward modern testing methods that had arisen since 1917. Lowell had disdained the use of such tests, but Conant had a chemist's predilection for the gathering of quantitative, empirical data, and what he admitted in *My Several Lives* was an "almost naive faith" that tests of verbal and mathematical aptitudes could be "the keys which would unlock all doors to a more promising future." Though he admitted to being "ignorant about the whole subject of objective testing," he characteristically moved to educate himself in his first year as Harvard's president by consulting several leading "psychometricians" and assigning two assistant deans, William Bender and Henry Chauncey, to investigate whether the recently created Scholastic Aptitude Test (SAT) could serve as a reliable measure of a youth's prospects for subsequent educational performance. They answered affirmatively, and Conant soon had a chance to accelerate the field's development as a member of the Carnegie Foundation for the Advancement of Teaching's board of trustees, to which he was elected in November 1934. To the foundation's existing interest Conant joined his own and Harvard's active support, deputizing Chauncey to cooperate in the development of a standardized nationwide graduate school entrance examination and an overhaul of the existing tests for college applicants. By late 1936, the historian Charles DeWayne Biebel reports, "thanks to James B. Conant and Henry Chauncey, Harvard was again moving back into the vanguard of the testing movement." And the following year, Conant headed a drive to consolidate several educational testing agencies into one, an effect that failed at first but led in 1946 to the creation of the Educational Testing Service under Chauncey's direction.[19] For all their many faults, the spread of mass standardized tests offered one more avenue for a wider pool of qualified youths to knock on the doors of Harvard and other elite schools.

Although it took World War II and the postwar GI Bill really to pry open Harvard and give it a more diverse student body and although rhetorical progress came more readily than real results—the bias in favor of alumni "legacies," for example, never fully disappeared[20]—Conant quickly set a new tone and direction. By 1936 he had gone beyond the initial program to bring exceptionally able midwestern youths to Harvard to initiate a "National Scholarships" policy to provide financial aid to selected applicants from southern and western states and to the graduate schools as well as the college.[21] And, although this scheme bore uncomfortable resemblance to Lowell's unsavory attempts to restrict the admission of Jews from northeastern city schools by stressing geographic diversity, Conant's administration chipped away at the residual anti-Jewish practices at Harvard, and they would largely collapse by the time he left. In racial matters, too, Conant eschewed Lowell's blatant prejudice. When an alumnus offered in 1934 to endow a fellowship limited to Kentuckians "preferably of predominantly white colonial descent, and necessarily of white northwestern European descent," Conant insisted that any Harvard fellowship must be awarded to "the most promising boys" regardless of other considerations[22] — a stand contrasting with Yale's acceptance in 1936 of funds for a scholarship memorializing "the Anglo-Saxon race to which the United States owes its culture" and restricted to "sons of white Christian parents of Anglo-Saxon, Scandinavian, or Teutonic descent, both of whom were citizens of the United States and born in America."[23]

But, as his critics have noted, Conant's liberal egalitarian philosophy, aimed primarily at the "academically talented," neglected some sectors of American society still on the fringes of educational acceptability:

> Conant argued that children from all social classes were to have an opportunity to reach the professions and become America's future leaders. Conant pretty much limited access to the professions to the upper fifteen to twenty percent of youth as determined by intelligence tests. Through testing knowledge thus became categorized and predetermined. The same was true for those who would have access to this knowledge. Out of this efficient technique emerged limited access to the professions. To his credit, Conant understood that the poor and culturally disadvantaged quite possibly were being discriminated against. To his discredit, Conant did little about it.[24]

His upbringing, while outside the Brahmin mainstream and adequate to inoculate him against most forms of bigotry, had not brought him into extensive contact with the Irish, blacks, Jews, or others still fighting for acceptance against racial or ethnic barriers, nor did he strain to seek them out.[25] During his presidency, Harvard traversed the path from enlightened ideals to classroom reality only in fits and starts, albeit faster than its Ivy League competitors. Dormitories remained segregated until World War II, the negligible black contingent grew at a glacial pace until a decision in 1950 to recruit it more actively, and Conant, reflecting the mores of his era, was not above racial jokes that, while not mean-spirited, were insulting or condescending.[26] Confronted with evidence of lingering anti-Semitism at Harvard, Conant rejected openly confronting the issue head-on on the grounds that this would be "dynamite" for the university, and as late as 1939 a faculty inquiry concluded that bias against Jews persisted in some departments and in housing allotments. As for women, Conant was a confirmed skeptic, "throw[ing] up my hands in complete despair and consternation" when it came to "the education of the fairer sex," and he once admitted that the "last thing in the world I desired when I took office was to open Harvard College to young ladies." But, like Churchill's boast about the British empire, Conant acquiesced in the collapse of Harvard's males-only classrooms, although he permitted coeducation only under wartime duress.[27]

Still, Conant had firmly realigned his alma mater, setting it on a course toward a goal implicit in his own philosophy ever since his collegiate visit to Wisconsin, if not earlier: the creation of a geographically balanced, national university, a microcosm of the "flexible classless society" he hoped would arise in the United States. In the vision he now began insistently to articulate, America's universities and public schools would assume the responsibility to seek out, sponsor, and cultivate the cream of each generation so as to train them as citizens, scholars, and leaders—"to cull," in Jefferson's words, "from every condition of our people a natural aristocracy of talent and virtue."[28]

Important as they were, Conant's tactics for the restructuring of Harvard in the 1930s paled alongside the issues he would face as a result of ominous international developments. In a decade of revolution, upheaval, and dictators, the rise of Hitler was only the darkest cloud on a stormfront of political and ideological extremism, intolerance, and uncertainty. In the Soviet Union, Stalin staged assassinations and show trials as his sweeping, murderous purge gained force; Japanese militarists threw a tight clamp on protectorates in China and eyed other areas vulnerable to incorporation in their Asian "co-prosperity sphere." European fascism seemed to have a bright future. During Conant's first six years in office, Hitler's Germany launched a rapid rearmament drive, remilitarized the Rhineland, and pushed for Lebensraum in countries to its south and east; Mussolini's Italy flexed its muscles by trampling on Ethiopia, thumbing its nose at the powerless League of Nations; both dictators cooperated in Spain to help fascists overthrow the leftist Republican government. In England and France, meanwhile, democratic governments dithered impotently, unable to rule effectively at home or forge viable defensive coalitions abroad.

With democratic forces, institutions, and ideas on the retreat overseas, the Depression also threatened cherished assumptions about the durability and utility of constitutional government in the United States. Even Franklin D. Roosevelt's inaugural address contained what the historian Frank Freidel describes as a "chilling analogy" to the totalitarian temptation. Assuming the presidency from Hoover on March 4, 1933, after a painful four-month interregnum during which economic confidence had plummeted to new depths, FDR spoke of taking command of "this great army of people" and alluded to the possibility of seeking "the one remaining instrument to meet the crisis—broad Executive power to wage a war against the emergency, as great as the power that would be given to me if we were in fact invaded by a foreign foe."[29]

The closest that President Conant came to a true inaugural address came at the close of his first academic year in office, in June 1934, when he spoke to the thousands of alumni and new graduates thronging Harvard's annual pomp-filled Commencement. Of the many singular dangers he could address, he singled out the menace to universities posed by the violent ideological squall raging abroad and at home, and he promised to do battle to defend academic freedom at Harvard. "Whatever be the outcome of the uncertain future which the whole world faces," he asserted, "the universities must stand firm by their principle which insures the right of free inquiry and free debate." Hoping to blunt alumni criticism of Felix Frankfurter and other professors aiding the New Deal, he vowed that "Harvard's stimulating atmosphere" would foster debate of current problems, and that "so far as possible all sides should be represented among the permanent members of the staff."30

How well did Conant fulfill his self-proclaimed role of defending academic freedom in an era of domestic and foreign crisis, ideological polarization, and ultimately war? Repeatedly, Conant defined and adopted lofty principles, but his actions uncomfortably blended principle and pragmatism, courage and squeamishness, personal integrity and concessions to the constraints of his position. As a leader of American education whose stature soared during his time in office, Conant represented more than himself, or even Harvard, each time he took a stand or failed to take one; his responses to great issues said much about the response of America's most prestigious and influential institutions to profound political, ideological, and moral challenges and questions. And until World War II, the two questions that most gravely tested Conant's moral leadership were how strongly Harvard would oppose the Nazi persecution of universities in Germany, and how fiercely Harvard would fight challenges to its own freedom and independence coming from forces hostile to the leftist opinions being expressed on its campus.

Though Conant loathed the Nazi regime that had taken over his beloved Germany, in his first six years as president of Harvard he attempted a delicate balancing act between outright expressions of distaste and the reticent tact he felt his position required. When he did give vent to public denunciation of Hitler's rule, he focused on the danger it constituted to German academic freedom and to the formerly proud institutions he had visited in 1925. The scholar who has studied the record most carefully has concluded that while his private views consistently reflected deep loathing for the Nazification of Germany's universities, Conant's timidity, inconsistency, and "unduly cautious actions" lent comfort to Berlin and typified a failure of American leaders to alert Americans to the dangers of Hitlerism.31

Conant's wavering stance in defining Harvard's "diplomatic relations" with Germany gives an early indication of the difficulties he faced. Until the moment he finally made up his mind in mid-1940 that Hitler needed to be stopped at any price, including war, his concern for propriety and public relations seemed to outweigh any recognition of the enormity of the menace Hitler posed; it fostered a short-sighted conception of solidarity for threatened colleagues and values which blunted the force of any clarion calls he might make for academic freedom.

Such, at any rate, was the impression Conant gave in several decisions during his first year in office. In one case, inherited from Lowell's final months (and glossed over in My Several Lives), he and the Corporation quietly voted to keep Harvard aloof from an Emergency Committee in Aid of Displaced German Scholars, a coalition publicly backed by the presidents of Cornell, Princeton, Stanford, and Williams, and many other colleges. Examining the credentials of the proposed visitors, Conant said he didn't see anyone the university could use and warned the committee's organizers to guard against the tendency "to mix up charity and education." Although Harvard eventually took in émigré scholars, this initial cold-blooded indifference showed Conant's serious underestimation of the contributions these refugees from Hitler would make to American scholarship, not to mention what historian William M. Tuttle, Jr., labeled his "failure of compassion and political sensitivity."[32]

In the spring of 1934, a far more public controversy sprang up over the class of 1909's decision to invite a wealthy German alumnus who had become Hitler's press secretary and confidant to officiate at its twenty-fifth-anniversary reunion during the June commencement week.[33] Among Hitler's camp followers, the lineage of Ernest F. S. "Putzi" Hanfstaengl stood out; his mother hailed from a prominent New England family, the Sedgwicks, while two generations of his father's ancestors belonged to the court of the dukes of Saxe-Coburg-Gotha and had a reputation as patrons of the arts. Hanfstaengl's singular social credentials, access to dollars during the Weimar inflation, and piano-playing skills had attracted Hitler, who was regaled by his playing Wagner and then by his composing a march derived from a Harvard football chant. "That is it," Hitler clucked, pacing, as he listened raptly to descriptions of how cheerleaders and bands had roused the crowds at Soldiers Field. "That is what we need for the movement, marvelous." Soon, "Fight, Fight, Fight!" was converted into *"Sieg Heil, Sieg Heil!"* Hanfstaengl also came in handy after the botched 1923 Beer Hall Putsch, when Hitler hid from the police in his friend's Munich house. In the late 1920s the two had a brief falling-out, but as the Nazis neared the pinnacle of German power, Hitler hired Hanfstaengl as press secretary, relying on him for advice on foreign affairs and for creative publicity-seeking stunts.[34]

True to form, Hanfstaengl constructed his sentimental journey to Harvard in the spring of 1934 to assure screaming headlines. Before departing from Berlin, he called in reporters to witness his signing of a bank note for 2,500 Deutsche marks made out to James B. Conant to endow a "Dr. Hanfstaengl scholarship" for Harvard students to study in Germany, and he kept newspapers wondering until the last minute whether he would actually sail across the Atlantic to attend the ceremony.

Undeterred by the protesters that greeted his arrival in New York or by press criticism of Harvard's designation of him to serve as an aide to his class marshal, and eager to spread propaganda for his master, the tubby, exuberant Hanfstaengl waded into the Cambridge festivities to join his classmates. Over the next few weeks, he lived it up at balls, weddings, even the Harvard-Yale crew races in New Haven, and assiduously offered gifts to prestigious recipients that would honor Germany and its new rulers. To the large right-wing faction of Harvard students and alumni, entertaining a representative of Europe's most notorious dictator brought no shame; the conservative *Crimson* even urged the college administration to confer an honorary degree on Hanfstaengl in view of his high government post. Tuttle has vividly described

the buffoonish high jinks of this Nazi flunky and the reaction of the many
Harvard graduates who seemed more bemused than offended by their fellow
alumnus:

> Hanfstaengl was front-page news almost every day in Boston, the newspa-
> pers picturing him as jovial and jocular—as Hitler's "court jester." Much of
> his free time he spent at the piano keyboard, drinking tumblers of gin and
> singing bawdy ballads upon request. His hair was dishevelled and his suit
> wrinkled, but his broad, toothy grin was indeed jolly and he looked like an
> overgrown clown. During the annual class day ceremonies in the stadium, he
> marched with his class in the parade and rendered the Nazi salute to his
> friends as the band struck up "Ach, du lieber Augustine." This brought roars
> of delight from the stands, as did the antics of the Class of 1924 who in
> imitation strutted in goosestep and extended stiffly their right arms Nazi-style.[35]

To those who felt it vital for Harvard to be at the forefront of U.S.
education's efforts to denounce Nazi abuses, the glow of Conant's honeymoon
was fast fading. In Cambridge and around the nation, scattered but intense
blasts of anger were directed at the country's most prestigious university for
awarding a place of honor to a man who sang paeans to Nazi and Aryan
supremacy and proudly paraded his anti-Semitism—Germany's Jews, Hanfstaengl proclaimed, were "leeches" feeding on his country's body politic,
"dead branches" destined to be chopped off by a "surgeon," *der Führer*, "so
that the tree could take on new life."[36]

Conant averred that as president he had no right to interfere with a
reunion committee's actions, but his only face-to-face encounter with Hitler's
lickspittle public relations man, a perfunctory handshake at a presidential
receiving line for alumni, revealed no warmth toward the guest who had
overshadowed Harvard's year-ending bash.

"I bring you greetings from Hönigschmid," said Hanfstaengl, referring to
the chemist who had escorted Conant around Germany in 1925.

But the carefully prepared line failed to break the ice. Uninterested in
banter and convinced in any case that Hönigschmid was a Nazi, Conant did
not return the greetings.

Hanfstaengl's farcical visit climaxed at Commencement itself, the university's annual graduation festivities held before a throng of more than ten
thousand graduates and guests packed into Harvard Yard and featuring the
presentation of honorary degrees and a speech by a distinguished visitor. In
1934, Conant's efforts to keep politics out of the show failed miserably, as two
women wearing red ribbons adorned with the words "Down with Hitler"
infiltrated the proceedings, shouted slogans against "fascist butchers," and
chained themselves to wooden bleachers where they remained, still screaming,
until police arrested them, a feat requiring the removal of several rows of the
stands. University authorities declined to press charges against the women,

but seven other anti-Nazi activists nabbed in Harvard Square by police later on during Commencement day received stiff sentences.

The Corporation deferred consideration of Hanfstaengl's scholarship gambit until the following fall, but Conant proved helpless to derail another Nazi attempt to exploit Harvard in September, when the University of Berlin announced that it would award an honorary degree to the dean of the Law School, Roscoe Pound. Germany's rulers had good reason to honor Pound; in two newspaper interviews following a recent visit, he had gushed admiration for Hitler's "new order" and discounted reports of persecution of Jews. Felix Frankfurter, disgusted by Pound's plan to accept the degree personally from a German envoy in a special public ceremony in the law school's Langdell Hall, with a reception to follow at a fancy downtown hotel, drafted a curt note declining to attend and expressing his "sense of humiliation" that "my beloved Law School, the centre of Anglo-American law, should even by indirection confer special distinction upon an official representative of enthroned lawlessness."[37]

Frankfurter set up a lunchtime appointment with Conant on September 14 to plead that he minimize Harvard's contribution to Hitlerist prestige. He found him highly sympathetic but unyielding.

"We're in a kind of a hole, and I don't see how we can get out of it," Conant told Frankfurter. While contemptuously terming Pound a pro-Nazi and a "pathological case," he nevertheless stated, fairly enough, that it would be inconsistent with academic freedom to order Pound not to accept the honorary degree. But, sliding down a slippery slope of rationalizations, Conant went on to say that he could not reject the German ambassador's request to make the presentation at the law school, and furthermore, "when I was asked to attend, I thought that as President of the University I could not stay away without insulting a friendly government." Unimpressed, Frankfurter noted in his memo of the conversation that he had refrained from "pointing out to Conant that to exercise a veto power on Pound's personal right to accept a degree from Germany is one thing; to allow Langdell Hall to be turned into a Nazi holiday is quite another."

Conant, perhaps sensing that his reasoning was not especially convincing, several times confessed uncertainty over whether he was doing the right thing, and chafed at the limitations his office placed on the outrage he could express. "If I were not President of the University," he assured Frankfurter, "I would write the kind of letter you are proposing to send to Pound, because I feel about the German situation the way you do. If I were a member of the Corporation and were asked to attend, I wouldn't feel I was called upon to attend. And so there is every reason why you should send Pound the letter which you have written."

Though committed to attend the award luncheon for Pound at the Ritz-Carlton Hotel, Conant worried that German ambassador Hans Luther might take advantage of the occasion to read a pro-Nazi homily, and he prepared a rebuttal, just in case. But he remained silent when the envoy delivered an innocuous speech, and let his discomfort show only when photographers attempted to corral him to pose with Luther and Pound. "I'm not in it," Conant snapped. "It's strictly a matter between these two gentlemen. I'm not in it."[38]

A week later, when Hanfstaengl's scholarship offer came up for consideration with the Corporation, Conant finally mustered the gumption to make a firm anti-Nazi gesture. Convinced that "Hitler's henchmen were trying to use Harvard as an American base to spread approval of the Nazi regime," he forthrightly insisted that the university reject the offer. "We are unwilling," he wrote to Hanfstaengl on behalf of the Corporation, "to accept a gift from one who has been so closely associated with the leadership of a political party which has inflicted damage on the universities of Germany through measures which have struck at principles which we believe to be fundamental to universities throughout the world."[39]

These clear-sighted words earned widespread applause from many enemies of Nazism, with congratulatory letters and editorials far outnumbering the anonymous hate notes he received with "Heil Hitler!" scrawled over them.[40] After the disappointment with the Pound affair, Frankfurter felt a surge of pride in Harvard. "Your response to the Hanfstaengl offer," he wrote Conant, "is a heartening and noble reaffirmation of the very basis of modern western civilization and of the university as its chief intellectual instrument."[41]

It did Conant good finally to stop equivocating, speak his mind about the Nazis, and put Harvard on the side of the angels. "I must admit that it is a load off my conscience to have come out in this way," he wrote to a friend. "I don't think that a university or the head of a university should attack foreign governments however much he may dislike what they do, but I do think universities have an interest which transcends national lines; and what the Hitler regime has done to learning is so frightful that we ought to protest. I felt that tolerance had gone as far as it possibly could at Commencement time last June and at the more recent ceremony in Langdell Hall."[42]

Harvard's awarding in 1935 of honorary degrees to two distinguished German refugees, Thomas Mann and Albert Einstein, strengthened Conant's new reputation as a stalwart enemy of Nazi abuses. That same year, he furthered his stature as a spokesman for academic freedom by leading a drive by Massachusetts educational leaders to oppose an effort by the state legislature to impose a mandatory teachers' loyalty oath. "We do not believe this oath will be of the slightest service," declared the presidents of Harvard, Radcliffe, MIT, Amherst, and other Massachusetts colleges in a public manifesto, since "no disloyal plotter or seditious conspirator, if any such indeed exist in our whole teaching force, would hesitate to take this oath and then violate it." Passage of the oath would be a dangerous precedent, they argued, that might be a first step toward the kind of state-imposed regimentation of education then taking place "in Russia and certain European countries."[43]

What a journal called Conant's "black hatred of the Communist, the Fascist, and the Hitlerite policies of oppression" increasingly laced his speeches and public pronouncements, as he eased into his new role as a self-proclaimed militant in the battle to preserve universities from outside pressure and, in the case of Germany, devastating repression.[44] "Scholarship is under fire to-day from many directions," he warned in a speech at Amherst College, later revised for the April 1935 *Atlantic Monthly.* "The ever-recurring suspicion of man's creative intelligence has once again become a powerful force and threatens to sweep all before it." Fed up with being "pestered from the reactionaries to take a strong stand against 'the dangerous radicals' in the universities, and particularly at Harvard," he unapologetically called for universities to serve as "an arena for combat" for a no-holds-barred debate on the vital social, political, and economic issues of the day. Rival doctrines and viewpoints in the humanities and social sciences, he insisted, must be ventilated for the benefit of students through vigorous controversies.

It seems to me that there is a certain tendency among our scholars to avoid debate. Perhaps a false analogy with the natural sciences has had a stifling effect. One seems to feel that the opposing forces are at times sulking in their tents, enjoying their own brand of orthodoxy, damning all heterodoxy in private, but not engaging in open discussion as freely as might be desired. Our colleges and universities must not only guarantee the right of free inquiry, they must also see that the various points of view are represented so that a conflict of opinion really takes place. From such clashes fly the sparks that ignite the enthusiasm in the students which drives them seriously to examine the questions raised. We must have our share of thoughtful rebels on our faculties.[45]

"Behold the turtle," Harvard's president liked to advise listeners, "it only makes progress when it sticks its neck out." But Conant's actions did not always match the militancy implicit in his encouragement of "thoughtful rebels" or rip-roaring campus controversies. His new authority emboldened him to follow a scorched-earth policy when it came to fervently held educational views, but his sense of propriety, responsibility, and caution also led him to actions—or inactions—that vitiated his principled rhetoric and laid him open to charges of inconsistency and expediency.

Conant's pragmatism often disappointed his more liberal friends. Once the Massachusetts legislature passed the teachers' oath bill in June 1935, he rejected advice that Harvard refuse to cooperate with the noxious measure, and told the faculty that he would obey the statute's provision that prohibited employing any teacher who failed to swear loyalty to the U.S. and Massachusetts constitutions. "I am taking the oath," Conant wrote, "and hope that all members of the various faculties of this University will do likewise."[46]

Notwithstanding Harvard's heritage of heresy epitomized by Henry David Thoreau, Conant's "treasured armory of liberal principles" did not include, as he put it, "the doctrine of passive resistance."[47] Chastely pronouncing himself "shocked and surprised" when some professors refused to sign the oath for political or religious reasons, Conant pleaded with them to give in, negotiated with the state attorney general to accept qualified compliance, and urged faculty members to await the election of a more favorably disposed legislature before launching a repeal campaign. Unyielding in his insistence that Harvard had an obligation to enforce even those laws with which it fundamentally disagreed, Conant's obeisance to order and authority foreshadowed the attitude he was to take when congressional panels would call during the McCarthy period:

> To my mind it is out of the question for the President of a semi-public institution, as I regard Harvard to be, to defy in any way the well organized method of the people of the state of expressing their will, namely by a law passed by the legislature. There is no question that the law intended to put the burden on the President of an institution to see that all the teachers did sign the oath, and I was unwilling to and should be unwilling again to do anything except carry out the intent and spirit of such a law, even when I opposed it. (The question of taking a test case to court is, of course, an entirely different matter.) I am afraid that on this matter I have as much of a conscience as our friend [Harvard theologian Henry J.] Cadbury, the Quaker who is now refusing to take the oath without qualification (after all, I had a Quaker grandmother myself!).[48]

Throwing more cold water on Conant's tolerance for controversy were the plans for a lavish birthday party in September 1936 to celebrate the three-hundredth anniversary of Harvard's founding, envisioned as a two-week scholarly saturnalia uniting the world's greatest minds, reaping a harvest of positive publicity, and capping a crucial three-year fund-raising drive. Like his counterpart in Washington, Conant had the responsibility to create a climate of confidence and optimism in the institution's basic solvency and stability, and the tercentenary was viewed as an audacious attempt to do just that. Still eager to prove himself to the old-money crowd that had permitted him to run the place, Conant was acutely conscious of the risks involved in an ambitious hat-passing effort during the Depression, and he fretted.

One sore point, he knew, was the anticipated presence at the festivities of President Roosevelt, who to many Brahmin alumni (as well as to the *Crimson*'s editorial board) was purveying a dangerous economic program that smacked of socialism. For rich graduates outraged by the New Deal's tougher taxation of wealthy persons and institutions, Roosevelt was a "traitor to his class." Already, Conant had been forced to face down an Overseers' revolt against the granting of an honorary degree in 1935 to FDR's outspoken secretary of agriculture, Henry Wallace, and he had stolidly ignored conservative alumni carping about Felix Frankfurter's moonlighting as a Roosevelt adviser.[49]

Conant's unobtrusive but unabashed sympathy for the New Deal elicited criticism from other quarters as well. In private conversation, Conant expressed admiration for FDR's goals, and on occasion was not afraid to show his angry dissent from the contempt toward the reformist president expressed by so many in Cambridge. (He gave less than unqualified support, however, arousing ire in the White House by openly opposing FDR's 1937 scheme to pack the Supreme Court, and he carefully refrained from public electoral endorsements.) In the spring of 1936 Conant and his wife welcomed Mr. and Mrs. Robert Frost to dinner during Frost's brief stay at Harvard to deliver the Charles Eliot Norton lectures. The evening feast turned sour when the poet and president sparred sharply over the difference between the scientific and humanistic outlooks, and then politics utterly destroyed it. Conant praised FDR for his having recently invited representatives of the Teamsters Union to the White House as a gesture of support for organized labor, Frost nastily criticized this as a sign of New Deal profligacy. Roosevelt's welcoming speech should be titled "Every Man's Home His Own Poorhouse," he tartly suggested, for soon those union members would all be relying on the government dole. Conant didn't laugh, replying acridly, "You have a bitter tongue."[50]

The irritation generated by quarrels with alumni and visiting bards was nothing in comparison to the headache that arose when Harvard's crusty president-emeritus, who was to preside over the alumni meeting that would cap the year-long tercentenary celebrations, balked at sharing center stage with a politician he despised. Lowell was soon persuaded that Harvard could not very well hold such an affair without inviting its most famous alumnus, especially since an invitation had already gone out and since presidents had been invited to address previous affairs of this sort.[51] But he remained fearful, as he told Conant in March 1936, that FDR might exploit the tercentenary "to make a stump speech" that would "ruin the occasion."[52] He peppered Roosevelt with condescendingly phrased invitations to limit his remarks to no more than ten or fifteen minutes, and to "divorce yourself from the arduous demands of politics and political speech-making" at a gathering dedicated to "the mutual congratulation of the graduates at the three hundredth anniversary of their alma mater." Roosevelt had accepted Conant's invitation with the jocular request that he be treated "as much like a member of the Class of 1904 and as little like the President of the United States as you possibly can," but he can hardly have expected to be taken literally. Yet Lowell did little to hide his heartfelt wish that the president would be treated *precisely* as just another graduate and no more. FDR relied on the "ca'm judgment" of his friend Frankfurter to draft some suitably dignified responses to Lowell, and refused to do more than to promise to speak in a manner "true to the requirements of the office which I shall represent on the occasion."[53]

Conant's handling of this titanic spat — connoisseurs of upper-crust tackiness may turn to *Roosevelt and Frankfurter* to savor the entire catty correspondence, published in 1967 to Conant's great annoyance — showed his improving sense of politics and personalities. While sympathizing with

Roosevelt's exasperation, he concentrated on soothing Harvard's crotchety
elder statesman, urging him to set aside his fears for a few months. By
August, he predicted, tempers will have cooled; and besides, he assured
Lowell, "it would be very bad politics for [FDR] to speak too long or to make
too much of a stump oration, and he is above everything else a politician."[54]
Thus did Conant successfully separate the quarreling giants, at least temporarily.
But pressure from Lowell and other right-wing alumni, together with the
battle about the teachers' oath and a general nervousness about his biggest
challenge since becoming president made him determined to keep the tercentenary free of political turbulence—as a young economist discovered to his
surprise.

Encouraged by Conant's Amherst address, Robert K. Lamb requested a
few minutes of Conant's time in the innocent hope of convincing him that
Harvard should not permit the tercentenary to pass without an opportunity
for the gathered scholars publicly to exchange views on contemporary political,
economic, and social crises. Alas, Lamb had no inkling that he was making
this reasonable request in the midst of Conant's efforts to defuse the secret
contretemps between Lowell and Roosevelt. On a blustery March afternoon,
Conant explained his refusal to go along with Lamb's idea as the two men
walked through Harvard Yard, and then sat in a parlor at 17 Quincy Street
while Mrs. Conant served tea to the irascible Frost in the next room.

Lamb's account of their remarkable conversation depicts a university
president fearful of taking risks in the name of free speech, and quickly
conceding that the planned celebration had degenerated from a congress of
openly exchanged views "into a great show where discussion would be out of
the question, a pageant in which no useful purpose would be served by
controversy."[55] But Conant encouraged Lamb to express his views, so he persisted. What about the Amherst speech? Was it only empty rhetoric? Did not
Conant also desire to have the university serve as a forum to explore vital issues?

> I said that I thought it unfortunate that the Tercentenary could not be used
> for public discussion of current controversies in the field of Society, since the
> world was not likely soon again to draw together so many eminent scholars in
> these fields, and it amounted to a lost opportunity. I recognized that the
> objects of the celebration included money-raising, and other non-controversial
> matters such as entertainment, and the celebration of Harvard's own history,
> and wanted only to register my regret.
>
> He said that I must realize how undesirable controversy would be at
> such a time, and I countered with the observation that it was undesirable for
> some reasons but that the cause of knowledge might be served. He seemed
> skeptical whether that was the way in which knowledge might be served.
> And he was quite firm on the danger presented by letting the press report
> such controversies. It would tend to involve the University's name, at a time
> when the oath bill had already involved the University community with the
> press, the patriots and the legislature.

I said that was the very matter which interested me most. How could he University expect to have such subjects discussed, even in the classrooms if it was not prepared to risk public clamor[?] He said he was prepared for clamor about subjects taught in the classroom, but not eager to invite such interest, for instance by encouraging outside speakers to use the University as a platform, or members of the University to use it either, for that matter.

The conversation then turned to another point of contention: Conant's attitude toward the social sciences. Many nonscientists on the faculty thought that Conant cared little for the cultivation of Harvard's writers, artists, economists, poets, or social analysts, intent instead to pour resources into bolstering the scientific departments. One economist recalls feeling that the brisk, businesslike Conant "fit the popular picture of the scientists as a severe, unfun-loving group of people."[56] And Frost, who jousted several times with Conant, left this jaundiced appraisal:

He was proud of being called Dr. James Bryant Conant, twenty-third president of Harvard College. To begin with, what place has a scientist as the head of a university? A scientist sees only science, his own. A researchist thinks all that matters is found in the precipitation at the bottom of a test tube. I told Conant once that it was mighty little he knew about humanities, or about poetry, or even about philosophy—with his nose stuck in a test tube. That's the trouble with scientists. They compute everything in milligrams on their tiny scales. They discount and discredit everything not reducible to an algebraic equation. But I've managed to slip in a little word of rebuttal in my books now and then, and don't you forget it, ever.

I remember one night at a party. Conant had been laying it on pretty thick, even for Conant. "The trouble with the nonscientific mind," he said, looking slyly at me, "is its inability to be practical. On the other hand, the scientist is a practical thinker." "Hold on, Conant," I put in, for I knew what he was driving at, slapping me over somebody else's shoulder. "Hold on. Don't tell me a poet is impractical or I'll get up and go home."

With all his science—research at Harvard, University of Chicago, Cal. Tech.—Conant was always a very "proper" individual, a Puritan and a prude if not a prig. He tried to regulate the lives of all his faculty—a task even a New Deal bureaucrat would have found strenuous. He tried to interfere with their mores. I have always felt that we should allow to every man his own manners. For myself I won't be shoved around. What's more to the point, I refuse to be directed by any outside force. My propulsion has got to come from inside myself. I'm a gyroscope, not a string top.[57]

Of course, some of this criticism was unmerited. Unlike Whitehead's prototypical chemist, Conant roamed widely in his reading, had thought seriously about issues in history and philosophy, and, as proof that he appreciated the need to transcend "thinking in a groove," had created interdisciplinary chairs to encourage scholars to transcend their specialties. But the social scientists' suspicions were not without foundation. Less comfortable with subjective analyses than with rigorous standards of facts and clearly defined, provable hypotheses, Conant found it difficult to credit such "unverifiable" disciplines as economics, psychology, government, history, and sociology. At least chemistry and astronomy had shaken off their superstitious shadows, alchemy and astrology, and medicine had similarly evolved into a respectable field worthy of university study. But the verdict was not in on whether the same could be said for the nonscientific studies in which more than half of Harvard's undergraduates received their degrees. "The real question which I keep turning over and over in my mind," he admitted to a correspondent in early 1936, "is whether or not the social sciences are the modern equivalents of astrology or of medicine."[58] A few years later he complained to a chemist friend that "many social philosophers are pretending to be scientists. As a result, the real scientists tend to get 'swamped.' "[59]

Even when a new project in the social sciences excited him, Conant's caution sometimes stayed his hand. Such had been the case some months before his conversation with Lamb, when two editors of *Fortune* magazine, Archibald MacLeish and Ralph Ingersoll, proposed that Harvard help launch *Fortune*'s latest innovation: using market research techniques to take public opinion surveys, a venture of special interest with a presidential election year upcoming. Hearing their pitch over breakfast, according to a somewhat breathless account by Ingersoll's biographer, Conant initially reacted enthusiastically, jumping to his feet and exclaiming that the polls could "revolutionize the functioning of democracy." And, indeed, the idea neatly accorded with Conant's yen for quantification, and he bubbled on, likening it to Watt's invention of the steam engine in cahoots with the University of London and promising to "turn the University loose" to develop public opinion polls on a broad range of subjects: "My God, this is immense!" But suddenly, he is supposed to have halted: "No! We can have nothing to do with it. *Nothing,* you understand, *nothing.* You haven't even discussed it with me!" "But Jim," MacLeish interrupted. "Archie, we couldn't even begin before we'd be in politics. And this university is a privately endowed institution. The slightest breath of involvement would destroy it. No, no, no . . . please leave me and don't ever say you've been here."[60]

Conant was more caustic about the social sciences to Lamb, and told him he was reluctant to spend a dime more than necessary on fields outside the purely scientific. "I consider the social sciences to be the new Theology," Conant was quoted as saying, alluding to the subject that Harvard's Puritan founders, "dreading to leave an illiterate Ministry to the Churches," had imposed on undergraduates until Eliot discontinued the requirement. Part of the problem with the social sciences at Harvard, Lamb replied, was that Conant seemed to favor as a typical appointment a "pretty tame middle-of-the-roader," afraid of controversy, to whom any supporter of Franklin

Roosevelt was a radical—in other words, hardly the sort of teacher who would inspire a lively debate. Well, Conant replied, who do you suggest, then? Lamb tossed out the names of a few radical economists, but Conant promptly cast a veto:

> He said that all those people would get Harvard into the headlines, and that the temper of the legislature and the alumni would not permit such appointments, even to visiting lectureships. Indeed, he had recently had a letter offering him a large sum of money if he would fire Professor Frankfurter. He added that of course he was prepared to fight endlessly on any individual case of that sort. I asked whether that meant he would fight for a new appointment, and he said that there greater caution was obviously required.
>
> I said that he seemed to me to be in a tough spot. As the presiding head of an endowed university he was bound to defer to his wealthy alumni, and that as far as I could see that made it practically impossible for him to take a bold stand on social questions. But that meant his Amherst speech would turn into mere pious wishes. He must either risk future gifts, or take the consequences in a limitation of free speech.
>
> He said that he considered the state universities somewhat better off on that score, but they had their troubles with legislatures. In his estimation, the problem was one of Machiavellianism. He had recently been reading 17th century history, and one head of an Oxford college had turned his coat seven times in the course of the Cromwellian revolution. He added, "I think I can do as well." "But," he laughed, "he married, I think it was Cromwell's niece, and that's out for me."

What Conant and Lamb spoke of next testifies to the gravity of the ideological crisis afflicting the United States in the 1930s—a matter-of-fact, straight-faced discussion of the possible rise of a fascist regime, and how Harvard would fare under it, financially and intellectually. With the Depression still shadowing the country, debates raged as to the relative merits of democracy compared to the ideologies of the rising dictatorships abroad. In the increasingly strident political atmosphere, conservatives watched with mounting alarm the proliferation of left-wing tastes and ideas around them—in the arts, where "proletarian literature" flourished, in commerce, where trade unions and strikes sprouted, and most of all in economics, where Roosevelt was relying on an infusion of state spending to create jobs, resuscitate growth, and mitigate suffering. To a significant if unquantifiable segment of Harvard's upper-class elite, the regimented efficiency of Italian fascism, which at least supposedly made the trains run on time and threw ruffians and radicals into prison camps, held an undeniable appeal compared to the scary alternative of socialism—there was, Conant later recalled, "quite an argument in and about Harvard" about Mussolini.[61]

To Lamb's charge that he seemed resigned to Harvard's going along with the tide and its rich alumni toward the "safe harbor" of fascism, Conant denied there was any immediate danger of that. But he hardly seemed a pillar of confidence in the staying power of American capitalism and democracy, either. When Lamb guessed that a fascist takeover was likely in five or ten years, Conant reportedly "shook his head and said he gave us twenty-five." Even if Lamb were to be proven right, Conant reportedly said, he was confident that "he could twist and turn his way through the maze of public opinion and maintain the only things in a University which were really important." To Lamb that implied protecting the integrity of the pure sciences and math, no sure thing in light of the treatment accorded those subjects in Germany and Italy. But Conant doubted the extent of the damage there, and voiced confidence that even under fascism Harvard could maintain its endowment intact. Lamb was skeptical, for Italian universities were hurting financially under the burden of state interference from Mussolini's officials. Conant said that was a new twist on him, glanced at his watch, thanked Lamb for an interesting talk, and wished him a pleasant spring vacation as he led his guest to the door.

"Well, good-bye," said Conant, "perhaps we shall meet in a concentration camp."

Conant's fear of igniting controversy also tempered his inclination to take a bold stand against academic abuses in Germany, and led him to a decision that dissipated much of the moral capital he had acquired in rejecting Hanfstaengl's scholarship two years earlier. At issue was Harvard's response to an invitation to attend Heidelberg University's 550th anniversary celebrations in June 1936.[62] Oxford, Cambridge, and numerous other British and European universities quickly announced their intention to boycott the ceremonies, disgusted by the ongoing purge of Jewish and dissident scholars and fearing the event would turn into a Nazi propaganda bash. But in March 1936, Harvard announced that it would send a representative, solemnly explaining that it was desirous of maintaining "the ancient ties by which the universities of the world are united" regardless of political exigencies. Amid a firestorm of criticism—pleading for a reversal, a disappointed Frankfurter quoted Oliver Wendell Holmes's dictum that "We live by symbols"—Conant cited high principle and derided the "confused thinking" of British universities that had spurned Heidelberg.[63] "[P]olitical, racial or religious matters" should not interfere with "academic or scientific relations," he declared. A "policy of ostracism" would "head . . . down the path which leads to the terrible prejudices and absurd actions taken by scientists and universities during the World War [I]." Despite "distressing" Nazi actions, he vowed, Harvard would continue to welcome visits by "German scholars here as scholars whether they be Nazis in their hearts or not."[64]

Privately, Conant conceded that his decision had been an expedient one; to snub Heidelberg would risk provoking a retaliatory boycott of Harvard's own fete, to which Heidelberg officials as well as several German scientists had already been invited, with the resultant publicity interfering with the planned fund-raising and self-congratulation. "What my views would have been if we had not been celebrating our Tercentenary, I cannot tell you," he admitted to Princeton's president, Harold Dodds, adding—in a turn of phrase that would suit many of his most controversial stands—that in accepting Heidelberg's invitation he may have been merely "rationalizing a situation into which circumstances forced us!"[65]

In the end, the presence of a Harvard delegate at Heidelberg dignified a crudely Nazified spectacle festooned with swastikas and choreographed by Joseph Goebbels's Propaganda Ministry. After an opening that featured a parade of goose-stepping storm troopers, speaker after speaker acclaimed Hitler's definition of scholarship as a servant of Aryan greatness. Conant, scanning the newspaper accounts, privately expressed disgust with such "nonsense," which he considered "not only absurd but dangerous." At least the orators had not mentioned the presence of delegates from American universities as a sign that U.S. educators approved of Nazi ideology; and on what Tuttle has justifiably called that "flimsy pretext," Conant and the presidents of Yale and Columbia, James R. Angell and Nicholas Murray Butler, shelved a joint press release they had prepared which criticized the perversion of the academic occasion.[66]

Conant's nightmares were not realized—the tercentenary celebrations went off without a serious hitch, surviving even the downpour that confounded three years of meteorological prophesying and drenched the more than twenty thousand alumni, students, and savants who descended on a banner-filled Harvard Yard on the morning of September 18, 1936. A bugle heralded the finale of months of parties, celebrations, evocations of Harvard lore and scholarly (and apolitical) discourses by Carl C. Jung, Sir Arthur Eddington, Arthur H. Compton, and other giants of science, history, philosophy, and literature. The morning's festivities centered on academic rituals acted out before a sodden crowd stretching across Harvard Yard from Widener Library to Memorial Church—the opening of messages sealed after a bicentennial celebration, the reading of odes to Harvard icons, and the bestowing on the international pantheon of scholars the honorary degrees whose citations had sorely tested Conant's vocabulary of superlatives. Representatives of educational institutions from around the world, led by Cairo's Al-Azhar University (founded in A.D. 970) and followed by emissaries from Bologna, Paris, Oxford, and Heidelberg ascended the stage. Heading a parade of 554 foreign delegates, Professor Saleh Hashem took his soggy seat after he was greeted by Harvard's genial president with a handshake and a twangy, "How do you do?"[67]

Meanwhile, Lowell warily eyed his nemesis, Roosevelt, majestically seated in a red velvet chair. A photograph printed the next week in *Time* magazine captured Roosevelt alone in the center of the stage, primly maintaining a solemn demeanor, garbed in silken top hat and black trench coat, bravely exposed to the pelting rain. Twice he declined proffered umbrellas—as if preternaturally aware of the symbolic images history would record of events still to come: Chamberlain shielding himself from a sprinkle at an airport outside London as he returned from Munich to proclaim appeasement's success, Roosevelt himself shivering in the drizzle at Yalta between Stalin and Churchill.

Conant spoke first—a speech he had been crafting for months. As hoped, the tercentenary celebration had avoided open controversy, the only dissenting footnote lodged by radical alumni who handed out a twenty-nine-page indictment of Lowell's role in the Sacco and Vanzetti execution. But for all his ardor to dodge political scandal, Conant knew the occasion required a message of the highest relevance to a profession, country, and world shaken by crisis, discord, and uncertainty. He had a unique audience—Roosevelt, the national and world press, leaders of American arts and letters, and a nonpareil international assortment of pedagogues and scholars, including refugees from Hitler and scholars, like Jung, who were still working in Germany.[68]

Speaking in a firm, clear voice, Conant delivered a ringing avowal of the reverence that Harvard and America held for intellectual freedom, rebuking the rising totalitarian ethos but recognizing the almost primal human emotions that seemed to be fueling a global resurgence of barbarism. "A wave of anti-intellectualism is passing around the world . . . " he declared. "But the anti-intellectualism of the present is in part a protest—a most ungrateful protest, to be sure—against the benefactions of the learned world. It expresses a rebellion against the very triumphs of applied science, against the machines from which we would not be separated and yet towards which we feel a deep resentment."

Peering through the mist, Conant echoed earlier his liberal pronouncements but to far greater effect. To foster the development of a "unified, coherent culture suited to a democratic country in a scientific age—no chauvinistic dogma, but a true national culture fully cognizant of the international character of learning"—he demanded that America's schools and universities permit "absolute freedom of discussion, absolutely unmolested inquiry." Even touchy topics like "the forces of modern capitalism" and the Constitutional separation of powers "must be dissected as fearlessly as the geologist examines the origin of the rocks.

"On this point there can be no compromise; we are either afraid of heresy or we are not . . . Harvard was founded by dissenters. Before two generations had passed there was a general dissent from the first dissent. Heresy has long been in the air. We are proud of the freedom which has made this possible even when we most dislike some particular form of heresy we may encounter."

Robust cheering greeted these bold assertions, as well as Conant's optimistic closing sentiment that a hundred years hence it may be "manifest to all that the universities of this country have led the way to new light, and may the nation give thanks that Harvard was founded."[69]

In the afternoon, Roosevelt proved up to the task of praising Harvard's contributions to the cosmos without incurring further wrath. Forced by the deluge to speak inside musty Sanders Theatre, with thousands listening outside via a hastily erected microphone hookup, FDR subtly snubbed Lowell by omitting him from the salutation—"President Conant, distinguished guests, my fellow alumni"—and then quickly disarmed his hostile audience. At Harvard's bicentennial party in 1836, he observed, "many of the alumni were sorely troubled concerning the state of the nation. Andrew Jackson was President. On the 250th anniversary of the founding of Harvard College, many alumni again were sorely troubled. Grover Cleveland was President. Now, on the three hundredth anniversary, I am President." He stopped—and a rolling wave of laughter greeted this good-natured allusion to the alumni antagonism toward him. "I told the boys afterwards that I had stuck out my chin and said 'hit me'—and nobody dared!" FDR merrily wrote "Felix," who immediately after the speech had wired the White House to enthuse that his friend had "turned a difficult situation into a triumph. He was at his very best."[70] After this audacious start, the rest of Roosevelt's speech went smoothly. Yale's president Angell dispelled any lingering tension with a celebrated quip, remarking with the architect of the New Deal seated a few feet away that the inclement weather had been "President Conant's way of soaking the rich."[71]

But if Roosevelt made a good impression, Conant had stolen the show. His youth, his graceful bearing in the rarefied company of social aristocrats, political bigwigs, and intellectual giants, and most of all his carefully crafted speech and sturdy vision impressed both Harvard and the national and international audience. "The Tercentennial Celebration at the start of his third year marked his emergence," friends remembered. "His fresh words and lucid presence set the American tone of the Tercentennial, dispersing any hint of ponderousness."[72] Not everyone in Cambridge liked Conant, but his bravura performance earned him unanimous respect.

The tercentenary signaled something even more profound and poignant than Conant's emergence as a national educational statesman, or the university's central position as the nurturing ground for New Deal movers and shakers. It "pointed up, as did no other event of the decade, the recent cumulative loss of Europe to America in research enterprise, intellectual leadership, and the pursuit of disinterested learning. In place of the Old, the New World now held primacy in the advancement of knowledge."[73]

Basking in praise, acclaimed in national magazines (a two-part *New Yorker* profile and a *Time* cover story, featuring a portrait of its subject wearing black academic robes and a kindly smile), Conant was finally casting off his predecessor's shadow and stamping his authority on the Harvard scene. But power had not come without cost—a visitor in the autumn of 1936 noticed a touch of gray and furrows on the brow of the still "astonishingly young" forty-three-year-old occupant of the austere office at 5 University Hall. "Under closer scrutiny, the Peter Pan look fades, although it persists in his photographs," wrote the *New Yorker's* Henry F. Pringle of a man who had clearly grown comfortable with authority:

> Conant is tall and thin. Years of laboratory work—spent over malodorous sinks and test tubes—have brought a permanent stoop to his shoulders. But he is very well tailored, now that he is President of Harvard—a marked change from the baggy comfort of his chemistry days. His eyes are blue behind rather pedagogical steel-rimmed spectacles. He has a large mouth which might, hastily, be called charming. Rather, it is warm and sincere and friendly. The President of Harvard is an affable gentleman who has already learned the first trick of all major executives—to give the impression of leisure even when his day is most pressing and he has fallen behind in his schedule of appointments. He can find time to tell a story or to explain to visitors the significance of the furniture and pictures in his office.[74]

A more touchy question than whether the university president could find time to describe for a visiting correspondent his office's decor—mostly functional Harvard hand-me-downs from Lowell and Eliot, an 1861 carved chest, a watercolor of the Yard—was whether Conant could offer adequate attention and affection to two teenage boys, and to an insecure wife privately worried that her identity was slipping away in the shadow of her famous husband. All too frequently, the answer was no. The combination of the presidency's pressures and obligations and the personal idiosyncrasies of the Conant family proved harrowing. Whether receptions, faculty dinners, undergraduate teas, speaking engagements, fund-raising junkets, or educational conferences in New York, Washington, or Chicago, there was always another in a never-ending succession of social and professional obligations to keep President Conant from spending more than a handful of purloined free evenings at home during each month of the academic calendar—and even then there were always books and reports to read or write, or informal politicking to be kept up with. Mrs. Conant plunged into the social obligations and opportunities of the president's wife, usually delegating responsibility for the children to a parade of maids, governesses, and student helpers, even during family summer vacations in Europe or the mountains of New Hampshire or the Rockies. "It was like living in a hotel," remembers Theodore Conant, likening the ambience at 17 Quincy Street to that of the British upper-class television series "Upstairs, Downstairs."[75]

Conant's elder son, Jimmy, is said by relatives to have remained earnest, studious, and polite and reverential toward his parents; according to his brother, Theodore, he was being "groomed for power" by his father, who encouraged him toward rough sports and allegedly took away his teddy bear out of concern that he might grow too sensitive. (Ted, a sickly child, was allowed to keep his.) Later, as an intelligent if reserved teenager, he would be invited upstairs to his father's study to read Milton with him as an illustration of the importance of using power to change the world. Conant rested high hopes on him.[76]

Ted, three years younger, was another story. Captivated by the radical ideas floating around Harvard Square at the time, he vented resentment at his father's emotional (and often geographical) distance by accusing him of selling out for power—"I told him he was a capitalist tool"—and by masterminding spectacular and sometimes embarrassing pranks. Once, Conant stepped into the presidential residence's high-ceilinged foyer only to be startled by the sight of his pet cat plummeting downward aboard a parachute of handkerchiefs that had been dropped from the balustrade three flights up. Fascinated with radio and other electronic and technical devices from an early age, Ted recalls that he once hot-wired his brother's bed with electric cables to avenge the elder boy's "goody-goody" personality, and scandalized the Yard by rigging up an antenna to the roof of 17 Quincy Street using whiskey bottles as insulation. By the age of eleven, Ted and a friend had learned how to rig a gramophone to the home's heating system and startle a reception for the crown prince of Norway with scratchy jukebox tunes like "Scrub Me, Molla, with a Solid Six," and "Three Little Fishes in an Itty Bitty Pool." Although the guests thought the president very daring to play modern music at such a dignified event, Ted recalls, "I got a thorough hiding and hair brushing and got sent to bed without any food."[77]

His father grew still more irritated when Ted's mischief began taking on a hard-edged political tinge, like playing Paul Robeson's "Long Live Our Soviet Motherland" from the top of Lowell's mansion or frequenting a radical Harvard Square bookshop, a habit gleefully publicized by a scandal-mongering Hearst newspaper, causing the furious father to extract a vow from his son that he would avoid the Bolshevik den in exchange for a subscription to the *Daily Worker*. Signing a petition in favor of aid to the anti-fascist Spanish Republicans also brought a fatherly scolding that such actions were "not good for business." Though the topics were political, Conant's son says the real intent of his actions was personal—to get the attention of both busy parents, as well as to jab at his father's own residual ambivalence over the position he had been unable to turn down.[78]

The venomous psychological troubles that wracked the family after Conant became president in 1933 were documented in Patty Conant's intimate, tortured, and often reproachful diary entries. Near the end of her life, she ripped out many pages of "introspective and lonely lachrymose broodings," but those remaining contain enough "self-lacerations" to disclose a dark underside to her outwardly storybook existence.[79] Increasingly estranged from her children, prone to reveries, fainting spells, and bedridden binges of morbid self-analysis, she nevertheless thrived as a hostess to famous visitors and as an organizer of faculty wives' teas and other gatherings. In any "conflict of claims," Patty privately conceded, she put her husband's, and sometimes her own, ahead of her children's—something Ted surmised after both parents had toured Europe in the summer of 1933 while he recuperated in a Cambridge hospital, watched over by his grandmother Richards. While preferring to leave the boys in the care of servants in order to fulfill her own social obligations—"You are reduced to just 'checking up' on their routine," she confessed to herself—Patty nevertheless grew furiously jealous when the hired help became too friendly. When one governess showered affection on seven-year-old Ted, his mother fretted to herself that "She wants him under his spell . . . caters too much to his fears . . . she is softening him . . . by such subtle and insidious ways . . . He mustn't be spiritually crippled by what seems to me her hothouse affection" and ultimately resolved to fire her, along with another servant described as "much too sweet & weak." While frequently enjoining herself not to harangue young Jim and Ted so much, she confessed her failure to establish a warm relationship with either son, and acknowledged that under the pressure of the her husband's job the family was imploding. "You have definitely changed to the children since this new job began," Patty admitted in 1936. "You 'lost' them when it came."[80]

Though she labored to maintain a façade of pleasantness and "serenity" to her myriad social acquaintances, Patty concealed dark musings about the corrupting influence of the constant exposure to fame and flattery, the "diet of frosting" and "charming fatuous popularity" accorded the wife of President James B. Conant. "This Mt. Olympus life is bad for you because it erects barriers around your only too-isolated self," she wrote less than a year after moving into Quincy Street, "& when you do come down from the mount you are sometimes surprised by ordinary human phenomena of every day life."[81] "Don't offer up incense to yourself," she implored on another occasion, "and don't fill yourself too full of 'nobility' and noble aphorisms . . . You soar too high and get intoxicated with your own nobility. . . . " But tragically, she could not wean herself away from the chimera of Cambridge popularity lent by her position. Desperately clinging to the shreds of independent identity afforded by the artistic interests absorbed in the Richards' household, Patty feared that she was becoming "a good deal parasitic" of her husband, copying his perceptions and "living in his mind" even though she was "not like him really, inside."[82]

More than anyone else, Patty had been able to observe her husband's single-minded devotion to the amassing and exercise of power since taking the presidency. One of James B. Conant's earliest command decisions at 17 Quincy Street had been to limit carefully the access to his household and children of Patty's neurasthenic, at times overbearing mother, Miriam Thayer Richards. A diary entry by Mrs. Richards, recording a conversation with her daughter revealing her son-in-law's "dictatorial" resistance to her intrusions, offers an incisive glimpse into Conant's psychological self-reckoning with his difficult choice to abandon the laboratory for the presidency and all it entailed.

Patty advised against my . . . returning from England with them this year. "It makes one person more for Jim. He is tense inside although he seems calm.

He is well when away but one day of work in his office sends him home so tired his food won't digest. It is the responsibility"... I spoke of his remark, "The Presidency is an awful job—If you take it you have got to be willing to knife your best friend." "Oh yes" said Patty "he has to do that all the time. He doesn't like it, but he knew he shouldn't. He says he may as well accept it & stop feeling like a martyr." Well, I don't like being pushed aside, but I may as well accept it too, instead of having heart ache & indigestion.[83]

From her husband, Patty received lessons in the disciplined ability to suppress emotion and spontaneity, to calculate and calibrate every utterance for political and social propriety. "Remember!" she admonished herself after receiving one tutoring session. "You can never afford to be flip or frank. You are beginning to forget this and blurt out your personal reactions instead of the proper official ones. You must not admit the comic side of any one to whom you have an official relation. You must remember that you have not got a personal life any more. Read this over, grit your teeth, & *do not* forget it."[84] In dealing with her children, Mrs. Conant admitted in a brutally frank 1938 diary entry, she could not help indulging her dictatorial desires to control her sons, especially Jimmy Conant, then fifteen years old and on the verge of leaving for boarding school at Exeter at the end of the summer. "There's poison in my will to power," she wrote.

I inject a little bit of poison in the conversation, in my advice to darling, dear Jimmy who is much too sweet and tempts me to walk on him; I "pick on" Teddy too often (he deserves it, goodness knows, but if I nag he will learn bad tricks from me). I am almost never the quiet well of love that a mother ought to be. Let the dears be late and inconsiderate and heedless; they are young. You thought the world revolved around you when you were young. Ought I to correct Jim's manners?: He will go away to school this fall—it's my last chance in a way, but it is also his last summer at home as a child. And I must constantly bear in mind this fact. Jimmy's misdemeanors are slight ... When I think so constantly of putting them in their places and overlook so little, that is a symptom of a bad, selfishness in me, that is jealous of them because they are young and strong and happy and unconscious of my needs or desires. Rubbing in small failings in oblique ways is the pettiest indoor sport of the privileged grown-up. They can't retort—but Jim unconsciously— both more or less consciously store up an impression of grudgingness and bitterness. There is a bitter taste in me—I seem to have given up self-pity and romantic reveries for aggressive tactics—persecution of the subtle sort that matriarchs indulge in ... martyring myself about laundry lists, etc. and then being cross because of my grievances. Nothing—no routine, no table manners, are so important as the quiet radiating of generosity and love. Maybe I am stale, maybe I did miss my fine vocation, maybe I do mind this muggy climate and feel rather lost without Jim in this place where I have nothing to do—hells bells, what if J. never came back, what if I didn't have 2

wonderful boys—and a most devoted, conscientious tutor who is tireless in
their interests—I must smile, and let them play, and forget about their
carelessness, and never, never, never nag. I ought to tie a knot in my
handkerchief or something. Teddy deserves scoldings—I don't scold Jim, but
my cold repressed voice is too much for him to bear—And yet of course the
reason it is cold is because I am tense and sore inside because he is grown
and out of my power. *Power.* I have got to look out. Thank goodness he is
going away. I have got to paint and paint and wear myself out—or pour
myself into social life.[85]

If her diary is any indication, Patty Conant deliberately hid these and
other lurid thoughts from her busy husband, vowing to "fine or punish"
herself each time she complained about maids or other domestic woes:
"Remember that's what you can give J.—refreshment and life."[86] It is, of
course, presumptuous to estimate the innermost feelings of a person from
documentary *desiderata,* yet one has the sense that Conant preferred being
insulated from Patty's woes to sacrificing the prerogatives of power he had
accumulated—which is not to say that Conant lacked parental concern for his
children; he closely monitored their progress, suffered over their illnesses,
encouraged their hobbies, took pride in their achievements, taught them
about birds, bees, and microbes, shared some good times, a train track laid
out across the presidential ballroom, touch football, a mountain hike. "It's out
of our hands—we've done all we can," he told his wife after Jimmy had gone
off to Exeter.[87] And he confided something close to terror to his diary in
recording one of Ted's frequent illnesses. "When he has a little something
wrong, don't think the end of the world has come," the jittery father scolded
himself. "You have lost several years over this cold quite unnecessarily. The
delicate people often last better than strong people."[88]

But a combination of Yankee starchiness, discomfort with emotions and
sensitive personal matters, and, most importantly, the sacrifices he willingly
made and the obligations he undertook to satisfy his thrusting ambitions—all
these conspired to deny Conant the affectionate closeness with his two sons
that he was able to establish with his wife. As Conant rose from successful
scientist to university president to national figure, harmonizing his career and
family became harder and harder. The boys poignantly encapsulated their
feelings in a drawing for their father. It shows two choo-choo trains, one with
a curl of smoke rising from its engine, chugging along parallel tracks in
opposite directions with arrows marked "Boston" and "Washington." From
one window a tiny stick figure waves. *"To Dad,"* reads the caption. "We don't
see much of him. But we think a lot of him."[89]

Only a few months after Conant's moment of glory at the tercentenary, the
tribulations of being Harvard's president magnified greatly. The *casus belli*
was the administration's refusal, in the spring of 1937, to renew the appoint-

ments of two young, popular, and left-wing economics teachers recommended for retention by the economics department. Alan R. Sweezy and J. Raymond Walsh were only the latest and most controversial victims of the robust faculty-slimming philosophy Conant had been advocating ever since he took office. At first he moved gingerly to implement this "up or out" policy, but as the years passed he displayed mounting gusto in his quest to solve what he delicately termed "the young man problem"—how to lighten the faculty of junior instructors, mostly hired under Lowell, who by Conant's rigorous scholarly criteria and the Depression's austerity budgets were unlikely to win tenure. Conant summarized his guiding principles to Clark in 1938:

> What it all comes down to in my mind is this: (a) the corps of young men doing tutorial and section work must be much smaller than in recent years; (b) the future of these men must be directed toward positions elsewhere and every possible mechanism devised to make their Harvard stay short, profitable and part of a journey elsewhere; (c) a complete reversal of the Murdock regime, namely, a realization throughout the faculty that only the exceptional man in the exceptional case would find a continuous career at Harvard. The usual course would be Harvard, elsewhere, and called back to Harvard if the man is the best of his age group.
>
> This is essentially a reversion to the Eliot policy and a reversal of the trend of the last fifteen years of Mr. Lowell's administration. I am absolutely certain (more than I was five years ago) that this reversal is essential not only for Harvard, but as an example for the other universities. It is the university principle of recruiting personnel compared to the high school method where once in, always in. I think a vigorous policy on the part of the President in such matters is essential, otherwise a faculty runs down hill.[90]

Conant's formula may have been laudable, even necessary to keep Harvard solvent and thrust it to the top of American scholarship, but his methods left much to be desired. Controversial actions, like the simultaneous denial of reappointment to a dozen English instructors, combined with a mysterious, autocratic decision-making process that yielded seemingly arbitrary fiats, stimulated intense resentment. Young untenured faculty members began to regard him as a hungry vulture circling vulnerable prey, waiting for the right moment to strike. "The waves of criticism are already beating against the doors of the President's office in University Hall," observed the generally admiring *New Yorker* profile months before the Walsh-Sweezy case erupted. But having expected "howls of disapproval" when he took the job, Conant did not appear especially troubled by his growing reputation for being "quite ruthless when it suits him to be."[91]

Nowhere had the animus toward Conant grown more intense than in the humanities and the social sciences, where any presidential decision to deny tenure or turn down funding hardened the notion that Conant harbored a pro-science, anti-leftist bias.[92] And Conant's occasional clumsiness in handling sensitive personnel (and personal) matters magnified the potential for misunderstanding and antagonism that is inevitably present when austerity budgeting leads to staff cuts, or when outside prospects are imported while old colleagues are let go. Even an admiring colleague like the historian Paul H. Buck, provost of the university from the onset of World War II until the end of Conant's presidency, recalls that his direct, no-nonsense mien sometimes seemed brusque or just plain rude. Though Conant "never meant to insult," Buck remembered the amazement of a university official who recounted what happened to him one morning during a rush for taxis outside South Station after the train from New York had arrived. Stepping into a cab, the man noticed Conant and invited him to use it if he wished, expecting him to say, "Let's go together" or "Go to your place first, and my place later." Instead, perhaps making an instant calculation that his work would lead to a greater societal good than the good will to be gained by courtesy, Conant hopped in alone and rode off to 17 Quincy Street, leaving the man fuming on the curb. In another instance, Conant shocked a dean who was wringing his hands over his difficulty in meeting a budget ceiling. "What you need is an epidemic," the president joked.[93]

Buck, then a professor in the history department, recalls that Conant's initial policies, including the trimming of the "sacred cow" of the tutorial system, were "sound, but no man bungled application of them more than Conant did."[94] In one celebrated case, the English tutor and lecturer Bernard DeVoto was invited to become the editor of the *Saturday Review of Literature* and, hoping to use the offer as leverage, went directly to see Conant to say that he felt obliged to accept unless Harvard could give him a permanent position. A popular teacher, speaker, and author of the "Editor's Easy Chair" column in *Harper's* magazine, DeVoto confidently expected to receive a better offer to stay. Instead, Conant told DeVoto he was welcome to remain at Harvard as a tutor but his scholarship was too "weak" to merit a permanent appointment and seemed nonplussed at the prospect of his departure. Taking a few days at DeVoto's request to hear assessments from colleagues, Conant retracted his comment about DeVoto's scholarship but reaffirmed his decision. "In view of this fact," he wrote, "I feel that I must urge you strongly to accept the position which you said had been offered to you." Enraged by the probably unintended insinuation that he might be lying about the *Saturday Review* offer, DeVoto felt duty-bound to accept the counsel of his friend Robert Frost, that even though his academic career had been unfairly aborted, if he "wanted to keep the respect of others and of himself, he should immediately resign his lectureship." DeVoto packed his bags and left, trailing a residue of ill-will toward the man said to have treated him so shabbily.[95]

Despite much grumbling, Conant avoided a head-on collision with the faculty until it was disclosed that the administration would release Walsh and Sweezy after two-year "concluding appointments" instead of granting them the three-year renewable contracts for which their colleagues had proposed them. Immediately, critics claimed that Conant had used the pretext of belt-tightening to evict two political irritants: aside from their mildly leftist economic views, both had been active in the Massachusetts labor movement and in organizing the Harvard teachers' union, which had a strong and sometimes dominant Communist bent. Conant inadvertently worsened matters by issuing a press statement explaining that the decision had been made "solely on grounds of teaching capacity and scholarly ability"—thus seeming to slur the two teachers' professional qualifications.[96]

Though Conant quickly apologized to Walsh and Sweezy and retracted the imputation of scholarly inferiority, his contrition came too late. Galvanized into revolt, 141 junior faculty members, unsure whether Conant's swinging axe threatened them and suspecting the president of acting haughtily and precipitously, dispatched a fifteen-page manifesto to nine senior colleagues expressing "misgivings" at Conant's action and requesting their "academic seniors" to "tell us after all necessary inquiry" whether the refusal to rehire Walsh and Sweezy was warranted. The depth of the resentment at Conant's modus operandi can be gauged by the size, breadth, and quality of the young scholars willing to rock the boat in this fashion. Members of virtually every department were on the list, including Crane Brinton, Paul H. Buck, Rupert Emerson, Merle Fainsod, John K. Fairbank, John Kenneth Galbraith, Talcott Parsons, Willard V. Quine, and E. Bright Wilson, Jr.

Even more tellingly, the petition was received sympathetically by the nine senior professors to whom it was directed. Aside from Kohler, Conant's old chemistry department tutor, the group's composition was slanted toward professors whose attitude to Conant ranged from lukewarm to hostile: Murdock, Shapley, the philosopher Ralph Barton Perry; the historians Arthur M. Schlesinger, Sr., and William S. Ferguson; and Frankfurter, E. Merrick Dodd, Jr., and Edmund M. Morgan of the law school. They went en masse to the president's office to urge an investigation. Conant's initial strategy had been to have the chairman of the Overseers' economics department visiting committee, Walter Lippmann, whose politics had cooled considerably since radical student days, convene a nominally independent inquiry. But, sensing that this move would only incur more suspicion, Conant instead named the nine-member delegation as his own investigatory panel to explore the circumstances of the Walsh-Sweezy case as well as the broader issue of criteria for faculty hiring and firing, promotion and tenure; he gave them free and full access to his office's records and facilities. "This evidenced that absence of self-pride—that willingness always to reconsider a decision—which characterized his make-up," one member recalled. "It is hard to think of Lowell ever so acting."[97]

Perhaps so—but the "Committee of Eight" (reduced by one after Kohler's death) was less than delighted by Conant's response to its initial eighty-six-page report, submitted in May 1938 after a year's study. It absolved the administration of any political or ideological prejudice in handling Walsh and

Sweezy, a conclusion that gratified Conant, but he and the Corporation flatly rejected the report's other principal finding, that Walsh and Sweezy had not received fair treatment and deserved reconsideration. Nevertheless, he thanked the group for its troubles and urged it to move on to the second phase of its probe.

This peremptory dismissal of the committee's recommendation for a re-hearing triggered more acrimony; even within the Corporation, doubts rose about Conant's tactics. Though most of the faculty agreed with his objectives and ideas, Charles Coolidge informed him, "these men don't feel they are dealing with a helping friend, but rather with someone who is trying single-handedly to add luster to the university." Repeatedly insisting that "young men must go" didn't do much for morale, he added.[98] If not for some wise advisers who persuaded him to compromise and then apologize to his contentious faculty, Conant might well have been forced to resign. His "unpopularity can hardly be exaggerated in that era," confided Buck many years later. "The faculty meetings were terrible experiences."[99]

In the spirit of Lowell's alleged description of Harvard administration as "tyranny tempered by assassination," there appears also to have been an actual conspiracy to topple the emperor, complete with a Brutus: Kenneth B. Murdock. According to one of the plotters, a former official of the teachers' union who confessed his role in a letter to Conant almost four decades later, the cabal known as the "Leverett House gang" schemed to push Murdock into University Hall by launching a new faculty inquiry leading to a censure of Conant's autocratic policies. Along with Walsh and other coconspirators, the plot revolved around Murdock and his close friend F. O. Matthiessen, a distinguished historian of American literature who had passed through Yale's Skull and Bones Club on the path to claustrophobic (and homophobic) Harvard. Caution should be used at assessing motives and actions in this murky story; but Matthiessen made little secret of his outrage at Conant's butchering of the English department, and Murdock was said to have resented his ex-friend's convincing the Corporation to choose the wrong man (though he had, to be sure, hand-written his friend a gallant letter of congratulations at the time).[100] Conant, meanwhile, with his own "*et, tu?*" to mutter, reportedly viewed his friend as a traitor for leading the charge of the Walsh-Sweezy brigade.[101]

Seeing further work as futile in light of the "impenetrability of the Administration's mind," several members of the Committee of Eight considered quitting. Reports of the ongoing crisis filled newspaper and magazine columns. Supreme Court Justice Louis Brandeis, a graduate of Harvard Law School, considered Conant's conduct so rash that he counseled a young scholar to avoid Cambridge unless he received an iron-clad assurance of tenure right at the outset. To his friend Clark, Frankfurter pronounced the outlook for Harvard "very ominous indeed" if Conant's rampage continued. "Unless you are vigorously on guard," he thundered, "there is great danger that the very evils of authoritarian rule in government which you so much deprecate, and rightly, may become operative where they are most mischievous, namely, in the government of a great university."[102]

The furor rose to an even higher pitch after the Committee of Eight grudgingly carried out the rest of its mandate and, in March 1939, handed in 167 pages of detailed guidelines for employment procedures. Though Conant expressed "keen satisfaction" with its findings, his stubborn refusal to allow the faculty a formal role in assessing the report provoked new charges of dictatorial rule. Even undergraduates got into the battle, forming a Committee to Save Harvard Education to protest the dismissal of ten young English department scholars, felled simultaneously as a result of Conant's calculation that this would remove any hint of discrimination among them; to many, the action looked more like a massacre than a considerate gesture to help the teachers with future employers. More protests greeted Harvard's failure to reappoint the literary critic Grenville Hicks, an avowed Communist who had been hired to a one-year advisory post; though Conant had staunchly defended Hicks's presence on a temporary post, his seeming reluctance to approve permanent appointments for controversial scholars seemed to confirm the view that his fearless defense of dissent and heresy had limits. Skeptics quoted a comment attributed to Conant: "If we want to preserve our academic freedom, we'll have to watch our promotions."[103]

With Murdock's supporters feeling they were closing in for the kill and sympathizers of the embattled president hoping for a miracle, the crisis had a dramatic, public conclusion at a series of jammed faculty meetings in the fall of 1939. On November 7, a record number of professors filled University Hall and trounced a motion favored by Conant by a whopping 140–6 margin; observers felt that a decisive ballot to launch a full-blown review of the university's governance was inevitable. Infused with an adherence to Harvard tradition "so dogmatic as to be almost blind," Conant recalls in his memoirs that he was "prepared for a knockdown fight if necessary" to preserve the governing board's prerogatives. His presidency teetering on the brink of disaster, Conant rose to speak in the old chamber lined with oil portraits of somber Harvard faces, and the faculty fell silent.

But instead of fighting fiercely, Conant swallowed his pride, confessed errors, and pleaded with the faculty not to make an emotional decision that might damage longstanding Harvard traditions. He had followed the almost desperate pleadings of several close advisers who had grown increasingly fearful that Conant had lost the faculty's confidence and that only a show of penitence could placate it. It did. The anger drained out of the room like the air from a pricked balloon; an elderly mathematician in the front row, breaking the silence after Conant's remarks, offered a motion, quickly carried by voice vote, to table the pending resolution for a new investigating committee.

Conant had survived; no comparable challenge to his authority emerged from the faculty for the rest of his presidency. Within a few years, Harvard had adopted a revised appointments system employing one of the Conant administration's most praised innovations, a system of ad hoc committees to evaluate new appointments, and settled on a complicated mathematical formula to determine the number of permanent positions per department. The Committee of Eight disappeared and its chairman, Ferguson, was made dean of the faculty to oversee the reforms. When the shouting ended, it was noticed that Conant's major point, that junior appointments should be of limited duration leading either to tenure or to another institution, had gained acceptance in American universities.

But the two years of academic trench warfare had left deep wounds on all sides. With a rare twinge of bitterness, Conant recalled in *My Several Lives* that the mood of many faculty members "was close to being vindictive."[104] Exhausted and exasperated by the intramural warfare, Conant was ready to turn his energies in other directions, to return to the transcendent issues that he had addressed at the tercentenary and grappled with inconclusively during the Hanfstaengl controversies. Suddenly, events across the Atlantic made even Harvard's palace intrigues seem petty.

CHAPTER 7

"I Believe That Actions
Speak Louder Than Words"

President Conant
Goes to War
1939–1940

O Scholars, schooled upon the books . . .
Rise from your labor now! Enlist
For warfare in this fighting age

There are none neutral in this war
There are but friends and enemies
— Archibald MacLeish,
"Speech to the Scholars"

I believe the United States should take every action possible to insure the
defeat of Hitler. . . . The actions we propose might eventuate in war. But fear
of war is no basis for a national policy.
— JBC, nationwide address, May 29, 1940

Expressed my views on U.S.A. armed to the teeth, belligerent and running
the world. A Pax Americana like the Pax Britannica of the 19th Century.
— Diary, June 29, 1940

A twenty-fifth college-graduation anniversary often evokes a mood of self-
reckoning before the serious moment is quickly drenched in a bibulous
festival of nostalgia and good cheer. But in February 1939, as he composed a
note to fellow members of the Harvard Class of 1914 in advance of their
reunion that June, Conant could not suppress his sense of bitter reflection and
melancholy foreboding in place of the usual expressions of astonishment over
the rapid passage of time; for him as others, Hitler's drive for Lebensraum
and irrational aggression had wrenched the heart and twisted the gut. Looking

back to the blithe summer of his college graduation, he wondered, "Must it all happen again? Have the last twenty years been nothing but a fruitless armistice?" Had his generation's sacrifices in the Great War been in vain? The world would long remain haunted, Conant concluded, "by questions born of that conflict which was *not* ended at Versailles. And when I come to think of it," he added, "through the last twenty-five years of my own personal experience the word Germany has kept recurring like a theme song. For many of our classmates the same motif has carried a far more poignant overtone and the final curtain has not yet fallen."[1]

Conant had been apprehensive throughout the 1930s over the consequences of Germany's descent into barbarism, yet even he was not immune to the lethargy, introspection, and isolationism that kept the United States from responding forcefully to the rise of fascism. In the second half of the decade, he devoted most of his non-Harvard efforts to articulating educational philosophy and singing paeans to intellectual freedom, repeatedly sidestepping chances to expand his public animosity to the Nazi regime beyond the parameters of academic concerns or to take sharp actions that would give muscle to his rhetoric.[2] Often, Conant behaved as if his one frank rebuff to Germany had permanently satisfied his and Harvard's moral ledger. "No one seemed to remember our letter to Hanfstaengl," he pouted in *My Several Lives* when he recalled the "shower of abuse" that fell on his decision to send a delegate to Heidelberg in 1936.[3] That year, Conant turned down an award from the *American Hebrew* magazine for "the Promotion of Better Understanding between Christian and Jew in America," explaining that his actions in turning down Hanfstaengl's scholarship had "been actuated solely by my conviction of the importance of academic freedom, entirely irrespective of consideration of race or religion."[4]

Even when nervousness over the tercentenary was no longer a factor, Conant shied away from resolute action. In 1937, a repetition of the Heidelberg dilemma cropped up when the university in Göttingen sent out invitations to its 250th anniversary celebrations. This time, all British and most American institutions openly boycotted the affair, but Conant tried another balancing act that satisfied no one, formally accepting the German invitation but not bothering to send a delegate.[5] In June 1937, he reacted skeptically when his friend, the poet Archibald MacLeish, whom he had two years earlier unsuccessfully tried to lure to Cambridge as director of Harvard University Press, called on scholars to contribute their talents to the battle against fascism and totalitarianism. Coinciding with the proxy war against Hitler and Mussolini then being waged in Spain, MacLeish's "Speech to the Scholars" called on academics to vacate their lofty perch of objective detachment and charge to the front:

> O scholars schooled upon the books:
> O skillful readers of the page:

Rise from your labor now! Enlist
For warfare in this fighting age!

No longer may your learning wear
The neutral truth's dispassionate peace
There are none neutral in this war:
There are but friends and enemies

I say the guns are in your house:
I say there is no room for flight:
Arise O scholars from your peace!
Arise! Enlist! Take arms and fight![6]

To Conant, however, the call to academic arms was premature and even counterproductive, a "call to the betrayal of what is important in the life of a university," and he criticized "Speech to the Scholars" both in his baccalaureate sermon and in correspondence with MacLeish. Where the poet perceived a unique and unprecedented threat to academic freedom from twentieth-century totalitarianism, Conant discerned only the latest relapse of the factionalism that had plagued universities in England, France, and Germany in preceding centuries, an ideological fervor best avoided if learning was to survive.[7] When MacLeish stood his ground — arguing that in the "battle of the human spirit against tyranny . . . the scholar who lives for the truth must take arms to defend his freedom to pursue it" and insisting that "the modern dictatorship and the modern totalitarian state *is* a new thing in history and an incredibly degrading thing"[8] — Conant parried with a lengthy response that revealed much about both his reluctance to take sides in the struggle in Europe and the position he would ultimately take:

I assume, and I think most of your readers will assume, that the warfare in which you urge the scholar to enlist and in which there "are none neutral" is essentially the world struggle between the right and left which appears to be reflected in Spain. Most of your readers would feel that you identify freedom with the Russian side rather than with the German or French; in this country with those who are for the President's Supreme Court proposal, and J. L. Lewis [the militant labor leader and head of Congress of Industrial Organizations] to bring the issue nearer home. That is the war most people are thinking about. I refuse to admit that the scholar should take up arms in this struggle even to the extent of joining a people's front (though personally I hardly need tell you that if I am forced to fight, I hope it will be on that side). The people's front, or its equivalent, may yet turn out to have sheltered as much spiritual and intellectual tyranny as the other side. I am as fearful of rough handling of the "dispassionate search for the truth" by the left as I am by the right.

. . . the things I think important in a university have suffered from the enemies of learning who may be either radicals or reactionaries. If you mean by friends or enemies, friends or enemies of learning . . . then, of course, I am all with you. If you mean that the scholar should stand by his arms and be ready to throw a bomb both ways at once, then there probably is only a slight disagreement between us.

I believe it is easy to lose the very things one wishes to preserve by declaring war in favor of them. (The late war to end war and preserve democracy would seem to indicate this.) I think above all the scholar *qua* scholar must be careful lest his very existence be lost by his becoming a combatant, and like most combatants or professional soldiers soon fighting merely for the joy of fighting.

I do *not* believe, as you seem to think, that a scholar should see his freedom extinguished before he fights; but I do believe he should hold his fire until he sees the whites of his enemies' eyes. And I am convinced above all that he should be on his guard against being drawn into a "preventive war." I think a scholar should have his gun ready to draw when he is immediately attacked; but his gun should be carefully kept apart from his books all the rest of the time, else the smell of powder corrupts his scholarship. Above all, I believe he must keep himself free from entangling alliances and let the weary world fight around him. In short, I am not a "peace at any price" pacifist but a very suspicious Yankee trader whose policy is "armed neutrality."[9]

Before any further escalation of the dispute, which was conducted in a spirit of mutual admiration, a mediator stepped in: the journalist Walter Lippmann, a member of the Harvard Board of Overseers and a friend of both men. It was all a misunderstanding, he wrote MacLeish after speaking to Conant and reading their correspondence, for Conant viewed the issue through the prism of the "war of ideologies in Europe and supposes that you are calling on scholars to enlist on the communist side against the fascists." In fact, as Lippmann correctly inferred, MacLeish's real interest was the defense of freedom against totalitarian regimes left or right, Russian as well as German and Italian, and in this he would find a firm supporter in Conant, who had been "firm and willing to make very great sacrifices" to defend academic freedom and had "conceived and planned" the tercentenary celebration "as a demonstration against the tyrannies in Europe."[10] MacLeish agreed that Conant must have twisted his poem's meaning due to a "preoccupation" with the "fascism versus communism" struggle that was "superficial and temporary" compared to "the profound conflict between the conception of intellectual and moral freedom on the one side and on the other, the conception of the totalitarian state."[11]

Conant's determination to "let the weary world fight around him" and to abjure preventive war against fascism remained steady even as Hitler's triumphs mounted. After German troops marched into Austria in March 1938, he continued to discount reports of Nazi savagery in Vienna and even in Germany itself. Responding to an alarmed appeal from Felix Frankfurter, whose eighty-two-year-old uncle had been among the many Jews roughed up and briefly imprisoned by Nazi thugs, Conant assured him that books in Vienna's library had not been destroyed and, moreover, that "in spite of some absurd remarks and one symbolic bonfire, there seems to have been no real damage done to the German collection of books, even at the times of the wildest orgies of German insanity."[12] On the eve of the Munich Conference, Conant recalled in his memoirs that he "hoped the British would stand firm" and judged Chamberlain "to be making an almost criminal error,"[13] yet his correspondence of that era suggests that he too was susceptible to the peace-at-any-price attitude that underlay appeasement policies, writing to Lippmann in August 1938: "I am beginning to think that any solution which does not involve a general European war would be highly satisfactory from my point of view."[14] Further Nazi outrages, including the Kristallnacht anti-Jewish pogroms in November, prompted Conant to issue a rare public condemnation and finally to consent, albeit grudgingly and under intense faculty pressure, to Harvard's sponsorship of a token scheme to grant fellowships to a limited number of refugee scholars to attend U.S. universities. And by the following spring, after Hitler's swallowing of Czechoslovakia, he had reluctantly concluded that the European fascists were "so irrational and emotional that no logical scheme can probably appease them at present." Yet in June, in his Commencement week speeches, though he alluded to the crisis in Europe and warned graduates against "complacent Pollyanna optimism," he devoted most of his words to the need to safeguard the ivory tower from the "feverish demands of the market place" and other temporal, utilitarian pressures. "Neglect the tumult of the moment," he advised graduates.[15]

On September 1, 1939, rusticating in the New Hampshire hills after a ski vacation in the Canadian Rockies, readying to return to Cambridge for the fall semester, Conant heard a radio broadcast reporting that German panzer tanks and infantry were steamrolling into Poland. Finally, his complacency shattered, he appreciated the military, and not merely ideological, nature of the German menace. Within a few days of Hitler's blitz to the east, Britain and France had fulfilled their vow to declare war rather than tolerate further Nazi expansion, while the Soviet Union lapped up the fruits of its nonaggression pact (and secret protocols) with Berlin by seizing eastern Poland. A generation after the "war to end wars," violence was again engulfing Europe. And once again, as in 1914, across the Atlantic a bitter debate raged between isolationists and interventionists.

Conant's reaction this time contrasted sharply from his blasé response to Sarajevo. In the two-year interregnum that preceded America's entry into the war following Pearl Harbor, he emerged on the national scene as a leading interventionist and in the Roosevelt administration as an apostle of military preparedness.[16] Unlike the isolationists, Conant did not believe that war never settled anything. He did not recoil at the suggestion of American intervention if necessary to save Europe from Nazi domination. No pacifist — as his World War I work had proved — Conant felt nothing but disgust for those who emotionally opposed even the slightest gesture of solidarity with Britain and France for fear that it would hasten U.S. involvement in the carnage. One of his first communications after the war broke out was to MacLeish, now Librarian of Congress, whose ardent interventionism no longer elicited Conant's strong disagreement. The American public's initial response to the European conflict seemed "ostrich-like, puerile, and pusil- lanimous," Conant wrote his friend. "But being the head of an institution with eight thousand young men under my direction who may get shot if we go into the war, while I shan't, I am a bit estopped from saying much. I don't like the moral dilemma I find myself in, but my personal emotions are a small matter in these times of world grief."[17]

Few could don the pretense of neutrality this time, he told Harvard students in late September 1939: "Every ounce of our sympathies" is on the side of those fighting the Nazis. The conflict will shape the future of everyone present in Memorial Church this Sunday morning, he preached. On America's response might rest "not only the fate of humanity's experiment with free institutions, but the potency of man's belief in a life of reason — in short, what we now venture to designate as modern civilization." Though Conant called for "education as usual" at Harvard, he concluded with words that held hidden significance in light of his subsequent activities. The "forces of violence," he warned, "must be beaten by superior violence and yet without engendering bitterness or hate. Reason must triumph over unreason without being converted to the very thing it would destroy."[18]

With the United States still officially neutral, Conant tentatively sought to advance the cause of preparedness. In late September he communicated in that vein with the head of one of the richest and most powerful of the handful of private philanthropies that played a central part in endowing prewar American scientific research, the Carnegie Institution of Washington. "I hope you are making progress with that plan for enlisting the scientific men of the country on a research basis for preparedness," Conant wrote Vannevar Bush. "Let me urge again the importance of this step."[19] He also discussed with scientists in the Boston-Cambridge area the possibility of organizing military research help for Britain, but the president of the Massachusetts Institute of Technology, Karl T. Compton, told him the plan would violate the Neutrality Act, and it was stalled, at least for the moment.[20] To fellow university presidents, beginning even a few days before Germany invaded Poland, he urged initial steps to identify personnel and departments that could help a war effort, and who should be protected in any new conscription legislation.[21]

Inside the White House, word quickly reached aides to Franklin Roosevelt that Conant could be counted on to rebut the loud calls from isolationists to keep in force the laws that forbade the United States to aid belligerent powers.[22] On September 28, Conant sent an open letter to the titular head of the Republican Party, former presidential candidate Alf Landon, strongly supporting a repeal of the arms embargo provision of the Neutrality Act and calling for a "clear-headed, realistic discussion" of the pros and cons of U.S. involvement in the war.[23] Privately, he wrote Republican Massachusetts Senator Henry Cabot Lodge to urge military support for Britain and France, for if Germany and Russia should triumph "the resulting world would be one in which our country would be bound to take up arms in a most desperate struggle."[24]

Conant's alacrity in prodding Washington toward a more belligerent stance markedly diverged from the role he had assumed in World War I. So, too, did the reaction of Harvard undergraduates differ from the previous conflict, when many students had avidly sought to enter the battle. Like their counterparts in Britain, whose pacifism had surfaced most famously in the Oxford Union's 1933 resolution refusing "to fight for king and country," Harvard's students had grown disillusioned with the results of the earlier slaughter and emanated hostile suspicion at the thought of being once again lured into a bloody war by old men who themselves could stand safely aloof—by governments manipulating emotions, or munitions-makers out for profit. A poll of 1,800 students in November found 95 percent against immediate U.S. entry into the war, and 78 percent opposed even if Britain and France faced defeat. The undergraduate *Crimson* mounted a strident campaign against American involvement; it opposed altering neutrality legislation, predicted a German military victory, and favored a U.S. peace initiative that would leave Hitler in power and in control of Poland and other ill-gotten gains; one pro-appeasement editorial (entitled "Peace in Our Time," and unsigned, fortunately for its author's future political career) was written by a twenty-two-year-old senior named John F. Kennedy, who echoed the defeatist views of his father, Joseph P. Kennedy, the American ambassador to the Court of St. James. Many of Harvard's professors took a contradictory view, tilting toward intervention in some form, but its president came in for some of the sharpest criticism. By encouraging measures to involve the United States in a conflict that was just another "balance of power war," the *Crimson* charged, Conant was "earning an unenviable place in the road gang which is trying to build for the United States a super-highway straight to Armageddon."[25]

Such charges stung Conant, yet they did nothing to lessen his convictions. With the Walsh-Sweezy controversy peaking ("I feel quite as though war had come to Cambridge!" he wrote one friend in early October) and attacks raining down on him for questioning the embargo on military sales to belligerents, he was developing something of a defiant bunker mentality. "How can a country debate its foreign policy," he asked his friend Harold Dodds, president of Princeton University, "when it starts with such a negative attitude as expressed by the premise, the only thing that matters is how to keep the United States out of war?" One could "not disregard the fact" that war, regrettably, might one day be the "best next step" for American foreign policy. Meanwhile, he maintained, the "present highly emotional drive against war" amounted to censorship through intimidation: "You and I know that many people, including ourselves, do not dare say what we think for fear of being called warmongers." Making clear that his own ardor for stern measures against Hitler rested on more than sentiment, Conant avowed that, should the United States ultimately come to London's rescue, he would be "as hard-boiled as anyone about a quid pro quo from the British Empire," and he expressed the hope that "if we fight again, we shall do so with more realism and less idealism than under Mr. Wilson." But Conant's first aim was to lift the whole discussion "from under the emotional shadow of the pacifist" lest present attitudes "snowball until we have another prohibition situation." To do so he vowed to prod the debate forward with his own provocations, jauntily predicting that he expected to "get a barrage of dead cats from the isolationists and the pacifists, but I am rather getting used to and even liking these missiles."[26]

It was some time, however, before he openly advocated U.S. intervention in the war in Europe. In the months of the "phony war" that lasted from the fall of 1939 until the spring of 1940, he also allowed himself to be distracted by events of lesser significance from the imperative of preparing America, and American public opinion, for the battle ahead. Aside from the fleeting amusement of being voted the "fifth-best dressed man in America," Conant had to deal with a succession of minor crises. There was, first of all, the tense conclusion of the Walsh-Sweezy affair, followed by continuing dispute over Harvard's tenure procedures. And two more controversies cropped up that further showed Conant's contradictory and cautious approach to academic freedom issues. In November 1939, with Conant's approval, the Harvard Corporation barred the Communist leader Earl Browder from speaking on campus, using as a pretext his recent indictment on a passport violation. To Grenville Clark, a sharp opponent of the decision, Conant rather sheepishly confessed chagrin at being "so wobbly about my own conviction" but refused to change his view that the decision did not constitute a violation of free speech.[27] In April 1940, however, Conant eventually decided to "stand firm" after a scandal erupted over Harvard's invitation to Bertrand Russell to deliver the annual William James lectures the following fall. A flurry of newspaper stories noted the decision to prohibit Russell from appearing at the City College of New York, and reminded readers that his views had caused him to be passed over for a chair at Harvard in Lowell's time. Hopping on the bandwagon, a prudish Massachusetts state legislator threatened to bring suit against Harvard (under a 1789 law that mandated the state senate to protect the public from violators of "chastity") to prevent the "immoral" British philosopher from purveying licentious sexual doctrines to Harvard's students. Initially, Conant hedged, but after canvassing the evenly split Corporation, and consulting outside authorities to verify that Russell "would behave in Cambridge," he opted to let the invitation stand. Russell gave the lectures, which had no particular bearing (or known impact) on the undergraduates' sex lives.[28] Personal distractions also preoccupied the busy educator. At the end of January, after a ski vacation in Canada (a broken collarbone sustained when skiing two years earlier had not dampened his enthusiasm), the Conants were traumatized by the hushed-up suicide of Patty Conant's brother, William Richards,[29] and in early March the couple embarked upon a month-long visit to California and Lake Tahoe.

Hitler's assault on Norway, the Low Countries, and France in the spring pushed Conant over the dividing line between observer and actor, and an "almost overpowering emotional reaction" turned him into a full-fledged interventionist.[30] The blitzkrieg's rapid success shocked Conant even more because on the very eve of the flanking assault around the Maginot line he had privately voiced confidence that the French forces' edge in mobility and officers would give them "manifest" superiority once they came into contact with the German troops.[31] Now the realization sank in that contrary to previous hopes, the Nazi military machine was so powerful that only America's industrial and military might could destroy it. "We all live to change our minds in 1940," Conant wrote in his diary in July.[32]

Depressed as he felt by the news of the lightning Nazi advances into northern France, Conant was equally alarmed by the virulent strains of pessimism and defeatism he discerned among Harvard associates at the annual meeting of alumni clubs in New York City over the weekend of May 17–19. His diary entry (reconstructed a couple of months later) captures the atmosphere, including his own conversion to a more activist pro-intervention stance and the dark prophecy of Harvard's treasurer, William Claflin:

> 1 PM to New York for Ass. Harvard Club meeting . . . Everyone much upset and excited by European news. Breakthrough of French at Sedan or Meuse. Black prophecy of French surrender. Bill Claflin particularly pessimistic after visit to Wall St. Told him I might urge U.S.A. to get in and help. He said no, be realistic, Hitler's going to win let's be friends with him. Dinner at Lamont's.[33]

Conant's surging commitment to what he now regarded as an inevitable battle assumed several forms. On May 20, shedding his self-imposed injunction against joining advocacy committees unrelated to Harvard or education, he enlisted in the Committee to Defend America by Aiding the Allies (CDAAA), an ad hoc collection of notables chaired by William Allen White that aimed to get the U.S. government to implement concrete steps—short of war—to oppose Hitler.[34] On May 29, as 340,000 British and French troops frantically fled the continent from the French port of Dunkirk and German troops closed the ring on Paris, he went on nationwide radio at White's request on behalf of the committee to urge Americans to write Roosevelt in favor of "immediate aid" to the Allies—a suggestion he followed himself with a telegram to FDR. Declaring that U.S. security could not tolerate the capture of the British fleet or a Nazi victory in Europe, he stated flatly, "I believe the United States should take every action possible to insure the defeat of Hitler . . . The actions we propose might eventuate in war. But fear of war is no basis for a national policy."[35]

Those words thrust Conant to the forefront of the interventionist movement. From May 1940 through the Japanese attack on Pearl Harbor, he was a key intermediary between the Roosevelt administration and public opinion, constantly doing his best to nudge both toward belligerence.[36] Conant's effectiveness as a pro-intervention lobbyist was enhanced not only by the prestige of leading Harvard but by his resolutely nonpartisan stature— nominally a Republican, he kept his votes to himself and his eyes on the ball of achieving a consensus between the major parties on aiding the Allies and preparing the U.S. military for war. Distancing himself by degrees from day-to-day involvement with internal Harvard business, he consulted closely with fellow pro-intervention activists like Grenville Clark, Clark Eichelberger, and Lewis H. Douglas, and relied for political advice on his closest Harvard associate, A. Calvert Smith, a college classmate who had been *Crimson* president in 1914 as well as a fellow member of the Signet and who fully shared his pro-Allied views. He went more and more often to Washington, too, for earlier in the year he had won a seat to two key educational lobbying and policy-making groups: the Problems and Plans Committee of the American Council on Education, and the board of directors of the Association of American Colleges, and in January 1941 he was elected to a four-year term on the elite National Education Association's Educational Policies Commission (EPC), which gathered educational leaders from around the country and whose deliberations were dominated by the draft and other war-related issues.[37]

The first task of the interventionist movement, and of a Roosevelt administration cognizant of the danger of war but leery of alienating isolationist public opinion, was the passage of laws on military conscription. In the summer of 1940, the difficulty of obtaining congressional approval of the unprecedented peacetime measure was exacerbated by the presidential electoral campaign, in which FDR promised to keep American boys out of the fighting. A vital figure in the campaign that led to the razor-close passage of the Selective Training and Service Act in September 1940 was Grenville Clark, leader of the Plattsburgh military training camps before World War I, liberal New York lawyer, and Harvard Corporation fellow. To further the conscription drive, Clark promoted the nomination of Henry L. Stimson, the venerable seventy-two-year-old Republican lawyer and former secretary of war (for William Howard Taft) and state (for Herbert Hoover) as FDR's secretary of war and helped to mobilize big names outside the administration to come out in support of the controversial measure.[38]

Enthusiastically joining Clark's campaign, Conant lobbied extensively behind the scenes and—beginning with a speech to the Jewish War Veterans on June 12—publicly to obtain passage of peacetime conscription legislation. Horrified by what he regarded as military and congressional ignorance of the need to mobilize scientists and medical personnel for the war to come, he urged a bill that would develop a military training system even before any actual involvement in the fighting, explicitly reserving deferments for members of key medical, scientific, and educational categories and preparing the educational system for inevitable dislocations.[39]

In promoting aid to the Allies and a peacetime draft, Conant not only put his name to public lobbying groups but became a charter member of an informal circle of powerful, well-connected pro-intervention activists known as the Century Group, named after the Manhattan "gentleman's club" where they met a few times each month during 1940 and 1941. Key members included a Virginia liberal and Council on Foreign Relations executive, Francis P. Miller; Lewis W. Douglas, disaffected New Dealer, Willkie adviser, and future ambassador to England; the theologians Henry P. Van Dusen and Henry Sloane Coffin; *Time, Life,* and *Fortune* publisher Henry Luce, and newspaper columnists Joseph Alsop, Elmer Davis, and Maj. George Fielding Eliot; the bankers Will Clayton and James Warburg; lawyers Allen Dulles and Dean Acheson; two dramatist-screenwriters, John Balderston and Robert E. Sherwood; and educators such as Dartmouth president Ernest M. Hopkins and Conant himself. Carefully plotting strategy, they tacked just ahead of the administration's own public statements, conditioning public opinion to the adoption of ever-stiffer measures to prepare for the conflict to come, and tugging on connections built up through their careers in business, law, clergy, media, academia, and government. Their activist, internationalist views transcended partisan affiliations and came to dominate American foreign policy for the next decade and beyond.[40]

Conant's May 29 broadcast provoked emotional responses from supporters and critics. FDR sent a brief but portentous reply, assuring Conant that he had "been thinking along these lines for the past several months," Frankfurter, now on the Supreme Court, complimented him for countering the "temper of irresponsibility and frivolity among our college-bred youth," and the poet Robert Hillyer telegraphed congratulations "on a wise and what is better in these days a manly speech."[41] But the most moving messages came from closer to the battle. From the panic-stricken French capital, the scientist André Morize broadcast a shortwave message to the United States begging for help and declaring that Conant's words had raised the spirits of Parisians outraged by Belgium's surrender without a fight. "I want him to know that we listened to him with tears in our eyes," he radioed his wife in Vermont, asking her to relay a translation of his defiant words to Conant. She did so after Germany had occupied Paris, adding a distraught cover letter: "Oh Mr. Conant, Mr. Conant, is there nothing more that we can do?"[42] Conant was especially touched by a long, poignant handwritten letter from a Jewish chemist in London whom he had briefly met in Berlin in 1925. Professor A. Loewenbein related the sad story of his life since the Nazi seizure of power; twice, he had been forced to flee the Gestapo, from Germany and then from his native Czechoslovakia. Often he had wanted to write Conant, but he had hesitated until the "brave words" of his May 29 speech had made him too proud to resist. Appealing to shared values of civilization and science, he implored Conant to rouse Americans to action: "If the ideals of democracy are in danger—and nobody can deny it—what have the American people to expect from the future? Can anybody in your country who values these ideals stay outside of this struggle and wait until these ideals are submerged in darkness? Are they waiting to witness the darkest funeral in modern history?" Conant's brief but emotional reply hinted at his inner realization that the world they had known was gone forever.

> I was glad to receive your letter which was like a voice from a distant time—from a time when progress in pure science, peace and democracy seemed assured; a time when I was still an active chemist. Those were warm and tropical days; now it is snowing hard and you have already known the horrors of the ice age.
>
> Your letter moves me greatly. What this country can or will do remains to be seen. There are many who feel as I do, but not enough as yet. We have been sleeping in the warm tropics and now refuse to believe in snow. If England can head off the attempt to storm the island by a frontal attack, we may still awake in time.[43]

Still, although more than two out of three of the almost four hundred letters received after his May 29 speech were supportive, Conant's stand encountered tenacious resistance. To Conant's office in University Hall postmen delivered dozens of anonymous, abusive, often illiterate letters accusing him of supporting the British out of warmongering bloodlust, Jewish manipulation, or mercantile desires. ("Would you be in the front ranks? No, you yellow son of a bitch—of course you would not . . . the young men would be dying so that a dog like you might live.") One correspondent, signed "FRANTIC, WORRIED MOTHER," wrote: "Do you consider yourself an educated and civilized man? Then why in the name of God are you screaming for war? You know perfectly well that if we abandon any more of the neutrality that we have so foolishly abandoned already we shall become involved in that foul devil's mess that is stewing on the other side of the water." Equably, Conant scribbled on the letter: "Well, well, that's one way of putting it!"[44] He also continued to draw vehement opposition from the isolationist *Crimson,* although John F. Kennedy, now a business board editor, wrote a letter (borrowed from his senior thesis, soon to be published as *Why England Slept*) urging America to learn from Britain's sad failure to rearm in time — a stance that reflected a dramatic evolution from his views the previous fall and one that dissented from not only his fellow editors but his isolationist father.[45] At class day, graduating seniors "booed and hissed" Conant when he gave a "pro-war" speech, upsetting the reveling reunioners from the class of 1915.[46]

Remembering his own youthful doubts about going to war, however, Conant defended the younger generation's right to skepticism — the isolationist misjudgments of young people, he declared, were "symptoms of their idealism," and he praised them for independent thinking and refusing to be rubber stamps. Their view of history, Conant believed, had been "poisoned" by malicious claims in the 1930s, especially those made by the Senate's Nye Committee, that munitions makers had dragged the United States into World War I, callously trading lives for profit. In the future, he resolved inwardly, the American public must be educated to accept global responsibilities. Aside from the isolationist right, also deserving of some blame for the "present muddled state of our younger generation," he suggested to MacLeish, were those whose "leftist propaganda" and "perpetual sneering at the profit motive and general assumption that anybody who has made money is thereby a crook" had "undermined" young people's faith in their country, its system, and leadership. "They have heard so much sniping at the status quo from all sides," he wrote Felix Frankfurter, "so many reflections cast on the past history of democracy in this country and so many questions raised about the future of democratic civilization that I don't blame them for being bewildered and disturbed."[47]

One of the most militantly cynical expositions of the younger generation's attitude came from Conant's own son, James Richards Conant, who graduated near the top of his class from Phillips Exeter in rural New Hampshire in late June, just a few weeks after the fall of France. While his younger brother, Ted, fourteen, remained fixated on his youthful preoccupation with radio and followed the news from Europe by shortwave, James Richards and his classmates realized that combat might soon be a far more imminent prospect for them. That bitter recognition colored his grimly serious class day oration, delivered to an audience that included his parents and other dignitaries. Scorning the older generation's squeamishness over Germany's actions, he shocked listeners by confessing "admiration" for Hitler's cold-blooded, calculated daring and ruthlessness — qualities he declared the United States must squarely face up to, if not emulate, if it had any hopes of ultimately defeating Hitler and surviving in a brutal, amoral world. Regurgitating in extreme fashion his father's pragmatic and "realistic" outlook toward power, the seventeen-year-old's speech starkly presaged the degradation of morality that would accompany the total war which America would before long be forced to wage against vicious enemies. For that reason, as well as for evidence of the searing impact of Germany's blitzkrieg on both Conants, it bears quoting here:

> The last few weeks have seen events which have changed the world. Hitler's invasion of Holland and Belgium; the German armies, sweeping down through France, marching under the Arc de Triomphe, outflanking the Maginot Line, forcing France to surrender—all these things have changed, and will change our lives.
>
> We of the younger generation have watched these events with a point of view totally different from that of our parents. We have not beheld Hitler's invasion of neutral Belgium and neutral Holland with the same horror that our elders have displayed. We have not groaned about the rights of neutrals or about German barbarism. Rather, we have been awed by the cold-blooded efficiency and daring of the Germans; Hitler, as a man who can strike quickly and accurately, has won our admiration.
>
> When, two and a half months ago, Hitler invaded Norway and Denmark, it was the same story. We of the younger generation wasted no tears on the plight of neutral Norway. We reviled British blundering, Chamberlain's ineptitude, but not Hitler's ruthlessness. Once again, we admired, in spite of ourselves, Hitler's initiative and resourcefulness.
>
> The reasons for our point of view are clear. We have grown up in an age of cynicism, in an age where with coolness and deliberation, treaties are broken, laws of warfare violated, covenants disregarded, allies betrayed. We view this age of brutality without the rose-colored glasses of our parents. We have come to expect nations to violate the laws of warfare with considered cruelty rather than to obey those laws. It is no wonder, then, that we are not stricken with moral indignation when Hitler invades a neutral country. That is what we expect from a nation towards another.
>
> Moral indignation, indeed, is a dead letter as far as we are concerned. For we have seen that so-called "moral issues" don't have a show against the hand grenade, we have seen that the florid phrases of 19th-century moral indignation just don't go anymore. Today, the machine gun rules; today, the only thing that counts when the chips are down is force.
>
> This prospect is a grim one. But we face it without trembling, for we have seen no other; we are not indignant about it, for we have seen that indignation is flaggy and helpless in our modern world. That does not mean that we are callous or cold-blooded. It means that we are realists, that we are willing to come to grips with the truth, no matter how bald and stark it may be.
>
> And the older generation could learn something from our attitude. For today we, in the United States, must discard our old ideas of how nations *should* behave, and base our policy on how they *do* behave. We must assume that the nations which are our potential enemies will break treaties and violate all laws of warfare; we must realize that the chances are good that our own allies will sell us down the river for a mess of pottage. In other words, we must face realities.

Above all, in dealing with Hitler we must face the truth. We must not repeat the mistakes of Britain and France. Whether we go to war against Hitler now, or whether we arm to the teeth and prepare to keep him out of our hemisphere, we must take him for what he is. We must not put any value on his promises. We must not make treaties with him and then expect him to keep them. We must avoid the criminal error that the British made, that of treating Hitler like an English gentleman he never was and will never be. . . .

In dealing with events abroad, then, we must take it for granted that nations are cold-blooded and selfish and ruthless, and forget about any previous standards of international morality. That does not mean we ourselves should adopt Hitler's tactics, that we should become ruthless. It means that to preserve our own institutions, our own standards, we must recognize and cope with the lack of standards and the brutality of other nations. For our own protection we must consider facts, and on the basis of these facts alone we must make our decisions.

And when we make those decisions, emotionalism, moral indignation, has got to be left out of it. We of the younger generation are tired of being exhorted. To prate about German barbarism, Hitler's hordes, while the Germans are triumphantly marching through Paris, seems to us to be a sheer waste of breath. We know that the world into which we are graduating tomorrow has no regard for "moral issues," for standards of international morality. We know that the only hope of preserving our democracy and our Civilization is to face the facts, to recognize that our destiny will be decided, not by treaties or by international law or by diplomatic gestures, but by bombs and hand-grenades and bayonets; to recognize that the lines of history are being traced with steel.[48]

Conant in his diary described his son's oration as "quite 'shocking' to many" and an "overstatement of 'hardboiled' younger generation's point of view," but he reassuringly expressed confidence that the praise for Hitler and rejection of moral standards were simply debater's tricks: "Don't think he really believes it and 'moral issues' a battle of phrases!"[49]

Nevertheless, the acute grimness of the outlook forced Conant, like his son, to radical conclusions. Though Churchill, by now prime minister, had reacted defiantly to the collapse of France ("We shall never surrender"), Conant had already concluded that the complete defeat of Hitler would eventually require direct American participation, even if England were able to resist a cross-channel invasion with U.S. aid. Careful not to take positions more extreme than the political traffic would bear, Conant kept this view to himself for the moment. But, strikingly, he was already constructing a vision of what the United States would demand of the *post-*war world. While resolutely determined to see Hitlerism vanquished, he by no means envisioned a war to preserve the British Empire. Concerned that in the previous world war Americans had "embarked on a purely moral crusade" that resulted in a peace settlement that left them wondering what they had gained from the killing and dying, Conant like his son believed that if the United States entered this war it should do so less on the basis of sentiment and sympathy than out of a clear-eyed, hard-headed self-interest. "We were too idealistic and it was too easy for a subsequent group of debunkers to say the United States got nothing from the War," he wrote Grenville Clark in January 1940. "I hope at the next peace and reorganization of the world, it can be shown that the United States is indeed a beneficiary of the disaster into which we would be forced."[50]

By late June, Conant's aspirations for postwar American supremacy had grown far more expansive. On a rainy Saturday, Conant bluntly told Princeton's president, Dodds, that the United States must assure its own safety by taking over the globe, in language reminiscent of his son's oration a week earlier: "Expressed my views on U.S.A. armed to the teeth, belligerent and running the world," he jotted in his diary. "A Pax Americana like the Pax Britannica of the 19th Century."[51]

Conant's views on the war had crystallized. Hitler must be decisively defeated, not merely contained, at all costs. Survival of everything he believed in — freedom and democracy — was at stake. Eventually, the United States must be ready to fight, and to win a victory that would allow it to reorder the world. So long as the world was at war, means no longer mattered, only ends, and means included devastating weapons. If he could make those weapons more deadly and effective, so much the better.

But how best to mobilize American scientists for the war? It was a question that had gnawed at Conant since the day he learned of the German invasion of Poland; for months he probed contacts and encouraged Harvard scientists to lay the groundwork for future work, but he kept running into the logjams created by the neutrality laws, by competing priorities, and by his own unfamiliarity with Washington's bureaucratic politics. The disintegration of the Allied armies in the spring of 1940 roused into action Conant and several other leaders of American science and education who gathered for lunch, once again, at the Century Club, on Saturday, May 24, 1940, after a meeting of the Committee on Scientific Aids to Learning, a panel established by the Carnegie Corporation and attached to the National Research Council; Conant had chaired the group since its inception in 1937. In attendance, besides Conant, were Vannevar Bush, the head of the Carnegie Institution in Washington, one of the country's leading scientific philanthropies; the New York lawyer Bethuel M. Webster; Frank B. Jewett, president of the National Academy of Sciences and chairman of the board of Bell Telephone; and the group's director, Irvin Stewart. Alarm but not despondency over the deteriorating military situation in Europe dominated the conversation — and Bush, a wily ex-engineer who had, despite Republican leanings, maintained a close friendship with FDR confidant Harry Hopkins, left the meeting determined to get Roosevelt's OK to get a federal effort going to enlist U.S. science into military research.[52]

Bush moved quickly, seeing Roosevelt with Hopkins's help, and on June 14 telephoned Conant to recruit him into the newly formed National Defense Research Committee (NDRC), established by Roosevelt at Bush's urging to mobilize American scientific contributions to military research. Since he had "urged this committee on Bush for some months," as he put it in his diary, Conant of course accepted, contingent only upon receiving satisfactory answers to two questions: "Is it real?" and "Are you to head the Committee?"[53]

Bush's affirmative replies marked the beginning of a collaboration that would come to dominate the U.S. government's scientific research establishment for the duration of the war and that would culminate in the effort to develop—and control—the atomic bomb. It was a likely combination. Both were quick-witted, ambitious, no-nonsense, middle-class Massachusetts Yankees who had taken to tinkering with gadgets as teenagers and had, as adults, become well versed in academic and scientific politics. They even had in common a chastening failure in youthful entrepreneurship, although in Bush's case no one died in the fire that destroyed an industrial test site under his supervision and caused his dismissal from General Electric.[54] Before leaving Cambridge to head the Carnegie Institution, Bush had known Conant slightly in his days as a university administrator at Tufts and MIT.[55] In June 1934, MIT president Karl Compton had detailed Bush to "look after" the neighboring school's new leader. "The more I see of this man," Bush reported back, "the more I am inclined to believe that we are very fortunate to have him as the President of Harvard University."[56] In subsequent years, the two tangled in inter-university skirmishes that Bush later recalled as "good vigorous battles from which we emerged friends."[57] Then, as Conant learned the administrative ropes at Harvard, the bespectacled, pipe-puffing Bush became a scientific power broker in Washington, wielding Carnegie's prestige and financial resources to promote basic and applied research and becoming chairman of the National Advisory Committee on Aeronautics. In the fall of 1939, as war overtook Europe, Conant and Bush corresponded to resolve a delicate personnel matter—how Harvard and Carnegie should share in paying the salary of the historian of science George Sarton, who held a joint appointment from the two institutions—and gradually discovered a concordance in their conviction as to the need to accelerate rearmament and scientific preparedness measures.[58]

From the inception of the NDRC, the complementary characteristics that were to characterize the Bush-Conant management of the atomic bomb program were already apparent. The organic chemist and the applied mathematician and engineer had personalities that allowed them to act as foils for each other. Neither had patience for what they saw as incompetence or mediocrity, both had a wry sense of humor, but while Conant rarely, if ever, lost his temper, Bush was known for his sharp tongue and bluster. Harvey H. Bundy, who as special assistant to War Secretary Henry Stimson dealt extensively with both men on atomic matters, described Bush as "impatient, perhaps a vain man, but a very, very remarkable human being." Conant, Bundy recalled, "kept Bush on the rails as much as anybody" and was a "much calmer man than Bush, who would explode."[59]

The NDRC opened a new era in another respect—rather than proposing to draft scientists out of universities and to build new military laboratories, as the military had done during World War I, the wartime scientific apparatus overseen by Bush broke with the past by carrying out most war-related scientific research under contract to civilian universities and institutes. Later accepted as a norm, this strategy led to thousands of separate research projects being conducted around the country and fostered a transformation of the relationship among American universities, government, and the armed forces that would long outlast the war for which the committee was created.[60]

The "four horsemen" of the NDRC—Bush, Conant, Jewett, and Compton, along with a senior physicist, Richard C. Tolman, of the California Institute of Technology—gathered on June 18 at the Carnegie Institution's baroque head-quarters at 1530 P Street, a few blocks from Dupont Circle in northwest Washington, for a preliminary organizational meeting. A week later, Conant returned to Washington for a second NDRC planning session, staying at the suburban home of fellow interventionist Acheson, and gossiping with him and MacLeish. On June 25, Conant received his first NDRC assignment—he was to be director of Division B, in charge of bombs, fuels, gases, and chemical warfare.[61]

Immediately, the other NDRC leaders began to recruit prospects from universities all over the country for the work they firmly believed would be necessary for America's ultimate participation in the war. Returning by train to Cambridge, Conant gathered Harvard chemists and physicists in University Hall to inform them of the new organization, still a week from being formally announced by Roosevelt, and to seek their cooperation.[62] Later, in October, he gave a more detailed exposition to a score of scientists interested in war work at the home of NDRC chemistry chief Roger Adams (the chemist whose sudden departure from Harvard in 1916 had given Conant his first break). As each investigator outlined ideas, projects took shape, and the chemistry labs and football fields of Harvard soon housed a fast-growing array of experiments to devise new explosives.[63] Those lethal efforts, in turn, complemented a range of committees, panels, and projects championed by Harvard faculty members, staff, and families to organize humanitarian aid to the Allies, most prominently a medical mission to Britain.

For Conant, this work for the mobilization of science was welcome for several reasons. At times exasperated by his administrative responsibilities at Harvard and the sometimes acrimonious academic political warfare there, it sent him back to the world of the laboratory he had left so regretfully, and placed him as a colleague alongside like-minded scientists and engineers who cared for nothing but getting the job done for a purpose they all believed in.

And, committed now to the defeat of Germany, Conant felt that in the NDRC he could contribute concretely to crushing fascism and laying the groundwork for U.S. global leadership. The job promised uniquely to challenge both his scientific and administrative abilities. "Jim says his work in Wash. is extraordinarily interesting, even if it seems like turning the clock back 23 years," Patty Conant wrote her mother in mid-July. "And of course it has got to be done. On the whole, this last week, he feels a good deal has been accomplished. If England can only hold out through the summer, he feels the world may possibly pull through."[64]

The first priority, before building weapons, was assembling manpower. In the latter half of 1940, Conant embarked on a job that would never quite finish until the war had ended—recruiting university scientists, securing permissions for leaves of absence and approval for use of facilities and contracts from university presidents, tapping the network he had been building since before World War I. Although he and Bush initially encountered resistance from isolationist administrators and scientists, particularly in the Middle West, the scientific mobilization dwarfed anything ever previously attempted by the U.S. government.

For all his new fervency and resolve, Conant's careful monitoring of political currents led him to pull punches in the actions he was recommending to support England and tug the United States into the war. His speech to the Jewish War Veterans in New York City on June 12, 1940, illustrates the degree to which he calibrated his public statements. At first, he had been reluctant to accept the group's citation, but had grudgingly consented to speak at the behest of the group's representative, Max Slater, an old Roxbury Latin classmate. He warned, however, that his remarks would be relatively innocuous. Why the reluctance? "Since he was all out for preparedness," recalled Slater, "he felt that his appearance before the Jewish War Veterans would simply give the Nazis additional ammunition for labeling the Jews as war mongers." A few days before, however, Roosevelt gave his most militant pro-Allied speech yet, telling a Charlottesville, Virginia, audience that the United States would rearm and "extend to the opponents of force the material resources of the nation." Emboldened by this rhetorical abandonment of neutrality, and after careful consultation with Calvert Smith, Conant excitedly told Slater that, after all, he could now "express his true feelings" by calling for congressional legislation, including compulsory military training, to implement the president's wishes.[65]

Given the resilient potency of isolationist views, especially in the election year, Conant calculated shrewdly, if resignedly, that U.S. public opinion would not support a serious military rescue effort until England had proved its mettle in resisting a direct assault by German sea or air forces. That assessment solidified in mid-July, after a disconcerting dinner conversation with Bill Claflin, Harvard's conservative treasurer, who was pessimistic about England's chances to hold off Germany but confident that America could

" 'get on' with a victorious Germany." Conant wrote disgustedly in his diary that Claflin's view seemed "typical of business appeasement group" but nothing could be done "about such defeatism till England weathers a real attack."[66]

Concentrating for the moment on convincing Congress to pass the Burke-Wadsworth conscription bill—he testified before the Senate Military Affairs Committee on July 3—Conant developed a public-relations strategy designed to exploit likely military developments. Though the Nazis, having swallowed the European continent, seemed poised to press their onslaught across the Channel, Conant counseled the CDAAA against immediately pushing for specific actions to arm Britain. Instead, the group should for the time being confine itself to sounding a "general note of alarm" directed to "warning the people and waking them up." In his diary Conant succinctly outlined his reasoning: "Until the German 'frontal' attack *en masse* of England has occurred and been repulsed specific measures to aid England hopeless politically here. After Aug 15 be ready to urge repeal of neutrality laws." Once the first German wave had been spent, the "warhawks" would be ready to introduce pro-intervention legislation.[67]

As Conant hoped, Americans were deeply inspired by the spectacle of the "Battle of Britain," and he listened along with the nation to the dramatic broadcasts of Edward R. Murrow from a London under attack in August and September. Unlike most, however, Conant soon learned of the secret advances in radar that were helping British pilots down the incoming *Luftwaffe* raiders, a scientific breakthrough that helped Britain fend off the assault, as did a German decision to switch from the costly but damaging strikes on air bases to the less militarily effective tactic of terror raids on civilian populations. Britain's courage under fire also made it easier for Roosevelt to inch toward providing Churchill's government with more aid, though on terms beneficial to U.S. interests and short of actually joining the war. In early August, Conant learned of a "great scheme being cooked up" to give England fifty old destroyers and cruisers, an idea that soon culminated in a trade of the old ships for long-term leases of British bases in the Western hemisphere.[68] Churchill, though grumbling at what he regarded as a one-sided deal, saw little choice but to accept Roosevelt's terms.

To Conant, eager to see popular opinion roused, word that Germany's attack on England had begun came almost as a relief. In fact, he regretted not being there to demonstrate his personal commitment to the battle. Keenly aware that many students resented their president for advocating a military draft for which he was far too old to be liable, he was disappointed to learn, too late to go along, that an expedition of Harvard public health specialists was en route to Britain to set up a Harvard–Red Cross hospital to treat infectious diseases. Chagrined at "missing the boat," Conant felt the dean had "a bit doublecrossed" him by hiding plans for the trip because he thought it too dangerous.[69]

Rushing back and forth between Cambridge, Washington, and New Hampshire, his back ailing him and his traditional summer vacation in shambles, by the end of the summer Conant found himself devoting more time to national defense and pro-interventionist activities and less to Harvard. Occasionally, his many hats got in each other's way. Conant soon realized that the NDRC's task of mobilizing science and launching projects required close cooperation with military officials. Loath to endanger cordial ties with them by openly criticizing what he regarded as their obtuse resistance to scientific and medical deferments, he lobbied indirectly to promote a draft bill that preserved exemptions for the trained personnel who would be needed on weapons research projects. In the ferocious congressional debate on this issue in August and early September, prospects for the conscription bill were helped by the absence of criticism from Republican presidential candidate Wendell Willkie, a silence procured in part through the nonpartisan (and bipartisan) efforts and contacts of the Century Group. Though a majority of Republicans and an avalanche of mail opposed the bill, Congress passed and FDR signed the Burke-Wadsworth bill on September 16. Pleased by what he regarded as a necessary albeit minimal step toward readiness, Conant had mixed feelings about the vague deferment provisions, but the law at least assured that by late 1941 the United States would have more than 1.6 million troops in the field.[70]

Despite such achievements as the draft law and the destroyers-for-bases trade, Conant's impatience with the incremental pace of U.S. policy and public opinion mounted in the fall of 1940 as his conviction hardened that America must enter the war to defeat the Axis. "War is not the worst possibility we face," Conant told returning Harvard students in September. "The worst is the complete triumph of totalitarianism."[71] Disappointed by what he saw as Willkie's politically opportunistic criticism of the conscription legislation and the destroyers-for-bases deal, Conant at the last minute decided to vote for Roosevelt, though, characteristically, he confided to his diary that he would "tell no one not even Patty thus preserving political neutrality!"[72] But in the weeks after the election, the country's volatile public opinion tilted back toward isolationism—a swerve made painfully apparent to Conant during halftime of the Harvard-Yale football game in late November, when the *Crimson* and *Lampoon* staged a skit ridiculing him as a warmonger. As the Nazis consolidated their grip on occupied Europe, the United States seemed content to stay on the sidelines, as neither Democratic nor Republican leaders were inclined to risk opprobrium by advocating belligerence. Conant, however, felt no such constraint. To the chairman of the CDAAA, William Allen White, and other leading interventionists, he wrote that the "fundamental issue" appeared to be whether the United States would settle for a "stalemate peace" that would leave Hitler and the Axis dominant outside the Western Hemisphere.[73]

By the end of the year, Conant was rapidly deserting the CDAAA's stance that Washington should provide the Allies with all aid "short of war." Roosevelt needed to take steps to deepen Washington's commitment, he urged publicly and privately, not only to resist but to strangle the Nazi onslaught, which he likened to Mohammed's sweep across Europe thirteen centuries earlier.[74] Americans needed to become emotionally prepared for battle, Conant declared. "We shall be rightly condemned by posterity if we needlessly become involved in war and squander life and treasure," he told a nationwide radio audience on November 20. "But we shall be yet more guilty in the eyes of our descendants if we fail to preserve our heritage of freedom."[75] His determination that the United States abandon its qualms about entering the war in order to establish global predominance was also hardening—to the point of advocating, at least in private, that Washington embark on an openly "expansionist" policy to impose, after the defeat of Germany, a "new world order" policed by an international assembly in which the United States "would have more than fifty per cent of the votes." Declaring that the United States sought to widen its "spheres of influence to include a large part of the civilized world," Conant privately advised Maj. George Fielding Eliot that the steps by which United States moved were "a purely National concern and must be considered from a hardboiled, selfish, national point of view."[76]

Still cautious about getting too far ahead of public opinion, Conant successfully convinced Eliot, a fellow Century Group interventionist, to insert these ideas verbatim into his own widely distributed foreign policy analysis.[77] (It would be inappropriate, the educator privately told another Century Group member, for a "person concerned with the education of the young [who] is supposed to have certain humanitarian considerations foremost in his mind" to embrace openly positions which many will consider "unduly harsh and cruel.")[78] But Conant's own more belligerent public tone was enough to evoke new protests. After hearing his November 20 radio speech, a lawyer friend from Chicago accused him of abusing his "high office in an effort to consign the youth of America to the most cruel and destructive war which the world has yet known," and predicted that the United States could not crush Hitler without losing its own freedom and democracy. Conant rejected such "clairvoyance," arguing that a compromise peace would neither protect those values nor satisfy Hitler's long-term lust, but such protests deeply alarmed him.[79]

In mid-December, Conant took his concern straight to the top, writing his most personal letter yet to Roosevelt. Prodding him to counter distressing indications of "lethargy" and a "defeatist spirit," he suggested a series of nationally broadcast talks to educate the nation to the "grave danger which the country now faces due to the possibility of a defeat of Great Britain by the Totalitarian Powers." Only "you and you alone," he reminded FDR, could disabuse Americans of the insidious notion that the United States might accept a compromise peace with Hitler.[80]

Roosevelt's response deeply gratified Conant. Welcoming his suggestion "that I inform the American people concerning the grave implications of the present situation," FDR vowed to "make a radio address along the line you propose before the end of the year."[81] Roosevelt's fireside chat of December 29, 1940, his first major statement since his victory over Willkie seven weeks earlier, came as the interventionist movement was riven by dissension — symbolized by a split in the Committee to Defend America by Aiding the Allies — between those who recoiled from advocating more than shipping guns, medicine, and aid to Britain and those ready to make the leap to full belligerence. Firmly enrolled in the latter camp, Conant and Lew Douglas organized a strongly worded circular letter to Roosevelt, signed by 170 prominent figures, to bolster his resolve. When FDR spoke over the radio, sounding his familiar avuncular tones, he exhorted Americans to assemble "more ships, more guns, more planes — more of everything" to contribute to the "Arsenal of Democracy," and closely followed Conant's counsel by warning that American democracy and Nazi totalitarianism could not peaceably share the globe.[82]

While the general tones and firm denial of any intent to send U.S. soldiers into the fray disappointed some interventionists, Conant wrote to Clark on New Year's Eve that FDR's speech had been "magnificent and went as far as it was possible for him to go" given the current political climate. At times, before and later, Conant's caution and coolness led him to weak or self-contradictory positions, but on this occasion he dispensed sage advice. An open split in the CDAAA between the militants and the group's founder, William Allen White, who was openly in favor of the "short of war" formula, might be necessary if the White House advocated actions likely to lead to war. White soon resigned, but rather than break up on a still hypothetical issue, Conant characteristically told Clark, the committee should avoid a public ruckus that would hurt the interventionist cause, and instead focus on firmly backing Roosevelt as he "played his entire hand" and moved the country to take action against Hitler. "Happy New Year!" he added after sounding this optimistic note.[83] Conant had high hopes that within a few weeks Roosevelt would introduce concrete measures, such as a naval convoys to ship arms to England, both to aid the forces fighting Germany and, more importantly, to condition public opinion to something approaching "belligerent action" by the United States. Within ten days, those were largely redeemed by FDR's announcement of Lend-Lease legislation.

Conant was also cheered, and excited, by the prospect of soon being able to demonstrate that his personal mettle matched his belligerent rhetoric. Hearing in November that the NDRC planned to dispatch a liaison mission to England, Conant pleaded to head the mission despite Bush's objections that the trip through the U-boat-infested Atlantic to a city under aerial bombardment was too dangerous. But, having missed this opportunity once, Conant argued strenuously that he was the right person now. When Bush and Jewett tried to talk him out of it, he wrote an impassioned letter making the case not only for his ability to speak with authority for the NDRC, but more importantly, for the good it would do the country to see a college president willing to risk danger. Given the steady charges of warmongering coming from inside Harvard, the trip would help there, too.

> We have all been concerned with the reluctance of some of the young people today to wake up to the realities of the present. I believe that actions speak louder than words. I have been quite active as a private citizen in urging a more belligerent policy for the United States. I think it has some value for a man who has taken such a position to show that he is willing to take risks, even if they are slight ones, provided that the President of the United States asks him to do it. I hate to use the phrase, but I would say that my going would have certain small advantages from the point of view of my moral leadership in this academic community which would more than offset the dislocation in Harvard life which would be the result of my not coming back. I suppose it is this last consideration plus my general desire for interesting and adventurous experiences that really motivates me in making this long plea.[84]

In fact, he acknowledged, the chances of being killed were "probably not more than one in a thousand"—and his inner motive rather resembled that which he ascribed to the Harvard volunteers for the ambulance corps in 1914–17: "a desire to come dangerously close to a dangerous adventure without running much risk of becoming a casualty oneself."[85] Conant's drive to taste battle firsthand, to experience what his generation regarded as the fiery, violent crucible of character, to witness that which had eluded his father in the Civil War and what he had missed in the previous European war, seemed almost to match his fervency in contributing to the struggle against Hitler.

Conant's arguments did the trick: Jewett replied on New Year's Day that he approved his making the trip to England, in part on the basis of his agreement, after checking with his son, a student at Harvard Business School, that "at Harvard at least there is a lot of cynicism about the older generation which would be offset by something such as you are proposing to do."[86] Exhilarated, Conant secretly began preparing for the February sailing that would take him on an adventure that was to prove the "most extraordinary experience" in his life,[87] and that gave him his first serious contact with the possibility of building an atomic bomb.

CHAPTER 8

"A Major Push Along the Lines Outlined"

Commitments to Belligerency and the Bomb

1941

In that summer of 1941, with recollections of what I had seen and heard in England fresh in my mind, I was impatient with the arguments of some of the physicists associated with the Uranium Committee whom I met from time to time. They talked in excited tones about the discovery of a new world in which power from a uranium reactor would revolutionize our industrialized society. These fancies left me cold. I suggested that until Nazi Germany was defeated all our energies should be concentrated on one immediate objective.
　　　　　—My Several Lives

With the news from Great Britain unofficially at hand, the two Academy reports and the favorable action of NDRC, it became clear to the director of OSRD and the Chairman of NDRC that a major push along the lines outlined was in order.
　　　　　—JBC, "A History of the Development of an Atomic Bomb"

This war is in many ways a race of scientific developments and devices . . . Grim necessity requires that the unconditional surrender of the Axis Powers be the first war aim of the United States . . . The day the Nazi regime collapses will be the beginning of a new era . . . At that moment the United States must be ready to assume political and economic leadership of the world.
　　　　　—JBC, "What Victory Requires," December 22, 1941

As Conant quietly prepared for his journey, keeping his wife in the dark until late January while arranging for inoculations against typhoid and conferring with NDRC officials, he had no inkling that the most momentous scientific topic that would arise would be not the radar that had been so crucial during the Battle of Britain, but a subject on the periphery of his concerns: atomic energy.

Like any other observant human being, Conant had been aware of what in retrospect seems like a perverse coincidence: the discovery of fission, in Germany in December 1938, precisely as Nazi aggression accelerated Europe and the world toward a cataclysm. Since early in the twentieth century, atomic weapons had been a staple of science fiction novels, most famously H. G. Wells's *The World Set Free* (1914), whose futuristic speculations included devastating wars during which combatants spread lethal radioactive dust. And in the decades preceding 1938, a revolution in theoretical physics forced the abandonment of the Newtonian model that had dominated the field for three centuries and led to a conception of a universe in which matter and energy were, at least in theory, convertible. Einstein's $E = mc^2$ established the relevant relationship: liberating the tiny particles bound up in the atomic nucleus could release tremendous amounts of energy. But how? Until 1939, the idea that nuclear energy could actually be used either for power or for explosives was widely dismissed as "moonshine," as Ernest Rutherford, the British Nobel laureate physicist and pioneer of nuclear theory, said in 1933. The atom, all but a few dissenting physicists presumed, could not be divided into its component parts; the energy bonding its particles would safely remain impervious to human meddling or exploitation.

That conventional wisdom was shattered, however, when scientists learned in the first days of 1939 that experiments at the Kaiser Wilhelm Institute for Chemistry in Berlin, conducted by the German physicists Otto Hahn and Fritz Strassman and elaborated by Lise Meitner, had demonstrated that a well-aimed neutron could split the nucleus of a uranium atom, fissioning it into two distinct elements.[1]

Nuclear fission was feasible, then, but the engineering and industrial challenges involved in actually building a workable power plant appeared enormous and perhaps insuperable. Through the first nine months of 1939, physicists around the globe engaged in a frenzied rush of testing and speculation to confirm and advance the Hahn-Strassman results. In America, the amazing news was disclosed in dramatic fashion by Niels Bohr and Enrico Fermi, the Italian-born nuclear physicist who had defected from his fascist-ruled homeland after receiving the 1938 Nobel prize. Their presentation to a January 26, 1939, meeting in Washington of the American Physical Society caused some listeners to bolt for their labs to repeat the experiments even before Bohr had finished speaking. Hearing the sensational reports, however, the hard-headed and skeptical chemist who was president of Harvard University discounted the breathless newspaper stories claiming that the physicists would fast transform (or destroy) the world via atomic power.

Still, the fact that Hitler's scientists had outpaced those in England and the United States deeply troubled a group of émigré scientists who grasped the potential for construction of a devastating weapon.[2] Leo Szilard, a brilliant, impatient, and iconoclastic physicist who had fled oppression in

Hungary, had taken out a secret patent on a design for an atomic explosive as early as 1934, assigning it to the British Admiralty. Now he had transferred his work from London to Columbia University, on Manhattan's Upper West Side, joining a steady stream of refugees in the United States who both energized scientific investigations and personalized political concerns over events in Europe. Late in the summer of 1939, as Germany threatened and then started war, Szilard and two fellow Hungarian escapees, Eugene Wigner and Edward Teller, quietly urged their fellow physicists to restrain publication of research on fission, and persuaded Albert Einstein to sign a letter to President Roosevelt warning of the terrible danger should Hitler get the bomb first. On October 11, the financier Alexander Sachs carried this warning to FDR, who, seemingly impressed ("This requires action"), appointed an Advisory Committee on Uranium, headed by Bureau of Standards director Lyman J. Briggs, to investigate the military significance of nuclear fission research.[3]

Conant was not one of the handful of scientific advisers initially officially designated by the government to keep track of atomic developments, but he must have followed them at least generally, both out of innate personal curiosity and from awareness of their burgeoning import for university research programs. And as early as the spring of 1940, the European war as well as his informal network of contacts with the scientific world seem to have given him an acute sensitivity to the risks of publicizing atomic fission's military implications — a sensitivity unwittingly detonated one day by his irreverent younger son, when Ted was going through the papers of his uncle, William Richards, after Richards had committed suicide in New York City on January 30, 1940.

The tall, lean, dark-haired son of the Nobel laureate Theodore Richards and younger brother of Patty Richards had taught chemistry at Princeton from 1926 to 1937 and then joined the staff of a mysterious, elaborately equipped private laboratory owned and run by Alfred Lee Loomis, an eccentric multimillionaire physicist. Richards had commuted to Loomis's Tuxedo Park, New York, facility from the late twenties to work on various aspects of physical chemistry such as the chemical actions of ultrasonic radiation in liquids.[4] Loomis's friends and admirers included Ernest O. Lawrence, the University of California physicist whom Conant had tried to lure to Harvard, and who in the fall of 1939 had won the Nobel prize in physics for his invention of the cyclotron, a device to study radioactive isotopes. Lawrence and Conant considered Loomis a valuable patron and a talented and creative experimentalist; to critics he was a something of a screwball; perhaps he was both. When he wasn't spinning deals on Wall Street, Loomis oversaw the operations of the Loomis Institute for Scientific Research atop an isolated hilltop in the Ramapo Mountains north of New York City. There, in an English-style mansion, Loomis sponsored investigations of topics ranging from brain waves to hi-fi; in 1940, he transferred his radar research to the MIT

Radiation Laboratory, which became the NDRC's primary facility for work on this crucial military technology.[5]

Conant's brother-in-law was, friends and relatives said, a witty, scintillating, passionate, creative, yet solitary man who lived and worked under many pressures — among them Loomis's political and social conservatism, and the private issue of his own sexual tensions and confusion. These pressures exacerbated what appear to have been long-standing physical and psychological problems; one friend who shared his intense interests in science and music speculated that Richards was doomed by his own rigorously perfectionist nature, for "No human being could be expected fully to satisfy such standards."[6] An affectionate set of memoirs by his Harvard classmates concludes sadly that Richards took his own life after a "brave struggle for ten years to overcome a serious neurosis, which in spite of treatment grew worse,"[7] and Conant wrote a close family friend that the suicide had been "shocking" to him and especially to his wife, but had not come as a complete surprise, "as her brother has been far from well for a number of years and his psychological condition was such that his ending seemed, in a sense, inevitable."[8] Although one friend wrote that Richards enjoyed "one of the keenest scientific pleasures of his career" working at the Loomis Laboratory, shortly before taking his life Richards had scathingly lampooned the laboratory and its "inmates" in the huge stone castle in Tuxedo Park in a roman à clef murder mystery entitled *Brain-Waves and Death* and published under the rather incriminating pseudonym "Willard Rich."[9] (Eerily, the novel also forshadowed the ingenious method he would use to take his own life: a contraption rigged to an alarm clock that released a lethal dose of poison gas that killed him while he slept.)[10] Loomis threatened to sue for libel, and Patty Conant, agreeing that the book stained the family's honor, urged her brother to recall all copies.

Ted Conant, however, had loved *Brain-Waves and Death*. And within a few months after his uncle's suicide, going through Richards's papers, he was excited to discover the typed, double-spaced draft of a speculative story called "The Uranium Bomb." An avid science fiction fan, he had lapped up gossip on war projects from electronics and engineering friends at Harvard and MIT, and he thought the manuscript would be perfect for *Astounding Science Fiction*, containing just the right blend of futuristic titillation and realistic science. In fact, the manuscript *was* astounding — the fictionalized story of Boris Zmenov, a Russian émigré physicist, who, afraid that Germany might construct an atomic bomb, desperately seeks to warn the president of the United States and to convince fellow scientists to suppress publication of studies on atomic fission. Richards's story contained an amazingly accurate description of the principles that were in fact to be used in the gun-type uranium weapon dropped on Hiroshima five years later. It also bore astonishing resemblance to the real-life activities of the Hungarian refugee scientists Szilard, Wigner, and Teller in 1939, right down to their frustration at the difficulty of persuading government officials of the weapon's potentially earthshaking importance. And in fact Szilard, who by March of that year had become convinced—from his experiments at Columbia on uranium fission—that an atomic bomb was possible, and was frantic with fear that the Germans might build it first, had approached Richards seeking funds ($35,000 was one figure mentioned) for his nuclear research experiments to "decide once and for all if a chain reaction can be made to work."

"I am on the verge of developing a weapon," Zmenov sputters at one point, waving his arms, "which will be the greatest military discovery of all time. It will revolutionize war, and make the nation possessing it supreme. I wish that the United States should be this nation, but am I encouraged? Am I assisted with the most meager financial support? Bah."[11]

Another likely source of inspiration for Richards's protagonist was his close friend, the chemist and Russian émigré George B. Kistiakowsky. The two scientists had become friends while teaching chemistry at Princeton in the late 1920s, before Kistiakowsky was lured to Harvard's chemistry department by its prestigious chairman, Conant, who in turn developed a lifelong professional and personal friendship with Kistiakowsky. By the fall of 1939, Kistiakowsky, along with colleagues in Harvard's physics department, had plunged into radioactive isotope research, largely for biomedical purposes, and were particularly eager to cooperate with Lawrence's ambitious cyclotron project at Berkeley. In fact, in early February 1940, a few days after his brother-in-law's suicide, Conant had approved the appointment of the New Committee on Nuclear Physics at Harvard whose members included future Manhattan Project participants Kenneth T. Bainbridge, Kistiakowsky, Shields Warren, and E. Bright Wilson. And to render financial and technical aid to his university's embryonic cyclotron effort, Harvard's president was ardently wooing none other than Lawrence, whose own cyclotron project was about to receive a breakthrough $1.15 million grant from the Rockefeller Foundation, won with the assistance of Conant, Bush, and the two Comptons, Karl T., the MIT president, and Arthur H., the Nobel-winning nuclear physicist at the University of Chicago; and Loomis, who in May 1940 wrote a check for $5,000 to sponsor Harvard's small-scale nuclear physics research![12]

The plot grew even thicker. On the side, Kistiakowsky was making an "independent study" for Loomis on the danger that the Germans might be the first to develop a "tremendously powerful war weapon" employing uranium fission—and by May, in a conversation with Karl Compton, Loomis relayed Kistiakowsky's fears, and the fact that German scientists at the Kaiser Wilhelm Institute were "concentrating major efforts on this problem." Compton's report, in turn, resulted on May 23 in the Carnegie Institution's appropriating $20,000 in discretionary funds to Bush—who kept Conant and Jewett apprised of the developments—"for a defense research project concerning uranium fission."[13]

From such interwoven personal and institutional connections and obligations—Conant also urged Lawrence to plead Harvard's case to foundations, and to convince Loomis to sign on at Harvard as a consultant—was the nation's nascent World War II science effort soon to be created. But Conant's thirteen-year-old son had had no idea that his late uncle's science fiction story, a copy of which was in the possession of Richards's literary agent, was a tiny thread in a much larger and tangled web. So he was puzzled and disappointed when his father, after opposing his wife's proposal to recall *Brain-Waves and Death*, sternly rejected the idea of having the short story appear in the leading pulp magazine.

But it's a good story, Ted insisted, and *Astounding* would love it.

No, his father replied, it's too outlandish.

It's great, the teenager persisted.

It's silly and crazy, steamed Conant, and it's impossible to have such a thing published.

"I really argued," Theodore Conant recalls, "and he really got angry at me. It was one of the few times he *really* got angry at me, so I dropped it, because I had not seen him that angry for a long time."

Only after Hiroshima did Ted realize the motive behind the mysterious temper tantrum—even in the spring of 1940, Conant evidently accepted the necessity to suppress any public mention of atomic energy's military potential. Though at first outraged that he had been lied to, Theodore Conant laughed many years later as he analyzed his father's behavior—"he blew up on me because he was on pretty weak ground and he knew it, so rage was an effective substitute for logic."[14]

When FDR appointed the Briggs committee in October 1939, bureaucratic wheels had been set in motion to assure American atomic preparedness, but they turned slowly at first. For almost two years, atomic research languished— at least so far as the U.S. government was concerned. The uranium committee plodded along with a negligible budget, little sense of urgency, and desultory organization; it never bothered to organize any serious experiments. Even a front-page story in the *New York Times* (on May 5, 1940) warning that German scientists were "feverishly" working to develop an atomic explosive failed to spur much new activity.[15] And, for some months after he joined the NDRC in mid-1940, Conant fully shared the prevailing strong skepticism about the potential usefulness of atomic energy in the war effort. Although Bush took the lead in trying to figure out whether the nuclear fission question needed a new approach, Conant also tried to stay abreast of developments. On June 15, 1940, a day after he accepted Bush's invitation to join the NDRC, he also accepted an invitation to chair a panel at a Conference on Applied Nuclear Physics to be held at MIT that fall, saying he was "deeply interested in the subject." The invitation had come from Columbia University's Harold C. Urey, the Nobel laureate nuclear chemist who was a member of Briggs's committee and who along with Kistiakowsky was investigating the gaseous diffusion method of uranium isotope separation, and in fact the conference featured many physicists and chemists who would figure in the American atomic bomb effort: besides Urey and Conant, other participants included Briggs, Frederick Seitz, Ernest Lawrence, Edward Condon, Lee DuBridge, Kenneth Bainbridge, and Enrico Fermi, who was scheduled to speak on "Nuclear Fission." Conant recorded laconically in his diary that he found the sessions "very interesting," but there is no indication whether the possibility of a bomb was raised. When the topic came up at NDRC meetings— discussed solely as a power source, he says—Conant considered the schemes the physicists put forward to be unrealistic and irrelevant. More obvious priorities included proven devices: radar, gas, and bombs. To invest substantial amounts of men and money on a project with such long odds of success and peripheral military value might sidetrack the defense effort just when time was at a premium.[16]

That was Conant's belief as he reached the Jersey City pier from which he sailed for Europe on the sunny, crisply cool morning of Saturday, February 15, 1941. Stepping up a gangplank to board the transatlantic steamer *Excalibur,* Conant discerned a "very gala" atmosphere reminiscent of "the gay 20's with everyone off on a Mediterranean Cruise" as passengers boarded the American Export Liner for a two-week cruise to Lisbon via Bermuda. Contributing to the air of excitement, and to Conant's sudden consternation, a flock of newsmen and photographers waited to pounce on them with cameras and notebooks. Alarmed, Conant and his NDRC associates—Carroll L. Wilson, Frederick L. Hovde, and Cheryl Haskins—huddled along with Harvard adviser Calvert Smith to decide on strategy. They settled, Conant wrote in his diary, on a "dignified though conservative policy of 'laissez-faire' and would neither seek nor avoid the flash of the photographic bulb." Soon, however, a "cloud of witnesses" surrounded them on the ship's deck, cutting off all avenues of escape.

"How did you hear of this?" the NDRC delegation asked, startled to see their hush-hush mission off to such a well-covered start.

"Oh, it's in all the papers," replied the a reporter, who promptly produced a *Sun* with a banner headline reading "Conant Heads Mission to London." Thus did he learn that, the night before, the White House had announced that Roosevelt had requested Harvard's president to lead an NDRC team to England "to facilitate the exchange of information on recent scientific developments of importance to national defense."[17]

The weeks leading up to the well-documented sailing had been filled with hectic activity for Conant. On January 10, Roosevelt had introduced lend-lease legislation to assure British access to American weapons, sparking a furious response mobilized in part by the America First Committee, the isolationist counterpart of the CDAAA. Though of course he had been publicly and privately urging FDR to take firmer steps to bind America to England's struggle, Conant's years of careful restraint from overt partisan affiliation served him well, and he testified as one of three final rebuttal witnesses for the administration—along with Wendell Willkie and Fiorello La Guardia—in favor of lend-lease before the Senate Foreign Relations Committee on February 10. When Conant had met with Roosevelt in the White House on February 1 to discuss his upcoming trip, the president's concern over the bill's fate dominated the conversation, to Conant's annoyance. "I had great difficulty getting the President to talk about my mission," he recorded in his diary. "Rather, he was anxious to outline the political strategy" for securing passage of the Lend-Lease Act. Peppered by talking points for the Capitol Hill appearance, afraid Roosevelt might usher him out of the Oval Office, Conant barely succeeded in distracting FDR long enough to get his agreement formally to request that Conant lead the NDRC liaison mission.[18]

Armed with a presidential order to undertake the task that he had campaigned for, Conant returned to Cambridge and finally broke the news of his imminent departure to the Harvard Corporation, which reacted with thunderstruck silence. "Well," Grenville Clark said finally, "if the President has asked you to go, there's nothing more to say, is there?" No, replied Conant, there seems not to be, hastening to add that his temporary absence should not unduly hamper university business. Unconvinced, the treasurer, Claflin, groused that Conant had "pulled every wire" to go on this trip and asked whether his "conscience didn't trouble" him—leaving Harvard in the lurch that way. "In general, there was little or no enthusiasm for my mission!" Conant noted privately.[19]

As a witness before the Foreign Relations Committee, Conant not only fulfilled FDR's hopes by effectively promoting lend-lease but cemented his own stature as a leader of the interventionist movement. Since the New Year's Day resignation of CDAAA's founder, William A. White, who had been unable to go along with the group's insistence on tougher pro-Allied measures, Conant along with Lew Douglas had been widely seen as chief organizers of the lobbying effort to push FDR toward belligerence. The publication of a compilation of Conant's pro-intervention speeches, *Speaking as a Private Citizen*, further burnished his national luster. What most lifted the imagination of those who wanted the United States to shed its inhibitions about confronting Hitler was Conant's unhedged willingness to declare that the "soulless creed" of Nazism must be conclusively defeated, regardless of the cost. "Suppose it required us to go to war to do it," prodded Michigan's isolationist Republican, Arthur H. Vandenberg. "Would you go that far?"

"I should," Conant replied without hesitation, "if it were absolutely necessary as the last step."[20]

The congressional appearance, for which Conant had received intensive coaching by Calvert Smith, proved a tonic for the bill, which had already been approved by the House and would receive Senate backing the following month, and it also ensured for him a rapturous reception in England, where the lend-lease debate was closely scrutinized. The act's fate was still uncertain, however, as the *Excalibur* sailed, and Conant carefully followed Smith's instructions not to wave for fear of providing photographers with an undignified pose. "The trip was on and I didn't have to make another speech for six weeks," he jotted down after the delayed departure. "God be praised!"

The next ten days gave Conant a chance to relax, read, savor sea breezes and sea food, and mingle with the eclectic crowd of travelers: an Austrian baroness, Norwegian aviators, American journalists and diplomats, British businessmen; one presumes there were spies and smugglers, too. Enlivening the nonstop war gossip, a false radio report that German troops had marched into Spain provoked a flurry of nervous excitement. Briefly, Conant and other Americans on official missions (to say nothing of the refugees from Hitler) wondered whether they should get off at the Azores to avoid the risk of being interned in Portugal. Subsequent reports relieved those worries, but the strong emotions churning through Conant as he approached the warring continent surfaced in a series of chatty, tender handwritten letters he penned faithfully to his "Dearest" Patty, pledging love from "Your adoring Jim." Reaching Lisbon, Conant found a noisy, chaotic, festive port, a "last oasis" of relative freedom in a "blazing" Europe under the fascist clampdown. With rumors flying that the air link with Britain would soon be cut off, military priorities restricted space on official transports, and Conant was forced to leave his NDRC compatriots behind, at least for a few days, when he hitched a plane ride to London with FDR's new ambassador to St. James's, John G. Winant, a replacement for his resigned isolationist predecessor.

Peeking through their window at a plane with a swastika emblazoned on the fuselage, Conant, Winant, and the ambassador's special assistant, Benjamin Cohen, flew from Lisbon airport at dawn on the morning of March 1, munching hard-boiled eggs "and some pieces of rather crude sandwiches" and cheerily greeting the Dutch pilot who at one point left the cockpit to black out the windows. Along with the wool sweater and heavy blanket he hoped would protect him from the damp English winter, Conant's luggage included some personal and official ambivalence about the nation toward which he was speeding.

For all his sympathy with England's fight against Hitler, Conant's long-term aim of postwar American dominance presumed leadership not only over defeated enemies but also over Washington's principal prospective ally. While he had developed genuine admiration for Britain's pluck under fire, a sympathy that would soon grow even stronger, Conant instinctively was "as opposed to British colonial policy and as suspicious of the long-run objectives of British foreign policy as any Midwestern farmer." The previous fall, he had privately urged that Washington's bargaining should be "hard-boiled and cruel" to assure that it did not make "undue sacrifices to protect the British Empire."[21] If Americans were to be asked to enter the war and to shoulder the responsibilities of a "world power," he wrote Lew Douglas in October 1940, they must be assured that in any Anglo-American military alliance the United States remain the "majority stockholder" and the " 'top dog.' " "I hope you will not be unduly shocked by my nationalism," he added.[22]

Conant's wariness of British motives mirrored that of many American military officers, who reacted coolly at best to the notion of sharing secret military weapons or techniques. Their feelings changed somewhat, as did Conant's, upon learning that in some areas, at least, American scientists might have more to learn from English colleagues than the other way around — especially in the new, still secret area of radar. After the fall of France, a British delegation headed by Sir Henry Tizard had come to America to open interchange on military-related scientific research. Over dinner at the Cosmos Club—the rarefied gentleman's club and watering hole for Washington's intellectual elite, then located near the White House on Madison Plaza, which Conant joined early in the war and utilized for gossip, meals, and business the rest of his life—Conant learned from Bush that the reluctance of the navy and army to cooperate with the visitors had collapsed only after the military, red-faced, realized that they were "five years behind on detection of planes." Suddenly, enthusiasm for a full exchange of information materialized.[23] In-bred military reluctance to open files remained, however, and Conant's thoughts as he neared England were further clouded by uncertainty, as a delegate from a neutral though sympathetic government, as to how he would be received.

Those fears started dissolving moments after his plane touched down in the drizzly, blacked-out British capital. From an effusive airport reception until his return trip via Portugal to New York six weeks later, the British hailed Conant as tangible evidence of "American might pausing on the brink" before coming to the rescue.[24] Feted at banquets, garlanded with awards and honorary degrees, spotlighted in newspapers, Conant conferred with leading scholars, educators, scientists, and politicians—including three talks with Churchill—and was granted an audience with the king. His reception was enhanced, naturally, by the final adoption of the Lend-Lease Act on March 11.[25]

Conant was deeply impressed by the courage, grit, and serenity displayed by residents of the "beleaguered fortress" under Nazi attack. When visiting Oxford, Cambridge, and other universities where wartime heroism and mundane academic routines incongruously coexisted, he felt pride at embodying the solidarity of Harvard with her sister schools. In London during the Blitz, he almost relished the sounds of battle—the nighttime shrieks of sirens, the thuds of bombs, and the *ack-ack* of antiaircraft guns. "Oh, yes, they are flying very low tonight," a waiter replied nonchalantly while serving Conant dinner one night when asked if those were German planes buzzing outside so close as to shake the windows of Claridge's Hotel. "I distinctly heard several whistling bombs land, exploding with a large bang," he recorded on Saturday night, March 8. "My feeling was one of incredulity that here at last I was actually in an air-raid." Writing his wife in the middle of the raid ("Here sounds one now! As though it were going to land in the courtyard!"), Conant reminded himself to practice distinguishing a "bomb-burst bang from a gun's discharge" and likened the spectacle to a cross between a fireworks display and a thunderstorm. "As far as I can see," he wrote as the explosions seemed to come nearer, "this is a game where no one knows the score unless the hit is so near or the hits are so many that all the possible spirit of curiosity has evaporated!" The next morning, Conant learned in the papers that bombs had hit within a half-mile of Claridge's. Walking through London, he saw the ruins of destroyed buildings and homes, the cratered streets, the "lower-income groups" crowded into "narrow, fetid, dirty" air-raid shelters.[26]

The belligerent educator had reached the front.

Chilly, dank conditions forced Conant to spend evenings shivering wrapped in blankets with his wool sweater and a hot-water bottle, but nonetheless he vigorously forged contacts with elite Britishers and American expatriates. When he lunched with Churchill on March 6 in a "bomb-proof basement dining room" beneath 10 Downing Street, he seemed to please the prime minister, who had been led to anticipate an "old man with a long white beard, exuding learning and academic formality," and who liked the tweed-suited, strong-minded person he encountered. Conant broke the ice, as Mr. and Mrs. Churchill and Frederick Lindemann (later Lord Cherwell) sipped sherry, by speaking of his testimony in favor of lend-lease. But Churchill was in a grumpy mood; despite the refrain of "Give us the tools and we shall finish the job" — a line he repeated to Conant — he yearned for full U.S. participation in the war, and his eloquent pessimism so upset Conant that after the meal he shot off worried missives to Cambridge to inquire whether the interventionists and Roosevelt were doing their utmost to nail down a final Senate victory. Ten days later, after the Lend-Lease Act passed, Conant found Churchill in a more relaxed mood, and the two established a philosophical bond in their distaste for inveterate pacifists who claimed that "war never settles anything."[27]

To Conant's surprise, an audience at Buckingham Palace turned out to be more than perfunctory, as King George discoursed on the most up-to-date radar techniques. After a fifteen-minute royal discussion, which Conant deemed the maximum permissible, he amused himself by backing out of the crowded room as a sign of respect. He obtained a still more revealing introduction to the still secret technology when he inspected an active center where operators were tracking a German attack, a sight that inspired him to come up with a scheme to send American technicians to aid the British and thus gain valuable experience themselves. But in transmitting to Washington his ideas for aiding Britain, Conant learned a lesson in the treacheries of bureaucratic warfare. Conant had recalled a recent American naval innovation that might be helpful to the British cause, but he blundered by sending a cable to NDRC headquarters via a navy communications channel; when an admiral in Washington dawdled before relaying the cables, evidently loath to collaborate in a plot to convey secret information to London, Bush exploded, suspicious that interchange between Americans might be more difficult than liaison with the British. It was not the last time that questions would be raised during the war about sharing American military data.

Conant's month-and-a-half survey of the British scientific program left him convinced that the NDRC office he had established in London under Hovde's supervision would have much to do, and his taste of research under wartime conditions alerted him to the importance of quickly dispatching Americans to test their military innovations and tactics under genuine battle conditions. On returning to Washington, he met with Roosevelt on April 25 and successfully promoted his scheme of creating a U.S. "Electronic Training Group" to cooperate with the British in their operation of "radio magic" to detect incoming planes—and, astonished to discover the president ignorant of radar, found himself tutoring FDR in the war's most crucial technological breakthrough to date.[28]

Neither in that conversation nor in his detailed twenty-nine-page report to Bush did Conant mention the portentous item that had unofficially popped up several times during his visit.[29] At a laboratory in Cambridge, Dr. Hans von Halban, an Austrian-born, French-trained physicist who had fled to England, had mentioned experiments with "heavy water," indicating the probability that a nuclear chain reaction for power production or a bomb could be achieved. Conant shut him up: "Look, you're not supposed to talk to me about this thing. That's not part of my work at all."[30] And over lunch at a London club, Conant heard the subject of atomic energy raised again, this time by Professor Lindemann, the "eccentric Christ Church physicist who had become Churchill's most intimate adviser."[31] To this, Conant reiterated his customary dim view of nuclear power as a war measure, and Lindemann agreed. But then, related Conant in a secret historical note written a year later, the prime minister's adviser noted that a "bare possibility" existed of atomic energy's "use as an explosive," and outlined "the theory of critical mass and the way the material might be used." Conant listened intently but, "[f]eeling that this was entirely an unofficial and private communication and represented a highly speculative scheme," did not press the subject—though he was startled a few days later when Ben Cohen also mentioned Lindemann's mysterious research toward developing a powerful new explosive.[32]

Displaying characteristic caution and discretion—and aware that Bush could be "very vindictive when people went out of channels"[33]—Conant kept mum about this piece of gossip until the news reached him properly. This occurred in May, when Bush sought his advice in considering a report prepared by a committee of the National Academy of Sciences on the progress to date in the American uranium research effort. He had asked for the report after hearing complaints from leading nuclear physicists, especially Ernest Lawrence, that it was bogged down, despite significant theoretical advances, because of excessive secrecy, the Briggs committee's passivity, and inadequate commitment.[34] (Dissatisfied by Bush's initial response, Lawrence had reportedly pressed Conant, after his return from London, to "light a fire under the Briggs committee," and then continued the offensive with Loomis and Karl Compton—prompting a rebuke from Bush for attempting an end run around him.)[35] Bush had two important questions to consider: was atomic energy of military value, and if so, how far had the Germans progressed? The academy committee, headed by Arthur H. Compton, called for a strongly intensified American effort over the next six months to determine the "possible military aspects of atomic fission."[36] But it listed prospects for a bomb only after such projects as dropping radioactive products on enemy territory and atomic-powered submarines.[37] While presenting optimistic timetables, the report failed to impress Conant, who was, in the words of an official history, "perhaps the most influential NDRC member."[38]

Still unconvinced, Conant disdained the arguments of physicists who "talked in excited tones about the discovery of a new world in which power from a uranium reactor would revolutionize our industrial society." Such "fancies" left him cold.[39] Only clear evidence of atomic energy's potential application to the current battlefield situation could raise his enthusiasm, especially with the predicament of England fresh in his mind. "Was there really any chance of a power development materializing during the next five years or so? Wasn't this a development for the *next* war not the present one?" On Conant's recommendation, the NDRC told the committee to add a few engineers—"some practical men"—and try again.[40]

Conant now began to assume direct and vastly expanded responsibilities for the American atomic effort. In June, Bush asked Roosevelt to create an enlarged and more powerful executive agency to oversee the use of science for military purposes, the Office of Scientific Research and Development, and Bush became head of the new agency with Conant in charge of the NDRC, which now became an OSRD subsidiary along with a newly formed Committee on Medical Research.[41] Conant retained the NDRC title for the remainder of the war, administering a vast, highly decentralized operation that produced numerous advances in weapons technology.[42] The new structure also put Conant in the number two slot at OSRD, but the job came to mean much more than keeping Bush informed of NDRC developments: from the late summer of 1941 on, he served as Bush's deputy for the atomic bomb program, responsible for "reorganizing and increasing the tempo of the work" and assuming for a time "the full burden of its administration." For the rest of the war, Conant later estimated, he spent three-quarters of his government work, and more than half of his entire time, on matters pertaining to the atomic bomb.[43] With the reorganization, the atomic effort, previously in the hands of Briggs's independent advisory panel, now became the OSRD's S-1 Section, and Conant became chairman of the S-1 section's Executive Committee.[44]

In that capacity, Conant plied his boss with information and recommendations while the OSRD director played politician, advocating the cause of military science in the Washington corridors, meeting rooms, and gentleman's clubs where priorities and budgets were determined. Bush, lacking the time and expertise to keep up with highly specialized and rapidly moving developments in nuclear fission, relied on Conant for his frank, coldly calculated appraisals of people, projects, and prospects, and Conant's detailed memos on technical matters, administration, and policy determined the contents of most of Bush's atomic reports to the president until late in the war. On all policy-related atomic questions, Bush and Conant conferred frequently and usually came to compatible conclusions.[45]

Conant's first priority was to clarify the enormous technical obstacles facing an all-out program. One question was whether a self-sustaining fission reaction of any kind could be conclusively demonstrated. Another was finding a sufficient amount of uranium-235 (U-235), a rare isotope of natural uranium (U-238). If enough "enriched" uranium, containing high proportions of the isotope, could be combined, the theory went, the emission of one neutron by a uranium atom would trigger a chain reaction when the pile "went critical." A slow reaction would produce power in the form of heat; with especially highly enriched uranium—or plutonium, a newly discovered element which physicists predicted would behave similarly—a *fast* chain reaction could be triggered, resulting in an enormous explosion.[46] However, the difficulties in producing sufficient amounts of the necessary material were staggering. Even Lindemann had told Conant that a successful isotope separation program would constitute "a heroic undertaking"; the scientific challenge involved resembled a doctor laboring to produce an eyedropper's full of a rare antidote and then trying to produce enough of it to pave the streets.[47]

A succession of events in the summer of 1941 dispelled Conant's pessimism, however. In July, he obtained a copy of a preliminary draft report produced by the MAUD Committee of British scientists working in uranium research. (The code-name MAUD derived from a cryptic reference in a telegram carrying a message from Niels Bohr in Denmark; it turned out to be the name of a governess in Kent to whom the physicist desired to transmit greetings.) Unlike the American evaluations, which while optimistic had wavered between stressing the value of using atomic energy for power and for a bomb, the British report came down squarely in favor of a crash program to develop a weapon. Better, it cited new, lower measurements of the needed "critical mass"—the amount of U-235—required for an explosive. Given the necessary support, the report stated, it should be possible by the end of 1943 to produce enough material for an explosive equal to 1,800 tons of TNT. Despite the large sums that they acknowledged would be needed, the authors concluded that "the destructive effect, both material and moral, is so great that every effort should be made to produce bombs of this kind." The focus on a goal of obvious military import added greatly to its appeal in Conant's mind, as did the authors' sober, hard-headed approach, evident in their opening paragraphs:

We should like to emphasise at the beginning of this report that we entered the project with more scepticism than belief, although we felt it was a matter which had to be investigated. As we proceeded we became more and more convinced that release of atomic energy on a large scale is possible and that conditions can be chosen which would make it a very powerful weapon of war. We have now reached the conclusion that it will be possible to make an effective uranium bomb which, containing some 25 lb of active material, would be equivalent to 1,800 tons of T.N.T. and would also release large quantities of radioactive substances, which would make places near to where the bomb exploded dangerous to human life for a long period.[48]

In fact, the MAUD Committee's projections, based in part on a secret analysis, previously unknown to the Americans, that had been prepared in England a year earlier by the German refugee scientists Otto Frisch and Rudolf Peierls, turned out to be in error, underestimating the difficulties involved in isotope separation. But that was in the future, and in July 1941 the report radically undermined Conant's resistance to the concept. "With the news from Great Britain unofficially at hand," Conant later wrote in a secret history of the Manhattan Project's origins, "the two Academy reports and the favorable action of NDRC, it became clear to the director of OSRD [Bush] and the Chairman of NDRC [Conant] that a major push along the lines outlined was in order."[49]

But the clinching factor, he recalled, came later that summer in consultation with his old friend and colleague at Harvard, George Kistiakowsky. Since mid-1940 Kistiakowsky had turned from working on the medical potential of radioactive isotopes to leading, at Conant's request, the NDRC division on explosives, and he had frequently spoken with Conant, in formal conferences and informal dinners, about NDRC matters, and explosives in particular. Now Conant conveyed to his trusted friend the idea that he had first heard from Lindemann and that Lawrence, Compton, and other physicists were pushing—that suddenly bringing together two masses of fissionable material would produce an explosion. In fact, after setting up their New Committee on Nuclear Physics, Kistiakowsky and several colleagues at Harvard had quietly investigated the problem of separating uranium isotopes, and had asked the Briggs panel for a thousand dollars to study thermal diffusion methods. But this was, Conant later claimed, the first time his friend had heard earnest talk of a bomb. Doubtful at first, "Kisty" came back convinced a few weeks later: "It can be made to work," he told Conant. "I am one hundred percent sold." At the sound of that unequivocal judgment, Conant's doubts "evaporated" and gave way to the "rather rugged optimism" beginning to take hold among Allied scientists. "If he was sold on Arthur Compton's program, who was I to have reservations?"[50]

Near the end of September, the process leading to an unqualified American commitment to build the bomb received impetus from an unusual cha-

rade in which Conant played the leading role. Visiting the University of
Chicago's fiftieth anniversary celebration, Conant found himself exposed to
an "involuntary conference" with two Nobel laureate physicists dissatisfied at
the slow pace of the U.S. uranium program: Berkeley's Lawrence and Chicago's
Arthur Compton. All present were aware of the recent encouraging experiments in England, but as they sipped coffee around the Compton fireplace,
Conant chose not to let the physicists in on either his still unofficial knowledge of the MAUD Report or his conversion to support for an intense
investigation of the chances for a bomb. Instead he allowed the two men,
both members of the National Academy investigating committee, to believe
he still planned to shelve atomic research for the rest of the war. Knowing
Conant controlled the fate of the program, they earnestly presented their case
for an all-out American effort. Finally, Conant appeared to come around.
Then he asked Lawrence point-blank if he believed in the idea of an atomic
bomb enough to devote the next several years of his life to a project to build
one. Taken aback, Lawrence sat silent for a moment, his mouth half-open. "If
you tell me this is my job, I'll do it," he replied.[51]

Satisfied, Conant reported the conversation to Bush, who was preparing
a recommendation for Roosevelt.[52] On October 9, the OSRD Director met in
the Oval Office with Roosevelt and Vice President Wallace and received
FDR's permission to speed work on all fronts short of actual construction.[53]
Having based his advice largely on information relayed by Conant, Bush
mentioned his worry at carrying such responsibilities alone as the program
expanded in size and importance. Roosevelt replied by naming a "top policy
group" to pass on major decisions and to whom full knowledge concerning the
effort would be restricted. Its members were Roosevelt himself, Wallace,
Secretary of War Henry L. Stimson, Army Chief of Staff George C. Marshall,
Bush, and Conant.[54] Unlike the leisurely Briggs panel, this quest for an
atomic bomb would be the real thing.

To Conant's intense frustration, the U.S. government's progress toward commitment to the anti-Hitler coalition had not advanced nearly so dramatically
as its secret atomic-energy endeavors. More impatient than ever to get public
opinion to support the war after witnessing so many inspiring scenes in
England, within a few weeks of his return to America Conant issued his most
militant pronouncements yet. America should enter the war now, he argued,
all but accusing his country of unconscionably saluting freedom while letting
another nation do the fighting. "In my opinion," he stated in a nationwide
radio speech on May 4, 1941, "strategy demands we fight tomorrow, honor
and self-interest that we fight before the British Isles are lost."[55] He issued a
similarly frank declaration later that month in Williamsburg to a meeting of
the Harvard Board of Overseers, whose blasé attitude infuriated him, especially after hearing Churchill's plaintive farewell at 10 Downing Street: "Here
we are, standing alone. What is going to happen?"

Conant recounted his frustrations with the alumni during a lunch with Roosevelt at the White House, and soon followed with a letter to FDR recounting a positive reaction by a different Harvard audience to a "highly belligerent" speech.[56] Like the rest of the interventionist leaders, however, Conant was fast concluding that only events, not speeches or petitions, could bring the country to make the terrible decision to go to war. The Roosevelt administration was equally impatient—in late June, Conant learned that a senior State Department official had secretly urged the CDAAA to come out for war now and to mobilize resources for a letter-writing campaign to the White House demanding belligerency against Germany; with British morale holding but liable to "crack" soon if the United States did not enter the battle the "most useful thing any American can do at present is to devote his time, thought and energy into getting us into the war."[57]

On June 22, 1941, Germany launched Operation Barbarossa, its massive surprise invasion of Russia, and Conant's reaction to the idea of supporting the Kremlin's defensive struggle paralleled that of FDR and Churchill, the two leaders with whom he was now on cordial personal terms. Like Churchill, who quipped that if Hitler invaded Hell the Devil would merit a favorable comment in the House of Commons, Conant counseled that the United States should welcome Moscow into the anti-Hitler alliance. Even if Communism and Nazism were "equally detestable," the crucial distinction lay in the fact that National Socialism constituted a "combination of a soul-destroying philosophy and a man-destroying army," whereas it was "inconceivable" that Russian forces could menace the Western Hemisphere. Since "the major concern of the United States must be to secure the military overthrow of the Nazi power," Washington should be encouraged to lend aid to Russia as well as England.[58]

Some Americans, however, took comfort from the sight of the two totalitarian giants fighting each other, with Senator Harry Truman voicing his hope that the Russians and Germans would kill each other off while the United States egged on whoever was lagging in the carnage. "The thing that worries me most," Conant wrote privately in early July, "is that if we do not start shooting by September, the British-American relations will deteriorate rapidly, and leave a long trail of bad feeling for the future. This is the one thing, however, that cannot be said publicly."[59] In August, as isolationist sentiment bubbled up again, the administration was able to win the renewal of Selective Service by only a one-vote margin, 203–202, in the House of Representatives. Soon afterward, Conant's call for an outright congressional declaration of war evoked little response.

The sagging interventionist fortunes alarmed Conant even more than might be expected because, significantly, his secret conversion to belief in the feasibility of atomic weapons had already begun to affect his outlook on the international situation. Already convinced that at the end of the war the United States should impose a "Pax Americana" and divide the European continent into "a series of small agricultural states,"[60] Conant now added a covert nuclear calculation—the chance that Germany might develop atomic weapons meant that the war had to be not only won but won quickly and decisively.[61]

Thus did Conant in the fall of 1941 become the first prominent American openly to call for the "unconditional surrender" of Germany as a basic U.S. war aim.[62] Roosevelt, too, had been aware from the start that the advent of atomic weapons would have consequences beyond the immediate conflict—at an October 9 meeting with FDR and Wallace, Bush told Conant, they had "discussed at some length after-war control"[63]—but the United States did not declare unconditional surrender to be an official strategic objective until FDR blurted out the phrase at a press conference at the Casablanca summit meeting in January 1943. Conant, however, used this formulation privately as early as October 22, 1941, in a letter to Grenville Clark, to whom, of course, he could not mention his classified atomic concerns. Rejecting the concept that the allies could "bring Hitler to reasonable terms," Conant instead endorsed the "Churchill-Roosevelt" position

> that peace can only come *when Hitler and his crowd are eliminated* [Conant's emphasis] from all question of making terms. But, let me add once more that unconditional surrender of Germany which I believe to be the first of our peace aims does not mean that the victors will impose a Carthaginian peace. It does mean, however, that Germany must be willing to surrender at discretion. Any other outcome of the war will only be an armistice in my opinion, and may easily lead to the final victory of Nazism. Even if we start shooting soon, the time will come, I am afraid, when weariness will overtake the people of both this country and Great Britain, and Hitler will launch a real peace offensive and ask us for "reasonable terms." When that point comes, we will once again be in the same jeopardy we were in during September, 1940, when the battle of Great Britain was in the balance.[64]

By November, events had driven public opinion closer to the recognition that American entry into the war was bound to occur, and the question now seemed to be how the entry would be precipitated. Inside the atomic program, too, a conviction that a uranium fission bomb was in fact possible was hardening among the most important American and British physicists looking at the subject, and among the leaders of the OSRD. In early November, a third secret National Academy report on uranium "not only radiated a more martial spirit than the first two," in Conant's words, "but was much more specific on the matter of a bomb." Relegating power generation to secondary status, the report firmly stated that "within a few years" atomic bombs using U-235 might be constructed that would "determine military superiority," and it recommended "urgent development of this program."[65]

On the first Saturday in December, a wintry but clear Washington morning, Conant convened a meeting of the S-1 Executive Committee around an oak table at the Carnegie Institution building. Relieving their suspense, Conant told the men who joined him—Briggs, Lawrence, and Arthur Compton— that FDR had approved an "all-out" research and planning effort to determine the feasibility of atomic explosives. Most importantly, Conant, now a firm advocate, made it plain that from that day forward, all efforts were to be directed toward producing a bomb, *not* power production, at the earliest possible time. That suited Compton fine, for he had chaired the National Academy investigation that had produced the November report.

After the meeting broke up, Conant and Compton strolled over to the Cosmos Club at Lafayette Square to meet Bush for lunch. There, for the first time, Compton mentioned the theoretical possibility of extracting plutonium from a chain reaction as a usable alternative to the rare uranium isotope. The contours of the project were still blurry, but coming into focus.[66]

The next afternoon, December 7, Conant and his wife were at 17 Quincy Street in Cambridge preparing to greet students at the weekly four o'clock tea when they heard the first radio bulletins of Japan's attack on Pearl Harbor. In an atmosphere that Mrs. Conant later described as "electric," students and faculty spent the next few hours listening to updates and speculating excitedly, with several scholars who were German refugees fearful that they might be interned as enemy aliens. One overriding fact shone through the confusing and fragmentary reports: at long last, America was at war. As armed guards began appearing around labs where NDRC projects were under way, Conant appeared at a mass rally attended by 6,000 cheering students the next evening to vow Harvard's full cooperation with the military and the government until a "speedy and complete victory" was achieved. Afterward, Conant wired FDR to pledge full support on their behalf, adding his personal hope that a declaration of war on Germany would shortly follow the one issued against Japan.[67]

With the great debate over intervention suddenly rendered moot by Japan's surprise attack, Conant now publicly expressed his ardent belief in a policy of "unconditional surrender," clearly alluding to his still secret nightmare that Germany might be ahead in the secret atomic rivalry.

"This war is in many ways a race of scientific developments and devices," he told the New England Society of New York on December 22, how much so "only those close to the secrets of the Army and Navy can really know."[68] Poison gas and tanks, if introduced earlier, might have changed the result of World War I, he noted, and it was common knowledge that without "the new radiolocator" Britain might have been left exposed to a Nazi invasion in the fall of 1940. But Conant hinted at his own worry by noting that for the future, "enormous changes in airplanes and aerial warfare are certainly in the cards." Nothing less than total victory was acceptable, he told the Plaza Hotel audience, because in "a state ruled by a dictator, covered by a Gestapo, new weapons can be devised, developed and manufactured with utmost secrecy.

During a period armistice it might well happen that such radical developments could occur as to make a complete victory possible in a few months once the fighting was resumed." "Grim necessity requires," Conant concluded, "that unconditional surrender of the Axis Powers be the first war aim of the United States."

The possibility that an atomic bomb could be built by Germany or any industrialized country reinforced Conant's already strong conviction that the United States could never again remain aloof from a fast-contracting globe. Two weeks after Pearl Harbor, he declared that after the Nazis were defeated and the war was won, isolationism would be "as extinct as the volcanoes on the moon" and "the United States must be ready to assume political and economic leadership of the world."[69]

CHAPTER 9

"This Scientific Delirium Tremens"

The Horse Race to the Bomb
1942–1943

The Germans can never win this war, and we shall win it unless they are ahead of us in the development of the atomic bomb.
—JBC to Harvey Bundy, Christmas 1941

I am sure you will agree with me that the record, which some day will be gone over with a fine tooth comb, is of importance, not because of its effect on any one of us, but because it will stand as to what American scientists can do under pressure ... It isn't faith we need now, Arthur. It's works.
—JBC to Arthur Compton, 1942[1]

How many times in all the scientific conferences of the last two years has it been said "I hope the thing won't work, but we must be sure it won't."
—JBC, "A History of the Development of an Atomic Bomb," Spring 1943

Around Christmas Day, 1941, Conant lay in bed at home with a heavy cold, but his guest had an even worse ailment: pessimism. The apprehensions of Harvey H. Bundy, War Secretary Stimson's chief liaison to the OSRD leadership, mirrored the nation's: As the first shock of Pearl Harbor had worn off and the United States confronted the scary reality of battle, the navy reeled from the crippling of its Pacific outpost as Japan stormed new targets, and the military outlook, at least for the short term, looked anything but bright. The news was so bad, Bundy told Conant, that he didn't see "how the devil we were going to win the war."

"Don't worry," Conant replied, trying to cheer up his holiday visitor. "We'll win the war unless the Germans get S-1 first." But his words sent a shudder through Bundy. Instead of being consoled, he left 17 Quincy Street more glum than ever.[2]

The conversation reflected the vision that would underlay Conant's passionate and deepening commitment to the rapid completion of the bomb project: a regnant Washington in a postwar world. The nightmarish long shot danger and defensive fear he expressed to Bundy—a German victory in the secret atomic race—translated into an offensive goal: building a U.S. weapon first.

The shock of war imparted new urgency to the "all-out attack" on the uranium program. In a major organizational rehaul, Briggs's old committee was phased out, replaced by a strengthened S-1 Executive Committee, still chaired by Conant but adding program chiefs Harold Urey, Ernest Lawrence, and Arthur Compton. The NDRC was officially cut out of the picture, as the top policy committee, restricting atomic data to the smallest possible group, transferred all S-1 research to OSRD's aegis. "Thus ended the connection of the NDRC with the uranium project," Conant recalled in 1943, "but not, alas, the connection of the Chairman of NDRC with this scientific delirium tremens."[3]

As the enterprise picked up pace, Conant's responsibilities mounted accordingly. Taking up residence in Georgetown at the Dumbarton Oaks complex—a Harvard-owned maze of ivy-covered, statuesque mansions, museums, and libraries known for its Byzantine, Medieval and pre-Columbian art collections, but borrowed during World War II for secret meetings to plan both the development of the atomic bomb and the United Nations—Conant commenced working in Washington five days a week, making frequent inspection trips to laboratories and universities around the country. In the months after Pearl Harbor, Conant also devoted much time and energy to lobbying Washington to establish a comprehensive program to use American colleges in the war effort and to create an equitable deferment system to ensure "a continuous and adequate supply of men and women trained in technical and professional skills and in leadership" without turning campuses into "refuges for draft dodgers." Fearing especially the drying up of scientific and technical talent in a war lasting several years, Conant's idea was for the federal government to select and subsidize a limited number of qualified high school graduates to receive training (to become officers and specialists in important war-related professions) at American colleges, which feared ruin due to falling enrollment. To promote his plan, Conant quietly mobilized a "conspiracy" of leading university presidents, gave speeches and published an article in the *Atlantic,* and conveyed his views to influential journalists like Walter Lippmann, War Department officials Harvey Bundy and John McCloy, with whom he worked on NDRC matters, and even Roosevelt himself. But after the president, on the advice of the army, the navy, and War Secretary Stimson, rejected his plan as impractical, Conant and other educators had to fight a rearguard battle to persuade the military to institute a rational deferment and training system.[4]

Engagement in these and other war-related activities forced Conant to discard most of his remaining Harvard obligations (to set an example for wartime austerity, he requested a forty percent cut in his annual salary of $25,000, though the Corporation only agreed to a twenty-five percent reduction) and to see less of his family, for he returned to Cambridge at longer intervals for shorter visits.[5] Inevitably, the national mobilization that followed Pearl Harbor also swept up his two teenage sons: James, after finishing at Exeter, enrolled in a submarine training course while attending the University of Michigan, and Ted, though still too young for the draft when the United States entered the war, vainly cajoled his father to allow him to help with radar work as one of the technicians sent to Britain under the scheme Conant had cooked up after visiting London. Though Conant vetoed the idea as too dangerous for a boy who was barely fifteen, Ted's eventual participation in the war effort seemed a foregone conclusion—and his obsession with radio and electronics, even if it complicated relations with parents and teachers, suited the needs of a fast-modernizing military.[6]

On top of the natural fears of a father whose sons were endangered, the imperatives of working on a top-secret project and concealing the potentialities of atomic energy clouded Conant's relations with his family and friends, especially those who did not have government security clearances. His family sensed that Conant's responsibilities went way beyond the norm when the army wired a special telephone line up the dirt road to the isolated summer cottage in Randolph to assure instant communications from Washington, and on occasion sent a special military plane to retrieve him from New Hampshire. But he never let on to what he was doing, even when he asked his teenage son Ted to buy a secondhand oscilloscope and help build a makeshift cloud chamber—the same sort of equipment used to monitor neutron emissions from radioactive isotopes of uranium—to give him a hands-on feel for nuclear physics. Patty Conant did not bother to contest her husband's lack of candor, although she had not been able to avoid a certain skepticism after finding a Santa Fe matchbox in one of his suit pockets after he had supposedly traveled no farther west than Chicago. But by then, Conant had already ascended into a highly classified realm which he never fully left, in which dishonesty in the name of national security was an occupational hazard and social habit. "The amount of bare-faced lying that was done in Washington in those days is beyond estimate," he later acknowledged. "Military secrets of all sorts were closely guarded. One just didn't ask an old friend whom one met at the Cosmos Club what he was doing. A statement that a person was working for the government on a confidential matter was a sufficient sign to change the conversation."[7]

A stickler for security, yet used to enthusiastic experimenters and campus politicos, Conant worried as much about the scientific instinct to blab about exciting research as he did about foreign espionage. In February 1942, he recruited a young security officer from army intelligence ("G-2"), John Lansdale, to infiltrate Berkeley undercover and snoop on the physicists there. Lansdale, a recent Harvard Law School graduate who was later to become Groves's chief security aide, had been oblivious to the secret atomic research until he was summoned to Conant's NDRC office. There, in what Lansdale recalls was a matter-of-fact, down-to-earth manner, Conant explained that the United States and Germany were desperately racing to build an atomic weapon, that "Whoever gets this first will win the war," and that it was necessary to learn whether the Berkeley physicists were talking too much, contributing to the danger that the Nazis might learn about the U.S. project and redouble their own efforts. Equipped with some background reading Conant had given him on atomic physics, Lansdale changed into civilian clothes, boarded a train to California, and, impersonating a law student, quickly discovered that atomic research on campus was common knowledge in the university cafeteria. During lunch in the Faculty Club, a law school dean pointed out Ernest Lawrence as the man who was trying to split the atom for use as an explosive. In a few weeks Lansdale filled a pocket diary with snippets of atomic gossip, and he returned to Washington and read them out loud to Conant. Normally unflappable, the administrator flinched in horror at each example of lax security, issuing what for him passed as expletives: "Oh! . . . Oh! . . . Oh my goodness!" On Conant's orders, Lansdale forthwith went back to Berkeley, summoned the atomic physicists there to a secret meeting, and, now in uniform, sternly warned them that the security breaches he had witnessed during his incognito visit were endangering the project's success.[8]

Conant had not expressed concern about the danger of espionage from any country other than Germany, Lansdale later recalled, but by then army counterintelligence specialists "knew the enemy was Russia," at least so far as spying against the United States was concerned.[9] And indeed, it appears—if one can assume the authenticity of secret Soviet intelligence files disclosed decades later—that Moscow was already astonishingly well-informed about both the political and technical aspects of the Anglo-American atomic collaboration. In October 1941, the People's Commissariat for Internal Affairs (NKVD) reportedly cabled from London that British officials had determined that it would be feasible to construct a uranium bomb by the end of the war but that U.S. aid was essential, and that Roosevelt had "endorsed an extensive exchange of scientific and technical information with Britain and suggested that any efforts in this important project be coordinated and pooled." And in March 1942, just as Lansdale was reporting security breaches to Conant, a secret top-level conference was called at the Defense Ministry in Moscow after the NKVD reported that German physicists, too, were developing nuclear weapons.

Meeting as Nazi forces occupied vast stretches of western Soviet Union and threatened Leningrad and Moscow itself, the Russian scientists agreed that a uranium bomb appeared feasible. But, they cautioned, the war's destruction and dislocation made any large-scale project even more daunting than would otherwise be the case, and it might take at least ten to fifteen years to finish a weapon. Stalin did not want to wait that long, declared that the USSR must seek an atomic bomb "despite the wartime hardships," and put the project under the head of the NKVD, Lavrenti Pavlovich Beria, who had supervised murderous purges and tolerated no obstacles when carrying his leader's baton. But Stalin also recognized that Russia's wartime privations meant that the bomb project should look for "short-cuts"—and here Beria's intelligence service came to the fore. The next day, Stalin ordered the NKVD in its espionage work in the United States to concentrate on four objectives: warning of any signs that Roosevelt and Churchill intended a separate peace with Hitler; War Department data on Hitler's military operations against Russia; estimates of U.S. and British war aims and, if possible, their planned date for opening a second front in Europe; and information on the development of secret weapons—specifically, on the atomic bomb.[10]

By 1942, Conant's incentive for clamping down on any potential security lapse, whether by garrulous relatives or scientists lacking a "need to know," had steeply risen due to his belief that only a Nazi A-bomb could alter the war's outcome. Roosevelt, influenced by reports from Bush and Conant, shared that calculation. "I think the whole thing should be *pushed* not only in regard to development, but also with due regard to time," FDR wrote Bush in March, authorizing the OSRD to hand over development work to the army "on condition that you yourself are certain that the War Department has made all adequate provision for absolute secrecy."[11] But the atomic project could not go to the War Department for construction until the OSRD determined which method should be used in the immense plants that would fabricate the few kilograms of highly radioactive mass making up the core of each new weapon. Conant still lacked a firm conception of the fastest route to success. Four contestants in the fissionable material "horse race"—the metaphor that quickly gained vogue—appeared worthy of serious consideration. Three (gaseous diffusion, electromagnetic separation, centrifuge) aimed to isolate quantities of U-235, and one to produce a new element, plutonium, known as element 94 after its predicted atomic number, that would be even more fissionable than the uranium isotope.

It was, effectively, up to Conant to place the government's bet. Yet, no obvious favorite had emerged by the time he met with S-1 Section program chiefs on May 23, 1942. Intensive conferences yielded informal predictions— optimistic, it turned out—that six bombs might be ready by July 1944, and possibly as early as January 1, 1944. But since there was no consensus on the best method to meet that timetable, Conant faced two choices, neither especially palatable. He could call for an intensive "Napoleonic" program on all fronts, costing hundreds of millions of dollars. Or he could place the project's hopes on one method, which might or might not prove preferable to the others, and might result in no bomb at all if he chose wrong.[12]

One factor complicating his decision, he admitted to Bush, was his awareness that unless he gave "a green light on everybody's hopes and ambitions," some "disheartened and discontented people" would "take the case to the court of public opinion, or at least the 'top physicists' of the country." Such a public stink, of course, would be disastrous. But the main argument in favor of a crash, "all out" program remained fear of German competition. Since it now appeared to him that several of the alternate methods for devising a bomb were likely to work, "the probabilities of the Germans eventually getting such a weapon become very high." As evidence to back this proposition Conant noted British intelligence information that the Germans had seized a ton of heavy water, needed for experiments leading to a self-sustaining chain reaction; reports as early as 1940 that German scientists were working on the problem; and, especially, "recent intercepted instructions to their agents in this country" showing interest in atomic weapons. Conant thus reasoned:

> If they are hard at work, they cannot be far behind since they started in 1939 with the same initial facts as the British and ourselves. There are still plenty of competent scientists left in Germany. They may be ahead of us by as much as a year, but hardly more.
> If the possession of the new weapon in sufficient quantities would be a determining factor in the war, then the question of who has it first is critical. Three months' delay might be fatal. For example, the employment of a dozen bombs on England might be sufficient to enable an invasion to take place.

If, instead, the military judged that possession of "a dozen or two atomic bombs" would be "not in reality determining but only supplemental," the need for haste and for "betting heavily" would be much less.[13]

But Conant didn't expect to get off the hook that easily and, not out of enthusiasm, but despair at the lack of consensus, he recommended continued work on all four processes. In his report to FDR, Bush "lifted verbatim" Conant's views, having first carefully obtained the approval of Wallace, Stimson, and Marshall. On June 17, Roosevelt approved ("VB–OK–FDR") this multiple approach, asking only one key question: "Do you have the money?" (Bush assured him that he did.)[14] The project then entered one of its most frustrating periods, as a somewhat sluggish transfer of authority took place between the civilian OSRD and the army's Manhattan Engineering District. Conant yearned during the summer of 1942 for signs of a clear winning method so the army could begin the job of constructing the factories that would produce the core material.[15] Meantime, in August and September he briefly detoured from weapons research to serve along with Bernard Baruch and Karl Compton on a special ad hoc panel appointed by FDR to investigate bottlenecks in rubber production. Confusion, bureaucratic turf battles, and scandal had plagued the government's program, threatening critical shortages of the militarily vital raw material (or usable substitutes) which before Pearl Harbor had largely been imported from Asian lands now under Japanese control. During the intensive six-week inquiry, headquartered once again at Dumbarton Oaks, Conant concentrated on issues relating to synthetic fuels and, Baruch records, served as an authority on all technical matters. The press quickly tagged the threesome as the "park bench committee," after the publicity-conscious Baruch staged a meeting in Lafayette Park, opposite the White House. In its final report, quickly adopted by FDR, the panel recommended the creation of a rubber "czar" to centralize production and distribution for maximum military efficiency. At a jovial Oval Office ceremony to hand over the final report, Roosevelt facetiously asked Conant whether he would be interested in the job, venturing that he already had experience in running a "pretty big show up in Cambridge."[16]

But Conant had another big show to oversee, and after the banter he left later that day to catch a train to California to inspect Lawrence's electromagnetic separation operation at Berkeley and other OSRD laboratories. Despite the shift to army control, he remained—due to S-1's rigorously enforced policy of "compartmentalizing" information—the only scientist in a position to assess the atomic data flowing from various research centers and thus the project's overall progress. Despite desperate pleas from his S-1 Executive Committee, and army incredulity over the resources that would be needed for across-the-board development, Conant stuck to his view that no production method should be abandoned unless it clearly became inferior to others.[17]

As the date for making a final decision on construction neared, and the problems in coordination between OSRD and the army became more and more apparent, a new joint group was formed to oversee development of the entire project. On September 23, 1942, the Military Policy Committee—with Bush as chairman and a representative each from the army and navy (Conant was named Bush's alternate and attended all meetings)—began to act as "a sort of board of directors" for the Manhattan District's new commander: the gruff, husky, ambitious, bumptious Gen. Leslie R. Groves.

At the outset, the selection of Groves had not aroused great delight. Bush's candidate had been Brig. Gen. Wilhelm D. Styer, the army's contact with S-1, and his first encounter with Groves on September 17 did not produce a good impression—"very seriously" bothered, he wrote Conant that "Colonel Grove" [sic] seemed "abrupt and lacking in tact." Although in a subsequent note Bush softened his view, the jury remained out. Groves, in turn, had been furious when he learned of his new assignment, having hoped for a post closer to the battlefield that would boost his career, and was hardly mollified by a quick promotion to general. Moreover, he did not think much of scientists. But he had a brass-knuckles reputation for getting things done fast, crashing through anything in his path, and so the army high command gave him the job. In a well-staged display of his energetic attitude, Groves excused himself from the first MPC meeting to catch a train to Tennessee to pin down the location for the first fission plant.[18]

Traveling to different sites to consult with top scientists working on various methods, Conant and his S-1 Executive Committee in the fall of 1942 took stock of the situation. In late October, Conant told Bush that the centrifuge method had proved the "weakest horse" and could be dropped, although strangling the project proved long and bitter, since its supporters repeatedly attempted to raise it from the crypt.[19] And Conant remained particularly dubious of Compton's plutonium project at the Metallurgical Laboratory at the University of Chicago. He still suspected the backers of this plan to produce plutonium—via a slow self-sustaining chain reaction in a uranium pile, or "boiler"—of being as interested in ascertaining the potential for nuclear power as they were in producing a bomb. He was also "boggled" by the complexities of planning a program around an element that had never been produced in visible quantities.[20]

In November, Compton's casual revelation that the prototype pile was being built under the stands of Stagg Field, the university's football stadium, allegedly caused Conant's face to turn white, but he thought it too late to stop the experiment for safety reasons.[21] Then Conant received conflicting estimates of the amount of impurities that could be tolerated in element 94 (plutonium) without spoiling its usability as a weapon; this disturbing and "extremely embarrassing" report prompted him to order a review of the entire Chicago program. "Now is the time for faith," implored the project's leader, Arthur Compton, a devout Christian, in a special-delivery letter to Conant. But Conant did not think highly of such an appeal. "It isn't faith we need now, Arthur," he replied. "It's works."[22] After seeing a pessimistic calculation from a British scientist, a "rather highly disturbed" Conant complained about the "present rather fuzzy state of our thinking" and forcefully reminded Compton of his duty to make honest estimates, even if they were discouraging. "I am sure you will agree with me," he added, "that the record, which some day will be gone over with a fine tooth comb, is of importance, not because of its effect on any one of us, but because it will stand as to what American scientists can do under pressure. I should very much hate to have the record show that under the enthusiasm of the chase American scientists lost their critical acumen and failed to be realistic and hardboiled about the chance of success."[23]

As it turned out, Conant's jitters over the purity issue stemmed not from incompetence or subterfuge but confusion caused by S-1's tight security restrictions.[24] And on December 2, 1942—only one day after venting his fears—Conant was in his Dumbarton Oaks room when he received a phone call from Compton, who in a security-conscious exchange used an improvised code to refer to Enrico Fermi, physicist in charge of the effort to create the first man-made self-sustaining nuclear chain reaction:

COMPTON: Jim, you'll be interested to know the Italian navigator has just landed in the new world.

CONANT: Were the natives friendly?

COMPTON: Everyone landed safe and happy.[25]

Buoyed up by this milestone achievement, which buttressed claims of the feasibility of transmuting U-238 into bomb-grade plutonium, the S-1 Executive Committee in early December still found itself unable to recommend the cancellation of any of the other remaining methods. Conant appended his personal assessment to Groves on December 9. In general he agreed with the committee, even though expenditures for multiple development might ultimately run to $350–500 million and even though perhaps a one-in-three chance existed that neither uranium nor plutonium would prove a feasible basis for a bomb. As for a time scale for production, Conant's hopes had slipped since May. Due to rising projections of the critical mass needed for detonation, his prediction was six months more pessimistic than the committee's: if the war ended by January 1945, he thought, no American bombs would have been employed; if the United States could be certain the war would be over by then without the Germans having produced an atomic bomb, "then there would be no justification for recommending this project as a war measure."

> We must consider, however, what the time schedule of the enemy may be. It is quite possible that the Germans are a year ahead of us, or perhaps have even eighteen months head start ... Taking this possibility into consideration and allowing for the intrinsic basic uncertainty of the whole project, I would judge there was an even chance that the Germans would produce a number of effective bombs by the middle of 1945 and a slight chance (perhaps 1 in 10) of their achieving the same result by the summer of 1944. However slight this possibility may be, the consequences would appear to be so serious that the possibility must be the determining factor in any decision. To my mind, it is this fear that the Germans may be near the goal which is the prime reason for an all out effort now on this gamble. This being so, it is clear that nothing short of a full-speed, all-out attempt would be worthwhile.[26]

Conant's apprehensions reflected his awareness of both the prewar prowess of German physics and a steady stream of ambiguous yet alarming intelligence — circumstantial evidence, snippets of conversations with scientists in Europe who maintained contacts in Germany, worst-case analysis and extrapolation — indicating that a German atomic project might be on the verge of success. Six months earlier, in May, he had guessed that the Germans were at most a year ahead. But then, over the summer, for example, prodded by Leo Szilard and other physicists at Chicago, Arthur Compton in great distress had passed Bush and Conant allegedly "reliable" information that German physicists had successfully achieved a self-sustaining chain reaction, and warned of an imminent threat of a German atomic weapon, either a method for spreading radioactive fission products "in lethal quantities," or a bomb ready for use on Allied targets "in 1943, a year before our bombs are planned to be ready." Compton urged Bush to step up "sabotage, air, or commando raids" to disrupt the German project, and to step up the pace of U.S. efforts. Cables shot back and forth between Washington and London, with Conant and the British atomic leaders trading rumors about the extent of German progress and showing special concern about the activities of Werner Heisenberg, the renowned physicist said to be heading nuclear efforts at the Kaiser Wilhelm institutes in Berlin-Dahlem.[27]

But in fact, the warnings of a German lead were false, often the product of garbled second- and third-hand conversations embellished by fear: German physicists had indeed been conducting research for the Nazi regime on atomic energy, reporting their results to Albert Speer and other top civilian and military officials, but by the spring of 1942 authorities concluded that the possible military uses were too distant to suit immediate war priorities, and relegated atomic research to a backwater behind other secret weapons projects. Although the motives behind the German physicists' assessments and ultimate failure remain disputed — scientific incompetence, bureaucratic bungling, or moral qualms about building the bomb for Hitler? — by December 1942 the Nazi government had already turned away from a crash program to develop nuclear weapons and the race that so obsessed Conant was essentially uncontested.[28] Much later, after the war, Conant claimed that he was "never convinced that the Germans were anywhere near getting a bomb," and spoke rather scornfully of "ghosts that were being seen by some of my scientific friends."[29]

But that was after-the-fact wisdom: he, too, resorted to the argument that the Germans might get the bomb first in order to pressure recalcitrant contractors or scientists, and as he summarized his estimate of the situation to Groves, and then to Bush for transmission to Roosevelt, he certainly seemed to take that fear seriously. On December 16, Bush forwarded to the president a detailed progress report on behalf of the Military Policy Committee asking his approval for the atomic program to "be vigorously pushed throughout," noting in his cover letter: "We still do not know where we stand in the race with the enemy toward a usable result, but it is quite possible that Germany is ahead of us and may well be able to produce superbombs sooner than we can." Two weeks later, the report came back with the customary "VB — OK — FDR," and the Manhattan Project entered its next phase: the construction of plants for the production of fissionable material.[30]

At the same time, in winter of 1942-43, the OSRD and the army hastily moved to create an isolated laboratory to centralize work on the bomb's eventual design, assembly, and testing, to be run under contract by the University of California. On the site of a boys' school in Los Alamos, New Mexico, atop a mesa in the Sangre de Cristo mountain range, a complex known by the official code name of "Site Y" and the more romantic appellation of "Shangri La" rose from the desert. Soon, after train trips of hundreds or thousands of miles, hundreds of professors, grad students, and freshly minted Ph.Ds. and their families, accustomed to urbane university towns like Berkeley, Princeton, and Cambridge, were squinting at the desert sun and gawking at the stark mountain scenery surrounding the tiny railroad station at Lamy.

The man who had chosen the obscure location and who was to direct the secret lab was the theoretical physicist J. Robert Oppenheimer, whom the Military Policy Committee had approved for the task in September 1942 despite a security file bulging with reports on allegedly "questionable" and "Communistic" activities and associations.[31] A tall, slender, charismatic polymath, then thirty-eight years old, Oppenheimer had already won legendary status at Berkeley, where devoted students assured standing-room-only status for his witty, dense, and scintillating lectures on modern theoretical physics. This son of wealthy, cultured German Jews on Manhattan's Upper West Side, a decade younger than Conant, had raced to scientific prominence along a route not entirely dissimilar to that taken by the Harvard president. Oppenheimer, too, had quickly gravitated toward science as a child, sped through Harvard, and then embarked on a pilgrimage to the great German universities, arriving at Göttingen in 1926 to share in the thrilling atmosphere around Bohr and Planck and Max Born, as the structure of the atom was being dissected. They also shared a love of the outdoors, treasuring the peace and healthy exertion of lonely mountain trails, though in temperament, Oppenheimer's intense emotional nature differed from Conant's caution and cool reserve. Since joining the University of California faculty in 1929, Oppenheimer, previously aloof to contemporary affairs outside the scientific world, had experienced a dramatic rise in political awareness, encouraged by left-wing colleagues, friends, and lovers. Sensitized to the dangers of international fascism and the injustices and suffering of the Depression years, Oppenheimer signed up to help Spanish refugees, migrant workers, émigré scholars fleeing Hitler, the teachers' union. Filling out a government security questionnaire in early 1942, he wrote that he had belonged to "just about every Communist Front organization on the West Coast,"[32] although a rather dunderheaded notice sent to Conant's office in May of that year after a War Department "field investigation" related only that:

> One J. Robert Oppenheimer, 16 Kenelworth Court, Kensington Park, California reported connected with radical organizations for years in and off the campus of the University of California.
>
> One J. Robert Oppenheimer visits 3031 Benvenue Ave., Berkeley, California, a hotbed of Communism for students of the University of California. He is either strongly communistic or pro axis.[33]

The army's decision in August to officially turn "thumbs down" on Oppenheimer[34] — who at that moment was heavily engaged in startling research into thermonuclear reactions — had only exasperated the OSRD leaders, who were increasingly irritated by the military's foot-dragging on clearances and its incomprehension of eccentricities considered mundane or at least tolerable in scientific and academic circles. Far more important to Conant was the judgment of Ernest Lawrence that Oppenheimer "combines a penetrating insight of the theoretical aspects of the whole program with solid common sense, which sometimes in certain directions seems to be lacking," and California Institute of Technology physicist and NDRC division head Richard C. Tolman's vouching for Oppenheimer's "integrity, discretion, and loyalty to the United States."[35] Nothing the military sleuths uncovered shook Conant or Bush sufficiently to resist claims that Oppenheimer, with his ability to juggle complex physics theories and Nobel laureate egos, was the right choice to head the weapons lab. Desperate for fast results and increasingly worried that the Army's "nervousness" on security might "seriously delay the S-1 work,"[36] Conant prodded Bush to recommend quick clearances for Oppenheimer and other scientists with admittedly "unusual" backgrounds who under normal circumstances would not be used. Appealing in early October to War Department aide Harvey Bundy to break the logjam, Bush cited the cases of Arthur Compton, at times indiscreet but learning, Fermi, Italian born but "probably the best man anywhere from certain angles," and Oppenheimer, "decidedly left-wing politically, but who has contributed substantially"—and elevated the whole clearance issue to the Military Policy Committee.[37]

They recognized, however, that the crucial question was how Groves and Oppenheimer would get on—and fatefully, united more than anything by their shared desire for the project to succeed, they somehow fast established a good working relationship and a genuine personal bond. Though temperamental, philosophical, and intellectual opposites in many ways, both men brooked no waste of time or effort or unnecessary interference in advancing the project—and at their first meeting, on October 8, 1942, they agreed on the need for an isolated, centralized laboratory to most effectively utilize scattered resources and on the best region to establish it, each having fond memories of traveling in the desolate, beautiful countryside of the southwest United States; rapidly arranged inspection tours yielded the Los Alamos site, and cemented the Groves-Oppenheimer collaboration.[38]

Once Groves made up his mind, that settled the clearance issue; and, on November 3, the Army formally notified the OSRD that it had no objection to employing Oppenheimer, "Due to further investigation and the fact that he is already well informed about the project."[39]

In fact, Oppenheimer had shed most of his ardor for international socialism after the Nazi-Soviet pact, and he accepted the Los Alamos assignment with an earnest desire to learn the ropes of administration and dealing with the new world of political and military bureaucratic warfare. For this task, Oppenheimer found Conant an ideal tutor. Between them flowered a strong mutual admiration that sprang from their complementary strengths. Conant was impressed by Oppenheimer's intellectual brilliance and range, and after the war he tried repeatedly if vainly to lure him to the Harvard faculty.[40] For his part, Oppenheimer, newly emerged from his academic cocoon, envied and sought to emulate his boss's savvy as a Washington administrator and operator. "Oppenheimer saw this faculty of Conant and wanted to learn from it," recalls the physicist John Manley, a close associate of both men. "I could tell by the way he talked of Conant that he was very fond of him and relied on him a great deal."[41] Over the next few years, Conant became Oppenheimer's "mentor in national policy matters" and, according to Manley, grew in his eyes into "a very wise, elderly person who in a normal sense of events he would like to have had as a godfather."[42] As work on the bomb progressed, these two tall, thin men—the chain-smoking Oppenheimer almost wispy, Conant lanky, brisk, businesslike and sufficiently youthful to be once mistaken for a graduate student[43]—conversed for many hours in the informal atmosphere at Los Alamos during Conant's numerous inspection trips there. By late 1944 their relationship had reached the point where Conant sent off letters to "Dear Oppie" and Oppenheimer affectionately addressed Conant as "Uncle Jim."[44]

Not one to suffer fools gladly, Oppenheimer was pleased to find in Conant a government bureaucrat who could speak his own language, who could both grasp technical intricacies and empathize with scientists' philosophical concerns even when they did not conform to traditional military procedure. Countless times, Conant would grease the government machinery to allay Oppenheimer's worries about restriction of information, military discipline, and most of all, recruitment, the highest priority as the new lab director began scouring universities and rival war projects for prospects.[45] By late October 1942, the two were closely collaborating to pry loose personnel; hearing that there had been trouble obtaining one Harvard physicist, John van Vleck, Conant vowed cheekily that "if it is true that Harvard has refused this request, as Chairman of NDRC I will raise cain with the President of Harvard University!"[46] A few days later, Oppenheimer wrote to Manley: "I have no idea what success Conant will have, or whether the men themselves will be fully cooperative, but I think Conant will bring a very sympathetic attitude to our personnel problems and that we may find fewer difficulties in all this than we anticipated."[47] The relationship was not without its rough spots, however, and Oppenheimer's sometimes undiplomatic aggressiveness in recruiting top-flight scientists from competing OSRD and NDRC projects (at Princeton, the MIT Rad Lab, and elsewhere) initially provoked so much irritation that Conant, who bore the brunt of the complaints, worriedly reported to Groves in late December that he and Bush were "wondering whether we have found the right man to be the leader."[48] Intent on assuring that S-1 triumphed in the ferocious personnel competition, Conant and Groves soon hammered out a strategy to smooth Oppenheimer's recruiting efforts by having Conant first make an approach at the highest level, then adding their own voice to pressure hesitant individuals:

> It was my arrangement with Oppenheimer that as soon as we had got the clearance from the top man in each organization who was likely to kick, — in this case, the President of the University, — Oppenheimer will then approach the man in question directly and try to sell him on the idea. If there was then reluctance, you or I, or both of us, would write a letter to the man in question telling him just how important it was for him to make this sacrifice in the war effort.[49]

Reassured the situation was improving, Conant recommended that Bush approve an initial $350,000 start-up contract with the University of California for the "Oppenheimer project."[50] But Conant soon ran into trouble, and it was indicative of the discontent among Manhattan Project scientists at other sites. He had already alienated many of those working under Compton on the plutonium project in Chicago, where scientists were upset at his enforcement of the hated compartmentalization policy, which they felt hampered progress, and because they were "left behind" when the army and industry (the Du Pont Company) took over much of the work in the fall. Disturbed, some Met Lab scientists felt the army's "conventional and routine" pace, and industrial considerations, were endangering the goal of the quickest possible bomb — and placed much of the blame on Conant. Compton dampened the dissension but "the sense of frustration and distrust did not disappear."[51]

Now another aspect of the security system that riled Chicago threatened to hamper recruiting at Los Alamos. Oppenheimer himself had no objection to military induction, but several top physicists whom he wanted — in particular I. I. Rabi and Robert Bacher, both working on other war projects at the MIT Rad Lab — raised serious objections to giving Los Alamos military status, fearing that suffocating security and a rigid, uninformed scientific hierarchy would inevitably foster friction and "social cleavage," kill morale, and generally render the atmosphere unsuitable for productive research. Regarding them as essential to carry on work at "anything like the speed that is required," Oppenheimer listed their conditions for joining Los Alamos to Conant on February 1, 1943. They included demilitarization of the lab and a role for scientists in deciding security matters. Without fulfilling the conditions, Oppenheimer wrote, Los Alamos might nevertheless "go, more or less," but only at a significantly slowed pace; the "solidarity of the physicists" was such that recruiting would suffer.[52]

Conant, recalling his World War I experience, did not share the scientists' visceral distaste for a military setup. Yet he could see that their dissension could cause serious problems for S-1 if not confronted. His solution was a letter, co-signed by Groves, for Oppenheimer to show recruits; in it was the assurance that the laboratory would not become militarized until January 1944 at the earliest (it never was). When work reached a particularly dangerous stage, Los Alamos civilians would then have the option of becoming commissioned officers. To assuage worries that compartmentalization might prevent researchers at isolated Los Alamos from learning needed information from experiments being carried on at other sites, the following rather presumptuous statement was included: "Through Dr. Conant complete access to the scientific world is guaranteed."[53]

This February 25, 1943, letter formalized an arrangement that had been in effect since the previous fall's reorganization: Conant's function as Groves's scientific adviser, and as intermediary among the scientists, military and OSRD.[54] It showed, Groves felt, Conant's "great experience in, and understanding of, the academic world, particularly its scientific element," and it helped to overcome the fears of potential recruits.[55]

It helped, but it was hardly sufficient. Obviously the arrangement in the Conant-Groves letter left much to be desired, Oppenheimer admitted to Rabi. If he agreed with Rabi's argument that the venture to build a weapon of mass destruction would be "the culmination of three centuries of physics," Oppenheimer might himself walk away. But the objective was less grandiose — to develop "in time of war a military weapon of some consequence," a choice of priorities dictated by the Nazis. Rabi came part-time to Los Alamos as a consultant, and with comparable cajoling and string-pulling, other scientists began signing up, lured by a combination of the challenge, adventure, the company, and the prospect of competing with Hitler's physicists.[56]

And, as they did, Conant shed his doubts about the selection of Oppenheimer, whose "patience, courage, and determination" had begun to show results. "Don't worry at all about the trouble which your activities may have caused me," he reassured him. "I am only sorry that I can't press a button and produce the men that I know you need and want."[57]

By the spring of 1943 the army had begun to implement Conant's agonized decision to back development of all three surviving "horses" — plutonium, electromagnetic separation, and gaseous diffusion — in secret plants and cities employing hundreds of thousands of workers for a purpose that few were permitted to know, in Tennessee, Washington State, New Mexico, and elsewhere. For the moment Conant had little to do but wait — and to scribble a "fragment of a strange scientific history," a forty-seven-page account of the project's inception and early stages.[58] Completed in May 1943 and declassified in 1979, this document offers both a firsthand recapitulation of the decision to build the bomb and clues to Conant's own thinking. "My story," he began, "starts with the report of a Committee of the National Academy dated May 17, 1941. When and where it will end no one can now foresee." He summed up the status of the project:

> The basic experimental program has been completed; the responsibilities of OSRD for the uranium program are nearly terminated; four large and

powerful chemical companies have undertaken a difficult and ambitious manufacturing program; the guidance of this gigantic undertaking is in the hands of Brigadier General L. R. Groves, responsible to a Military Policy Committee of which Dr. V. Bush is Chairman (with the writer as his alternate). For eighteen months this highly secret war effort has moved at a giddy pace. New results, new ideas, new decisions and new organization have kept all concerned in a state of healthy turmoil. The time for "freezing design" and construction arrived a few weeks past; now, we must await the slower task of plant construction and large-scale experimentation. The new results when they arrive will henceforth be no laboratory affair, their import may well be world shattering. But as in the animal world, so in industry: the period of gestation is commensurate with the magnitude to be achieved. For the moment, those in charge of policy must wait for new events. Hence this appears an appropriate moment to review the past.[59]

The most revealing section of the history comes in the conclusion, where Conant bares his fear of the Manhattan Project's *success*, rather than its failure. This corroborates Arthur Compton's 1954 recollection that many in the atomic project, himself excluded, "hoped sincerely that atomic explosions would never become a reality! Then we should be free of the fear of such weapons coming first from Germany, or from some other potential enemy. I believe James Conant would have counted himself among those who had this hope."[60] On the other hand, Conant knew well that it was he who would shoulder the blame if the bomb did not go off. He and Groves joked about buying houses on Capitol Hill if the project ended in failure because they would spend the rest of their lives testifying before angry congressional committees.[61] Compton notes that even aside from the potentially fatal consequences for his own career, Conant had to be concerned that an erroneous decision could mean "incalculable damage to the nation's respect for its men of learning."[62]

It was not too late to pull out, he knew. In March 1943 it seemed to Conant that the difficulties had increased over the past eight months and at least part of the project might have to be cancelled. "The one important point," he wrote Bush, "is to review frequently that nature of the gamble and estimate the odds to see if the game is still worth the candle."[63] Even the troubles encountered so far were, in a way, comforting: "At least every difficulty that develops means probably an equal difficulty for the Germans!" Writing not just to himself but also for any subsequent investigators, Conant noted that "one cannot emphasize enough the fact that everyone at every stage realized that all the prophecies were gambles, all the time schedules studded with 'ifs' and 'ands,'—they represented 'the best' one might hope to do; the worst was some unforeseen block,—a complete failure."

As of his writing, no such block had appeared. Except for the centrifuge, the methods Conant had approved remained competitive and promising. In that respect the predictions of 1942 still "look good," Conant wrote; from the point of view of the resources and time necessary to build the plant, however, "those prophecies now seem far too rosy. What the future a year hence has to say is still another story."

Despite the consequences, and the ever-decreasing odds, Conant still held out hope that the future would bring that "unforeseen block" that would prevent the Manhattan Project—or any attempt to build atomic weapons—from success. Since the previous summer, Conant had also been aware of research, conducted by Oppenheimer and colleagues at Berkeley, showing the possibility of using atomic fission bombs to trigger fusion explosions of a theoretically unlimited size; at one point, concern was even raised that an atomic blast might detonate a thermonuclear reaction in the atmosphere, destroying all life on the planet. That fear had faded after hurried studies, but Conant's secret history reveals his already profound belief that the existence of any sort of atomic weapons boded poorly for human survival. Though Conant's responsibility and commitment were to the completion of a bomb, he wrote that "everyone concerned with the project would feel greatly relieved and thoroughly delighted if something would develop to *prove* the impossibility of such an atomic explosive." His closing words described an idyllic scenario (shortly afterward to die in a series of experiments at Los Alamos) that seemed an effort to quell his rising fear that humanity and atomic bombs could not long coexist.

How many times in all the scientific conferences of the last two years has it been said[,] "I hope the thing won't work, but we must be sure it won't." With the establishment of a slow neutron self-sustaining chain reaction the chances of the "thing not working" have greatly diminished; yet it may be that a self-sustaining *fast* neutron reaction may be impossible,—civilization would then, indeed, be fortunate,—atomic energy for power a reality, for destruction an impossibility![64]

CHAPTER 10

"The International Complications of S-1"
Anglo-American Atomic Angst
1943

Does it make any difference which among the Allies manufactures the munitions?
> —Memorandum to Vannevar Bush, October 26, 1942

[If you see the President you should] point out that if the by-product of the power plant is a "super-explosive," the implications of that for the future of civilization are even graver than you predict in your report . . . it is of the utmost importance that these facts be established before the question of policing the post-war world comes up for debate.
> —Memorandum to Bush, December 15, 1942

It seems to me of the greatest importance to be sure that the President understands the basic issue . . . From the point of view of the security of the United States, knowledge of the design, construction and operation of these plants is a military secret which is in a totally different class anything the world has ever seen if the potentialities of this project are realized. Therefore, the passing of this knowledge to an ally under conditions whereby the ally cannot profit directly in this war would seem to raise a question of national policy comparable at least to alienation of control of a fortress or strategic harbor. . . . The major consideration must be that of national security and post-war strategic significance.
> —Memorandum to Bush, March 25, 1943

On the Friday before Christmas 1942, a cold, rainy, sleety afternoon, two Harvard administrators jostled through crowds of holiday shoppers on the sidewalks of midtown Manhattan to catch the five o'clock Merchants' Limited for Boston. The faculty dean, Paul H. Buck, and Calvert Smith had made the trip down to New York City from Cambridge just in order to ride back with the university's busy president, who had boarded the train in Washington and was making a rare visit to see his family. Ever since mid-1940, and especially since Pearl Harbor threw America into the war, Conant had delegated

day-to-day responsibility for running the university to his underlings, especially Buck and the treasurer, Bill Claflin. On this occasion, Buck and Smith
calculated that joining Conant on the Merchants' would be the only chance to
steal a few hours to transact a historic piece of business: after more than three
centuries of male exclusiveness and years of delicate negotiations, Harvard
had reached a tentative agreement with Radcliffe College to merge classroom
instruction. They came prepared for a laborious discussion that would probably eat up much of the trip.

When they found Conant, however, he had his head buried in a book on
foreign policy and seemed distracted. After dinner, as the train changed
engines at New Haven, Buck had just begun laying out the terms of the
arrangement when Conant interrupted. I have one important question, he
said. Has Claflin approved it?

"Wholeheartedly," replied Buck, "and so has Radcliffe's treasurer."

Good, the president nodded. "I have no questions, go ahead with it," he
told them, and dove back into his reading.[1]

Conant had more important matters on his mind that day. A week earlier
he and Bush had been present in Secretary of War Stimson's office to hear an
alarming report from Chief of Staff Gen. George C. Marshall, who cited
intelligence cables to warn that Germany might soon launch gas attacks
against the Allies. A "gas Pearl Harbor" might be imminent, and the Germans might have solved the problems that had hampered their use of mustard gas in the last years of World War I. Fearful that a major escalation in the
scientific war might come any day, the OSRD advisers had sent Stimson an
urgent inquiry to find out whether the War Department was fully prepared to
provide gas masks for American soldiers, to retaliate with U.S. toxic fumes
should gas warfare start, and to handle the public relations should the
Germans gain the upper hand; the message spurred a full-scale review of
Chemical Warfare Service's contingency planning, leading to new training
programs and a stepping-up of production of gases that could be used in a
retaliatory blow.[2]

But Conant also worried about another sub rosa race for scientific superiority in advanced weapons—this secret rivalry, however, involved not America's
enemy but its principal ally, Great Britain, and the weapon in question was
the atomic bomb. Before leaving Washington on Friday afternoon, Conant
had received the latest report from Bush on a brewing Anglo-American crisis
over the terms of the Allied nuclear partnership. Over the previous month,
Conant had engaged in difficult and at times testy negotiations with an envoy
from Britain, Wallace T. Akers, over the terms of joint cooperation; now
Conant awaited the fate of his advice to FDR, relayed by Bush, on how to
handle this delicate matter.[3]

Though the two countries were united in their battle to defeat the Axis,
Conant had privately decided that the Anglo-American atomic relationship
needed to be dramatically constrained as the Manhattan Project passed from

laboratory research to large-scale industrial manufacturing and production. His recommendations, in turn, once they were approved by FDR and communicated to the British in January 1943, set off a bitter secret dispute that disrupted Anglo-American atomic cooperation for eight months and left long-term scars on relations between the wartime partners. This was the first instance of the capacity of atomic bombs to exacerbate tensions even between friendly countries, and it crucially marked the intellectual transformation of nuclear weapons from a short-term military factor to a political and diplomatic bargaining chip. For the handful of officials in the know on both sides of the Atlantic, the struggle to control the fruits of the Manhattan Project forced to the surface the ambitions of both British and American officials to achieve maximum benefit for their respective nations in the postwar world.[4]

Despite Conant's citation of German progress as the primary motive for a "full-speed, all-out attempt" to build an atomic bomb, it was not entirely mysterious that he would pay closer attention to the Manhattan Project's longer-term ramifications. A year after Bundy's gloomy Christmas visit a couple of weeks after Pearl Harbor, Allied battlefield successes had encouraged him to devote increasing thought to the shape of the postwar world. As U.S. forces began to turn the course of the battle during 1942, prospects for eventual victory brightened; on both the European and Pacific fronts pressure built steadily against the Axis powers, though years of hard fighting clearly remained. It was, therefore, by no means obvious to Conant that the United States needed S-1 to win the war.

Yet fears about both the domestic and international repercussions of a prolonged struggle now grew more prominent in Conant's public and private statements. At an emotional January 10, 1943, early graduation ceremony for Harvard undergraduates heading off to battle, Conant concentrated on the difficulties of restoring peacetime moral standards rather than on the task of winning the war. His expression of concern that wartime pressures might inculcate a "totalitarian virus" in the United States showed his awareness both of the inherent dangers in a society energized to run a military machine, and his own war-induced support for measures normally anathema to him. America had the same objectives in peace and war, he said, but the methods employed had to remain distinct. "Indeed," he warned, "the winning of the war could engender such conditions in our minds that we would be unable to preserve liberty when the time of peace had come."[5]

It was paramount, Conant believed, that a post-victory America promote maximum social fluidity, and he began to advocate the emergence of what he called an "American Radical," a "fanatic equalitarian" who would work to undermine social stratifications born of inherited wealth. Conant had long believed in a "free and classless, or casteless, society," though he had spelled out his ideas only gradually. But his sense that the war created opportunities for serious social change and widened the boundaries of politically permissible discourse emboldened him to state the case more sharply than he had previously thought advisable. In an article entitled "Wanted: American Radicals" in the May 1943 *Atlantic Monthly,* he suggested that victory over the Axis would necessitate a broad rethinking of past shibboleths in both foreign and domestic policies, and urged Americans to shed the old labels of liberal and conservative, to welcome a new "third force" in U.S. politics rising out of the New World's soil of libertarian individualism and egalitarianism rather than European models of totalitarian or aristocratic rule. While "respectful but not enthusiastic about Marx, Engels, and Lenin," Conant's postulated radical would be an intellectual and spiritual descendant of Andrew Jackson and Jefferson, Thoreau and Emerson, and Walt Whitman. He would fanatically uphold, Conant wrote,

> equality of opportunity, not equality of rewards; but, on the other hand, he will be lusty in wielding the ax against the root of inherited privilege. To prevent the growth of a caste system, which he abhors, he will be resolute in his demand to confiscate (by constitutional methods) all property once a generation. He will demand really effective inheritance and gift taxes and the breaking up of trust funds and estates. And this point cannot be lightly pushed aside, for it is the kernal of his radical philosophy.[6]

"Wanted: American Radicals" delighted and intrigued many liberals and leftists, even genuine Marxists like Harold Laski with whom Conant disagreed, but the article went over like a lead balloon with Harvard's Brahmin hierarchy. To many guardians of this private university—whose endowment relied heavily on inherited wealth and trust funds and whose student body still included a large proportion of rich alumni's offspring—the article seemed little short of blasphemy. Giving the state the right to "reorder the 'haves and have-nots' every generation to give flux to our social order," as Conant's "hypothetical gentleman" advocated, reeked of totalitarian socialism to these conservative critics. Among those most disturbed were members of the Harvard Corporation, who found fault both in the views of Conant's "American Radical" and the author's coy evasion of responsibility for them—"I urge the need of the American radical not because I wish to give a blanket endorsement to his views," Conant had hedged, "but because I see the necessity for reinvigorating a neglected aspect of our historical development." Fumed one Corporation fellow: "Now this is not a dignified or sportsmanlike way to put yourself on the record." Even Grenville Clark, whose effusive recommendation of Conant for every major war post in the Roosevelt administration provoked another Corporation member to accuse him of messianic hero-worship, agreed that JBC's advocacy of wholesale confiscation was excessive and ill-considered.[7]

A particularly vigorous dissent was lodged by Thomas W. Lamont, the chairman of J. P. Morgan, one of the wealthiest men in America, and a

Harvard alumnus (Class of 1892) upon whom Conant counted for major contributions to the university (he had already pledged to underwrite the construction of a new undergraduate library at the end of the war).[8] The Wall Street banker admired Conant, and had warmly welcomed his pre–Pearl Harbor interventionist activities, but the *Atlantic* article provoked him to draft a sharp letter denying the existence of a "caste system" in the United States and charging that the confiscatory inheritance task advocated by Conant's "American Radical" would cripple private universities and lead to state domination of education.[9] On reflection he decided to file the letter until he had a chance to speak personally with Conant at Harvard commencement ceremonies in June. To Lamont's pleasant surprise Conant cheerfully welcomed his polite inquiry as to whether he might write a memorandum expressing disagreement with the article, and seemed generally unruffled: "Conant was not in the least bit sensitive apparently about the paper," Lamont reported to a friend, "although the Harvard crowd was generally buzzing with the whole thing, and most of the Back Bay–Somerset Club comments, where I had been dining with classmates, were very vociferous and not easy. Without meaning to, he apparently stirred up a hornet's nest."[10]

After gathering ammunition from associates, Lamont on June 22 dispatched an eight-page critique disputing Conant's analysis of the role of class divisions in either American society or the European crisis, and asserting that his "American Radical" was "a destructive sort of chap," since his ideas, particularly the inheritance tax, would foster the growth of a "monster State" and strike a "death blow" at the free enterprise system by undermining incentives for the accumulation of wealth.[11] Conant, in response, retaliated with a seventeen-page letter arguing in detail his case that America still did not live up to its promise of a fluid society bereft of caste and class barriers to advancement and was desperately in need of new measures to assure social mobility. "My American radical . . . fears that the clash of the 'haves' and 'have nots' will destroy freedom in the post-war world unless a majority of the American people *believe* in the *reality* of the American dream—equal opportunity for all." And Conant, unlike Lamont, saw that dream becoming more rather than less distant. Viewing the future with an admittedly "jaundiced" perspective, Conant speculated that their disagreement boiled down to a fundamental divergence in "diagnosis of America of the present and prognosis for its future"—having stayed relatively optimistic during the Depression years, he now found himself "in the unhappy position of being much more pessimistic than some of my friends as to the intensity of the social forces now pulling against each other in the American scene." Regarding the sentence which had most offended Lamont, Conant acknowledged that in using the word "confiscate" he was representing the radical "in his most extreme mood," and disclaimed any desire to enhance governmental power or authority. Yet he still found the basic idea sound enough to elaborate that "to be effective" any new system of inheritance taxes would require elimination of loopholes to avoid them through trusts and gifts, prompting the astonished Lamont to scribble in the margin: "Sic! From the President of *Harvard!*"[12] The debate petered out in the fall, neither Conant nor Lamont having given much ground.[13]

In fact, though Conant disavowed the most extreme suggestions of his "American Radical," the article well expressed his carefully modulated antipathy to the "perpetuation of wealth, power and privilege in the ruling class" and his ardent support of state-supported public schools as the vital engine of democracy. Complementing his public recommendations for egalitarian reforms, Conant since at least 1940 had been privately urging a stiff inheritance tax, together with a gift tax ("except for gifts to charity and universities!"), as an "effective weapon to keep society fluid" and for "breaking up large trust funds passed on by individuals for the benefit of their heirs." The trouble, Conant told the Republican statesman Alf Landon in 1940, was that most government officials viewed taxation as a device to fill state coffers rather than to foster social mobility, and "very few people seem to do more than lip service to the ideal of an American type of classless society."[14]

Much of Conant's advice was not really that "radical"—"the language of the Left in order to express the ideas of the Center," one critic charged.[15] To some degree Conant would have gladly pleaded guilty to that charge; even before Pearl Harbor, he had prophesied that in the postwar world class tensions might require the United States to steer a middle course between "an American brand of fascism and an American brand of socialism." America's destiny, he then asserted, must be to strive for political freedom *and* social fluidity, in contrast to the Soviets ("classless but not free"), England ("free but not classless"), and Germany ("neither free nor classless").[16]

Long before his *Atlantic* article, Conant knew that his eyebrow-raising rhetoric might alienate powerful Brahmin power centers. After a 1940 speech in Ohio, a surprised local educational official had complimented him as a new kind of Harvard president, as a real democrat, adding, "I hope they won't make you repudiate those doctrines when you get back home." Acidly JBC added in his diary: "I hope they won't try! I think Charlie Coolidge would like to and Bill Claflin if they understood them!"[17]

Certain Corporation members, grumbling over the *Atlantic Monthly* piece, had a sense that Conant, burned by the Walsh-Sweezy turmoil, had been happily and irrevocably bitten by the Potomac bug; and soon they started a quiet move to edge Conant permanently out of the Harvard presidency. Nothing was put in writing, but though it amounted to less than an outright coup attempt it was far more than a wishful daydream, Buck recalled privately many years later. Reportedly, the Corporation's Harry Shattuck spearheaded the move, which envisioned asking Conant formally to submit his resignation and putting Buck in the post.

Conant was horrified when he got wind of the idea—not because he cherished the title so much as because he feared that without the aura of the

Harvard presidency behind him he would lose much of his clout as a Manhattan Project administrator, both within the government and with the university presidents whom he was constantly nagging to release key personnel. Of course, having kept S-1 secret from even his wife, Conant could not tell Buck or the Corporation about it, but he made it clear that FDR, an old Harvard College man, agreed that his NDRC work necessitated clinging to the most prestigious post in the educational world. "I've got to have the title in order to get this important work done," Conant pleaded to Buck, who had been deputized by Shattuck to smoke him out.

"Well," the pudgy, good-natured historian replied, "that's very simple, then." Buck refused to go along with Shattuck, who dropped the idea.[18] But Conant's discomfiture endured, and the knowledge of the Corporation's impatience added yet another incentive to assure that the Manhattan Project visibly repaid the time, resources, and personal commitment that were daily being gambled on it.[19]

Though unable openly to identify the source of his deepest fears, Conant warned Harvard students in January 1943 that every month "adds to the chaos with which the postwar world must deal."[20] In private, his thinking about the bomb already ran along two parallel tracks: the immediate task of finding the fastest route to a bomb; and the equal if not more important challenge of discerning the weapon's immense, but unclear, long-term political and diplomatic consequences. The dispute with Britain challenged Conant to balance these dual imperatives — to assure that the United States produced the atomic bomb in the shortest possible time, taking maximum advantages of British scientific resources, yet at the same time preserve U.S. national atomic prerogatives for the postwar era.

Reflecting a deep, broader change — as during World War II the United States supplanted Britain as the West's predominant power — the OSRD's nationalistic calculations simmered beneath the polite surface of the transatlantic partnership until Akers's talks with Conant in the fall of 1942. Churchill's envoy had arrived in Washington at a sensitive juncture. In 1940–41, British progress in atomic research, as in radar, had outstripped U.S. efforts. It had been the MAUD Committee rather than the National Academy of Sciences, that had decisively dispelled Conant's skepticism about a uranium bomb, and initially the OSRD leadership had accepted as a given that the S-1 project stood to gain from maximum interchange. At the October 9, 1941, White House meeting at which FDR first okayed an urgent investigation of the feasibility of atomic weapons, the president and Bush had completely agreed on the idea of a collaborative U.S.-British project, to be based in Canada. Two days later, FDR had written Churchill to suggest that the two countries open discussions "in order that any extended efforts [toward making an atomic bomb] may be coordinated or jointly conducted."[21]

But then the British, still thinking in terms of an independent program to produce "Tube Alloys," their code name for the atomic bomb, or at worst an Anglo-American project in which London was the leader, played hard to get. On the surface Churchill responded cordially to Roosevelt's entreaty—"I need not assure you of our readiness to collaborate with the US administration in this matter"—but the fact that he had taken two months to write showed Britain's reluctance to give up its edge. The prime minister's atomic advisers were loath to sacrifice what they mistakenly believed would be a ticket to preserve Britain's endangered status of a preeminent imperial power far beyond the conflict then in progress, and they grossly underestimated the speed with which Washington could and would plunge massive resources into the bomb project once politically committed. As a result, they missed the boat—and blew their chance to get FDR's signature on an ironclad, fully collaborative atomic-production pact.[22]

In early 1942, the British diffidently consented to pooling research efforts for producing fissionable material, and Anglo-American interchange proceeded in a relatively productive manner. The Americans, newly energized by Pearl Harbor, accelerated their efforts on all fronts in the search for the fastest route to the bomb, but they still gratefully sought and accepted help from across the sea. In April, Bush wrote to his British counterpart, Sir John Anderson, to urge that particular attention be devoted to assuring "adequate interchange" in the construction of pilot plants, at which stage the OSRD head "strongly" felt that it was "highly desirable that future action should be considered jointly."[23]

At their June 1942 summit at Hyde Park, FDR and Churchill genially if vaguely agreed on the concept of a joint project, with the plants to be located in the United States—"I talked with Mr. Churchill in regard to this whole matter and we are in complete accord," FDR assured Bush.[24] But by the summer, the clandestine balance was fast shifting. In Washington, FDR approved an all-out program, and mandated the army to devote all necessary resources on a top-priority basis to construct the bomb. In London, meanwhile, Churchill's advisers despairingly conceded the impracticability of a solely British atomic program. England was financially drained and still threatened by German aerial assaults. On July 30, Anderson jealously informed the prime minister that the Americans were "applying themselves with enthusiasm and a lavish expenditure, which we cannot rival, to experimental work over the whole field of Tube Alloys." Sadly, he admitted, insurmountable wartime handicaps required that atomic plants be constructed in the United States rather than England. Therefore, he advised, Churchill should expeditiously conclude arrangements to pursue "a combined Anglo-American effort" while the "dwindling asset" of British scientific cooperation was still something to offer. "We now have a real contribution to make to a 'merger,'" he judged. "Soon we shall have little or none."[25]

Conant and Bush, in turn, knew that as time passed they had more cards to play. Having laid down strict guidelines to "compartmentalize" access to atomic information for U.S. scientists and industrialists—and provoking a good deal of grumbling as a result—Conant resented the idea that British collaborators would gain that information, even on sectors of the project which they could not directly aid, valuable data that would assist their own long-term military and industrial atomic enterprises. The "fundamental difficulty" of having English scientists working on S-1 in the U.S., he grumbled in May, lay in their not being "essentially responsible to anyone in this country."26

By the end of the summer, as Groves and the army took over the implementation phase of the Manhattan Project and it moved into higher gear, OSRD skepticism about the usefulness of British aid was rising quickly. Now it was Bush who responded leisurely and vaguely to anxious inquiries from Anderson aimed at acquiring data from U.S. experiments and cementing arrangements for joint projects. In October, Conant congratulated Bush on a "masterly evasive reply" that, without a single misstatement, deferred Anderson's principal requests until later discussions.27 In conferences and memos, Conant indoctrinated Bush, Stimson, and through them, FDR with his reservations about exchanging data with the British, pointing out that the importance of their potential contributions to the project had shrunk to the point that it was not needed in most areas and dispensable in others. Conant wrote to Bush on October 26 that he saw "no reason for a joint enterprise as far as development and manufacture is concerned," since American taxpayers were footing the bill and Britain was unable to profit from its knowledge to advance the war. "Does it make any difference," he concluded, "which among the Allies manufactures the munitions?"28

In the case of the atomic bomb, it certainly did, as Conant well knew. What he had attempted to highlight was his contention that no *military* justification existed for full interchange: if American participants in the project were expected to adhere to a "need-to-know" security policy, why should an exception be made for the British? Were an agreement to be reached that allowed the British to gain the fruits of American efforts in all areas of the atomic project, that entailed a careful political decision made with awareness of potential postwar consequences.29

Informed by Bush of the OSRD views, which were wholeheartedly supported by the Anglophobic Groves, Stimson duly informed Roosevelt at the end of October that the United States was doing ninety percent of the work on the bomb project, and that the OSRD leadership was anxious to discover just how far the president had committed Washington to a full exchange with Britain.30 The answer was that interchange rested on a series of vague, general oral and written statements that had included enough ambiguity for each side to interpret to its own advantage.

There the matter rested, in uneasy limbo, when Akers and Conant sat down together in late November. Conant had been chosen to represent the American side because as chairman of the OSRD's S-1 Executive Committee his status was most nearly analogous to that of Akers, a senior engineer on the board of the giant Imperial Chemical Industries (ICI) conglomerate whom Churchill had tapped to head his government's uranium research program (reporting to Anderson at the cabinet level). Before the talks had started, Bush had instructed Conant to insist on terminating interchange except where the British could clearly help to advance the bomb's completion, and to put off all consideration of after-the-war relations.[31] Conant, who was used to tough bargaining with faculty over budgets and hiring, adopted what seemed to be a sure-fire negotiating stance: like any other scientists or agency, the British should be permitted access only to those aspects of the Manhattan Project to which they could contribute—on all other areas, they would be cut out.

Neither man initially admitted that his respective government's positions on interchange reflected postwar interests. But slowly, the delicately concealed mutual uneasiness about the other side's long-term motives began to creep into their conversations. Conant, like Groves, exasperated Akers by declaring that secrecy required rigid enforcement of compartmentalization even between Allies. Firmly rejecting his arguments, Akers insisted that top-level understandings between FDR and Churchill entitled Britain to full information on all aspects of the project; Conant, in turn, was willing formally to acknowledge the importance of early British research to the project, but now adamantly stuck to narrow war-related criteria. Personal distrust further soured the atmosphere. Akers wrote to his associates in London that he was "wasting his time" by talking with Conant, who didn't understand physics, being only an organic chemist, lacked influence with the army, and was little more than a "post-box," and "tries to keep to himself, without delegation, the execution of higher policy matters and, at the same time, tries to run Harvard and half a dozen other whole time jobs."[32] In fact, Akers seems to have fallen victim to a typical Conant snow job, in which he shrewdly hid his knowledge to avoid exposing his position. (Eight months later, Akers advised British officials that "the most important thing really is to get into really good relations with Conant" who, he now concluded, strongly influenced the decisions of Groves and Bush.)[33] Another corrosive factor was Akers's well-founded hunch that the protestations by Conant and Groves that wartime secrecy was their paramount consideration masked other goals, the most important of which was a "desire to build up a monopoly in this field for the USA."[34]

For his part, Conant more than reciprocated Akers's suspicions, rapidly concluding that his attitude showed just how much the British were angling to exploit the Manhattan Project to bolster their postwar position. For one thing, there were close relations in Britain among the government, the official atomic establishment, and the industry most likely to profit from peacetime applications of nuclear power. Imperial Chemical held a virtual monopoly in the chemical field, would undertake any government work in atomic energy development, and, given full interchange, stood in an ideal position to exploit U.S.-supplied information; in the United States, by contrast, firms competed for assignments on the various aspects of the project, and worked under the compartmentalization rules; no one company would have advantages comparable to ICI's when the war ended. That Akers and another British atomic delegate "have both been high in the I.C.I. Councils" further irked Conant, who believed (probably mistakenly) that the entire controversy might have been avoided had the British negotiators been scientists comparable to Bush and himself.[35] A clue to his reasoning in the secret dispute seeped into public view in a speech he gave in February 1943, "Science and Society in the Post-War World," delivered to a New York City educational group. Noting the necessity of large investments for the development of a new scientific idea or discovery, he added: "No one will risk the capital necessary for this development work . . . unless he is assured that a commercial rival will not enjoy the financial benefits which come from this investment."[36]

When Akers learned that the OSRD leaders felt he had acted out of postwar commercial interests, he vehemently denied the charge. Some historians have attributed Conant's chilliness toward Akers to his surmise that the ICI employee was hoping to further his firm's postwar commercial prospects,[37] but Conant may have been even more troubled by a different postwar motive to which Akers *did* admit. The official British atomic history relates that Akers argued that "America might become isolationist again after the war and might tell Britain to accept responsibility for keeping peace in Europe; Britain must therefore have full knowledge of the manufacture of probably the main really effective police weapon."[38] Or, in Akers's own words: "I made it clear that Britain would want to have full knowledge of any large scale plant put up in America, as we would very likely be left with the job of keeping order in Europe, and we would want the best weapons for this purpose."[39]

Even at a distance of half a century, one can hear the alarm bells sounding in Conant's brain. Miscalculating disastrously, Akers made the argument most likely to alienate his audience. For all his admiration for British pluck, nothing had changed Conant's determination, firmly held since mid-1940 at the latest, that the United States should emerge from the war in the driver's seat of what he described as a "new world order," with isolationism dead and replaced by a new American "expansionism."[40] Moreover, he remained firmly convinced that Washington must be the "top dog" and "chief shareholder" of any Anglo-American military alliance, willing to engage in "selfish," "hard-boiled and cruel" bargaining with London to receive a quid pro quo for any concession. "I share the suspicion of many on the other side of the fence," he had written during the pre-Pearl Harbor debates against the isolationists, "that we might be called upon to make undue sacrifices to protect the British Empire."[41] Perhaps Akers, reasonably enough, had figured that his gambit would neatly fit the Rooseveltian conception of Britain as a partner in an Anglo-American international police force (later expanded, with the Soviet Union and China, to "Four Policemen") to guard the peace of the postwar world, a concept FDR had communicated to Churchill as early as the Atlantic Conference in August 1941.[42] But so far as Conant was concerned, "Give us the tools and we shall finish the job" was the wrong line to take when the "tools" were atomic bombs; equating the prospective weapons with the attributes of global leadership, he disdained to help Britain cling to American coattails as it was edged aside.

Yet Conant knew that he had no right to decide such policy issues. Heedful that they required consideration at higher political and diplomatic levels, he found it more expedient, and more than sufficient, to base a strong recommendation for restrictive interchange solely on the grounds of wartime security—and by the time his talks with Akers had been suspended, the success of Fermi's chain reaction experiment in Chicago bolstered Conant's confidence that the United States was well headed toward a successful nuclear project for power and weapons whether or not the British cooperated. In a December 14, 1942, memorandum to Bush, he laid out what he considered to be the alternatives for a presidential directive to settle the whole tangled matter. Bush should tell FDR, Conant wrote, that "there is presumably only one reason for free interchange of secret military information between allied nations, namely, to further the prosecution of the war in which both are engaged." As neither England nor Canada had the capability or intention of constructing plants to manufacture fissile material, "our passing our knowledge to them will not assist the British in any way in the present war effort." Using the classic bureaucratic technique of bracketing a favored option by two seemingly extreme ones, Conant said the president could select one of three courses: "(A) Cessation of all interchange"; "(B) Complete interchange not only in the research field but in development and production, including free interchange of personnel"; or "(C) Restricted interchange along clearly defined lines," meaning that the British would be permitted access to information only in areas in which they were already working. Excluding international complications outside of the atomic project, Conant argued that restricted interchange, alternative C, was in the best interests of the United States; failing that, he preferred a complete break in the relationship.[43]

"British may not *accept* C," Bush scrawled across the memo.[44] Recognizing that possibility, Conant minimized the effects of choosing A: a group of British scientists working on "heavy water" manufacture of plutonium could certainly be utilized, but their departure "would not hamper the effort greatly"; knowledge of British development of the diffusion process would be "helpful" but "not vital" for Americans working on a diffusion plant. In sum, he wrote, "there would be no serious hindrance to the whole project. . . ."[45] Bush incorporated Conant's analysis and advice, almost word for word, in a December 15 report to Roosevelt. More than six weeks earlier, after being told that the United States was doing "nine-tenths of the work" on the bomb as compared to Britain, the president had agreed with Stimson that it was "better for us to go along for the present without sharing anything more than we could help." More recently, his confidence in Britain's discretion had been shaken upon learning of a recent Anglo-Soviet pact to exchange scientific data related to weapons research, and on December 28 he approved the OSRD recommendation, also endorsed by Groves and Stimson, sharply to curtail interchange with Britain.[46]

Conant moved briskly in the first days of 1943 to secure U.S. national control of the fast-growing atomic effort. To put the new policy into effect, in early January he drafted a memorandum that bluntly set out Washington's terms for a revised Anglo-American atomic collaboration:

> This memorandum sets forth the general rules and regulations for interchange of information with the British and Canadians. It derives from the basic principle that interchange on design and construction of new weapons and equipment is to be carried out only to the extent that the recipient of the information is in a position to take advantage of this information in this war. Since neither the Canadian nor the British Governments are in a position to produce elements "49" [Plutonium, or element 94] and "25" [Uranium-235], our interchange has correspondingly been restricted by orders from the top.

Accordingly, he continued, the British and Canadians were to be excluded from most of the scientific and industrial work of the Manhattan Project—from all manufacturing and bomb design data, details of the electromagnetic method, the production of heavy water, and fast neutron reactions—and to be let in on restricted aspects of the diffusion process and the heavy-water research at Chicago and Columbia only insofar as the work could directly aid the American centers. Transmission of "basic scientific information" to Britain and Canada, in all but a few categories, would be permitted "only on direct approval of the chairman of the S-1 Executive Committee"—Conant himself.[47]

When they got wind of Conant's long-awaited new policy directive, Britain's atomic leaders seethed with anger and consternation, and enlisted Churchill to go over the heads of what they perceived as a hostile Manhattan Project praetorian guard composed of the army and OSRD. "This development has come as a bombshell and is quite intolerable," Sir John Anderson minuted the prime minister. "I think that you may wish to ask President Roosevelt to go into the matter without delay." One could not help suspecting, he wrote, "that the United States Military Authorities who are now in complete control wish to gain an advance upon us and feel that having benefited from the fruits of our early endeavors they will not suffer unduly by casting us aside." Erroneously presuming that Conant had acted without presidential authorization, the British sent out feelers to Washington to discern the motives behind the new policy, and beginning at Casablanca in late January Churchill lobbied Roosevelt and his chief confidant, Harry Hopkins, repeatedly over the coming months to restore full collaboration. A series of telegrams expressed his anguish over the breakdown in collaboration and hinted that Britain would soon have no choice but to resort to an independent program. "I am much concerned at not hearing from you about Tube Alloys," he wired Hopkins on April 1. "That we should each work separately would be a sombre decision."[48] Meanwhile, science administrators in both countries worked to pressure the other side into capitulation and to compile a respectable-looking record should the secret squabble erupt into a gargantuan public scandal.

Confident that working-level U.S. scientists opposed the restrictive policy, London refused to permit British-sponsored scientists to cooperate officially with the Manhattan Project under the guidelines set down in Conant's memorandum and, with more bravado than realism, threatened to prosecute an independent project. The maneuvering had commenced even before Akers left Washington, when Conant invited Rudolf Peierls and James Chadwick to visit the United States to meet Manhattan Project physicists who were about to go into isolation at Los Alamos, though Akers had already forewarned him that London would veto any such trip until the interchange issue was clarified; he deemed it wise to put the request on the record anyway as a display of enthusiasm for continued cooperation, albeit on U.S. terms.[49]

A far more nettlesome point of contention involved a planned visit to New York City by Hans von Halban, the head of a British-Canadian scientific team in Montreal that was investigating problems in the use of heavy water, which the Americans eagerly sought to use as a moderator for the nuclear core of chain reactors used in the production of plutonium. Under Conant's memorandum, complete interchange was to be permitted between Halban's Montreal team and the scientists working at the Met Lab in Chicago. Instead of relying on the British-Canadian heavy-water plant in Trail, British Columbia, however, the OSRD elected to contract with the Du Pont Company to erect an American heavy-water plant that would assure self-sufficiency in plutonium production. With that plant still in its early stages, Manhattan Project scientists working in Chicago under Fermi and Glenn Seaborg and at Columbia under Harold Urey, as well as Conant, expectantly looked forward to a March 9 review meeting in New York City to compare experimental results with Halban, who had conducted pioneering work on heavy water at Cambridge University in England. But rather than seem to acquiesce in the new ground rules, London ordered Halban to cancel the visit in order to "bring home to the United States authorities the very serious view which we take of their present attitude."[50]

Conant effectively countered with a sly maneuver—ardently wooing the Canadian leadership by dangling promises of cooperation, expressing sympathy for Ottawa's balancing act between London and Washington, and cultivating what Akers derisively described as a "very active mutual admiration society" with the head of the Canadian project, C. J. Mackenzie.[51] Reading over a series of missives enticing Mackenzie to break the ranks of the British boycott, a peeved Sir John Anderson wrote to the British high commissioner in Ottawa, "I trust that Mackenzie will not lend himself to this blatant attempt by Conant to divide ourselves and the Canadians in this matter."[52] Yet Britain could only watch in frustration as Canada drifted closer to her southern neighbor.

The calculated British refusal to cooperate with Conant's memorandum did succeed, however, in the intended goal of riling some Manhattan Project scientists. The March 9 meeting at Columbia went off without Halban and with Conant, Groves, Urey, Fermi, and a Du Pont representative in attendance, and all present, especially Fermi and Urey, voiced sharp regret at Halban's absence, especially as it was hoped that the Montreal team could perform critical experiments to resolve uncertainties over the heavy-water plant; Conant, however, miffed by London and unimpressed by the Montreal operation, determined that the OSRD would refuse to follow through on a plan to send Halban heavy water, and instead arranged for Du Pont to conduct the experiment.[53] These disruptions deeply angered Urey, who fired off a series of irate letters to Conant, climaxed by a blast on June 21 charging that the failure to establish a cooperative relationship with the British and Halban had damaged critical research on barriers needed for the diffusion method, delaying his heavy-water investigations by six months to a year or more. The cutoff in ties with Britain "had no justification on scientific or technical grounds," Urey wrote, and if the decision to eschew full cooperation with Britain were made "on nationalist grounds by the highest authority, I hope that this authority was advised of the possible delay that might result from our not being able to use the only considerable supply of heavy water available."[54]

Urey's letter infuriated Conant, for he knew why the British had vetoed Halban's trip to New York.[55] Fearing that Urey was building a record that would be used against the Manhattan Project if the war should end before a bomb was built and used, Conant quickly rebutted him in a long letter and met with him to try to persuade him that his complaint stemmed from "misinformation and erroneous analysis."[56] Although the two men subsequently exchanged "Dear Jim" and "Dear Harold" letters affirming undying trust in each other's sincerity,[57] the disagreements were rancorous. A decade later, Halban still steamed about the incident, as a visitor recorded:

> Halban said Conant was a son of a bitch. During the war when he, Halban, had been working on the British atomic scientists team, Conant, the great liberal, had gotten up and made a speech saying: "In this business it is necessary to double-cross your own brother." Later Halban saw Conant on behalf of the British government to arrange to have American heavy water sent to Canada to help the British experiments. Conant was most affable and

promised to do everything possible to cooperate and send an adequate supply immediately. Halban later found that Conant had gone to see Vannevar Bush afterward and arranged that no single drop of heavy water would be sent.[58]

Urey, equally, could hardly contain his ire, and aside from writing to Conant directly vented his spleen to his fellow Manhattan Project scientists, spreading the perception that the OSRD leaders put nationalistic political concerns ahead of the most rapid completion of the bomb. In July, Conant was outraged to learn that Urey had commiserated with a disgruntled scientist from the Met Lab, agreeing with his complaint that the OSRD's inept administration and hand-over to Du Pont had delayed the reactor project by six months. "I must say," he huffed to Bush, "that Dr. Urey's statements to a man who he knew was acting in this dissenting capacity . . . seemed to me an extremely disloyal way for a member of the S-1 Committee to behave. . . . "[59] Conant on various occasions grudgingly acknowledged that a complete severing of atomic ties with Britain might harm certain aspects of the Manhattan Project, for some useful personnel would be lost. From this and other memoranda, the historian Martin J. Sherwin in *A World Destroyed* concludes that Conant and Bush "did not regard rapid development of the atomic bomb as the primary concern" in recommending interchange policy, but were instead more interested in ensuring a postwar American monopoly of the weapon.[60]

Certainly, Conant had from an early date grasped the potential postwar military and diplomatic significance of atomic weapons. It was "of the utmost importance," he had written Bush in December 1942, that the bomb's capabilities be determined "before the question of policing the postwar world comes up for debate."[61] Even more than fears of British commercial exploitation, fission's long-term military implications made Conant wary of an overly tight Anglo-American collaboration. To permit Britain total knowledge of the design, construction, and plants necessary to produce material for atomic weapons—"a military secret which is in a totally different class from anything the world has ever seen if the potentialities of this project are realized"—might be "the equivalent to joint occupation of a strategic harbor in perpetuity rather than alienating complete control!"[62] In deciding the extent of the partnership, Conant told Bush on March 26, 1943, "The major consideration must be that of national security and postwar strategic significance."[63] Transmitting these views to the president's attention a few days later, Bush stressed to Harry Hopkins that the president must not commit himself to a permanently binding relationship to Britain "simply as incident" to the bomb project.[64]

Did Conant now believe postwar considerations sufficiently important to justify possible delay of the Manhattan Project's completion? Was the man who calculated that Germany might have a year and a half's lead on the United States and stood an even chance of using atomic bombs by mid-1945 willing to take such a gamble? The evidence shows that Conant already looked beyond the defeat of Germany and Japan to "policing the post-war era," but not that he was willing to sacrifice the earliest completion date for a usable bomb in World War II. A key assumption in Conant's thinking during the controversy was that a total cessation of Anglo-American ties would not damage his favorite "horse" in the fissionable-material production race: the electromagnetic separation process under Lawrence's direction at the University of California Radiation Laboratory. In contrast to his qualms over other, more ambitious methods, Conant waxed optimistic over Lawrence's slower but relatively straightforward project, which used cyclotrons (dubbed "calutrons" in honor of the University of California) to whirl uranium atoms in a circle and methodically accumulate traces of the rare, lighter U-235 isotope. In the fall of 1942, Conant told Lawrence he was "truly thankful" for his method, for it would "surely work."[65] The S-1 Review Committee examining the different routes "overemphasizes the difficulties of the electromagnetic method and underestimates the advantage of having at least one bomb by the end of 1944," Conant wrote Groves on December 9. "The Committee, I understand, admits that the electromagnetic method is the one sure bet of producing material and agrees that even with its present limitations one can 'pull through' such a program to give enough material to try out one bomb by the end of 1944. I believe this is of the utmost importance. . . ."[66]

Unlike the diffusion method—where British exclusion could hurt—Conant believed that electromagnetic separation would yield enough material for a weapon even before completion of an entire plant. And even one bomb, he believed, "would be of great comfort" and a "great psychological advantage if the Germans were to start the use of such material before our complete production."[67] He evidently did not believe that lack of British help would actually push back the date of the first completed bomb, even if it did slow down overall production.

So long as there were no serious threats to the success of the bomb project, then, Conant's objective was to safeguard U.S. interests against what he regarded as British encroachment in the commercial sphere and, more importantly, against a partnership that would foreclose American foreign policy and military options after the war. He and Bush were acutely conscious, moreover, of the danger that Congress, still in the dark about the project, might well repudiate any secret agreement that extended beyond wartime imperatives.

Roosevelt's priorities differed. He knew that the Allies still faced years of arduous battle against Japan in Asia and the Pacific, and an enormous land war against Germany, including the planned invasion of the European continent, and he desired a harmonious Anglo-American alliance and a smooth relationship with Churchill; both appeared endangered by the quarrel over restricted interchange. Moreover, he sympathized with Churchill's desire to retain a strong postwar Britain to counter Russian influence in Europe.[68] Unwilling to alienate his closest ally and without informing his OSRD atomic advisers, Roosevelt consented at the Trident summit in Washington in May 1943 to Churchill's urgent requests to resume full atomic collaboration.[69]

A few more surprises remained before the curtain came down on the altercation. Having promised cooperation, Roosevelt took his time before taking action, moving only after Hopkins confirmed that he had given his word to Churchill. By late July, when FDR transmitted a message to the OSRD to "renew, on an inclusive basis," interchange with Britain, the matter was already being discussed in vigorous fashion at 10 Downing Street in London by Churchill, Anderson, and Cherwell (Lindemann) on one side, and, on the other, three Americans well-placed to dispose of the matter—Stimson, Bush, and Harvey Bundy. The British officials and scientists were desperate to get back in the Americans' good graces, having considered and dropped the idea of an independent nuclear project. After months of evasions and double-talk, these Americans and Britons spoke straightforwardly about the issues that had separated them for almost a year. Churchill recited the sorry history of broken American promises of full collaboration, but then he cleared the air by stating openly that he disclaimed any rights to postwar commercial exploitation; at the same time, he set forth the other postwar motive, as Akers had to Conant: possession of the atomic bomb would be "necessary for Britain's independence in the future," since otherwise the Soviet Union—the absent ally against Hitler—might one day be in a position to wield the weapon as a tool of "international blackmail" unless the United States and Great Britain "worked together." At that juncture Stalin's massive army was heroically turning back the German army on the Eastern Front while the British remained bogged down in a slow-moving campaign in North Africa and Sicily, and this only enhanced a sense of future insecurity. That dark intimation of a postwar falling out among the Allies receded into the background, however, when Churchill proposed a new Anglo-American atomic pact enshrining joint control over the bomb's use and ceding to the U.S. president the authority to limit Great Britain's commercial or industrial rights to atomic power.[70]

That sounded reasonable to the Americans, who had not yet received FDR's instructions to renew atomic interchange on an "inclusive basis." Back in Washington, however, the president's message had gone to OSRD head-quarters at 1530 P Street, where an upset Conant dictated for the record his conviction that complete interchange would be a "mistake" and, outside of those areas already specified in his earlier memorandum, a "pure waste of time as far as the job of winning this war is concerned."[71] Fearing that Bush and Stimson had also given their blessing to resumption of full interchange, he grumped that perhaps he should join the staff of the rabidly anti-British *Chicago Tribune*.[72] But his mood brightened considerably when he and Bush saw Anderson in Washington on August 4, and discovered that the British now seemed willing to accept the original American terms for restricted interchange, with the exception of the provision for communications at the head-of-state level.[73]

On August 19, 1943, Roosevelt and Churchill buried their eight-month disagreement, at least temporarily, when they initialed the Quebec Agreement providing for the resumption of "full and effective collaboration" on Tube Alloys. Under the accord, Roosevelt and Churchill pledged that the United States and Great Britain would never use atomic weapons against each other, and would obtain mutual consent before employing "this agency" against, or communicating any information regarding it to, any third party. But Churchill also accepted that "postwar advantages of an industrial or commercial character" would be stipulated by the president of the United States to the prime minister of Britain, "in view of the heavy burden of production falling upon the United States." More immediately, the agreement provided for an atomic interchange along the basic lines acceptable to Bush and Conant. Rather than allowing full British participation in plant construction and development, it established a high-level joint Combined Policy Committee to review overall project progress and resolve lingering questions.[74] The OSRD advisers had won something of a pyrrhic victory at Quebec (to which they were not invited). Churchill later defended the pact by saying that while it "may be judged to have been too confiding on our part," his actions could be understood only by "those who knew the circumstances and moods prevailing beneath the [U.S.] Presidential level."[75] However, the pact also formalized and strengthened the Anglo-American military and political bonds in a manner that seemed to promise nuclear collaboration beyond the immediate conflict: Conant's pleas for the United States to retain maximum flexibility for the postwar period had been ignored.

The whole episode exposed a growing rift between Roosevelt and his atomic energy advisers: on technical issues Bush's and Conant's recommendations still went unquestioned at the White House, but when atomic matters entered the diplomatic realm, that was Roosevelt's exclusive territory. The Quebec pact—not publicly revealed until 1954, and partially repudiated by the Truman administration—had contained several clauses with which Conant and Bush had "nothing to do and which had postwar implications."[76] Specifically, although they knew the British wanted them, Bush and Conant expressly did not recommend presidential agreement to the clauses requiring joint action on the bomb's use or on transmitting information to third parties, and were not told that Roosevelt had accepted the British draft without changing a word.[77]

Roosevelt never again brought up the subject in his conferences with Bush. Not until a year later—September 1944—did Bush and Conant discover just how little Roosevelt had relied on their advice. But it is apparent that by the time of the Quebec Conference they already suspected that their views on the diplomatic implications of the atomic bomb were not in great demand in the Oval Office. Certainly the dispute had not made for more comfortable relations between Roosevelt and the officials he ostensibly turned to on atomic matters, or encouraged them to speak up on potentially explosive diplomatic issues that might be considered beyond the purview of technical advisers.

Bush and Conant worried that Roosevelt did not completely grasp the meaning of their opposition to complete interchange, and they tried to limit the damage to their influence. Shortly before Roosevelt left for Quebec, Bush urged Bundy to tell Stimson to relay a message to the president. It was "vital," he implored Bundy, that Roosevelt "understand that what Dr. Bush and Dr. Conant are really trying to do is to work out the agreement for interchange of information so that nobody, including the political opponents of the President, will be in the position to say that he acted otherwise than under the war powers and for the sole purpose of winning the war." Bush and Conant strongly favored an arrangement reached on a quid pro quo basis and aimed solely at expediting the bomb project; they were "trying to avoid at all costs the President being accused of dealing with hundreds of millions of taxpayers' money improvidently or acting for purposes beyond the winning of the war by turning over great power in the postwar world to the U.K. without adequate consideration and action by both Executive and Legislative authority."[78] Whether or not Stimson conveyed this message to Roosevelt is not known.[79] But its substance and tone—a plea for understanding that appealed to the president's political sensibilities—shows they recognized the dangers of steadfastly supporting a position not in line with the President's views.

Anglo-American interchange resumed quickly with British scientists trickling into Manhattan Project labs at Los Alamos, Berkeley, and elsewhere by late 1943, but the eight-month secret dispute left ruffled feelings on both sides. To one of the several English physicists dispatched to the United States after the Quebec Conference, Conant confessed that one reason behind "the general coyness" of the Americans had been a feeling that the British were "so much more adroit in negotiation" that they tended to get the better of any deal. "It is all very flattering and it may even have some basis of truth," sniped Akers privately to his colleagues in London, "as there seem to be a surprising number of stupid Americans about if one judges from what they say about each other, as reported in their Press."[80]

But the most impressive coda was delivered obliquely by Winston Churchill, with Conant beside him, only two weeks after the Quebec Agreement restored Anglo-American atomic harmony. On September 6, after an overnight train ride from Washington following late-night talks at the White House with FDR, Churchill and his wife were greeted in Boston by Mr. and Mrs. Conant and escorted to Harvard, where a special convocation was set—secretly, for security reasons—to award the visiting prime minister an honorary doctor of laws degree. Though "the PM" was running a temperature from a cold, he had taken the speech he was to deliver seriously and had stayed up until a quarter to three in the morning preparing it. FDR, too, took a keen interest in the ceremony, "sticking pins into Conant" to assure that Harvard matched "English standards in pomp and color."[81]

On reaching Cambridge, the Churchills were brought by their hosts to the colonial Dana Palmer House in a corner of the Yard serving as the temporary presidential residence (the navy had commandeered 17 Quincy Street). Along with having lunch at the Fogg Museum and inspecting Harvard military units from the steps of Memorial Church, the cigar-smoking states- man had an opportunity to chat with Patty Conant of his plans to write a history of the war, to dispense advice on oratory technique (improvisation works best because "you have a sense of your audience"), to declaim poetry, and to complain that he had been too busy to paint since the war started. He also had a few moments to converse privately about the atomic bomb with Conant, whom he had last seen in blacked-out London in 1941.[82] Though the substance of their exchange is not known, the subject formed a secret subtext to Churchill's public utterances that afternoon from the stage of Sanders Theatre. Like the tercentenary seven years earlier, it was a moment instantly burned into Harvard history—the ruddy-cheeked British leader, resplendent in a black coat, gray flannel trousers and bow tie beneath a scarlet robe, holding a black velvet hat and flashing a V-for-Victory sign, and Conant a few steps away in formal cap-and-gown, as the hastily assembled crowd of more than six thousand uniformed men studying in army and navy training courses roared.

Stressing the "ties of blood and history," of law, language, and literature uniting Britain and the United States, Churchill captured considerable public attention by proposing a common Anglo-American citizenship, proclaiming the death of isolationism and urging a continuation of military and political alliance even beyond the end of the war. But for Conant, one of the very few people there who were aware of the atomic project, Churchill's words had an extra meaning—from his opening quip, a twinkle in his eye, that he was glad to return to "academic groves—groves is, I believe, the right word—" to his prophecy that "the empires of the future are the empires of the mind," which Conant took to refer to the twentieth-century battles to come over ideology and weaponry that had supplanted nineteenth-century struggles over ter- ritory.[83] And he surely discerned the hidden agenda in Churchill's heartfelt plea to preserve the closely intermingled Anglo-American military relationship, including a combined chiefs of staff committee, on an indefinite basis:

Now in my opinion it would be a most foolish and improvident act on the part of our two Governments, or either of them, to break up this smooth- running and immensely powerful machinery the moment the war is over. For our own safety, as well as for the security of the rest of the world, we are bound to keep it for a good many years, not only until we have set up some world arrangement to keep the peace, but until we know that it is an

arrangement which will really give us that protection we must have from
danger and aggression, a protection we have already had to seek across two
vast world wars.[84]

Conant, however, doubted whether in a world endangered by atomic
weapons an Anglo-American alliance would best serve the goal of preventing
future world wars. Even as he bore down on Manhattan Project scientists to
complete the bomb in time for use in the war, Conant now began to devote
increasing attention to the question of how the United States should seek to
control the bomb—through national monopoly, international control, or limited alliance—in the postwar world. And if the interchange dispute had
shown how difficult resolving atomic issues could become between the closest of allies, how much more troublesome it would be to establish good
relations between the United States and the third member of the Grand
Alliance—the Soviet Union.

CHAPTER II

"Another Experimental Arrangement"

Conant, Bohr, and Fears of a Postwar Nuclear Arms Race

1944

> Alternatives[:] race between nations and in the next war destruction of civilization, or a scheme to remove atomic energy from the field of conflict.
> —JBC, "Some Thoughts on the International Control of Atomic Energy," May 4, 1944

International disputes aside, the Manhattan Project's technical and administrative problems gave Conant plenty of headaches, and the optimistic timetables dilated as the war dragged on in Europe and the Pacific.

Concerns over Germany's atomic enterprise lingered, especially as intelligence reports streamed in that Nazi engineers and scientists were building rockets that could conceivably deliver a nuclear warhead across the Channel to London. During 1943 the OSRD leaders investigated options for suitable "S-1 targets" in Germany for Allied bombers to strike, and Conant, who accorded the highest priority to destroying the Kaiser-Wilhelm institutes of physics and chemistry in Dahlem, where Werner Heisenberg and Otto Hahn worked, collected and passed to the War Department data on the identities and locations of German scientists likely to be laboring on atomic weapons; in June Bush promised Roosevelt that arrangements to hit German atomic sites were "now under way."[1] As Thomas Powers has noted, Conant during this period also "very probably knew" of Manhattan Project plotting to kidnap or assassinate Heisenberg, plans which in late 1944 led to the sending of an agent to neutral Switzerland with instructions to shoot the visiting physicist should he seem close to finishing an atomic weapon.[2]

Nazi vows in late 1943 to end the war "by one fell, drastic stroke,"[3] meanwhile, only intensified the nervousness and grumbling among some Manhattan Project scientists about the apparently slow pace of the U.S. effort. And their complaints, particularly at the Met Lab in Chicago, quickly translated into resentment of the project's top administrators: Groves, Conant, and Bush.

Conant received numerous signs of the volcano simmering below him. As the chairman of the S-1 Executive Committee he had helped to lay the structure and chart the direction of the project, and, Leo Szilard later recalled, many disgruntled scientists believed Conant's views always prevailed, "and so the committee's decisions were mostly regarded as Dr. Conant's decisions."[4] Szilard, one of a growing number of Chicago scientists whose direct and indirect criticisms of Conant filtered up to OSRD headquarters, wrote to Bush repeatedly requesting interviews to discuss the widespread and "keenly felt" dissatisfaction he perceived.[5] "My guess is Szilard will not be satisfied with seeing me," Conant noted after reading one such missive. "He thinks I am one of the evil doers."[6] Clearly, the feeling was mutual. "I think Szilard is interested primarily in building a record on the basis of which to make a 'stink' after the war is over," Conant wrote to Bush at one point. "He & [Eugene] Wigner are very anxious to build a record against the management and I want a full hearing on that when the time comes!"[7] Szilard's gripes ranged from principled concern over postwar atomic dangers to a violent contempt for what he regarded as the absurdities of the compartmentalization system, to alleged managerial defects that were delaying the bomb's construction, to an exhaustive battle over patent rights — and they were so exasperating that in the spring of 1945 Groves once seriously proposed interning Szilard. When Stimson vetoed that idea, he instead suggested to Conant that he hire Szilard on the Harvard faculty to "get him out of my hair," with the U.S. government footing his salary, since the reassignment so obviously aided the national interest. Conant refused, telling Groves that the government "couldn't pay him enough to take on the headache of having Szilard at Harvard," and he didn't know any other university that would take him, either.[8]

Bush, Conant, and Groves sidetracked Szilard's complaints before they reached the Oval Office, but in 1943 a well-connected young Met Lab physicist, Irving S. Lowen, managed to obtain an interview with FDR to air his concerns over mismanagement of the project, and over the course of several months fretted to a wide assortment of Washington figures, including Felix Frankfurter, Bernard Baruch, and Eleanor Roosevelt. Conant received requests from FDR on several occasions to calm the worried scientist but met with limited success. In meetings in July and December 1943, Conant found Lowen "obviously sincere," but learned nothing besides new details of the scientists' resentment at how he had handled the transfer of plutonium production from the University of Chicago to Du Pont as the work progressed from laboratory experiments to mass production. The scientists who had accomplished the world's first controlled nuclear chain reaction did not want to lose control to military and industrial officials, and they fumed over what they considered avoidable logjams; it was "common knowledge" at Chicago,

Lowen reported, that Du Pont had delayed the project as much as six months. "[Lowen's] story reflects the dissenting opinion of certain physicists in the Chicago group who seem to me to fail to understand the difficulties of large scale [manufacturing] and the responsibilities of the duPont Company," Conant recorded in his "S-1 Diary," adding, "Human nature as well as nuclear physics cause their difficulties."[9] Conant found even less pleasant the report that Urey had confided to Lowen resentment at being "constantly overruled in this project and, in general, agreed with the bill of complaints" against the OSRD managers.[10] With few exceptions, Conant later insisted in *My Several Lives,* his Manhattan Project critics "did not know the score." But resentment over his actions in the spat with Britain had surely exacerbated the atmosphere of backbiting and resentment, especially among scientists working at the Met Lab and with Urey at Columbia.

More significantly, these bitter internecine disagreements generated a distrust among many atomic scientists toward the Manhattan Project's leadership that increased the prospects for subsequent misunderstanding when the issue concerned the weapon's postwar diplomatic and political significance. Critics who regarded Conant's management as unenlightened assumed that his understanding of atomic energy's potential for the future — both its threat and its promise — to be similarly limited.

For the time being, however, most of the agitation revolved around concern over the future of nuclear research, security restrictions, and resentment of industrial inroads into the Manhattan Project.[11] Only scattered voices were heard regarding the bomb's long-range dangers: appropriately, given his prescience in calling attention to the possibility of constructing the weapon, Szilard was one of the first. In a January 1944 letter to Bush, the iconoclastic Hungarian wrote that with expected advances "this weapon will be so powerful that there can be no peace if it is simultaneously in the possession of any two powers unless these two powers are bound by an indissoluble political union," and that some system of international control, "if necessary by force," would therefore be essential.[12] Though Szilard heard nothing from Bush to assuage his concern that the Manhattan Project's administrators were failing to grasp the bomb's long-range dangers, in fact Conant's views on the issue were developing in a comparably radical direction. But Conant neglected to communicate his awareness of the long-range peril to the scientists, and as a result of his secretiveness, historians have overlooked important aspects of the origins of U.S. policy on the international control of atomic weapons.

To date, most accounts of the initial wartime efforts to control the atomic bomb have centered on Niels Bohr, the illustrious Nobel prize–winning Danish physicist who was smuggled from Nazi-occupied Denmark to England in the fall of 1943 and subsequently traveled to the United States. Recognized the world over as the decipherer of the atomic nucleus, Bohr also derived stature from being widely acknowledged as a premier scientific spokesman on social issues. As Groves, Bush, and Conant hoped, Bohr lent his expertise and inspiring presence to the secret lab at Los Alamos; but the assignment he most took to heart was his own personal mission to alert the British and U.S. governments to what he saw as the bomb's revolutionary impact on the basic structure of international relations, and the danger of a postwar nuclear arms race between the United States and the Soviet Union.[13]

Bohr believed that the only chance of preserving peace once the bomb had been introduced lay in an open world devoid of military secrets: otherwise, suspicion would drive governments to build their own nuclear arsenals. The new weapons would necessitate a new approach to relations among nations, he believed, and unless an agreement could be obtained to bar atomic bombs, "any temporary advantage, however great, may be outweighed by a perpetual menace to human security."[14] In England in late 1943 Bohr discussed his ideas with Sir John Anderson, who was sympathetic; on visiting the United States that winter under the alias "Nicholas Baker," he confided them to British diplomats in Washington, who soon came to share his sense of urgency about creating a basis for postwar atomic cooperation.

But after the earlier tensions, the British had little confidence in the judgment, sympathy, or open-mindedness of the Manhattan Project's administrators, least of all Conant, whom they perceived as the culprit who disrupted Anglo-American atomic ties. FDR, by contrast, had overruled his advisers and taken Churchill's side. So, understandably, London's ambassador in Washington, Lord Halifax, advised Bohr that to have any chance of successfully promoting his views, he needed to somehow get directly in touch with the U.S. president, circumventing the OSRD.[15]

Conveniently enough, in mid-February 1944, Bohr encountered just the person for such a mission: Supreme Court Justice Felix Frankfurter, an old prewar acquaintance.[16] Nominally in the dark about the Manhattan Project, Frankfurter had already learned, from scientists seeking his counsel on the weapon's long-term political implications, that an atomic bomb was secretly under construction. A wary overture about a topic Frankfurter and Bohr called "X" established that both men were in the know. The justice quickly warmed to the Dane's arguments and promised to tell FDR, whom he predicted would be sympathetic. Like the British, however, Frankfurter had limited esteem for Conant, the most obvious target of such advice. Even before his departure from Harvard for the Supreme Court in 1939, the Walsh-Sweezy episode had convinced him that Conant was dogmatic and unimaginative, though he admired his interventionist activities. Though Frankfurter was now corresponding with Conant on various political and educational questions, and politely discussed getting together for dinner one evening when their busy schedules permitted, he had little inclination to approach Conant on the profound issues that Bohr had raised, or to recommend that Bohr do so.[17] Consequently, for the next eight months, Bohr relied on

Frankfurter as his intermediary to communicate and arrange meetings with
Roosevelt.

Bohr's failure to approach Conant is ironic, for Conant privately had
already come to many of the same conclusions and basic premises on what
needed to be done to prevent a postwar nuclear arms race. Several historians
have cited the ideas in Bohr's memoranda of the summer of 1944 as the basis
for U.S. postwar international control policy as expressed in the 1946 Acheson-
Lilienthal and Baruch plans, and suggest that Bohr's views, peremptorily
rebuffed by Churchill in May and gently brushed aside by Roosevelt a few
months later, did not gain currency with Conant and Vannevar Bush, until the
end of September.[18] In fact, the evidence shows that as early as in the spring
Conant had independently developed, in greater detail, many of the basic
features that characterized most of the postwar international control proposals.
Like Bohr—albeit with "optimism tempered by a realistic appraisal of inevitable opposition and with a natural tendency to a more prosaic embodiment
of ideas," as one historian has put it[19]—Conant recognized that nuclear
weapons raised fundamental questions about the very nature of international
organization. He initially laid down his thoughts on international control in an
informal handwritten document, dated May 4, 1944, which he apparently did
not circulate.[20] What stirred him to jot down his ideas is uncertain, though he
left a clue in an exchange with Bush two weeks earlier. Bush had briefly
summarized "our plans" for the postwar period—an official Manhattan Project
history (a document, suggested by Conant and Richard Tolman, that would
foster informed public discussion without disclosing military secrets), and a
domestic atomic energy commission with civilian and military representation.
In handwritten comments on the memo, Conant promised to draw up an
outline for domestic legislation and concluded: "Of course, for the very long
run, I'm inclined to think the only hope for humanity is an international
commission on atomic energy with free access to all information and right of
inspection."[21] On May 4 he elaborated on that sentence, beginning with a flat
statement indicating that he believed the bomb offered humanity a stark
choice: "Alternatives: race between nations and in the next war destruction
of civilization, or a scheme to remove atomic energy from the field of
conflict."

On general acceptance of that assessment rested Conant's hopes for the
organization whose structure he now sketched out—a powerful supranational
body with complete authority over all work on atomic energy conducted
anywhere on the globe. Run by a fifteen-member commission—including
three representatives each from the United States, Great Britain, and the
Soviet Union—Conant's hypothetical commission would license and finance
all atomic energy research and development. It would have full authority to
inspect laboratories and factories to ensure that no material was being diverted
for weapons. Commission members would act as "trustees and custodians" of
a nuclear arsenal, to be located in Canada (a location that perhaps reflected

Conant's progress in wooing Ottawa from London). The commission would control a force of airplanes and 10,000 men pledged to the international organization and to "prevention of seizure of supply." Interference with the commission's actions and freedom of movement, for any reason, would be considered an act of war, and commission members were required to declare war against any violator. With the offender disqualified from voting, the remaining members would decide whether or not to employ atomic bombs for this purpose. Any discovery of a nation secretly assembling prohibited weapons would be publicly announced, and the commission could then (presumably by force, if necessary) remove the weapons to its own arsenal. Conant then anticipated an obvious Soviet query: "What is to prevent Canada or U.S. or British seizing [the commission's] arsenal[?]" Answer: the arsenal's guards, and "use of bombs by arsenal guards on Canada or U.S."

An essential feature of Conant's plan—and the concept central to Bohr's thinking as well—was his provision that the commission would publish all information relating to atomic energy, including "full publicity as to raw materials, potential weapons, etc." In contemplating such basic alterations in the nation-state system—the abandonment of military secrecy, a sharing of national sovereignty in some respects tantamount to world government[22]— Conant did not figure on a sudden surge of idealism but on a cold, realistic analysis of the situation by statesmen. Once they perceived the threat represented by nuclear weapons, even politicians might recognize the need for, in Bohr's piquant phrase, "another experimental arrangement."[23]

Conant's private thoughts in May 1944 are particularly startling in light of the outward pessimism he had recently displayed. Many Americans, he had told Harvard alumni a few months earlier, were too utopian in hoping that a United Nations organization would be sufficient to prevent a third world war.[24] Conant frowned on utopianism—he considered himself a "tough-minded idealist" who shunned a "roseate view of human nature" and whose mode of action was the "calculated risk"[25]—but he apparently did not reject the idea that atomic weapons afforded at least the possibility of a breakthrough that might even extend beyond control of the bomb to total disarmament. "If this works what next?" he wrote after describing his proposed atomic commission.

> Next step, after a decade [would] be to enlarge scope of agreement and include all armament inspection and publication of figures.
>
> If eventually why not at start? Perhaps so. Might try International Commission on Military Science with powers above on atomic powers but powers of inspection and publication on all armaments problems and military secrets.
>
> What would be the result: Everyone would know where each nation stood???

The question marks perhaps expressed Conant's doubts that such radical ideas could ever be implemented. Significantly absent from the document, however, is any discussion of the problems of putting his system into operation. No mention occurs, either, of "stages" — the piecemeal approach that the U.S. government, and Conant, eventually adopted toward international control.

Surely he did not believe that gaining approval for such an audacious scheme would be easy. Yet Conant lacked the sense of urgency that drove Niels Bohr to all but plant himself on the doorsteps of No. 10 Downing Street and 1600 Pennsylvania Avenue. And unlike Bohr, Conant did not yet feel the circumstances justified the immediate diplomatic step of notifying the Soviet Union of the Manhattan Project's existence in hopes of gaining Moscow's confidence and thus easing the way toward an eventual agreement.

Nevertheless, Conant's outline suggests that Bohr's views would have touched a sympathetic chord had he presented them to him at this point. The sorry history of what actually occurred instead is well known. In mid-May Bohr had a "terrible" conversation with Churchill at which the British leader, distracted by Bohr's accent and manner, brusquely rebuffed the idea of revealing the secret of the Manhattan Project to Stalin. Bohr had somewhat better luck in changing Roosevelt's outlook, though not nearly as much as he first believed. In a meeting on August 26 set up by Frankfurter, and unknown at the time to Bush and Conant, Bohr received an outwardly cordial hearing without receiving any commitment of substantive action.[26]

In fact, Roosevelt's reaction to the session was far from enthusiastic. To begin with, he was disturbed by what he regarded as a possible breach of security, having learned of Bohr's interest from Frankfurter, who had no business in the matter, and this colored his impression of the physicist.[27] Having held no discussions with or received any recommendations on the subject of international control from his putative atomic advisers Bush and Conant, Roosevelt pliantly acceded to the urgings of the far more suspicious Churchill when the two met at Hyde Park a few weeks later. On September 19, they secretly signed an *aide-mémoire* pledging to continue the exclusive Anglo-American atomic alliance beyond the end of the war, rejecting Bohr's proposal to inform Stalin of the bomb's existence (which they misunderstood as informing "the world"), and even, in a gratuitous insult, ordering surveillance to assure that Bohr did not leak atomic data to the Soviets.[28]

Ignorant of this top-level intrigue over and rejection of Bohr's ideas, Conant in the summer of 1944 concentrated on other atomic matters. The long-awaited invasion of Nazi-occupied Europe by Allied forces in June had followed a year of secret fears that Germany might use radioactive material against the attacking forces on D–Day. In the summer of 1943 Conant had headed a secret S-1 Committee inquiry, along with Arthur Compton and Harold Urey, that urged the army to develop countermeasures should the Germans employ radiological warfare, leading Groves to order "Operation

'Peppermint' " to prepare for that contingency. They also had not neglected the possibility that the United States might retaliate in kind, delicately stating that "*if* military authorities feel that the United States should be ready to use such weapons in case the enemy started to use it first, such studies should be initiated immediately."[29] Conant's qualms about going first appear to have been not moral scruples but worries about the practical obstacles of uniformly or efficiently distributing radioactive particles or gas over enemy territory. (Oppenheimer, whom Conant consulted on the problem, did not think the results would be worthwhile "unless we can poison food sufficient to kill a half a million men," since the number actually affected would be far smaller.)[30] Based on such calculations, Conant, in contrast to Urey and Compton, believed it "*extremely* unlikely" that Berlin would use radioactive warfare—a prediction that turned out to be correct.[31]

Similarly, Bush and Conant were not greatly concerned that the Germans would employ chemical warfare (C.W.), as they had in World War I, as a defensive measure. Their belief that poison gas was, in Conant's words, "not an effective military weapon"[32] helps explain their negative reactions to probes by the Office of Strategic Service to obtain OSRD backing for C.W. work. James Grafton Rodgers, an O.S.S. agent, made several such pitches during 1943, urging backing for the clandestine agency, "if only for the War-to-Come we speak of so often."[33] Conant's general attitude toward the O.S.S.'s chief, Col. William J. Donovan, was not unfriendly: he had enjoyed a lunch with "Wild Bill" at Claridge's in London in March 1941, soon discovered he was "organizing some kind of a superintelligence service for the Government," and helped the new outfit recruit Harvard history professors.[34] And he occasionally shared relaxed suppers at the Cosmos Club with Rodgers, who found him "spry, quick, always too sure and cocky like most Harvard leaders, always alert for a job at Yale but likeable and genuine." But Conant and Bush rapped O.S.S.'s scientific performance as desultory and disorganized, and protested its interest in offensive chemical and biological weapons preparations—"all toxics are taboo as attack measures," Rodgers quoted them. "I agreed. We had best avoid this ugly business."[35] Conant's main objections were pragmatic rather than moral. Aside from skepticism about C.W.'s effectiveness—unlike that of the atomic bomb—Conant vividly understood the opprobrium heaped on those linked with poison gas; how lucky he was, he reflected to Calvert Smith in 1943, that "Lewisite was first discovered in [chemist W. Lee] Lewis's lot and not mine!"[36] Mostly, though, Conant already knew that the NDRC was already working closely with the Army's Chemical Warfare Service to assure that, as he later wrote, "there would have been a big payoff on the battlefield" had gas warfare started.[37] As the invasion approached, Bush assured Groves that the Germans would be foolish to contaminate the beaches with poison gas because they knew the Allied air superiority would enable decisive retaliation.[38]

Nevertheless, Stimson and Roosevelt were understandably engrossed for

months by the progress of the Normandy invasion, and Conant quietly
developed plans for postwar military research and, per Bush's request, in late
July 1944 submitted an outline for legislation on the domestic control of
atomic energy. The two-page memorandum contained no references to international complications.[39] Meanwhile, the constant and massive flow of reports
emanating from Manhattan District plants and laboratories brought disquieting and unexpected news—that a plutonium gun-type weapon had proved
impossible, that relations with Chicago continued to be strained, that there
was progress on some fronts, disappointment on others, and no let-up in
intensity—despite the clear signs of Allied victories in both Europe and,
though more slowly, the Pacific.[40]

The news of the liberation of Paris in August was exhilarating, but
Conant and Bush, like other U.S. officials, found their excitement tempered
by rising apprehension about the future intentions of the Soviet Union. With
German forces finally diverted by the opening of a second front in the West,
the Red Army pushed into central Europe, advancing into Poland, Romania,
Bulgaria, and Hungary as the Allies closed their vise on Hitler from opposite
directions. To the casualty-conscious American public, the achievements of
the forces under the command of "Uncle Joe" were welcome news, raising
hopes of a rapid capitulation of Nazi defenses. But English and American
officials concerned with postwar geopolitical considerations dreaded the prospect of Soviet power overwhelming the Continent as Germany, its traditional
counterweight, collapsed. As early as the August 1943 Quebec Conference,
high-level U.S. military strategists were privately predicting that "Russia's
post-war position will be a dominant one," with "no power in Europe to
oppose her tremendous military forces." Taking the most optimistic tack, they
had deduced that the "obvious" implication was that Washington should
render Moscow "every assistance and every effort must be made to obtain her
friendship."[41] Cooperation among the Big Three, both in military strategizing
against Germany and in tentative theorizing about the postwar makeup of
Europe, reached a high-water mark at the Teheran Conference in November
to December 1943, remarkable for the good cheer and relative frankness and
informality characterizing exchanges among Stalin, Roosevelt, and Churchill.
"We came here with hope and determination," they declared. "We leave here,
friends in fact, in spirit, and in purpose."[42]

But by the spring and summer of 1944, Soviet conduct in Eastern Europe,
especially Poland, had deeply troubled American officials and cast new
doubts on the likelihood of long-term cooperation. Besides resolutely insisting
on installing a Communist government in liberated Poland, Moscow outraged
Western opinion by first seeming to encourage an uprising among the bedraggled partisans of Warsaw against their Nazi occupiers, then standing by on
the opposite banks of the Vistula River as the Germans viciously crushed the
rebellion; the inescapable conclusion was that Stalin callously let Berlin do
the dirty work of exterminating Polish patriots who might resist Kremlin

domination. Other disagreements, largely hidden from public view, also flared over indications of Soviet efforts to extend political influence into the Balkans and Italy. "Evidently we are approaching a showdown with the Russians about their Communist intrigues in Italy, Yugoslavia, and Greece," Churchill minuted his foreign secretary in May. "I think their attitude becomes more difficult every day."[43] Instead of a soft-pedaled, conciliatory approach, the exasperated U.S. ambassador to Moscow, Averell Harriman, now strongly advised Roosevelt to start playing tough to keep Stalin in line. "When the Soviets do not like our proposals they certainly do not hesitate to be abrupt with us," Harriman cabled. "We may look forward to a Soviet policy of playing the part of a world bully if we don't follow this procedure of firmness now in connection with each incident."[44]

Though they were not privy to all these diplomatic demarches, Conant and Bush could not escape alarm at the ominous harbingers of tension among the Big Three. Discussing postwar matters during an inspection trip to Los Alamos in August 1944, they agreed that the time had arrived to start prodding the government to give serious attention to the atomic bomb's likely future impact on foreign policy.[45] In September, after returning to Washington, they finally began taking up these matters in earnest—just as some concerned activists among the Manhattan Project's rank-and-file also turned in that direction. Already, in Chicago, the percolating ferment had resulted in the formation of a group headed by Zay Jeffries to formulate a long-range "prospectus on nucleonics."[46] But as Conant and Bush drafted their memoranda, Roosevelt and Churchill were already privately reinforcing the long-term alliance made at Quebec a year earlier, favoring a postwar Anglo-American atomic monopoly in preference to international control or an early overture to Stalin. In the Hyde Park pact of September 19, Roosevelt acceded to Churchill's desire that "full collaboration between the United States and the British Government in developing Tube Alloys for military and commercial purposes should continue after the defeat of Japan unless and until terminated by joint agreement."[47]

In keeping with failure fully to coordinate such forays with his atomic advisers, FDR did not inform Bush and Conant of the *aide-mémoire*. Already aware of their lack of influence on the president, the OSRD leaders had decided in early September that their best entrée to him was through Secretary Stimson's office, where Harvey Bundy had proved a reliable and compatible liaison.[48] On September 19—the day the Hyde Park meeting symbolized their impotence—Conant and Bush cosigned the first of a series of documents addressed to Stimson containing proposals for the handling of atomic energy in peacetime. The first memo stressed the need for prompt action following an initial announcement of the bomb's use, and it listed three items atop the government's agenda: release of a "rather detailed" history of the Manhattan Project, including basic scientific information; introduction of legislation for a domestic atomic energy commission; and a treaty with Great Britain and

Canada assuring similar controls in those countries. In arguing for the first point, Conant and Bush recognized the uselessness of trying to keep the matter under wraps. "We cannot emphasize too strongly the fact that it will be quite impossible to hold the essential knowledge of these developments secret once the war is over ... Furthermore we should like to emphasize that the progress of this art and science is bound to be so rapid in the next five years in some countries that it would be extremely dangerous for this government to assume that by holding secret its present knowledge we should be secure." Yet Bush and Conant did not recommend a comprehensive international control pact or raise the question of a Soviet contribution.[49]

On September 22, however, Bush attended a revelatory session in the Oval Office that disclosed unexpected intimations of FDR's thinking on postwar issues and spurred him and Conant into spelling out their concerns over the international prospects explicitly and forcefully. Bush was chagrined and "very much embarrassed" to hear Roosevelt, with Lord Cherwell present, discuss aspects of the bomb's effect on postwar international relations that he had never brought up with his own advisers. Speaking "quite generally" on the subject, FDR for the first time in Bush's hearing revealed his desire to have Britain and the United States be joint atomic postwar policemen, and his statements favoring continued indefinite dual collaboration "went very far," Bush told Conant. Discovering for the first time how isolated from atomic diplomacy Roosevelt had kept him, Bush now garnered the essence, if not the specifics, of the president's discussions at Quebec the previous year and at Hyde Park a few days earlier. Conant, too, was "much disturbed," both by the apparent direction of American atomic policy and by the realization that it had been hurtling forward unaided by those most knowledgeable. "Conant and I feel that the very broad world-wide implications of this subject need careful evaluation," wrote Bush, "and that while good relations with Britain are certainly important in this it is certainly far from being the entire story."[50] Hurriedly approaching Stimson about this "highly dangerous situation," the two men found the war secretary sympathetic but harassed, and doubtful he could have any better luck getting FDR's ear.[51]

To focus the issue, Bush and Conant delivered a package of memoranda to Stimson on September 30. In two detailed documents, they gave a vivid, admittedly "lurid" view of the grave threat the administration would be facing in the not so distant future. Before August 1, 1945, they wrote, atomic bombs would be demonstrated, each as powerful as up to 10,000 tons of high explosive or the equivalent of a raid by 1,000 B-29s. In the future — perhaps as soon as a year after the first atomic bomb was constructed — a new category of weapons might come into existence on an order of magnitude more powerful than the atomic bomb itself: a hydrogen or "super-super" bomb, detonated by fission bombs. Delivered by guided missile, the super-super bomb could threaten any city with immediate devastation. The present Anglo-American monopoly was only temporary; any nation with good scientific and technical resources could catch up in three or four years. It would thus be the "height of folly" to count on the unchallenged continuation of U.S. atomic superiority. With total secrecy impossible, any attempt to impose it was likely to induce the advisers' worst-case scenario: a secret U.S.-Soviet arms race ultimately leading to an apocalyptic conflict. To avoid this fate, they called for drastic measures: a wholesale interchange of scientific information at the conclusion of the war, and the creation of an international commission to preside over the inspection of laboratories, and perhaps of all technical military installations.[52]

Because of the timing of these memoranda, and their close resemblance to Bohr's advice, it has been assumed that the OSRD advisers had only recently come to these ideas, perhaps as a result of contacts with Bohr or reports on his activities. The fullest and most eloquent articulation of this interpretation is Sherwin's influential *A World Destroyed*, which credits Bohr with the "first serious attempt to analyze the postwar implications of the atomic bomb for relations with the Soviet Union" and asserts that Bush's and Conant's thinking on this subject remained virtually "embryonic" until the last week of September 1944, when they composed their multiple memos to Stimson.[53]

Though his May 4 memorandum reveals that Conant grasped those connections at least five months earlier, Sherwin is absolutely correct in stressing the critical difference between Bush's and Conant's calmly reasoned proposals and Bohr's passionate quest to instill U.S. and British leaders with a vivid appreciation for the immediate necessity of taking action before it was too late. "Beyond urging a general commitment to international cooperation," as Sherwin writes, Conant and Bush "suggested no diplomatic initiatives likely to increase the probability of such cooperation." And, as he notes, "they certainly did not propose that Roosevelt inform Stalin of the existence of the Manhattan Project, as Bohr and the Chicago scientists had urged."[54] In fact, Bush and Conant ultimately *did* urge Truman to "mention S-1" to Stalin before the bomb was used against Japan, but only in a last-minute reversal shortly before the Potsdam summit in July 1945, and as a general comment without any specific commitment to international control.[55]

A more distorted interpretation appears in Richard Rhodes's *The Making of the Atomic Bomb*. Apparently overlooking Conant's May 4 memo, Rhodes attributes to Bohr the ideas at the heart of the Bush-Conant proposals to Stimson. At a loss to explain the congruence between Bohr's ideas and the OSRD administrators' promotion of "free interchange of all scientific information on this subject [atomic energy]" after the war, Rhodes simply *invents* a meeting which never took place! "Bush and perhaps Conant had talked to Bohr" before writing to Stimson, Rhodes states, explaining in a footnote that Bohr's influence on the two men "can be traced by careful reading." Rhodes reasoned that since the Bush-Conant memorandum of September 30 "contains and endorses all [of Bohr's] basic ideas," therefore Bush and perhaps Conant must have spoken to Bohr during the week after September 22 — when Bush had been alarmed to hear Roosevelt discussing postwar atomic policy with Cherwell—but had found it "politic not to credit him as their source" to Stimson since they knew Bohr was "in the doghouse" with FDR.[56]

But Rhodes missed evidence that Conant and Bush had derived their views on international control and formulated their proposals to Stimson *independently* of Bohr, and that they did not learn of the physicist's ideas until October 11—almost two weeks later. That afternoon, Bohr saw Bush at the behest of FDR, who had steered them together after turning down Bohr's request for a second conference to follow up the August 26 session arranged by Frankfurter. For the first time, Bohr explained to Bush the history of his past friendship with the Supreme Court justice and how the first meeting with FDR had been set up. But Bush's more important discovery concerned the substance of Bohr's views on how to establish a postwar international control regime. Conant would be "glad" to hear, he related, that while there were some "points of departure," Bohr's proposed method "is extraordinarily close to the point of view that you and I arrived at a week or two ago."[57]

This confirmation that Conant and Bush, on the one hand, and Bohr on the other, had unknowingly traveled parallel courses during the spring, summer, and early fall of 1944 raises previously unasked questions about the circumstances surrounding the birth of the nuclear arms race. Given that at least Conant had come to the convictions expressed in the September 30 memos in early 1944, what explains his reticence to press them for nearly five months? Beyond, of course, the huge matter of the invasion of Europe and beyond his ignorance of Bohr's meetings and FDR's private views, various factors militated against urgency: Conant's sense that the bomb was still too distant to command serious attention from high officials, his natural tendency to wait for opinion to build before committing himself to a cause or position (in this case the impetus was the groundswell for postwar planning at the Met Lab), his fear that premature airing of unorthodox ideas might actually hurt their chances of acceptance. Regardless of the specific reason, Conant's caution betrayed him. For, rather than disdaining Bohr's ideas, as the British presumed, he would likely have responded very favorably. What if Bohr had brought his ideas to Conant in early 1944 rather than going through Frankfurter? Perhaps Conant and Bush would have been spurred to communicate to Stimson their strong concern about the dangers of a postwar atomic arms race with Moscow prior to late September. At a minimum, a concerted lobbying drive might have convinced Stimson to raise the issue with Roosevelt, heightened the secretary's own awareness of the dangers many months earlier, or sparked a serious high-level study of the bomb's meaning for postwar foreign policy at a time when the State Department had no inkling of its existence. At the most, Roosevelt might have responded to Bohr's proposals in a more positive frame of mind had Bohr's visit gone through normal channels, or had the proposals been conveyed in a more intelligible form through Bush and Conant.

Such a counterfactual scenario is, of course, highly speculative. Conant himself had no great faith in Roosevelt's handling of the bomb's diplomatic complications and had been irritated by the "somewhat cavalier" way the president had dealt with the British during the earlier controversy about atomic exchanges. Convinced that FDR possessed "only fleeting interest in the atom, and that the program never got very far past the threshold of his consciousness" and that he "really had no idea of the enormous importance of our [atomic] secrets," Conant might have remained skeptical of the efficacy of an early approach to Stimson or FDR, even had Bohr's urgency infected him.[58] Moreover, Roosevelt might well have followed Churchill's lead at Hyde Park even had Bush or Stimson already presented the case for keeping an open door to Moscow on international control. Still, the arguments for international control would have stood a better chance with FDR had they been straightforwardly, if bureaucratically, made by his top advisers.

It is naturally impossible to know whether a Bohr-Conant meeting in the spring of 1944 would have materially improved the chances to prevent a postwar U.S.-Soviet nuclear arms race, or changed FDR's outlook prior to his crucial summit conferences on the subject with Churchill. But Conant himself seems to have also believed that an opportunity was missed—although he did not realize it until more than three decades later. In his personal copy of *A World Destroyed,* published three years before his death in 1978, there are only two handwritten comments in the margins. Next to Sherwin's assertion that the interchange controversy had left Churchill's principal atomic administrator "skeptical about the likelihood" of the Manhattan Project's administrators sharing Bohr's ideas, Conant penciled a question mark. And alongside a passage relating that Bohr had deliberately sidestepped the OSRD leadership to contact Roosevelt directly, Conant wrote "XX" and one word: "mistake."[59]

CHAPTER 12

"The Animate Scheme"

The Quest for Postwar Planning
October 1944–May 1945

Modern science and technology have so transformed the art of war as to require us to rethink many of the problems involved in an international attempt to keep the peace... Either we must play our part in a world organization to preserve the peace, or we must convert this Nation into an armed camp bristling with weapons. Either we must have confidence in an international arrangement in which we are vigorous partners and plan our military program in terms of such an arrangement, or else we must go it alone and arm to the teeth to defend our national independence.
　　　　　　—JBC, "The Effective Disarmament of Germany and Japan,"
　　　　　　October 7, 1944

I for one am ready to accept her [the Soviet Union] as a peace-loving nation, though I should be very realistic in my attitude as I am sure she will be. The alternative, to my mind, is much too dreadful to contemplate, namely, starting down a road which will lead to war with Russia in the course of twenty-five years.
　　　　　　—JBC to L. W. Douglas, October 11, 1944

We are to spend our money and our scientific manpower on a feverish race but when we have the ultimate what do we do with it? And if we can't answer that question, why enter the race?
　　　　　　—JBC to Bush, May 9, 1945

The fall of 1944 was a time of personal and political anxiety for Conant. To the top-secret technological and diplomatic problems of the atomic bomb, and the presidential burdens of leading Harvard as its students went off to war, was added the gnawing uncertainty of having two sons engaged in hazardous wartime duty.

Both, coincidentally, were serving in the Pacific. James Richards Conant, the elder, had joined the submarine corps after rushing through an accelerated academic schedule at the University of Michigan while writing a column for the school newspaper and enlisting in a navy ROTC, training as a deck officer. Graduating Phi Beta Kappa, the lanky, rawboned officer was assigned duty in August 1943 to the U.S.S. *Halibut,* a hunter-killer patrol sub which over the next fourteen months went out on ten missions in south Pacific waters infested with Japanese shipping. With anti-submarine warfare technology steadily growing more astute, survival was an iffy business: One in five sailors in the submarine patrol never returned, the highest casualty rate of any branch of the armed service. Amidst the vessel's claustrophobic camaraderie and repeated brushes with disaster, all recorded in the primitively printed *Halibastard Herald,* Lieutenant (junior grade) Conant rose to a senior command position. On November 14, 1944, the *Halibut* faced its most perilous crisis as it engaged an enemy convoy in the Luzon Strait off the Philippines. Suddenly, a series of depth charge concussions dented the hull and forced the sub to the ocean floor; for hours, as the desperate crew chain-smoked, frantically struggled to repair the damage, and evacuated compartments during a frightening (though false) poison gas alarm, Conant operated the key instruments on which hope for rescue depended. Ultimately, the *Halibut* managed to limp to safety and contact a friendly ship to lead her home. But it had been a harrowing, scarring experience — and the Silver Star for "gallantry and intrepidity in action" could not calm the twenty-one-year-old's jangled nerves, especially since the navy immediately shipped him out for additional combat action.[1]

Conant's alienated younger son, Ted, entered the war in the fall of 1944 by taking advantage of his precocious electronics expertise. He put in a stint as a warrant officer for the U.S. Maritime Service, then became a radio operator for the merchant marine, transmitting from cargo ships crisscrossing the Pacific, where he had chosen to go rather than joining the lend-lease shipping mission in the frigid north Atlantic. To join the service, the eighteen-year-old had dropped out of a boarding school in Vermont, the latest in a series of educational institutions to which he had been shuttled as the Conants searched for an environment they hoped would temper his rascality and indiscipline. According to Theodore Conant, his father had "pretty well written me off as a guy who would dabble in the arts and flunk out and end up in an institution." Uninterested in conforming to his father's expectations or emulating the well-rounded behavior and ambition of his brother, Ted threw himself with fanatic energy into self-designed radio and film projects, outraging some teachers by flouting regulations while impressing them with raw talent. In early 1944, his father consented to Ted's desire to sign up for the maritime service rather than finish boarding school.[2]

Heading off to the Pacific turned out to be Theodore's ticket to freedom and independence. After completing boot camp with a fresh FCC radio license, he went via railroad to California, where he spent Christmas 1944 visiting Ernest Lawrence, a family friend, and sniffing around the Berkeley lab where the electromagnetic separation progress was secretly being carried out. In a guided tour, Lawrence judiciously avoided mentioning S-1, but when the gawky teenager impudently mentioned that gossip about secret nuclear power work was all around MIT, the Nobel laureate allegedly fixed him a withering stare, grabbed his lapels, and barked: "You just keep your mouth shut!"[3] Then it was time to sail—and the sea breezes, adventure, rough-housing revelry of fellow sailors, and eye-opening exotic ports of the Far East liberated the rambunctious teenager. To his mother, he cabled poems describing sultry tropical sunsets and the spooky wreckage of battle on Guadalcanal, though he prudently omitted a ditty describing adventures with buddies in a honky-tonk port. While the merchant marine's missions mercifully were not as consistently life-threatening as the *Halibut*'s, Ted quickly absorbed the sobering proximity to combat and death so alien to Cambridge or Washington, braving the sudden terror of kamikaze attacks and surveying the decomposing corpses of Japanese soldiers. Visiting his son during a port call in Portland, his father discerned some palpable maturation. The two were walking near the harbor when they were accosted by a carload of drunken sailors, whores in tow, shouting uproariously; Ted's casual and comfortable handling of the situation seemed a sign of impressive social skills.[4]

In Cambridge, meanwhile, isolated from her family, Patty Conant tried to participate vicariously by comforting returned casualties in the psychiatric ward of a local hospital—a satisfying yet disturbing experience fictionalized in May Sarton's novel of wartime Harvard, *Faithful Are the Wounds*.[5] The Conants had news of their boys though sporadic letters, shortwave radio broadcasts, and snippets of intelligence data clandestinely passed on to the OSRD, but the reports could only hint at the perils the young men faced.

Forebodings about the bomb dwarfed Conant's personal concerns, however. He and Bush were deeply distressed by the phenomenon of administration officials earnestly endeavoring to draw up a blueprint to preserve the world's future tranquillity in blithe ignorance of the greatest threat to peace. By then, the two advisers had become a single working unit in campaigning for postwar planning; the gap in knowledge which had made Conant's decisions preeminent in technical matters and Bush's on political tactics was no longer critical. They aimed not at enhancing their own importance in formulating postwar policy, but at imparting their knowledge to those who were in a position to integrate the bomb into military, political, and diplomatic calculations.[6]

But Conant's delay in bringing the issue of international control to the fore had not helped their cause. The September 30 documents were intended to jolt Stimson, and the administration, into a serious look at atomic energy's implications. Bush hoped the war secretary would just add his comments and pass the papers on to Roosevelt, but Stimson, distracted by other matters and uncertain where the bomb might fit into them, read the memoranda but for nearly two months did nothing with them.[7] Bush wrote to Conant in late

October after an inconclusive conference with Stimson: "Of course what the President needs is a good solid group to study the implications of this affair and advise him as to possible moves, but I judge this is too much to hope for just at the present time."[8]

Conant's overriding priority, of course, remained making sure that his $2 billion bailiwick reported in before the war ended. Though Groves ran the show, Conant remained intensely involved as S-1 Executive Committee chairman, scientific adviser to Groves, and deputy to Bush, and he stayed up-to-date through a steady succession of inspection visits and meetings with key scientific and industrial managers. Though unexpected glitches kept unnerving Conant right up until the bomb was tested, it turned out that he had had good reason in mid-1942 for not eliminating any of the three leading contenders for producing fissionable material: they all were working.[9] Now the question became: would they work fast enough? By the late summer and early fall of 1944, the success of the Normandy invasion, whose troops rapidly broke out from their beachheads to advance eastward toward Berlin, prompted high hopes that Nazi Germany would soon be defeated, probably before the first atomic bombs would be ready for use the following summer. Moreover, the nightmare that Hitler would get the bomb first was fast vanishing. On the heels of the Allied armies in liberated Paris in late August, army scientific intelligence officials working with Project Alsos (code-named by the Manhattan Project's top officer after the Greek word for "grove") soon discovered documents and sources that tentatively established that the German uranium effort had been a miserable failure.[10]

Yet this reassuring discovery did not slow work in the Manhattan Engineering District—the pace, if anything, intensified, as Conant and his colleagues now viewed ending the bloody, grinding war against Japan as the most likely test for the first use of the bomb. Although Allied forces were also making progress in the Far East—reclaiming enemy-held island strongholds in New Guinea and the Marianas, pressuring occupation forces in China and Southeast Asia, and triumphing in sea and air battles in the Pacific as they prepared to invade the Philippines and close in on Japan itself—the desperate battles continued to exact a high toll and the timetable for victory remained uncertain.[11] For over a year, there had been suggestions that S-1 might be used first against Japan. As early as May 1943 the Military Policy Committee had designated the well-defended Japanese fleet at Truk in the Caroline Islands, a major obstacle to the U.S. "island-hopping" campaign, as a suitable target for the first atomic bomb. Discussing that idea with Roosevelt, Bush himself seemed rather disconcerted by the notion, recording that "our point of view or our emphasis on the program would shift if we had in mind use against Japan as compared with use against Germany." But Groves signaled his thinking later that year when he ordered the modification for atomic delivery of a B-29 bomber, used primarily in the Pacific.[12]

By the fall of 1944, the OSRD leaders, too, had fully shifted gears, substituting worries about outpacing German physicists with concern that the bomb be finished in time to terminate the war against Japan. Racing to finish the weapon, Manhattan Project administrators now concentrated on the final stages of delivering fissionable material to Los Alamos and determining the design of the bomb itself. To give the enrichment process a head start before the treated uranium was then converted to weapons-grade quality, the Army rapidly built a thermal diffusion plant; one afternoon at Oak Ridge, Conant urged a group of startled soldiers to volunteer to work on it. "I'm James Conant," he introduced himself simply—but the troops, in their early twenties, had already recognized him and gasped when he walked into the room. Soon he was enticing them by saying their task would involve "probing the unknown" and could win the war sooner. But he also added that it would be highly dangerous work—and he wasn't kidding. The dozen or so troops, who had received special scientific training and grasped from "scuttlebutt" that the job would be part of a project to build an atomic bomb, immediately accepted Conant's proposition, and a few days later, on September 2, two of them were killed in an explosion at a pilot plant at the Philadelphia Navy Yard; nevertheless, the thermal diffusion plant went ahead and pushed the schedule for a gun-type uranium weapon forward by a few days.[13] Visiting Los Alamos in December 1944, a month after receiving the now definitive word that Germany's atomic program had failed, Conant still applied pressure: "Gun method seems sure but needs a little pushing which it got," he reported. "I bet Oppie it would be used first."[14]

Besides defeating Japan, Conant now devoted increasing energy to figuring out how nuclear weapons might complicate the already daunting task of "policing the postwar world," which he had long assumed would be an American responsibility.[15] And even his knowledge that a Nazi atom bomb no longer posed a threat in the current conflict failed to dispel Conant's worries that Germany might one day rise from the ashes of defeat to embark secretly on an atomic construction program. To forestall that possibility, Conant proposed to reduce drastically Germany's industrial capacity and reorient the country along pastoral lines for at least two decades. His speech at an October 7, 1944, luncheon meeting of the New York–based Foreign Policy Association, "The Effective Disarmament of Germany and Japan: The Menace of a Third World War to Our Civilization," was consistent with his early advocacy of unconditional surrender as the chief U.S. war aim. In many respects it resembled a far more famous plan that had been secretly advanced at the Quebec Anglo-American summit a month earlier by Treasury Secretary Henry Morgenthau, who also envisioned dismembering German industry and reconstituting the country's postwar economy along pastoral lines.[16]

Press leaks about Morgenthau's proposals had put ideas for Germany's postwar status in the headlines as he spoke, but Conant had a different motive behind his plan: the atomic bomb. "Defeated enemies secretly planning to once again give battle present an obvious danger," Conant warned the group, using general phrases about the "mounting curve of aerial offensive power" and "potentialities of the robot bomb." "Is it not the lesson of history," he asked, "that a once powerful and strong nation, badly defeated in war, will cherish the aims of renewing that war at the first opportunity, at least for a generation?"

> There is little doubt that a considerable proportion of the German youth today are convinced believers in all that Germany has stood for in the last ten years. It would be a miracle indeed if bitter defeat suddenly changed their minds. One has to be an incurable optimist to believe that any process of education—particularly one sponsored by other nations and imposed from without—will change the views of these youths hardened by the party discipline. In time, of course, we can hope for modification of this attitude. But the time is not ten years or even twenty, it is the span of life in which those now young become old and in which new social forces arise to influence a new generation of German people . . . if the disarmament of Germany is to be effective for a generation I believe that it can be demonstrated that a drastic change in the German industrial scene and a considerable degree of redistribution of European industry will be required.[17]

Unless his plan were adopted, Conant warned his audience, factories built for peaceful purposes could be quickly converted to military use, and "the interval between the rise of a new Hitler and the ability to strike with terrific force may be as short as a single year."

The notions Conant proposed for postwar Allied collaboration to contain Germany closely accorded with the scheme for an international atomic armaments commission he and Bush had communicated to Stimson a week earlier. For more than three years, Conant had privately favored what he now urged publicly—a "profound alteration" in the economies of the Axis countries so as to make impossible a rearmament drive in the event that cooperation among the victorious Allies collapsed. His public prediction that young Germans would deify Hitler for a generation was in his mind all the more ominous alongside his private conviction that the essential know-how behind atomic weapons would be widely known within a few years of the war's end; and building a plant to produce the necessary material, he realized, was "by no means a prohibitively difficult, expensive, or laborious undertaking."[18] In a letter to a friend a few days later, Conant wrote that "the threat inherent in Germany's desire to start a new war after this war is so great that we must put safety measures on this point above all else," and advocated the creation of a German economy based on "light industries and specialties." Unconsciously echoing FDR's wartime comment that it might prove necessary to "castrate the German people," Conant conceded that his plan would lead to a low standard of living and a drop in Germany's birth rate, which he thought would be a good thing. He conceded that a "period of extreme suffering," including "many deaths in the civilian population," would follow in the months or years after an Allied victory.[19]

Not revenge or hatred but a sincere estimation of the dangers of secret German nuclear rearmament lay at the heart of Conant's proposals. He saw no plausible alternative to redistributing the Ruhr Basin's steel industries, for example, so as to inhibit the industrial capacity necessary for isotope separation or plutonium plants. And he had no faith in the ability of any international alliance to act quickly or effectively enough to restrain a resurgent Germany or to control it by restricting its access to raw materials.[20] Concerned that top policymakers did not grasp that their worries about a secret Soviet postwar nuclear effort were equally applicable to Germany, he wrote Bush in May 1945, shortly before V–E Day, "Unless you stop Germany and her steel industry, we are in for trouble and in about 10 years."[21]

In his Foreign Policy Association speech Conant coupled his support for draconian postwar measures with an airing of what he admitted might be called "Utopian dreams"—his (and Bush's) proposal for a worldwide armaments commission with powers of inspection staffed by an international corps of experts. An effective, united international organization in which the United States took an active part was Conant's preferred solution to preventing World War III. One purpose of his speech, then (and a reason to republish it the following spring in *Life* magazine), was to condition public opinion to accept the idea of postwar collaboration with other powers and to drive another nail in the coffin of isolationism.

Essential to the success of any system of international collaboration was, of course, the cooperation of the Soviet Union. Bush and Conant, like other policymakers, now recognized that U.S. relations with Russia posed the biggest potential obstacle to the stability of the postwar peace. An exclusive postwar Anglo-American atomic monopoly to "control the peace of the world," Bush worried in September 1944, might lead to a "very undesirable relationship on the subject with Russia," and perhaps a war in twenty years.[22] Conant also saw that the bomb might exacerbate the tensions underlying the makeshift alliance against Hitler—or it could, conversely, be the glue that bound the Soviets to a postwar order, inspired and designed by the United States, in which the nuclear threat was eliminated. How could the Soviets be made to go along with this idea? "It appears to us that Russia would be the most reluctant to enter into this combination," Bush and Conant observed after describing their proposal for an international commission, "but since we hold the advantage, if only temporary, in this art it would seem that the quid pro quo was evident."[23]

The quid pro quo was to be the hallmark of the American discussions regarding Russia on the international control issue as the war drew to a close. From Conant and Bush to Stimson to Averell Harriman, the U.S. ambassador to Moscow, the byword of bargaining on the subject of atomic energy was that the United States should not give up something for nothing; that in exchange for giving up its monopoly, it should demand a concomitant sacrifice from Moscow. But, wearied enough from the strains of overseeing the war and coping with worsening health, Roosevelt believed that to engage in a strenuous give-and-take on difficult postwar issues when it could be put off might interfere with the immediate job of winning the war.[24] Thus when he met strong resistance from Churchill to the idea of informing Stalin about the Manhattan Project, even so near the end of the conflict as the February 1945 Yalta Conference, he allowed himself to be dissuaded.[25] In general, Roosevelt felt in no particular hurry to tackle the problems the bomb might cause for Soviet-American relations, partly because of his confidence in his own personal diplomacy, partly because until the bomb was actually detonated—an event that seemed to recede into the future with each revised timetable—it still seemed to represent only a potential complication. The day before his death, Roosevelt wrote to Churchill: "I would minimize the general Soviet problem as much as possible, because these problems, in one form or another, seem to arise every day, and most of them straighten out."[26]

By late 1944, Conant learned, the Met Lab in Chicago was clamoring for an immediate study of the bomb's future political implications. Indirect assurances to the effect that the matter was being looked into did little to satisfy the growing number of atomic scientists who had come to believe, as one historian put it, that "the preoccupation of Washington (meaning Groves, Bush and Conant) with the immediate objective of completing the bomb appeared to be needlessly exclusive."[27] The scientists were divided on what overture, if any, should be made to Moscow, but they repeatedly sought to compel attention to the ominous indications of a postwar nuclear confrontation. In November 1944, a report compiled from five committees of Met Lab researchers by the metallurgist Zay Jeffries warned that "the inevitability of the development of nucleonics by some if not all nations shows compellingly, because of its potential military consequences, the necessity" for an international control administration.[28] The Jeffries Report also described the dangers of a surprise attack by a nation that had secretly developed atomic weapons, estimated that Germany was well along in its atomic program, and observed that it "would be surprising if the Russians are not also diligently engaged in such work." That last possibility prompted twenty-two Chicago scientists, including the Met Lab director Samuel K. Allison, to transmit to Washington in early November their hope that the United States would prevent suspicions from arising in the Alliance by issuing a general statement revealing the Manhattan Project's existence in advance of the bomb's use.[29]

Conant thought such a step premature. His cautious policy of "carefully guarded trust"[30] toward Russia derived from his strong distaste for the Kremlin's repressive totalitarianism and his sense that steps had to be taken to contain Russian expansionism in Europe. Like Churchill, who was secretly scribbling his famous "percentages" on the back of an envelope during a summit with Stalin to delineate their nations' respective spheres of influence in various European countries, Conant hoped that the Kremlin's territorial ambitions could be limited in as friendly and agreeable form as possible, with an understanding that committed Russia and the United States to refrain from using either military, financial, or political pressure in internal ideological contests in other countries. There were four key exceptions. In Germany, France, Belgium, and Holland—the heart of Western Europe—the United States would "stand committed for the next decade to supporting a democracy based on a capitalistic economy." As for possible postwar tensions among the Allies, as Conant put it in a letter to a friend, "in any of our foreign transactions which might tend to embroil us with Russia, we should act in partnership and with constant consultation" with Great Britain.[31]

Conant's concerns about future conflict with the Soviets by no means reflected an implacable animus, for he, like many Americans, had come grudgingly to admire their tenacity and courage in staving off the German invaders, and even to wonder whether the "Russian experiment" might offer valuable lessons. The "vast contributions of the Russian people under a collectivist dictatorship to the defeat of Hitler are almost immeasurable," he acknowledged to Tom Lamont in 1943. "The question must rise in our minds whether, if we fail to work out a satisfactory adaption of the American system to the needs of the post-war years, the influence of Russian success will not be profound in our search for an answer." Still, however impressed he might be by the Soviet Union's energetic technological efforts, and empathizing with the Marxist-Leninist hostility to class stratifications, Conant did not ignore Moscow's brutal suppression of political and intellectual liberties. He had no doubt, for example, as he wrote Lamont, that the "chief glory of Harvard as an institution of free and untrammelled inquiry would disappear under any such system as prevails in Russia."[32] And, commenting favorably on the reported entry of many young men into Soviet scientific and military ranks, Conant had written Walter Lippmann in 1943 that "I suppose that if we were to drive out of the country or shoot everyone who in the 1930's was paying an income tax we too would have a situation which once stability was assured would be open to the talented."[33] But despite his misgivings, Conant now recognized that living with Russia was no longer an option but a necessity. "I for one am ready to accept her as a peace-loving nation, though I should be very realistic in my attitude as I am sure she will be," Conant wrote Lew Douglas in October 1944. "The alternative, to my mind, is much too dreadful to contemplate, namely, starting down a road which will lead to war with Russia in the course of twenty-five years."[34]

Since he expected Russia to obtain atomic weapons long before that, Conant knew that failure to create an effective world peacekeeping organization meant disaster—if not global war, then the conversion of America into "an armed camp bristling with weapons" and the likely extinction of domestic personal freedom. "Only if we were convinced that in spite of our best efforts all hope through international collaboration had failed could we embark upon such a course of action."[35] The goal was obvious, but the means to achieve it elusive: Could the Russians be induced to cooperate in an international control association and if so, how?

To Bohr and the Chicago scientists, the likelihood that Russia had already embarked on an atomic program invalidated the contention that informing it of the Manhattan Project's existence represented an untenable security risk. For the United States to refuse to notify its ally of such a portentous development merely meant that Russia would find out by other means (it had), and, as Bohr argued in June 1944, "the present favorable opportunity of inviting confidence may be forfeited."[36]

Whether that favorable opportunity ever in fact existed cannot be determined, of course—at least until the Kremlin archives are fully opened and explored—and Stalin's record offered few grounds for optimism. It does now, in retrospect, seem clear that the Soviets possessed detailed knowledge of the U.S. bomb project through espionage sources at Los Alamos, which seems to support the argument that the United States really didn't have much to lose from a candid approach, even if the chances of success were slim. Conant in any case had grave doubts that the effort would prove fruitful. He believed strongly that a good-faith attempt must be made, and sincerely desired international control. But he also was guided by caution.

That go-slow attitude is apparent in a letter Conant wrote on January 29, 1945, to Maj. George Fielding Eliot, who had solicited his views in preparation for a magazine article. In "Strict Confidence," Conant disclosed some of his views on a subject that had "been disturbing my thinking for some months." Interchange with the British was then complete and "no problem," he stated. But the same situation did not exist with Moscow, "and from what I have learned of the way Russia is operated it is going to be difficult indeed to break down the Chinese wall that surrounds that country." Conant then rejected the notion that the United States and Britain should unhesitatingly welcome Russia into their military partnership. Without directly mentioning the atomic bomb but clearly thinking of it, he agreed that it would be desirable eventually to bring Russia into the Anglo-American joint-chiefs-of-staff arrangement, to be followed by exchanges of "scientific research of a military nature. But in proceeding to such a goal, which must appear somewhat utopian, I should require a series of quid pro quos at every step. We certainly would not want to be in the position of giving a lot of information to the Russians and getting nothing in return either in the way of facts or open channels of communication."[37]

Like Stimson—who had known since 1943 that the Russians were spying on the Manhattan Project but had told Roosevelt in late December 1944 that it was essential "not to take them into our confidence until we are sure to get a real quid pro quo for our frankness"[38]—Conant still felt the United States could get more "in return" from the Russians by holding back knowledge of the bomb. After the war ended, he believed, the United States should disclose all basic scientific information relating to atomic energy and try to expand that bridgehead to full *two-way* interchange with the Soviets across the full range of scientific and military subjects. "Unless we can crack the Chinese wall, the prospects of good relations between our two countries seems to me to be in grave danger," he wrote to Eliot, adding that "every effort" should be made to, at a minimum, begin a free flow of nonmilitary scientific information. "Whether it is possible to meet this nightmare in advance," he wrote, "I do not pretend to know but I should like to try."[39]

Conant staked the success of any effort to gain Soviet acquiescence to international control on the bomb's ability, once demonstrated, to instill fear. Alongside an atomic stick, Conant hoped, the United States would offer the carrot of scientific cooperation and, more to the point, the end of the Anglo-American monopoly and a genuine sharing of power.

In trying to devise a U.S. policy that would simultaneously prepare for both success and failure—for a solution that would preclude an arms race and remove atomic weapons from U.S. arsenals, and for the collapse of negotiations and the beginning of an arms race in which the United States must stay in the lead—Conant faced an impossible task. No policy could fully embody two such divergent objectives. Conant recognized the incompatibility of the clashing precepts—but could not escape the logic pointing toward both.

The deep, probably irreconcilable dichotomy in both Conant's thinking and in American policy is starkly captured in a letter Conant wrote to Bush on May 9, 1945. Reacting to an appeal from the Chicago scientists to continue atomic weapons research at wartime intensity after the defeat of Germany and Japan because of the danger that other nations were working on such programs, Conant wrote, "We are to spend our money and our scientific manpower on a feverish race but when we have the ultimate what do we do with it? And if we can't answer that question, why enter the race?" Since true peace in a world with atomic-armed superpower antagonists appeared impossible—sooner or later one side or other would surely pull the trigger, he believed—Conant recognized that logic led to a preventive war: "Furthermore, *ex hypothesei,* the other fellow will also have the ultimate some years later unless we propose to use the ultimate to eliminate him." But Conant could not stomach the idea of a preventive war to preclude the threat of Soviet atomic weapons, and conceded that the U.S. must enter the race even as it tried to stop it. "I am inclined to back an all out research program for the super-duper [hydrogen bomb] as first priority (leaving industry second role)," he wrote Bush, "and at the same time with equal priority push for an international armament commission. We have about 5–10 years to do both!" And, he insisted, "I refuse to be a defeatist about the animate scheme any more than we were about the inanimate."[40]

It would not be easy to lure the Soviets into an international agreement, as Conant well knew. To have any chance of gaining Soviet acceptance, a U.S. proposal for international control would have to appear as more than a means of consolidating the American atomic advantage. But, as several historians have shown, U.S. leaders wanted to pocket the obvious immediate gain to American military strength supplied by the bomb and to exploit that advantage in their relations with the Soviet Union.[41]

Was Conant an adherent of "atomic diplomacy," the proposition that the threat, implicit or explicit, of atomic weapons could be used to modify Soviet behavior? He was. But his aims were more limited than those of officials who believed Washington should use its atomic monopoly to impose changes in Soviet domestic policy (as Stimson suggested to Truman in July 1945) or to make Moscow "more manageable" in Eastern Europe (as Truman's future secretary of state, James F. Byrnes, told Szilard in May 1945). Conant could accept the continuation of Communist rule in Russia, and a fair contest between Communism and capitalism in Eastern Europe, because of his abiding faith in the long-term strength of democracy to overcome ideological competitors.[42] In pressing for the quid pro quo of an opening in the Soviet "Chinese Wall" of secrecy, Conant hoped that step would be the first step in a general liberalizing of the Soviet system,[43] but this hope was secondary— removing the danger of atomic weapons was the first priority. Conant's lack of confidence in the bomb's long-term usefulness as a diplomatic instrument led him to hope that the U.S. could use its short-term advantage to gain a settlement that would leave it free to pursue its goal of world leadership through other avenues. With or without the bomb—so long as the Soviets did not develop it—the United States would naturally ascend to the top, he believed.

The same factors that made Conant overestimate the atomic bomb's ability to frighten the world and the USSR into an international control agreement also caused him to downgrade the efficacy of conventional diplomatic approaches before the bomb had been tested or used. By his reckoning, any action reducing the bomb's shock value decreased the chances that its significance would be recognized. This held for its capacity to induce the Japanese to surrender—which is why he argued that no advance warning should be issued before using it against Japan—and for its impact on the Russians and on Americans who might otherwise not recognize the need for international control. Conant and Bush first addressed this aspect of the problem in their September 30, 1944, message to Stimson. Complete interchange of military secrets, they acknowledged, "would presumably be violently opposed in this country as well as Russia since it would mean in the last analysis the opening of all industrial plants to officials of an international organization." But such drastic steps might be accepted, the administrators stated, "if people in this country and in other countries are convinced of the terrific potentialities of the new weapons which now lie just over the horizon."[44]

Still, wartime attempts to gauge Soviet receptiveness to international control were not necessarily excluded. Though they never pushed for a full-fledged effort to begin talks with Moscow, Conant and Bush, frustrated by Stimson's slow approach, in late October 1944 tried a different tack aimed at the same goal. Biological warfare (B.W.) was another rapidly advancing technology that posed a future danger of uncertain but possibly immense proportions. A nation that secretly developed biological weapons might suddenly loose a virulent agent on the world; open international scientific cooperation on the subject might ease the world's fears. An obvious incentive therefore existed for all nations to join in an effort to eliminate that danger. Bush thought a U.S.-sponsored venture on B.W. could be a dry run for atomic-energy control, an "entering wedge," and noting that interchange with England had already begun, wrote to Conant to "suggest that we immediately advocate full interchange on all aspects of the subject with Russia. We might learn a great deal from the way in which this worked out."[45]

Conant agreed. He and Bush then sent the secretary of war a "camouflage" of their September memo—this time recommending that the Allies be approached regarding the establishment of a B.W. interchange agency within the framework to establish a postwar United Nations organization agreed to by the Big Four at the Dumbarton Oaks conference in Georgetown that met from late August through early October.[46] Participating governments would provide full information to this Office of Scientific and Technical Development; its inspectors would have free access to all laboratories and plants concerned with biological warfare in all countries; complete publicity would be given the results. Using arguments virtually identical to those behind their plan for the international control of atomic energy, Conant and Bush acknowledged that critics might contend that such a plan would hurt U.S. interests and that "in particular Russia with its peculiar form of tight control could not possibly be an effective partner." Their response: "Granted that evasion on the part of Russia might take place, is not the scheme proposed less dangerous to the security of the United States than to assume that Russia would proceed with this development without any reference to the activities of the other nations?" Besides, the United Nations should have at its disposal combined weaponry at least equal to that of any potential violator. One shouldn't in any case be too pessimistic. Given time, the exchange of information and, "above all," the compatibility of scientists working together without reference to national boundaries, barriers of secrecy could be broken down.[47]

Their memorandum implicitly called for quick action; as in their previous documents, however, Bush and Conant aimed at stimulating discussion and consideration of the issues as much as instigating any diplomacy. Faced with evident bureaucratic inertia, they were asking for attention to be directed to the problem as much as recommending a course of action. Conant's devotion to the processes of bureaucracy, to operating "inside channels,"[48] meant that he conceived of his responsibility as consisting of putting the international issues before the State Department and convincing the president that they deserved special attention in the form of "a good solid group to study the implication of this affair and advise him to the possible moves."[49]

On December 8, 1944, Bush and Conant urged Harvey Bundy and Assistant Secretary of War John McCloy to begin postwar planning on S-1 "at once."[50] Five days later, Bush repeated this in a talk with Stimson himself; the secretary, however, had not yet made up his mind about international control and thought "enormous care needed to be used in arriving at a policy."[51] Just before the New Year, Stimson twice discussed with Roosevelt the atomic program's relations to the international situation, in particular a threatened leakage of information to France and the recent heightening of tensions with Russia, but no move was made to form the advisory group Bush and Conant envisioned.[52] The OSRD leaders felt virtually hamstrung: "I can think of no aspect of this subject at the present time on which it seems to be my move," Bush wrote Bundy on January 30, 1945.[53]

Then, after Yalta, on the first Saturday in March, Bush and Conant buttonholed Bundy for a "considerable time" and told him that "confusion and turmoil," and "almost public hysteria" would result if the bomb was tested and used without the government having made adequate plans. Statements and laws were needed; the international aspects required "intensive study."[54] Bundy successfully conveyed their profound anxiety to Stimson, who wrote in his diary, "Our thoughts went right down to the bottom facts of human nature, morals, and governments, and it is by far the most searching and important thing that I have had to do since I have been here in the Office of the Secretary of War because it touches matters which are deeper than even the principles of the present government."[55] Shortly thereafter, he recorded that S-1 matters were "taking up a good deal of my time and even then I am not doing it justice. It is approaching the ripening time and matters are getting very, very interesting and serious."[56]

Bush and Conant had finally accomplished their immediate mission. Stimson now grasped the issues created by the bomb's development, not just as a weapon but as a force in the postwar world. When Stimson next met with Roosevelt, he "went over the two schools of thought" on future handling of atomic weapons—either international control, or national control combined with an attempt at "close-in" secrecy—and emphasized the need for advance planning.[57] Roosevelt agreed. As scientists at Los Alamos hurried their preparations for a first test explosion in the late spring or early summer, Stimson also disposed of a suggestion from Director of War Mobilization James F. Byrnes that the Manhattan Project be reviewed by a group of "outside" scientists. "Rather a jittery and nervous memorandum and rather silly," thought Stimson, who pointed out to Roosevelt that practically every eminent physicist in the Allied world was engaged in the project, including four Nobel-prize–winners.[58]

* * *

While making progress in his own thinking, the septuagenarian secretary of war had failed to advance the plans for postwar control of atomic weaponry when the death of President Roosevelt on April 12, 1945, assured further delay. His vice president, Harry S Truman, had remained officially in the dark until the day he was sworn in, and not until April 25 did he receive a full briefing. But Stimson then relayed to the new president many of the atomic scientists and administrators' chief concerns: the United States could not indefinitely retain its monopoly; if determined to do so, Moscow could produce the weapon within a few years; provisions for inspection and control must be adopted to handle the problem both domestically and internationally; if not controlled on an international basis, atomic weapons might destroy civilization.[59]

Truman recalls that he listened to Stimson's briefing with "absorbed interest."[60] However, he had spent most of his first two weeks in office receptively absorbing advice that he take a harder line toward the Soviet Union, and two days earlier he had given the Soviet foreign minister a tongue-lashing that expressed the friction now dominating relations.[61] Harriman had rushed home from Moscow to tutor the new president in Stalin's duplicity but was pleased to find that Truman didn't need any convincing. He already intended to express U.S. displeasure over Soviet actions in Poland "with rather brutal frankness," and to warn them if they did not cooperate with American plans for the upcoming San Francisco Conference "they could go to hell." "I have never been talked to like that in my life," Molotov is said to have complained. "Carry out your agreements and you won't get talked to like that," Truman supposedly shot back.[62] Soviet-American relations had taken a sharp turn for the worse; against this background the new president received the news that the U.S. would soon possess an awesome new weapon.[63]

Ironically, just as the Alliance began to fracture, Bush and Conant were coming around on the question of advance consultation of the Soviets on S-1. After meeting with Bohr on April 25, Bush once again strongly petitioned Stimson's aides to begin advance planning, and enclosed a memorandum from Bohr laying out the case for an early approach to the Kremlin. At last, after further prodding from his aide George L. Harrison, Stimson acted, and on May 2 obtained Truman's consent to the creation of a seven-member advisory group on atomic issues—an "Interim Committee," so-named to forestall congressional charges of executive usurpation of authority—to be chaired by Stimson (with Harrison as his alternate), and including three scientist-administrators, Conant, Bush, and MIT president Karl T. Compton; navy undersecretary Ralph A. Bard; Assistant Secretary of State William L. Clayton; and James F. Byrnes as Truman's personal representative.[64]

Conant had mixed feelings about joining the group; on May 5, he wrote to Stimson expressing "serious doubt" whether he and Bush could be proper representatives of the project's scientists "for we have been primarily distant administrators rather than active participants."[65] By this time Conant was fully cognizant of the strong feelings of the Met Lab scientists, who continued to suspect that Washington was abjectly ignorant of the dangers to peace posed by the bomb. On April 21, a leading Chicago scientist, James Franck, had personally conveyed some of his colleagues' forebodings in a meeting with Secretary of Commerce Henry Wallace.[66] And Szilard and Urey, convinced there was "no point" trying to alert Conant, Bush, or Groves of the peril they perceived, in late May arranged an out-of-channels meeting with Byrnes to press their case for postwar international control. Trying to explain this breach of procedures to Groves, Arthur Compton blamed their initiative on the fact that the atomic scientists believed that they had lost control of the bomb, were "uninformed" on future plans for its use and development, and had received "little assurance that serious consideration of its broader implications is being given by those in a position to guide national policy." Their apprehensions were magnified, Compton added, by the knowledge that "scientists will be held responsible, both by the public and by their own consciences, for having faced the world with the existence of the new powers."[67]

Acknowledging the "growing restlessness" among Manhattan Project scientists, Conant told Stimson that many "are now deeply concerned about the international problems arising from the use of this weapon," and about U.S.-Soviet relations in particular. "They suppose that there has been no transmission of any information on this subject to our Russian allies, and they fear lest this fact endanger the future of our relations with that country and that we may be soon involved in a secret armament race with that nation, —particularly if use should occur before the Russians were notified of the existence of the weapon."[68]

Conant now shared those apprehensions, and his conversion to the idea of prior notification to the Russians appears to have come about partly due to the pressure from other scientists. He knew of Bohr's conversation with Bush, and the physicist Richard Tolman, also advising Groves, had told Conant of the argument that such a move would improve chances for gaining subsequent Soviet cooperation.[69] The disparity between Conant's view and that of the Chicago scientists concerned only the means to be used, not the end, on which they agreed. But so far as most project scientists knew, their administrators still thought of the bomb solely in terms of a military weapon.

Conant hoped Stimson would take steps to assure the scientists that their views were being considered. It was "essential," he wrote, that the government have the full support of the scientific community and "that there be no public bickering among experts after the bomb became public knowledge."[70] Before he agreed to join the committee, Conant had two requests. First, he wanted to show the material he and Bush had given Stimson in September to a few key scientists and assure them that the gist of their argument on international control had been communicated to Truman. And he recommended that the Interim Committee solicit their views on the international situation. (This led to the creation of an Interim Committee scientific advisory panel, an unprecedented example of scientific participation in the U.S. government's national-security policymaking process.)[71] Worried about his continued absence from Harvard, Conant still doubted the "wisdom" of participating on the committee, but this was not an insuperable obstacle and he promised to serve if reassured on the points he had raised. Stimson quickly dispatched a soothing letter agreeing that Conant's relations with the scientists were "exceedingly important" and consenting to the creation of the scientific advisory group, though he suggested that Conant wait before discussing his memorandum on international control.[72]

Conant now had an opportunity to take part directly in the postwar planning he and Bush had been advocating for the previous nine months. The Interim Committee's mandate was "to study and report on the whole problem of temporary war controls and later publicity, and to survey and make recommendations on postwar research, development, and controls, as well as legislation necessary to effectuate them."[73] But the item for which it would be most remembered did not even appear on the agenda, nor did it receive extensive consideration. As Conant has recalled, the committee had not formally planned to examine "what, in retrospect, was the most important matter on which an opinion was to be recorded"[74] — whether or not the bomb should be used at all.

CHAPTER 13

"... Like the End of the World"

Hiroshima and Alamogordo
Summer 1945

> At the suggestion of Dr. Conant the Secretary agreed that the most desirable target would be a vital war plant employing a large number of workers and closely surrounded by workers' houses.
> —Interim Committee minutes, May 31, 1945

> I was quite aware of the potentialities for global destruction which were inherent in the project in which we were engaged.
> —JBC to his editor, 1968

"Let us freely admit that the battlefield is no place to question the doctrine that the end justifies the means," Conant told Harvard students in 1943. "But let us insist, and insist with all our power, that this same doctrine must be repudiated ... in times of peace."[1]

The atomic bomb severely tested Conant's neat division of doctrines. For, with the bomb, the means threatened to overwhelm the end: the new weapon might end the war, but it might also lead to a new war that would make the previous victory meaningless. Did the weapon's immediate value — a *deus ex machina* end to hostilities, a resounding assertion of American might — outweigh the long-term dangers it posed to civilization?

In Conant's views about using the atomic bomb against Japan, one may discern the contradictory impulses both in his own thinking and in American atomic policy more broadly considered. Conant fully supported, and never subsequently showed regret over, the decision to bomb Hiroshima.[2] With the exception of Ralph Bard, who expressed post hoc reservations, the entire Interim Committee endorsed the conclusion that the bomb should be dropped on a heavily populated Japanese city, and dropped without prior warning.[3] Of those sanctioning the action during the committee's meeting of May 31, 1945, Conant has captured a special place in accounts of the decision for the minutes record that *"At the suggestion of Dr. Conant the Secretary* [Stimson] *agreed that the most desirable target would be a vital war plant employing a large number of workers and closely surrounded by workers' houses."*[4] Conant's suggestion, it has been pointed out, "enabled the maximum number of civilians to be killed with the maximum moral rectitude."[5]

Conant believed that no credible alternative existed, and wrote later that his only regret was that the bomb wasn't ready sooner.[6] His position mirrored that of Secretary Stimson, who claimed that from 1941 to 1945, he never heard it "suggested by the President, or by any other responsible member of the government, that atomic energy should not be used in the war."[7] That is not quite true: although they mentioned it only in passing, Bush and Conant in their September 30, 1944, memo to Stimson had said the first weapon might be demonstrated "over enemy territory, or in our own country, with a subsequent notice to Japan that the materials would be used next against the Japanese mainland unless surrender was forthcoming."[8] A week earlier, Bush had informed Conant that Roosevelt himself, at a September 22 meeting, had speculated whether the bomb "should actually be used against the Japanese or whether it should be used only as a threat with full-scale experimentation in this country."[9] And in their September 1944 Hyde Park *aide-mémoire*, which Stimson finally saw in June 1945, Roosevelt and Churchill had agreed that a bomb "might perhaps, after mature consideration," be used against Japan.[10] In 1942, Conant had spoken of the bomb in terms of "insurance" against German success, noting that "the knowledge that such a bomb *could be made to work* [emphasis added] would have great psychological advantage" if the Germans began use of atomic weapons.[11] On the other hand, the clear weight of evidence does support Stimson's assertion: the atomic bomb was built as a weapon of war, to be used; once the project had been set in motion (and particularly after $2 billion had been wagered on its timely completion), high officials had no significant doubts that the bomb would be used at the earliest possible date.[12] Byrnes put the matter crudely: "How would you get Congress to appropriate money for atomic energy if you do not show results for the money which has been spent already?"[13] To scientific and industrial associates, to government officials, to the Harvard Corporation, to future historians, and most of all to the prospective congressional investigating committees, Conant felt an acute desire to justify his wartime labors.

Conant's support for using the bomb never seriously wavered, but the motives underlying his commitment to the Manhattan Project did undergo a subtle transformation. Initially, his primary reason for supporting an all-out push had been his fear of a German head start. From the start this negative incentive had been complemented by the realization that atomic energy and weapons, if practicable, held such revolutionary power that the United States might want them regardless of whether other nations possessed them. Roosevelt, Bush, Conant, and others involved fast recognized that atomic weapons would have a significance far outlasting the immediate conflict, and after his momentous White House conference on October 9, 1941, Bush had reported to his deputy on a lengthy discussion of the problems of "after-war control."[14]

Postwar potentialities alone, though, would not have prompted the government to embark on a highly speculative, astronomically expensive venture without the tangible threat of being beaten to the mark by a wartime enemy. By 1945, however, Conant knew that threat had, for the time being, disappeared. Germany was defeated. Japan had no chance of building atomic weapons. The race was over. Conant nevertheless found other justifications for using the bomb as soon as possible. Most of those reasons boiled down to the argument that the bomb, sprung on the Japanese without warning, seemed likely to bring the fastest end to hostilities with the minimum loss of American lives. In May and June 1945, the United States was clearly headed for victory in the Pacific, but Conant and other scientists on the Interim Committee were informed that a long and bloody path lay ahead. Stimson told the Interim Committee that plans called for an Allied invasion of the Japanese mainland beginning in November.[15] Supporters of the decision, most prominently Truman, Stimson, and Churchill, later asserted that an invasion would have cost from a half-million up to a million Allied casualties, plus (a lesser consideration) many more Japanese losses.[16] After the war, serious doubts were raised about these casualty estimates, and the assertion was made that Japan desired to surrender anyway, and would have done so without a bomb.[17] In defense, Conant answered that the signs of impending Japanese collapse (including peace feelers extended to Moscow) did not become evident until after June 21 when the Interim Committee reaffirmed its recommendation, and in any case his knowledge of the battlefield situation came from Stimson and did not include a full-fledged military briefing.[18]

Like Stimson and others on the committee, Conant counted on the bomb's uniqueness to *shock* Japan's leaders into surrender. One plane could wipe out a city in a flash—a "brilliant luminescence," Oppenheimer told the panel, "that would rise to a height of 10,000 or 20,000 feet." The suddenness, ferocity, and spectacular nature of the blow would aid the goal of making, as Stimson put it, "a profound psychological impression on as many of the inhabitants as possible."[19] Conant believed it might allow the Japanese army and navy, as a point of pride, to attribute their surrender to a mysterious new device, "that scientific stuff," rather than to a defeat on the battlefield.[20] In early May, he wrote privately that the "essence of war is not slaughter but *impressing your will upon the enemy.*"[21] Any demystification of the bomb might reduce the effect: its aim was not to exterminate the entire population of Japan but to raise that specter, so that its leaders would act to avoid it.

No technical demonstration, Conant believed, would produce the same result as actual military use. The Interim Committee flirted with the idea only once—over lunch on May 31—and Conant "threshed over" the idea informally with Bush, Karl Compton, Harrison, and perhaps others on several occasions.[22] He subsequently detailed his reasons, however. One major factor was the limited availability of the weapons at Los Alamos: only two would soon be ready, and it would be several more weeks before a third. "Therefore," he wrote to McGeorge Bundy in late 1946, "a maximum effect had to be obtained with the few at our disposal. Nothing would have been more disastrous than a prior warning followed by a dud, and this was a very real possibility." It should be remembered, he added, "that never before in the history of war had a weapon been used on a large scale which had not been proof-tested; that even the success of the test at Alamogordo Proving Grounds did not give 100% assurance that the first bombs in combat would actually be successful; that there was certainly in the minds of the Interim Committee or at least those most cognizant with the development of the weapon a conviction that it was only a matter of probability that the first bombs used would be successful."[23]

To those who later argued that dropping the bomb on Hiroshima was immoral, Conant replied with arguments that reflected a basic philosophical strain running through his whole life; in an imperfect world, one has to deal with greater and lesser evils, and make unpleasant compromises, to get anything accomplished. All war was immoral, he believed, so therefore almost any action was equally permissible or impermissible—a clear, unbroken chain of logic led inextricably from the contention that atomic weapons were in some way more immoral than other weapons to a belief in total disarmament. And that, to Conant, was a philosophically defensible but utterly unrealistic point of view.[24]

Dealing with morality on a relative plane, accepting that desirable ends from time to time required heinous means, Conant could accept the use of the bomb as a grim necessity: the war had to be ended. In later years, even on long summer days in New Hampshire, in talks with his family, he never expressed misgivings over his recommendation as a member of the Interim Committee—although late in his life he conceded that the bombing of Nagasaki, which did not come before the panel as a separate choice, may have been a mistake.[25] On the essential decision, based on the information available to him at the time, he believed he had no other alternative and saw no use in agonizing afterward. More than two decades after Hiroshima, Conant bristled when his editor nudged him to include an account of his soul-searching prior to the decision. Disdaining "those scientists who have paraded their sense of guilt," he replied: "You speak of the conflict in the minds of those who were working on the bomb before Hiroshima . . . Probably because of my connection with the use of gas in World War I and my close connection with the sections of the NDRC which were developing napalm incendiary bombs so devastatingly effective against Tokyo, the conflict of which you speak hardly existed in my mind."[26]

But that is not the whole story. Conant appreciated that the existence of atomic weapons—the irrevocable fact of the explosive potential bound up in the atomic nucleus—presented moral dilemmas that, if not entirely unrelated, raised issues on a wholly new scale. "On the other hand," he admitted to his editor, "I was quite aware of the potentialities for global destruction which were inherent in the project in which we were engaged." Atomic explosives ultimately threatened civilization, perhaps even human existence. These were weapons "in a totally different class from anything the world has ever seen," as he had written in March 1943,[27] and he had also been alerted early in the war to the potential for vastly more destructive fission bombs, as well as to the possibility of hydrogen bombs perhaps a thousand times more powerful. When Conant first heard of the idea in 1942, prospects seemed good for rapid development of fusion weapons; the chances were somewhat dimmer in 1945 but it was still estimated that they could be built in a few years.[28] Examination of hydrogen fusion theory spawned an even more terrifying concept: could an atomic bomb trigger a chain reaction in the nitrogen of the atmosphere, exploding it?[29] Tense calculations in late 1942 showed that danger to be negligible, but it haunted Conant anyway.

Such considerations made him hope that atomic weapons would prove to be an impossibility, although if they could be built, the United States must do so before any other nation. This was a violent clash of short-term and long-term imperatives—ending the war and preserving the peace. Ideally, in Conant's view, they could be separated. He warned repeatedly that the means, the mindset, and the dehumanized values of war must not outlive the battle: peacetime must guarantee secrecy ended, liberties restored, individual rights revalued. Victory could then truly be won; ends could be divorced from means.[30] But atomic weaponry threatened to invalidate that separation. How could genuine peace—or a free, open American democracy—exist under the constant peril of devastating surprise attack, with no defense possible? In a nuclear world, customary warning signs would no longer apply; without mobilization, numerical superiority of forces, geographical proximity, or warning, one country could suddenly wreak overwhelming destruction on another.

Conant therefore tried to find a framework in which rapidly completing and then using atomic weapons in the war represented not merely an unavoidable evil but a positive good. If such weapons were feasible, they would be built sooner or later, he reasoned—the basic scientific knowledge was already known—and if the war ended before the United States used the bomb, the danger of its future development would be just as great but much less obvious. To impress both on Americans and on other nations the need to control it, the bomb's terrible force had to be starkly evident. "We have had some skeptics express doubts as to whether it is indeed a revolutionary weapon," Conant said in 1947, "but what skepticism there would have been had there been no actual use in war!"[31] He later insisted that use of the bomb had been "part and parcel" of the war's total operation, but believing that using it would have a beneficient influence on the postwar control efforts allowed him to integrate his short- and long-term objectives into a single, consistent, integrated viewpoint.[32]

In the weeks and months leading up to Hiroshima, however, a group of Chicago scientists took the opposite view. In June the members of the Met Lab's Committee on Political and Social Implications wrote a report (known as the Franck Report) stating that if the United States launched a surprise atomic attack on Japan "she would sacrifice public support throughout the world, precipitate the race for armaments, and prejudice the possibility" of international control.[33] Far from becoming more accommodating, Russia would speed its efforts at catching up. For, they pointed out, it would be very difficult for America "to persuade the world that a nation which was capable of secretly preparing and suddenly releasing a weapon as indiscriminate as the robot bomb and a million times more destructive, is to be trusted in its proclaimed desire of having such weapons abolished by international agreement." The Franck Report urged that any bomb demonstration take place on a desert or deserted island before representatives of all the United Nations.

The Interim Committee received the Franck Report on June 11, but the document was kept away from President Truman and diverted to the scientific advisory panel, which came down on the side of those, like Conant, who believed that a surprise attack on Japan would improve chances for an eventual agreement: "We can propose no technical demonstration likely to bring an end to the war; we see no acceptable alternative to direct military use," the panel reported to the full Interim Committee on June 16.[34] Oppenheimer, Fermi, Arthur Compton, and Lawrence—the foursome Conant had recommended[35]—did, however, strongly endorse the suggestion that the Allies, including Moscow, be informed of American progress on the bomb.

When the issue came up at the Interim Committee's June 21 session, Conant and Bush now reversed the skepticism they had shown toward Bohr's key contention. At the upcoming Big Three Conference in Potsdam, they urged, "there would be considerable advantage, if suitable opportunity arose, in having the President advise the Russians that we were working on this weapon with every prospect of success and that we expected to use it against Japan." If Stalin pressed for more information, Truman should not volunteer any data but promise future discussions in the hope that after the war this "new means of warfare will become an aid in preserving peace." Finally, at the eleventh hour and in diluted form, Bohr's initiative won the day. Altering its May 31 position—when Byrnes had supported continued secrecy out of fear that Stalin would ask to be an atomic partner—the Interim Committee now agreed that such a step might be conducive to postwar control efforts, and Stimson so informed the president.[36]

Truman and his top advisers, however, perceived a potential usefulness in the soon-to-be-tested atomic bomb that outweighed their desire to devise arrangements to control it. Quite aside from its capacity to end the war with Japan, the weapon promised, they believed, a fervently desired diplomatic and, if necessary, military counterweight to Soviet truculence. An enthusiastic apostle of the bomb's diplomatic utility in this regard was Byrnes, soon to be named secretary of state. In late May, two weeks after Germany's surrender, Byrnes reputedly told Leo Szilard that a demonstration of American atomic might could make the Kremlin "more manageable" in a showdown over Red Army occupation forces in Hungary and Romania.[37] Secretary of War Stimson in the spring had also come to see S-1 as "powerfully connected" with and in fact "dominant" over Washington's chances of trumping Soviet aggression or even forcing a liberalization of the Communist system, and he spewed glowing metaphors into his diary such as "master card," "royal straight flush," and "ace in the hole" about the weapon's potential prowess. "We must find some way of persuading Russia to play ball," he told Truman on May 16—observing, in view of the upcoming S-1 trial, "We shall probably hold more cards in our hands later than now."[38]

In a meeting with Stimson on June 6, Truman fully agreed that the Soviets should not be allowed into the nuclear partnership unless it substantially moderated its behavior in, for starters, Poland, Romania, Yugoslavia, and Manchuria.[39] Yet the president, like his secretary of war, grasped the frustrating fact that the bomb was still only a theory, even though "every prophecy thus far has been fulfilled by development."[40] Loath to pursue a high-stakes diplomatic strategy without the sure knowledge that it rested on reality and not a scientific boondoggle, Truman deliberately postponed and delayed the Potsdam Conference—and the showdown with Stalin it might bring—"to give us more time" to test the bomb. Another motive to wait for the results before seeing Stalin involved the war in the Pacific; if the secret weapon could quickly end it, that might negate the need to cajole the Russians into the war against Japan. Truman gave the Manhattan Project's leaders a deadline of July 15, the day he was scheduled to arrive in the devastated capital of the defeated Nazi Reich, now in the firm control of the Red Army, to discuss the shape of postwar Europe with Churchill and Stalin.[41]

On Sunday, July 15, as the Big Three converged on Berlin, Conant flew to New Mexico to find out whether four years of frantic efforts and mind-numbing expense had paid off. Groves had put the screws on to meet Truman's deadline. And under Oppenheimer's code name, Trinity, the first test—of a "gadget" with a core of plutonium, the method about which Conant had initially been so skeptical—was planned for before dawn Monday morning.

Though Conant rarely mentioned his experience at Alamogordo, the 1982 declassification of his secret eight-page handwritten account prepared the next day for the files of the OSRD permits a detailed reconstruction of his actions and emotions.[42] The bomb project's top echelon—Bush, Conant, and Groves—reached the Los Alamos base camp at eight o'clock Sunday night, where Conant found the atmosphere "a bit tense as might be expected" but confident. A pool on the size of the anticipated explosion drew guesses from zero (a postponement) to Rabi's estimate of 18,000 tons (18 kilotons) of TNT to Teller's 45,000. Conant, who had for some time expected the initial atomic weapons to start at relatively low levels, figured on 4,400 tons, but didn't sign up. At the Alamogordo test range, in a lonely desert region known as the *Jornada del Muerto* (Journey of Death), Conant sustained a sleepless night, kept awake by excitement and the battering of high winds against his tent. Thunderstorms punctuated by lightning delayed and threatened to postpone the test: "What the hell is wrong with the weather?" Groves roared at the site's meteorologist. Fermi, in a bit of black humor that unnerved some listeners, offered to wager on the chances that the detonation would ignite the atmosphere, with a side bet on whether the event would destroy the entire world or merely New Mexico; less jocularly, Groves secretly informed the governor of the state that he might need to declare martial law should something go wrong. Scientists fidgeted, rechecked calculations, played poker. Finally, conditions allowed for a countdown aimed at 5:30 a.m. As the time approached, Conant took up position at an observation point 17,000 yards from the plump implosion device, nick-named "Fat Man" after its squat spherical shape (in contrast to the cylindrical gun-method uranium bomb, known as "Little Boy").

Conant lay on his stomach between Bush and Groves on a tarpaulin laid over the sand, his feet pointing toward the bomb. Against advice, he kept his eyes open and intently watched the dark horizon opposite ground zero, streaked with the first faint rays of dawn. Breaking the tense silence, a scientist shouted the final countdown over a loudspeaker. Leaning over to Groves, Conant whispered that he never imagined seconds could last so long. Minus 40, minus 30, 20, 10 . . .

> Then came a burst of white light that seemed to fill the sky and seemed to last for seconds. I had expected a relatively quick and light flash. The enormity of the light quite stunned me. My instantaneous reaction was that something had gone wrong and that the thermal nuclear transformation of the atmosphere, once discussed as a possibility and jokingly referred to a few minutes earlier, had actually occurred.

Though calculations had supposedly dismissed the danger that an atomic explosion could set off an uncontrolled chain reaction in the atmosphere's nitrogen, the thought had lurked in Conant's subconscious, dormant until the incredibly powerful light had activated the sudden, "irrational" thought: "The whole world has gone up in flames."[43] A scientist more than twenty miles from ground zero, twice as far away as Conant, left a cogent description of that eerie illumination:

> Suddenly and without any sound, the hills were bathed in brilliant light, as if somebody had turned the sun on with a switch. It is hard to say whether the light was less or more brilliant than full sunlight, since my eyes were pretty

well dark adapted. The hills appeared kind of flat and colourless like a scenery seen by the light of a photographic flash, indicating presumably that the retina was stimulated beyond the point where intensity discrimination is adequate. The light appeared to remain constant for about one or two seconds (probably for the same reason) and then began to diminish rapidly.[44]

As did Brig. Gen. Thomas F. Farrell, located 10,000 yards south of the explosion:

> The lighting effects beggared description. The whole country was lighted by a searing light with the intensity many times that of the midday sun. It was golden, purple, violet, gray and blue. It lighted every peak, crevasse and ridge of the nearby mountain range with a clarity and beauty that cannot be described but must be seen to be imagined. It was that beauty the great poets dream about but describe most poorly and inadequately.[45]

Momentarily blinded, Conant quickly turned and, lying on his back and raising his head, observed the fiery maelstrom ascending from the desert, holding in front of his eyes a small, thick piece of darkened glass. He later described the sight as "an enormous pyrotechnic display with great boiling of luminous vapors," a ball of flame rapidly billowing into a giant, reddish-purple mushroom cloud, fueled by secondary explosions, resembling a giant oil fire. "Watch out for the detonation wave!" someone shouted. Forty seconds after seeing the flash, the silently awed Manhattan Project leaders heard a thundering growl reverberate off the surrounding mountains—a sound described by Farrell as a "strong, sustained, awesome roar which warned of doomsday and made us feel that we puny things were blasphemous to dare tamper with the forces heretofore reserved to the Almighty."[46] Before rising to his feet, Conant turned to shake hands with Bush and Groves. "Well, I guess there is something in nucleonics after all," the burly general told him.[47]

The bomb had not only worked but had exceeded all expectations. Aside from the visual effect, the test-firing had produced an enormous yield, ultimately calculated at 18.6 kilotons—Rabi won the bet. The shock wave toppled Kistiakowsky and two others observing from 10,000 yards south of the device, which vaporized an adjacent steel tower. A minute after the explosion, Conant recorded, a spontaneous cheer arose from the assembled scientists and military policemen. Harvard's Kenneth Bainbridge had a more ambivalent reaction: "Now we are all sons of bitches," he told Oppenheimer, whose face was observed to relax into "an expression of tremendous relief"; the philosopher-king of Los Alamos conjured up a suitably melancholy and awe-filled sentence from the *Bhagavad Gita,* the Hindu scripture: "I am become Death, the destroyer of worlds." Seemingly immune from the tumble of conflicting emotions, Groves proudly wired news of the successful test to Stimson in Potsdam, where the venerable statesman perversely employed the code of childbirth ("Babies satisfactorily born") to inform an overjoyed Churchill.[48]

For Conant, however, the apocalyptic image of the first moment of the nuclear age overshadowed even his relief at the project's success. Never before, one may assume, had a human being who was awake, sober, with an intellectual justification for what he believed, and responsible for the event, believed that he was literally witnessing the end of the world. Many at Alamogordo recall that they *thought of* the end of the world—"I am sure," said Kistiakowsky, "that at the end of the world—in the last millisecond of the earth's existence—the last men will see what we saw"[49]—but for a split second, Conant believed that he *was* one of the last men. According to one account based in part on interviews with Conant, his reaction

> was almost violently intense, although not nearly so dramatic as the second-hand reports which describe him as "embracing those around him and weeping for joy." If he wept, as he may have done, it would not have been for anything so simple as joy; for that word, read relief, hope and fear, exhaustion, gnawing responsibility, a compound of stresses and emotions which might make even the formulas of atomic energy seem relatively simple.[50]

One person present at Trinity said it was "difficult" to carry on a coherent conversation with Conant after the bomb went off.[51] It is not surprising that on the flight back to Washington he and other scientists—Bush, Lawrence, and Tolman—were "still upset by what they had seen and could talk of little else," to the annoyance of Groves, whose thoughts were already "completely wrapped up" in preparing the details of the "upcoming climax" in Japan.[52]

For Conant, the test had been a traumatic reminder that the future hinged not on defeating Japan but on mitigating the suspicion that suffused the summit meeting at Potsdam. In Washington, he wrote up his notes of the test for Bush. "My first impression remains the most vivid," he concluded, "a cosmic phenomenon like an eclipse. The whole sky suddenly full of white light like the end of the world. Perhaps my impression was only premature on a time scale of years!"[53]

CHAPTER 14

"My Fingers Are Still Crossed on the Bomb"

Ominous Fallout

1945

It seems to me that you do essentially threaten or bargain if you do anything short of "blandly giving away the secret," and I think we should bargain and bargain very hard.
> —Letter to Vannevar Bush, September 27, 1945

It might be advisable to select the printed material that would preserve the record of our civilization for the one we can hope will follow, microfilming it and making perhaps 10 copies . . . In that way we could ensure against the destruction that resulted from the fall of the Roman Empire.
> —To Harvard librarian Keyes D. Metcalf, September 1945

Looks as if the conference were headed for a large success. But my fingers are still crossed on the bomb and will be until the commission is set up.
> —Diary entry, Moscow, December 24, 1945

For Conant, Hiroshima was an anticlimax. On July 19, 1945, three days after Trinity, he sketched out his long-range plans on a piece of blue Harvard notebook stationery: "What JBC would like to do before death or senility overtakes him." The list included books on chemistry, on science philosophy, and poetry, on public education and American society; an intensive study of the advancement of knowledge in post-Renaissance Europe; teaching, studying, writing. No mention is made of the atomic bomb.[1] With relief, one must presume, he and Mrs. Conant headed off at the end of July for several weeks of rest (twice interrupted by urgent summonses to Washington) and relaxation at "Ravine House" in Randolph, his latest summer base in the New Hampshire hills.

After years in the pressurized, looking-glass world of the Manhattan Project, Conant happily looked forward to resuming life as a full-time educator. Finally, he could divulge to associates and to Harvard's governing boards the secret explanation behind his detachment from university affairs for the past four years, though one close aide, Calvert Smith, died before learning the news his boss had so carefully hidden since 1941. There was plenty of business awaiting Conant's return to University Hall for the fall semester: welcoming home students and faculty from wartime assignments, commemorating those who had died in battle, and debating a just-released report on "General Education in a Free Society" which he had commissioned from a special faculty committee shortly after Pearl Harbor. A reflection of Conant's oft-voiced wartime implorings to nurture "the liberal and humane tradition" and democratic values for the post-victory world, the three-year study under the chairmanship of Provost Paul Buck recommended that undergraduates receive a broader exposure to the advancement of knowledge in different fields of thought—the natural sciences, humanities, and social sciences—and better training for life as informed citizens in a democracy and in a dangerous, complex world, as well as narrow specialists.[2] Finally, students and faculty streamed back to Cambridge from their wartime assignments and reclaimed classrooms, labs, and dorms commandeered by the armed forces. It was time, Conant told an opening chapel convocation in September, for Harvard to carry out a "psychological conversion no less important than the readjustment of our economic life." Harkening back to the moral dichotomy he had proclaimed during the fighting, he asserted that with victory achieved, the "moral imperatives of the battlefield must be transformed into those of a free society which believes in the supreme significance of each individual man or woman."[3]

But Conant could not easily escape the indiscriminate killing machine that he had labored to construct for four years. Nor, finally, could the rest of the world, after President Truman's announcement on August 6, 1945, that the United States had "loosed" a weapon "harnessing the basic power of the universe" against Japan.[4] At 8:15 that morning, local time, a noiseless flash bursting from a point 1,800 feet above downtown Hiroshima incinerated the port city. Two days later, the Soviet Union declared war on Japan and blitzed into Manchuria. On August 9, a second American atomic bomb seared Nagasaki. Carried out without warning, the two attacks killed or wounded close to 300,000 people—figures comparable to those produced by the fierce firebombing raids that continued until Japan surrendered on August 14, but achieved with a striking economy of forces.[5] Reactions encompassed every emotion from anger and horror to the comment of President Truman when he heard of *Enola Gay*'s success while he sailed home from Potsdam. "This is the greatest thing in history," he said.[6]

Conant decidedly disagreed. As with many others, his emotions mingled dread and hope. The alternative to an international agreement controlling atomic weapons, he believed, was an arms race ending in disaster; on July 18, a day after returning to Washington from Alamogordo, Conant and Bush had reaffirmed to the Interim Committee their support for a global commission to exchange scientific data as a prelude to a full sharing of the bomb. "To avoid a secret armament race and strengthen the United Nations Organization must be the prime objective of every sane man," they wrote, the vision of Trinity still fresh in their minds.[7]

But Truman's reaction to Trinity, as the inexperienced president nervously awaited the opening session at Potsdam, had differed markedly from Conant's. Truman, too, was moved to profound reflection, wondering whether the force released in Alamogordo might be the "fire destruction prophesied in the Euphrates Valley Era, after Noah and his fabulous Ark." But, thankful that the United States had beaten "Hitler's crowd or Stalin's" to the punch, he speculated that the weapon might be the "most terrible thing ever discovered, but it can be made the most useful."[8] Thrust into the stratospheric company of Churchill and Stalin and shadowed by FDR's ghost, Truman suddenly perceived a chance to undercut the fierce resistance he expected from Stalin on a range of vexing disputes, including Soviet political and territorial claims in eastern Europe, Germany, and the Far East. The spectacular descriptions of Trinity inspired Truman to take a tougher position with "Uncle Joe." The news "tremendously pepped up" and "evidently greatly reinforced" him, Stimson recorded, and Churchill noted that after reading Groves's report the "fortified" American president had "stood up to the Russians in a most emphatic manner and decisive manner . . . he was a changed man. He told the Russians just where they got on and off and generally bossed the whole meeting."[9]

Now hopeful that America's atomic edge could boost its postwar diplomacy, Truman (warmly backed by Churchill) did not believe it necessary to make a serious overture to Stalin regarding control of the bomb or to inform him explicitly of American atomic progress or plans, as the Interim Committee, and Conant and Bush, had hoped. Instead, he waited until near the end of the conference, on July 24, during a break between meetings, before nonchalantly mentioning that "we had a new weapon of unusual destructive force." Stalin replied just as casually, Truman recalled in his memoirs, that "he was glad to hear it and hoped we would make 'good use of it against the Japanese.'"[10]

Neither Truman nor Churchill, closely observing the informal exchange from a few feet away, believed that Uncle Joe had understood the cryptic reference, and Soviet sources are divided on the subject. A recent biography based on partial access to Soviet archives (Dmitri Volkogonov's *Stalin: Triumph & Tragedy*) asserts that Stalin cabled Beria that same evening ordering him to "speed up the work" on the bomb, but the author provides no specific source for this claim. But either then or a couple of weeks later, Stalin got the message clearly enough, and ordered his own atomic scientists to step up their efforts. Like their colleagues around the world, Soviet physicists had been investigating fission since 1939, and Stalin had approved a low-level uranium weapons development effort as early as 1942. Through the espionage of Klaus Fuchs, a German-born physicist working under British auspices at Los Alamos, and a still uncertain number of other sources, Moscow had kept up-to-date on Manhattan Project progress despite the official silence on the subject from FDR and Churchill. The dislocations and urgent priorities of fighting a bloody rearguard war against the German invaders had hindered the Soviet effort and distracted the Kremlin, however, until the American accomplishments in the summer of 1945 generated new political will to catch up at any cost. "A single demand of you, comrades," Stalin told his weapons and scientific chiefs in mid-August, "provide us with atomic weapons in the shortest possible time. You know that Hiroshima has shaken the whole world. The equilibrium has been destroyed. Provide the bomb—it will remove a great danger from us."[11]

But Stalin had kept poker-faced at Potsdam, and Truman had no desire to volunteer any information that would lead to a candid discussion.[12] Thus, the era of nuclear diplomacy opened in the fashion in which it would continue for decades to come: under a cloud of mistrust and obfuscation, with both sides maneuvering for advantage and relying on the accumulation and brandishing of nuclear might to buttress their political strategies.

On August 10, the day after his ship docked after the crossing from Europe, Truman met with Conant, Bush, Groves, and senior military leaders at the White House to decide what the public should be told about the bomb. Overriding some concern about military security, the Manhattan Project leaders convinced him to release the Smyth Report, a document intended both to present a general narrative of the bomb project and to delimit for atomic scientists the boundaries of permissible public discussion. Conant hoped the Smyth Report, a faint echo of his original aim of open scientific interchange, would help to quash the misguided notion that the United States possessed an "atomic secret" that would indefinitely preserve a monopoly.

Detached from the diplomatic and military intrigue surrounding Japan's final defeat, Conant grappled with the difficulties of formulating a plan to prevent a postwar atomic race that would realistically conform to the more skeptical and assertive attitude that Truman and other policymakers seemed to be taking toward Moscow. His originally quite radical conception of May 1944, watered down by the time he and Bush put it in written form to Stimson, had undergone additional alterations by the time the bomb was used.

Those changes can be seen in an exchange of letters in the first days after Hiroshima and Nagasaki between Conant and Grenville Clark. "Congratulations on the bomb!" the lawyer wrote Conant on August 13. Clark thought it had been wise to use the weapon, otherwise "hardly anyone would have believed it; or been moved to do anything adequate to control its use," and that the atomic bomb offered the most dramatic evidence yet of the correctness and urgency of his long-held belief in a "real measure of world government."[13]

Clark's letter reached Conant at a moment of deep anguish—on top of the trauma of Alamogordo, bad personal news had arrived from the Pacific front where his sons were serving. Within forty-eight hours of Hiroshima, Ted had recognized an opening to exploit years of snooping into secret military projects, and launched an impromptu lecture tour on the new weapon for high-ranking naval officers, who repaid the favor with surplus electronic gear or the occasional crate of whiskey. Soon a gift copy of the Smyth Report arrived from his father to supply more material for his booming lecture business. A few months later, hitching around Asia aboard military transports and weather planes, Ted was "horrified" at the sight of the destruction wrought on Hiroshima and came to doubt the decision to use the bomb. But on August 6, his initial reaction, like that of many U.S. soldiers and sailors in the Pacific, was gratitude at deliverance from an invasion of the Japanese home islands, plus something more personal and, for him, unusual: he was proud of his father.[14]

His brother Jim, however, was not so fortunate. As the *Halibut* headed for the scrap yard, its chief deck officer was ordered out on additional submarine missions in the final months of the murderous island-hopping campaign against Japan. The tension proved too much. Using military intelligence channels to keep track of his sons' fortunes, Conant learned "just as the news of the atomic bomb arrived" that Jim had "'cracked up' just before going out on his 6th patrol" with what doctors diagnosed as "a severe case of 'combat fatigue'" and was being returned to the United States for hospitalization. "Coming just at this time, the news was a kick in the teeth," Conant wrote "Grennie" on August 17. "These psychoneurotic cases are bound to be long and distressing for all concerned but we hope for the best." Besides, he added bravely, it was "nothing" compared to the news many families had received.[15]

To Clark's congratulations on the bomb, Conant confined himself, in this first letter, to a thank-you and a significant comment that Clark's reasons for supporting the bomb's use were "exactly mine."[16] In another hand-scrawled missive two weeks later, cheered by an upbeat letter from his hospitalized son,[17] Conant elaborated on his current thinking about international control.

He began by mentioning to Clark that some of their "leftist friends" in America and Britain were arguing that the "atomic bomb . . . makes an international police force for using it imperative." He had thought so too, privately, fifteen months earlier, but now he ridiculed precisely this idea, having completely lost faith that such an organization could or should be established. On the contrary, he asserted,

> this weapon makes the creation of a United Nations force to handle weapons a very dangerous proposition. To put such power in the hands of a relatively small force alone, would be to live with a Damocles sword over one's head. What is to prevent the corruption of this force and its control by a few men bent on power or fanatically on the side of some ideological argument?

Of course, the world government supporters would respond, that sword would soon be over our heads in any case through national rivalry; it was simply a matter of which poison was preferable. But Conant now saw national sovereignty as an insuperable obstacle to world government, and cited the failure of the United States' strong federal government to prevent a civil war. The same kind of consideration had applied at the founding of the United States. Suppose in 1789 "all power to wage war had been concentrated in the hands of a small professional group and all power to resist removed from the states." Would anyone have accepted the plan, even if the professional group had "sworn an oath to the Federal Government on a stack of Bibles a foot high"? Conant's central point became a common refrain of skeptics of international control in the months to come: A strong central authority could not render war extinct, Conant maintained, "so long as the local loyalties could conflict with the sworn allegiance."[18]

Whatever the reasons—a darker view of Soviet intentions, a more skeptical view of what the political traffic would bear after months of exposure to high-level bureaucratic politics, instinctively cautious second thoughts overwhelming his initial revelation—Conant's transition from an innovative believer in a radical transformation of the international system to a skeptical opponent of world government illustrates the general pattern of psychologically integrating nuclear weapons into familiar and conventional ways of thinking that Einstein described when he commented that the "atomic bomb has changed everything, except the nature of man."[19]

In the fall of 1945, watching the public try to come to grips with the atomic dilemmas he had been secretly considering for four years, Conant felt the very survival of civilization resting on his shoulders. An intimate knowledge of the workings of atomic weapons, reinforced by the transcendentally terrifying vision of Alamogordo, spurred him again to campaign forcefully for two diametrically opposed positions, both of which were more radical than the government was willing to adopt. One was an intensive effort to see if an effective international control agreement with the Soviets was possible; the other was to take urgent actions to prepare for World War III—the First Atomic War.

Even before Hiroshima, Conant himself had become a firm adherent of the proposition that atomic weapons would be so effective that they would inevitably dominate future wars. "For us to plan otherwise," he wrote Grenville Clark in early October, "would be the height of folly."[20] Within weeks of the bombing of Hiroshima, Conant had urged War Department officials to launch intensive studies of atomic warfare and the best methods of preparation for it. As a first step, in view of the "general muddying up [of] the waters" occurring as a result of uninformed public discussion, he suggested that the War Department issue a public statement acknowledging that other industrialized countries could develop their own bombs in five to twenty years and therefore this "revolution in warfare" necessitated a complete rethinking of military strategy as well as of "the important problem of location of civilian industry and the nature of American cities."[21] In letters to Clark and Vannevar Bush in October, he spelled out the specific and far-reaching steps he felt should be taken to ensure that no matter how terrible an atomic war might be, the United States would survive in some form. Characteristically, he viewed the situation in coldly practical, utilitarian terms.

"I see no escape from the conclusion that a drastic change in our industrialized pattern is in order if we are to have adequate defense," he wrote. Even if an atomic attack destroyed the ten largest American cities, "considerably more" than half the population would be left to carry on. "At the worst, the use of the atomic bomb does not add up to the destruction of the United States or civilization. But unless precautions are taken in advance, an attack would destroy our power of resistance to an enemy. It would seem wise to arrange matters so that survivors of a holocaust could carry on some sort of national life in spite of the devastation." If this was done, he concluded, an "intelligent enemy" might not consider the ten largest cities important targets.[22]

But even these comments only hint at the flabbergasting proposal Conant flirted with privately in those days to save civilization from itself. While publicly criticizing the rampant "manifestations of panic and alarm in the press and on the air"[23] in the weeks following Truman's announcement, the private record shows that Conant himself was not immune to panic. In September or October, he took a first, highly secret step toward enabling "survivors of a holocaust" to "carry on some sort of national life," or to at least provide them with adequate reading material. He called in the librarian of Harvard University, Keyes DeWitt Metcalf, who had not seen the president for a one-on-one meeting since before the war. Metcalf didn't really know what to expect when Conant requested the meeting—and found it hard to believe his ears as Conant began explaining what he had in mind.

"We are living in a very different world since the explosion of the A-bomb," Metcalf later recalled Conant as saying. "We have no way of knowing what the results will be, but there is the danger that much of our present civilization will come to an end."[24] Conant reminded Metcalf that "the greatest disaster" of the fall of Rome fifteen hundred years before was "the destruction of a large part of the information that was then recorded only in manuscripts that were destroyed or lost." To head off that danger this time around, Conant then suggested this plan: "It has seemed to me that, in the world's present situation, it might be advisable to select the printed material that would preserve the record of our civilization for the one we can hope will follow, microfilming it and making perhaps 10 copies and burying those in different places throughout the country. In that way," he added, "we could ensure against the destruction that resulted from the fall of the Roman Empire."

Presumably alluding to his government connections (he could hardly start an alumni fund-raising drive for this purpose), Conant assured Metcalf that the "funds required, even if very large, can be found," and asked him to report back in two weeks with his recommendations on how much material would have to be preserved and how it should be selected and organized.

Two weeks later, the shaken but dutiful librarian reported back, telling Conant that "to preserve the material on which our present civilization is based" would require microfilming 500,000 volumes averaging 500 pages each for a total of 250 million pages. Ten copies meant 2.5 billion pages.

"This would include," Metcalf said, "the great literature of all countries that should not be lost, such as everything written by Shakespeare, Tolstoy, Dante and Goethe" although in a snub to literary critics Metcalf noted that "there would be no need to preserve more than a few of the thousands of volumes written about these writers and their works." Also to be inscribed on microfilm were "other great authors, music, books about the fine arts, the important records of world history, philosophy, economics, sociology, etc., and, perhaps especially important, our scientific developments in the broadest sense of that term." (Whether that included the blueprints for separating uranium, Metcalf apparently didn't say.) "It would be difficult to select the material," Metcalf summarized, "but I think it could be done reasonably well."

Nevertheless, Metcalf urged Conant not to go ahead with the project. For one thing, he said, "it could not be done without the world learning about it, and everyone would be so upset at the idea . . . that it would be unwise to undertake the task." A second reason given by Metcalf was that even if nuclear war wiped out all major cities, "copies of practically all of this material" would survive in the libraries of "Dartmouth, Stanford, Iowa State College, Oberlin and other institutions at a distance from large cities." Metcalf later recalled that Conant "accepted my report. We did not discuss costs, and I heard nothing more about the proposal."[25] Conant never spoke of it publicly and of course omitted it from his memoirs.

Conant in the first years of the atomic age was slow to learn that matter-of-fact, unemotional references to the unpleasant notion of planning for the apocalypse were not easy fare in his public utterances, and he was slow to erase them. In his first public statement on the bomb in November 1945 he admitted that a nuclear war would deliver a "crushing blow, perhaps a fatal one" to industrial civilization but expressed confidence that "the human race would survive even an atomic war. The Chinese or Indian cultures, for example, might be untouched and soon replace our own."[26] "Perhaps the fated task of those of us now alive in this country is to develop still further our civilization for the benefits of the survivors of World War III in other lands," he stated when the atomic threat refused to disappear. "It would not be an inglorious mission."[27] Understandably, he always quickly reminded listeners that these grim alternatives were by far inferior to his preferred future scenario, the course of action vocally advocated by numerous scientists and commentators in the United States and elsewhere: internationalizing the atom. He still regarded the establishment of an international agency as absolutely vital. But increasingly, due both to suspicions about Russia and awareness of domestic political constraints, Conant as well as Bush urged hard bargaining with Moscow before handing over the bomb or key industrial information needed for its production. Their July 18 memorandum had highlighted the necessity of a staged process in any control plan, and for at least the first five years of their proposed commission's operation, they specifically exempted inspection of American laboratories directly connected with manufacturing fissionable material. No other country would receive such an exemption; during its monopoly, however, the United States would release information on the number and power of bombs in its arsenals.

Five years was a long time to expect Stalin to twiddle his thumbs, but Conant and Bush expressed the tougher mood that was in favor in the Truman administration. "It is too Utopian to hope for complete interchange with the Russians now," they wrote. "We must test out their good faith. The above scheme does so." If the plan failed after a year or two because a nation backed out, they admitted, the third world war would be just over the horizon — but at least the situation would be clear.[28]

In the months following Hiroshima, however, the situation was anything but clear, and Conant watched in frustration as secrecy prevented many informed persons from publicly debating the bomb's significance — scientific, military, political, diplomatic, social, commercial. The Truman administration, he believed, for whatever reason, seemed unable to develop a coherent policy or, at a minimum, even to launch a serious study of the bomb's implications on a multitude of issues. Conant, still formally a member of the Interim Committee, OSRD, NDRC, a U.S.-British Combined Policy Committee, and probably other secretive bodies no one had bothered to disband, could exert influence by transmitting his exceptionally well-informed opinion to decision-makers — principally Bush, who retained considerable though waning power in atomic matters more by dint of his expertise and experience than any formal position or closeness to Truman or his associates — and to opinion-shapers in finance, the media, and academia.

Occasionally, however, Conant tried more directly to sway policy. On September 25, he joined in an appeal by educational leaders to Truman to appoint a blue-ribbon independent commission to analyze the impact of atomic weapons on military strategy and planning, in particular the question of universal military training, a subject dear to students' and educators' hearts. The bomb's rendering "obsolete much of our previous thinking" and "the current confusion in the public mind" compelled a wholesale reevaluation, they argued.[29]

Part of the confusion, as Conant saw it, stemmed from people's inability to grasp the utterly revolutionary nature of atomic weapons. To his dismay, even Bush seemed susceptible. In late August 1945, when Bush had sent some tentative notes for his first substantial post-Hiroshima public pronouncement, Conant recoiled from the statement that, "[d]evastating though the atomic bomb is, it does not compare in horror with other weapons which we declined to use in the war"—a "hideous catalog" ranging from "plant hormones to be sprayed from airplanes to kill all the enemy's crops and impose man-made famine on an entire population" to "poison gases of such penetrative power that no protection of masks or special clothing can withstand them and of such deadly potency that a single drop brings instant death."[30] Conant chided Bush for "play[ing] down the atomic bomb too much as a new weapon of war, and tend[ing] to mix up ideas of barbarism with military effectiveness," a tack that would only "confuse the issue still more." Biological warfare and poison gas, to Conant's mind, were just "not in the same category with the atomic bomb" or even incendiary bombs "from the point of view of military effectiveness." By tossing in the atom bomb with other new and diabolical, but far less momentous, devices, Bush would "play into the hands of those who want to ignore the atomic bomb as a weapon and proceed with defense along the old-fashioned lines."[31]

Those who suggested that the bomb, like poison gas, could be eliminated by international covenant were engaged in wishful thinking, Conant believed. Gas had not been used during the war, despite its possession by both sides, not out of ethical considerations but because "few if any in positions to determine overall strategy believe" gas was an effective weapon against an enemy with gas masks.[32] Against atomic bombs, he felt, no such defense existed. The only method of reducing the impact of an atomic attack was dispersal of industrial and population centers. Even without expected improvements, a few bombs could destroy a hundred square miles. Unless all air traffic was to be banned over cities and antiaircraft guns surrounded each potential target, nothing could prevent a surprise attack. "One plane will do the work of an armada. But defense against a single plane, *particularly against a surprise attack*, is vastly more difficult than defense against a thousand."[33]

Considering these attributes, Conant believed the bomb represented an ideal weapon against industrialized nations, and that no power with great security interest, least of all Russia, would want to be without it. And Conant had no doubt the Russians would manufacture atomic weapons. Then, by his definition, the atomic age would truly have begun. "If a situation were to develop where two great powers had stacks of bombs but neither was sure of the exact status of the other, the possibility of a devastating surprise attack by one upon the other would poison all our thinking," Conant told the Cleveland Chamber of Commerce in November. "Like two gunmen with itchy fingers, it would be only a question of who fired first." And, as Conant presumed (in terms that seem quaintly anachronistic a generation later) that the United States would "never attack without prior warning through a declaration of war," such a state of affairs would put the United States at a severe disadvantage as compared to "a totalitarian state in the hands of a ruthless dictator [who] might well follow the notorious example of the Japanese."[34]

In private and, beginning in mid-November, in public speeches, Conant's despair at finding any conventional way of countering atomic weapons impelled him to hammer home the message that "the first line of defense against atomic attack" was an effective system of international inspection and ultimately control of the production of atomic bombs.[35] Its most essential feature remained the publication of weapons information garnered by agents granted free access to laboratories and factories in every country. Without inspection, he wrote privately, war would be inevitable when "one great power or another (which may mean a handful of men)" believed it had secretly attained atomic superiority.[36]

In public, Conant claimed that in seeking Soviet agreement to an American-inspired plan "we are not using our present knowledge as a threat."[37] Privately, however, he wondered whether at least some arm-twisting might in the end prove necessary to obtain Russian agreement or acquiescence. "It seems to me," Conant wrote Bush in late September, that "you do essentially threaten or bargain if you do anything short of 'blandly giving away the secret,' and I think we should bargain and bargain very hard."[38]

U.S.-Soviet relations had drifted into an uncomfortable limbo since the war's end, with the already strong undercurrent of discord more and more in public view. Amid reports of the heavy Soviet hand in occupied Eastern Europe, Moscow's complaints of "capitalist encirclement," and the unbridgeable disagreements on a host of issues between Secretary of State Byrnes and Foreign Minister Molotov at the Council of Foreign Ministers meeting in London in September, even the most optimistic U.S. officials and commentators were acknowledging that dealing with the Soviets was exhausting and frustrating. The administration's suspicions about Soviet motives grew even stronger after the White House learned secretly in mid-September that Canadian police had obtained hard evidence of a Soviet spy network, based at Moscow's embassy in Ottawa, charged with the primary objective of acquiring "complete information regarding the atomic bomb" in advance of the "next war" with the Anglo-American allies. Worse, FBI director J. Edgar Hoover informed Truman, inquiries had identified a British scientist who had visited the Met Lab in late 1944, Dr. Alan Nunn May, as a "paid Soviet spy of long standing" and Communist Party member who had regularly furnished Manhattan Project data and even specimens of uranium-235.[39] Though the news would not become public for another five months, the sense of getting ready for a tough diplomatic confrontation with Moscow extended even to those officials who, like Bush and Conant, genuinely wanted international control.

Already, by late September, Conant had begun to think of a fallback plan—a limited nuclear alliance of the form that was to emerge four years later in the North Atlantic Treaty Organization. Of all the pronouncements tossed about by pundits, politicians, and scientists that autumn, the one that struck Conant as the most sensible came from a surprising source: the bridge expert Ely Culbertson, who peddled his "Quota Force" plan to whomever would listen. "I hate to admit it," Conant wrote Bush, "but the stuff that Ely Culbertson has sent me . . . makes the best sense of anything I have read on the subject."[40] Under Culbertson's scheme, a World Federative Body weighted in favor of the Big Three and without veto power would establish a yearly ratio of permitted military forces and major weapons allotted to each country— say, twenty percent of the world's annual military production to Russia, Britain, and the United States; ten percent to France and China; and twenty percent to the rest. To monitor compliance and to act against aggressors, the group would create a World Peace Force consisting of national forces from the major powers as well as an "International Contingent" from the "lesser member-states," which would be the first to move against any violator of the quota. Like other plans, Culbertson's aimed at total abolition of nuclear weapons and strict inspection to assure compliance, although in a rather prescient provision he noted that if this was impossible then a quota could also be established for producing atomic weapons.[41]

What evidently caught Conant's eye was not so much Culbertson's ideal scenario but his advice on how to proceed if Russia was unwilling to cooperate. If Moscow refused to join this Federative Alliance, the United States should go ahead and establish the alliance anyway—and Culbertson had no doubt that "four-fifths of the world," including Britain, France, and China, "could be effectively organized even without Russia." While Culbertson specified that Moscow should not be "threatened or coerced" to join, either at the start or later, Conant could not fail to spot the implications inherent in forming a military coalition lacking one principal power. Urging Bush to delete a renunciation of "threatening the world with our present power" from an upcoming speech, Conant said he hoped that the United States would push for a tough deal with Moscow "pretty soon," and "in terms of a strengthened United Nations organization and very much along the lines Culbertson has in mind."[42]

While Culbertson's formula of idealistic internationalism mixed with realistic recourses to national alliances appealed to Conant, Grenville Clark's steady movement toward outright world government caused the two to part ways. The gap, evident in August, grew even wider after a conference organized by Clark in mid-October issued a statement calling for the creation of a World Federal Government to replace the existing United Nations Organization. Since the first week of the war, Conant had been a friendly if sometimes skeptical observer of what he called Clark's "save the world" campaign, and the two had consulted frequently on foreign policy questions ranging from military preparedness to plans for postwar peace.[43] As a personal assistant to Stimson, Clark had learned about the atomic bomb's development in the spring of 1944 and resigned his War Department position with Stimson's blessing ("Go home and try to figure out a way to stop the next war and all future wars") to formulate a plan for a world organization to keep the peace;[44] organizing the October 1945 Dublin, New Hampshire, conference was his first postwar step in this direction. Unable to attend due to a previous commitment, Conant had spent a weekend at his friend's home at the end of September and, Clark recorded in his diary, "talked atomic bomb for 5 hours."[45] It was their first chance to talk at leisure since the end of the war, and Conant confided that he was thinking of resigning as Harvard president[46] — perhaps out of awareness of the Corporation's earlier plot to unseat him, or because he already suspected that he would be asked to take a major government post related to atomic matters. When the two discussed controlling the bomb, however, communication apparently broke down, although neither man realized it. Judging from the account of the meeting that Clark gave to Stimson, Conant spent much of the time explaining why he felt a tough inspection system under an international authority offered the only chance for a workable control arrangement. But while Conant said international inspection, all Clark heard was world government, limited, to be sure, but "really effective world government."[47] Clark's conference went off as scheduled, highlighted by an off-the-record reading of Conant's six-page "personal and confidential" memorandum analyzing the international control issue and stressing the essential roles of inspection and interchange while equivocating on the issue of an atomic-armed international police force.[48] Clark enthusiastically sent Conant a copy of the conference's final declaration, but got a cold shower in return. "I am sorry that I cannot go along with you on this," Conant replied. "It did not turn out the way I thought your mind was running when I last saw you."[49]

For all his tough talk, however, Conant simultaneously recognized the need for a suitable inducement for Russia to accept any proposal that left the American advantage intact and infringed upon Soviet sovereignty. The lure he counted on was a general immediate offer of American scientific and technical know-how on atomic energy and as many other subjects as possible, always exempting the detailed specifications of weapons and plants to produce fissionable material. Opening the door to scientific exchanges prior to final agreement, Conant wrote optimistically to Bush, "may well prove that international inspection would be acceptable to Russia because of the great technical advantages that would flow from her assumption of a place in a scientific world of free interchange."[50] In his Cleveland speech, Conant likened U.S. scientific and technological resources to "a series of cargoes which we would gladly ship to Russia for her later use," in exchange for her acceptance of American experts to set up an inspection apparatus. Nothing sinister in that, he insisted, merely a "series of partial payments" agreed to in advance, that would serve as a "frank basis for present negotiation."[51]

But how badly did the Soviet Union think it needed such aid? Conant's assessment of Russian industrial and technological prowess had altered subtly but significantly since the spring of 1945, when he had warned the Interim Committee that the Russians might catch up in three or four years.[52] Now, both publicly and privately, he was "quite certain" that it would take them between five and fifteen years from August 1945 before they began steady production.[53]

What caused that shift? The answer is worth close examination, as historians have cited predictions of the length of the American monopoly as a key factor in determining the urgency of U.S. efforts to establish international control.[54] Conant gave little weight to one of Groves's arguments: that Russia would not explode an atomic bomb for at least twenty years, partly because it could not acquire sufficient amounts of uranium. "My answer is a categorical no," Conant replied to the idea that control of raw materials could be an adequate method for enforcing international control, since, he said in October 1945, Russia "in all probability" already possessed the requisite ores.[55] On the question of Russia's industrial potential, in May he had thought it "highly unsafe" to assume "a very poor view."[56] But when four industrialists who briefed the Interim Committee on June 1 predicted a slightly longer American monopoly than he believed, he appears to have trusted the experts and adjusted his timetable accordingly.[57]

Conant acknowledged that immediate disclosure of nonmilitary scientific information related to atomic energy might advance the due date of a Russian bomb by up to two years, but believed that if there were any hope to avoid an arms race the precise date of Russian entry did not matter very much.[58] "The really crucial time interval," he stated prophetically on November 20, 1945, "is between today and the date on which the international political situation might become frozen in so ugly a pattern as to make impossible any control of the atomic bomb. This might occur long before another country were militarily prepared as regards to this new weapon."[59]

For this reason, Conant regarded it as vital that ultimately the United States made every effort to satisfy Soviet concerns. For that reason, also, he was not an enthusiastic believer in a doctrine subsequently called "linkage" —the linking of weapons reduction to diplomatic issues not directly related to arms control. In contrast, Byrnes, who at Potsdam had expressed to an aide his hope that the atom bomb "would control" the outcome of any U.S.-Soviet showdown,[60] seemed to entertain that hope as he traveled to the first postwar U.S.-U.K.-Soviet Foreign Ministers Conference in London in September, a session that was dominated by unbridgeable disagreements over the status of Soviet-occupied Europe, as expected.

Conant, however, accorded the problem of controlling the bomb the highest priority. He and Bush agreed completely with the views expressed in a memorandum prepared by Secretary Stimson for his final cabinet meeting on September 21, which reversed the advice he had given Truman at Potsdam.

Stimson now urged that the United States negotiate with Moscow on the merits of the bomb question alone and without attempting to use the issue to change the USSR's internal political makeup. If the United States should "fail to approach [the Russians] now and merely continue to negotiate with them, having this weapon rather ostentatiously on our hip, their suspicions and their distrust of our motives will increase," Stimson wrote.[61]

Conant, by now back at Harvard full-time, was kept informed of Washington developments, and Bush wrote him that Stimson's memorandum—"a fine state document"—was "right down the path that you and I have many times discussed."[62] After the cabinet session, Truman asked those in attendance to write up their thoughts on the matter: Bush, after consulting Conant, echoed Stimson's prescription. It might be argued that the bomb gave the United States a gun on its hip, Bush acknowledged, but "there is no powder in the gun, for it could not be drawn, and this is certainly known."[63]

Still, the administration was in no hurry to prepare plans for international control. Stimson's presentation met energetic opposition from Secretary of the Navy James V. Forrestal (who thought the Russians were "Oriental" in their thinking and could not be trusted) and from Byrnes.[64] Bush's and Conant's ally then departed government service. As for Truman, though he had—much to Byrne's displeasure—hesitantly committed himself to the principle of international control (in a message which drew Conant's cautious approval), he quickly backtracked. Possession of the bomb, he said, was America's "sacred trust," and if other nations wished to "catch up" they would "have to do it on their own hook, just as we did."[65] As an Anglo-American-Canadian summit approached in November, Bush reported to Conant that he was no longer consulted, no specific American plan existed for proceeding toward international control, and the administration's atomic energy policy was in a "thoroughly chaotic condition."[66]

Bush's suspicions that the administration was not taking arms control seriously, as well as criticism from atomic scientists still unaware of his secret actions to promote international control, heightened Conant's desire to sever his formal ties to the government so he would be free to speak out publicly. "It is getting to be a disgrace that the Administration doesn't give the country 'a lead' on this issue," he complained to Bush in late October, indicating his own intention to "break silence" before long.[67] Appearing on November 2 before a Senate committee to testify in favor of a federal science scholarship program, Conant was miffed to be on the receiving end of questions critical of administration atomic policy. "It is not for me to comment at this time on the policies of the Government in regard to the atomic bomb," he replied, "because, frankly, I don't know what they are."[68]

Returning to his Washington office, he immediately sent the new secretary of war, Robert P. Patterson, a formal resignation from the Interim Committee, blaming the press of his Harvard duties—Conant's all-purpose white lie when he didn't wish to undertake a task, or to cite a more sensitive

reason—and appending a more truthful explanation to "Bob." It was necessary to clear the record, he explained, because he planned a speech on the
subject and wished to be able to say that he no longer had close contact with
atomic bomb work and had "not been in a position to influence policy matters
for several months." As a private citizen, of course, Conant stressed, he would
be glad to continue to assist as desired.[69]

When Conant finally did put his views on the record on November 20,
the situation was looking up slightly. Due largely to Bush's efforts, the
Truman-Attlee-King meeting five days earlier produced a declaration calling
for the creation of a United Nations commission that would exchange basic
scientific information, ensure only peaceful uses of atomic energy, and institute safeguards against violations and evasions. Proceeding in stages, the
commission would aim ultimately at the elimination of atomic weapons
already assembled.[70] Calling the tripartite declaration the "first steps" toward
preventing an atomic arms race, Conant wired Truman a telegram of congratulations and called on the administration to convert "rapidly" its words
into diplomatic deeds.[71]

Almost unnoticed, however, was that this declaration, drafted by Bush,
had bypassed the course urged by Stimson (with the backing of Bush and
others) in September of approaching Moscow directly so as to reach an
agreement on international control bilaterally before bringing the issue to the
United Nations. Instead, Truman and Clement Attlee had satisfied themselves with a haphazardly organized conference and a communiqué laden
with generalities and rhetoric which hardly gave serious consideration to the
implications of appearing to cut the Soviets out of a direct approach.[72] The
final declaration, with its avowed commitment to international control, did
not much impress the Soviet ambassador to Washington, Nikolai V. Novikov,
who secretly cabled Moscow that it

> represents a new tactical approach in relation to the USSR, the substance of
> which can be reduced to the following: on the one hand, to use the atomic
> bomb as a means of political pressure to oblige the Soviet Union to accept its
> [Washington's] will and to weaken the position of the USSR in the U.N.,
> Eastern Europe and so on, but on the other hand, to accomplish all of this in
> such a form as to somewhat ameliorate the aggressive character of the
> Anglo-Saxon alliance of "atomic powers."[73]

Following the goings-on in Washington via newspapers, gossip, and Bush's
frequent letters, Conant suddenly found himself in the center of the whirlwind when Byrnes, in an abrupt change of strategy that signaled conciliation
toward the Soviet Union, called a Council of Foreign Ministers meeting for
late December in Moscow at which the proposal for creating a UN commission could be discussed.[74] Bush, who was to have gone, came down with the
grippe, so on December 10, Byrnes placed a call to Conant's NDRC office,

where the Harvard president and George L. Harrison were discussing legislation to establish a domestic atomic energy commission. "What in the world does he want of me?" said Conant, half to himself, when his secretary said Byrnes was on the line. "He probably wants you to go with him to Moscow," guessed Harrison. "My God," Conant sputtered.[75]

Sure enough, Byrnes asked Conant to accompany the American delegation leaving in two days. Wondering what he was getting into, Conant asked for an explanation of U.S. policy before agreeing. Assured that Byrnes's policy was "paving the way for a scheme of international control and release of our information as the scheme develops," he signed on for the trip. Byrnes said they would be back by Christmas, but Conant thought him a cheerful liar, he noted in his diary.

Byrnes's last-minute invitation gave Conant a front-row seat at one of the most curious performances in the early history of postwar U.S.-Soviet relations, a conference held in the twilight zone between alliance and enmity. Fresh from his failure to wrest concessions at the previous foreign ministers' conference, despite the atomic bomb "on his hip," in Stimson's phrase, Byrnes now embarked on a quixotic effort to score a personal triumph by obtaining some highly visible semblance of Kremlin cooperation in establishing international control over the bomb.[76]

To share in such an accomplishment—if it represented a genuine step forward, not a mere public relations exercise—was one of Conant's fondest wishes. But Conant's liberal calls for international control and the release of scientific information did not gibe with either congressional or public opinion, or with the views of some of the government's leading Soviet specialists. The American chargé d'affaires in Moscow, George F. Kennan, had harshly advised against sharing atomic energy information with the Soviets—for they would not "hesitate for a moment to apply this power against us if by doing so they thought they would materially improve their own power position in the world."[77] A poll taken in late October 1945 found that more than seven out of ten Americans opposed the idea of putting the bomb under UN auspices, even though almost the same percentage predicted that the United States would not retain its monopoly for more than five years.[78] On Capitol Hill the members of the Joint Committee on Atomic Energy, with the backing of Senate Republican leader Arthur H. Vandenberg, feared that Conant's presence at the conference meant that Byrnes planned to disclose atomic energy data to the Russians. Angrily they confronted Byrnes on the eve of his departure to deride his lack of consultation and his employment of "college professors"[79] for such a sensitive mission, and after he had left they demanded and received an audience with Truman to emphasize their strong view that the United States should not impart any atomic information to the Soviets until after a firm inspection system was in place. Truman fervently assured them that he had no such intention—an extracted promise urgently cabled to Byrnes in Moscow.[80]

Historians have pointed out that Byrnes's initiative met more troubles from the U.S. Congress than from the Soviet government. And, though the senators misjudged Conant if they thought him a wild-eyed idealist, they had not been far off the mark in sensing that he was eager to begin releasing scientific information to the Russians. He was: but Conant's view of what could safely be transmitted was far more expansive than that of the security-obsessed senators, who had evinced little ability to distinguish between genuine secrets and basic scientific knowledge. In Berlin, on the way to the conference, Conant learned of the congressmen's fears that Byrnes might "give away too much too soon," and he got reassurances from Byrnes and State Department aide Benjamin Cohen that the "partial payment" concept of information for inspection was "well fixed in the minds of both of them."

Though bedraggled by a head cold and chills, Conant, for his part, expectantly looked forward to a firsthand look at top-level diplomacy and viewing Russia for himself. The Americans touched down in Moscow on December 14 after a frightening plane ride from Tempelhof airport in Berlin that ended with their C-47 slicing through a blizzard after running low on gas and getting lost for an hour.

After sightseeing through the cold Moscow streets and ingesting "lots of aspirin and some brandy (not a good combination)," Conant arranged as a priority matter a conference with Ambassador Averell Harriman on Sunday, December 16, about "getting information about Russian industry and science" —advancing his secret, and ultimately futile, side mission to learn what he could about the extent of Soviet progress toward an atomic bomb.[81]

That evening, after a day of "horsetrading" over procedural matters, conversation among Conant, Cohen, and Byrnes led to a "fairly drastic revision" of the draft U.S. position prepared by the Military Policy Committee, mostly to assure that it conformed to the tripartite declaration's insistence that any international control plan went in stages. A December 17 memorandum by Conant outlined a "step by step" procedure under which immediately after a treaty was signed the United States would provide "full details of the electromagnetic method of separating Uranium 235," and six months later, if the control system was functioning properly, "full details of the gaseous diffusion process." If all went well, a year later, the Americans would hand over their most treasured accomplishment, the plutonium production blueprints and then "dismantle all its bombs and place the material in storage or in industrial power plants, if it has been agreed that no other nation will construct atomic bombs."[82]

Intense and sometimes tense wrangling ensued as the Americans, with Conant principal drafter, and the British tried to coordinate their positions on the atomic matter, which they presumed would be a leading item of contention at the conference. Speculation on the Soviet attitude tended to be pessimistic, with Conant recording in his diary, "Most observers in the embassy feel the Russians cannot accept inspection and the scheme will bog down somewhere as a consequence." Byrnes, he noted, "plans to go ahead with the plan in the UNO [United Nations Organization] anyway Russian sponsorship or not."[83]

To help Byrnes prepare for the conference, the British had forwarded an analysis from their ambassador in Moscow of the Soviet Union's evolving psychology regarding the atomic bomb. Four months earlier, he recalled, before the news from Hiroshima had arrived, Russians were full of exultation, pride, and relief over the defeat of Nazi Germany and the Red Army's conquering of a vast buffer zone in Eastern Europe that would provide "the immense benison of national security" after four years of horrific struggle.

> Then plump came the Atomic Bomb. At a blow the balance which had now seemed set and steady was rudely shaken. Russia was balked by the west when everything seemed to be within her grasp. The three hundred divisions [of the Red Army] were shorn of much of their value. About all this the Kremlin was silent but such was the common talk of the people. But their disappointment was tempered by the belief inspired by such echoes of foreign press as were allowed to reach them that their Western comrades in arms would surely share the bomb with them . . . But as time went on and no move came from the West, disappointment turned to irritation and, when the bomb seemed to them to become an instrument of policy, into spleen. It was clear that the West did not trust them. This seemed to justify and it quickened all their old suspicions. It was a humiliation also and the thought of this stirred up memories of the past. We may assume that all these emotions were fully shared by the Kremlin. . . . If my interpretation of the state of mind of the Russians is anything like right we may I think expect them to approach the proposal to discuss Atomic Energy in the first instance in the open forum of the General Assembly with all the prickliness of which they are capable.[84]

The Russians were in no hurry to end the suspense. At an early session, Foreign Minister Molotov requested that atomic energy be dropped to the bottom of the agenda, arousing "great speculation and curiosity" among the Americans and British.[85] Conant, who had hoped to return to Harvard after an early disposal of the atomic issue, had to sit instead through ten days of discussion on unrelated subjects. During one droning debate, he leaned over to the secretary of state and whispered: "I think the President of every university in the United States should be forced to attend a conference of the Council of Foreign Ministers. They might then appreciate the patience required to reach agreement with our Soviet friends."

"I felt like accusing him of harboring some secret animosity toward his fellow university presidents," Byrnes remembered, "but I appreciated the thought."[86]

Pressing their "reverse atomic diplomacy" strategy of minimizing the bomb's importance, the Soviets not only gave the topic short shrift, but took several opportunities to chide Conant about it. At an evening reception on December 20, he recorded in his journal, "Molotov quite floored me by joking about atomic energy and asking if I had an atomic bomb in my pocket," and then inviting him, "half in jest," to give a lecture on the subject to the Soviet Academy of Sciences. (Conant offered to deliver the address, then found out the suggestion had been fully in jest.)

Molotov and Stalin "certainly 'make like' " they aren't interested in the bomb, Conant noted that night, and Byrnes was "of two minds" about it. Perhaps the Soviets really were not interested, he thought, "because the top has not been properly briefed as to the real significance of the bomb . . . or else they will demand all the know-how at once as the price of coming along."

The Soviet delays gave Conant an opportunity to see Moscow, and his impressions did nothing to alter his prediction that the Communist state would not be exploding atomic bombs for at least five years. "Terrific disorder and squalor everywhere," he wrote, not an unexpected sight considering the devastation during the war. "There is an enormous job to be done here to make this even a halfway modern capital of an industrialized nation. In ten years it will look very different." But while the country needed rebuilding, the Russians themselves impressed Conant, who described them in terms akin to those he might use for hardy New England Yankees. After a companion pointed out that none of Moscow's residents had "the vacuous look of certain American urban dwellers," Conant noted: "Here everyone has character. They are a toughened race (by war, climate and revolution). No foolishness in this nation, nothing soft." Conant came expecting to find a police state "and I have no reason to doubt it"; however, no police were in evidence, and all was "rather chaotic."

Despite a nagging sore throat, Conant filled his spare hours. He joined a rump Harvard alumni gathering of embassy staff; quizzed diplomats, military attachés, businessmen, and journalists about the state of Soviet science, engineering, and industry; visited the deputy minister of education to promote U.S.-Soviet exchanges; rode the subway ("Very grand indeed; no wonder they are so proud of it!"). Attending the Bolshoi Ballet, he heard the crowd cheer lustily when the three foreign ministers appeared in the dignitaries' box, a "very genuine" reaction that reminded him of the comment that he had heard Harriman make, that the Russians were worried about another war.[87] One of Conant's first stops, of course, was Red Square, and a visit to Lenin's mausoleum. Americans in Moscow had been debating whether the body on display was the genuine embalmed corpse or a wax substitute, and there was hope that Conant, as a trained chemist, might be able to resolve the mystery. Robert C. Tucker, then a young embassy staffer and translator (who later wrote a multi-volume biography of Stalin), accompanied Conant on that gray afternoon as the long procession was ushered through the silent chamber, guards watching every move. As they emerged, Tucker looked questioningly at Conant, who shrugged; he couldn't tell, either.[88]

If the Soviets' delaying tactics nonplussed Conant, their next move pleasantly stunned him. On December 22, Molotov finally dealt with the proposals to create a United Nations atomic energy commission submitted earlier. "To my utter amazement, and contrary to all the predictions in the Embassy," Conant wrote, Molotov accepted the proposals with the sole proviso that the commission be responsible to the Security Council rather than to the General Assembly. Though he objected to the provision for separate stages, he gave in to Byrnes's insistence that they be retained.[89]

It was just a first step, but at least the Russians had agreed to join the process. A joint communiqué, written by Conant, reiterated the basic principles of the Truman-Attlee-King declaration of November.[90]

At a raucous Kremlin Christmas Eve state dinner before the conference closed, the Soviets even permitted themselves to take Conant—and the bomb—seriously. Deep into a series of toasts, Molotov again implored Conant to display the A-bomb in his "waist-coat pocket" and wished him and the commission success. As all raised their glasses, Stalin brusquely interrupted Molotov's revelry. Earlier in the evening, Byrnes had described Conant's accomplishments as atomic administrator to the Soviet leader, eliciting words of admiration. Now Stalin voiced those sentiments to the entire gathering. Dr. Conant and the American scientists were to be congratulated, he said quietly. The bomb was "too serious a matter to joke about," and "we must work together to see that this great invention is used for peaceful ends." The diplomat Charles Bohlen, who witnessed this scene, later wrote: "There in the banquet hall of the Kremlin we saw Stalin abruptly change Soviet policy without consulting his number two man. The humiliated Molotov never altered his expression. From that moment on, the Soviets gave the atomic bomb the serious consideration it deserved." Looking back on the incident, others, including Conant, suspected Stalin had staged the burlesque.[91]

Conant's immediate task, however, was to formulate a suitable toast in response. He stood, raised his glass, and uttered the following words (as he later reconstructed): "The fine words of the Generalissimo about Science and Mr. Molotoff's [sic] humorous remarks about science embolden me fortified by the molecular energy of your excellent wine to prepare a toast to Russian science. I have no atomic energy in my pocket but I can say that the scientists of Russia and those of the other countries represented here tonight worked to win a common victory. I trust they may cooperate equally effectively in the tasks of peace which lie ahead."

As the banquet ended, Conant approached the Generalissimo—"much shorter and smaller than I had imagined," resembling "a shrewd but kindly and humble old peasant, sort of shuffles"—to say good night. Through an interpreter, Stalin repeated the sentiments of his toast, sending his "heartiest congratulations to the American scientists for their accomplishment" and stating that it was "very important" that atomic energy be used only for peace. Fishing for polite conversation, Conant mentioned that American scientists who had visited Russia the previous summer had had a wonderful time.

"Yes," Stalin replied, "Russia is famous for its hospitality, but it is also behind in science!"

"Which made me think," Conant wrote in his diary, "that I should *not* want to be a Russian physicist at this moment!!!"[92]

Conant's astute reaction indicates that, unlike Bohlen or Byrnes, he did not believe the Soviets had not taken the bomb seriously, only that they had admittedly gotten a late start.

The Soviets' unexpectedly cooperative attitude at the Moscow conference made Conant more optimistic about whether they would agree to international control. "As it turned out," he wrote Bush upon his return, "neither of us was really needed for much to everyone's surprise the Russians did not argue or talk back."[93] Ironically symbolizing his hopes for cooperation, Conant planned to present Mrs. Molotov with a copy of the Smyth Report for her daughter to use for a school assignment on atomic energy.[94] And, recalled Tucker, he solemnly did hand the volume over to Molotov—with both men wearing wry smiles that may have reflected their mutual awareness that the Russians had already translated and reprinted the document.[95]

Still believing that Byrnes's strategy might yet bear fruit, Conant prepared a five-page memorandum for the secretary of state while still in Moscow, urging the immediate initiation of scientific interchange with Russia. Completely misjudging public opinion, not to mention the suspicious congressmen, he predicted that "Pressure within the United States will certainly build up" for such interchange "long before" the UN commission was set up. Infused with the spirit of the occasion, he went on to stress the "unique position" of Soviet scientists, who, while clearly government agents, were "the nearest approach to informed public opinion with high standing that exists in that country." The United States and Soviet Union should begin bilateral exchanges and annual joint conferences in hard science (physics, chemistry), medicine, and agricultural sciences. Indiscretions by U.S. scientists were inevitable, but they would accelerate Soviet development of atomic power by at most six months, Conant assured Byrnes. Significantly, he emphasized the importance of establishing *bilateral* exchanges, cautioning that Washington should not neglect the "unique position of Soviet science" and the positive effect that quick action along these lines could have on relations between Washington and Moscow. "I feel this is a matter of great urgency," he concluded.[96]

Byrnes ignored his suggestions, but the optimism which had spurred Conant did, in fact, infect public opinion in the U.S. and Britain when the results of the conference—what one historian later termed "the one moment of accommodation and compromise in the otherwise bleak history of postwar polarization"[97]—were announced. The outcome seems excellent, Bush wrote

Conant, since there was "much satisfaction in the feeling that at least the whole show is started down the right path."[98]

At the close of the conference Conant had a brief chat with the British philosopher and diplomat Isaiah Berlin about the chances of getting the Soviets to agree to inspection. "No chance," Berlin replied candidly, "but we must act 'as if.' " Putting the UN atomic energy commission under the Security Council, where Soviets retained veto power, "might mean it wouldn't work at all," Conant well knew. And another incident in Moscow had demonstrated to Conant just how tenuous the U.S.-Soviet friendship was. The Russians treated their guests to a nationalistic propaganda film that implied that the United States had been only tangentially involved in the defeat of Japan. Yet, Conant noted, no American could afterward approach a Russian and say, "That was a bit thick, you know."

Just as revealing was a discussion Conant held with Byrnes on December 24. The secretary of state had been a recent convert to the cause of international control. Was he sincere? Conant didn't believe it, and his private assessment (omitted from *My Several Lives*) was that Byrnes was motivated more by ambition and public relations than by a genuine belief that progress with Moscow on the atomic bomb was either possible or even desirable.[99] "Byrnes is really very skeptical and a little cynical about the whole business," Conant wrote.

> The danger is too long-range to worry him. He is right as an individual as the chickens won't come home to roost in his lifetime or perhaps mine. "And what possible chance is there of getting the USSR or even the USA to accept adequate inspection," say[s] he? About 1 in 5 or 1 in 10, given time, says I, but it is so important as to be worth doing all we can even against such long odds. Right says he, if it[']s our duty we must do it even if we think it hopeless. But he hasn't his heart in the business and I don't blame him. But the other issues are being compromised fairly successful[ly]. Looks as if the conference were headed for a large success. But my fingers are still crossed on the bomb and will be until the commission is set up.[100]

Two decades after the Moscow Conference, Conant looked back with incredulity at his enthusiastic advocacy of U.S.-Soviet scientific interchange. "I find it hard to realize now that I and many others ever believed what I subscribed to as the year of 1946 opened," he wrote in *My Several Lives*. "My ascent into the golden clouds of irrational hope can only be explained by my honest appraisal of the world-wide catastrophic consequences of a failure to attain international control. Some scheme just had to work. And who is prepared to say my basic belief was wrong?"[101]

CHAPTER 15

*"The Only Possible Solution
of a Desperate Problem"*

Trying to Control the Bomb
1945–1946

The Harvard Corporation will never know how much the existence and
ambitions of one Lewis Strauss saved them a lot of trouble in 1946!
—Letter to Vannevar Bush, August 1946

I feel that even a rickety bridge out of the shadow of the Superblitz is better
than none.
—Speech to the National War College, September 1946

I believe I speak for the scientific community when I say that your attitude
on this bill will determine whether you are with us or against us.
—Edward U. Condon to Conant, Fall 1945

Conant's energetic promotion of international control of atomic energy in
1945–46 coincided with a bitter, related controversy over domestic control.
Eyed with suspicion by senators who thought him too accommodating with
Moscow, he found himself simultaneously assailed by many atomic scientists
for taking too militaristic a view of atomic energy and supporting measures
that they believed would endanger prospects for a UN agreement.

This dispute finally brought into the open the feud between the wartime
Manhattan Project administrators and some of the scientists who had worked
on the project. In this instance, the focus of their discontent was a bill,
strongly backed by the Manhattan Project leadership, to establish a U.S.
atomic energy commission to control both civilian and military development.
Conant himself had begun to formulate that legislation in a July 27, 1944,
memorandum proposing a twelve-member commission composed of three
civilians, five scientists or engineers, and two army and two navy officers, all
of whom would serve part-time. Necessary because of atomic energy's potential threat to "safety, health and welfare" and because of "the importance of

its further development," the new agency would regulate nuclear materials, construction and operation of power plants, even, if it was agreed after further discussion, small-scale experimentation.[1]

In July 1945, those plans were developed into draft legislation by two War Department lawyers, Kenneth C. Royall and William L. Marbury.[2] While Truman, Byrnes, and Stimson dueled with the Soviets at Potsdam, members of the Interim Committee who were not at the summit with them considered this War Department draft. Conant saw that the lawyers had incorporated his earlier ideas, but "had, if anything, done too good a job"[3]: with the end of the war imminent, Conant wanted a return to peacetime methods and, along with Bush, now favored an all-civilian commission.[4] In addition, he expressed concern over the sweeping powers that the proposed commission would have over basic research and urged a minimum of interference in scientific freedom consistent with preserving "national security."[5]

Like Conant, the atomic scientists wanted action simultaneously to develop and regulate nuclear energy, and they wanted swift movement toward international control and a commitment to a strong, well-funded research program under peacetime conditions. The Chicago group had frequently spoken of the need both for control and for further development, especially since it was likely that other countries would launch their own large-scale programs. Conant had been skeptical, describing one report from Arthur Compton as "transparently a 'brief' by a bunch of scientists for more support for research — nothing subtle about this approach."[6] But he too concluded that the United States had to cultivate a thriving atomic program if it expected to remain preeminent, and the scientists who had long believed this now pinned their hopes on the bill the government was preparing.

The Truman administration acted sluggishly on these issues in the weeks after Japan's surrender, but movement finally came, and with a vengeance, in early October. The War Department introduced the Royall-Marbury Bill (soon renamed the May-Johnson bill, after its Senate cosponsors) on October 4, and five days later the House Military Affairs Committee, without advance notice, "rushed its public hearings to completion in five hours," as one news account put it, "and prepared to send a bill to the floor by the end of the week."[7]

All four witnesses heard on October 9 — Bush, Conant, Groves, and War Secretary Robert Patterson — emphasized the urgency of the bill. Conant said Manhattan Project scientists were in a state of unrest and uneasiness, and the delays already incurred were "costing the country, from the point of view of getting ahead in further development of this weapon" and in the development of atomic energy. The commission would have unprecedented peacetime powers, he admitted, but atomic energy "is so new, so extraordinary and so powerful," that unusual measures were necessary. Perhaps, he added, only someone who had seen "that tremendous illumination that burst all over the sky" in New Mexico could realize the potential dangers or the potential good.

The senators could be assured that the views of everyone involved in the project, including the scientists, had been taken into account.[8]

But scientists in Chicago and elsewhere quickly began to express their "near unanimous opposition" and poured much of their wrath on Conant, who had come to epitomize bureaucratic red tape, due to the restrictions of his policy of compartmentalization and his seeming obliviousness to the bomb's wider implications (few knew of Bush's and Conant's memos to Stimson).[9] Among those who were especially critical of Conant were those who had feuded with him during the war, notably Szilard and Urey.

A sharp exchange of correspondence between Conant and an old friend and fellow statesman of the scientific establishment, Frank B. Jewett, president of Bell Telephone Laboratories and the National Academy of Sciences, illustrates the intensity of anger generated by the way in which the May-Johnson bill had been handled. One of the "four horsemen" who had gathered at the Century Club over lunch five years earlier to conceive the NDRC and a member of its executive committee, the occasionally cranky sixty-six-year-old Jewett had already been rubbed the wrong way by the NDRC leader's management style in the past.[10] But any of Jewett's previous complaints of high-handedness must have seemed minor compared to the way he hit the roof upon reading newspaper accounts of Conant's and Bush's testimony on October 9. You and Bush, he wrote Conant, in trying to rush through the legislation, were likely to be remembered "either as very great farseeing statesmen or as men who may be looked upon as having done the country and the world a great disservice. I wouldn't know how to bet on the matter."[11] Conant's mild reply, blithely predicting that before long "we will have all the scientists back of" the bill, utterly failed to mollify Jewett, who if anything sounded even angrier in his response. "I think the Bill atrocious and the high-handed way it was handled in the House Military Affairs Committee more so," Jewett declared. "If this is what the past four years has brought us to, I wonder why we have been so hot and bothered about Fascism, Nazism and the Japanese."[12]

Conant, who was also under assault from the *Washington Post*, which had named him as responsible for the mishandling of the bill,[13] discerned a bright spot in the downpour of criticism. All the uproar, he wrote Bush in a handwritten postscript, "doesn't bother me in the least but it does indicate in a small way just what a storm would have broken over our heads if the bomb hadn't gone off. I hope that thought cheers you up. It does me."[14]

The atomic scientists had expected—and now demanded—an opportunity to help determine the future of their field. Many were disappointed and enraged to see that the May-Johnson specifications were that military representatives could serve as administrator and deputy administrator; that meant, in their minds, a continuation of the reign of Groves. And, they deduced, the provision that the commissioners would serve part-time on a per diem basis would allow Bush and Conant to retain control over atomic policy without sacrificing their prestigious, full-time jobs.[15] Herbert Anderson, a Met Lab physicist, wrote angrily to a Los Alamos colleague: "Could it be that James B. Conant would be loath to yield the presidency of Harvard in order to serve so vital a position as Commissioner of Atomic Energy in the United States?" If atomic energy were the world-shaking force they believed it to be, he continued, the scientists could not allow it to "rest in the hands of a body so flippantly conceived." Just as disturbing were the bill's security provisions, which threatened jail sentences or fines for unauthorized disclosures of information, and could have a chilling effect on scientific discussion. "The war is won, let us be free again!" Anderson concluded.[16]

The congressmen hastily scheduled a second round of hearings on October 18 to hear additional testimony on May-Johnson; and while Urey and Szilard blasted the bill, two physicists who had formed a more comfortable relationship with the OSRD leadership, Arthur Compton and Robert Oppenheimer, avoided rocking the boat and endorsed May-Johnson. Reflecting his high esteem for Conant—who a few weeks after Hiroshima had vainly sought to entice him to Cambridge with promises of a university professorship and a large-scale nuclear physics program[17]—"Oppie" expressed confidence in the OSRD leaders. "I think no men in positions of responsibility, who were scientists, took more responsibility or were more courageous or better informed in the general sense than Dr. Bush or Dr. Conant," he testified. "I think if they liked the philosophy of this bill and urged this bill it is a very strong argument. I know that many scientists do not agree with me on this, but I am nevertheless convinced myself."[18] However, rather than raising confidence among the angry Manhattan Project rank and file, the fact that four of the project's top scientists—Oppenheimer, Fermi, Lawrence, and Compton—had approved the bill only cast suspicions on them. "I must confess," wrote Anderson, "that my confidence in our own leaders ... is shaken. I believe these worthy men were duped."[19]

Conant had been aware of, but underestimated, the scientists' anger. He had hoped Truman would approve of "letting them loose" for public discussion prior to October 9, but he had overlooked passages in the bill that were certain to rile them.[20] He was visited by a delegation of Cambridge scientists who feared that the bill's security provisions would shut down all nuclear research except in government-run "monasteries," and Conant agreed that the wording was overly restrictive and that clarification was necessary.[21] He insisted that the bill's object was not to preserve military control, but he now supported the idea of military representation.[22]

Regardless of his intent, the effect of the controversy over the May-Johnson Bill was to magnify the ill will between Conant and many of the Manhattan Project scientists. Ironically, the security system which Conant had enthusiastically enforced during the war now boomeranged against him. Compartmentalization had not only fueled the scientists' resentment of impediments in the flow of information but meant they were unaware of Conant's and Bush's advocacy of international control.[23] Unfortunately, Conant was either unwilling or unable to convey his concern informally, running as it did against his belief in adhering to "channels," but this might have saved him considerable ill will. Instead, the internecine warfare grew ever more personal and acrimonious. Szilard, Urey, and others with whom Conant had jousted during the war now rose to the forefront of a new coalition opposing the scientific bureaucrats. In one dramatic face-to-face confrontation shortly after the first hearing in October at a luncheon in Stimson's private Pentagon dining room the temperamental Edward U. Condon warned Conant dramatically: "I believe I speak for the scientific community when I say that your attitude on this bill will determine whether you are with us or against us."[24]

The atomic scientists' movement took Washington by storm, though events would qualify its success. Enveloped in an aura of power, given their wartime accomplishment and godlike mastery of the universe's mysterious energies, the scientists vigorously lobbied senators and the press and rode the crest of a wave of public admiration. Ironically, this even rubbed off on Conant. "Whatever the effect of this controversy," noted an admiring profile, "Harvard's President stands as mentor to the powerful science-in-government element that has Washington more or less in awe."[25]

Senior administration officials, however, were perturbed by the atomic scientists' desire to influence atomic control policy. To war secretary Patterson, Byrnes grumbled at "the overemphasis placed on the view of the scientists," and recounted that when Oppenheimer had urged an immediate overture to Stalin on the atomic bomb, he had bluntly replied that "while he had great admiration for Dr. Oppenheimer's scientific attainments, he did not believe that he knew the facts or had the responsibility for the handling of international affairs." Patterson noted that "he had brought Dr. Oppenheimer back on the track"—he had, after all testified in favor of the May-Johnson bill—and that while the Manhattan Project's "smaller fry" were "less stable," the "scientists with experience in public affairs like Dr. Bush and Dr. Conant are all right."[26]

But Conant also found himself opposed by some members of the Truman administration. His original framework for a domestic atomic agency recommended that the president directly appoint three of the twelve commissioners, with the other selections restricted to people nominated by the National Academy and the military services.[27] Conant, like Bush, wanted to insulate control of science and atomic research from partisan politics. And his idea for part-time commissioners also expressed his view that no presidential administration should be in a position to control atomic energy.[28] But Truman's advisers now took steps to make the proposed commission more responsive to presidential command. As opposition stalled May-Johnson, the Bureau of the Budget drew up a substitute bill more to the liking of both the scientists and Truman, who had become persuaded that May-Johnson would lead to eventual army control. Introduced on December 20, 1945, by Senator Brien McMahon, chairman of the special joint congressional atomic energy committee, the alternative bill allowed the president to appoint directly five full-time commissioners and it explicitly eliminated military participation.[29] By the time Conant returned from his whirlwind Kremlin adventure, the future of domestic atomic energy was mired in a controversy part ideological, part a struggle over turf.

Conant's detractors had claimed that his backing of May-Johnson proved his lack of faith in international control. Pressing for a commission with such militaristic and security-conscious overtones seemed to be admitting that the arms race had already started. But as 1946 opened Conant had a chance to prove his preference for international solutions to atomic problems and personally to help the process along. By agreeing in Moscow to the formation of a United Nations Atomic Energy Commission, the leaders of the postwar world—the United States and Russia, with Britain tagging along—had taken their first collective step toward the international control of atomic energy, a small step, but one more than many expected. The Truman administration now decided to undertake a serious examination of the issues involved, and Byrnes took the natural step: he named a committee, headed by Under Secretary of State Dean G. Acheson. The mandate was to formulate guidelines for the then unnamed American delegate to the UN Atomic Energy Commission talks agreed on at Moscow. On January 7, Acheson asked Conant to join the group; assured it would not be a full-time job, he accepted. Also joining were Bush, Groves, and John J. McCloy, the New York lawyer and ex-War Department aide who had worked with Conant on various matters since early in the war, and who had helped Stimson develop his farewell memorandum in favor of international control the previous autumn.[30]

Not long after the invitation from the State Department, Conant received a virtual command from the secretary of war and the secretary of the navy to sit on another panel connected to the atomic bomb: the Joint Chiefs of Staff Evaluation Board for the first series of peacetime tests of the weapon, scheduled to be held at Bikini Atoll in the Pacific Ocean beginning in May 1946 and stretching into the summer.[31] "We . . . request that you accept appointment as one of the members of the board," Robert P. Patterson and James V. Forrestal wrote Conant on January 25.[32] But Conant responded with an equally clear definition of priorities. Two weeks later he declined this forceful invitation. There was, he pointed out, a "certain degree of incompatibility" between the work involved in evaluating new and improved forms of atomic weapons, and the assignment to study methods of controlling and possibly eliminating those weapons from national arsenals. Conant left no doubt where his preference lay. "I have become particularly concerned with the international aspects of the atomic bomb," he explained, "and feel that either in speaking as a private citizen or serving as an adviser to the Federal Government, as I am for the moment, I should like to concentrate my attention on this phase of the problem."[33]

Conant's decision accurately reflected his belief that there remained a reasonable chance of preventing a postwar nuclear arms race, and his conviction that he should devote himself to that cause. He had never doubted that his involvement with the bomb would extend beyond the war, whether he liked it or not, and the State Department committee seemed to offer at long last an opportunity for qualified persons—himself included—to give sustained attention to the issue of international control. Moreover, he had been on good terms with Acheson since before the war, and knew that he had fully endorsed Stimson's international control memorandum to Truman the previous fall.[34] Here was a chance to sit alongside men who had known the atomic business long enough to have informed ideas, and to participate directly in shaping policy.

Conant missed the group's first meeting in Washington, but suggested to Bush and Groves that two panels be created: one, given all information on atomic energy, to work out technical details of control, the other to devise a plan "solely on the basis of public information concerning the atomic bomb and by reference to existing experience in other fields of international inspection and detection."[35] Instead it was decided to form a single subcommittee to examine the technical questions and report back with its findings. Named to chair the "Board of Consultants" was former TVA director David E. Lilienthal, who turned to Oppenheimer for scientific advice; along with Charles A. Thomas, vice-president for engineering for General Electric; and Chester I. Barnard, president of Bell Telephone. Conant's old NDRC traveling partner, Carroll L. Wilson, would act as secretary, assisted by Herbert S. Marks.

Conant took up Acheson's invitation with a fairly clear idea of the general principles on which an international commission should operate. Wrote the Atomic Energy Commission's official historians: "No one had thought longer about international control. In his definition, an effective system of inspection was one which gave a danger signal—flashed a red light—when some power moved toward manufacturing an atomic weapon." Warning against getting bogged down on sanctions—they could leave punishments to the Security Council—Conant urged his colleagues to concentrate on elucidating the specifics of the staged process by which the United States would release sensitive information.[36]

Like Moses disappearing to Mount Sinai in search of divine guidance, the consultants sequestered themselves at a hotel for five weeks in search of a workable plan. Inspection had been at the core of Conant's ideas about international control since his earliest consideration of the issue, but the consultants came up with other ideas. To Oppenheimer, the kind of global FBI that Conant envisioned was unappealing. Would top-flight people really want to devote themselves, he wondered, to "such a dreary, sterile and repressive job?"[37]

On March 7, Lilienthal's board of consultants returned to the Acheson committee with their solution. The United Nations international commission, they suggested, should be not a policing agency that gave spot checks to nationally run facilities, but an Atomic Development Authority that would itself take on major responsibility for the development of atomic energy, licensing and inspecting production facilities and also constructing and operating power plants. The basic idea was to emphasize the appeal of development rather than the necessity for control and, in so doing, enhance the incentives for Russian cooperation.[38] Conant saw the sense in this, but still insisted on more emphasis to the right of the agency's international staff to "go anywhere and see anything." It was vitally important, he reiterated, for the inspectors to have "guaranteed freedom of access."[39]

Other sections of the draft report pleased Conant, particularly the differentiation between safe and dangerous activities — between basic and applied physics research — a distinction that had been clear in Conant's and the scientists' perspectives but frequently blurred in public debate.[40] In addition, though he was not keen on the prospects for atomic power, the provision for direct operation of power plants rather than mere inspection solved a problem that had bothered him for some time: it was "important to realize," he had written the previous October, "that the manufacture of atomic bombs cannot be divorced from the use of uranium as a source of atomic energy for industrial purposes. Any nation which had atomic energy power plants would have the wherewithal to make bombs; the larger the power plants, the larger the number of potential bombs.[41] Under the panel's plan, an international staff would operate the plants. Seizure of a plant would thus be a clear danger signal.

However, Conant did not approve of the panel's omission of the step-by-step approach. Although no one on the Acheson and Lilienthal panels considered the Soviets especially trustworthy, Conant, like the consultants, wanted a plan that would have a chance at Russian acceptance. But, while the consultants thought spelling out the stages before negotiations started would be "bad tactics" and would "blight the spirit" of a proposal that assumed the good faith of other nations, Conant believed that the Russians still needed to be tested, and that public and congressional opinion would not permit a stageless offer in any case.[42]

Conant had good reason for this belief: in the two months during which the Acheson panel had met, the "spirit of Moscow," restrained as it was, disappeared entirely, and U.S.-Soviet relations plummeted. The brief flowering of optimism for international atomic collaboration vanished in late February with the belated disclosure of the Soviet spy ring in Canada, along with the arrest of twenty-two suspects on espionage charges. To the American public, watching a debate often framed in terms of whether the United States should magnanimously reveal the "secret" of atomic energy, this shocking news undermined Conant's efforts through the Smyth Report to have an informed public discussion, and to explain that Americans had built the atomic bomb on the basis of generally available physics research, largely generated in Europe, rather than through a secret U.S. breakthrough. Few congressmen had ever grasped or accepted Conant's contention that pure nuclear physics research could be safely shared with Russia, while exchanges of *applied* physics data required stiffer safeguards. All the talk about spies now seemed to vindicate the restrictive security measures which Groves and the army had sought in the May-Johnson bill. Immediately, the supportive mail that had flowed into the headquarters of the liberal Federation of Atomic Scientists' Washington office halted; speculation that the army was embellishing the Canadian story to advance its position did little to stem public concern.[43]

This was only the tip of a fast-expanding Cold War iceberg. In Congress, in the general public and especially in the White House, the view that Russia was no longer an ally was becoming predominant. Soviet occupation policies in Eastern Europe had convinced many that the Russians did not know how to behave properly, and its tardiness in withdrawing troops from Iran precipitated a showdown. In February and early March, as the Byzantine complexities of atomic energy cooperation absorbed the Acheson-Lilienthal group, a crisis atmosphere enveloped Washington, as reports circulated that the Soviets were massing to attack Turkey, Iraq, and Iran; abandoning the conciliatory approach favored by Byrnes at Moscow, Truman now threatened dire consequences if the Soviets did not pull back.[44]

They soon agreed to, but the episode battered Soviet popularity in the United States—and the dangers were underlined by Stalin's bellicose rhetoric and, on March 5, by Winston Churchill's landmark speech in Fulton, Missouri. "From Stettin in the Baltic to Trieste in the Adriatic," the defeated statesman declared, with Truman nodding silent approval, "an iron curtain has descended across the Continent."[45] Churchill's weighty pronouncement came on the heels of an equally pessimistic private analysis of Soviet foreign policy that reached Washington in late February. In a "Long Telegram" from Moscow, the diplomat George F. Kennan, the U.S. embassy's number two man, declared, in authoritative tones, that Soviet distrust of the West could not be overcome by conciliatory gestures or diplomatic initiatives, that Soviet foreign policy bore little relationship to Western actions, that the policy of seeking quid pro quo concessions was hopeless.[46] Though Kennan would not become a celebrity for more than a year, his prescriptions quickly gained wide acceptance in official circles and among the foreign-policy elite.

Unlike Churchill or Kennan, Conant did not yet consider good relations with Russia a completely lost cause. Hard-line pronouncements like the Fulton speech, he felt, simply "rocked the boat," and might even encourage an unnecessary but irretrievable break.[47] But he, like Acheson, Groves, McCloy, and Bush, also distrusted Moscow and pragmatically evaluated the direction of opinion. On March 7 the panel asked Lilienthal's board to beef up their plan's safety provisions and to insert the staged-process idea. The consultants were depressed by the conservatism of the Acheson group but reluctantly made the changes, and spent the weekend of March 16 and 17 at Dumbarton Oaks arguing. Conant thought the revisions helped, but Groves and Bush were concerned about the lack of a definite timetable, even though general stages were now described. On Saturday night, a weary Lilienthal wrote of the "animadversions of Conant, Bush, Groves" but was "determined to keep working with these men until they saw that their objections were simply a refusal to face the inescapable price of international action, or a step in that direction." Commiserating until midnight with his fellow consultants, who had developed a deep consensus feeling over the previous six weeks, Lilienthal feared that "all our works might be wasted, and some cheap alternatives offered, for reasons that would be cowardly and could only lead to the certainty of atomic warfare." Yet the next day, the Acheson Committee agreed not only to send the report on to Secretary Byrnes but warmly to endorse it. A pleasantly surprised Lilienthal thought the change in attitude "nothing less than a miracle. Such praise of the report and of those who developed the plan!"[48]

A certain amount of Conant's contentiousness was probably due to his taking the devil's advocate position, which he also adopted in ad hoc committee hearings at Harvard and in other discussions. But most of it was real. Not only did he want to test the Russians, but he felt the upcoming United Nations negotiations would be long and difficult, perhaps impossible: it didn't make sense to start bargaining from anything less than the most hard-line position. Like Truman—who later professed to have believed in January 1946 that "unless Russia is faced with an iron fist and strong language another war is in the making"[49]—Conant thought American military might could intimidate the Soviets. In an early expression of the philosophy animating Cold War and nuclear policy (and justifying massive military expenditures) from the Truman to the Reagan administrations, Conant invoked the philosophy of "peace through strength" in dealing with the Soviets. He stated this clearly, though not publicly, at an off-the-record black-tie dinner and talk sponsored by the Council on Foreign Relations in New York on April 12, 1946. The discussion turned to the atomic testing that the administration had scheduled in the Pacific for July, allegedly to gauge the effectiveness of the new weapon on ships, the same tests that Conant had been invited to analyze for the military. Asked whether he thought the Bikini tests would hurt or help chances for securing international control, Conant replied, according to a digest of the meeting, that "the Russians are more rather than less likely to come to an effective agreement for the control of atomic energy if we keep our strength and continue to produce bombs."[50] Why would the Soviets bend to this pressure? Because Conant believed they needed the bomb more than ever. He had not found out anything in Moscow to indicate progress that the Russians had made toward their own atomic weapons—encouraging the erroneous assumption that the Russians "know nothing"—and his estimate of the time it would take before the Russians began production had risen.[51] In 1945 his guess had gone from three to four years in May to five to fifteen years in the fall. Now, in April 1946, he told the CFR that "scientists" agreed the range was five to twenty years, and if he had to guess, Conant would pick fifteen.[52]

Conant was in tune with the top echelons of the Truman administration in putting faith in the atomic stick, and he believed that the Acheson-Lilienthal plan, released by the State Department to mostly favorable reviews in late March, was an adequate and generous carrot. But the plan's positive tone, as well as its strategy of trading off American atomic superiority for improvements in Soviet behavior, quite contradicted the prevailing winds in Washington. By early 1946, the historian John Lewis Gaddis has concluded, the quid pro quo strategy had "not only failed to produce results: but it had become a domestic liability as well"—and in the coming months, Truman discarded it.[53]

An unmistakable sign of the administration's attitude came in its selection of a negotiator to the upcoming United Nations negotiations. Speculation in the weeks following the Moscow Conference had encompassed a wide range of figures, including Conant. The leaders of the atomic scientists' movement had worried about just that possibility. In late November 1945, the Association of Los Alamos Scientists had drafted a statement stressing the need to supplant Bush and Conant with "men about whose views there is less doubt."[54] The head of the Federation of Atomic Scientists echoed those concerns a few months later. "For UNO delegate we should shy away from a scientist because too likely to get Bush or Conant," wrote W. A. Higinbotham, who optimistically hoped for Lilienthal, Stimson, or Gen. George Marshall.[55] But Truman had no intention of naming anyone likely to appeal to a liberal constituency and on March 16 selected Bernard M. Baruch, the crusty seventy-five-year-old financier and self-styled adviser to presidents who radiated conservatism and caution and unabashedly paraded his ignorance of atomic energy; Baruch disdained procuring scientific advice, he told Bush, because all he needed to know about the bomb was that it "went boom and it killed millions of people."[56]

Considering what happened, the scientists would have been lucky to get Conant. Still doubting his commitment to international control, they had been upset when Conant was appointed to the Acheson panel, but joined in applauding its report.[57] Unlike Groves, who considered it softheaded and later blamed Baruch's failure to reach an agreement on the document's premature release, Conant actively defended its tenets.[58] Reversing his previous position, he now vocally opposed plans based solely on inspection as insufficient and embraced Oppenheimer's vision of an active, thriving international development agency. "The great thing about the proposal," he said, "is its positive aspect."[59] Although careful to qualify his statements, Conant even appeared to absorb some of Oppenheimer's enthusiasm for atomic energy's peacetime potential. Such uses might be developed in three to fifteen years, he told a meeting of the Carnegie Endowment's committee on atomic energy on April 13, and efforts for control should assume that the atom would have an industrial function.[60] To the Council on Foreign Relations he predicted that "real peacetime uses" appeared to be in the "near future" in regions where fuel costs were high, "though apparently not in the United States."[61]

Conant used his influence to promote the Acheson-Lilienthal report and to sway Baruch in its direction. But like the scientists, Conant was surprised by Truman's choice, which he guessed had been made to assuage congressional opinion.[62] Though on reasonably good terms with the "Chief"—with whom he had served on the 1942 rubber panel—Conant knew Baruch's outlook diverged sharply from the idealism of the Acheson-Lilienthal group, most of whom reacted with barely concealed disgust to Truman's choice. "When I read the news last night, I was quite sick," wrote Lilienthal in his journal. "We need a man who is young, vigorous, not vain, and whom the Russians would feel isn't out simply to put them in a hole, not really caring about international cooperation."[63] Oppenheimer thought any chance for a settlement with Russia vanished the day Baruch was chosen.[64] With Acheson and Bush not feeling much better about it, Conant delicately tried to convince Truman's designated negotiator that the Acheson-Lilienthal report, which had been submitted on an advisory basis, should become official policy when the UN commission convened in three months. "I hope that the Secretary of State, the President and yourself will like the advice we tendered," Conant wrote. "To my mind it is the only possible solution of a desperate problem."[65] When a Carnegie Endowment panel drafted a confidential alternate control plan emphasizing inspection over development, Conant sent Baruch a detailed critique of its "fatal defects," "argued very strenuously and persuasively" in favor of the Acheson-Lilienthal approach to the Carnegie group, and tried to dissuade its organizer, James T. Shotwell, from publishing the report.[66] Carroll Wilson, bemused to discover that Conant criticized the Carnegie plan for overstressing police functions, confided to Herbert Marks, "When I see Conant I shall remind him that it was he who felt that we had labored this point unnecessarily."[67]

Despite a public invitation from Baruch, perhaps repeated at a private meeting between the two men in New York in late April, and prodding from Byrnes, Conant declined to join the U.S. delegation to the UN commission as an adviser. As with other scientists who also turned Baruch down, Conant probably refused out of disagreement with Baruch's approach to international control.[68] During April and May, the Acheson-Lilienthal group and Baruch's "Wall Street Gang" tried vainly to bridge the gap between their philosophies, but Baruch made it clear that the only reliable system depended on swift and "condign" punishment, and brought his mistrust of the Russians into the open with his insistence that in running the commission the Security Council must drop its provision allowing a veto by any of the big powers.[69]

Baruch's confession that one of his objectives was "preparing the American people for a refusal by Russia" did little to alleviate the sharp personal hostility between Baruch's crowd and the remarkably cohesive Acheson-Lilienthal group; tapping Oppenheimer's phones, the FBI recorded and forwarded his slighting references to the "old man." Soon Baruch was accusing Acheson of recording *his* conversations (Acheson indignantly denied the charge but took it as evidence that Baruch "deeply distrusted me"); Bush and Baruch had a falling out; and Lilienthal concluded that the negotiator had cut him out of consultations "because I refused just to yes-yes him and feed his vanity."[70]

Despite the rancor, Baruch wanted Oppenheimer as his chief technical adviser; he was torn over whether or not to accept. Deeply committed to international control, yet fundamentally distrustful of the Baruch group's motives and ability, he turned the job down in early May.[71] A few hours later, riven with self-doubt, Oppenheimer telephoned Conant at Harvard, seeking the older man's wisdom in bureaucratic and academic politics. Confessing he had been foolish, Oppenheimer asked if should change his mind and have Baruch take him after all. Conant told him not to bother: Baruch had already lost confidence in him.[72]

By keeping his temper and by flattering and humoring him, Conant stayed on speaking terms with Baruch even as relations between the two panels collapsed. After Oppenheimer and Charles Thomas had turned down Baruch, Conant promoted a substitute candidate for technical adviser, the senior Caltech physicist and former OSRD stalwart Richard C. Tolman, who might prove acceptable to Baruch and his team while opening a reliable back-channel route for Conant to gather and convey information. "Unofficially, Conant agrees to give every help," Tolman jotted in his diary after accepting the job.[73] And Conant continued to try to swing Baruch around to the Acheson-Lilienthal point of view. On May 23, he wrote urging Baruch not to allow talks to get snagged on the veto issue. Rather, the United States should simply declare that it was prepared to act unilaterally against any member of the UN commission that "commits an overt act in regard to atomic energy."[74] He suggested to Baruch — and, after a conversation at the Harvard commencement in early June, to Dean Acheson — that the United States insert a clause into its plan deeming any prohibited move against a UN atomic commission as tantamount to an act of war, allowing member nations to take whatever action they saw fit.[75]

In a follow-up letter to Baruch shortly before the talks opened, Conant hinted at his fear that a gratuitously negative attitude might guarantee a catastrophic failure. Arguing that a declaration by the United States to attack any violator would suffice, he underlined the perilous consequences of letting the commission live or die on the veto. "I have listened to the arguments of those who feel we should take many steps towards a world federation or world government and then put it up to Russia to take it or leave it," he wrote. "Although there are some attractive features of such a scheme, on balance it seems to me a highly dangerous line of procedure unless we are prepared to wage a preventive war. And after we had won such a war what would we do then?"[76]

The United Nations negotiations in New York opened on June 14 and quickly settled into a stalemate, with Baruch and Soviet delegate Andrei Gromyko presenting mutually unacceptable proposals. The American called for the gradual, phased establishment of working controls, after which the United States would relinquish its "monopoly." The Russian demanded the outlawing and destruction of all atomic arms; then he would discuss controls. Gromyko insisted on retaining the veto; Baruch insisted on eliminating it.[77]

With the international picture cloudy, Conant fretted over the delay in establishing a domestic atomic energy commission. Mired in legislative and bureaucratic infighting, and the continuing military versus civilian dispute, the McMahon bill had inched ahead during the spring.[78] Conant, worried that if it was not passed quickly the United States' position in atomic energy would "deteriorate greatly," decided that though it was far from perfect, it was better than no bill at all. Setting up the governmental machinery to supersede Groves's still-functioning Manhattan District was a matter of the "utmost importance," he told Baruch in late May, since Washington needed to effect a smooth and rapid transfer of authority in order to remain preeminent in both peaceful and military atomic energy—at least until an international organization came into existence.[79]

By the summer, the bill to establish the U.S. Atomic Energy Commission neared final congressional approval, and in late July, not altogether unexpectedly, Conant found himself considering an offer from Truman to become its first chairman. Among those urging Truman to appoint him was Baruch, who had heard privately from Tolman that Conant was likely to accept the post.[80] When Acheson phoned to say the president would like to talk to him in Washington, Conant had a good idea of what was in store. He was tempted, well aware that taking the job could place him in one of the most important positions in the world.

Not one to make a hasty decision, however, Conant consulted carefully with some well-placed friends before making up his mind. In some respects the decision was a litmus test of his prognosis for the talks under way in New York. If he thought of the position "in terms of being head of a vast arsenal for improving and manufacturing weapons (which is what the job actually became), I doubt if I would have spent long in declining," Conant wrote in his memoirs. On the other hand, if the UN commission succeeded, Conant would expect his influence to be both great and rewarding. But an even more important consideration was a frank "appraisal of the relative strength of the friends and enemies" he would encounter in Washington.[81]

Conant had gained a number of the latter during the May-Johnson fight, but business friends strongly counseled him to avoid one person in particular: Lewis L. Strauss, a Wall Street financier and wartime Navy Department aide, whom they said was out to make a name for himself by whatever means were necessary.[82] One almost certain source of caution was William Marbury, the War Department lawyer who had helped to draft the atomic energy legislation with Conant and had become his close friend. During the war, while working on maritime reconversion legislation involving the several military branches, executive agencies, and congressional committees, Marbury and other young lawyers in the complex negotiations had been enraged when Strauss clandestinely met with House Committee on Naval Affairs chairman Carl Vinson and "made a deal without consulting any of the rest of us which in our view would have created great complications in administering contract settlements." Marbury and his cohorts successfully scrambled to recoup the situation, but Strauss then compounded his transgression (and his colleagues' scorn) at the bill's signing ceremony in the Oval Office by eagerly accepting Roosevelt's congratulations.[83] To Conant, no greater sin could be imagined than out-of-channels angling for vain personal glory in a collegial setting at the expense of effective results. And during the war, he later told Lilienthal, he and Bush had been exasperated when Strauss, while at the navy, "kept poking his unauthorized nose into things we were doing about atomic matters [at the OSRD]. . . . We told him off; in fact Van and I didn't speak to him after that. We didn't trust him and never did."[84]

Concluding that he would not be able to work effectively with Strauss on the five-member commission, he gave Truman a blunt him-or-me offer when the two met in the Oval Office late on the morning of July 29. Truman replied, according to the account Conant later gave his son, that he had promised Senator McMahon that Strauss would be named, and could not change his mind.[85]

That settled the matter. On August 2, Conant telephoned the White House with the message that after considering Truman's offer it had been "difficult to make a decision, and unfortunately I am sorry it had to be No." In a polite note, Conant declined the president's "flattering proposition" because the "pull of the educational world and all it means has been too great." But in an August 17 letter to Vannevar Bush from his summer cottage, Conant left a clue to his real reason. "The Harvard Corporation," he wrote in a postscript, "will never know how much the existence and ambitions of one Lewis Strauss saved them a lot of trouble in 1946!"[86]

Over the summer of 1946 Conant prepared a major secret speech on atomic energy and warfare that he delivered to officers at the National War College in Washington on September 16. "The Atomic Age" is a full exposition of

Conant's hopes, fears, strategies and tactics regarding the new world he helped to bring into being. In the spring, at the suggestion of Grenville Clark, Conant had started a manuscript on the atomic bomb's strategic implications but had dropped the project after receiving an advance copy of Bernard Brodie's *The Absolute Weapon,* a book that quickly won acclaim as the prototypical expression of nuclear deterrence theory.[87] Apparently thinking along the same lines, Conant had broken off his own work, he explained to Clark, because the "best I could prove was a stalemate with both sides in a bad way—maybe Stalin would like this"; and because Brodie had done a "much better job than I can."[88] Although the contents of that discarded "rough draft" remain unknown, Conant was able to draw on this earlier analysis in producing the War College speech, which he asked the few friends to whom he sent numbered copies to treat as a "classified" document and return after reading.[89]

One can see why. Assured that his views would remain secret, Conant simultaneously urged the United States to make concessions in its stance on international control in order to enhance chances for Soviet agreement, and to initiate rigorous planning for what he termed "the age of the Superblitz"— when two enemy countries possessed stocks of deliverable atomic weapons.[90]

Military planners, Conant recommended, should be divided into three separate groups, each studying a different set of circumstances: the current period of uncertainty, lasting a few months or years; a world free of nuclear weapons, contingent on the success of the UN commission; and the Superblitz age. The Superblitz planners should be kept "entirely separate in order to be radical beyond measure," for in that age "all preconceived ideas should be thrown out of the window" and "these men must rethink every branch of the military art." Operating on the premise that another power had sufficient atomic bombs to destroy major cities and plants in a surprise attack—"the essence of the age"—the Superblitz planners needed to consider four interrelated strategic principles: information, dispersion, retaliation, and survival. The threat of retaliation, Conant stated, probably represented the "one chance of preventing the actual destruction of our cities." But although he had calculated that an atomic "stalemate with both sides in a bad way" was the "best" future scenario he could "prove," he still did not put much faith in nuclear deterrence. It was, in any case, he said, "a very poor and grim alternative, let me say, to that of *not* living in an age of Superblitz."

If the UN commission should fail, however, the military should face the fact that "the world will enter this age one of these days"—ten years at the most. "And in such an age war may well be inevitable. It is hard to see a peaceful way out. . . . "

And what of war in the Superblitz age? Conant doubted those who said that in a future atomic war, fighting would return to conventional military operations following a surprise nuclear attack and subsequent retaliation. For one thing, a superblitzed nation probably wouldn't be in a position to support a conventional military offensive; and against a superblitzed enemy, what operations would be required? If the enemy were Russia, occupation would be neither desirable nor possible, Conant said. Rather, strategic bombing could keep Russia "deindustrialized" from the air. With this in mind, Conant said, "I think the case still has to be made for the existence of each arm of the combat service in the age of the Superblitz: a case *de novo* for the need for ground forces, navy, a conventional air force—in short, for anything except the means of delivering atomic bombs in retaliation and organizing a Superblitzed nation for survival."

Conant's belief that atomic weapons had revolutionized warfare had confounded his thinking on military draft policy: previously a strong supporter of compulsory conscription, Conant had startled fellow educators during World War II by voicing equally strong objections to FDR's proposal to institute a draft after victory, and a similar peacetime draft act put forward by Truman in October 1945 had struck him as ill-considered.[91] In the angry interservice rivalry under way in Washington, Conant's views put him for the moment squarely on the side of the Air Force, which in early 1946 he had called "the only branch of service looking to the future realistically."[92]

To his War College audience, Conant accurately predicted that failure of the control negotiations and the entry into the Superblitz age would leave the United States in a limited nuclear alliance. Disadvantages of joint international control of an atomic stockpile without Soviet membership included loss of American freedom of action, seizure of the stockpile, political complications, loss of intelligence, and "the lining up of the world against Russia and her allies which might make war inevitable."

But, Conant then outlined the advantages of such a scheme: dispersion and addition of targets, an increased retaliatory capability, and better chances of survival. "Could even Russia and her satellites hope to Superblitz the entire urban population of the world? I doubt it very much."

Conant expressed his preferences for a nuclear alliance of some kind even if the UN approach failed, picturing a combined joint chiefs of staff that would control the atomic bombs; the question of who gave the order to fire would "hinge on the principle of retaliation." Limited international control, Conant acknowledged, went "to the heart of every suggestion for international action by force to eliminate war." But it shouldn't be too difficult to set up an alliance composed of a few members, or to assure a top military council dominated by the United States and the British Commonwealth. ("I haven't heard even the bitterest Anglophobe suggest that the British might revise the Declaration of Independence by a Superblitz with atom bombs," he noted.) The limited plan might lead to war, but if it worked, "and the doors were always held open for Russia to come in, then there would be hope."

Then Conant dealt with the psychology of living under the threat of nuclear war—"the time, let me repeat, when we are fairly certain our cities could be blown up, but before they have been!" Conant didn't like living in this Superblitz age. It was difficult to predict how the American people would react, but he explored a likely scenario. First, "there will be a frightful controversy as to whether or not the age has begun." Without a firm international program in place, "Russia might well claim to have 'enough bombs' to do in the United States or Britain alone, and yet they might well be bluffing." But convincing the public of this would be difficult. "The city dwellers will begin to shout and demand all sorts of protection. You military men will be under strong temptation to be overoptimistic in what you promise. Personally, I think the Superblitz planners may have to write off the cities, but any such plan would be extremely hard to sell the city dwellers."

In 1946, then, Conant had anticipated, dreaded, and yet acknowledged the need for the alarmed public reaction that three years later greeted the Soviet Union's first atomic explosion. The atmosphere of secrecy would create "all sorts of spy stories and saboteur stories . . . In short, to the normal benign chaos of a democracy will be added an almost hysterical chaos, the result of fear. *Or else* we will do nothing adequate in the way of dispersal, retaliation and survival. All this and no way out but war. A very bad picture."

The inescapable progression which had burned into Conant's mind, leading inevitably to disaster, now exposed the logical corollary of his grim scenario. Starkly contradicting the general opinion in Washington, he expressed the hope that "the United States will eventually be willing to take considerable chances to get the Acheson-Lilienthal scheme (or its equivalent) in operation." Of course, he added judiciously, as a basis for negotiation the Baruch proposals were one hundred percent correct, and he would not suggest publicly that the United States should settle for anything less. "Yet I hope we would," he said. "I feel that even a rickety bridge out of the shadow of the Superblitz is better than none. And I hope that a start could be made and then the bridge built stronger. If it collapsed, we would be no worse off than before." Certainly, he hoped, the United States should not let "the verbalism involved in some of the talk about the veto" destroy the negotiations: the United States just needed to state that a violation of the treaty would be cause for war.

Conant's sine qua non for an agreement remained inspection—despite his Acheson-Lilienthal flirtation with development. He was willing to trade all U.S. industrial know-how and the remaining secrets of the bomb for a two-year inspection of Russia, including a raw-materials survey; he thought a firm base of information on Russian resources and industrial development was worth the trade. Why? Conant still thought the Russians would not explode a bomb for another four to fifteen years ("too wide a spread to be useful"). "But the value of this know-how of ours decreases rapidly with each year. It is an asset like a cake of ice on a hot day." Fast action thus was necessary.

Conant's views were jarringly out of synch with those of officials in Washington. As Conant advocated renewed flexibility in dealing with the Russians, Truman had on his desk a 100,000-word report from special counsel

Clark Clifford (prepared with the aid of George Elsey) dedicated to the proposition that long-term military might—specifically a willingness to use weapons of mass destruction—represented the only language that Moscow understood. The report assumed that the Kremlin fully embraced as a fundamental tenet of Communist philosophy the impossibility of coexistence with the West. Only preparedness "to wage atomic and biological warfare if necessary" had a chance of deterring Soviet aggressive action. Therefore, the report continued, the United States "should entertain no proposal for disarmament or limitation of armament as long as the possibility of Soviet aggression exists." Any arms-control talks, it cautioned, "should be pursued slowly and carefully with the knowledge constantly in mind that proposals on outlawing atomic warfare and long-range offensive weapons would greatly limit United States strength, while only moderately affecting the Soviet Union."[93]

With the awkward exception of Commerce Secretary Henry Wallace, who publicly challenged Baruch in September 1946 for his alleged intransigence toward the Russians, the top echelons of the U.S. government now largely subscribed to the principles embodied in the Clifford Report.[94] Though Conant did not yet realize it, the administration was placing the atomic bomb closer to the center of its long-range national security planning and had no intention of compromising the perceived advantage it represented.[95]

Conant carefully avoided public criticism of Baruch's performance and of the U.S. position in the talks, acutely conscious of the danger that public opinion would swing dramatically against the government, but as the stalemate at the United Nations persisted into the fall he privately indicated his dissatisfaction to Tolman and other close friends in the nuclear business. Publicly supporting Wallace's emotional and polemical critique was, of course, unthinkable for Conant, but privately he could understand why Wallace (who would be fired by Truman for his sins) criticized the United States for failing to agree in advance to a clearly defined series of stages leading to destruction or disarmament of America's nuclear arsenal: Acheson-Lilienthal had been flawed for not spelling that out, he thought.[96]

When Conant attended a New York banquet in honor of Baruch on October 8, his private discomfort with Baruch's handling of the atomic talks grew still more acute. Conant delivered of himself a flowery tribute to the guest of honor, "a unique American institution and a very human individual for whom we have great affection," and laid it on thick: "Mr. Baruch's life epitomizes in many ways our ideal of a wise and distinguished citizen in a great republic . . . keen analyst . . . largeness of mind and bigness of heart," etc., etc. And as for that great endeavor in which Mr. Baruch was now involved, Conant had one clear message: "I suggest that from here on out he and his counselors be left alone! Surely we are concerned with a situation which is not entirely dissimilar to that which occurs when a case is before the court, and all of us like visitors to the courtroom might well cultivate patience and silence as our virtues."[97] In his first draft of his remarks, Conant had included the line: "If one has views on how Mr. Baruch should proceed, let the advice be given privately." But he had crossed out that loophole for critics.

Even as he issued this singularly undemocratic call for self-censorship in the name of unity, though, Conant could not stifle some critical thoughts of his own as he listened to Baruch's cronies. A few days later, he confided to Tolman: "Just between ourselves, I was rather unhappy at the dinner. I didn't like the Freedom House group rubbing in the veto, and I didn't like his emphasizing it in the reply. But he is playing the cards, so I shall try to keep as quiet as I can."[98] Nonetheless, he enclosed a copy of his National War College address with its criticism of the "verbalism" of the veto stand and willingness to settle for less than Baruch was asking for, and rather timidly left it to Tolman to "use your own judgment whether or not you would want to show it to John Hancock and the Chief, or if you think it advisable I could send a copy to the Chief myself." Tolman would understand after reading it why Conant was "loath" to put a copy in Baruch's hand.

Despite his best efforts, his misgivings still popped up. In early October, a colleague involved in preparing the Acheson-Lilienthal report was taken aback at the lengths Conant seemed willing to go in the negotiations. "One thing that Jim said disturbed me a little," Carroll L. Wilson wrote Bush. "We were discussing the Wallace-Baruch controversy and Jim expressed the view that Baruch would probably be willing to settle for less than he is now requiring. Jim indicated that he, himself, would be willing to settle for quite a lot less." Some items were open to compromise, Wilson agreed, but he was "convinced that if concessions involve sacrifice of principle, there may be nothing left."[99]

Bush was similarly alarmed at the prospect of Conant's defecting from the atomic establishment's tradition of closing ranks when it came to international controversies. Though no admirer of Baruch, Bush pronounced himself "very much disturbed" at the news that Conant seemed to be backsliding from total support for him: "Here I think resides a great deal of danger." The wartime science baron had actually been relieved by Wallace's attack: he thought the Wallace position "might indeed have secured quite a following in this country if it had not been advanced so poorly and clumsily." Bush hoped that the United States would "sit tight as long as necessary" in the talks, even for years, in order to convince the Russians that it had advanced a "sound" position at the outset, not a mere negotiating platform from which to retreat. Such an uncompromising stand, "if exercised rigorously and without hesitancy," might pay off, and Bush strongly opposed any "inclination to soften up."[100]

He quickly dispatched a long letter to Conant stressing the same message he had recited to Wilson: maintain a united front, support Baruch's negotiating position, and, most important, condemn Soviet inflexibility as a mere negotiating tactic best countered by long-term U.S. steadfastness, and not by a slippery slope of concessions. As Bush put it, Moscow at first "looked behind [the Baruch plan] for some sinister motives" and now had entered a stage of creating "confusion, delay, and opposition on all sorts of technicalities with the expectation that they can wear us down and hence force the compromise which they regard as inevitable far in their direction." The United States had to be on guard to prevent the talks from degenerating into "a nibbling process in which we would be at great disadvantage." This was, indeed, a succinct summary of traditional Soviet negotiating etiquette as understood in the West. Running through Bush's letter was an undercurrent of concern that Conant, by misjudging the situation, might fall into Moscow's trap.[101]

But he need not have worried. Conant, too, felt a keen awareness of the need to "synthesize steadfastness," in Bush's pungent phrase, in the American public. And he did not break ranks throughout the fall of 1946, as the Baruch Plan went on to a meaningless adoption by the United Nations Atomic Energy Commission at the end of December, doomed to irrelevance by an abstention by the Soviet Union that stood for continued rejection. Already, in fact, he had embarked upon his own campaign to assure that the American public neither turned against the U.S. position on international control nor against the atomic bomb itself.

Harvard's president in his Massachusetts Hall office after World War II. On Conant's desk, his souvenir from the Trinity test: a glass-encased fragment of ground zero

James Scott Conant

Conant, at age one, watched by
his mother, Jennett Orr Conant

Dressing up: the son of a Union Navy sailor, eight-year-old Conant dons a
Yankee soldier's uniform.

With classmates at Roxbury
Latin School's 1910 production
of *Maître Corbeau*. Conant
(*in gown, center*) played
the female lead.

Harvard College senior,
class of 1914

Conant at Harvard as a Ph.D. candidate in chemistry (*top row, second from right*); in the center is Theodore William Richards, the first American Nobel laureate in chemistry, later to become Conant's father-in-law.

Grace "Patty" Richards

In the lab: the boyish
assistant professor of
chemistry, 1921

Patty Conant with sons
Jim (*left*) and Ted, 1930

Exploring the Sierra Mountains in 1937 and mountain-climbing with his son Ted in 1939

On a park bench across the street from the White House in 1942 with members of the rubber survey committee, Karl T. Compton (*left*) and Bernard Baruch

The S-1 Executive Committee, then overseeing the atomic bomb project, at the Bohemian Grove Club, Berkeley, on September 13, 1942. From left to right: Harold C. Urey, Ernest O. Lawrence, Conant, Lyman J. Briggs, Edgar V. Murphree, and Arthur H. Compton

(*Above*) Inspecting the Hanford, Washington, plutonium production plant at the time of the Manhattan Project. From left to right: Bush, Conant, Gen. Leslie R. Groves, Col. Franklin Matthias

Shortly after the two opposed each other in a secret Anglo-American dispute over atomic collaboration, Conant presented Winston Churchill with an honorary degree from Harvard in September 1943.

CHAPTER 16

Making History

Shaping Hiroshima's Legacy

1945–1947

[Criticism of the decision to bomb Hiroshima] is bound to have a great deal
of influence on the next generation. The type of person who goes in to
teaching, particularly school teaching, will be influenced a great deal by this
type of argument . . . a small minority, if it represents the type of person who
is both sentimental and verbally minded and in contact with our youth, may
result in a distortion of history.
— Letter to Harvey H. Bundy, September 23, 1946

You have to get the past straight before you do much to prepare people for
the future.
— Speech to National War College, October 2, 1947

Visit Hiroshima today, and it's hard to distinguish the city from any other of
Japan's noisy, thriving, bustling, overcrowded metropolises. The busy citizenry,
a million strong, is devoted to the national pastime: work, leavened by
outings to cheer the local baseball team, the Carp, or to gobble a *bigu maku*
at one of the few surviving bastions of American influence, the ubiquitous
golden arches. Surrounded by the sights and sounds of prosperity, visitors
must make a special effort to seek out a reminder of the event that branded
the city's name onto history. Along the banks of the Motoyasu River, a stretch
of green is preserved from the post-1945 urban sprawl. There one finds a
memorial park, a museum, and assorted monuments devoted to the victims of
the devastation wreaked a few seconds after 8:15 a.m. on August 6, 1945. Of
the scattering of buildings that withstood the atomic blast, only one still
stands: the eerie gray exoskeleton of the domed Industrial Promotion Hall.

Yet despite Hiroshima's astonishing recovery, it is the eidetic image of a
nuclear fireball and an incinerated city that endures. Nearly a half-century
after the fact, *that* Hiroshima — the mushroom death shroud, the grainy
black-and-white newsreel of ruin, human shadows baked into stone, 100,000
victims charred or slowly corroded by radiation — lives in modern memory.

Testament to past horror, harbinger of present and future peril, Hiroshima persists as the symbol of a grim age.

But a symbol of what? Of America's firmness in resisting and defeating aggression? Or its moral depravity in committing mass murder? "This atrocious action places 'us,' the defenders of civilization, on a moral level with 'them,' the beasts of Maidanek [a Nazi death camp]," wrote one outraged commentator days after the bombing.[1] By contrast, U.S. policymakers who are reliant on nuclear deterrence have regarded the decision as a useful reminder to potential adversaries. A State Department official, asked in a 1980 television interview whether Washington might initiate the use of nuclear weapons to block a Soviet thrust into Iran, answered, "We make no comment on that whatsoever, but the Soviets know that this terrible weapon has been dropped on human beings twice in history and it was an American president who dropped it both times. Therefore, they have to take this into consideration in their calculus."[2] A decade later, the Bush administration made a comparable excursion into history to signal Saddam Hussein. During the early weeks of the air war against Iraq, fears ran high in Washington that Baghdad might use chemical weapons to repel American ground forces poised to charge into Kuwait. In a nationally televised interview, Defense Secretary Richard Cheney pointedly agreed with the conservative columnist George Will that Harry Truman had acted morally, saved lives, and "made the right decision when he used the bomb on Hiroshima." Though Cheney disclaimed any intention to use atomic weapons "at this point," his historical allusion sent a crystal-clear message to Hussein: the United States stood ready, able, and willing to more than match any escalation to weapons of mass destruction.[3]

Among the handful of men positioned to decide Hiroshima's fate, Conant was one of the first to grasp its totemic significance for his own and future generations. And after the fallout settled, when doubts arose over the atomic bombing's efficacy and morality, he actively joined the battle to define the event's meaning. "As you know," he wrote J. Robert Oppenheimer in early 1947, "I feel that a great deal turns on this point in regard to the future."[4] The stakes were high: on the outcome, he believed, hung not merely history's verdict on one of the most momentous decisions ever made by the U.S. government, but the atomic bomb's potency as a peacetime American political and diplomatic tool—and the instrument for obtaining Soviet agreement to Washington's plan to internationalize nuclear weapons and head off an apocalyptic secret arms race.

Conant's fear that the American public might repudiate the bomb stemmed from the same considerations he had employed as a member of the Interim Committee in the summer of 1945 in recommending the weapon's use. Beyond the military rationale, Conant had convinced himself that dropping the bomb on Japanese cities represented the best, perhaps only, chance to stop a postwar arms race. His position in 1946 and 1947 represented a logical, if ultimately futile, extension of that earlier calculation and assumption—and deep hope—that brandishing the atomic bomb, even as an implicit threat somewhere down the road if negotiations failed, could have a salutary and sobering effect on the Soviet Union's own atomic aspirations.[5]

Conversely, he believed, rejection of the atomic bomb by the U.S. public, on moral or other grounds, could cripple America's bargaining position in the talks at the United Nations and foreclose the chances of producing what he hoped would be a dramatic reversal in Moscow's position. The U.S. public's attitude about the bomb, he feared, could go either way, and so those who had worked on atomic weapons faced a dilemma. "Clearly we have a duty to impress on everyone the extreme gravity of the threat to Western civilization inherent in the atomic bomb, and at the same time we do not want to produce hysterical reactions by dwelling too exclusively on the devastating effects of an atomic war." The fluctuating condition of public sentiment Conant likened to that of a man with diabetes before the discovery of insulin:

> The physician, therefore, had to frighten the patient sufficiently in order to make him obey the dietary rules; but if he frightened him too much, despondency might set in—hysteria if you will—and the patient might overindulge in a mood of despair, with probably fatal consequences.[6]

The medical analogy was perhaps more revealing than Conant intended: the patient, the American public, needed close observation and careful treatment. To prevent the onset of atomic angst—and, in his mind, to preserve the possibility of success in the negotiations with Russia—Dr. Conant prescribed a strong dose of "boldness and vision," a stiff drink to ward off the knee-weakening specter of nuclear doom and to allow Americans successfully to walk along the "tightrope of the atomic age." Only if the Kremlin (i.e., Stalin) believed the United States possessed not only the wherewithal but the *will* to produce and use nuclear weapons, would it see the light, drop the fruitless polemics, and bargain for acceptable terms for atomic control. As Bush wrote Conant in October 1946, in order to win the diplomatic "trading game" with Moscow the task was to "synthesize a steadfastness" among "well informed people who guide public opinion." Thus, Bush concluded, the "cue at the present time" for "any of us that have any influence is to emphasize patience and steadfastness."[7]

Conant's generally low opinion of the Truman administration's competence in promulgating a coherent policy made him feel that the task of private initiatives to galvanize public support for the bomb was all the more critical. "It is really getting to be a disgrace," he had told Bush in late 1945, "that the Administration doesn't give the country 'a lead' on this issue."[8] A year later, he was still complaining—privately—that Americans could "smell" the uncertainty and discord among government officials, who "ought to have a policy worked out, and then sell this policy to the public if it can."[9] Now no longer operating from within the government, but at the zenith of his prestige as educational and scientific leader, Conant seized that cue and, from the Harvard president's office, he carefully aimed several shots.

Conant's actions and motives in combating criticism of the Hiroshima bombing set the pattern for subsequent attempts by supporters of America's atomic-reliant foreign policy to manipulate public opinion and ward off periodic surges of anti-nuclear sentiment.[10] "For the moment it would seem that the pressure groups ought to operate on the Kremlin rather than the American public," Conant chided Lilienthal, Truman's new choice to head the U.S. Atomic Energy Commission, after he had painted a depressing picture of the consequences of failure in atomic negotiations. "Am I right about that?"[11] But on a human level, Conant's actions may have masked suppressed feelings of guilt about his atomic involvement, an emotion which he never did acknowledge. If he felt guilt, it derived not from the deaths and suffering inflicted by the actual bombings of Japan so much as from dread that the weapon he had helped bring into being might end up as the destroyer of humanity.[12] In any case, the criticism of Hiroshima rubbed a raw nerve in this usually unemotional man. His bristling, his anxiety, and his marshaling of support for the decision to use the bomb reveal an intense personal sensitivity over how history would judge his role in the event, and a yearning to believe that Hiroshima's destruction had been necessary to win both the war *and* the peace.

Well before August 6, 1945, Conant's acute sensitivity to public attitudes toward the atomic weapon had motivated his sponsorship of the Smyth Report, the official account of the Manhattan Project, and his and Bush's warning that "almost public hysteria" and a political uproar could result if the bomb became general knowledge before the government had devised detailed plans for its future handling.[13] When Americans finally did learn of the secret, the pent-up shouts of celebration that greeted Japan's surrender all but drowned out the scattered voices raised against the bombing of Hiroshima. A Gallup poll taken in late August indicated that eighty-five percent of Americans approved of the bombing, and Conant for the most part drew plaudits for his role.[14]

But a few others charged him with original atomic sin. "Is there nothing to make you science men say: 'This far and no further!'?" asked a private-school French instructor who fulminated against "the greatest scientific crime in history."[15] A clergyman, Bradford Young of Grace Church, Manchester, New Hampshire, also refused to join the chorus of approval. In an emotional exchange in late 1945, the Reverend Mr. Young grudgingly conceded the validity of Conant's rationale equating the (im)morality of atomic and conventional bombing, but still felt a demonstrative atomic blast before obliterating Hiroshima "would have done more for the remnants of human decency than any other act." Conant's proposition that destroying the Japanese cities was also the "best way to arouse public opinion to control the A-bomb in the future" failed to impress him, for it was based on "so many uncertainties that only God could make it." "What bothered me," Young added, "was to see you preparing and participating in such a Godlike decision with *apparently* no sense of presumption, no fear and trembling, no feeling of tragic involvement in a horrible deed."[16]

Conant refused to admit to presumption, fear, or trembling. Instead, he sought ecclesiastical imprimatur for his relativistic view of wartime morality by citing the religious figure he admired most: Reinhold Niebuhr, the worldly, hard-edged "crisis" theologian whose political liberalism was stiffened by what Conant considered a refreshing realism about man's sometimes dark nature.

Conant had reason to expect Niebuhr's intellectual support; born only a year apart, both reaching the height of their powers and prestige as they reached their mid-fifties, the two men were tracing parallel courses at the top of their professions. The tall, self-assured Conant and the gaunt, intense Niebuhr increasingly came to personify their respective realms; acclaimed on *Time* covers, widely quoted as authorities to buttress the nation's new view of itself as global guardian in an age of twilight struggle, they were the quintessential educator and theologian of the tense early postwar years.

They held in common a pessimistic conception of human beings as fallen and flawed, but equipped to fight against enemies on both right and left for the values of freedom and individual rights embodied in liberal democracy. Unlike most of America's religious leaders, Niebuhr had unabashedly defended the use of military force to confront totalitarian "barbarism," whether Hitler's or Stalin's. An ardent internationalist—like Conant, he had spoken out for early U.S. entry into World War II on the Committee to Defend America by Aiding the Allies—Niebuhr eschewed the strain of evangelical pacifism that Conant, too, found naive and even dangerous, if well-intentioned. Pragmatic, tough, nondoctrinaire, politically and intellectually engaged, occasionally impious (he once fashioned himself as an "unbelieving believer"),[17] Niebuhr struck a sympathetic chord in Conant, who advocated a "secular basis for moral conduct" and rarely attended services at Memorial Church except to deliver rationalist Sunday sermons. God, at least in a literal sense, did not loom large in Conant's universe. His own Swedenborgian upbringing had instilled dissent, tolerance, and empiricism rather than faithful adherence to scriptural injunctions, ultimately producing what he rather tepidly characterized as a "cautious but optimistic theism."[18]

But if Conant saw no need to bring God to Harvard Yard, Niebuhr was another story. Early in the war he had tried in vain to lure the fiery preacher to Harvard from Union Theological Seminary with a prestigious University Professorship.[19] And in Niebuhr's *The Children of Light and the Children of Darkness* (1944), which firmly stated the imperative to fight to defend civilized values, he found a congenial moral defense for his own conduct in making and using the atomic bomb.[20] It was, Theodore Conant later recalled, probably his father's favorite book—"If he had an equivalent of the Old Testament for an orthodox Jew it was *The Children of Light and the Children of Darkness.*"[21] Read that book and see if you still disagree with me about Hiroshima, he had told the Reverend Mr. Young.

Conant was thus all the more jarred when he picked up the *New York Times* on the morning of March 6, 1946, to find Niebuhr's name among the signatories of a statement by a Federal Council of Churches special committee condemning the atomic bombings of Hiroshima and Nagasaki as "morally indefensible" and asserting that regardless of whether or not the destruction of the two cities had shortened the war, by its action the United States had "sinned grievously against the law of God and against the people of Japan." Singling out the weapon's employment without advance warning as "illegitimate," the panel's twenty-two prominent Protestant philosophers, ministers, and commentators declared themselves "deeply penitent" for the "irresponsible use already made of the atomic bomb."[22]

Conant had anticipated criticism of the atomic decision from "professional pacifists" and "certain religious leaders,"[23] but he was shocked by this harsh and seemingly unequivocal blast from the Protestant mainstream—and from Niebuhr. It took only a few hours for the educator to fire off a sharply worded protest to his putative kindred spirit. "At the risk of having this letter considered a highly personal reaction by one who has a guilty conscience," Conant challenged Niebuhr to justify the Council's moral condemnation of the atomic bomb as distinct from other, equally heinous military means used against the Axis. Use of the bomb, Conant claimed, was "part and parcel" of the war effort, and it made no sense to condemn the atomic bomb as morally more egregious than strategic bombing.

> If the American people are to be deeply penitent for the use of the atomic bomb, why should they not be equally penitent for the destruction of Tokyo in the thousand-plane raid using the M69 incendiary which occurred a few months earlier? (I may say that I was as deeply involved with one method of destruction as the other, so at least on these two points I can look at the matter impartially.) If we are to be penitent for this destruction of Japanese cities by incendiaries and high explosives, we should have to carry over this point of view to the whole method of warfare used against the axis powers.

Appealing to Niebuhr's consistent rejection of pacifism, Conant reasoned that the *reductio ad absurdum* of the statement's argument was to "scrap all our armament at once"—a "logical and defensible position, but to my mind unrealistic." He concluded by admonishing Niebuhr for straying from the path he had set out in *The Children of Light and the Children of Darkness:* "I can't reconcile this book with your signature on the document in question."[24]

Conant's arrows found their target. Niebuhr's conciliatory reply stressed that the statement's drafters were primarily disturbed by the lack of advance warning to the Japanese rather than the use of the bomb itself, but he acknowledged that the Council's statement "does not make sufficiently clear what was the conviction of most of us—that the eventual use of the bomb for the shortening of the war would have been justified."[25] Noting that he had "consistently" argued that use of the bomb would have been appropriate "to save the lives of thousands of American soldiers who would otherwise have perished on the beaches of Japan," Niebuhr promised to ask the group's chairman, Yale professor Robert L. Calhoun, to redraft the statement before final publication so that it would no longer be subject to "justified criticisms such as you have made."[26]

But on the question of guilt Niebuhr stood his ground somewhat more firmly, though he seemed to dilute the outright admission of sinfulness contained in the Council statement. He echoed the more general argument he had made in *The Children of Light and the Children of Darkness* that while admittedly America's "first task" was to win the war, once victorious there would be a need to "establish moral checks upon its power lusts" and inculate "self-criticism . . . informed by the humble realization of the fact that the possession of great power is a temptation to injustice for any nation."[27] Citing an army captain's comment, "How much evil we must do in order to do good," as a "very succinct statement of the human situation," Niebuhr wrote Conant that there was "too general a disposition to disavow guilt because on the whole we have done good—in this case defeated tyranny." He had endorsed the expression of guilt "because I thought it important from the Christian standpoint to admit the moral ambiguity of all righteous people in history, who are, despite the good they do, involved in antecedent and in marginal guilt."[28]

Conant was in no mood to swallow the charge of even "antecedent" or "marginal" guilt, but Niebuhr's clarification considerably relieved his fear that Niebuhr had defected to pacifism. "I imagine we are still in disagreement," he wrote the theologian, "but not as completely so as I feared."[29] And for a time he comforted himself with the notion that any religious figures who turned their back on the bomb were "cutting themselves off from a vast body of American opinion . . . a very large majority" that regarded the destruction of Hiroshima and Nagasaki as necessary to the prosecution of the war.[30]

Precisely to assure that American public opinion remained supportive of the government's promotion of atomic weapons, in the months following his quarrel with Niebuhr Conant grew increasingly anxious to see to it that the images of Hiroshima and the Manhattan Project were placed within the most appropriate context. In mid-century America, with television still in its infancy, most citizens saw the world in newsreels projected on the screens of movie theaters across the country. Conant "never liked mixing the grim matter of atomic energy with Hollywood romance,"[31] but like it or not it was inevitable that the entertainment industry would latch on to the atom—and in late 1946, Conant became enmeshed in efforts to influence the making of two motion pictures that for many Americans would represent the "true" story of the bomb.

The first case involved an attempt at *cinema vérité.* In the early summer of 1946, "at the suggestion of" the still-functioning Office of Scientific Research and Development, Time Inc. set out to produce a "March of Time" newsreel documentary re-creating the Manhattan Project story through a mix of genuine footage and staged scenes.[32] After initial hesitation about whether to "play ball" with the production, Conant and Bush agreed to reenact their witnessing of the Alamogordo explosion, lying prone and solemnly shaking hands inside a dirt-filled warehouse in Harvard Square.[33] But beyond cooperating with the production, they and other officials took care to see that the film—due for a summer release in the midst of the UN negotiations over the Baruch plan—promoted a favorable impression both of the decision to use the bomb on Japan and of official U.S. attitudes toward postwar international control. "If the script turns out to be for a good factual narrative stressing the necessity for action looking toward international collaborative control, the picture can, I think, turn out to be a very useful thing," Bush wrote Conant in June.[34]

But although "March of Time" producers had insisted that their "purpose" in making *Atomic Power* was to "put science's own message forcefully and factually before the public and to help ensure achievement of the goals of the Acheson-Lilienthal Committee and the United Nations,"[35] after viewing a rough cut in late July OSRD officials felt the film's portrayal of Conant and Bush was "weighted too heavy in the development of the bomb and not enough in seeking its contributions to the peace of the world." To guard against that impression, the editors inserted narration about their "major contribution in the establishment of a plan for peace-time use"—the Acheson-Lilienthal report—over a scene shot in the Harvard president's office.[36] "It is necessary," NDRC official John H. Teeter wrote to Conant shortly before the newsreel's August 1946 release, "to depict you as men of peace."[37]

And so they were. When *Atomic Power* reached theaters across the country, starring the Manhattan Project's leaders "as themselves" (Oppenheimer, Fermi, Rabi, Szilard, and even Einstein made stiff acting debuts), it showed Bush and Conant at the Trinity test but also stressed that the two men, "cognizant of the potential threat to humanity in the unrestricted use of atomic power," had helped draw up the Acheson-Lilienthal report and continued to endeavor to achieve a peaceful solution to the atom. The film concluded with the ringing declaration that the United States "is prepared to cooperate fully in eliminating by world agreement and for all time the nightmare of atomic war."

Unenthusiastic as they were about the newsreel, Conant and Bush hoped the documentary might at least mitigate the impact of the other motion picture on the atomic bomb then in production: Metro-Goldwyn-Mayer's *The Beginning or the End,* Hollywood's first stab at an A-bomb blockbuster.[38] Doing their best to reduce the subject's profound scientific, political, and moral complexities to timeworn moviemaking convention, MGM execs billed the film as the "romantic, dramatic story behind the story of the making of the atomic bomb,"[39] and cast handsome matinee idols to impersonate the Manhattan Project's leading lights (Hume Cronyn played Oppenheimer, but Spencer Tracy turned down a chance to play Leslie Groves) and issued publicity posters of the clean-cut stars and their girlfriends resolutely facing the atomic age under a mushroom cloud. Amid much fanfare, *The Beginning or the End* premiered in February 1947 at an opulent Washington gala (Conant and the Soviet ambassador were among those who sent regrets).[40] But as far as box office and critical reception was concerned, the beginning *was* the end. The film was a flop. *Time's* reviewer berated its "cheerful imbecility," and those familiar with the real thing sneered at the celluloid version's scientific and historical whoppers.[41]

But the offscreen drama, while perhaps less glamorous, was at least as interesting as the film itself. Conant, Bush, and other prominent scientists, military officers, government officials, and opinion-makers, including the journalist Walter Lippmann, had maneuvered quietly to influence the content of the MGM film, and in Conant's case even to block its distribution. Their backstage machinations offers a fine illustration of how keenly the foreign-policy insiders cared to fashion public perceptions of the atomic issue.

The Manhattan Project and the White House were able to exercise considerable leverage over the form and content of the film due to a law requiring signed releases from all those portrayed in the movie. Sensitive to charges of censorship, President Truman declined personally to request changes, but others had no such inhibitions, and they ultimately forced numerous stylistic and substantive alterations in the film.

From their first contact in March 1946, the MGM moviemakers had managed to rouse the suspicions of Bush and Conant. The producer, Sam Marx, claimed that the project had Truman's personal blessing (and promised that it could render "a great service to civilization"), but they could not have been reassured by reports that the movie's genesis came from members of the atomic scientists' movement, long critical of the OSRD, who hoped a popular film would further their message of international and civilian atomic control. And the studio got off on the wrong foot with Bush by pressing him to sign a release form or else suffer the indignity of seeing an actor playing Alexander Sachs receive primary credit for "selling the entire [atomic] program to FDR." True to form, the temperamental Bush "violently" exploded at what he took as a sign that the studio was not above making a film that was "historically incorrect and admittedly so," and told Conant the incident "disturbed me greatly."[42]

Though Marx later made peace with Bush, adopting to the letter his suggested changes, the squabble set the tone of relations between the bomb project's dubious old guard and the moviemakers, who believed (in the words of a 1946 memo from MGM chief Louis B. Mayer to Albert Einstein) that "dramatic truth is just as compelling a requirement on us as veritable truth is on a scientist."[43]

Conant consistently "inclined" against cooperating with the moviemakers,[44] but in early May the studio contacted him to seek his consent to be depicted in a few brief scenes. Forewarned of Conant's coolness, the screenwriters, Robert Considine and Frank Weak, had already done their best to minimize his role—just one line of inane dialogue, when Conant tells Groves after the test blast at Alamogordo, "I'm glad you'll not be busted to sergeant," to which the general responds, "And I'm glad Harvard is not looking for a new president."[45]

Conant turned up his nose at the script itself, which ran real and fictionalized scientists and army officers through a hokey simulacrum of the atomic story, but he may have been unnerved by the far-out opening scene. Set in the year 2446, it purports to show the burial five centuries earlier of a silvery, bullet-shaped time capsule containing "a message to future generations!" and the "enduring record" of a past civilization—that is, the movie the audience was about to see. The screenwriters had no inkling that Conant himself had seriously flirted with a similar idea only a few months before.[46] Nor, for that matter, did they know that Conant, like an army officer shown in the film, had for a moment wondered if the Alamogordo explosion might be igniting a chain reaction in the atmosphere.[47]

Stalling for time, Conant sought guidance from Bush, who was busily sounding out Truman aides and Groves to see if they were cooperating. But Bush's confusion only deepened after presidential press secretary Charles Ross told him the White House "neither approves nor disapproves the film," and Groves, by contrast, seemed to be preening for stardom.[48] In the meantime, MGM sent Conant a steady stream of personal entreaties aimed at prying a signed release form from him. One studio official assured him the actor cast to play Conant, Frank Ferguson, "does you no discredit" (and would not wear the mustache gracing his publicity photos), and Marx flattered Conant's wartime exploits and "exalted position . . . in American life." The film wished, he vowed, to "salute . . . the contribution of America's great universities."[49]

The studio's increasingly cozy ties to the administration disillusioned some liberal scientists who had previously supported the movie, but helped to convince Bush (still holding Conant's proxy) of MGM's apparent readiness to be "sensible" and "cooperative" in correcting obvious historical errors.[50] After conferring with Bush in late July, the moviemakers inserted (and then rewrote) a new scene in which Bush gives FDR the briefing that leads to the Manhattan Project's creation. Several revisions later, on December 6, Bush informed Conant that since the scenes which portrayed him no longer egregiously distorted the historical record, he had signed the release form, albeit reluctantly.[51]

Even that was further than some others were willing to go. Citing "fundamental objections" and threatening a lawsuit if his wishes were ignored, Niels Bohr firmly refused MGM permission to portray him, forcing major script revisions, while Oppenheimer grudgingly signed a release in May but ceased further cooperation, citing aesthetic revulsion over the film's characters, who seemed to him "stilted, lifeless, and without purpose or insight."[52]

But the most important approval sought by the filmmakers was from the man in charge the summer of 1945—and who still sat in the White House. Though Truman did not openly intervene in the editing process, Ross did, and pressed for "considerable changes" before he was satisfied that the president's appearances were "handled properly."[53] Perhaps the most revealing change concerned the film's depiction of how Truman reached the decision on Hiroshima. Initially, Truman was shown unhesitatingly issuing the order, snapping, "I think more of our American boys than I do of all our enemies."[54] But at a preview to a select Washington audience in October, the scene reportedly disturbed Truman,[55] and it outraged Lippmann. It was hardly the image either man wanted to have projected, either domestically or abroad at a time when criticism over the bomb's use persisted, the Russians disputed America's fitness as custodian for the weapon, and the United Nations negotiations over international control hung in the balance. Lippmann felt the "shocking scene" would "disgrace" Truman (whose role was reduced to "extreme triviality in a great matter"), Stimson, and the United States, and privately conveyed his dismay to a few well-placed insiders able to influence the White House and War Department. "Serious people abroad," he warned, "are bound to say that if that is the way we made that kind of decision, we are not to be trusted with such a powerful weapon."[56]

John McCloy, on sabbatical from government service to refresh his bank account at an elite New York law firm but still keeping a hand in high-level matters,[57] agreed that the imputations of cavalier treatment of the atomic decision could cause trouble for the government's efforts to maintain public support for its atomic policy. "I can readily see how such a misrepresentation would greatly complicate some of the thinking which is now current about the bomb . . . and I can see how it might complicate some of Baruch's problems," he wrote War Secretary Robert P. Patterson.[58]

Lippmann's angry protests produced quick results. An MGM official, "deeply impressed by your feeling that we were showing our country's Chief Executive deciding a monumental matter in what was a much-too-hasty fashion," informed him a few days later that the offending scene had been cut from the film.[59] (You see, Lippmann wrote Conant in enclosing the exchange, "sufficiently drastic criticism does have its effect upon the producers.")[60]

What millions of moviegoers eventually witnessed on the screen instead was a misleading suggestion that Truman spent "sleepless nights" agonizing over whether or not to use the bomb on a Japanese city. In fact, Truman himself frequently insisted that he "never had any doubt" about the decision.[61] To the actor who portrayed him in *The Beginning or the End,* he asserted that he had felt "no qualms" about the two atomic bombings because they forced an end to the war and saved American lives, and because the Japanese had been "vicious and cruel savages" in their own wartime conduct.[62] "I never lost any sleep over my decision," he declared on another occasion.[63] In an even more egregious invention, the film also intentionally created the false impression that American planes had dropped leaflets warning the residents of Hiroshima of the impending atomic attack.

Conant's already negative attitude to the movie was further exacerbated when Lippmann wrote of his fear that this "bad example of the vulgarization and commercialization of a great subject by Hollywood" would damage America's image abroad. (And if that wasn't bad enough, he told Conant, after attending the October preview, "whereas General Groves has been transformed into a dashing, romantic cavalier, you have been de-glamorized in a most unfair way!")[64] While Conant believed responsibility for dealing with the matter lay "squarely" with the War Department and the Chief of Staff[65] — and Groves, still officially head of the Manhattan Engineering District until the Atomic Energy Commission began operations, was raising hackles with MGM to make sure the movie did not compromise security restrictions[66] — he stealthily opened his own gambit to stop the movie.

After lunching in late November with Lippmann (who had journeyed to Cambridge to see Yale trounce Harvard, 27-14, in "The Game"), Conant settled on Bernard Baruch as his best hope. Conant sent the "Chief" (via aide John Hancock) a copy of a November 27 letter from Bush (which perhaps Conant got him to write for just this purpose) voicing agreement with Lippmann's concern over "the bad effect . . . this film may have in other countries," and pointedly noted that it was a matter on which the State Department should advise the White House.[67] And in December, he pressed Baruch to take action. Conant broadly hinted to Hancock that he "certainly hope[d] that the combination of his [Bohr's] action and other forces will end in having the picture withdrawn. That will be the best thing that has happened along this line for some time."[68] Soon afterward, he took his case directly to Baruch. He could "hardly pass judgment" since he hadn't seen the film, but what he had heard, he didn't like. Raising the possibility that the film might "endanger the international solution of the atomic energy problem," Conant rued that, under the "misapprehension" that the White House and War Department had given their approval, he had not forcefully protested when he first heard of the movie the previous summer. Now he felt "morally committed" to allowing the use of his name since Bush had given his consent. "I can say most sincerely, however," Conant added, "that if you would find some way of having the film held up and kept out of circulation, I for one would feel greatly relieved."[69]

That Harvard's president would resort to this backhanded attempt at censorship, and even seriously suggest that a movie might sway the United Nations negotiations, revealed just how sensitive he was to the whims and shifts of public sentiment over the bomb. But in this case he need not have worried. While it is not known what, if any, action Baruch took—he promised Conant he would look into the matter—the film ultimately released by MGM had no discernible effect on public opinion. Conant rested easier after hearing in early January from Lippmann, who had just seen the latest revised "cut" at a special screening for the War Department, that the movie was "still embarrassingly vulgar, but it is not so dangerously bad as it was." Better still, his journalistic informant related, Conant, along with Stimson, Bohr, and Lise Meitner, had "made an effective 'get-away' and was no longer mentioned by name in the film.[70] The film thus rendered innocuous, Conant finally begrudged his permission for impersonation a few scant weeks before it premiered.[71]

It was, in the end, no accident that *The Beginning or the End* gave the moral issues evoked by the bomb a "once-over lightly," in the words of one reviewer, and "shunned" controversies over international and domestic atomic control "like the plague."[72] Critics gave the filmmakers high marks for earnestness in trying to present the subject of atomic peril to a mass audience, and oohed and aahed at the reenactments of Alamogordo and Hiroshima, but it was equally clear that a unique, timely opportunity to provoke the public into a serious examination of the bomb's mystery-enshrouded genesis had been missed.[73] In laboring mightily and bringing forth a cinematic mouse, in blithely rubber-stamping the administration's moral rectitude in using the bomb, one historian has concluded, Hollywood had "contributed its bit to the larger cultural process by which Hiroshima and Nagasaki gradually sank, unconfronted and unresolved, into the deeper recesses of American awareness."[74]

On August 31, 1946, the usually wry, above-it-all *New Yorker* magazine shed its customary mien and format to devote an entire issue to a report from devastated Hiroshima by the journalist John Hersey.[75] This powerful portrait of shattered lives and a devastated city evoked an immediate and overwhelming response that went far beyond the publication's readership. Simply yet movingly written, centered on individuals rather than abstract concepts, Hersey's article was reprinted widely, read over national radio, discussed in public meetings. For the first time, the same American public that had hailed the destruction of a Japanese "military base," as Truman's press release described Hiroshima, saw the victims of the atomic bomb depicted as distinct and identifiable individuals with hopes, dreams, and mundane concerns rather than the undifferentiated subhuman mass commonly portrayed during the war in the Pacific. Like a delayed aftershock, the realization that the "Little Boy" and "Fat Man" had wiped out *cities* filled with people not so different from Americans stimulated a sudden rush of second thoughts and questioning about the atom bomb's morality.[76] Now that the war had ended and the boys had come home, doubt begun to fester in a wound previously salved in certitude.

Conant, returning to Cambridge for the fall semester from his annual summer escape to the cool breezes, placid lakes, and green hills of New Hampshire, was also troubled—but for a different reason than those horrified by Hersey's depiction of atomic ruin. And Conant's response, only now coming to light, was ultimately to have a profound effect on the way Americans understood Hiroshima throughout the postwar era.[77]

It was not so much Hersey's account that alarmed Conant—the thirty-one-year-old Pulitzer-prize–winning *Time* war correspondent deliberately abjured blatant moral condemnations or policy prescriptions—but the surrounding clamor questioning the bomb's use.

Shortly before Hersey's article appeared, the government had released the results of the U.S. Strategic Bombing Survey, a high-powered report sponsored (to its subsequent chagrin) by the air force, on the effectiveness of the Allied aerial attacks on Germany and Japan. Among the economists culled from government and academia to take part in the detailed study were George Ball, John Kenneth Galbraith, and Paul Nitze, who led the group assessing the results of the Hiroshima bombing. To Conant's dismay, the analysts concluded that "certainly prior to December 31, 1945, and in all probability prior to November 1, 1945, Japan would have surrendered even if the atomic bombs had not been dropped, even if Russia had not entered the war, and even if no invasion had been planned or contemplated."[78]

Conant did not contest that judgment but considered it to be "Monday morning quarterbacking," and he groused at the implication that dropping the bomb had been unnecessary and mistaken. "After all," he reminded a Buffalo newspaper editor, "I doubt if anyone in the United States or Great Britain was in a position to find out the facts which the United States strategic bombing survey found out after the war was over."[79] Conant was further riled, in the late summer of 1946, by a book by the commentator Leland Stowe decrying the "error" of using the bomb, and by remarks by navy admiral William F. Halsey, Jr., commander of the Pacific Fleet, claiming that the bomb was dropped because the scientists "had a toy and wanted to try it out" even though "the Japs had put out a lot of peace feelers through Russia long before."[80]

It was an editorial in the September 14, 1946, *Saturday Review of Literature,* written by its activist-editor Norman Cousins, that finally drove Conant to respond.[81] Praising Hersey, Cousins blasted those who had approved the atomic bombings and demanded an accounting. "Have we as a people any sense of responsibility for the crime of Hiroshima and Nagasaki?" he asked. Why had those in power "refus[ed] to heed the pleas of the scientists against the use of bomb without a demonstration" and to issue instead an ultimatum? And what about claims that Japan was ready to surrender even before Hiroshima? What of the lingering death that doomed "thousands" of

Japanese? To bring home implications for readers, Cousins wondered aloud if Americans yet recognized that the atomic bomb was ideal for use against *them,* and "that by our use of it—at a time when no other nation had it—we have almost guaranteed its general use in the next war?" A small but growing number of commentators, including Cousins and a fellow world-government advocate, Thomas K. Finletter, also charged that a major underlying motivation for using the bomb had been to intimidate Moscow.[82]

On reading Cousins's editorial, Conant first telephoned Vannevar Bush and then wrote with unusual passion to his old friend and colleague Harvey H. Bundy, who had returned following the war to the Boston law firm of Choate, Hall & Stewart, enclosing the *Saturday Review* piece. "I am considerably disturbed about this type of comment which has been increasing in recent days," he wrote, for nothing had come to light to change his view, expressed on the Interim Committee, that the use of the bomb was justified "on the grounds (1) that I believed it would shorten the war against Japan, and (2) that unless actually used in battle there was no chance of convincing the American public and the world that it should be controlled by international agreement." Of course, he continued, he had expected "professional pacifists and perhaps certain religious leaders" to condemn the weapon's use, but he was "disturbed" to see "nonreligious groups and people taking up the same theme."[83]

Conant doubtless agreed with Cousins's assertion that the moral and political questions raised by the bombing of Hiroshima "are not moot, they are not marginal, they are not to be separated from the problem of building a workable peace." Both also shared, more than they realized, the goal of internationalizing the atom and ameliorating the ever-deepening U.S.-Soviet enmity. But the two men diverged profoundly in their vision of Hiroshima's lessons: where Cousins interpreted the bomb's use as a symbol of the American government's moral bankruptcy and as the starting gun for a postwar nuclear-arms race, Conant considered it vital that the decision be understood as a firm yet justified use of American strength, and as a result translate into a psychological edge in influencing Soviet behavior. Now was the time to ensure that historical judgment served to underpin the twin objectives of international control and U.S. military strength. Losing the struggle over Hiroshima's meaning, in Conant's view, threatened not only to undermine America's negotiating leverage but to presage an abdication of its historic destiny as a global political, military, and economic leader. Acutely conscious of history as a subjective and fluid process, susceptible to shifting influences, Conant sensed that the lessons and implications of Hiroshima would have an enduring, perhaps decisive impact on the hopes for postwar peace. He wrote Bundy:

> You may be inclined to dismiss all this talk as representing only a small minority of the population, which I think it does. However, this type of

sentimentalism, for I so regard it, is bound to have a great deal of influence
on the next generation. The type of person who goes in to teaching, particularly school teaching, will be influenced a great deal by this type of argument.
We are in danger of repeating the fallacy which occurred after World War I.
You will recall that it became accepted doctrine among a group of so-called
intellectuals who taught in our schools and colleges that the United States
had made a great error in entering World War I, and that the error was
brought about largely by the interests of the powerful groups. Of course,
there is little relation between these two types of fallacies, but I mention the
history after World War I only to emphasize that a small minority, if it
represents the type of person who is both sentimental and verbally minded
and in contact with our youth, may result in a distortion of history.[84]

To prevent this "distortion," Conant hoped to do more than carp—he
plotted a preemptive strike. It was of "great importance," he wrote to Bundy,
that "someone who can speak with authority" issue a clear-cut statement
explaining the circumstances behind the decision to drop the bomb. The best,
indeed the only, man for the job, Conant felt, was the retired secretary of war,
Henry L. Stimson—then working on his memoirs at his estate at Highhold, on
Long Island, with the assistance (as Conant well knew) of none other than
Harvey Bundy's son McGeorge. Could not the senior Bundy and his old War
Department cohort George Harrison together convince Stimson to write a
short article "pointing out the conditions under which the decision was made
and who made it?"[85]

Shrewdly, Conant sought to exploit Stimson's unrivaled prestige and
respect to defend the legitimacy of bombing Hiroshima and, though less
explicitly, to preserve its usefulness in the ongoing UN international control
talks. Not incidentally, Conant also was anxious to protect his own role in the
events of 1945; though he remained "quite unrepentant" as to his endorsement of the bomb's use, talk of the "crime" of Hiroshima and Nagasaki
further sensitized Conant to the dangers of ending up on the wrong side of
history.

There was another personal element to his concern: his mounting resentment at the widespread impression that the atomic scientists themselves had
not been permitted a say in the decision to use the bomb. Stimson should be
sure to mention in his article, Conant noted, the still secret role of the Interim
Committee's scientific panel, which had "raised no protest" to the proposed
use of the bomb and had even sat in on target meetings. "I think it unfair for
the scientists to try to dodge the responsibility for this decision, although of
course they were not in a position to influence greatly whatever was done at
Potsdam." In conclusion, it was "a matter of real importance and considerable
urgency" to get this side of the story out.

Conant's missive produced the desired effect—the old-boy War Department network went to work. Bundy called Harrison, who contacted McGeorge

Bundy on Long Island, set up a lunch with Conant, and put the idea to Stimson, who reluctantly agreed to write the article.[86] Stimson hardly relished the assignment. Wearily, he explained to Justice Felix Frankfurter that the "history of it is that Jim Conant felt very much worried over the spreading accusation that it was entirely unnecessary to use the atomic bomb" and that "I was the victim" who should correct the record. "I have rarely been connected with a paper about which I have so much doubt at the last moment," he confessed. "I think the full enumeration of the steps in the tragedy will excite horror among friends who heretofore thought me a kindly-minded Christian gentleman but who will, after reading this, feel that I am cold blooded and cruel."[87]

The drafting of the article was largely to be the work of Stimson's amanuensis, McGeorge Bundy, who solicited aid from several key participants in the original decision: his father, Conant, Groves, Harrison, and Interim Committee secretary Gordon Arneson.[88] (Harvey Bundy's supporting brief defended the decision on military grounds ["the belief that the use would save American lives by terminating the war as rapidly as possible"], but it also contained what may well have been allusion to Conant's dualistic rationale; "at least some" members of the Interim Committee, Bundy wrote, thought that "unless the bomb were used it would be impossible to persuade the world that the saving of civilization in the future would depend on a proper international control of atomic energy.")[89] The army historian Rudolph Winnacker contributed background data and his own fusillade in a military journal.[90] Truman also gave his seal of approval; annoyed at speculation that the decision to bomb Hiroshima was "arrived at hurriedly and without consideration," the president urged Stimson to "straighten out the record on it."[91]

In effect, the universally venerated, statesmanlike figure of Stimson served as the medium through which the men behind the decision tried to safeguard their place in history and to nip in the bud what a latter generation might have termed a "post-Hiroshima syndrome" among Americans. Conant was not the only one who worried about the need to do this. Days after Hersey's article appeared, General Thomas F. Farrell urged Baruch to see if he could get the *New Yorker* to print a comparable article "by a writer with Hersey's skill in drawing word pictures" about six allied prisoners of war in Japan, their mistreatment at the hands of their captors, and how *they* felt about the atomic bomb—"America forgets so quickly," rued Farrell, who was "much more moved by starved American soldiers who had been continually beaten by baseball bats than I was by the wounded Japanese in Hiroshima."[92] John McCloy noted to War Secretary Patterson in early November that McGeorge Bundy and George Harrison had worked on Stimson's draft just as, on other fronts, Lippmann tried to prevent *The Beginning or the End* from spreading the impression that Truman had made the decision to bomb Japan with little or no consideration. "Both of them feel," related McCloy, "that it is supremely important that the people of the country should not gain such a false impression as this film creates."[93] After Halsey's remarks, Baruch had protested angrily to navy secretary James V. Forrestal, declaring that those who claimed the use of the bomb had been unnecessary were giving "aid and comfort to the minority in this country who seek to weaken our national security by putting America in the wrong on moral grounds in the eyes of the world."[94] By late September 1946 the Navy Department and the U.S. delegation to the international control talks were quietly cooperating to turn the tide of the debate over Hiroshima. Cautioning that the controversy "might go very far afield and the emotional responses would be very difficult to control," a Baruch aide reported, "We are doing all we can" to "help clarify this moral problem," including efforts "to secure the support of the leading thinkers in this field and particularly, of all church organizations."[95]

Conant now moved to open another front. At the other end of Cambridge's Massachusetts Avenue, MIT president Karl T. Compton had just returned from a visit to Japan, where he had observed the ruins of Hiroshima and spoken with counterparts in the defeated nation's scientific establishment. The trip left him more convinced than ever that the bomb had been responsible for bringing about the war's rapid conclusion, that its use had saved "hundreds of thousands, perhaps several millions of lives, both American and Japanese," and, clearly thinking of the Strategic Bombing Survey, that criticism leveled by "after-the-event strategists" reflected "much delusion and wishful thinking." Contemplating the carnage that lay ahead if the war continued, Washington had had no choice but to use the bomb, Compton believed.

Conant urged Compton to express his views on Hiroshima in an article for the popular press. At his suggestion Compton wrote a short, sharp essay for their mutual acquaintance Ted Weeks, editor of the *Atlantic Monthly*.[96] The December issue of the *Atlantic* featured Compton's "If the Atomic Bomb Had Not Been Used," which rehearsed the arguments for the bomb's use and received President Truman's personal, public endorsement in a letter to the magazine.[97]

As Compton's article hit newsstands in late November, Conant was orchestrating a second, more powerful salvo. Stimson and McGeorge Bundy had completed a first draft of the *Harper's* article. Late on the afternoon of November 29, Bundy gave Conant a preliminary draft detailing the events leading up to Hiroshima and Nagasaki.[98] Asked to comment, Conant responded with unusual gusto. Scrawling his blue pencil "pretty freely" over Bundy's draft, Conant within twenty-four hours mailed off a "mutilated manuscript" and an eight-page letter explaining his suggested revisions.[99] His editing concentrated not on stylistic polishing but on substance; his aim was to craft an effective piece of advocacy that would appeal to informed readers yet present a difficult target for critics. Stressing that the article should stick to a "mere recital of the facts," Conant urged Bundy to drop sections in which Stimson appeared to be "arguing his case or justifying his position." Recasting the article in a less argumentative form, he predicted, would make it impossible for the "other side" to "attack Mr. Stimson in such a way as to make him feel that he should reply."

Rather than a neutral, informative article, what Conant really envisioned was a "mere recital" of only those "facts" that would bolster Stimson's case—and ignoring, or discounting, information that might raise uncomfortable questions. Specifically, Conant implored Bundy to avoid a lengthy discussion of the pros and cons of modifying the U.S. requirement for Japan's unconditional surrender prior to Hiroshima—a key point in arguments that Japan's capitulation could have been obtained without dropping the bomb by assuring the survival of the Emperor. Introducing "the problem of the Emperor diverts one's mind from the general line of argumentation," wrote Conant, and would be "unnecessary and unwise."

Conant also proposed revealing additions. He wrote in a new section—incorporated almost verbatim in Stimson's published version—that elaborated on the Interim Committee's reasons for rejecting a demonstration blast or an explicit advance warning before the bomb was used, since "both these points are stressed strongly by the people we are trying to impress with this article." And, Conant convinced Bundy to mention the "similarity in destruction brought about by the fire raids over Tokyo and the damage done by the atomic bomb," a favorite argument. While equating the atomic bomb and strategic bombing in terms of their moral value and military damage, however, Conant also hoped Stimson would note that the atomic weapon seemed the "ideal" device to obtain Tokyo's surrender. Since "one plane and not many hundreds would be involved in the attack," he reasoned, "it would be clear to the Japanese that defense against such a raid or even a conventional air raid warning would be impossible." Carefully qualifying his praise, Conant told Bundy that "on a revised basis" the article "would do a great deal to correct certain misunderstandings now current in the American public" if published in a major national magazine.[100]

The younger Bundy wired back that he was "personally delighted" at Conant's suggestions—and a fortnight later, like a student handing in a revised term paper, he returned to Cambridge bearing a new draft that incorporated most of Conant's ideas.[101] This time, Conant gave the paper a passing grade, dashing off a note to Stimson on December 14 expressing enthusiasm for the new version and urging him to publish it "as soon as possible," since there continued to be a "great deal of misinformation widely circulated in the United States" to the effect that a warning should have been issued.[102]

Despite a relative lull in the acrimony that had come to characterize U.S.-Soviet relations, the failure of the United Nations atomic energy negotiations in New York that month to nail down a unanimous accord only deepened Conant's conviction that a public consensus behind America's stand on the bomb was the last best hope to gain eventual Soviet acceptance of the Baruch

plan or something like it. Writing to Stanford University president Donald
Tresidder on January 22, 1947, he predicted that *"if the American people will
stay tough* in regard to the use of the bomb I think we may be in for a period
of peace and that there are fairly good chances that the bomb can be put
under international control; of course if that happens we are well on the road
to a long period of world order."[103]

In elevating U.S. public opinion to this decisive role in determining the
success or failure of the negotiations, Conant foreshadowed a persistent strain
of postwar American policy: the belief that a perceived advantage in nuclear
weapons could translate into tangible political and diplomatic gains by virtue
of the implicit threat of their possible use—so long as that threat rests on
credible public support. Of course, as with the hoped-for diplomatic consequences of the bomb's initial use, this presumed that the Soviets so badly
trailed the United States in technology and economic development that they
would be forced to concede nuclear inferiority and a major loss of international political prestige—a perennial postwar dream.

Conant clearly expressed this credo in late January 1947 after Stimson
sent him a preprint of the forthcoming magazine article. "It seems to me just
exactly right, and I am sure will do a great deal of good," he said. The article
would "play an important part in accomplishing" Stimson's goal of forever
abolishing war, he predicted, because

> if the propaganda against the use of the atomic bomb had been allowed to
> grow unchecked, the strength of our military position by virtue of having the
> bomb would have been correspondingly weakened, and with this weakening
> would have come a decrease in the probabilities of an international agree-
> ment for the control of atomic energy. I am firmly convinced that the
> Russians will eventually agree to the American proposals for the establish-
> ment of an atomic energy authority of world-wide scope, *provided* they are
> convinced that we would have the bomb in quantity and would be prepared
> to use it without hesitation in another war. Therefore, I have been fearful lest
> those who have been motivated by humanitarian considerations in their
> arguments against the bomb were as a matter of fact tending to accomplish
> exactly the reverse of their avowed purpose.[104]

When Stimson's "The Decision to Use the Atomic Bomb" led the cover of
the February 1947 *Harper's* magazine, its impact far exceeded Conant's
original expectations.[105] His alarm—not a request from Truman, as one
historian has suggested[106]—had set in motion a chain of events leading to the
publication of the most influential statement on the atomic bomb ever made,
immediately recognized as historic. Stimson's article evoked an outpouring of
praise not only from predictable quarters (such as Truman) but also from
many erstwhile critics. The editors of the *New York Times* accorded it lavish
front-page treatment and, in a separate editorial, hailed it as "not a mere

memoir" but "a stage in an evolving national foreign policy."[107] To spread the word, *Harper's* followed the example the *New Yorker* had set with Hersey's article by granting blanket permission to reprint the article free of charge because of its "exceptional public importance."[108] Ironically, in defending the bomb's use as a military necessity, Stimson successfully borrowed Hersey's strategy of a sober, understated narrative rather than argumentation—precisely as Conant had advocated. Readers were struck not only by his forceful marshaling of facts to underpin the reasoning behind the decision and by the revelations of the Interim Committee's deliberations and other previously unknown events and information, but also by Stimson's stern yet humane tone, melancholy over the tragedy of war but not apologetic over the measures that had been necessary to end it. The paramount motivations for using the bomb had been to finish the war and save "over a million" American lives. And given the alternative of prolonged fighting leading to a land invasion of Japan, Stimson wrote, "no man, in our position and subject to our responsibilities, holding in his hands a weapon of such possibilities for accomplishing this purpose and saving those lives, could have failed to use it and afterwards looked his countrymen in the face." His powerful concluding paragraphs rammed home a dual message—the decision's unavoidability ("this deliberate, premeditated destruction was our least abhorrent choice") and the identification of war itself, as opposed to any particular weapon, as the enemy facing humanity.

This first and seemingly definitive account of the atomic bomb decision stood for almost two decades as the authoritative historical record of the events of 1945. Its carefully calibrated defense of the decision on military grounds—and Stimson's claim that the only alternative was an invasion of the Japanese mainland at an estimated cost of "over a million casualties, to American forces alone"—instantly became the basis of the orthodox defense for bombing Hiroshima and Nagasaki.[109]

From the perspective of forty-five years, Stimson's article seems in some respects as notable for what it left out as for what was included. There was no mention of postwar relations with the Soviets as a consideration in the calculations and deliberations preceding the bomb's use; no mention of the Strategic Bombing Survey's claim that Japan would have surrendered even without the bomb or an invasion; no explicit mention of the arguments raised against the decision; only the barest grazing of the issue of why Truman rejected proposals to modify unconditional surrender so as to leave the Emperor on his throne; no explanation other than Stimson's desire "to record for all who may be interested my understanding of the events" as to why he wrote the article; and of course, no mention of Conant's overriding belief that the article was necessary in the contemporary context of atomic negotiations with Moscow, not merely to correct the historical record.

But Stimson was out to sway minds, not to expand discourse. As McGeorge Bundy (the invisible, uncredited co-author) himself later acknowledged, the article was "not a piece of history—it's Stimson the advocate, who has an advantage because he was there."[110] Stimson explained to Truman that he had intended to rebut the criticisms of the Chicago scientists, and, relaying Conant's concern without explicitly citing him, also "to satisfy the doubts of that rather difficult class of the community which will have charge of the education of the next generation, namely educators and historians."[111] The range of laudatory letters preserved in Stimson's papers at Yale extends from Groves and Truman to Ralph A. Bard, the Interim Committee's sole dissenter against the bombing of Hiroshima without warning, and W. A. Higinbotham, the executive secretary of the liberal Federation of Atomic Scientists. In a rather smug report from Cambridge, McGeorge Bundy noted that among those who approved of the article were "one or two of my friends who fall into Mr. Conant's unkindly classification of the 'verbal minded.' I think we deserve some sort of medal for reducing these particular chatterers to silence."[112]

Not everyone was satisfied with Stimson's version, of course. Former ambassador to Japan Joseph C. Grew, who as acting secretary of state (and unaware of the Manhattan Project) had urged Truman in the spring and summer of 1945 to modify the requirement of unconditional surrender, noticed immediately that Stimson had conspicuously omitted a full discussion of whether Washington could have ended the war several months earlier by doing just that. He reminded Stimson a few weeks after the *Harper's* article appeared that "I and a good many others will always feel" that if Truman had issued a "categorical" promise to leave the Emperor in place, as Grew had recommended, "the atom bomb might never have had to be used at all." And, he added, "If surrender could have been brought about in May, 1945, or even in June or July, before the entrance of Soviet Russia into the war and the use of the atomic bomb, the world would have been the gainer."[113]

When his memoirs, *On Active Service in War and Peace,* appeared a year later, Stimson all but conceded the point, acknowledging that "history might find that the United States, by its delay in stating its position, had prolonged the war."[114] In the book, cowritten with Bundy, Stimson also dealt explicitly with another central issue the *Harper's* article had elided: the intermeshing of the atomic bomb, in the summer of 1945, with U.S. diplomatic and military policy toward the Soviet Union. In a frequently overlooked comment, he now acknowledged, "[E]ven the immediate tactical discussion about the bomb involved the Russians," i.e., the bomb was seen as obviating the necessity of Soviet intervention to force Japan's defeat in the Far East. Moreover, Stimson and Bundy now added, British and American leaders at Potsdam greeted the news from Alamogordo "with great and unconcealed satisfaction" because they believed the weapon would "give democratic diplomacy a badly needed 'equalizer'" to counter Soviet truculence in Europe and Manchuria.[115]

These rather significant modifications—presaging revisionist charges a generation hence of "atomic diplomacy"—attracted little contemporary notice. By the spring of 1948, the mood of atomic doubt had dissipated and public opinion had crystallized behind the administration's policies. With Czechoslovakia's government recently toppled in a brutal Kremlin-backed coup, and Berlin besieged by Soviet troops, Americans were hardly in a mood to criticize their government for scheming to use the atomic bomb to restrain Russian ambitions. Timing had been everything. The magazine article, rather than the book, had had by far the more dramatic impact on public attitudes. When Truman later related his own version of the events, in correspondence with historians and in his own memoirs, *Year of Decisions* (1955), he and his aides took care to assure that the narrative did not contradict Stimson's account, even to the extent of revising upward Truman's casualty estimates to "half a million lives" from 300,000 in an earlier draft.[116]

Not until the opening of Stimson's private diary and other sources in the early 1960s disclosed incontestable evidence that postwar considerations vis-à-vis Russia had influenced Stimson and Truman about the bomb prior to Hiroshima, could a documented revisionist interpretation of Truman's actions clearly emerge, as it did most notably with the 1965 publication of Gar Alperovitz's *Atomic Diplomacy*.[117] His and other subsequent accounts strongly challenged Truman's assertions that Japan's surrender could not have been brought about without a large-scale American invasion of the Japanese mainland, and emphasized political and diplomatic as well as purely military rationales for the bomb's use. Still later, in the 1980s, historians would charge that Truman, Stimson, and Churchill had grossly exaggerated claims that military authorities had expected half a million, or a million, American casualties in the invasion of Japan planned to commence on November 1, 1945; debunking the "myth" that the bomb had saved 500,000 lives, several historians cited June 1945 military staff documents presented to Truman predicting that roughly 40,000 U.S. soldiers would die and 150,000 would be wounded in a full-fledged invasion.[118] But by then, the justification for Hiroshima initially promoted by Stimson and Conant had become firmly embedded in the psyche of a generation of Americans who had not yet learned to question their government's explanation of controversial events.

Conant hastened that process of acceptance. In public appearances in early 1947, Conant pointed to Stimson's account to demonstrate the government's judiciousness in using the bomb only after "the most careful and searching appraisal" and slyly left unmentioned his own role in promoting the article. He must have felt a *frisson* of satisfaction in being able to quote Stimson's recitation of his own views. "I should like to call your attention to that extraordinarily interesting article by Mr. Stimson in the current issue of *Harper's* magazine," Conant told a University of Texas audience on February 21. "This article deals with the past and clears up, I hope, a certain confusion in the public mind." (Incidentally, he added, Karl Compton had also written an "interesting" article on the same subject in the *Atlantic*.[119])

Conant also masked his concern that public debate over Hiroshima might sap America's military and diplomatic prowess—a stance that did not exactly accord with the principles of an exponent for free and unfettered exchanges of controversial or heretical views. Rather than voicing elitist-sounding irritation at popular criticism of a secret decision in which he had played a part, Conant used more moderate language. "The discussion of whether or not the United States should have used the bomb has been a necessary, even a healthy discussion, to my mind," he averred. "If no voices had been raised against the use of the bomb, this would not have been the America our youth was fighting to defend."

But enough arguing about the past—now was the time to end the debate and leave the weighty decisions about international control in the able hands of government negotiators. For the moment, he declared, "there appears to be little that we citizens of the United States can do" to further the UN discussions. "When an agreement is reached and the treaty comes before the Senate for ratification, then if there be any who think this is the wrong road, these people will need convincing. But for the present there is no matter for debate."[120]

Conant's efforts countered those of the atomic scientists advocating a more forthcoming U.S. position on international control. The Emergency Committee on Atomic Scientists (ECAS), founded in the spring of 1946 and chaired by Albert Einstein, was the most prestigious of the assortment of organizations that sprang up after the war to give Manhattan Project participants a vehicle to influence public opinion on nuclear issues, and, Conant worried, it was rife with opponents of the Hiroshima bombing. Closely associated with the Chicago-based *Bulletin of the Atomic Scientists,* a new journal that was quickly established as *the* forum for hashing out bomb-connected issues, the ECAS numbered among its driving forces two men who had feuded most bitterly with Conant during the war and after it—Szilard and Urey.

When Conant heard in early March from an old friend and "well-to-do lawyer in Chicago" (who himself believed that the bombing of Hiroshima and Nagasaki exemplified "the Nazi philosophy which supposedly we were fighting against") that at a recent meeting of the Emergency Committee all present shared his view that the use of the bomb "should have been avoided," Conant was "quite distressed" if perhaps not completely surprised.[121] The lawyer's report merely reinforced his impression that opposition to the atomic decision had grown "fairly prevalent" in certain circles, if still a minority in the population as a whole. Rather than confront the scientists directly, however, Conant quietly asked Oppenheimer, now back at Berkeley, to "find out whether indeed it is true that the Committee officially or the majority of the individuals believe that the decision to use the bomb was wrong."[122]

What Conant did not know was that the Emergency Committee at that very moment was anxiously trying to appease him. Internal ECAS correspondence reveals that the group's leaders viewed him as a nagging impediment to their goal of mobilizing public opinion to put pressure on the American atomic negotiators. Most recently, they blamed Conant for sabotaging "three months of labor" to establish a branch in Houston. Urey and Einstein had invited Rice University official Dr. Harry Hanszen to finance and house an ECAS chapter. After assiduous cultivation by a local attorney representing the committee, Hanszen seemed to be on the verge of cooperating. But, the lawyer reported disconsolately in mid-March, Hanszen had suddenly changed his mind after hearing Conant tell the Harvard Club "that the time has not yet come for the civilians to participate in atomic knowledge to any great extent" and advocate "the so-called 'get tough' policy" toward the Russians. "Mr. Hanszen was present at that dinner as he also is a Harvard graduate. That being the case, he may have interpreted the committee as being opposed to the views of Conant."[123] Nor was this an isolated case. An ECAS organizer wrote Urey soon afterward, "This question of Conant's attitude towards the Committee crops up in various places and causes difficulty when there is not some person of at least equal stature and reputation, like yourself, to reassure the doubters."[124]

In financial straits, seeking endorsements from "distinguished scientists," and trying to concentrate on building support for international control rather than resuscitate the ebbing controversy over the 1945 decisions, the Emergency Committee was in no mood to alienate Conant further. When on March 22 Oppenheimer telephoned the MIT theoretical physicist Victor F. Weisskopf, one of the Emergency Committee's founders,[125] and a scientist personally convinced that the bombing of Hiroshima had been a "mistake" and that of Nagasaki a "crime," Weisskopf quickly sent Conant a conciliatory note stressing that while Urey's and Szilard's criticism of the decision were well known, the Emergency Committee "has not taken, and never intends to take, a stand on this question."[126] The news that the Emergency Committee had no appetite to reopen the secret battle of 1945 buoyed Conant. Having "heard indirectly to the contrary," he responded that he was "very glad indeed" to learn of ECAS's true attitude.[127] Oppenheimer also reported that while some members, such as Urey, Szilard, and perhaps Einstein, deplored the bomb's use, "there are other members—I would suspect a majority—who feel about things very much as you and I do."[128]

The crisis had passed. The vast majority of public opinion still stood firmly behind U.S. atomic policy and its decision to use the weapons on Japan. The "March of Time" newsreel, the MGM film, the Compton and especially the Stimson articles had all helped to project the image of U.S. officials, military leaders, and Manhattan Project participants as decent, humane, patriotic, and compassionate; the image of President Truman as careful, informed, and deliberate in his decision to use the bomb; and the image of the United States as sincerely desirous of achieving peaceful control of the atom as a basis for world peace—but willing, if necessary, to use the weapon again to defeat aggression.

Perhaps, as some analysts have concluded, there really was no danger of the American people turning against nuclear weapons in the autumn of 1946, and the intense but brief reaction to Hersey's article represented no more than a blip in the overall postwar pattern of consistent support for the government's dependence on and initial use of them.[129] "*Hiroshima* neither reenergized the international-control movement nor launched a vigorous public debate over the bombing of Hiroshima and Nagasaki," observes the historian Paul Boyer, who suggests that Hersey's book functioned as "less a stimulus to action and reflection than a cathartic end point."[130]

Conant's reaction, however, and that of others around him, revealed the depth of the fear among those responsible for the birth and maintenance of America's nuclear policy that the lurking, inchoate, anomic terror of living in the strange new atomic age might coalesce into an unstoppable demand for the elimination of America's nuclear arsenal—or, almost as damaging, vitiate its diplomatic usefulness. Then as later, anti-bomb sentiment was seen as playing into the hands of the Russians and their infernal, expedient demands for immediate nuclear disarmament.

What Conant, Stimson, and other defenders of Hiroshima and Nagasaki aimed to do was to convince Americans that "the problem now before the world is to stop war rather than to ameliorate the weapons which are used in war."[131] America was heading into a period marked by U.S.-Soviet rivalry, not one of unlimited global cooperation, and if the negotiations were doomed to fail, then it was time to resume the job of building atomic weapons, not dismantling them. The bomb's defenders wanted to shift the political damage created by fear of atomic weapons—a fear exploited by the scientists—to a more suitable target: the threat to peace represented by Moscow. Their efforts helped to reassure the American public that their leaders could handle atomic decisions morally and judiciously, and to stave off inquisitiveness about nuclear policies (which were still shrouded in secrecy).

Though Conant's initial rationale for pushing Stimson into writing his article had been to promote the idea of international control of nuclear weapons, he developed a different reason for relief that the debate over Hiroshima had subsided when Cold War tensions banished that hope: assuring that the American people would support the use of the nuclear weapons in a war against the Soviet Union. "I have always wished some official source would make the statement that if war occurred we should certainly order our battleships to fire and if it was militarily advisable the first thing that we would do is to drop [atomic] bombs," he told a secret gathering of military officers at the National War College in October 1947. In this regard, Conant added, the Stimson article had "helped a great deal." "You have to get the past straight," he explained, "before you do much to prepare people for the future."[132]

CHAPTER 17

"Back in the Atomic Harness"

Building Bombs, Again

1947

Bush and Conant were still on the scene, their authority somewhat concealed
from public view but with the same firm hands in control of the project they
had guided since the black days of Pearl Harbor in 1941.
— Hewlett and Anderson, *Atomic Shield*

Discussion of the relative emphasis on weapons and reactors followed, with
rather general final agreement that weapons were of first priority.
— Minutes of General Advisory Committee to the
Atomic Energy Commission, February 2, 1947

An hour before midnight on Thursday, January 1, 1947, Conant stepped
aboard a Pullman sleeper car at Boston's cavernous South Station for the
overnight ride to Washington. The journey on "The Federal" was by now
numbingly familiar — Conant estimated that he had covered half a million
miles on that rail route during the war[1] — but this trip evoked a sense of déjà
vu for a different reason: scarcely fifteen months after Hiroshima, the educational statesman was returning to the netherworld of nuclear policy-making.

The first hours of 1947 ushered in a new chapter in the American
government's nuclear weapons program. The old year had closed with the
ominous image of a poker-faced Andrei Gromyko signaling Moscow's abstention from the U.S.-sponsored international control plan and ringing down the
curtain on the world's first diplomatic effort to prevent a postwar nuclear
arms race. (Unbeknownst to the Americans, earlier in December 1946 the
Soviets had secretly achieved their first self-sustaining chain reaction, almost
exactly four years after the first U.S. "pile" had started operating in Chicago.)
The new year began with Washington formally shifting its emphasis to
winning that contest. Following Truman's formal signing of a New Year's Eve
executive order, the civilian Atomic Energy Commission displaced the army's
Manhattan Engineering District as custodian of the nation's atomic bombs,
labs, and factories.[2] Its mission — and Conant's, as a charter member of the

AEC's powerful General Advisory Committee (GAC)—was to develop atomic technology as quickly as possible, both for weapons and for industry. If any doubt had lingered over which objective would enjoy top priority, the dead end of the international control talks quickly clarified that the AEC's success or failure hinged on one supersecret measure of performance: the number of bombs in the American nuclear stockpile. "By 1947 it took more optimism than most anyone had to expect international control as proposed earlier," former AEC commissioner Robert F. Bacher recalled later. "I think it was a unanimous view of the GAC that the AEC should do its job, and in particular to develop and produce nuclear weapons."[3]

But the Manhattan-to-AEC transition was messy. General Groves was still reluctant to give up his powers, few top AEC officers had taken their posts, and a bitter and prolonged battle loomed over the Senate confirmation of the man Truman had chosen as chairman: former Tennessee Valley Authority chief David E. Lilienthal, an articulate, idealistic manager who had displayed energy and concern in atomic matters by helping to draft the State Department's international control plan. In the meantime, confusion and disorganization reigned, made worse because among the five nominated commissioners only one had any substantial nuclear experience: Bacher, a Cornell University physicist who had been one of Oppenheimer's division leaders at Los Alamos. Joining him were the Wall Street financier and patron of the sciences Lewis Strauss, a wealthy, ambitious Republican with close ties in the armed forces and Congress who had been chosen over Conant's objection; Sumner T. Pike, a businessman; and the *Des Moines Register*'s editor-in-chief, William W. Waymack.

The disorganization and confusion, the uncertainty over future priorities, their own inexperience, the enormity, complexity, and unfamiliarity of the technical challenges, and the thick blanket of secrecy covering atomic matters and precluding informed public or congressional input—all assured that from the start the AEC's leaders looked for guidance and direction to its nine-member advisory panel, drawn from the core of the wartime atomic program. In fact, assesses one historian, the GAC "largely determined A.E.C. policy during its first few years."[4] Chaired by Oppenheimer, it had a list of members that read like a "Who's Who of wartime physics,"[5] including Conant, Nobel laureates Fermi and Rabi, Glenn T. Seaborg (a pioneer in plutonium research who was to win his own Nobel a few years later), and Caltech's president, Lee A. DuBridge, who had headed the OSRD Radiation Laboratory at MIT. Filling out the roster were the metallurgist Cyril S. Smith, who had worked at Los Alamos; Hartley Rowe, an NDRC division chief who was now a director of United Fruit Company; and Hood Worthington of the Du Pont Company. If only Truman's cabinet "were made up of men who in general philosophy of administration and policies had the distinction and brain power of this group!" sighed Lilienthal after one session.[6]

Although the Atomic Energy Act of 1946 (the McMahon bill) had mandated the GAC to advise on "scientific and technical matters relating to materials, production, and research and development," its effective charter was far broader.[7] At first Lilienthal and his fellow commissioners eagerly sought and usually followed its recommendations on administration, policy, and organization as well as on purely scientific or technical issues. Since most government officials (including the members and small staff of the Joint Committee on Atomic Energy, Congress's newly created watchdog panel) lacked the knowledge or the clearance, and many of those who were entitled to atomic data were deathly afraid of possessing it, the GAC had a virtual monopoly on experience and information. Scientific prestige was also at a very high point in Washington and the country. The GAC thus epitomized a pattern of the government's entrusting vital public matters to small groups of experts, a pattern that was repeated again and again in the postwar years, as America turned to its technocratic elite to solve complex social and technological problems.[8] Opponents eventually clipped its wings, but the GAC for years threw its weight around like no other advisory panel; their Olympian, almost mystical standing as wise men of the strange new force of atomic energy inspired one later chronicler to dub them "the Nuclear Oracles."[9]

Scurrying from Union Station on the morning of January 2 for a breakfast appointment with Vannevar Bush, Conant could anticipate playing an especially exalted role in the atomic inner sanctum. In addition to accepting Truman's invite to join the GAC, Conant had also, as he told DuBridge, "agreed to do a little job for Bush on this atomic business"[10] — to chair the Committee on Atomic Energy of the Joint Research and Development Board. Another acronym in a jumbled alphabet soup of early postwar weapons work, the JRDB was a combined military-civilian board, later codified in the National Security Act of 1947 as the Research and Development Board under the authority of the National Military Establishment, to coordinate top secret war-related scientific research on a government-wide basis (the "Joint" was later dropped, leaving it the RDB).[11] Truman had requested Bush to head the JRDB and generally keep tabs on weapons research, and in December, Bush persuaded Conant to head the board's three-member atomic-energy subcommittee, which would be responsible for reviewing atomic programs and those involving other methods of mass destruction, such as biological and radiological warfare.[12] Two other members of the nuclear fraternity joined Conant on the atomic subcommittee, Oppenheimer and Du Pont vice president Crawford H. Greenewalt.

With the dual appointments, Conant and Oppenheimer were both poised to assume the role of behind-the-scenes nuclear baron: Bush informally told Conant that he could expect to be named chairman of the Atomic Energy Commission advisory group as well as of the JRDB panel.[13] When Truman had announced the group's members, no chairman was named and the question of who would lead it had been left to them to determine. Misled by erroneous news accounts that Conant had the chair, Kitty Oppenheimer indignantly asked her husband why he hadn't gotten the job; Robert supposed that Conant or he would be elected, "and it is not a major issue."[14] In fact, a subtle campaign on Oppenheimer's behalf ensured that he won the chairmanship. Conant had received an inkling of the strong pro-Oppenheimer sentiment when DuBridge—prodded by Rabi—wrote to him on December 17. Oozing bonhomie, DuBridge congratulated Conant on his appointment and assured him, "Needless to say, every one would agree that the most logical and obvious plan would be to have you named [chairman], and this is a move that I, myself, would certainly support." But DuBridge, a newly installed university president himself, felt that given the chores of his full-time job, Conant might prefer not to shoulder an additional burden. If so, he had just the man to fill the slot: Robert Oppenheimer "stands out" even among so lofty a group as the GAC, he wrote, as a man of ability and relative freedom from administrative duties whose beneficent influence would profit from some official recognition of his proven usefulness. "You will understand that I am not electioneering for him to serve as Chairman instead of yourself, for there are many reasons why you should serve as Chairman," he went on. "But, as I have said, if you have already come to the conclusion that you could not serve in this capacity, or if in this capacity you would feel the need of an able lieutenant, Robert might fit the bill."[15] Picking up the spirit of mutual admiration, Conant had agreeably responded that he had thought of urging *DuBridge's* selection as chairman, allowed that "Robert would be excellent" as chairman or executive vice-chairman, and confessed that he, Conant, would "prefer to duck the job" especially in view of his impending work for the JRDB. On the other hand, Conant did not pull himself entirely out of the running; he was sure the matter could only be settled "without embarrassment, let alone hard feelings" when the committee actually met.[16]

As the members gathered in Room 5136 of the New War Department Building on 21st Street on January 3, the new AEC general manager, Carroll L. Wilson, took Conant aside for a moment, and delicately reiterated the same pro-Oppenheimer arguments DuBridge had.[17] Sensing that the message "clearly had come from Lilienthal"[18]—who had established a fast friendship with Oppenheimer while collaborating on the State Department report a year earlier—Conant gallantly gave way to, and effectively declared himself head of, the "Elect Oppie" campaign. After Lilienthal ceremonially presented members with formal presidential commissions—jokingly handing Conant the "diploma" with "all the privileges and headaches thereto"—Conant immediately nominated Oppenheimer as chairman, a motion adopted without dissent.[19] Watching the scene, the conspiratorial Lewis Strauss thought to himself that Conant's "railroading" of the Oppenheimer nomination foretokened the physicist's powerful influence, and the inauguration of an alliance between the two.[20]

Though Oppenheimer got the chairmanship, Conant's initiative reflected his senior status on the GAC. Though not so equipped as the full-time scientists and engineers to judge purely technical issues, his national stature, prior experience, and contacts throughout the scientific and academic worlds, as well as his close relationship with Oppenheimer, left him well positioned to exert a strong pull on GAC deliberations—deliberations, as Lilienthal proceeded to tell them, that would extend well beyond technical questions to "major policy and program determinations."[21]

A general discussion of issues and problems consumed the rest of Friday's and Saturday's sessions. GAC members requested more information on the status of AEC programs and expressed concern over cumbersome security procedures that hampered declassification of scientific data and, because of the lengthy FBI background checks required of all personnel, slowed down work at laboratories. On Conant's motion, the group requested Oppenheimer to name standing subcommittees to produce reports on existing capabilities and future plans for R&D, materials, and production. Talk soon turned to managerial and administrative appointments to oversee the AEC's far-flung operation: huge facilities and construction projects around the country, hundreds of thousands of workers, massive research programs. The scientists picked their brains for possible candidates to fill such posts as directors of research, production, engineering, and "military applications."[22]

To Conant, who had been present at the creation of an array of large-scale projects started from scratch by the NDRC, OSRD, and Manhattan districts, the talk had a familiar ring. "It would not have been hard," the AEC's official historians noted, "for Conant to imagine as he sat there that he was reliving one of the many conferences he had attended during the war project."[23]

In fact, the whole fast-paced weekend of GAC and JRDB meetings was a working preview of the more boisterous reunion of the OSRD's wartime upper echelons, set to take place in Washington later that month: despite the new faces at the AEC, to direct the nation's atomic future the Truman administration still looked to the men who had built the bomb in the first place. Those statesmen now confronted a wider, more complicated set of issues than merely completing a bomb, and a more crowded, competitive bureaucratic landscape than the one in which they maneuvered before the secret exploded over Hiroshima.

But to a capital, a country, and a government still adjusting to the changed atomic world, they personified continuity, caution, and wise counsel. In contrast to the four years of nearly constant duties during the war, Conant expected to ride the Pullman to Washington for secret conferences only once every month or two. "Bush and Conant were still on the scene," recalled the AEC's official historians, "their authority somewhat concealed from public view but with the same firm hands in control of the project they had guided since the black days of Pearl Harbor in 1941."[24]

Conant and his fellow Manhattan Project veterans already looked back with nostalgia to the camaraderie—and clarity—of their earlier association. "It was a great experience, this business of fighting a war," Vannevar Bush wrote to a friend in 1947.[25] Although few phrased it so crassly, many in the government's high command shared those emotions, which were to prove so elusive during subsequent wars in Korea and Vietnam: the unalloyed "common cause," the sense of a nation firmly united, the exhilaration of flexing new sinews of American power. The ambiguous battles of the Cold War promised few such consolations, and the official phasing out of OSRD/NDRC afforded a welcome chance to celebrate past success before plunging too deeply into new responsibilities.

All fall Bush and Conant had plotted a gala black-tie stag bash to mark the occasion, and on January 20, after some words of presidential praise at the White House, the OSRD top brass—Bush, Conant, Compton, Jewett et al.—joined military leaders (including War Secretary Patterson) in the ball-room of the Carlton Hotel for an evening of nostalgia, booze, jokes, and good humor. Truman's refusal to sign a gag memo failed to poop the party, code-named "Operation Pay-Off." At one point, Pacific war hero Adm. Chester Nimitz delivered a long-winded mock presidential nominating speech, which caused Conant and Dwight Eisenhower to "squirm uneasily," before concluding with an endorsement of Bush. And in a symbolic acknowledgment of strained military-scientific relations and in a gesture of friendship, too, Conant made Stimson's former aide Harvey Bundy an "honorary scientist," presenting him with a mock cap-and-gown and diploma. Seated next to Conant was Navy Secretary James V. Forrestal, who would succeed Patterson later that year, and whose service had become a nexus for weapons research, since efforts to establish a federal science agency were languishing. "Buy whatever he recommends," Conant was urged in a whimsical program which described the Harvard president as an "undercover operative . . . affiliated with erudite elements seeking government by intelligence."[26]

Returning to Cambridge, Conant knew he was "back in the atomic harness."[27] His new status as part-time adviser hardly precluded him from jumping into other national issues only tangentially tied to education, however— those efforts, if anything, intensified, as Conant never quite returned to his prewar level of engagement in day-to-day Harvard affairs. He took a particular interest in one proposal that was a subject of persistent national debate and had more than passing connections to his secret views on atomic weapons: to institute Universal Military Training (UMT) or Universal Military Service (UMS). Conant had been a leading proponent of a peacetime draft before Pearl Harbor, but he subsequently adopted the view that atomic weapons had "blown away" most of the arguments for it, since they relegated conventional warfare to the periphery of strategic concerns. The anticipated centrality of nuclear weapons in future military planning (or in a U.S.-Soviet war) seemed to make the tough draft legislation he had fought for in 1940 and 1941 irrelevant to the United States' postwar security needs.

Even as the U.S.-Soviet alliance fractured, he initially doubted the long-term need to maintain large conventional military forces, except to man occupation contingents or, more pessimistically, to sort out the chaos of a future nuclear conflict. In 1945 and 1946, to the dismay of some fellow educators who had fought alongside him for conscription before Pearl Harbor, Conant opposed the administration's proposals for a peacetime draft. In concert with other university presidents—Princeton's Harold Dodds, Stanford's Donald Tresidder, and Deane Malott of the University of Kansas, as well as the members of the American Council on Education's Committee on the Relationships of Higher Education to the Federal Government—Conant had instead pressed Truman to appoint an independent commission to study military needs and strategy in the context of atomic warfare, a factor which had "made obsolete much of our previous thinking."[28]

Though Conant favored a continuation of Selective Service for the short run to deal with the immediate problem of occupying Axis territory and to shoulder "our share of international responsibility,"[29] he believed that atomic weapons delivered by long-range bombers would be the determining factor in any future U.S.-Soviet conflict, and he had not yet considered that the two powers might channel their rivalry into peripheral conflicts or bolster their political commitments with massive conventional forces. But in the spring of 1947 his views began to change, a transformation hastened when the blue-ribbon commission, chaired by MIT President Compton, concluded that a need for UMT did indeed exist. Compton had been on the other side of the conscription debate since 1945, but Conant judged the commission sufficiently qualified and balanced to hand down a fair verdict that he would feel honorbound to support.[30]

Nevertheless, Conant remained doubtful of the relevance of a large-scale army in the age of atomic warfare, a viewpoint he disclosed in a revealing letter to Tresidder of January 22. Conant stuck to his thesis that apart from manning occupation forces in Germany and Japan and cleaning up the debris from a nuclear exchange if World War III broke out, there seemed little point in maintaining a large peacetime army. At a meeting of the Association of American Colleges in Boston in mid-January, he reported, he had heard the case for UMT presented by "some generals" who argued that, given the increased importance of air power and atomic bombs, "when the next war came there would be no time to train an army." But in Conant's view, UMT wouldn't help the situation because in an atomic war "there would be no time even to call up the trained reserves."

My own strategic analysis, for what it may be worth, runs something as follows. The chances of a war are very slight until such time as our potential enemy, presumably Russia, was able to obtain weapons of "mass destruction" in sufficient quantity to make an all-out sudden attack well worth while. Today there would be nothing in it . . . If we can't get the bomb under control and come down in twenty years to a period of "Superblitz" warfare, then I don't see how trained infantry are going to play any role. It may be, however, that some kind of organization of trained men will be necessary in order to take care of all the internal problems of health, communication, and keeping order which would result in a Superblitz[ed] nation. To my mind this is the strongest case for some kind of organization of universal military training for a few months.

When Conant testified to the Compton board, convening in the East Wing of the White House on Saturday afternoon, March 1, he still adhered to his anti-conscription views but also promised to make good on his pledge to back any measures, including UMT, unanimously endorsed by a qualified commission.[31] And, three months later, when the commission unanimously favored UMT in its final report on May 29, 1947, he publicly endorsed its conclusions.[32]

Conant's access to secret nuclear data gave him special reason, however, to question the assumption that nuclear weapons gave Washington an easy route to military security. Like all the GAC members, he knew that the nation's atomic program was hampered by disorganization, technical problems, and low morale, that the scientists who had powered the Manhattan Project had largely disbanded, and that "no real exploration of new weapons" had taken place despite the highly publicized tests at Bikini.[33] Seeking data on AEC projects, facilities, and raw materials in order to make specific recommendations to improve this situation, the advisers at their second meeting, on February 2, asked Lilienthal for the hard raw-material and production-rate numbers. These were the most closely guarded secrets in the land—most of the country's military leadership had not been given the figures, and even Truman would not receive a full briefing until April.[34] Lilienthal turned to Bacher, the only scientist commissioner, to give a verbal briefing; for security's sake, the information would only be accurate to within twenty percent. "It was rather dramatic," Lilienthal recorded in his diary, "for [the meeting] began by their formal request for certain very highly secret information needed in their work. . . . I stated that information was to be imparted by word of mouth, by Bacher, and that no notes were to be taken. The staff was sent out and the recital made, in the huge, three-story high, paneled conference room with its long table."[35]

Had any doubt remained about the principal objective of the atomic program, the revelation of the lackluster production rate and the scarcity of available fissionable material removed it. According to figures declassified only in 1981, the United States then possessed components for somewhere between nine and thirteen atomic bombs of the "Fat Man" implosion model used on Nagasaki; none was assembled or ready for use.[36] It is not certain precisely what data the nuclear advisers received that Saturday morning when they had (in Conant's phrase) their "peek behind the curtains"—better informed in this matter than their commander-in-chief, they probably did not react with "shock," as Truman did when he was told two months later—but they could not help being disturbed by the contrast between the dismal reality Bacher described and the popular image of atomic prowess perceived by American, and international, public opinion. When discussion resumed in the afternoon following reading of technical reports, Oppenheimer put in a good word for the importance of reactor development as a demonstration of atomic energy's peaceful dimension, but Fermi sharply rebutted him. Maximum effort must be on testing and developing new explosives, including the "super" or hydrogen bomb, on rebuilding Los Alamos, and on increasing production of raw materials. The international situation, he declared, demanded fast action. Fermi's impassioned plea won quick agreement around the table. "Discussion of the relative emphasis on weapons and reactors followed," the minutes relate, "with rather general final agreement that weapons were of first priority."[37]

Their goal set, the advisers devoted most of the rest of the two-day meeting to preparing recommendations for Lilienthal and the AEC commissioners. Their greatest challenge was to revitalize and bolster Los Alamos in order to develop new and more powerful and usable forms of atomic weapons, and to attract top-flight scientists back to the program despite its increasingly grim character. While mindful of what Oppenheimer termed the "prejudice against weapons among our colleagues," the advisers strongly agreed on the need to "greatly strengthen" thermonuclear work at Los Alamos; the physicist Edward Teller, it was noted, had filed an "optimistic report" on the prospects for developing such a weapon. The topic underlined the import of the assignment Oppenheimer gave Conant near the close of the working weekend to chair the GAC subcommittee on weapons.[38]

In melancholy language the soft-spoken Oppenheimer summarized the talk around the table. "It seems to me that the heart of the problem has been reached with surprising speed: The making of atomic weapons is something to which we are now committed," he said. He added plaintively: "It must be recognized that within our hearts we have been hoping that the world will be the world it was ten years ago. This is no longer possible and we must try in ourselves and in our colleagues to find some way of obtaining public service."[39]

In the next few weeks, Conant watched with mounting frustration as the controversy surrounding Lilienthal's nomination prevented the commission from getting down to business. On Monday afternoon, February 4, Conant went to Capitol Hill to put in a good word for the embattled AEC leaders, who needed confirmation from the Senate section of the Joint Committee on Atomic Energy. During an executive session the previous Friday, Bernard Baruch had suggested that the senators seek Conant's counsel, and Senator Bourke Hickenlooper had called him to the Hill.[40]

The subject of the day was the nomination of Carroll Wilson as AEC general manager, but before testifying, Conant had a bit of personal business to transact with Lilienthal. Conant blamed Lilienthal for simultaneously dragging him into the middle of a sudden controversy and getting the commission off on the wrong foot on the issue of secrecy. For during public hearings the previous week Lilienthal had criticized Truman's release of the Smyth Report—the government's official account of the Manhattan Project—as "the principal breach of security since the beginning of the atomic energy project," a "ludicrous" act that had made a "laughing stock" of security regulations.[41]

In fact, Lilienthal had intended to prove his fitness as guardian of the atomic "secret" by discrediting Groves, who had approved the report's release and whose supporters loudly claimed that control of the bomb program should remain with the allegedly more security-conscious military. But the jab had landed squarely on Conant as well, since he had been a driving force behind the Smyth Report.[42] Lilienthal realized he had "stepped on [Conant's] toes" but found that a price worth paying in order to "stop the hysteria" over secrecy and to swing the confirmation hearings in his direction. Learning indirectly of Conant's ire, Lilienthal jotted in his diary that that was "too bad; the Smyth Report is a sacred cow with him."

Conant held his tongue until Monday morning, when, as he waited to testify, a recess in the hearings provided a chance to buttonhole Lilienthal. "Carroll has told you that I was upset about what you said in your testimony about the release of the Smyth Report," Conant said. "I have read your full testimony and I continue to feel the same way about it. What you may not have understood was this: that [Senator] McMahon's question to you was part of the line of dissenters among the scientists in the Manhattan Project, led by such fellows as Szilard. Their purpose is to discredit Bush, Groves, and myself for the conduct of the work, and since they can't criticize the results—because the bomb did work—they concentrate on such things as the Smyth Report. You didn't realize that McMahon had set a trap for you with that question." And he implored Lilienthal to make a fuller statement after his confirmation clarifying that he did not regard those behind it as having jeopardized security.

Conant's outburst dumbfounded Lilienthal. "I had no idea," he responded, "that there was a feud of this kind so deep-seated that it would disturb the president of Harvard in this manner." He tried to explain his view of the military's hypocrisy about security—but Conant seemed uninterested. The unexpectedly chilly encounter reminded Lilienthal of the sensitivities and hidden landmines he could expect to face after he was confirmed. Some grinding of gears is inevitable in any bureaucracy during a changing of the guard, but Lilienthal now gathered that behind Conant's pique lay "a great deal of painful history"—suppressed emotions, tensions, rivalries, and egos that could flare up to disrupt the atomic program.[43]

Despite the dispute over the Smyth Report, Conant remained anxious to see the AEC leadership confirmed. And upon stepping up to the witness stand after the lunch break, he kept the morning's argument to himself, and tried to confine himself to a brief but firm endorsement of his young wartime colleague, Carroll Wilson. But he quickly became ensnared in a nasty vendetta on the part of Tennessee senator Kenneth D. McKellar to scuttle Lilienthal's nomination. Vindictive, stubborn, nearly senile, ignorant of atomic energy (and not a member of the committee) but obsessed by desire to avenge a decade-old grudge against Lilienthal dating from the nominee's days as head of the TVA, McKellar had gained permission to attend the hearings by virtue of senatorial courtesy. From the start he had dominated the proceedings, hurling innuendos and unsupported charges against Truman's nominee, accusing the Harvard Law School graduate of belonging to a Communist espionage cell, of incompetence, of ideologically suspect New Deal leftism.

Conant stayed on his politest, most deferential behavior as McKellar tossed a series of rhetorical queries designed to elicit agreement that the new agency chairman should be a man of unquestioned loyalty and "Americanism," untainted by "Russian proclivities, Communist proclivities." He placidly seconded these platitudes and carefully avoided getting drawn into any testy exchanges. At one point, McKellar evoked titters from the gallery by asking if Conant were "acquainted with the historic fact" that Alexander the Great "2,300 years ago had some Macedonian scientists working on the splitting of the atom."

"I wouldn't want to challenge you, sir, on your history, but it would be news to me," Conant answered drolly, restraining whatever private musings he had about the usefulness of an electoral process that would thrust such buffoons into high office.

When McKellar finally got around to asking his opinion of Lilienthal, Conant firmly if rather passionlessly testified to the nominee's loyalty, citing their brief but intense contact when they "threshed over" the Acheson-Lilienthal Report. It did not take long for McKellar to bring up General Groves and win Conant's acknowledgment that he had "indeed done a splendid job; no doubt about that."[44]

Lilienthal, watching the testimony before returning to the stand himself, feared that Conant had "made a good impression but not a very strong one."[45] The days of relentless, arcane, innuendo-filled interrogation were grating on him; McKellar, he had written in his diary a few days earlier, "can be so ugly and mean that it is not always easy to stay relaxed; and one slip of anger or a wisecrack and I could be in considerable Dutch."[46] Tired of twisting in the wind, he sensed the need to do something dramatic. Conant had already left when Lilienthal turned the tide with an eloquent, heartfelt, impromptu affirmation of his belief in democracy, freedom, and fair play.[47] This burst of emotion won widespread praise from congressmen, press and public alike, including a handwritten note from Conant "to say hurrah! and offer my congratulations."[48]

Despite Lilienthal's effective counterpunch, the all-out brawl over his nomination, complete with sinister undertones of anti-Semitism, had spilled across editorial pages and into radio commentaries across the country.[49] This exasperated his supporters on the GAC, who were acutely aware of the price the AEC was paying for its lack of effective leadership as the nomination wavered. Hoping to shift the battle in Lilienthal's favor, Conant lobbied hard with three fence-sitting New England Republican senators to get them behind the nomination, stressing the grave damage Lilienthal's rejection could do to the national defense. Even if he were not the greatest administrator in the world, Conant considered it "nonsense" to leave dangling such a vital post when it was only, after all, a two-year appointment.[50]

But Conant drew the line at resigning in protest, and he bristled when word reached him on February 17 that some of Lilienthal's fellow commissioners were seriously considering that drastic step if the senators voted against Wilson or Lilienthal. Oppenheimer, distressed, was calling Conant in San Antonio, where Conant was in the midst of a tour of Harvard Clubs of Texas; and as the FBI, which had placed a bug on Oppenheimer's Berkeley office, listened in, Oppenheimer urged Conant to do all he could with his congressional contacts. Conant assured him he was doing just that, and then launched into a mini-lecture on the need to stay on the job no matter what happened. When Oppenheimer replied that not all the AEC leaders would go along with that — probably thinking of Bacher, his closest friend on the commission — the pragmatic educator "said it was very vital [to stay on the job] and he felt that much more than before he had been taken behind the curtains, and that this thing must go on; that they should say the Constitution has operated and that Democracy was this way. He said he thought the other members of the Commission would make a great mistake resigning."[51]

Lilienthal's drawn-out predicament — which lasted until the Senate finally approved his selection in an anticlimactic 50-31 vote on April 9 — only underscored the authority of the GAC, which in the absence of an established leader of the new agency constituted the AEC's most powerful source of guidance and experience.[52] In early March, however, as the furor over Lilienthal's nomination was beginning to subside, Conant received a jolting secret reminder of just how tenuous the atomic project's position was in the renewed frenzy over security. On Monday, March 10, when Conant was in Washington for a meeting at the Pentagon of the Committee on Atomic Energy's civilian members with air force officials on better procedures for sharing atomic information, he received an urgent summons to Lilienthal's office.[53] There, Conant found Bush, who also happened to be in town, and the AEC commissioners.

The mood in the closed meeting was grim: Over the weekend, the FBI had forwarded a "rather voluminous file" of "derogatory information" concerning J. Robert Oppenheimer, charging that the nation's most famous atomic physicist was probably a Communist, or at least a former Communist, and could represent a dangerous security risk. The FBI reports recited a litany of contacts and associations that Oppenheimer had had with Communists, most dating from his days as a professor at Berkeley in the 1930s; among those listed was his brother, Frank, now a physics professor at the University of Minnesota, and his wife, Kitty, whose first husband had died fighting for the Loyalists in Spain. In June 1943, it was noted, Oppenheimer had spent the night at the home of a former woman companion, Jean Tatlock, an active party member. Then there was a wartime incident involving a left-leaning Berkeley specialist in French literature named Haakon Chevalier, who in kitchen conversation at a faculty cocktail party had suggested to Oppenheimer a way to pass information on his work to Soviet officials; the physicist had told varying and inconsistent accounts of this exchange to security officers. J. Edgar Hoover and his minions already distrusted Oppenheimer; and now the commissioners, too, concluded that the files, although largely based on reports from confidential or anonymous informants, could "seriously impeach" his reputation and effectiveness.

It did not take much calculation for the AEC chiefs to recognize that they had a potential disaster of major proportions on their hands, in both a public relations and practical sense. Anti-Communist sentiments were running high, what with news reports of a pro-Soviet insurgency in Greece and rumors of espionage agents in America. Allowing the news to leak out that the "father of the atomic bomb" might be a "red" would fling a match in a tinderbox. And how would this affect Lilienthal's chances, as well as that of civilian control over atomic energy? A suspicious Lilienthal wondered whether the FBI had deliberately chosen this sensitive moment to whip up fears. But there was also an immediate, pragmatic problem: Oppenheimer occupied a central place in the AEC's planning and development, hardly less vital than his position at Los Alamos, and to lose him when morale was already low among the scientists working at the commission's facilities would be devastating.

All Monday morning and into the afternoon, the commissioners pored over the FBI materials.[54] Lilienthal did not believe that Oppenheimer represented a security risk, but he hardly carried the political weight to make his view stick, and seeking guidance and support, he had placed emergency calls to Bush and Conant, both fortuitously in Washington on other business. That Oppenheimer once had leftist tendencies hardly came as a surprise: while they had not reviewed the investigatory files, Bush and Conant had informally discussed the physicist's "decidedly left-wing" political background with Groves when they approved Oppenheimer's selection to head Los Alamos back in the fall of 1942. And Bush had already assured Lilienthal in a phone conversation on Saturday that he never regretted the choice. Conant, while occasionally doubting Oppenheimer's "judgment and discretion," had also come to trust the physicist's loyalty and patriotism completely as well as to admire his brilliance as a scientist and thinker. Neither Bush nor Conant felt a need to examine the FBI dossier after Lilienthal summarized its findings, and both quickly expressed full confidence in his essential reliability. More cautiously, however, they also noted that Groves, who had been primarily responsible for choosing Oppenheimer, should be consulted. Lilienthal tried and failed to find the general, who was vacationing in Florida. Considering the poor relations between Lilienthal and the Pentagon, Conant and Bush agreed to take on the delicate mission of seeing War Secretary Patterson after the meeting in order to obtain statements from him and Groves vouching for Oppenheimer. And they strongly reaffirmed their view that Oppenheimer's record of wartime leadership and postwar advice had been "so outstanding" as to leave "no doubt" of his loyalty—or of the fact that his loss would deal "a very serious blow" to the country's atomic program and alienate other scientists considering government service.

Later in the month Conant put his position on the record in a letter to Lilienthal that lay quietly in the commission's files for seven years until questions were again raised about Oppenheimer's security clearance:

> I can say without hesitation that there can be absolutely no question of Dr. Oppenheimer's loyalty. Furthermore, I can state categorically that, in my opinion, his attitude about the future course of the United States Government in matters of high policy is in accordance with the soundest American tradition. He is not sympathetic with the totalitarian regime in Russia and his attitude towards that nation is, from my point of view, thoroughly sound and hard headed. Therefore, any rumor that Dr. Oppenheimer is sympathetically inclined toward the Communists or toward Russia is an absurdity. As I wrote above, I base this statement on what I consider intimate knowledge of the workings of his mind.
>
> At the time of Dr. Oppenheimer's entering the work on atomic energy, I heard that there was some question of his clearance by the security agencies. I understand that was based on his associations prior to 1939 and his "left wing" sympathies at that time. I have no knowledge of Dr. Oppenheimer previous to the summer of 1941, but I say unhesitatingly that whatever the record might show as to his political sympathies at that time or his associations, I would not deviate from my present opinion, namely, that a more loyal and sound American citizen cannot be found in the whole United States.[55]

Lilienthal now had what he needed to recommend Oppenheimer's continued participation in the atomic program to the president. On March 11, the AEC commissioners, acting "on the basis of" what they had heard from Bush and Conant, unanimously agreed that there seemed to be "no immediate hazard" requiring the convening of an official investigatory board, a step that would almost certainly have crippled Oppenheimer's ability to conduct government work. Lilienthal asked White House counsel Clark Clifford to relay the AEC's position to Truman, and Clifford reported back the next day that Lilienthal had done the right thing in consulting Bush and Conant and in reporting to the president, and that he was not obliged to inform the JCAE or convene a board of inquiry.

Engrossed in the crisis about U.S. aid to Greece and Turkey, Truman did not immediately act, and for the rest of the month, unknown to the public and probably to Oppenheimer himself, the physicist's future hung in the balance. Then, to Lilienthal's great relief—and Hoover's disappointment—word came down from the Oval Office that Truman had no desire to pursue the matter. Ironically, Oppenheimer's reprieve arrived only days after Truman had announced a sweeping federal loyalty program that instituted strict procedures for investigating the political backgrounds of government employees. Not lacking for work, the FBI soon reluctantly dropped its investigation of Oppenheimer and its surveillance, including telephone taps, of his day-to-day activities. The AEC's fledgling leaders had dodged a bullet, at least for the moment. Even screaming newspaper headlines in July about Frank Oppenheimer once belonging to the Communist Party failed to shake the commission's judgment that Oppenheimer did not currently pose a security risk.[56] On August 6—thanks in large measure to the confidence expressed in Oppenheimer by Bush, Conant, and Groves—the AEC formally granted the wartime director of Los Alamos a "Q" clearance giving him access to all atomic secrets.[57]

While the AEC struggled to get on its feet, the Cold War was taking shape. Two Truman administration foreign-policy pronouncements in the first six months of 1947—the Truman Doctrine and the Marshall Plan—charted the United States' long-term strategy. Although uninvolved in the secret State Department deliberations preceding these actions, Conant supported them to the hilt, especially the Marshall Plan. When, on March 12, President Truman officially declared America's determination to support through economic or military means any country around the world threatened by armed Communist insurgencies, Conant was one of few citizens who realized just how flimsy was the military strength upon which this commitment rested. The immediate spur behind Truman's pronouncement was the news that Britain could no longer afford to support the pro-Western governments in Greece and Turkey; fearing that the Soviet Union would inexorably move to fill the power vacuum there, U.S. officials, led by Under Secretary of State Dean Acheson, concluded that Washington must act immediately and firmly to prevent countries throughout the entire eastern Mediterranean from falling under Kremlin domination, "like apples in a barrel infected by one rotten one."[58] Truman told a joint session of Congress that U.S. policy must henceforth be to "support free peoples" against the forces of totalitarianism who, "by direct or indirect aggression," sought to impose regimes based on "terror and oppression." This open and formal declaration that Washington had dropped the pretense of maintaining the wartime alliance and had chosen to confront the Soviet Union head-on gave practical form to the policies and ideas put forth a year earlier in Kennan's "Long Telegram" from Moscow. The speech, and Truman's request that Congress vote $400 million in military and economic aid to Greece and Turkey, inaugurated a dramatic expansion of America's traditional peacetime foreign-policy objectives. To gain congressional and public support, Truman had depicted the global struggle as an apocalyptic, Manichaean one between opposed "ways of life." Inevitably, albeit without actually naming his foe, he raised the prospect of direct military conflict with Moscow.

Truman's grim alarum deeply depressed Conant, causing him to "lose almost all the hope to which I still clung."[59] Yet Conant seemed concerned less with the military danger supposedly emanating from the Kremlin than with its ideological and political threats; even after such polarizing and ominous events as the Communist coup in Czechoslovakia in February 1948 and the imposition of a blockade of West Berlin a few months later, he continued to regard the Soviet armed forces as "defensive troops to support political gains . . . not to be used as the spearhead of the forward movement."[60] At the same time he strongly believed that the United States should make it clear to the Soviets that it would draw the line at further military advances, would act decisively to strengthen surrounding democracies from internal Communist movements, and—in the broadest sense—stood ready to enforce the "Pax Americana"[61] he had envisioned even before U.S. entry into World War II. By taking over from the British in the Mediterranean the United States had finally, as Conant had advocated as early as 1940, become the unquestioned "majority shareholder" and "top dog" of a postwar alliance intended to ensure "a world order which makes safe the American way of life in cooperation with the other democracies."[62]

It was only a quirk of fate that had Marshall making his momentous declaration at Harvard's 296th commencement ceremonies, for he had declined Harvard's invitation to receive an honorary degree for the previous two years running, and until the final week of May it had seemed that he might decline the honor once more.[63] Plans for a massive U.S.-funded reconstruction program in Western Europe had been churning within the State Department for several months, and Acheson had proof-tested the idea in early May to an obscure gathering in rural Mississippi. Then, on May 28, when the time came to nay-or-yea Harvard's invitation, Marshall suggested that he might use the opportunity for the long-discussed official unveiling of the European reconstruction program, though Acheson "advised against it on the ground that commencement speeches were a ritual to be endured without hearing."[64] Innocuously, Marshall informed Conant that he could, after all, be present to accept the honorary degree and to "make a few remarks in appreciation of the honor and perhaps a little more."[65]

During the plane trip from Washington to Boston the day before his speech, Marshall crafted the still incomplete "little more" into final form, rewriting the critical passages that constituted the core of the plan that would bear his name. Meanwhile, Acheson still worried that newsmen, their acumen dulled by generations of platitudinous commencement speeches, would not give Marshall's remarks the prominence they deserved. So, over lunch, he tipped off a handful of trusted British correspondents to the significance of the Harvard address and suggested that their editors immediately slip a copy to Foreign Minister Ernest Bevin, thereby assuring that Britain would get the message that the European powers should, on their own, put together a plan for U.S. aid.[66]

Mr. and Mrs. Conant knew nothing of such machinations that evening as they presided over a dinner for the Marshalls and hosted them for the night. Even after applauding Marshall's brief comments from the steps of Memorial Church, Conant had "no suspicion that his speech would turn out to be so epic making"[67]—nor, it appears, did most of thousands of students and spectators thronging the grassy quadrangle in Harvard Yard that mild spring morning. Nor did Marshall's call for a European recovery program attract special notice from the American press the next day: not for nothing had Acheson feared that the speech would fall on deaf ears![68]

Marshall was careful to leave an outstretched hand open to the Soviet Union, at least rhetorically, but the division of the postwar European world into Soviet and Western spheres was becoming painfully evident. Conant still clung to the optimistic hope that some form of global cooperation could be effected, so long as the United States displayed economic and social vitality and proved wrong the Marxist-grounded predictions of capitalism's collapse.[69] For long-term amity, Conant still believed that the international control of atomic weapons was essential—that with it, it would be "an easy step" to a peaceful world—and he was searching, at that moment, for a new approach to achieve that receding goal.

CHAPTER 18

"The Conant Alternative"

A Secret Plan to Stop the Arms Race

1947

They say you can't turn clocks back but everybody who has clocks knows that you can . . . What is needed is a self-denying ordinance . . . people who have a mania for suicide aren't permitted to use razors. If the human race has this mania perhaps we had better put all this atomic fuel underground.
— Speech to National War College, October 2, 1947

Coupled with some generous offers on our part toward the Soviet Union, I really believe there is a chance for a grand international settlement of our outstanding troubles with that nation along these lines.
— Letter to J. Robert Oppenheimer, November 1, 1947

Although a generation hence Conant described himself as, by mid-1947, "one of the first of the Cold War warriors,"[1] contemporary documents show that, at least when it came to nuclear weapons, Conant refused to join the growing majority of U.S. government officials ready to "drop the pretense of one world" and to abandon the negotiations aimed at a comprehensive international atomic control pact.[2] But as East-West relations deteriorated during 1947 and 1948, that hope grew increasingly forlorn, and Conant grew correspondingly desperate.

Not that Conant rejected the essential tenets of the Cold War. On the contrary, he forcefully and consistently condemned Soviet behavior and Communist ideology, fully supported the administration's "containment" strategy as it emerged in the Truman Doctrine and Marshall Plan, and donated much time and expertise to government military programs. Like most foreign-policy experts at the time, Conant in the late 1940s and early 1950s viewed America's nuclear weapons as essential to a military balance of power with the Soviet Union, at least in the short run, and he unflinchingly supported the American use of atomic weapons in the event of World War III. But unlike many of his peers, Conant refused to accept nuclear weapons or energy as being in the long-term national security interests of the United States.

Historians have incorrectly assumed that Conant, like other formulators of the Acheson-Lilienthal proposals, steadfastly stuck by the U.S. position after the international control talks fell into stalemate in 1946.[3] And it is true that in public he did so. But secretly, he fought an against-the-wind battle to promote his own, radical alternative plan to save international control at the expense of what he disdainfully described as the "mirage" of nuclear power development. His call fell on deaf ears, as would his equally fervent private campaign to liberate atomic information from the straitjacket of secrecy; indeed, his more iconoclastic views, especially his pessimism about nuclear power, perturbed friends and created enemies among the military and scientific figures more enthusiastic about the atom's potential to revolutionize society and to serve as America's "winning weapon" in the Cold War.

Conant's consternation over the seemingly unbridgeable impasse in the U.S.-Soviet atomic control negotiations began to fuse with his doubts about the feasibility and advisability of nuclear power in the spring of 1947. Over the course of a few months, he reversed the position he had taken since the war's end and when he had endorsed the Acheson-Lilienthal report's lofty vision of global nuclear power development by an international agency that would simultaneously run the new industry and keep it from cloaking secret weapons construction. In fashioning their plan in early 1946, the State Department's consultants had recognized that the distinction between peaceful and dangerous atomic activities was a blurry one; Conant and others involved in the Manhattan Project had also quickly realized that power-generating reactors could also churn out the plutonium and enriched uranium needed for the cores of nuclear weapons. In November 1945, in his first public comments on the bomb, Conant had directly addressed this issue: "There are those who argue that all use of atomic power should be prohibited since the peacetime and war uses can be only slightly separated. This idea should be debated, but I do not like the idea of such a self-denying ordinance aimed against our technical development."[4] And rather than deterring the State Department panel, the inescapable realization that atomic energy for peace and for war easily overlapped had impelled it to recommend the maximum promotion of nuclear power, reasoning that an active, industrializing outfit would have both the pretext and the need to oversee all phases of nuclear-power generation, from mining uranium to operating reactors. It disdained creating an international agency devoted solely to negative inspection and policing functions. According to the idealistic scheme of Oppenheimer and his colleagues, reactor development and operation would be at the "heart"[5] of the new Atomic Development Agency (ADA), which would forge bonds of international cooperation to "develop the beneficial possibilities of atomic energy and encourage the growth of fundamental knowledge, stirring the constructive and imaginative impulses of man rather than merely concentrating on the defensive and negative."[6] Successful atomic energy development in the United States, Oppenheimer believed, would, by demonstrating its feasibility and rousing popular support, further the chances of ultimately constructing an international arrangement for the same purpose.[7]

The grand scenario of a world knit together by the thread of nuclear energy never truly enthralled Conant. From the beginning, he had been left "cold" by the "fancies" of physicists who "talked in excited tones" about the revolutionary potential of nuclear power,[8] and his skepticism had become well known among some Manhattan Project scientists after word spread that he had expressed doubts about the theoretical basis of nuclear power on the very eve of Fermi's demonstration of a controlled chain reaction. (Years later, one physicist present at Stagg Field in Chicago still vividly recalled hearing of Conant's "shocking" last-minute jitters, and claimed Conant was the only prominent scientist who "really seemed surprised" when the experiment succeeded.)[9] But in the end Conant had swallowed his qualms, at least for a while, and affixed his name to Acheson-Lilienthal, a conversion resulting from respect for the force and unanimity of Oppenheimer and his fellow consultants, who argued that only a forward-looking, idealistic plan had a chance of winning public support and international adoption.

For a time, Conant, too, flirted with the comforting notion that nuclear power would develop a cornucopia of benefits that would compensate for the destructiveness of its weapons. The "great thing" about the State Department report was its "positive aspect," Conant had told the Council on Foreign Relations in April 1946, adding that there appeared to be "real peace-time uses for atomic energy in the near future" in locations where power costs were already high.[10] Peaceful uses might be reaped in as soon as three to fifteen years, he told a private session of a Carnegie Endowment atomic energy panel around the same time, and all international control efforts should proceed on the assumption that industrial development would go forward.[11] Conant repeatedly declared that nuclear power represented a "promising development of a new source of energy for peaceful purposes," even if the required technology "unfortunately" could also be used for weapons, and he dismissed as "no real alternative" the idea of achieving international control by abandoning "all the possible advantages" of peaceful nuclear energy, shutting uranium and thorium mines and assuring that no nation secretly obtained weapons-grade ores. "I cannot imagine," he said, "that any country would be willing to forgo research and development in a field which *may* (and I underline the may) mean so much for an industrial civilization."[12]

Conant often cited an allusion to cosmic ambivalence postulated nearly a century before by one of his spiritual (and Harvard) forebears, Ralph Waldo Emerson. In his essay on the "Law of Compensation," Conant recalled, Emerson had observed that " 'Every excess causes a defect; every defect an excess. . . . With every influx of light comes new danger . . . There is a crack in every thing God has made. It would seem there is always . . . this vindictive circumstance stealing in unawares ... this back-stroke, this kick of the gun, certifying that the law is fatal; that in nature nothing can be given, all things are sold.' " "If, following Emerson," Conant added, "we think of the potential power of destruction of the atomic bomb as the price we pay for health and comfort in this scientific age, we can perhaps more coolly face the task of making the best of an inevitable bargain, however hard."[13] Conant seemed to be trying to project the scientist's fundamental faith that fearlessly pursuing knowledge ultimately benefits mankind.

But, in fact, this boldly optimistic sentiment was largely a front, concealing Conant's intensifying private conviction that the danger of atomic warfare reversed the prenuclear assumptions about the inevitability and beneficence of scientific advance. More fundamentally, it masked Conant's sense that human nature and history offered little hope that mankind could handle the atom without destroying itself. Emerson had declared that "every jet of chaos which threatens to exterminate us is convertible by intellect into wholesome force,"[14] but Conant entertained no such comforting belief about the convertibility of atomic energy, and had a "more practical" view of human nature. His brief subscription to the dream of nuclear abundance expired, replaced by a far more dubious appraisal of the risks. "People who have a mania for suicide aren't permitted to use razors," he remarked in a closed-door meeting in October 1947. "If the human race has this mania perhaps we had better put all this atomic fuel underground."[15]

Conant later explicitly disclaimed any belief in the inevitability of human progress, and one can infer that his journeys on the border of science and death helped to extinguish whatever belief he once held in the intrinsic goodness of knowledge. Sharply distinguishing his own optimism in America's future from "the belief in progress so characteristic of liberal theological writing in America and England before World War I," Conant in 1948 cautioned,

> No evidence appears to be at hand for any trend in the universe toward a goal where human misery is any less than in the past or the sum total of human happiness is greater. In fact, one may question whether on critical analysis such phrases have real content. Progress in techniques and skills and certain types of knowledge has been enormous over the centuries. But the relation between accumulated knowledge and skills on the one hand and human satisfaction or lack of satisfaction (suffering) on the other is very complicated and uncertain. In short, I see no need for believing we are living in a world which automatically is getting better and better; there is no evidence that we are on a roller-coaster where one can relax and think of the inevitable goal of sweetness and light that lies ahead. Instead, it would appear that modern man can be sure only that tragedy has always been, and for centuries to come is likely to be, a constant aspect of the human drama.[16]

So Conant was hardly ready to trust humanity safely to "harness the atom," as the cliché of the day went. And several less philosophical and more immediate factors encouraged him to discard nuclear power promotion as the keystone of international control: Moscow's adamant rejection of the Baruch plan led him to seek alternatives that might be more acceptable to the Russians, but even when Conant granted the presumption that they seriously desired to join an international atomic control and development agency, there also remained the "stumbling block on which I stubbed my toe so often"—how such an agency would divide its bounty of atomic weapons and plants among rival nations.[17] Also, the steady stream of pessimistic evaluations received by the GAC in early 1947 eroded whatever sense Conant might have had that atomic power might satisfy a significant fraction of mankind's needs in any but the longest-range projections—it would take fifty years, Fermi predicted in March.[18]

These new predictions left Conant more convinced than ever that developing a nuclear energy industry was neither realistic nor important enough to stand in the way of a potential agreement with the Soviet Union to prevent a nuclear weapons race. He acted on this conviction by lobbying—secretly—for a dramatic new U.S. offer to forswear forever the development of atomic power as part of a general plan to prohibit the international manufacture or stockpiling of atomic weapons.

While easily the most prominent insider supporting a power moratorium, Conant was not the first to suggest it. Before the outbreak of World War II, Leo Szilard had tried to keep secret the possibility of an explosive nuclear chain reaction by voluntarily restricting scientific publication,[19] and even during the Manhattan Project some scientists had argued that the evil inherent in nuclear energy overshadowed the imperative of scientific progress— such sentiments of mingled doubt and disgust allegedly prompting Oppenheimer to remark that Los Alamos should be "given back to the Indians" when the project was concluded.[20] More commonly heard, however, were the sentiments expressed in the secret 1944 Jeffries Report by Met Lab scientists on "The Impact of Nucleonics on International Relations and the Social Order," which briefly considered and then discarded as suicidal the "backward-looking" idea of calling for a "moratorium on the progress of science and industry, and in particular nucleonics, in order to give social, economic, and political development a chance to catch up."[21]

One of the earliest and most anguished voices to raise the option of shackling science to save civilization was that of Norman Cousins, editor of the *Saturday Review of Literature*. Cousins's "Modern Man Is Obsolete," written a few days after Hiroshima, pleaded for the establishment of a world government and warned "in all seriousness" that if a global authority were not created, then man's only remaining alternative was to

destroy, carefully and completely, everything relating to science and civilization. Let him destroy all machines and the knowledge which can build or operate those machines. Let him raze his cities, smash his laboratories, dismantle his factories, tear down his universities and schools, burn his libraries, rip apart his art. Let him murder his scientists, his doctors, his teachers, his lawmakers, his mechanics, and anyone who has anything to do with the machinery of knowledge or progress. Let him punish literacy by death. Let him abolish nations and set up the tribe as sovereign. In short, let him revert to the condition in society in 10,000 B.C. Thus emancipated from science, from progress, from government, from knowledge, from thought, he can be reasonably certain of safeguarding his existence on this planet.[22]

What Cousins termed the "primordial apprehensions" lifted by the bomb "out of the subconscious and into the conscious" also produced less drastic and, proponents hoped, more practicable proposals to curb the scientific exploitation of atomic energy. A plan advanced in early 1946 by a prominent international-law specialist at the University of Chicago (a hotbed of world government schemes) featured a five-year prohibition on power production.[23] In late 1946 and early 1947, David F. Cavers, a Harvard Law School professor, privately circulated a memorandum recommending that such a moratorium be incorporated into the U.S.'s international control proposal.[24] Cavers's plan would have permitted use of isotopes for scientific and medical research, but natural uranium would remain unmined and reactors unbuilt. Such a change, he argued, would greatly ease the task of international inspection. It would also avoid the problem of handing over American nuclear factories to international control, since instead they would be destroyed. Mankind would sacrifice the benefits of atomic power, but Cavers did not see this as a great loss. Reactions to early drafts of Cavers's idea, solicited by a Harvard Business School colleague advising the U.S. delegation to the UN talks, ranged from skeptical to almost contemptuous. Declaring himself in "rather total disagreement," Oppenheimer labeled it poorly conceived and "extreme" and argued that restricting the agency's purview to the "grim machinery of purely negative policing and inspection" would dash hopes for establishing a cooperative enterprise that would foster better U.S.-Soviet ties.[25] When Cavers submitted his moratorium proposal to *Fortune* magazine, an editor there, John Kenneth Galbraith, sent a regretful rejection slip that cited the prevalent feeling "that we have gone too far down the road with one idea of control to reverse the field with another."[26] Two atomic scientists who also favored a power moratorium as a method for international control, Cuthbert Daniel and Arthur M. Squires, had better luck, publishing their plan in the April 1947 *Bulletin of the Atomic Scientists.*[27] But it, too, elicited a largely negative reaction, with Oppenheimer terming the plan a "sour note" and insisting that effective international control could not be established "unless there is something for an agency to do besides snoop."[28]

Though what influence these proposals had on Conant's thinking is not known, sometime in 1947 he began to part company with Oppenheimer over the question of nuclear power promotion's centrality in fostering international control. The UN talks were in a dreary cul-de-sac, and the idea of striking out in a different direction seemed appealing; Conant now began seriously to consider possibilities for moving the official U.S. stance away from the confines of Acheson-Lilienthal and Baruch. In his memoirs, Conant writes blithely that he "lost all touch with the plans for the control of atomic energy" after the submission of the Acheson-Lilienthal proposal in early 1946.[29] But in the first week of May 1947, a chance to participate directly in shaping American policy landed in his lap. The phone call to Cambridge came from the new U.S. representative to the UN Atomic Energy Commission, Gen. Frederick H. Osborn, who knew Conant from the time when he had been running the army's wartime information and education branch and as a trustee of the Carnegie Corporation, a major Harvard benefactor.

In January 1947, after the adoption of the American plan over Soviet objection, a frustrated Baruch had resigned with a flourish—essentially, he declared victory and went home. But it was obvious to everyone concerned that if there remained even a ghost of a chance for a genuine agreement—which was more and more doubtful, even, to many U.S. officials, undesirable— difficult months of negotiation and compromise lay ahead. Some insiders suggested Conant for the job, but considering the prospects for success he probably would not have been interested if asked.[30] Conant would have been in a strong position to influence events had his close friend William L. Marbury taken the job, but Marbury declined Acheson's offer.[31] Instead, in March 1947, Marshall persuaded General Osborn to take over day-to-day control of the U.S. negotiations, reporting to Ambassador Warren R. Austin. The departure of Baruch and his Wall Street crowd, never comfortable with the administration or with the atomic scientists, offered a chance for Conant and other proponents of the Acheson-Lilienthal plan to reassert a measure of influence. Now, in early May, Osborn telephoned Conant with a proposition: would he join a select group of outside consultants that would periodically review the American position—in effect, serving as a kind of "visiting committee" to the U.S. atomic control negotiators?

Conant was inclined to accept—in late April, he had implored Americans not to give up on a U.S.-Soviet atomic agreement, telling a convocation of the Virginia Polytechnic Institute "I still cling to the belief" that international control "will eventually succeed"[32]—but his views were already shifting. On May 1, addressing the U.S. Chamber of Commerce, he opened with a pointed warning that despite gossip and press speculation to the contrary, from an industrial standpoint the atomic age "lies over the horizon."[33] And before accepting the consultancy, which would imply public endorsement of the U.S. policy at that moment, Conant wrote Osborn that he had "some definite ideas" about what the plan should include, and confessed his own misgivings about the way the United States had handled the talks the previous year.[34]

In Conant's view, the standing American proposal was incomplete.[35] It had been a mistake, he now believed, for the United States not to commit itself more firmly to a definite, clearly defined staging process for revealing atomic information, turning over nuclear material, and ultimately destroying its stock of atomic bombs as the international control plan went into effect. Conant now told Osborn that the failure to make that commitment more explicit, either in the Acheson-Lilienthal plan or at the United Nations talks, had handed Henry Wallace and his supporters ammunition in criticizing Baruch.[36] For there to be any chance of Soviet acceptance, and to table a proposal "with a clear conscience," Conant believed that the next U.S. plan needed to spell out "in great detail the actual steps" leading to the elimination of the U.S. atomic monopoly, as opposed to the carefully hedged Baruch formula of assessing compliance after each stage was completed and only then determining how to go forward.[37] A second "valid criticism" of Acheson-Lilienthal, Conant went on, was that it had failed to explain how the proposed international agency would allot its assets — raw materials, fissionable products, plants, etc. — among various countries, each naturally wanting the largest possible slice of the atomic energy pie and ready to seize those assets if hostilities broke out and the arrangement collapsed.

These qualms notwithstanding, Conant pronounced himself "anxious" to contribute "on this vitally important matter." And in his reply, Osborn enthusiastically welcomed him as a consultant while carefully avoiding any specific endorsement of a firmer schedule. "Your letter clearly indicates how great your help can be," Osborn wrote. "The problem of stages needs to be dealt with, at least in general terms, in the report we hope to get out."[38]

On May 6 Osborn announced that he had appointed Conant as a consultant, joining Oppenheimer, Tolman, Groves, Bacher, Chester I. Barnard, and Maj. Gen. Thomas Farrell, who had formerly advised Groves and Baruch.[39] As with the GAC's relationship to the AEC commissioners, this high-powered group possessed far more experience in atomic matters than the negotiators themselves, and Osborn told them flat out that if they could achieve a consensus, their views would undoubtedly determine the U.S. position.[40]

By stature and experience, the group's two most influential members were Oppenheimer and Conant. But the divergence in their approaches to international control persisted; the two disagreed over whether the United States should continue to try to reach a control agreement with the Soviets through talks at the United Nations; and while both earnestly shared the ultimate objective of eliminating atomic weapons, Conant favored further development of the U.S. proposals, even considerable concessions, whereas Oppenheimer wanted to break off the negotiations until relations with Moscow were more favorable.

Oppenheimer, in fact, had been forcefully pressing that idea on Osborn for months. In March, as soon as he learned of Osborn's appointment, he had urgently requested an interview and flown cross-country from Berkeley to spend a Saturday night at Osborn's country home outside New York City. Ironically, at precisely the same moment that the FBI was forwarding its report of suspicions to the AEC, Oppenheimer was warning the new U.S. negotiator that any international atomic control agreement would be "exceedingly dangerous to the United States" since, he now felt certain, the Russians would never accept a plan that required "lifting the Iron Curtain." Continuing the talks therefore seemed to him to present twin dangers: the United States might get snookered into a flawed agreement, or the Soviets might exploit the talks for propaganda gain.[41]

Osborn himself, like many Truman administration officials, "never had, for a moment, expected to reach any sort of agreement with the Russians."[42] But he and the administration, unlike Oppenheimer, had to take into account the sensitivities of America's West European allies, who had nearly given up on the Baruch Plan in December 1946 because of objections to the negotiator's stand over the veto and his "take it or leave it" tactics.[43] Now these same allies vehemently opposed any idea of breaking off the talks, claiming that that would put them in an untenable political position.[44] Truman's advisers grudgingly permitted Osborn to remain at the negotiating table, but only after the negotiators had argued that taking a lone stance against the talks "would be very injurious to our international position" and promised to stay "properly on our guard."[45]

From the outset of his $10 per day consultancy, which lasted from May 1947 through September 1949, Conant allied himself with Osborn's view that the United States should continue negotiating with the Soviet Union, and he treated a comprehensive U.S.-Soviet international control agreement as a real, albeit remote, possibility. At his first conference with Osborn, on May 14, Conant reviewed "all drafts of working papers" with the American delegation, offered "many suggestions for staffing, stages, etc.," and—so Osborn recorded in his diary—"[t]horoughly approved what we are doing."[46]

By late June, however, Conant had started informally to float a personal proposal among U.S. atomic and government officials that for the first time united his doubts about nuclear power and his desperation to find a workable international control formula.[47] At first Conant and Oppenheimer apparently acted in concert. The "Conant-Oppenheimer Plan," as Paul Fine, one of Osborn's advisers, dubbed it in an internal memo, "would in effect restrict the use of nuclear fuel to research and limited development" in contrast to the Baruch proposal's provision for full-scale production and exploitation of nuclear power. Fine instead suggested a compromise that would permit only sufficient development of nuclear power to determine its feasibility for future exploitation—and in fact the American negotiators, prodded by Conant, now began to adopt a less expansive vision of the power-related activities of a proposed international atomic agency.[48]

But Conant himself now began to move well beyond the U.S. delegation—and Oppenheimer—in his willingness to discard atomic energy altogether. A confidential meeting in mid-June with the physicist Sir George P. Thomson, a British delegate to the United Nations talks, may have accelerated this. Thomson's name rang a bell as a result of his previous service, in 1940–41, as head of the MAUD committee of British scientists whose optimistic report on uranium fission had helped convince the skeptical Conant that an atomic bomb could be built before the war ended. Now, six years later, Thomson informally conveyed to Conant, Tolman, and Osborn what he described as his own, personal idea to bring the whole atomic energy enterprise to a screeching halt: a plan under which all nuclear power development would be prohibited for, say, twenty years, or until small-scale experimentation proved atomic energy's economic value. If that were too bold, he added, then at least the contentious issues revolving around the strategic balance and disposition of nuclear fuels—the same issues that so vexed Conant—could be kicked into the far future by proceeding more slowly. The Americans gathered that Thomson wasn't certain that his plan would actually work, but felt it offered "the only hope" for inducing Moscow to sign a treaty.[49]

Encouraged by such views and discouraged by the unveiling of the latest, clearly unacceptable Soviet proposals, Conant adopted the moratorium plan as his own. On Saturday afternoon, June 28, his ideas popped up in the course of a troubled conversation between Lilienthal and a tired Dean Acheson, about to leave the State Department for private law practice (temporarily, as it turned out). Lilienthal mentioned a "Conant alternative" to the standing Western atomic proposals "whereby power development is forsworn, and hence not part of international development and operation, and everyone agrees to raw material international control and limiting themselves to nondangerous research." Lilienthal had learned of Conant's plan from Bacher, "who didn't care for it," but had heard that Oppenheimer "rather" favored it. Conant's reported motivation for advocating this 180-degree turnabout from Acheson-Lilienthal "was that since it was obvious that Russia wouldn't agree to our proposal we must find something else they might agree to, and this might be it."[50]

Conant carefully kept his proposal secret, though hints of his lack of enthusiasm about nuclear power occasionally seeped out. The idea of shunning atomic energy, after all, flew in the face of the optimistic public predictions advanced by journalists, social commentators, and some scientists. It also ran directly counter to Lilienthal and the AEC commissioners' philosophy of capturing the public's imagination by promoting atomic energy's allegedly bright future—in power, medicine, transportation, agriculture, and other areas. In its "search for a silver lining," and especially in Lilienthal's tireless invocation of nuclear power's ultimate wonders, the AEC leadership aimed to secure vital popular and congressional support.[51]

In late July—shortly after CBS journalist Edward R. Murrow, at Lilienthal's behest, hosted an hour-long radio broadcast on the "Sunny Side of the Atom"[52]—Conant's dissatisfaction with nuclear power plans came to a head during an intensive week in Washington and New York.

❖ ❖ ❖

On Monday and Tuesday, July 28 and 29, the tension inside the AEC conference room on Constitution Avenue matched the uncomfortable heat of the sweltering dog day outside. In the sharpest dispute yet between the AEC commissioners and their scientist-advisers, the GAC strenuously advocated that the AEC warn publicly against overoptimism about nuclear power. Conant and Oppenheimer, backed firmly by DuBridge and Rabi, were in the lead. For months, Conant had read with distaste the newspaper reports suggesting that atomic paradise was just around the corner and asking why the AEC was taking so long to get there, and now he and the others favored a sober, authoritative retort. On Conant's motion they drafted a statement declaring bluntly that the current status of nuclear power efforts was "not fully understood," that it "does not appear hopeful" to use uranium as a power source, that the costs of nuclear reactors made them "economically prohibitive." The only practical way of synthesizing adequate amounts of nuclear fuel would be to develop "breeder reactors" that would convert uranium into plutonium rather than using it up in normal operations. But that last idea remained only a distant dream. Even under the most favorable projections, "decades will elapse" before nuclear power contributes significantly to the industrialized world's energy resources.[53]

Lilienthal and his fellow commissioners were horrified. "Had quite a blow today," Lilienthal wrote in his diary. "The General Advisory Committee drafted a statement that, as written, not only discouraged hope of atomic power in any substantial way for decades, but put it in such a way as to question whether it would ever be of consequence. This pessimism didn't come from nobodies, but from a top group—Oppenheimer, Conant, Rabi, Seaborg, etc."[54] Already being sharply criticized by other atomic scientists, notably Compton and Lawrence,[55] for allegedly not doing enough to promote the private industrial development of nuclear power, Lilienthal was now catching flak from the GAC for being too enthusiastic. But he and the other commissioners feared the marring of the carefully nurtured positive image for the AEC which, Lilienthal hoped, would belie its increasing emphasis on weapons production, and, as Strauss warned, the loss of congressional support. Even if the news was bad, why spread it?

Conant and Oppenheimer strongly dissented, arguing that the public needed a dose of realism, and that it was in the commission's own best interests to give it. "If one did not release the facts," the notes of the meeting record Conant as saying, "the prevalent optimistic impression would continue," and with the lack of results in actual power production, scientists would conclude that "either the Commission was incompetent to carry on a power development program or was completely military-minded." The two men insisted that the statement lay out the discouraging truth as they saw it: that nuclear power as an important factor in the national economy was a generation away at best. They did consent, however, to soften the morose tone, and grudgingly accepted Strauss's suggestion that it would be "prudent" to defer issuing a public statement until after the GAC's next meeting, in October.[56]

This tenuous compromise did little to smooth ruffled feelings. Oppenheimer wrote to his friend Bacher, the only AEC leader unable to attend, that he had been "very much appalled" at the commissioners' reaction to the draft, not so much at their sensitivity to public reaction but because none of them "appears to have the least idea as to whether this was a true or false statement, whether it was a wise or foolish one; nor did any of the Commissioners evidence any sign of familiarity with the [technical] issues which we tried to raise." And besides exposing underlying differences in the GAC's and commissioners' approach and philosophy, the sessions opened a rift between Conant and Lilienthal. Oppenheimer tried to play peacemaker between the two, but to no avail. "I had a terrible luncheon with Dave and Conant in which the gulf between them looked very broad and Dave manifested no great desire to bridge it," he reported to Bacher.[57] (Lilienthal might have had a more benign view had he known that Conant, despite his misgivings, was loyally defending Lilienthal's performance. That same day, responding to Arthur Compton's charge that the commission had failed to encourage private industrial interest in atomic energy, Conant expressed "in strong terms my belief that your suspicions are absolutely groundless." The "trouble with the atomic power project rests in technical matters," he wrote, not AEC opposition— "quite the contrary." An hour's conversation with Oppenheimer, he suggested, would clear up Compton's "misunderstanding.")[58]

On Wednesday, July 30, Conant chaired a meeting of the JRDB's atomic energy committee. In attendance were air force and navy representatives seeking support for nuclear-powered long-range bombers and submarines, respectively. Since first learning of the project in March, Conant, Oppenheimer and Greenewalt had all quickly concluded that the nuclear plane (known as NEPA, for Nuclear Energy for the Propulsion of Aircraft) was a boondoggle primarily designed to give the air force a berth on the atomic energy gravy train. Since then, with growing irritation, Conant had been resisting military entreaties to ramrod JRDB approval of advanced projects in order to obtain quick congressional funding.[59] Pouring cold water on the NEPA enthusiasts' dream of completing an atomic plane in five years, Conant's panel now urged a low-key research effort in place of the rapid development program under way at Clinton Laboratories at Oak Ridge. It also put the brakes on a proposal, promoted by, among others, Ernest Lawrence, to build offensive weapons using nuclear fission by-products to "dust" enemy territory with the poisonous materials. Finally, it rather wanly okayed further research and development of the navy's pet project, the nuclear-powered submarine.[60] The meeting over, Conant and Oppenheimer caught the four o'clock train to New York, where they were expected the next morning at the U.S. delegation's Park Avenue offices for the first full-dress gathering of outside advisers to the UN talks.

Conant had little reason for optimism as he walked from the Harvard Club on West Forty-fourth Street for his third session with Osborn. Signs were even more inauspicious than for the previous two meetings. A few weeks earlier, Soviet Foreign Minister Molotov had angrily stalked out of an East-West conference in Paris, denouncing the Marshall Plan as an American plot to divide Europe. Soon afterward, Moscow announced its own rival economic program, and in a heavy-handed fashion leaned on Poland and Czechoslovakia—neither of which was quite accustomed to being treated like a Russian satellite—to drop any thoughts of joining the Marshall Plan.[61] With the last remnants of the wartime alliance crumbling, prospects for attaining a workable compromise on the overarching issue of atomic weapons control seemed bleaker than ever.

At the United Nations, the outlook was equally gloomy. The latest Russian proposal, unveiled on June 11, struck the Americans as "wholly inadequate" because of its lack of effective safeguards against cheating.[62] For their part, the Soviets did little to conceal their belief that the American proposals were no more than a propaganda masquerade for Washington indefinitely to maintain its nuclear monopoly. The diplomats at Lake Success went on thickening the mound of opposing blueprints, but a sense of futility, if not unreality, had descended over the proceedings.

Nevertheless, Osborn had copies of the latest American draft proposals to hand Conant and the other consultants as they assembled on Thursday morning. The six documents, all highly classified, contained nothing startling, for they were largely devoted to setting the agenda for the upcoming fall United Nations debate and to delineating U.S. positions on the proposed atomic agency's structure, financing, staffing, hierarchy, functions, and sanctions. Their significance lay not so much in their content but in their signal that the United States was persisting in the negotiations.

The U.S. plans met with a mixed, though on balance favorable, response from the advisers. As Osborn recounted to Bacher afterward, the discussion, "full of ideas and fireworks," pitted the odd makeshift alliance of Oppenheimer and Groves—both of whom opposed further U.S. participation—against Tolman and Barnard, "with Conant taking an independent line."[63] Conant not only "most strongly" supported Osborn's plan to go forward, but urged additional steps to make the American plan seem more credible. Tolman, Barnard, and Farrell also backed Osborn's plans to continue developing the American proposals. Like the rest, Conant agreed with the U.S. insistence on explicit provisions for on-site inspections and controls, but he added his own twist—"in order to write either the 'strategic balance' or the 'stages,' it would be necessary explicitly to provide for the destruction of nuclear fuel and nuclear plants and the cutback of the level of ADA activity previously suggested by him."[64]

Conant's impassioned endorsement of that idea sparked sharp opposition, for the other consultants believed that adequate inspection would be impossible without an international agency running atomic development in all countries; that dispute masked a deeper division of views between Conant, who favored completing the U.S. proposal and modifying it to improve chances of acceptance, and others who believed the conflict with Moscow had already rendered international control a dead letter. Testy exchanges ensued.

To Conant's urging that Osborn should propose the "initial machinery" that would effect the ultimate destruction of U.S. atomic stocks, once an agency went into operation, Groves countered that the United States could not destroy its nuclear fuels because of a global scarcity of uranium and thorium—the only two materials that could be used to generate the enriched fuels for use in nuclear weapons. Conant, to put it mildly, looked at that prospect from a different perspective: destroying the fuels would be a "great contribution to humanity," he declared. But, rejoined Groves, destroying America's painstakingly produced nuclear fuels would leave the sources for nuclear energy and weapons available to others—in mines and clandestine plants, perhaps—"and not under our control." This obstructionism irritated Conant. Groves was "merely arguing against any treaty," he shot back, urging Osborn again, as he had in May, to see to it that the next American proposal included provisions for stages and strategic distribution of assets. "These two questions should have been decided before now," Conant told the group.[65]

Already up against Groves and General Matthew B. Ridgway, Conant now ran into opposition from an unexpected quarter: Oppenheimer.[66] While "pleasantly astonished" that Osborn's staff had drawn up relatively "sensible" proposals at a time of unprecedented public U.S.-Soviet acrimony, Oppenheimer nevertheless believed that with no real chance of success in the talks, it was time to terminate the charade. To go ahead with U.S. plans for collaborating with the USSR on atomic controls, Oppenheimer argued, would be dishonest— an "act of bad faith"—and worse. The "real danger," it seemed, was the unlikely possibility that the Russians might actually accept the American proposal at a time when neither the U.S. government nor people favored international control.

Conant also saw the danger in disingenuously advancing a nonserious proposal—but his solution was to advance a *more* serious one. "If someone really sees this box and makes a stink about it we're in a horrible position," he warned. The U.S. government, he insisted, needed seriously to decide whether it still really favored international control and the unitary global structure that would result, and to educate the public on its decision.

Conant also clashed with his fellow advisers over the possibility of monitoring a control scheme that did not include international participation in development. Chester Barnard feared that the Russians would cheat, but Conant, who felt that even a flawed agreement was better than none, took a more philosophical view. "All governments have bad faith," he said, it was merely a "question of degree." But, since "all nations are rascals," he agreed with Barnard and other skeptics in the room that any staging process leading to eventual U.S. relinquishment of its atomic monopoly must include tough provisions to prevent cheating and prove good faith. Even that went further than Groves, who strongly opposed even bringing up stages at a point when the very idea of international control attracted waning support among Americans.

Groping for common ground, Osborn canvassed the consultants to see if they would endorse the completion of an American proposal with everything up to—but not including—the issue of stages. Oppenheimer and Conant went along with this tentative truce, and Osborn reported proudly to Austin on Friday, August 1, that except for disagreement over staging and one minor clause on inspection, his team of consultants had "thoroughly" approved the U.S. proposals and "recommend them unqualifiedly."[67]

That shaky consensus barely survived the weekend: a few days later, the dispute between Conant and Oppenheimer over whether to pursue the UN talks sharpened. Before the New York meeting ended, Oppenheimer had grudgingly allowed that going forward with the U.S. proposal might be worthwhile to keep alive the slender hope for agreement and to boost America's international image. But "much thought" over the weekend changed his mind, and late on Monday afternoon he sought out Osborn in his office to emphasize that he was "very disturbed" about the idea of continued participation in the control talks.[68] Osborn listened with considerable chagrin as Oppenheimer warned that it would be "unwise, not altogether honest, and exceedingly dangerous to the American position" to keep negotiating.[69] In Oppenheimer's view, Osborn's approach sacrificed long-term prospects for short-term appearances and risked giving Moscow a chance to string the Americans along—"to make us out both fools and swindlers if the Russians play their cards somewhat more skillfully than they have in the past." Given "the rapid past and probable future deterioration" in U.S.-Soviet relations, the "deep and fully justified suspicion with which the people in this country regard Russia, the sharp even if temporary alignment, and the always present threat of war in the not remote future," it was no longer feasible "to undertake a cooperative enterprise" such as the Acheson-Lilienthal plan. No alternatives, and "certainly not that of Conant's," seemed to Oppenheimer "either hopeful or salable either to us or to the Russians."[70]

Oppenheimer claimed that Conant supported his position—citing an alleged comment that the U.S. government should "make it clear that no treaty on atomic energy would be acceptable until world conditions of peace are assured."[71] But Osborn doubted that Conant really went along with Oppenheimer's negative approach—and his skepticism was vindicated the next morning when he received a letter from Conant.[72] Precisely contradicting Oppenheimer, Conant expressed his "hope that people in Washington will take an optimistic view even in this grim world and *complete* the American proposal. I think you understand," he added, "that my specific position is that the United States made a proposal, but an incomplete one."[73]

While no more optimistic than Oppenheimer about the chances of success, Osborn still rejected his arguments because of his keen awareness that an

American walkout would be a diplomatic blunder. "Strong propaganda by Russia that we had never intended the offer seriously" would be the result, he told Austin, and suggested that if Washington desired a clean break with Moscow, it should take that step elsewhere. As for Oppenheimer's fear that the United States, by staying in the talks, might end up signing a disadvantageous agreement, Osborn assured Austin that it should be easy to stall consideration of a detailed staging process for destroying or handing over the U.S. stockpile.[74]

This strategy satisfied neither Oppenheimer nor Conant, who had urged more candor about the stages, since a firm timetable for ending the monopoly would make the American offer more plausible. While rebuffing Oppenheimer's suggestion to break off the talks altogether, Osborn and the State Department also turned a deaf ear to Conant's plea for a more conciliatory and credible proposal.[75]

Osborn's mixed response expressed the administration's increasing negativism about the control talks through 1947 and 1948: Soviet rejection of the Baruch Plan, the military and police repression in central and southeastern Europe and ideological truculence that had inspired the Truman Doctrine, the rising domestic "Red scare," and especially Moscow's brusque dismissal of the Marshall Plan all helped convert the government's policy on international atomic control from wary but serious interest into a desultory waiting game, keyed to public relations rather than diplomatic progress. International control itself, never unanimously favored, was increasingly viewed as irrelevant to and even inconsistent with the more critical aim of building up the U.S. atomic stockpile and integrating atomic weaponry into a coherent military strategy for confronting the USSR. Although they discarded as implausible the notion of issuing an atomic ultimatum to Moscow, U.S. policymakers sought subtle methods to exploit the American monopoly for geopolitical advantage. Soliciting Oppenheimer's aid in July 1947 for a Voice of America program to be beamed into Russia, the State Department's "special consultant for Russian broadcasts," OSS veteran Charles W. Thayer, explained that its purpose would be two-fold: to explain U.S. policy on international control, and "to counteract in so far as possible, the view now being disseminated in the Soviet Union that an atomic bomb is hardly worse than a bad head cold. This second objective must, however, be achieved by rather gentle methods since otherwise it will be discounted as saber-rattling or atomic diplomacy propaganda."[76] The following month, a report by the State Department's Policy Planning Staff declared that "under present circumstances the effort to achieve international control affords less hope for protecting our national security than other means," the principal alternative being to "materially improve the United States position in a world in which others possess atomic weapons."[77]

As with Washington's shrewd offer to include the USSR in the Marshall Plan, few U.S. officials believed the Soviets would respond positively to the prolonged offer at the United Nations of plans for the international custody of nuclear weapons. In refusing to take the bait, Stalin unwittingly assisted Truman's efforts to rally American and Western opinion behind his tough anti-Soviet policy; in the view of later historians who mark the summer of 1947 as the "point-of-no-return" in the emerging Cold War, he assured the polarization of Europe into opposed power blocs.[78] Simultaneously, *Foreign Affairs* published State Department aide George F. Kennan's famous pseudonymous "X" article in July, warning that the Soviet Union's addiction to expansion and aggression could only be "contained" by American might — what Kennan termed the "adroit and vigilant application of counterforce at a series of constantly shifting geographical and political points."[79] Rapidly, despite qualms by commentators such as Walter Lippmann who worried about the administration's apparently limitless commitment to restrain communism wherever it threatened, U.S. public opinion coalesced behind the Truman administration's policies.

Conant, too, fell in line. As in 1940 and 1941, when he ardently called on citizens to back American intervention in the war against Germany and Japan, he transmitted and reinforced the thrust of shifting government policies. In numerous public speeches before elite audiences, he dramatized the differences between capitalist democracy and the totalitarian society ruled by the Kremlin, and called for support for the administration's European Recovery Program. Making an exception to his rule of refusing membership in public advocacy groups, he enthusiastically joined the Committee for the Marshall Plan, composed of prominent internationalists, headed by Stimson, who rallied public support for the plan's huge foreign aid bill.[80]

But he also stubbornly railed against the idea that war with Russia was inevitable, and insisted that international control of atomic weapons remained a realistic possibility "in a relatively short time" once Moscow came to its senses. After a three-week hiking vacation in the Canadian Rockies, Conant embarked in September 1947 on a "rather strenuous" speaking tour of alumni clubs on the Pacific coast and in the farm belt. In his speeches, he admitted to mystification at the Soviets' intransigence in the atomic talks and, still more exasperating, their studied indifference to the dangers of atomic war.[81] "Perhaps they do not appreciate the military value of the bomb," he wondered. "Perhaps they do not realize that until atomic bombs are abolished by international agreement they remain a method of waging war if war should come." Publicly, at least, Conant did not dwell on the ominous conclusion already reached by many government officials — that the Soviets were stalling until they had perfected their own atomic weapons. Instead, he surmised that it was "more likely" that the "hard headed realists" in the Kremlin were engaging in some Marxist-inspired wishful thinking. Soviet leaders, he speculated, confident that the capitalist West was destined to "disintegrate in a whirlpool of internal troubles," were in no hurry to remove the atomic "sword of Damocles hanging over our industrialized civilization." They would cooperate on controlling the atom, he believed, only when convinced that the West—principally meaning the United States—had proved itself "prosperous, strong and democratic."[82] Citing various sources, including the "X" article's challenge to Americans to promote a vital society "capable of holding its own among the major ideological currents of the time," and an analysis by a former government official, John Fischer, Conant made a double argument about ultimately triumphing in the Cold War—which to him meant not military victory but holding firm until the Soviet Union cooperated in sustaining peace—including both a "firm and enlightened foreign policy," with the Marshall Plan bolstering Western Europe, and the assurance of "a healthy and vigorous growth of democracy" within the United States. As to the latter, the two key factors in Conant's analysis were public education, the engine of social mobility that would ensure Americans from stratifying into antagonistic economic classes, and political liberty as guaranteed by free speech and free elections, which, he said, must be preserved uncompromisingly "even in days of an armed truce."[83] Only thus, Conant told alumni clubs, local chambers of commerce, and journalists from Seattle to Omaha, could the United States hasten "the successful solution not only of the control of the atomic bomb but of the larger problem of achieving peace in our divided world."

Conant's speeches were covered by the *New York Times* and other newspapers, assuring that his ideas reached a mass audience. At a moment of widespread unease about America's sliding toward a harsher conflict with the Soviet Union, his pronouncements helped to calm frayed public nerves and inculcate a steely determination to face the uncertain future, while studiously avoiding the appearance of second-guessing administration policy. But in private, to a more select audience, Conant offered blunter advice for banishing the atomic "sword of Damocles"—and hinted at a darker appraisal of the chances for survival should that sword remain hovering over a divided world.

On Thursday, October 2, Conant made a second annual pilgrimage to address the National War College's training seminar on postwar weaponry and strategy. His appearance there afforded him a rare chance to elaborate views he considered too "explosive" for public consumption, although, he noted wryly to the officers, even in this "highly secure audience" it was impossible fully to express himself "without breaking security regulations." In a speech that ranged from Strangelovian prescriptions for dispersing American industry the better to survive a nuclear attack to an idealistic plea for a non-nuclear foundation for long-term military policy, Conant presented his controversial scheme to scrap Acheson-Lilienthal and Baruch, and substitute in their stead "not the maximum development of atomic energy for peaceful purposes but the minimum."[84] He derided the "emulators of Jules Verne (or should I say H. G. Wells)," who were having a "field day" describing the imminent "atomic age of plenty." "What bedtime stories we have been told about that age!" he told his War College audience, dismissing a previous speaker who had spoken favorably about nuclear power prospects as "by temperament an optimist."[85]

But Conant himself confessed to being a "hardy optimist" in his advocacy of international atomic control, well aware that many in his audience had long since given up hope for Soviet participation in a U.S.-sponsored plan, if they had ever backed the idea in the first place. He refused to "write off" the possibility of an eventual pact with Moscow, "however gloomy the prospects now appear." And he reviewed the same grim landscape of the coming "Superblitz age" he had painted in his War College speech the year before, again glumly endorsing the idea of a limited U.S.-West European nuclear alliance as the best hope to deter war should the Soviet Union begin producing its own atomic bombs.

Then he came to the heart of his presentation, which included two propositions that were heresy to many Pentagon and AEC officials: "First, it is in the interest of the military security of the United States to enter into an agreement even if the scheme breaks down during the operation. Secondly, in the long run the United States would from a military point of view be very much better off if there were neither atomic bombs nor their equivalent in existence anywhere in the world." If the USSR agreed to allow American inspectors to do a two-year survey of raw materials and industry, he suggested, the United States in return should be willing to hand over "all its industrial know-how and remaining secrets about the bomb."[86] This was, Conant admitted, "an extreme statement." But, he warned, the nuclear monopoly on which so much depended—and which he predicted would last for another three to twelve years—was quickly diminishing in value, "like a cake of ice on a hot day." Why not cash in while it was still worth something? Of course, it should be the first step in a longer-term process leading to full international control; the difference between his line and the standard U.S. policy was offering far more atomic information far more quickly, in exchange for the intelligence that inspection of Soviet territory would supply.

Even if Moscow were willing to go along—unlikely, considering Stalin's aversion to on-site inspection—Conant conceded that such an agreement would take years to negotiate, and even longer to put into operation. What would Washington do about its steadily growing stock of fissionable, weapons-grade material in the meantime? That was the "springboard" for Conant's second radical proposition: "that the United States would be better off in a world which contained no separated isotopes or plutonium." He frankly acknowledged that formally proposing this idea would require a drastic revision in U.S. policy. But, he pointed out, the American people were hardly likely to approve of handing over a growing stock of nuclear materials to other countries, including the Soviet Union, once the new agency had been set up, as the existing U.S. plan called for. "Therefore," Conant concluded, Acheson-Lilienthal must be "amended or extended," although he quickly added that it was "not my business to say so publicly and I am holding my peace behind closed doors."

In fact, Conant's skepticism toward the future of nuclear power had already pushed official U.S. policy away from the previous emphasis on atomic energy promotion. On September 11, with the USSR casting the lone dissenting vote, the United Nations Atomic Energy Commission had approved its Second Report to the Security Council on the structure and program of the proposed international atomic control agency. In contrast to its statement nine months earlier, which had spoken optimistically of the "straightforward development" of peaceful nuclear energy "competitive" with other sources of power such as coal, the new report echoed the private assessments of the GAC in conceding that atomic power "probably cannot become an important factor in the world's existing power resources for some decades."[87] And, in a provision that attracted little public notice, it actually mandated that the international agency limit the production of nuclear fuel to "the minimum required for efficient operating procedures" of research plants already under construction.[88]

In his talk to the War College, Conant wanted to go still further, urging the total elimination of all atomic power plants. To do so he outlined a three-stage plan. First, the United States and the Soviet Union would trade basic information on atomic energy and industrial resources. In the second stage, the United States would trade more information for a "trial run" at joint ownership, management, and operation of all uranium mines in both countries. Then, in the final stage, all existing stocks of plutonium and uranium-235 would be "denatured"—rendered unusable for weapons—or "dumped into the sea." The mines would be worked and inspected just enough to make sure no one was "bootlegging uranium." So much for the difficult task of monitoring a wide range of "dangerous activities" provided for in the final stage of Acheson-Lilienthal, for there would be no "dangerous activities" to monitor.[89]

"There would likewise be no prospect for the development of atomic energy for peaceful purposes," Conant conceded. "Being a skeptic about the value of this energy anyway, I cannot weep at the prospect of having the door shut on the prospects of what I think has been to a large extent only a mirage: the alleged atomic age of plenty."[90] "I do not believe the benefits of atomic energy are worth the price," he stated firmly. "Atomic fuels can be too readily turned into atomic bombs to be safe for the civilized world to handle. A self-denying ordinance is needed."

During a lively question-and-answer session, the military officers challenged Conant, and while failing to shake him much, they drew out some unusually candid and revealing statements that illuminated Conant's emotional and intellectual struggle over atomic weapons. Asked if the United States should "consider preventive war" against the Soviet Union—a notion whose popularity in certain quarters came increasingly to alarm him in the months to come—Conant raised several warnings. Americans, he asserted, were unlikely to support a "preventive" attack. But, he frankly admitted, he had no idea "what is going to happen to the American psychology, or my psychology, when I am convinced the Russians really have the bombs." Even thinking about the issue was premature, except perhaps in one's "innermost thoughts," he said. "Perhaps I am just kidding myself in thinking [the USSR] won't have [atomic bombs] during the next ten years," he went on (they would have them in two). "Perhaps I am in the mood of a gentleman over seventy who said, 'If you give them ten years I am out anyway.' Perhaps we are all hoping it is beyond the age of our own survival."

Conant acknowledged that his moratorium scheme was "idealistic" and "assumes you have some chance" of obtaining an international agreement, an admittedly distant prospect. But he hoped to provoke fresh consideration of international control as a laudable goal among an audience he probably suspected had long grown cynical about the idea. "I am addressing this proposal to those of you who are going to be making the military decisions in ten or fifteen years," he stated frankly. "I am trying to plant the seed of an idea in your mind. I don't think the issue will come up within five years. But sometime there may be a chance of getting back on the road toward an international scheme."

To an objection that his plan might leave the United States militarily vulnerable should the Soviets surreptitiously manufacture atomic weapons, Conant first answered somewhat unconvincingly that non-nuclear forces would have to be used, then contended more vigorously that in a world of sharply curtailed, tightly monitored atomic activity, it was highly unlikely that a nation could produce more than a few bombs on the sly—hardly a decisive number. He agreed that if hostilities broke out even after the moratorium the atomic weapons race would start again, but why would that be any worse than the situation now? After all, he pointed out, if the Acheson-Lilienthal plan went into operation and "the world went sour again, or shall we say continued sour, and everybody started in and grabbed the plants, bombs would be made awfully fast." At least if war broke out after fissionable materials and atomic plants had been destroyed, there could be no specter of an atomic Pearl Harbor, and a time lapse before the fighting nations could build up large stockpiles. "In other words," Conant admitted frankly, "you are trying to turn the clock back to 1940 or before. They say you can't turn clocks back but everybody who has had clocks knows that you can."[91]

This yearning to erase the irrevocable reality of atomic weapons surely struck many in his audience as not only futile but indicative of an unwillingness to confront unpleasant truths; yet Conant, like Bohr before him, insisted that his radical thinking in fact stemmed from a hard-headed appraisal of the consequences of not eliminating nuclear weapons from the world's arsenals. "I am afraid I am a pragmatically minded fellow," he responded to one listener, who had asked Conant to comment on the observation that, throughout history, mankind had always "directed his greatest genius to his own destruction," and now at last appeared on the verge of accomplishing that fatal goal. Startlingly, for a man who made endless public appeals for courage and steadfastness, Conant seemed to accept this premise of a species bent on its own extinction, comparing his plan to prohibit atomic-energy development as akin to denying razors to "people who have a mania for suicide." He admitted that people had told him that a "self-denying ordinance" was all wrong, and that efforts should instead center on cultivating a climate of opinion in which nations would never resort to nuclear war despite their possession of the devastating weapons. But Conant had little faith in the possibility of an everlasting nuclear peace. "Between the two proposals," he said, "I think mine is the more practical. That is according to the past history of the human race, assuming there is not going to be a sudden mutation."[92] In his typically unemotional, logical manner, Conant had simply derived a lesson from history that spelled doom unless the bomb were controlled—and he was at best ambivalent about humanity's ability to change its spots. "Perhaps the fated task of those of us now alive in this country is to develop still further our civilization for the benefit of the survivors of World War III in other lands," he speculated in public speeches around this time. "It would not be an inglorious mission."[93]

For the record, Conant refused to succumb to pessimism. He loudly exhorted Americans to eschew fear and panic and to be patient, determined, and resolute in facing the future in a divided, nuclear-armed world. He tried passionately to instill confidence in America's—and civilization's—ability to avoid a nuclear armageddon, to survive and flourish in perilous times. Few knew he was laboring no less fervently to convince himself of the same thing.

Conant quickly gathered that his War College speech had created a stir in Washington. Within days, tantalizing indications of high-level interest in his remarks began filtering back to Cambridge. His emphasis on coordinated planning had appealed to the secretary of defense (the title of secretary of war had been abolished), James Forrestal, who as the head of the newly created National Military Establishment was trying to enforce order on the constantly squabbling services. On October 8, Forrestal congratulated Conant on his "provocative and thoughtful paper" and said he would recommend that President Truman, as well as Secretary of State Marshall and Under Secretary Lovett, "read it at some time when they have plenty of leisure to digest its implications. For me," Forrestal added, "it was a breath of mental fresh air in an atmosphere which seemed to me to be becoming extremely thick in the past twenty-four months."[94]

Conant's "outstanding performance" had "so favorably impressed" Forrestal that he had also made sure the address reached the three service chiefs, as Maj. Gen. Alfred M. Gruenther of the army, the new director of the Joint Chiefs of Staff, told Conant.[95] Bush also received a copy from Forrestal, returning it with a scrawled message ("A remarkable paper") that barely hinted at his startled reaction; he told Conant later in October that his "bully" speech "has gone all over the National Military Establishment."[96] Finding the speech both stimulating and fear-inducing, Army Chief of Staff Dwight D. Eisenhower lost his appetite after reading a copy, writing to Conant that it moved him to sympathize with those "who at the time of the building of the railroads expressed a longing for the 'good old days.' "[97] War College commandant Adm. Harry Hill handcarried a copy to British atomic adviser Sir Henry Tizard, and at the AEC, Lilienthal, though in fact less than enthralled by the speech, distributed copies to his fellow commissioners.[98] UN negotiator Osborn, sent a copy by Conant, responded obliquely that his speech had been "most provocative to our thinking" and thanked him for his "new ideas."[99]

All this upper-level attention left Conant pleased but puzzled. "I seem to have started something as I get reactions from high quarters in Washington that they liked the address very much," he wrote Oppenheimer, "but I cannot find out to which of my ideas they were referring."[100] The only idea that Conant knew had already produced results was his recommendation—also contained in his 1946 speech—that the Pentagon organize three independent groups of military planners to examine U.S. strategy, forces, deployment, weaponry, etc., in the event of three divergent alternative atomic futures: continued U.S. monopoly, international control agency, or a "Superblitz age" of rival nuclear-armed powers. It was the glaring failure of Pentagon planners to tackle the dangers and problems posed by this last scenario that most distressed Conant.[101] Again, as in his first appearance at the War College, he had exhorted listeners to "think afresh" when planning for the "revolutionary" Superblitz age to come, to justify from scratch the need for any military branch other than that responsible for atomic warfare. Conant's remarks foreshadowed what, by the late 1950s, became a permanent fixture of U.S. military policy: the nuclear "triad," in which the air force, navy, and army control separate nuclear delivery systems, the survivability of each being deemed essential. In seeking congressional funding, each service stressed its centrality in assuring the ability to employ atomic weapons.

Dining with Bush after the speech, Conant learned that General Gruenther wanted him to brief Pentagon planners on his ideas. Two weeks later, Gruenther confirmed that the War Department had decided to launch the parallel planning groups Conant had advocated. "My own conviction is that you have given us a very fine blue print to guide our future action," Gruenther enthused, "and my ambition is, with respect to the Joint Staff part of your plan, to follow your suggestions almost in their entirety."[102]

Conant soon learned, however, that the more radical and controversial proposals in his speech had not fared so well. Despite a personal appeal during a lunch with the defense secretary and Under Secretary Lovett on November 21, his efforts to convince Forrestal to widen public dissemination of classified atomic data had no apparent effect, though they may have influenced him later to appoint Conant to oversee a (largely fruitless) top-secret study of classification strictures.[103] Yet even that questionable measure of success was more than Conant achieved with his bold twin contentions that it was in the United States' military interest to enter into even a flawed international control plan, and that in the long run America would be militarily "very much better off" in a world without nuclear weapons or power. He probably anticipated that these propositions would fail to move administration and Pentagon officials, for they were all becoming more and more reliant on atomic weapons, but even his closest nuclear collaborators, Bush and Oppenheimer, found these assertions difficult to swallow. "Your two points ... brought me up short and I have not quite recovered," wrote Bush, explaining that he could not for the life of him see the advantage of the United States entering into an agreement that might break down when implemented. Of course, he added, their disagreement on this point was probably moot since there existed "little chance" that the U.S. Government or Congress would agree to an international control plan that was viewed as less than foolproof. Bush also had his doubts about Conant's second proposition, although he allowed that perhaps at some future date the United States would be better off in a world without atomic bombs or separated isotopes. "I want to get with you and argue some of the points on which I am not fully clear," he ended.[104]

As for Oppenheimer, he wrote a letter that was a model of diplomatically couched criticism. He had found the talk "wonderfully stimulating and rich" and could "well understand why it should have attracted attention in the Big City." Predictably, he strongly endorsed its calls to revamp ("re-enlighten") secrecy policy and to instigate fresh thinking on military planning in the "Superblitz" age ("the answers we have today are full of sloth and the misreading of history"). More warmly than Bush—who was "decidedly pessimistic" but "unwilling to dismiss the possibility" of an atomic agreement should the Soviets become more moderate—he also welcomed Conant's "spirit of hopefulness and open-mindedness with regard to the ultimate prospects of international control."

But Oppenheimer also registered three protests. First, he explicitly recognized the divergence in their estimation of nuclear power's potential, still believing as he did in the Acheson-Lilienthal theory that "constructive uses of atomic energy" could ultimately contribute "strength and vitality" to international control. It was "far from clear," he reminded Conant, that the industrial potential of atomic energy would remain as "trivial" as it was then.

Oppenheimer also chided Conant for blurring the distinction between a general international atomic control authority as envisioned in Acheson-Lilienthal and a "limited nuclear alliance" in which the United States would share control over atomic weapons with its political supporters. Secrecy, insecurity, and "preparations for military offensive" would dominate a limited alliance, whereas an international control agency, predicated on mutual security and free exchanges of information, could devote itself to peaceful atomic development. On balance, Oppenheimer favored a limited nuclear alliance, with the rather wan hope that it would represent a step toward full internationalization.

Oppenheimer dryly added one "very minor" final objection, flowing from their months-old dispute over whether a flawed international control effort was better than none. "It has often been our concern," he wrote, "that if we embarked on international undertakings and they collapsed, that could only mean war. In my own fumbling way I am an advocate of postponing war, at least for a little while. I should be worried about embarking on a scheme whose collapse is probable and . . . would face us with the necessity for immediate military action."[105]

Conant's quick response to Oppenheimer's critique revealed an almost Wilsonian faith in the possibility of a breakthrough in U.S.-Soviet relations, and a pragmatic recognition that political circumstances militated against such a development. Hinting that he might elaborate his ideas in a more formal memorandum, Conant clearly did not believe that his proposals were merely an "academic exercise," as Bush had implied. Envisioning a less militaristic Western alliance than the one that actually came into existence in 1949—following the Russian blockade of Berlin and other events that made U.S.-Soviet relations far more hostile—he remarked with only mild irony that if a limited atomic bloc were set up, the "right hand of welcome" should be constantly extended to the "our friends in the Soviet Union to come in and join the party." "Coupled with some generous offers on our part toward the Soviet Union, I really believe there is a chance for a grand international settlement of our outstanding troubles with that nation along these lines," he wrote.

But Conant hardly wanted to develop a reputation for soft-headedness. Convinced that "nothing can be done for the next few years anyway," he confessed that he was "not particularly anxious to push this idea even in private." Lest Oppenheimer conclude that he had "gone Utopian," Conant assured him that he had not "ascended in the stratosphere too far even in my own thinking!"[106]

Conant had taken care to keep his proposals private, but he could hardly have failed to notice the strongly negative reception that greeted the idea of a "self-denying ordinance" against nuclear power when, quite by coincidence, Cavers published his own plan for such a thing in the *Bulletin of the Atomic Scientists* the same week as the War College speech.[107] Most commentators condemned the proposal as unrealistic and unacceptable, given the international situation and the public's determination to explore atomic energy's promise. "Professor Cavers, we fear, is being academic," scorned the *New York Herald Tribune;* "unnecessarily shortsighted," the *Providence Journal* chimed in. "The public may not understand the difference between fast and slow neutrons and the part that they play in an atomic pile, but it knows what it wants," declared the *New York Times.* "From the very beginning its imagination was fired by the prospect of smokeless cities and of wheels turned in some mysterious way by the heat given off in a pile as neutrons do their work. It is willing to wait a decade or so for the development of the first big atomic central station . . . but it is not willing to wait until the scientists have decided when a moratorium on atomic power should be abandoned."[108]

Conant got a taste of this sort of reaction when he took his case to Washington for the November 21–23 GAC meeting. By then, word of his War College remarks had reached the nuclear power enthusiasts within the Atomic Energy Commission. A State Department adviser who quietly canvassed a scientific conference at Princeton in late November had found "almost no support" for a moratorium.[109] Bacher, a strong supporter of international control, remonstrated scornfully, "This is the way of the Middle Ages." And an equally appalled Lilienthal privately likened Conant's proposal to "trying to put the genie back into the bottle" and complained that it went "against the whole spirit of science." He personally conveyed his concern over lunch during a recess in the GAC sessions. Don't worry, Conant assured him, I don't plan to talk about it publicly, and anyway this is no time to propose anything in this direction, anything at all. "He certainly is right about that," the AEC chairman muttered to his diary.[110]

Conant apparently sensed that it would be futile to put much energy into promoting his moratorium scheme. When Osborn's consultants gathered on December 12 for their first session since July, most of those present spoke of the UN talks as an exercise in futility, and Conant alone pressed strongly for a serious American effort to work out the details on staffing and operating an international agency, as well as for a unilateral U.S. offer of better terms for the stages. But he did not mention the moratorium concept this time — nor did he at a subsequent session two months later.[111] A secret State Department analysis in early 1948 noted that the "most important reason" the U.S. could not accept the moratorium concept lay in the difficulties in guarding against clandestine atomic activities, but it also highlighted the future promise of atomic energy as another major reason: The appeal of an international agency remained its "positive and constructive nature," and while atomic power was not an economic necessity in the United States, American science and industry had "considerable interest" in the subject. The State Department officials asserted that a moratorium on atomic power

> would face the general philosophical objections that this was a move of retrogression rather than progress, that it might be extended to other fields of science, that the present difficulties are not due to advances in science and technology but to the destructive purposes for which they are used, that Western civilization cannot be saved by calling a halt to these advances, and that the solution must lie in the field of international relations.[112]

Conant's plan was additionally doomed by the fact that its ultimate target — the USSR — seemed bent on developing nuclear power, had never evinced the slightest interest in a moratorium, and seemed unlikely to accept its stringent inspection provisions, the State Department reported in late 1948. Proposals to prohibit peaceful nuclear energy development, claimed an article in the officially sanctioned Soviet press, were nothing more than "reactionary nonsense."[113] Passing Conant's suggested detour with hardly a glance, neither Washington nor Moscow cared to turn from the road to an atomic future.

CHAPTER 19

Secrecy and Security

Conant, Atomic Energy, and the Public

1948–1949

I am afraid we are heading toward a major national catastrophe, not through lack of information, but through false information coming from apparently reliable sources; information which will lead to both ignorance and panic.
— Letter to David Lilienthal, December 4, 1947

At the risk of shocking this audience . . . I think the time has come when in the interests of military security we should release a great deal more information to the general public . . . articles and books are . . . full of misinformation about atomic energy and atomic bombs . . . The public mind is getting confused, to put it mildly.
— Speech to National War College, September 1948

Conant's interest in the public debate over Hiroshima had stemmed from his acute concern that the unprecedented, unpredictable phenomenon of atomic weapons might render U.S. public opinion dangerously volatile. In the years thereafter, he was profoundly troubled by what he regarded as the pernicious effects of government secrecy on the public understanding of nuclear weapons and nuclear power. With security getting ever fiercer and anxiety about the Cold War mounting, in his dual capacity as Harvard's president and as an adviser to the government on nuclear policy, he continued to influence public attitudes about the bomb even as he feared that those attitudes were becoming dangerously warped.

The late 1940s marked the advent of a supremely important weapons technology that, "born secret," posed new questions and challenges to American democracy, threatening traditional ideals of public involvement in and awareness of governmental policies and decisions about issues of peace and war. How did the government and elite opinion shapers respond to the public, psychological dimension of nuclear weapons? Why was the official secrecy regarding anything about atomic power so pervasive? Were government officials motivated primarily by considerations of national security or expedience and paternalism in excluding the public from debates over nuclear policy? What efforts were made to challenge the secrecy from within the government? How did members of the tiny coterie of persons entitled to secret information react to, and attempt to influence, public discussion? What effect did secrecy have on public attitudes to nuclear power or preventive war? How seriously was talk of a preventive war taken?[1] To what extent can subsequent attitudes, assumptions, and actions be traced to the events of this period? Conant's activities in 1948-49 shed light on all these questions. Rushing between public, educational, and secret realms, alternately combating and exploiting the suffocating secrecy about nuclear energy, he labored to mold official policy on, and American society's adaptation to, atomic energy and weapons at a time when the fragile postwar peace seemed on the verge of giving way to another, still deadlier conflict.[2]

As East-West relations steadily worsened, Conant's priorities shifted. He turned to devising a strategy and philosophy with which Americans could endure the Cold War without provoking war, or, alternatively, cringing in the face of nuclear terror and prompting a collapse of national will. Amid war scares and spy scares, he worried constantly about the American public's psychological health, and the debilitating effect of atomic secrecy inside and outside the government. Dissatisfaction, even contempt, permeated his private attitude toward government public-information policies, and in particular those of his part-time employer, the Atomic Energy Commission.

That a certain tension had arisen between Conant's views on nuclear secrecy and the preferences of the AEC had become clear by the summer of 1947. With Lilienthal doing his best to stress the "peaceful atom," and getting heat from other scientists for not doing *enough* to promote cooperation with industry, by November Conant had further alienated himself from the AEC leadership with his plan for a "self-denying ordinance." Even as he called civilian nuclear power a "fraud" and "mirage" that would probably never prove cost-effective, he also criticized as inadequate the AEC's plans for reactor development, and proposed methods of speeding the process. At a GAC meeting on October 3—the day after his speech at the War College—he urged the creation of a "quick and dirty" reactor program, headed by Ernest Lawrence, the "only" man who could accomplish the job. His motive appears to have been to meet military, rather than civilian, requirements of the atomic program, and to correct the shortcomings stemming from the AEC's uncoordinated and excessive decentralization. That a skeptic on nuclear power would advocate such a program on such grounds indicates to what extent the fortunes of commercial nuclear power were tied to military rationales.[3]

Although the GAC had deferred further consideration of its statement that had caused so much dispute in July, its pessimism compelled Lilienthal to tone down his public prognostications about nuclear power, though not nearly so much as it wanted. In October he warned that large-scale peaceful uses of atomic energy were "not just around the corner, not around two corners."[4] Ironically, by then the GAC was itself moving toward a slightly less pessimistic view. By the group's meeting of November 21–23, Enrico Fermi had sharply reduced his estimate of how much it would cost to mine low-grade uranium ores. At a cost of one-tenth or one-hundredth his previous calculations, "the whole picture is changed," he believed, and Rabi thought Lilienthal's more realistic statements had accomplished the purposes of better public understanding. But Conant still strongly favored a draft statement written by Fermi and Cyril Smith over the one prepared by Oppenheimer and Rabi. Lee DuBridge described it as "more optimistic," and, puzzled, asked Conant to explain the apparent shift in his position. Conant agreed that "there had been change in the climate of opinion" since July, but it had not yet been sufficiently appreciated, he thought, that there existed no evidence to show that atomic power in a given locality could "revolutionize the social life in that area." Oppenheimer had a more mundane reason for favoring a public statement: to lower public expectations so the commission could avoid blame when the timetable for atomic power slipped beyond the short-term; Fermi wanted to dampen the "so very appalling" military speculation in the area.[5]

As the draft statements were returned for further revision, Conant aired his other motives for favoring a relaxation of the secrecy standards, both within the government and for the general public. Secrecy regulations barred important scientific data from reaching university researchers in public journals, and, in secret laboratories, even properly "cleared" physicists could not learn relevant information because of a rigid adherence to the compartmented, "need-to-know" system imposed during the Manhattan Project. Primarily, Conant wanted to facilitate pure research, a goal shared by his GAC scientific colleagues who with his ardent support had urged the AEC to fund a fellowship and scholarship program as well as general, nonprogrammatic studies "especially in the universities and other research establishments."[6] Excessive classification hampered the basic research underpinning the development of future weapons systems, Conant and the other scientists argued, and thus actually damaged long-term national security. So in October the GAC recommended that research on thermonuclear weapons, including the physics of tritium, be downgraded from "Top Secret" to "Secret," thereby permitting wider distribution of classified scientific reports on the subject. "It would be far better," DuBridge told a skeptical military official, "to have a secret weapon in a decade than a 'Top Secret' paper forever."[7]

Conant also believed that excessive secrecy obstructed vital military planning, although he cautioned that the GAC should avoid "telling the military how to run their own business."[8] Few Pentagon officials possessed the requisite security clearances to know even rudimentary facts about America's stock of atomic bombs—their number, explosive power, production rate, or anticipated future developments.[9] How could those responsible for drawing up plans and strategy for a possible war with the Soviet Union do their jobs without such information? From what he learned on the JRDB's atomic energy committee, Conant was already convinced that the tangled web of military and civilian bureaucracies, clouded by interservice rivalries, made the circulating of classified information even harder.

But Conant's deepest concern centered on what he considered to be an abysmal paucity of authoritative information on atomic power reaching the general public. This popular ignorance could lead to disaster, he feared, since an uninformed or misinformed public could hardly criticize or check the AEC's policies, let alone have intelligent opinions on national defense matters or cast votes realistically. Worse, the strict secrecy created fertile territory for rumors, scare stories, and unpredictable and potentially uncontrolled gyrations in public opinion. At the close of his War College speech, he had addressed a special plea to the secretary of defense to release "a great deal more information" on atomic matters in order to rebut the "many wild stories that appear in the daily press." Advocating relaxed guidelines for releasing information, he made a concerted effort to educate his secrecy-conscious audience. Whatever the future holds, he told the officers,

> we must be in a position to know as soon as anyone the new developments. . . . Furthermore, we must be in a position to take advantage of those new discoveries in a technical way both for industry and for military use. Now it is a strange paradox that the only way we can do that is by living in a world in which the maximum amount of information is transmitted freely on these scientific matters. . . . The only way to be prepared scientifically is to have as many excellent men of science available as can be. . . . The time has come when in the interests of military security we should release a great deal more information to the general public as well as to the scientists. . . . Articles and books are appearing almost daily that are full of *mis*information about atomic energy and atomic bombs. These documents are beginning to be dangerous. The public mind is getting confused, to put it mildly. . . . Perhaps a pronouncement from the Secretary of National Defense if he felt it possible to make one could clarify the situation to some degree. However, it may be felt that the over-all strategy of an armed truce—for that is what we are living in—cannot be revealed to the public. Yet the general lines, it seems to me, must be very evident to those who sit in the Kremlin. Indeed, perhaps all I am arguing for is that the American people be as well informed about our own alleged secrets as are those who direct Russian foreign policy. . . . I have been told that at times during the last war security was often sacrificed for speed by one side or the other with good results. When we are dealing with the peoples of a democracy—either the voters or a professional class like scientists—we may need to sacrifice some degree of security, not for speed but for confidence based on understanding.[10]

Conant was unsure about how to go about correcting the errors that arose because of oversecrecy. Under questioning at the War College, for example, he suggested that the U.S. government state officially its readiness to use atomic weapons in any conflict if "militarily advisable," yet conceded uncertainty as to whether such a statement would advance global peace and, apparently, never formally pushed the idea.[11] Similar indecision marked his views on whether the U.S. government should disclose that most sacred of secrets—the size of its atomic stockpile, whose level was far lower than the public probably assumed. The United States possessed components for two atomic bombs at the end of 1945; nine in July 1946; thirteen in July 1947; and fifty in July 1948. None of the bombs had been assembled as of April 1947.[12] Members of the GAC were acutely conscious that, as Fermi put it, America's defense system "rested on the pillar of the atomic bomb,"[13] yet few members of the public were sufficiently informed to discuss it intelligently. At least as disturbing, however, was their knowledge that disclosure of the true state of affairs might undermine whatever political or diplomatic benefit the temporary U.S. monopoly was providing.

The tension over this issue, and Conant's unsureness on how to proceed, was expressed during the GAC's debate on the afternoon of November 22, a day after he apparently suggested a "re-examining" of secrecy policies to Forrestal.[14] When Conant suggested that one method of piercing the fog of secrecy would be to disclose the number of bombs available to the U.S. government "or their size or their probable effect," DuBridge countered that this would "reveal in a general way the strength of this nation." Whereupon Conant, "on further reflection," shifted to say that while disclosing the number of bombs would not be "possible or desirable," perhaps more data concerning the effectiveness of the weapons could be released "to good purpose."[15]

And what would that good purpose be? Gen. James McCormack, the AEC's director of military applications, insisted that Pentagon planners were receiving "adequate" atomic information, but Conant asked about public involvement in "defense planned against atomic attack." Misunderstanding the question, McCormack warmly agreed that Conant had "put his finger on" a key problem—something ought to be done to design structures better able to withstand a nuclear attack! But Conant feared the bomb's impact on people's minds, not their shelters. "He was concerned," the minutes relate, "that the public, as the result of ignorance arising from secrecy, would adopt a fatalistic attitude of do-nothing in their belief of the existence of superbombs capable of wiping out a large community. It seemed to him that public education is presently hampered by excess secrecy, both from this viewpoint and that of the need to be realistic about the effects of present atomic weapons."

Later in the meeting, he argued that it was "dangerous to our security to have the public and the military misinformed as to the strength of this country in atomic weapons."[16] But the idea of releasing the data went nowhere.

The GAC's long-debated power statement, finally approved on November 23, outlined some of the technical and engineering difficulties in translating the theoretical basis for atomic energy into a practicable resource for industrial and civilian uses. Progress would be slow and gradual, not swift and dramatic, it warned. Unless breeder reactors were perfected—a far-off prospect—other, conventional methods of producing electricity, such as coal and gas, would remain cheaper than atomic power. Therefore, the GAC members declared, they "did not see how it would be possible under the most favorable circumstances to have any considerable portion of the present supply of the world, replaced by nuclear fuel before the expiration of twenty years."[17]

Two major speeches given by Lilienthal in late November and early December, the first to the American Education Fellowship and the second to the American Society of Mechanical Engineers, gave the AEC leader a chance to spread this cautionary message and, in the process, to mend one badly broken fence with one touchy adviser. The latter mission Lilienthal accomplished by finally praising, as a useful educational step, the Smyth Report, whose release he had criticized during his confirmation hearings as a "serious authorized breach of security."[18] Lilienthal's comment had deeply angered Conant then, and subsequent repetitions of this allegation by others had only intensified his displeasure. "I don't think we gave the Russians anything they didn't know, anything of importance," he insisted when challenged at the War College by a colonel who thought it had given Moscow a two- or three-year head start. And asked to justify the presence in the report of photographs of Oak Ridge's exterior, he snapped: "I can't imagine the Russians haven't some sort of intelligence service. . . . If they didn't pick up the looks of the outside of the plants and the approach map they would be incredibly dumb."[19]

Conant was now "enormously pleased" by Lilienthal's favorable words about the Smyth Report, which Lilienthal combined with criticism of the "illusion" that everything connected with atomic energy was a "closely held military secret." And Conant must have been pleased that the press played up his message that an electorate informed about atomic energy was essential for democracy to function.[20] But he seems to have been less than fully convinced that Lilienthal now appreciated the urgency of deflating public expectations of atomic energy's imminence or importance—and it's not hard to see why. In step with the GAC's wishes, Lilienthal told the mechanical engineers on December 2 that commercial nuclear power was "not just around the corner or anywhere near the corner," but he continued to insist that "in an industrial sense nuclear power's ultimate importance can hardly be exaggerated" and passionately exhorted businessmen and industrialists to help it develop.[21] With soaring rhetoric, he spoke of the "wholly new and almost boundless sources of atomic energy that in time will be ours," the "great advances in the conquest of disease," the "radical improvements in agriculture and in nutrition"—all of "vast significance" and achieved or on the way. "It is hardly possible to exaggerate the role of atomic energy for weapons, for energy, and for research," he declared, doing exactly that, in Conant's view.[22]

Instead of reopening a personal dispute with Lilienthal, Conant did his best to keep up the pressure by directing fire at his *bête noire* in the educational world, University of Chicago chancellor Robert Hutchins, who in a magazine article fulsomely hailed a future in which the atom would provide "the cheapest energy the world has ever known" and put hospitals out of business by curing "most human ailments . . . as quickly as they are diagnosed."[23] Alerted by Harry Smyth, who resented Hutchins's assertion that the Smyth Report had shown the way for other nations to build atomic weapons, Conant read the article "with horror" and concluded that its author was "even more dishonest than I thought possible!" and perhaps even "a sick man."[24] Blasting this "frightful" and "most disturbing" essay, Conant urged Lilienthal to use the AEC's leverage—Chicago had a contract with it to oversee the Clinton Laboratories at Oak Ridge—to calm down the pronouncements of "this self-appointed expert on atomic energy and somewhat reckless writer." In a letter of December 4 he warned: "I am afraid we are heading toward a major national catastrophe, not through lack of information, but through false information coming from apparently reliable sources; information which will lead to both ignorance and panic. In short, we need to mobilize the 'enemies of error' in a very large way."[25]

It was, Lilienthal thought, "an intemperate letter as one could receive, from so well contained a man," and reinforced his impression that Conant "hates Hutchins, in an active way." But the AEC head had been equally put off by Hutchins's article ("Such poor taste, in its tone, and so shockingly wrong in facts and inference!"), and had promptly written to Conant to say so.[26] But scarcely had he mailed the letter when Conant sent another outraged missive, this time citing a credulous *New York Times* article trumpeting radioisotopes as an agricultural breakthrough that would end hunger. "What with the exaggeration about atomic energy and atomic bombs and now the extrapolation from the use of tracer materials in biology to the enrichment of the soil," Conant wrote on December 18, "I feel that a great deal of negative education has been the product of the attempts of the first year or two to tell the American people about nuclear fuels."[27]

Nor did Conant feel that those inside the government had necessarily received a better education. If he had achieved a tenuous alliance with Lilienthal on the need to pop the overblown atomic-energy balloons—"I feel sure you are trying to correct this situation," he wrote—he remained sharply at odds with military enthusiasts who were losing patience with his caution. One project viewed by Conant as a boondoggle and by the air force as a matter of the highest national import was the nuclear-powered airplane. By January 1948 the air force chief of staff, Carl Spaatz, considered Conant's skepticism—he was reluctant to promote the project as head of the Research and Development Board's atomic energy committee as well as on the GAC—to be "a matter of very serious concern," and sought Bush's help to convince Conant of the error of his ways. Obviously exasperated, Spaatz complained that the problem of developing nuclear propulsion for the aircraft, "for some reason or other" still gave pause to Conant, who inexplicably did not appreciate the "urgency" of NEPA's development or the importance of fostering ties between the aircraft industry and the AEC. What Conant needed, Spaatz added without irony, was something "to balance his strictly scientific approach to the problem."[28]

Another project that Conant tenaciously resisted as impractical and unnecessary was radiological warfare, an idea championed by the air force and by Ernest Lawrence, who vainly made a special trip to Harvard to lobby for it after the skeptical Conant, at a February 1948 GAC meeting, turned back a recommendation to accelerate military research in that area.[29] His attitude toward plans for a nuclear-powered submarine, the navy's pet project, was also colored by disdain for what he regarded as uninformed, politically motivated overeagerness. Navy pressure to ram the project through the JRDB/CAE in mid-1947 mostly produced irritation, an emotion still evident a year later in his refusal to support a proposal by General Electric that the company abandon its work on a power reactor in favor of one intended for submarine use. Conant suspected that GE's request resulted from "military pressure," adding that his past experience with the nuclear-powered airplane had not led him to "favor military interest as a motivation when the practicality of the objective was so unclear."[30]

The GAC's first year was summed up in a report to President Truman, transmitted over Oppenheimer's name on New Year's Eve 1947. In industry, military problems, and technology, Truman was told, "the fruits of secrecy are misapprehension, ignorance, and apathy," a key Conant point, and its results had already harmed "the common defense and security." But Conant's deep skepticism about nuclear power vanished in Oppenheimer's carefully hedged formulation that atomic reactors "may, within a time which will probably not be short, and which is difficult to estimate reliably, be developed to provide industrial power, and so make important contributions to our whole technological and economic life."[31]

Although the GAC reported "great progress" in the commission's work in its year-end report to Truman, Conant as a professional administrator found much to fault in the nuclear weapons program's organizational structure. And a major impediment to improving the situation, he believed, was Leslie Groves, who seemed determined to preserve his waning influence from AEC encroachment at any cost.

Several months earlier, fed up with Groves's sniping at the commission, Lilienthal had gone to Army Secretary Kenneth Royall to urge the general's ouster from his positions as head of the Armed Forces Special Weapons

Project (AFSWP) and as military representative on the Military Liaison Committee (MLC). Before doing so, he had enlisted the support of General Eisenhower, the army's chief of staff. But the effort was doomed to be frustrated, as it became clear that Groves still had strong allies. Royall refused to push Groves off the two groups despite Lilienthal's pleas that the general's continued refusal to ease relations between the military and civilian atomic programs made it impossible for the commission to work effectively. Royall claimed that Groves was the "best-qualified man" for the job, but he also feared a political backlash if the general was forced out, since Groves had successfully managed to identify himself publicly as the military's stalwart protector of atomic secrecy and strength; to Lilienthal's disgust, Eisenhower timidly went along with Royall's edict. Lilienthal threatened to take his and the commission's complaints about Groves directly to Truman, but as the year ended Groves remained entrenched in his posts and as convinced as ever of the commission's unfitness to control the bomb.[32]

Then Conant stepped in where Lilienthal had failed. Since joining the GAC and CAE, he had grown increasingly convinced that the structure set up to oversee military atomic research had degenerated into an unwieldly, cumbersome mess; his admiration for Groves's brusque, assertive leadership of the Manhattan Project, moreover, did not extend to the general's tactics or to his views on atomic weapons in peacetime, particularly his insistence on military custody. Quietly, in cahoots with Oppenheimer, General McCormack, the GAC's military liaison, and Bush, he plotted to push Groves aside. During a special GAC meeting in Chicago in late December 1947, and in a long telephone conversation a few days later, he hashed out with McCormack the problem of streamlining the weapons research bureaucracy.[33]

Conant enlisted Oppenheimer's support, sending him a detailed "personal and confidential" analysis of the situation and the "drastic" personnel and structural changes he envisioned. It was essential, he advised, to trim deadwood from the committees, and to replace those whose personal qualities or bureaucratic loyalties hampered cooperation with energetic, able, and responsible members who could "work out a real plan for a decade involving research and development." To unclog communications within the weapons research bureaucracy, he proposed rearranging the MLC to include top-level planners from all services, and dissolving altogether the AFSWP. Groves, he stressed, "should be eliminated by all means from this picture." Conant knew these were only stopgaps, and that eventually an under secretary, "and perhaps a whole department," would be needed to handle weapons research and development. Yet, as he wrote to Oppenheimer, if the GAC and RDB could present "a united front" to the Defense Department leadership, "something important could be accomplished."[34]

On Saturday, January 17, 1948, Conant, Bush, and Oppenheimer confronted Secretary Forrestal with their case for evicting Groves, a case which accorded with advice Forrestal had been receiving from his own staff. The three representatives of the atomic establishment, Oppenheimer told Lilienthal afterward, bluntly "insisted that Groves must get out." Even Royall agreed. At the conclusion of the four-hour talk, Forrestal seemed ready to act, and a few days later, Groves announced his retirement, much to Lilienthal's relief.[35] Conant remained on ostensibly cordial terms with Groves, but his actions showed that he knew how to cut a backroom deal behind an associate's back when the need arose.

The focus of Conant's concerns about public attitudes toward atomic weapons and national security changed dramatically early in 1948. The previous fall Conant had thought that no wide-ranging settlement of differences with Moscow could occur for at least the "next few years,"[36] but as the year opened he could still, remarkably, speak seriously of negotiating an international control agreement with the Soviets. The disparity in Conant's and Oppenheimer's views on this was still evident when the two saw Osborn in New York on February 18. In contrast to Conant's willingness to walk even a "rickety bridge" with the Russians to avoid an atomic arms race, if only they would accept strict inspection, Oppenheimer told Osborn that pervasive U.S.-Soviet hostility precluded any full-fledged cooperative venture. Osborn wrote in his diary,

> Conant indicated his belief that if the Russians would extend their proposals to permit of full and real inspection and drop the proposal for prohibition first, then their plan might be better than no plan at all. In checking this with Oppenheimer on the telephone next day, Oppenheimer does not agree with Conant. He thinks that the substitute of the Russian plan — however strengthened and improved — for the majority plan would be impossible, dangerous and unacceptable in the present state of the world. He feels that the weakness of the Acheson-Lilienthal Report is that it did not sufficient[ly] define the state of the world necessary for any effective plan of control. If an ideal state of the world were attained — unlikely in our generation — then he might go along with Conant. Otherwise, [Oppenheimer considers] Conant's position absolutely untenable.[37]

For a U.S. atomic adviser even to consider accepting a *Soviet* plan at this stage was an astonishing heresy. When another Osborn consultant and Acheson-Lilienthal alumnus, Chester Barnard, learned of Conant's views a week later, his response was apoplectic. Expressing "violent disagreement" with this "folly," he complained that basing an agreement on inspection rather than joint operation was a "phantom Conant has pursued from the beginning."[38] A generation later, of course, that phantom became the basis of every major U.S.-Soviet nuclear arms control agreement. But within days, a dramatic worsening in U.S.-Soviet relations turned Conant's thoughts, like those of his countrymen, from long-range hopes of peace to possibly imminent dangers of war. In February 1948, a Communist coup overthrew Czechoslovakia's demo-

cratic government and forced Prime Minister Eduard Beneŝ to resign; though
George Kennan had predicted this, as a consolidation of Soviet control in
Eastern Europe in response to the Marshall Plan's success in Western Europe,
the clampdown immediately evoked comparisons to Hitler's occupation of the
Sudetenland a decade before. Meanwhile, worries mounted over the possibil-
ity of Communist election victories, sabotage, or other actions in Western
Europe as a next stage in Moscow's aggressive design; talks over the future of
Germany had already collapsed, leaving the country divided into Soviet and
Western zones. Desperately seeking American military protection, Britain,
France, and the Benelux nations formed a mutual defense treaty (the Brussels Pact) and looked across the ocean for support. Truman wrote to his
daughter on March 3: "We are faced with exactly the same situation with
which Britain and France were faced in 1938–9 with Hitler," and with an
enemy in the Kremlin that was "a Frankenstein dictatorship worse than any
of the others, Hitler included." Two days later, a cable from the commander of
U.S. Occupation forces in Germany, Gen. Lucius D. Clay, created new
anxiety. Clay, once quite dismissive of the danger of war, now professed to
have detected an unnameable "subtle change" in Soviet behavior and believed
that a clash could now occur with "dramatic suddenness." This alarmist cable
was quickly leaked, and the crisis tone in Washington was further darkened
by the news on March 10 of the death of the popular Czech foreign minister,
Jan Masaryk, killed in a fall—or push—from a building in Prague where he
was being detained by Communist forces. On March 11, Truman acknowledged that his faith in world peace had been "somewhat shaken," and six
days later he grimly asked Congress for passage of Marshall Plan and conscription legislation (immediate universal military training and preparations for
selective service) to help defeat the "ruthless" Soviet "design" to wipe out the
"remaining free nations of Europe."[39]

Some historians have concluded that the Truman administration manufactured, or at a minimum exploited, the March crisis to obtain congressional
passage of its legislative program; Clay's cable, in particular, is believed to
have deliberately exaggerated the danger of an imminent clash.[40] Whether
this is true or not, there can be no doubting the war scare's strong effect on
Conant. The news from Prague dashed the hopes of those who, like the
Harvard literary critic F. O. Matthiessen, had hoped that Czechoslovakia
might somehow tiptoe along the East-West fault line and unite the best
aspects of capitalism and socialism. Not only the geopolitical and ideological
but the academic aspects of the Czech action—in addition to what was
happening to the government, intellectuals, professors, and writers who were
adjudged unreliable were being summarily arrested and some killed—shook
Conant.[41] A decade before, he had hemmed and hawed about whether to
send Harvard delegates to academic festivities in Hitler's Germany; now he
acted without hesitation to pull Harvard out of a comparable ceremony in
Prague.[42] Like many other liberals and centrists, Conant also hardened his

views about American "fellow-travelers" and Communists, seeing in the conduct of the Czech Communists a brutal confirmation that Communists could not be trusted to abide by democratic rules and that attempts to collaborate with them were therefore naive and pointless. "Frankly, I think the British Labour Party is barking up the wrong tree, and likewise the Socialists in the European countries," he wrote the theologian Reinhold Niebuhr on March 12. "Just how much they are being deceived on the political front has been shown by the recent tragedy. But more fundamentally, I think they have been deceived in ideological terms."[43]

Still, Conant discerned essential differences between the threats of 1938 and 1948. He did not deviate, at least in public, from his frequently voiced conviction that the Soviets, unlike the Nazis, desired to conquer the world by ideological rather than military means. He "inclined to think," he wrote to Niebuhr, that Soviet leaders "really swallow the whole [Communist] doctrine," including the "utopian objective" of Marx's envisioned "withering away of the state," and therefore saw no need to attack the capitalist world, only to wait for its historically predetermined collapse. And Conant had no doubt that the West could outwait them, for it was precisely on this point that he perceived the "fundamental fallacies in Marx's thinking," which flowed from

the fact that Marx knew no anthropology, and neither he nor his intellectual contemporaries had faced up to the problem of human organization and motivation. I believe the official Soviet philosophy is weakest when it talks about the ultimate "withering away of the State" . . . [A]ny analysis of modern industrial society makes it clear that there must be some type of organization which has to have a collective base, and therefore, does involve the machinery of the State. Furthermore, I think that recent experience as well as all of history shows that human beings are moved by a variety of incentives. Under the transitional form of Socialism in the totalitarian state the incentive is based on the rather immediate application of force. We still live in an economy where the rewards and punishment are on a more flexible and humane basis. If we can show that it is possible to have a fluid society with a variety of social hierarchies and incentives, I think we have an answer to both present Communist practice and their utopian dreams.[44]

Since Conant viewed the Soviets as ideological competitors rather than "ruthless gangsters bent on capturing the world by military force," it followed that World War III was by no means inevitable—and calming war jitters was one of Conant's two principal public concerns during the March crisis. On March 19, two days after Truman's speech, he predicted the crisis would pass without military conflict. "Conant Sees: NO WAR, BUT ARMED TRUCE," screamed the banner headlines of the March 24 Boston Globe after he had spoken at the Boston Rotary Club. Instead of war, Conant no longer mentioned the now fanciful notion of international control but a long, ideological "armed truce."[45] His other major public effort was to urge support for Truman's legislative goals, especially passage of the European Recovery Program, which he had vocally supported since Marshall's speech at Harvard the previous June. If these measures were not enacted, Conant warned—and quickly, with the days before the Italian elections on April 18 "rapidly slipping by"—then his reassuring prophecy might not hold. "We must do all in our power," he said, "to see that the 16 nations in the European plan preserve an economy which will keep these countries immune from the virus of the Soviet philosophy; for if governments should come to power in these strategic countries which were puppets of Soviet foreign policy, I must admit that I would become a pessimist with regard to the possibility of avoiding World War III."[46]

Privately, Conant already sounded like a pessimist. In a remarkable letter written on March 19 to Vannevar Bush—who apparently destroyed the original at Conant's request but the carbon of which remained in Conant's files—he confessed alarm at the administration's failure to face up to the practical problems involved in confronting Russia militarily or to give the American people a frank discussion of strategy and tactics "during the first few months of war." In contrast to the calming public persona, *this* Conant sounded like the bellicose interventionist of 1940–41, pushing Americans to rearm. Among the ideas that Conant did not care to voice publicly was his belief that if pro-Soviet parties won in the Italian elections, U.S. armed forces should reoccupy southern Italy to assure American control of airstrips within bombing range of Moscow. Only absolute control of the Mediterranean and the secure threat of atomic retaliation might make the Soviets "stop and think" before marching to the English Channel, he calculated. Although he wrote this while Washington was actively engaging in its first major covert operation (urged by Kennan and marking the debut of the newly created Central Intelligence Agency), to assure a Communist defeat in the balloting, open U.S. military intervention in Italy in response to an unfavorable vote would have been a drastic escalation with potentially violent repercussions.[47] Yet it was not out of step with ideas being raised in the highest councils of the government, throughout which there was a mounting recognition of the importance of securing and maintaining air bases ringing the Soviet Union to assure a capability for strategic bombing.[48] A week before, the National Security Council had endorsed using U.S. military power, if necessary, to maintain a pro-American government in power in Italy and prevent a Communist takeover.[49] Kennan even proposed provoking civil war if the Communists won, so as to provide a pretext for military intervention.[50]

Conant's letter also shed light on his evolving stance on universal military training. Despite his public switch to approval of a peacetime draft, strategic nuclear bombing was still central in Conant's notion of countering the USSR militarily in Europe; rapid mobilization would be necessary only to seize and defend air bases. With the international situation at a flash point, Conant lamented what he presumed to be political timidity in an election year. In public he insisted, "I am not criticizing anyone," but went on to complain about the "inability of our leaders to be frank" on how the United States proposed to counter Russia's "three or four million men under arms." Maybe, he hoped, the politicians could speak more frankly after November."[51] But in private, to Bush, he felt less constrained. Complaining of the "tremendous amount of fuzziness" in official statements, Conant sharply criticized Truman for not taking stronger concrete measures to respond to the new, more dangerous strategic situation, and most of all for not telling the public what would be required "to make [his] threats something more than words." The flavor and substance of Conant's candid prescriptions are worth reproducing in full:

CONFIDENTIAL

Dear Van:

This is a letter for your wastebasket, or better, for the incinerator. You being the only person in the Administration whom I know well enough to blow off to, I am venturing to do what many citizens would like to do at this time, — tell the Government how to run its own affairs in a time of crisis!

After having listened to the President Wednesday, and read Walter Lippmann and other unofficial advisers, it seems to me there is a tremendous amount of fuzziness in the present planning, or at least in the exposition of the plans as far as the general public is concerned. It is all very well to talk of being prepared, mobilizing, strong from a military point of view, et cetera; but just what does this add up to in terms of strategy?

Why not explain to the people just how the military plans to meet the Russian tactics? I cannot see how Universal Military Training is the answer to the problem; certainly not for the next five years, and it now seems clear that the next five years will be crucial. Perhaps Selective Service is the answer, but I think the American people are first entitled to know why with the higher rate of pay and the changes in regulation the armed services could not get more men through a voluntary enlistment system.

But what annoys me more comes in your area as a planner from a scientific point of view. It is the failure to show the importance of our meeting on a manpower basis the Russian military potential in Europe. Our only chance of balancing their threat with an equal one is by means of an air offensive, including use of the atomic bomb. This in turn means bases, which in turn means control of the Mediterranean, which in turn means we must occupy Italy — at least the lower half — if there is a threat that a government sympathetic to the Soviet can come into power. What this all adds up to in terms of manpower is certainly something other than Universal Military Training.

The situation having deteriorated to the point it has, I should think we could begin to talk frankly about bases, strategic lines of communication, the number of men required to man the bases and hold them during the first few months of war — during which time we would presumably deliver a devastating barrage which would be the answer to the Russian march to the channel ports. Just where anybody goes after that, I do not know; but I think that knowledge on the part of the Russians that they would have to trade devastation in their own country for the privilege of marching to the channel would make them stop and think.

As I said, this is all intended for your wastebasket. It is written in dogmatic form as though I knew something about the situation, which I obviously do not. However, I am afraid the American people are going to get more and more confused unless some clear-cut statements are made about what we can and can not do in the way of military action in the next few years; and what it takes in the way of money, men and geographical positions to make these threats something more than words.

As ever, [JBC][52]

Conant's views on the draft acquired immediate significance as the country's educational establishment rushed to formulate a response to the crisis. Of course, he had been there before, having been deeply involved in public and private maneuvering about conscription legislation and student and scientist deferments before and after the United States' entry into World War II. Now he received a summons to Washington to attend an emergency meeting of the American Council on Education's Committee on the Relationships of Higher Education to the Federal Government, which was seeking a unified position on the draft.[53] Though unable to attend, Conant laid out his position in a long letter to the group's chairman. Two points stood out. One was Conant's "strong conviction" that students, like scientists, deserved no special privileges — and that any attempt by colleges to obtain educational deferments would only incur resentment. The other was that any draft laws should be designed to permit immediate full mobilization if war broke out:

> Of course, what I would like to see is a provision in the act that if we should become engaged in a war while the act was in effect, there would immediately be an over-all manpower clause evoked similar to the one which was embodied in the bill which people quarreled over towards the end of the war, and which was never passed, — a total mobilization bill, if you will. But I assume this is too much to expect at this stage.[54]

Although a strongly worded presentation by Secretary of Defense Forrestal to the Senate Armed Services Committee on March 25 requesting funds for specific military programs made him "feel a little better," Conant still anxiously awaited an "over-all strategic plan which comprises military and political objectives, and to use Walter Lippmann's phrase, limited objectives." Perhaps such a plan existed, "but if so, it has not been made clear to the public," Conant wrote to Bush on March 29. In fact, a highly classified plan did exist by the time Bush received the letter: National Security Council memorandum 7, dated March 30, concluded that to defeat the "forces of Soviet-directed world communism" the United States would embark on a "world-wide counter-offensive" employing a range of political, economic, covert, and military tactics just short of open warfare.[55] But that document was secret: Conant wished the United States government would, as soon as practical, issue a statement "to the world" declaring something like the following:

> Until such a time as there can be a frank disarmament conference between the United States and Soviet Russia, we must be in a position to protect the 16 nations in the Marshall Plan against military aggression by Russian ground forces which, according to our information, are X millions of men fully mobilized for war who could overrun Europe on short notice. To this end we insist that the Mediterranean be under our control, and we will not allow a government under Soviet domination to come into power in Greece, Italy or Turkey. To that end, we are ready to supply arms and troops to these countries to prevent this happening. (At the same time we shall do all in our power to enable these countries to develop a free and prosperous economy in a democratic society.) We are establishing bases for strategic bombing of Soviet Russia in the following places. The threat of this bombing is our way of balancing the Russian manpower. To maintain our supremacy in the Mediterranean, we need a standing army of Y men, a navy of X men, and an air force of Z men. We are prepared to consider a reduction of this balance of military power any time Russia opens up and demobilizes her own armed forces, but until that time we match strategic bombing poised to devastate Soviet industry against ground forces poised to overrun Europe.

"All of which may make no sense at all," Conant added to Bush, "and certainly not for public presentation at the present."[56]

Conant's sudden burst of armchair strategizing bespoke a new stage in his attitudes toward the Cold War. While not abandoning his contention that the conflict was essentially ideological, the crisis touched him no less than other Americans. But he was determined, at least in his public utterances, to help stabilize public opinion. It was of surpassing importance to prevent the American public from becoming "hysterical or panicky as the long years of the armed truce continue" and as a consequence produce "something foolish on the international scale."[57]

In Conant's dry lexicon, two prime examples of "something foolish on the international scale" were launching a preventive war (or sliding into an unnecessary one), and abdicating international great-power responsibilities. In either case, Conant saw irrational fear as the most likely culprit. He did not claim that masses of citizens secretly lusted for a nuclear Pearl Harbor against Moscow, only that certain ideas and emotions sowed the seeds for such a plan to sprout rapidly given the proper conditions, especially if cultivated by an organized political movement. In his typically centrist mode, Conant argued that extremes of right and left could have comparably pernicious effects. To

emphasize either the horrors of nuclear war if proposals for world government were not accepted, or the inevitability of military conflict with the
Soviet Union, only encouraged anxious Americans to search for desperate
solutions. And the two ideas in combination, Conant warned the United
World Federalists president Cord Meyer, Jr. (later, after a political conversion,
a prominent CIA official), could easily lead people who were convinced that
"we are all going to be blown to pieces if we wait more than a couple of
years," to conclude that preemptive war represented the "least of the many
evils." "You stop just short of saying if after due notice they fail to accept this
proposal, then it means war initiated by us," he noted. Meyer denied that his
organization favored force to achieve its aims, but a few putative world-
government enthusiasts, notably the British philosopher Bertrand Russell,
actually did take the position that if world government were not possible,
Moscow should be given an ultimatum to forswear atomic development or
face preventive attack.[58]

On the evening of April 28, attending a charity banquet at the Waldorf-
Astoria Hotel in New York City, Conant received an unexpected reminder
that atomic bombs were not the only weapons that threatened to trigger
dangerous emotional reactions. Following him to the dais was Brock Chisholm,
a Canadian doctor who had been a major general during the war and was, as
Conant put it in a worried letter to Bush the next day, "presumably a person
of intelligence and consequence." Dr. Chisholm's remarks terrified Conant—
for the twelve hundred persons in the audience "roundly applauded" them
after Chisholm painted a devastating portrait of the suicidal consequences of
any future war, and asserted that bacteriological warfare ("not the atomic
bomb, which he more or less pooh-poohed") could easily wipe out humanity:
"Biological warfare renders the atomic bomb childplay," Chisholm said. "Its
potentialities for destruction are vastly greater than those of the atomic
bomb. It . . . permits any small country which becomes belligerent equality
with any other country. All that is necessary is a few technicians and a few
fanatic distributors."[59]

Bacteriological or biological warfare was by no means a new subject for
Conant. After all, the National Defense Research Committee had experimented
during the war with every form of destruction known to American science,
and had authorized a major biological-warfare research effort in which two of
Conant's old college chums from Mrs. Mooney's Pleasure Palace, George
Merck and John Marquand, had been key.[60] But Conant's wartime experience
had left him unconvinced that "B.W.," as it was called, would prove a
particularly useful military weapon. When Bush likened B.W. to the atomic
bomb in a draft of his first post-Hiroshima public statement, Conant had
chided him for pointlessly confusing the issue and "play[ing] into the hands of
those who want to ignore the atomic bomb as a weapon and proceed with
defense along the old-fashioned lines."[61] To his closed-door audiences at the
National War College, he had described himself as the "[Maj. Gen. Alexan-

der] de Seversky of bacterial warfare," after the author of several articles minimizing the effects of atomic bombs.[62] When a brief flurry of press notices raised the biological warfare issue late in 1946, Conant had sought counsel from a long-time chemistry colleague, Roger Adams, now a professor at the University of Illinois at Urbana. "I am a skeptic about B.W.," Conant wrote. "But I may be wrong[;] if so I want to know it . . . if B.W. is just as compact a weapon against cities [as the atomic bomb] we have another equally bad problem."[63] Adams, also an NDRC veteran, was "astounded" to read in the papers of what he thought was still a top-secret subject, but had no information to change Conant's previous opinion: "Nothing that was done before [the end of the war] gave me the slightest promise of producing a weapon for effective distribution," Adams recalled.[64] Conant, who periodically encountered the subject inside the classified world of the JRDB, probably stopped worrying about its public impact after army chief of staff Eisenhower declared the entire subject under censorship early in 1947.[65] Since then, work had progressed behind a comfortably thick shroud of secrecy.

So the vision of a movement of Chisholms terrifying Americans into submission via lurid tales of bacteriological genocide shocked Conant into a sharp plea for action: "If Dr. Chisholm were correct on his technical facts," he wrote to Bush, "then there would be no choice but to vote for Mr. [Henry] Wallace and dismantle our present inadequate Navy, Air Force and Army. I submit," he continued, "that the United States Government has got to tell the people one way or another whether this man is totally misinformed, possibly right, or clearly correct. Any secrecy that now surrounds the development of bacteriological warfare and defense against it should be given secondary consideration." For unless an answer to Chisholm's argument were found, and quickly, "all intelligent people will end by being on Mr. Wallace's side as far as armanent and military policy are concerned." Conant had a request and a warning:

> You are the one person in a position to evaluate the whole field, with the aid of some tough-minded, unprejudiced experts. I urged you to do that in the interest of military security some time ago; now I urge the Secretary of Defense and the President to appoint a civilian committee to review the potentials of bacteriological warfare and to tell the truth to the American people. To do otherwise is to play directly into the hands of Stalin and Molotov. Dr. Chisholm's arguments are worth a fifty-group air force to the Soviet rulers![66]

Conant's sharp letter, it appears, had the desired effect. "This morning we had a meeting of the [Research and Development] Board and I read it to them," Bush wrote back two weeks later. "I realize it was written as a personal letter to me, but it hit the nail on the head so completely that I read it just as it is. I found the Board entirely in agreement with your viewpoint that a statement of some sort is now indicated." Bush intended to give Conant's letter and a few others to Forrestal with the advice that a special board be created by the president to review the entire B.W. field.[67]

When no action was taken, over the next few months, Conant followed up his earlier request. In September, in a secret speech forwarded to Forrestal, he blasted the "wild statements" about biological and other weapons.[68] A month later he reminded Forrestal: "I trust something is going to be done to knock down the wild men who talk about the destruction of the human race if there should be another war and by means not only of atomic bombs but RW [radiological warfare], BW, and various and other sundry weapons of mass destruction. Whatever happened to my plea for a frank statement from the Government about the present status of these subjects?"[69] Ultimately, Conant's persistence paid off. On March 12, 1949, the *New York Times* reported the next day on its front page, Secretary Forrestal "broke an official three-year military silence . . . on the use or discussion of the term 'biological warfare,'" and condemned "much of what had been written about the germ weapons as 'fantastic,' 'exaggerated' and 'unduly spectacular.'"[70]

On June 24, 1948, the gravest East-West crisis yet erupted as the Soviet Union imposed a blockade on West Berlin. The action capped months of acrimony and hostile incidents between the former Allies, climaxed by the initiation of a U.S.-sponsored currency reform in the American, British, and French zones of Germany (and in West Berlin) that Moscow, suddenly deprived of access to hard currency, bitterly charged was a violation of an agreement undertaken at Potsdam to treat the defeated country as a single economic unit. As the Soviets severed rail, road, barge, electricity, and food links to West Berlin, the United States, backed by Britain and France, launched a massive airlift to the besieged city; in Washington, the National Security Council debated the advisability of sending in ground troops to break the blockade and of transferring atomic bombs from civilian to military control, and dispatched B-29s to England as a sign of resolve and commitment should the standoff escalate.[71]

A new war seemed nearer than ever, and as the "Red scare" surged at home, Conant's fears increased that the national psyche might spin out of control. His treatment of international Cold War issues in his book *Education in a Divided World* showed his desire both to recognize Soviet totalitarian brutality and to explain to readers that Moscow's leaders, as devoted Marxists, did not need military victory to be triumphant. He dissented from the increasingly popular Hitler-Stalin, or Nazi-Soviet, parallel:

> I am convinced that there is little or no analogy between the Nazi menace and the Soviet challenge. The former, to my view, had to be met by force of arms because it was an immediate military threat. The latter is an ideological and political thrust supported by military means; the Russian armies hidden behind the Iron Curtain are defensive troops to support political

gains by the advanced fifth column within another nation; they are not to be used as the spearhead of the forward movement. I recognize I am being very dogmatic about a highly debatable subject. Not only will many experts on foreign affairs prove me wrong within this diagnosis, but history may prove me wrong within the next few months. However, I am bold enough to predict that, unlike Hitler, Russia will not take aggressive military action by invading a nation without an invitation from a *de facto* government. I make this prediction in July 1948, in spite of the gravity of the situation in Berlin. If Great Britain, France, and the United States are firm in their determination to hold positions recognized as just by world opinion, I doubt if the Soviets will force the issue. The proper pattern for preventing the outbreak of another global war would seem to involve readiness to answer coercion by the use of force coupled with the willingness to negotiate at any time on matters of broad policy.[72]

How did the U.S. government propose to balance strategically Russia's ability to use surplus manpower "on short notice [to] overrun Europe with her armies (which as far as we know may be mobilized to spring forward at any moment)"? Conant knew that the presidential election—"this four year oratorical hazard inherent in our system"—precluded an open discussion of the question until after November. Still, he urged the administration openly to disclose the nation's military strength, since "the Russians must have an extremely poor intelligence service" if they didn't know already. "We might as well be frank about it to ourselves and to them. We must assume the worst from the military point of view about their readiness and we must balance them quite openly with a counterplan."[73]

Moderately, and presciently, Conant predicted that, given the United States' strong support for the sixteen European nations participating in the Marshall Plan, "even a fanatic believer in the Marx-Engels-Lenin doctrine may be able to see a road block when he meets it." Once that recognition has taken place, "a frank talk" with the Soviets could take place, leading eventually to a "gradual demobilization on both sides; and the first step in this program must be the raising of the Iron Curtain . . . From gradual and open demobilization one may hope in time to come to a gradual disarmament beginning, I hope, with the atomic bomb. But, as things stand, that is a prospect at least five years away."[74]

By September 1948, Conant believed that the risk of a domestic movement favoring preventive war was "the most dangerous thing in the immediate future, outside of the Berlin crisis."[75] Demands to beat Russia to the punch were broadcast widely, and rightwing intellectuals such as James Burnham openly advocated conquering Russia and suggested that U.S. nuclear weapons were potentially useful for this purpose.[76] Then there were multitudes who did not thirst for war but were firmly convinced that Moscow was fanatically intent on taking over the globe and had to be stopped sooner or later. In the September 1948 *Harvard Alumni Bulletin,* an air force intelligence officer and reserve colonel speculated on the most likely moment for World War III in an article entitled "When Will the Shooting Start?"[77] For those who believed it only a question of when, not whether, the shooting started, logic compelled the conclusion that the U.S. government should assure that the conflict took place at a moment of maximum advantage— preferably before the USSR had atomic bombs or the capability to deliver them.

Conant elected to use his third consecutive annual speech to the National War College to make the case against preventive war. On each of his previous appearances—his only chance of the year to unwind on nuclear subjects before a large audience that was cleared to discuss them—officers had raised the option during questions-and-answers, and Conant had strongly rejected it on pragmatic grounds. "After you Superblitz Russia, what do you do then?" he had asked in 1946. Occupying Germany was hard enough, and occupying Russia would be even tougher: "You would have the question of keeping Russia Superblitzed every now and then to keep the production down." Not to mention the troubles at home: Conant estimated that "with the great mass of left-wing thinkers, twenty-five or thirty percent in the country perhaps— not communists but left-wing liberals—an attack on Russia would mean civil war." Preventive war, Conant said, would be a "counsel of complete despair."[78] Returning to the War College in October 1947, Conant cited similarly "hardboiled" considerations, but seemed a bit less steadfast in his confidence that the American people could be counted on firmly to oppose such a venture. It had been difficult to rouse the public to war in 1940 and 1941 "when the case was clear-cut," yet no one could predict what would happen when Americans learned that the Russians had atomic weapons. In any case, even to save American cities from destruction, it didn't strike Conant that a preventive war was "the best approach to the problem, certainly not for the present."[79]

In 1948, instead of waiting for questions, Conant got quickly to the heart of the matter. Three alternatives to acknowledging the inevitability of Soviet atomic acquisition existed, he said: international control was a "closed chapter"; world government was a "panacea"; that left preventive war—the " 'smash 'em now' " policy, whose supporters said, "in effect, We are now rearmed, Europe is strong, let's take on the Soviets before they get the bomb rather than wait and be destroyed by their surprise attack." The aggressive right-wingers, in turn, were "given support unconsciously by those utopians who are advocating an immediate world government." World federalists, Conant said, "paint a black picture of the atomic age with an avowed purpose of scaring people into accepting their remedy," but actually were "more likely to be the agents of a panicky rush into a deliberate attack on the Soviet Union."[80]

Rather than arguing from a frankly moralistic point of view—that preventive war was *wrong*—Conant tried to turn the tables on supporters of preven-

tive war "who pride themselves on being realistic." Conant recited his familiar
theme that the Soviet leaders "do not dream of a military victory over the United
States which would result in an occupation and control by Russian commissars,
but rather a revolution in this country which would result in a totalitarian
socialistic state with native American rulers." Therefore, he continued,

> the over-all strategy of the United States must be aimed primarily at preserv-
> ing the type of free society we have inherited from the past and now enjoy.
> Our open society rests on a fundamental moral basis, and once we destroy
> this basis we have destroyed the essence of this nation. Therefore, for us to
> develop a Machiavellian foreign policy culminating in our launching a sur-
> prise attack on the Soviet Union or declaring war for the sole purpose of
> waging destruction would negate the very premise on which our culture
> rests. In short, it seems to me the moral argument against a preventive war is
> by no means soft-headed, but rather a realistic appraisal of the fundamental
> issue which divides the world.[81]

When a copy of Conant's speech reached Secretary of Defense Forrestal,
he was struck by its fervent warning against the rise of a "preventive war"
movement, and wrote to Conant "to inquire whether you would object to my
making use" of his words. He, too, detected "a growth, more among the
civilians than among the military, of this thesis," he explained, "and it seems
to me it needs to be dealt with."[82]

Forrestal had more in mind than flattery. He contacted Edward Weeks,
editor of the *Atlantic Monthly* and a mutual friend of Conant's and Forrestal's,
and urged him to publish the broadside against preventive war in that
influential journal, whose current number featured an excerpt from *Education
in a Divided World.* Forrestal believed that the American press "should be an
instrument of our foreign policy," and this was not the first time he had
moonlighted as a literary agent in the service of U.S. foreign and military
policy: a year earlier, he had helped midwife the publication in *Foreign
Affairs* of Kennan's epochal "X" article, a paper initially prepared for the then
navy secretary's "private edification."[83]

Conant was understandably gratified by this support from such an authoritative quarter. "I am delighted to hear that you are going to attack the
preventive war theory," he wrote Forrestal on October 27. "Coming from the
Secretary of Defense it would be heartening to many."[84] By then Conant had
already heard from Weeks. Dreading from dismal experience the red tape
required to get his War College remarks formally declassified, Conant sent
Weeks a speech incorporating the preventive war arguments he was already
planning to deliver that night in Memorial Church to commemorate the
"300th anniversary of the Cambridge Platform of Church Discipline"—or what
this unshakably rationalist chemist contemptuously described as "a rather
stupid celebration arranged by the Unitarians and the Congregationalists."[85]

In tune with the theme of retrospective introspection, Conant used the chance "to amuse myself in connection with my avocation in the 17th century" and likened the Americans' current dilemma to that of Cromwell's New Army scrapping its way to victory in the English civil war. More fundamentally, Conant fleshed out his moral philosophy, in addition to recapitulating some sections from his War College speech. He still clung dearly to the distinctions between ethics or morality in wartime and peacetime, and dwelled on the seeming impossibility of maintaining a "moral basis of personal freedom" in a "world of force."[86]

In fact, Conant was dealing with the essential contradictions and tensions between moral ends and immoral means that bound his nuclear career, and strapped him into iron-bound rationalizations to justify his actions. For the atomic bomb cast the starkest shadow on the questions he now raised: "How can we reconcile the doctrine of military force—the idea of killing men in war—with any moral purpose? How are we to accommodate our thinking and our emotional reactions to an abomination of war on the one hand and a love of freedom on the other—when, as a matter of history, freedom has so often emerged from the successful use of force?"

The foundation of Conant's moral framework was his "deep-seated conviction that war is not always wrong but is always morally totally different from peace." In amplifying his doctrine, he performed the neat trick of criticizing Communists and (implicitly) preventive-war advocates simultaneously:

Only those who believe that they are divinely led or that history is on their side can maintain that the issue between themselves and their opponents demands that the rules of war should operate even in time of peace. Only fanatics who regard political action backed by force as a kind of holy war can maintain that the end justifies the means. The fact that this same doctrine must be invoked in time of war by all but pacifists should not confuse us. Freedom has more than once been won by war, but once won it can only be protected by adherence to those moral principles which were repudiated in its achievement. The distinction between the ethics of war and peace, I submit, is a fundamental postulate of Western ideas of democracy and freedom. It is of the utmost importance to emphasize this distinction in these confused and gloomy days.

Leaping out from Conant's distinction is the question: Where does a cold war, neither war nor peace, fit into this moral scheme? Significantly, he conceded implicitly that the struggle with Moscow forced a moral standard that was lower than the peacetime one for judging international conduct: because of the importance of the moral distinction between war and peace, he "object[ed] to the use of the words 'Cold War' to represent the present struggle with the Soviets: Something more than a matter of words is involved when we insist that we are living not in a cold war but in a period of an armed truce."

Conant quickly set about whipping the talk into publishable form, and within weeks had mailed a draft to Weeks, who quickly approved publication without a single cut. Weeks sent a copy of the proofs to Forrestal, and warmly told Conant in December that the defense secretary considered it "a valuable contribution to the nation's thinking on the vital subject it treats." Weeks himself told Conant the piece was "the most far-reaching contribution you have yet made to the *Atlantic,*" a judgment he backed up by commissioning a dramatic artist's rendering of a pensive Conant contemplating a fiery night-time atomic explosion for the cover of the magazine's January 1949 issue.[87]

"Force and Freedom," reprinted in full in the *Washington Post,*[88] was a milestone in Conant's struggle to relate his moral philosophy to the problems of atomic warfare. Forrestal enthusiastically recommended the article as the definitive word on the preventive-war thesis, describing it as "possibly the best presentation of the way any thoughtful person must react toward such an idea."[89] Press commentary was also favorable, and Conant's reputation grew as an important national articulator of controversial themes or partially gestated consensuses. "It is quite possible that when looked at in retrospect this essay may appear as significant as William James' 'Moral Equivalent of War,'" wrote a Vermont paper. " . . . It is an authoritative reply to the Devil, and that answer is a resounding 'No.'"[90]

Conant remained committed to curbing what he regarded as unwarranted optimism toward the future of civilian nuclear power. Only one allusion to atomic energy can be found in his most prominent public writing of this period—his book *Education in a Divided World*—but his reference to its "somewhat dubious and far distant prospects" expressed the view he was forcefully arguing behind closed doors.[91] It was, he argued, "atomic lunacy" that no one had convincingly demonstrated a need or utility for civilian atomic energy, and yet the public resolutely failed to appreciate the necessarily slow rate of progress involved in its development. "The combination of secrecy, technical uncertainty, and difficult physics has brewed a veritable witch's cauldron of atomic misinformation," he told the War College in 1948.[92] "On no subject since we were told that the stock market would never crash has there been so much nonsense said than about atomic energy," he told fellow educational leaders that September, adding a dig at the Republican presidential candidate: " 'The Golden Age of Atomic Energy'—I see Mr. Dewey has fallen for some of it."[93]

Conant did his best—and it was quite successful—to transmit his skepticism to the country's educational establishment and to influence the nation's curricula. That the educators would turn to Conant, the only one among them intimately involved in nuclear policy, is hardly surprising. Conant helped the NEA's Educational Policies Commission to develop guidelines for a national educational program on atomic energy, after first scorning the government's efforts. "[M]ay I say that I am not at all in sympathy with the educational policy so-called of the Atomic Energy Commission," he wrote William Carr, the EPC's secretary, who had asked Conant to head a committee on the subject. "Just between ourselves, I have never understood what they were trying to say or the point of a great deal of their talk. So you will find me as usual in a very skeptical mood. This warning perhaps is unnecessary, but it will prepare you for my very critical appraisal of nearly everything concerning education that I have heard or seen coming from the Commissioners individually or collectively!"[94]

When the educational subcommittee met on March 11, 1949, Conant's viewpoint dominated their conclusions:

1. The importance of atomic energy is great, but it has been exaggerated both with respect to its use as a weapon and its use in industrial developments.

2. It is estimated that the cost of the fuel is perhaps five to ten percent of the total expense in the delivery of electric power. Hence, if atomic fission could supply fuel at no cost whatever, the consequent cost of power would not be dramatically changed.

3. Since the United Nations discussions of atomic energy have reached an apparent stalemate, and since domestic control of atomic energy, research, and development is settled at least for the time being, it appears opportune to review information policies about atomic energy.

4. It is necessary to make a distinction between those things that can be stated for sure, or reasonably surely, and those which are simply guesses. The confusion of established facts with speculation is a serious hazard to public understanding and to the development to critical thinking. Facts, informed opinion, and phantasy should be clearly differentiated.

5. No one need be criticized for the present state of affairs, but it is important to develop a more critical approach to education and public information about atomic energy. The schools should not become automatic adjuncts to the "informational" programs of federal government agencies. . . . [95]

Precisely at this juncture, in early 1949, after two years of carping at the absurdities of official atomic secrecy, Conant received what appeared to be a perfect opportunity to do something about it: an invitation from Secretary of Defense Forrestal to chair a top-secret panel of prominent civilians who would explore the whole issue of secrecy in relation to atomic weapons and other weapons of mass destruction, and advise the government on ways to improve the system.

CHAPTER 20

The "Fishing Party"

The Conant Committee
on Nuclear Information Policy

1949

Why is it necessary, because you spend public money, to go out and blah, blah all over the country about these bombs?
— Senator Tom Connally of Texas to AEC
Chairman David Lilienthal, 1949

I believe that this report may serve you in two ways. First, as a sampling of high-level, intelligent judgment regarding the advisability of releasing substantially more detailed information; second, as a possible protection to you in the event that pressure again builds up on you to release such information.

If the latter eventually should take place you could, if you wished, point out that you had secured the advice of this group of well-known representative citizens, who were given full access to all information available in coming to their conclusions on this subject.
— Secretary of Defense Louis Johnson to President Truman,
October 31, 1949

If ever an information policy needed an outside review, this was it. To the public the entire subject of nuclear weapons remained shrouded in mystery, secrecy, and rumor, while inside the government a maze of classification impeded the flow of information even among persons responsible for dealing with atomic matters. The decision to review the secrecy policy was taken only under duress and at a time when the government's attitude to public involvement in nuclear decision making was characterized by paternalism, exclusion, and just a hint of nervousness, all of which were evident in the most authoritative policy statement yet issued on the subject. According to National Security Council 30, a top-secret directive approved in September 1948, public debate or decision on nuclear policy—on, for example, whether

or in what circumstances to use atomic weapons—could not be risked because
it "might have the effect of placing before the American people a moral
question of vital security significance at a time when the full security impact
of the question had not become apparent."[1] So the creation of the "Fishing
Party," as Conant's top-secret committee was code-named, was due to the
government's—and its chief executive's—reluctance to foster public debate
on a "moral question of vital security interest." Ironically, the dispute arose
over a document produced by a group of which Conant was initially supposed
to be a member: the civilian Joint Chiefs of Staff Evaluation Board, which
had monitored Operation Crossroads, the U.S. atomic weapons tests at Bikini
Atoll in the Pacific Ocean in July and August 1946. (Conant had turned down
appointment to the board in order to concentrate on the Acheson-Lilienthal
report.) Out of the JCS Board came a classified report assessing the tests'
military implications. Though a version of the report had been approved for
public release by the JCS and the Atomic Energy Commission in late 1947,
the government had balked,[2] and declassified documents now explain why:
the Truman administration sat on the Bikini report because of its explosive
political content rather than any dangerous technical data.

The Bikini evaluation panel first painted a bleak picture of the devastation a surprise atomic attack could cause, predicting that atomic bombs could
"not only nullify any nation's military effort, but can demolish its social and
economic structures and prevent their reestablishment for long periods of
time." If used in conjunction with biological weapons or other weapons of
mass destruction, atomic bombs could quite possibly "depopulate vast areas
of the earth's surface, leaving only vestigial remnants of man's material
works." Given the bomb's tremendous destructive power, the side that struck
first stood to gain a decisive advantage—an advantage that the United States
could not afford to lose.

That conclusion led the JCS Evaluation Board, in turn, to call for a
"revision of our traditional attitudes toward what constitute acts of aggression
so that our armed forces may plan and operate in accordance with the
realities of atomic warfare." In perhaps its most politically sensitive recommendation, the panel urged Congress to enact special legislation to circumvent the Constitutional provision vesting in Congress the power to declare
war—a provision rendered anachronistic by the imperatives of the nuclear
age. A new law should be passed, the report stated, giving the president the
authority to unleash a first-strike attack against any nation "preparing an
atomic weapon attack upon the United States." To keep the legislation
up-to-date, the board suggested that Congress periodically redefine what
would meet the standard of an "aggressive act" and thus trigger an American
attack.[3]

The Joint Chiefs of Staff, who evidently saw no harm in stressing the
need for urgent development of all forms of military hardware and bolstering
the military's role in policy making, presented a ready-for-publication copy of

the report and an accompanying press release to Secretary of Defense Forrestal in January 1948, with the caveat that certain portions, including the proposal for a revised definition of aggression, were "of a political nature and thus beyond their purview. . . . "[4] But both the State and Defense Departments gave the idea of releasing the report a frosty reception, and on April 6, following a War Council session at which the Bikini report was "extensively considered," Forrestal forwarded a copy to Truman with the recommendation that it "not be released at this time." The hawkish defense secretary, whose own zeal for security had been expressed a week before when he requested a National Security Council study on the danger of Communist subversion in the United States in the event of war,[5] cited objections by State Department officials, who were said to believe the report "might be misinterpreted both here and abroad, and considered as a preface to some brusque action which we do not, in fact, intend." Referring to the JCS position, Forrestal noted that while the service heads considered the report "suitable" for release from "a purely military standpoint," they had "emphasized that there were non-military considerations which should be taken into account before making a final decision to publicize all or any portion of it."[6] There the report rested, in limbo, until Bradley Dewey, a member of the JCS Evaluation Board, wrote an article in the December 1948 *Atlantic Monthly* highly critical of government secrecy.[7]

A year before the magazine article appeared, Dewey, an industrialist who had directed the wartime rubber program and chaired a JCS study on guided missiles, had warned Karl Compton, head of the JCS Evaluation Board and chairman of the National Military Establishment's civilian-military Research and Development Board (RDB), that he refused to be silent on atomic-policy issues if the Bikini report were indefinitely suppressed. His article finally forced into the open a dispute that had been simmering internally in government circles since the JCS submitted its final report in June 1947.[8] In revealing to the public that the report was being kept under seal, it put the administration on the spot—and triggered the creation of the "Fishing Party."

"Information has been sleeping in the White House, gathering dust there for many months—information which is vital to the development of an atomic weapons policy and its acceptance by the American people," Dewey told the *Atlantic*'s readers. He also pinpointed an issue noted by NSC-30 but by no means resolved. "If the United States is forced into another war," he asked, "will we use our atomic weapons, and to what extent will they help to restore peace?"

"There is no clear, authoritative answer to these questions," he added. "Three years and more have passed since the first atomic bomb was launched against Hiroshima; yet the United States has no high policy—that is, no publicly proclaimed and endorsed policy covering its use of atomic energy in war." To address widespread "fears and uncertainties and anxieties which only facts can dispel," Dewey called on the Truman administration to release the necessary information, including that contained in the Bikini report, for public discussion and approval of atomic policy. "The American people must participate in this policy, must accept it and be willing to support it," he concluded. "To do this they must have the facts which have been kept from them by the White House."

Support for a U.S. declaration of willingness to use atomic weapons now came from Vannevar Bush, who wrote to Forrestal on December 20, 1948, in response to his inquiry on how best to handle the controversy stirred by Dewey's article.[9] Bush, who had recently left the JRDB to concentrate on the presidency of the Carnegie Institution, saw two main advantages in an official American statement on policy for employing atomic (as well as biological, chemical, and radiological) weapons. First, "there is a good deal of unreasoning fear in this country and we are likely to do strange things when we are fearful. I believe that a factual statement about the possibilities and limitations of these weapons would tend to quiet fears rather than otherwise, would tend in fact to replace unreasoning terror with a calm determination to face unpleasant facts."

The second aspect of the issue, Bush continued, involved

> the very important task of clarifying national policy in regard to the use of new instrumentalities. There is not the slightest question in my mind that if we were attacked, or if freedom-loving peoples elsewhere were attacked by a powerful aggressor and we came to their support, we would use atomic bombs. We would do so reluctantly, and primarily against military targets, but we would use them. The danger is that we might hesitate, use them only in extremis, and use them too late.

Bush predicted that U.S. public opinion would support a policy explicitly favoring the use of atomic weapons "if necessary to protect our freedom." He added that "if this were known to be our position, and if it were known that this had the full support of the American people, it would greatly aid to preserve the peace of the world."

Though asked initially to comment simply on the advisability of releasing the Bikini report—an action the Carnegie president favored, though he had qualms about Truman's appearing to release it solely because of Dewey's article—Bush raised the level of discussion by asking for a document of national policy. He suggested gathering a small and distinguished group of "five or six well-trusted individuals" (the matter was "altogether too flammable for more") that would "gather without fanfare to examine all of the pertinent technical information and the like and prepare in consultation with government officials a document" for the president "summarizing the situation for his benefit." What the president did with the report would be up to him, but Bush did think it evident that if it were "sufficiently wise and so regarded by the President" he would use it for "other purposes than merely his own enlightenment" and release it or a modified version to the public or Congress. To chair the group, Bush suggested Conant, "for I believe there is no better qualified man from the standpoint of sound judgment."

Bush's suggestion apparently found favor with Forrestal, who knew that during the winter of 1948–49 charges of excessive secrecy were mingling with allegations of insufficient security. For example, Lilienthal's release of a detailed report on AEC activities had provoked howls of protest from the powerful congressional Joint Committee on Atomic Energy (JCAE). "Why is it necessary, because you spend public money, to go out and blah, blah all over the country about these bombs?" asked Democratic senator Tom Connally of Texas. Several senators complained to Truman that too much information had been released. Controversy also flared anew over the granting of AEC fellowships to scientists whose backgrounds some commentators deemed too left-wing. At the other extreme, the influential JCAE chairman, Democrat Brien McMahon of Connecticut, wondered whether it might make sense for the government to disclose the size of the U.S. atomic stockpile in order to facilitate intelligent public discussion; Truman quickly vetoed the idea.[10]

These events formed the backdrop to the War Council meeting of February 8, 1949. With Forrestal's and Truman's approval, the council decided to establish the ad hoc committee suggested by Bush; Conant would chair it.[11] On February 14, Forrestal instructed RDB chairman Compton to

> call together a small group of private individuals which, without any public-ity whatsoever as to its formation or purpose, will prepare recommendations for the War Council as to:
>
> (a) The information which should be released to the public concerning the capabilities of, and defense against, the atomic bomb and weapons of biological, chemical and radiological warfare;
>
> (b) Such other related questions which I may refer to it.

Absent from Forrestal's directive, though not beyond the reach of an ambi-tious or unified committee, was Bush's idea for a statement of policy concern-ing the willingness of the United States to use these weapons; but the latitude available to Conant's committee to deal with broad policy issues was evident, since each of the eight members selected (plus Conant) was given a copy of Bush's letter to Forrestal as well as a background memorandum from Compton outlining the events leading to the creation of the group and the competing arguments on the subject of releasing information.[12]

In any bureaucratic exercise in which a bristly topic gets dumped into the lap of an ad hoc committee, the power to choose membership can predeter-mine the outcome. The "Fishing Party" is a classic example of this axiom, for its composition destined the group to frustration and stalemate. For Lilienthal, the subject matter itself seemed impervious to rational solution. "It is doubtful," he memoed his fellow commissioners after learning of the panel's creation, "how much good comes from these hashings and rehashings of problems that can never be 'solved' by any formula or report, since there are no objective criteria that can be developed to cover these matters, and since public opinion and Congressional opinion, are the final arbiters."[13]

Forrestal, Bush, and Compton seem to have intentionally balanced advocates and opponents of a liberalized information policy and firmly excluded radicals of any stripe: the middle-aged white males chosen for the "Fishing Party" shared high-level status in the academic, business, or political worlds, membership in elite social establishments like the Cosmos and University clubs, and, in most cases, previous experience in government or advisory posts. There was no "man in the street"—the person whose opinion was the ultimate target of nuclear information policy. Joining Conant were: Isaiah Bowman, president of Johns Hopkins University; Erwin D. Canham, editor of the *Christian Science Monitor;* John Foster Dulles, then a New York lawyer who was to serve a brief Senate term in the second half of 1949; Eisenhower, then president of Columbia University; Crawford H. Greenewalt, president of E. I. duPont Nemours and Company; James L. Morrill, president of the University of Minnesota; the industrialist Arthur W. Page; and Charles A. Thomas, vice president of Monsanto Chemical. To assemble this busy crew for periodic meetings and assure that they actually fulfilled their task, the Pentagon's advanced planning unit loaned Lt. Col. Edwin F. Black to be the group's chief staffer.[14]

The "Fishing Party"'s first outing was a briefing by Pentagon officials on current and projected weapons capabilities. On Thursday, April 7, 1949—three days after the signing of the North Atlantic Treaty formally committed the United States to the military defense of Western Europe—the panel convened in Room 3E 679 of the Pentagon. Conant and Black, on the basis of what they heard that day as well as "subsequent individual consultations with qualified experts," then drew up a five-page, single-spaced working paper intended to "frame a reasonable estimate of the capabilities of, and defenses against," atomic, biological, chemical and radiological weapons.[15]

Though expressly not an official Defense Department statement—perhaps due to a reluctance to be pinned on chancy predictions, doubts about modifications by Conant, or both—the capabilities paper merits close inspection for the clues it provides to the then current projections of the U.S.-Soviet atomic weapons balance, of the ability of each country to withstand atomic attack, and of trends in advanced military hardware. In its section on the atomic bomb, the paper estimated that in the next ten years it was "conceivable that within this period Russia might accumulate a stockpile of approximately 100 atomic bombs, although those who are thoroughly familiar with the production problems consider this a maximum and believe that the actual figure will probably be considerably less."[16] It dismissed claims by "alarmists" that a

Soviet surprise atomic attack would cause the "destruction of all our major cities and the killing of 40 million civilians," declaring that a "more rational statement of the resulting damage would probably lie between 1 and 5 million casualties, and from 3 to 10 key areas destroyed. Obviously, such an attack would result in a severe blow to the warmaking capacity of the United States, but it certainly would not be decisive, particularly if morale remained high."

Similarly reassuring predictions were made on the presumption of likely improvements in air defense techniques — which might force even a surprise attacker to "launch up to 10 atomic bombers to insure that at least one delivers its bombs successfully on the designated target" — and on what were judged the slim chances that intercontinental missiles would materially alter the situation: "It appears unlikely that within the next 10 — or even 20 years — new carriers, such as intercontinental controlled rockets, will greatly alter the capabilities of the offense. On the other hand, if a proper effort is made in the development of a ground-to-air missile, it should be possible within 10 years to make it prohibitive for an enemy, except in an initial surprise attack, to bomb adequately defended critical installations." The report also pooh-poohed the idea of thermonuclear or hydrogen bombs:

> Talk of superbombs of the order of magnitude of 50 or 100 times more powerful than the Nagasaki bomb are not based on fact. There is no evidence that within the next 10 years the effectiveness of our atomic bombs will be improved by anything more than a factor of 3 or 5 times that of the Nagasaki bomb. This applies not only to our own weapons, but also to any which might be produced in the USSR.

Still, the paper conceded there was "no escape" from the conclusion that, barring some "strikingly effective" improvement in air defenses, "it would be possible for Russia to strike a severe blow at our civilian economy and destroy a number of key industrial or administrative centers within the United States." Just how nuclear weapons would affect the course and outcome of a World War III could not be known, of course, but the group hazarded some rough scenarios, predicated on a Pearl Harbor–like opening strike:

NUMBER OF ATOMIC BOMBS DELIVERED ON TARGET	CAPABILITY
10	Neither the United States nor Russia would be in a position to do much damage to the other. However, this number would permit Russia to launch a heavy, but indecisive, attack on Great Britain.
Somewhere between 10 and 100	Russia could render Great Britain completely incapable of any further war effort.

Both Russia and the United States could strike a serious, but indecisive, blow on the other's warmaking potential.

Somewhere between 100 and 500	The effect on either the United States or Russia of an initial attack of this magnitude would probably be so great as to prevent any effective continuation of an offensive war effort.
More than 500	The number of bombs delivered on target which would be required to completely destroy Russia's capacity to wage war, except on a guerrilla basis, may well exceed 500. In the case of an attack on the United States, an even larger quantity than that required for the USSR appears indicated. A more accurate estimate of this upper limit would require extensive study. There are so few facts to go on that not even an approximate figure can be ventured at this time.

What stands out most strikingly in these predictions is their underestimation of the future rate of Soviet atomic bomb production and the pace of technical advances such as the hydrogen bomb and intercontinental ballistic missiles; the paper also grossly miscalculated the flow in the offensive-defensive balance, opting for defense when offense was to dominate the arms race for three decades.[17] The desire to deflate "alarmist"—if ultimately more accurate—public speculation seems also to have influenced the optimistic calculation that in a surprise attack with 100 atomic bombs the Soviet Union could inflict no more than "1 to 5 million casualties, and from 3 to 10 key areas destroyed," and in the sharply negative tone of the section dismissing the possibility of a hydrogen bomb.

The paper's pessimism about rocket delivery vehicles also showed a curious complacency among the presumably well informed. Like Vannevar Bush's book *Modern Arms and Free Men,* published a few months later in 1949, which doubted the rise of intercontinental missiles "for a long time to come . . . if ever," the Conant committee document doubted that new carriers would "greatly alter the capabilities of the offense" prior to 1970. In fact, the first tests of ICBM would be carried out by both the U.S. and Soviet Union by 1958.[18]

As for the H-bomb, which both the United States and Soviet Union would develop by the mid-1950s, the paper's sharply negative prognosis reflected Conant's fervent opposition to the idea on both technical and moral grounds, and foreshadowed his stand in the subsequent secret debate that occurred after the first Soviet A-bomb was detected. Conant's strong views on the subject had also surfaced in March 1949, shortly after the "Fishing Trip"'s formation, when Lieutenant Colonel Black went to Cambridge for dinner at 17 Quincy Street to be filled in on his new assignment. Black vividly recalled a lengthy tirade: "I got the impression that [Conant] wanted to squelch what he considered to be a scientifically unsound concept. He had a preconceived notion that the hydrogen bomb was unfeasible and he was determined to shape the committee's report in that direction."[19]

The paper's assessments of other weapons of mass destruction also showed a desire to slap down "alarmist" predictions that might upset public opinion. Biological warfare remained, despite "rapidly accelerating" scientific advances, "nowhere near as effective as the atomic bomb" from a military standpoint; its "chief danger," the paper stated, was "clandestine employment" through deliberate infection of crops and livestock or the spreading of "debilitating diseases through the contamination of nationally marketed food staples or metropolitan water supplies." Even if the enemy tried to do this, however, the damage "should be no greater" than the toll exacted by smallpox, yellow fever, and other more orthodox wartime scourges. Thus, the "current crop of fantastic statements made about biological warfare are clearly gross exaggerations of any potentialities that now lie above the horizon of scientific knowledge." Radiological warfare, while useful for "area-denial purposes," was outclassed by the atomic bomb and "can hardly be regarded as an instrument of mass destruction, particularly since radioactivity is easily detected and it should be possible to arrange for the evacuation of a contaminated area within a reasonably short time." The report commented only cautiously about the biological and genetic effects of radioactive fallout, urging further study, but noting that one investigation had concluded that "the extent of such undesirable effects would be small." Despite advances, chemical weapons, too, could not challenge atomic bombs, and "would still be used to accomplish tactical rather than strategic ends."

From this analysis, the report deduced that for the next ten years "any attack by Russia on the United States calculated to inflict the maximum damage to our industrial centers or to decimate our population would, for maximum effect, certainly be based largely on the use of atomic bombs." Regardless of whether Washington or Moscow launched a first strike, one bomb in three was likely to reach its target. While conceding a large degree of uncertainty, the report reflected the Pentagon's confident projection that "our ability to successfully deliver atomic bombs should be higher than that of the USSR because of the superior training and equipment of our strategic bombing forces and the distribution of our advanced bases."

With this rather provocative and speculative document as a basis for discussion, the Conant committee set to work in the spring of 1949. But after two meetings, the group found itself split down the middle. "Two opposing points of view have been expressed," Conant wrote Compton on July 22, 1949, "which stem from such entirely different philosophies regarding the release of information that it seemed unlikely they could be resolved by subsequent extended discussion." Favoring the release of atomic data in some way were Conant, Canham, Morrill, Page; arguing for a restrictive policy were Dulles, Bowman, Greenewalt, Thomas, and Eisenhower. Rather than producing an "emasculated compromise report," Conant explained to Compton, the two opposing factions submitted statements explaining their positions.[20]

Those against any public declaration on the capabilities of atomic or other new weapons argued:

a. As far as has been determined, there appears to be no public demand for additional official information of this sort. In their opinion, the position taken by certain well-known and probably well-meaning pressure groups who have been clamoring for releases of atomic energy information do not spring from any general public sentiment in this regard and should, therefore, be ignored. The public would seem to be more concerned lest their officials release too much classified information, rather than too little.

b. Any official statement of this nature would set a precedent for subsequent official releases containing information as to the over-all status of our national security.

c. From the standpoint of the existing world situation and general trends in the field of international negotiations, the release of such a statement at the present time would be ill-advised.

d. It was felt by some of the members that the very nature of these weapons permit such a wide variation in estimates of their capabilities, that even a carefully reasoned statement attempting to narrow the area of uncertainty might have a very disturbing effect on the general public and could be misinterpreted by pressure groups in support of any extreme position which they were currently advocating.[21]

Notably missing from this list is any indication that they were worried that the Soviet Union might derive military benefit from the release of data under consideration. Rather, the majority took the elitist view that the government has no obligation to inform citizens so that they may act intelligently in public affairs. The observation that the "public would seem to be more concerned lest their officials release too much classified information, rather than too little" may have been accurate, but would the attitude have been the same if it were known the government was hiding information not from Moscow, but from its own people because it did not trust them? How else to explain the fear that "even a carefully reasoned statement . . . might have a very disturbing effect on the general public and could be misinterpreted by pressure groups in support of any extreme position they were currently advocating"?

Generally endorsing this majority stand were four prominent public figures whose views were sought out by the committee: Secretary of State

Acheson; the powerful Republican chairman of the Senate Foreign Relations Committee, Arthur H. Vandenberg; former Supreme Court justice Owen J. Roberts, now dean of the University of Pennsylvania Law School, and the previous year a member of the AEC's Personnel Security Review Board; and Reverend Henry P. Van Dusen, president of Union Theological Seminary in New York.[22] Between July 7 and 19, Black had showed each the capabilities paper.

Their reactions, a snapshot of high-level views, exemplified the widely held belief that the American public didn't need to know, didn't want to know, and couldn't be trusted with the details of the atomic weapons program then being assembled. None of the four recommended a comprehensive public release; in fact, noted Black, "they were unanimous that the fewer people who saw this document, the better." Roberts thought the best idea would be to "file" the paper, while Van Dusen and Vandenberg warned that any distribution beyond selected members of the National Security Council would invariably leak to the public in some, possibly distorted, form. "Nothing should be given to Congress as a whole that you do not want to go to the press," cautioned Vandenberg, who added that, speaking "cold-bloodedly," even members of the relevant congressional committees (e.g., Foreign Relations, Appropriations, Atomic Energy) could not be relied upon to keep the information to themselves. Acheson, Van Dusen, and Roberts thought only the president, the secretary of state and the secretary of defense should see the paper, with Roberts noting that even distribution to the full cabinet would be "both unwise and unnecessary."

None of those interviewed expressed surprise at the report's estimates of the new weapons' capabilities, though Roberts and Van Dusen called them more "reassuring" than they had expected — Van Dusen because of the report's overall tone, Roberts because of its prediction that Russia would possess no more than 100 bombs over the next decade. Indeed, all but Acheson feared the document was too reassuring for public release, as it could encourage complacency rather than alertness to the Soviet threat. By contrast, the secretary of state was concerned lest it was too alarmist. First, he feared that "even though the paper does considerably reduce the popular estimate of damage from these new weapons, it still presents the picture of a disaster of the first magnitude should we be subjected to an atomic attack. As such, it might persuade a considerable number of people that war is so dreadful that any concessions, political, economic, or moral, are better than the consequences of such a war." Second, Acheson thought, an even larger group might conclude "that since these weapons are technically capable of inflicting such damage on the United States, it would be far better, if the Russians continue their uncooperative and recalcitrant attitude in international negotiations, to wage a preventive war rather than to wait for them to obtain an atomic capability." This option Acheson found abhorrent, because "while it will not wipe out civilization as the alarmists have prophesied, (a war) will nonetheless be a terrible struggle, exhausting to the victor as well as to the vanquished."

The minority on the Conant committee favoring a more open information policy found only limited support in the four responses. Acheson and Van Dusen did react positively to the idea of calming fears of biological weapons (and radiological weapons, Van Dusen felt). Acheson thought a public information program designed to "take the 'magic' " out of biological warfare was desirable. And three out of the four — Roberts took no stance — intimated that their opposition to publishing the paper might change depending on future events. Vandenberg, for instance, who warned that he was "ultra-conservative" on the issue, acknowledged that public information might be "a useful 'shot in the arm' " to counteract either "sensational press reports [resulting] in public jitters," or "a lessening in international tension (which) might lull the public into lethargy."

Acheson showed cautious interest in an informal proposal, backed by Conant, to have an "annual report to the public on the present status of national security" and the capabilities of the new weapons. The idea required "a great deal of thought," he said, admitting that "perhaps useful information could be given out concerning the technical capabilities of the new weapons." But, skeptical that experts could agree on any assessment of the offensive-defensive atomic balance or any "broad appraisal of the status of national security," he believed that a detailed treatment incorporating these uncertainties and disagreements would be too complex and confusing to be of much help to the "average layman." Moreover, Acheson warned, a regularly issued report "would give the man in the street the erroneous impression that he would then possess *all* the necessary factual data to make sound judgments in matters of national security [emphasis in original]."

Before the Conant committee's third and final formal session, to be held in New York City on July 28, members reviewed a draft final report[23] containing majority and minority opinions that sharply defined the wide gulf separating the two factions among them. With the exception of a "general program of public information in biological warfare, dealing particularly with the civil defense aspects," the majority recommended against any public statement "at this time" on the capabilities of, and defenses against, the new weapons, and thought estimates of weapons capabilities should be distributed only to those members of the National Security Council whose duties required them to have the information. It opposed release of the Joint Chiefs of Staff Evaluation Board's Bikini report on the grounds that it was, "for the most part, obsolete, and not of particular usefulness to the general public."

The pro-release minority bluntly accused the majority of having misinterpreted the "Fishing Party" 's purpose. Forrestal had given them a broad mandate to make recommendations that would have "positive and far-reaching effects" on the government's information policy, it argued, but the majority's conclusions were "essentially negative in character. In effect, they endorse the present haphazard methods of keeping the American people informed whereby the public receives its information on these critical matters through a process of osmosis involving intentional or unintentional 'leaks' to the press from individuals having access to classified data." The minority pointed out that the original working paper had after all not been intended for public release. They had hoped "that during the discussion it would become apparent that certain areas outlined in [it] were directly related to the broad problem of civil defense and as such, merited release as part of a general public information program. We feel strongly that this can be done without provoking an emotional public reaction and without endangering national security."

The minority gave five arguments favoring a more open information policy. First, the public was faced with conflicting appraisals from a variety of "informed and uninformed" sources and "is at present completely confused," with no prospects for clarification. Second, a practical civil defense program was needed urgently, and the voters had to be able to instruct their congressional representatives to act on this issue. Third, "the people are entitled to know" the information needed to protect themselves in the event of an attack employing these weapons. Fourth, present restrictions on the dissemination of classified information inside the government

> appear to be blocking satisfactory progress in national security planning, and as such, weaken rather than strengthen our national security. What appears to be needed is a bold, new philosophy. Instead of following the principle whereby the higher levels within the government give the lower levels access to that information the former deem necessary for the latter to perform their duties, the policy should be to distribute information to the maximum extent that it can be absorbed by the working levels.

Fifth, there existed "ample precedent" for regular reports to the nation on national security issues, e.g., the president's State of the Union address and semiannual economic report to Congress. (Given the ideological competition with Russia, the minority added, "vital economic statistics may be even more useful to the enemy than carefully considered statements of weapon capabilities.")

The minority used these arguments to recommend that the secretary of defense issue an annual report on the potentialities of the atomic bomb and of chemical, biological, and radiological weapons, giving the public "as much information as possible about the capabilities of, and defense against, these weapons, being limited only by the obvious prohibition against giving potential enemies clearly vital military information." (Any disputes about what constituted "clearly vital military information" should be resolved on the basis of advice from an ad hoc military-civilian panel and the Joint Chiefs of Staff, they suggested.)

In the end, the July 28 meeting led to a substantial watering down of this candid clash of views—yielding what may fairly be described as (to borrow Conant's phrase to Compton) "an emasculated compromise report."

Gone were the competing statements of reasoning and explanation; gone was the minority's call for a "bold, new philosophy" and disclosing the "maximum" possible information. In their place was an innocuous paragraph in the letter of transmission embracing the "well-recognized principle" that government officials have an obligation to keep the public informed on vital issues "provided, of course, such information does not endanger the national security." As for the substantive disagreements, these were boiled down to compromise recommendations on biological and radiological warfare, and terse contrasting recommendations on atomic and chemical weapons.[24]

On the atomic bomb, a majority in the new draft final report recommended that "In view of the large areas of uncertainty which exist with respect to the capabilities of the atomic bomb, and taking into account both the offensive and defensive problems related to its delivery, it is undesirable, and perhaps dangerous, to give any official statement on this subject at the present time," though it thought this could be reconsidered if circumstances changed. The minority urged that

Information should be released about the atomic bomb, stating essentially:

(a) The capability of doing damage by an atomic bomb attack cannot now be assessed with accuracy, as there is a wide area of disagreement among experts as to the probable effectiveness of delivery of the bomb on well defended targets.

(b) Atomic bombs have not been developed and are not now in the process of development which are in any way in the category of the super-bomb popularly discussed in the press.

On biological weapons, the committee deferred to another ad hoc group Forrestal had already established, but it wanted information made public "which would insure support of pertinent national defense policies, including civil defense measures." Moving to chemical weapons, the majority held that since there "seem to be no new developments of critical significance in the field," no release was necessary; the minority thought "this fact in itself is significant," and should be released. Minimizing the effects of radioactive fallout and radiological warfare, the committee claimed that "essentially all well-informed biological opinion agrees that the deleterious genetic effects of exposure to radiation, including that of the atomic bomb, *likely to be experienced by large population groups in the event of war* are essentially negligible" (the italicized phrase was added in the final version). This information should be released to the public, the two sides agreed, if confirmed by "proper competent authorities."

They also met halfway in unanimously recommending that "the information which is released should be made part of a regular document, such as the next annual report of the Secretary of Defense," and suggesting that such a statement could "establish the practice of annual reports to the public on the changing capabilities of these weapons of mass destruction as a paramount consideration of national defense." In a shift from the earlier majority view, they agreed that "such a procedure would serve to protect our population against hysteria or defeatism, avoid the growth of public complacency, and enable our people to act intelligently if exposed to sudden attack with these weapons."

On August 1, Conant forwarded this draft to committee members for individual approval.[25] Consultations resulted in minor clarifications and editing changes which were reflected in a third draft, dated September 28 but completed prior to Truman's September 23 announcement of an atomic explosion in the Soviet Union.[26] For the first time, the draft included the identities of the rival factions: in the two cases where an official release (in regard to the atomic bomb and chemical warfare) was mentioned, identical coalitions emerged: Bowman, Dulles, Eisenhower, Greenewalt, and Thomas opposed; Conant, Canham, Morrill, and Page in favor.[27] The news of a Soviet atomic explosion did not prompt a full reassessment by the Conant committee, though Conant asked specifically "whether this announcement changes your views or not, and if so, to what extent,"[28] and only one member altered his recommendation as a result of the news. Tersely, Eisenhower told Conant, through Black, "The announcement seems to me to change the situation." Ike's change of heart reversed the majority and minority positions and put the committee on record as favoring an official statement that: 1) the damage inflicted by an atomic bomb attack "cannot now be assessed with accuracy," due to disagreement among experts; and 2) weapons "in the category of the super-bomb popularly discussed in the press" neither had been developed nor were under development.[29] With that major recommendation reversed, the Conant committee's final report was submitted to Compton on October 15 and by the end of the month was in Truman's hands.[30]

The "Fishing Party" report made barely a ripple in the turbid debate roiling the highest levels of the U.S. government after the announcement of the Soviet bomb. Its dismissal of the "superbomb" would be swallowed up in the debate that ended with Truman's laconic announcement on January 31, 1950, that H-bomb research would, in fact, go forward. And the report's divided, minimalistic form assured that it would have virtually no impact on the pervasive atmosphere of secrecy in which the H-bomb debate took place—a debate that, in Conant's view, displayed the worst effects of the secrecy regime he so opposed. In opposing the H-bomb, he continued to argue strongly that the public should be involved in what was in large part a political rather than a technical decision. On October 29—three days after Compton forwarded the committee's report to Secretary of Defense Louis Johnson (who had replaced Forrestal)—he made that "firm point" at the outset of the General Advisory Committee's all-day debate on the H-bomb: "Can this be declassified—i.e., fact that there is such a thing being considered, what its effect would be, if it succeeded, etc.[?]"[31]

Conant's plea went nowhere. As McGeorge Bundy later noted,

the need for secrecy was so deeply felt and so widely accepted that in principle all the participants in the debate fully accepted Mr. Truman's insistence that the very existence of the issue be kept a secret.

The president succeeded in his objective. He made his decision before there was a debate. So the process of that decision is deeply different from what we see in such matters today. Our own public debates may be full of error and ignorance; they may often be late and feeble. But we have them, and we can have more if men and women are alert. All this was missing in the case of the H-bomb decision—no sermons pro or con, no dire public warnings from defenders of security or Cassandras of nuclear catastrophe—no public discussion at all, careful or irresponsible. And when the decision was made there was no audible complaint at the way it was made. By habits that had first been set in wartime and then set in concrete by the belief that the secrets of the atom were crucial to national survival itself, the decision was left to the president.[32]

It is clear in retrospect that the report of a high-level special committee charged with reviewing the government's nuclear secrecy policy could scarcely have chosen a more important moment to make its views known; yet in this case, the Conant committee brought forth a mouse. Considering the magnitude of the question it was created to address—what should the U.S. government tell the American people about weapons of mass destruction? —its recommendations were trivial, unsupported by significant philosophical discussion. In addition, events overtook its efforts and rendered them almost irrelevant. Besides its complete evasion of the critical issues raised at the time—the question of the Bikini report (which remained classified until 1975), whether the United States should give the public a frank accounting of its policies on the possible use of the atomic bomb, and so on—its failure to render strong or germane judgment on the matter helped to bury the secrecy issue for years. Not until the Operation Candor report of 1953—in which Conant played a different role—did a move toward a more open policy occur.

Instead of Conant's strongly expressed views on the national security drawbacks of excessive secrecy, eloquently argued in his War College speeches, the committee's final report had confined itself to the perfunctory statement that it took "as a basic premise" the "well-recognized principle" that the government had an obligation to provide the people with all significant information that did not endanger national security. But in fact, this principle was not widely recognized in the government, not even within the committee itself, where half the members opposed releases on the grounds that there appeared to be "no public demand" for them. Had Conant stuck to the idea of issuing strong competing statements of philosophy—incorporating the minority's plea for a "bold, new" policy of "maximum" information dissemination—at least the final report could have stimulated serious debate. Instead, its "emasculated" compromise precluded the significant expansion of public knowledge regarding the government's arsenal of mass destruction. The only positive results were minor and incremental—the inclusion in the defense secretary's semiannual report for 1950 of a ten-page section on radiological and biological warfare, stressing the need for preparedness and the avoidance of alarmism.[33]

By allowing the first major high-level reconsideration of nuclear secrecy to have such little effect, the Conant committee by default contributed to the perpetuation rather than amelioration of excessive secrecy. Officials and elites who did not trust the public were permitted to dominate, and it is clear that they were concerned far more with political sensitivity than with disclosure of valuable technical information.

Though the chairman and members of the "Fishing Party" received the usual compliments for an important job well done, Conant recognized that it had not been a sterling performance. "I am not very proud of the results but am glad if they proved helpful," he wrote Compton, who had assured him that the group's conclusions were, despite the lack of unanimity, "nevertheless, helpful."[34] He would have felt even less pride had he known of the value accorded the report at the White House. Defense Secretary Johnson transmitted it to Truman on October 31 with this comment:

> I believe that this report may serve you in two ways. First, as a sampling of high-level, intelligent judgment regarding the advisability of releasing substantially more detailed information; second, as a possible protection to you in the event that pressure again builds up on you to release such information.
>
> If the latter eventually should take place you could, if you wished, point out that you had secured the advice of this group of well-known representative citizens, who were given full access to all information available in coming to their conclusions on this subject.[35]

In short, Conant had given the administration "protection" for continuing the pattern of secrecy he so deplored, and this in the midst of the most critical national-security decision regarding nuclear weapons since Hiroshima. As news of the first Soviet atomic bomb came, Conant failed to achieve a more rational public understanding of nuclear arms or a more open government policy on secrecy. It is hard to avoid the conclusion that the principal cause for that failure was that, with a few muffled and belated exceptions, and lacking the nerve to do otherwise, Conant made all his strongest statements on the subject—in secret.

CHAPTER 21

Cold War Educator, Part I

"A Dark Shadow Has Been Cast"

1946–1948

I think we are in for a period of witch-hunting and red-baiting and I shall be very glad to do what I can to help in bringing sanity into the situation.
— Letter, October 11, 1946

Another consequence of an armed truce which could be most disastrous in its effect on our universities . . . is an interference with their freedom as a consequence of panic . . . Without free inquiry universities cannot flourish. . . . No compromise with this principle is possible even in days of an armed truce.
— Speech to Commonwealth Club of San Francisco, September 8, 1947

You can't kill an idea by making martyrs of its disciples.
— Comments to Massachusetts State Legislature, February 9, 1948

A shock awaited some of James Conant's friends when they glanced at the front pages of the morning papers on June 9, 1949. Harvard's president, they learned, had signed a statement declaring that Communists should not be employed as teachers in the United States. "Conant, Eisenhower, 18 Educators Urge Ban on Communist Teachers," blared the headline of Cambridge's "Only Breakfast Table Daily," the student-run *Harvard Crimson.* Page one of the *New York Times* also directed readers to the two most prominent members of the National Education Association's Educational Policies Commission: "Eisenhower and Conant in Group Barring Communists as Teachers." It was, observers agreed, the most authoritative and unequivocal statement on the subject yet issued by the country's leading educators.[1] Before the day was done, President Truman and his commissioner of education, Dr. Earl J. McGrath, had strongly endorsed this newsworthy conclusion. "Well now, the teachers know more about that situation than I do," Truman told reporters. "I don't think that anybody ought to be employed as instructors for the young people of this country who believes in the destruction of our form of government."[2]

Conant's new stand gladdened inveterate anti-Communists who had long clamored for a tighter clampdown on what they alleged was a far-reaching "red" campaign to poison young minds by penetrating institutions of higher learning. Even William Loeb's rabidly right-wing *Manchester* (New Hampshire) *Union* grudgingly yielded a compliment: "A dim ray of light appears to be breaking slowly into the head of President Conant of Harvard."[3]

But Conant's conversion disappointed those who had looked to him for leadership in the struggle to preserve academic freedom on the nation's campuses. Over the previous three years, despite sensational espionage charges and exposes, congressional inquiries into "Un-American activities," and mounting apprehension that domestic "Fifth Columnists" were plotting to support a decisive Kremlin thrust against the West, Conant had stubbornly defended civil liberties and free speech as essential to American democracy. His views had even won the disdain of FBI director J. Edgar Hoover, as well as criticism from conservative Harvard alumni who threatened to withhold contributions and from legislators who angrily demanded the removal of left-leaning Harvard professors. Still, Conant had stuck to his guns, affirming that "no compromise" with the principles of free speech and academic freedom could be tolerated "even in days of an armed truce."[4]

Now, suddenly, Conant seemed to be advocating the very political vetting of academics that he had promised would never intrude upon Harvard—to be putting himself, in the words of the *Crimson's* disapproving editors, on the side of the "men of little principle and no discernment, men who are attempting to stifle ideas and change our constitutional guarantees of civil liberties to suit their purpose."[5] The Educational Policies Commission's members were not wild-eyed reactionaries spotting Commies beneath every bed—"no band of diehards and anti-progress fanatics," as one paper put it[6]—but some of the soberest, most distinguished leaders of American education. Now they, too, had solemnly declared that the Communist danger required making a prospective teacher's politics, as well as his professional competence, an issue in his or her employment.

What had happened? How and why did Conant, America's leading educator, change?

The answers illuminate a critical intellectual, political, and social evolution and polarization that was occurring throughout America at every level of society, from national politics to local school boards. He, too, found himself under pressure to choose sides, to respond to competing pressures from varying constituencies and from his own, sometimes contradictory, impulses. The result, for Conant no less than for America's other leaders and institutions, was not clarity but inconsistency, as rationalization, compromise, and expediency overwhelmed principles and ringing rhetoric.

✧   ✧   ✧   ✧

Following the passionate battles of the 1930s, controversies over America's civil liberties and academic freedom had subsided during World War II. Pearl Harbor eradicated the friction between isolationists and interventionists, and the common imperative of winning the war muffled partisan discord for the duration of the conflict. That held true at Harvard as well, where the urgency of war work displaced the nastiness of the Walsh-Sweezy era. And Conant spent most of the time in Washington, leaving day-to-day control of the university in the hands of other administrators.

When the fighting stopped, however, the arguing resumed. Conant interpreted the blossoming "Red scare," evident as early as 1946, as a "period of passing excitement in this country as a consequence of the reactions which almost always follow a war and the tensions created by a divided world." The pressures directed at Harvard and other educational institutions as a result he termed merely the latest in a succession of attacks stemming from "a total misunderstanding of the nature of university work."[7]

Flaring phobias over Communists and other foreign agitators had long been a part of the American landscape; they were present in the xenophobia, the chauvinist "populism," and anti-labor activity of the turn of the century, and in the "Red scares" of the 1920s, from which Lowell's Harvard had not been immune. But, Conant recognized, the situation after the World War II "Red scare" was significantly different. Never before had the United States wielded such global influence or interpreted its security so broadly; now, events in distant lands such as Iran or Greece or China could be viewed as harbingers of lethal danger. Nor, of course, had Washington previously confronted a Communist adversary as vast and militarily powerful as the Soviet Union seemed to be, openly wedded to a revolutionary philosophy that hailed the inevitability of its global success.[8]

The experience of World War II had yielded a jumbled, contradictory mixture of emotions among Americans: it simultaneously intensified their feelings of confidence and fear, ambition and suspicion, attraction and repulsion, when they looked at their nation's place in the postwar world. Hitler taught that a vicious dictator could devise a secret timetable for military conquest and could not be appeased by concessions, as at Munich. Pearl Harbor implanted the lesson that polite diplomatic discussions could conceal preparations for a devastating surprise attack. Conditioned by Munich and Pearl Harbor to imagine an enemy characterized by diabolical deceit and demonic designs, attuned to the need for peacetime vigilance, the public was newly susceptible to claims that spies and subversives were a genuine threat.

But the most important difference lay in the unprecedented threat of the atomic bomb, which loomed over these concerns and lent them a mystique and awe that struck a deep psychological nerve. Not only the new nightmare of a nuclear Pearl Harbor at some future date but the "most deadly illusion" that the United States could protect its atomic "secrets" produced a paradoxical combination of arrogance and vulnerability, bluster and insecurity.[9]

Soviet conduct lent credence to the fear that something of value was being threatened. Communist parties imposed new governments in the nations of Eastern Europe that the Red Army had occupied, Stalin gave speeches that were interpreted as bellicose, and shock waves were set off when Soviet-sponsored atomic espionage in Canada was revealed in early 1946. J. Edgar Hoover secretly warned Truman of "an enormous Soviet espionage ring in Washington operating with the view of obtaining all information possible with reference to atomic energy." Unbridling his paranoia, the FBI director described a vast conspiracy whose tentacles extended to every branch of the government and whose witting masterminds included Dean Acheson, John J. McCloy, Herbert Marks, Henry Wallace, Edward Condon, and others in the executive branch, Congress, and the press.[10]

As we have seen, Conant to a remarkable extent anticipated the corrosive effect that nuclear danger and secrecy could have on the political climate of the United States. But he, too, found the news about the espionage disturbing, making a point of reading the detailed official report of the Royal Commission investigating the Canadian case, for example.[11] Yet he considered an overreaction inevitable—a regrettable price to pay for maintaining public support for the measures needed to safeguard the country's national security in the atomic age. At the National War College in 1946, Conant had confessed that he thought it hopeless and, therefore, pointless to try to prevent the Russians from gaining access to U.S. atomic "secrets," but political realities dictated that the attempt would be made. The inevitable result would be the flourishing of "all sorts of spy stories and saboteur stories ... In short," he predicted, "to the normal benign chaos of democracy will be added an almost hysterical chaos as the result of fear. *Or else* we will do nothing adequate in the way of dispersal, retaliation or organization for survival." In either case—assuming the failure of international control—he envisioned "a very bad picture, indeed."[12] And during the 1946 congressional election campaign, Conant had felt helpless to stem the exaggerated fear of domestic Communism and could only hope to ameliorate its most harmful effects. "I think we are in for a period of witch-hunting and red-baiting," he wrote a colleague then, "and I shall be very glad to do what I can to help in bringing sanity into the situation."[13]

In deciding how far to go in combating the security scare, Conant faced difficult choices. In the fall of 1946, former NDRC colleague Ralph Connor sought his aid in helping a fellow chemist who, despite an unblemished wartime service, had inexplicably been denied clearance to work on classified projects. The specifics in Dr. Martin A. Paul's dossier formed a pattern that was to become depressingly familiar—and Conant's response foreshadowed his own conduct in the stormy years ahead. Even as he rued the excesses of a security system that sometimes equated dissent with disloyalty and as he acted to shield Harvard from those excesses, Conant balanced the impulse to fight for civil liberties against other considerations: timidity, caution, political calculation, and pragmatism, and, ultimately, his own mounting concern over Communist advances.

Connor described the man at the center of this case, Dr. Paul, as a Roosevelt liberal, a loyal American, "completely antagonistic" to Communism. Paul had worked effectively for Connor—and indirectly, for Conant—at NDRC Division 8's Naval Ordnance Laboratory, yet after the war, for unknown reasons, the Office of Naval Intelligence refused to grant Paul clearance to work on classified projects. Connor told Conant that the navy's action undoubtedly stemmed from anonymous allegations that Paul had befriended a Communist Party member on the faculty of the City College of New York and signed a petition backing a Communist gubernatorial candidate in New York (a charge he denied), and because "a couple of reactionary staff members" regarded him as a "troublemaker." Since the navy, in 1946, dominated military-funded research, its ruling threw Paul's career into limbo.[14]

Conant did not know Paul personally but agreed that it was unfair to deny a man clearance without a chance to rebut or even know of the evidence against him. He offered to bring the case to the attention of high Navy Department officials, an offer "purely of a transmitting agency" that gratified his friends.[15] On October 31, 1946, he forwarded to Secretary of the Navy Forrestal three strongly worded testimonials to Paul's reliability and patriotism from NDRC stalwarts still involved with military-related projects, along with a cover letter urging Forrestal to assure that no "injustice" occurred. He coupled his appeal for a review of the case with a thinly veiled warning that the military risked creating a perception of unfairness that could further impair the already difficult task of recruiting able scientists to work on defense projects.[16]

The navy responded brusquely. Acting Secretary John L. Sullivan wrote Conant emphatically reaffirming the rejection of Paul's clearance, explaining that "derogatory information" available to the navy left a "reasonable doubt" as to the scientist's "complete subscription to the principles on which this Government is founded, and there is reason to believe that he has followed the Communist Party line." Regrettably, Sullivan added, he could not disclose the nature and source of the information, even to men who had safely kept the secret of the atomic bomb for several years, but he felt sure that if they could only see the damning reports, Conant and the "eminent gentlemen" who had vouched for Paul would agree with the navy's verdict.[17]

Far from mollifying Paul's supporters, Sullivan's response further outraged them, both by its condoning the "completely un-American" idea of "blackening a man's reputation without a hearing or an opportunity to defend himself," and by its holier-than-thou implication that loyalty required that every employee demonstrate "complete subscription to the principles on which this Government is founded." One of Conant's colleagues confessed that Sullivan's letter had "done very little to reassure me about the conduct of the Intelligence Office."[18] Conant's own response seems rather more deferential than necessary.

He went as far as propriety dictated, and no further. Apologizing to Sullivan for taking up his time, he declared himself "entirely satisfied with your own personal assurance" that the government had acted properly. "Whether we like it or not," Conant wrote Paul's supporters, there was no alternative but to accept the Navy's decision.[19]

The Paul episode reminded Conant of the troubles and tensions inherent in classified scientific projects, and of the vast chasm between the scientific and national-security mindsets.[20] After five years immersed in the secrecy of S-1, with all its accordant personality and bureaucratic conflicts, Conant had seen more than enough to be convinced that the potential benefit of having classified scientific research on the Harvard campus during peacetime would simply not be worth the price. Given his own and Harvard's prominence in the scientific world, the work of both in wartime weapons research, and the new priority accorded to basic science for military purposes, Conant knew well that the university stood to gain not only money but prestige by taking in its share of big-dollar secret projects in hard science. During the war, Harvard had received $31 million in OSRD contracts, ranking third behind Caltech ($83 million) and MIT ($117 million) and just ahead of Columbia ($28 million).[21] By the end of 1946, not counting those projects winding down from the war, it had already gathered an estimated twenty-eight army and navy research contracts, all for unclassified work, totaling more than $3 million.[22]

Scientific research funded by the armed forces took on even greater importance, at this point, as a result of the failure to establish a civilian National Science Foundation, which Conant regarded as a more appropriate conduit for peacetime government funds to universities. Proposals to create such a federal agency had proliferated at the end of the war, with the atomic bomb dramatizing the assertion that promoting the country's security required a flourishing scientific estate. Vannevar Bush, convinced that the OSRD had proven the government's capacity to promote and finance civilian research at universities, had written a detailed report, *Science: The Endless Frontier,* laying out the rationale and proposed structure of such an agency. Prepared with FDR's OK (and with help from Conant and other wartime scientific leaders), Bush's report had been applauded upon its release in June 1945, and prospects for rapid legislative approval seemed rosy.

But by early 1946, despite vigorous lobbying by Conant, Bush, and other science and university leaders, the science foundation idea had become mired in political infighting, mostly due to ideological qualms about government control over science and, even more important, a power struggle over where authority for the new agency would lie. The fight in some respects replicated that over domestic atomic energy legislation: While Bush, Conant, and other wartime leaders favored an agency insulated from partisan political influence and governed by a part-time board of directors selected by outside bodies such as the National Academy of Sciences, the Truman administration just as resolutely insisted that the president retain control over what was, after all, a part of the executive branch. The controversy dragged on through 1946 and 1947, and two annual NSF bills died in succession, the first to a House vote, the second to a Truman veto; only in 1950 did a compromise measure finally pass congressional and presidential muster.[23]

Meanwhile, abhorring a vacuum, the Office of Naval Research (ONR) stepped in to fund scientific research with potential military applications, and began shoveling out money to universities so fast that Conant smelled a rat. It seemed to him that almost any scheme, no matter how harebrained, qualified for lavish naval assistance, with few or no strings attached. "The recipients are glad to get it, of course," he wrote Bush in October 1946, "but are wondering just why it is flowing in that particular channel, and rather suspect there is a joker somewhere." Conant had heard that some of the grants went to "very second-rate people in third-rate institutions" and that the army was chafing to compete with the navy in subsidizing both hard and social sciences. "All this looks bad to me," he wrote, admitting frankly that he had "dodged" questions about whether Bush was responsible for these dubious expenditures "as I frankly don't know the answer."[24] Bush, who was trying to set up a system to bring some order to the chaos of military subsidies for scientific work, defended the navy's largesse as a stopgap measure to support basic research, but agreed: "The real answer is that we must get a Foundation."[25]

But even without the assurance of a government mechanism to back university science, Conant grew convinced that Harvard should avoid the feeding frenzy for classified government contracts. He first expressed that view—a pathbreaking position in the still-uncertain relationship among universities, the military and the civilian government—in December 1946, in a "Crimson network" radio broadcast and a speech to American Association for the Advancement of Science (AAAS). Conant lauded wartime cooperation among scientists, universities, and the armed forces, but now that the fighting had ended it seemed to him "highly inadvisable for universities which are dedicated to free investigation" to conduct the classified work that they had undertaken "for patriotic reasons" during the war. "All secret research in days of peace," he declared, "should be done in government laboratories, arsenals and proving grounds."[26]

Conant did not, then or later, consider military research on campus to be intrinsically evil, as demonstrated by his robust support of university contracts during his tenure as head of the NDRC. By the same token, he did not believe that government support invariably corrupted research agendas or university scientists' quest for truth. He was, after all, an ardent supporter of efforts to establish a federal science agency. "If the National Science Foundation is properly set up and properly managed," he said, "I have no fear myself that there will be any deleterious effects to the universities even if they receive very large sums of money for the support of scientific research by this

398   JAMES B. CONANT

route from the Federal government."[27] But Conant deeply feared the effects on a university of the rigid, voracious, snooping security apparatus he had witnessed (and helped to create) during the war, the FBI investigations and clearances, the locked and barricaded laboratories, safes, and offices, and the pall of suspicion over the politics and personalities of faculty and students. In the words he used in 1949 to denounce plans to investigate the political backgrounds of student scientists awarded Atomic Energy Commission fellowships, the "atmosphere thus created among students in scientific departments would cause far more disturbance than any possible gain."[28]

Under Conant's guidelines, as later formally adopted, individual faculty members at Harvard remained free to conclude personal consulting arrangements for classified work (and some did so with gusto). But the university authorities frowned at secret research on campus. The behavioral scientist B. F. Skinner recalls cloaking the real reason for experiments on pigeon visual acuity—they were part of his admittedly "crackpot" project (enthusiastically funded by the navy) to teach pigeons how to guide missiles by pecking the correct target coordinates while sealed inside the nose cone—because "classified projects were taboo at Harvard."[29]

Not that Conant barred close cooperation between Harvard and the federal government as the Cold War intensified. By late 1947, less than a year after renouncing classified work at Harvard, he had no choice but to acknowledge the "dark shadow . . . cast upon our institutions of advanced education by the unfortunate turn of events in the postwar world." Given the changed situation, Conant stated, "today as during the war" there were many tasks, "neither entirely peaceful nor pleasant" and "all part of the grisly business of military armament," that "the universities must perform and gladly do so to assist the government of the United States."[30] For the most part, however, he never altered his early, clear position against accepting classified contracts, even as lucrative contracts for secret military and atomic work flowed to other institutions such as MIT and the University of California. If anything, his conviction that universities needed to be protected from the harmful effects of the security apparatus grew as the national obsession over secrecy widened. On March 29, 1949, Harvard's faculty pondered the "calculated risks involved in its own future freedom, its budget, and its tenure" entailed in accepting major government contracts. Aided by a "cool head" as well as several veterans of secret wartime scientific work (George Kistiakowsky, Percy Bridgman, and Bright Wilson), Conant won the day, and he officially proclaimed that "the University will accept no contracts which involve classified work, thus obviating the kind of security which was required during the war period."[31]

A few months later, a quiet attempt to get Conant to change only gave him another chance to stick to his guns. The case involved plans by Harvard and the University of Colorado greatly to expand their jointly run solar observing station in Climax, Colorado, in the Rocky Mountains.[32] Harlow

Shapley was expected to be a leading member of the project—director of the Harvard College Observatory and an unapologetic leftist who had campaigned the previous year for Progressive Party presidential candidate Henry Wallace and who had recently captured headlines for chairing a peace conference widely condemned as a pro-Soviet propaganda forum. The observatory's trustees privately complained to Conant that it would be "impossible" to raise funds, and military support would be endangered, if Shapley were involved. Suppose, they asked fearfully, militarily useful data obtained from the observatory were leaked to Russian agents, "unwittingly or otherwise"—through disloyalty or mere incurable scientific talkativeness?[33]

Conant refused to be cowed. Harvard's official attitude, he affirmed to Colorado's president,

> (and I take it of the University of Colorado) is that all their scientific work, whether supported by government funds or not, is freely open to anyone. We are advancing science, and the information might be immediately available to the Kremlin and it would not make any difference to us. If the National Military Establishment feels they do not want to put money into any university which has this attitude, that is their affair. But we can accept no responsibility in regard to the ultimate use of the scientific information which is collected in order to advance science which is, in times of peace, the sole concern of the two universities.[34]

It was Conant, the psychologist Jerome Bruner later recalled, "supported by a handful of scientists who had been at Oak Ridge, Los Alamos and other places where the action had been—who brought Harvard into the era of Big Science without at the same time turning the 'other side of Kirkland Street' into a no-go area of national defense fortresses."[35]

Beyond these university issues, Conant also plunged into the public debate over how Americans should interpret and react to what John Fischer, one of his favorite foreign affairs analysts, described as the "present grinding adjustments to the new two-power arrangement."[36] His principal intellectual contribution was his integrating of traditional arguments in favor of political freedoms within a larger thesis that highlighted the importance of political, economic, and social fluidity if American society was to attain ultimate victory in the ideological rivalry with the Soviet Union. By simultaneously defending civil liberties and condemning Communism, Conant embodied and helped shape what Arthur M. Schlesinger, Jr., called the "vital center" in American politics: a zone of political belief peopled by war-hardened, tough-minded yet idealistic anti-Communist liberal internationalists. Typified by the people who helped to create the Americans for Democratic Action in early 1947, this was a breed that fought with equal passion the totalitarian extremes of right and left, and wanted to strengthen the values of capitalist democracy.[37] A less

exalted description would be "middle-of-the-road liberalism." But with liberalism decried by one conservative military intelligence officer as "only a hop,
skip, and a jump" from Communism,[38] its practitioners sought to redefine
democratic principles in hardnosed terms.

In late 1946 and early 1947, Conant gave voice to this emerging position
in a series of pronouncements and public speeches. In an impressive feat of
ideological versatility, he cobbled together a synoptic programmatic response
that meshed everything from increased federal aid to education to international control of atomic weapons. He would ask, "How can we put our minds
on long-range plans for improving public education when the atomic bomb,
like the Sword of Damocles, hangs ominously over our heads?" And he would
answer: The two problems are connected.

Sharply telescoped, Conant's argument went something like this: the
future peace and survival of Western civilization depended on a U.S.-Soviet
accommodation on nuclear weapons; the Russians were likely to be obstinate
and skeptical about negotiating an atomic pact with Washington until they
were convinced that their rival would never collapse as a result of internal
atrophy and attendant internecine strife;[39] the key to America's long-term
social, economic, and political health, in turn, lay in maintaining a fluid social
structure and a framework of political and economic freedom that afforded
universal opportunity for talented citizens to advance, thereby dissipating the
social and economic stratifications that fostered class tensions on which
extremist ideologies preyed. The engine for America's social mobility and
capitalist energy had always been its system of free public education, "ladders
of opportunity" that allowed the cream of each generation to rise and prevented
the entrenchment of a hereditary aristocracy. Public schools faced massive
new challenges: war-caused demographic upheavals; training students to
cope with complex scientific, technical, and industrial advances; and, perhaps most daunting, an anxious future dominated by the United States'
unprecedented assumption of global leadership, the ominous prospect of
long-term rivalry with the Soviet Union, and the threat of nuclear annihilation.
Public education, to have a chance of adequately meeting these responsibilities,
required new infusions of federal funds. In other words: the survival of
civilization might hinge on the pending bill to increase federal aid to public
education.[40]

Conant's analysis, with its emphasis on the centrality of a vibrant democracy marked by social mobility to America's foreign and domestic prowess,
responded to a peculiar crisis of confidence that afflicted U.S. society in
1946–47, at precisely the moment when the country was seen internationally
as ascending to new heights of greatness.[41] In the words of one historian, "a
sense of insecurity and a feeling of competitive disadvantage vis-à-vis the
Soviet system coexisted in the minds of American policymakers with a
contrasting sense of aggressive overconfidence stemming from America's
great industrial power and monopoly of the atomic bomb."[42] The unity that

had been inspired and imposed by war disintegrated under the weight of strikes, inflation, and partisan bickering over Republican charges that the Truman administration was allowing the country to drift, and had passively countenanced Soviet aggression abroad and left-wing agitation at home. The Soviets, by contrast, seemed purposefully and brutally to be tightening their grip on power throughout Eastern Europe and advancing wherever disorder or weakness opened new opportunities. In the summer of 1946, Henry Wallace had observed scornfully that "for the first time in our history defeatists among us have raised the fear of another system as a successful rival for democracy and free enterprise in other countries and perhaps even our own."[43] To respond to this challenge, many Americans feared that a drastic curtailment of traditional democratic protections would be required. Bernard Baruch, for instance, privately predicted that the United States would "have to limit lots of freedoms" to outlast the Soviets in the Cold War.[44] In a September 1946 report, White House counsel Clark Clifford warned that to compete with the Soviet Union—"a highly-centralized state, whose leaders exercise rigid discipline and control of all government functions, [and whose] government acts with speed, consistency, and boldness"—Truman needed to improve the U.S. government's unwieldy machinery in order to produce "consistent and forceful" policies in spite of the tendency of democratic governments to be "loosely organized" and impeded by policies that are "confused, misunderstood, or disregarded by subordinate officials."[45]

In contrast to these pessimistic appraisals, which were not so different from his own occasional private views, Conant repeatedly affirmed America's ability to prosper and survive by recognizing and exploiting "those elements of strength in our chaotic democracy which like taproots reach back into our history."[46] Warning of the dangers of imitating the "stratified" social structures of the European powers, he argued that America's strength depended on preserving its unique "way of life"—a system whose combination of "diversity and flexibility," he insisted, "in education as in many other matters, allows for fruitful experimentation."[47] Rousing listeners to preserve liberal democracy during peacetime was a good deal harder than hailing democracy's "fighting faith" while the bullets were flying. But Conant often quoted the sign said to have hung in a restaurant of a rough 'n' tumble Old West mining town: "If you find our steak too tough, take your hat and leave. This is no place for weaklings."

Like George Kennan, whose "Long Telegram" and "X" article had highlighted the opportunity offered by the rivalry with the Soviet Union to prove the worth of American society, Conant even professed to welcome the prospect of ideological competition with Soviet Communism. And he drew a sensible distinction between Nazi and Soviet tactics and aims, between Hitler's megalomaniacal global power lust and Stalin's brutal, ruthless, yet still cautious probing. In a commencement speech at Ohio University on June 9, 1947—even as East-West tensions deepened and the Truman administration moved to block Communist political gains in Europe through the newly announced Marshall Plan—Conant explained the basis for his relative optimism. To critics who claimed that the war had merely traded a German hegemony for a Russian one, Conant responded that while "an armed truce between Nazi Germany triumphant in Europe on the one hand, and the United States on the other," could never have led to a permanent peace, "I believe . . . that given patience, intelligence, and courage on the part of this country we may within your lifetime, if not mine, work out a basis for a real peace with our former ally, the Soviet Union."[48] It was precisely this analysis of Soviet ambitions and motives, this belief that the Cold War was primarily ideological rather than military, and Conant's view of what he called the "mutual interaction between the new world order . . . and the domestic policy of the United States," that enabled him to advocate policies consistent with his long-standing educational and political philosophy.

While Conant had "no doubt" that the Soviet Union was every bit the police state Nazi Germany had been, he also believed that the Cold War rivals would vie for world predominance not through "brute force matching brute force" (although he supported Washington's maintaining a prudent level of armament) but by "competing for the allegiance of the dispossessed of the world, the ill-fed underdog. We both promise that our way of life means increased prosperity and greater personal happiness for the wretched peoples of this planet." Despite such rhetoric, Conant rarely showed much interest in or concern for what would later be called the Third World nor, in any urgent sense, toward the systematic poverty and racism still prevailing in large sections of the United States, an issue he only began to tackle later. But his successful encouragement of a more meritocratic, a socially, ethnically, and geographically more diverse student body at Harvard—probably his most significant legacy to the college—and his recurrent stress on eliminating class barriers to educational opportunities expressed his hope that the U.S.-Soviet rivalry would "increase the rate at which we move within this country toward the realization of those goals which historically have characterized our unique brand of democracy."

Conant's own rise from non-Brahmin middle-class Dorchester to the presidency of Harvard, traversing a path of professional achievement rather than class credentials, epitomized his ideal of the educational opportunity he believed could keep American society from stratifying into classes and vindicating Communist critiques.[49] "Wanted: American Radicals," his 1943 *Atlantic* polemic, had been the most pointed expression of his gradualist, pragmatic goal of attaining Jeffersonian democracy for his country and university—open to all classes and creeds, in which the most talented of each generation could rise according to their ability, unhampered by barriers of entrenched wealth—and it recognized the opportunity represented by the war, with its mobilization of millions of soldiers from all classes. Now, in the postwar era, it became clear that without the boost provided by the conflict's massive social changes, his well-meant prewar reforms and gestures would have produced only plodding progress. The single most important factor favoring a more diverse student body at Harvard and other elite schools was, of course, the G.I. Bill, which permitted thousands of soldiers to attend private universities who otherwise would have lacked the money to do so. For those who had survived the war and profited from the experience, training, and social contacts, Harvard offered an attractive respite and an avenue for further economic and social advancement. At first skeptical of them, Conant later glowingly praised the veterans who attended Harvard College as "the most mature and promising students Harvard has ever had."[50] He ardently advocated (and where feasible instituted) scholarship programs to bring promising scientists and others from around the country to Harvard, and directed resources toward a new School of Education.[51]

Under Conant's philosophy of "democratic education," well-funded public schools were not a side-product of American political culture but the central driving force separating it from the rest of the world—precisely the absence of an egalitarian educational system in Germany, he charged, had "cultivated attitudes of superiority in one small group and inferiority in the majority, making possible the submissions on which authoritarian leadership has thrived."[52] Public education, he declared repeatedly in 1947 and 1948, represented the key to America's future since "our survival depends on a vigorous demonstration in the next decade that we can make our form of democracy function even in a war-torn world."[53] While not openly urging the confiscatory inheritance tax backed by his imaginary "American Radical," he consistently urged Congress not only to increase federal aid to public education but to impose special taxes to redistribute resources from wealthy states to poorer ones.[54]

Critics claimed that Conant's focus on America's alleged tradition of social mobility derived in part from a too favorable reading of the country's history and sociology, that it underestimated the class, racial, political, and ethnic barriers arrayed against his meritocratic ideal.[55] In fairness, though, Conant was trying to serve the laudable function of making American democracy at home live up to the standard it tried to package for export, chiding those who showed more concern for social justice and civil rights in countries behind the Iron Curtain than at home.[56] While less than enthusiastic about women's rights, Conant did frankly recognize and condemn discrimination against ethnic and religious minorities, in particular what he called "two particularly distressing problems" in the United States: the "future role of our Negro population" and "anti-semitism," areas in which, he acknowledged, "our national idealism and our social practice are in head-on collision." America's vaunted "belief in a society with the minimum of class distinction is contradicted every time we segregate Negroes or discriminate against those of Mexican, Japanese, or Jewish ancestry." These regrettable "social mores" were "perhaps the most vulnerable spots in our armor."[57]

Yet one wonders whether Conant might not have responded more ener-getically to these national embarrassments. He believed in racial justice and equality, but he did not seem to take an especially strong interest in it. His recommendations, dependably, stressed caution over action, careful planning over moral indignation, and of course disdained outright civil disobedience — the method by which, a few short years later, the civil rights revolution would finally make fast progress. "No one but a utopian or a revolutionist can sincerely hope for a change of public opinion overnight," Conant wrote — and he was clearly neither. Instead, he advised a "set of limited objectives," "careful studies and well drawn plans rather than broad pronouncements," and acceptance that "abolishing social hostility and intolerance is clearly an instance where we must recognize ideals as goals" to be achieved over decades of gradual progress.[58] Going slow was the only practicable solution, as Conant saw it — and he showed little inclination to confront head on those who believed that solutions could wait until some indefinite future.

Conant's vision of a classless, fluid democracy was mildly liberal and comfortably mainstream, progressive in concept and rhetoric yet at times overly abstract and euphemistic in both description and prescription. It could inspire but not rouse; and his muffled criticisms of American failings were more likely to generate social science research projects than the moral out-rage that could, and would, galvanize political will.[59]

On March 21, 1947, under severe pressure from a "bitterly reactionary"[60] Congress elected five months earlier, Harry Truman instituted a sweeping government-wide loyalty-security program. Issued only nine days after his call to send arms to Greece and Turkey, Executive Order 9835 represented the domestic side of the administration's suddenly tougher line against Communism, and showed the rhetorical overkill that was characteristic of Truman's campaign, in line with the advice of Senator Arthur Vandenberg, to "scare the hell out of the country" in order to assure public support for Cold War programs.[61]

There is no reason to doubt that Truman hated the Soviets, whom at times he likened to Nazis, and he believed at least some of the claims that a pro-Soviet Fifth Column, composed of "Reds, phonies and 'parlor pinks,'" genuinely represented a potential "national danger."[62] But since existing security regulations gave ample means to find spies, Truman's primary motive in creating the Federal Employee Loyalty Program was political and partisan — to pull the rug out from under right-wing Republican critics who were demand-ing even more drastic measures, and to rally public support for potentially controversial and costly policies.[63] Whatever his intent, his order institutional-ized and exacerbated the postwar "Red scare" and its consequences. When more than 2 million federal employees instantly became eligible for FBI political and personal background investigations, Hoover's agency reaped a windfall in funds and influence.

In addition to setting up the machinery for thousands of security probes, the order allowed for the attorney general to label certain groups as "totalitarian, fascist, communist or subversive"—broad designations that permitted many abuses, as individuals were subjected to imputations of guilt by their "membership in, affiliation with, or sympathetic association" with any "foreign or domestic organization, association, movement, group or combination of persons" named on the attorney general's list. In practice, despite its initial narrow focus on the Communist Party and associated organizations, the list effectively functioned as an instrument of political thought control, as organizations risked being publicly stigmatized merely for opposing Cold War policies (such as military aid to Greece) or supporting civil rights or criticizing other social ills marring the "American way of life." Hundreds of such groups were eventually so designated (or threatened with designation), casting suspicion on thousands of Americans and deterring others from expressing controversial views. "It was the Truman Administration that manured the soil from which the prickly root of McCarthyism suddenly and awkwardly shot up," wrote the historian David Caute. "The manure was called the Attorney General's list."[64] Periodically, Truman would denounce some of the more extreme manifestations of the Red hunt, but the process was difficult to control. And as the security apparatus expanded, often run by persons to whom civil liberties placed a distant second to the imperatives of "loyalty," the fear and paranoia spread—although few genuine espionage agents were discovered.

Reacting cautiously to the signs of this harsh new security regime, Conant lamented its excesses and shielded his own realm, education, rather than frontally attacking Truman's approach as flawed, irresponsible, or overblown. He couched his criticism in veiled allusions and general rhetoric—intensified pleas to preserve freedom of speech, cautions against exaggerated and emotional political rhetoric and against unfairly branding individuals as "disloyal" when they merely did not meet criteria for government employment.

As the "Red scare" gained momentum in 1947 and 1948, Conant made some of his most straightforward and stirring defenses of academic freedom.[65] While conceding that the Soviets might well engage in "vigorous secret intelligence, sabotage, and even planned disruption of the basic philosophy of a nation," he warned Americans to take care that "any steps we take to counteract such activities of a foreign power within our borders do not damage irreparably the very fabric which we seek to save"; to avoid hurling labels like " 'Fascist' and 'Communist' at those who do not like our views"; and to distinguish between treasonous, criminal espionage activity, on the one hand, and "the expression of opinions no matter how repugnant they may be to the majority of this nation," on the other. "Only the enemies of American democracy," he stated, "could desire a witch hunt as a consequence of our attempt to protect our security from a military point of view."

Without explicitly referring to Truman's order, Conant acknowledged that the government should employ only "persons of intelligence, discretion, and unswerving loyalty to the national interest. But in disqualifying others," he added, it "should proceed with the greatest caution lest unjust and false accusation deprive many not only of employment but a reputation." Besides a generalized apprehension at the ongoing congressional inquests, his comment suggests that he was disturbed by cases such as the State Department's abrupt dismissal (on June 23, 1947) of ten employees who were not given benefit of hearing or access to the evidence against them and who subsequently "found themselves stigmatized as disloyal" and unemployable—and the Department's cravenly preemptive crackdown on internal "security risks" in early October, taken with a clear eye to appeasing congressional watchdogs.[66] By the fall of 1947, Conant was publicly warning of "a grave and immediate danger that we may jeopardize the morale of our government officials" and "perhaps even create the atmosphere of a witch hunt which could adversely affect our democratic institutions."[67]

The historian Richard Freeland points out that Conant's cautionary words echoed those of other prominent Americans who tried, with only limited success, to dampen the signs of panic over internal security: George Kennan "deplore[d] the hysterical sort of anti-Communism which . . . is gaining currency in our country," while Archibald MacLeish denounced "political pressures" on educators to indoctrinate students with anti-Communist philosophy. Arthur Schlesinger, Jr., publicly called on political leaders and opinion shapers, especially liberals, to heed Conant's admonition that the search for subversives must not turn into a self-destructive political purge. But short-term political considerations overrode predictions of long-term danger, Freeland notes. On the national level, "powerful forces" both in domestic and foreign affairs pushed the nation toward McCarthyism and they "did not seem part of any general pattern, and there was no conclusive reason to regard MacLeish, Kennan, Conant, and Schlesinger as the prophets to be heeded."[68]

Conant's more limited objective was to insulate the university—"an independent, self-governing community of scholars bound together by loyalty to the truth"—from outside interference, and from the security scare's more damaging effects. "Above all," it struck him as "important for the whole country to realize" that some persons "temperamentally unsuited" for government employment nonetheless deserved "full respect as citizens" and might nevertheless deserve places on university faculties. "The criteria for joining a community of scholars are in some ways unique," Conant reminded audiences and readers repeatedly. "They are not to be confused with the requirements of a Federal bureau." A conscientious objector on religious grounds, for example, while "automatically disqualified from service to the country in matters pertaining to the use of force," might nevertheless "be an intellectual and moral leader of the greatest importance for the welfare of our society." By the same token, a "naive scientist or a philosopher" committed to world government might make a "questionable" diplomat but, if competent in his or her specialty, an "excellent" professor. Interference with the freedom of universities "as a consequence of panic" could be "disastrous," he warned, because without a "charter of free inquiry" genuine scholarly endeavor was impossible:

> Without free inquiry universities cannot flourish. We must have an objective analysis of every phase of our national life. No compromise with this principle is possible even in days of an armed truce. The community has a right to demand of its educational institutions that the teachers dealing with controversial subjects shall be fearless seekers of the truth and careful scholars rather than propagandists. But granted honesty and sincerity, there must be tolerance of a wide diversity of opinion. Indeed, this diversity of opinion is not only basic for the welfare of our universities but for that of the entire nation.

Conant's wish to safeguard the university from outside or state interference, consistently expressed since the 1930s, was reinforced by his sense of the postwar changes in traditional relations between the university and the state, between the university and society. After the war, an unprecedented range of problems faced America and the world — recovery from devastation, atomic weapons and energy, demographic, political and economic upheavals, the need to reconstitute the global economy and international organization, and countless more — and concurrently a new respect for intellectual and academic expertise developed. To Conant, an exemplar of the technocratic "power elite" who were making major societal decisions, the implications were clear: more than ever, "the nation and different groups within the nation, geographic, social, or economic, must look to the university scholars for guidance in handling basic social and economic problems."[69] Partly in response to this sensed need, Conant became an enthusiastic supporter of establishing a strong social sciences program at Harvard, and had sought increased funding for and acceptance of scholarly investigation of contemporary social and political problems, the "burning questions of the day."[70]

Conant's work on the Manhattan Project had crystallized his view that the public needed a better understanding of science and scientific ideals, and it impelled him now to reinvigorate the still embryonic advanced program in the "History of Science and Learning" that he had initiated at Harvard in 1936. The man who had been the driving force behind the program was George Sarton, author of the pioneering multivolume *Introduction to the History of Science,* the founding editor of the journal *ISIS,* and in many ways the father of history of science as a modern academic discipline.[71] Along with Henry Black, Theodore Richards, and L. J. Henderson, Sarton had also been an important influence on Conant's own developing intellectual interest in the history of science, growing out of his initial fascination with the history of chemistry. In later years, Conant credited a "great deal" of his writings, ideas, and investigations in that field to the "deep impression" left by Sarton, dating back to a conversation Conant (then a graduate student) had with the older scholar at an evening party at Harold Laski's house.[72] "As a specialist in one very special department of a somewhat narrow science," the chemistry professor had written Sarton in 1927 after reading a draft chapter of the first volume of his opus, "your undertaking brings most needed intellectual refreshment and stimulant."[73]

When Sarton had returned to Harvard in the mid-1930s to oversee the new major program, setting up in his office in the Widener Library stacks, he had expansive hopes of turning the fledgling history of science discipline into a major field of study. But to his disappointment, despite assurances of "real interest, I might almost say faith, in the importance of the doctrine you have been preaching for so long," Conant before World War II gave Sarton scant financial or administrative support, repeatedly vetoing (in the politest terms) ambitious schemes for library acquisitions, publications, staff hirings, or an institute devoted to the history of science. Later, Conant explained that aside from austerity budget limitations he was reluctant to encourage young scholars to enter a field with so little prospect of future advancement.[74] But the outbreak of the war, on top of the "scientific basis" claimed for various totalitarian ideologies, raised the stakes. "For twenty five years or more," Sarton wrote Conant in July 1940,

> I have claimed (and I believe proved) that the best if not the only way of bridging the widening abyss between science and the humanities is the study and teaching of the history of science . . . science is now more than ever under fire. In their despair many good people are led to consider it as one of the main sources of all our evils, economic or political. The scientist is put on the defensive. He sometimes answers that his only concern is to find the truth and that he can not be held responsible for the applications, good or evil, which other men may make of his discoveries. That answer is not convincing. We have claimed credit for the beneficial applications of science and have been boasting endlessly about them; if so, we cannot have it both ways and escape responsibility for the evil applications.[75]

Even without Conant's privileged knowledge of the Manhattan Project, Sarton worried that the carnage of war would generate an anti-science backlash that would deepen the breach with the humanities. After the "fantastic abuse of science caused by the war I fully expect a violent revulsion of feeling against it," he wrote to Conant in early 1943.

> There are already many humanists who speak tenderly of the Middle Ages as if that was a golden age of peace and love; there will be many more after the war. It will be more necessary than ever to explain that science does not conflict with the best mediaeval ideals but on the contrary brings us nearer to their realization. Neither humanists nor scientists can explain that, cer-

tainly not as long as they are unable to understand one another. The widening abyss separating them must be bridged, or our culture will be jeopardized and defeat itself.[76]

Conant sympathized with Sarton's contention that the history of science "must build a bridge between the humanities and the technicalities of science" in the postwar world,[77] but it was not until after Hiroshima that he began taking real steps. In a privately circulated memorandum in the fall of 1945, he described having witnessed from the vantage point of the OSRD "the bewilderment of lawyers, business men, writers, public servants (and not a few Army and Navy officers) when confronted with matters of policy involving scientific matters." Conant now proposed creating a commission to study how to teach the "tactics and strategy of science" within the larger context of "General Education in a Free Society." The goal, he explained, would be to inculcate among lay students not the content or principles of science "but rather an appreciation of how scientific research is really done . . . the difference between controlled and uncontrolled observation and experiment; the difference between basic research and applied research; and the relation of both to development and production."[78] To raise funds for this project, he approached the Carnegie Corporation in New York, which soon signed on to the venture, now scaled down to a plan to instigate the teaching of college-level courses and the development of suitable research materials.[79]

At Harvard, Conant volunteered to take on this assignment himself, and inaugurated a new undergraduate course, Natural Sciences 4: "On Understanding Science," which became the basis for a book of the same name.[80] Building on a set of case studies, the course emphasized the cultural, intellectual, and political contexts of major advances in scientific knowledge and theory, and conveyed some of the confusion, uncertainties, ambiguities, false starts, and blind alleys that commonly precede or accompany important conceptual breakthroughs. Conant's major contribution to the "Harvard Case Histories in Experimental Science" series was an account of the overthrow of the "phlogiston" theory, an eighteenth-century notion to explain chemical reactions involved in combustion, which was discarded when oxygen was discovered; expressive of its author's skepticism, the study demonstrated how an utterly erroneous theory can gain wide acceptance among scientists until disproven by an experimenter with a fresh perspective.[81] Conant's tactic contrasted with the usual method of teaching science at the time, which depicted a smooth, grand, inexorable march of knowledge and theory toward higher plateaus of understanding.

For the next three years, Conant annually taught Nat Sci 4, reprising his old table-top demonstration lecture techniques, collaborating with up-and-coming scientists and historians of science (including I. B. Cohen, Thomas S. Kuhn, Gerald Holton, and Leonard K. Nash) who helped to design and teach the course, providing an unusual opportunity for Harvard students to get more than a passing glimpse of their distinguished president.[82] The course and accompanying case studies, conferences, and workshops for university and high school instructors stimulated further efforts, as Conant hoped, as well as thoughtful criticism. Oppenheimer was doubtful whether teachers could "re-create the experience of science as artifact" without slipping into "antiquarianism," preferring instead an effort to transmit those "general features of the scientists' work," such as cooperative labors and rigorous scrutiny that roots out errors.[83] And Conant's larger vision of scientific knowledge as a grand edifice, rising stone by stone like the Gothic cathedrals of Middle Ages, would fifteen years later come under fire from one of his protégés, Kuhn. In his controversial *The Structure of Scientific Revolutions* (1962), Kuhn credited Conant for initiating the "transformation in my conception of the nature of scientific advance," but instead of viewing scientific progress as an "incremental or cumulative activity," Kuhn postulated the radical notion of a revolutionary "paradigm shift" to explain the rise and fall of scientific theories through giant leaps and violent overthrows. Scientists, philosophers, and historians of science still passionately debate Kuhn's theory, basic to understanding how knowledge and understanding change in science and other fields, with many critics echoing the skeptical view of the "paradigm" theory that Conant sent its creator after reading a draft.[84]

By personally attempting to integrate the teaching of science into the broader task of transmitting knowledge, Conant was, in part, actualizing the implications of a philosophical movement with whose ideas he had found sympathy. This movement had arisen in Central Europe in the early 1900s and then taken root in the United States, its seeds transplanted by American disciples as well as by refugee scholars who had crossed the Atlantic to escape Hitler and, in some important cases, found refuge at Harvard. At the turn of the century and in the years immediately before and after World War I a collection of scholars influenced by the Austrian physicist and philosopher Ernst Mach—a group ranging from the Harvard philosopher William James to Albert Einstein and Sigmund Freud—began to coalesce behind scientific and philosophical ideas they regarded as modern and civilized. Revolting against the mystical, metaphysical, anti-intellectual, absolutist, and religious dogmas that had long clogged so-called scientific discourse, the group embraced pragmatism, empiricism, logical positivism, and the identification and promulgation of universal and "unifying" premises, methods, and principles underlying scientific inquiry and all intellectual enterprises aimed at expanding knowledge. The movement's precepts were most clearly articulated in the classrooms and cafés of the Vienna Circle (and an associated society in Berlin) of the late twenties and early thirties. In turn, admirers in the New World published and contributed to journals and organized meetings around the themes of "Unified Science" and the "Unity of Science." At Harvard the movement's proponents included the philosopher W. V. Quine and the physicist Percy Bridgman, a close friend of Conant's; and as fascism overwhelmed the European continent, important members of the Vienna Circle made their way to Cambridge: Rudolf Carnap arrived to receive an honorary degree at the tercentenary celebration in 1936, and Philipp Frank and others came literally on the eve of the war—September 3-9, 1939, the week Germany invaded Poland—to attend the fifth International Congress for the Unity of Science, a gathering chaired by Bridgman, welcomed by Conant, and described by Quine as "the Vienna Circle, with accretions, in international exile." During and immediately after World War II the movement gained further momentum as its commitment to logic and empiricism dominated science. In the Boston area, Frank founded an Institute for the Unity of Science that the American Academy of Arts and Sciences took under its wing; the institute became a fulcrum of activity for scholars in many disciplines committed to overcoming specialization, seeking a "synthesis of knowledge," and broadening the understanding and use of scientific methods. Conant made common cause with those basic objectives, as indicated by his experiment in teaching science "as part of a general education": "If we are going to give the lawyer, the statesman, the business man, the newswriter some understanding of science, we educators must ourselves endeavor to understand the method of science."[85]

Whether the Harvard program appreciably bridged the gap between science and the humanities is debatable. For Conant, however, Nat Sci 4 may have served other, more personal aims—exercising his old, never vanquished hankering for science, and salving a troubled conscience for having been a central participant in the revolutionary increase in science's potential for mass destruction.

In other ways, too, Conant wanted to make Harvard (and U.S. education generally) more responsive and relevant to the immediate concerns of the postwar world. That implied both opportunity and risk—the chance to feel the heady satisfaction of influencing national policy and determining, rather than just analyzing, the course of history, but also the danger of getting embroiled in temporal disputes: "The world cannot have it both ways," he said, "either the professors live in ivory towers and their thinking and teaching have no relevance to the times in which they live, or the professors are going to have views that somebody will not like." Universities would receive criticism, "sometimes for being too unorthodox, sometimes for being too conformist"—for harboring professors that were "too radical" or "too conservative."[86] Other less evident dangers also lurked: external pressures from funding sources, and the self-limiting choices of intellectual conformism and consensus. But the importance of the task before the universities, Conant asserted over and over again, only underlined the need to preserve professors' "absolute freedom of discussion and absolutely unmolested inquiry . . . We are either afraid of heresy within our universities or we are not," he declared, echoing his tercentenary rhetoric of a decade before. "If we are afraid, there will be no adequate discussion of the great questions of the day, no fearless exploration of the basic problems forced on us by the age in which we live."[87]

In late 1947, Harvard took a step toward Conant's goal of "relevance" by founding the Russian Research Center (RRC), established with an initial $100,000 grant from the Carnegie Corporation. Carnegie and Harvard, in turn, were prodded to go ahead with the venture by U.S. government analysts in the State Department, the military, and the newly created Central Intelligence Agency, who welcomed the creation of a new, high-powered source of experts and expertise to supplement and collaborate with their own efforts to understand their Cold War adversary.[88] An additional incentive for Conant to support a Harvard role in studying the sources of Soviet conduct was his frustration over Moscow's behavior in the UN talks about international control of atomic weapons: the U.S. negotiator in the talks, Frederick Osborn, was a Carnegie trustee, and strongly backed the research center proposal. "Our last hope [for peace with Russia] lies through the social sciences," said Osborn in October 1947, assuring one Carnegie official that "if any question arose at Harvard as to the interest of the State Department or the U.S. Delegation to the United Nations in having more systematic information about Russia, we were free to use his name without reservation." Osborn volunteered to lobby Conant, his consultant on atomic affairs, in favor of the project, but that proved unnecessary.[89]

Initially envisioned as temporary, the country's first major academic institute dedicated to studying contemporary Soviet affairs quickly grew into what one historian, Sigmund Diamond, has described as "the locus of fruitful collaboration between the intelligence agencies and Harvard."[90] Carnegie money, supplemented by air force grants, poured in, totaling about $1.5 million during the next ten years,[91] and from the center's inception, ideological and national policy goals complemented and influenced the "straight research" that Paul Buck later described as its sole work.[92] According to contemporary press reports, the center planned to make its work "available to the State Department and other federal agencies, including the central intelligence groups, through informal channels long before publication by the university,"[93] and the wartime connections of many center staff—including its director, Clyde Kluckhohn, an anthropologist who had analyzed Japanese morale for the War Department prior to the use of the atomic bomb—facilitated ongoing government contacts. (Several of the center's staff and researchers were veterans of the Office of Strategic Services, which had also bequeathed much of its collection of materials on Slavic studies.)[94]

Not surprisingly, despite a Harvard press release vowing that the center's "research will be entirely independent of governmental agencies,"[95] given the provenance of its funding and the political temper of the times, the RRC coordinated its research activities with the agendas of State Department, CIA, and military intelligence analysts concerned with the Soviet Union. A prime example of this symbiotic relationship was a massive, multiyear study (the Harvard Project on the Soviet Social System), designed to satisfy both open scholarly and covert governmental curiosities, to explore the Soviet political, social, and military scene by interviewing and collecting detailed questionnaires from thousands of Soviet émigrés, defectors, and refugees in Europe; center researchers were instructed to compile "poop sheets" to send directly to intelligence officers in the air force, which was providing major funding and had a special interest in "social science" data to help it prepare for another world war—for example, how to select bombing targets in the Soviet Union that would "maximize positive psychological reactions toward the attacking force."[96] Other center-government connections and contracts multiplied: Conant personally approved special arrangements to make research results directly available to the FBI, CIA, and other government agencies; RRC specialists bartered information and contacts with various government agencies, which in turn tapped the center to fill permanent and temporary positions, to the point where Kluckhohn complained that government consulting assignments were draining his staff's energies[97]; by 1950 Osborn would estimate that the RRC "constituted an appreciable fraction of our country's intelligence potential on Russia,"[98] and consequently urge the State Department to assure that its personnel were exempted from military service in Korea. Thus the center symbolized the tightening web of connections between state and university as the Cold War dominated the national agenda and as Conant showed his readiness, in certain circumstances, to use Harvard to promote the national interest and his own conception of education's ideological mission.

It also represented a test case of the constraints on academic freedom. Inevitably, friction sometimes arose as the center's staff and scholars tried to balance their academic objectives with pressure, either implicit or explicit, from funders and potential critics to influence research, conclusions, or personnel decisions.[99] And from the start, the FBI took an interest in its activities, and began to scrutinize the political backgrounds of affiliated scholars and to look for informants.[100]

> There is no doubt about it—a dark shadow has been cast upon our institutions of advanced education by the unfortunate turn of events in the postwar world.
>
> —Speech to San Francisco Commonwealth Club,
> September 8, 1947

The threat to academic freedom at Harvard and other universities grew more palpable in late 1947. Encouraged by the administration's loyalty program, state governments rushed to impose their own procedures; schools, and especially universities, were a popular target. Were they not, after all, teeming with intellectuals, some of whom had unorthodox ideals and agitated for labor unions, who were perfectly positioned to indoctrinate gullible youngsters? Here, claimed the fearful, was one of democracy's many weaknesses. Between

1946 and 1951 fifteen states joined the twenty-one who by 1940 had already put loyalty oaths on the books, with many requiring teachers to disavow membership not only in the Communist Party but in any organization on the attorney general's list of front groups or adhering to any radical doctrine.[101]

Twelve years earlier, Conant had spearheaded a drive to knock down a teacher's oath bill. Now he took a position that seemed equally straightforward when Massachusetts assistant attorney general Clarence Barnes propounded similar legislation in November 1947. At first Conant had hoped to use the old-boy network to convince Barnes to withdraw the bill, but after quiet inquiries by Harvard officials into Barnes's background (Yale Republican) proved inauspicious he launched a skillful behind-the-scenes lobbying campaign to scuttle the legislation. He and MIT president Compton worked through late December and January to line up key educators to testify when the Barnes bill came before state committee hearings in February.[102]

Conant also moved swiftly to secure the help of Harvard's foremost expert in civil liberties, the law school's professor Zechariah Chafee, Jr. Chafee knew from personal experience the dangers faced by controversial faculty members in times of political tension: in 1921, he had come under fire during another generation's "Red scare" for opposing harsh anti-sedition measures, prompting president Lowell to lead his defense before a swarm of angry overseers; by a narrow 6–5 vote, Chafee had escaped unscathed.[103] Since then, he had gone on to establish himself as "probably the most respected civil libertarian in America."[104] In December 1947, in response to Conant's appeal, Chafee prepared a forty-three-page legal memorandum outlining arguments and precedents against the Barnes bill.[105] To test the bill's constitutionality should it become law, Chafee concluded, Harvard might have to sue the attorney general.[106] Swallowing hard, Conant set about ensuring instead that it never got on the books. Assisted by Corporation secretary David Bailey, he saw to it that a hundred copies of Chafee's memorandum were mimeographed and distributed to leading university presidents to "quarry material for their objections," to university officials and faculty members interested in academic freedom issues, such as Arthur M. Schlesinger, Jr., and Kirtley Mather, and to selected lawyers, friends, and organizations such as the local Civil Liberties Union.[107] At the same time he sounded out other prominent and respectable social and commercial figures to speak out against the bill.

As he organized the counterattack against the Barnes bill, Conant used his 1947 annual year-ending president's report to advance his defense of academic freedoms. In the statement, which received wide press coverage, he repeated his warning against political intrusions into universities, solemnly affirming that "no compromise" with academic freedoms could be tolerated "even in days of an armed truce."[108]

Testifying against the Barnes bill on February 9, Conant again cited lofty principles of academic freedom and independence from state interference, but shrewdly chose to emphasize *Realpolitik* arguments to explain why the law would be an ineffective and even counterproductive tactic. In telling the Joint Committee on Education that the Barnes bill would be both unconstitutional and unwise, Conant stressed the importance of maintaining the independence of private universities from state control, but, more important, he also contended that loyalty oaths actually hurt the United States in its battle against the Soviet Union and international Communism. To display signs of "fear approaching panic" during a period of "armed truce" with the Soviet Union could, he warned, "destroy the whole basis for our success in a worldwide competition with an alien and hostile ideology." The "gentlemen in the Kremlin," he surmised, anxiously sought confirmation of their ideological prediction that capitalist bourgeois democracy was doomed to fail. "And if I were in their place I should seize on every bit of evidence that tended to support this view. I should eagerly await news that indicated that the American people had begun to succumb to panic, that they had lost confidence in those historic principles which had guided their development in the past." Passage of the loyalty oath would bring just such "welcome news to the rulers of Soviet Russia," he predicted:

> Once we depart from our robust belief in those ideals which have been our goals for a century and a half and our confidence that these ideals will win in any ideological conflict in a free society, we may well be on the road to ruin. It is this possibility—a very remote but still real possibility—which makes me so determined in my opposition to this bill or any similar type of legislation. Once we start altering the basic framework of our society . . . once we start showing alarm at people's opinion and legislate against any views short of advocacy of criminal action . . . we have given the world a danger signal. We have proclaimed to ourselves and to our neighbors, our friends and hostile critics that we have lost confidence in our future, that a wave of fear is mounting.[109]

Conant even opposed sanctions against teachers found to be Communists because, as he put it, "You can't kill an idea by making martyrs of its disciples."[110]

Stirring, forceful, and deliberately calculated to appeal to hard-line sensibilities, Conant's arguments also contained a danger: if such measures were judged not on principle but on their effectiveness as Cold War stratagems, then changed circumstances, or a different cost-benefit analysis, might necessitate the opposite conclusion. In engaging the practitioners of *Realpolitik* on their own turf, Conant subtly moved closer to a compromise of his purist insistence on academic freedom.

How important the opposition of Conant and other educators was in sending the Barnes bill to defeat is uncertain. His conciliatory attitude— frowning on overt noncooperation with constituted authority, he had gone out of his way to commend "the patriotism and sincerity" of Barnes and his supporters—contrasted with the unvarnished outrage of University of Chicago chancellor Robert Hutchins, who sheltered professors who defied state investigations and blasted the official inquests as "the greatest menace to the United States since Hitler."[111]

Still, his sharp rebuke of the loyalty watchdogs attracted national attention and evoked warm applause from the academic community at Harvard and from others. Roger Baldwin, director of the American Civil Liberties Union, congratulated Conant on his "magnificent" statement, which was "in the best Harvard tradition, and in what I have come to know also as yours," and ventured the hope that it would "go far to stiffen some pretty weak academic back-bones."[112]

Not all were so pleased with Conant's steadfastness, however. At the Federal Bureau of Investigation J. Edgar Hoover and his associates kept track of his remarks on Communists, loyalty, and security, even after Conant easily passed an FBI background check in early 1947 following his appointment to the GAC; FBI files declassified decades later show that Bureau officials thought Harvard at a minimum coddled dangerous subversives if it did not wittingly serve as a tool of the international Communist conspiracy. It is hardly surprising that they disdained Conant's unabashed opposition to loyalty oaths and his principled defense of the idea of hiring as faculty members persons who might be considered by security agencies as unfit for government service. When a summary of Conant's 1947 annual report was circulated at the FBI, its defense of academic freedom inspired fresh contempt. "Intellectual freedom is not license and when it is slavery is around the corner," Assistant Director D. Milton Ladd scrawled at the bottom of the report, under which Hoover himself added: "I agree. I now understand some strange things about Harvard."[113]

Conant's firm opposition to the loyalty oath bill and Red-baiting did not always translate into strong and effective action, however, and his attitude toward individuals upon whom suspicions had been cast varied from case to case. His vouching for Oppenheimer in March 1947 showed that his backstage intervention could help to blunt excessive zealotry, yet his timidity in the Paul case exposed the limits of his willingness to make a nuisance of himself to constituted authorities even when questionable rationale was employed to deny clearance. Controversial tenured faculty members at Harvard could count on Conant to reject demands that they be fired or silenced, even if he despised their politics. This was the case in 1948 with two eminent faculty members, the literary critic F. O. Matthiessen and the astronomer Harlow Shapley, who were both vocal supporters of Henry Wallace. Despite dozens of complaints from conservative watchdogs, Conant held to his position that they were free to engage in lawful political activity outside the classroom. He also stuck up for liberal non-Communist Harvard scholars, as in 1948–49 over the tenuring of the economist John Kenneth Galbraith, and in his refusal to apply pressure on a controversial China specialist, John King Fairbank. As Republicans blasted Democrats for "losing" China to Communism, Fairbank earned right-wing enmity by denying the divinity of Chiang Kai-shek and acknowledging Mao Tse-tung's popular legitimacy; yet Fairbank reports that he never received any pressure from Harvard's administration to alter his critical views.[114]

However, in the spring of 1948, two cases suggested that Conant could also respond equivocally or even succumb to political pressures.

The first case involved the new Russian Research Center and centered on a young Harvard historian, H. Stuart Hughes (the grandson of Chief Justice Charles Evans Hughes), who had resigned from the State Department in 1947 out of disillusionment with the Truman administration's hard-line policies.[115] Although promised a senior staff position at the center, Hughes was pressured by Carnegie and Harvard officials to resign early in 1948 because of objections to his politics, which included support for Wallace, though this did not affect his junior appointment in the Harvard history department.

"Although barred from administrative responsibility," Hughes recalled in his memoirs, "I was able to teach at Harvard for another four years, and in that sense my freedom was not abridged. So far as I could tell, the prevailing view among those in the know was both that the Carnegie Corporation had gone too far and that I had shown commendable institutional loyalty in resigning. But in less tangible fashion I was given to understand that in supporting Wallace in the first place, I had behaved like a bad boy . . . people at Harvard made me feel ashamed."[116]

The details of the Harvard administration's role in collaborating in Hughes's removal are uncertain, owing to the university's fifty-year secrecy rule, but the available evidence suggests that Harvard authorities expediently interpreted the issues so that the high matters of principle so often invoked by Conant could be ignored. The result was an acceding to outside pressure and a shrinking conception of academic freedom. By controlling the purse strings, Carnegie was able to exert additional pressure on Harvard: Hughes was told that he was "the stumbling block" in the way of a five-year grant from Carnegie for the center's operations to supplement the initial $100,000 start-up funds.[117]

Carnegie's request to sever Hughes landed on the desk of Conant's right-hand man in faculty matters, the provost, Paul Buck, who candidly described the incident in an oral history interview in 1967. "I didn't like it," Buck recalled. "It violated some of my principles. And yet, on the other hand, I had authority to remove him because, according to our statutes, administrative officers can be removed from their administrative offices at will, as distinct from faculty tenure as a professor." So instead of rebuffing Carnegie's request as improper, Harvard implored Hughes to restrain his political activities. "Stop sticking your neck out on issues too soon in life," Buck recalls telling

Hughes. For his own good, Buck told Hughes to do some academic "grubbing" and to "stick to his knitting as an historian for a while and then develop into some position, and then when he's in his forties and fifties he could make his real impact."[118]

After listening to Buck, Hughes resigned from the center, though he continued campaigning for Wallace and went on to build a considerable reputation as a European intellectual historian. An often sympathetic study of Harvard's conduct during this period concludes that Hughes "never received any suggestion that the University was prepared to fight out the issue with the foundation as a matter of principle," although the center did later play host to radical and Marxist scholars.[119]

Conant's personal role here is unclear,[120] but it seems safe to assume that he approved Buck's actions; and the hairsplitting rationale cited by Buck is quite in the Conant tradition when faced with an uncomfortable dilemma. Buck's advice may, indeed, have been in Hughes's best interest—his political activities apparently did not endanger his history department appointment, and a head-on challenge to Carnegie might well have triggered a public scandal that would not only embarrass Harvard but cast a shadow over Hughes. (Buck had no doubt that if the news had leaked, the press would have jumped all over a controversy pitting the grandson of a Chief Justice of the Supreme Court versus a Corporation whose board of trustees included the sitting secretary of state, General Marshall.) Moreover, Buck notes, Hughes continued campaigning for Wallace, unencumbered by any tie to the new center.

Yet Harvard's coercing of Hughes's resignation purely because of peaceful, legally expressed political views—an action not revealed publicly until the publication of Seymour Martin Lipset's and David Riesman's *Education and Politics at Harvard* in 1975—made a mockery of Conant's rhetoric about the need for scholars to be "fearless seekers of the truth," free to plunge into controversial topics in an environment of "absolutely unmolested inquiry." Buck later claimed that Russian Research Center scholars voluntarily reached a "self-determination" that they "would not participate freely in politics that would bring them into controversial positions in regard to present government policy," and that "there was nothing here in university policy that would have ever suggested that."[121] Indeed, restrictions on political activities were not yet, in 1948, formally written into "university policy." But at the same time, the message imparted by Harvard officials to Hughes also applied to other young scholars: Don't rock the boat—at least, not until you get tenure.

That Conant's overly abstract, timid or aloof approach to defending academic freedoms could impede timely action was demonstrated by his response in the second case, a controversial March 1948 allegation by the House Un-American Activities Committee (HUAC) chairman J. Parnell Thomas that a prominent government scientist represented "one of the weakest links in our atomic security." The target of Thomas's remarks, Edward U. Condon, director of the Bureau of Standards, was not one of Conant's favorite scientists. Never one to pull punches, the sharp-tongued, strong-willed theoretical physicist, one of the early recruits to the S-1 Section on Uranium, caused migraines for the Manhattan Project's administrators, ultimately fleeing Los Alamos in disgust after clashing with Groves over compartmentalization restrictions. When the war ended, Condon had emerged as one of the leaders of the atomic scientists' political movement, and battled Conant from the other side of the barricades during the controversy over domestic atomic energy legislation. However, neither Conant nor other scientists had the slightest reason to suspect Condon of disloyalty, or to believe that Thomas was concerned about anything more than generating publicity. Beyond that, Condon's defenders deeply resented the fact that Thomas had leaked the charge to reporters without presenting supporting evidence or giving Condon a chance to defend himself. Without elaborating on the "derogatory" information it claimed to hold, the committee catalogued Condon among "other Government officials in strategic positions who are playing Stalin's game to the detriment of the United States." Appalled by what they regarded as character assassination through unsupported smears, scientific organizations moved to stem the attacks before less prominent scientists fell victim.[122]

Towering in prestige over the rest of American science, the National Academy of Sciences debated how best to respond. Its president, Alfred N. Richards—selected to replace Frank Jewett after Conant had declined the post in early 1947—sought out Conant's response to a draft statement condemning HUAC's tactics and warning that a repetition would "threaten the ability of Government to induce able scientists to enter into or remain in Government positions," a development that could cause the country "incalculable harm."[123] But Conant was far from enthusiastic about rallying to Condon, though he thought he had been "most unjustly accused and is an entirely loyal citizen and, as far as I know, a first-rate Director of the Bureau of Standards." Not that he sympathized with the attackers, but Conant wondered "whether the National Academy charging into this won't do more harm than good." Like Bush, he worried about the public reaction if scientists seemed to be seeking special privileges or exemptions from investigations, or seemed to be threatening to blackmail the government by withholding services.[124] Instead, he proposed asking for a careful legal inquiry into the entire issue of smear tactics and congressional investigations—an idea grander in scale and far less likely to influence the immediate controversy. Conant's explanation sheds light on the unemotional, orderly approach he adhered to:

What I don't like about the whole business is this. We are witnessing the use of a smear technique by Congress in an area to which as scientists we are particularly sympathetic. This technique is not new. It was used very successfully by Senator Nye and the pacifists in the 20's—or was it the early 30's—to smear the munition manufacturers, and I am inclined to think did irreparable damage to the United States in connection with the crises of 1938–41. The same technique was used quite deliberately by Mr. Roosevelt and his advisors to "get" the public utility people when the New Deal came into power. After they had been sufficiently smeared, the S.E.C. legislation was enacted. In this case I am not prepared to say that the final end wasn't a good one, but I am quite sure it didn't justify the means.

The real problem before the American people is not Condon or the scientists but trying to find some method of holding in check Congressional inquiries. I have urged every lawyer that I have come in contact with for the last half a dozen months (before the Condon case came up) to try to work on this problem. It is an extremely difficult one from a technical point of view. No one wants to abridge the right of Congress to investigate. We couldn't if we wanted to. But it is important somehow to protect not only scientists and Government officials but all manner of citizens in private and public life. Therefore, it seems to me you ought to broaden enormously the point of view of this statement reciting the whole history of the national scandal of Congressional smearing techniques which has been going on for more than a decade. If you do this, and then show how it will affect scientists who have been in touch with the Government and are, therefore, open to the charge of being weak links in security chains, and finally urge the appointment of a commission of lawyers to do something about it in the way of improving procedures, I think you might make a contribution.[125]

After Richards rejected his idea, however, Conant endorsed "without any great enthusiasm" a revised academy statement that urged "full and impartial investigation of legitimate charges" but denounced a "procedure by which a man is represented to the public as guilty before having been given opportunity to answer."[126] He chose not to speak out as an individual on the case, at least not in any forum that attracted press notice. On May 3, 1948, after Richards privately expressed concern to Thomas, the academy released a statement expressing "grave concern" that the committee's unfair attack on Condon "may diminish the respect with which citizens regard opportunities for service to their Government."[127]

Thomas and HUAC, having thrown Condon's loyalty into doubt, turned their attention to a more titillating arena: allegations of Communist penetration of the Hollywood movie industry. But the academy's belated and meek protest had had little if any effect on the outcome: "No newspaper has seen fit to make the slightest allusion" to it, Richards reported ruefully.[128] The experience disappointed both the academy leadership and Conant. Both returned later to the issue in the year, hoping for more concrete and more sweeping action to protect the civil liberties of scientists and others while according due weight to the growing suspicion of subversion.

Pleading for tolerance even as he strongly denounced Soviet actions, fearful that volatile swings in public opinion would lead to potentially disastrous foreign policy decisions, Conant tried to ameliorate the effect of the worsened international situation on American attitudes toward educational and political freedoms; he rebuffed fatalistic predictions of a third world war and simultaneously staked out a position as a "hard-headed idealist" dispensing cool, tough-minded advice in uncertain times.[129] The October 1948 publication of his book *Education in a Divided World: The Function of the Public Schools in Our Unique Society* cemented Conant's reputation as a national educator who clearly discerned the dangers and debacles of Soviet Communism yet retained confidence in democratic ideals. Conant aimed his book not at a highbrow audience but at a large readership of educators and the intelligent, literate, reasonably informed public, and he succeeded. Praised in reviews in leading newspapers and journals, *Education in a Divided World* was listed as one of the 1948's ten most influential books.[130] As suggested by his choice of subtitle, Conant devoted much of the book to his familiar argument that publicly funded education constituted the key to a fluid, socially mobile, economically and politically vital American democracy that would triumph in the long-term ideological contest with the Soviet Union. Predictably, however, most public interest centered on his analysis of the most immediate and controversial issues of the Cold War. Along with his blast against the "criminal folly" of preventive war, his prediction that Soviet leaders sought victory by ideological appeal rather than by military conquest, his views on universal military service, and his support for U.S. foreign policy, that meant Conant's views on American education's proper response to the Communist menace.[131]

Conant now responded more directly to concerns of "alarmed" and "excited" citizens that " 'communist infiltration' " was turning universities into "centers for fifth column activities." The proper response of educators to such fears, Conant insisted, was to

> emphasiz[e] again the central position in this country of tolerance of diversity of opinion and [to] express confidence that *our* philosophy is superior to alien importations. After all, this is but one version of the far wider problem . . . : how are we to win the ideological conflict if it continues on a non-shooting basis? Clearly not by destroying our basic ideas but by strengthening them; clearly not by retreating in fear from the Communist doctrine but by going out vigorously to meet it.[132]

Conant's affirmation of the right of scholars to study whatever subjects they wished was resolute yet defensive, framed in terms designed to reassure anti-Communists that he did not intend to permit Marxist study sessions in Harvard lecture halls. "Studying a philosophy does not mean endorsing it, much less proclaiming it," he stressed. "We study cancer in order to learn how to defeat it. We must study the Soviet philosophy for exactly the same reason." Banning Communist literature, he argued, would only give it, like pornography, an "underground" appeal to the immature. In Conant's view—

once again defending the independence of universities by citing their potential usefulness in the Cold War struggle for young minds—Communist ideas
should be vigorously "combated in the classroom." And if a teacher proved to
be an "avowed supporter of the Marx-Lenin-Stalin line," Conant still adhered
to his opposition to bans, loyalty oaths, or firings: The best response was "to
force him into the open and tear his argument to pieces with counter
arguments."[133] Not yet was Conant ready to endorse an open ban on party
members.

Conant's blend of sharp anti-Soviet rhetoric with a defense of traditional
democratic freedoms, his provocative, challenging, yet politically safe analysis
won praise from mainstream reviewers, including a fulsome paean from a
young Caspar W. Weinberger, ten years out of Harvard. "President Conant of
Harvard has, in this small volume, written one of the sanest, best-reasoned,
most logical, tolerant and wisest expositions of the crisis now faced by
America that has appeared in this or any other year," wrote the future
Reagan administration secretary of defense in the *San Francisco Chronicle.*
The *New York Herald-Tribune* found Conant's book "far-reaching" and
"intelligent," while the *Saturday Review of Literature* praised him for bringing a "toughness and freshness of outlook" to themes that might "in less
capable hands seem threadbare and platitudinous." One reviewer called
Education in a Divided World not "an alarmist's trumpet call" but "nevertheless
a call to arms."[134]

But no endorsement was more significant than that bestowed by that
paragon of the American establishment, the *New York Times,* and its reviewer,
the New York University philosopher Sidney Hook, the one New York
intellectual with whose ideas Conant found a strong, growing, and reciprocal
resonance. Perhaps the most distinguished Marxist scholar of the 1930s, Hook
had violently and vocally abandoned Stalinism and Communism and now
(supporting "democratic socialism") engaged in regular and sometimes nasty
guerrilla warfare with intellectuals he considered insufficiently condemna-
tory of Soviet atrocities, well on the way to filling his "quasi-official role" as
"the premier anti-Communist of the 1950s."[135]

In Conant, Hook discovered to his pleasure an example of what to him
seemed an endangered species: a "plain-spoken," pragmatic, unapologetically
anti-Communist academic, in tune with "current thought trends in this country"
and willing and able to do battle with a "noisy group of American educators—
who cry havoc at the slightest lapse from American ideals, but remain silent
before, when they do not condone, police methods in Soviet education." Hook
hailed Conant's "realism" as a "[p]articularly encouraging sign of possible
change in educational thinking," a refreshing departure from the professional
educators' "stock-in-trade" of "vague, high-order abstractions" susceptible to
conflicting interpretations. Better still, in an implicit allusion to the atomic
scientists' movement, Hook detected "little trace in Mr. Conant's position of
that political naivete which has marred the thinking of most scientists outside

their laboratories." Contrasted to those scientific and educational colleagues who were "urging a policy toward Stalin which failed toward Hitler," Hook wrote, Conant's "common sense appraisal of what the world Communist movement is about seems like extraordinary acumen."

Hook's laudatory review inaugurated a significant ideological alliance between the Harvard educator and the New York intellectual. "It is hoped," Hook concluded, "that this book will reach all educators—not least his own faculty."[136]

Despite its solidly anti-Soviet stance, *Education in a Divided World* had offered, in Hook's words, "small comfort for reactionaries who under the guise of defense against Soviet aggression would like to relinquish our liberal traditions." But in fact, although only a handful of persons knew of his shift, even before Conant's book reached the shelves its author had abandoned his uncompromising insistence on preserving unfettered freedom of speech and excluding political loyalty tests on teachers. Conant had sent his manuscript off to Harvard University Press's printers after completing his introduction on July 7, 1948; the official publication date was October 14. In that three-month interval, events dramatically intensified the anti-Communist atmosphere in the United States—and Conant's reaction to it.

CHAPTER 22

Cold War Educator, Part II

"Nobody Is Safe"
August 1948–May 1949

I would think you stood a much better chance of defending the right of
inquiry into things and people having a variety of political opinions if you
once got defined that small coterie who hardly need protection and declare
them out. That would create a clear-cut issue . . . A lot of people would say
that I sold myself down the road to the reactionaries.
> — To fellow educators, urging a ban on Communist teachers,
> September 1948

But it should mean something to you that professors in our colleges and
universities are being fired for nonconformist ideas, that it's becoming a
crime to subscribe to the *Nation*, that everywhere in this country fear is
taking the place of reason.
> — Harvard professor to student, in May Sarton's
> *Faithful Are the Wounds*

In the summer of 1948, the postwar "Red scare" escalated into a "psychodrama
of mystery and revelation, imputations of guilt and protestations of innocence,"
in the phrase of one historian.[1] The international situation lent an ominous
backdrop to the production. Soviet troops blockaded West Berlin, which
subsisted from supplies dropped by U.S. planes; Moscow's stranglehold on
Eastern Europe tightened; and voices claimed with increasing frequency that
an East-West war was only a matter of time. "COULD REDS SEIZE DETROIT?"
asked *Look* magazine, providing a grim fanciful description of the city under
Kremlin occupation.[2]

Domestic politics fueled this hysteria. Eager to unseat Harry Truman, the
"accidental president," and to end sixteen years of Democratic rule, Republican
leaders searched for a way to exploit the internal security issue as the fall
elections neared. It may seem farfetched that the administration responsible
for the Truman Doctrine, the Marshall Plan, and a strict internal-security
program would face the charge of being soft-on-Communism; but political

opportunism and public fear was a potent mix—and partisans on both sides of the aisle quickly recognized that fact.

Egging on the search for Communist infiltrators and spies, the House Un-American Activities Committee (HUAC), the spearhead of the Republican drive to elevate the internal security issue, set late-summer hearings to investigate charges by FBI informer Elizabeth Bentley that a Communist spy ring had operated in the Roosevelt administration in Washington in the late 1930s—a not-so-subtle attempt to discredit the incumbent president by attacking the New Deal. Not to be outdone, the Truman administration acted to demonstrate its own alacrity in rooting out domestic Communists. With Hoover's FBI aggressively leading the charge the Justice Department named the Communist Party as a legal criminal conspiracy, thus giving prosecutors the right to move against party members at will. In late July, a federal grand jury in New York indicted twelve members of the American Communist Party's national board under the little-used Smith Act for conspiring to overthrow the government and for membership "in a society, group and assembly of persons who teach and advocate the overthrow and destruction of the United States by force and violence."[3]

Concerned by the frenzy and acutely aware of its political pitfalls, Truman treaded a perilous middle path, scorning Communists and "fellow travelers" like Progressive Party candidate Wallace, yet at the same time defending the civil rights of those unfairly smeared. His harsh words for Wallace and stern policy toward the Soviets in Berlin gave Truman political room for maneuver and helped undercut Republican hopes of painting him as a coddler of Communists, but he still faced increasing pressure to divorce himself from those elements now regarded as unacceptably tainted by allegiance to, or even contact with, the manifest evil of Communism.[4] In this charged atmosphere, failing to support hard-line Cold War verities implied not just dissent but something close to treason.

Enter Alger Hiss. In newsreels, radio, and newspapers, the most effective spectacle yet produced by the House Un-American Activities Committee kept the nation on tenterhooks as it followed the hearings into allegations that the ex-State Department official, now president of the prestigious Carnegie Endowment for International Peace, had belonged to a Soviet espionage ring in Washington from 1934 to 1938. Hiss's presence at the Yalta Conference as an aide to FDR gave the charge a special resonance, fitting neatly into right-wing conspiracy theories that Roosevelt had sold out Eastern Europe to Stalin. A walking embodiment of the East Coast liberal establishment—upper-class, aristocratic, a Harvard Law School graduate, a striped-pants diplomat—Hiss offered an appealing target for Republican anti-Communists eager to prove that traitors, subversives, and fellow travelers had been "boring from within" the top echelons of American society and government since the "socialist" New Deal. This perfectly fit the Republican election strategy (although the presidential candidate, Thomas Dewey, tried to stay above the fray), which featured charges that the Truman administration had fostered a rise in Communist influence abroad and at home. The fiery president retaliated by charging that the HUAC hearings were nothing but a "red herring" to divert attention from the Republicans' refusal to tackle inflation.[5]

Throughout August, the congressional crusade, led by a freshman California Republican named Richard M. Nixon, captured headlines. Quietly aided by Hoover's FBI, which since 1946 had put Hiss at the nexus of a Communist conspiracy inside the executive branch, Nixon thirsted for the opportunity to make his mark as the capital's foremost anti-Communist sleuth. The drama began on August 3 when HUAC produced the mournful, husky, sepulchral figure of Whittaker Chambers, a *Time* magazine senior editor and Communist apostate now turned informer. Chambers appeared as a supporting witness for Bentley, but his allegation against Hiss quickly became the focus of the hearings when Hiss demanded a chance to clear his name and took the witness chair two days later. HUAC members knew they had a good thing going, and soon established the Hiss-Chambers duel as the centerpiece of their investigation. Skillfully blending open hearings and leaks from executive sessions to stimulate public interest, Nixon and the committee united accuser and accused for a dramatic private encounter, then hauled Hiss back on the stand later in the month to hear new charges of Communist contacts he had allegedly made during the New Deal.

Later events—including a 1950 conviction (after a first trial ended in a hung jury) on perjury charges for his denial of involvement in the espionage ring—threw the question of Hiss's guilt or innocence into dispute, where it has remained ever since.[6] Initially, however, Hiss's defenders, including Conant, had little doubt where the truth lay. Though he did not know Hiss personally,[7] Conant felt "certain that he was an innocent victim of a vicious Red hunt."[8] And one of Hiss's staunchest supporters was none other than William L. Marbury, who as a War Department lawyer had helped draft domestic atomic energy legislation in the summer of 1945 under Conant's supervision. Marbury's admiration for Conant had rapidly skyrocketed; of all those on the Interim Committee, he later declared, "I found Jim Conant to be the most sensible, in that he could match wits with Oppenheimer, was as far-seeing a statesman as Bush, and his ability to handle people seemed equal to that of George Harrison."[9] Their mutual admiration society continued beyond the war's end. Marbury and his wife joined the Conants at their summer retreat for mountain climbing and schmoozing, and Conant scouted out Marbury in 1946 as a possible new dean of the law school, at the suggestion of their mutual friend the war secretary, Robert Patterson. That idea fell through, but when Harvard Corporation member Henry James announced his intention to retire in 1947 Conant fixed on Marbury as a reliable candidate to fill the vacancy and thereby consolidate his control of the powerful body over the conservative State Street faction headed by the strong-willed treasurer, Bill Claflin. The nomination of Marbury touched off a private *bataille royale,* a knock-down, drag-out power struggle brewing ever since Conant first became president of Harvard and privately vowed to break the back of the entrenched Brahmin aristocracy.[10] While Conant could count on Grenville Clark's firm support, Claflin and Charles Coolidge favored Ralph Lowell, a "right sort" Brahmin, and they choked at seating Marbury, who besides being an obvious Conant ally and a non-Bostonian to boot, had not even attended Harvard College! That Marbury had been graduated from Harvard Law School hardly compensated for Conant's effrontery, since the notion of an outsider on the alumni-dominated Corporation had been unheard-of since the body was formed in Puritan times. Nor was the old guard pleased by Conant's remark that he had not nominated a Bostonian because, after looking over the field, "we didn't find anyone."[11]

In October 1947, faced with a loyalty test to Conant, the Corporation approved Marbury's appointment by a 5–2 vote, but Claflin refused to concede defeat and instead carried the battle to block ratification to the Overseers, the larger alumni body which routinely rubber-stamped Corporation decisions. Determined to have their way, Conant and Clark pulled out all the stops in a behind-the-scenes lobbying campaign for Marbury, calling in pro-Marbury endorsements and testimonials from Dean Acheson, John McCloy, George Harrison, Robert Patterson, and other notables in Washington. In a blunt private memorandum to the Overseers shortly before the decisive January 12, 1948 meeting, Conant threatened to resign if they failed to back him and a majority of the Corporation: "If this election is not confirmed, it will be apparent to the Treasurer and to the President that a majority of the Overseers think that the Treasurer and not the President ought to run the University."[12] In the end, Conant prevailed and Claflin departed, climaxing a bitter duel that left scars for the rest of his presidency—and in early 1948 Marbury joined the Corporation, to a mixture of applause and grumbles from Conant's supporters and rivals. Felix Frankfurter congratulated Clark both on Marbury's election and the "stiff fighting" that it required, observing that "Convictions and reason, like all other functions, rust unless they are exercised, and an issue such as that raised by Bill Marbury's election keeps spiritual muscles from becoming flabby."[13] From the opposite corner, overseer Bobby Cutler was said to have overheard the following remark at the Somerset Club: "By God, the place has gone to hell under Conant. Did you see who the class marshals were? A Jew, a Negro, and a Roman Catholic. And they say this fellow Marbury isn't even a college man!"[14]

One issue that hadn't arisen, however, had been that Marbury had been a schoolboy chum of Alger Hiss and a close friend for two decades. After Chambers first testified before HUAC, Marbury instantly volunteered his legal services. "If you and Alger are party members," he wrote the accused's brother, Donald, the next morning, "then you can send me an application." On August 5, Marbury accompanied Alger Hiss when he appeared before the committee to declare his innocence. Satisfied that Hiss had impressed the congressmen and the trouble seemed to be waning, Marbury departed for Europe for a month of unrelated State Department business. Instead of cooling off, however, the case heated up again by the end of August. HUAC called Hiss back for private testimony and then public hearings on his activities during the New Deal, and at the latter Nixon seemed to shake Hiss's insistence that he and Chambers had barely known each other by getting him to admit that he had loaned Chambers a car. Suddenly, some of those who had vigorously defended Hiss began to wonder if, indeed, he had something to conceal.

Conant, who had followed the developments with growing unease, gave Marbury the bad news of Hiss's slipping fortunes when the lawyer returned from Switzerland on September 12 for a Harvard Corporation meeting. At 17 Quincy Street that Sunday night, Conant, Marbury, and Grenville Clark discussed the case for several hours.[15] Conant and Clark feared that unless Hiss effectively refuted Chambers's claims, "a flood of similar charges against political and academic figures would soon follow, which would have a very serious impact on our foreign policy and on academic freedom generally."[16] "Nobody is safe and great public harm will be done," Conant warned, if Hiss were unjustly smeared and ruined.[17]

It was for reasons that far transcended the fate of one enigmatic former official, therefore, that Conant and Clark impressed upon Marbury the importance of retaking the public offensive quickly by filing a libel suit against Chambers. Like Hiss, who had challenged his accuser to make his charges outside the privileged forum of a congressional hearing room, Conant had heard Chambers on the radio program "Meet the Press" two weekends earlier repeat his accusation that Hiss belonged to a Communist cell in the 1930s, and might still belong. Conant believed those unprotected remarks constituted sufficient grounds for a suit, and Marbury, whose admiration for Conant was boundless and whose own career had profited from his unstinting support, was swayed by his and Clark's arguments.

It was a decision he would later regret. While in Cambridge, Marbury learned from another local eminence, Judge Charles Wyzanski, that Hiss had so far been dissuaded from filing a suit by attorneys who urged him to wait until his case was better prepared. That was in fact the state of affairs Marbury found on his return to Baltimore, with Hiss itching to face down Chambers in court but wary of countermanding the advice of his distinguished New York lawyer, Edward McLean. Alarmed that Chambers might "take the offensive" by lodging his own slander suit first, Marbury strongly urged Hiss to file despite his other lawyers' misgivings, and sought endorsement for this course of action from other advisers such as John W. Davis, the new president of the Carnegie Endowment for International Peace; Arthur Ballantine, a former Treasury Department official; and Robert Patterson. Troubled by his reading of the record of HUAC hearings, which had established the existence of a Hiss-Chambers relationship of some sort a decade earlier, Marbury also interviewed Alger and Priscilla Hiss (getting the "mystifying" impression that the latter, while insisting on the couple's innocence, felt somehow responsible for getting her husband into trouble). Faced with conflicting legal advice, Hiss backed Marbury, saying he had "nothing to hide" from a full-blown court trial. And on September 27, Hiss sued Chambers for slander in U.S. District Court in Baltimore.

"We have a hard road ahead of us," Marbury wrote Conant in enclosing a copy of the suit, "but I am reasonably hopeful of the outcome."[18]

Conant's fears about the danger of witch-hunts spreading to the academic realm were not without foundation. The Hiss case coincided with a turning toward educational institutions as a new target for investigation. The list of areas of American society already under the microscope was growing steadily: the atomic energy program, labor unions, TVA, Hollywood, and now, especially at the local and state levels, high schools and universities.[19]

The efforts to purge the classroom of the Communist taint took many forms, varying from region to region and campus to campus. There was the loyalty oath tactic, spreading from state to state; California was the site of the next major battle. Campaigns to force the firings or resignations of professors accused of "Red" connections was another favored technique. Throughout 1948, the University of Washington had come under the scrutiny of a state legislative committee—the Joint Legislative Fact-Finding Committee on Un-American Activities, headed by a right-wing Republican chairman, Albert Canwell—in search of Communist organizers and sympathizers. Rather than stand up to the inquisitors, the university's administration, led by president Raymond B. Allen, had promised to cooperate fully in vetting the politics of faculty members, launched its own internal investigation to pressure suspected Communist professors to disclose their political affiliations, and vowed promptly to dismiss anyone found to have participated in subversive activities. In July, the state panel held a week of highly publicized hearings in which witnesses described alleged on-campus Communist activities. Several professors refused to testify, and some went to jail. On September 8, the university administration officially began proceedings to evict six scholars who had refused either to disclose whether they had been Communists or to inform on others.[20]

There were also accusations that certain assigned readings spread "un-American ideas" or were written by authors who were party members, had made pro-Soviet statements, or belonged to "subversive" organizations on the attorney general's growing list. Even scholarship on Soviet and Communist history and philosophy—which Conant now described as "the number one educational need of the present moment"[21]—became a suspicious activity, warranting close monitoring by off-campus watchdogs, whether self-appointed investigators, legislative committees, or police authorities. The chairman of the House Un-American Activities Committee, Representative J. Parnell

Thomas, announced his intention to look into public school personnel and textbooks—a comment that sent shivers down the spines of scholars who envisioned an orgy of book-burning. How long would it be before the investigators ransacked Widener Library for offending titles?

While Harvard had yet to feel the brunt of the campaign, the issues hit close to home for Conant. The university had its share of controversial characters: Shapley and Matthiessen were actively involved in the Wallace campaign. Pressures resulting from the Russian Research Center persisted as well; its officers prudently informed the FBI before making purchases from Communist bookstores so as, in Buck's words, "to save the trouble of being hounded," and also told Hoover's men of contacts they made with Russian and Polish sources to obtain materials.[22] As public hostility grew toward anything "Russian," the center attracted negative attention: Adam B. Ulam, a scholar there and later its director, recalls that postmen sometimes refused to deliver copies of *Pravda* and other Soviet publications.[23] State Department, air force, and Central Intelligence Agency officials also took an increased interest in its personnel and research topics ("What will happen when Stalin dies?"),[24] but the center was less constrained than some research institutions with more direct federal links—it secretly agreed to obtain certain books on Communism and Soviet affairs for the Library of Congress, which feared that congressional investigating committees might notice its own purchases of such materials.[25]

By late September 1948, Conant was ready to support a move he had previously resisted: the banning of Communists from the teaching profession. It is usually assumed that Conant held back from a total bar on Communist teachers until June 1949, when he and the rest of the members of the Educational Policies Commission of the National Education Association publicly took that stand.[26] But it was in fact nine months earlier that Conant first argued that in order for the educational establishment to protect itself against further state inquests, to preserve the right to study and teach controversial subjects, and to defend leftist faculty members and others who were not actually party members—it needed to throw a bone to the anti-Communists. On September 22–25, as Hiss and Marbury prepared to sue Chambers, Conant joined twenty of the country's leading educators at the National Education Association's Washington, D.C., headquarters near Dupont Circle for the thirty-second meeting of the Educational Policies Commission (EPC). Conant had joined the EPC in 1941, instantly attaining *primus inter pares* status by virtue of his Harvard post, and had taken advantage of the group's meetings to nurture alliances with other educational leaders as well to help shape the group's pronouncements on federal aid to education, military conscription, and other issues. His first term, from 1941 to 1945, he described as an "apprenticeship in the realities of public education." Besides Conant, members included presidents of universities and colleges, school superintendents, a representative of the U.S. Office of Education, the president of the Carnegie Foundation for the Advancement of Teaching, and other educational pooh-bahs. The EPC had "affected significantly the course of public education" in America, Conant believed, and had come to occupy a "unique role in the educational world."[27]

On this occasion the pressing issue was how to react to the anti-Communist crusade sweeping the nation, and by the time the meeting ended, Conant had forged a consensus that the commission should support a ban on Communist teachers; this reached the public in a report on "Education and International Tension" the following June.

Strikingly, the verbatim transcript of the meetings[28] does not record Conant making the arguments that he later used publicly to support the ban. Both after the statement's publication and in his memoirs two decades later, Conant cited the Communists' alleged intellectual surrender to party discipline, their conspiratorial plotting, the danger of their doctrines penetrating the classroom.[29] In his closed-door comments to fellow educators, however, Conant justified the step on purely tactical grounds. Perhaps he left unsaid his derogatory assessments because they no longer needed saying and had become an accepted article of faith. But the tone and substance of his remarks leave little doubt that expediency and calculation figured far more prominently with him than any genuine alarm at the danger posed by Communist teachers. He first raised the possibility when the group was discussing a proposed policy statement that would help teachers now catching flak merely because they wanted to teach *about* the insidious doctrine. Some of the educators sensed there would be a price to pay for such support. "If we are going to be truly zealous for democracy," one cautioned, "we better decide to be against something else."[30]

EPC vice chairman James M. Spinning turned to Conant and asked his opinion.

"It is a tough question," Conant began cautiously. "Just at the risk of sticking my neck out and admitting that I might reverse myself, I am inclined to think that you would not employ a member of the Communist Party. That is a different thing than some vague phrase. And it might be coupled with a statement that it was important to study the doctrines of Marx, Engels and Lenin and others of that group. Then you would be on about the best ground."

Conant added that he had reached this position "with great regret." But, he went on, he had settled on it as necessary and appropriate—not only in elementary and secondary schools, but, although he was less sure about it, in universities as well. Genuine worry about Communist teachers hardly constituted a principal motive: in fact, he emphasized that banning party members would affect only a "terrifically small number" of teachers, perhaps one in a thousand.[31]

Not everyone at the table jumped at Conant's initiative.

Spinning could not "see the logic" in barring Communists from the classroom on the grounds that they seek a violent overthrow of the U.S. government, while at the same time they are permitted to run for elective office, a well-known point.[32] A year earlier, the ruling council of the American Association of University Professors, of which Conant was a member, had declared that so long as the Communist Party remained a "legal political party" in the United States, membership "in and of itself should not be regarded as a justifiable reason for exclusion from the academic professions."[33]

But times had changed. Conant pointed out that banning Communists from holding office created political and legal complications. Besides, just because certain people can run for office doesn't qualify them to teach. "Politics is one thing and teaching school is another," he insisted. "I wouldn't think those went along together. I would be opposed to outlawing the Communist Party, but I wouldn't be in favor of having communists teaching in our schools."[34]

"Suppose you have them in your school system, would you dismiss them?" asked George A. Selke.

"It is different and makes it much tougher," Conant replied.

What about Wallace supporters? somebody else asked.

"Disenfranchise everybody who voted for him in the last election," cracked Spinning.

No ivory tower innocents, the educators were far from ignorant of the political consequences of their actions—especially with a presidential vote just six weeks off. Spinning worried that a statement about the small percentage of Communists in the school system might be interpreted as backing Truman against the congressional investigators.

"You can wait until after the election," responded Conant.[35]

Conant's comments illuminated why the educational leaders believed they could better defend non-party liberals, leftist, and Wallacites—who, they averred, deserved full protection—if the EPC took a stand against Communists. "If you were willing to take the stand against members of the party," Conant explained, "you could make a strong defense against anybody who is being persecuted as belonging to popular front or front organizations, which is a different thing."[36] Repeatedly, the educators had raised recent headline-grabbing cases of government pressure on teachers accused of sympathy or associations with subversive organizations, doctrines. Alluding to HUAC's threat to investigate public school textbooks, one EPC member predicted that the watchdogs would "take a sentence up here and down here and put the different sentences together and say, 'This shows Russian bias.' "[37]

Conant advocated the prohibition on Communist teachers as a tactical move that would cast pro-academic freedom arguments in the most favorable light. School authorities could then concentrate on assuring the survival and health of a far larger and more defensible group of teachers, courses, and textbooks:

I would think you stood a much better chance of defending the right of inquiry into things and people having a variety of political opinions if you once got defined that small coterie who hardly need protection and declare them out. That would create a clear-cut issue. That would be my view. A lot of people would say that I sold myself down the road to the reactionaries.[38]

After hearing all the arguments, the EPC members approved by a show of hands a motion to include in their upcoming pamphlet the statement "that a Communist Party member should not be employed in the schools."[39]

The tentative decision was not made without second thoughts—but Conant did his best to quell them. One EPC member asked whether firing a teacher because of party membership would "stand up in the courts?"

In reply, Conant backed off and set the stage for confusion nine months later:

> I said not to employ, not anything about discharging. Whether you can discharge in a given school system is a matter of the particular law. You can implement it where there are temporary certificates. If you say you do not think they should be employed, you make a policy statement, and I think you would be all right. If you say they should be discharged, you are making an operational statement. *You are ducking the issue, but you would want to duck it in a policy statement.*[40] [emphasis added]

Conant alluded to his philosophical grounds for banning Communists, using language that implied a quasi-religious belief in education's ideological function in the postwar world. Communism's philosophy was so "inconsistent" with that taught in U.S. schools, he argued, that having one of its adherents as a teacher was "like having a Protestant teaching in a Catholic school or a Catholic teaching in a Protestant school. You have different articles of faith."[41]

Although the EPC decided that its statement would also include a condemnation of smear tactics and Red-baiting, Professor John K. Norton of Teachers College, Columbia University, and chairman of the commission, knew the group was crossing a dangerous line. "I have come with great reluctance," he said, "although I am there, to what appears to be a reversal of the traditional American policy that you are not going to cause trouble to an individual because of his political beliefs or affiliations.

"The fact is that the Communist Party is even a legal party in some states and yet we are saying something that appears to be a reversal of one of the most fundamental tenets in American life."[42]

The surging controversy over loyalty and security also continued to raise difficult questions about Conant's other chief constituency, the scientific community, the target of magnified popular suspicions with each revelation of alleged espionage. "Fired by an ambition to discover the Alger Hiss of science,"[43] the House Un-American Activities Committee and its chairman, Thomas, still disseminated new and rehashed charges that leftist scientists working on atomic energy and other government-funded projects had spilled secrets in the past and were still an ongoing major security risk. And while there had been, indeed, espionage during the Manhattan Project and after, HUAC's sense of imagination was sometimes evident: noting that the Belgian Congo was a known source of uranium ore, it suspiciously noted Shapley's involvement in an astronomical observatory there.[44] No longer the toast of Washington for having won the war against Japan, the scientists were now cast in the role of gullible, utopian, dangerously talkative political waifs who needed close watching to make sure they didn't give away the secrets they themselves were responsible for producing.[45]

Conant encountered this anger toward scientists when he went back to the National War College on September 14, 1948, just as HUAC was hurling (and leaking) charges that Manhattan Project scientists had passed atomic data to Moscow during the war.[46] "There is quite a lot of suspicion about those physicists right now," one officer complained. "From what was in the papers this morning you wonder just who they are working for."[47]

Conant was philosophic. He thought the present scare was an "inevitable" outgrowth of the growing tension with Moscow, "and [of] the perfectly obvious fact that I suppose everybody realistically knew in an armed truce they are going to do what everybody does in war, that is, espionage, sabotage, and so on." Still, he insisted, government officials had to strike a balance between "security measures that will insure that their vital information doesn't get out" and draconian measures that would discourage scientists from working for them.[48]

The National Academy of Sciences and its president, Alfred Richards, also worried about the cloud of suspicion hovering over the scientists. Disappointed by their ineffectiveness in rebutting the smears against Condon earlier in the year, the academy's leaders had decided in June 1948 to create a committee to "investigate, study and report . . . regarding civil rights, includ- ing clearance of scientific personnel, secrecy, and loyalty investigations," and the relationship of these questions to federally supported scientific research.[49] The proposed panel bore a strong resemblance to the group Conant had urged Richards to establish three months earlier, so it was no surprise that he asked Conant to be chairman when it was finally formed in November. To assist him, Richards turned to two familiar faces: Robert Oppenheimer and Bell Telephone Laboratories president Oliver Buckley.[50] Both, like Conant, sat on the AEC's General Advisory Committee and could speak with author- ity on the contrasting demands of science and security.

They were also quite busy. It took six weeks for the three men to arrange a meeting—over lunch at the Century Association in mid-town Manhattan on December 29—where they could draft a statement for Richards to bring before the academy's leadership. By then, the political atmosphere had hardened, and the result was a heightened perception that Soviet espionage represented not just the paranoid fantasies of right-wing conspiracy-mongers but a genuine threat of uncertain dimensions.

One intervening event did the most to multiply suspicions: a series of stunning developments in late November and early December had blown the Alger Hiss case wide open and cast serious doubts on his innocence. Requested by Hiss's lawyers to document his contention that their client had belonged to a Communist spy ring, Chambers had produced decade-old internal State Department memos that he said Hiss had provided him, as well as contemporaneous notes written by Hiss. When Marbury recognized his friend's handwriting, he suffered a shock that never quite wore off: suddenly, he realized, the issue was not whether Hiss could successfully press his libel suit, but whether he could defend himself against a suit brought by Chambers; worse, his own faith in Hiss was shaken. Many others who had jumped to Hiss's defense replicated Marbury's reaction when the documents were made public. And to assure maximum impact, Nixon made sure they were made public in the most sensational fashion, convening new hearings to announce the existence of what would be immortalized as the "Pumpkin Papers," after the unusual place used by Chambers to hide some of his evidence. On December 15, a New York grand jury indicted Hiss on two counts of perjury, mooting the libel suit against Chambers.[51]

Although Hiss was not a scientist, the startling new evidence against him signified a victory for Nixon, HUAC, and all those who had ardently insisted on the reality of the Soviet spy menace. The possibility that Hiss might actually be guilty dumbfounded many of his supporters. Future espionage charges lodged against academics, intellectuals, and diplomats now seemed to merit more serious consideration—especially from liberals who were chastened by having passionately defended a man once regarded as a martyr but now as suspect.[52] The political atmosphere turned dirty and sordid; there were lies in the air: "There was nothing quite like sworn testimony to make life look trivial and mean ever after," laments the narrator of Kurt Vonnegut's *Jailbird,* modeled after Chambers.[53] No one knew whom to trust: The "intense personal betrayal" of discovering that a trusted campus colleague had been a closet Communist, recalled the sociologist David Riesman, then at the University of Chicago, was comparable to finding out that someone was sleeping with your wife.[54]

Precisely when Conant grew convinced of Hiss's guilt, or lost confidence in his innocence, is not clear. He writes in his memoirs that after Hiss's conviction on perjury charges, in January 1950, "it was hard to maintain that there was no possibility of Communists being in positions of responsibility."[55] Hiss's defenders' faith actually eroded in stages, and a good chunk of it vanished when the "Pumpkin Papers" were made public in December 1948. Some of this seems to have affected Conant; though he does not mention Hiss specifically as a factor, his attitude toward security matters had taken on a noticeably harsher cast when he wrote to Oppenheimer on December 22 to present "a few random thoughts about what Buckley, you and I might advise Richards to do."

Conant urged that the academy couple a condemnation of smearing and guilt by association with an explicit affirmation that scientists were not claiming privileges not held by other citizens—or else not comment at all on the "loyalty" issue. He advocated relaxing security standards where government offices not handling confidential information were involved; prewar measures in these cases were sufficient, and therefore the academy ought to express the hope "that the loyalty order of the President as a blanket order may be modified or revoked."[56]

But where secret information was concerned, Conant took a much tougher line. He showed little tolerance toward scientists suspected of indiscretion or political naivete (i.e., an excess of sympathy for world government, or for Soviet policies), using language that set a standard that later haunted both himself and Oppenheimer. Six months earlier, in June 1948, Oppenheimer had ventured the belief that in the clearance procedure there should exist enough hope to "take a reasonable risk in favor of an individual."[57] But courageous defiance of public and political opinion was becoming more and more difficult. Conant wrote on December 22,

> It must be recognized that we are today faced with an international situation in which a small number of residents of this country are nevertheless connected by strong emotional ties to ideological doctrines which transcend their loyalty to the nation. While the evidence indicates that their number is small, the presence of something approaching international conspiracy can not be ignored. Furthermore, it must be recognized that quite apart from the possibility that some individuals might be connected with this conspiracy, others who are quite innocent of any such ties are nevertheless temperamentally naive and indiscreet and can not be trusted with confidential information in spite of their excellent intent and high ability. *The government, in resolving doubts on these matters about employees, including scientists, must settle the case in favor of the government rather than the individual. If a shadow of doubt exists, the individual should be prevented from having access to confidential information.*[58] [emphasis added]

Conant added that even in cases where clearance is withheld the government should "protect the individual and his reputation, unless acts of espionage have been committed." Someone suspected of being a "poor secrecy risk" might still be transferred to another, less sensitive government position, he suggested, adding the constructive point that the term "loyalty investigation" should be dropped because it might not be a person's "loyalty . . . but his discretion and judgment that are at fault."

Nevertheless, by acknowledging that "a shadow of doubt" could be enough to bar scientists from government, Conant gave voice to a mentality in which the slightest taint of leftism, past or present, or unpopular views on political matters, could be used by zealous inquisitors to disqualify loyal citizens. The "shadow of doubt" standard, in fact, came chillingly close to the obsessive mentality that would, less than six years later, move the majority of the board investigating Robert Oppenheimer, in a proceeding which Conant abhorred, to state that the government reserved the right to "search . . . the soul" of employees to assure their loyalty and reliability.[59]

At their long-delayed December 29 lunch at the Century, Conant, Buckley, and Oppenheimer drafted a statement that they subsequently revised in a flurry of phone calls and letters over the next week.[60] Clearly bearing the imprint of Conant's ideas, it cautiously balanced an endorsement of a strict system for clearing persons handling secret data with a plea for mild reforms to lessen the chances of injustices against those caught in the security system. Taking the increasingly common tactic of flashing hard-line credentials before seeking some mild reform — toughness before softness — the statement first "explicitly . . . repudiate[d]" the notion that scientists "should be accorded any preferred treatment," and firmly endorsed the proposition that security investigations for those dealing with secret data "must resolve doubt not in favor of the individual but in favor of security." At the same time, the three-some pleaded for a clearer distinction between doubts about an individual's loyalty and the more frequently invoked concerns about "character, experience and temperament"; between security requirements for federal employees using classified materials and those who did not (in the latter case, the group felt, there existed "no reason for, and many reasons against, applying elaborate investigative machinery, or the criteria of loyalty and security clearances"). They also asked that persons who were deemed unsuitable for jobs requiring clearance but were not involved in espionage should not be further "penalized, stigmatized, deprived of livelihood, or exposed to public shame."[61] They should instead be transferred to less "hazardous" positions; there should in general be a "more careful separation of the punitive from the preventive aspects of the problem of disloyalty in government service."[62]

This product of hurried consultations among worried but instinctively cautious men represented an effort to make the security problem "more manageable" rather than to spark a wholesale reform. Its equivocating, incremental nature may have been calculated to strike Truman as judicious, but it also ensured that it would have no dramatic impact. The New York lawyer John Lord O'Brian, a frequent adviser on Harvard business who had published a long article on the impact of loyalty investigations in the *Harvard Law Review*, responded to the draft statement — Conant had sent an advance copy — with lukewarm praise: he couldn't see how the statement could hurt, and thought it might help.[63]

Conant sent the statement on to Richards on January 13, writing that he hoped it "might have a very salutary effect."[64] But it didn't exactly set the academy ablaze: Oppenheimer's impression was that the academy's council thought it was "not very hot stuff and that many members would have wished to say more and deeper things."[65] Still, the council unanimously approved it on February 3, and sent it to Truman a week later with "the hope that you will find it of interest and possible usefulness."[66] Truman's perfunctory acknowledgment, drafted by a mid-level aide, gave scant indication that the president had read the two-page statement, let alone modified his views.[67]

Conant's efforts continued in this vein—vociferous but narrow expressions of concern that had little effect. In May and June 1949, joined by his General Advisory Committee colleagues, Conant publicly blasted a proposed congressional requirement that the FBI investigate the political backgrounds of young scientists awarded Atomic Energy Commission fellowships for pure— and unclassified—scientific research. (The uproar had been stimulated by the discovery that the AEC had given a stipend to a graduate student at the University of North Carolina who belonged to the Communist Party.) In telegrams to the Joint Committee on Atomic Energy chairman Brien McMahon, and in a joint GAC statement, he vigorously supported the AEC and Lilienthal policy that the education of the most promising young candidates, not political vetting, should be the sole criterion.[68]

Here again, Conant emphasized a "clear distinction" between scientists engaged in secret work and those doing open research, and he tried to be level-headed in a debate that had passed the no-return point of hysteria. Putting all fellowship recipients on the same basis of government employees working on classified projects, he wrote to McMahon, would not only add an unnecessary burden on the security system but foster a smothering atmosphere of tension on campus—exactly what he had hoped to avoid by banning classified research at Harvard. And, in any case, he added, "If occasionally a member of the Communist party should accidentally obtain one of these fellowships, no great harm would result as any demand on his part to obtain access to confidential information would automatically involve checking and personal investigation." Even a Communist scientist might make "important contributions," and there was a "good chance that as in the past a certain number of young Communists would have a revulsion of feeling and leave the party."

Conant also warned the congressmen not to alienate the nation's scientists from government service by "creating an atmosphere of distrust and suspicion in the scientific world as I feel certain the loss to the country will far outweigh the possible hazards involved in the calculated risk of the method now used."[69] But congressmen such as Republican senator Bourke Hickenlooper, eager to prove Lilienthal's "incredible mismanagement" of the AEC, showed far more interest in scoring political points and in discrediting the administration than they did in Conant's reasoned distinctions and arguments. In August 1949, bowing to congressional pressure, Truman signed the FBI provision, tacked on to the AEC appropriation bill, into law.[70] In science as in education, political and professional excommunication was becoming routine treatment for those who still dared to identify themselves as Communists.

By the end of 1948, Conant's still-private conversion to a supporter of a ban on Communist teachers—known only to fellow members of the Educational Policies Commission—was only one aspect of a more general, Cold War-inspired hardening of his outlook toward U.S. education. The Conant who from 1946 through mid-1948 had stressed tax-supported public education, political and academic freedom, economic health, and fluid social mobility as the true path to America's domestic well-being and international strength, had reached a turning point. His earlier position, in spirit and content, bore close resemblance to the "Zeal for American Democracy" program fitfully promoted by the Truman administration's Office of Education in 1947 and 1948 to "vitalize and improve education in the ideals and benefits of democracy and to reveal the character and tactics of totalitarianism." The historian Richard Freeland, an acerbic critic of Truman's internal security policies, has observed that the "Zeal" programs—intended to "strengthen national security through education," in the words of Truman's education commissioner, John Studebaker—"flowed from a challenge to Communism entirely distinct from the Truman Doctrine, the attorney general's list, and the deportation [of leftist radicals] drive"; they emphasized democratic values and international awareness ("world-mindedness") rather than "militant patriotism or anti-communism," and extolled "the principles of the United Nations, not realpolitik."[71]

But now, as these programs faded away and international and domestic tensions reached a higher pitch in late 1948 and early 1949, Conant's sense of the proper role of American education also seemed to shift. He still spoke in centrist terms, of guiding public opinion along a "dangerous knife edge" between equally unpalatable extremes—right and left, naivete and cynicism, complacency and despair, etc. But his center point in that balance had drifted. On his right, Conant took a harder line on security measures, as we have seen, laid the groundwork for taking a public stand against Communist teachers, roused support for a military draft, and tried to steel Americans for an indefinite rivalry with Moscow. And to his left, after publishing *Education in a Divided World*, Conant devoted himself to damage control: preventing new attacks on "liberals" in universities and laboratories, defending the teaching of courses on Communism and the Soviet Union, keeping the security system away from the campus, and forestalling the rise of a fatalistic acceptance of the inevitability of war or a mass movement favoring a preventive nuclear strike against the Soviet Union.

The preparation of the Educational Policies Commission report in the months following the September 1948 meeting reveal the extent to which Cold War ideology had come to dominate Conant's educational perspective. Conant deeply believed that U.S. education in general (and Harvard in particular) needed to inculcate American students, from "the kindergarten on," with the ethos of democratic capitalism and a centrist, mainstream, unthreatening political perspective comfortably within the emerging consensus. At times, Conant sounded more like a social engineer, psychologist, or philosopher—or perhaps the screenwriter of *Casablanca,* dreaming up Humphrey Bogart's pragmatic yet principled Rick—than a university administrator. In light of the "grim world in which we live," he had declared in late 1947, teachers should aim to achieve a "transformation" of young students into idealists of the "tough-minded" rather than the "visionary" sort—in other words, into "tough-minded idealists" of Conant's own mold.

> To increase their number and nourish their faith is high on my list of the educational aims made urgent by the times. Of course, it may be said that such individuals are born, not made. Granted to a considerable degree that it true, nevertheless, formal education can strengthen the idealism of the hardheaded skeptic and, conversely, it can greatly increase the powers of critical analysis of those who temperamentally are the starry-eyed. Admittedly, we are dealing with a question of a nice balance of mentalities and moods. We can all recognize the lopsided individuals; on one side of the fence stand the cynics and skeptics who pride themselves on being hard-boiled and scoff at "do-gooders" and debunk all social goals; on the other side we have the gullible but earnest souls bent on improving the lot of men, but forever dodging stubborn facts. Metaphorically speaking, we need to pick one from each of those groups and fuse the two into a single man. Surely when you do find the constructive features of each type combined in any one individual you find almost the ideal proponent of human freedom and a stout fighter for the rights of man.[72]

Nowhere is the urgency and depth of wish to link the educational and foreign-policy spheres more evident than in a letter he dashed off on January 3, 1949, to EPC chairman John K. Norton to aid the staff who were drafting ideas for the group's forthcoming report, "American Education and International Tensions." To obtain the "requisite synthesis between the two opposite blends of temperaments and points of view," Conant prescribed an "alternate hot-cold treatment" of students:

> The realities of the divided world in which we find ourselves make it necessary for all who temperamentally have been on the anti-militaristic side in the past to reexamine their position. As I have said on more than one occasion, I think the times demand the education of "tough-minded idealists." This means that our educational process should take those who by temperament and by home environment are apt to be on the starry-eyed idealistic side and make them more tough-minded by the exposure to the hard facts of life and emphasis on the empirical point of view; on the other hand, those who are all too hardboiled in their approach, cynical in their attitude, defeatist in their idealism should be given the opposite treatment by expo-

sure to portions of history and philosophy and literature which strongly emphasize the importance of the ideals of a free society as a moral basis on which this community must rest.[73]

Complementing Conant's concept of how American students should view themselves was his concept of how they should view the world. Believing that foreign policy decisions should be entrusted to educated experts (in and out of government) and then dispensed down to the public in simplified form,[74] Conant favored steps to enhance the educational preparations of America's postwar internationalist elite; during the war, for example, he had enthusiastically supported Paul Nitze, Christian Herter, and others in establishing a graduate school for international studies in Washington, an effort that led to the creation of Johns Hopkins University's School of Advanced International Studies.[75] But his earlier hopes that U.S. internationalism would be integrated within a global United Nations organization had waned, and Conant wrote to Norton in 1949 that the altered international situation and America's new role in it "force a change in education." U.S. education, he stated, now needed to attune students to the realities of a divided world — and to breed an "enlightened selfishness" regarding the political, economic, and military requirements of American global leadership, as opposed to the idealistic multilateralism characterizing the United Nations, world government, international control, or other starry-eyed schemes of dubious practicality. While students might remain "hopeful" that international organizations could be useful — and Conant himself, of course, had spoken optimistically of chances for international control of atomic energy until the fall of 1947 — they should be conditioned against believing that internationalization or world government offered "a magic formula that is going to get us out of this tough period rapidly."[76] Instead, he urged, education must prepare a new, enlarged, firmly nationalistic foreign-policy elite to run the world and cope with its complexities. "From the kindergarten on," Conant wrote,

> we have to give future citizens of the United States the same concern with the problems on the other side of the Atlantic and the Pacific that the British for centuries have been giving to their young people of the upper classes. This will have to be done, I believe, in terms of enlightened selfishness from the point of view of the United States and not too much in terms of Utopian goals embracing the future of all humanity. I believe we are more likely to do harm than good by propagandizing our schools for too distant goals or objectives.

Conant's vision suggested a curriculum keyed to contemporary politics and ideological goals, a kind of peacetime educational mobilization:

> The enlightened selfishness of the United States position first of all requires an understanding of the problems of the entire world which we face. These are for the first time, alas, military as well as economic and cultural. World

geography in terms of transport by ships and by air must be brought up to
date. Accuracy in these facts will be hard to achieve since it is very easy to
overstate the significance of the airplane when looking into the future. In
short, the logistics of both war and peace should form the basis of world
geography.

But his prescription also had a strong humanistic, nonmilitary dimension.
Convinced that "by the time a person is a young man he is a product of a
cultural pattern and his thinking and acting is heavily conditioned by this
pattern," he thought that international studies should be based on social
sciences, economics, anthropology, religion, and culture. Only by "understanding
the significance of different cultural patterns and disentangling these from
so-called racial characteristics," he observed, could one "hope to build up the
tolerance necessary for peace and good will in a divided but closely congested
world." As in *Education in a Divided World,* however, Conant's central
motive in stressing the social sciences was the need to study "the Communist
philosophy as exemplified by the writings now made official dogma in Russia
and the satellite states," as well as differing Marxist interpretations, "for
example, by the British Labor Party." The EPC's report should emphasize
two main objectives, he recommended: "First, a thorough study of our own
cultural patterns with a clear recognition of our historic goals, and second, a
careful study of the cultural pattern which is developing in Russia as the
consequence of (a) its history, and (b) the ruthless importation and indoctrination in the Marx-Engels-Lenin notion."

For all his advice, however, Conant remained torn—and his most impassioned recommendation lay in the hope that American educators would at
least be able to foster a "frank discussion" of the dilemmas facing those who
"believe in a moral basis of our society and who hate war," yet who also
recognize the need for the use of force. Borrowing arguments from the article
("Force and Freedom") he wrote for the *Atlantic* decrying preventive war,
Conant underlined "the importance of facing up to the issues of peace and
war on a totally different basis from those in which most of us were brought
up in the early days of this century." The EPC statement, he urged, must try
to convey the moral complexity and ambivalence of life in the imminent,
uncertain era of nuclear deterrence—imbuing students with philosophical
and ethical sensibilities to reconcile the seeming contradictions of threatening
war and mass destruction to preserve peace.

"I believe," he wrote, "we must take the illogical position of drawing a
distinction between the ethics of war and the ethics of peace, or to put it
another way, we must not destroy our fighting capacity by taking a position
that the use of force is always immoral or destroy our free society by grasping
the other horn of the dilemma and saying that since we admit war may be
necessary and right, therefore, always force must rule and the ends justify the
means."[77]

＊　＊　＊

Conant had not mentioned the issue of Communist teachers in his January letter to Norton—nor did he divulge it in public comments that winter—but the subject reared up again when Conant attended the Educational Policies Commission's session in Washington on March 11-12, 1949. There was one significant new face at the table: Gen. Dwight D. Eisenhower, who had left the army to become president of Columbia University and whose decision to join the commission had been "greatly influenced" by a strong letter from Conant.[78] A national hero already bandied about as a likely future presidential hopeful, Eisenhower by his presence assured additional prominence for any EPC pronouncements.

Otherwise it was much the same group as in September that examined, for the first and only time, the draft report that commission staff members had prepared. Again, Conant found himself a chief spokesman for the view that it include a statement barring Communist teachers—and again, Conant tied himself in knots trying to figure out a position on whether this also meant that already employed teachers should be fired, or what means the group proposed for school and university administrators to discover the political affiliations of teachers under suspicion. The outcome was a conscious decision to fudge the issue, yielding a report flawed by what Conant fully realized were internal contradictions and unclear implications.

But first, the educators fully backed Conant's strong emphasis on what he variously described as the "first job of American education," the "chief educational task" and "the major job of our schools and colleges": to help schools and universities turn out "tough-minded idealists" who were informed about the Soviet Union and Communism and ready to "face up" to the "pretty bleak" prospect of living in a fear-ridden, nuclear-armed, Cold War world. Or—though this was implicit—ready for war. "How do you somehow show that you are living in a situation which is the equivalent to living in a country which is full of geological faults?" Conant asked. "There may be an earthquake at any moment. But you have to get used to it."[79]

Among those who enthusiastically allied themselves with Conant's conception of a nationalistic, ideologically infused education was Eisenhower. The pair was now on an "Ike" and "Jim" basis after the "General" had wondered "[h]ow long I, as a freshman in the ranks of College Presidents, have to serve before my associates adopt the undergraduate practice of using nicknames?"[80] And Eisenhower assented to the need to get the "facts about communism" before students around the country, even those in isolated places like his dusty, isolated hometown of Abilene, Kansas:

> What I want to know is just exactly how do we get at these kids, and I believe that the facts of communism can be presented in such a way, as Dr. Conant says, so that they can, as they must, become accustomed to the fact that this is going to be a world of terrific fears, and some thread of hope to

which we are holding, and get them so trained and so thinking that they say, "We have something we are going to hold on to."[81]

When the issue of Communist teachers arose — after EPC secretary William G. Carr proposed omitting the controversial statement "from this particular pamphlet"[82] — Conant explained that he would favor firing Communist teachers as well as a ban on hiring them "if it means nearly the same thing — Should not be given employment as teachers." But at the same time, he thought universities should not themselves work to discover who actually belonged to the party:

> I feel that, if you take the point that under no condition should they be teachers, somebody may say, "Then you are under an obligation to find out under any possible method whether there is any member of the Communist Party on your staff."
>
> On that point I would disagree, because I think the damage you do to a university trying to find out — it wouldn't be easy — trying to ferret out these Communists would far outweigh the good you would get by getting rid of a couple.[83]

This was a tactical, not principled, distinction; for Conant's next words countenanced investigations and inquisitions for tax-supported educational institutions if they would hold up in court:

> I am not sure it holds in the public school system. There seems to be a difference. Some of you raised the question of whether you can legally fire a teacher under the state laws. We could not fire a communist without being subject to a suit, I am pretty sure, under our statutes at the present. I suppose we could have them give up teaching, but we are under a contract which gives the reasons for the dismissal, and I don't think you could show that being a member of the Communist Party would be a ground for dismissal. I would prefer "should not give employment."
>
> You are in a better position. To most people it means the same thing. Maybe it is a subtle point. Maybe it is too subtle.[84]

At this point Eisenhower came to the rescue, with a semantic rather than a philosophical escape hatch: "Why not add the word 'knowingly'?" he asked. "Make it read: 'should not knowingly' [employ Communists as teachers]."

Conant answered, "I am afraid that someone will push us."

"I go along 100 per cent," said Eisenhower. "We ought not to be Gestapo agents."[85]

As the two took refuge in calculated ambiguity, Eisenhower again backed up his Harvard colleague, disavowing SS tactics, but even going further than Conant to speak of the "responsibility" to fire a known Communist:

GENERAL EISENHOWER: I agree with [Conant's] view. I have seen enough Gestapo. I would like to see some word like "knowingly" and cover that.

DR. CONANT: The difference between taking them on and firing them must be covered if you said "should not be given employment."

C1HAIRMAN NORTON: Or "offered employment."

GENERAL EISENHOWER: There I go further than you do. If I know that a man is a communist, from my viewpoint, I could not be relieved of the responsibility, but, on the other hand, I would not conduct an investigation and establish a Gestapo to find out what the people are.[86]

Conant and Eisenhower, clearly in charge now, then united to squelch a tentative reference to what critics would pinpoint as a major logical flaw in the EPC's stand. To fire a teacher who belonged to the party, one educator recalled having heard, "you would have to prove that it [party membership] interfered with his objectivity and impartiality in presenting his views."

Here, indeed, was an important argument. The historian Ellen Schrecker has pointed out that Communist teachers were "almost unanimous in refusing to use their classrooms for purposes of indoctrination." Nevertheless, she notes, arguments such as Conant's rested on the "explicit assumption that all communists followed all of the party line all of the time."[87] But of what relevance were the political views of a music instructor, say, or a mathematician, or language specialist? Did not Conant believe that even Communists could "make important contributions" to science and often ultimately left the party out of disillusionment?[88] And furthermore, was it not necessary to establish professional misconduct, using the classroom as a political platform, before firing or refusing to hire a teacher?

This would clearly have been a more difficult—if better—standard to use. But Conant and Eisenhower, citing University of Washington president Allen's authority for stating that party membership by itself constituted grounds for dismissal, quickly rejected such a test. It might be "easier," Conant said, to leave unchanged the statement that members of the Communist Party "should not be employed" as teachers, "and let everybody interpret it."[89]

And by "everybody," Conant and the rest of the EPC understood perfectly well that this meant not only educators but the general public, especially hard-line critics. Carr made clear that "public relations" was a major consideration in the EPC's stand against Communist teachers. "You can say, 'Oh, you are just writing this for teachers,' but the Educational Policies Commission material won't just go to teachers. The newspaper boys are out there now and they will be around tomorrow."[90]

If a desire to protect politically controversial but non-Communist faculty had motivated Conant, that concern sharply intensified in the spring of 1949, as new attacks on Harvard professors thrust the issue into the spotlight.

In late March, Harlow Shapley was back in the headlines as the chairman and leading organizer of a tumultuous "Cultural and Scientific Conference for World Peace" held at New York City's Waldorf-Astoria Hotel.[91] During the weekend gathering, he and F. O. Matthiessen were among numerous speakers criticizing U.S. foreign policy as aggressive and imperialistic and calling for improved relations with Moscow. Along with a great deal of press coverage of the many literary and cultural celebrities who attended or protested the conference, it drew a barrage of accusations from critics who derided it as a pro-Stalinist, fellow-traveling propaganda spectacle. A number of liberal intellectuals, led by Sidney Hook, organized an ad hoc group called the American Intellectuals for Freedom to picket the meeting, and Arthur M. Schlesinger, Jr., railed against the "Lost Weekend" at a curbside protest rally.[92] For his part, Shapley solidified his reputation as a fellow traveler and was especially criticized for denying a request from Hook to address the group.[93] Right-wing critics of Harvard were enraged. "Men like Shapley and others at Harvard are not living up to their obligations in maintaining Americanism," raged one Massachusetts official; "Shapley has been commie-conned by the Russians," claimed another.[94]

Anger over Shapley's political outspokenness inspired one alumnus, a Baltimore lawyer named Frank Ober, to do more than complain. Ober, head of the Maryland Bar Association, had recently spearheaded a successful campaign to enact a loyalty oath act similar to the proposed Massachusetts law Conant had so ardently opposed. Ober's ire over Shapley merged with fury over another Harvard instructor, associate professor of English composition John Ciardi, who had appeared at a Baltimore meeting demonstrating against his loyalty legislation. Though Ober did not actually know what either Ciardi and Shapley had said, to him their mere presence at such meetings constituted "aid and comfort to Communism." Worse, he admonished Conant in a letter on April 26, they were exploiting Harvard's name in the service of a criminal conspiracy. Ober warned that Harvard needed to take prompt and drastic measures to rid the campus of any professor about whom existed "reasonable grounds to doubt his loyalty to our government," regardless of whether "he can actually be proved guilty of a crime." In the meantime, Ober told Conant, he had decided not to contribute to the Harvard Law School fund.[95]

It was neither the first nor last time that Conant's "fan mail" contained an alumnus's attempt to coerce Harvard by economic means. But Ober's epistle struck him as especially alarming because he feared that any response would unwittingly supply fresh ammunition to an anti-Communist activist who might "push the crusade into other states." Anything Ober could "attach to the signature of the President of Harvard might well be used in an unscrupulous way against us."[96]

Conant's response ran along at least two tracks. First, he sought a quiet avenue to influence Ober. On May 10, Conant discussed this delicate mission with Zachariah Chafee.[97] Chafee knew Ober personally, but he and Conant agreed it would be fruitless to write to him directly—Chafee preferred not to further strain their friendship. Instead, Chafee offered to write to one of Ober's law firm partners, Robert W. Williams, an old friend and fellow World War I–era graduate of Harvard College and Law School. That night, Chafee wrote "Bob" a lengthy personal letter recounting Ober's "most extraordinary" missive to Conant, and wondering what had happened to their seemingly "obsessed" mutual friend: "Is he letting this Anti-Communist Commission of his capture his whole personality the way Captain Ahab in Moby Dick let the White Whale he was chasing drive every other thought and emotion out of his life?" Chafee discreetly inquired whether Williams knew someone who could "get to" Ober. Did "Frank" have "any heroes, any Harvard or Princeton men whose achievements he admires who could perhaps persuade him to stick to Communists and the practice of law, and leave the colleges and universities to save their souls in their own way?"[98]

This back channel response to Ober failed, for Williams responded to "Zech" by acidly seconding his partner's concerns about Harvard's and Conant's "tolerance" of Shapley and other Soviet apologists on the faculty. "Would it not have been fortunate if there had been a few in Germany 'obsessed' with the need of immediate action when Hitler started taking over ... ?" And anyway, why didn't President Conant speak up "for the American way and the American ideal" as conspicuously as Shapley had spoken in Soviet-sponsored forums?[99] With considerable understatement Chafee confessed: "Probably [Williams] was not a good choice."[100]

Conant's second plan was more productive. It was time, he felt, for Harvard's authorities to issue a full and forthright public statement explaining its philosophy on academic freedom. Conant had just the man in mind to compose it. On May 9, he sent a copy of Ober's letter to Grenville Clark and tried to prime his veteran verbal sparring partner for battle. Ober's efforts raised anew the danger posed by state regulation to the independence of universities, he observed, and Harvard's response would be crucial. But a "forceful brief" from Clark explaining Harvard's refusal to discipline or monitor its faculty members' outside activities might make Ober "stop, look and listen." "Would you like to take on the job?" Conant asked his friend.[101]

Clark jumped at Conant's suggestion, and for the rest of May labored over the lengthy (eleven single-spaced typewritten pages) statement in consultation with Conant, Chafee, Marbury, Shattuck, and David Bailey.[102] All of them thought it a "splendid manifesto," with Chafee taking special delight in Harvard's authorities shielding controversial faculty members in light of his own brush twenty-eight years before.[103]

Clark made good use of that history in asserting that Harvard's refusal to knuckle under to Ober accorded with proud university custom. Not only had Lowell defended Chafee's status despite disagreeing with his views, but Conant's predecessor had also stood up for Harold Laski, then a junior lecturer who had aroused conservative ire by siding with Boston police strikers in 1919. Again, despite detesting Laski's socialism, Lowell had firmly rejected calls for his dismissal. More recently, Laski, now a professor at the University of London, had been permitted to speak at the Harvard Law School forum.

There was no doubt, wrote Clark, that Conant would continue to act in this fashion—even if Harvard lost money in the process. Citing the case during World War I when the Corporation, under Lowell, had contemptuously rejected a bribe of $5 million to fire the Germanophile philosopher Hugo Munsterberg, Clark confidently declared that "nothing is more certain" than that the Corporation would react the same way if someone offered $5 million for the removal of Ciardi or Shapley (a statement that caused the latter to muse that Harvard had finally comprehended his true dollar value to the university).[104]

Clark waxed lyrical about the spirit of free and open discourse, "a tradition that must and will be upheld as long as Harvard remains true to herself." That tradition, in Clark's retracing, ran straight from Eliot—"A university must be indigenous; it must be rich; but above all, it must be free" (1869)—to Lowell—"If a university or college censors what its professors may say, if it restrains them from uttering something that it does not approve, it thereby assumes responsibility for that which it permits them to say . . . a responsibility which an institution would be very unwise in assuming" (1917)—to Conant: " . . . there can be no compromise: we are either afraid of heresy or we are not" (1936).

And Clark linked the status of civil liberties on campus to their health in the nation as a whole. "The professor's right to speak his mind and to espouse unpopular causes should not be regarded as something separate and apart from the maintenance of our civil rights in general," he wrote. "I think what is usually called academic freedom is simply part and parcel of American freedom,—merely a segment of the whole front."

From Ober's statement that the administrators of Harvard and other colleges must "police themselves" and maintain "a closer watch on what its professors are doing" in order to "avoid aiding and abetting sedition or peacetime treason," Clark inferred a whole system of investigations, censorship, and review boards for faculty and students. "What sort of a place would Harvard be if it went down this road?" Clark asked. "It would, I think, not require six months to destroy the morale of both our teachers and students, and thereby our usefulness to the country. I think one need do no more than state the necessary implications of what you ask to demonstrate that nothing could be more alien to the principle of free expression that Harvard stands for."[105]

When published in the *Harvard Alumni Bulletin* in late June 1949, along with the letters from Ober and Conant, Clark's eloquent defense of Harvard's tradition deservedly attracted national attention and acclaim. But by then, its message clashed discordantly with other, equally weighty messages from Harvard's chief spokesman.

CHAPTER 23

Cold War Educator, Part III

Commencement
June 1949

In small, the University was the world. The same splits broke it into pieces, the same tensions were working inside it, like fine fissures which might suddenly gape.

— May Sarton, *Faithful Are the Wounds*[1]

In this period of a Cold War, I do not believe the usual rules as to political parties apply to the Communist party . . . as far as I am concerned, card holding members of the Communist party are out of bounds as members of the teaching profession.

— Speech, June 22, 1949

Like a boorish intruder crashing a dignified party, in June 1949 the Communism-in-academia controversy permeated and overshadowed that most sacred of months on the Harvard calendar. As the month opened, and Conant dropped down to Washington for a GAC meeting, action developed swiftly on several fronts. Two Massachusetts loyalty oath bills went down to defeat. In the mail came Conant's advance copy of the green-covered EPC report, which the commission on April 29 had unanimously approved for publication, with the request that the findings be kept confidential until its public unveiling on June 8.[2] Conant must have been comforted by a *New York Times* survey reporting a virtual consensus of educational leaders that party members were beyond the pale as teachers,[3] and he hailed a statement by MIT's new president, James R. Killian, Jr., that resolutely defended freedom of inquiry while at the same time denouncing Communism.[4] Up at Dartmouth, Grenville Clark put the finishing touches on his broadside—and the *Harvard Alumni Bulletin* made preparations for a special issue on the subject to appear later in the month. Conant himself publicly blasted the proposal that the FBI investigate recipients of AEC fellowships.[5] Among members of Harvard's governing boards, the strategizing intensified in a secret struggle over the proposed tenuring of a young economist named John Kenneth Galbraith. And on June 1, the chairman of the House Un-American Activities Committee, Georgia Democrat John S. Wood, sent a letter to Harvard and seventy other U.S. universities urgently requesting lists of textbooks—"with names of authors"—assigned for all courses in "American literature, geography, economics, government, philosophy, history, political science and any other of the social science group."6 The terse two-paragraph letter did not specify the purpose for which the lists were requested.

Wood's letter sent Conant and other university presidents into a tizzy. Hurriedly they consulted each other in search of a coherent response: Should they accede to the request? Temporize? Plead impracticality? Issue a forthright rejection? All these alternatives received consideration over the next few weeks as Conant, serving that year as chairman of the American Council on Education, checked with fellow educational leaders such as ACE president George F. Zook and Cornell president Edmund E. Day, and trusted advisers such as Clark and O'Brian. Some outraged faculty primed for battle—"we shall fight them on the beaches...[and] not yield an inch," vowed Chafee7—but Conant's response was, as usual, cautious. On O'Brian's advice Conant elected on behalf of the ACE to send Wood a short letter noting that the request had raised "very grave issues" and that further communications would be forthcoming pending advice from counsel.8

When Wood's letter became public on June 10, his accompanying explanation was hardly reassuring. The request for textbook lists, he said, applied to all U.S. grade and high schools, colleges, and universities. The committee had not decided yet what to do with the information, which, he said, no institution had refused to provide. "We have received an avalanche of mail from responsible people saying that subversive doctrines have been allowed to creep into our schools," he explained. "We just felt that we should have these textbook lists for our files."9

With Conant still silent, it was Cornell's president Day who found the courage to respond forcefully to HUAC's challenge. While fully endorsing the exclusion of Communist teachers, Day declared that "a witch-hunt is developing in this country" and that universities stood in danger of "infiltration, not by those attacking Communism, but by those who, under the guise of attacking Communism, attack something quite different."10 Academic opinion then "suddenly solidified" against the request, the *Harvard Alumni Bulletin* reported.11

By then, a new controversy had arisen. On June 8, amid considerable fanfare, the EPC released *American Education and International Tensions*. Read in its entirety, the fifty-four-page booklet conveyed a reasonably balanced and moderate agenda for the country's teachers at a time of high emotion and stress. It was also a quintessential Cold War document, firmly reinforcing the by now orthodox U.S. government's foreign policy and ideological orientation.12

Though it is, of course, impossible to discern precisely the relative contributions of a score of EPC members to a committee-written and -reviewed document, Conant's views shone through. A section on "Psychological Tension," for example, emphasized the need for emotional adaptation to long-term engagement "in a war that is not war," and for a "basic psychological reorientation" of the American people so as to better handle life "under an oppressive shadow of fear." This was pure Conant. Faced with the unnerving threats of atomic and biological warfare, Americans were admonished to resist the twin temptations of naive internationalism and preventive war, and be alert to the symptoms of tension that threatened to "sap the nation's strength": divisive activities by "[i]rresponsible persons . . . with selfish or malicious intent," and "public susceptibility to propaganda and demagoguery, spread of prejudice, scapegoating, witch-hunting, and the prevalence of crime, divorce, and mental illness."[13] Conant's influence was also apparent in the report's warning that a depression "would create extensive unrest in which appeal to prejudice and violence would find a ready audience," and thereby "lend plausibility" to arguments that "the American economic and political systems are moribund."

"There is no better way to prevent the spread of communism and other forms of dictatorship than to show the people that they can achieve a maximum of freedom, justice, and well-being by actively supporting and improving American democracy," the educators wrote. "Amelioration of economic injustice, psychological insecurity, racial discrimination, substandard housing, and other evils that beset us will help to produce a soil in which the seeds of communism cannot thrive."[14] And repeatedly, the report echoed Conant's strong advice to Norton that America's youth be taught to appreciate their country's new global stature.[15] The EPC exhorted teachers to "give the American people an awareness of their power — plus mature attitudes of responsibility with respect to use of their power — plus the ethics, wisdom, and skill to use their power effectively for good ends." Indeed, the report's overriding message was a nationalistic call to moral, political, and ideological arms, aimed at galvanizing young Americans with a love of their country and its system, an understanding of and hatred for totalitarianism and Communism, and a "high state of national and individual morale."[16]

The educators knew well that the endorsement of a ban on the employment of Communist teachers, a tactic described as one of four "main lines of strategy" for U.S. education in winning the "continuing ideological conflict," would attract the most attention, and they paid homage to free speech and the doctrine of academic freedom even as they severed one segment of their profession from entitlement to its traditional protections:

> At the same time we condemn the careless, incorrect, and unjust use of such words as "Red" and "Communist" to attack teachers and other persons who in point of fact are not Communists, but who merely have views different from those of their accusers. The whole spirit of free American education

will be subverted unless teachers are free to think for themselves. It is because members of the Communist Party are required to surrender this right, as a consequence of becoming part of a movement characterized by conspiracy and calculated deceit, that they should be excluded from employment as teachers.[17]

American Education and International Tensions was widely praised for the eminence of its sponsors, the sobriety of its arguments, and the correctness of its recommendations. And the National Educational Association did its best to ensure that its findings reached every corner of the country, distributing 15,000 copies to the press, to the professions, and to the delegates to the upcoming NEA national conference, which endorsed the report by a 2995–5 vote.[18] In its merging of toughness toward Communism and rhetorical praise of democratic ideals, the report ratified and articulated a new centrist consensus which education, under attack for insufficient patriotic vigor, was eager to join. "Education can and should be a powerful factor in national security," an NEA official told a national radio audience on the day of release,[19] and recognition of the report's significance did indeed emanate from across the spectrum of mainstream media and politics, up to President Truman.[20]

Despite the accolades, almost immediately Conant began to have worries about the prohibition of Communist teachers. Naively, if not disingenuously, he had counted on the report's strong condemnation of Red-baiting and smear tactics to mitigate the effects of its declaration against Communist teachers. Instead—predictably—every front-page story featured the ban in its headline and lead. And now support for Conant flowed from vehement anti-Communists who welcomed him as a new convert to the cause—among them his erstwhile nemesis Frank Ober. "Mr. Conant's joinder in a splendid public statement on Communist teachers today gives the reassurance I was seeking—that Harvard *is* alive to that menace," Ober wrote on June 8. "Appropriate steps to implement that policy are now in order."[21]

In expecting Conant to "implement" the EPC's report, Ober seized upon the very issue the Harvard president had hoped to "duck," as he had put it at the September 1948 EPC meeting. Others, too, also noticed the missing link in the statement. The *New York Times* had breezily dismissed the dangers of enforcement: "Surely we can rid our schools of the Communist and the indubitably subversive without paying in that process the far too costly price of losing our most cherished heritage, freedom of thought and expression." The crosstown *Post*, however, then among the city's leftist papers, seemed less sanguine. "Communist teachers conceal their affiliation," it pointed out. "How can they be investigated unless the techniques of FBI investigation . . . are imposed on the campus? How can that be done without imperilling the innocent?"[22]

Conant's evasion of these crucial questions was pounced on by the undergraduate editors of the *Harvard Crimson*. The paper had undergone a political transformation since 1945, a result not only of changing times but of the college's more diverse, urban, and Jewish enrollment.[23] Featuring many bylines familiar to later readers—Anthony Lewis, Michael Maccoby, Michael Halberstam (soon joined by his younger brother, David), et al.—the *Crimson* of the late 1940s had moved to a liberal perspective and had begun printing comprehensive annual national compilations of controversial academic freedom cases. A three-part exposé by David E. Lilienthal, Jr., had detailed excesses by local anti-Communist investigating committees, and in the first week of June, the *Crimson* reported that FBI snooping had produced a climate of fear at Yale University, eliciting an indignant protest from J. Edgar Hoover demanding a retraction; the paper firmly if nervously stood by its story.[24]

On the night the report was released, the president of the *Crimson,* John G. Simon (a junior who after graduation would go on to aid the army's defense against Senator Joseph McCarthy and to a career as a Yale Law School professor), first spoke to Paul Buck and found the provost surprised at his boss's action and curious to learn its significance. Simon read Buck the sentence about Communist teachers and asked what Conant had in mind. Did he intend to investigate the Harvard faculty's politics? I don't know, replied Buck, why don't you ask him yourself? Buck even seemed supportive when Simon told him the paper planned to run an editorial critical of the EPC statement.[25] Simon next telephoned Conant, who tried to continue dodging the enforcement issue, noting merely that the report "did not attempt to discuss legal and procedural aspects of the appointment and possible dismissal of teachers in schools and colleges."[26]

These blurry comments hardly satisfied Simon and his colleagues, who had looked up to Conant throughout their crusade for academic freedom, meeting him for weekly or biweekly off-the-record chats in Buck's University Hall office. More in sorrow than in anger, therefore, they roundly denounced him in an eloquent editorial, expressing disbelief, regret, and disappointment that Conant and the EPC, whose motives the paper accepted as sincere, had aligned themselves "with men of little principle and no discernment." "The *Crimson* believes," the editors wrote, "that competence alone should be the standard for hiring or firing a teacher. A political standard is irrelevant; it is dangerous; it is a repudiation of the traditional American principle that an individual be judged for what he is, and not for what he belongs to." Bitingly, they called on Conant and the Commission to explain frankly how they thought the ban should be implemented: "To be plain, how much of our civil liberties are we expected to surrender?"[27]

On Friday, June 10, as it happened, Conant had another one of his periodic background conferences with the *Crimson* executives. A spirited argument ensued between the fifty-six-year-old university leader and Simon, the sort of intellectual jousting Conant enjoyed, far preferring a contentious but good-natured test of wits and ideas with alert undergraduates to glad-handing alumni at a football game or fund-raiser. "He never pulled rank on you, conversationally," Simon recalled. But on this occasion he seemed less comfortable than usual. On the unfitness of Communists to teach, he held his ground firmly, defending on its merits the claim that they had surrendered their intellectual integrity by joining the party. At one point, countering Simon's insistence that individual Communists might retain sufficient independence of mind to be competent teachers, at least in certain subjects, Conant reached for a new edition of the *Communist Manifesto* to read aloud from British socialist Harold Laski's introduction attesting to the party's invariably deceitful and conspiratorial nature. If even Laski, with his impeccably radical credentials, thought this there must be something to that point of view![28] But Conant was defensive when confronted with arguments that the EPC report would be interpreted as endorsing procedures to discover and root out faculty subversives, with all the abuses such inquests would bring.

Agreeing to disagree, the reporters returned to the *Crimson*'s debris-strewn Plympton Street headquarters and wrote a second editorial for Saturday morning's paper. While somewhat reassured as to Conant's intent, they accused him and the rest of the EPC statement's signers not of malevolently scheming to slash civil liberties but instead (giving them more benefit of the doubt than they deserved) of a less heinous sin: naivete. Due to its signers' ignorance of "newspapers, or, more fundamentally, what is considered newsworthy," the EPC report had "completely backfired." Worse, the paper observed, "this backfire goes far deeper than the average newspaper reader; it goes down to the average educator, to the school board member in Green Bay, Wisconsin," who "will probably never read the complete statement" but conclude from abbreviated news accounts "that top educators believe in tossing out the 'Reds'—'Reds' exactly in the 'incorrect, unjust use'" which the EPC condemned. Unsatisfied by off-the-record explanations, the editors demanded that

> President Conant must go beyond opposition to "witch-hunts." He must state categorically what criteria will, and what criteria will not be used for keeping Communists off the faculty. He must do all this first, because until he does, there will be room for doubt within the Harvard academic community. Second and most important, he must do this to re-establish Harvard as a leader in this fight to preserve the faltering integrity of the American university.[29]

Conant now started to get the message, and to recognize that oblique assurances would not suffice to reassure the jittery Harvard community—not only liberal undergraduates but also many faculty members who opposed hiring Communists but feared the debilitating effects of a campus-wide political inquest.[30] One way or other, he decided, the enforcement issue had to be faced.

At first he assumed the protective mantle of the EPC, and sheepishly suggested to EPC secretary Carr that the commission issue an additional statement clarifying that the group did *not* endorse any particular procedure to investigate teachers' political activities and pointing out that exhaustive inquests could cause "a great deal of harm."[31]

Maybe so, the EPC leaders agreed, but it was too late for second thoughts. Largely on public-relations grounds, they vetoed Conant's proposed special statement. A hastily issued amendment would appear "defensive" and "would not be good for the prestige of the Commission or for the degree of respect which its statements command," argued the two EPC leaders who considered and rejected Conant's request.[32] Conant must have been pleased to escape the heat and hurly-burly for a long-planned fishing trip in the Adirondack lakes of upstate New York with his old OSRD colleague and Harvard class-mate, James Phinney Baxter III, now president of Williams College. But after four days of splendid isolation, Conant learned to his dismay that, the plaudits of the White House and the *New York Times* notwithstanding, the controversy over the EPC report had expanded rather than abated. Questions persisted during his appearance on June 17 at Yeshiva University graduation ceremonies, where he received an honorary law degree. Asked what he would do if a prominent Harvard professor walked into his office and declared himself a Communist, Conant answered: "I would send for a psychiatrist."[33]

Harvard's campus also displayed symptoms of schizophrenia on the issue of Communist teachers, Conant discovered upon returning to Massachusetts Hall on June 18 and plunging into the customary heavy schedule of Commence-ment Week—varsity track meets, House dinners, class reunions, baccalaureate speeches, and Overseers' meetings. Taking the pulse of two major controversies-in-progress, the HUAC textbook letter and the Galbraith appointment,[34] he read *Crimson* surveys taken during the previous week that found campus opinion sharply split, with students opposing by a two-to-one ratio the idea that otherwise qualified Communist teachers should be barred from the classroom, but faculty members approving Conant's stand by a comparable margin.[35] (The president had not filled out or returned the newspaper's mailed questionnaire card.[36]) It then fell to one of the Law School's most distinguished faculty members to deliver the most incisive and measured rebuke to him yet—on June 20, the same day the *Harvard Alumni Bulletin* printed Grenville Clark's paean to Harvard's commitment to academic freedom, when Professor Zechariah Chafee delivered the annual Phi Beta Kappa address on the subject of "Freedom and Fear."

While Chafee had helped Conant prepare responses to the teacher's oath and Ober controversies, here the country's leading civil liberties expert found himself in the position of advising Conant after the fact. Like Grenville Clark, Chafee had not known about the EPC report until it was a "fait accompli." And, like Clark, Chafee had deeply regretted Conant's action, immediately predicting that it would "be interpreted with a very much wider scope than he intended."[37]

Now Chafee had a chance to argue his side of the issue with Conant listening attentively in the front row. Mounting the stage in the Gothic, multi-tiered Sanders Theatre at eleven o'clock on a muggy Monday morning, the white-haired, stern Langdell Professor of Law launched into a magisterial attack on the prevailing climate of fear and dissected "with the meticulous precision of a great surgeon" the latest internal security measures proposed in Congress.[38] As an audience of five hundred waved fans and listened, Chafee recounted previous panics over internal subversion from the Alien and Sedition Acts of 1798 to the "Red scare" of 1919–20, and termed the present rumors of Communist penetration of the United States to be, like those of Mark Twain's death, "greatly exaggerated." That the Communist Party represented an abomination in Moscow, a proven disaster in Czechoslovakia, and perhaps a dire threat in Italy and other places, he acknowledged, but it did not therefore follow that such a danger existed in the United States, where only "one-tenth of one percent of our population" had opted for CP membership. What was all the fuss about, then? Why pass vaguely worded, fear-inducing, sweeping legislation—such as Truman's security order (especially its noxious offshoot, the attorney general's list), or the most recent restrictive bill, championed by the rabidly anti-Communist South Dakota senator Karl Mundt—penalizing political speech as if it represented criminal behavior? "To pass the Mundt Bill in order to hit communists," declared Chafee, "is like using a hammer to swat a wasp on a baby's head."

Chafee gradually neared the issues at the center of the controversy over Conant's position on the "non-employment" of Communist teachers. Communists were individual human beings, and it was "absurd to go on assuming that every communist is the spitting image of every other communist." One imagines that Chafee paused for effect before uttering his next line:

"Even distinguished university presidents have fallen into this fallacy. It is the same fallacy," he went on, as that "displayed by Harold Laski when he talks about American businessmen as if they were interchangeable parts like the bolts in a Ford car."

"We must choose, and choose very soon, between freedom and fear—we cannot have both," the scholar concluded.

In quintessentially Harvard fashion, Chafee had politely avoided naming Conant. But none present could fail to catch the barb—least of all its intended target. After Chafee stepped down from the lectern, Conant buttonholed him and the two men argued over the meaning of party membership as they strolled through Harvard Yard on the first day of summer.

Conant carried on the debate that afternoon in a letter to Chafee that took full advantage of the latest sensation.[39] The previous week, Frank Oppenheimer, Robert's brother, had appeared before HUAC, admitted lying to Manhattan Project security officers about his Communist Party membership, and refused to name his former compatriots. Before the day was out, the University of Minnesota had obtained his resignation. While Robert avoided getting ensnared in his brother's woes, and although Frank denied current party membership or any espionage activities, the incident offered fresh evidence that party members had occupied sensitive positions and still refused to be forthcoming about their past.[40]

Conant now added the "recent sad case" of Frank Oppenheimer to other evidence—his wartime experience ("when I knew something of the espionage work of party members"), the Canadian atomic spying affair, and Communist doctrine "in which it is frankly stated that the ethics of war are the prevailing ones"—to explain his "reluctant conviction that we are dealing not with a political party but something more akin to a fanatic religious movement." Oppenheimer's evident lying about his party membership prior to the most recent hearing not only justified his firing by the University of Minnesota, in Conant's view, but demonstrated anew "that this kind of deceit is in accord with the indoctrination of party members, and the calculated policy of conspiracy."

Congratulating Chafee on "what was from my point of view a ninety percent excellent speech," he added, "When on the other hand you challenge this diagnosis of Communist activities, though admitting those in Czechoslovakia, it seems to me you alienate the sympathy of a great many of your readers and hearers."

The quarrel with Chafee occurred, ironically, just as Conant and Harvard were being showered with praise—from many of the same establishment media that had welcomed the EPC report—for Clark's pro-academic freedom rejoinder to Ober, and it added to the pressure on Conant publicly to clarify his position on the Communist teacher issue. The coincidental juxtaposition of the EPC declaration and the Ober-Clark correspondence "had placed me in an almost indefensible position," he recalled many years later. "The charge of inconsistency was not easily answered."[41]

On Wednesday, June 22, he tried to do that, in a luncheon speech to Harvard's Foundation for Advanced Study and Research in the dining hall of Dunster House, one of the undergraduate houses Lowell had built along the banks of the Charles River. After preliminaries and pleasantries Conant quickly got to the point:

> In this period of a cold war, I do not believe the usual rules as to political parties apply to the Communist party. I am convinced that conspiracy and calculated deceit have been and are the characteristic pattern of behavior of regular Communists all over the world. For these reasons, as far as I am concerned, card-holding members of the Communist party are out of bounds as members of the teaching profession.

Conant promised his audience that except for party membership—this "single exception which is the unique product of our century"—Harvard's administration had no interest in a professor's political views or private conduct. "As long as I am President of the University," he promised, "I can assure you that there will be no policy of inquiry into the political views of the members of the staff and no watching over their activities as private citizens." Nor would Harvard institute security procedures comparable to that required for secret government work, a concept Conant found "utterly repugnant to my concept of a university." Even the benefit of discovering that a few faculty members maintained secret party affiliations, he declared firmly, would not compensate for the harm such an investigation would cause.[42] He spoke not a peep, naturally, about the *Realpolitik* justification he had used at the EPC, that excommunicating Communists would ease the burden of defending controversial nonparty teachers.

Even in this declaration of principles, Conant hedged. In phrases that surely did not get there by accident, he stated that he "should not want to be a party to the appointment of such a person to a teaching position *with tenure* in any educational institution [emphasis added]." Would the appointment of a party member to a nontenured post or as a visiting fellow be acceptable? One Harvard professor later suggested that Conant probably wanted to preserve a loophole: "We used to wonder: 'What if Tito was overthrown and we wanted to make him a visiting professor?' "[43]

Conant also fudged the question of what Harvard would do if a tenured faculty member got up and "suddenly announced" his party membership. Would the university then be obliged to fire him? On what grounds? (Under Harvard's bylaws, the Corporation could remove instructors "only for grave misconduct or neglect of duty.")[44] Conant merely gave thanks that "no such problem exists here at Harvard" and elided the question of what he would do if that "difficult problem" arose. But merely because Harvard, at that moment, lacked known Communists on the faculty did not mean other universities would not have to face the issue. Conant's failure to come to grips with that issue constituted an abdication of the educational leadership he had so carefully cultivated.

In one scene from May Sarton's *Faithful Are the Wounds*, Professor Edward Cavan—modeled after Matthiessen—complains to his wife that he and other leftist faculty members were being politically castrated.

> "They're making eunuchs of us, Grace, that's what it amounts to," says Cavan.
> "That couldn't happen at Harvard, Edward . . . ," his wife begins.
> "That's it," Cavan replies angrily, "that's just what Goldberg [a university official bearing a suspicious resemblance in philosophy and manner to Conant] said. As long as it doesn't happen at Harvard, all's well. As long as it doesn't touch *us,* it isn't real."[45]

It is hard to avoid the conclusion that, as pressures on academia closed in, exactly that mentality began to shape Conant's calculations.

But as he had hoped, Conant's speech served the intended purpose of allaying the fears of his Harvard friends and admirers. Chafee correctly interpreted it as in part a response to his own, and wrote warmly: "You have no idea how deep a satisfaction it is to me to be spending my life in the free atmosphere of Harvard."[46]

One final private act remained to be played out as the 1949 Commencement month concluded: Conant collaborated in a maneuver to save a controversial faculty appointment from going down to defeat at the hands of a censorious Board of Overseers who had balked at confirming the virtually unanimous decision of the Economics Department to give tenure to John Kenneth Galbraith. On Commencement morning, June 23, the Overseers seemed to be on the verge of sinking Galbraith—until a sympathetic Overseer, Judge Charles Wyzanski, shrewdly exploited the diversion of the noisy ruckus in the Yard outside to move to delay consideration of the nomination until the fall semester, giving Conant and other Galbraith supporters time to marshal their forces.[47]

It was, a friend reported shortly afterward, a "tired out" Conant who fled Cambridge for his annual summer retreat in the New Hampshire hills.[48]

What would have been the impact had Conant, with equal prestige, held fast to his original, long-held views on academic freedom, and had not repositioned himself to follow the shifting political center? Would the consequences for universities have been worse than actually occurred?

In his memoirs, and in public speeches and private correspondence at the time, Conant explained his revised stand as motivated solely by his "evaluation of the nature of membership in a Communist Party" in the United States.[49] Since membership, he claimed, required a surrender of intellectual integrity and ironclad adherence to an anti-democratic doctrine and to Soviet orders, this was "not a question of heresy; this is a question of a conspiracy which can only be likened to that of a group of spies and saboteurs in an enemy country in time of war. . . . I have reluctantly come to the conclusion that they must be considered as essentially a group of persons who have declared war against American society and whose ethics are therefore exactly comparable to those of spies and saboteurs."[50]

This explanation is repeated without challenge by several analysts, such as Seymour Martin Lipset in *Education and Politics at Harvard* and Richard Norton Smith in *The Harvard Century*.[51] But other, more critical accounts, have emphasized baser motives and more damaging consequences. In a 1977 exchange with former Harvard dean of the faculty McGeorge Bundy in the *New York Review of Books*, Sigmund Diamond accused Bundy of having pressured scholars to name names to congressional investigators after Conant's departure from Harvard in January 1953. He concluded that "Harvard's policy during the McCarthy period was based to an important degree on political expediency, rather than on notions of justice, academic freedom, or any moral principle."[52] Diamond later wrote that "the James B. Conants separated themselves from the Frank Obers, but their notion of Realpolitik—based in part on their conviction that Communism posed a mortal threat, in part on their concern to safeguard their institutions—required them to proceed part way down the path of the purge to justify not going all the way."[53]

The evidence presented here—in particular the transcripts of the Educational Policies Commission meetings of September 1948 and March 1949—weighs heavily in favor of Diamond's conclusion that political expediency, not moral or philosophical considerations related to Communist Party membership, were central to Conant's advocacy of a ban on Communist teachers. To the worried EPC members, narrowed standards of academic freedom seemed a reasonable price to pay for favorable publicity about the rest of their worthy agenda.

Conant's genuine and informed loathing of Communism and totalitarianism was an important component of his hardening stand on Communist teachers.[54] But when he so chose, Conant could discuss Communism with perfect equanimity and detachment. Conant's views on Communism, at least in 1949, were strong but hardly fanatic. Barely two weeks before the EPC report appeared, he had told his close friend Vannevar Bush to tone down an "oversimplified" and "too emotional" condemnation of Soviet philosophy in a draft chapter of his *Modern Arms and Free Men.* One had to account for the existence of socialist scientists such as J. B. S. Haldane and Frederic and Irene Joliot-Curie, Conant wrote, adding, "You do not spell out enough that after all, corrupted as it is by a tyranny in the Kremlin, nevertheless, the religion of the Marx-Engels-Lenin creed still has an enormous sway on many people."[55] But once he had opted, for tactical reasons, to support the expulsion of Communist teachers, it no longer seemed prudent to depict Communism as an interesting though flawed philosophy, deeply corrupted in one country, attractive to some intelligent and even brilliant men and women and not to others. The tenor of the rhetoric had to match the severity of the proposed action. When it came to defending the move to the public, to critics, and to history, Conant and the rest of the EPC needed an intellectually respectable argument—or at least one more dignified than self-preservation—hence the unanimous and consistent emphasis on the argument that all Communists had already surrendered their intellectual freedom. Conant may even have believed it. It would not have been the first time that he was, as he had admitted in an earlier academic controversy, "rationalizing a situation into which circumstances forced us!"[56]

In succumbing to fear Conant fulfilled the prophecy he had made so often that in fanatically trying to protect America from its enemies it risked adopting some of their tactics. (As the taint of Communist thought became sufficient for exclusion from the academic world, John King Fairbank has recalled, it became "second nature to indicate at the beginning of an article, by some word or phrase, that one was safely anti-Communist. This of course was the mirror image, in subtler form, of the Soviet custom of quoting Marx, Lenin or Stalin in the first footnotes of any publication.")[57] Simultaneously, Conant was also violating the "deep-seated conviction" he was ardently urging on the American people in 1949, "that war is always totally different morally from peace."[58] For the ban on Communist teachers, a kind of intellectual censorship usually resorted to only during a wartime emergency, was a tacit admission that traditional peacetime civil liberties could not be maintained.

Conant never admitted to error about the position he took in 1949, yet an incident two decades later suggests that perhaps he recognized, at some level of consciousness, that he had not really satisfied the criteria that the EPC itself insisted on for changes in educational policy: that they "should not be made for trivial and transient reasons."[59] In 1970, in the midst of campus protests against the Vietnam War, a lawyer for the University of California at Berkeley asked Conant, in connection with unspecified "litigation on the subject matter," whether his 1949 statement expressed his "current view on this question."

"The 60s are another story," Conant replied. "Therefore, if I had to answer your question in one word, it would be 'no.'"[60]

CHAPTER 24

"Over My Dead Body"

The Battle over the H–Bomb
1949–1950

This whole discussion makes me feel I was seeing the same film, and a punk
one, for the second time.
> —During General Advisory Committee meetings on
> the hydrogen bomb, October 1949

When I am in Washington, it seems as though I were in a lunatic asylum, but
I am never sure who is the attendant and who the inmate. Nor am I even
sure whether I am a visitor or a potential patient.
> —Letter to Bernard Baruch, February 1950

Shining sun, brisk mountain air, spectacular landscapes with soaring, snow-
capped peaks, alpine meadows flecked with gold, lavender, red, and white
flowers, rushing cataracts, sparkling lakes swimming with trout, exhilarating
mountain paths trod by rigorous hikers and the occasional grizzly—these
were among the attractions that Patty Conant counted on to relax and divert
her husband during the family's month-long outing to Glacier Park in the
Canadian Rockies in August and early September 1949. After a few weeks in
an isolated mountain chalet, she cautiously reported signs of success. While
Patty happily scribbled a note to her mother, "After washing out a crop of
wool socks," the husband she had once described as a "jet-propelled missile"
placidly stood on the balcony of their hotel room working on a watercolor of
mountain peaks soaring over and reflected in a nearby lake. "I always feel a
bit dubious about vacations with Jim," Patty wrote, "because he is theoretically 'against' them, and expects so much from any outlay of his precious time
that I'm never sure that the best-laid plans will turn out satisfactorily! I'm
glad to say, however, that to date this trip has turned out very well. After the
usual early stages of suspended judgment and adjustment to the holiday
spirit, he has become so absorbed in fishing and sketching that the days just
aren't long enough."[1]

Already, the trip had yielded memorable moments; a few days earlier, the couple had saddled a pair of "gentle and amenable" horses and ridden beside a towering cliff with an elderly retired forest ranger who spun anecdotes about the "wild and woolly early days" of Canada's old west, finally reaching a crystal-clear lake where Jim had hooked "some beautiful and delicious fish" and Patty had counted "*seventeen* white Rocky mt. goats capering about the summits above us!"

The presence of their son Ted, who had traveled cross-country during his summer break from Swarthmore, soon added to Patty's happiness. Gushing over the relief of having escaped "all the pressures that have sometimes complicated home life at 17 Quincy Street," she reported that the younger Conant son, just turned twenty-three years old, was "having the time of his life," showing unexpected passion for mountain scenery, devouring modern authors like Sartre and Wolfe, eating like a horse, hiking eighteen miles a day, and best of all, spending time with his father. "You can imagine how happy it makes me to see them having such fun together . . . Jim is getting a great deal of pleasure out of [Ted's] enthusiasm, and the two of them are having an experience of shared exhilaration and companionship that is unique for both of them." While unable to join the happy campers, James Richards Conant, twenty-six, was also reported to be flourishing, writing enthusiastically of his new job as a reporter in Chicago; the psychological breakdown that had traumatized him at the war's close seemed, for the moment at least, to be in abeyance.

In short, the Conant clan's complex, often strained web of relationships, personalities, and circumstances had mercifully permitted a rare halcyon interlude. "We are all in fine health and spirits," Patty informed her mother on September 4, describing a fire of huge logs in their cozy communal living room while a rainstorm raged outside. Her husband, after three hours of fishing and a twenty-mile hike, was catching some well-earned sleep. "Our vacation has been a great success," Patty summed up. "Jim & I have never known such uninterrupted sunshine, and goaded by our eager son we have been outdoors long days and taken (esp Jim) a good deal of healthy exercise. We have all had great fun."

The next day, Conant left the mountains for a packed series of speaking engagements in San Francisco. The troubles of the autumn term were still far away when, a week or so later, en route to Cambridge by transcontinental railroad, Conant was urgently summoned from the train to receive a telephone call from Washington. Picking up the receiver, he heard a voice relay the cryptic message, camouflaged in scientific double-talk, that he had been dreading for four years: *They have it.*[2]

The news that the Soviet Union had detonated an atomic explosion surprised Conant, like almost everyone else in the United States, especially since the lack of advance warning had raised hopes that the interval before Moscow's first bomb might last longer than the three to five years he and most other scientists had predicted near the end of the war. "I am more and more inclined to think," Conant had written Leslie Groves early in 1949, "that history will record that you had the best of the guesses when you gave the twenty-year end of the target rather than the five years which I put as the short end!"[3] Arriving when it did, the news darkened an already grim horizon: a divided and militarizing Europe; the imminent triumph of a Communist revolution in China; and at home, panicky fears of internal subversion. The "age of the Superblitz," of which Conant had warned, in which two hostile powers possessed substantial nuclear arsenals, now loomed inescapably.

Conant had long known that this moment would be most dangerous, both for the world and for the American public's psychology, and his first reaction was to transmit popularly the same message that Robert Oppenheimer privately gave Edward Teller: "Keep your shirt on."[4] In early October, two weeks after Truman's September 23 public announcement of Soviet atomic capability, Conant helped to prepare a statement issued by the Educational Policies Commission calling for calm, criticizing state-imposed loyalty oaths, and reiterating the group's warning against Red-baiting and the "careless application" of the Communist label to "those who merely have views different from those of their accusers"—though it reaffirmed its stand against employment of party members.[5] Domestically, he feared the Russian achievement would polarize public opinion between proponents of preventive war and of nuclear disarmament at any price. Recalling past analogies likening the U.S. atomic edge to "a cake of ice in an open field on a hot day," Conant confessed to Niebuhr that the "day has proved to be hotter than we thought; the last of the ice is melting fast." In two to five years, once they realized "that the Russians could play us a game of tit for tat with atomic bombs, the American people would "split into two camps, those who will say, 'Let's hit them now before they can hit back too powerfully' and those who will look for some kind of negotiations to reduce armaments and particularly to get the bomb out of the picture." Public opinion had to be "mobilized to discuss this issue realistically and unhysterically but with real concern," lest internal instability lead the country into disaster. But Conant also discerned that Moscow's success had transformed the global East-West strategic equation, and endangered the hard-won nuclear advantage on which Washington and its allies had counted to balance the Red Army's conventional might in Europe. "The explosion of the Soviet bomb," one profiler wrote a few years later, "blasted Conant out of the contentious debate he was then engaged in as to whether the salvation of the American way of life depended on public or private schools. Soon he was speaking on the theme that 'the frontier of American freedom lies somewhere east of the Rhine.' "[6]

Though he favored acceleration and intensification of U.S. efforts to modernize and diversify its nuclear arsenal, Conant continued to oppose adamantly the development of the hydrogen bomb—a weapon, still on the drawing boards, that would increase the destructive capability of nuclear explosions by several orders of magnitude. If the serious theoretical and practical obstacles to developing the weapon could be overcome, it was thought that a single H-bomb, employing the thermonuclear reactions that take place in the center of the sun and using a smaller fission weapon as a "trigger" to generate the conditions of heat and pressure necessary to initiate fusion, could generate thousands of times the explosive force that had destroyed Hiroshima. I. I. Rabi, a fellow member of the AEC's General Advisory Committee, recalled Conant's expressing the view that building the hydrogen bomb would only "louse up the world still more."[7]

But with increasing frequency, others in a position to influence U.S. nuclear policy latched on to precisely that idea as the proper American response. The temptation of regaining a clear advantage in destructive capability over the Soviet Union—combined with the (apparently justified) fear that Moscow too might be working on an H-bomb[8]—overwhelmed worry about escalating the nuclear arms race.

In the fall of 1949, then, national-security policy was at a crossroads: Should Washington launch a crash program, modeled after the Manhattan Project, to build thermonuclear weapons capable of wiping out entire cities, or look to smaller atomic bombs to use against military forces? Should the United States plan a long-term military strategy that depended on weapons of mass destruction, or attempt to match Soviet strength in conventional troops? Was the nuclear arms race to accelerate and escalate, or should one more effort be made to head it off? The answers came only after four months of intense, mostly secret, sometimes bitter debate among a small number of civilian and military officials, scientists and congressmen, leading up to Truman's decision on January 31, 1950, to endorse a program to develop thermonuclear weapons.[9] On a personal level, the battle over "the Super," as it was colloquially known, was a conflict that touched the deepest chords of a man some associates considered cold and unemotional, and it also climaxed Conant's relationship with Oppenheimer. The physicist and the university president ten years his senior bonded together in events that "recorded more than a political struggle; they seemed to involve the very destiny of man."[10]

The potential use of atomic fission weapons to set off thermonuclear reactions had darkened Conant's thoughts since the summer of 1942, when research conducted by a team at Berkeley that included Oppenheimer, Hans Bethe, Edward Teller, and John H. Van Vleck had explored the possibility of fusion weapons. "After these studies," Oppenheimer later recalled, "there was little doubt that a potentially world-shattering undertaking lay ahead."[11] When it learned of the ideas being discussed, the alarmed OSRD leadership hastily tried to limit the knowledge to as small a group as possible. When the question of man-made fusion initially arose, Conant had two principal concerns. First, the theoretical possibility was raised that an atomic fission explosion could ignite the earth's atmosphere, causing a thermonuclear chain reaction that would wipe out life on the planet. Hasty calculations determined that this danger was a "red herring," in the later words of Hans Bethe, but Conant was reminded of this apocalyptic scenario at Alamogordo when for a breath-taking instant the end of the world flashed before his eyes.[12] Conant's second, more enduring concern about hydrogen fusion was that it might allow for the construction of thermonuclear bombs producing yields of a far larger magnitude than fission weapons. Memoranda he wrote during the war indicate that his estimate of the prospects for building an H-bomb diminished between 1942 and 1945, but its eventual likelihood influenced his assessment of future developments in a possible secret U.S.-Soviet atomic arms race. Informed by an appeal from Oppenheimer urging that "the subject of initiating violent thermo-nuclear reactions be pursued with vigor and diligence, and promptly," for political and scientific reasons "of profound importance" for the postwar world, Conant and Bush in September 1944 speculated to Secretary of War Stimson that a thermonuclear weapon (a "super-super bomb") might be built "within six months or a year after the first atomic bomb is constructed."[13] A few weeks later, however, Conant sounded more pessimistic, after a visit to Los Alamos at which he heard a report on thermonuclear developments from Edward Teller, whose fascination with fusion was already well known at the lab and a source of occasional friction with scientists more interested in completing a fission device in time to use in the war. "It seems that the possibility of inciting a thermonuclear reaction involving heavy hydrogen is somewhat less now than appeared at first sight two years ago," Conant wrote to Bush on October 20, 1944. Noting that the explosion produced by such a weapon could reach 100 million tons of TNT—compared to the Hiroshima bomb's later yield of 20 *thousand* tons—Conant acknowledged that this "real super bomb is probably at least as distant now as was the fission bomb when you and I first heard of the enterprise," i.e., about four or five years off.[14]

Conant was still seeking clarification when the Interim Committee convened. On May 31, 1945, in the same meeting at which the group endorsed using the atomic bomb on Japan, the minutes note that Conant "mentioned a so-called 'third stage' of development (of atomic weapons) in which the products of the 'second stage' would be used simply as a detonator for heavy water." Asking Oppenheimer "for an estimate of the time factor in developing this phase," he received the reply that this "far more difficult" stage would require a minimum of three years.[15]

The uncertainty and confusion clouding prospects for hydrogen bomb development did nothing to recommend it to Conant, who prided himself on level-headedness and cold-eyed resistance to physicists' "fancies."[16] But an even more important factor in his lack of enthusiasm for the H-bomb was his steady (with one apparent exception) conviction that boosted fission weapons would prove more than adequate for U.S. military strategy. "[T]he purpose of this memorandum," Conant had written Bush in late 1944, "is to show that even without [thermonuclear weapons] the potentialities of a bomb of tremendously devastating effect are not far off if the efficiency of the fission bomb can be increased, as it undoubtedly can, by straightforward research and development along the lines now in progress."[17]

The destructive power of fusion weapons further dramatized to Conant the transcendent moral and political dilemmas posed by far smaller fission bombs. Yet, while fearing a catastrophic conflict once the Soviets acquired their own bomb, Conant had conceded that the United States must enter the race for nuclear supremacy even as it tried to halt it. "I am inclined," he had written Bush in May 1945, "to back an all out research program for the super-duper [presumably the hydrogen bomb] as first priority (leaving industry second role) and *at the same time* with equal priority push for an international armaments commission. We have about 5–10 years to do both!"[18]

On this one occasion, Conant seemed to endorse building the H-bomb; but over the next four years he reverted to more cautious views, even though hopes to establish an international atomic-energy control commission dimmed. The GAC encouraged research on the Super from its earliest sessions and made no move against such work prior to October 1949[19] — in part out of prudence, since total secrecy on the concept of the Super had proved impossible despite the high classification accorded the subject since the end of the war and surely the Russians had taken note. "I find it is being rediscovered every day by people quite outside of our tight little circle," I. I. Rabi told Stanislaus Ulam in December 1945, noting that he "would very much dislike to have it worked on hard by a group at the present time, since it might discourage a political solution."[20] A year later, John J. McCloy gave a speech (reprinted in the *Bulletin of the Atomic Scientists*) predicting the development within a decade of hydrogen bombs a thousand times more powerful than those dropped on Hiroshima and Nagasaki.[21]

But among atomic scientists involved in weapons work, opinions about the feasibility (and desirability) of the Super remained sharply divided and the GAC accordingly gave H-bomb studies low priority. Several reasons compelled caution. First, research had not progressed much since the war, and critical theoretical problems still needed to be solved before the weapon's feasibility could be established, and before testing or construction could begin.[22] (Nor did Edward Teller's persistent investigations make much of a dent in the GAC's skepticism: "Every time he reported," recalled Lee DuBridge, "we thought he'd taken a step backwards.")[23] Second, the AEC initially concentrated on improving the efficiency of its program to stockpile Hiroshima-type bombs, given its limited financial, material, and manpower resources.[24] But underlying these practical barriers was the fact that for Conant and other GAC members, there seemed no obvious military or political need to jump from fission to fusion; as Oppenheimer was to say later, eerily, even if the Super had been available during the war the United States would not have used it on Hiroshima because the "target" was "too small."[25]

Finally, at the root of Conant's opposition was his recognition of the horrendous potential of thermonuclear weapons to destroy far more than military objectives might ever justify. At a GAC meeting in April 1948, he had "wondered in regard to the super bomb, how many bombs it would be sensible to consider from the point of view of the contamination of the atmosphere, since he felt the stockpile of any such weapons should be well below this limit."[26] These qualms about the H-bomb hardened into firm opposition as early as March 1949 — *not* only after the shock of the Soviet atomic blast, as is usually assumed[27] — and before Oppenheimer had made up his mind on the issue. With good reason, he had strong doubts about the scientific and technical basis for the Super as it was then envisioned by its supporters.[28] The Conant "Fishing Party" committee's April 1949 working paper, accurately conveying the assessment of physicists such as Oppenheimer and Bethe, had flatly declared that "talk of superbombs of the order of magnitude of 50 or 100 times more powerful than the Nagasaki bomb are not based on fact."[29] During the summer Conant helped to draft a recommendation urging the government publicly to declare, "Atomic bombs have not been developed and are not now in the process of development which are in any way in the category of the super-bomb popularly discussed in the press."[30]

Conant's position in the debate on the hydrogen bomb cannot be understood without also understanding his perception of the political and diplomatic landscape. While detesting Communism, distrusting the Soviet government, and lacking faith in the short-term chances for negotiating an international control agreement with it, he continued to believe that the Soviet Union hoped to "further . . . the world-wide spread of totalitarian socialism" primarily through political and ideological rather than military means. Yet at the same time, he also took steps to prepare for what many believed was the increasingly likely possibility of all-out war. Conant, the evidence suggests, thought the Super would be unnecessary in the strategy of promoting a nuclear standoff yet disastrous in an actual war. For a time, with the atomic bomb, he had believed that technological advance would intimidate the Soviets and thus lessen the dangers of an atomic arms race, but he could not believe that a superbomb would help the prospects for international control. By 1949, it was clear that the U.S. atomic monopoly had failed to coerce the Soviets into agreeing to international control, and the disintegration of the wartime alliance into hostile armed blocs rendered the issue moot. Recognizing these harsh realities, Conant and other consultants in March 1949 had urged the U.S. delegation at the UN talks to break off the discussions with the Russians; the Acheson-Lilienthal plan was "no longer applicable," he acknowledged. Truman "should make announcement that conditions have deteriorated," Conant urged. "We are playing with dynamite now since the Soviet might accept . . . When and if the Soviet is a friendly government we will have to make a new plan."[31]

Conant grew simultaneously exasperated with the herky-jerky progress of the U.S. Atomic Energy Commission and with the pressures exerted by scientific and military enthusiasts to accelerate civilian and military nuclear power. The GAC's mounting frustration with the commission had erupted into the open at a turbulent June 1948 meeting at which the panel recommended a major reorganization. "We certainly have a wealth of advisers and watchdogs," a depressed and irritated Lilienthal wrote in his journal, adding: "I feel pretty *low*, frankly."[32] Conant had helped to write the GAC's "undeniably sharp" statement, which cited a lack of imagination and foresight on the commission's part, urged a large-scale decentralization of operations and authority, and concluded tartly: "We are afraid we can be of little use to the Commission under the present organization. We despair of progress in the reactor program and see further difficulty even in the area of weapons and production unless a reorganization takes place."[33] Even decades later, Lilienthal wrote angrily of "the kibitzers on every hand, most of them arrogant and ignorant (the effrontery, for example, of the scientific geniuses of the General Advisory Committee, Oppenheimer the worst of the lot, telling me — an experienced manager — how to manage a large organization!!)"[34]

Conant, for his part, was increasingly finding his nuclear work a burden. Writing to Oppenheimer in March 1949 to suggest the GAC be more actively investigatory — for "from the point of view of the general public until such time as individually and collectively we are ready to resign as a protest because of what we find, we are by our silence giving our blanket endorsement of the work of the Commission" — he admitted that "in recent days I have taken what may have seemed a rather defeatist attitude about the work of the Committee."[35] And his disillusionment showed again that summer during a drive from Berkeley to San Francisco with physicists Luis W. Alvarez and Ernest Lawrence. "Dr. Lawrence was trying to get a reaction from Dr. Conant on the possibility of radiological warfare and Dr. Conant said he wasn't interested," Alvarez recalled. "He didn't want to be bothered with it. I have the strong recollection that Dr. Conant said something to the effect that he was getting too old and too tired to be an adviser on affairs of this sort. He said, 'I did my job during the war' and intimated that he was burned out, and he could not get any enthusiasm for new projects. So when Dr. Conant disapproved of the hydrogen bomb, I interpreted it in light of that conversation."[36] The historian Robert Jungk considered it "staggering" that Alvarez regarded Conant's behavior as evidence of being "burned out" rather than an expression of deep moral principles,[37] but Conant was fed up, that much is clear — and in the ensuing debate, he had an opportunity to show that principles, not fatigue, motivated his actions.

In early or mid-October 1949, after learning that the superweapon was being broached in some circles as *the* American reply to the Soviet atomic advance, Conant vented his feelings in a strongly worded letter to Oppenheimer vowing that if the hydrogen bomb were built it would be "over my dead body."

It was natural that Conant should confide in Oppenheimer, for the two had "definitely" the closest tie of all the members of the GAC, according to the physicist John H. Manley, the group's secretary. "They were kindred spirits, very sharp and perceptive, and that drew them together," and the relationship grew "most intense during the H-bomb period. That cemented them together."[38]

While Oppenheimer was and is often depicted as the central figure in opposition to the hydrogen bomb—and was portrayed as such by the AEC during the probe that revoked his security clearance—the evidence suggests that, rather than being swayed by Oppenheimer, Conant led the opposition and emboldened Oppenheimer to make a stand in the controversy.[39]

Although the GAC met in Washington on September 22–23—just as Truman was breaking the news of the Soviet test to the nation—the advisers did not make any formal recommendations for the AEC in light of the changed situation, because, Oppenheimer explained to Lilienthal, so much hinged on public response to the news, and they had not been asked to assess the event.[40] Another opportunity for Conant and Oppenheimer to assess the situation arose on October 9–10, when Oppenheimer and three other new members of Harvard's Board of Overseers were in Cambridge and stayed at 17 Quincy Street; afterward, Oppenheimer wrote an associate that he and Conant had had a "long and difficult discussion having, alas, nothing to do with Harvard," but Oppenheimer, alas, did not say what their conversation *did* concern.[41] The two communicated by terse telegrams between October 11—when Lilienthal wrote Oppenheimer requesting that he call a special GAC meeting to determine whether the AEC could do more for the "common defense and security" in light of the Soviet explosion—and October 14, when Oppenheimer replied and set the date for the weekend of October 29–30, the first days on which "both President Conant, who is quite busy," and Fermi, could attend.[42]

On Friday, October 21, physicists Edward Teller and Hans Bethe visited Oppenheimer in his office at the Institute for Advanced Study in Princeton. In concert with Alvarez, Lawrence, and other Berkeley scientists, Teller had traveled cross-country from California to lobby for an all-out effort to build the Super, his pet project for nearly a decade. Unlike Oppenheimer and Conant, these scientists had few qualms about exploiting to the fullest the destructive potential of the atom; they believed arms control was a chimera, and that American security therefore depended on maximum military might, and specifically in aerial striking power to counter Soviet manpower advantages; finally, they shared a romance with the intrinsic technical and scientific challenge of thermonuclear weaponry, a lure to which not even Oppenheimer was fully immune.[43]

As part of his recruitment drive, Teller had called on Bethe, one of the pioneers of fusion research, at Cornell, but Bethe was torn over the prospect of returning full-time to weapons work. The two decided to visit Oppenheimer to solicit his views on the subject. As evidenced by a letter that Oppenheimer wrote to Conant dated that same Friday, Oppenheimer had grave doubts about the feasibility, morality, and military efficacy of the Super, but on this occasion he did not express a strong position; instead, Oppenheimer showed or read his visitors a letter from Conant "which he said he had just received." Teller later told the Oppenheimer board that "one phrase of Conant's sticks in my mind, and that phrase was 'over my dead body,' referring to a decision to go ahead with a crash program on the thermonuclear bomb."[44]

Bethe, in his testimony, corroborated Teller's account. Finding Oppenheimer "equally undecided and equally troubled in his mind about what should be done," Bethe said Oppenheimer disclosed that "one of the members of the General Advisory Committee, namely Dr. Conant, was opposed to the development of the hydrogen bomb, and he mentioned some of the reasons Dr. Conant had given. As far as I remember, he also showed me a letter he had written to Dr. Conant. As far as I remember, neither in this letter or in his conversation with us did he take any stand."[45] In a 1985 interview, Bethe clarified that he was shown a "very strong" letter written by *Conant* rather than Oppenheimer and that "the gist of it was just like the sentence Teller quoted." He added: "The letter showed me that Conant and Oppenheimer were in very close contact."[46]

Had Oppenheimer displayed Conant's letter while cloaking his own view because he was still unsure of what stance he would take when the GAC met? Or, instead, did he prefer to preserve an air of impartiality as the panel's chairman while nevertheless hoping to sway opinion away from a crash program? Bethe, who in the end rejected Teller's overture to come work on the hydrogen bomb at Los Alamos and publicly criticized Truman's decision (though he changed his mind and worked on the Super after the Korean war broke out in June 1950), believes the latter interpretation more likely: "Probably Oppenheimer wanted to influence us against the development of the hydrogen bomb and didn't want to do it in his own words, so he used Conant's letter instead."[47]

Two other atomic physicists also report that, shortly before the GAC met, they learned from Oppenheimer of Conant's strong opposition to the Super. Kenneth S. Pitzer, then the AEC's director of research, remembers that when he visited the physicist's Princeton home for a small dinner party, which Oppenheimer's appointment book indicates took place on October 22, Oppenheimer took him aside and either showed or described to him a letter containing Conant's views on the H-bomb and suggesting that he was taking a "similar" position.[48] And on Thursday, October 27, the eve of the GAC gathering, Oppenheimer told the physicist Robert Serber, a former student and old friend who was in Princeton on a visit from Berkeley, that Conant had been the originator of a broad proposal to block the development of the hydrogen bomb as a means of slowing the U.S.-Soviet nuclear weapons race.[49]

Were Conant and Oppenheimer collaborating to oppose the H-bomb prior to the GAC meeting? If so, their efforts were not very extensive compared to those made by pro-Super scientists to lobby politicians and military leaders. But the incidents lend further evidence to the view that Conant's opposition to the H-bomb exceeded Oppenheimer's in intensity. "Felt Oppie was lukewarm to our project and Conant was definitely opposed," was Teller's impression after the meeting, as recorded in Alvarez's diary.[50] In any case, the accounts of Teller, Bethe, and Pitzer tend to indicate (as Oppenheimer's lawyers pointed out) that Conant forcefully transmitted his opposition to the Super *before* receiving Oppenheimer's October 21 letter to him. As Oppenheimer later testified, Conant "told me what his views were before mine were clearly formulated."[51]

Still, Oppenheimer's cogent, cautious letter likely impressed Conant, for its reasoning echoed his own concerns over the excessive influence he believed atomic weapons were coming to have in U.S. military planning:

> What concerns me is really not the technical problem. I am not sure the miserable thing will work, nor that it can be gotten to a target except by ox cart. It seems likely to me even further to worsen the unbalance of our present war plans. What does worry me is that this thing appears to have caught the imagination, both of the congressional and of the military people, as the answer to the problem posed by the Russian advance. It would be folly to oppose the exploration of this weapon. We have always known it had to be done; and it does have to be done, though it appears to be singularly proof against any form of experimental approach. But that we become committed to it as the way to save the country and the peace appears to me full of dangers.

The Super, Oppenheimer wrote, remained a "weapon of unknown design, cost, deliverability and military value," as it had been in 1942, but the human, rather than the technical, conditions had changed: two "experienced promoters," Teller and Lawrence, were hard at work selling the weapon, and the congressional Joint Committee on Atomic Energy, "having tried to find something tangible to chew on since September 23rd, has at last found its answer. We must have a super, and we must have it fast."[52]

The most powerful ally that Conant and Oppenheimer had in preferring an expanded fission program to the hydrogen bomb, AEC chairman Lilienthal, was aghast at the enthusiasm of the pro-Super scientists. "Ernest Lawrence and Luis Alvarez in here drooling over [Supers]," Lilienthal wrote in his journal on October 10. Earlier he had conferred with Truman, still anticipating final presidential approval for a reinvigorated, "whopping big" AEC weapons program *sans* Super.[53]

The GAC itself was split as it assembled in a conference room featuring a fine panorama overlooking the Potomac at AEC headquarters on Constitution Avenue on the final weekend of October 1949. It was the group's eighteenth gathering since January 1947, and only one change had taken place in the membership: Oliver E. Buckley, director of Bell Laboratories, had replaced Hood Worthington in August 1948. Conant missed the Friday afternoon session, when the panel heard a briefing from George Kennan, also opposed to the Super, and conferred informally with Bethe and Serber. Discussion began in earnest on Saturday morning, with eight of the GAC's nine members present: Oppenheimer, Conant, DuBridge, Fermi, Rabi, Buckley, Rowe, and Smith; only Glenn Seaborg, the Berkeley chemist, was absent. During the marathon sessions over the weekend, Conant emerged as the leader who built a consensus against the H-bomb. The most lucid record of his views of the hydrogen bomb came later, in his testimony before the 1954 Oppenheimer hearings, when he said he opposed the weapon "as strongly as anybody on a combination of political and strategic and highly technical considerations." He went on to explain,

> Some of us felt then, and I felt more strongly as time went on, that the real answer [to the Soviet atomic bomb] was to do a job and revamp our whole defense establishment, put in something like Universal Military Service, get Europe strong on the ground, so that Churchill's view about the atomic bomb [that it prevented the Russians from reaching the Channel] would not be cancelled out.
>
> One of the considerations was that [the hydrogen bomb] was sort of a Maginot Line psychology being pushed on us. On the technical ground the question was the investment in preparing certain materials which I am not going into, which are restricted, which seemed at the time necessary; the use of materials which I don't want to mention, which would be used up.
>
> The question was when you expended a certain amount of manpower and energy and material, would you actually from the point of view of delivering blows against a potential enemy be very much better off even if this line worked?[54]

Contemporary accounts of the GAC discussion suggest, however, that moral qualms, far less fashionable in the atmosphere of October 1949 (or April 1954) than political or military or technical considerations, were central to the arguments against the Super. According to Gordon Dean, an AEC commissioner who attended some of the sessions, those opposing the weapon displayed a "visceral" reaction that emerged as the "moral implications were discussed at great length."[55] And Lilienthal wrote in his diary that Saturday night that Conant, "looking almost translucent, so grey," had come out "flatly against it [the H-bomb] 'on moral grounds.'" (Interestingly, the last three words were omitted in the published version but appear in Lilienthal's original journal entry.) Oliver Buckley argued that there was no moral difference between scales of weapons, between "x and y times x." But Conant was sensitive on precisely that point: "Conant disagreed—there are grades of morality." Receiving support from Rowe and at least tacit backing from Oppenheimer—who as chairman did not express his own view until the others had spoken—Conant again stressed morality when Lewis Strauss, who as a commissioner sat in for part of the discussion, commented that the final decision would not be made by a popular vote but "in Washington." Conant replied, according to Lilienthal: "But whether it will stick depends on how the country views the moral issue."[56]

Conant's moral arguments appear to have had a pivotal influence on Oppenheimer, who despite profound misgivings about the Super had written in his October 21 letter that it would be "folly to oppose [the Super's] exploration." Now, nine days later, he joined the rest of the group in forthrightly opposing the weapon's development. Why the shift? "Conant was really the mover in this and Oppie followed," recalls Serber, who accompanied Oppenheimer on the train from Princeton to Washington and spoke with several of the GAC's members (as well as H-bomb proponent Luis Alvarez) that weekend.[57] Oppenheimer himself explained, according to notes of an off-the-record 1957 interview, that his change "was a result of Conant's intervention. Conant said he just wouldn't have this, and pointed out that a firm stand could be expected to meet with the approval of various groups, churches." It had been, he concluded, "a mistake to go along" with his long-time mentor.[58]

For the often stolid Conant—described by his long-time friend George Kistiakowsky as an "unemotional, cold Yankee," by another chemistry colleague, Bright Wilson, as a man with a "cold logical approach" to important decisions, and by Rabi as "brisk," "business-like," "not much of a sentimentalist," "a red-tape man"—this stand on the hydrogen bomb involved an unusual degree of passion.[59] Also, his position on atomic weapons was coming full circle. At first dubious that any atomic bomb could be built, by the war's end he had come to believe that a few nuclear explosions and the threat of more could work diplomatic wonders; now that hope was gone. At the outset of World War II he had been a vocal proponent of the draft; by 1945 and 1946 he had decided that the atomic bomb blasted away the need for a large conventional army and considered the air force "the only branch of service looking to the future realistically";[60] now he lamented the Pentagon's emphasis on nuclear strategic bombing and favored rehabilitating conventional capabilities and reinstituting the draft. Having witnessed one weapon inspire such great expectations, and beaten back other weapons projects he regarded as harebrained, he was appalled by the sight of another fearsome gadget inspiring undue confidence: "This whole discussion makes me feel I was seeing the same film, and a punk one, for the second time," he muttered disgustedly at one point in the GAC discussions.[61]

Why did Conant feel the moral issue was so significant? After all, even Reinhold Niebuhr, Conant's favorite theologian and a person he looked to as an authority on moral issues, who had alarmed him only a few years before by raising moral questions about the use of the atomic bomb on Hiroshima, was now ruefully but firmly backing H-bomb development on the grounds that the Russians would build one, too; "no absolute line can be drawn on any weapon," Niebuhr was quoted as saying, just as Conant was doing his best to draw one.[62] William L. Borden, who was to accuse Oppenheimer of disloyalty in part because of his opposition to the H-bomb, conjectured privately to the FBI and AEC in 1954 that Conant "never quite recovered from his World War One experience of working on poison gas; that he, Conant, had an emotional reaction to developing a horror weapon, and that has colored Conant's viewpoint ever since."[63] But this is unconvincing for several reasons. For one, there is scant evidence to indicate that Conant had any moral or emotional misgivings (as opposed to pragmatic qualms) about his work on poison gas, which in fact was not completed in time for use in the war.[64] Second, one must remember that Conant helped to develop a vast array of "horror" weapons during World War II. And perhaps most significantly, neither Conant nor the other members of the GAC were pacifists: the panel's report opposing the Super also urged an "intensification of efforts to make atomic weapons available for tactical purposes, and [for the AEC] to give attention to the problems of integration of bomb and carrier design."[65] As Herbert York points out, Conant, Oppenheimer, and other critics of the H-bomb, while finding nuclear weapons "repugnant," nevertheless "explicitly recognized the need to possess nuclear weapons, especially for tactical and defensive purposes, and they regularly promoted programs designed to increase their variety, flexibility, efficiency, and numbers."[66]

Like other GAC members who had worked on the atomic bomb, Conant differentiated the hydrogen bomb on the grounds that it "might become a weapon of genocide," in the words of the majority annex to the GAC report, written by Conant and DuBridge and cosigned by Oppenheimer, Rowe, Smith, and Buckley. Because the Super was too big for use on military targets alone, the GAC said in its main report, signed by all eight attending members, "Its use therefore carries much further than the atomic bomb itself the policy of exterminating civilian populations." The majority annex stressed: "Let it be clearly realized that this is a super weapon; it is in a totally different category from an atomic bomb."[67]

But one must delve further to understand Conant's rationale. He had, after all, not shied away from the wholesale destruction of cities during World War II, helping to produce not only the atomic bomb but other weapons used in strategic bombing, and about Hiroshima and Nagasaki Conant only expressed regret that the atomic bomb hadn't been completed and used earlier.[68]

A crucial moral distinction, for Conant, between the decisions to build the atomic and the hydrogen bombs was their respective contexts. One of his guiding dictums was that during war one had no choice but to employ whatever means were needed or available to win. "Let us freely admit," he had said in 1943, "that the battlefield is no place to question the doctrine that the end justifies the means." After the war, however, must come a restoration of morality: "But let us insist, and insist with all our power, that this same doctrine must be repudiated . . . in times of peace."[69] That same theme had been sounded in his January 1949 *Atlantic* article, which affirmed his "deep-seated conviction" that "war is always totally different morally from peace" and suggested that "acceptance of the doctrine that the end justifies the means would be the moral equivalent of dropping atomic bombs on a dozen of our own cities."[70] Even more than atomic bombs, thermonuclear weapons posed the problem of the means threatening to overwhelm any conceivable end for which they might be employed, and whereas Conant had rationalized the dropping of the atomic bomb on Hiroshima not only on military grounds but in the hope that it would promote postwar international control efforts, he had no illusions that this would be the case with the Super.

Conant had overseen S-1 with a war in progress and fearing, until almost the close of the conflict, that the Nazis were frantically competing. (In fact, Conant had been startled, if relieved, to find out just how little progress the Germans had made, perhaps because the discovery implied that it had been unnecessary for the United States to build the bomb in the first place.) Echoes of that experience were sounding in Conant's mind as he opposed the H-bomb; despite the explosion of "Joe One," he was more skeptical of Soviet than American chances for producing a fusion bomb, and he was *quite* skeptical of the American chances.[71] Could 1949 represent a chance not to repeat the fateful turn taken in 1939?

The majority annex, co-written by Conant, implies that the Soviets would not have completed an atomic device by August 1949 without the successful example of the American atomic bomb; and that therefore it might prove possible to forestall the advent of the new weapon simply by not proving that it could work. It also expresses Conant's deep-set pessimism about the capacity of human beings to handle their technological creations safely:

> We believe a super bomb should never be produced. Mankind would be far better off not to have a demonstration of the feasibility of such a weapon until the present climate of world opinion changes.
>
> It is by no means certain that the weapon can be developed at all and by no means certain that the Russians will produce one within a decade. To the argument that the Russians may succeed in developing this weapon, we should reply that our undertaking it will not prove a deterrent to them. Should they use the weapon against us, reprisals by our large stock of atomic bombs would be comparably effective to the use of a super.
>
> In determining not to proceed to develop the super bomb, we see a unique opportunity of providing by example some limitations on the totality of war and thus of limiting the fear and arousing the hopes of mankind.

The main body of the report also reflected the priorities as set by Conant, Oppenheimer, and the rest of the GAC, as well as Lilienthal: accelerated production of fissionable materials, increased emphasis on tactical atomic weapons, and the production of freely absorbable neutrons for experimental and military purposes. As for the Super's feasibility, the panel frankly acknowledged that "an imaginative and concerted attack on the problem has a better than even chance of producing the weapon within five years." While noting that there was no theoretical boundary to yield of superbombs, the GAC nevertheless stated flatly that "there appears to be no chance of their being an economical alternative to the fission weapons" on a dollar-per-damage basis.[72]

The full GAC also adopted Conant's "firm" proposal that the government declassify enough information about the Super to facilitate public debate and to state clearly where the government stood on the issue. Ideally, the GAC hoped, Truman would forswear development of the Super, explain its destructive potential, and specify that no nonmilitary benefits would be sacrificed by not going ahead.[73]

From Lilienthal's account at the time, as well as the recollections of key participants, it appears that Conant played a critically important part in swinging the GAC into firm opposition against the Super. During the Saturday discussion as many as five of the eight members present ("less than half of the 8, never more than 5") seemed to favor an all-out development program for the H-bomb, Lilienthal wrote, but on Sunday all agreed to sign the report, and only two, Fermi and Rabi, signed a minority annex making their renunciation of thermonuclear weapons conditional on Soviet agreement to do the same.[74] (In 1982 interviews, DuBridge said Conant's arguments were "forceful, but so were some of the others," while Rabi recalled that "Oppenheimer followed Conant's lead" in the discussion.[75]) On Monday, October 31, convinced the decision might have gone the other way had Conant not stood his ground, Lilienthal telephoned him to congratulate him on the outcome of the meeting.[76]

Yet the GAC report also galvanized the supporters of the Super, as the battle lines in the secret debate emerged. Advocates of the weapon longed for a return to the sensation of superiority enjoyed during the years of monopoly, feared the Soviets might beat America to the weapon, and, conversely, hoped for the gains available if Washington won the race. To Lewis Strauss, the hydrogen bomb represented a "quantum jump" in atomic weapons and "the way to stay ahead" of the Russians.[77] The Joint Chiefs of Staff confidently predicted that U.S. possession of the Super would "grossly alter the psychological balance between the United States and the USSR," at least until the Kremlin developed its own H-bomb.[78] These positive sentiments were shared by two other significant forces rallying behind the weapon: a calvacade of nuclear physicists who went to Washington in October to lobby sympathetic figures in Congress, the government, and military; and Senator Brien McMahon, the powerful chairman of the Joint Committee on Atomic Energy, who told Teller that the GAC's report "just makes me sick,"[79] and soon sent Truman a lengthy letter rejecting the "false, horror-inspired logic" of the GAC and urgently demanding an "all-out effort" to produce the H-bomb.[80]

Meanwhile, on November 9, the Atomic Energy Commission itself had backed up the GAC's recommendation against the H-bomb in a split 3–2 decision, with Lilienthal, Pike, and Smyth against development, and Strauss and Gordon Dean in favor, Dean having defected from the majority view despite a concerted effort by Conant, Oppenheimer, Rabi, and Fermi to defend their conclusions during a hastily arranged special meeting with the commissioners at AEC headquarters on November 7, which, with Strauss absent, had centered mostly on Dean's objections. To Dean's skeptical inquiry as to what positive purpose would be served by a unilateral renunciation by the Super—for U.S. public confidence, the allies' security, the Soviet assessment of American resolve—Conant responded by reversing the question. "What effect would a decision to go ahead have?" he asked, presuming a wave of popular opposition. Dean stuck by his view that building the H-bomb could have a healthily deterrent effect on the Soviet Union.[81]

The GAC members' stress on the benefits of a public declaration of intent *not* to proceed, and the arguments they used to support it, show a number of conflicting elements: their naivete about U.S. public opinion; their desperation to prevent the nuclear noose from tightening around the neck of civilization; their concern over the moral deterioration of U.S. national-security policy; and their hope that, much as the Interim Committee had hoped that using the atomic bomb would "shock" Japan into surrendering, Washington could now strike an equally stunning blow for disarmament by a dramatic abjuration of this frightening new weapon.[82]

One may suspect that the GAC's arguments concealed uneasiness over the scientists' own contribution in having already created one monstrous weapon: "Conant, like all of us," Oppenheimer recalled in 1957, "felt a certain onus for his part in ushering in these weapons."[83] But they also boldly suggested a "new thinking" in international politics in which a dynamic of disarmament would replace the Cold War's deadly trend toward escalation and would produce, as Oppenheimer wrote cryptically to Niels Bohr in early November, "great and hopeful changes . . . within the next months."[84] To optimists in international politics, this tactic of wresting long-term mutual diplomatic gain by initiating a process through a preemptive concession would seem eminently plausible—Mikhail Gorbachev later explored its possibilities with mixed results. But to those who thought it hopeless to anticipate reasonableness from Stalin's Soviet Union, it must have smelled of appeasement, if not treason.

Conant, in fact, quickly became aware that suspicions were being cast on scientists who were not taking an adequately hard line. On December 1, he received a memorandum from his former "Fishing Party" aide, Lieutenant Colonel Black, purportedly describing two conflicting viewpoints "being expressed by highly qualified and, I believe, sincere scientists in this country." Black didn't explicitly mention the secret H-bomb controversy, but he didn't need to. "Group A" believed that advances in weaponry threatened the destruction of civilization, discounted the idea that the Soviets wanted war and sought a *"modus vivendi"* with them, anticipated long-term capitalist-communist convergence, and believed that "Since weapons exist which could destroy civilization, we must avoid a total war at all costs." This group recommended a reduction in U.S. military spending and a retraction from foreign influence. But "Group B," which Black preferred, considered Moscow to be "irrevocably committed to the destruction of Capitalist Society and to a program of world domination" at any cost, including "all-out aggressive war once she has achieved a clear-cut position of military superiority"—a position likely to occur, if present trends continued, within three to five years; therefore, America's "only deterrent" was "military superiority," requiring "radical increases" in defense spending, "greater boldness" internationally, and "above all a clear understanding by the American people of the imminence of danger and the necessity for immediate and drastic countermeasures." Black's covering letter suggested that Pentagon officials worried that "Group A" was getting too much clout. "As *one* [emphasis added] of these groups has already begun to express its ideas to the public, it is important that both concepts be summarized and brought to the attention of the appropriate authorities and, if possible, to the press."[85]

Conant recoiled from this reading of the situation. Black was describing two points of view that were "grotesquely fallacious," he replied, warning him against trying to divide such a varied group as scientists into simple categories. "Perhaps there has been too much discussion in the last five years about what the scientist thought or did not think." If Defense Department officials worried about the morale of government scientists, that was a problem of "leadership" in official laboratories. But, he continued,

> If we were talking about the various views expressed by citizens—these can be widespread and would have to be thrashed out in public debate. As you know, I have always thought that this debate would lead to more sensible answers if better information about some aspects of our national security were made available to the citizens. In short, I am afraid that my only advice is that anything you can do to expedite publication by the Administration of sober and reasonable statements about the future of modern arms will be of great value.[86]

By the GAC's next meeting on December 3—when the group reaffirmed its anti-H-bomb stand, with Seaborg now present and Conant ardently reiterating his previous arguments[87]—the secret debate was raging. To make a final recommendation, Truman had appointed a special three-man committee of the National Security Council: Lilienthal, Secretary of State Dean Acheson, and Secretary of Defense Louis Johnson. Of the three, Lilienthal strongly supported the GAC's position, now coming under increasing fire, and Johnson was just as clearly determined to develop the weapon.[88] That left Acheson as the potential swing man.

At the State Department, the viewpoint espoused by the GAC and Lilienthal had one strong advocate: George Kennan, in his final months as director of the Policy Planning Staff, searched anxiously for alternatives to building thermonuclear weapons, and, like Conant, flirted with the notion of proposing to the Soviets a moratorium on nuclear power development as part of a new emphasis on international control; he worked hard on a passionate seventy-nine-page report for Acheson decrying the increasing reliance on nuclear weapons in U.S. national security policy.[89] At a Policy Planning Staff meeting in early November, Acheson had shown some sympathy for Kennan's animus to the H-bomb, suggesting an 18–24-month moratorium on developing the weapon ("bilateral if possible, unilateral if necessary") to explore the possibilities for lessening international tension before going ahead with full production and stronger public support.[90]

But Acheson and Kennan, not unlike Conant and Grenville Clark four years earlier, were drifting in different directions. In November and December, as Kennan grew more convinced that nuclear weapons were dragging the United States and the world toward catastrophe, the secretary of state was becoming increasingly responsive to mounting pressures on Truman to go forward with the H-bomb.[91] But before he made up his mind, Lilienthal asked him to see some opponents of the weapon—and one of them was Conant, whom Acheson hosted for lunch on Wednesday, January 18, 1950.[92] By then he had all but decided to back the Super's development—he had been unable to fathom how Oppenheimer and the GAC believed the U.S. could "persuade a paranoid adversary to disarm 'by example.' "[93] Precisely what arguments Conant employed are not known. Acheson did not mention the meeting in his memoirs, though he may well have had Conant in mind when he wrote that die-hard opponents of the superweapon may have been moved less by logic than by "an immense distaste for what one of them, the purity of whose motive could not be doubted, described as 'the whole rotten business.' "[94] It does seem from one surviving document that Conant came tantalizingly close—as close as anyone—to luring Acheson into the anti-H-bomb camp. Yet for all his eloquence, Conant fell short. The next day Acheson wrote that while he had decided to recommend pushing ahead with the Super, "after listening to Conant it would be very easy to arrive at the opposite conclusion, except that in arguing against the position I had come to, he admittedly could not suggest an alternative."[95]

Listening to Conant's impassioned arguments against the H-bomb, Acheson grew fearful that the educator might publicly oppose a presidential decision to develop the weapon. He may have heard the rumor secretly reported to the JCAE a week earlier by Chairman McMahon that Conant had privately declared that if the H-bomb were approved he would "take the decision to the country" rather than silently acquiesce.[96] Now Acheson begged Conant not to resign from the GAC or promote a public debate on the H-bomb, claiming that such an action by him or Oppenheimer would be "contrary to the national interest."[97] "For heck's sake," he is said to have told Conant, don't "upset the applecart."[98]

Like his secretary of state, Truman also saw no alternative to going ahead, nor did he seek one after being told that the Russians would probably be able to develop their own hydrogen bomb. The option of resurrecting international control in the form of a mutual pledge not to build or test any

H-bombs he considered neither feasible nor desirable. Building up military power seemed the most prudent policy, since unilaterally forgoing or offering to negotiate the fate of the Super might, he feared, be perceived as a sign of weakness. Even if there was no clear military requirement for the weapon, as the GAC believed, its chief value, as General Bradley had said, was "psychological." And with anti-Communist fears and passions rising—it was the fortnight of Alger Hiss's conviction and Klaus Fuchs's confession, and the country was in the midst of the debate over "Who lost China?"—even the appearance of conceding any advantage to the Soviets was politically unacceptable. When the Acheson-Johnson-Lilienthal committee met with the president on January 31, he told them that "there has been so much talk in the Congress and everywhere and people are so excited he really hasn't any alternative but to go ahead and that was what he was going to do."[99] That day, the White House announced that Truman was directing the AEC to "continue"—Lilienthal's euphemism—"its work on all forms of atomic weapons, including the so-called hydrogen or superbomb."[100]

Truman's decision to go forward on the hydrogen bomb sharply curtailed the GAC's influence. Though it continued to meet regularly to offer technical advice, there was a widespread perception that the president's sharp rebuff on so important an issue had irretrievably damaged its stature within the government. Gathered for its scheduled January 31 meeting, the GAC was plunged into gloom when Lilienthal relayed Truman's decision. Not only would research on the Super go ahead, but Truman had rejected Conant's "firm" view that the matter should be publicly debated and had slapped a secrecy order on them. "It was like a funeral party—especially when I said we were all gagged," Lilienthal wrote in his journal. "Should they resign? I said definitely not, on the contrary. This would be very bad. Though before long a number of them may, just because they feel their standing is impaired."[101]

Ironically, in view of the accusations later hurled at the GAC for allegedly delaying the H-bomb program even after it had become official policy, Conant later wrote to a friend that he and Oppenheimer "didn't [resign] (or at least I didn't) because I did not want to do anything that seemed to indicate we were not good soldiers and did not do what we could to carry out orders of the President!" But in retrospect, he felt, the two should have departed immediately after the decision.[102] Whether he felt equally regretful about obeying the injunction against arousing public debate on the H-bomb, against "upsetting the apple cart," democracy notwithstanding, is not known.

In any event, instead of taking his case to the country he watched gloomily as a state of virtual hysteria descended upon the capital and the nation. Within two days of Truman's announcement, Klaus Fuchs, the German-born British physicist and a participant in discussions of thermonuclear weapons at Los Alamos at least through 1946, was revealed to have been a Soviet spy. Suddenly, the speed with which Moscow had obtained an atomic bomb became more explicable.[103] Fears spread that the entire American nuclear program had been compromised, and any lingering doubts in the White House about the necessity for rushing ahead on the H-bomb vanished.[104] The revelation that Fuchs had committed espionage hit Conant especially hard. Almost four decades after the event, an undergraduate who saw him in a Harvard office on the afternoon of February 2, 1950, vividly remembered the ashen expression on Conant's face as he reeled from the news of Fuchs's confession. "That man knew everything," Conant muttered repeatedly, as if in shock. "That man knew everything."[105]

Gleefully exploiting the widening pall of paranoia, Wisconsin Republican senator Joseph McCarthy gave a speech in Wheeling, West Virginia, during which he waved a sheet of paper supposedly listing the names of 201 (or 57, or 81) Communist traitors working in the State Department. An edgy press and Congress pounced on his sensational charges, and bloodhounds clamored to expose the traitors who were selling out the country and its secrets.[106] The new crescendo of fear and suspicion not only drowned out the GAC's futile pleas for self-restraint in the quest for new weapons but gave such views an aura of disloyalty. "I hope you are standing up under the strain of these trying times as well as usual," Conant wrote Oppenheimer on February 14, enclosing a copy of a letter he had received from a friendly Washington reporter disclosing that a Republican senator on the JCAE was spreading the story that the GAC had opposed the H-bomb program "on moral grounds."[107] Later that month, after McCarthy had choreographed "one of the maddest spectacles in the history of representative government,"[108] as the journalist Richard Rovere described it, by ranting and raving on the Senate floor from afternoon until past midnight about alleged State Department Communists, Conant hinted at his own disgust in a private letter to Baruch:

> When I am in Washington, it seems as though I were in a lunatic asylum, but I am never sure who is the attendant and who the inmate. Nor am I even sure whether I am a visitor or a potential patient. However, I am trying to keep my sanity and will do what I can with the others.[109]

On March 2 Conant had a chance to insert his views directly into the policy-making process when he was called in for consultation on a major internal review of Soviet-American relations in light of the new developments. The document that emerged, National Security Council 68 (NSC-68), recommended a major U.S. military buildup to forestall the danger of Soviet superiority within four to five years, defined in stark terms Moscow's "design for world domination," disdained immediate prospects for negotiation, and issued a clarion call for the U.S. to "bring about an internal change in the Soviet system" and liberate those under Kremlin domination.[110] Disturbed by this sweeping definition of U.S. objectives, Conant engaged in a sharp debate with NSC-68's architect, Paul Nitze, Kennan's new replacement as the

State Department's director of policy planning.[111] The goal of rolling back and eventually eliminating Soviet rule could not be achieved short of war, he suggested, and had Nitze "considered the fact that in World War III, we might, in winning the war, lose our freedom"? As before, Conant's sights were set more narrowly; rather than the "Utopian objective" of uprooting Communist rule, he felt "that for the next 20 years our objective should be to live on tolerable terms with the Soviet Union and its satellites while avoiding a war." Nitze responded, foreshadowing the rhetoric of John Foster Dulles's "rollback" schemes, that "if we had objectives only for the purpose of repelling invasion and not to create a better world, the will to fight would be lessened."

Disagreement also flared over the advisability of arms negotiations. While NSC-68 expressed grave doubts about the wisdom of seeking international controls over nuclear weapons, Conant refused to concede the defeat, or irrelevance, of the view that it was in America's long-term security interest to shift away from them, and asserted that "the atomic bomb is a bad weapon from the United States point of view." Despite Truman's decision, and the grim state of U.S.-Soviet relations, he still pushed for negotiations with the Russians, perhaps to rein in atomic energy development. To Nitze's claim that a failure in talks could raise tensions to a flash point, Conant argued pragmatically that even the failure to reach a settlement "would be a very strong argument for the necessary sacrifices on the part of the United States" and "might put the Soviet Union in a hole in the cold war."

What America needed to do, Conant felt, was to build up Western Europe economically, to put a million troops on the ground there to defend it—an idea that Nitze considered "politically impractical," in view of the problems already encountered in gaining support for a peacetime draft[112]— and to avoid squandering resources on new and costly weapons such as the hydrogen bomb. Disdaining visions of moving to the "offensive" in the Cold War, he stressed the more limited but, in his view, more practical and sensible goal of avoiding global war for the next few decades. By 1980, he predicted, the Soviets' "absurdities and static system would cause them to grind to a stop. He repeated that if we can hold what we have, especially the United Kingdom, and avoid war, then the competition between our dynamic free society and their static slave society should be all in our favor, or if not, we deserve to lose[!]" And, he added presciently, his guess off by only a decade, "By that time, Russia may Balkanize or Byzantinize itself."

That the GAC, though down, was not yet out of the picture continued to rile the scientists who strongly favored the most rapid possible development of the H-bomb and nuclear power. Some of that acrimony emerged when Conant was nominated for a post that would have crowned his position as leader of America's scientific community: the presidency of the National Academy of Sciences.

Seeking a replacement for President A. N. Richards, who had announced his plans to retire, a nominating committee in early 1950 selected Conant, perhaps the most illustrious figure in U.S. science but not the most active figure in academy affairs. In the past, such selections had been routinely rubber-stamped by the full membership. The post carried immense prestige, a $15,000 annual salary, and both ceremonial and substantive responsibilities.[113] In the spring of 1947, freshly embarked on new atomic responsibilities, Conant had quietly turned down a summons to succeed Frank Jewett as academy president, but now, three years later, tired of the battles over nuclear issues, he welcomed the honor and the chance for a new identity as scientific statesman. Upon receiving word that the nominating panel, "with a high degree of unanimity," desired to put his name before the academy, Conant after a few days' thought replied that he would be "very happy to serve" as president.[114]

As planned, Conant's name was placed into nomination at the April 24 meeting (which he did not attend). But, the original minutes of the meeting read, "From the floor, Mr. W. M. Latimer nominated Detlev W. Bronk as candidate for President. Mr. V. K. LaMer seconded the nomination."[115] Bronk, president of Johns Hopkins University and chairman of the academy's National Research Council, had urged Conant to stand for president and disclaimed any foreknowledge of the uprising from the floor. But it was quickly evident that a "revolt of the chemists" was under way: both Wendell Mitchell Latimer, the dean of chemistry at the University of California at Berkeley and chairman of the academy's chemistry section, and Victor LaMer, a Columbia University chemist, were right-wing scientists who had worked under Conant in the NDRC during the war, and Latimer in particular was known to be unhappy at Conant's performance.[116] And a number of other chemists had been nursing resentment over what they considered Conant's wartime misadministration and "authoritarian" behavior.[117] "They ganged up on him behind his back" is how the chemist George Kistiakowsky put it, still angry more than three decades later.[118]

Confusion erupted on the floor of the convention, during which Bronk requested his name be withdrawn; instead, another chemist rose to make a "very effective . . . 'drafting' " speech in his favor.[119] After emotional speeches for and against Conant, a vote was then taken among the 201 members in attendance "with the result that a majority of votes was cast for Mr. Bronk—77 to 71, by one account."[120] Reached by telephone at the home of William Marbury in Baltimore—at a dinner to which Bronk, too, had been invited— Conant withdrew and endorsed Bronk.[121]

Though Conant refused to speak of it publicly, the humiliation suffered at the hand of fellow chemists left a bitter aftertaste. "What the hell has gone on?" Kistiakowsky recalled Conant asking right after the academy meeting. He was "terribly upset by this dirty deal that was engineered by the chemists" and "furious about what he regarded as a revenge by a few West Coast

chemists feeling slighted in W.W. II and a real doublecross by Detlev Bronk."[122]
After Conant's death in 1978, Kistiakowsky wrote to Mrs. Conant:

> Probably the most painful incident of Jim's life as science leader occurred
> without warning to me and without my being able to take any steps to
> prevent it, an event which I see as a tragedy to American science as well as a
> disappointment I know to Jim. I refer to Jim's withdrawal from nomination
> as the next president of the National Academy of Sciences, when suddenly
> confronted by a small but secretly well organized group of little men who
> resented Jim's wartime leadership. The rest of us were unaware of what was
> being organized and thus were unable to demonstrate to Jim in good time the
> strong support which in fact would have been his. Jim's sensitive personality,
> of course, led him to withdraw rather than wage a political battle, which for
> his opponent was largely that for status and position. Had Jim become the
> president of the Academy, I know he would have raised its influence in
> Washington and made it into the center of science policy leadership in
> America and abroad, an objective the realization of which largely escaped
> . . . the men who led the Academy since those days.[123]

Though he made no such charge in his memoirs, Conant believed, according
to Kistiakowsky, that Bronk "urged him to stand for election but then conspired with the malcontents . . . without warning Jim . . . until post factum,"
but in fairness to Bronk—described in one account as the "innocent beneficiary"
of the anti-Conant revolt—it must be stressed that no hard evidence has
emerged to support this contention.[124] One scientist reported privately several months later that Conant's opponents "picked Bronk more or less
whimsically," and the Academy history notes that Bronk was elected "over
his protests as a friend of Conant."[125] But doubts sprang up almost immediately.
One scientist wrote a month after the event of "ugly rumors going around
Harvard and Hopkins and presumably elsewhere that *Bronk* himself conspired & assented in advance to the *coup,*" but added that "if he did he is a
more perfect dissembler than anybody I ever saw in action . . . he asked that
the floor nomination of his name be withdrawn and when the Academy went
ahead and elected him he was so completely taken aback that he lost all his
aplomb for just once in his life and was determined to decline the election"
had not Conant endorsed him and withdrawn his own candidacy.[126]

For seventeen years the incident remained a family secret of the scientific
community, until the appearance of an article in *Science* magazine in 1967
attributing Conant's defeat to "vengeance . . . exacted in a vendetta seething
since World War II."[127] Other motives have also been cited to explain the
uprising, the most innocuous of which was concern over the fact that Conant
would inevitably be a part-time leader since the bulk of his time would still
be spent at Harvard. "Undoubtedly the spearhead of the opposition was
personal, but I heard later that cogent arguments were used," Conant wrote
in his memoirs.[128] "No one is in a position to assess the motives of the

individuals who voted to elect Bronk," declared one of Bronk's supporters, Berkeley chemistry professor Joel Hildebrand, in a letter to *Science* vehemently rebutting the idea that a "vendetta" against Conant had occurred.[129] Concern that Conant would only be a part-time president, genuine support for Bronk, and a residue of resentment toward Conant still festering among certain Manhattan Project veterans were all factors.

There is, however, a chain of evidence, both circumstantial and direct, linking the crisply planned and executed maneuver to the controversy over the hydrogen bomb. The nucleus of the opposition to Conant, centered at but not confined to the Radiation Laboratory at the University of California at Berkeley, consisted of scientists whose prior dissatisfaction with him was now reinforced by strong antipathy to his position on the Super and his close ties to Oppenheimer. This largely overlooked connection suggests that the events at the academy were a harbinger of the quiet campaign to expel Oppenheimer and Conant from the GAC two years later, and of the open cleavage of the scientific community in the Oppenheimer security case in 1954, reflecting the ascendance of the faction of scientists ardently favoring the hydrogen bomb, nuclear power, and reliance on nuclear weaponry as the long-term mainstay of U.S. national security policy.

The prime agitator against Conant was Latimer, dean of chemistry at Berkeley, delicately described by Conant as "a California chemist to whose ideas I had not always lent a sympathetic ear."[130] According to Kenneth Pitzer, a colleague in the Berkeley chemistry department, Latimer had resented Conant's hiring of "second-rate Harvard people" to fill chemistry posts during the war when "more technically expert people were available whom Conant didn't happen to know personally. . . . This caused a certain amount of resentment . . . such things never completely disappear."[131] As Alvarez put it, Latimer was "a little paranoid about Conant,"[132] and, like LaMer,[133] he had acquired a reputation as an bellicose militarist.

Latimer later revealed his almost pathological dislike of Oppenheimer, whom he saw at the center of a diabolical conspiracy of scientists, and his lesser distaste for Conant, whom he considered one of Oppenheimer's henchmen.[134] In the fall of 1949, Latimer had helped to organize the scientists from Berkeley — Teller, Alvarez, and Lawrence — who descended on Washington to lobby for the H-bomb prior to the October meeting of the GAC, a group he regarded as under Oppenheimer's spell. "You know," Latimer told the 1954 hearing about Oppenheimer, "he is one of the most amazing men that the country has produced in his ability to influence people. It is just astounding the influence he has upon a group. It is an amazing thing. His domination of the GAC was so complete that he always carried the majority with him, and I don't think any views came out of that Committee that weren't essentially his views."[135] Specifically including Conant as "under the influence of Dr. Oppenheimer," Latimer averred that Conant's technical reasons for opposing the hydrogen bomb "sounded pretty phony to me . . . I doubt it was a free judgment on his part."[136] (Conant testified that he relied on Fermi rather than Oppenheimer for nuclear expertise.)[137] And he acknowledged the link between his feelings about the GAC and the National Academy incident when he was secretly interviewed by an FBI agent and AEC attorney Roger Robb as they prepared for the Oppenheimer hearings: "Latimer stated he had helped defeat Dr. Conant in the election for President of the National Academy of Sciences and elect Dr. Detlev W. Bronk since he knew that Oppenheimer 'had Conant in his hip pocket' and was promoting Conant's candidacy."[138]

Latimer was not the only H-bomb proponent who in the spring of 1950 knew of and rued the influence of Oppenheimer and Conant on American nuclear policy: Pitzer himself appears to have been a leader of the revolt against Conant at the academy, according to Lawrence Hafstad, a close associate at the AEC, where Pitzer was director of research from 1949 to 1951.[139] "I do not know what Pitzer felt about the explosion," another scientist wrote Bronk a week after the academy meeting. "He took no public part in it; but he did not appear downcast after it."[140] In a 1985 interview with the author, Pitzer—who told the FBI he had been "amazed" when Oppenheimer did not share his H-bomb enthusiasm, "surprised" to learn from Oppenheimer that Conant agreed with him, and "suspected Oppenheimer had persuaded Conant," and who also resented Conant's skeptical view of nuclear power prospects—confirmed that he "was of the Latimer viewpoint at the Academy" and, while citing other reasons to oppose Conant's nomination, added, "You can say that Conant's position on the hydrogen bomb . . . may well have been a significant motivation for a minority of the voters."[141]

Another leader of the anti-Conant movement, Hildebrand, fully backed Latimer's view on the H-bomb, lauding the fiery chemist's "wisdom and foresight" in lobbying government officials and fellow Berkeley scientists to oppose the GAC viewpoint.[142] Less clear are the positions of several other scientists who, as strong H-bomb advocates actively engaged in the development of the weapon, may have disapproved of bolstering Conant's prestige. Lawrence and Alvarez, who had joined the lobbying expedition to Washington, had been disappointed by Conant's lukewarm response to new possibilities for radiological warfare, and believed Oppenheimer had shown bad judgment in atomic policy matters and had dominated the GAC. According to FBI documents, Alvarez thought "Oppenheimer and his group had put the University of California on the black list."[143] But Alvarez, while recalling talk about the academy revolt against Conant, said he did not participate, and Pitzer believes Lawrence was not "an active conspirator."[144]

One Berkeley physicist whose view of the academy's action seems clear even if his own action, if any, remains mysterious, was Edward Teller. By April 1950 Teller considered Conant as an enemy in the struggle for control of U.S. atomic policy, an impediment to the H-bomb program, and an Oppenheimer ally. He told the FBI in 1952 that Conant "is outspoken in his opposition to the H–Bomb and even to the atomic bomb [and] against further work in atomic energy for peace-time use as he is of the opinion that better results can be accomplished through the use of solar energy."[145] A month before the National Academy meeting, he wrote to the executive staff director of the Joint Committee on Atomic Energy, William L. Borden, "I feel the attitude of the members of the GAC has been a serious difficulty in our recruiting efforts. . . . A man like Conant or Oppenheimer can do a great deal in an informal manner which will hurt or further our efforts."[146] And his dim view of Conant's candidacy was explicit in a March 1954 interview with an AEC agent shortly before the Oppenheimer hearings:

> Teller talked . . . about the "Oppie machine" running through many names, some of which he listed as "Oppie men" and others as not being on his team but under his influence. He says the effort to make Conant head of the National Academy of Sciences is typical of the operation of the "Oppie machine." He adds that there is no organized faction among the scientists opposing the "Oppie men."[147]

More definitively linked to the move against Conant was Harold C. Urey, the Nobel laureate in chemistry from Columbia University and leading scientist-activist who had been a member of the wartime S-1 Executive Committee chaired by Conant. Urey had sharply criticized Conant for alleged bureaucratic bungling, and Conant believed he had disloyally complained behind his back to other dissatisfied project scientists.[148] At the war's end Urey had been on the opposite side of the controversy over atomic energy legislation, and strongly opposed the idea of Conant's being appointed to head the AEC.[149] Having split with Conant over the decision to use the atomic bomb, Urey in 1950 also opposed Conant on the hydrogen bomb, vocally promoted the "Strauss-Lawrence" line, and, Lilienthal wrote in his diary, spread "innuendo on [the] GAC."[150] Conant, according to his son, in turn "had very little use" for Urey, who, Conant believed, "shot from the hip and acted emotionally."[151] As with Latimer, LaMer, and Hildebrand, Urey was described by one academy member present as being "in active revolt" against Conant's selection.[152]

Willard F. Libby, a chemistry professor of the University of Chicago who joined the GAC in 1950, shared the perspectives of the anti-Conant cabal. A protégé and close associate of Latimer's, and a friend of LaMer's, Libby had been a group leader during the Manhattan Project in the section on isotope separation at Columbia University, a source of discontent with Conant's administration; Urey in particular had been dissatisfied with Washington's handling of the research that Libby conducted.[153] In the fall of 1949, both Urey and Libby had been contacted by Latimer shortly after the announcement of the Soviet atomic bomb, and they responded favorably to his pro H-bomb pleas.[154] Described by one liberal colleague as a militant right-winger who "saw Communists under every bed," Libby also shared Latimer's

490 JAMES B. CONANT

view that Conant (and Lee DuBridge) usually backed Oppenheimer on atomic matters and "perhaps . . . were taken in or persuaded in their views" by him.[155] But whether he joined Latimer's crusade to block Conant at the academy is not known.

The outcome of the struggle for the presidency of the NAS had immense consequences for American science, and for Bronk and Conant personally. Bronk headed the institution until 1962, a twelve-year term that included the Korean War, the spread of McCarthyism, the reaction to the Soviet Sputnik, and the Oppenheimer case; during that same time the academy, and U.S. science generally, vastly expanded its activities vis-à-vis the government; how the academy would have fared under Conant is a matter of speculation.[156] It is clear, however, that the event marked a turning point in Conant's life, for had he gotten the job he doubted he would have been invited by Eisenhower in 1953 to go to West Germany as U.S. high commissioner (and later ambassador), or would have embarked on his subsequent career as self-appointed ombudsman of public education; "in other words," he concluded many years later, "my career after 1950 would have been totally different."[157] While he continued to serve on government science panels, he made a sharp break with the scientific establishment and, according to one report, "never again set foot in the Academy building."[158]

Outwardly, Conant professed nonchalance. When a mortified representative of the NAS nominating committee wrote to him expressing astonishment and regret over what had happened—"I was astounded when opposition developed in the lobby . . . a small group did a lot of electioneering"—he replied gallantly that "everything had come out for the best," Bronk would "make a fine President," and that, in sum, "this is a case where the electorate proved to be wiser than the bosses!"[159] In his memoirs, Conant characteristically downplayed the affair, claiming that as the years went by he grew "happier and happier with the outcome and soon almost forgot the incident."[160] But he had felt sharply wounded by being denied an expected laurel for a career of scientific statesmanship,[161] and, worse, the academy affair, coming so shortly after the bitterly contested fight over the hydrogen bomb, revealed a vein of bitterness flowing beneath the collegial exterior of American science—an early symptom of divisions that soon deepened.

CHAPTER 25

"Paul Reveres of the Atomic Age"

The Committee on the Present Danger

1950

Get a group of distinguished citizens together, put it before the public, get people to write Congress and, in general, respond to the gravity of the situation. From what I have just heard, I judge the country is asleep. You should wake it up.
— To Tracy Voorhees, August 1950

In the uncertain technological arms race now in progress, the dwellers in the Kremlin may consider themselves the winners on paper somewhere in the period 1952–54 and having made this decision will start a global war if they can be sure of marching to the Channel ports.
— JBC, "A Stern Program for Survival," in *Look* magazine, December 1950

Dean Acheson and James Conant eagerly anticipated the last week of June 1950. After a winter of tribulations—the Communist victory in China, the Hiss case, the H-bomb decision, Fuchs, the secret struggle over NSC-68, and the "revolt of the barbarians," as Acheson termed the rise of McCarthy and his allies—the secretary of state savored a chance to trade Washington's grim atmosphere for the convivial air of Cambridge, to bask in the pomp and splendor of the springtime Harvard graduation ritual, to receive an honorary doctorate of laws, and to pass an evening at the presidential residence at 17 Quincy Street. His host, in turn, endured the hectic duties of Commencement week while quietly relishing the prospect of a long-planned summer voyage to the British Isles; he and his wife had reserved two seats aboard a transatlantic flight leaving Boston at Friday afternoon, June 23, the day after Commencement.

On Thursday, everything went according to plan. In the morning, Conant donned cap-and-gown to confer degrees on graduating seniors, condemned Communist abuses of education, and awarded honorary degrees to a dozen notables, including Acheson. That afternoon, the graduates and their families assembled in the outdoor, elm-shaded Tercentenary Theater for the annual Commencement address. Before Acheson stepped to the microphone, another honorary degree recipient, Foreign Minister Carlos P. Romulo of the Philippines, warned that events in Asia might well determine whether the world headed toward peace or war. But Acheson accentuated the positive. At the rostrum from which his predecessor had launched the Marshall Plan three years before, Acheson hailed Western Europe's ongoing economic recovery as well as the West's progress in containing the Soviet Union's "inordinate ambitions." As the sunny afternoon faded into dusk, the graduates who four years earlier had strode into Harvard Yard through a gate whose inscription admonished them to "enter to grow in wisdom," now streamed out beneath an exhortation "to serve thy country and thy kind." And Conant and Acheson headed off to respective summer holidays.[1]

Disaster awaited both men. Early the next morning, Conant awakened with a sharp pain coursing through his abdomen. His wife summoned a family physician, and he soon found himself rushing not to Logan Airport but to a branch of the Massachusetts General Hospital. Doctors diagnosed him as suffering from diverticulitis, "an acute inflammation in a loop of the intestine," and immediately performed emergency surgery, removing six inches of Conant's large intestine.[2] Late the next evening, Saturday, June 24, as Conant recuperated in "good" condition, Acheson readied for bed after a relaxing afternoon of gardening and a hearty dinner at his Maryland farmhouse retreat. Then the phone rang, and a crisis halfway around the world shattered his weekend repose: North Korean forces had stormed across the 38th parallel into South Korea.

Even in those first sketchy reports, the meaning of the Far East attack seemed obvious. Attuned to the "lesson of Munich," Acheson and most of the rest of official Washington interpreted the invasion as a Soviet-supported military thrust, a carefully plotted move in the Kremlin blueprint for world domination. "The attack upon Korea makes it plain beyond all doubt," Harry Truman told the nation, "that Communism has passed beyond the use of subversion to conquer independent nations and will now use armed invasion and war." Intervention on behalf of South Korea, he declared, was required to avert "a third world war." Although some aides feared that Stalin had staged the Korean assault as a diversion from a planned move against Western Europe, Truman ordered U.S. forces to the Korean peninsula, and the grinding three-year "police action" began.[3] With the Soviets boycotting United Nations sessions to protest the exclusion of Communist China, they missed a chance to cast a veto when the Security Council endorsed the use of force to repel the North Koreans; thus the United States was able to lead a military effort that was officially under the banner of the world body.

On June 28, between crisis conferences, Acheson spared a few moments to dictate a note to the stricken Conant: "Before I could write you to thank you for all you did for Alice and me last Wednesday and Thursday, two catastrophes occurred—your own and the Korean one—and the latter has taken every minute of my time."[4] But a full week elapsed before Patty Conant decided that her husband had recovered sufficiently to let him read the newspapers and learn of the events in Korea. "I never had a chance to form an opinion unbiased by the *fait accompli* as to whether President Truman had made the right decision," Conant judiciously noted in his memoirs. "I like to think I would have been among the majority who applauded."[5]

Yet it's by no means clear whether Conant would have been an ardent interventionist in Korea had the choice been his: Asia did not loom large in his view of the world, and his sense was that the decisive moves on the Cold War's strategic chessboard would be made in Europe. Four months earlier, he had agreed privately that the United States must "decide on a line [the Russians] cannot cross," yet added that Indo-China and even Finland might be on the other side so long as the United Kingdom was protected.[6] (He was always rather cool toward what became known as the Third World, tending to regard it as little more than an arena for superpower intrigues; he had given India's prime minister Nehru a tepid reception in Cambridge the previous fall, despite Grenville Clark's insistence that India was vital in the struggle against Communism in Asia, and he opposed U.S. aid to developing countries beyond that "needed to combat the Communist menace.")[7] Later, in fact, in arguing against rearming West Germany, Conant cited South Korea as an example of the "dangers involved" when America was allied with a "nationalistic government [with] an independent army."[8] But there could not be, and was not, any hesitation about Conant's jumping into line behind the president's decision to fight in Korea once it had been made. As soon as he learned what had happened Conant dispatched a note of support to Truman (who had sent his own telegram of concern to Conant), and a warm letter to Acheson expressing admiration for "the way you and the President have handled the South Korean situation."[9]

By his release from the hospital on July 12, Conant had recovered sufficiently to joke about his ordeal: "I am beginning to be superstitious about what happened Commencement Day," he wrote to MIT president James Killian. "[M]y emergency operation occurred within twenty-four hours . . . and what has happened to poor Dean Acheson about South Korea hardly needs to be underlined."[10]

The outbreak of the Korean War consummated Conant's conversion to Cold Warrior, and that is the role to which he devoted his energies for the next half-decade. As educational statesman, as scientific adviser, and—by founding and heading the Committee on the Present Danger (CPD)—as propagandist, Conant lobbied for a sharp increase in military spending, for a drastic domestic emergency mobilization, including a mandatory two-year military draft, for the unprecedented long-term peacetime commitment of U.S. troops in Western Europe, and for an ideological appeal to the American people to win a cold war of indefinite duration or else to triumph in a hot war.

A number of related, interconnected themes emerge from these efforts. Though he urged moderation as against extremist demands for a preventive or inevitable war against the Soviet Union, his own interpretation of the United States' rivalry with the USSR changed significantly. Formerly he had seen it as a political and ideological struggle whose outcome would be determined by each system's economic and social vitality; now it appeared to him as a military confrontation whose outcome would depend on relative armed might and the willingness to use it. Stalin and the Soviets were now portrayed as totalitarian menaces bent on world conquest, and even ambiguous indications of Communist expansion required, as Hitler's had, an immediate military response in order to avoid repeating the disastrous example of Munich.

Tracing Conant's views during this most dangerous phase of the Cold War suggests the wider perceptual shift among influential Americans in and out of government. Looking back, chroniclers of this era have wondered why, after the Korean invasion, so many leading Americans believed in a "real danger of the Soviets unleashing in the fairly near future, what would have been World War Three."[11] After all, border clashes had occurred sporadically for several years on the artificially divided peninsula, and in fact, subsequent historical accounts of the still murky decision-making process leading up to the North Korean invasion—including Khrushchev's memoirs, published in 1990—and documents located in Soviet archives suggest that while Stalin endorsed Kim Il Sung's attack, he neither initiated it nor envisioned it as an initial step toward all-out war with the West.[12] Nevertheless, Conant, like most other opinion-shapers and policymakers in the United States, presumed or worried that it might be just that. Truman regarded the Korean attack as part of a carefully orchestrated Kremlin plot to weaken the West. "From the very beginning of the Korean action I had always looked at it as a Russian maneuver, as part of the Kremlin's plan to destroy the unity of the free world," Truman wrote in his memoirs. "NATO, the Russians knew, would succeed only if the United States took part in the defense of Europe. The easiest way to keep us from doing our share in NATO was to draw us into military conflict in Asia."[13]

Conant consistently (although more firmly in public than private) inveighed against the notion of an inevitable third world war. Yet, by spreading the idea that Moscow sought to dominate the world through military conquest, and by helping to coordinate and coalesce the views of the "leaders in American life" (as the *New York Times* described the CPD's membership)[14] to ratify this new consensus, he encouraged the American ideas that nearly laid the basis for a "terrible misunderstanding"[15]—a global war precipitated by an incorrect assessment that the Soviets plotted a military assault on Western Europe.

Conant's intellectual and emotional gyrations were also a response to another significant aspect of life in this period—America's forced adjustment to the threat of nuclear destruction. Since 1946 he had prophesied that the "Age of the Superblitz" would arrive only when the Soviet Union had offensive nuclear capabilities, and now that this was fast becoming true he feared that only a miracle would allow humanity, or at least Western civilization, to survive. But Conant came to rely on a new hope, named nuclear deterrence, to replace the discarded dream of international atomic control and the diabolical temptation of preventive war. And, like other Americans, he grew accustomed to what he described as "living under the shadow of the 20th century volcano—atomic bombs."[16] Until North Korean troops stormed across the 38th parallel, he clung to the notion that the Soviet challenge to the United States was "primarily ideological," to be resisted by revivifying America's economic, social, and political vitality rather than by preparing for a "fighting war," which struck him as both unlikely and contrary to Kremlin strategy.[17] He had told the drafters of NSC-68 in April 1950 that "a far greater danger" was a "series of coups *à la* Czechoslovakia."[18]

Sticking to that view meant resisting the mounting clamor to confront the Soviets militarily, a demand that intensified as alarmism pervaded public discussions as well as the still secret NSC-68. Conant tried to be, as ever, a voice of "cautious optimism"—optimism now being defined as assuming that a third world war was neither inevitable, imminent, nor desired by Moscow. "I believe with intelligence, patience and good luck we can get through the balance of this century without another global war," he told educators in May. "And if we can, I have every confidence that the free peoples of the world will win the ideological struggle of our times!!"[19]

The fighting in Korea strained even Conant's cautious optimism, however. "The aggression of the North Koreans established a new pattern," he told Americans. Now it had become clear that the Kremlin intends to "use military means" to achieve world domination.[20] Modern weapons and technology, wielded by a superpower of seemingly implacable hostility, threatened for the first time to overwhelm the great oceanic moats that had protected the United States since its birth. Conant believed the country's very existence was gravely threatened—and sought a way to transform his private frustrations into practical deeds.

Through July and August 1950, Conant convalesced between operations at his Randolph, New Hampshire, summer home. His intestinal woes were exacerbated by peritonitis and his doctors, who had already scheduled additional surgery in October to finish their work, advised complete rest. On July 12, Conant wrote a friend that by Thanksgiving he hoped to be "as good as new." In the meantime he was "trying to possess my soul in peace as best I can."[21]

By mid-August, the situation in the Far East had momentarily stabilized. Despite heavy fighting, American troops were holding on to the "Pusan perimeter" on the southeastern tip of the Korean Peninsula, and Acheson judged the military situation safe enough for him to "escape" for a family vacation at a lake in the Adirondacks. In Washington, meanwhile, the emotional response to Korea that had first plummeted the nation into depression in early July under the intense North Korean offensive now started to veer toward the fatally attractive idea of "liberating" all of Korea, North as well as South. After a succession of what seemed to be defeats—the Soviet atomic bomb and espionage successes, the "loss" of China—some officials were eager to score a dramatic total victory that would "roll back," rather than merely contain, Communism.

But Conant still worried more about Russian threats to Europe than he was tempted by the allure of gains in Asia. And his concern mounted one evening in mid-August when he dropped by the Randolph summer home of an old friend and sometimes golf partner, the Boston lawyer R. Ammi Cutter, for an after-dinner chat (a restricted post-surgery diet forced him to miss the main course). There Conant met Cutter's guest: another lawyer, Tracy S. Voorhees, a former under secretary of the army. A few months earlier, Voorhees had been involved in preparing a secret report to Truman about the unfavorable military balance in Europe; among his collaborators in the report, prepared concurrently with and complementing the conclusions of NSC-68, had been Vannevar Bush, who had told Conant about Voorhees. More recently, Voorhees had written an article for the *New York Times Sunday Magazine* on the need "to prevent another Korea in Europe." As Conant was about to learn, when Voorhees "was alarmed about a public situation, he became the enraged citizen ready to argue his case to anyone who would listen."[22]

Conant made a ready listener. "I was all ears that night," he recalled. "What I heard reminded me of the cries of alarm in Washington and New York when France fell in 1940." The agitated Voorhees quoted army general Alfred M. Gruenther (a mutual friend, whom Conant had secretly advised on advanced weaponry) as saying that "All the Russians need to march through to the Channel is shoe leather." Unless the United States immediately led a massive rearmament drive and sent a large contingent of U.S. ground forces, Voorhees warned, the Soviets could overrun Western Europe virtually at will.

This was music to Conant's ears, for since his reversal on UMT after the Compton commission report in mid-1947 he had, to no avail, advocated stronger steps toward a comprehensive peacetime draft; now could be the time to try again. Moreover, he shared Voorhees's low regard for Truman's secretary of defense, Louis Johnson, whose ill-concealed political ambitions alienated associates and whose tightfisted fiscal policies frustrated supporters of increased military spending. Having "no doubt that they had solid grounds for their apprehension," Conant agreed that if Cutter and Voorhees "were only half right, the nation was once again, as in June 1940, in extreme danger."[23]

That the fall of Seoul should evoke the same fears as the fall of Paris—

when Conant's "overpowering emotional reaction" to the Nazi onslaught, which he likened to the sweep of Mohammed, had impelled him to campaign actively for intervention—shows the extraordinary extent to which the still fresh memories of Adolf Hitler colored American perceptions of the Soviet threat. Here was Conant stepping into a Churchillian role, alerting countrymen to the danger of a barbarian threat to civilization, raising a call for the sort of drastic military measures for which the British statesman had vainly pleaded in the 1930s.

It is likely that Conant had already read the recently published first volume (*The Gathering Storm*) of Churchill's magisterial World War II memoirs, which helped to ingrain the Munich analogy by recounting in damning detail how "the English-speaking peoples through their unwisdom, carelessness, and good nature allowed the wicked to rearm." Together with Churchill's postwar warnings, from the "Iron Curtain" March 1946 Fulton speech to subsequent claims that only the atomic bomb had stopped the Russians from marching to the English Channel, his book radiated a clear contemporary message: Western statesmen risked repeating the same failure to confront militarily an aggressive, expansionist, totalitarian dictatorship.[24]

Conant believed it was already too late to stop "the wicked" from rearming: Since "no sane man would advocate the use of an atomic bomb now that the Russians had one of their own," he now considered preventive war impractical as well as immoral. But there remained the option of erecting a military roadblock to further Soviet expansion, which Conant believed required a million-strong American force in Western Europe, a sharp increase in military assistance to anti-Soviet allies, and a willingness to bear huge financial as well as political costs. Such an unprecedented, costly peacetime commitment, he knew, required firm congressional and public backing. Ten years earlier, he had been appalled when public opinion lagged behind the Roosevelt administration in its readiness to face up to the prospect of war against Germany, and he had thrown himself behind powerful pressure groups to prime the public for war and, by doing so, to assist FDR. Now, too, Conant's thinking dovetailed with an administration's private inclination: the need to obtain a national "consensus" had been a central theme of the discussions leading to NSC-68, which had bemoaned the supposed advantage of totalitarian dictatorships "acting in secrecy and with speed" compared to "vulnerable" democracies dependent on public opinion and riven by partisan bickering.[25]

Acheson well comprehended the importance of public support for expanded foreign military commitments. In 1940–41, he had joined Conant in the interventionist campaign, and in 1947, he had followed congressional advice to "scare the hell out of the American people" into supporting the Truman Doctrine. In drawing up NSC-68, Acheson later acknowledged, its authors had purposely inflated the Soviet threat to "so bludgeon the mass mind of 'top government'" that Truman's orders would be carried out.[26]

But "top government" still depended upon appropriations voted by congressmen, who were guided by public opinion. And since gaining mass support for an unlimited increase in military spending, with a consequent slashing of myriad competing domestic priorities, was to be no easy task, NSC-68's planners envisioned a "scare campaign" to create the proper atmosphere. "[I]f we can sell every useless article known to man in large quantities," reasoned Robert Lovett, "we should be able to sell our very fine story in larger quantities."[27] And it's far from clear that Harry Truman was rushing to the cash register; at a background White House press conference in early May, he told reporters he expected to *reduce* defense spending in fiscal 1951.[28] But then, "Korea saved us," as Acheson candidly said later.[29] By condoning North Korea's invasion, even if he did not instigate it, Stalin unwittingly provided a ringing celebrity endorsement of NSC-68's "very fine story" and very expensive product. Once the fighting broke out, Truman asked for everything NSC-68 had asked for and more—arms and men not only for Korea, but also for Europe (and a grudging acquiescence in West German armament), and a sharp acceleration in production of all types of weapons, both nuclear and conventional.[30]

But not fast enough for Conant. Well aware of NSC-68's secret prescriptions, he thought the Truman administration was moving too slowly to capitalize on the opportunity given by the Korean War to mobilize public opinion behind universal military service and troops to Europe; he agreed with Voorhees and Cutter that a distinguished "citizens' group," along the lines of the ones he had worked on in 1940–41, could guide the public, especially the articulate, news-following, vote-casting, middle- and upper-class public whose support was essential.

"Get a group of distinguished citizens together," Conant urged, "draw up a program, put it before the public, get people to write Congress and, in general, respond to the gravity of the situation. From what I have just heard, I judge the country is asleep. You should wake it up."[31]

"Would you be one of the leaders in such a committee?" Voorhees asked.

I might, Conant replied, but he would be a "semi-invalid" for a few months and faced another operation in October. Fatigued, he ended the conversation without formally agreeing to anything, yet he had set the ball—and Voorhees—rolling. "Without being aware of it," Conant later recalled, "we had just participated in forming the Committee on the Present Danger, which was to fulfill a useful function until the Korean War was over."

That Voorhees should court Conant to chair the proposed group was natural, for educational leaders possessed unique credibility and authority, and Conant more than any other (with the momentary exception of Eisenhower) commanded attention on a national level. Although he had his share of critics, Conant's status within the profession once prompted another university president, Berkeley's Robert Sproul, to be characterized as "one of those who thinks that the voice of Conant is the voice of God."[32]

Also pushing Conant to lead the proposed group was William Marbury, his man on the Harvard Corporation and a fellow Randolph summer vacationer. Proselytized by Voorhees during a round of golf, Marbury enthusiastically supported the idea of Conant's leadership, and offered to help in Washington. With Cutter and Marbury now on board, and two days after his first conversation with Conant, Voorhees pledged to work full-time for as long as it took to do the job if Conant "would give the prestige of his name to head such a committee."[33] Voorhees later wrote that for Conant to "trust his name to someone who was virtually a total stranger" was an "adventure in faith."[34] But he did so, with the proviso that the program accorded with the Truman administration's own policies.

In fact it fit almost perfectly. The administration had already been urged to create a "citizens' committee" to gain public approval of NSC-68's program. In February and March 1950, State Department consultants Robert Oppenheimer, Henry DeWolfe Smyth, Chester Barnard, and Robert Lovett had all stressed the importance of convoking a panel of "worthy citizens" to endorse NSC-68's message publicly, and several named Conant as a likely member or leader of such a group.[35] Lovett, later Truman's secretary of defense, said a "vast propaganda campaign" to implement NSC-68 would be necessary, and to do that "a group of paraphrasers" should be gathered to "audit and certify our findings and thereby back up the Administration's statement of the facts." But he also recommended that this citizens' group should not be appointed officially by Truman "because it might thereby be tarred with the Administration's brush in the eyes of the people."[36]

It was precisely this demimondish role that Conant wanted his lobbying group to fill—combining outsider standing with insider connections, ostensibly independent, nonpolitical and "non-partisan," yet closely coordinating behind the scenes with, and acting as an unofficial propaganda arm of, the government. Voorhees again: "Dr. Conant's basic conviction—which I fully shared—was that such a citizens' committee could be really effective only if it were welcomed by the Administration."[37]

With Conant's approval, Voorhees in early September quietly held preliminary conversations with top U.S. officials—including State Department foreign policy adviser Robert Bowie, General Gruenther, and High Commissioner to Germany John J. McCloy, who had been privately complaining about the administration's failure to move swiftly toward a European defense plan with major West German participation[38]—and found ready support for a dramatic rise, on the order of several hundred thousand to several million troops, in American ground forces in Western Europe.[39]

But even before the administration could respond to Voorhees's informal inquiry, Conant conscripted the nation's educational establishment—and through it the foreign policy elite and the general public—in an effort to mobilize "the youth of this nation in a time of unparalleled crisis." "Sitting on a mountaintop between hospitals" in early September, Conant wrote to

Brown president Henry Wriston that the crisis offered the Association of American Universities (AAU), which Wriston then headed, a "special opportunity" to "show real leadership" by coming up with "a long-range, sensible scheme for universal military service (*not* training). If a group of university presidents came forward with such a scheme within the next few months, it might be a matter of great importance."[40] In Conant's view the AAU and the American Council on Education (ACE) should back immediate enactment of a bill to draft "every male" for two to three years of military service, with virtually no student deferments. "Since I believe the sooner we have a million combat troops in Europe the better," he reasoned, "I am naturally on the side of immediate action to raise the armed forces to 3–5 million men." On September 18, Conant wrote in a similar vein to the EPC's William Carr, stating that he had "with much reluctance" reached the conclusion "that I do not see how we can avoid drafting all able-bodied young men for a couple of years service."[41]

By so sternly advocating a mandatory draft, with minimal exemptions for students, Conant found himself, not for the first time, taking a minority view, for most educators and students preferred to insulate universities as much as possible from military mobilization. Educators who opposed UMT during this period "plainly outnumbered their professional colleagues," according to one study,[42] and Conant ran into rough water soon enough. But he hoped to find powerful allies—and it did not require deep calculation to figure out that the educator whose opinion on military matters mattered most was Columbia University president Dwight D. Eisenhower. Conant viewed his support as essential, and in fact, Eisenhower shared Conant's dissatisfaction with the Truman administration's handling of military affairs and with Defense Secretary Johnson in particular.[43] Conscious of Eisenhower's enormous prestige, Conant "inclined to agree in advance to anything to which he would subscribe, but judging from past experience, he and I might find ourselves in a minority on some questions involving education and military affairs!"[44]

At the end of September, a special mini-summit of college and university presidents held at the Waldorf-Astoria Hotel in New York City to discuss the international situation offered Conant a chance to probe Eisenhower's position and to launch the campaign that soon would be taken up by the CPD. Of the seven university presidents sponsoring the "Citizens' Conference"—among them Wriston, Eisenhower, the University of Pennsylvania's Harold Stassen, Princeton's Harold Dodds, and MIT's Killian—he had collaborated with several on UMT and other issues and soon would again on the CPD. In line with its organizers' desire to promote its message as widely as possible, the off-the-record session also attracted "about fifty industrialists, heads of communications services, representatives of the press, radio, newspapers, magazines, financiers, educators, heads of farm organizations, life insurance companies, and railroad presidents"—in other words, a cross-section of the kind of opinion-shapers who were to populate the CPD.[45]

By the time the conference opened, events had eased slightly the summer's atmosphere of disaster. General MacArthur had made his dramatic landing at Inchon, behind North Korean lines, and U.S. forces pushed north from Pusan. Reversing earlier statements, Truman had acknowledged for the first time that he had approved "substantial increases in the strength of the United States forces to be stationed in Western Europe." At a NATO foreign ministers meeting in New York City, Acheson had unveiled new proposals for West European defense that presumed major U.S. participation, an overall U.S. commander and, for the first time, a substantial West German contribution in some still-to-be-determined form. And on September 12, Truman had fired Louis Johnson and announced that George Marshall would step out of retirement to become the new secretary of defense, with Conant's friend Robert Lovett as his deputy. Conant wrote to Marshall that he greeted his appointment with "a sense of relief."[46]

Nevertheless, alarm, not relief, permeated the message Conant drafted for the New York conference. Unable for health reasons to attend in person, he set down his thoughts in a seven-page, single-spaced memorandum to be read to the group by Harvard Business School dean Donald K. David. Ostensibly addressed to "the need for mobilizing the youth of the nation in this time of unparalleled crisis," the memo seems most interesting now for its barely qualified endorsement of the new orthodoxy that pictured the Soviet Union as rapidly approaching a nuclear capability equal to America's, enabling it to march into Western Europe without fear of atomic retaliation, and its repetition of the still secret NSC-68's claim that within two to four years, the United States would face a period of "maximum danger" of a Soviet surprise attack.

Although Korea still dominated the headlines, Conant's memo fixed squarely on the imperative that "Western Europe be held against Communist domination." He predicated his assertion that this task was a military problem on three assumptions:

1) "that Churchill is correct when he states that the Russians would now be in the Channel ports but for the U.S. strategic air force armed with the atomic bomb";

2) "that the ability of the Russians to retaliate with atomic bombs and their ability to thwart strategic bombing of their cities will increase rapidly in the coming years"; and

3) "that in the uncertain technological arms race now in progress, the dwellers in the Kremlin may consider themselves the winners on paper somewhere in the period 1952–54 and *having made this decision will start a global war if they can be sure of marching to the Channel ports.*" [emphasis added][47]

While these premises may be questioned, Conant conceded, he insisted they were "at least extremely probable" and in any case the safest guide to policy-making. This analysis mirrored not only the Nitze-Acheson view expressed in NSC-68 but one that was rapidly gaining adherents within the administration—NSC 73/4 of August 25 had argued Korea might represent "the first phase of a general Soviet plan for global war," and the CIA now estimated that the Kremlin might "deliberately provoke . . . a general war" by 1954, with the "peak" danger point reached by 1952.[48]

To deter the threat to Western Europe, Conant went on, would require a conventional force able to stop a Russian onslaught, and a substantial American troop presence for at least a decade. That, in turn, would necessitate raising an army of 3–3.5 million men by the "time of maximum danger" (1952–54) through a system of mandatory military service for two years for all eighteen-year-old-men—with "absolutely no exemptions" or deferments. Five years after the end of World War II, he admitted, it was again time to mobilize America's universities, requiring "drastic readjustments," including a "great sacrifice in the area of general or liberal education," a sacrifice "demanded by the extreme peril which the free world faces."

Conant tried to conclude on a hopeful note. "Peace time conscription is a bitter pill for the American people to swallow," he acknowledged, but he saw "no other way of responding adequately to the dangers of the times. What we fail to do in 1950 may come home to roost in 1953." He insisted his proposals were not meant to prepare for an "inevitable" global war, but, rather, "addressed to the task of bringing about a real global stalemate." And if that stalemate "can be achieved in spite of the technological progress of the Soviet Union in the 1950's," Conant added, "the 1960's might see important steps taken toward a gradual disarmament and an approach to peace."

Henry Wriston later observed that those present at the closed session gave Conant's memo "a mixed response, but an impromptu talk by General Eisenhower on the need for a stronger American military position [in Europe] generated more enthusiasm."[49] Eisenhower's off-the-cuff remarks, in fact, largely echoed Conant's gloomy analysis: the Soviets were bent on world domination and ready to use armed force to achieve it but did not want a global war now; preventive war would be "stupid and futile"; Korea was a Russian-inspired test of American will, and more would follow; a U.S. force of at least 3 million men must be raised within eighteen months; "this country, if it is to survive, must have universal military service." Confidential notes of the meeting recorded that the university presidents in attendance generally favored Conant's plan but thought a year-and-a-half of mandatory military service, rather than two, might suffice; more importantly, they show, "General Eisenhower agreed with Dr. Conant in the main," and "unreservedly" backed his insistence on UMS.[50]

The Harvard and Columbia presidents, who had shared headlines a year earlier by rejecting the employment of Communist teachers, were again allied on a major issue linking education and national security. Before the meeting, Conant had sent Eisenhower a copy of his statement—"You will see that I have ventured to intrude into affairs of which you know a great deal and I next to nothing. . . . If you can persuade me that my drastic suggestions are unnecessary and unwise, I shall be more than delighted"[51] — and Eisenhower dispatched a cordial private endorsement: "Your memorandum rings the bell with me!" Ike especially lauded the "crux" of Conant's argument, the advocacy of universal military *service* rather than training; a "promptly enacted and earnestly executed" UMS or even UMT program, he averred, might have prevented the Korean War (presumably by deterring Moscow).[52] "The particular satisfaction I get out of your memorandum," he added, "is the fact that someone of your standing in the academic world should have written [it]. It reveals a lot of soul searching."[53]

The outcome of the New York meeting—a "great success," he wrote Eisenhower[54]—encouraged Conant to press the battle for mandatory conscription on other fronts. Over the next month, Conant arranged for his memorandum to be presented in October to the Association of American Universities annual meeting in Rochester, and to be published in *Look* magazine in December.[55] At the same time, he solicited Eisenhower's aid in persuading the EPC to take a firm line on universal military service, or at least not to muddle the issue by settling for universal military *training,* in a forthcoming report on "Education and National Security." Otherwise, he warned the EPC's William Carr in late September, he would make his dissent public and perhaps resign from the commission, an act that for him represented an extremely serious step.[56]

Most importantly, Tracy Voorhees had been making the rounds in Washington to determine whether the administration would back up Conant's proposed "citizens' committee" with its own program of universal military service. In early October, Voorhees and Marbury sounded out the Pentagon, and got an assurance from Lovett that Secretary Marshall would be eager to see such a group come into existence. Conant had reason to hope that his multipronged propaganda campaign to "wake up" a "sleeping" America was falling into place. On October 9 he began contacting the prominent figures he wanted on the citizens' committee to sign a formal entreaty to Marshall explaining the group's raison d'être and seeking informal support.

Two weeks later, a collective letter went out to Marshall from Cambridge over Conant's name, signed also by Bush; the educators James P. Baxter III (Williams College), Dodds, and Wriston; former secretary of war Robert Patterson and ex-State Department official William Clayton; the advertising mogul Stanley Resor; and three well-connected attorneys—Marbury, Voorhees, and John Lord O'Brian. Despite efforts to raise public awareness of the need to defend Western Europe, the letter warned, "even yet the gravity of the civilized world's peril is not adequately understood," and the administration might well face problems gaining support for "the hard decisions necessary" for a "realistic defense" including a "hard core of American troops" in Europe. This "small group of interested citizens" offered to enlarge their circle into "a citizens committee wholly nonpolitical in character" that "might be of help in strengthening the public support of such stern measures as may be necessary." In an attached statement, the signers proposed a "very substantial U.S. ground force of several hundred thousand men under arms in Europe for a long period," as well as a two-year mandatory draft "both to train a manpower pool should war come, and to make possible rotation of personnel to maintain our requisite military strength."

Conant ended by putting the ball squarely in Marshall's court—they "would not wish to proceed," he wrote, "if you felt that it would not be constructive to do so." The general's quick reply looked like an official imprimatur: "Your proposal is an undertaking of great importance," he wrote each signer of Conant's letter.[57] Meanwhile, army secretary Frank Pace told Voorhees that both the envisioned group and its program were "splendid."[58]

With what seemed like the administration's private blessing, Conant, Voorhees & Co. went forward. And it was Conant finally who made a firm decision to chair the group and to name it "The Committee on the Present Danger" (over "The Committee to Strengthen the Defense of the Western Democracies" and "The Committee to Strengthen the Defense of Freedom").[59]

In the fall of 1950 Conant had other matters to take up, and the most immediate of these was a second surgical operation to complete his "internal repair job." The importance he placed on chairing the CPD, in fact, is all the more apparent when contrasted with his almost complete withdrawal from other duties and responsibilities. His desk calendar is virtually devoid of its normal clutter of trips, meetings, speeches, and appointments for weeks before and after his operation for diverticulitis on October 16, and he remained under doctor's orders not to stay away from home overnight (although he did take a week off in Tennessee to recuperate) and in general to keep to "a pretty restricted schedule." Doubtless he considered it a silver lining in the cloud of his medical predicament to have this socially acceptable excuse for turning aside the endless invitations to address alumni associations, chambers of commerce, conferences, convocations, and the like, to minimize his administrative obligations—which, in any case, he had already largely delegated to Paul Buck, David Bailey, and other trusted underlings—and to throw himself into the more challenging task of alerting his countrymen to the Communist menace.[60]

The survival of civilization, in the late fall of 1950, seemed more in doubt than at any time since the end of World War II. For Americans, the soaring highs of September's Inchon landing, the success of which tempted the Truman administration into authorizing General MacArthur to push into North Korea, gave way to shock and despair as the nightmare of an all-out intervention by "Red China," whose warnings against crossing the parallel had been ignored, now became reality. At first a trickle, then a flood of hundreds of thousands of Chinese "volunteers" swept southward across the Yalu River and, beginning with a violent attack on November 25, overwhelmed the United Nations forces.[61] For many Americans, the shock was even greater because their expectations had been unrealistically raised by MacArthur's proclamation of a "win the war offensive" intended to "bring the boys home by Christmas." Instead, by the end of November, the American troops, heralded as victors only a few weeks before, surrendered, fought, died, and retreated in a frantic, desperate struggle.

At the peak of the crisis, on November 30, Truman set off more global shock waves by telling reporters that use of the atomic bomb in Korea was under "active consideration" (he quickly backed off from the threat after a hurried visit by British Prime Minister Clement Attlee). The Pentagon that week, Acheson later recalled, collapsed into "deepening gloom" as the U.S. position in Korea neared "a crash state."[62] The prospects of defeat in Korea, war against China, or an escalation to a full-scale East-West war all loomed. On December 9 Truman wrote in his diary: "[I]t sure looks like World War III is here."[63] To make matters worse, the atmosphere of anger and recrimination was further poisoned by the just-concluded, bitterly partisan congressional elections, in which Red-baiting had surged.

In some quarters, the reaction to the unstable world situation verged on panic. At the Harvard Law School, Dean Erwin N. Griswold confidentially circulated a detailed memorandum prepared by a faculty member who proposed urgently establishing a research project to investigate and perhaps mitigate the "serious legal problems" that would result from a nuclear attack on the United States.[64] In Washington, a senior official addressed a memo to Truman urging him to issue an ultimatum to Moscow that any further aggression "would result in the atomic bombardment of Soviet Russia itself."[65] Eisenhower wrote in his diary of "hysteria" in the nation's capital, of a floundering president ("poor HST, a fine man who, in the middle of a stormy lake, knows nothing of swimming. Yet a lot of drowning people are forced to look to him as a lifeguard"), of something "terribly wrong" afoot in the country.[66] The theologian Reinhold Niebuhr saw no exit from the quagmire: "The international situation seems to me to be hopeless," he wrote his friend, the historian Arthur Schlesinger, Jr., on December 1. "I don't see anyone with enough moral authority, or statesmanship, to extricate us out of a deep involvement in the vast convulsion of Asia."[67]

Moral authority and statesmanship, together with a concrete program, were precisely what Conant and the founders of the Committee of the Present Danger hoped to supply. By proposing the military and political measures America needed to face a "struggle for survival," and by professing to voice the considered, informed consensus of a distinguished, apolitical coalition from all walks of American life, they tried to fill the void that Niebuhr had complained of. And by coming into existence in the midst of the worst military disaster that the country had sustained since Pearl Harbor, the

CPD sensed an opportunity to exploit the perception of peril for their own foreign policy aims.

The CPD's widely reprinted inaugural statement, drafted by Conant, Patterson, and Sherwood and released by Conant and Bush at a press conference in Washington on December 12, struck a tone of grim alarmism leavened only slightly by hope. On the psychological level, Conant once again, as with his earlier effort to mold public perceptions of Hiroshima, sought to steel the nerves of a rattled American public, to prepare it for either World War III or else a tense, grim, twilight struggle of uncertain duration. And again, this meant quelling any panicky rush toward preventive war or, conversely, a retreat toward isolationism; the strategy of withdrawing from overseas commitments and creating a "Fortress America" the CPD rejected as "a counsel of despair and defeat" that would, in Conant's words, leave the country in a "terrific mess."[68]

While the CPD denied that war was inevitable "unless the Soviet so wills it," its rhetoric and analysis were clearly intended to rouse Americans to prepare psychologically as well as militarily for a climactic battle with the enemy. The "naked aggression by powerful Communist forces" in the Far East constituted a "grave threat to the survival of the United Nations and a peril to the very security of these United States," and the atomic deterrent that had kept at bay Moscow's "aggressive designs" was fast being undermined by Soviet advances in atomic bombs and air defenses. The CPD quite openly likened the Soviet threat to the Nazi menace of a decade earlier, in both aggressive intent and boundless immorality:

> Unless an adequate supplement for the atomic potential of the United States is brought into existence, the time may soon come when all of Continental Europe can be forced into the Communist fold, and the British Isles placed again in even graver peril than in 1940, at sacrifices in blood and wealth that the Kremlin would accept. No scruples of conscience will stand in their way.

Of course, the "adequate supplement" Conant and the CPD had in mind to defend Western Europe was large-scale military aid plus a "powerful contribution of troops" culled from a U.S. armed force of "at least" 3.5 million men, double the size at that time. Here, on the practical level, the CPD wanted to channel fear into a practical program that had as its centerpiece Conant's sine qua non for a practicable defense scheme, UMS for two years for all males upon turning eighteen or graduating from high school. Universal military training should be not a substitute for but complement a program of universal service.

To meet "the danger of all-out war," the CPD warned, Americans must accept not only UMS but also vastly expanded military spending, "submission to economic controls more exacting than those now in effect, particularly in the field of credit, Government and private," and "a sharp reduction in

Government spending for non-defense purposes." For all this pain, the CPD contended that the program might still not be "arduous enough," since it represented "the only chance of averting a war of world dimensions" or winning it if necessary.[69] A kind of an anti-Communist flip side to Trotsky's concept of "permanent revolution," this vision of a Cold War "permanent emergency" helped to enshrine a new American political orthodoxy in which constant readiness for war (a "fully loaded pistol," in C. Wright Mills's phrase), with all of the activities later subsumed under the category of the "military-industrial complex," would be viewed as a natural, necessary, and perhaps eternal precondition for "peace."[70] A profound departure from past American behavior, this state of affairs depended on a pervasive and ongoing public appreciation of foreign military menace.

While the CPD's twenty-five founding members (the membership later rose to about fifty-five, plus a West Coast branch of about forty) were agreed on the fundamental nature of the new, militarized situation, that consensus did not extend to all issues, and they tended to eschew positions on controversial subjects that threatened to divide them. The December 12 statement, for example, failed to take a position on the subject of what part, if any, West Germany (still disarmed and under occupation) should have in a plan for West European defense. "If we were even to embark on a discussion of the question of the rearmament of Germany I am sure we would break up!" Conant wrote to a friend later that month.

> For the time being my attitude as a member of the Committee would be "We'll discuss the rearmament of Germany later; let's get ahead with strengthening the American contribution." Maybe it will turn out that we will arm Western Germany, maybe it won't. But for the time being the problem is to get Europe armed without waiting for a decision on this tough point.[71]

This occasionally mealy-mouthed approach brought the CPD criticism, as liberals denounced the group for its reluctance to take on McCarthyite civil liberties abuses, and inevitable internal disagreements: some CPD members, for instance, vainly urged a more forthright stand against General MacArthur in his showdown with Truman during the spring of 1951.

Nevertheless, the favorable press reaction to the CPD suggested that the group had struck a chord in the nation's political establishment. The *New York Times* reprinted the CPD's December 12 statement in full, as it would many other subsequent CPD pronouncements, and in a glowing editorial — alongside a masthead bearing the name of VP and General Manager Julius Ochs Adler, a CPD stalwart — applauded the committee's "exceptionally distinguished membership" for its "heartening awareness of an imminent danger . . . at least as great as it was in those terrible years of 1939–45." The *Washington Post* also endorsed the CPD's call for UMS, and *Time* and

Newsweek printed positive accounts. One newspaper headline hailed the members as "Paul Reveres of the Atomic Age."[72]

The CPD's timing, it seemed, could not have been better. The military disaster in the Far East had concentrated the country's mind on proposals for national security. In the week before the committee's debut, *Look* spotlighted Conant's "Stern Program for Survival" (a revised version of his memorandum to the "Citizens' Conference" in September). Although it was criticized by parents and by other educators (Conant later termed it an "initial and not well-aimed shot"), it put in the hands of millions of readers his somber appraisal of the Soviet military peril and the measures needed to confront it.[73] And on the same day as the CPD's official appearance, an off-the-record "study group" at the Council on Foreign Relations, that traditional watering hole of the internationalist East Coast establishment, weighed in with a private letter to Truman. Chairing a group that included Allen Dulles, Hamilton Fish Armstrong, and the ubiquitous Henry Wriston, Dwight Eisenhower drafted the panel's final conclusions, which closely paralleled the CPD's assessment of the Soviet threat and its call for a program of mandatory conscription and expanded U.S. military forces (twenty divisions) in Western Europe.[74]

In his original draft, Eisenhower included a recommendation that Truman convene a blue-ribbon "Citizens' Committee . . . comprised of respected leaders of American business, professions, education and religion" in support of this program—but he omitted the idea after Wriston, who had prodded him to write the letter, pointed out that the CPD made the suggestion redundant.[75] In fact, the Pentagon had already begun providing the CPD "confidential information which it is believed will be of great assistance in its work," and then emphasized its supportive attitude with a publicized background briefing for a CPD delegation on December 13.[76]

That day, Truman exhorted congressional leaders to vote for a fourth supplementary budget increase for fiscal 1951 (NSC-68/4) to cover military spending increases, and followed that up the next day with a declaration of national emergency. And on December 15, in a nationwide radio address that borrowed liberally from the CPD's vocabulary, Truman explained that a rapid military build-up, including a 3.5-million-strong U.S. army (the CPD's number) and an upgraded and integrated fighting force in Western Europe, would be necessary to face "the present danger" presented by the Soviet Union to "our homes, our nation, all the things we believe in."[77]

So, three days after its premiere, the CPD could feel well launched, its own semiprivate initiative and the president's actions interacting in the synergistic fashion Conant had intended. And, of course, the quality that had enabled the committee to attract such rave opening-night notices was not so much its script but its cast, which radiated moderation, credibility, prestige, judiciousness. As the *New York Times* later put it, the group was calculated to "give anti-communism in the United States the respectability and authority which it deserves but sometimes lacks, because of abuses by well-meaning zealots, more or less cynical demagogues and those who make anti-communism a profession."[78] Among the "twenty-five leaders in American life"[79] signing the CPD's founding statement were college presidents (Conant, Baxter, Dodds, Sproul, Wriston, Frederick A. Middlebrush, Raymond B. Allen) and the chairman of the board of trustees of the University of Chicago, Laird Bell; former government officials (Bush, Clayton, Patterson, Voorhees); leaders of the Carnegie Institution of Washington (Bush) and the Carnegie Corporation (Charles Dollard) and Council on Foreign Relations (Frank Altschul); the chairman of General Mills (Harry Bullis); influential lawyers (Marbury, O'Brian, Cutter, Edward S. Greenbaum, Monte Lemann); and key mass communications figures (Julius Ochs Adler of the *New York Times;* the author and speechwriter Robert E. Sherwood; and Stanley Resor, head of J. Walter Thompson).

In the months to come, more heavy hitters would join the CPD's line-up. Several were swayed by friendship with and admiration for Conant: CBS broadcaster Edward R. Murrow signed up despite his customary rule of avoiding affiliations that might taint his hard-won image of journalistic objectivity, and personal lobbying by Conant brought Oppenheimer aboard, though not before a typically talmudic inquiry that subtly expressed the physicist's preference for ground forces and tactical atomic weaponry over strategic nuclear power to counter the Soviet threat. "I take it that the principal theme of the Committee is the defense of Western Europe, and that its subsidiary themes are that neither the timidity, nor the discretion of the Kremlin, nor the atomic bomb are adequate guarantees of this defense," Oppenheimer wrote. "With all this I fully agree. Does this qualify me for membership?" Indeed it did: "I am enrolling you forthwith," Conant promptly telegraphed."[80]

Other prominent figures taking CPD membership in early 1951 included William J. "Wild Bill" Donovan, formerly head of the Office of Strategic Services; Ford Foundation director and former Marshall Plan administrator Paul Hoffman; the economist Richard Bissell, later a high-ranking CIA covert operations overseer; the Hollywood studio head Samuel Goldwyn; Boston Trust Company's president (and later Eisenhower's national security adviser), Robert Cutler; the head of the International Ladies' Garment Workers' Union, David Dubinsky; the psychiatrist William C. Menninger; FDR adviser Samuel I. Rosenman. A separate California branch opened in April 1951 that featured numerous business, Hollywood, and defense industry titans as well as Walt Disney, Conrad Hilton, California Institute of Technology president Robert A. Millikan, *Look* publisher Gardner Cowles, and a B-movie matinee idol and Screen Actors Guild president named Ronald Reagan.

The biographies of most charter CPD members followed similar paths to or along the upper levels of American society, and to fully disentangle and explain the web of interlocking connections among them would require a computer program, a flow chart, and a separate book (one exists: Jerry W. Sanders's *Peddlers of Crisis*). Oozing respectability and status, they were comfortably situated within a well-heeled, Europe-oriented, urban, foreign policy elite largely headquartered along the Boston–New York–Washington corridor. Although this putatively nonpartisan group featured some Democrats, its ideological focus was on the internationalist wing of the Republican Party—Conant was a Republican, and most CPD members enthusiastically supported Eisenhower's 1952 presidential bid (though the CPD made no formal endorsement), with many graduating into high positions in Ike's administration. A typical CPD résumé bulged with listings of previous public service, in government, the military, or both. Many members had manned previous internationalist lobbying campaigns such as the Fight for Freedom, the Committee to Defend America by Aiding the Allies, and the Committee for the Marshall Plan. They retained numerous and overlapping memberships on corporate and foundation advisory boards and boards of trustees of universities, legal, educational, philanthropic, and business organizations, on local chambers of commerce and foreign policy associations, on public, private, federal, scientific, and/or military committees, commissions, boards, and of all shapes, sizes, and purposes. (Several, including Cutler and Oppenheimer, sat on Harvard's Board of Overseers, and of course Marbury was one of five members of the Harvard Corporation.) They were accustomed to running their respective shows, and believed their social and business positions would give their pronouncements credibility with a national audience that seemed to be losing faith in elected political leaders. They could be found in boardrooms, elite metropolitan clubs, expensive town houses and summer cottages in New England or Long Island, at or near the top of social, professional, and corporate hierarchies. Overwhelmingly, they were white, middle-aged, male, wealthy. They were gray men in gray suits with a gray message, solemnly reprinted in the good gray pages of the *New York Times.*

To preserve its public image as a "spontaneously organized, nonpartisan group of citizens,"[81] as Conant put it in testimony to Congress, the committee barred membership to persons holding full-time government posts, though many members had once held high-ranking government positions, would move into them in the near future, or served in part-time capacities that gave them access to highly classified information—Conant himself was a prime example. The result, naturally, was that CPD members comfortably glided in and out of government offices and agencies, and the Truman administration felt no compunction about sharing classified information with and giving frequent classified briefings to the members on varied subjects relating to the draft, military plans, and foreign policy. Its interest in coordinating programs to manipulate public opinion at home and abroad was shown, for example, in the State Department's arranging, on May 23, 1951, of a "special presentation" for CPD representatives "of some of its classified psychological warfare activities."[82]

One of many examples of the hand-in-glove relationship between the government and CPD concerned the Psychological Strategy Board (PSB), an outfit created by Truman in the spring of 1951 for the purpose of coordinating secret efforts to triumph in the ideological struggle for the hearts, minds, and souls of people around the world — but especially in territories under Communist control in the Soviet Union and Eastern Europe. In the last years of the Truman administration and the first year of Eisenhower's presidency, the PSB promoted covert psychological and political warfare against Moscow to, if possible, pave the way toward "liberation" of the so-called captive peoples. A natural outgrowth and supplement to the operations of the CIA, created in 1947, the PSB derived from NSC-68's ambitious goals to roll back Communist influence through all means short of actual war, and it coincided with efforts by the CPD to promote "unconventional warfare" abroad.[83]

In the late summer of 1950, with Conant ailing, provost Paul Buck promised Harvard's full cooperation in a secret study undertaken at State Department request and headquartered at the Massachusetts Institute of Technology: Project Troy was supposed to explore how the U.S. government could utilize advances in communications technology to penetrate the Iron Curtain. But the project, which got under way that fall, quickly expanded to a general investigation of political and psychological warfare; the interdisciplinary crowd of physical and social scientists, engineers, and humanities scholars included prominent Harvard representatives such as the Nobel prize–winning physicist Edward Purcell, the anthropologist, OSS veteran, and Russian Research Center director Clyde Kluckhohn, and the social scientists Jerome Bruner and Samuel Stouffer. In February 1951, Project Troy handed in a detailed classified report on political and technical techniques to circumvent Soviet controls on information, jamming of foreign broadcasts, and defenses against Western intelligence collection efforts.[84]

Conant kept track of Project Troy's results through contacts with James Killian and through the Committee on the Present Danger's own quiet studies of the use of unconventional and psychological warfare. In January 1951, as head of the CPD's Committee on Modern Weapons, Bush reported to Conant that the United States suffered from a "chaotic or nonexistent" program in psychological warfare, while Moscow employed subversion, coups, and propaganda to extend its sway and perhaps lay the groundwork for an attack on the West. Reporting that Acheson had expressed "keen interest" in this problem, Bush complained that while the United States "feebly attempt[ed] to penetrate the Iron Curtain," the "raucous voice of the Kremlin penetrates the entire world." Though shunning "extreme forms of skullduggery," Bush advocated the creation of a new government agency that would enable Washington to take the offensive in the ongoing "unconventional war" with Russia.[85]

In response to various pressures, including charges from McCarthyites that leftist taints precluded the State Department from properly administering

propaganda activities, the Truman administration created the PSB in April
1951 under the aegis of the National Security Council. Though the CPD's
precise role in its establishment is uncertain, the group's insider membership
and parallel objectives assured close relations. The first PSB director, Gordon
Gray, had ties to both Conant and Tracy Voorhees; as a former secretary of
the army, he had worked closely with Voorhees, and as president of the
University of North Carolina, he had traded views with Conant in late 1950
regarding military conscription legislation. The links to Gray's successor were
tighter yet: University of Washington president Raymond B. Allen, a CPD
member, took over the PSB at the start of 1952.

This sort of tangled web was the norm, not the exception. The committee's
membership, with its octopuslike contacts and affiliations, incarnated what
C. Wright Mills termed the "power elite"—the occupants of "the strategic
command posts of the social structure." It fit perfectly Mills's theme of an
"interlocking directorate" at the upper levels of American life—"circles" that
were not some demonic "conspiracy," but rather "a set of overlapping 'crowds'
and intricately connected 'cliques'" that, in their cumulative and interactive
behavior, accounted in large measure for major national policy decisions and
directions.[86]

With his simultaneous membership in educational, scientific, social,
communications, corporate, and national security organizations, Conant neatly
exemplified this "power elite." It was therefore especially apt that Mills cited
the Interim Committee's deliberations over the atomic bomb as a prototypical
example of how small circles of well-connected figures had replaced mass
politics in making society's critical choices. "The creation of pivotal roles and
their pivotal enactment occurs most readily when social structures are undergoing epochal transitions," Mills wrote. "It is clear that the international
development of the United States to one of the two 'great powers'—along with
the new means of annihilation and administrative and psychic domination—
have made of the United States in the middle years of the twentieth century
precisely such an epochal pivot."[87]

It would be a mistake, of course, to take a view that is Conant-centric. By
late 1950, all but a fringe minority of Americans swore opposition to
Communism, even if their battle plans varied. Yet it is clear that, by lending
his (and Harvard's) name to the CPD crusade, Conant significantly helped to
foster the rise of a more militaristic, Europe-first Cold War consensus in the
upper levels of the American foreign-policy establishment, to give this consensus a new, flexible institutional form, and to articulate it to millions of
Americans.

To reach that mass audience, the Committee on the Present Danger over
the next two years embarked on an all-out propaganda effort, taking full
advantage of its media, advertising, educational, and Hollywood connections.
Operating as unpaid individuals and through a Washington staff office run by
Voorhees, the CPD corps

- spoke at scores of fund-raisers, rallies, seminars, roundtables, commencements, and press conferences;
- wrote newspaper articles, editorials, columns, advertisements, and letters-to-the-editor;
- appeared before congressional committees and lobbied individual legislators;
- met frequently with Pentagon and administration officials for strategy sessions and classified briefings;
- held background briefings for journalists;
- gave radio and television interviews and speeches, including a series of weekly nationwide radio broadcasts in early 1951 during the "Great Debate" over sending U.S. troops to Europe;
- wrote detailed briefs (culled in part from classified information from government sources) for the administration and Congress on such issues as military manpower procurement and foreign military assistance;
- sponsored a theatrically released film adapted from Vannevar Bush's "Modern Arms and Free Men";
- published 100,000 copies of an anti-isolationist cartoon-illustrated pamphlet entitled "The Danger of Hiding Our Heads";
- disseminated publicity to other internationalist groups (such as the Foreign Policy Association, a nationwide organization with regional chapters)[88] eager to spread its message.

In trying to sell its "very fine product," the CPD insistently reiterated the theme that the United States faced a grave military threat, requiring drastic and immediate sacrifices. Otherwise, with the bomb and "the mass armies of Red China" on their side, the Soviet Union would one day attack Western Europe and take over "any state that is weak enough to be defeated or terrorized into their empire." Information or arguments that might muddle the clarity of that message—uncertainty regarding the likelihood of a Soviet attack against Western Europe, say, or the USSR's actual military strength relative to that of the United States, or its precise involvement in the North Korean attack, or its relationship with Communist China—were scorned, glossed over, or ignored. The CPD, including Conant, at times resembled Mills's "crackpot realists" who "in the name of realism have constructed a paranoid reality all their own."[89] But if the committee at times engaged in rhetorical overkill, it was simply trying to accomplish for the general public what NSC-68's authors had attempted within the "top government," and vindicating Acheson's after-the-fact justification for NSC-68's purple prose:

The task of a public officer seeking to explain and gain support for a major policy is not that of the writer of a doctoral thesis. Qualification must give way to simplicity of statement, nicety and nuance to bluntness, almost brutality, in carrying home a point . . . *If we made our points clearer than the truth, we did not differ from most other educators* and could hardly do otherwise [emphasis added].[90]

The Committee on the Present Danger was poised to be a major influence on the hard-fought, sometimes bitter disputes that were to erupt in the first half of 1951 about the direction of U.S. foreign policy. Battle was joined over issues that decisively affected America's posture toward the world for the next several decades. Should American foreign policy be isolationist or interventionist? Should it aim to achieve a near-term political or military victory over Communism (rollback) or to sustain a global balance of power short of war (containment)? Should it be oriented principally toward Asia or toward Europe? Should its military force be structured to emphasize strategic nuclear air power or ground forces drawn from a semipermanent national mobilization? Who would fight when America went to war?

CHAPTER 26

"The Great Debate"

1951

The United States is in danger. Few would be inclined to question this simple statement. The danger is clearly of a military nature. On this much we can all agree.

—JBC, nationwide radio broadcast, February 7, 1951

I too am troubled by the implications of my argument. It comes up in every discussion that I have. I've presented my point of view to no less than ten student audiences since January first and in every case have had questions either from the floor or personally with a small group after I had finished. There is almost sure to be someone who says, in effect, why not get it over with now.

—Letter to Walter Lippmann, March 5, 1951

Got up to date on MacArthur story. Apparently the U.S.A. has been on an emotional binge.

—Diary, May 6, 1951

The Committee on the Present Danger's appearance on the American political scene did not overjoy everyone, least of all those opposed to the United States' becoming committed to the military defense of Western Europe. World War II and the atomic bomb had dealt mortal blows to the traditional isolationism and "continentalism" that had molded U.S. foreign policy since Washington's Farewell Address. But distaste for entanglements in the corrupt, sordid Old World persisted, fed by the stubborn, visceral feeling that the Europeans' troubles stemmed from their own cynical maneuvers over "spheres of influence" and the "balance of power," in contrast to the alleged American ideal of a foreign policy based solely on truth, justice, and morality. Though the Senate in 1949 approved the North Atlantic Treaty, the Truman administration's avowed intention in the winter of 1950–51 to dispatch at least four divisions of U.S. ground troops (with the likelihood of more to follow) to back up the NATO forces under Eisenhower's command resuscitated the fading isolationist impulse and aroused a sharp if brief controversy.

At the forefront of the movement against an expanded U.S. military role in Europe stood, somewhat paradoxically, not Stalinist apologists or leftists fearful of provoking Moscow, but some of the most rabidly anti-Communist voices in the country. Fearing anything that smelled of an open-ended U.S. military commitment to Europe, they instead preferred rooting out Communist subversives at home or combating them not across the Atlantic but in the Far East. They were not pacifists but Pacificists, in contrast to the pronounced Atlanticism of the Committee on the Present Danger. It is therefore something of a misnomer to characterize the "Great Debate" as pitting internationalists versus isolationists, when many of the latter actually applauded foreign military escalation against Communism in Asia. Thus did traditional adherents of "Fortress America" and "America First" isolationism join forces with the so-called Asialationists who championed Douglas MacArthur; accused Truman, Marshall, and Acheson of harboring traitors in their midst; and spoke of the need for military "victory" not only in Korea but in China, which they believed had "fallen" to Communism as a result of the Truman-Acheson policy of "cowardly containment."[1]

Just as the Committee on the Present Danger reunited many activists from the pre–Pearl Harbor interventionist lobby—among them Conant, Acheson, Bush, Clayton, Wriston, Donovan, Dubinsky, and Sherwood—so too their opponents gathered many familiar faces together from the debates of 1940–41. In the leading ranks of those tagged as "new isolationists" and "Asia Firsters" stood Republican senators William Knowland, Kenneth S. Wherry, Everett Dirksen, and, most importantly, Robert Taft, who voted against the NATO treaty and who was priming to contest the 1952 Republican presidential nomination; former president Herbert Hoover, who counseled Americans that the loss of Europe to Communism would be "no reason for hysteria," and implored them to reject UMS and NATO and concentrate instead on defending the United States as a "Western Hemisphere Gibraltar of Western Civilization"; and former ambassador to England Joseph Kennedy, once blasé about the prospect of a Nazi-dominated Europe, now calling for America's withdrawal from Korea, from Berlin, and from a "suicidal" and "morally bankrupt" policy to risk American lives defending ungrateful West European allies.[2] Isolationist newspapers also blasted the committee. To the *Washington Times-Herald,* the committee was a bunch of "windbags who have publicity value through corporate, banking, legal, or academic connections" and persistently "assail the public" with pro-Truman manifestos; Colonel Robert R. McCormick's *Chicago Tribune* branded Conant (who was "coddling Reds in the Harvard professoriat and within the student body") as a "globalist and red-hot interventionist" and described the CPD as "a group of influential interventionists . . . committed to ever greater American intermeddling abroad, to increased militarization of the country, and to alarmist attitudes toward perils said to confront Western Europe. . . ."[3]

Let the Europeans defend themselves, the committee's opponents argued, and we can rely on strategic nuclear air power to ward off or wipe out anyone who dares infringe on American territory in the Western Hemisphere or the Pacific. Rather than waste money and men on a vast land army to oppose the Russians in Europe, better to "arm to the teeth and stay home," as Ferdinand Eberstadt, a Wall Street friend of Bernard Baruch and Herbert Hoover, put it.[4] According to MacArthur and his supporters, the true front line against world Communism was the Yalu River, not the Elbe, and the final showdown against the Red Menace was not looming in Europe but had already begun in the Far East. And if escalating the Korean War meant risking World War III, so be it.

This kind of blood 'n' guts "isolationism" appealed to the McCarthyites, the MacArthurites, the right wing of the Republican Party, and the vocal, influential, and stridently anti-Truman China Lobby, which dreamed of a U.S.-backed counteroffensive by Nationalist forces on Taiwan to recapture the mainland. But some isolationists also advanced arguments that, ironically, revealed their common ground with leftist opponents of NATO and rearmament. They expressed skepticism about the gravity of the Soviet military threat to Europe, and the belief that the presidency was growing too powerful and that Congress (having permitted Truman to fight an undeclared war in Korea) should reassert its rightful Constitutional role in any dispatch of troops to foreign lands. Some feared that Moscow would be provoked into rash action, that excessive military spending would hurt social programs, and that a mandatory draft and other long-term mobilization steps might be the beginning of a domestic "garrison state."

A decade earlier, Conant had hoped that Pearl Harbor had rendered isolationists "as extinct as the volcanos on the moon." Now he discovered to his distress that the species, while endangered, still showed signs of life. One of Conant's objectives in forming the CPD, therefore, was to administer a *coup de grâce* to isolationism, the resurgence of which had caused him to write Voorhees in late October 1950 from his hospital bed of his worry

> about the growing attitude apparently sponsored by Mr. Hoover. For my money, we have to defend the present line in Europe not for the sake of the Europeans but for our own selfish interest! Whether the Europeans will help or not has little relevance to what we must do. The idea that we "won't play if they don't" seems to me preposterous. Do your military friends really believe we could withdraw to England and make our stand there? If they don't, this is one of the red herrings our committee must destroy.[5]

When Conant wrote those words, he feared principally that a quick victory in Korea, where the United Nations forces under MacArthur were then marching northward to the Chinese frontier, would foster "a return to complacency and above all a retreat to neo-isolationism."[6] But instead of rapid victory, MacArthur's "win the war" and "get the boys home by Christmas" offensive ended in disaster and recriminations, disputes over past and future conduct of the fighting, and fears of an imminent global war dominated the increasingly rancorous political landscape of the winter of 1950–51.

The CPD initially found its hard-line prescriptions for full mobilization and arming Western Europe welcomed as minimal steps to respond to the crisis. Simultaneously, however, a contradictory current of opinion arose in opposition to its program: "Troops for Europe, UMS (Universal Military Service) and foreign aid were all parts of one package," Conant later recalled, "and all three proposals were highly distasteful to the new isolationism which emerged at the end of 1950." Rather than diverting new resources to NATO, Asia Firsters rallied behind MacArthur's strategy of escalating the fight against Communism in the Far East by strategic bombing of air bases, troop concentrations, and industrial targets in Manchuria, and by "unleashing" Nationalist forces on Taiwan against the mainland. "Even without Europe, Americans have no reason for hysteria or loss of confidence in our security or our future," claimed Hoover in a December 20 nationwide radio address that opposed UMS and ridiculed the idea of using America's "sparse ground forces" to counter the Soviet land armies.[7] In such statements, Acheson smelled the "stench of spiritless defeat, of death of high hopes and broad purposes."[8]

On January 5, 1951 — the same day Taft opened the isolationist offensive on the Senate floor against sending ground troops to Europe — Conant led a CPD executive board meeting at the capital's Metropolitan Club to consider its next moves. Voorhees gloomily reported that Hoover's policy had "received wide public acceptance," with congressional mail "running very heavily in this direction." Yet he also discerned opportunity for the committee in the charged foreign policy debate:

> The thought is that — in addition to effective support of universal military service, which still has a difficult path to travel — the importance of combatting the new isolationist doctrine has created a great and unexpected need for just the kind of non-partisan advice and counsel to the public which this Committee is in an almost unique position to furnish.[9]

It did not take long for the committee to recognize that in its battle with the isolationists and Asia Firsters, and its desire to appear nonpartisan, it had one ideal symbol: Eisenhower. With the Truman administration's political stock at a nadir, the shining hope for both the administration's Eurocentric rearmament program and the CPD campaign was Ike's appointment — rumored all fall and finally announced on December 19 — to become supreme allied commander of NATO forces in Europe. The end of Eisenhower's (brief and uneasy) fling with academia resulted from a fairly desperate sense in Washington and in Western Europe that only this heroic figure could, by sheer prestige and willpower alone, stabilize the West's tottering confidence in its ability to face the Communist behemoth. In fact, Eisenhower accepted the post despite his considerable exasperation with the administration's "vagueness" about what military forces it wanted to put on the ground to stop the Red Army—"the answer is 'In Europe Eisenhower can solve all the problems,' " Ike wrote disgustedly in his diary.[10]

Eisenhower and Conant recognized that they could fruitfully coordinate their actions. Having learned from Truman in late October of his impending NATO appointment, Eisenhower never formally joined the CPD, but he considered the committee a "fine program" and, as NATO commander, even solicited Conant's help to work behind-the-scenes to establish a similar group in Britain.[11] "To most Americans your appointment came as the first piece of good news in a long time and gave us all a sense of relief," Conant wrote "Ike" on December 21, expressing the hope that "we have hit the low point of disunity, and if we can be united behind a policy based on reasonable military and political considerations, it will be in no small way due to the inspiration of your example."[12] "I am on your team," Eisenhower replied, congratulating Conant on his stand in favor of Universal Military Service, a measure he had already endorsed in the report of the Council on Foreign Relations study group.[13]

Conant and Voorhees, meanwhile, labored assiduously to align the committee with Eisenhower in the public mind. In the words of an internal CPD memorandum: "With the wide appeal of the isolationist philosophy in various forms which took such a hold on the country about January 1st, and with the appointment of General Eisenhower to the command in Europe, it became apparent that education and support of General Eisenhower's mission had to be carried to the public."[14] The administration fully shared the CPD's analysis. When Acheson met with Eisenhower just before he set off for Europe on January 6 on an initial inspection tour, the secretary of state observed that the "Supreme Commander's greatest handicap was being created at this very moment here at home in the current debate, carrying to Europe with every new broadcast doubts of American constancy toward its defense. This we must terminate as soon as possible."[15]

A more succinct précis of the CPD's intended function purpose could not be devised: to muffle the "current debate" over aid to Europe, as Acheson hoped, the CPD could act as a high-profile, respected, yet nonpartisan oracle, in contrast to the beleaguered administration, and it could wade into the political fray more straightforwardly than the uniformed, dignified Eisenhower. Ike's departure for Europe occasioned a good example of the CPD's cheerleading, when it issued a widely republished statement (given front-page treatment by the *Times*) urging full public support for Eisenhower's mission and for the creation of a ten- to fifteen-division NATO army in Europe.[16]

Comparable statements followed, and on the evening of February 7, after Ike had returned to Washington and reported to Congress and the country, Conant went on NBC radio to deliver his first nationwide address as CPD spokesman.[17] Doing his utmost "to wrap General Eisenhower's mantle around me," as he put it later, Conant quoted the new NATO commander, "whose

professional competence no one can challenge," in rendering the firm judgment that Western Europe could indeed be militarily defended "against the
vast manpower of Russia and its satellites"—provided, of course, that America
helped its friends "build a secure wall for peace." Blasting the Hoover-Taft-
Kennedy line, Conant stressed that "the defense of Europe" was "essential for
the survival of a free United States," and quoted Eisenhower's argument that
"our safety would be gravely imperiled" should Europe be lost to the Soviets.
In Conant's analysis the only reason that the Red Army had not already
reached the English Channel was "the overwhelming destructive power of
the United States strategic air force armed with the atomic bomb"—but that
advantage was rapidly waning as the Soviets assembled their own nuclear
arsenal and perfected their strategic defenses. "Therefore," he reasoned, "the
danger of a third global war, I am convinced, turns on the fact that a few years
hence the handful of men who rule Russia may decide that the power of our
strategic Air Force has been largely canceled out. If at that time Europe is
defenseless on the ground, the Russian hordes will begin to move."

To prevent this from happening, Conant pleaded (again quoting Eisenhower
for authority) for troops and military aid for Western Europe: "Strengthening
the defense of Europe in terms not of a deterrent threat against Russian cities
but in terms of armies to stop an advance—this seems to me the top item on
the agenda of the free nations of the world. Only then can we achieve a true
global stalemate." And as a necessary step, Conant put in a fervent plug for
UMS, since partial mobilization and a standing force in Europe might be
required for one, two, or three decades—as long as it took to convince
Moscow that world domination was impossible. If these steps were adopted,
Conant told listeners that there remained "a chance, a good chance, of
avoiding World War III."

Conant finished his speech—and other addresses he gave at this time—by
carefully blending long-term hopefulness with short-term alarmism. Once
again, Conant tried simultaneously to soothe and to steel the nerves of the
American people, to prepare for war yet not provoke it, to seek peace yet not
make hasty concessions for it.

> I venture to conclude on a note that I trust will not seem unduly optimistic. If
> the United States will show leadership, be both calm and strong, prove that
> freedom can endure even long years of partial mobilization, then there is
> hope for the second half of the twentieth century. I see a radically altered
> international situation a decade or more hence, a free world secure on its
> own frontiers, a Soviet Union with diminished ambitions and pretensions,
> yet itself secure against invasion. Under such conditions, the United Nations
> might well function as those who founded it first dreamed. Under such
> conditions, steps toward disarmament would no longer be regarded as utopian;
> the terror of modern weapons might slowly vanish from the skies.
>   But while the present danger lasts the peoples of the world must be
> armed and ready. As General Eisenhower has so well said, we must meet

the fearful unity of totalitarian force with a higher unity—the unity of free men that will not be defeated.

Such confident public declarations about Western Europe's defensibility were warmly greeted by Truman and Eisenhower, who in private was far more pessimistic but who, like Conant and the CPD, stressed the importance of unity above all else. "I believe it is silly for the United States to send me or anyone else to France—you had better throw me in the middle of the ocean—if you are sending me on a completely divided basis," Ike had told a closed-doors session of the House of Representatives Foreign Affairs and Armed Services committees. "There has to be some unanimity of opinion and that unanimity of opinion is expressed only through Congress."[18]

The CPD bolstered Eisenhower's appeals for bipartisan support for limited U.S. troop deployment in Europe, and in so doing helped turn the Great Debate. Conant later recorded that "the way General Eisenhower handled his assignment seemed to silence for the time at least those advocating a policy of hemispheric defense."[19] Although the orientation of U.S. national security policy—Europe or Asia?—remained bitterly contested, a number of previously skeptical congressmen began to concede that at least a limited deployment of American troops on the Continent might be worthwhile.

Besides endlessly quoting the venerated Eisenhower—"an old rhetorical tactic," Conant later acknowledged—he and the CPD occasionally resorted to another tested method of rousing public support for stern military measures: scare tactics. Just as NSC-68 had warned of the Kremlin's "design" for world domination, Conant and the CPD repeatedly supported Truman's line that the Korean invasion—"clearly directed" by Moscow—proved that the Soviet Union was a "menacing despotic power, bent on conquering the world." While denying the inevitability of World War III, the committee stressed that Western Europe was "the next great prize that Russia seeks," and could only be kept from further military conquest through a massive, rapid, U.S. armament of NATO.[20] Conant rammed home this message of military peril in the opening words of his radio address. "The United States is in danger," he said. "Few would be inclined to question this simple statement. The danger is clearly of a military nature. On this much we can all agree."

As news from the battlefield improved during the spring of 1951—by March the United Nations forces had fought their way back to the 38th parallel—the emotional pendulum swung back, and the committee (and administration) once again grew concerned that the end of the fighting in Korea would permit a rise in complacency. That the Russians had not borne out the fearful prediction that the Korean attack would be followed by aggression in Europe only increased that anxiety.[21] It was therefore a consistent CPD objective to keep the public alarmed about the Soviet peril and the threat to European, and therefore American, security. No chance was missed to emphasize that America's "survival" and "existence" were at stake, or to stress the catastrophic consequences of failing to support a massive Western military build-up.

In late March, the Truman administration had to overcome some savage political warfare in Washington to squelch what one historian has called the "last hurrah of isolationism."[22] In the days leading up to the congressional vote on the sending of ground troops to Europe, the CPD accelerated its campaign, spewing out statements and speeches; diehard congressional opponents of Truman's policy scorned it: the American public was "being sold a bill of goods" by the same people who had advocated aid to the allies before Pearl Harbor, Everett Dirksen said in the final hours of the Senate debate, angrily (and correctly) charging that the CPD's members unabashedly used Eisenhower's name to support its goals, while barely whispering Truman's. Rep. John T. Wood of Idaho branded the CPDers as "potential traitors" who were "whooping it up to draft eighteen-year-olds, send an army and unlimited supplies to Europe, and thereby hasten the day, so fervently hoped for by Joe Stalin, when we will have spent ourselves into bankruptcy."[23]

All to no avail. The battle ended on April 4, when the Senate passed a resolution approving Eisenhower's appointment and the deployment of four ground divisions (about 100,000 troops) to NATO. The 69–21 vote, in which even Taft grudgingly fell in line with the administration, capped the postwar transformation of American foreign policy—and the consolidation of a consensus on foreign military commitments that would survive until Vietnam.

Conant and the CPD could justly claim a substantial share of credit for the success of the Truman policy. Under the banners of unity, anti-Communism, Eisenhower, and preparedness—and constantly repeating the same few themes, in accord with advice given to Conant by one supporter, that "there is no such thing as plagiarism in the propaganda field"[24]—the committee had helped to rally public and congressional opinion behind the American commitment of troops and military aid to Western Europe. That much accomplished, the CPD now turned its efforts to garnering public and congressional support for vastly increased foreign economic and military aid to Western Europe and other bulwarks of the "free world."

While the committee's effectiveness in the Great Debate stemmed from many collective and individual activities, no tactic better illustrated its ability to blanket a mass audience than a series of twelve nationwide radio programs broadcast in prime time on Sunday evenings from March to June 1951, a barrage that the CPD organized after the success of Conant's February 7 radio speech. By the final broadcast on June 3, when Conant spoke on "The Defense of the Free World in the Atomic Age," Bush, Patterson, Clayton, and other prominent CPD members had spread the gospel over 550 stations belonging to the Mutual Broadcasting System. Each distinctive presentation was reprinted and distributed in pamphlet form, and received wide press coverage. On March 4, Bush discoursed on "The Atomic Bomb and the Defense of the Free World." A week later, Patterson explained why Europe represented "The Defense Line of Freedom." Ex-spymaster Donovan on March 18 called for "unconventional" defense — covert actions short of war to roll back Communist influence — to "regain the initiative in the Cold War." (Prophetically, Donovan listed Iran as one likely target, two years before a CIA operation launched by the Eisenhower administration overthrew the Mossadegh government.) Anxious to avoid being tagged as biased toward one side in the "Europe versus Asia" argument, the group sponsored an April 29 broadcast from London by Sherwood on "England and the Present Danger" and two weeks later spotlighted the Far East with an interview with a retired general who had led one of the Pacific campaigns. Devoutly anti-Communist Protestant and Catholic clergy jointly preached "Faith to Meet the Present Danger." Americans troubled by atomic peril could hear Dr. Menninger psychoanalyze "Our State of Mind and the Present Danger." And so on.[25]

"I have always cherished the thought," Conant wrote later, "that the Committee on the Present Danger by its statements and the broadcasts of several members played an important part in shaping public opinion on this issue."[26] Conant's assessment was if anything too modest, the sociologist Jerry W. Sanders concluded in the only full-length study of the group, although in terms that would have riled its chairman. "The CPD played a critical role — perhaps *the* critical role," Sanders wrote. "The Committee's efforts severely undercut the popular base of support which the isolationists in Congress desperately needed if they were to mount a successful challenge to the Administration in the field of foreign policy. Thus, just as NSC-68 had bludgeoned the 'mass mind' of the national security elite, as Acheson so felicitously put it, so the CPD bludgeoned the aspirations of the conservative political elite through its scare campaign to the mass public."[27]

Before the administration had any chance to savor its hard-earned victory, an even nastier controversy erupted: after months of rising exasperation with his military commander in the Far East, Truman fired General Douglas MacArthur.[28] The shocking news reached the bitterly divided nation first in leaks, then in a dramatic post-midnight White House announcement on the morning of April 11. It came after the latest of a long series of public statements — *pronunciamientos,* in the words of one critic — in which MacArthur had disparaged the administration's handling of the war, and it set off a first-class national crisis.

Not that the stolid, undramatic president of modest bearing and background and the charismatic, messianic SCAP (supreme commander of Allied forces, Pacific) had ever enjoyed a cozy relationship. Hero of World War II campaigns, overlord of occupied Japan, famous for his trademark sunglasses, cigar, and frayed battle cap, his frontline bluster and daring, his larger-than-life image and ego to match, MacArthur had amassed a following and reputation that placed him in a position seriously to challenge his putative commander-in-chief. They met only once, on October 15, 1950, when Truman made a pilgrimage across the Pacific to Wake Island to hold an awkwardly staged, two-hour summit meeting that he claimed was to discuss strategy and that his critics attributed to his desire for pre-election publicity, with news photos of the smiling president proudly pinning medals on the hero of Inchon. Whatever brought this odd couple together, they managed to have a pleasant enough conversation, and Truman recalls that MacArthur contritely pledged not to make any more unauthorized policy statements and generally "kissed my ass."[29]

But when the UN offensive failed, the "spirit of Wake Island" quickly vanished. Communications between the two men lapsed from surface cordiality to cold testiness. With everyone involved running for political cover, MacArthur openly chafed at Truman's refusal—backed up by the Joint Chiefs of Staff—to permit attacks against the enemy's "privileged sanctuary" north of the Chinese border, to blockade the Chinese mainland, or to permit the use of Taiwanese forces to open up a second front. Such restrictions, MacArthur told a long parade of journalists and other interlocutors, were "an enormous handicap, without precedent in military history," that had crippled his ability to prosecute the fighting. In repeated interviews that infuriated the White House, MacArthur made it clear that he rejected and scorned Truman's entire strategy of backing away from the objective of "liberating" North Korea and refusing to widen the war to China. Even worse, in his view, was the pusillanimous "Munich attitude" of West European allies such as Britain and France who opposed a fight to the death against China and Communism in the Far East.[30] The only alternatives MacArthur considered valid were total victory or surrender and withdrawal from Korea; a "limited war" that ended with Korea divided—the status quo ante—struck him as tantamount to surrender and appeasement.

Truman, meanwhile, was compiling his own list of grievances. He faulted MacArthur for misjudging the likelihood of Chinese intervention; for raising unrealistic expectations for winning the war even after the gravity of Peking's intervention became clear; and for waging guerrilla warfare through the press—even after a presidential gag order—in an effort to deflect blame for military setbacks onto the White House. And MacArthur's repeated requests to expand the war into China also convinced Truman that a fundamental difference separated the two men: "General MacArthur was ready to risk general war. I was not."[31]

MacArthur sealed his own fate in late March, after Truman had secretly approved a diplomatic overture proposing peace talks and a cease-fire in place—with the two armies facing each other roughly along the prewar border. No longer wedded to the seductive chimera of unifying Korea, Truman was ready to compromise. But in a statement that struck Truman and his advisers as clearly intended to sabotage the peace initiative, MacArthur on his own issued a virtual ultimatum to the Chinese, ridiculing their military prowess and implying that his force might "depart from its tolerant effort to contain the war to the area of Korea," expand operations to China's interior and coastline, and "doom Red China to the risk of military collapse." He graciously offered to meet face-to-face with "the commander-in-chief of the enemy forces" to negotiate an end to the fighting on the United Nation's terms, i.e., Korean unification. In other words, fully aware of Truman's plans, MacArthur called on Peking to surrender or else.[32]

A furious Truman finally decided that the mutinous general had to go: "By this act MacArthur left me no choice—I could no longer tolerate his insubordination." Acheson, who along with most other White House, State, and Defense Department advisers strongly supported evicting MacArthur, recalls finding Truman the next morning "in a state of mind that combined disbelief with controlled fury." Long frustrated by MacArthur's imperious actions and no longer under the spell of his alleged military genius—especially since most of the military successes in the drive northward since mid-January had been under the on-site leadership not of MacArthur but of Eighth Army commander Gen. Matthew B. Ridgway—Truman regarded the March 24 statement as a flouting of U.S. policy, an act "in open defiance of my orders as President and as Commander in Chief," and "a challenge to the President under the Constitution," endangering the basic principle of civilian control of the armed forces.[33]

Truman knew that firing MacArthur would ignite a political firestorm among the general's legions of admirers, but "the last straw" that erased any doubts about his "rank insubordination" or about the correctness of the decision to relieve him was the disclosure on April 5 of a telegram that MacArthur had written on March 20 to a prominent Capitol Hill critic of the administration.[34] Replying to the GOP House minority leader Joseph W. Martin, MacArthur endorsed the idea of opening a "second front" employing Chiang Kai-shek's Nationalist forces on Taiwan, in direct opposition to Truman's policy. And in a clear insult to those who emphasized the importance of troop commitments to NATO, he commented that it seemed "strangely difficult for some to realize that here in Asia is where the Communist conspirators have elected to make their play for global conquest . . . here we fight Europe's war with arms while the diplomats there still fight it with words. . . ." MacArthur added: "As you point out, we must win. There is no substitute for victory." The administration's policy, he said in an interview published the same day, "would be ludicrous if men's lives were not involved."[35]

While Martin read MacArthur's incendiary letter on the floor of the House of Representatives—it was only a day after the Senate vote on NATO troop appropriations—the CPD released a statement it drew up to consolidate the bipartisan consensus behind the NATO vote. United by "the deep conviction that the United States and its way of life are gravely threatened by Soviet aggression," this "non-partisan, non-political group of private citizens," pledged to work for:

1. An American public opinion which will wholeheartedly support the joint defense of Europe, without neglect of the Far East.

2. The firm support of General Eisenhower's mission.

3. A determination not to allow political differences at home to obscure our vision of the Soviet menace to our existence as a free people.

4. Full realization of the peril to the United States arising from its current spirit of complacency, while the Soviet power grows and its stock-pile of atom bombs increases.

5. Adoption of the principle of universal military service and training through appropriate legislation and administrative action.

6. Adequate legislative measures to make the United States and its Allies strong.

7. Rejection of any thought of preventive war.

8. A national policy of averting World War III by confronting the aggressors with a strong free world, attacking their weaknesses by non-military means and supporting the United Nations.[36]

Conant learned of Truman's impending action against MacArthur on the afternoon of April 10, as he set off for Europe to take the trip to England and France postponed by emergency surgery the previous summer. Waiting for a flight from New York's Idlewild Airport, Conant rebuffed a reporter who requested comment on stories in the morning papers that Truman had "fired" the recalcitrant general. But when his plane landed in Boston to refuel, Conant had an unpleasant surprise when he dashed for the newsstand: "Harvard to Give MacArthur Honorary Degree" blared the front-page headline of the *Boston Globe*. A five-year-old Honorary of Laws degree conferred by the university in 1946 but which MacArthur had been unable to accept in person was at issue: now that MacArthur was returning to the United States for the first time in fourteen years, the Harvard Corporation secretary David Bailey had confirmed, he remained eligible for the accolade if he chose to attend Commencement ceremonies.[37]

Of course, Conant realized immediately that honoring MacArthur at that moment would put Harvard smack in the middle of the donnybrook between the general and the president, and on the wrong side: MacArthur could exploit an award from Harvard politically—and although a majority of Americans immediately rallied to MacArthur's side, boosting his standing was the last thing Conant or most Harvard faculty desired.[38] On the other hand, the university could hardly openly retract the degree or tell the war hero to stay away. Whether MacArthur actually intended to show up to claim his degree was unknown, but for the moment Conant had only one notion: he telephoned Bailey to "tell him to keep quiet!"[39]

For the next few weeks, Conant toured Britain and France, visiting fellow educators, scientists, and opinion-makers in both countries, probing elite opinion on current issues, and delivering public addresses stressing the CPD's message of U.S. solidarity with Europe and Eisenhower. Most of Western Europe, terrified for months that MacArthur might embroil them in an unnecessary global war and aghast at his Napoleonic challenge to civilian government, breathed a sigh of relief at Truman's decisive action.

But across the Atlantic the United States was in a political convulsion. "It is doubtful if there has ever been in this country so violent and spontaneous a discharge of political passion as provoked by the President's dismissal of the General and by the General's dramatic return from his voluntary, patriotic exile," wrote Richard H. Rovere and Arthur M. Schlesinger, Jr.[40] In a sort of national primal scream, Americans lavished hero worship on MacArthur and spewed bile on the president who had cashiered him in the middle of the night. Polls found that seven of ten citizens backed MacArthur and opposed Truman. Conservatives around the country demanded Truman's impeachment or, better yet, his scalp. Rage-filled telegrams (125,000 in two days) and telephone calls flooded the White House. Several state legislatures voted angry condemnations, Michigan's declaring solemnly that "at 1 a.m., of this day, World Communism has achieved its greatest victory of the decade...." Officials in several cities, including Los Angeles, lowered flags to half-mast. Truman and Acheson were burned in effigy around the country, and baseball fans booed the president when he showed up to throw out the first pitch on opening day. And of course, congressional Truman-bashers had a field day— Senator Jenner said the country was being run by a Kremlin spy ring, Senator Knowland lambasted a "Far Eastern Munich," Senator Nixon said "the Communists and their stooges" welcomed Truman's move, and Senator McCarthy, not to be outdone, charged "treason in the White House," said Truman must have been drunk on "bourbon and benedictine," and added, "The son of a bitch ought to be impeached."[41]

When he flew back to the United States, MacArthur was accorded, in the words of one historian, "a welcome that would have made Caesar envious."[42] Millions of cheering, weeping, awestruck, confetti-showering admirers thronged ticker-tape parades in San Francisco, Los Angeles, Washington, New York, breaking attendance records set at comparable events for Eisenhower and Charles Lindbergh. Prayers, calls, letters, flowers, gifts, honors surrounded MacArthur as he toured the country, ending at his headquarters in a donated luxury suite at New York's Waldorf-Astoria Hotel. The climax of this triumphant procession came just after noon on April 19, when MacArthur addressed the joint houses of Congress and a national radio and television audience. In an impassioned oration interrupted thirty times by ovations, MacArthur unrepentantly defended his conduct and strategy, including his advice to blockade and bomb China and encourage Chiang Kai-shek to attack. Stressing again that there could be "no substitute for victory," he ripped into "some" (meaning Truman) who had limited his military actions and who would "appease Red China" due to fear of precipitating World War III. In a clear retort to the "Europhiles," as he had once called them, MacArthur warned: "You cannot appease or otherwise surrender to communism in Asia [i.e., accept Korean partition], without simultaneously undermining our efforts to halt its advance in Europe." Through his commanding presence and firm voice, his militaristic bearing and patriotic fervor, and his bathetic tear-jerker finale— "'Old soldiers never die; they just fade away'... Good-bye"—MacArthur succeeded in converting the House chamber into an evangelical prayer hall. Whipped into a frenzy, his supporters bawled, bayed, sobbed, shouted his praises, mobbed him, grabbed his sleeve, bowed, and scraped. "We heard God speak here today, God in the flesh, the voice of God!" yelled Representative Dewey Short.[43]

Less impressed by the spectacle of "damn fool Congressmen crying like a bunch of women," Truman told Acheson that the speech was "nothing but a bunch of bullshit"[44] (an opinion shared a generation later by gonzo journalist Hunter S. Thompson, who cackled uncontrollably upon hearing what he presumed was some sort of parody but was actually a grainy recording of the "Old Soldiers Never Die" speech). In the category of mawkish sentimentality in a political address, MacArthur's farewell set a standard challenged only by Nixon's Checkers Speech the following year. At the time, however, a vast majority of Americans responded with reverence, and paeans to the martyred gladiator reverberated through the country. "Apparently the U.S.A. has been on an emotional binge," wrote Conant in his diary after flying home on May 5 from a rainy and far more sedate London. Welcomed back to Cambridge, he was shocked to hear the members of the Harvard Corporation assert that "'Everyone is on McArthur's [sic] side.'" "Are you?" Conant asked. No, they assured him, they were not.

Conant now worried more than ever at the prospect of the general's storming Harvard Yard to capture his honorary degree. There had still been no word from MacArthur, and in Conant's absence Bailey had loyally obeyed instructions to muzzle university officials, telling underlings to rebuff all press inquiries regarding honorary degrees and "if we incur criticism on this subject in a time of near hysteria we are just to damn the torpedoes and sail ahead without paying any attention."[45] Rejecting the idea of holding a special convocation to honor MacArthur, on May 7 Conant proposed to the Corporation that it informally pass word to MacArthur that "he needn't come" to the mid-June Commencement ceremonies. Instead it decided simply to "stall" and, like soldiers fearing an attack, hope that MacArthur would direct his fire elsewhere.

A week later, a letter from MacArthur arrived saying that the general had a "complicated" schedule and Harvard "better not count on him." Reversing the Trollope ploy—in which the heroine interprets an ambiguous profession of love as a marriage proposal which she promptly accepts—a greatly relieved Conant took "maybe" for "definitely not" and instantly responded "that we will assume he wasn't coming." He didn't.[46]

Conant's cautious handling of the MacArthur mini-flap at Harvard paralleled the CPD's gingerly response to the larger maelstrom in Washington. Deeply concerned that the controversy would divert attention from its first priority and for the most part largely immune to the general's maudlin theatrics, it shied away from frontal attacks on MacArthur for fear of alienating public opinion and tarnishing its own bipartisan image. "To take on a nation-wide basis a strong, sharp position apparently contrary to MacArthur at this time would be to gain nothing but brickbats, mudslinging, and wind from the Wherry-Martin-McCarthy axis," warned Robert Cutler. "Our effort would be called a 'smear' on MacArthur."[47] Voorhees later wrote: "In the end we were able to keep the CPD out of the MacArthur controversy, which was essential for the Committee's continued usefulness."[48]

For a time, however, the committee's hesitancy in confronting MacArthur caused at least some members to question just how useful it was. In the initial hullabaloo, with Conant gone in Europe, the CPD seemed paralyzed. Private correspondence among members in late April, just after MacArthur's speech to Congress, was frustrated and uncertain. The American people, wrote Sam Goldwyn to Voorhees, were "literally waiting for someone to express for them at least the minimum objectives on which the nation as a whole can unite."[49] Edward R. Murrow strongly urged publishing a statement reaffirming the U.S. troop commitment in Europe, notwithstanding MacArthur's fervid call for escalation in Asia. "If such a proposal would split the Committee, then I say let's split it," Murrow wrote. "If other members of the Committee have been caught up in the MacArthur hysteria to the point where they are forgetful of where the main interest lies and where the solemn commitments have been made then we would be better off without them."[50]

The strategy ultimately designed by Voorhees in May and adopted by the CPD was, as before, to emphasize unity, "to close the ranks" behind the basic tenets of containment and troops-for-Europe, with its brand-new Senate stamp of approval.[51] Like a marriage counselor trying to calm a bickering couple, the CPD's approach to the high-pitched squabble required discovering, defining, highlighting, and even inventing common ground between MacArthur's advocates and those lined up behind the administration and Eisenhower. Since participants on both sides loathed Communism even more than each other (although it was sometimes a close call), the CPD could frame the debate as being merely over tactics in fighting Communism, not about irreconcilable differences in basic objectives.

Perhaps the CPD's shrewdest tactic was to enlist MacArthur himself involuntarily in the committee's cause and against his own right-wing, isolationist supporters. This occurred even though a secret, direct approach to MacArthur had failed, when on May 23, Julius Adler had met with MacArthur on behalf of the committee, but found him combative rather than conciliatory, interested more in blasting the Truman administration's focus on European defense than in publicly endorsing the CPD's agenda of UMS and support for

Eisenhower.[52] Still, that didn't stop committee members, and Conant in
particular, from selectively quoting the great man's words for their own
purposes. In two key statements—a May 17 address to the Chicago Association of Commerce and Council on Foreign Relations, and a national radio
broadcast two weeks later—Conant solemnly cited MacArthur's statement to
Congress about the various aspects of the conflict with Communism being
"global and so interlocked" that they should be dealt with together, not in
isolation. By saying that, of course, MacArthur had intended to stress that the
battle in Asia must be won first or else Europe would fall, but Conant turned
MacArthur's argument on its head; he also invoked MacArthur against traditional isolationists who advocated a "purely hemispheric stand against Communist aggression."[53]

For all his caution, Conant did align himself squarely with the anti-
MacArthur coalition when he went on record in mid-May. He may have felt
on slightly safer political terrain by then, since the pro-MacArthur wave had
ebbed and public opinion had begun to slip away from the general. Among
the events helping the process along were the publication of a leaked transcript of the Wake Island conference, showing that MacArthur had incorrectly
discounted the risk of Chinese intervention, and extensive Senate hearings
that offered a calmer forum for administration and Pentagon witnesses to
make their case for a limited war in Korea.

That Conant and MacArthur found themselves in opposition should
hardly come as a surprise: in style, temperament, strategy, and foreign-policy
orientation, the two presented starkly contrasting profiles. MacArthur radiated
bombast, patriotism, faith, pride, glory, victory, Hollywood, overstatement,
extremism. Conant emanated measured tones, calmness, committees, steadi-
ness, Cambridge and Washington, centrism; he regarded emotional appeals,
or "sentimentalism," with distaste.

Now project those differences onto the big screen of American strategy
during the 1950s. First priority for Conant was the military containment of the
Soviet threat in Europe, the continent that had been his intellectual locus since
youth. MacArthur not only fixated on "rollback" in Asia but was willing to break
the taboo against the use of nuclear weapons to achieve it.[54] He chomped at the
bit to lead his troops and country into World War III, since there could be, he
intoned, "no compromise with atheistic Communism—no halfway in the preser-
vation of freedom and religion. It must be all or nothing."[55] Conant preached
not "victory" but "global stalemate," and, in the short term, he believed that
an aggressive policy in the Far East risked a global war that would leave West
Europeans "exterminated or enslaved," as Voorhees put it.[56] In the long run,
he consistently condemned the idea of an inevitable U.S.-Soviet war.

In psychological terms, Conant was ready to delay the gratification of
victory in the Cold War; MacArthur wasn't. Or, to put it another way, Conant
had learned the lesson of the nuclear age that MacArthur had refused to
accept—that deterrence and containment might be an emotionally unsatisfying

"substitute for victory," but that trying to crush Communism through military means was simply too dangerous. Not that Conant rejected resorting to nuclear weapons in any case; he endorsed their use if the Soviets attacked Western Europe or Japan. But that willingness did not extend to battles over what Conant viewed as peripheral confrontation zones such as Korea. He fully identified with the view pithily expressed by Chairman of the Joint Chiefs of Staff Omar Bradley, that spreading the Korean War into China would "involve us in the wrong war, at the wrong place, at the wrong time, and with the wrong enemy."[57]

If global war must come, Conant firmly believed, let Moscow, not Washington, start it. But he could not easily ignore the impulse for preventive war that hovered on the fringes of the pro-MacArthur camp—a sentiment that Conant had feared and warned against repeatedly since 1945. It sprang from more than simple bloodthirstiness or emotionalism, involving as it did a recognition that the Soviets were about to achieve both a substantial arsenal of nuclear weapons and the means to deliver them on the United States, frustration with the prospect of fighting indecisive wars against Moscow's "puppets," like North Korea, and the pervasive apprehension that Moscow had a master plan or timetable for global military conquest.[58]

In using the rhetoric of NSC-68 to get the public to support rearmament measures yet understand that global war was avoidable, Conant tied himself in knots trying to distinguish himself from preventive-war advocates, as a flurry of letters with Walter Lippmann showed. "The Russians are certainly making atomic bombs and perfecting their own defenses against strategic bombing," Conant wrote Lippmann in February.

I can imagine a time three to five years hence when the people sitting in the Kremlin could say, "We have X atomic bombs, very good methods of delivery (possibly by water rather than by air), our own defenses against the U.S. bombers are now in position to cost them many duds for every one delivery; let us proceed with the first phase of a global war." This phase, I believe, would be to open up their propaganda as Hitler once did and tell their enemies of the destruction lying in store. Up to now, you will notice, the Russians have said that anyone who used an atomic bomb was an enemy of mankind. I venture to predict that within the next three years you will find them threatening Great Britain, possibly France, and certainly the United States with destruction from the air. Now it seems to me that with no ground forces in Europe such threats would be far more effective than otherwise.[59]

Conant meant his analysis to support the idea of a large U.S. conventional force in Europe, which Lippmann also supported, but his belief that the Russians were fast developing defenses against strategic bombers alarmed Lippmann. The journalist had a "fierce conviction" that unless the Red Army withdrew from Eastern Europe within "a relatively few years," war was "certain and unavoidable," and while for the time being U.S. atomic air power could be relied on to deter a Soviet attack, if Moscow could soon neutralize this retaliatory capability, then, Lippmann asked, "Does not the logic of this argument support the doctrine of preventive war within the next three to five years?"[60]

"I too am troubled by the implications of my argument," Conant confessed in reply.

It comes up in every discussion that I have. I've presented my point of view to no less than ten student audiences since January first and in every case have had questions either from the floor or personally with a small group after I had finished. There is almost sure to be someone who says, in effect, why not get it over with now. I take it the answer is that trading the destruction of Russia's industrial potential for their overrunning Europe would be a bad trade from our point of view quite as much as from theirs. This is the most hard-boiled argument, but there is a still deeper one, namely, that war is by its very nature an incalculable catastrophe and one to be avoided in a modern age of technology by anything short of surrender of first-line positions.[61]

Conant correctly sensed that the great deterrent in the nuclear age was not intricate calculations of "victory" and "defeat," but a basic awareness of the catastrophic consequences of nuclear war regardless of who "won" and "lost" and knowledge of the cosmic and diabolical uncertainty implicit in using the weapons. Convinced, unlike Lippmann, that a "stalemate on the ground" in Europe was attainable even before the Russian army left, he acknowledged that for the moment realistic disarmament negotiations were precluded: the United States "cannot possibly forgo the advantages of the atomic bomb." And while it was "an open question" whether "the Russians and the free world will start devastating each other's cities from the air, once a defensive line has been established in Europe," he hoped that "the dread of mutual disaster will prevent our taking that course and likewise restrain the men in the Kremlin." Admitting that his arguments "may be shot to pieces within the year for there is a distinct possibility the Russians have decided to move in Iran, or against Yugoslavia, or to precipitate the issue in the Far East," he banked on "the power of the strategic air force" and based his long-term optimism on the critical truth that,

In a highly technological arms race such as the world has never seen before, the area of uncertainty is very great. The admirals and the generals and the statesmen who make war plans and calculate risk are up against uncertainties unknown in previous days. On the assumption that rarely have wars started in modern times except as one group or another felt there was a good chance of winning, then since no such chance can be assured with modern weapons, there may be a long though extremely uneasy period of no war. (I would hesitate to call it peace.)[62]

Conant used unusually blunt language in his Chicago speech to condemn those who urged early preventive war before the Soviets built up their atomic stockpile. "Such argumentation borders on the treacherous," Conant declared. "It is flirting with high treason, treason against all that is best in Western civilization." But characteristically, when it came to criticizing MacArthur, he chose less inflammatory language and more narrow, politically expedient grounds. Careful not to incur the wrath of the powerful China lobby, he said not a word about the wisdom or foolishness of "unleashing Chiang" or about the risk that an aggressive military offensive against Peking might set off a global war. Judiciously refraining from judgment on MacArthur's recommendations—"these are matters it seems to me that must be left to responsible military authorities"—Conant seized on the general's statement to Congress that if European allies "haven't got enough sense to see where appeasement leads," then the United States should "go it alone" in the Far East.[63] That Conant could not countenance, not because of the risk of a wider war in Asia, but because a fracture in the North Atlantic alliance might result.

That Conant stressed this of all issues supports the view of one historian that the CPD opposed MacArthur's proposals not "on principle" but because of concern that "rollback in Asia not interfere with the remilitarization of Europe."[64] In fairness to Conant, he clearly opposed "on principle" any action that might set off a global war, but it is nevertheless true that, fearing controversy, he declined explicitly to endorse Truman's unpopular accusation that MacArthur's policies unacceptably risked inciting World War III. Instead, he warned that undertaking a unilateral U.S. offensive in Asia without the support of Britain and France "would make impossible the unity required in the extremely difficult matter of rearming Europe—an operation which by its very nature touches sensitive nerves in every country."

Conant then put forward his own notion for preserving Allied unity, a vaguely defined joint mechanism for coordinating U.S.-U.K.-French strategy in the Far East. "France, Great Britain and the United States must hammer out a twentieth-century policy which will yield wise political, economic and military decisions as to every critical area on the entire globe," he declared, in a throwback to Roosevelt's "Four Policemen" rhetoric—only now he was speaking of three policemen, and one of the ex-cops had turned criminal.[65] This insistence on "United Action"—like Eisenhower's and Dulles's similar insistence three years later as a prerequisite for U.S. intervention to help the French in Indochina—camouflaged a simple opposition to MacArthur's proposals for expansionist military operations, for Conant knew full well that the European allies would oppose provocative actions in any Far East "supplement" of NATO, even while laying the foundations for cooperative military planning in an actual global war along the lines of the combined Anglo-American Joint Chiefs of Staff during World War II.

Better still, Conant hoped that united efforts made by the Western allies in Asia, complementing their European armament drive, could be extended to address some of the festering economic and political grievances that, as in Europe a few years before, he feared were facilitating Communist advances. Conant elaborated to Voorhees in late May that the U.S.-British-French group could also recognize the nationalist aspirations of "the Asiatic peoples," admit that "old-fashioned colonialism" was outdated, and propose diplomatic and economic initiatives designed "to give some hope to these peoples of a better life without yielding to Communism."[66]

Conant's proposal for an Asian NATO was typical of U.S. foreign policy efforts during this period to address the dilemma of how to pursue Cold War objectives in parts of the world where poverty, colonialism, and Western imperialism, not Communism, were commonly perceived as the enemies. Washington in the 1950s dreamed of creating a "Third Way" democratic alternative to Communism and European colonialism, and Conant's idea paralleled discussions among U.S. and Allied officials about a "Pacific Pact" that would contain Communism in Asia and make at least a token bow toward decolonization. Such ideas recurred in the form of U.S.-led regional security alliances in the Far and Near East championed in the Eisenhower administration by Secretary of State John Foster Dulles. But it was difficult to square the circle by opposing Communist threats in the Third World without being seen as complicit in the labored efforts of Britain and France to preserve their empires. Faced with the choice of propping up European empires or backing nationalist movements against them, Washington, in most cases, grudgingly but firmly tilted toward the Europeans, and in some cases, then integrated various doomed neo-imperial regimes into its own empire. To take two examples that were in the headlines when Conant spoke: Iran's efforts to nationalize British oil interests led two years later to a CIA-sponsored coup against its leftist government that tied Washington to Shah Muhammad Reza Pahlavi for the next quarter-century; and in Indochina, the stepped-up military struggle in Asia led the United States to align itself firmly behind the sanguinary, futile French battle to suppress Ho Chi Minh's nationalist forces in Vietnam, to embrace Ngo Dinh Diem as a nationalist "George Washington" after the French were defeated, and finally to disastrous direct military intervention.[67]

It was, Conant understated, far easier to profess than to implement "a liberal anti-imperialist policy" in the Far East, and he anticipated objections to the idea that the United States, "with its enlightened anti-imperialistic attitude towards the peoples of Asia," should collaborate with colonial powers in their imperial domains. But, freshly sensitized to European views after his recent travels, Conant urged Americans to "examine more sympathetically" British and French concerns and assured them that public opinion in those countries, too, accepted the need for "a totally new approach": "Old fashioned colonialism," he declared, "must admittedly be replaced by a policy frankly recognizing the aspirations of the Asiatic people." And he added—in a passage from his Chicago speech dropped from his nationwide radio address two weeks later—an unusually candid allusion to the pro-MacArthur China lobby:

> We Americans have had at times a tendency to be a bit self-righteous about our Far Eastern policy, extremely critical of the conduct of other nations. . . . We would do well to recall that there have been and perhaps are now spokesmen for what amounts to an American Imperialism in Asia, before we launch too vigorous a criticism of the policy of France and Great Britain in the East.

Of course, as we have seen, Conant had nothing against what historians have variously dubbed a "protectorate" or an "empire by invitation" in Europe, where he believed the stakes were higher, the probable costs lower, and the cultural, historical, and social affinities and political common interests clearer.[68] His European priorities meant that concerns about colonial "past errors" were secondary, since the "common danger which now confronts us all, the existence of an aggressive Communist Russia and its satellites in an atomic age," made it imperative to maintain the closest possible alliance with Britain and France as well as burying the political hatchet at home.[69]

By the summer of 1951, such appeals were beginning to have some effect. Like a fever that had run its course, the MacArthur hysteria was subsiding. Although the domestic political battlefield still had frequent skirmishes and was littered with victims that included a wounded presidency and Democratic Party, U.S. military support for NATO proceeded apace with little serious opposition. The dispatching of American troops to Europe "now seems to be accepted on all sides," noted Conant, who added in an internal CPD memorandum that U.S. policy toward Europe had consistently "moved in the direction sought by the Committee."[70] Only the seemingly imminent prospect of a halt to the fighting in Korea, where American forces had dug in around the 38th parallel and a feared Chinese spring offensive had failed to materialize, marred this prospectus. "That the spirit of defeatism about securing the frontiers of freedom is still strong is evident," he cautioned in another internal CPD memorandum before departing on a two-month trip to Australia and New Zealand. "If the Korean war ends at an early date in an armistice which lasts, the reaction of the United States may once again be one of complacency."[71] No evidence was found in the archives to suggest that Conant was so callous (or tactless) as to state that it "was necessary to keep the small war going until rearmament was complete"—which is the historian Stephen Ambrose's explanation of the Truman administration's diffident handling of initial cease-fire overtures[72]—rather, he believed that if peace broke out, "a few well chosen statements on behalf of the Committee" might help keep the public firmly along the path of militarization laid down by NSC-68.[73] He needn't have worried. The Korean War dragged on for two more years, and the new American troop presence in Western Europe became

JAMES B. CONANT

so firmly entrenched, both politically and literally, that by the fall the commit-tee even seriously considered (but voted 15-5 against) disbanding. "NATO today compared to a year ago is a miracle," Conant told CPD members at a dinner meeting at the University Club in Manhattan that October. "Credit for this must go to the Russians primarily, not to this Committee. But we have at least, in our judgments and positions, been with the tide of events."[74]

CHAPTER 27

"Doublecross" and Defeat

Campaigning for Military Conscription

1950–1952

I see no escape from having some kind of draft. I think it is much better that it be uniform, because I think it best for morale and for the democratic system . . . I would think that one of the questions as to whether we can survive this challenge of the Soviet and all it implies, is whether we can put into practice what we preach. I would say part of that was equality of sacrifice as well as equality of opportunity.
— Remarks to Educational Policies Commission, March 1951

What is amazing and might be brought out in your article is the widespread deepseated objection by the American public to a fair system.
— Letter to William Marbury, February 20, 1971

The rapid expansion of the U.S. military machine simultaneously to fight in Korea and defend Western Europe was accompanied by intense diplomatic efforts to negotiate the terms of Allied cooperation in NATO operations under Eisenhower's command, and to secure West German military participation in an integrated West European army, to be known as the European Defense Community (EDC), simultaneous with that country's elevation from the status of occupied enemy to respected ally;[1] but both these efforts advanced only ploddingly, while at home the Truman administration faced a political, and ethical, quandary over how to obtain the military personnel for this vastly enlarged global mission. Its success (and the CPD's) in marshaling public support for deploying U.S. ground troops to NATO was, after all, only a partial victory — to achieve the across-the-board military build-up envisioned in NSC-68, it still had to draft or otherwise attract into the armed forces the additional 2 million personnel needed to increase their size from 1.5 million before Korea to 3.5 million by the end of 1952, in accordance with Pentagon plans.[2] While Congress was now ready to appropriate funds and technical breakthroughs were quickening the pace and variety of nuclear weapons production, the issue of who should go to the front lines proved more controversial—and in that controversy, Conant took a strong and sometimes unpopular position.

In championing the cause of universal military service, Conant culminated an engagement with the conscription issue that had started during the isolationist versus interventionist debate on the eve of America's entry into World War II; his goals then had been two-fold: to gain congressional approval for a general military training program, and, knowing how important it was to mobilize American science for war, to protect scientists doing critical weapons research from induction into battle-line service (though after Pearl Harbor, his "annoyance" shifted from overzealous draft boards to colleagues who sought "wholesale" student deferments which, he feared, would give colleges a reputation as sanctuaries for draft dodgers).[3] The atomic bomb compelled Conant temporarily to downgrade the importance of a military draft in favor of concentrating on strategic air power, but after 1947, and especially after the Czech coup and Berlin blockade in 1948, he loudly if vainly advocated a tougher system of universal military training, proposing the creation of a kind of national militia in which every male high-school graduate would have to enlist and opposing occupational or educational deferments for men under twenty-two years old. Truman proposed such a bill, but a reluctant Congress instead adopted a limited selective service bill laying out guidelines in the event the draft was reinstituted, a measure Conant derided as "an unsatisfactory stopgap."[4] The issue lay dormant until the Korean conflict exploded—and from the late summer of 1950 Conant urged universal two-year eighteen-year-old conscription as necessary to mobilize an army adequate to defend Western Europe on the ground, and the Committee on the Present Danger made UMS its "first legislative objective."[5]

Why was the issue of the military draft so important to Conant? The answer involves a web of motives that included both considerations of fairness and equity in Conant's consistent emphasis on democratic education, and his political, military, and ideological calculations of how best to wage the Cold War.

Conant always championed public education as the engine of social mobility in America, the potential leveler of class divisions that might otherwise harm the social fabric and make Communism attractive. When the Korean War convinced him that the Soviet Union constituted a grave military danger, at least in the short term, he also continued to maintain his principle of democratic burden-sharing in military service, seeking to forestall charges that educators sought to protect college students as a "privileged class" excused from the hardships and perils of war. Even a delayed draft of men aged twenty to twenty-two who had completed two years of college, rather than an across-the-board induction of eighteen-year-olds, would mean that "the inevitable 'class distinctions' between college men and non-college men will already have been formed," Conant warned Defense Secretary Marshall, when the administration and Congress skirmished in 1951 over the terms of military manpower legislation.[6] The draft policy then on the books, administered by local draft boards under the authority of the federal Selective Service System, struck Conant as "erratic and unfair."[7] To fellow educators, Conant explained that his fervent support for a comprehensive draft rather than "selective service" flowed from concern for "social justice" and the "democratic system." A democratic draft would fuel social mobility and class mixing, enabling a "widening of horizons of experience in the Army for those from localities and homes where college education has not been seriously thought of." With the aid of a "modest educational bonus" from Congress, though not a "prohibitively expensive" G.I. Bill, the United States might "come nearer to being a society with true educational opportunity."[8] To Conant, that goal had seemed a higher priority than ever, for he perceived grave dangers in the "social cleavages" already evident in Washington "between labor, management, and agriculture. I would think," he told fellow members of the Educational Policies Commission in March 1951, "that one of the questions as to whether we can survive this challenge of the Soviet and all it implies, is whether we can put into practice what we preach. I would say part of that was equality of sacrifice as well as equality of opportunity."[9] So pivotal did Conant consider the draft question that he warned the EPC that if the military measures recently enacted did not meet the test of democratic fairness and shared sacrifice, then America might not "continue as a free society" and would instead "go down the totalitarian road."[10]

Still, it was of immediate concern, Conant believed, to counter both the imminent and long-term Soviet military threats to Western Europe. While conceding that the United States "cannot forgo the potential use of the atomic bomb, frightful as such use might be, as long as there is no way of stopping the movement of Russian troops by adequate defense," Conant hoped UMS would enable the United States to avoid a permanent reliance on nuclear weapons and strategic airpower, which he feared had increased with the decision to build the hydrogen bomb. Also, he thought UMS was the best way to prepare for both the best- and worst-case scenarios for the future. Should deterrence fail, he calculated, it would supply the manpower reserve needed to maintain and replenish an army to fight in Europe.[11] More optimistically, he hoped that by deploying a large ground army there, any Soviet dreams of taking over the continent would be extinguished, and a new global "stalemate" would lead to eventual disarmament and real East-West peace. Conant's "thesis" postulated that if Western Europe were secured and a military clash deterred, "then in the course of years negotiations with the Soviet Union could begin to take a realistic turn." On the other hand, should "by subversion or aggression Communism reach the Channel ports," the United States would face global war or surrender before "the might of the whole Eurasian continent under Soviet rule." Therefore, he insisted, "paradoxical as it may appear, I believe the steps now being taken to build up the ground forces for the defense of Europe are steps away from a global war and towards the goal of peace."[12]

In Conant's view, then, UMS was a prerequisite both for avoiding World War III and for preserving American democracy.

By the summer of 1951, despite all the Committee on the Present Danger's unassailable credentials and well-orchestrated appeals to Congress and public opinion, Conant sadly conceded that the group had suffered a "complete defeat" in its bid to achieve UMS.[13] CPD activists watched disgustedly as Congress and the Pentagon fashioned a watered-down bill, preserving deferments and loopholes opposed by the committee and entrenching a system that inducted, as one member put it, "the poor, the stupid, and the friendless, while the smart, the influential and the rich are getting out."[14]

That the relationship between the committee and the administration would eventually unravel over the draft issue was not unpredictable, but Conant failed to appreciate how sensitive a political nerve his pleas for a comprehensive draft were striking. In fact, the CPD's leaders nearly aborted plans to announce the group's creation due to well-founded eleventh-hour suspicions that the Pentagon was less than wholehearted in its commitment to UMS. According to one account, in order to assure a long-term ability quickly to mobilize mass armies, Defense Secretary Marshall preferred universal military *training* to maintaining "large, burdensome, and potentially dangerous regular armed forces,"[15] but he kept those views close to the vest. Still, even as he welcomed inquiries as to whether he would favor the CPD's creation, in October 1950 Marshall complained to Acheson, Nitze, and Harriman that a "group of prominent educators including James Conant" were preparing a statement in favor of compulsory military service; he preferred a more politically viable solution to the military manpower shortage.[16] Eisenhower, who supported Conant's pro-UMS stand, wrote in his diary on November 6, a week after Truman had privately invited him to be NATO's first joint commander: "Have urged universal military service of two years duration, without pay for all eighteen-year-olds. Jim Conant is in general agreement. Marshall does not agree, ditto Lovett."[17]

Doubts about the administration's willingness to stand behind UMS flared on November 20, during a sometimes tempestuous series of meetings between CPD organizers and senior Pentagon officials, one of a number of contacts designed to clarify the administration's position before the CPD went public.[18] Conant, in Tennessee recuperating from surgery, could not attend, but Voorhees, Bush, Marbury, and Patterson hoped to hammer out an agreed plan of action when they met with Marshall, Lovett, and top advisers. Due to the news from Korea, where MacArthur's Thanksgiving offensive was beginning to falter amid alarming reports of Chinese infiltrators, a nervous and dour mood prevailed, and the CPD delegation fidgeted restlessly as Marshall embarked on a rambling statement that left uncertain just what the Pentagon proposed to do to raise a vastly larger army to defend Western Europe as well as to fight in Korea. When asked directly whether he backed the group's firm position in favor of a mandatory two-year draft for all eighteen-year-old males, with no student deferments, Marshall equivocated, replying (according to Marbury) that "even if the Department decided to ask for a more limited program, the fact that our committee had come out for the stronger program would help in the process of educating the public and the Congress." That response infuriated Marshall's predecessor, Robert Patterson, and detonated what one person present in the room described as an "Homeric clash" between him and the sitting defense secretary. Speaking for the disappointed CPD delegation, Patterson declared "that he would not be willing to advocate universal military service if the Department was going to come along afterwards and ask for some 'watered down' program" and that "under the circumstances our committee had better just mark time." Princeton's president, Harold Dodds, agreed that the proposed citizens' committee "would certainly not want to do anything which would not be in complete harmony with the position of the Defense Department."

The CPD activists' restrained disappointment exploded into outright anger after Marshall left and the visitors sat down to lunch with Assistant Secretaries of Defense Anna Rosenberg and Marx Leva, and Defense Department lawyer Felix Larken. "Van Bush opened on them with both barrels," recalled Marbury. "He told them that as a result of the meeting in General Marshall's office, our committee had come to a standstill and that it was not easy to get this sort of thing started again once it stopped. He said that we had been shocked and disheartened by the atmosphere of 'defeatism' and 'timidity' which seemed to us to pervade General Marshall's remarks."

Marshall's aides, according to Marbury, "immediately fell over themselves to say that it had all been a terrible mistake." They had not had a chance to prepare Marshall for the meeting. Rosenberg "said point blank" that universal military service represented "the only possible solution for the present situation," and expressed confidence that Marshall and Lovett could be quickly convinced to commit themselves to support UMS for all eighteen-year-olds without deferments. Larkin promised that the Pentagon's plans coincided with those outlined by the committee. Assuaged, the CPD activists cautiously resumed planning for their public unveiling—and ten days later, on December 1, in the depths of gloom over the defeat in Korea, Rosenberg and Leva assured Bush, O'Brian, and Voorhees that the Defense Department would stand behind the Committee on the Present Danger's mobilization measures.[19]

Convinced, at least for the moment, that the administration would support them, the CPD organizers went ahead with their plans to announce the committee's formation on December 12, but by then Conant's position on the draft had become a subject of controversy among the public in general and among educators and students around the country and, naturally, at Harvard in particular. Until mid-November, he had maneuvered quietly, hedging his public statements and explaining his position in off-the-record meetings and private letters and memorandums. Some educators were already gathering forces to secure deferments for students in specialized fields and would be taken aback when Conant failed to take a similar stand. John Kenneth Galbraith, now safely ensconced in the Harvard economics department after his tumultuous tenure battle, recalls sending Conant a proposal for a military draft and being surprised when Conant replied by curtly criticizing its provisions for student deferments.[20] But as at universities around the country, at Harvard the renewed threat of a military draft overshadowed academic concerns in that fall of 1950. "If Professor Samuel Eliot Morison ever finishes another volume of his history of Harvard," the *Crimson* had told arriving freshmen that September, "he will undoubtedly point out that the University fully recovered from World War II for precisely three days—the period between the Class of 1950's commencement and the invasion of Korea. 1950 was a war-baby class, largely veteran and thoroughly overcrowded; until it left, the University could not settle down to what Harvard likes to call its 'pre-war normalcy.' For your Class of 1954, it looks very much as if that normalcy has gone up in battle-smoke."[21]

All fall and into the winter, students rode an emotional roller coaster about the likelihood and requirements of a military draft. Whether conscription would be universal or selective, whether it would induct or exempt students already in college, what would be the length of service required and the ages of eligibility, what categories of students might get deferments—all these questions were up in the air. ROTC units on campus, not surprisingly, reported a surge of students betting that their enlistment would put them in a good stead to avoid frontline combat. In October, Selective Service System director Maj. Gen. Lewis B. Hershey announced a plan under which student deferments would be awarded according to class ranking, prompting scornful comments about the unfairness of such a system and the inevitable resultant rat race for easy A's; the inclusion of compulsory midterm grades on a list of possible university mobilization measures increased speculation that the army planned to "hack away at each class from the bottom up."[22] The Selective Service scheme, known as the Trytten Plan after the chairman of the agency's Scientific Advisory Committee, quickly won endorsement from the American Council on Education (ACE) and other educators who backed a deferment policy as "in the national interest."[23]

Conant's own preference for two-year UMS for all eighteen-year-old males, able-bodied or not, with "absolutely no exemptions," finally jutted into public view in early December, with a publication in *Look* of his "A Stern Program for Survival." Its appearance in that particular magazine was more than happpenstance: its publisher, Gardner Cowles, had attended the

September Citizens' Conference at the Waldorf-Astoria, heard Conant's memorandum presented and agreed to print it, and would himself shortly join the California branch of the CPD.[24] Widely publicized through advance releases to opinion-leaders and media figures, Conant's *Look* article was timed to coincide with the December 12 debut of the Committee on the Present Danger, whose platform declared:

> The time has come for a new concept that universal service in defense of our freedom is a privilege and an obligation of our young men. To accomplish this with the least interference with education, with business and professional careers, and with family life, this service should commence at the age of 18 or upon graduation from high school, whichever is later. Two years of such military service, including training, will be necessary, and the program should embrace radically broadened standards of fitness.

Though plotted for months, Conant's and the CPD's prescriptions for UMS reached readers precisely at the nadir of American fortunes in Korea, a moment when pessimism dominated the global outlook and drastic mobilization measures could expect support from a desperate public. Besides the promised albeit vague endorsement from the administration and the Pentagon, the committee's advocacy of UMS accorded with proposals advanced by the Association of American Universities and the Association of American Colleges. Conant, of course, had for months actively sought to push the AAU and its head, Henry Wriston, to back UMS, and had written at length to the University of North Carolina's president, Gordon Gray, head of an AAU panel to examine the subject of conscription legislation, to urge a requirement that draftees be inducted at age eighteen for two years, rather than having the option of deferring service until after college; the final AAU report reflected that change.[25] Nevertheless, Conant's views was considerably tougher than that of many educators, both because it required universal military *service* rather than *training* and because it flatly rejected all deferments or exemptions. For reasons that did not exclude self-interest, many educators protested that this would irreparably disrupt careers in such vital professions as science, medicine, and engineering, damage American security by depriving the armed forces of trained specialists, and shock the economy. Conant's plan was "short sighted" and fatally defective because of its "rigid provision" for service prior to college, charged the New York State Association of Colleges and Universities, while the president of Notre Dame University also dissented, citing the need for military personnel with advanced skills.[26] Responding in the next issue of *Look* — "A Reply to Harvard's Dr. Conant: A Total Conscription Will *Hurt* America" — Amherst's president, Charles W. Cole, a member of the Selective Service's Trytten advisory panel, instead urged deferment of college-age men "who show by tests, like the Army aptitude test, that they can profit from further training."[27]

Conant's enthusiasm for mandatory conscription and for a full-scale domestic mobilization precipitated a firestorm of criticism from isolationists, pacifists, and others, reminiscent of the ire generated by his pro-interventionist speeches in 1940–41; some excoriated his seeming callousness in coolly calculating the need to make young men go off to fight distant battles. "Have you sons to send into this mess?" asked one angry correspondent, evidently unaware that Conant's sons had already faced travails in the Pacific during World War II.[28] "May I ask, please, who will survive in your proposed Stern Program for Survival?" inquired another. "Certainly not the young men and women you propose to send out for training to kill and be killed. . . . "[29]

Condemning Conant's plan as "a step away from peace and in the direction of another catastrophic war," the American Friends Service Committee, an influential pacifist and Quaker organization, circulated a letter by the novelist Pearl Buck criticizing Conant for taking an excessively militaristic approach to international Communism, rather than addressing social and economic ills, and accusing him of "panic or recklessness."[30] The *Chicago Tribune,* alluding to Conant's recommendation to "radically broadened" physical standards for military service, editorialized that the CPD "blueprint seems to be for a sweeping militarization of the country, with almost any young man able to limp, blink, or jerk through the motions being outfitted with a uniform and not only trained but put into combat wherever the opportunity might offer."[31]

The apocalyptic tone of Conant's *Look* article prompted some critics to claim that his prescription for addressing the conscription quandary did not match his diagnosis of the world situation. Cole pounced precisely on this point. "Dr. Conant's plan seems based in some degree on the belief that we are facing all-out war in 1952–54. If that is in prospect, UMS is not nearly enough. We should mobilize at once, step up war production, eliminate luxury goods, put factories underground and disperse our city populations." But, he went on, if such a war was not in the offing, if the more likely prospect was a "long, sullen, cold war with hot Korea-like flashes," then the most important priority was to preserve a "healthy economy, our scientific and technological advantages over our prospective enemies." And even should war break out, he insisted, the key to victory lay not in simply raising a much bigger army but in preserving (with the aid of student deferments) the advantage of trained specialists needed to develop, produce, and operate advanced weaponry. "*We cannot compete with Russia (much less Russia plus satellites plus China) in raw man power,*" Cole argued. "*Where we can compete is in trained, educated, skilled man power.*"[32]

Cornell's president, Edmund E. Day, raised similar objections. Agreeing with Conant that the Soviet Union posed a serious military threat, Day strongly disputed his presumption that the Russians would strike when they calculated that they had gained the technological edge. After all, he reasoned, the Kremlin already appeared to be winning the Cold War through a shrewd strategy of manipulated crises and fear-mongering. If a drawn-out struggle rather than a convulsive shooting war lay ahead, Conant's plan would unduly militarize American society and education and, in the long run, "actually weaken our defenses." Conant's idea of drafting every American eighteen-year-old male for two years, able-bodied or not, struck Day as "too simple, and in consequence too rigid." Better to institute a more flexible system that preserved deferments to assure trained personnel for the military and to avoid too drastic a disruption of the country's economy, education, and society, and better for Americans to "keep our heads," Day argued, rather than play into Stalin's hands by panicking.[33]

Inflated rhetoric aside, though, Conant really did seem to have convinced himself that the Russians intended to attack Western Europe. Gravely concerned by the implications of the Soviet atomic bomb and the North Korean attack, Conant had assumed in his September memo to the Citizens' Conference and December *Look* article that "somewhere in the period 1952–54" the Soviet leaders would "start a global war" if they had an advantage in the arms race and could feel confident of "marching to the Channel ports." The escalation of the Korean conflict pushed him still further toward the view that a U.S.-Soviet showdown could not be avoided. He preferred to plan "on the arbitrary assumption" that war wouldn't break out within the next year, he told William T. Golden shortly after China intervened. " 'Maybe there won't be any war at all,' " Golden recorded Conant as feeling, "but he didn't seem very hopeful on this as he had been some three years ago when he expressed optimism that there would be no world conflict in the foreseeable future."[34]

That there had been no quick realization of the worst fears of an imminent World War III, fears which peaked after China's intervention in Korea, meant that whatever public willingness had existed to make the kind of sacrifice inherent in Conant's hard-line UMS plan quickly began to fade. And in fact, Conant later conceded that he had "made a mistake in rushing into print" and that Cole had "had much the better of the argument."[35] Conant soon shifted his argument to reflect a belief that a long period of "partial mobilization," rather than imminent or near-term global war, was the most likely challenge requiring military preparedness.[36] Indeed, by the time his article appeared Conant's watertight rejection of college deferments had already begun to spring leaks. In what he later acknowledged was a tactical error, Conant and the CPD had endorsed the Association of American Universities' plan for full conscription despite its provision for "feeding back" a small percentage of draftees to colleges for additional specialized training, including ROTC, once they had completed basic training;[37] and fencing politely in correspondence with Cole, Conant tried vainly to get him to support this program as a compromise scheme merging the principle of universal service with the flexibility of selective service.[38]

Conant remained adamantly opposed, however, to several aspects of the

Trytten Plan. With true universal service "the fundamental postulate" of his thinking, he strongly believed that using local draft boards rather than a uniform standard would inevitably lead to inconsistent deferment decisions.[39] Wholesale exemptions of college-bound students who planned to go into science, engineering, and medicine threatened to create a "privileged class" and to inspire an unseemly rush by leaders of various professions to proclaim their own respective central roles in national security so as to merit deferment status. And Conant despised Trytten's use of academic standing to determine eligibility for students in universities — while perhaps able to separate "the brilliant from the dull," such a process would foster grade-mongering and poison the atmosphere for students and faculty.[40]

Not that Conant discerned much brightness in the mood on campus as 1950 drew to a close. He wrote to Van Bush on December 26 that as a result of uncertainty over the draft, student morale had "pretty well gone to pot," and he recruited a reluctant Bush to start "mixing into this manpower problem" by joining a Defense Department advisory panel on scientific and military mobilization issues. Outlining a detailed list of tactics and arguments to use in pressing for UMS, Conant told his old atomic-policy collaborator that "the colleges have been very much upset" by December's events. "We shall have to do something to try to steady [students] when they return after Christmas," Conant concluded. "Nothing could do more for them than a clear-cut statement from the Government as to what was going to be the policy in regard to student deferment."[41]

Doing his own part to steady the Harvard community's raw nerves, Conant tried to sound a more optimistic note than in his *Look* article as he drafted his annual presidential report to the board of overseers, declaring at the outset his assumption that the United States was not yet engaged in a global war requiring total mobilization, and would not be "for many a year to come." He admitted noticing a "certain harsh resemblance" to the situation at the board's meeting a month after Pearl Harbor, but found the analogy "superficial," for in January 1942 the imperative of defeating the Axis was arduous but clear-cut, whereas now the future challenges seemed so murky that, he admitted, his assumption might already be invalidated by events by the time his report (completed on January 8, 1951) was printed later that month. But since it was, in his view, "far more likely" that the future would bring a long, drawn-out Cold War stalemate, and since all-out preparations for global atomic war would shatter U.S. education's normal functioning and likely be ineffectual if such a conflict did in fact occur, Conant proposed, unless "directed otherwise by the Governing Boards," to chart the university's course on the assumption that World War III was not imminent.[42]

But the uncertainty persisted into the new year, and Conant sensed a spreading malaise among students who anxiously wondered whether the Cold War would suck them into the abyss. "Boys only concerned about the draft," he jotted in his diary on January 9 after a "difficult" evening of "amicable if forceful" questions from undergraduates. "When I used to visit the Houses," Conant remarked later, "they asked me to lower the board rates or to have a hockey rink built. This year all the students' questions seriously concerned themselves with the present crisis."[43] While some students, including the *Crimson*'s editors, supported UMS, others resented Conant's enthusiasm for a no-deferments draft; strolling through Harvard Yard one day, he heard "good-natured booing" from a line of students filing into a draft deferment exam.[44] Perplexed and depressed by the welter of conflicting proposals and provisions, many students reportedly displayed a " 'What's the use?' attitude" as their futures hung in the balance.[45]

To the disappointment of Conant, the CPD, and of course the students themselves, the Truman administration's long-awaited bill, released on January 17, 1951, only increased the confusion. Instead of two years' service for all eighteen-year-old males, the proposed "Universal Military Service and Training Act" ostensibly stipulated twenty-seven months of military service between the ages of nineteen and twenty-six. But—besides being wide open to erosion, criticism, and counterproposals from Congress—the bill also preserved deferments for seventy-five thousand entering college students who theoretically would be obligated to serve after graduation, and, worse, it left unclear whether existing deferments would remain in effect.

Conant and the CPD swallowed their qualms and warily endorsed the administration's bill as a reasonable alternative to absolute UMS. Conant now backed the AAU "feed-back" proposal because full universal service was, "for the moment at least, impractical," and agreed that if a UMS bill were enacted students already enrolled in colleges and professional schools could postpone service until after graduation "without damage to the democratic principles of our educational system."[46] This milder position reflected in part his awareness of the political opposition to hard-line UMS, and in part his desire to preserve some semblance of educational "normalcy" so long as global war did not start—thus he organized a petition of Ivy League presidents to Marshall opposing the resumption of wartime "accelerated" year-round college schedules, and accepted the argument that instant mobilization of all eighteen-year-olds would cause an unwarranted disruption of the nation's educational system.[47] Stung by criticism that his original plan would overly militarize American society, he acknowledged that "a nice balance" existed between "getting enough military strength to prevent a World War" and "getting so much military strength we destroy the country in the process of defending it."[48]

Conant's grudging departures from his prior absolutist position on deferments confused some admirers. Wasn't his new stand "diametrically opposed" to his earlier position? asked Indiana Representative William G. Bray, adding that his views "carried considerable weight in Congressional as well as educational circles."[49] (Responding that he could "readily understand that I might seem inconsistent," Conant insisted that excluding college students from the draft until after graduation reflected his "firm conviction" that college careers should not be interrupted.)[50]

But despite adjusting their position to support the administration bill and loyally trooping up to Capitol Hill to support it, Conant and other CPD members were enraged when Pentagon aides could not guarantee that the murkily written law would indeed provide for universal military service. "Their answer seemed to me to be negative," recalled Marbury, "and at this point I exploded, reminding them of the fact that the Committee on the Present Danger had gone out on a limb in reliance on the assurances of Mrs. Rosenberg that the Administration bill would be clear and unequivocal on this point. My rudeness was startling to Jim Baxter, who rightly thought that nothing could be accomplished by such a display of anger and disappointment."[51]

A disappointed Conant held back from public criticism, at least for the moment, but as the debate turned into "confusion doubly confounded" and various congressional and administration plans tangled on Capitol Hill in February and March, he tried to tug Marshall toward UMS. When the defense secretary asked him if he had any suggestions for an upcoming speech Marshall was to give at an educators' conference, Conant "venture[d] to write frankly," supplying a long manifesto designed "to offset the very bad publicity" the administration's draft bill had received. "It seems to me the argument has gone off the track badly," he observed, exhorting Marshall to declare that the new draft legislation would not merely extend selective service but establish a "democratic, fair system" without "privileged groups." Like public schools, he argued, an army drawn from eighteen-year-old males of all walks of life would open avenues of opportunity to the poor: "Some young men who might never have realized that they could handle college work or failed to realize what careers college opened up will be educated as to the world by their two years in the army. Their horizons will be expanded; their ambitions awakened." But inducting older men would mean that "the inevitable 'class distinctions' between college men and non-college men will already have been formed."[52]

Marshall admitted that the administration bill was "not exactly what we wanted" but insisted that it was "a great step in the right direction."[53] Not seeing much choice, Conant strongly plugged it at a sparsely attended hearing of the House Armed Services Committee on March 8; but the panel's chairman, Conant noted in his diary, while "very amiable but made it clear he was interested in UM_T_ (only!)."[54] An encounter with Anna Rosenberg on March 13 further shook Conant's confidence. Near midnight, at a buffet supper after he had addressed a forum sponsored by the *Philadelphia Bulletin,* she too seemed interested only in universal military *training.* "What is going on?!" Conant wondered.[55] (At best only a "very lukewarm supporter" of UMT, he soon came to wish the CPD "had never got tangled up with this issue" since it confused the objectives of general preparedness and building up a 3.5 million-man army requiring two years of actual service.)[56]

From there, things only went downhill. Within days, the administration decided to discard UMS and instead support conscription with extensive deferments for college students or high-school graduates with high test scores.[57] General Hershey testified that the revised bill would not affect existing exemptions or occupational deferments, would not endanger student deferments, and would allow all students with satisfactory grades to defer service. On March 31 Truman confirmed that the administration had adopted the modified Trytten Plan, a stand that outraged the CPD members, Conant included. "You will recall that at the time we met Secretary Marshall last November we did our best to urge simplicity and directness," wrote Robert Patterson to a fellow CPD member. "Little by little these points have been chipped away. It makes me fairly sick."[58]

In private, Conant heaped scorn on the administration for vacillating, "backing and filling," between UMS and UMT, between a comprehensive draft and selective service, and among various proposed lengths of required service—two years, twenty-seven months, three years. Students, he told fellow educators in late March, felt "double-crossed," and he couldn't blame them. "I don't think the Administration has played fair with the young people ... If they had deliberately set out to demoralize the youth of the country, I submit they could [do] no better than they have done within the last six months."[59] Publicly, Conant vented his anger against General Hershey and the Selective Service System while avoiding direct criticism of Truman. In a nationally broadcast April 8 CBS radio interview with fellow CPD member Edward R. Murrow—what Conant characterized in his diary as an "'ad lib' broadcast" but in fact a carefully rehearsed exchange—he responded with unusual emotion when asked to comment on the new measure: "You asked me what I think of it? Well, I can tell you. Less than nothing. In fact, my reactions are so negative that I'd like, if I may at this point, read a prepared statement, lest my language become too violent." He then read a paragraph blasting the proposed draft measure as undemocratic and unfair, and reaffirming the CPD's support for UMS.

"Well, President Conant, would it be fair to say, in wholly unacademic language, that in your opinion General Hershey's directive stinks?" asked Murrow.

"Well, I ... I shouldn't disclaim that word," replied Conant, evoking the journalist's laughter for this uncharacteristic dash of incivility.[60]

Conant's campaign took other forms. Beyond the speeches and statements, he also tried to use his status as Harvard president to align the divided educational establishment behind UMS; and in one skirmish, he again turned to his most powerful ally: Eisenhower, whose stature was high after his appointment as NATO commander, was already arousing speculation about a possible presidential candidacy.

A report on education's place in defense issues was being prepared by the National Educational Association's Educational Policies Commission, and

Conant threatened to resign from the EPC rather than go along with a statement that failed to "face up to the real issues" and evaded the mobilization question.[61] It would be "like publishing Hamlet without the Prince of Denmark," Conant told the EPC in late March.[62] The EPC promptly agreed to a redraft of the report (by *Christian Science Monitor* editor Erwin Canham, a veteran of the "Fishing Party"), convinced Conant to stay, and elected him chairman. At that point, Conant solicited help from Eisenhower, still formally an EPC member despite his NATO assignment, when he saw him at SHAPE headquarters during his delayed spring 1951 visit to Europe, and urged the EPC to hold off on its final report until it had Eisenhower's comments.[63] But Conant remained pessimistic: "I despair of getting all the educators to agree with us but I am hoping we can narrow the area of disagreement so that subsequent discussions will be more rational and informed," he wrote Eisenhower on June 19. "Of course I would like to have it all come out agreeing with UMS, but that is hoping too much."[64]

EPC secretary William Carr quietly supported Conant's efforts, believing that Ike's support was essential.[65] After making a pilgrimage to Paris, Carr told the EPC in October that Eisenhower had gone "like a homing pigeon to its nest" to the question of student deferments. Like Conant, Eisenhower strongly opposed them, citing the democratic principle of "equality of sacrifice," and like Conant, he believed in conscripting all eighteen-year-old males. "What does Dr. Conant think about this?" Eisenhower asked Carr, adding that "he had great confidence in Dr. Conant's opinion and would be prepared to be influenced very much by what Dr. Conant thought."[66]

Of course, "Dr. Conant" had already seen to it that Ike knew full well what he thought about the report, and the combined efforts of the two men assured that the final report on "Education and National Security"—a joint product of the EPC and the American Council on Education—took a harder line on higher education's contribution to the military effort. When finally published in December 1951, "Education and National Security" endorsed UMS for "*at least* two years" (emphasis in original) for all eighteen-year-old males.[67] "Not too happy about it but it may do some good," Conant felt.[68]

Conant's class-conscious vision of a democratic draft fell in battle and did not rise again. Instead of UMS, the law finally voted on by Congress in June 1951 contained, as Marbury bitterly wrote, only a "promise to consider in future a program of universal military training"—training, not service—"which has no practical significance as far as the present struggle against communistic expansion is concerned." Worse, "no one will be selected for military service except those too poor to afford to go to college, too stupid to stay there, or too lacking in initiative to avail themselves of some of the other manifold avenues by which military service can be avoided."[69] Although the administration tried to sugar-coat the result, profusely thanking the CPD for its "wonderful work," Conant realized that the Pentagon's assurances—that the continuation of the deferment system was only a "temporary expedient" on the path to "the concept of universal service"—were only hollow rhetoric.[70] In a somber address at the Harvard Commencement ceremonies in late June, he told the graduating seniors that "the bill which the President signed on Tuesday settles nothing" and imposed the "great injustice" of continuing uncertainty for draft-age young men. "The American people" would soon demand that Congress take action to recognize the "obligation of universal service," he predicted.[71]

But Conant had badly misread public opinion, and he seemed reluctant to accept the ever more obvious proposition that UMS was doomed in large measure because those powerful enough to decide its fate simply did not want to send their children into war, while those who were most vulnerable to selective service lacked the political power to change the system. The "Universal Military Service and Training Act" led to nothing of the sort, and succumbed to the age-old fate of death by committee: a panel was established to draft a law for six months of mandatory military training, but in 1952 the House of Representatives soundly voted down the proposal.[72]

Though the Committee on the Present Danger continued to press for UMS until it went out of existence in 1953, passing on its recommendations to a sympathetic but cautious president-elect Eisenhower, universal service never became law.[73] And just as Conant had feared, the CPD's inability to win approval for the principle of a comprehensive draft established a precedent that was followed not only in Korea but subsequently, from Vietnam to "Desert Storm": an undemocratic system determined who would fight and kill and die for their country.

During the Vietnam War, Conant believed that the recurrent spectacle of students evading the draft proved the correctness of the CPD campaign. Once again, the fairness of the Selective Service System was a matter of angry public controversy, and General Hershey's name evoked contempt on campuses around the country. At the height of the war, Conant wrote that the Vietnam experience demonstrated the difficulty of mobilizing the country to face an unclear or unconvincing threat. "If large numbers are asked to prepare to fight and, if need be, die in defense of the United States, the nation must be at war or face serious outbreaks of disloyalty among the young," he wrote. "I am sure Selective Service was never intended to provide combat troops for military action that was less than an all-out national effort." Still convinced that UMS represented the fairest way to share the burden of military service, he concluded that attempts to tinker with Selective Service had been "a continuous but fruitless process." As for the earlier debate over the draft, at the time of the Korean War, Conant in his memoirs blamed the defeat primarily on public opinion and Congress. "The arguments of worried parents," he wrote, "proved more powerful with Congress in 1951 than the reasoned opinions of the educators who supported the program of the Committee on the Present Danger."[74]

A man who, in his son's words, rarely fought battles he did not expect to win, Conant continued to be keenly disappointed over that defeat. And not long after publishing his memoirs in 1970, his ire was aroused by a retrospective of the controversy written by William Marbury. In responding to the draft Marbury sent him, he told his old associate that what struck him as "amazing" about Marbury's account was "the widespread deepseated objection by the American public to a fair system. Congress responded to pressure groups," Conant observed, and many, especially "academic people" and "the scientists," believed that "an unfair system was o.k. if you didn't talk about it." He now conceded that the CPD had erred in embracing the AAU plan with its "feed-back" provision.

"My own view, now," he wrote to Marbury, "is that we were beaten in large part because (a) the mothers would never go along with the 18 year [old] provision and (b) the colleges forced us (me in particular) to put in the 75,000 provision," and as a result, the CPD's record was "not as clear cut as it should have been. . . . " It had also blurred its stand, he concluded, by endorsing a whittled-down administration bill that emphasized UMT rather than UMS, and he thought the committee had been too passive and timid between April and June 1951, when the conscription bill was undergoing its final revisions—and when Conant was visiting Europe and the MacArthur paroxysm distracted the nation. "Were we all asleep?" Conant wondered. "I am afraid so."[75]

But what rankled Conant most was the idea that the Truman administration had been deceitful at his own expense. Now Conant believed that the CPD had not merely suffered a political defeat, but been hoodwinked. "From the evidence you present," he wrote to Marbury, "it looks as if Gen. Marshall, a fanatic proponent of UMT, was using the Committee for his purposes which were not UMS." It seemed hard to avoid the conclusions that Marshall and his top aides had deliberately given the CPD "the run-around." "I think the General's staff gave us the double cross. No wonder the Senate and House Committees produced the 'fake' document they did." The venerated Marshall, in Conant's revised judgment, was "a smarter politician than we took him for and not as honest and open hearted as often depicted . . . [the] forces of evil (i.e., Gen M's staff) seem to have led us down the garden path."[76] Marbury disagreed, believing that Marshall and his aides had sincerely advocated UMS but were outmaneuvered by Congress and blindsided by public opinion, and he blamed Hershey, who "had no superior in detecting which way the wind was blowing," for helping to doom universal service.[77]

Perhaps acknowledging that his egalitarian concept of a democratic army was politically impractical—indeed, his explicitly class-related argument for using the military as a force for social justice might today cause him to be labeled a radical—Conant ultimately transferred his allegiance from UMS to an all-volunteer army. "You probably won't agree," he wrote Marbury in 1971, "and I imagine Congress won't either. So our scandalous system will continue."[78]

In fact, however, after the Vietnam War the government did turn to an all-volunteer military service, and it was an all-volunteer force that fought in the Persian Gulf in 1991. Yet the troubling questions Conant vainly sought to raise remain relevant. So long as the United States professes to be a democracy, one may question the fairness of a system that allows its wealthy and college-bound youth to avoid national service while it essentially bribes, with promises of economic and career advancement, poor and underprivileged citizens to do the dirty and dangerous work of war. The basic dilemma of who should fight and die for the United States at war still awaits an equitable resolution.

CHAPTER 28

"I Told You So"

Conant and the Militarization of American Science

1950–1952

It seems to me something like the old religious phenomenon of conversion. As I see it now, the military, if anything, have become vastly too much impressed with the abilities of research and development . . . at times they seem to be fanatics in their belief of what the scientists and the technologists can do . . . the Defense Department is now like the story of the man who sprang on his horse and rode madly off in all directions.
— Speech to the National War College, February 1, 1952

I had hoped that after World War II was over, the universities of the United States might be spared the burden of secret or confidential research. For secrecy and the pursuit of knowledge for its own sake are uneasy bedfellows.
— President's Report, 1951–1952

Since 1933 I can't claim to have advanced the barriers of science one millimeter.
— 1952 interview

The cartoon in the September 30, 1951, issue of the Soviet humor magazine *Krokodil* showed a conclave of obese, medal-laden, cigar-chomping generals around a conference table. Underneath read the caption: "A meeting of the educational council of Harvard University, America's greatest university." The claim that military brass ran Harvard — inspired not only by Conant's exploits but also by the appointment of Corporation member Charles A. Coolidge as assistant secretary of defense — accompanied the journal's assertion that the "leadership of the educational and scholarly activities of the institutions of higher learning falls more and more into the hands of the military." *Krokodil*'s caricature embellished an undeniable reality: military patronage was fast coming to dominate scientific research in U.S. colleges and universities.[1]

As military research and development soared to more than twenty times the pre–World War II standards, money for defense-related work saturated campuses. Military research chiefs signed up scientists and waved dollar signs in front of university presidents like Hollywood studio moguls enticing movie stars to sign exclusive contracts. By 1949–50, federal expenditures for weapons-related research had topped $1 billion, exceeding 1946 levels by $300 million, with the Defense Department budget supporting more than 15,000 separate projects, the majority in industry but a rising percentage at universities. Then, when the Korean War added urgency to this activity, Pentagon spending for science instantly ballooned, almost tripling in the next two years to reach $1.6 billion in fiscal 1952. Many people and institutions that had previously resisted the Pentagon's blandishments now succumbed. A 1951 survey discovered physicists at 750 U.S. colleges and universities devoting seventy percent of their time to "defense research." By the time of the cease-fire in 1953, which signified no let-up in the Cold War, 98 of every 100 dollars spent by the government on academic physics came from the Defense Department or the AEC. Lured by Faust and Uncle Sam, vast battalions of American scientists, never really demobilized after World War II, gratefully accepted a lucrative commission to reenlist.[2]

Inevitably, Conant was sucked into the vortex of this transformation. In addition to retaining a position of considerable, if lessened, influence as a GAC adviser through 1952, he participated in the creation and early development of two milestones in science-government relations: the creation of the National Science Foundation, and the establishment of a federal Science Advisory Committee (SAC), which by the end of the decade led to the appointment of a single science adviser to the president, positioned to offer counsel on arms, space travel, nuclear energy, pollution, and other politically charged issues.[3]

Conant's concerns about the relationship between science and politics were principally in two broad areas: first, the problems that occurred when nonscientists, especially politicians and military officers, had to make scientific and technological judgments about the development and production of new weapons; and second, the dangers to pure scientific inquiry when the armed forces and federal government so massively sponsored basic and applied research. His frustrating experience in the hydrogen bomb controversy had only deepened his sense of unease over what he regarded as a new and unhealthy relationship between science and the Pentagon. In a wide variety of forums during 1950–52, in and out of government—from an article in *Foreign Affairs* to secret defense advisory boards—he championed the idea of establishing juridical-style review boards in the Pentagon to resolve technical disputes, in which at least one person would be designated to ask "all the dirty questions," to make the skeptical taxpayer's case against any new venture—to act, in Conant's wry description to a military audience, as "a devil's advocate, if one may speak of the taxpayer in that sense."[4] The "worst way" to make weapons decisions, he declared, was to "resolve conflicts in favor of those with the loudest voice or the closest approach to political leaders." Writing to the *Washington Post*'s publisher, Philip L. Graham, in March 1950 declining an invitation to contribute an article on the H-bomb decision, he lamented the "great fallacy" in the minds of many military leaders, scientists, and engineers, that in technical matters "there must be a right or wrong judgment and that it is rather indecent to have proponents present a clash of opinion and betray their prejudices. . . . The fact of the matter is that one cannot examine any proposal for future technical work without getting into an area in which prejudice and opinion are bound to have their influence. What I want to do is to have them come out in the open." One of the "distressing aspects" of the H-bomb decision, he added, had been that both inside and outside the government "the discussion was so ill-informed" about a grave matter that was "far more technical both from a military and a scientific point of view" than the public thought. He feared that same pattern of decision on nuclear policy would repeat itself "time and time again for the next decade which from my point of view is likely to be increasingly grim."[5]

It was in large part as an effort to dampen this excessive zeal for and belief in scientific wonder toys to win wars, not to mention his long-standing desire to educate the citizenry about science, that Conant wrote *Science and Common Sense,* published in early 1951 by the Yale University Press (a choice that evoked some general bemusement). Begun as a revision of his earlier *On Understanding Science,* and as a summation of his postwar Carnegie-supported science education project, *Science and Common Sense* expanded into a full-blown discussion of the rift between what C. P. Snow a decade later called the "two cultures" of science and of literary intellectual life; in Conant's more inclusive formulation, he wanted "to bridge the gap to some degree between those who understand science because science is their profession and intelligent citizens who have only studied the results of scientific inquiry—in short, the laymen."[6] Long before this issue became a *cause célèbre,* Conant had agonized over the problem Snow succinctly described: "It is dangerous to have two cultures which can't or don't communicate. In a time when science is determining much of our destiny, that is whether we live or die, it is dangerous in the most practical terms. Scientists can give bad advice, and decision-makers don't know whether it is good or bad."[7]

Science and Common Sense was intended to demystify science and scientists and thereby integrate them into normal political processes and discussion. Trying to correct the flourishing belief that scientists, and experts generally, held magic keys to unlocking natural, human, or military mysteries, Conant noted dryly that his "own observations" had led him to conclude that "as human beings scientific investigators are statistically distributed over the whole spectrum of human folly and wisdom much as other men," and warned that anyone who claimed that the solution to social, political, or economic ills lay in something known as the "scientific method" would have a "very dubious" hypothesis to defend.[8] In taking this stand so assertively, Conant now seemed to be putting some distance between his views and the tenets of the "Unity of Science" movement he had formerly embraced and for which he still felt considerable sympathy. He had subtly signaled this gap in his greetings to an April 1950 national conference in Boston of the Institute for the Unity of Science, founded three years earlier "to encourage the integration of knowledge by scientific methods." Opening the conference, Philipp Frank had unhesitatingly declared that "the elementary operations of which our scientific knowledge consists" were "essentially the same ones in all fields of science and learning" and could "serve as the building stones for the synthesis and integration of our knowledge in all fields." Frank quoted a 1946 American Academy of Arts and Sciences report endorsing the view "that the spirit, purpose and essential logical and instrumental methodology of science can be applied more or less readily and successfully to any and every form and aspect of knowledge." But then the friendly yet skeptical Conant took a mild dig at that view. It seemed to him that the most accomplished scholars he had encountered were bound not by "a unity of method, but a common agreement as to certain premises that almost unconsciously guide their actions" — most crucially the importance of contributing new ideas and new knowledge. Across-the-board theoretical constructs could not replace, and might even impede, the dynamic advance of science based on common sense and empirical observations. Moreover, since scientists were as susceptible as nonscientists to emotion, bias, "pride of authorship," and other subjective traps, Conant suggested that "exhortations to people to be 'scientific' or to substitute 'controlled inquiry' for judgments based on mere opinion would seem to be somewhat beside the mark."[9] In fact, convinced that "a great deal of nonsense" was being taught along these lines, Conant presented the case studies in *Science and Common Sense* precisely to demolish the voguish idea that there was such a thing as "the scientific method," some impartial and objective process to tackle any dilemma.[10] Rather, he argued, breakthroughs resulted most often from the insights, accidents, coincidences, and creative thoughts of scientists with "prepared minds," who freely indulged their intellectual wanderlust and followed up hunches, as opposed to occurring with the application of brute force, governmental or industrial pressure, or the accumulation and taxonomy of empirical data. Conant's view was that the field should be defined not as some storehouse of knowledge and information but as a tentative and fluid endeavor: "Science is an interconnected series of concepts and conceptual schemes that have been developed as a result of experimentation and observation and are fruitful of further experimentation and observation."[11]

Conant's lucid accounts of earlier conceptual breakthroughs and the debunking of once sacrosanct theories led to his immediate message — about the insidious consequences of the accelerating trend toward applied research, and his hope for a "persistent and effective campaign" to persuade Americans to support basic scientific research. A note of wistfulness crept into his words as he bemoaned the passing of the "uncommitted investigator," a species he said was nearly as extinct as the American buffalo. "The amateur scientist of a century ago and the lone inventor were free as the wind in choosing from day to day the subject on which to focus their intellectual energies," but now this noble figure had given way to the vast industrial research project, the federally financed lab, the lucrative military consultancy. The consequences, to Conant, were both ominous and obvious: "Once the expenditure of money becomes justified in terms of specified aims, the investigator is no longer uncommitted: programmatic research is at hand." Any scientist, laboratory, or institution that contracted to explore a particular problem would work under limitations, implicit or explicit, practical or intellectual, that might cause unanticipated discoveries to be missed—a peril he illuminated in the parable of an unfortunate American chemist who failed to discover argon in the 1880s because the crucial evidence lurking in his data seemed trivial compared to his government assignment.[12]

While it was true that large, well-funded research projects occasionally yielded useful results, Conant insisted that the "pendulum is in danger of swinging too far toward organized programmatic research" directed toward solving "practical problems," and he scorned the massive expansion since 1940 of government laboratories. If it were indeed true that "the significant revolutions, the germinal ideas" of science originated with uncommitted investigators, he observed ominously, "then the present trend holds grave dangers for the future of science in the United States."[13]

In a passionate final chapter (mysteriously omitted a decade later, after Sputnik had shot defense research to the top of the national agenda, when Yale reissued *Science and Common Sense*), Conant fervently warned that the hungry wolf of military domination must not devour the lamb of basic research (support of which was described in a 1952 Defense Department directive as an "integral part of programmed research committed to specific military aims").[14] Given the existence of a "continuous chain running from the laboratory to the battlefield," he asked whether American science—as an open, independent, uncensored, globally collegial enterprise—could make progress when more and more of its activities fell under the aegis of national security. Once again he rode his "hobby horse," which was that each new military program should receive a "quasi-judicial review." And while he carefully balanced criticism of the Pentagon's secrecy and censorship with an attack on Soviet manipulation of science, he flatly asserted a "fundamental incompatibility in having the progress of an international public enterprise [science] closely related to preparation for national defense." The country's "overriding priority is now effective and rapid rearmament," but that did not absolve Americans of the obligation to foster basic science and safeguard its free, open, international nature—the receding nineteenth-century ideal of Conant's youth.[15]

In *Science and Common Sense*, Conant expressed the hope that the soon-to-be established National Science Foundation would support uncommitted investigators pursuing basic research, but he recognized that "in a period of tension and rearmament" this policy would be difficult to stick to, since "almost all the political and social pressures act in a contrary direction."[16] By then, of course, the Korean War had firmly focused "political and social pressures" on military hardware and national security, and the resultant stronger military tone to the government's relationship to science came precisely as perceived shortcomings were causing the government to redefine that relationship. Dissatisfaction ran high over the armed forces' unwieldy research-and-development bureaucracy, a constantly reshuffled deck of committees, agencies, boards, offices, and "groups" racing to carve out fiefdoms in military science, a category that now included basic research, neglected in the delay in establishing NSF.

The Pentagon's Research and Development Board (RDB) was primarily responsible for what James Forrestal called "the application of science to war"; by 1949 it boasted 250 full-time staff members, 1,500 consultants, and hundreds of committees coordinating research projects averaging several hundred thousand dollars each.[17] At the same time, the Office of Naval Research had become academic science's chief bankroller: by 1949, it was signing checks to the tune of $29 million a year to support 1,200 projects at two hundred universities engaging more than 5,000 faculty and graduate-student scientists, in what the National Academy of Sciences later termed "the greatest peacetime cooperative undertaking in history between the academic world and the government."[18] But concerns over the RDB's size, complexity, halting leadership, and diffuse authority had prompted proposals both from Congress and an executive branch panel (headed by ex-NDRC aide Irvin Stewart) to hire a presidential science adviser and to create a new, civilian-run umbrella organization comparable to the wartime OSRD.[19] And the patronage role of the ONR and the National Institutes of Health, the two federal agencies that had stepped in most briskly to support academic scientific research since 1945, fell into doubt when both houses of Congress finally passed—and, on May 10, 1950, Truman finally signed—a bill to create a National Science Foundation to "develop and encourage" scientific research and education and to devise federal science policy.

The five-year mission to create the NSF did not arrive at the goal Bush had described in "Science—The Endless Frontier." He had envisioned a comprehensive civilian-run agency to spearhead the federal government's promotion of basic scientific research, including long-range military research; he wanted it protected from political intrusion, and therefore overseen by an independent board of part-time directors chosen solely for their scientific distinction—precisely the elitist provision, of course, that had elicited Truman's veto of the 1947 NSF bill, since it precluded direct presidential supervision and control. Compromising what in retrospect seems like a rather arcane dispute, the NSF Act of 1950 provided for a largely independent board of directors (the National Science Board), to be named "on the basis of established records of distinguished service," which would in turn nominate candidates for NSF administrator, with the final choice up to the president. Wanting to avoid a politicized or rogue "science czar," the bill tried to bind presidential, legislative, and foundation authorities in a web of mutually balancing checks; in practice this tended to produce confusion and paralysis. More importantly, by 1950, having already voted funds to the Defense Department and Atomic Energy Commission to contract for research, Congress drastically scaled down the foundation, slapping a $15 million ceiling on annual appropriations and dribbling out a token start-up budget of $250,000; this effectively prevented the NSF from competing with far more generously funded rivals for illustrious scientists and research efforts. Rather than subsuming federal science policy under a single agency, as originally envisioned, the NSF only added yet another contestant to an already crowded field.[20]

In October 1950, facing a welter of science-policy dilemmas, Truman deputized the Wall Street investment banker William T. Golden to make sense of the muddle and report back. Golden, a close associate of Lewis Strauss, for the next few months talked to scores of leading figures in science, academia, government, and the armed forces. Not surprisingly, Conant's name soon emerged as a candidate for a top post—Carroll Wilson suggested him for presidential science adviser, Stewart and Rabi considered him a logical NSF chairman—but Golden also heard reports that the old OSRD leadership had made some enemies. Several sources told him that Conant was "too opinionated" and "not sufficiently well-liked," and mentioned the revolt at the National Academy. Better Conant should remain an "elder statesman," Golden was told, than be put in a formal position where he would alienate key scientists. As for Bush, he himself confessed that Truman, unlike FDR, rarely consulted him, and as a result he clearly would be wrong for the adviser's job; another of Golden's contacts reported that Bush had "left scars both on the President and on the military which he feels eliminates him."[21] Still, in November, Conant accepted membership on the National Science Board, and at its first meeting, on December 12, in the "Fish Room" in the West Wing of the White House, he was elected chairman "by a considerable margin" over none other than Detlev W. Bronk—an ironic role reversal that must have tasted bittersweet.[22] He still had no stomach for a full-time defense science post, however, writing a friend that even if a "new OSRD" were formed, "Bush, Compton, and myself are retired veterans and should not be called back into service for this purpose."[23]

Two days later, during a whirlwind visit to Washington that gave him a taste of the panicky atmosphere in the capital after the Chinese intervention in Korea, Conant spent an hour and a half with Golden discussing possible strategies for scientific remobilization. Reluctantly, he recognized that the public clamor for tangible action might necessitate the appointment of a presidential science aide. If such a job were created, Conant told Golden, the job should go to a "younger man," as he and Bush would be more valuable as consultants. He recommended Lee DuBridge—who in fact was too busy at Caltech to take a full-time outside post. But Conant feared a single presidential counselor would be a lightning rod for attacks and appeals, and, almost alone among those Golden consulted (except for Oppenheimer), he strongly preferred a part-time panel to advise the president: this solution expressed his life-long predilection for committees, as well as being a formula that preserved his own influence. Conant doodled some pencil drawings of possible new arrangements for defense research, suggesting that a "new OSRD" might be located in the Defense Department, reporting on a "pari-passu basis" with the ineffectual RDB. It was more advisable to "strengthen the RDB" than to create a new agency, he thought, and gave Golden proofs of *Science and Common Sense*'s last chapter containing his review board proposal. When the subject of the embryonic NSF came up, Conant sadly recognized that "under present mobilization conditions it would be illogical to expect additional funds" for basic research when the foundation was expected to take over ongoing projects from military-related agencies such as ONR and AEC.[24]

Conant seems not to have realized fully to what extent his own promotion of the NSC-68 depiction of the Soviet Union as a grave military threat inflamed precisely the public attitudes that exacerbated the rush to militarize science that he so deplored. On the same day that he met with Golden (and also with Pentagon chiefs to urge universal military service), his friend the Harvard chemist George Kistiakowsky wrote to him warning that his plan for mandatory conscription—headlined that week both in *Look* and in reports about the Committee on the Present Danger—had reawakened fears among college scientists that research and careers would be disrupted because of the draft. There was "already quite a movement underway to sign up for military research 'to hold the department together,'" he told Conant. Kistiakowsky worried that the "present stampede" to wrap the mantle of national security around scientific research would produce "chaos and more than a tolerable amount of boondog[g]ling." Conant rather complacently responded that since there should be no problem protecting qualified scientists from the draft—by then he had amended his no-deferments stand[25]—then "there ought not to be a stampede into military research." Perhaps, he added hopefully, the next meeting of the National Science Board could do something to "create the proper 'climate of opinion.'"[26]

Conant could not have been more wrong about the January 3, 1951, National Science Board meeting, over which he presided after rushing from a late-arriving overnight train from Boston. Truman by then had on his desk a

December 18 report from Golden on the issue of scientific mobilization recommending the appointment of "an outstanding scientific leader" as a presidential adviser who would coordinate military research and "stand ready promptly to initiate" a new Scientific Research Agency comparable to the wartime OSRD. Golden presumed that the NSF, on the other hand, would "concentrate its attentions on basic research, essentially of a non-military character."[27] But at the meeting, the discussion veered off toward military involvement. "Things just snowballed," DuBridge later told Golden (who inferred that Conant "did not have the meeting under as close control as one might have looked for");[28] the board believed that, "given a continuation of international tension," military research and development might be "one of the most important concerns of the Foundation for some time to come."[29] Explaining this unexpected view to White House budget officials, Conant said that the board feared that "opportunities for recruiting good people and arousing real enthusiasm would be seriously limited" if the foundation were excluded from military work.[30] Or, in the more down-to-earth language Golden used: "Somehow National Science Foundation needs a National Defense label to get appropriations and manpower (and hold off General Hershey) and keep its Board happy."[31]

To make matters still more awkward for Conant, among those favoring a greater defense role for NSF was Bronk, who a few hours earlier had won the board's overwhelming endorsement (by secret ballot) as the top choice on the list of nominees for executive director to be passed to Truman. Conant was probably reluctant to challenge Bronk openly, for he reportedly desired the NSF job only if, as his views were paraphrased a few days later, "the military stuff were included."[32] "Bronk unanimous choice but indicates he will serve only if President makes a real job of it," Conant wrote in his diary. "Members feel it should be *the* scientific job and NSF should be in on Defense Research."[33]

So Conant went along. And in a lunchtime Oval Office conference with Truman two days later, he obediently relayed the board's preference for Bronk, whom he didn't much care for, and for a major NSF military role, which he privately opposed. The peppery Truman, known to be lukewarm to NSF, evidently wanted to impress Conant with a display of alacrity and enthusiasm. Clearly surprised, Conant wrote in his diary that Truman had "jumped at Bronk," "wanted NSF in on Defense work," and even "wanted [the NSF] Director to be his adviser!!!"[34]

In fact, and probably to Conant's relief, none of Truman's three stated wishes came true. Truman left the ambitious and reputedly overworked Bronk twisting in the wind for weeks as opposition to him built within the White House staff. By the board's next meeting, on February 13, he had gotten the hint and dropped out of the running.[35] As intrigue over the NSF directorship persisted, Conant's and Bush's already low estimate of the insidious effect of Washington politics on scientific matters dropped still further. Bush told Conant that DuBridge would be called in "to head a new office on part time, that he will take it & 'ball everything up' and the Boys around the White House will double cross him!"[36] And Conant was shaken by a minor incident that testified to the fragility of the new agency and to the power of McCarthyism. As Conant put it in his diary, there was a "last minute hitch on security!" that nearly ruined his hopes for the NSF post going to his next choice: the physicist Alan T. Waterman, a cautious, respected ONR administrator and OSRD veteran, to whom the White House turned after another one of Conant's friends, the chemist Roger Adams, turned Truman down.[37]

On Friday morning, March 9, with Waterman's appointment a virtual *fait accompli,* Conant got an urgent summons to leave a National Science Board meeting and proceed "posthaste" to the White House. There, he recalled vividly many years later,

> I met a man who was acting as special counsel to President Truman. He said in effect that the security check on Waterman was unsatisfactory; the appointment could not be made. I was flabbergasted. What could be wrong? Waterman had had access to all sorts of highly classified material in his work in the Naval Research Laboratory. I knew him well, as did Dr. Bush; it was unthinkable that the administration would balk at this late date.
>
> "The trouble is with his wife," was the answer. "The file shows that Mrs. Waterman has been to the Soviet Embassy twice for tea." I almost exploded with annoyance. "Can such a trivial report block an excellent appointment?" I exclaimed. "It seems ridiculous." "So it may to you," President Truman's spokesman said, "but with the atmosphere what it is on the Hill, we cannot proceed with this appointment unless you can personally guarantee the man and stand ready to give full public endorsement." I gave the assurance, and the matter proceeded as scheduled. The words "with the atmosphere what it is on the Hill, we cannot proceed," remained with me; the incident I would never forget. "Against what follies must the executive branch struggle?" I thought.[38]

The allegations that nearly torpedoed Waterman's nomination included "social" contacts with the Polish embassy, attendance at Paul Robeson rallies, a daughter who once visited Warsaw, and a wife who was "generally held to be 'ultra-liberal,'" although—thank heavens!—not a "fellow traveller or communist."[39] In other words, as Conant wrote in his diary: "Not much there! But the 'climate of opinion' has the boys scared!"[40] Nonetheless, Truman, his political backside protected by Conant's testimonial, announced Waterman's nomination. A White House aide quickly hand-delivered the wire-service ticker-tape to Conant, back at the National Science Board, whose members greeted the news with "audible relief and enthusiasm"; at 4:30 p.m., Waterman met "at long last" with the board, and then joined Conant and Bronk for a working dinner.[41]

Their conversation revealed a distinctly changed atmosphere since the tense days of early January, when it had appeared almost inevitable that the new foundation would gallop down the path of military research. Then, Conant had argued to Truman's staff that NSF should "take over a substantial portion" of ONR's massive research empire—"the sooner the transfer is made, the better," he insisted, brushing aside suggestions that this required "careful, if not extended, consideration"[42]—which reflected his long-standing assumption that a proper National Science Foundation would reclaim studies that had been supported by the armed forces and the AEC since the end of the war on a supposedly provisional basis.[43] But neither the military research sponsors nor their generously funded scientists wanted to break off the affair. Both were equally aghast at the prospect of seeing their flourishing enter- prises dropped into the hands of an uncertain, untested, meagerly funded new agency, subject annually to the whims of penurious congressmen certain to scrutinize taxpayer-supported "pure science" while happily voting gold buckets for "national security." Insisting that it needed to keep abreast of current developments in many fields, ONR reneged on its earlier commit- ment to transfer research to NSF, and many educational leaders, notwith- standing their high-sounding statements about the importance of scientific independence, feared what would happen if the Pentagon stopped paying for basic research. In 1949, Lee DuBridge had eloquently extolled the virtues of a civilian NSF devoted to basic research, wringing his hands over military and AEC funding of science and proclaiming: "When science is allowed to exist merely from the crumbs that fall from the table of a weapons development program then science is headed into the stifling atmosphere of 'mobilized secrecy' and it is surely doomed—even though the crumbs themselves should provide more than adequate nourishment."[44] But simultaneously DuBridge was "busily sweeping up those crumbs for the nourishment of his demanding brood of scientists," as one writer has put it—there were numerous Pentagon- backed projects at Caltech, including intensive studies on rocket propulsion— and he fretted that Caltech would go broke if the NSF gained responsibility over the military's basic research programs.[45]

Such concerns were shared by many academic leaders and scientists and complemented by the military's own well-developed turf-protecting instincts, and they could be rationalized in the loftier context of a commitment to the NSF's sacred mission of promoting fundamental science. A memo that Golden wrote to Truman in mid-February (and Conant circulated to the National Science Board) exemplified this new viewpoint. Heavy involvement in defense research, Golden argued, "would seriously impair the long-term mission of NSF without materially contributing to the war effort, since such work can better be done by other agencies." Besides, since the Pentagon planned to double its investment in short-term applied weapons work, rather than in basic research, NSF didn't stand to gain much from buttering it up. Moreover, the improved military situation in Korea was easing fears of global war and, consequently, pressures for full scientific mobilization. Finally, Truman had by then rejected the idea of a personal science adviser and endorsed instead the creation of a defense science advisory panel.[46]

Thus, when they dined on March 9 Conant, Bronk, and Waterman agreed that while NSF should be willing to undertake defense work if the Pentagon requested it, it should emphasize sponsorship of "really fundamental research" and definitely "should not be put in position of becoming another OSRD." The problem was to make basic science "seem valuable to the taxpayer" and avoid "ever diminishing budgets." (Earlier in the day the board had optimistically presumed that the foundation would receive its maximum $15 million allotment for 1952, and projected an operating plan that included $7.5 million for research and $6.5 million for a generous fellowship program.)[47]

Convincing Congress to fund a defense-less NSF turned out to be difficult, to put it mildly. "You may have trouble getting money out of those fellows over in Congress," Truman had told the National Science Board at its first meeting. "I will help."[48] But cautious White House budget officials considered the board's budget package a "very crude affair" and opposed rushing ahead with a "half-baked" and "over-ambitious" fellowship program despite Conant's admonition that the need for it was "so clear and so strong that a major beginning should be made at once."[49] Their skepticism was nothing, however, compared to that shown by the House of Representatives, which in August 1951 slashed the proposed budget for 1952, the NSF's first full year of operations, by ninety-eight percent, from a requested $14 million down to $300,000 on the grounds that the new agency was "unlikely to provide assistance to the country in the immediate emergency."[50] Scientists across the country, as well as the *New York Times* and *Washington Post,* shrieked in outrage at so blatant a sign of congressional contempt. Hearing the bad news during a summer tour in Australia and New Zealand, Conant publicly excoriated this "severe blow to the cause of science" and helped to organize NSF's counterattack when he returned.[51] Leading a phalanx of science notables— including Waterman, Bronk, Buckley, and Oppenheimer— who trooped up to testify before the House Appropriations Committee, Conant delivered his best sales pitch. Predictably, he stressed the "enormous role" of science and technology in "arming the free world," and the NSF's potential contribution to national defense: "The point I should like to emphasize is that the development of new weapons and new industries to produce new weapons depends on (a) having a supply of well-trained scientists and engineers, and (b) having new scientific discoveries." Asking for a $12.6 million appropriation for 1952, Conant also noted ominously that the Soviets were sponsoring "a great deal" of useful scientific research.[52] But even loaded Cold War arguments had only limited effect, and the foundation got a mere $3.5 million.[53] Conant consoled Waterman that the "important thing" was that at least it could now "get off the ground" and into operation with a complete staff.[54] But both men well understood that while its exclusion from the high-stakes defense R&D business might help the NSF avoid onerous restrictions—and indeed, it bravely fended off FBI investigations of fellowship recipients, censorship, and classification restrictions—its negligible funding ensured that it remained a sapling among redwoods in the dense forest of federal science support. Lacking budgetary or political power, moreover, NSF would be in no position effectively to influence the direction, utility, or ethics of military-funded research.[55]

Not that this disappointed most of the academic world. "After Korea, few complained about the predominance of the military's presence in civilian science," the historian Daniel J. Kevles has observed, adding that America's scientific leadership "breathed a collective sigh of relief when it became clear that very little basic research would be transferred to the NSF and that most such research would continue to be supported in the pluralist system that had grown up since 1945 under the military's generous and predominant patronage."[56] The five-year delay in establishing the NSF, as well as the bruising battle over its initial budgets, only reinforced the scientists' preference for the defense establishment. "While old men in congresses and parliaments would debate the allocation of a few thousand dollars," wrote the approving authors of one study, "farsighted generals and admirals would not hesitate to divert substantial sums to help the oddballs in Princeton, Cambridge, and Los Alamos."[57]

Although "not happy about the way the support of science and the armed forces were becoming closely connected," as chairman of the National Science Board Conant felt constrained, as he later wrote, "to make the best of a situation which had developed in many institutions."[58] That regret applied equally to his tenure on the Science Advisory Committee (SAC), which Truman established in April 1951 in part to keep a watchful eye on the developing science-military relationship. Formed when jockeying bureaucrats and scientists arrived at Conant's preference for a committee rather than a single presidential adviser, the ten-member group reunited the usual suspects: SAC included five GAC members (Buckley, Conant, DuBridge, Oppenheimer, and Walter G. Whitman) and five NSF board representatives (Waterman, Conant, DuBridge, Bronk, and Robert F. Loeb). Named to chair the group was Buckley, the recently retired head of Bell Labs, who, along with Monsanto president Charles A. Thomas, lent industrial connections; RDB chairman William Webster, navy alumnus Waterman and ONR consultants Oppenheimer and DuBridge assured military research links; Hugh Dryden represented the executive branch's Interdepartmental Committee on Scientific Research and Development; Bronk, Conant, DuBridge, and Killian skimmed the elite of academic science.

Notwithstanding its prestigious provenance, SAC had a difficult birth as well as a tenuous early childhood. Due to Buckley's reticence as well as bureaucratic intriguing by "the Truman palace guard," as Killian later recalled, it initially was put outside the White House in the Office of Defense Mobilization (ODM), reporting to its director, Gen. Lucius D. Clay, instead of directly to Truman.[59] Shortly before its first meeting, defense secretary Robert Lovett confessed to having only "fragmentary knowledge" of what it was supposed to do, and complained of "too many super level groups in existence."[60] Indeed, the Science Advisory Committee failed to live up to its creators' and members' expectations of serving as a source of firsthand advice for the president. In his April 1951 message establishing the group, Truman stated his intention to consult "from time to time" on scientific aspects of defense, foreign, and intelligence policies,[61] but the part-time committee rarely if ever drew Truman's notice, served only as a low-key liaison, generated vague, unexceptionable, roundly ignored reports, and waited for a crisis—e.g., World War III—to call them into a more active mode. Under Buckley's diffident leadership, the group met sporadically, eschewed publicity, hired only a minimal staff, and showed little initiative, neither influencing executive policy, curbing the military sponsorship of academic research, nor promoting Conant's idea (which he advanced to the group in January 1952) of a "quasi-judicial" board to referee major military research and development programs.[62] "Buckley didn't want the committee to do anything except figure out what scientists might do in another war emergency," DuBridge later recalled. "The rest of us were frustrated. We didn't see much point in just writing reports for a file drawer."[63] Oppenheimer believed it had perhaps helped "keep some balance" between military and civilian scientific research interests—"a balance," in the words of one committee statement, "appropriate to the times, between the normal functions of academic science, and the abnormal and immediate demands of military problems."[64] But Conant soon grew impatient, and became convinced in a matter of months that by refusing to assume leadership in screening big defense projects for universities the committee was "shirking its responsibility."[65]

In a May 1952 one-year progress report to Truman, Buckley noted that the SAC had not assumed an "operating function," had developed into an "excellent forum" to exchange opinions, and had provided informal advice to educational associations on screening huge defense projects.[66] For the most part, however, it functioned as an elite watering hole, seminar series, and "skeleton OSRD" in search of a mission.

When DuBridge became SAC's chairman in mid-1952—after Buckley resigned because of poor health—and Eisenhower was elected president that November, the exasperated members were galvanized to reassess the desultory existence of what Oppenheimer bluntly called "our good-for-nothing committee."[67] DuBridge was a more dynamic political operator than Buckley, and at his first meeting as chairman, on June 15, he and Oppenheimer suggested elevating SAC from the Office of Defense Mobilization to the more powerful National Security Council—so, in DuBridge's words, "the President can get better scientific assessments of the situations behind the decisions which he has to make; for example, the 'H' bomb"[68] — but Truman rejected the idea.[69] Just after Election Day, most of the group (Conant was in Cambridge with a bad cold) assembled at the Institute for Advanced Study, Oppenheimer's lair in Princeton, for a "leisurely" three-day conference "away from the hurly burly of Washington" to draft a statement to be conveyed to Eisenhower's transition team. All those present agreed that the group should either be put out of its misery and disbanded or, conversely, elevated to a more powerful position. Since SAC had had "few — if any" occasions to advise the president, their report to Eisenhower stated, as then structured it was "not needed in the national interest" and could be safely eliminated. However, the government needed scientifically literate decision-makers and, therefore, a more powerful, better staffed and financed, and "truly deliberative" presidential science advisory body: obviously the SAC members preferred the latter course, and argued that a beefed-up SAC should have an active part in policy formulation: "Experience has convinced us of one general point. It is not enough for planning bodies to be 'briefed' on scientific matters before making their decisions. Men conversant with the scientific background must participate in the process of making these decisions."[70]

Conant made his views known in a phone call and a memorandum agreeing with the idea of dissolving SAC and with the "urgent need for more effective use of science and technology manpower in the rearmament effort"; he presumed the place for a new overall director and coordinator of military research and development would be in the Defense Department.[71] He warmly applauded the put-up or shut-up message, though he expressed concern, quickly dispelled by DuBridge, that SAC might evolve into an "incipient NDRC" and complicate an already tangled situation if it tried to "experiment," i.e., sponsor applied research.[72]

Eisenhower and his aides, while not instantly transferring SAC to the White House as DuBridge hoped, responded favorably to the entreaty to take science and technology more seriously. Not only did SAC stay in business but, under DuBridge's more active tutelage and with the creation of a technological capabilities panel headed by Killian, it initiated important studies on ballistic missiles, long-range aerial reconnaissance (leading to the U-2 program), and (at Ike's personal request) the dangers of surprise attack. Equally important, it preserved an institutional base that Eisenhower could use in 1957, when Sputnik propelled science to the top of the political agenda: amid great fanfare, he rechristened SAC the President's Science Advisory Committee (PSAC) and named Killian his personal science adviser — a post later filled by George Kistiakowsky and, in the Kennedy administration, by Jerome Wiesner.[73] By then, Conant and Oppenheimer were long gone from the scene — for differing, but related, reasons that were, in fact, foreshadowed at the November 1952 Princeton meeting.

With Oppenheimer, Conant, and DuBridge by then already evicted from the General Advisory Committee, the SAC represented a last bastion of relatively liberal scientific advice in the executive branch—perhaps one reason it had fallen into disuse. Acutely aware of the hostility of some scientists to his skepticism about nuclear energy, the H-bomb, and nuclear weapons development in general, Conant had frankly expressed a desire to bow out of the science-advisory scene and, if possible, to take some enemies with him. Any SAC statement, he had urged Oppenheimer, must frankly recognize the "present cleavage of opinion among some of the older scientists of the country . . . and if and when a reorganization of research and development is attempted, the avowed partisans on both sides should withdraw or be eliminated from the picture, [and] younger men not identified with the present bitter feeling should be introduced as the leaders."[74]

Conant soon learned that the tensions were even sharper than he imagined. At lunch at Killian's house on November 25, he found out what his well-connected host had told the other SAC members at the Princeton conference, during which, over cocktails at Oppenheimer's house, Killian had "the distasteful responsibility" of reporting rumors emanating from the air force that the physicist's security clearance might be challenged. Now he passed word to Conant, who wrote in his diary afterward of a "Long talk on the 'split' among the scientists about national defense and the 'dirty ball' being played on Oppenheimer."[75]

This unsavory scuttlebutt coincided with the long-dreaded first test of the hydrogen bomb, and made Conant all the more anxious to give up his positions in the government's administration of military research. By now, he sounded even more profoundly disturbed by the direction that military sponsorship was taking science than he had two years earlier in *Science and Common Sense*. Even in February 1952, when he returned to the National War College for another address to officers, this was amply clear: his scorn of the Pentagon's faith in technology would resonate decades later in debates over "Star Wars" and other military proposals whose technical sophistication and complexity sometimes overwhelmed calculations of feasibility and utility. Before the atomic bomb, Conant recalled, a principal hindrance to weapons development had been the "technological conservatism" of military officers who were "perhaps unduly slow in some cases to take up new ideas developed by the civilian scientists, full of enthusiasm who came down here with many wild ideas." But since then the situation had completely reversed:

It seems to me something like the old religious phenomenon of conversion. As I see it now, the military, if anything, have become vastly too much impressed with the abilities of research and development. They are no longer the conservatives. I don't know what I should say—at times they seem to be fanatics in their belief of what the scientists and the technologists can do. As I see it, in a word, the Defense Department is now like the story of the man who sprang on his horse and rode madly off in all directions; in other words, some of your colleagues have become infected with the virus that is so well known in academic circles, the virus of enthusiasm of the scientist and the inventor.[76]

During the spring of 1952, Conant elaborated his dour appraisal in a series of widely publicized speeches. On March 17, during a two-week visit to Europe, he delivered the third annual Stevenson Memorial Lecture to the London School of Economics and Political Science and the Royal Institute of International Affairs. It was a delicate moment to be speaking under the heading of "Anglo-American Relations in the Atomic Age." Those relations, as Conant knew better than anyone, had been fraught with hidden strains of distrust and suspicion—mostly still secret—even during the publicly hailed wartime collaboration. After the war the two countries had angrily divorced their nuclear programs: Congress had been outraged at Roosevelt's wartime agreements at Quebec and Hyde Park to continue atomic collaboration with Britain after the war and to obtain its assent before using the weapon, and in short order it had induced the administration to abrogate those commitments and sharply curtail U.S.-U.K. atomic ties. Meanwhile, both Labour and Tory politicians agreed that national glory as well as geopolitics required Great Britain to have an atomic bomb, with or without the United States' blessing, and in 1947 the British government launched an all-out effort to build and explode one. In early 1949, Conant, Oppenheimer, and other U.S. atomic advisers had vainly tried to revive closer coordination with London rather than to block a British bomb—with Conant chairing a high-level meeting at the Institute for Advanced Studies of State Department, military, and AEC officials that secretly recommended that the administration seek a U.S.-U.K.-Canada agreement to restore full atomic interchange among the three countries [77]—but the talks bogged down and Washington's enthusiasm plunged in 1950 after learning that Klaus Fuchs, who worked at Los Alamos under British auspices, had betrayed secrets to the Russians.[78] The Americans' mistrust then multiplied in the summer of 1951, when two British diplomats who had served at their country's embassy in the United States, Donald D. Maclean (posted to Washington from May 1944 through September 1948) and Guy Burgess (August 1950 to April 1951), defected to Moscow; aghast, U.S. officials concluded that Maclean, in particular, had been able to inform the Kremlin of details of American atomic policy making and even stockpile information at key junctures such as the Berlin blockade crisis, and worried that a "third man" inside the British government had tipped the two spies off to growing security suspicions about them in time for them to make a hasty getaway.[79]

It had been Maclean, coincidentally, who in 1948 had officially informed the State Department of Britain's independent atomic bomb project, and now, as Conant spoke in March 1952, London's effort was nearing fruition (the first fission blast would take place in Australia on October 3). Familiar as he was with the secret history of Anglo-American atomic acrimony, Conant had vowed that he would graze this "ticklish" subject only obliquely. "I shall be discreetly silent," he wrote to Oppenheimer, "except to indicate that the very mystery and secrecy that surrounds these developments can cause difficulty not only across the Iron Curtain but also between the best of friends." He also hoped to "kill the idea so prevalent, I'm told, in England in certain circles that they, and they alone, are the targets for a possible atomic attack."[80] To his hosts before the talk, Conant worried that a frank airing of the U.S.-U.K. atomic dispute would be inadvisable, not because of security restrictions, but because "of the difficulty of saying publicly some things which could be misused by the propaganda agencies within the Soviet Union." With Anglo-American relations "at a rather low point, alas," he hoped to reduce tensions. "Whether I shall succeed remains to be seen."[81]

True to form, Conant praised Anglo-American collaboration in NATO, expressed regret over the breakdown in Anglo-American "co-operation in all aspects of applied nuclear physics," recommended a renewal of joint studies — an ironic position for the man perhaps most responsible for curtailing such cooperation during the Manhattan Project — and judiciously chided "malicious whispering on both sides of the Atlantic about the alleged carelessness of the British in keeping secrets and the alleged hysteria as to Communist spies in the United States."[82]

The crux of his lecture was a topic "heavy with grief" — the "highly unpleasant revolution" in science and international affairs since World War II. "Write down the words 'science' and 'international relations,'" Conant challenged his audience, "think of the events of the past six years and envision the immediate future; if after this you aren't subject to at least a momentary fit of depression, you are a hardy character indeed." Harking back again to the convivial, noble profession that had won his heart as a youth, Conant plaintively recalled the bygone days of universal scientific fraternity, when a British chemist honored by France during the Napoleonic Wars could invoke the duty of scientists to "soften the asperity of national war." But the advent of the atomic bomb, equating a branch of science with national security, had slammed the door on that era: "Whether we like it or not, we must face the fact that today, as in the Second World War, a large proportion of the scientific skill of the heavily industrialized nations of the world is concerned with improving the killing power of weapons." In what he described as a "new type of social machinery," Conant disparagingly noted the unprecedented emergence of a scientific field — applied nuclear physics — as a virtual government monopoly, dependent on large taxpayer funds, shrouded in secrecy, and "justified in terms of the destructive power of a weapon required in a desperate global struggle."

Another "post-Hiroshima cultural problem" that troubled Conant — and here the Anglo-American atomic rivalry came through clearly — was the crude identification of national and political prestige with the nuclear physicists' terrible achievements. Given the dramatic claims that atomic power could vest the virtual power of the gods in the hands of man, Conant asked,

> Is it strange that politicians in free nations as well as totalitarian States have felt a peculiar possessive pride in the advances in applied nuclear physics made by their compatriots? Quite apart from military considerations, therefore, pre-eminence in atomic energy developments has become a matter of national pride—and pride in an undertaking that was born and raised in secrecy.[83]

In late April, Conant delivered the prestigious Bampton Lectures at Columbia University—over four nights, to packed houses, stitching together strands from his earlier speeches to continue his exegesis of the radical social and cultural alterations in science induced by modern warfare and weapons.[84] (Between the lectures, which he had originally agreed to deliver when invited by Eisenhower, then still at Columbia, Conant took advantage of the prolonged New York stay to catch up with old acquaintances; at dinner one night with an ailing Reinhold Niebuhr, he recorded in his diary, the two men and their spouses pondered "presidential candidates and the Book of Job!")[85] These lectures were still another attempt to communicate a coherent philosophy of science to a lay audience, another chance for Conant to impart a skeptical view of scientists and "experts," to reject reliance on a "scientific method" to resolve social or moral quandaries, to decry the pernicious effects of government and military secrecy, and to plead for a more sober assessment of atomic energy and weapons development. More poignantly, they also expressed his grief at twentieth-century science's radical departures. Fear of the atomic bomb and other new "awesome" weapons, he declared, had helped instill universal dread and apprehension, spurred a "wave of enthusiasm for religious worship that has been mounting in the English-speaking nations in the last dozen years," and introduced a "novel and highly significant element into the complex relations between science and society." Even if fear of nuclear devastation should wane, as he hoped, he admitted reluctantly that the old relations of science and society would not automatically return. "Let me make it plain—I wish they would: I do not like the atomic age or any of its consequences. To learn to adjust to these consequences with charity and sanity is the chief spiritual problem of our time."[86]

The bomb merely marked the thunderous climax of an evolutionary process that wove science together with wider societal forces, Conant explained. From around 1700, when modern science "first reached the walking and talking stage," until World War I, each generation gathered up the beneficial inventions of previous ages and looked forward expectantly to further progress. Then the twentieth century's two global wars and the development of atomic weapons had completely changed the social role and context of science— changes that paralleled those in Conant's own life, though he did not mention them, from teenage tinkerer to World War I poison-gas maker to Du Pont consultant to top-secret wartime administrator. The Second World War, he asserted, taught the general public about a new reality that modern industry already appreciated: the old-fashioned scientist, a long-haired loner working "in an ivory tower gradually unravelling the secrets of nature for his own spiritual satisfaction," had turned into an inventor, relied upon by state, business, and society alike for destructive weapons, miraculous cures, and "tremendous transformations of man's relation to his material surroundings."[87]

World War I's chief innovation, poison gas, had only a limited effect on science, because it failed to open any significant vistas for research. "How completely otherwise it was in the manufacture of the atomic bomb!" Conant remarked. The government constructed previously unimaginable and prohibitively expensive tools to test the dreams, theories, and extrapolations of nuclear physicists and chemists, but participating in this bonanza required scientists to dive into a "turbulent and, at times, a muddy stream" where science, technology, and politics merged—and to accept a regime of secrecy that endangered their tradition of free exchanges and discussion, essential to the flowering and cross-fertilization of new theories.

"Destroy the social nature of scientific research in the sense of destroying the intercommunication of scientists, and the advance of science would almost cease," Conant warned. "Recognizing this fact, one must ponder on the consequences of the vast sums of money now being spent on secret military research and development undertakings. One cannot help wondering how long a large fraction of our scientific manpower can be employed in this atypical scientific work without threatening the traditions that have made science possible."

Though Harvard tried to maintain a "business as usual" atmosphere, even Cambridge could not remain cloistered as the pressures of the Cold War closed in. Driving west from the city, Conant would pass a sign by the highway reading: "In case of enemy attack, this road will be closed to all but military vehicles." What disturbed him was the fact that it wasn't a rusting reminder of World War II, but a fresh notice put up after the first Soviet atomic blast in 1949.[88] When Russian bombardiers drew up target plans for Cambridge, they presumably concentrated on the other end of Massachusetts Avenue, where MIT's defense work boomed, but Harvard, too, responded to the stimulus of federal and military support for science.

One episode in Harvard's astronomy department testifies both to the skepticism many scientists felt about the NSF and to the incentives to devise research agendas in the physical sciences tilted toward the Pentagon funders. In the late 1940s and early 1950s, two senior Harvard astronomers, Fred Whipple and Donald Menzel, won handsome contracts from the signal corps and air force, respectively, while a third, Bart J. Bok, resisted military funding for his "pure" observational studies of the Milky Way and instead looked for support from the fledgling NSF. Eventually, Bok recalls, he left

Harvard in disgust, primarily because "my colleagues made me feel that Milky Way Astronomy was a silly field to be involved in, when there was plenty of military money in other areas." According to his bitter retrospective account,

> Whipple made very strong points in our faculty meeting that Harvard couldn't afford to keep Bart Bok any longer. Bart Bok had that silly interest in the Milky Way and he wanted to do radio astronomy of the Milky Way. That was so expensive, and he had some hope in that silly National Science Foundation that was never going to amount to anything. What you should have is military funding, he thought.
>
> My colleagues had the nerve to tell me to get out of Milky Way astronomy, and to go into meteor astronomy. "Because meteors," says Whipple, "are the cheapest slugs that God almighty sends for the Signal Corps, and they all love it, and they would support your research. You can do your radio astronomy, but for God's sake, man, get away from your silly Milky Way. There's no point to that. What you ought to do is get into meteors. They are running through the atmosphere. They want to study deceleration, that's the way to study.[89]

Although the university never formally overturned Conant's injunction against classified work on campus, the Korean War sharply changed the atmosphere there, as elsewhere, and by 1951 Harvard had made an exception for a Business School study for the Defense Department and signed nearly a hundred contracts with more than twenty-five government agencies totaling more than $4 million annually in military-related research.[90] It enthusiastically cooperated with "summer studies" and other short-duration national security projects undertaken at MIT, and carried out a 1951 investigation for the navy on infrared detection (Project Metcalf).[91] Beyond institutional contracts, individual Harvard faculty made consulting arrangements that often included classified work. At the urging of the Harvard physics department, to which he was a member of an Overseers' visiting committee, Robert Oppenheimer personally urged Conant to allow members of the department to take leaves of absence to work on defense projects.[92] Among senior faculty members who had toiled during the war for the government and were called back into service were the historian William L. Langer, the OSS veteran who was summoned in late 1950 to set up the CIA's new Office of National Estimates, described in the agency's official history as "the heart of the national system of intelligence";[93] Buckminster Fuller, using ONR dollars to train pigeons to guide missiles; experts at the Russian Research Center; and the physicist Norman Ramsey and law professor Walter Barton Leach, both air force consultants. "Numerous members of the university staff are heavily involved as consultants in highly confidential scientific matters connected with the armed forces," Conant reported in January 1952. "Indeed many professors here and elsewhere find themselves perplexed as to how to divide their time between calls from the government and their responsibilities as scholars and teachers."[94] Conant pressed the Association of American Universities to approve guidelines restricting the time spent by and benefits accorded to faculty who engaged in military activities, but in the process he crossed swords with presidents of institutions heavily involved in defense work, such as MIT and Caltech; also, he closely monitored military contracts to assure that they did not impose onerous security requirements or clearance procedures, and tried to assure that Harvard's teachers and departments did not become dependent on outside funding.[95]

Conant devoted much of what was in fact his final annual Commencement address, on a rainy afternoon in June 1952, to warnings against what he called "elephantiasis" in the natural sciences—a disease characterized by bigger budgets and bigger projects (of which Lawrence's cyclotron was the prototype) directed at applied and "practical" results. Too many scientists, he warned the throng in Harvard Yard, bent to the force of uncontested pressure for "practical and immediate" rather than "fundamental and enduring" research. Biologists scurried for a cure to cancer rather than probing fundamental processes, and in physical sciences "some of our best men are now spending long hours on military problems. This is a national necessity," he conceded, "but a loss to the advance of science." Fearing that such tendencies "threaten the long-term contribution of the Harvard company of scholars," he valiantly praised "those scholars whose work will be remembered a century hence even if it may have little relevance for these grim and trying days."[96]

Conant at times sounded melancholic as the tilt toward applied work became more and more pronounced—he conceded morosely to the *Harvard Crimson* in late 1952 that "since 1933 I can't claim to have advanced the barriers of science one millimeter."[97] And the following January, the physicist Percy W. Bridgman put this tribute to him into the record at a faculty meeting:

> There are many threats to our universities; among the most formidable of these is domination by Government. This is especially true in President Conant's own area, the physical sciences. All of us, scientists and nonscientists, will continue for many years to be indebted to President Conant's insistence that Government support for projects in this University be kept to a minimum.[98]

Yet, Conant accepted and endorsed the need for his faculty's participation in the Cold War, and he joined in the SAC's statement that regretfully but firmly supported a strong academic contribution to military work and wholeheartedly endorsed faculty leaves for participation in defense studies. "It is our view," SAC held in September 1951, "that under present circumstances the major part of our academic research effort should continue to be devoted to fundamental research but that a substantial portion of the effort, and particularly that of those best qualified by experience and abilities, should be applied to defense research in a way to meet present urgent defense needs and at the same time build up throughout the academic community a widespread knowledge of the scientific problems of defense and a reserve of scientists to meet extreme emergencies should they arise."[99] By 1952, SAC told Truman, only ten percent of Pentagon research funds went to colleges and universities, yet many academic institutions were "now dependent to a great degree on this source of funds"[100] — a dependency that only increased for the remainder of the decade. As one historian has summarized it:

> The university administrator, however seriously concerned for his institution's independence, could hardly resist the combined pressures of the would-be sponsors dangling contracts, his own scientists — first and foremost, the physicists — pressing for such facilities as only the military could provide, and not least important, the leading spokesmen for science — again nearly all physicists, electrical engineers, applied mathematicians — invoking and promoting continuation of the wartime "partnership" with the military.[101]

Although in the mid-1950s the Defense Department tried to cut back on fundamental science and transfer projects to NSF — with Secretary Charles E. Wilson issuing the derisive verdict that "Basic research is when you don't know what you are doing"[102] — the frenzied reaction to Sputnik and the alleged "missile gap" reinvigorated the government's devotion to sponsoring military research and development in all forms, proportionately exceeding, by the end of the decade, World War II peak spending levels.[103] And at the end of his presidency, Eisenhower, in the same January 1961 Farewell Address that immortalized the phrase "military-industrial complex," also sounded a note of alarm, with which his friend Conant strongly agreed, about government-financed academic research. The "revolution" in research at universities, "historically the fountainhead of free ideas and scientific discovery," Ike warned, had created a situation where the "prospect of domination of the nation's scholars by Federal employment, project allocations, and the power of money is ever present — and gravely to be regarded."[104]

It is still unclear, almost a half-century later, to what extent the mutual embrace of academic science and government (particularly military) funding has borne out Conant's fears that it would inevitably distort scientific progress. In 1970, when there were mass protests against secret Pentagon research on America's campuses, Conant looked back ruefully at the history of the "close connection between university research and the armed forces" and tried to show that the entire development "was in a sense an accident." The fault lay, he claimed, in Truman's failure to press Congress to immediately enact into law Vannevar Bush's 1945 proposal (in *Science — The Endless Frontier*) for a national research agency that vested *all* support of basic science in civilian hands. Harvard had endorsed Conant's proposal to ban classified research, but "Few if any other universities followed Harvard's lead." ONR and other military agencies had made arrangements to have classified research done at universities all over the country. "Truman signed [the bill to establish NSF] but it was too late," Conant lamented. "The armed forces had taken over."[105]

This analysis has been faulted on several grounds. First, not only Truman but an unruly Congress contributed to the deadlock that delayed NSF's creation by five years.[106] More importantly, the key impetus behind the expanded military involvement in the sponsorship of American science since World War II was not any particular administrative or institutional arrangement but Cold War imperatives, mindsets, and priorities—which Conant himself had actively promulgated.[107] Nevertheless, Conant's concerns remain cogent, and the debate persists whether American scientists have exploited the Pentagon to expand the frontiers of knowledge or whether the military has manipulated American science. "What *direction* of the advance of science, and thus what *kind* of science, resulted from military sponsorship?" asked Paul Forman in 1987, arguing that American physicists had "blinded themselves" to the fact that, by narrowing their research ambitions to fit the Pentagon's grant criteria, they had "lost control of their discipline [and] were now far more used *by* than using American society, far more exploited by than exploiting the new forms and terms of their social integration."[108] Less contemptuous but equally critical, Daniel J. Kevles responded that the Cold War quickened "not the seduction of American physics from some true path but its increased integration as both a research and advisory enterprise into the national-security system." The Korean War, Kevles concluded, "along with further enriching civilian science, had tied its laboratories and advisory apparatus closer to the state in ways that, at least in the mid-1950s, amplified the opportunities and, in some respects, the incentives to intensify the arms race."[109]

In his memoirs, Conant reaffirmed his stand against classified research at universities during "peacetime" yet disagreed with critics of the war in Vietnam who claimed that "since war is evil a university should have nothing to do with" weapons research.[110] But some months later, speaking when he was nearing eighty, he gave a blunter account. Considering the sight of students angrily picketing university labs doing secret work, he was unable to resist saying "something which old men should be forbidden to say, namely: 'I told you so.' "[111]

CHAPTER 29

God and Man at Harvard

To equate secular with godless and then godless with immoral, or at least amoral, is surely a fallacious line of argumentation.
—Baccalaureate sermon, June 18, 1950

I am frankly very much disturbed by the turn which President Conant's thought has taken.
—Reinhold Niebuhr, letter, June 22, 1950

Religion I believe is not primarily a basis for ethics but an attempt to organize metaphysical speculations and historical traditions in a way to enable people to handle situations.
—JBC, course outline, 1952

Conant's philosophy of science—a "mixture of William James's *Pragmatism* and the Logical Empiricism of the Vienna Circle with at least two jiggers of pure skepticism thrown in," as he put it himself—explicitly rejected claims that science or a "scientific method" was better as a guide to ethical human conduct than spiritual beliefs or that it could discover the "minimal assumptions" common to the moral tenets of the world's great religions.[1] But in firmly denying science's supremacy in the conduct of human affairs, the "skeptical chemist" was hardly in agreement with ecclesiastical leaders like Pope Pius XII, who in a 1951 address to the Pontifical Academy of Science interpreted modern cosmology to mean that "true science to an ever-increasing degree discovers God as though God were waiting behind each closed door opened by science."[2] For behind each door opened by science Conant expected to discover—indeed eagerly anticipated discovering—another closed door with a lock for scientists to pick, not an omnipotent deity impervious to understanding. Science offered sublime opportunities for the expansion of the human mind and spirit, yielding theories and advances every bit as monumental as the Parthenon or the cathedrals of the Middle Ages. But in seeking answers to the philosophical, theological, and political quandaries troubling Americans in the atomic age, Conant used the bully pulpit of the Harvard presidency to make clear that he vested his faith in neither science nor religion but in secular institutions that would give Americans the means to develop their full potential and to "serve better thy country and thy kind," as Harvard sternly demanded of its graduates.

❖ ❖ ❖

One controversy that focused Conant's position on matters theological, on the Cold War, and on Harvard's purpose in American society concerned whether the university should extinguish or expand its Divinity School. The dispute squarely pitted the rationalist, secularist, scientific Conant, formally committed to studying plans for enlarging the school yet privately dry-eyed at its possible consignment to the hereafter, against a coalition of Divinity faculty and alumni, fund-raisers and outsiders, an influential crowd that included Henry Stimson, Reinhold Niebuhr, Jerome Greene, and John Lord O'Brian.

Founded in 1816, the Divinity School had long languished in relative obscurity, once being described as consisting of "three mystics, three skeptics, and three dyspeptics." Some disgruntled Divinity faculty, frustrated by years of inconclusive debate over its status, were also critical of the Conant regime's emphasis on scientific and general-education instruction. "If they want to kill a department," complained one, "why don't they come out and say so?"[3] Conant, for his part, did not see inculcating sectarian faith as an appropriate mission for Harvard. He threw cold water on a 1940 suggestion by Corporation member Charles A. Coolidge to hire a new instructor to teach religion by saying, "I think if we were to give a course in religion by a man who in his faith does justice to the central convictions of Christianity, as seen from the Protestant point of view, we should also give a course for similar credit by one who sees religion from the Catholic point of view and one who sees it from the Jewish point of view."[4] Critics pointed to the school's falling enrollment and prestige, and Conant groused about its annual $20,000 operating deficit paid out of general university funds.[5]

To make a recommendation for the school's future (or lack thereof), Harvard authorities in 1946 appointed a committee headed by O'Brian which reported back a year later with an ambitious proposal to expand the school and establish "a new center for religious learning capable of exerting a nationwide spiritual influence." The battle was then joined, with partisans lining up on both sides. Easily the weightiest alumnus of Harvard (Law School Class of 1890) enlisted to support the project was that most eminent elder statesman Henry Stimson, who sent Conant an emotional three-page epistle stressing "with my whole heart" the need for Harvard to create a "living Christian spirit" rather than a mere facility for the study of "theology and philosophy." Ruefully, Stimson recalled his own experience in Cambridge, where irreverence prevailed:

> The young men of that time who were, like myself, seeking to find the summum bonum of life were not being led to religion by that atmosphere. I do not wish to criticize Harvard; she gave me many of my dearest friends, as well as my admirable instruction in the law, but I was a young man of 21 troubled by religious doubts which young men are troubled by in their search for the living truth of life, and I got none of that from Harvard.

In 1949, with Communism seemingly on the ascendancy, Stimson reasoned that the frightful international predicament only augmented Harvard's obligation to "express" and "father" Christian faith; without "that religious feeling," he feared, the "dire prophecies" of a third world war would be fulfilled. "Every successive war is becoming more dreadful in its mechanism and its brutality, and with those elements is likely to come national callousness and materialism." It was up to Harvard and other universities, he declared, to produce prophets and spiritual leaders who would satisfy the "feeling of religious need [that] is abroad in our people today."[6]

But Conant reacted to such appeals as he had to Arthur Compton during the Manhattan Project: What was needed was not faith, but works. He gave grudging endorsement to the expansion of the Divinity School, but only if supporters could raise $5 million. And he made clear that instruction should be directed to scholarly theological research rather than to pastoral work, suggesting that the training of ministers be done at other seminaries. In part, Conant's skepticism accorded with the austere fiscal outlook he had been compelled to take since assuming the Harvard presidency in the depths of the Depression. Firmly believing that each department of the university had to be self-supporting (he approvingly quoted a predecessor's maxim that "Each tub at Harvard stands on its own bottom"),[7] Conant had shown himself more than willing to sever Harvard's connections to individuals or ventures that he regarded as financial or administrative burdens, or peripheral to the university's mission, no matter how unpopular the decision. That attitude, so evident in the troubled Walsh-Sweezy epoch, had more recently motivated Conant during the war to threaten the "liquidation" of the School of Education unless it raised more funds,[8] and to try to eliminate the Harvard University Press, despite the fact that Harvard had been in the publishing business as early as the 1640s, when it "owned and operated the first printing press in British North America,"[9] although the Press itself was established in 1913. Conant concluded that the Press was a losing proposition and did his best to convince the Corporation that Harvard should get rid of it, but his hostility engendered such a vociferous response from the house's partisans, who included such prominent faculty as Zechariah Chafee and Ralph Barton Perry, that he wearily but grudgingly gave in. "Much as I feel if we were honest and brave, we would give up the Press, we cannot undertake the gruesome slaughter," he wrote to the Corporation's Henry James. "The death agonies would drag out for many years because of the nature of our contracts and many commitments."[10]

Conant acknowledged to James that, were it up to him, he "might well be the executioner of the Harvard University Press"—and now, many thought, he had his axe out for the Divinity School. To some, his attitude showed not only financial prudence but a general chilliness toward religion, but this went over well among most of the Harvard faculty and community. Enthusiasm for religious belief and ceremony seemed passé amongst the coolly analytic, scholarly Harvardians, and Conant's secular tone also suited the increasingly diverse student body.

But to others, Conant's attitude was impious at best, blasphemous at worst. (One particularly angry local Catholic critic blamed Conant's secularism for the atomic bomb, and predicted "a Third World War and another one after that because of these 'skeptical chemists' like Conant.")[11] The argument over the Divinity School expansion was coinciding with a national campaign spearheaded by the anti-Communist right against secular and "progressive" education; a symptomatic and well-publicized expression of this critique made a youthful celebrity of its author, an editor of the *Yale Daily News* who later became a staff aide to Senator Joseph McCarthy. In *God and Man at Yale* (1951), William F. Buckley, Jr., directed most of his fire at his alma mater, but he also blamed Harvard for undermining the Christian faith and morality of its students by failing to mandate or encourage religious instruction, and he claimed Conant's *General Education in a Free Society* had fostered anti-religious bias among American educators.[12] Conant already knew about this *enfant terrible* on the radical right as a result of sharp ideological skirmishes between the *Daily News* and Harvard's more liberal *Crimson* over Cold War policy and the FBI. At a February 1950 banquet in New Haven for outgoing Yale president Charles Seymour, Conant wryly acknowledged Buckley after hearing him criticize Ivy League educational practices. "In all my years in education," he good-naturedly told the diners, "I had come to the conclusion that most bright young men were liberals at twenty–twenty-five and conservatives at thirty-five or forty, but I wonder what will happen to William F. Buckley, who is more conservative at twenty or twenty-five than most Harvard graduates I have known at thirty-five or forty."[13]

Conant's sensitivity to the rising criticism of secular schools led him to organize a counterattack. One prime opportunity was provided by a report on "Moral and Spiritual Values" in American schools being drafted by the NEA's Educational Policies Commission. The report should explicitly declare, he urged the group in early 1950, that "sometimes secularism has been used as a smear word and has been assumed to equate a school with taking a position that was antireligious, but that secularism is not antireligious."[14]

To his religiously inclined critics, however, Conant's baccalaureate sermon on June 18, 1950, offered little reassurance. His homily on "the place of religion in a secular society" was probably his fullest public exegis of his personal religious philosophy.[15] Only a week before his own brush with mortality under a surgeon's scalpel, Conant spoke amid reminders of troubles in this life and the next one. Looking out from the altar of Memorial Church, he could see freshly inscribed stone plaques on the walls, bearing the names of Harvard fallen, as well as the dark-suited undergraduates, many battle-scarred vets on the G.I. Bill, packing the wooden pews. Not surprisingly, even this most spiritual of talks could not escape reference to the ubiquitous stresses of the Cold War and the atomic age, to which he attributed the religious revival he perceived sweeping the country. Admitting the truth of the old saw that "there are no atheists in foxholes," he allowed that in these "grim days" it felt as if Western civilization itself were in a foxhole. It struck him as natural for America to be "witnessing an ever-increasing interest in matters theological." And given recent history, it seemed understandable that demands should arise for a new theology to replace an outdated "gospel of progress." Taking the long view, he predicted that historians

> viewing the scene a century hence will readily identify the factors which give ammunition to the opponents of secular education at this moment. All the overtones of the words "Iron Curtain" and "Atomic Bomb" tend to make people fearful; these and similar phrases often repeated evoke in us the lonely apprehensions of a solitary soldier dug in a forward post. The fact that the most vituperative attackers of the aims of our free society—the Communists—also denounce dogmatically every form of religious thought has likewise had its repercussions.

"Yet," he preached, "we cannot answer dogma with dogma." Like a visitor to the Kremlin quoting Marx to support capitalism, Conant proceeded to quote the Gospel according to John—"In my Father's house are many mansions"—to bolster his argument that secular education could transmit values "inherent in our American tradition" (honesty, integrity, loyalty, etc.) and constituting a "common denominator of all religious faiths." Disdaining moral relativism as "nonsense," he nevertheless insisted that the basis for moral conduct did not belong exclusively to "this or that theology" and could even "be translated by an agnostic into a code of ethics." And by choosing "the secular path," nonreligious schools such as Harvard had not forfeited the ability to foster the moral, ethical, and even spiritual development of their impressionable charges.

> There are those, of course, who believe that education divorced from formal religion is bad. Indeed, zealous proponents of religious schools miss no opportunity of attacking secular schools and colleges. Their right to do so is unquestioned. But so, too, I take it, is the right of the rest of us to defend our point of view. To equate secular with godless and then godless with immoral, or at least amoral, is surely a fallacious line of argumentation.

Conant declared his own adherence to what he called a "cautious but optimistic theism," rationalizing this wan belief on the grounds that "the surprising aspect of the world" was to be found not in the pervasiveness of evil but in "the existence of good, the consistent strain of self-sacrificing behavior in human beings." It was possible, therefore, that "the sum total of the human drama seen over a sufficient span is not 'a tale told by an idiot full of sound and fury,' but on the contrary, has a purpose, though it be hidden from us."[16] But the thrust of Conant's remarks, with their emphasis on "a secular basis for moral conduct," and his efforts to delay the Divinity School expansion, alarmed those lobbying to revitalize Harvard's involvement in religious instruction—and especially his friend Niebuhr, whom O'Brian kept informed of the behind-the-scenes wrangling. "I am frankly very much disturbed by the turn which President Conant's thought has taken," Niebuhr wrote O'Brian. "His baccalaureate sermon was an explicit disavowal of any historic faith and practically an assertion that only ethical humanism was compatible with modern education. I don't understand just what has happened to his thought, but I thought the sermon was definitely a revelation of a defensive attitude upon this whole project."[17]

Fearing that Conant's opposition ("which I cannot understand") might doom the Divinity School, Niebuhr tried to convert him over lunch on September 19. The theologian bluntly shot down Conant's minimalist idea that Harvard could leave the preparation of pastors to Oberlin or other schools and, crucially, convinced him to permit a successful endowment drive to go forward with a $2 million target, instead of the unattainable $5 million.[18] Aided by Niebuhr's intervention, proponents raised this sum over the next few years, and the expansion plan went forward—although Harvard's faithful who still longed for an openly pious leader would have to await the coming of Nathan M. Pusey.[19]

For the rest of his presidency, Conant grappled with the questions of how to reconcile religious and secular values in modern American life and education. In the postwar boom years, the men and women looking to "get ahead" and "make it" in an environment of intense competition and rapid change looked for guidance to new oracles—technocrats, scientists, managers, consultants, businessmen. Conant was skeptical of this new cult in any case, and the Divinity School controversy further sensitized him to the charge that secular education left a void in the moral development of the nation's youth. In September, a week after seeing Niebuhr, Conant sharply criticized the latest draft of the Educational Policies Commission report (he gave it a C+) for failing to give due weight to the "reality of spiritual values." Merely citing moral and ethical precepts, he wrote to William Carr, would leave the group "wide-open to attack from the religious groups by such smears as, 'See, the Educational Policies Commission gets out a book on moral and spiritual values, and what it all boils down to is the recognition of a set of cold, dispassionate ethical precepts for making a materialistic civilization work!' "[20] "Offsets to the materialism and the 'success complex' of America today must be in terms other than pure humanitarianism to be effective," he asserted, recommending that the report stress biblical axioms such as "What profit a man to gain the whole world and lose his soul?" and "Things that are unseen are eternal."[21] For public educators to spread spiritual values without seeming to endorse religion was admittedly tricky, but teachers "should be aware of and allow their students to become aware of the reality of those emotional experiences which are the basis of many forms of religious expression," even if the EPC considered it "impolitic frankly to admit" the relationship between the "Judeo-Christian tradition" (ethics, values, and morals defining right and wrong conduct) and its underlying religious doctrines.

"In short," Conant urged, "without getting into formal religion, I believe some recognition and discussion of the nature of the 'inner life' of a dedicated individual can be undertaken." Groping for secular euphemisms, he defined "spiritual 'truth' " as "channelizing one's emotions toward ideals which are in conformity with certain moral principles," and "spiritual 'error' " as "treating one's emotional life as a succession of immediate appetites." Perhaps, he ventured, the educators could enshrine a sort of "secular sainthood"—eschewing an existence centered on scratching materialist and physical itches, devoted to the pursuit of "moral beauty"—that might substitute for the divine pantheon.

When finally released, amid much fanfare, in February 1951, *Moral and Spiritual Inquiry* quickly shot to best-seller status, aided by Conant's and Eisenhower's seals of approval. Exhorting Americans to rededicate themselves to "moral reconstruction," and to emulate such apple-pie values such as honesty, integrity, and self-discipline, the report incorporated Conant's sharply felt concerns by strongly defending secular, publicly supported schools as "hospitable to all religious opinions and partial to none," and capable of inculcating the "moral and spiritual values" that would help America win the Cold War.[22]

But Conant had only begun to fight. His championing of the cause of secular education soon brought him into open conflict with the religious right in general and the politically powerful Catholic hierarchy in particular, for they strongly supported parochial schools, which Conant believed should not be favored in the tax code, and they were suspicious of any increased federal role in education as smacking of socialism.

In early 1951, the firing of a nationally prominent school superintendent, Dr. Willard E. Goslin of Pasadena, roused Conant to action. Pressure groups had forced Goslin's removal because he dared to advocate "progressive education," which was actually a fairly bland and watered-down philosophy emphasizing practical skills rather than rote memorization and classical texts. While many critics thought that the real danger in public education was that it tended toward minimum-common-denominator learning and propagated conformist, mass-culture values, the anti-Communists seemed to smell a conspiracy in the very idea that government-supported schools were the proper place to teach America's youth and to the fearful right wing, even the term "progressive education" had a suspicious ring: "How Red is the Little Red School House?" asked one pamphlet. In the public schools, Cold War zealots found a target vulnerable to tax revolts, textbook censorship, and pressure against controversial teachers and administrators.[23]

Conant discerned the broad issues raised in the organized crusade against Goslin, and his belief that "what happened in California in 1950 could happen in almost any community in the United States" inspired him to take steps to alert the public to "certain reactionary forces at work in our democracy in these days of uncertainty and fear." A journalist named David Hulburd had written a book about the Goslin affair and Conant wrote a lengthy and laudatory review of it, printed on the front page, for the *New York Times Book Review*. Such a review was a departure for Conant in several ways— since becoming Harvard's president, he had rarely written book reviews, let alone controversial ones, and it was equally unusual for him to focus on a specific case or personality rather than on a lofty general issue or principle. But at just about this time, he had seen administration officials cowering at making Alan Waterman head of the National Science Foundation for fear that Congress might discover that Mrs. Waterman had sipped tea at a Soviet-bloc embassy, and now his disgust at the paranoia gripping Washington and the nation had mounted to the point where he felt compelled to denounce "government by intimidation."

Though he did not mention McCarthy or HUAC, Conant's review showed his willingness to confront, at least rhetorically, everything the Wisconsin senator stood for. He denounced the "irrational mob spirit" animating the anti-Goslin forces (whom he likened to the posse in *The Ox-Bow Incident*) and compared the "venomous" smear tactics of people attacking progressive education to those employed by Nazis and Communists. One had to confront "the reactionary temper of our times" in the 1950s:

> The tide of reaction is flowing strong; there are sincere opponents of all forms of non-denominational schools and colleges; there are others far from sincere who, as in every age, like to exert power by causing trouble, by urging the posse to lynch the victim, the mob to burn the dissenter's house, the school board to fire the "progressive" administrator. All this is made clear in the story of what happened in Pasadena; the more who read it the better, for these are days when those who believe in tolerance and rational discussion of public matters must realize the consequences of passivity and inaction on their part.[24]

By now recognized as America's leading educator—of his only competitors for that title, Columbia's Nicholas Murray Butler had died and the University of Chicago's Robert Maynard Hutchins had retired[25]—Conant had long planned to leave his position after two decades, in September 1953. Given the direction of science in the Cold War and the comeuppance he personally had received at the National Academy, Conant's interests beyond his immediate station turned more toward education than science. His first goal, before leaving Harvard, was to write a sequel to *Education in a Divided World* that would examine public education and whose egalitarian message was evident in its proposed title: "The Principle of Equality (The Unique American Answer)."[26] To gather the comparative data he needed for his study, he

embarked on a series of meeting-packed intercontinental tours of public
education systems in English-speaking countries, visiting Britain in the springs
of 1951 and 1952, and in the summer of 1951 touring (with the bill footed by
the Carnegie Corporation) universities and institutes in Australia and New
Zealand.[27] These far-flung investigations were summed up in lectures he gave
at the University of Virginia in February 1952, later published as *Education
and Liberty: The Role of the Schools in a Modern Democracy.*[28]

Thinking ahead to the needs of what was later called the "baby boom"
generation, the children being born to World War II veterans, he argued for an
expansion of government funding of public schools, and used his studies to
explain why American education and society (as compared to that of Great
Britain and the antipodal Commonwealths) would thus be best served rather
than by giving a wider role to private or parochial schools. Conant had
anticipated that his denunciation of a "dual system" of education would draw
fire from religious critics, but his Virginia talks attracted little notice.
Unperturbed, he accelerated his offensive against private school enthusiasts
and clergymen to whom "secularism and communism are equal dangers,"
arguing in deliberately provocative terms to a Boston conference of the
American Association of School Administrators that federal aid to private or
religious schools was suicidal for democracy, and for that Tocquevillian and
Jeffersonian equality he so ardently believed in, "not parity of status for
adults but equality of opportunity for children." While in England, Scotland,
and much of Australia public funds were used for church-connected schools,
those models were not suitable for the United States, given its constitutional
separation of church and state. The greater the proportion of U.S. children
attending private denominational schools, he warned, "the greater the threat
to our democratic unity. Therefore, to use taxpayers' money to assist such a
move is, for me, to suggest that American society use its own hands to destroy
itself."[29]

From pulpits around the country, religious leaders hurled brimstone at
Conant's blasphemy, which coincidentally fell just before Easter, and many
holiday sermons challenged his contention that education should stress secular values and good citizenship rather than spiritual instruction. "Let those
who have no king but Caesar arrange for an education in which 'Americanism'
is the ultimate unifying reference," the Very Rev. James A. Pike, the new
dean of the Cathedral of Saint John the Divine, told twelve thousand worship-
pers crowding Manhattan's Saint Patrick's Cathedral for Good Friday services.
"Some of us will continue to give our backing to schools in which the
Christian world-view is the unifying principle."[30] Boston's politically powerful Catholic archbishop, Cardinal Cushing, denounced him at length on
Easter Sunday, declaring his statement "a sign of the times" and of the
"campaign of secularism against independent schools, above all religious
schools;" Conant must be "indulging in high humor or in something considerably less attractive" for condemning private schools while heading one himself.

(Conant later clarified that his criticism referred to secondary education, not universities.) And in mid-April, the annual convocation of the National Catholic Educational Association in Kansas City quickly turned to Conant-bashing. Promoting "government-controlled education" would pave the way to an American dictatorship, the keynote speaker warned, ripping Conant for "trying to scare the American people into believing that religious education is harmful to American democracy."[31]

Having provoked the debate on the merits of federal aid to private schools, Conant quietly backed off—at least for a moment. As he later wrote in his memoirs, "after firing my shots against the target I had so carefully defined, I could then withdraw from the field of battle." His diary discloses that there was one exception to this tactical retreat, a July 1952 off-the-record dinner at the MIT faculty club with a delegation of private school scholars. "Quite a tense evening but I think I carried [it] off OK," he wrote after the meeting, which ended in "Amicable but earnest disagreement."[32] But for the most part, he confined his response to revisions and footnotes to *Education and Liberty.* Rushing to finish the manuscript during the summer of 1952, he worked hard to gather comments from sympathetic clergy that would buttress his contention that newspaper headlines and stories about his Boston speech had misrepresented his real position: truly, he insisted, he held many private and parochial schools in high esteem but simply opposed the use of public moneys to support them.[33]

During the summer and fall of 1952, Conant also distilled his thoughts on religion, education, and science for undergraduate courses at the summer school at Dartmouth College, still seeking to "formulate a philosophy of science that will be compatible with a concern for those values deemed significant to philosophic theologians," and, happily accepting an invitation from the philosophy department of his own university, for Harvard undergraduates as well. That he should take on regular teaching tasks twice weekly on top of his myriad other jobs for Harvard, the government, and the Committee on the Present Danger testifies to the intensity of his Puritan sense of duty and his desire to edify "people [who] are needlessly confused about both the nature of scientific inquiry and the basis of ethical behavior." In fact, a few weeks into the Harvard course (Philosophy 150, "A Philosophy of Science"), he confessed in his diary to being "really up to my neck! (in many spots over my head)" but soon began to "see light!" with the aid of an informal tutorial from two philosophy professors.[34]

A lively public debate had broken out on the theological import, if any, of new theories about the universe's structure and origins—especially those of relativity, quantum mechanics, and the recently popularized Big Bang origin of the creation (or Creation, to one side of the argument)—and Conant intended to address this in his course. His plans for Philosophy 150 show how he saw religion through empiricist and positivist lenses, as a phenomenon arising from and perhaps useful for human relations and emotions rather than as a window on the divine. In a long memorandum he wrote outlining the course, he faulted logical empiricists for their lack of interest in cosmology (as well as their "jeering remarks about metaphysics"), but on the other hand he remained distinctly unimpressed by teleological inferences of God's design from astronomical hypotheses or observations. In the spirit of Descartes's historic compromise, which held that theologians and physicists could amicably coexist in separate, independent realms, Conant appealed for a cease-fire in the war between Science and God:

> Finally we come to the highly controversial and most difficult area in which religion, art, poetry, ethics, and cosmology appear to merge. The thesis I propose to maintain is that they don't have to merge. . . . Religion I believe is not primarily a basis for ethics but an attempt to organize metaphysical speculations and historical traditions in a way to enable people to handle situations. The realm of spiritual values I shall bound as best I can and suggest that just as all sane, literate people believe in a three-dimensional world, *approximately* the same for all, so all people in a culture believe in approximately the same framework to which they relate emotional reactions involving other people. That this framework has to be fitted to the cosmological conceptual scheme of science I shall deny. (This ought at least to start a heated discussion!)[35]

Conant's minimalist definition of religion might have displeased Niebuhr, yet it captured Conant's conviction that "Actions not words are the test of the reality of a belief and thus, for me, the reality of objects."

His skepticism extended equally to social scientists who quested after laws of human behavior as predictable and reliable as Newtonian physics. Forewarned that his class would expect a "personal credo" on the intersection of science and ethics, Conant wrote that he intended to state a view

> largely negative and completely skeptical in regard to the immediate prospects for a unified world hypothesis. Evolution, the origins of life, the history of nature in general are problems which can be handled by increasingly satisfactory conceptual schemes (*not* increasingly true schemes). These theories have no relevance to the question of whether or not a person should lie or steal, commit murder or suicide except so far as their successful development, like acts of heroism and self-sacrifice and the music and art of a handful of persons, differentiates man from other animals.

Conant could live with an eternal search for satisfactory conceptual schemes, not Truth, and he was content to probe the mysteries of creation through experiment and intellect rather than through faith. This was an ethos that he helped sustain at Harvard for a generation. But in trying to devise a generally applicable secular canon to replace spiritual and religious instruction in moral and ethical values, he frankly admitted to having "only vague and nebulous suggestions." And these suggestions, while admirable for their awareness of the alienation and moral tension lurking beneath America's material and political ascendancy, could not salve the anxiety of an accelerating, out-of-kilter century—rattled by Freud and Einstein, Auschwitz and Hiroshima, fearing World War III, haunted by the question of whether or not God was dead. Still, his efforts to arrange a tenable twentieth century mixed marriage of theology and secularism do offer valuable clues to his own "search for the living truth of life," as Stimson had put it, or, in his own phrase, "the spiritual trials involved in the formation of character through a series of internal struggles."[36]

While careful not to question the validity of the intense inner experiences that inspired many people to religious faith, even as he discounted the "metaphysical speculations" of scripture, Conant apparently never had any such experiences himself—perhaps only his glimpse of the apocalypse at Alamogordo, which, if anything, seems to have turned him not toward religion but away from it. In *Homo sapiens* he saw not God's reflection but a flawed, imperfect species rather impressively advanced on the evolutionary chain but by no means incapable of improvement or replacement. Conant's one true love, science's unbounded inquiry into the nature of things, had produced not permanent progress or revelation of divine handiwork but, most spectacularly, the bleakness of the atomic bomb. If anything, the knowledge that nature had thus facilitated the possibility of humanity's destruction must have deepened Conant's doubts in the existence of a beneficent deity. "There is a crack in everything God has made," he often said, quoting Emerson—and by the early 1950s that fissure seemed to be widening daily. Unable to trust Providence or science to stay mankind's folly, yet unwilling to despair that World War III was inevitable, he chose the alternative of hoping—and preaching—that rational behavior, a delicate political-military high-wire act, and a spot of luck, might yet rescue civilization from itself.

CHAPTER 30

"A Bad Business Now Threatening
to Become Really Bad!!"

Conant and Nuclear Weapons
1950–1952

> Finally, Oppie, Lee DuBridge and I are through as members of the GAC!!
> 10½ years of almost continuous official connection with a bad business now
> threatening to become really bad!!
>   —Diary, June 14, 1952

> I no longer have any connection with the atom bomb. I have no sense of
> accomplishment.
>   —Quoted, *Newsweek*, September 22, 1952

Already anxious to leave the atomic business after losing the H-bomb fight,
Conant had planned to depart the GAC in the spring of 1950 when he had
expected to become president of the National Academy of Sciences. That
new burden would have offered a convincing public excuse to resign without
arousing speculation that he had left due to a policy dispute. For, in line with
Acheson's plea that he avoid a resignation that would spark a "debate on a
matter which was settled"—and with Truman's gag order on the GAC—
Conant was looking for a graceful exit.[1] Ironically, however, the participants
in the academy revolt unwittingly helped prolong Conant's tenure as an
official nuclear adviser: a few weeks after the climactic meeting, he wrote to
Oppenheimer in typically euphemistic fashion that, "since certain plans
miscarried, I propose to stay with this assignment for an indefinite period of
time."[2]

I. I. Rabi recalled that Conant's interest in nuclear matters seemed to
wane after the H-bomb debate, although he continued to attend GAC meetings and chair the panel's weapons subcommittee until his six-year term
expired in August 1952.[3] Early in 1951 the mathematical calculations that
would make thermonuclear weapons a reality—that Oppenheimer would
describe as "sweet and lovely and beautiful" technical concepts to build a

"dreadful weapon"—were worked out by Teller and Stanislaus Ulam and presented at a special conference hosted by Oppenheimer at Princeton that June. For Conant, the breakthrough merely reduced the "degree of empiricism" involved in devising thermonuclear weapons, and he shunned the conference for reasons that can be surmised from a letter he received from Oppenheimer. "From the first it seemed to me unlikely that you would come to the thermonuclear conference, or for that matter that you would much want to," Oppenheimer wrote. "There are some new thoughts which may be important for you to know; and I will tell you about them when I see you. . . . "[4]

By early 1951, Conant searched for a means to provide a strategic counterweight to the purported Soviet menace to Western Europe—and he found it in the rapidly emerging prospect of tactical nuclear weapons. He had counted on building up a 3.5-4 million-man army to negate the Soviets' huge land forces, but universal military service was lagging. Something had to be done quickly, he calculated, because Moscow, by building up its own stockpile of atomic weapons, would soon be able to neutralize the strategic nuclear edge wielded by the United States since 1945. If the Soviets attacked Western Europe, how could the United States plausibly threaten to bomb Moscow and Leningrad with nuclear weapons when Moscow could retaliate by wiping out New York and Washington? This logic struck Conant as "fantastic," suicidal. "It might be fair to compare the arguments presented with that of the man who, placing a stick of dynamite in his pants pocket, said, 'Now the next fresh guy who slaps me will have his hand blown off!' "[5] Such reasoning had helped Conant (and Oppenheimer) to justify their opposition to the hydrogen bomb, and the Korean War helped to concentrate their minds still further on the question of how to devise quickly a panoply of smaller, more usable nuclear weapons for use in "tactical or defensive" campaigns instead of the permanent reliance on the mass destruction of cities.[6] In late December 1950, amid the dark news from Korea, a high-level panel headed by Oppenheimer secretly urged the government to concentrate for the next two years on a rapid build-up of fission weapons suitable for tactical or defensive use in Western Europe, and the GAC, whose members remained skeptical of the hydrogen bomb's feasibility and usefulness, quickly and unsurprisingly endorsed the report's conclusions.[7] Those views, presaging the subsequent arguments made by "defense intellectuals" against the "massive retaliation" strategy advocated during the Eisenhower administration, further alienated proponents of the hydrogen bomb and of strategic bombing, especially in the air force and the Strategic Air Command (SAC).

Oppenheimer helped to promote a strategy of using tactical nuclear weaponry in Europe combined with continental defense in the Western Hemisphere—as opposed to relying on strategic bombing—by influencing Project Vista, an army-sponsored study of military priorities conducted by scientists and strategists at the California Institute of Technology during 1951 and overseen by DuBridge. (Vista prompted a migration to sunny southern California of many scientists who had just participated in an MIT-based study, Project Charles, which to the air force's displeasure had delivered a favorable judgment on the feasibility of defending the United States against long-range enemy bombers—implying that defense, rather than strategic offense, could safeguard U.S. security.) Though a latecomer to Vista, Oppenheimer helped to draft its key chapter and, in December, helped DuBridge and the physicist Charles Lauritsen to brief Eisenhower and his staff in Paris on the wonders that tactical atomic weapons could achieve in support of NATO ground forces.[8] Issued in early 1952 but quickly suppressed by the air force, Project Vista's final report strongly endorsed the principle of "bringing the battle back to the battlefield" through tactical nuclear weaponry.[9]

Conant did not take part in Vista, but he took a sympathetic interest in its progress. In December 1951, for example, he received a report from "Oppie" of the Vista presentation to Eisenhower and wrote in his diary: "Much encouraged by what he said. Keep our fingers crossed for another ten months"—perhaps referring to the hope that a military confrontation in Europe could be avoided long enough to deploy effective tactical weapons (which later reached NATO in substantial numbers in 1953–54).[10] Conant used his stature as chairman of the Committee on the Present Danger to spread the view that tactical nuclear arms promised "an enormous advantage" to the United States that might make Western Europe defensible on the ground, even with relatively few ground troops (a likely prospect, as UMS foundered), even if the Soviet Union had the technological edge in offensive striking power and defenses against bombers, and perhaps even "without calling on [West] Germany to rearm"—an idea that Conant continued to regard with considerable suspicion even as it became official U.S. and NATO policy. The United States in particular had much to gain by emphasizing tactical weapons, he wrote Oppenheimer, because they suited the power "holding the line against an offensive" as well as the one that "first started manufacturing atomic weapons, for presumably their stockpile would for some time be greater than that of an enemy."[11] Here he adopted the guiding principle of U.S. strategy for the defense of Europe for the remainder of the Cold War: "We shall not meet hordes with hordes."[12]

Conant dutifully kept mum in public about his distaste for the H-bomb, but his skepticism of civilian nuclear energy finally burst into the open in 1951. During his summer tour in Australia, Conant spoke of the hopes for industrial atomic energy as "exaggerated in the United States," and in far more widely publicized comments to the American Chemical Society in New York on September 5, he vented the instinctive doubts he long felt about "fancies" of a nuclear-powered world.[13] He entitled his address "A Skeptical Chemist Looks into the Crystal Ball"—an allusion to Robert Boyle's seventeenth-century *The Sceptical Chymist* —and told his chemistry colleagues that he followed in

Boyle's footsteps by "questioning the prophecies of some of the modern alchemists — our friends the atomic physicists."

Imagining other accomplishments of science a generation hence, Conant had some startling visions, at least by 1951 standards, that even four decades later have not lost their relevance: While the desalinization plants that he hoped would turn deserts into gardens are still prohibitively expensive outside a few Persian Gulf oil sheikhdoms, he forecast that oral contraceptives would be tremendously important, and this antedated widespread use of the Pill by more than a decade. He had been encouraged by Nehru's advocacy of birth-control clinics, and was disappointed later that religious opposition to contraception did not fade away and that "harmless anti-fertility components" added to diet did not rapidly improve living standards in overpopulated nations. His prediction that this would occur prompted Robert Frost to compose a sardonic limerick to science's "mouthpiece Prexy Conant," who had "undertaken for it to make the planet less uncomfortably crowded with a new kind of manna (manna from Hell not Heaven, a religious friend, Al Edwards calls it), a contraceptive to be taken at the mouth so we can stop breeding without having to stop futution." Frost, confined to a hospital bed while recuperating from cancer surgery, acknowledged a debt to science for prolonging his life — "We ought not put on humanistic airs to make fun of science because though it can postpone death, it can't do away with death" — but he couldn't resist a jab:

> Pares Continuas Fututiones
>
> Says our Harvard Neo Malthusian
> "We cant keep the poor from futution;
> But by up to date feeding
> We can keep them from breeding."
> Which seems a licentious conclusion![14]

Conant's most controversial prediction, concerning nuclear power technology, contrasted with his remarkably optimistic vision of the political landscape in future decades. Still privately scornful of the "World Government or Bust" views of Grenville Clark, and of scientific "scareheads" who predicted nuclear disaster if disarmament were not rapidly achieved, Conant nevertheless judged some form of atomic controls necessary to retrieve the world from a "ridiculously dangerous situation."[15] Foreseeing "neither an atomic holocaust nor the golden abundance of an atomic age," he hoped that "worried humanity" would tiptoe safely through the nuclear minefield to reach a "great settlement" and gradual disarmament. Neither totalitarianism nor world government triumphed in his envisioned future. Even the Orwellian year 1984 did "not glare with menace," for although "the Marx-Lenin dogmas" persisted, democracy and freedom thrived. "Men and women still continue to be unregimented in many portions of the world," he predicted. "Paris, Berlin,

London, New York, Moscow still stand physically undamaged by any enemy action since World War II." Though Cold War disputes had "time and again nearly precipitated World War III," Conant postulated that "the industrialized nations" had avoided "de-industrializing each other by atomic bombs." How? "Only by the narrowest of margins . . . and only because time and again when one side or the other was about to take the plunge during the period of intensive armament . . . the expert military advisers could not guarantee ultimate success."

By the 1960s, in Conant's crystal ball, "People in the United States and in Russia had become somewhat accustomed to living under the shadow of the twentieth-century volcano—atomic bombs." Yet, though the U.S. commitment to the collective defense of Western Europe had preserved peace, pressures built to seek a "way out of the atomic age." Industrialized nations stressed conventional armed forces to safeguard their frontiers and worried less "about the existence of a few bombs more or less in another nation's arsenal." And sometime between 1960 and 1980 the superpowers stepped back from the nuclear brink, the West's rearmament having served its purpose:

> When that day comes the fear of communist aggression will cease to haunt Western Europe. When that day comes, one can begin to talk about a real settlement of the international situation. Ideas that must now be regarded as Utopian will once again have vitality and meaning. All this may seem to the pessimists among you,—those who believe a third world war to be inevitable, —as so much wishful thinking. But because I have so much confidence in what free men can accomplish when once aroused, I believe that in spite of grim years ahead this second half of the twentieth century may yet prove to be a period of gradual disarmament and peace.

Conant believed that a consensus would grow to reject civilian nuclear power as too unsafe, too costly, and too intertwined with nuclear weapons technology. A "sober appraisal of the debits and credits of the exploitation of atomic fission had led people to decide the game was not worth the candle," as he put it. While experimental plants pumped out a modicum of useful atomic energy, "the disposal of the waste products had presented gigantic problems, problems to be lived with for generations." Heavy capital investment was made in nuclear power generation, but "quite apart from the technical difficulties" the deleterious military applications of atomic energy overwhelmed the supposed beneficence of the new technology. "A self-denying ordinance seemed but common sense," Conant predicted, faintly echoing the secret international control plan he had advocated in 1947-48. "Once the illusion of prosperity for all through the splitting of the atom vanished from people's minds, the air began to clear."

And where would the world turn for energy sources as it eschewed the atom? Far before its time, Conant advanced an alternative that still remains underexplored: a "vast technical undertaking," modeled after the Manhattan Project, to develop solar energy, which he predicted by the end of the century would be "the dominating factor in the production of industrial power." This last idea intrigued one State Department official, who asked George Kennan, then retired from government service at the Institute for Advanced Study in Princeton, whether "the free countries in partnership" ought to organize a solar-energy effort along the lines of nuclear energy collaboration.[16] Kennan passed the inquiry to Oppenheimer, acknowledging that this sunny suggestion "may evoke some bitter reflection."[17] Oppenheimer responded:

Memorandum to Mr. Kennan

In re Solar Energy

It seems to me that we should immediately take the following steps:

(a) Classify the sun as Top Secret;

(b) Establish a commission to manage it for the benefit of all mankind;

(c) Give appropriate high-level indications of a super weapon based on the sun;

(d) At the same time, make an official policy pronouncement indicating that we wish to use the sun, not for devastation and war, but for the betterment of mankind.[18]

Others failed to find humor in Conant's irreverence toward nuclear power. It affronted those who believed that America's leadership in developing atomic energy, like its dominance of the nuclear arms race, could ensure the nation's global preeminence. One consultant to the Psychological Strategy Board even argued that by increasing world energy resources, "perhaps in geometric progression," and negating Marxist arguments that social justice would be limited by "scarce" resources, a "far reaching" international U.S. atomic power enterprise could invalidate Communist ideology. Through an "American sponsored atomic revolution," declared the writer of this well-received paper, "the free world will be immunized against the Communist infection."[19] Others complained that Conant's optimism about the possibility of avoiding a third world war—projections that were given front-page treatment by the *New York Times*—might lull Americans into complacency and, worse, endanger support for military spending. His remarks gave Americans "a false sense of security," scoffed Federal Civil Defense administrator Millard Caldwell. "The public read the headline, 'Conant unworried about an atomic war,' but it probably did not see that Dr. Conant used a plastic crystal ball as his authority. Not many people will stop to realize that Stalin may not be using the same crystal ball nor getting the same answers."[20]

His views also jarred the sensibilities of the hawkish staff members of Congress's Joint Committee on Atomic Energy (JCAE), already disturbed by his opposition to the hydrogen bomb. Now they peppered Chairman Brien

McMahon with arguments to disparage his speech. "Dr. Conant's crystal ball is necessarily beclouded because he looks so far into the distant future," wrote one JCAE aide. "He presents an attractive future but leaves the immediate problems unanswered."[21] And McMahon's fervently anti-Communist chief assistant, William Liscumb Borden (whose November 1953 letter charging Robert Oppenheimer with being a Soviet spy was to trigger the removal of the physicist's security clearance), advised him to emphasize that Conant's prescriptions reflected "professional jealousy" of physicists.[22] "Perhaps it is only fair in judging Dr. Conant," observed another aide, "to remember that he is an outstanding chemist and that the chemists generally are smarting from the fact that the world which they once held in the palms of their hands has been snatched away by the physicists."[23] Borden urged McMahon to argue that Conant's belief that the "a-bomb is not magical" is precisely why "we need this weapon in huge numbers," and to crack: "We could all wish that Dr. Conant would advise us how to act in the next two or three years with the same clarity that he sees the future from 1980 onward."[24]

Public criticism of Conant soon came from a comparably influential voice: Kenneth Pitzer, the dean of chemistry at the University of California at Berkeley, who had been the AEC's director of research in 1949–51 and a leader of the move to prevent Conant from becoming president of the National Academy of Sciences. Conant's speech gave Pitzer an opening to say what he and other critics already believed about the GAC. In a March 1952 speech to a section of the American Chemical Society in Los Angeles, Pitzer charged that "serious and unnecessary delays" had occurred in the U.S. atomic energy program as result of scientific "kibitzers." Singling out Conant as one of those advisers who should be replaced by scientists "with faith and enthusiasm in the job to be done" and who would give the AEC "more constructive advice," he claimed that more than several GAC members had shown "remarkably little enthusiasm for the primary goals of the Atomic Energy Commission."[25]

Pitzer's attack sounded publicly the opening of a concerted campaign to convince Truman not to reappoint the three surviving charter members of the GAC—Conant, Oppenheimer, and DuBridge—who were deemed to lack the appropriate zeal for the hydrogen bomb, strategic bombing, and nuclear power and whose terms were due to expire in the summer of 1952. (In the summer of 1950 the terms of three other original advisers, Enrico Fermi, Glenn Seaborg, and Hartley Rowe had expired, and the AEC had rejected all three of the group's suggested replacements, naming instead Edgar V. Murphree, Walter G. Whitman, and Willard F. Libby, a University of Chicago chemist and enthusiastic H-bomb proponent.)[26] A number of related issues contributed to the growing antagonism between the Oppenheimer-led GAC and a rival group of nuclear scientists, many of them (including Pitzer, Edward Teller, Ernest Lawrence, Luis Alvarez, and Wendell Latimer) associated with the University of California at Berkeley's Radiation Laboratory.

(Several others, such as Urey and Libby, worked at the University of Chicago.) Veterans of the successful guerrilla war to neutralize the GAC's opposition to the H-bomb, some of these scientists now believed that the GAC had obstructed development of thermonuclear weapons even after Truman's decision to authorize it, and thus lobbied friends in the air force, Congress, and the Defense Department to establish a new weapons laboratory to compete with Los Alamos, which they saw as dominated by pro-Oppenheimer scientists. (Ultimately their efforts led in June 1952 to the creation of the Lawrence Livermore Laboratory, run by the University of California, but this occurred only after they overcame the GAC's determined resistance.)[27] Conant's skepticism toward the second lab did not endear him to this California crowd, nor did his part in cancelling a massive accelerator project to be built under Lawrence's supervision at Berkeley.[28]

Although Conant did not see Pitzer's broadside until after he returned from Europe, DuBridge angrily leapt to his defense. His "blood began to boil" when he read the *New York Times* account of Pitzer's speech, and he hurriedly drafted a letter expressing shock that Pitzer had elected to "air in public your grudges against the G.A.C. and especially against Dr. Conant." Vigorously defending the GAC's record in encouraging civilian atomic power despite admittedly disappointing results, he went so far as to accuse Pitzer of cowardice. "To single out Dr. Conant for attack is especially unfair," DuBridge wrote acidly. "I assume that if your talk had been given in Boston instead of Los Angeles you would have singled out me. Actually the G.A.C. advice in this field has been the combined judgment of all its members and we all take equal blame—or equal credit." And to claim that any GAC member had "remarkably little enthusiasm for the primary goals of the A.E.C." was "to misrepresent the situation inexcusably." "That you dislike the G.A.C. and many of its actions—and its members—is not news to me," DuBridge's draft ended. "That you would be so indiscreet [a]s to parade your feelings publicly in such a fashion is a great disappointment."[29]

Oppenheimer warmly welcomed this tough response. "Your note to Pitzer did make me some pleasure," he told DuBridge, adding that Pitzer had "finally" sent him a copy of his talk, "as he had previously done to practically everyone, including lots of journalists." While the full text struck Oppenheimer as "a little more balanced and less intemperate" than the newspaper summary of it, he was justifiably convinced that Pitzer intended a frontal attack on the GAC and correctly concluded that "at least part of" this animus had germinated in the "rather tense atmosphere that still prevails in Berkeley."[30]

After reading the "much less sensational" text of Pitzer's actual remarks, DuBridge, too, settled down, and he discarded the first draft of his letter and sent instead a keenly regretful but more measured complaint. The GAC advisers had served "at considerable personal sacrifice" out of patriotic duty, he noted, and would have resigned already if they had genuinely "lost enthusiasm or interest in the work of the Commission." Besides, he added, the terms of Oppenheimer, Conant, and himself were about to expire, "a fact of which you are no doubt happily aware." DuBridge still maintained that the AEC should hear varied points of view on atomic energy, "rather than, as you suggest, to listen only to the advertised enthusiasts," and he firmly denied that it had done anything to retard progress. The three departing members didn't expect Pitzer to agree with them on these matters, DuBridge wrote, but were "only sorry that you saw fit to give us a kick in the teeth at this time."[31]

Pitzer belatedly sent Conant a copy of his speech with a handwritten note explaining that he had interpreted Conant's speculative "crystal ball" gazing of the previous fall "as an indication of your real opinion about atomic power."[32] On April 10, Conant replied politely but firmly. Pitzer had "left out half the story," he said; he had disavowed the peaceful use of nuclear energy in the context of a simultaneous cut in nuclear weapons which, he believed, would be possible only with the removal of atomic power plants that could supply the raw materials for bombs. "Therefore," he concluded, "it is hardly fair to say that I have 'remarkably little enthusiasm for the primary goals of the Atomic Energy Program' until you are prepared to consider yourself the very explosive (forgive the pun) subject of the relationship of atomic power to the future of an industrialized society."[33]

In a reply whose cordial form ("best regards . . . sincerely yours") did not mask their harsh disagreement, Pitzer castigated Conant for remaining as an atomic adviser, and he acknowledged that his principal motive had been not to express disagreement over the feasibility of atomic energy but to evict opponents of the H-bomb from positions of influence in the American nuclear program. Two areas of dispute separated them, Pitzer wrote. On the future prospects for international control of atomic weapons, he argued that any future U.S. reduction in nuclear arms should take place "only because of assurance that all others had done likewise" and under a system of international inspection and agreement "which would permit constructive uses of atomic energy to go forward." But the second disagreement was the key one: on the issue of who should oversee programs to accomplish AEC "objectives that are officially accepted as desirable. I feel very strongly," wrote Pitzer,

> that the technical leadership should be in the hands of those who, in addition to their technical qualifications, also believe in the objectives. If any individual lacks enthusiasm for the objective, he should drop off of the team that is trying to do the job and voice his objections from the outside. It was in this sense that I believe certain members of the G.A.C. have been open to criticism.
>
> As a matter of restraint and good taste, I have emphasized power reactors and avoided explicit mention of the H-bomb, although, to reuse your pun, the latter is the more explosive question. While it may be possible in principle to separate one's opinions on general social policy from judgements on technical questions, I do not believe this distinction has been clearly made

and I doubt if it is practical to expect it to be made. I think the only
satisfactory arrangement is to select the technical team from among those
who want to win the game.[34]

Pitzer did not mention in this collegial correspondence the fact that he
and other scientists who "want[ed] to win the game" were fervently lobbying
the government to remove Oppenheimer, Conant, and DuBridge from the
GAC. Several weeks earlier, in fact, he had been to Washington to plead with
McMahon and AEC commissioner Gordon Dean not to reappoint Conant and
Oppenheimer, citing Conant's "Crystal Ball" speech as the reason he had
criticized him publicly.[35] Nor did he mention that earlier in April he had told
FBI agents that he was "now doubtful" as to Oppenheimer's loyalty, and had
written Truman directly to charge that Oppenheimer, abetted by other GAC
members, had "dragged the brakes" on the H-bomb program and should "be
eased out of his position of influence."[36] Other scientists had also written to
Truman in the same vein, and in his speech Pitzer had suggested as possible
GAC replacements, among others, Harold Urey, Conant's nemesis since the
Manhattan Project, and Farrington Daniels, president of the American Chemical Society.[37] In a GAC meeting the previous December, Urey had already
"deplored" Conant's public skepticism about civilian atomic power, and had
urged encouragement of the program so "young men [will] be attracted into
it"—Conant, who arrived late, had noted in his diary: "Missed a good briefing
also an attack by Harold Urey which was a good bit of luck!"—and to
Truman, Urey now claimed that the GAC under Oppenheimer's "domination"
had caused years of delays and urged him not to reappoint him or the other
advisers who "follow him almost blindly"; as replacements he suggested
Pitzer, Latimer, Teller, or Arthur Compton.[38] Daniels, meanwhile, agreeing
with Pitzer that the GAC needed leaders who would "emphasize optimism"
in civilian nuclear power, advised Truman to appoint Pitzer and Latimer—
who in turn cautioned Truman that it would be a "tragic mistake" to reappoint
a man with Oppenheimer's "mystic pacifist philosophy."[39]

The anti-Oppenheimer forces had important allies in the top ranks of
the Defense Department, FBI, and AEC. Not only Pitzer but Teller, Libby,
Latimer, and other scientists gave detailed interviews to the FBI, arming
J. Edgar Hoover with ammunition against Oppenheimer to pass to the
attorney general and to Truman's national security adviser.[40] The campaign
for a GAC shake-up also gained momentum when Lewis Strauss reportedly
went directly to Truman to argue his case, and Thomas Murray told the FBI
that his efforts to bar Oppenheimer's reappointment were "proceeding very
well."[41] In certain quarters of the Pentagon, too, anti-Oppenheimer vitriol
overflowed, particularly in the air force and its new research institute, Rand.
The air force's single-minded priority: to banish Oppenheimer and his supporters from power so that their baleful influence, whether in the GAC or in
officially supported "summer studies" in Cambridge or Pasadena, did not

further undermine SAC or weapons production. In one particularly dramatic episode, the air force's bellicose chief scientist, David T. Griggs, confronted Oppenheimer face-to-face at his Princeton office and accused him of lying by spreading the story that air force secretary Thomas K. Finletter had boasted that with 200 H-bombs the United States "could rule the world." Griggs said that Oppenheimer's stand against thermonuclear weapons could bring disaster to the United States.

"Do you think I'm pro-Russian or just confused?" Oppenheimer asked, according to Griggs's account.

"I wish I knew."

Had Griggs "impugned his loyalty?" Oppenheimer demanded.

Indeed he had, Griggs claimed to have responded.

"You're paranoid," said Oppenheimer. And after some difficult-to-imagine "pleasantries" the conversation ended.[42]

On Capitol Hill, the campaign to overhaul the GAC also accelerated. Urging that careful checks be conducted to ascertain whether prospective nuclear advisers were "on Oppie's team or on the team that wants to build H-bombs,"[43] JCAE staff aide Borden drafted an emotional appeal for McMahon's signature imploring Truman not to reappoint Conant, DuBridge, and especially Oppenheimer, all of whom were alleged to have "bitterly opposed, in 1949 and 1950, any real attempt to build the hydrogen bomb," and to have "played a part in keeping the hydrogen issue away from your desk prior to the first Soviet explosion." McMahon elected not to send that particular draft but instead (according to Borden's notation) opted to "take this up verbally" with Truman while sending a toned-down letter that omitted explicit mention of Oppenheimer but called for a "bold decision" to speed production of the still-untested H-bomb and appending a damning chronology of delays in the thermonuclear program. The president, never a fan of the "'cry baby' scientist" who once confessed in the Oval Office to having blood on his hands for building the atomic bomb, did not need much prodding, and assured McMahon that his views would receive "the careful study which they deserve."[44]

A whispering campaign of this magnitude could not escape its intended targets, and by late April 1952 the GAC was struggling to defend itself from defense secretary Lovett's "strong dissatisfaction" with H-bomb development and from what Oppenheimer termed "high pressure methods" used by the Berkeley scientists to lobby for a second nuclear weapons laboratory.[45] By May, well before they seeped out into the press, rumors of the impending GAC purge had reached Conant during a visit to Washington:

Lunched w V. Bush at Cosmos Club. Talk with Jim Fisk [former AEC aide, government science adviser], Oppie, Lee DuBridge. Some of the "boys" have their axes out for the three of us on the GAC of AEC. Claim we have "dragged our heels" on H Bomb. Dirty words about Oppie!![46]

Thus, by the time of his last GAC meeting on June 13–14, Conant knew well that what one top Truman adviser privately termed a "clean sweep" of the group was imminent.[47] As a parting shot, Conant suggested that the panel prepare a report for the president reviewing the commission's progress since 1947,[48] and his handwritten suggestions to Oppenheimer showed how aware he was of the criticism of the panel, as well as his deep unease about the future. He defended his determined opposition to a rapid reactor program on the ground that proposed power-generating plants would not prove cost-effective compared to existing methods, and reiterated his "grave doubt as to whether mechanisms exist for an adequate review of the pros and cons in regard to broad strategic questions involving the military and the AEC." He believed that advances in basic science had been minimal, and noted that the postwar atomic program was "living off the scientific ideas of [the] pre-1940 era." Clearly thinking of the imminent testing of thermonuclear devices, scheduled for the fall, he wrote: "The President should be aware of the lack of clear evidence as to the number of bombs that can be exploded without . . . endangering life. More accurate estimates must be obtained and should be in the mind of the President and his advisors."[49]

The GAC's final report—a somber recital of both the achievements and dangers of the atomic effort—incorporated Conant's long-term fears (and his long-term hope for arms control) and tried to set the record straight about the technical basis for its earlier stand against the Super: "[A]tomic armament, which is now held to be the shield of the free world, may in a foreseeable time become the gravest threat to our welfare and security. . . . [It has been] only for about a year, since the spring of 1951, that we have had promising and practical schemes for very large-scale thermonuclear weapons."[50] On the evening of Saturday, June 14, the thirty-first meeting of the General Advisory Committee adjourned after a final session devoted to polishing the final report, and as he left the home of Commissioner Henry Smyth to catch the overnight Federal Express to Boston, Conant was also leaving a momentous, sometimes exhilarating, sometimes painful, but finally grim stage of his life. His nuclear career was over, and his relief, even glee, was palpable: "Finally, Oppie, Lee DuBridge and I are through as members of the GAC!!" he scrawled in his diary. "10½ years of almost continuous official connection with a bad business now threatening to become really bad!!"[51]

But he was not quite finished. Five days later he quietly made an appearance that, although previously unnoticed by historians, constituted a coda to Conant's own atomic career and significantly influenced a report often cited as a key document of the nuclear arms race. On the evening of June 19, after presiding over Harvard graduation rites, Conant strolled a few blocks from the Yard to the leafy Cambridge street on which sat the spacious nineteenth-century house of McGeorge Bundy, by now a tenured professor in the government department. (It was said that Bundy's being given tenure the previous year, continuing a stratospheric path leading from the coauthorship of Stimson's memoirs to Harvard's Society of Fellows, had raised Conant's eyebrows. When a government-department representative asked approval for the appointment, Conant is said to have examined the dossier and asked, in apparent incredulity, whether it was true that Bundy had never taken an undergraduate or graduate course in government. "That's right," the official is supposed to have replied. "Are you sure that's right?" "I'm sure." "Well," Conant harrumphed before giving his okay, "all I can say is that it couldn't have happened in chemistry.")[52]

But this overcast June evening it was Bundy's appointment as secretary to a "panel of consultants on disarmament" by the State Department that occasioned Conant's visit. It had been named by Dean Acheson to investigate alternatives to an endlessly escalating nuclear arms race.

Conant was not formally in the group, despite initial reports to the contrary,[53] but it gathered several of his close friends and members of the dwindling corps of advisers who still hoped—even desired—that the world could escape the shadow of nuclear weapons. Chaired by Oppenheimer, the panel included Vannevar Bush; Dartmouth president John S. Dickey; Joseph Johnson, head of the Carnegie Endowment for International Peace; and the New York lawyer Allen Dulles, soon to become Eisenhower's CIA director.

Reports about the group had circulated around Washington in the spring, just as the battle over the GAC appointments neared a climax; predictably, linking Oppenheimer and, to a lesser extent, Conant to such an enterprise only gave their critics further confirmation of their unsuitability as nuclear advisers. Some air force and JCAE officials quickly blamed Oppenheimer, Rabi, and Lauritsen, whom they scornfully dubbed "The Committee to Save the World," for what they saw as perhaps the most ludicrous and outrageous attempt yet to stymie the H-bomb.[54] Conant knew that in some ways the State Department disarmament panel was just that: a last desperate effort to stop the H-bomb, an eleventh-hour initiative, spearheaded by Bush, arguing that the first thermonuclear test, set for the fall of 1952, should be postponed for several months to give the newly elected president (expected to be Eisenhower) a chance to ponder the ramifications of such a fateful step. As a potential alternative, the panel suggested approaching the Soviet Union to see if it might agree to even a tacit moratorium on the testing of thermonuclear weapons, a "self-policing" idea that could be easily monitored by both sides. Bush seems to have told Conant about his plan at the same lunch on May 9 at which he relayed gossip about the anti-Oppenheimer campaign. "Bush on panel to advise State Dept about disarmament," Conant had jotted in his diary: "Has an idea."[55]

Conant appears not to have mentioned Bush's proposal on the June evening in Cambridge when he visited a rump meeting of the disarmament panel (Bundy, Johnson, and Oppenheimer were present, Bush and Dulles absent), but he certainly expressed his deep concerns about the American public's response to the nuclear arms race. In lectures in London and New

York, and in *Modern Science and Modern Man,* he had passionately condemned
what he described as the "gross distortion of the facts" of nuclear energy and
weaponry caused by excessive military and government secrecy and deliberate manipulation. "It is impossible today or in the foreseeable future to have a
frank, rational, searching discussion of the industrial uses of atomic energy,"
Conant had written. "The general public might as well stop reading anything
in the papers about atomic energy or atomic bombs. By the nature of the case
it is almost certain to be misleading."[56] And now in Bundy's comfortable
downstairs living room, amid convivial (and security-cleared) company, he
went into further detail about the importance of educating the American
public to the increasing destructiveness of nuclear weapons. Americans, he
pointed out, did not understand that the United States, with its large and
expanding cities, was especially vulnerable to atomic weapons. "Leaving
aside the possibility of a thermo-nuclear weapon," Bundy's minutes of the
meeting paraphrase Conant as saying, "developments in the field of fission
weapons had so multiplied the power of the atomic bomb since 1945 as to
make a single bomb capable of the total destruction of all but a very few of
the largest American cities."[57] Conant feared that "the ordinary American"
focused on the capacity of atomic bombs to assist a U.S. attack on the Soviet
Union, "while the more significant fact was that now and in the future such
blows could be delivered by others on the United States." Only when the
general public appreciated this point would the United States government be
willing "to participate effectively in disarmament planning and in disarmament itself." Public education on the *mutual* danger of nuclear destruction
could be a "first step" to arms control. "Once the danger of atomic weapons
was sufficiently widely recognized, it might become possible to get a further
development in American strength in conventional weapons, and if this
strength should become sufficient to balance the Soviet strength in the same
kind of weapons, it would become possible for the United States to dispense
with its present reliance on atomic bombs."

An even greater roadblock was "the attitude of the leaders of the American military establishment." It would be "very difficult," Conant said, "for the
United States to give energetic and genuine support to proposals for disarmament in the field of atomic weapons as long as the chiefs of the American
military relied almost exclusively upon the atomic weapon as their principal
means of retaliation against major aggression and as their principal hope of
victory in the event of all-out war." But to induce military leaders to accept
the idea of relinquishing their "Sunday punch," he recognized, "they must be
persuaded that atomic weapons in the long run are on balance a danger to the
United States." To this end he thought the State Department panel should
recommend that a supersecret high-level civilian-military committee con-
tinuously review the "over-all weapons position" and in the process "be useful
in developing an awareness, throughout the defense establishment, of the
character of the race in weapons of mass destruction." This was, of course,

reminiscent of the "quasi-judicial" panel he had urged on the Defense Department, and, similarly, he thought it should keep watch on the U.S.-Soviet balance and remind Pentagon leaders that they were "equally responsible for both overseas attacks and the domestic defense of the United States." At the moment, he observed—and here he was clearly alluding to the Strategic Air Force and its hostility to continental defense—"it seemed as if many of those having high authority were more concerned about what they could do to the other fellow than they were about what the other fellow could do to us."

Conant grew more "reticent and tentative" when asked for specific suggestions to alleviate the problem of improving public understanding of atomic weaponry. Perhaps some "press cooperation in commenting upon prospective atomic developments" could be obtained. But his most arresting and heretical proposition was not to gain prominence for another three decades—the idea of a "No First Use" declaration; in Conant's case it was consistent with his steady support of universal military service to balance Soviet conventional might in Europe. It "might be a good sign," as he put it, "if the United States could reach a stage in its military position in which it would become possible for us to announce officially that we would not be the first to use atomic weapons in any new war." By itself such a statement "might well be unwise," but Conant's real point was that one should work to strengthen the still tentative taboo on using nuclear weapons—he was implicitly admitting that, notwithstanding his earlier approval of the bomb's use on Japan, he now placed this method of destruction in a separate category. Present military plans made it difficult for the public to draw a "sharp distinction" between nuclear and conventional weapons, but he hoped that eventually it "might still be possible to separate atomic weapons from 'bayonets.'"

Conant's insistence on the importance of educating the American public to the realities of nuclear arms impressed the State Department group, for its final report, delivered to the incoming Eisenhower administration in January 1953, is remembered primarily for a section that closely corresponded to Conant's prescriptions, and that finally raised to the highest levels the arguments submerged during the "Fishing Party" expedition.[58] Its principal recommendation, that the U.S. government "adopt a policy of candor toward the American people" on the subject of nuclear weapons, soon filtered into public view (even though the report itself remained classified for several decades) via an article by Oppenheimer in *Foreign Affairs,* and it inspired the Eisenhower administration's 1953 Operation Candor and "Atoms for Peace" proposals, though under the influence of less idealistic advisers the State Department panel's profound concerns (with which Eisenhower had genuine sympathy) were converted into something more akin to Cold War public-relations and psychological-warfare exercises.[59]

As for the Disarmament Panel's hopes to restrain the arms race by invigorating U.S.-Soviet negotiations and considering a moratorium on H-bomb testing, they fared considerably worse. Though Conant's reaction to Bush's proposal to delay the fall 1952 thermonuclear test is not known, there can be no doubt that he supported it. Indeed, from the moment of Truman's announcement that the United States would go forward with the weapon in January 1950, he had warned the GAC about "the grave security problem presented by the proposed test of a thermonuclear weapon"—an apparent reference to the potential danger that the Soviets would reap a harvest of technical data by analyzing the fallout from a test explosion, thereby advancing their own H-bomb project.[60] And of course he also agreed with Bush's strategic rationale for postponement, since any test would inevitably hasten the day when both superpowers possessed thermonuclear weapons, with an edge to Moscow.[61] Nevertheless, happy to escape the atomic business, depressed by and resigned to the advent of the H-bomb, feeling his advice already rejected, Conant took no apparent part in Bush's last-gasp campaign.

Whether Bush's plan would have had any hope of success if conveyed to Moscow in 1952 will never be known—the slim odds of a positive reception would surely have improved after Stalin's death the following March—but the response couldn't have been much colder than the one it actually received in Washington. On October 9, the National Security Council quashed the proposal before it ever reached Truman, with Defense Secretary Lovett spluttering that "any such idea should be immediately put out of mind and that any papers that might exist on the subject should be destroyed."[62]

Three weeks later, on the evening of October 31, a man-made volcano—a 10.4-megaton thermonuclear explosion—vaporized the Pacific Island of Elugelab, leaving a charcoal-black, two-mile-wide, half-mile-deep scar on the ocean floor. The era of thermonuclear weapons had irrevocably opened, and the "age of the Superblitz" became even more terrifying than Conant had imagined.

Harry S Truman, whose only evident concern about the H-bomb test was that it not interfere with the presidential election, acceded to the clamor around him and allowed the terms of Conant, Oppenheimer, and DuBridge to expire on the General Advisory Committee. Rabi, the last surviving charter member, became chairman of a panel now much diminished in stature and influence; Strauss succeeded Dean as AEC chairman the following year. On September 27, Truman dispatched valedictory letters to Conant, Oppenheimer, and DuBridge expressing "real regret" at their departure from the GAC and admiration for their "long period of conscientious service."[63] But earlier that month, Conant had already uttered his own epitaph to his nuclear career. A *Newsweek* reporter preparing a cover story on "U.S. Education's No. 1 Man" asked Conant for his views on the government's atomic policies. "I no longer have any connection with the atom bomb," he answered. "I have no sense of accomplishment."[64]

CHAPTER 31

Cold War Educator, Part IV

McCarthyism and the Crisis of the Liberal Educator

1950–1953

War and threats of war sear into a university community like a red hot iron.[1]
— Commencement address, June 21, 1951

It would be a sad day for the United States if the tradition of dissent were driven out of the universities. For it is the freedom to disagree, to quarrel with authority on intellectual matters, to think otherwise, that has made this nation what it is today.
— Harvard president's report, January 12, 1953

When I said that I believed there are no Communists at Harvard, I went on to say that the university could not undertake, in my opinion, the kind of investigation which would find the really hidden Communists without destroying the life of the university.

On the other hand, if the Government has evidence that there are such people there, I say I hope they will ferret them out by FBI methods and prosecute them.
— Congressional testimony, February 3, 1953

Conant personified the crisis of liberal educators who struggled to balance the competing imperatives of academic freedom and Cold War orthodoxy as McCarthyism entered its most virulent phase. The liberal educator was a species scathingly indicted in Mary McCarthy's novel of campus intrigue of the time, *The Groves of Academe*, in which she skewers the hypocrisy of the "fearless administrator" who caves in when the going gets tough. A year after proudly hiring a left-wing literature professor who has fallen victim to "ordeal by slander," the president of "Jocelyn College" quietly decides not to renew the controversial scholar's appointment. In one particularly sordid episode, President Hoar, proud author of a *New York Times* magazine article condemning "The Witch Hunt in Our Universities," stoops to using false pretenses to interrogate a visiting poet about rumors that Mulcahy once belonged to the Communist Party. "We're all liberals, believe me," Hoar piously assures him, "and there's not one of us who isn't shocked and sickened by the reign of terror in our colleges." Speaking fondly of "the fight for academic liberties," he promises that he seeks the information only "for Mulcahy's own protection," though his real goal is to find some clinching excuse to rid his institution of a nettlesome presence. In the novel's David-beats-Goliath ending, Mulcahy quickly discovers this seamy subterfuge, storms into Hoar's office, and successfully blackmails him by threatening to expose him to educators' groups "and to every liberal magazine and newspaper in the country." Shaking his fist in his boss's face, Mulcahy vows "to write a sequel to the President's magazine article that would reveal to the whole world the true story of a professional liberal: a story of personal molestation, spying, surveillance, corruption of students by faculty stool-pigeons." Shaken by this confrontation, Hoar has a sudden *crise de conscience* — "Maybe our behavior did have an ugly little kink in it" — and impulsively resigns in penitence and shame. Little wonder, then, that the critic Bernard DeVoto (who as a boat-rocking junior literature instructor at Harvard fifteen years earlier had left Harvard in a huff after a chilly encounter with Conant) should find *The Groves of Academe* "brilliant, savage, fascinating, expert, oddly tender, and most satisfying."[2]

Conant never, so far as is known, resorted to such crude contrivances as personally investigating the political backgrounds of Harvard faculty members. Yet, like Maynard Hoar, this prototypical liberal educator found himself facing charges from his own faculty that he could and should be more zealous in combating the enemies of academic freedom. As with Jocelyn College's leader, Harvard's twenty-fourth president nobly uttered paeans to academic freedom, to rational discussion, to the toleration of unpopular views, and criticized "reactionary forces" that were harming American democracy, and this fostered the impression that he and Harvard stood steadfastly against any and all, including Senator McCarthy, who would trespass the hallowed citadel of free inquiry and expression. "Your presidency has seen in the Faculty of Arts and Sciences a vigorous advocacy of academic freedom," Provost Buck complimented Conant in November 1952, two months before the end of his reign. "Harvard remains a bulwark to other Universities in this respect."[3] And Harvard's most prominent chronicler, Samuel Eliot Morison, glowingly judged that Conant had "kept the flag of academic freedom flying 'through change and through storm.' "[4] Yet such proud claims were somewhat overdrawn. While Conant shielded the tenure process from blatant political manipulation and struggled to educate the public to the value of preserving academic freedom and independence from state control, he also took actions and positions that tarnished his sterling record. He consistently and publicly reaffirmed his position that party members should be excluded from the teaching profession.[5] Despite public and private pledges that Harvard would not collaborate with government investigations of political activities on campus, and Conant's clear distaste for such inquests, there is some evidence, uncorroborated but impossible to ignore, that his administration secretly passed confidential information to the FBI. And in the waning days of his presidency, the nation's most prominent educational statesman endorsed the principle that professors should be summarily fired for refusing to "name names" to congressional committees.

From mid-1949 on, the proposition that Communist Party membership disqualified otherwise competent teachers from practicing their profession constituted a veritable loyalty oath, an accepted starting point for educators and faculty in subsequent controversies. Conant's putative rationale for taking this stand—that Communists had sacrificed their rights by surrendering their intellectual freedom—was adopted by academic administrators around the country wanting to justify the ridding of their institutions, offices, or professions of politically troublesome individuals. While a handful of prominent educators (notably Alexander Meiklejohn, Henry Steele Commager, and Robert Hutchins) still insisted on the rights of academics to engage without penalty in peaceful, legal political activity, increasingly the debate gravitated toward the arguments of intellectuals like Sidney Hook, who regularly cited Conant to support his contention that Communism should be studied, but that adherents of its noxious doctrines were "unfit to teach in American schools" and that party membership by itself constituted "professional misconduct."[6]

This was the virtually unchallenged position of the educational establishment when Senator Joseph McCarthy burst upon the scene in February 1950. The profession had unilaterally disarmed just as its most powerful enemy neared the battlefield. Ironically, in their efforts to prove they were hardliners, the educators had failed to learn the vaunted lesson of Munich: Appeasement doesn't work, it encourages. And it encouraged, as the *Crimson*'s editors warned, "men of little principle and no discernment, men who are attempting to stifle ideas and change our constitutional guarantees of civil liberties to suit their purpose."[7]

Under Conant Harvard avoided some of the inquisition's worst excesses, but since Conant's influence extended well beyond Harvard, one cannot judge his performance simply by what occurred there. During the last few years of his presidency, as pressure on universities to purge radicals mounted, instead of coalescing to fight the threat, most academic leaders rushed to prove that they could do the job even more effectively than outsiders. Leaders of the University of California took that approach, with Conant's quiet backing, in its handling of one of the bitterest and best-known controversies, the battle over a state-imposed loyalty oath. Along with most faculty and staff, Robert Gordon Sproul, president of the huge UCal system since 1930, campaigned strongly against the measure, but also accepted the Conant-Hook thesis that Communist Party members were *ipso facto* unqualified to teach. The California oath, quietly adopted by the state board of regents in March 1949, caused an uproar later that spring when faculty learned that their employment now depended on their pledging that they neither endorsed nor belonged to "any party or organization that believes in, advocates, or teaches the overthrow of the United States, by force or by any illegal or unconstitutional means." When classes began that fall, only half the faculty had completed the required forms. Amid heated arguments, meetings, compromise proposals, Sproul's administration supported the no-Communist provision but hesitated to fire permanent staff. In December the regents imperiously dismissed a teaching assistant in the physics department at Berkeley who had signed the oath but then taken the Fifth Amendment before HUAC.

By the spring of 1950, exasperated by what it regarded as delaying tactics and unimpressed by a faculty vote in favor of a self-policing ordinance against Communist teachers, the hard-line faction on the regents handed down a "Sign-or-Get-Out Ultimatum." Sproul pleaded with the regents to allow the university to police itself, promising that any Communist faculty member would be dismissed—a request that fully accorded with the stand of Conant and the Educational Policies Commission, which had criticized state-imposed loyalty tests as harmful to educational freedom.[8] Worried by news reports that Sproul might resign, Conant privately tried to stiffen his friend's fortitude: "You are the commanding general," he telegraphed Sproul, "and we are looking to you for victory."[9]

The months of controversy exacted a high toll on the dispirited faculty. Academics around the country wrote letters of protest, initiated boycotts, or retracted applications to teach at UCal, while scores of teachers left in disgust or completed the oath under protest. The fighting in Korea inspired a patriotic surge that further reduced the number of nonsigners to less than a hundred, most of whom willingly assured a special faculty tenure review board that they were not Communists. On July 21, Sproul and the governor of California, Earl Warren, urged the regents to accept a compromise proposal framed on the principle that the main point was to cleanse higher education of Communists, not of independent-minded teachers. Under Sproul's formula, the university would retain thirty-nine nonsigners who had been cleared by the tenure review board, but dismiss six who refused to divulge their political beliefs to fellow teachers on the grounds that the proceedings represented an abridgement of academic freedom. The badly divided regents voted 10–9 to accept this compromise and then at the last minute decided to reassess the matter at a later session.[10]

Recuperating in New Hampshire from his recent operation, Conant congratulated Sproul on the meeting's outcome. "If an onlooker may say so it seemed to me the line you and Gov. Warren took was just right and very helpful to all of us in the academic business," he wrote. "More power to you

and I hope any attempt to reconsider or reverse the decision will be defeated."11
But the California regents did reverse their position and later that month
ordered the dismissal of professors who refused to sign the oath, regardless of
the faculty board's recommendations. And, though ultimately overturned by
the courts in 1952, the result of the California oath controversy accelerated
the purging of allegedly dangerous teachers, classes, texts, and thoughts
across the country. California, in turn, was one of many state governments
that proposed or passed loyalty oath measures, often modeled on Maryland's
Ober Law (named after Harvard alumnus who had inspired Grenville Clark's
June 1949 defense of academic freedom, who chaired the committee that
drafted the act) which barred state funds from any institution that failed to
enforce the oath-signing requirement.12

The Massachusetts state house also annually threatened to pass "anti-
subversive" statutes requiring college presidents to fire "red" teachers, and
held inquisitorial hearings that on one occasion in April 1951 nearly erupted
into a fistfight when an affronted Harvard chemistry lecturer hauled in for
questioning accused the representatives of treating witnesses "like prisoners
in a concentration camp."13 But each year the fulminations ended in a
watered-down bill that avoided a head-on collision, and in any case Harvard,
as a privately endowed institution independent of state financing, could
afford to take a relatively disdainful view of these Procrustean proceedings.

Conant had a far harder time shrugging off an internal challenge to
traditional Harvard personnel procedures that merged Cold War pressures on
education with a largely secret intra-university power struggle. As in the
Walsh-Sweezy case a decade before, the battle's flash point was the department of economics, which was especially scrutinized by right-wing businessmen who opposed all forms of government intervention in economic affairs.
And once again, as in the squabble over Marbury's appointment to the
Corporation, the anti-Conant forces were centered among conservative alumni
on Harvard's Board of Overseers. The internecine brawling divided into two
distinct campaigns—a year of trench warfare over giving John Kenneth
Galbraith a full professorship, followed by a counterattack by conservative
alumni who wanted to force the naming of a right-wing economist more
"sympathetic" to business interests. In both episodes, Conant showed considerable gumption in defending the inviolability of the tenure process from
encroachment by the Overseers, a group Galbraith has drolly described as
follows:

This liturgically august body numbering thirty members is elected by the
Harvard alumni and, with the smaller Corporation, comprises the bicameral
government of the university. Not for some decades prior to 1948 had the
Overseers risen above ceremony, and, to their credit, they have not done so
since. Dignity, shared presence and generously shared self-esteem are often
a substitute for function. But no pattern of behavior is wholly predictable;

my proposed appointment turned gentlemanly contentment and torpor into ardent and eloquent indignation.[14]

In *My Several Lives* Conant characteristically omitted all mention of the Galbraith drama—which though secret at the time has entered Harvard lore—as well as the fact that in both controversies in the economics department he threatened resignation at critical junctures to get his way. He even (misleadingly) wrote that until 1950 none of the Overseers had challenged the high-toned 1936 statement of the then chairman of the Board of Overseers' visiting review committee to the economics department, Walter Lippmann: "In the task of recruiting a new member of the faculty, the question of his views on controversial public issues is now, and we believe should continue to be, left aside; insofar as it arises at all, the question is whether or not he arrived at his views by thorough scholarship and by intellectual processes which command the respect of his peers."[15]

Being good sons of Harvard, of course, Galbraith's accusers disclaimed any notion of undermining academic freedom. But their animus clearly flowed from political controversies of the Cold War, and it reflected divisions on issues of national concern. First, many Overseers scorned Galbraith's participation in the New Deal, his unabashed liberalism (he had recently helped found the Americans for Democratic Action) and, worst of all, his professed admiration for John Maynard Keynes, whose blessing on deficit spending had helped to underpin FDR's economic-recovery strategy. In the glare of the ideological duel with Moscow, some conservatives discerned treason in virtually any endorsement of government intervention in the economy. "To a certain type of businessman," Conant later recalled, the British economist "was like the proverbial red rag. In the eyes of many economically illiterate but deeply patriotic (and well-to-do) citizens, to accuse a professor of being a Keynesian was almost equivalent to branding him a subversive agent."[16] Clarence B. Randall, a Midwestern steel magnate and president of the Harvard alumni association, who had tangled with Galbraith in a wartime turf battle with the Office of Price Administration; the financier Thomas W. Lamont; and Sinclair Weeks, the Republican Party's national finance chairman, former senator, and in Galbraith's considered judgment "the most resolutely regressive influence in the Commonwealth of Massachusetts"[17]—these men were all opposed to Galbraith.

A second strain of opposition arose from a controversy of some personal interest to Conant. Along with such noteworthy and later prominent scholars as George Ball, Paul Nitze, and Walt Rostow, Galbraith had helped to research and write the 1946 report of the U.S. Strategic Bombing Survey (USSBS), which after detailed on-site inspection had concluded that the air force's strategic bombing of German industrial targets had failed to match expectations; indeed, plant production had recovered promptly and even increased within weeks of the heavy aerial assaults.[18] Not surprisingly, these conclusions did not sit well with some air force officials, who feared that it cast aspersions on their service's wartime effectiveness and also damaged their prospects in the perennial interservice budgetary rivalries. (Indeed, Galbraith had joined the study against the advice of a Harvard faculty member working for the OSS who had warned that the final report might be manipulated in the air force's favor.) Among those affronted by Galbraith's findings, and his tenacity in arguing for them, was the panel's secretary, Judge Charles Codman Cabot, a member of the Board of Overseers' Executive Committee, who in 1946 had prepared a draft USSBS report that lauded the air force's accomplishments in Germany; it had been shelved in favor of the version written by Galbraith. In early 1949, Cabot told a special faculty committee investigating the Overseers' objections to Galbraith that the economist's conduct revealed "personality defects" and "intellectual dishonesty" that "made him unworthy" of a Harvard professorship.[19]

"He was not a mean man nor one to carry a grudge," Galbraith later recalled of Cabot, a quintessential Proper Bostonian, "with clipped mustache, well-cut hair, lean figure, quiet, good suiting," whose brother, Paul C. Cabot, sat on the Corporation. "But he had seen me behaving in an admittedly uncouth way and, as he saw it, on the wrong side. No brash civilian should have placed himself in opposition to the experienced wisdom of the Air Force or shown such a lack of respect for the acknowledged heroes of the Republic. This Charles Cabot knew, and therewith he knew his duty as a Cabot."[20]

However, Judge Cabot's claims did not move the faculty committee, which after interviewing several USSBS participants failed to substantiate the charge of intellectual dishonesty against Galbraith and endorsed his appointment.[21] Nor did they impress Conant, who thought the Overseers' effort to block Galbraith's advancement despite the support of his department not only an unacceptable intrusion into a sacrosanct tenure process that was vital to the university's survival, but a politically motivated challenge to his own authority that, if successful, would damage both Harvard and universities everywhere.

That challenge almost succeeded at the closed-door Overseers' meeting on June 23, 1949, at which pro-Galbraith Overseers, led by Charles Wyzanski, barely managed to put off until the fall a formal vote on his appointment. In an emotional personal memorandum to the Corporation the next morning, a shaken Conant showed his determination to fight hard to resolve on his own terms what he called the "very ticklish issue" of the relative functions of Corporation, Overseers and faculty in making permanent appointments. Fearing the emergence of a dictatorial cabal if he gave in, he noted the slight but real possibility that the Overseers, nominally restricted to reviewing matters of procedure rather than of substance, might seek "still greater responsibility and the enlarging of their inspectorial powers" and bar other appointments, perhaps springing a comparable surprise on a new president less willing to take them on. In an unmistakable hint that defeat might cause his departure, Conant warned that his position could become "literally untenable" if the anti-Galbraith forces triumphed:

> 4. If the case should finally go against the administration in October and if nothing is done between now and October, I think the situation would be very tough for the President of the University vis-à-vis the faculty. I won't elaborate on that again, and it may be that I am unduly worried about it, but I submit that the man who would have to take the gaff on this matter is the one who has some reason for considering the position pretty carefully in advance. I would point out that by the nature of the case there could be no formal statement of the reasons why the Board of Overseers failed to confirm; I should be bound by the secrecy of the proceedings and would have to return an evasive answer to all questions given by members of the faculty either in private or in a faculty meeting, except to say that from the debate the opposition appeared to be a combination of unfavorable judgment on character and an unwillingness to appoint a New Dealer. There are no responsible officials on the Board of Overseers to take the rap. The whole thing would be confused and disagreeable beyond measure. It would be said that the President in spite of his fair words about the integrity of the faculties, had knuckled under to "Wall Street" and the independence of the faculty had been sacrificed; whereas if he had had the guts, he would have backed up his words by making the alternative of resignation.[22]

Conant also left himself an escape hatch, however, outlining a plan to improve his "formal and distant" relations with the Overseers by allowing them more intimate leeway in governing Harvard while simultaneously limiting their power to block appointments. If that failed to save Galbraith's appointment, he calculated, at least he could tell the faculty that he had done his best to resist the Overseers.[23]

For some months the matter drifted. As both sides lobbied intensively, the Overseers formed a special committee to investigate accusations relating to Galbraith's "personality and character."[24] Galbraith himself, at the hurricane's eye, fidgeted uncomfortably, relying on what a sympathetic Provost Buck told him. Then, one morning in early October, he came to Edward S. Mason, his friend and dean of Harvard's School of Public Administration, "in a state of considerable turmoil" to complain that, while the whole episode had stayed out of the newspapers, slanderous gossip about his character and honesty had begun reaching his wife and friends. Like Galbraith, Mason blamed the whispering on the Overseers, as well as on a Boston attorney, Col. Guido R. Perera, who had helped to organize the bombing survey and, along with Cabot, had vainly attempted to ensure a pro–air force final report. Deeply angered, Mason warned Buck and the Corporation that if the Overseers should quash Galbraith's appointment because of his valor in preventing an air force whitewash of the bombing report, "A lot of dirty linen would be washed in public, and I feel certain it would not be Galbraith's linen."[25]

Galbraith drafted a detailed defense of his participation in the bomb survey to give Buck, and solicited effusive testimonials from USSBS colleagues attesting to his conduct and contribution.[26]

Armed with this new ammunition—which, ironically, reached Conant on the eve of his own climactic clash with strategic bombing enthusiasts over the H-bomb—Galbraith's supporters mounted a decisive offensive to get him appointed by late November, and they were aided by an unflinching Conant, who sternly informed the Overseers that they were unqualified to judge the merits of a nomination to the faculty, merely the procedure by which it was made.[27] The charge that Galbraith distorted the bombing survey report clearly had failed to impress Conant, and perhaps even contributed to his later assessment that air force generals "could be extremely dogmatic and even unscrupulous in respect to questions which challenge their premises."[28] Galbraith, looking back on the controversy after gaining national prominence for the liberal views, political shrewdness, and entertainingly acerbic prose displayed in his books and in his diplomatic service, sardonically related its personal aftermath: "Often in academic and public life one wonders whether one must speak out on some issue where the emotions or pecuniary interests of the reputable are in opposition to the public good. Perhaps this time one can pass and accept the pleasures of a tranquil life. Always when faced with this decision, I have thought of Sinclair Weeks, Clarence Randall and Thomas Lamont. Surely I must do whatever might be possible to justify their forebodings."[29]

Typically, Conant never discussed his role in the struggle, letting Buck serve as intermediary. That ingrained New England tight-lippedness still prevailed a decade later when he came to see Galbraith at Harvard while working on his study of U.S. public schools. Galbraith, eager to express his thanks and more than a bit curious to see if Conant would let his hair down and reminisce, spotted a suitable point in the conversation to express his gratitude. Conant was apparently discomfited, paused and perhaps muttered a few words of acknowledgment—before quickly and firmly steering the conversation back to a less personal plane. Galbraith got the message: busy men have no time to indulge in sentimentality.[30]

The Overseers' conservative faction soon regrouped for round two. Clarence Randall, presiding at the June 1950 Commencement rituals as the president of the Associated Harvard Alumni, could not resist the temptation to avail himself of this exalted platform and, departing from the banter usually dished out by the master of ceremonies, chided Harvard for inadequate enthusiasm for free enterprise, wondering "why it was that professors who were so jealous to preserve academic freedom were often the first to threaten freedom of enterprise for the businessman."

When Randall returned to his seat next to Conant's, he found the president wearing an expression "midway between smile and frown."

"Very good, very good," Conant said stiffly.

"But you didn't like it," Randall replied.

At this Conant broke into a restrained laugh: "Well, I guess it is all right, so long as it doesn't happen too often."[31]

He found the alumni's next move less risible. On November 27, a visiting committee to the economics department chaired by Randall and including several other disgruntled veterans of the Galbraith affair issued a blistering report denouncing its alleged left-wing tilt. It noted sadly that while Economics harbored "one or more Socialists, some zealous followers of British economist John Maynard Keynes, and some who advocate the extension of economic controls by Government," at the other end of the "social spectrum" the department seemed to lack "men of equal ability and zeal who hold opposing views and are prepared to teach them."[32]

Conant had run into this sort of complaint before—at a 1949 dinner gathering, he had strongly rebuffed a suggestion that Harvard have a "compulsory course in the American free enterprise system"[33]—but this challenge was more serious. His later account of this controversy generously ascribed high motives and concern for academic freedom to Randall, but a contemporary report by a newcomer on the visiting committee offers a more vivid taste of the stormy feelings animating the protesting members. In January 1951, David Lilienthal found himself surrounded by "sincere men and also genuinely conservative, so much so that if a man is called 'New Deal,' that disposes him as practically a Communist." They had complained, he wrote disgustedly, that the economics department

> does not have any right-wing professors capable of giving enthusiastic indoctrination to the students, and giving Harvard a good reputation in the country. This is called "lack of balance," and what they insist on are appointments in the future that will restore the balance. Sinclair Weeks, an overseer, undertook to grade the writings of the faculty by a system in which zero was center, plus was right, minus left of center, and he had it down to a science, with a score: In one year, the score of the writings for the year was plus 16; the next year minus 6. (This is just hard to believe among obviously intelligent, well-intentioned men.) Provost Buck and Dean Mason gave a spirited response, but it did nothing but arouse suspicion about them, too.[34]

Lilienthal, appalled—"I actually can't see why in hell I should give my further time to such a futile business"—recognized that the really important issue was "whether the faculty is to be independent and self-contained, or run by the varying views of the overseers," and confidently predicted that "Harvard's tradition has been strong on this, and I can't see Conant standing for any great change."[35]

He wouldn't. "More trouble in the offing," he noted in his diary in the spring of 1951 after recording another "blast" by Weeks and a "Flare up on

Economics" over an effort by Randall to block a new appointment.[36] "More trouble" arrived that fall in a proposal to create a new tenured slot in the economics department for a professor specializing in "the economics of enterprise." To Conant this suggestion "had an all too familiar sound," evoking the prospect of a barrage of requests to hire new professors to obtain "balance" in other departments, and he decided that the time had come to draw the line. On November 5, after a routine Corporation meeting, Conant met with Buck and Business School dean Donald K. David and, he recorded in his diary, "layed [sic] down the law about a professor across these two faculties. Showed some emotion which was necessary. Threatened to resign if there was a real row! Both took it well."[37]

Fiscal prudence may have motivated this resignation threat,[38] but forcefully stated concerns about academic integrity colored Conant's more considered response to the Overseers' campaign. "Started to write special confidential report on Economics department," Conant jotted in his diary on December 19. "Dynamite!" In quintessential empiricist style, Conant had decided to take the pulse of economics instruction personally at fourteen leading universities around the country (not to mention Britain, Australia, and New Zealand), and to consult scholars and financial figures such as David Rockefeller, Jr. (the value of whose opinion was not lessened by a recent $5 million donation to the Business School), and members of the Committee for Economic Development, a New York–based establishment assemblage of money and business power on whose board of trustees Conant comfortably sat. Conant reported to the Corporation and the Overseers in January 1952 that his autodidactic exercise showed that Harvard's department comprised a mix of teachers typical of that found in similar establishments throughout "the English-speaking world." He firmly rejected the claim that "one or more Socialists" taught economics at Harvard, and noted mildly that given the wide range of definitions of the term, it might not be such a bad idea if one did. He disputed the whole concept of rating economists on a "social spectrum" or cubbyholing them in radical or conservative categories, "Keynesian or anti-Keynesian, or 'socialists.' " Rigid enforcement of a departmental "balance" would limit candidates and "encourage the appointment of 'good' rather than 'excellent' men"—the most egregious possible sin to an educator given to quoting Lowell's admonition that the surest way to ruin a university faculty is to fill it with "good" men (in tune with prevailing social stereotypes Conant presumed the ideal candidate for the job would be male—"the man in question" would be chosen from "men of high character"):

> One could classify economists [Conant wrote], at least theoretically, in terms of their political beliefs, but except for communists and socialists this is a very difficult matter in the present flux of political opinion. Furthermore, people's political convictions, like their religious beliefs, are often subject to violent change. Everyone speaks of the dangers of introducing political

criteria into the consideration of academic appointments. If analyzed, I believe these dangers stem largely from the fact that political views do not represent a bias relevant to an academic intellectual discipline as does a philosopher's adherence to a philosophic doctrine such as idealism or logical empiricism. Political opinions are temporary, emotional, and subject to change under social duress; it is to avoid such duress that politics and religion are considered "out of bounds" in judging persons for academic posts in the United States in the mid-twentieth century.

Conant then threw a sop to the conservatives, Solomonically apportioning equal blame to the Overseers and to the economics department for the dispute, and proposing the tripartite appointment (to be shared among Harvard's Economics, Business, and Public Administration schools) of a tenured professor who would, among the usual qualifications, possess "an awareness of the positive role of business enterprise in a changing and developing economy."[39] Though Conant left Harvard before learning the fate of his compromise proposal, to his "astonishment" and pleasure both the Corporation and Overseers unanimously accepted his confidential report, with even Randall and Weeks voting aye after prolonged grumbling. "Issues still foggy but believe it helps and will help my successor," a cautiously optimistic Conant wrote in his diary.[40]

In fact the sparring over "balance" in economics dragged on for most of the decade—an "intellectually dreary affair," recalls McGeorge Bundy, dean of the faculty from 1953 to 1961, as he had to "fend off the crude but zestful efforts" to impose a conservative appointment.[41] To Galbraith's horror the Overseers successfully wrested an honorary degree for Sinclair Weeks, by now Eisenhower's secretary of commerce. But they failed to secure a guaranteed haven in the Department of Economics for a pro-business professor, though one member of the department in that era reported a case of a candidate who would have received tenure had he not been a Marxist.[42]

Other brushfires also smoldered—and a rancorous subterranean conflict in Harvard's restive astronomy department illustrates how the pressures of McCarthyism could shatter personal relationships and academic camaraderie even in fields ostensibly far removed from politics. Until he resigned in September 1952, controversy constantly swirled around the Harvard Observatory's flamboyant long-time director, Harlow Shapley. Shapley unapologetically continued to promote left-wing and pacifist causes, as well as himself, despite steady criticism from conservative alumni and from Red hunters in Congress, the Boston State House, and elsewhere, who routinely cited his presence as proof of Harvard's laxness about subversive influences. To the FBI, even routine academic contact with Shapley could put a colleague under suspicion. He had even won the supreme honor of McCarthy describing him as one of four dangerous spies singled out by name (albeit incorrectly, as "Howard

Shipley") in his famous February 1950 speech in Wheeling, West Virginia, which catapulted McCarthy into the national spotlight.[43]

Conant judiciously refrained from open criticism of Shapley's political activities, but he found him personally arrogant, politically naive, and an inept administrator; he expected his retirement to afford a chance to stream-line Harvard's astronomy program. Shapley, in turn, thought Conant officious, unimaginative, militaristic. (Apparently little had happened to raise his estimation since the night he dined with Felix Frankfurter in March 1933 when rumors first began spreading that Conant as well as Shapley himself was under consideration for Harvard's top job. Gossiping about the succession struggle, Shapley had noted that no one under serious consideration would harm the university if selected. "Including Jim Conant?" Frankfurter ventured. "Well," answered Shapley, "he is the only one who really would not do. But I don't suppose there is any danger of that.")[44] Their relations hardly improved after Conant, in October 1951, dashed Shapley's expectations of being made a university professor, the most prestigious title Harvard can bestow, leaving the astronomer, Conant thought, "very disappointed but not bitter or sullen."[45]

Inside the department, meanwhile, what one veteran calls a "hostile unpleasant atmosphere" developed as the tenured astronomers polarized into pro- and anti-Shapley factions and jockeyed for position to succeed him. Critics, led by professors Frederick Whipple and Donald Menzel, faulted Shapley for bringing the department into disrepute and neglecting administrative duties for the sake of quixotic political causes and his own ego — "Shapley could never resist the temptation to accept a speaking engagement when somebody would phone him at two in the morning," Whipple recalled.[46] Worse, they fumed that his politics would prevent Harvard from obtaining military funding; after all, merely appearing on the same stage with the notorious "leftist" could be used as evidence to deny security clearance for secret work.[47] Shapley's leading partisan, Bart J. Bok, charged that his enemies ridiculed colleagues who did research unlikely to attract Pentagon dollars, ganged up on Shapley when he came under investigation, and pressured Bok and his wife to abandon him as well.[48] In one unpleasant incident, as told by Bok, a "very old and close friend" stopped by his Cambridge house, "and before dinner we stood on the verandah and looked at Boston and saw the lovely lights of the evening, and suddenly Otto [Struve] said, 'I bring you a message from your colleagues. They have asked me to come and tell you that life would be so much simpler all around Harvard if you and Priscilla would stop supporting Shapley.'"[49]

The struggle climaxed in 1952–53, when the Corporation opted to sever Harvard's ties to Boyden Station, a major observatory facility in South Africa, and to name one of Shapley's adversaries as the new director. Boyden's termination shocked several Harvard astronomers, none more than Bok, who had counted on a southern hemispheric viewing site for his research on the Milky Way, and who also hoped to succeed Shapley. Bok blamed Conant for acting out of "spite" to punish Shapley for years of embarrassment.[50]

Did a vengeful Conant abuse his power because of a vendetta against Shapley? No doubt Shapley exasperated him, and the turbulent status of the observatory was a major irritant. Evidence of that can be found in the files of Robert Oppenheimer, who in 1952–53 chaired the Overseers' astronomy visiting committee. "What is worrying me most now," Conant wrote his friend after determining to go ahead with a drastic reorganization of the observatory, "is the internal public relations problem, namely, how I can hit the astronomers over the head without revealing the source of my doubts and worries."[51]

But Conant was not a petty man, and the evidence in Oppenheimer's correspondence—Harvard's records are closed until 2003, of course—suggests that the principal reason for his desire to bash the astronomers over the head was the unflattering assessment of the department's work attested to by Oppenheimer's visiting committee. As Conant told the Corporation in August 1952, the committee had frankly stated that none of Harvard's astronomers classed nationally in the "front rank" of the profession, and the department had grave shortcomings in graduate instruction, modern experimental and observational experience, and state-of-the-art equipment; the university might be better off dropping astronomy altogether were it not for the harm that would inflict on the prestige of Harvard science and U.S. astronomy.[52]

In his February 1950 after-dinner speech to the Ohio County Women's Republican Club in Wheeling, West Virginia, Joe McCarthy, in addition to waving a sheet of paper he claimed contained the names of Communists working for the State Department, reportedly vowed to name a State Department consultant as "the top Russian spy in the country." Reading the credulous newspaper stories, Conant was mystified by the reference to the subversive consultant. Do you have any idea who he's talking about? he asked Bill Marbury, who happened to be in Cambridge for a Corporation meeting. The Baltimore lawyer did indeed. Not long before, he had been asked by Gen. "Al" Wedemeyer if Professor Owen Lattimore of Johns Hopkins University, a prominent China specialist who had advised FDR—and who had sharply questioned the general about his hard-line stance on policies in the Far East during a recent public appearance—was a "Red."[53]

This afforded Conant his first inkling of a new phase in the Cold War "Red scare." He already knew that congressional investigations into subversion was taking aim at schools and scholars, but now, on the heels of the Fuchs and Rosenberg cases, a new thesis received a serious hearing and massive press attention: that a band of Sinologists had conspired to undermine U.S. policy and cause the "loss" of China as part of a master Kremlin plot. In 1951–52, the newly created Senate Internal Security Subcommittee (SISS), chaired by the rabidly anti-Communist Republican Pat McCarran, held months of publicized hearings into the Institute of Pacific Relations, directed by Lattimore; though he had been exonerated in an initial probe of

McCarthy's charges, they considered him the ringleader of scholars who had slandered Chiang Kai-shek. With Far Eastern studies so politicized, it was hardly surprising that leading scholars of Asian studies at Harvard such as the historians John King Fairbank and Edwin O. Reischauer also found themselves accused of being Communist stooges for daring to acknowledge the legitimacy of the new regime in Peking or failing to display suitable enthusiasm for the Nationalist cause.[54] "Chinese coolies and Harvard professors," charged one McCarthyite journal, "are the people . . . most susceptible to Red propaganda."[55] Once named, however unfairly, professors like Fairbank encountered trouble obtaining passports, clearance for government work, grants, previously available publishing opportunities, or invitations to lecture. For less prominent scholars, especially graduate students and non-tenured faculty, such accusations jeopardized job prospects, recommendations, careers.

At the same time, attacks proliferated against other alleged contaminants threatening the ideological purity of America's youth. The Girl Scout handbook was pulled because it contained a favorable reference to the United Nations, decried as a body reflecting dangerous internationalist views. Calls went up to censor textbooks and vet libraries. The McCarran-Walter Immigration and Nationality Act arrayed barriers to prevent those foreigners holding allegedly dangerous views from entering the country. Guilt-by-association became a common criterion in judging teachers or nominees for government service, and among students, analysts were already pointing to the emergence of a "silent generation"—conformist, cautious, more traditional than their parents or professors. A "subtle, creeping paralysis of freedom of thought and speech . . . limiting both students and faculty in the area traditionally reserved for the free exploration of knowledge and truth" was the result. A survey of seventy-two institutions of higher learning disclosed "a widening tendency toward passive acceptance of the status quo, conformity, and a narrowing of the area of tolerance in which students, faculty and administrators feel free to speak, act and think independently," the *New York Times* reported. Symptoms included:

1. A reluctance to speak out on controversial issues in and out of class.
2. A reluctance to handle currently unpopular concepts even in classroom work where they may be part of the study program.
3. An unwillingness to join student political clubs.
4. Neglect of humanitarian causes because they may be suspect in the minds of politically unsophisticated officials.
5. An emphasis on lack of affiliations.
6. An unusual amount of serio-comic joking about this or that official investigating committee "getting you."
7. A shying away, both physically and intellectually, from any association

with the words, "liberal," "peace," "freedom" and from classmates of a liberal stripe.

8. A sharp turning inward to local college problems, to the exclusion of broader current questions.[56]

Students and faculty at Harvard, with its exalted sense of itself and its inveterate tradition of daring to be heretical, suffered less from such self-imposed constraints. Yet, Conant rose to defend universities against what Zechariah Chafee described as a "barbarian invasion," warning that "those who believe in tolerance and rational discussion" must stand up or face the consequences of "passivity and inaction."[57] Conant's desire to oppose McCarthyistic demagoguery shone most eloquently during his last two Commencement ceremonies as president of Harvard. In June 1951, Conant carefully distinguished conservatism, which "stands for the *status quo* but leans heavily on due process of law," from reaction, which "appeals to mob spirit," operates by fear-mongering and intimidation, and sweeps all "progressive" views into one basket. "To some of you," Conant told the graduating class,

> this tide of reaction which has been rising in the last few years will be more shocking than to others. To the extent that it results in smothering ideas under a blanket of silent fears, it is as distasteful to the conservatives among you as to the liberals. You will recall better than those who follow you the more tolerant, more courageous, pioneering temper of the days immediately following the close of World War II. You will have a particular responsibility, therefore, as citizens to guard not only the letter but the spirit of the Bill of Rights, the spirit of tolerance, and due process of law.

Conant went on to say that, notwithstanding the hopes of "many sincere, patriotic, optimistic liberals," Russia had proven herself to be an unregenerate enemy of freedom and the U.S. Communist Party had been revealed as "something other than a political party . . . something far more in the nature of a world-wide conspiracy based on deceit and directed from the Kremlin." To that extent, history had "proved the pessimistic conservatives of the war years to have been more accurate prophets than the optimistic liberals," but this did not mean it was in America's best interests for "the enemies of all progressive ideas" to be given a free hand. Within twenty-five years, he predicted, both conservatives and liberals would "join in condemning the reactionary as opposed to the conservative temper of these days." Schools and colleges "flourish only in an atmosphere of wide tolerance," and any restriction of freedom of inquiry, "by laws or by intimidation," would lead to disaster. So long as "the tide of reaction is running strong," he urged his listeners to join in the "defense of tolerance, of free discussion, of honest debate, of diversity of opinion," against attacks spearheaded by a small minority "who, distrusting these principles, use the fears generated by anxious days to provide the smoke screen to cover their operations."

Defending these basic principles served a cause even more important than liberty or democracy, Conant argued: preserving the chances for long-term peace and nuclear disarmament. For the immediate future, Conant conceded that talk of a negotiated settlement with Russia "must be regarded as Utopian," but he confidently declared that

> if World War III can be avoided, the time will come when the prospects for peace will seem far brighter than in these days of 1951. Some time within your lifetime, if not in mine, I am convinced the chances will once again favor those who work to minimize the military expenditures of an industrialized world. A concerted attack will be made on the problem of eliminating the threat to the major cities of the world that is inherent in modern weapons. That the opportunity will be presented to you and your contemporaries I feel certain. What use you will make of it, only a bold prophet would venture to declare. But the probability of constructive international action some years hence will be increased if in the intervening years the American people keep their heads. Disunity at home is a bad omen for peace abroad. The spirit of the lynching party to the extent that it gains ascendancy in these fearful days is working against the hopes for eventual peace. For the mob spirit is essentially a spirit of blind fear and the road out of the atomic age, the road towards eventual disarmament, can be built only by men of courage.[58]

The following June, Conant continued to speak out in a tone that ran counter to popular fears of an imminent Cold War showdown. He eulogized two endangered species—the practitioner of basic scientific research, who was being lured by big money into large-scale military- and government-funded projects; and the social reformer, who had fallen under the same suspicion being directed by "the reactionaries" at all activities even remotely left-wing. Since the Hiss and Fuchs cases, he told the graduating seniors, the reformer had been forced to "struggle against a dark blanket of public suspicion woven by the same types of persons who have always fought him but now are aided by the revelations of the traitorous actions of a few fanatics." Nevertheless, despite these "benumbing" events, he beseeched them to enter public and community service.

> Unless all Western civilization is wrecked by the whirlwind of a third World War, it seems certain that there will be in your lifetime a reaction against the present reaction. And when this occurs, some of you will wish to take up the work of the American reformer. . . . To your college generation and succeeding classes will be given, I feel sure, the privilege of making of the reformer once again a highly respected though bitterly controversial figure [who] will once again take his place alongside the conservative in the front rank of public spirited Americans.[59]

These were, indeed, courageous and far-sighted statements, but whether Conant's actions matched his high-sounding words is a murkier subject, and there are considerable data to support the view that, as he had in the 1935–36 Massachusetts loyalty-oath controversy, when he had opposed the legislation but then enforced it after enaction, Conant valued obedience to constituted state authority over fealty to principles of academic freedom. And his handling of two contentious academic-freedom issues—the FBI and the Fifth Amendment—during his final years at Harvard raise the question whether a further erosion of principle occurred.

The precise relationship of Harvard and the FBI in Conant's time remains unclear: partial access to Harvard and FBI records does not yield a conclusive answer; and this incomplete record is sometimes contradictory. After his many frustrating run-ins with security personnel during his work on the Manhattan Project, Conant clearly hated the idea of G-men snooping into the private lives of Harvardians, and he resisted FBI requests for the university to take on police functions on its behalf. In October 1949, responding to an appeal from Los Alamos to vouch for a Harvard mathematician whose clearance to work on secret projects was being held up for seemingly "trivial" reasons, Conant insisted that on principle he could not get involved:

> Frankly, as a matter of policy I feel that I cannot answer the question which you raised ... I make it a point not to know anything about the political opinions or activities of the members of the Harvard staff. To show to what extent I carry it, when an F.B.I. agent comes into my office, I always say, "If you want to ask me questions about any member of my staff, I won't answer your questions." It has always turned out, as a matter of fact, that they want to find out about somebody who was in the NDRC, for example.
>
> This may seem an awfully strong attitude for me to take, but in these days of alarms in academic freedom I am afraid that you will have to turn elsewhere about the clearance of any member of the Harvard faculty.[60]

Conant's claim of ignorance concerning the political views of faculty members—hardly credible given the wide newspaper coverage and persistent alumni criticism of controversial professors such as Matthiessen, Shapley, Fairbank, and Galbraith—could be read as a mere reaffirmation of his firmly stated policy that the Harvard administration would not act as watchdogs over the faculty's outside activities. And Conant insisted, at least in private, that his declared belief that Communists should not be employed as teachers applied primarily to public schools, not private universities:

> So great is my desire to keep the atmosphere of the University free for all manner of heresy that I would be quite willing to run the risk that is involved in having clandestine members of the Party on the permanent staff and I should be adamant in my refusal to make any inquiry or allow any inquiry to be made which would uncover crypto-communists.

I think our public schools are in a somewhat different category, and it was with the public school in mind that the N.E.A. statement was published, though here again I would be very cautious in my actions in regard to any people who have tenure.[61]

But Conant's adamant refusal to "allow any inquiry to be made" to uncover any Communist activities of faculty members seems to have been contradicted soon afterward by an assurance given by his closest associate on the Harvard Corporation, William Marbury, that the university had instituted at least an informal policy of helping FBI investigations in at least one respect: trying to soothe a right-wing critic, he confided in December 1949 that the university might turn over to the FBI any information it had indicating that a faculty member belonged to the Party, though he reiterated that Harvard would refer persons complaining about the politics of faculty members to legally constituted authorities since "the responsibility for rooting out subversives must rest with the FBI and the police and not with University authorities."[62]

The more sensitive and morally troublesome issue is whether Harvard turned over confidential information such as medical files, personal correspondence, or peer evaluations to the FBI with the aim of keeping the bloodhounds at bay. (Harvard records show that the university had, on the eve of America's entry into World War II, volunteered derogatory and confidential background information on teachers and students.)[63] In May 1951, the dean of the college assured undergraduates active in liberal political groups that their names would not be handed over to the FBI despite many requests for such information, and the FBI quickly disavowed interest in seeking information from student files.[64] "We stone-walled 'em!" Frank Keppel, dean of the School of Education, proudly declared decades later when asked whether Harvard gave in to requests for confidential student or faculty files from Hoover's agency.[65] But declassified FBI documents obtained by the most tenacious investigator of this issue, Sigmund Diamond, tell another story, and suggest that Harvard, indeed, gave the Bureau data from confidential files. The documents describe close but scrupulously concealed contacts between the Boston FBI agents and a university official whose name is blacked out and state that Harvard's authorities were "desirous of cooperating with the Bureau," but feared lest "some independent agency of the government," such as a congressional committee, gain access to FBI records "and thus cause embarrassment to the University in its cooperation." By June 1950, in any event, FBI agents believed they had established a "most cooperative and understanding association between the Bureau and Harvard University." Hoover himself proudly noted that "arrangements have been perfected whereby information of interest will be made available to the Bureau on a confidential basis . . . in connection with Harvard College and the Graduate School of Arts and Sciences."[66]

Was Conant the Bureau's valued confidential informant? Did he approve "arrangements" with the FBI to secretly hand over "information of interest" from Harvard's student or faculty files? If not, who was it? The answer lies buried in confidential FBI and Harvard records. Diamond adduces circumstantial evidence pointing to Conant as the Bureau's source—a February 1949 memorandum from the chief FBI agent in Boston to Hoover noted that Conant had "indicated his respect for the Bureau's work and his understanding for its many and varied interests"[67]—but whatever cooperation he may have offered seems not to have impressed Hoover, who snubbed Conant after he became Eisenhower's envoy to Germany and in 1959 complained that he "had more or less condoned the employment of professors who might have communist backgrounds."[68]

The record is clearer when it comes to Conant's stand on professors taking the Fifth Amendment when testifying under oath; in his final months as Harvard president, he endorsed a policy of automatically dismissing any faculty member who refused to answer the questions of congressional investigating committees, who refused to "name names" of associates who had attended Communist meetings. Historians have largely overlooked Conant's view on this policy for several reasons: his initial actions and statements were made secretly, then overshadowed by the publicity surrounding his resignation and departure from Harvard, and most importantly, because the men who succeeded him in early 1953, more sensitive to faculty concerns, quietly repudiated his policy and refused to fire scholars solely because they refused to cooperate fully with congressional inquisitions.

The question of how to treat Fifth Amendment cases rose to the forefront for Conant and most other university presidents only in late 1952, as the pressure on universities to eradicate Communist influence increased. No longer was it a question of whether Communists had the right to teach; now the issue was whether a scholar's fitness to teach might be also forfeited by "taking the Fifth." In *My Several Lives,* Conant was to claim that in resigning Harvard's presidency to go to Germany, he could not be faulted for abdicating his responsibility to "stay at home and defend academic freedom," because when he made the decision he was unaware of "the growing momentum of the witch hunt Senator McCarthy and a few of his associates were mounting nor of its ultimate impact on Harvard."[69] And it is true that the crystal ball on Conant's desk could not have shown that the congressional hearings in Boston and Washington that began in late February 1953 would embroil the university and McCarthy in a tense confrontation. Yet the record shows that weeks before Conant accepted Eisenhower's offer on December 22, 1952, he and Harvard had anticipated trouble. The Senate Internal Security Subcommittee had turned for the first time to education, and to alleged Communist infiltration among New York City teachers. In New York in September 1952 a star witness, an apostate party member, named former associates and listed Harvard as one university at which Communist cells had operated. It quickly became evident that both Senate and House committees saw profit in opening all-out investigations of academic radicals, and an especially attractive lure in the prospect of hearings in Boston about Communist influence at the "Kremlin on the Charles." "Harvard was an obvious target," one historian has noted. "Its prestige ensured publicity."[70] Conant hoped that Harvard could somehow evade becoming a focus of the approaching investigations, and stay silent until (and unless) that happened, but three days before he was tapped for the Germany job, Buck warned him that the faculty was rife with concern over a possible congressional inquest, and Harvard Law School Dean Erwin N. Griswold bluntly told him that it was "almost inevitable that the University will be involved" if the investigatory committees undertook "any serious activity." Predicting that "you are almost surely going to have to participate if there is anything more than a skirmish," Griswold complimented the "fine affirmative job" done by Robert Hutchins in standing up to official boards and added, "You can do a better job, and it may be of very great importance that you should do so."[71]

The dilemma was the degree of cooperation the Harvard administration expected of faculty members called to testify. Congressional watchdogs could ruin careers with a single subpoena or press release, so scholars hauled in to talk about past left-wing activities faced intense pressure to "name names" of friends, acquaintances, and colleagues who had attended the same political meetings or even cocktail parties back in the 1930s. Often, the investigators employed this degrading technique not so much to obtain useful information but as a ritual loyalty test intended to punish, humiliate, and "expose" reluctant witnesses and intimidate future ones, to show off their browbeating investigatory tactics to voters, and to spread the moral lesson that anti-Communism superseded considerations of friendship or personal loyalty.[72]

For those witnesses who refused to name names, the principal strategy was to plead the Fifth Amendment barring self-incrimination, or a "diminished Fifth"—agreeing to describe one's own activities but refusing to answer questions about others. But Senator McCarthy, who was unmoved by claims that witnesses refusing to testify might have moral scruples about discussing private beliefs or imperiling themselves or others for what they regarded as protected political activity, taking the Fifth could only mean one thing: "A witness's refusal to answer whether or not he is a Communist on the ground that his answer would tend to incriminate him is the most positive proof obtainable that the witness is a Communist."[73]

The Fifth Amendment raised a tricky issue for educators in the mainstream who decried McCarthyism but who believed it legitimate to expel Communists from the teaching profession. Now the question became: If CP membership rendered someone unfit for the profession, did a refusal to answer congressional questions also constitute grounds for dismissal, whether or not one belonged to the party? Conant thought so—a position that he rationalized on legalistic grounds and that belied his shining words in defense of academic freedom. In adopting that stand, his innate caution appears to have been strengthened by his reaction to the handling of a comparable case at Rutgers University in New Jersey that was decided as Harvard's authorities contemplated their own strategy toward the imminent investigation.

At Rutgers, a state-owned university, the trustees on December 12, 1952, unanimously voted to fire two tenured faculty members who had invoked the Fifth during the IPR hearings, though both had voluntarily told university administrators that they had not belonged to the Party.[74] Overruling a special faculty committee that had defended their colleagues' performance as scholars and teachers and their prerogative to assert their constitutional rights, the publicity-conscious trustees sternly laid down the policy that

> The refusal of a faculty member, on the grounds of possible self-incrimination, to answer questions as to his present or past membership in the Communist party, put to him by a properly constituted investigatory body, impairs confidence in his fitness to teach. It is also incompatible with the standards required of him as a member of his profession.... [and] is cause for the immediate dismissal.[75]

Conant closely monitored the Rutgers saga, and he knew that a pivotal figure in it was none other than Tracy Voorhees, a Rutgers trustee who had become Conant's close friend and who met frequently with him on Committee on the Present Danger business during the fall of 1952. Voorhees had also chaired a special advisory panel at Rutgers which had reported in October that faculty members' silence when asked about Communist ties "inevitably raises in the mind of the average man a reasonable question concerning the witnesses' loyalty to the United States" and, in the case of a state-supported institution like Rutgers, tarred the university's reputation with the public and the state legislature.[76]

As a wealthy private institution independent of state funds, Harvard had greater latitude—and yet Conant endorsed Rutgers's blanket policy. He swung into action just as the Rutgers ruling came down, after receiving a confidential warning from Marbury, dated December 8, that any Harvard faculty member who invoked the Fifth Amendment in response to questions about Communist Party membership "would create the justified impression either that he was at one time high in party councils or that he is still a party member"; and that therefore, since taking the Fifth was tantamount to "admitting criminal activity," it followed that any Harvard faculty member who did so would be committing an "injury to the University (for such it is) in order to salve his own conscience without suffering the penalty which the law demands from those who defy it for such reasons or because he is in fact what his actions make him appear to be." Marbury's clear implication was that recalcitrant Harvard professors could and should be fired for taking the Fifth. On December 9, Conant reviewed the issue with Oscar Shaw, an attorney with the prominent Boston law firm of Ropes, Gray, Best, Coolidge & Rugg, the Harvard Corporation's regular counsel, and three days later received from Shaw a seven-page legal analysis summarizing the "tentative conclusions reached at our discussion." Given that joining the Communist Party constituted "grave misconduct" meriting dismissal under the University's Third Statute, it concluded, if a professor took the Fifth Amendment or refused to cooperate when asked by a congressional committee about CP membership (at least for the period after 1940, "when the climate in this connection began to change"), "certainly one of the inferences is that the witness is in fact a member of the Communist Party and would be found guilty upon a trial under the Smith Act." Thus the Corporation would be "put upon notice" to investigate the case, and "if after investigation the Corporation is not satisfied that the refusal to answer was in fact based upon other grounds than membership in the Communist Party, we thought that it should act under the Third Statute of the University."[77] Conant distributed Shaw's memorandum to the Harvard Corporation and explained his belief, as one member of that body described it to the FBI, "that the invocation of the Fifth Amendment by a faculty member constituted grounds for dismissal but that each individual case should be reviewed by whatever university was concerned."[78]

Eager for faculty approval of the policy he planned to adopt, Conant then set about lobbying Zechariah Chafee, Jr., to publicly urge Harvard professors not to take the Fifth. He ardently sought Chafee's support not only because he was the foremost civil liberties authority on the campus and in the country, but because he had recently alarmed Conant by endorsing the use of the Fifth Amendment as a last resort to resist the "mean and unworthy thing" that congressional investigators were doing ("in the name of Americanism") in trying to coerce witnesses to name names of friends or comrades. "The only sure way to evade this dirty question," Chafee had written in the *University of Kansas Law Review*, "is to remain silent throughout the whole hearing, through claiming a privilege against self-incrimination regardless of the very damaging effect of such a claim on a person's career." Pronouncing himself "shocked" by this advice, which had "done a lot of harm to the cause of freedom already!", Conant sent Chafee for "comment & return" the first two pages of Marbury's three-page analysis—omitting the explosive final paragraph explicitly drawing conclusions for Harvard faculty members who took the Fifth—with the notation, "I must say I like his argument better than yours." Rather than urge the use of the Fifth, Conant admonished Chafee, he should have advocated (as did Marbury) that an "innocent" witness who refused to testify about associates simply "decline to answer and accept the penalty of punishment for contempt." On Tuesday morning, December 16,

Conant invited the eminent Law School professor to his office and, disputing the notion that an innocent man "could in honesty" employ the constitutional protection against self-incrimination, tried strenuously to convince Chafee that such a person was effectively either admitting guilt or obstructing justice. Two weeks later, with Conant's encouragement, Marbury also implored Chafee to come out openly against use of the Fifth Amendment, arguing that it could only be invoked by witnesses who had "actually participated in criminally subversive actions."[79]

The Conant-Marbury campaign to sway Chafee paid off handsomely. On January 8, 1953, the *Harvard Crimson* printed a letter cosigned by Chafee and Arthur Sutherland, a solidly Republican law professor, stressing "the duty of the citizen to cooperate in government," and rejecting the use of the Fifth Amendment to avoid naming names or to protest political or personal harassment. This widely reprinted and influential manifesto effectively lent Harvard's blessing to other universities that wanted to encourage faculty members to cooperate with HUAC and SISS.[80]

But the rather painful personal climax of Conant's maneuvering within the jittery Harvard community came two days earlier, on January 6, when he met behind closed doors with thirty or forty Law School professors to present his position on the congressional investigations. "Not too well received," he admitted sadly in his diary.[81] There had been "a failure of communication, or a real division of views, or both," Conant reported to the Corporation.[82] The scholars had reacted coolly when Conant warily rejected their demands that he "take the offensive" against the Congressional investigators, and when he announced that since Harvard had traditionally drawn a "sharp line between activities of faculty as citizens and activities as members of the teaching staff," the Corporation had decided that the University would not hire or pay for legal counsel for faculty members asked to testify about activities not directly related to their teaching.

A few weeks earlier, Conant had argued a similar line to Chafee. But Chafee had questioned the practicality of trying to maintain that distinction against the onslaught of hostile investigators. "It may be a situation," Chafee had written Conant, "where if we do not all hang together, we shall all hang separately."[83] Now several of Chafee's Law School colleagues passionately objected to Conant's narrowly framed position, which ignored the truth that in most if not all cases the witnesses would be dragged into the spotlight because of their association with Harvard, or so as to discredit Harvard, whether or not they were specifically charged with indoctrinating students.

If much of his audience was distressed by Conant's position on this point, they were downright shocked to hear that he agreed with the Rutgers trustees about dismissing Fifth Amendment–takers. The Law School's dean, Erwin Griswold, relayed this to Conant in a dour postmortem: "Griswold reports," Conant wrote the corporation, "that in general the reaction of the faculty was that I was more interested in defending the Corporation than in defending the University, that my whole attitude had been neutral and cold instead of being warm and helpful, and that I seemed to be willing to let any and all of the professors be maltreated by the Congressional committees and would raise no finger to help them."

Part of the trouble, Conant believed, had stemmed from a misunderstanding—that in making a distinction between a scholar's professional and private activities he had been thinking of politically active scientists like Shapley or Kirtley Mather, while the Law School professors were thinking of their own faculty. He conveyed his uncertainty on this issue in his report to the Corporation: It might be more difficult to "hold the line" between a professor's activities as a citizen and those as a teacher for a law or economics professor than for an astronomer, he acknowledged, but insisted that despite "borderline cases" the distinction could be maintained. "If I am wrong," he admitted, "that is a fundamental point, and any efforts that might be made quietly to persuade a majority of the Un-American Activities Committee that there was a sharp line would be worse than useless."

Reflecting that same day on this "fundamental point," one Law School professor tugged at Conant's deepest loyalties to the spirit of academic freedom—and the confidential letter that resulted eloquently captured the deep divide between Harvard's cautious president and those scholars who wanted the university to charge into combat against congressional investigators with guns firing. At Griswold's urging, Professor Mark DeWolfe Howe expressed the profound concerns shared by many Harvard scholars and the hopes they vested in their leader to take a principled stand.

I am seriously concerned by the formula which you laid before us, not only because I think it will prove unworkable if the Congressional investigations are pursued with vigor but because I think it endangers an essential tradition of the academic community and jeopardizes a commitment of the nation. The community of scholars, I like to think, is dedicated to the principle that free inquiry and free expression of conviction are essential not only to a creative intellectual life but to a vigorous democratic society. The university's concern is not merely with the intellects of its teachers and students but with the society in which these teachers and students are responsible citizens. Any attempt to dissociate the university from the effort of its faculty members to discover the answers to the pressing problems of our time and as citizens to express freely their opinions, will imply that the university is indifferent to that effort—and in the minds of many will suggest that the university is distressed that the effort has been made. If the university does not manifest its conviction that the scholar's free inquiry and free expression of opinion is an indispensable element in human liberty it will tacitly have conceded that inquiry and expression involve unacceptable risks. Giving my conviction a somewhat different emphasis, I should assert that the university owes a responsibility not simply to the faculty as a corporate body but to the cause of free thought and free speech in general.

The serious danger which your suggested formula seems to me to entail is not simply that it will lead the public to believe that the universities regret the indiscreet efforts of the scholar-citizens to discover and proclaim the truth as they see it but that it will lead the teachers to feel the university regrets their occasional proclivity to assume the responsibilities of articulate citizens. One of the greatest dangers of our time is that the young teacher can no longer afford to be an energetic citizen. The risks which free expression today entails came no less, I suggest, from the obscene excesses of Senator McCarthy than from the cautious proprieties of the universities which, acting on the advice of public relations and legal counsel, have been persuaded, apparently, that the tranquility of an orthodox faculty is preferable to the ferment of dissent and questioning. If the universities express no concern that Congress looks upon teachers as citizens who should be silent partners in the democratic venture, the teachers not unnaturally will assume that professional advancement is to be achieved by discretion rather than by valor. That Harvard should, by silence, give justification for that assumption seems to me to violate principles to which this University is dedicated. To make my feeling clear by an example I would suggest that when Professor Chafee was named a University Professor Harvard did not accept the formula which you are now proposing to apply. Professor Chafee secured the appointment, I assume, not simply because of his essays on bills of interpleader and his mastery of law of negotiable instruments but because of his vigorous and distinguished career as scholar-citizen. Surely Harvard did not consider that Mr. Chafee's activities outside the class-room were of no concern to the institution. Rightly it honored the man as an individual and did not pretend ignorance of the fact that the distinguished authority on equity was also a valiant citizen.

These considerations lead me to believe most fervently that when and if an official announcement is made that Congressional investigations of communism and subversion in American universities are to be initiated the universities have a clear responsibility to state the ground of their concern. Certainly no claim of academic sanctity and immunity should be made, but a vigorous assertion that free inquiry and free speech by every independent citizen, even by the teacher, is essential to the intellectual and spiritual life of the nation might serve a most useful purpose. It would remind the nation that it is in danger of surrendering the traditions of our civilization to fear and it would revive in teachers a diminishing faith that the universities are whole-heartedly committed to these traditions.[84]

In a sense Howe wanted to have it both ways: to have the university keep its nose out of a professor's outside activities, and yet to stand up for him when those activities attracted hostile interest. That, at any rate, is how Conant saw it. And yet the expediency of his own position, and Howe's basic point that a hands-off attitude sent a signal of indifference about the state-sponsored suppression of citizens and scholars who dared to engage in nonviolent political or intellectual dissent, could not be easily ignored. Conant answered Howe rather lamely and observed, "It would take a long time for us to sit down and argue out details of our two positions."[85]

After the news broke on January 12 of Conant's resignation and imminent departure for Germany the press never bothered to investigate the behind-the-scenes maneuvers that marred Conant's last days at Harvard — quite the opposite. The sudden revelation of his impending exit stunned most of the faculty, who despite their qualms about him had come to depend on his leadership in the battle for academic freedom, and doubted that any successor could wield comparable prestige or force of intellect in what promised to be a nerve-wracking test of wills with the congressional committees. "The news about Conant was so disturbing to me (and to almost everyone else) that I have thought of little else since," one professor wrote Buck. "It is a tremendous loss to Harvard and even more so to the nation. It is surprising how, despite a certain aloofness, he has won such a place in the affection of his Faculty."[86]

Conant's final annual presidential report, released later that month, helped to solidify his reputation as a stalwart defender of academic freedom.[87] He branded many of the charges leveled against American universities — from coddling Communist teachers to indoctrinating students with leftist economic ideas such as nationalization of industries or "socialist schemes for health insurance" — as "malicious" and "ridiculous," and declared that "universities must be prepared to battle for their independence." Defending the right of scholars to advocate "unorthodox and hence unpopular doctrines," he acknowledged that "a few (a very few) professors" had foolishly laid themselves open to charges of being Soviet apologists because of their "completely unrealistic" appraisals of the "global struggle with Communism" and their earnest desire for global peace, but he urged critics to recall the disorienting postwar transition in U.S.-Soviet relations from alliance to enmity, "and also how long it took for many of us who became fully aware of the true nature of the Communist party in the United States." "It would be a sad day for the United States if the tradition of dissent were driven out of the universities," Conant declared; any attempt by school administrators to investigate professors' private activities would surely destroy the "life of the university." He reiterated his usual exception to this rule — he would never, he promised, "be party to the appointment of a Communist to any position in a school, college, or university" — and expressed confidence that Harvard's staff contained "no known" party members, "and I do not believe there are any disguised Communists either. But even if there were," he added — this was the sentence that attracted the most notice from journalists — "the damage that would be done to the spirit of this academic community by an investigation by the University aimed at finding a crypto-

Communist would be far greater than any conceivable harm such a person might do."

Still, these liberal-minded proclamations were balanced, both in the report and in Conant's confirmation hearing before the Senate Foreign Relations Committee on February 3, by statements endorsing the government's right, indeed duty, to "ferret out and prosecute" any subversives at universities. Eager to appease senators who disliked his opposition to any university investigation of faculty politics, he went further in his Capitol Hill remarks. In his presidential report, Conant had fudged the Fifth Amendment issue, remarking that a professor's private activities and statements were "of no concern to the university administration, provided he is not acting illegally as determined by due process of law"[88] — a carefully hedged formula that on the one hand would permit a scholar to remain on the faculty during a long appeals process but would also allow for the dismissal of anyone convicted of contempt of Congress. To the senators he took a sterner view. In an exchange with J. William Fulbright, Conant discounted the effect on higher education of McCarthyism, which he said was less severe than the intimidation of pro-German professors had been during World War I. "I do not know of any breach of academic freedom that has occurred in any first-rate university," Conant claimed, "and by that I mean somebody being fired because of what he said." When pressed, however, he admitted such firings had occurred:

> SENATOR FULBRIGHT. There have not been any firings because of procommunism that you know of?
>
> MR. CONANT. No, except in the cases which I think, quite properly, men called before a committee, have refused to testify as to whether they were or not members of the Communist Party. Personally, I think the trustees were right in that case although that is very disputable.[89]

Questioned about charges that his administration had tolerated Communist professors at Harvard and about his much-discussed assertion that a university investigation of faculty political views would cause more damage than an undiscovered "crypto-Communist," Conant resorted to his usual balancing act, defending the retention of naive liberal professors, even those who had become "unwitting tools" of the Kremlin, while excommunicating actual Communists from academic protections:

> As I have made evident on more than one occasion, and as I say in my report, I would not be a party to the appointment of any Communist to a position in any college, university, or school for which I was in any way responsible.
> The question that you have raised is the question of whether those

professors who are on permanent appointment, because of their public statements and their joining certain organizations (which I may say I have no sympathy with myself), have therefore branded themselves as being essentially members of the party or of being of the party's apparatus.

In my judgment they have not. Professors, as private citizens, particularly in periods of tension, may say many things and take many stands that many other private citizens will not agree with.

I think the record will show that the professors to whom attention has been drawn were people who were concerned with peace on one hand, better relations with Russia, and liberal causes on the other — their judgment as private citizens, the wisdom of their statements, is not for me either to condemn or condone, as president of a university.

They are free agents. It is my belief that, as I said before, there are no members of the Communist Party, either openly or disguised, on the Harvard faculty.

On the other hand, I recognize and know full well from my experience with the Government agencies during the war, particularly with the Manhattan District, that it is by no means an easy matter to find a Communist.

I used the word "crypto-Communist," as was brought out yesterday. I believe it is a somewhat academic term. The records of the Fuchs case and others show how difficult it is to discover a truly hidden Communist. Therefore, only the instigation of a police state within a university itself could possibly find such people.

Therefore, when I said that I believed there are no Communists at Harvard, I went on to say that the university could not undertake, in my opinion, the kind of investigation which would find the really hidden Communists without destroying the life of the university.

On the other hand, if the Government has evidence that there are such people there, I say I hope they will ferret them out by FBI methods and prosecute them.[90]

Conant said that, on balance, he did not welcome the SISS or HUAC probes, though he conceded the absolute right of congressional panels to investigate whatever they pleased, but he subtly shifted ground in admitting the *desirability*, not merely the right, of the state to root out Communists at universities. If, he hypothesized, a congressional committee had "a hot scent, a strong lead as to the existence in some academic community of a cell, an apparatus of Communists, and can with due process, and under proper safeguards, find the members of that cell and discover that these people are, in fact, members of the Communist Party, and then turn their names over to the Department of Justice, then that would serve a useful purpose."[91]

Afterward, Conant felt twinges of unease about his Senate testimony. To Marbury, he wrote that he hoped his replies, "when I read them in cold type," would "help rather than hurt the cause of maintaining the independence of the universities and Harvard in particular."[92] Probably they helped the cause of Conant's nomination more than they helped the cause of academic freedom. Conant's advice around this time to Yale president A. Whitney Griswold, who was preparing a statement for the Association of American Universities (AAU), offers additional clues to the tactics he was advocating as the universities prepared for the onslaught of congressional investigators, and underline both his distaste for the Fifth Amendment and his willingness to let controversial professors defend themselves, if necessary, in order to get the universities off the hook institutionally. According to Griswold's notes, Conant hoped to maintain a distinction between the investigation of individuals and the investigations of "institutions and what they are teaching"—Congress had not crossed that line yet, he said, and "May not do so." In the meantime, the educational community's objective must be "to observe tactical line, *not* to defend indiv. martyrs, screwballs etc. but [. . .] to defend basic procedures of univs." Counseling Griswold to disregard Chafee's "very bad advice" in the *Kansas Law Review*,[93] he held that it was better for scholars appearing before congressional committees to "fight perjury or contempt charges than refuse to answer." The final AAU statement, written largely by Griswold and Brown's Henry Wriston, accorded with Conant's prescription, stating use of the Fifth, while not in itself illegal, "places upon a professor a heavy burden of proof of his fitness to hold a teaching position and lays upon his university an obligation to re-examine his qualifications for membership in its society."[94]

It is, of course, impossible to know whether Conant would have stuck to his position on the Fifth Amendment had he still been Harvard president when HUAC and then McCarthy himself conducted extensive hearings at the university later in February 1953. But his exchange with Chafee, his meeting with the Law School faculty, his testimony on the Hill, and his advice to Griswold support the speculation of one historian that "Conant would have taken a hard line" and demanded the removal of several Harvard faculty members who did take the Fifth, most prominently physics professor Wendell Furry.[95]

What actually happened is that Conant's sudden departure threw most of the responsibility for determining Harvard policy upon Provost Buck and dean of the faculty McGeorge Bundy, who instead of invoking the Rutgers precedent decided that taking the Fifth constituted "misconduct" but was not in itself adequate cause for dismissal.[96] The three faculty members who refused to name names—Furry; Leon Kamin, a teaching fellow in the Department of Social Relations; and Helen Deane Markham, an assistant professor of anatomy at the Medical School—were disciplined but retained, and the new president, Nathan M. Pusey, defended that decision when it was, invariably, denounced by McCarthy. Given that Conant had no complaints with how the Corporation and Pusey ultimately handled the Furry case, it is equally possible that he would have softened his position on the Fifth Amendment issue. (To Marbury he conveyed "all strength to all of you in holding the fort on the line of independence and freedom of universities, even when they have to suffer with such fools as an Associate Professor of Physics.")[97] But the historical indications are that his resignation, mourned at the time as a grievous blow to academic freedom, actually facilitated Harvard's much-celebrated refusal to kowtow to McCarthy, who howled in outrage at the "smelly mess" in Cambridge, where America's youth were vulnerable to indoctrination by "Fifth Amendment Communists."[98]

Conant's successors at Harvard did, however, put pressure on faculty to name names and to get a political stamp of approval from the FBI; it refused to hire lawyers for accused scholars; and it reaffirmed his prohibition against Communist faculty members. And while Conant had never had to live up to his policy of dismissing faculty who belonged to the Communist Party or took the Fifth Amendment, many university presidents not in that enviable position did their best to get there as soon as possible, either through dismissals or refusals to renew appointments.

A comment attributed to Conant in the 1930s — "If we want to preserve our academic freedom, we'll have to watch our promotions"[99] — accurately expresses his caution in maintaining Harvard's independence without flouting congressional authority during the McCarthy period. When essential prerogatives of university governance seemed threatened, as in the appointment of Galbraith or demands that he fire outspoken tenured professors like Shapley, he stood firm, but he tried earnestly to keep American higher education in the orthodox mainstream which during the Cold War exaggerated the threat of domestic subversion and foreign attack, and he made it clear that the university looked askance at radical dissent or defiance of government authority. Senior professors felt secure at Harvard, but it is impossible to measure the impact of papers not written, persons not hired, subjects not taught, ideas not discussed, because scholars and students feared being tainted with charges of leftism.[100]

One can discern here something of the safely centrist spirit that shaped American education in the 1950s — a decade, in the words of one historian, when an intimidated profession "surrendered," when students, teachers, and professors "steered away from controversial and radical readings," and when a "sterile, unblinking conformity settled over American schools for an entire generation."[101] Denying any desire to curb democratic freedoms, extolling the virtues of reform and heresy, but yearning all the same to draw boundaries on discussion and behavior, to channel the energies of the potentially discontented in unthreatening directions, Conant and many other leaders of American education moved toward a subtle yet pernicious form of thought control. Alarm over the potentially apocalyptic dangers of the Cold War moved Conant, like others, wittingly and unwittingly to contribute to an atmosphere that penalized open dissent and rewarded and encouraged conformism. Just as the cause of victory in World War I and World War II had justified poison gas, strategic bombing, and the atomic bomb, Conant calculated that his country's political imperative of consolidating a Cold War consensus and his university's need to preserve its institutional independence required him to abandon previously sacrosanct tenets of academic freedom. In allowing his faith in democratic rights and freedoms to falter, in seeking an expedient compromise rather than unflinchingly standing up to McCarthyism, Conant, too, was guilty of the failure of nerve that afflicted so many leaders of U.S. politics, culture, and education.

CHAPTER 32

"Tired of Flexing Old Muscles"

Educator to Diplomat

1950–1953

The Day! Oh Boy! . . . Where will I be 4 years from now? Heaven knows, but at least not on *this* job.
—Diary entry, December 22, 1952

Typical of the physical scientist! To give up something very difficult so as to try the impossible.
—Robert Oppenheimer

I wanted to try my hand at one more tough task before I die.
—Letter to Percy Bridgman, January 21, 1953

By mid-century, at the age of fifty-seven, Conant outwardly seemed to be at the crest of national esteem and prominence, repeatedly in the headlines for his pronouncements on education, science, and national security. Despite his persistent disclaimers of any interest in electoral politics, he heard himself repeatedly touted as a dark horse presidential candidate, and in late 1951 a Gallup poll rated him fifth behind Eisenhower for the GOP nomination.[1] He was showered by honorary degrees, awards, and attention, from the Presidential Medal for Merit with Oak Leaf Clusters for his atomic-bomb work, to the Freedom House award for his championing of the defense of Europe; in September 1952 *Newsweek* published a cover story on "U.S. Education's No. 1 Man."

Privately, however, Conant had grown weary of the Harvard presidency, tired of "flexing the same muscles all the time."[2] His restless nature sought new challenges—by rising to become one of the country's leading organic chemists and president of Harvard, he had, after all, satisfied only two of the ambitions he had confessed to Patty Richards in 1920 ("a Cabinet post" was the third). As ever, he hated the mundane chores of glad-handing, chit-chatting, and extracting pledges from football-addled alumni. Most of all he hated fund-raising. "Getting money for divinity, geography, a theatre, or a hockey rink sounds a lot easier than it is," he carped. "When it comes time for actually writing out a check people can find a lot of excuses."[3] "My last or next to last appearance thank God!" he confided to his diary in January 1952 after his annual hat-passing speech to the Harvard Club of New York.[4] "The record is wearing thin," he felt another night after confronting yet another university audience.[5] He vowed to himself to resign the Harvard presidency after two decades, in September 1953, at the pension-qualifying age of sixty, rather than wait until his ideas as well as his welcome had been worn out.[6]

But he had fresher reasons for seeking an escape from his gilded rut. Bruising battles with the Overseers still cropped up from time to time, as did conflicts within the Corporation, though Conant's appointment of Marbury had given him an ally. And, though his wartime service and international reputation had won him Harvard's unquestioned respect, Conant had never fully recovered from the wounds sustained during the bitter 1930s battles with the faculty.

His principal, largely successful method of dealing with faculty issues was to delegate day-to-day administration to underlings, in particular Provost Buck, whose sharp tactical sense for faculty politics and jocular down-to-earth manner earned widespread affection and a reputation as "Harvard's Harry Truman." For more than a decade, Conant observed graciously in 1953, he and Buck "have been a team. I happened to have worn the ranking hat, but he carried the load. The initiative, imagination, accomplishment were his."[7] Conant could be "chilly, publicly remote, lofty in argument—not an accessible figure," while his provost was "personal, literally rather gossipy, warm, good humored," recalled the Harvard psychologist Jerome Bruner. David Lilienthal observed in early 1951: "Buck seems to be an ideal provost; takes things as they come, easy, relaxed, and the real head of the university so far as faculty matters are concerned."[8] Buck himself considered that assessment to be an exaggeration, for Conant did not always confide in him on major decisions (such as the Marbury nomination), but many at Harvard thought that Buck ran the show and instinctively understood faculty concerns.[9]

By contrast, Conant sometimes had to relearn painful lessons. A perennial source of exasperation was athletics, and especially the slumping football team. If Harvard sports one day disappeared into a Cambridge sewer, one suspects that President Conant would not have shed a tear. But from the day he took the job he had to deal with "football-crazed alumni," and in February 1951, a seemingly inconsequential foul-up—a mundane matter compared to the weighty subjects of national security and education which consumed much of his time, thought, and energy—reminded him of his still-vexing occasional tendency to ruffle feathers in the interests of efficiency. Irritated with the athletics department for running up a deficit, a sin compounded by disastrous football records, the Corporation decided to ease out its director, an outspoken and temperamental man named Bill Bingham, and replace him with a quieter, more malleable underling.[10] But Conant botched the announcement of Bingham's "retirement," neglecting to ensure that the victim learned of his demise before the press did. Then he paid scant attention to headlines about Bingham being "fired without warning" after twenty-five years of loyal service, and soon the flap escalated into a major row. University officials all over the place were pointing fingers and running for cover. "On the 'affair Bingham,' " Conant wrote in his diary, "everyone is mad. Bill thinks Buck to blame, Buck Bill, George W[hitney, president of the Overseers] distrusts Buck, general bad blood!"

Ultimately, as local sportswriters delightedly stirred the brew, Conant had to apologize publicly. In his diary, Conant considered his failure to alert Bingham "not only *bad* but an incredible administrative error." Ruefully, he remembered faculty criticisms during the Walsh-Sweezy affair—"What we object to is not your *ideas* but your *manners*" and "we object not to your aims but your methods!"[11]

Given the amount of time Conant found he had to spend on financial and policy woes related to athletics, it is not surprising that he should, in his farewell presidential report, vent some spleen, even going so far as to cite collegiate football scandals as a source of popular resentment toward institutions of higher learning that in turn contributed to McCarthyism![12]

Other Harvard controversies not only sorely tried Conant's patience and rattled his personal relationships but seemed more and more marginal alongside the national and philosophical issues that truly engaged him. One long-running wrangle, both obscure and intense, was a four-year battle over the Arnold Arboretum, a nature preserve in the Boston suburb of Jamaica Plains that had been bequeathed to Harvard in 1872. Somehow a subject of major interest to botanists and horticulturists turned into a cliff-hanging test of wills between the Corporation, led by Conant, who wanted to transfer the facility's library and collections of plants and shrubs to a new botanical building in Cambridge, and a coalition of outsiders led by Grenville Clark, who led the opposition to the proposed move even after retiring from the Corporation in 1950. Clark thought Conant had an aesthetic blind spot that caused him to favor scientific botanists at the expense of horticulture, while Conant vowed that he would not (as his son put it) "let a looney conservationist determine university policy." When the Corporation rejected Clark's arguments in late 1952, he and his supporters appealed the decision to the state courts—an action Conant is said to have considered "dirty pool." In the end, Conant's position triumphed over Clark's but only after a bitterly contested court battle ended their two-decade long friendship.[13]

A loss of composure during a meeting with a faculty member, a startling event with the normally unflappable Conant, offered a sure sign that the routine irritations of administering Harvard were taking a toll. Conant regarded the biochemist Edwin J. Cohn, a nationally prominent pioneer in blood transfusion techniques, as an "empire-builder" when he began peppering the Harvard administration with requests for funds to expand lab facilities and establish a foundation to promote patent profits. The two men had once been friends, worked side-by-side in the Chemistry Department, and cooperated on war-related research, but their relations had cooled during the Walsh-Sweezy affair. On the afternoon of October 20, following a tense Corporation meeting about the arboretum, Conant walked over to Cohn's office to hear his latest requests. His skepticism mounting, Conant demanded justifications from Cohn for the proposed expenditures. William Marbury, whom Conant had asked to be in on the meeting, recalls what happened next: "He started cross-examining this guy, and the fellow got pompous and haughty, and Jim flung the papers down and walked out of the room."[14] "Lost my temper with E.J. more than I intended but 'broke' with him I hope forever," Conant wrote in his diary after this outburst. "Corporation will have to handle his megalomania from here out."[15]

As Conant's exasperation with his job waxed, a chapter in his personal life was drawing to a close. His two sons, after troubled, war-interrupted youths, seemed to be embarking on new, promising paths: in August 1952, Ted, twenty-six, after being graduated from Swarthmore and taking courses for teaching audiovisual studies at Columbia, went to South Korea to make newsreel and documentary films for a United Nations relief agency. And on October 10, James, twenty-nine, who after his medical troubles had gone into journalism, reporting from Montreal for a Detroit newspaper and for *Time* magazine, married Norice O'Malley (née Maloney). After a "merry-go-round" of last-minute planning, and elaborate (and futile) strategies to evade press coverage, the two exchanged vows in a small Unitarian service at 17 Quincy Street before escaping cold Cambridge for a honeymoon in Barbados. Despite complications with her family, who refused to attend the wedding, the bride struck the concerned father-in-law as "remarkably mature and very nice."[16] She also made Conant a grandfather, bringing a four-year-old daughter, Clark, from a previous marriage.

What was Conant to do after the Harvard presidency? Conant cautiously weighed the informal offers for government service that inevitably came his way. Shuttling as he did between Boston, New York, and Washington, respected by leaders of both parties, in Congress, and in the executive branch, Conant knew that his nonpareil status as politically attuned educational and scientific statesman ensured that his name would come up frequently when important jobs were doled out. Moreover, his leadership of the Committee on the Present Danger had reflected a desire to participate in the shaping of U.S. foreign policy, to further American values in the Cold War, and to try to reduce the chances of World War III. *Conant oblige*, whether to science, nation, or species, came naturally.

Not any assignment would do, however. In September 1951 Conant gave the cold-shoulder to one government agency seeking his help: asked over lunch at the Mayflower Hotel by the CIA director, Walter Bedell "Beetle"

Smith, to take a month off to review the agency's "scientific set up"—the agency was at the time dueling with the military over who would control scientific and technical intelligence estimates—Conant begged off, suggesting he instead call Karl Compton.[17] A few months later, Conant received another, more exotic CIA proposition. Over late afternoon drinks at the Cosmos Club, Kermit ("Kim") Roosevelt, the aristocratic spy who had profiled him for the *Saturday Evening Post* in 1949, tried to recruit the president of Harvard for an undercover mission to assist the agency's Middle East directorate, then engaged in a clandestine effort to topple Egypt's King Farouk. But Conant had a dim view of covert operations of this kind. "K. Roosevelt of CIA wanted me to be one of a 'front' on Egyptian affairs," he wrote in his diary. "Said no!"[18]

Dignified diplomacy, however, was another matter. In October 1951, the Truman administration quietly sounded him out about replacing John J. McCloy (who had decided to retire) as U.S. high commissioner in Germany. Since going to Bonn two years earlier, McCloy had concentrated on the gradual strengthening of West Germany (the Federal Republic, established in 1949 and comprising the former U.S., British, and French occupation zones), and its pro-American chancellor, Konrad E. Adenauer, on solidifying the country's westward orientation as a reliable partner for Western Europe and the NATO alliance in the Cold War; to advance those goals, McCloy also did his best to put the legacy of the war behind them, refurbishing the image of the "new Germany" and granting clemency to Alfred Krupp and others who had helped the Nazis but whose assistance was now desired in West Germany's economic revival and military rearmament. The Korean War had only speeded up these processes, of course, raising fears of a Soviet attack against Western Europe once it had built up its nuclear arsenal; but until the allies concluded and ratified a treaty providing for West Germany's rearmament, presumably as part of the European Defense Community (EDC), the country remained formally under Allied occupation.[19]

Impatient to return to private life, McCloy had recommended Conant to Acheson, who in turn received Truman's approval to go forward and urgently summoned Conant to a private lunch one Saturday. Shortly before noon, a State Department limousine retrieved an intrigued Conant from downtown Washington and transported him to Acheson's farm in Maryland, where he joined Acheson and his wife for a pleasant meal and innocuous conversation. Then the secretary of state took him aside. Conant's excited diary entry: "Dean asked me to be the new Ambassador to Germany!!! Was I surprised." Although he candidly admitted to Acheson that he planned to leave Harvard "in the not too distant future," his instincts compelled a cautious response. Voicing "grave doubts" that he was the right person for the job, he tentatively declined but agreed to return for dinner a few days later to talk the matter over. After this initial probe, Acheson told McCloy he had found Conant "most interested, somewhat tempted, but somewhat alarmed by the possibility of entering a field so foreign to all his previous experience."[20]

Actually, Conant had been tempted: the idea of helping to rebuild a democratic Germany, the nation that had alternately impressed and horrified yet never failed to fascinate him, seemed almost irresistible. So did the implicit dare to the chairman of the CPD to put his money where his mouth was by serving on the front lines of the Cold War in Europe, as he had urged his countrymen to do. "Inclined to accept," Conant felt after a heart-to-heart talk with his wife. The next day appears this jaunty note: "Felt more encouraged about my fitness for the job!"[21]

Still, when he showed up at the Achesons the following Thursday, Conant played hard to get. After dinner, Conant confessed to the secretary of state uncertainty about his "ability to conduct the negotiating side of the work" and fretted over the difficulties his sudden departure would cause Harvard. But his most serious qualm was a substantive one—and it stemmed from his deep private doubts that a country that had given rise to Hitler could be trusted again so soon. Conant told Acheson he had "doubts about rearming Germany," despite his support for a strong European military counterforce to the Soviet Union, and suggested that smaller and more efficient U.S. tactical nuclear weapons under development "made this unnecessary." Acheson found this argument impenetrable, and told McCloy:

> The third element of our discussion revolved around policy. At first it was expressed by [Conant] as disagreement with the idea of rearming the Germans. After we had gone into this in some detail, the difficulty rather changed to one of the speed of doing this. The argument seemed to be that in no event could German forces large enough to affect the whole power problem be organized within two or three years, whereas within that time perhaps the development of new weapons would change the intensity of the problem. I did the best I could with this discussion, but it was a difficult one. He was more interested in stating his point of view than listening to any answers. I felt that in the conflict between convincing him and becoming overwhelmed by weariness myself, the latter got the upper hand.[22]

By the end of the long evening's conversation, Conant sensed that Acheson was growing "chilly" and didn't like his "line," and a little before eleven o'clock he formally declined the offer to take over from McCloy the following summer, but he "imprudently left the door a crack open if later he found no one else can do it and I was convinced by him and Gen. Eisenhower this was call of duty. . . . I doubt if I ever hear of the matter again."[23] Conant's formal reason for rejection was for "personal reasons"—that he had planned to stay on another year at Harvard.[24] More likely, Conant like everyone else could read the political tea-leaves for the Democrats, and did not want to accept a post in the waning days of a lame-duck administration. Still, he wondered with his wife "what kind of experience it would have been to connect our German memories of 1925 with the realities of the present," and resolved to say yes if asked again.[25]

Since going to Paris at the end of 1950 to head the NATO command, pressures had been building steadily on Dwight Eisenhower to run for president in 1952. And while power brokers in both major parties fancied him as their candidate, the political locus of his support was the moderate wing of the GOP, which wanted a consensus candidate that could both roust the Democrats from the White House for the first time in two decades, and at the same time preserve the party from its extremist, isolationist faction typified in different ways by Taft, McCarthy, and MacArthur.

One quarter of quiet but firm support of Eisenhower was Conant's Committee on the Present Danger, and especially its executive director, Tracy Voorhees, who during lunch at 17 Quincy Street on December 1, 1951, asked Conant's advice on whether he should resign to work full-time for a draft-Ike campaign. Conant, a registered Republican, also favored Eisenhower over the available alternatives—"We all breathe easier because of your leadership," he was to write Ike a few months later, expressing "great admiration" for his accomplishments[26]—but his sense of propriety told him that to preserve the CPD's nonpartisan image members should not take posts with presidential campaigns. In any case, he argued, Voorhees "might be more useful to General Eisenhower by supporting through the Committee the steps necessary for the success of General Eisenhower's mission in Europe than . . . by working for his nomination as President."[27] Voorhees agreed, and in the coming months many CPD members hailed the NATO commander's work at every opportunity and promoted UMS and more U.S. aid for European defense; they functioned as a cheerleading squad for Eisenhower, and upon his election many were to graduate into the new administration.[28] Eisenhower, for his part, expressed his continued esteem for the CPD's work.[29]

Meanwhile Conant, who had only reluctantly agreed to stay on as CPD chairman, spent much of 1952 mulling over his private intention to retire and wondering whether he would get a second chance to take the job in Bonn. Reading newspaper reports in January that State Department official Robert Murphy, rumored to succeed McCloy as high commissioner, was now instead expected to be named ambassador to Japan, he could not resist a flicker of hope that Acheson might turn back to him. A month later, hearing of a crisis in negotiations among the NATO allies on an EDC treaty—France, which had first suggested the idea, was now balking—Conant thanked his lucky stars that he had said no, since his predictions of trouble had come true and "I *would* have looked silly if I had accepted his offer for Feb. 1 with no sign of a treaty yet!" A few weeks later, however, he flip-flopped again after hearing an optimistic report, and spent the day debating with his wife what to say if Acheson rang.[30] But any thoughts of taking a post with the Truman administration evaporated when Eisenhower entered the presidential race. On the afternoon of March 22, during a three-week swing through Europe, Conant stopped in for tea at the NATO commander's quarters in Paris. Though Eisenhower was still playing hard to get, refusing openly to declare his candidacy despite a write-in victory over Taft in the New Hampshire Republican primary, organized by a draft-Ike campaign squad, Conant correctly scented "some political overtones in the General's remarks."[31] Shortly thereafter Truman publicly announced the decision his staff had been keeping secret for six months, that he would not seek another term; Eisenhower ended the suspense and returned to the United States to contest the Republican nomination.

With the Democrats in disarray, he quickly emerged as the front-runner, not only in the country but among the Harvard elite. Dining at Conant's house in May 1952, a group of Overseers held a straw poll of presidential preferences. Of the twenty-five or so present, virtually all cast their secret ballots for Eisenhower—the most notable exception, whom Judge Wyzanski suspected was Oppenheimer, marked his ballot for Aristides.[32] The Democrats, however, unable to woo the just Athenian statesman, settled on another erudite politician, Adlai Stevenson; the Republicans, as expected, nominated Eisenhower at a convention marked by frenzied receptions for MacArthur and McCarthy.

Like millions of other Americans, the Conants followed the 1952 conventions on live television for the first time, watching the flickering black-and-white images at friends' homes in New Hampshire. During his annual summer escape from Cambridge for contemplation, rigorous physical exercise, and personal writing, the question of his future plans nagged at Conant. Hiking and fishing ("No fish but many many bites of black flies & midgets!!"), teaching a philosophy class at Dartmouth, finishing the manuscript for *Education and Liberty,* Conant tentatively decided to retire from Harvard sometime between September 1953 and June 1954, though what would come next remained up in the air.[33]

Eisenhower's landslide victory (to Conant's apparent satisfaction, though he recorded in his diary on election night that his wife was "*not* happy") at first did not figure to change that timetable. When McCloy dropped by Harvard in late November to "pick the brains of some professors," Conant told him that he was still interested in the high commissioner's post but to himself he doubted that McCloy had much influence with the incoming administration.[34]

With Eisenhower's election, Conant and the Committee on the Present Danger leadership believed they had largely accomplished their mission, and they set about preparing detailed proposals for Ike's staff for an increase in military and economic aid to the West European allies, as well as yet another plea for UMS, though they had little hope of seeing the idea enacted. On December 12, Conant, Voorhees, and Donovan presented drafts of the CPD proposals to Harold Stassen, who was working with Eisenhower on the transition, and arranged a follow-up conference with the president-elect. Ten days later, on December 22, a CPD delegation headed by Conant briefed Eisenhower for more than two hours at the Commodore Hotel in New York.

But for Conant, the main event came afterward, when the incoming secretary of state, John Foster Dulles, took him into a side room and offered him, again, the high commissioner's post. Inwardly elated—"I had made up my mind to accept before I had even been offered the job"—but outwardly as cautious as ever, Conant noted his political liabilities, as he had to Acheson fourteen months earlier: Catholic leaders would object to his nomination because of his opposition to state aid to parochial schools, and he retained "very grave doubts" about German rearmament.

How did that square with the statements of the Committee on the Present Danger on the defense of Europe? wondered Dulles.

Conant hedged—perhaps it was just a matter of timing.

"Well, we don't have to agree on everything," Dulles replied.[35]

Why would Eisenhower name to this critical position a man with "very grave doubts" about German rearmament, who was half-hearted or even resistant to the objective of making West Germany a powerful military bulwark against Soviet expansion even while dutifully supporting EDC? The answer apparently lay with the favorable impression Eisenhower had of Conant's stands on national-security issues, dating from the alliance the two had struck during Eisenhower's short interlude as president of Columbia University and after, when Conant's campaign in favor of sending U.S. troops to Europe as CPD chairman had coincided with Ike's urgent request for NATO ground reinforcements. Eisenhower judged Conant, unlike many of his educational peers, to be hard-nosed and realistic, and speaking a no-nonsense language which made sense—a conviction supported by Conant's friendships with Ike's close aide, Gen. Alfred Gruenther, and with McCloy, who had an opportunity to inform Eisenhower of Conant's willingness to be high commissioner, and of West German chancellor Adenauer's desire that an "American personality of high prestige and importance" be appointed to the post, when he lunched with the president-elect and Dulles in New York City on December 15.[36]

Notwithstanding his carefully guarded aloofness from partisan political activities, Conant received "political clearance" after Massachusetts's rock-ribbed Republican senior senator, Leverett Saltonstall, attested to Conant's GOP affiliation.[37] So it was done, and Conant was thrilled. "The Day! Oh Boy!" he wrote in his diary. "Where will I be 4 years from now?" he wondered in his diary. "Heaven knows, but at least not on *this* job."[38] The next day,

Dulles telephoned to confirm that the offer still stood: "You are hooked," he said. "There is nothing in the objection you raised."[39]

Hating the ideas of long good-byes at Harvard—and told by Dulles to hold the news until mid-January—Conant told only his wife and a very few friends and colleagues about the impending change, and he quietly made arrangements with Roger Lee of the Corporation for the university to set up a transitional leadership. During the Christmas vacation Conant "readjusted plans," brushed up on his rusty German, wrote his final annual presidential report, worked on a left-over "case study" on Pasteur he had promised to write, and enjoyed holiday cheer with friends—"dissembled very well," he confided cheerfully to his diary after one party.[40]

In early January, Conant spent a weekend writing dozens of handwritten notes to friends and colleagues telling them of his new occupation, timing these letters to arrive just before the official announcement was made, and on New Year's Day he officially broke the news to the full Corporation, which (he wrote in his diary) greeted it with "Thunderous silence." Once the White House let the cat out of the bag on January 12, hundreds of tributes poured in to Massachusetts Hall to mark, or mourn, the passing of an era, and to applaud Eisenhower's choice of a man emblematic of American culture as envoy to Germany. Though some Catholic and anti-Communist activists registered predictable objections, the vast majority of newspapers, educational leaders, and faculty paid tribute to Conant's wartime service and to his egalitarian influence on Harvard and U.S. education; as *Time* put it, he was "an outspoken brand of liberal to whom democracy was a sort of religion and citizenship apparently the highest aim of man." Some wondered why he had voluntarily relinquished his prestigious post—it seemed ten steps down, remarked McGeorge Bundy, for the president of Harvard University merely to run Germany.[41]

But Conant had no such feelings—merely an eagerness to get on with his new job. Twenty years as a university president, he wrote Kistiakowsky, was "long enough to serve a sentence for youthful indiscretion."[42] In those twenty years, Conant had pushed Harvard into becoming a more meritocratic, international, professionalized, diverse, and ambitious institution, and he personified these qualities to the nation and the world. Becoming the U.S. representative in Germany seemed an appropriate sequel, the logical consummation of the ambitious prophecy he had confessed to his fiancée four decades earlier; it connected him to the land that had sounded throughout his life "like a theme song," and it promised an opportunity to further the policies he advocated in Europe. And, as they had with his ascent to the Harvard presidency, events on the global political stage neatly synchronized with Conant's departure: one chapter also seemed to be closing and a new one opening. Having come into that office with Hitler and Roosevelt, Conant left it as a nominee of the first Republican to reach the White House in two decades and just weeks before the death of Stalin.

Yet, as he hurried through a series of hastily arranged farewells to faculty, friends, and alumni groups, Conant knew that the new task posed immense challenges. The EDC treaty, the centerpiece of Western hopes to make the continent militarily defensible, remained in limbo, trapped in a web of political maneuvering. American relations with the "new Germany" were complicated by still vivid memories of its recent Nazi past, as well as by continuing tensions over the country's division. With McCarthy still on the rampage, moreover, Conant anticipated close and not friendly scrutiny by Congress, both in confirming his nomination and (assuming passage of that ritual) in overseeing his activities. Above all, of course, loomed the threat of a U.S.-Soviet war, liable to be triggered by a German crisis and likely to take place on German soil. Conant, as one of four Allied high commissioners in a still functioning occupation regime, would have to deal on an equal basis with the Kremlin's emissary. But Conant didn't take the job because he thought it lacked challenges—quite the opposite. "I would like to be frank with an old friend," he wrote the physicist and philosopher Percy "Pete" Bridgman, "and to say that one of the primary reasons for my undertaking the difficult assignment is the feeling that I wanted to try my hand at one more tough task before I die."43

Walking Cambridge's snowbound streets with a Harvard colleague after hearing the news of Conant's decision, Robert Oppenheimer shook his head: "Typical of the physical scientist! To give up something very difficult so as to try the impossible."44 But the classicist John Finley, serenading Conant at a farewell dinner at one of the Harvard houses,45 more accurately captured the departing educator's own frame of mind:

> Dealing with Stalin will be easy
> After Walsh and Sweezy

Toward the end of his last working day in Cambridge, however, Conant permitted himself one sentimental gesture. From the president's office in Massachusetts Hall, he telephoned Paul Buck and asked if he was free to come over; he was, and walked across the Yard. It was, Buck recalled later, a "curious interlude for two men who were normally frightfully busy"—Conant having wound up his affairs at Harvard and ready to leave for Washington and then Germany, Buck gearing up to add the load of Conant's job to his own. Ever since they had struck up their partnership during the war, in their innumerable conferences, it had been a rare occasion for them to talk without some critical decision pending. They chatted about various subjects, none of great import, for about forty-five minutes. Neither mentioned what they both knew, that it was their last conversation as president and provost, and both were reluctant to say the last word. Finally, Conant broke an awkward silence.

"Well, Paul, I guess this is the end," he said. They gathered up their hats and overcoats, and as they were about to go Conant turned to him and said: "I wanted you with me at the end. I shall never again enter this office as President." For once, Paul Buck could see the emotion on his friend's face. As a student held open the green door beneath the sign reading "Massachusetts Hall—Offices of the President and Fellows," Conant followed Buck out of the ivy-covered brick building into the gray, overcast, late January dusk.[46]

CHAPTER 33

"Explosion in the Offing"

Intrigues in Bonn, Berlin, and Washington

1953–1955

CIA briefing. Tough! Almost hope the Senate won't confirm.
——Diary, January 29, 1953

The basic German political situation is too unstable and the German governmental structure is too new to trust the final command of a national army to the hands of the unknown German leaders of the future . . . the crucial decision of these months is whether we can bind West Germany to the West politically, economically, and militarily.
——Letter to John Foster Dulles, October 28, 1953

Eisenhower's choice of Conant as America's ambassador-level high commissioner to Germany came at a moment of sharp tension. Domestically, McCarthy and his allies badgered and intimidated enemies wherever they could be found or invented, and the Wisconsin senator threatened to oppose Conant's nomination—on the grounds that he allegedly coddled leftist professors at Harvard, that he opposed federal aid to parochial schools, and because his 1944 plan for the postwar disarmament of Germany was draconian. Internationally, the war in Korea was still continuing, Cold War fears and Stalinist purges and show trials kept Europe on edge, and the European Defense Community treaties providing for West German rearmament and sovereignty within the context of an integrated West European army remained mired in allied bickering and negotiations. In late January 1953, just before Senate hearings on his nomination, Conant wrote in his diary: "CIA briefing. Tough! Almost hope the Senate won't confirm."[1]

He might have realized that hope had not Eisenhower made a strenuous effort to extract a private pledge from McCarthy to hold his fire, despite having pusillanimously refrained from criticizing McCarthy during his election campaign (a reluctance that persisted into his presidency). The senator had long made Harvard the target for his charges that the Eastern Establishment was soft on Communists, and his most precocious staff aide, William F. Buckley, Jr., had prepared a lengthy tirade against Conant for him to give on the Senate floor. But Eisenhower was determined to wrest a measure of cooperation from him not only about Conant but also about Charles "Chip" Bohlen, a veteran foreign service officer whom Eisenhower wanted to become ambassador to Moscow. To dissuade McCarthy, then at the peak of his powers, the president enlisted his erstwhile rival Senator Robert Taft, then Vice President Nixon, and finally, telephoned McCarthy himself. Sensing that opposition to the widely acclaimed Conant would be a lost cause, and seeing a chance to gain a few points with a popular new president, McCarthy relented.[2] On February 3, when Conant testified before the Senate Foreign Relations Committee, he marveled at the silence of the senator from Wisconsin. "Just for the moment, Senator McCarthy's hostility to me was under wraps," he later wrote. "Just how this was accomplished, I never knew." In a largely uneventful two-day proceeding, his nomination survived its toughest hurdle, helped along by Massachusetts' senior senator and Conant's old college friend Leverett Saltonstall, whose support was considerably more enthusiastic than that of the state's recently elected junior senator; under pressure from Catholic constituents, John F. Kennedy had stated that he would oppose Conant's becoming U.S. commissioner of education but he backed his nomination as high commissioner in Germany.[3]

Still, McCarthy had not entirely repressed his virulent animus toward Conant and Harvard. In a letter to Eisenhower drawing on the arguments Buckley had prepared for him to deliver on the Senate floor, McCarthy strongly condemned Conant, opining that his "innocent statements about Communist activities in education and about the presence of communism in his faculty indicate a woeful lack of knowledge of the vicious and intricate Communist conspiracy."[4] Normally, he would "put up an all-out fight" to thwart Conant's nomination and "would do that now if I thought there were any possibility of defeating him." But since the Senate seemed likely to vote aye, rather than "furnish the Communists in Europe with a vast amount of ammunition for their guns" McCarthy magnanimously consented to remain quiet as "the lesser of the two evils," a speedy but intense FBI background check failed to uncover any serious black marks, and Conant's nomination swiftly received full Senate approval.[5]

Shortly thereafter, Conant left for West Germany's "temporary" capital to take stock of his new domain. Bonn, a tidy Rhenish village, was serving as a holding company for governmental functions during the ostensibly brief interval before Berlin could be disentangled from the complications that had left it a metaphor for the Cold War, a divided city under quadripartite occupation, its western sector a tiny island of capitalism surrounded by a Communist sea. His new address was the high commissioner's headquarters in a segregated (no Germans allowed), comfortably serviced American compound in the verdant, sleepy diplomatic enclave of Bad Godesberg, an "amiable sanatorium settlement" built beside a spa outside Bonn's town walls to accommodate the unexpected influx of outsiders.

At his new job, Conant faced an array of conflicting pressures and administrative woes that quickly evoked comparisons to the multiplicity of competing constituencies of the Harvard presidency. "This is worse than any meeting of professors," he said to himself after one staff meeting, and the personnel problems he encountered struck him as "so reminiscent of the Walsh-Sweezy days at Harvard as to be comical." He drew in his journal a diagram showing the high commissioner being assaulted by arrows representing various groups—a skeptical and critical American press corps, the State Department upper echelon, a worried and demanding local staff, Congress and McCarthy, the Soviet Union, the Allies, and the Germans. But all those troubles, he comforted himself, were preferable to the headaches of the Furry case he had left behind in Cambridge![6]

As high commissioner, Conant represented the United States in dealings with the three other occupying powers—the Soviet Union, Great Britain, and France—that maintained residual rights in determining Germany's future and still uncomfortably shared occupation duties in Berlin, where Conant was now considered the senior U.S. official, and where he paid frequent visits to "show the flag" and consult with local authorities. In Bonn, his principal day-to-day work was to establish close ties with West Germany's pro-American chancellor, Adenauer, the courtly, tough-as-nails septuagenarian former mayor of Cologne. Since the three Western powers had formalized the creation of the Federal Republic in 1949—after the year-long Berlin blockade quashed any lingering hopes of rapid reunification with the Soviet-controlled eastern zone—the "old man" (der Alte) had emerged as West Germany's preeminent politician, a symbol of stature and hope lording over a bruised nation from his modest fiefdom along the Rhine.

"In Bonn, even the flies are official," a spy sighs to himself on a dank, misty night in John le Carré's novel of 1950s Cold War espionage A Small Town in Germany. And as Conant would discover during his four years as Eisenhower's envoy—first as high commissioner, then ambassador—the makeshift capital of the Federal Republic was rife with subterranean plots, tensions, scandals, defections, undercover operations, double crosses and shady schemes. Bonn had been chosen more because of its convenience as Adenauer's political power base than because of any intrinsic grandeur or traditions. "[P]ermanently committed to the condition of impermanence," in Le Carré's phrase, it had a dour, grim, leaden air, a condition accentuated by the charmless sprawl of hastily erected drab gray concrete structures, along with an "indefinable hint of Nazi architecture, just a breath, no more."[7] In Bonn, and even more in Berlin, the anxiety was augmented by a sense of being caught at the intersection of the globe's two rival blocs, grinding together like tectonic plates that rumbled and threatened to quake with devastating force. Controlling the fault line was at the top of the geopolitical agenda for both superpowers. "Germany," judged one analyst, "once more returned to power as a first-class force in world affairs, elevated from her cataclysmic defeat by the irony of history to a key position between East and West, holds the balance of power in the cold war."[8]

Conant's assignment put him at the front of not only World War III's most likely flash point, but of the Cold War's most hotly contested battlefield. The crucible of that confrontation was the volatile issue of Berlin, with its still permeable frontier through which up to a hundred thousand residents of the Soviet-controlled East Zone slipped each month during the cold winter to claim asylum in the West in an exodus that strained West Berliners' supplies, facilities, and nerves.[9] And looming in the background, always, was the fear that through miscalculation, provocation, or attack Berlin might kindle a new East-West crisis or military conflagration—or that economic or political instability might once again awaken German nationalism. "Inflation and unemployment and the Russians are the three dangers that threaten Europe," Conant calculated privately in March 1953. "The refugee problem adds to the possibility of unemployment and social unrest. . . . Neonazism will take a different form if it emerges, more of a nationalistic reactionary capitalistic bias. Communism within Fed. Republic is hardly any danger *now*. But totalitarian government always will hang over this nation as a threat for years to come."[10]

One of his less publicized responsibilities would be to keep track of the CIA's massive anti-Soviet operation in Germany, an enterprise that promised to expand in accord with Republican vows to press for the "liberation" of Soviet-ruled Eastern Europe and East Germany (the German Democratic Republic, or GDR) by all possible means short of war. From Munich, the CIA directed anti-Soviet broadcasts throughout Eastern Europe, and Berlin, a hundred miles into "enemy territory" behind the Iron Curtain, was a prize listening post for Soviet-bloc activities. During this period, according to a 1976 Congressional report, "The CIA station in West Berlin was the center of CIA operations against Eastern Europe, and the German Branch of the European Division was the Agency's largest single country component."[11] As Conant arrived, U.S. officials were scrambling to dampen a minor furor that had erupted over one covert operation gone awry: local police had stumbled upon evidence of a secret U.S. intelligence program to arm, train, and finance right-wing extremists, including veterans of Nazi groups, to become anti-Communist guerrillas in the event of World War III; among the papers they discovered, embarrassingly, was a list of leftist West German political leaders to assassinate in that contingency.[12] Conant's message to the CIA station chief, Lt. Gen. Lucian K. Truscott, Jr., was blunt, one former agency man recalls: You created this mess, you straighten it out.[13]

But Conant's most important and pressing task was to encourage Bonn's parliament to ratify the voluminous, intricate Paris and Bonn treaties which the allies had concluded in 1952 to provide for West German rearmament within EDC's integrated army and its reacquisition of sovereignty, and which also awaited final approval from French legislators. Though the allies had granted Bonn self-government in all areas other than foreign and military policy in 1949, West Germans still yearned for full sovereignty and the end of the Occupation regime. At the same time, they feared that endorsing EDC and firm membership in the West's military alliance would doom their prospects for reunification with the millions of Germans in the Soviet zone, whose desperate plight was dramatized by the huge refugee exodus. Rather than abandon their suffering countrymen, some West Germans preferred the alternative of negotiating with the Soviet Union for a neutralized, demilitarized but reunified Germany—a notion stridently resisted in Washington (and by Adenauer himself).

In short, despite West Germany's rapid economic recovery from wartime ruin, the uncertain prospects for reunification, rearmament, and sovereignty, combined with the nationalistic passions unleashed by the refugees and their compatriots under Communist rule, raised major questions—about the tenuous "peace" of a divided Europe; about the health and future stability of a post-Nazi German democracy; about Adenauer's odds of winning reelection later in 1953, a goal to which Washington and Conant were firmly, albeit unofficially, committed; and about U.S. plans for consolidating the West European nations into a unified, well-armed, capitalist bastion capable of deterring or resisting Soviet encroachment.

At this juncture, the selection of the sixty-year-old Harvard president embodied the Eisenhower administration's confidence in the cultural rebirth of Germany, its return to international social, intellectual, and political acceptance, and its full membership in the Western alliance. Conant was also another distinguished figure in Washington's progression of plenipotentiary proconsuls. First had come military commander Gen. Lucius D. Clay, who symbolized the Allied conquest and occupation of Germany (and, during the Berlin airlift, its military defense). Then High Commissioner John J. McCloy, a lawyer fit for the diplomatic negotiations and corridor politics involved in the contracting of the new postwar relationship. And now Conant, educator and scientist, embodying esteem and respect for German culture. Conant was also the first "atomic diplomat"—realizing the advice of the Science Advisory Committee that officials "conversant with the scientific background," not merely briefed on it, must participate in decision making.[14] It did not take him long to gain the nickname of "Professor Atom" or to awe listeners by dropping casual allusions to being the only person in the room actually to have seen an atomic bomb explode.

Despite the smooth partnership usually depicted by historians between the Eisenhower-Dulles and Adenauer administrations,[15] events would demonstrate that Ike's appointment was perhaps most apt because Conant personified the deep ambivalence felt by many Americans toward a miraculously transformed "good Germany" confronting a suddenly "evil Russia."

Conant, of course, had become involved in the Manhattan Project out of fear that Germany might be the first to develop the atomic bomb, had promoted a Morgenthau-like plan to dismember German industry and reconstitute the country's economy along pastoral lines to ensure against a secret postwar atomic effort, and he had continued to voice doubts about the wisdom or necessity of rearming Germany. Shortly before leaving office, in fact, Acheson had warned his successor that Conant's reservations about German rearmament should be "carefully explored, because such an attitude on the part of the High Commissioner at a time when the Chancellor was in a very bitter battle might be disastrous."[16] And Conant himself had reminded Dulles of the need "to have a person over there who agrees with your fundamental policy." "Well, maybe," demurred Dulles.[17] But he was in Bonn without a clear idea of Eisenhower's general policy objectives beyond full support for EDC and for Adenauer — and indeed the new administration itself was muddled and divided over its true objectives. Was Washington genuinely committed to German unification? At what price? Did "liberation" rhetoric imply concrete measures to incite and support popular uprisings in Eastern Europe (and Eastern Germany) against Soviet-backed rule? In what form, if any, might Washington find German rearmament acceptable should EDC fail? With what safeguards? Should Conant plan for a rapprochement with Moscow leading to a settlement of existing problems in Europe, or a deepening of the division on the Continent and a likely East-West war?

These questions were critical to the shape of Europe and of U.S. foreign policy. But the Truman and Eisenhower administrations' ability to address them was hampered throughout much of the early 1950s, by the orthodox anti-Communism enforced by Senator McCarthy and his supporters in Congress and the State Department — where Dulles, in an effort to palliate him, had appointed a McCarthy crony named Scott McLeod as head of security. It was a time when veteran diplomats like John Carter Vincent and John Paton Davies were being hounded out of the department for accurately reporting bad news, and when Dulles would admonish Charles Bohlen for flying to Moscow two weeks before his family because it would allegedly nourish rumors that he was homosexual.[18] Dulles made several highly publicized dismissals that pleased the rabid anti-Communists, and he warned upon taking office that anything less than "positive loyalty" from foreign service officers was "not tolerable at this time."[19] Many career diplomats felt abandoned by superiors willing to sacrifice loyal and competent aides to appease McCarthy and his allies.

These pressures were felt nowhere more acutely than at the U.S. diplomatic mission in Germany. Since McCloy had left the previous July, leaving it under the temporary stewardship of deputy chief of mission Walter Donnelly, the high commissioner's office had been rudderless. Morale was already low because of severe budget and personnel cuts made in anticipation of the Occupation's official end, and now Conant found the staff reeling from the McCarthy and now McLeod attacks. Conant had barely arrived when, on March 13, he received an order from the State Department to request the resignation of one staff aide (Charles Thayer) who had incurred McCarthy's wrath.[20] In April, the main event was a whirlwind visit made by two McCarthy sidekicks, Roy Cohn and G. David Schine, on a crusade to root out Communist influence from the State Department—a trip that did nothing to enhance U.S. security but produced a media circus and a growing sense of paranoia. Conant—in Washington at the time with Adenauer—had learned through intelligence channels just as he was leaving Bonn of the impending Cohn and Schine visit. (State Department cables were considered "open" to McCarthyites; on at least one occasion Conant presumed McLeod was wiretapping him.[21])

Soon after Conant's arrival, McCarthy made the high commissioner's office a prime target, smearing several officials with "pinko" labels and charging that the USIA libraries there, as elsewhere, circulated books by Communist authors. Observers in Bonn reported pervasive fear, distraction, caution, and suspicion, as a flurry of coerced departures by key personnel began in March with Thayer and continued in April with the resignation under pressure of USIA aide Theodore Kaghan, who had had the temerity to criticize Cohn and Schine openly as "junketeering gumshoes." Bonn, wrote one American journalist in August, "was a peculiarly depressing place for a peculiarly American reason," with the U.S. mission substituting "dogma for policy and the official line for serious original thought."[22]

While Conant was appalled by McCarthyism, knew it "badly shattered" State Department morale, and in several cases fought its excesses, he was a Dulles-Eisenhower appointee, and believed he could not go beyond the administration's cautious, politically determined line; propriety, expediency, and fear of controversy sometimes triumphed over moral indignation and principle. As a result his standing suffered among American reporters who thought he was not doing enough to stand up for his colleagues. "General feeling I am too cautious and cagey," Conant wrote in his diary.[23] C. L. Sulzberger of the *New York Times*, "horrified" when Sam Reber, a veteran diplomat and Conant's deputy, was forced from office in mid-1953, "asked our correspondent to call up Conant and have him say something to the effect that he regretted to have his great friend and able assistant, Mr. Reber, retire. Conant refused."[24] A scathing *Washington Post* report alleged that senior West German officials' estimates of the high commissioner had plummeted after seeing that he was "unable or unwilling" to stop his key advisers from being "snatched away on loyalty or security charges." Conant brushed the charge aside as a "highly slanted" exaggeration.[25]

Characteristically, Conant's strongest efforts to stem the hysteria were behind-the-scenes efforts yielding mixed results. Lunching with Eisenhower on June 9, he decried "the useless 'public executions' that were going on" but also reiterated "my unwillingness to fight publicly with Senator McCarthy as long as I was working for the President," as he put it in his diary.[26] A confrontation with McCarthy at a Senate Appropriations Committee hearing one week later epitomized this ambivalence. Unaware that Eisenhower had just publicly denounced "book burners"—he had done so moments after hearing a damning report from John McCloy about the situation in Bonn[27]—Conant allowed himself to be maneuvered by McCarthy into endorsing the "de-shelving" of books by Communist authors in USIA libraries, lamely suggesting that it be done "without too much publicity." Under McCarthy's browbeating, Conant waved a white flag in the morning session: "I certainly don't object to anything that congressional committees do, sir." His explanation for kowtowing to McCarthy? In *My Several Lives,* Conant explained this by saying that he had vaguely remembered a State Department cable dictating cooperation with congressional committees: "I snapped to attention mentally and expressed what I thought was the official line, which was not far from my own official thinking."[28]

After lunch, however, during which he learned that Eisenhower had taken a firmer stand against this kind of censorship, Conant mustered a bit more nerve, cautiously defending two aides (Kaghan and Lowell Clucas) whom McCarthy labeled as security risks. That measured display of independence gave the senator an opening to scorn Conant for doing "infinite damage" to U.S. interests—a burst of opprobrium that actually did much for Conant's image among dispirited staff members in Bonn and critical newspapermen.

Soon after, when Conant heard that another trusted aide was being threatened, he contacted his friend McCloy, who passed the word to Dulles that "there was a feeling in the staff that the Department did not support them" and that the continuing inquisitions were hurting anti-Communist efforts in Germany. Conant crowed in his diary that he could claim credit (but wouldn't) for the fact that the State Department "seems to have come to life on the issue of McCarthy versus personnel." But his efforts were for naught: despite a plea from Conant that Glenn Wolfe, his chief administrative officer, should "not be tossed to the wolves," Dulles replaced him with a long-time McLeod associate.[29] Conant sympathized with the pressures Dulles and Eisenhower faced, but he considered Dulles insensitive to the needs of the diplomatic corps, and later said that he "never got any encouragement" from the State Department's top level in dealing with McCarthy. "It might have been wonderful if both of them—the Secretary and the President—grabbed white horses and tried to ride down McCarthy," Conant recalled. "But they didn't. They lived through it. And it's certainly not a very great glory for the Secretary, the way he came through it."[30]

Nor was it for Conant.

✿ ✿ ✿

The reign of McCarthyism at home reinforced militant tendencies in U.S. foreign policy, in particular Dulles's stern, moralistic, evangelical anti-Communism, and his declared intention to move from defensive containment to what he called "a psychological offensive, a liberation policy, which will try to give hope and a resistance mood inside the Soviet empire."[31] But the sails were taken out of this initiative by Stalin's death in early March, followed in May by a proposal by British prime minister Winston Churchill (who had been returned to power for a last hurrah) to hold the first East-West summit conference since the leaders of the Grand Alliance had met at Potsdam in 1945. These slender signs that there might be a nascent thaw also threatened the likelihood of getting final approval from France and West Germany of the EDC treaties—whose enaction, Moscow darkly warned, would squander hopes for German reunification, finalize the division of Europe, and increase the prospects for war.[32]

In April, Eisenhower sought to project an image of reasonableness by delivering his hedged but hopeful "Chance for Peace" speech while at the same time he sought more seriously to consolidate West German rearmament within the Western alliance and secure EDC ratification. The first tangible indication of the new administration's desire to cement a strong relationship with Adenauer and to boost his political fortunes at home was its hosting of the chancellor's symbolically crucial visit to Washington in April 1953—the first such journey by a German leader since the war. Accompanying the chancellor to Washington, Conant ardently sought to convince U.S. officials to accede publicly to Adenauer's request that the United States moderate procedures for prosecuting alleged Nazi war criminals. "Largely at my insistence," Conant wrote privately, Washington "was willing to push this matter vigorously" in talks with British and French HICOGs. Those talks led to the creation of mixed German-Allied tribunals to consider clemency and parole requests—a political boon for Adenauer that enabled him to outflank right-wing critics, who charged that the chancellor had sacrificed German interests to appease the American occupiers.[33] Even before Adenauer's arrival, the atmosphere had improved with the ratification by the West German Bundestag (although complications remained regarding ratification by the Bundes*rat*, the parliament's upper house, which considers certain constitutional questions) of the EDC treaties—pleasing U.S. officials, who pointedly linked cooperation on the clemency issue to final West German parliamentary ratification of EDC[34]—and then the trip itself marked a watershed in postwar U.S.-German relations as well as a personal triumph for Adenauer. Easing into the job of rehabilitating Germany in the eyes of the American public as well as supporting Adenauer at every turn, Conant hosted him at Harvard. Beneath the surface, however, Adenauer's and Conant's relationship already showed signs of trouble. Twice in the weeks preceding the visit, Adenauer had dispatched a personal envoy to Washington—circumventing annoyed officials at the high commissioner's office—to see how the Americans would react to a secret plan to begin early training of West German military cadres before France had ratified EDC. Dulles promptly vetoed the idea, which Adenauer had concealed from Conant "because of his fear of leaks," and was disturbed by this early indication that the German leader did not find it worthwhile to present his idea to Conant. Telephoning McCloy to see what could be done about "getting the German thing back in diplomatic channels," he voiced concern that the Conant-Adenauer relationship was getting off to a rocky start. "We want to build up Conant," Dulles said, "and this sort of thing weakens his position."[35]

Engrossed in their own complicated maneuvers in Moscow, Soviet leaders in April and May lifted hopes for a breakthrough toward German unification and East-West reconciliation by instructing East German leaders to relax hard-line Communist economic and political controls, halt farm collectivization, cease persecution of churches, and in general deemphasize socialist ideology. Recent information emanating from Soviet and East German sources tends to support the hypothesis that these adjustments did not represent a full-fledged shift by Moscow toward accepting a unified, non-Communist Germany, but rather a tactical measure to raise popular support for the East German government, to sow divisions between the Western allies and to undercut Adenauer and EDC by fostering belief in a reunified Germany, and to achieve breathing room for the Kremlin internationally as it sought to consolidate domestic authority.[36] But the reform gambit backfired, in part because the East German leaders imposed stricter industrial work norms, effectively reducing wages, just as they were implicitly conceding the failure of their economic and political policies (and the validity of Western criticisms) and allowing a greater venting of dissent. "In short, they did the one thing a dictator should not do, they played it both 'hard' and 'soft' at the same time," Conant privately concluded. "As a consequence, I believe, the riots of June 17 occurred."[37]

The first major revolt against Communist rule in Soviet-dominated Europe since the end of the war, the June 17, 1953, workers' protests in East Berlin and throughout the GDR compelled the Soviets to use tanks, machine-gun fire, and widespread arrests to reimpose order; scores or hundreds of dissidents were killed in the clampdown. One of the first major foreign policy crises of Ike's presidency and Conant's tenure in Germany, the events also exposed the bankruptcy of the new administration's blithe "rollback" and "liberation" rhetoric, for when the so-called captive peoples actually revolted, as Dulles and Eisenhower had been confidently predicting they would, they took the U.S. government completely by surprise, and its reaction was hesitant and ineffectual. On the night of the uprising, aflame with visions of forcing a humiliating Soviet withdrawal, the CIA station chief in Berlin cabled Washington asking permission to arm rioters in the East Zone with rifles and Sten guns. But the administration limited the U.S. response to asylum, commiseration, and symbolic gestures.[38] The crisis "left our State Department not knowing what to do," Conant admitted some years later.

"We were all caught unawares, without any plans, for which all of us got sufficient blame . . . There really wasn't much to do."[39]

The tentative way in which the United States responded to the Berlin crisis demonstrated to the Soviet Union and the world that Washington would not risk World War III to accomplish the liberation of Eastern Europe. Conant, who was in Washington testifying on budget matters and jousting with McCarthy, did little to dispel the impression of disorganization and unconcern by appearing to take his time returning to Germany.[40] He put on a show of U.S. resolve by driving through the east sector of Berlin in a limousine flying the Stars and Stripes, but he could offer little to assuage the outrage of West Berliners at the treatment their fellow citizens were suffering— and his mood wasn't helped much when he was sidetracked by a mini-crisis involving a recently graduated managing editor of the *Harvard Crimson* who was reported missing after being arrested by East German police; the young reporter, who was free-lancing for the Boston *Traveler*, was soon released (just as the high commissioner's office was preparing an official *démarche* to the Russians on his behalf), but received a stern lecture on irresponsibility from a harried and distinctly unamused Conant before being sent home with a firm instruction to stay out of trouble.[41]

On first coming to Germany, Conant had dutifully if unenthusiastically echoed the administration's promise of a Cold War offensive, telling a West Berlin audience that "the frontiers of freedom will peacefully expand and Berlin will then no longer be an isolated citadel."[42] But while the National Security Council in August (NSC 160/1) endorsed continued covert operations to "nourish resistance to Soviet power in East Germany,"[43] Conant and other American envoys in Europe urged Dulles and the president to cut back on the more aggressive forms of anti-Communist subversion, fearing that they could spin out of control. "I assume that our objective in the East Zone is to keep the pot simmering but not to bring it to a boil!" wrote Conant in a handwritten postscript to an August 8 letter to Dulles (a strange place to raise a fundamental policy question).[44] On the same day, elaborating his cautionary message, Conant cabled Washington that

> US policies toward East Germany while aimed at encouraging and keeping alive the intensified spirit of resistance awakened in mid-June should still carefully avoid and if necessary endeavor to restrain East Zone resistance from taking such overt form as would give Commie authorities excuse for brutal and bloody repression of population and particularly their leaders. As long as western world unable contribute effectively to East Zone freedom, and there is no reason believe such freedom brought into sight by recent events, US propaganda and other initiatives (essential and timely though they are) must continue be governed by restraint. Otherwise smouldering fire East German resistance may be prematurely fanned up and stamped out; and the fetters of Communism tightened again and Commie propagandists given opportunity to fasten responsibility upon USA.[45]

Conant's missives to the State Department were aimed primarily at those he privately dubbed the "P.W. boys"[46]—the plotters and planners of "psychological warfare," one of the mainstays of the early Eisenhower administration's Cold War strategy. Until supplanted in September by the Operations Coordinating Board (OCB), the Psychological Strategy Board (PSB) was responsible for developing policies to manipulate events, people, and opinions around the globe. Presidential assistant C. D. Jackson, a veteran of psychological warfare operations in World War II recruited from Henry Luce's *Time* magazine, wrote that Eisenhower considered psychological warfare as the way to "win World War III without having to fight it" and "not . . . the pet mystery of one or more Departments of the Government, but . . . the entire posture of the entire Government to the entire world." All that psychological warfare needed in order to triumph, he averred, was "(1) money, (2) no holds barred and (3) no questions asked."[47] The Berlin revolt showed, Jackson thought, that the "slaves of the Soviet Union" were moving "past the riot stage, and . . . close to insurrection," and the National Security Council turned to the PSB to come up with "policies and actions" to "exploit the unrest in the satellite states" (there were also reports of rioting in Czechoslovakia).[48] It was with Jackson in mind that Conant recalled several years later that in early 1953, judging from what he had heard both in public statements and privately from General Clay and "some of the CIA boys," a rollback was in the "in the mind of some" Eisenhower administration officials "though whether it ever got Pres. OK is another matter."[49]

Conant, by contrast, took a generally dubious view of covert schemes to roll back Communist rule or to prepare for World War III, and remained privately convinced that "responsible Republicans" (like himself) supported the containment strategy in practice even if they might denounce it in principle.[50] Fostering political and economic strength and stability in West Germany, he believed, would prove far more important to winning the Cold War over the long term than high-risk clandestine operations or aggressive psychological warfare programs. On several occasions, Conant clashed with Washington over proposed or functioning U.S. covert operations that he felt might endanger Adenauer's political standing or U.S.–West German ties if exposed—and just a few weeks after the Berlin revolt, he was instrumental in short-circuiting a provocative top-secret scheme to create a "Volunteer Freedom Corps" (VFC) composed of right-wing anti-Communist émigrés (including members of groups that had collaborated with the Nazis) from areas under Soviet domination who would be covertly assembled in West Germany and armed, trained, and financed by Washington. These forces were to be ready for guerrilla missions behind the Iron Curtain or for use as substitutes for U.S. soldiers in Korea or other limited wars or as shock troops for World War III.[51] Strong proponents of the VFC concept included the U.S. ambassador to the United Nations, Henry Cabot Lodge; C. D. Jackson; and Eisenhower himself, who shortly after taking office said it should be feasible "in these days of tension, with a zeal equal to the need, to recruit up to 250,000 men."[52] Instructed to sound out the West German government, whose approval was essential for the VFC's creation, Conant informed Washington on July 11 that Bonn was likely to reject the idea and that its very existence, if it became public knowledge, could damage Adenauer politically. The idea was reluctantly put aside, at least for the time being.[53]

Conant's skepticism about covert operations and the yen for rollback reflected and reinforced the general assessment of senior U.S. diplomats throughout Europe. Meeting in Luxembourg in September 1953, he and the other U.S. ambassadors in Western Europe and NATO issued a stinging top-secret rebuke to "psywar" tactics, a manifesto echoed a few days later by the U.S. envoys posted to Eastern Europe, meeting for an annual conference in Vienna.[54] If not more carefully tuned to political objectives, they warned, psychological warfare might "start to make policy rather than serve it." Already, West Europeans had grown "generally distrustful" of American objectives, and showed "fear and anxiety" that U.S. "impatience and implacable hostility" toward Moscow might lead to war. Citing the U.S. operations in Berlin following the Berlin riots — perhaps alluding to the "unattributable" anti-Soviet broadcasts urging revolt (invoking the example of 1848!)[55] as well as the short-lived program of food aid — the envoys underlined the need for closer coordination with West European allies, who, while they did not object to keeping "the Eastern European pot lukewarm or even simmering," worried that U.S. political warfare kept it "at a constant boiling point." By raising the specter (and perhaps likelihood) of disaster, the diplomats charged, psychological warfare had already proven counterproductive. "American unilateralism in this field is dangerous and serves devisive [sic] forces within the Western alliance," they asserted. "Our psychological operations at times serve to increase fears on the part of our allies that we were prepared to break in the windows; to bring the pot to a boiling-over condition, the grave consequences of which we have perhaps not weighed and carefully considered."[56]

The diplomats counseled instead a more realistic appraisal of the prospects for freeing Eastern Europe and a general toning-down of U.S. information programs, which they felt should be "as quiet and as subtle as possible." Implicitly — but only implicitly — referring to Senator McCarthy, they said the most important factor in improving America's position abroad was foreign perceptions of "the American domestic scene" and Washington's actions abroad rather than its rhetoric. "Propaganda," they emphasized, "begins at home."[57] As Conant had already written in an earlier cable, many Germans compared McCarthy to Hitler and cited his power as evidence that the United States had no right to give lectures on democracy or tolerance.[58]

This diplomatic broadside stirred a sharp debate in the White House when in late October it and a countering memorandum from Jackson ("Just what did the Ambassadors expect American psychological warfare to do? Tell the rioters to go home and be nice to the Commies?") reached the president.[59] Eisenhower had, at least to some degree, maintained hopes that rollback could work in Germany. He had believed that a strong and advancing West Germany could be such a strong magnet to East Germans that, as he put it in a draft private letter, it might "become impossible for the Communists to hold the place by force."[60] So he reacted dubiously to the envoys' criticism of the liberation strategy and its vaunted secret weapon, psychological warfare. They were interpreting the term "in too narrow a fashion," Eisenhower stated. "After all, psychological warfare can be anything from the singing of a beautiful hymn up to the most extraordinary kind of physical sabotage."[61] Still, the "revolt of the diplomats," which Conant helped to catalyze, showed the strain of internal resistance to the much proclaimed vow to discard the hated "Truman-Acheson line" of containment and move to the "offensive" in the Cold War. Washington was reluctantly concluding that rollback was not an immediately feasible option, at least in Europe.[62]

A second major consequence of the abortive East German uprising was to thrust the reunification issue to the forefront of the election campaign in West Germany, in which the United States was firmly backing Adenauer's Christian Democratic Union (CDU) against Social Democratic Party (SPD, for *Sozialdemokratische Partei Deutschlands*) opposition. Adenauer "obviously thought it was my duty to help him get re-elected," Conant recalled many years later, and in fact it was; the need for a CDU victory, he said, determined U.S. policy throughout the campaign.[63] (And that Eisenhower and Dulles enthusiastically supported Adenauer's election was no secret — the secretary even remarked publicly a few days before the vote that an SPD victory would be "disastrous," an unsubtle intervention that had Conant fretting.)

When the June 17 revolt in East Berlin forced Adenauer to deal with the issues of unification and of a possible parley with Moscow—issues he had preferred to duck until the Federal Republic's sovereignty had been fully established within the Western alliance—the matter of assuring his political success in the upcoming elections became trickier. Both Adenauer and Washington gave a higher priority to the rearmament of West Germany and opposition to Moscow than to German reunification, and were willing to postpone the latter indefinitely rather than accept Soviet terms that precluded German membership in the Western alliance. "A 'neutralized,' unified Germany, with or without armed forces, would entail sacrifices and risks to the West incommensurate with any possible gains," the National Security Council declared in August. "It would deny German strength to the West, wreck present and prospective plans for building augmented European strength through union, and open up the whole of Germany to Soviet intrigue and manipulation which would aim at the absorption of Germany into the Soviet bloc."[64] But reunification as a political problem was another question. The opposition SPD, though no longer using the neutralist *"ohne mich"* (count me out) slogan, chided Adenauer for being the "Chancellor of the Allies" and demanded that rearmament and integration into Western military and political structures be delayed until every avenue leading to reunification had been explored with Moscow. Adenauer could hardly ignore this challenge when polls taken after the June uprising in Berlin found that four of ten West Germans listed reunification as their number-one issue, though they supported even more strongly a continued tight association with the West.[65]

Largely to mollify pro-SPD domestic critics, to "neutralize neutralism," Adenauer grudgingly uttered what Conant described as the "magic words" — a politically expedient expression of support for the four-power foreign ministers' conference that the Soviet Union had been advocating in the "war of the notes" since Stalin's letter of March 10, 1952, to take up the problems of a German peace treaty and reunification. Whether or not Stalin was seriously interested in a settlement, or merely in scoring propaganda points and disturbing West German politics, was unclear at the time and has never been fully clarified.[66] Adenauer did not want to find out — he had grave doubts that he could depend on either London or Washington to preserve West German interests, which he saw as being firmly embedded within the Western alliance. But the "groundswell of demand" for such a parley from the Social Democrats and other Germans calling for the negotiated "liberation" of their East Zone countrymen forced Adenauer in July publicly to appeal to Eisenhower to "do everything in your power," to restore German unity, even though he himself was steadfastly opposed to quadripartite talks prior to September.[67]

From the start, U.S. officials had regarded the Soviet proposals as a cynical propaganda ploy intended, as an intelligence report put it, to "play upon the nationalism of the West Germans, to retard West German integration into the Western defense system, to divide the Western Powers, and, in general, to obstruct implementation of Western defense plans."[68] Washington's policy, nearly as cynical, was to profess support for negotiations and reunification while hoping that the evident futility of these efforts would refocus attention on ratification of EDC; the means of doing this was to respond with counter-notes that insisted as a prerequisite on a restoration of full democratic rights and genuinely free voting in Soviet-controlled East Germany, which the CIA concluded the Soviets were unlikely to allow despite their avowed support for the concept of "free all-German elections."[69] Since U.S. officials believed, as Acheson put it in October 1952, that the "present Commie drive for four-power 'talks' is phony, with ulterior motives," intended to "befuddle and confuse" West German and West European public opinion, they argued that the most prudent course lay in building up Western military strength "so as eventually to bring about real talks with honest aims and some prospect of resolving tensions instead of fanning propaganda war."[70]

Adenauer "does not in the least desire a 4-Power conference before the German elections," Conant had written Dulles on June 25. "Indeed, nothing would be less helpful to him in the coming campaign and more helpful to the opposition."[71] And a week later, Adenauer was still telling Conant that a four-power conference "would merely provide a propaganda platform for [the] Russians and lead to never-ending talks" and suggesting instead that Washington confine itself to harshly worded protests and insistence on political liberalization in the Soviet zone as a precondition to a general conference.[72] Indeed, Conant, too, liked the idea of delaying high-level talks: he urged Adenauer and Washington to stick to Eisenhower's "deeds not words" formulation and insist on a mid-level preliminary conference to settle terms for East Zone elections.[73]

But by July 9, Adenauer had completely reversed his position—his aides told a U.S. diplomat that he was "absolutely certain" that Moscow was brewing some bold offer on reunification in order to help the SPD—and he now urged Washington to upstage the Soviets and "take the initiative" in requesting a four-power conference "by September."[74]

Adenauer's wish was quickly granted: on July 14, U.S., British, and French foreign ministers called for a four-power conference to consider steps toward "a satisfactory solution of the German problem, namely, the organization of free elections and the establishment of a free all-German government."[75] Eisenhower and Dulles had another vital motive to support a four-power conference after all—convincing French public opinion that the West had done its utmost to reach a settlement with Moscow before resorting to the EDC—but helping Adenauer and European rearmament, rather than negotiating an East-West settlement, was the real reason for Dulles's willingness to change his policy.[76] Declaring the intention "to make a new effort so as to bring to an end the abnormal situation to which the German people is subjected," Washington's note to the Kremlin not coincidentally specified that the meeting "might begin about the end of September"—*after* the September 6 elections, in conformity with Adenauer's precise instructions.[77]

Conant was not entirely pleased with Adenauer's about-face, and unsure whether it came after a calculated delay or an impulsive decision, but he acknowledged that the "whole outcome was a political triumph for the Chancellor . . . Even playing his 4 power card so late in the game proved most effective."[78] To Dulles, he wrote that Adenauer had superbly "spiked the Opposition's claim that he was not doing all he could to bring about unification. I think everyone must admire the skillful way in which he has turned the flank of the SPD."[79]

Paradoxically, Adenauer's overwhelming September 1953 reelection victory, which required increased power for right-wing factions in his parliamentary coalition, led to a secret crisis in U.S.–West German relations that brought Conant's doubts about German reliability to the surface, and illuminated the deep-set mutual ambivalence about the relationship and about the United States' commitment to defend Europe on the ground with conventional forces.

This ambivalence had existed from the outset of the Eisenhower administration, which tilted toward "big bomb" supporters enamored of the idea of using the Strategic Air Command to defend Western Europe "on the cheap" rather than getting sucked into the messy and expensive business of maintaining American ground troops in Europe and into the political morass of EDC. This strand of policy ran counter to the assurances that had been given of a long-term conventional U.S. ground presence in West Germany, and the well-publicized arrival of tactical nuclear weapons at U.S. bases in Germany, beginning only days after the September election, fed Adenauer's fears of a U.S. troop withdrawal from central Europe, as well as general public concern over NATO's seeming willingness to permit Germany to become an atomic "killing ground" in the event of war. Such sentiments escalated U.S.–West German tensions, which would increase with each revelation of German civilian casualty estimates from NATO war game exercises.[80] Some years later, Conant recalled that he was "firmly convinced" that from "almost the beginning" the Eisenhower administration had "planned to rearm Germany and pull American troops out." The impetus for substituting German troops for American troops, in Conant's recollection, came from administration officials, led by Treasury secretary George M. Humphrey, who were convinced that the continued deployment of U.S. forces in Europe constituted an intolerable economic burden. "If any hint of such a thing had got to the Germans, it would have been impossible for the Chancellor to have rearmed the Germans," he remembered. "Therefore, we were dealing with a very, very delicate situation in which hypocrisy verging on straight prevarication was the only thing that could be used."[81]

In the weeks following his reelection Adenauer faced the unsettling prospect of high-level East-West negotiations that he had publicly supported but still privately dreaded. Notwithstanding subsequent claims by historians that Adenauer's "cordial reception and assurances" during his triumphant April visit to Washington had "dispelled his fears" of an East-West détente at Germany's expense, and despite fervent denials from Eisenhower's minions, the notion of a superpower summit evoked Adenauer's "Potsdam nightmare" —his fear that the wartime Allies would settle Germany's affairs on their own, thus enabling the United States to withdraw its forces from Europe's heartland.[82] Adenauer urged U.S. officials to restrict the talks to the terms for holding free German elections as a prerequisite for progress toward reunification. But on October 12, when Conant showed him the latest draft of an Anglo-American-French letter to the Soviets, Adenauer was "very much upset" to note a willingness to conduct broad discussions, and argued that they would give Moscow a chance to "drive a wedge" between the Allies and further delay French EDC ratification.[83] But Conant believed Adenauer's explanation masked a deeper foreboding that "some commitments" on Germany's final status might be made, whether through betrayal or unanticipated results in a freewheeling bargaining session, and Dulles concluded that Adenauer was putting up a smoke screen, and was "still basically afraid" of four-power talks.[84]

Adenauer might have feared the four-power talks even more had he been able to read the correspondence between Eisenhower and Dulles. For in fact it had been his decisive reelection that emboldened Dulles to raise the idea of a U.S. troop withdrawal most dramatically. In a top-secret September 6 memorandum to Eisenhower, Dulles proposed "a spectacular effort to relax world tensions on a global basis," including a mutual pullback of U.S. and Soviet troops in Europe as well as major agreements to reduce conventional and nuclear weapons. The timing was right because the United States would be "speaking from strength rather than weakness," he declared, citing Adenauer's victory, the Korean armistice, the pro-Western coup in Iran, renewed indications of French determination in Indochina, and the United States' substantial if diminishing edge over Moscow in nuclear arms.[85] In response, Eisenhower claimed to be in "emphatic agreement" that efforts should be launched to reduce global tensions, and allowed that mutual withdrawals of U.S. and Red Army forces from Europe "could be suggested as a step toward relaxing these tensions." But Eisenhower also recognized that while "the semi-permanent presence of United States Forces (of any kind) in foreign lands is an irritant, any withdrawal that seemed to imply a change in *basic* intent would cause real turmoil abroad."[86] This was, he knew, particularly relevant in Germany's case.

After this passing glance at a dramatic disarmament initiative, later expressed in watered-down form in Ike's December 1953 "Atoms for Peace" speech to the United Nations, Eisenhower and Dulles returned to the strategy of convening (rather than indefinitely delaying) East-West talks in order to convince West European, especially French, public opinion to support EDC before the French Assembly voted on it. Dulles recognized, as he wrote to Conant, that Adenauer's "smashing victory" enhanced his personal influence "to a point where it will be very difficult — and perhaps undesirable — to deal with the German problem except on the basis of treating him as a full partner."[87] Yet he assumed that, with a new popular mandate, Adenauer would be in a "much more reasonable mood" and that he would go along with Washington's strategy of palliating French public opinion through East-West talks and West German concessions on the disputed coal-rich Saar border territory, which though historically German had been under French control since the war.[88] But Dulles miscalculated. The vote, while endorsing Adenauer's pro-American and pro-EDC foreign policy, had reflected and intensified a general rise in West German self-confidence, feelings fueled by the country's rapid economic growth and the evident disarray both of the Communist regime to the east and the French government to the west. "Obviously the Germans are on the move again," a visitor wrote in his diary after meeting Adenauer and his military aides a few weeks after the election. "They are either going to get EDC and gain control of it or pull out and act on their own if such control isn't granted. Or they are going to set up a national army with full American approval."[89] Detecting "signs of a recrudescence of 'right radicalism,' " Conant noted that after the election it seemed "as though the nationalistic [forces] had bounded up," with Adenauer's government engaging in a "flexing of muscles" when it began to appreciate the extent of its victory.[90]

The clearest expression of the changed mood in Germany was a hardened determination not to make concessions to France over in the deadlocked Saar negotiations, which Washington regarded as the "crucial" obstacle blocking Paris's approval of EDC and European integration in general.[91] For three years, U.S. and West European officials had been seeking a formula to create supranational safeguards over the region's coal and steel resources, which were vital to German military industries, and a major ingredient in Paris's foot-dragging on West German rearmament. Like Dulles, Conant had erroneously supposed, on hearing the voting results, that Adenauer was "now in such a strong position that he should be able to make concessions to France on Saar."[92] And at precisely this moment, Washington launched a new effort— deliberately delayed until after the elections to forestall any public friction[93] —to get Adenauer to be more forthcoming. Dulles was simultaneously putting pressure on the French, but he believed that the solution lay "squarely in Adenauer's hands," and in early October instructed Conant to have "a frank talk" with the chancellor on the subject.[94] But Conant, citing an "inferiority complex" on the part of the chancellor's smaller coalition partners, warned Washington that the position of the emerging Adenauer government on the coal, iron, and steel industry center "appears stiffened rather than relaxed following elections."[95] Adenauer had gained great power by his victory and effectively vanquished the opposition, but "this power in turn means he may have to wrestle more vigorously or compromise more readily with some members of his Cabinet or the different party leaders."[96] Later in the month a top State Department officer on a special arm-twisting trip to Europe was more explicit: he warned State Secretary for Foreign Affairs Walter Hallstein that recent anti-French statements from Bonn were "very damaging" and the West German government would have to "give till it hurts" to reach a Saar settlement.[97]

Conant's work on these delicate diplomatic issues was complicated by the deterioration of his personal relationship with Adenauer. The two had never established more than a formal bond. Conant was professorial, didactic, proper, sometimes elliptical or abstract; Adenauer, an ex-*Bürgermeister* fifteen years his senior, was a masterful political operator who relished the conspiratorial jockeying and maneuvering for power that Conant disdained. "I don't think [Conant] stacks up against shrewd, tough Germans like Adenauer," was one American journalist's conclusion.[98] Adenauer was unimpressed with Conant's political acumen, and he also quickly recognized that Dulles had given Conant far less independence or influence in shaping policy than Acheson had given McCloy; consequently he repeatedly bypassed the high commissioner's office and dealt directly with Dulles and his close associates.[99]

Conant was not oblivious to this development, but felt powerless to reverse it. Uneasily observing the comings-and-goings of Adenauer's envoys, in early September 1953 he had sent an anguished "personal—eyes only" letter to a friend in the administration confessing insecurity about his policy-making role.[100] And when he called upon Adenauer to congratulate him on the election results, Conant noticed that the chancellor seemed "pleased but distant"—a coolness due, he discovered later, to his failure to bring a "message from the President!"[101] An incident in mid-September lengthened that distance, and also cast a shadow over Conant's view of Adenauer's political maturity. After lunching with SPD chairman Erich Ollenhauer as part of his post-election consultations, Conant got a letter from Adenauer objecting to the meeting and inquiring as to what had been discussed. Conant, offended, answered with a sharp note telling Adenauer, in effect, to mind his own business; he viewed this impertinent request as lending credence to warnings from American journalists that the chancellor was "going reactionary" or, at a minimum, getting too big for his britches. "What insolent behavior," Conant fumed in his diary. "I'm afraid the critics are right. The old gentleman doesn't understand democracy and the victory has gone to his head. . . ."[102]

In October and November, Conant became convinced that Adenauer, frustrated with France's delays in ratifying EDC and bolstered by more assertive public opinion, was secretly plotting a political heresy—the creation of a national West German army instead of the integrated, multinational EDC army officially supported by the United States as the "only" way for the West to arm West Germany. On October 28 he noted to Dulles the "remote possibility" that Adenauer, despite repeated declarations of loyalty to EDC, might be swayed by "the more nationalistic elements in his coalition" and "be flirting with the idea of a national German army within the NATO framework." His own alarmed reaction showed his grave concern over the fragility of West German democracy and loyalty to the West. While recognizing that in some quarters—in the Pentagon, in Congress, and in London—people were so impatient with French dawdling on EDC that they favored rapid West German rearmament, Conant wrote that he would

> consider the creation of a national German army a most dangerous undertaking. The basic German political situation is too unstable and the German governmental structure is too new to trust the final command of a national army to the hands of the unknown German leaders of the future. It could well be that such a national army would find itself allied with the East against the West. In short, the crucial decision of these months is whether we can bind West Germany to the West politically, economically, and militarily. If in the coming months there should be serious discussion in Washington of an alternative involving a national German army, I hope I may be permitted to

return to argue my case at the highest level. If worse came to worst I myself would prefer the withdrawal of all but token forces from Europe and a so-called peripheral defense rather than a German national army.[103]

Conant's reference to a "peripheral defense" was exactly what Adenauer most feared, and his foreign secretary was making that clear in Washington. Despite swearing fealty to EDC and receiving in return personal assurances from Eisenhower and Dulles that Washington remained committed to West Germany's defense, Hallstein had confessed informally to State Department officials Geoffrey W. Lewis and Robert R. Bowie that Bonn had "the jitters" that the Americans were "thinking seriously of withdrawing from Europe and perhaps adopting some kind of peripheral concept."[104] He doubtless grew even more jittery when he returned to Bonn on October 24 and met with the State Department counselor, Douglas R. MacArthur II, who (in addition to laying down the law on the need for German concessions on the Saar) warned that if EDC went down the drain, he "did not believe US Congress or public would pour further resources and treasure into a Europe which seemed incapable of unity which is essential to any real strength."[105]

U.S.–West German tensions worsened over the next few weeks. Bonn and Paris continued to trade inflammatory statements and charges over the Saar, and the State Department urged Conant to turn the screws even tighter on Adenauer to reach an agreement. Dulles, who read Conant's October 28 letter "with intense interest and considerable disappointment," apparently only now really appreciated the serious post-election trouble Adenauer had run into, and he was sufficiently alarmed by Conant's comments on the signs of renewed German nationalism to read them to Eisenhower. Sticking obstinately to his EDC guns, Dulles reaffirmed that a German army in NATO would be "a most unsatisfactory alternative" to EDC. "No doubt we are at the crossroads," he wrote to Conant, "and if EDC fails, the consequences may have to be a change more radical than merely to bring Germany into NATO."[106]

On November 13, Conant received a report from a Central Intelligence Agency source inside the Bonn government reporting flatly that Adenauer was preparing a national military alternative to EDC. Shocked, he urged Dulles and Eisenhower to warn Adenauer that he was flirting with disaster.

Dear Foster: When I wrote you on October 28 that I believed there was "even a remote possibility" that the Chancellor, under the influence of the more nationalistic elements in his coalition, might be flirting with the vague idea of a national army, I was giving expression to only a vague suspicion. I am sorry to say that events which occurred yesterday, and of which you have heard through other channels, have now thoroughly alarmed me. It seems clear that the Chancellor is interested in exploring an alternative to EDC. This can only mean a national army, presumably within the framework of

NATO and in close collaboration with the United States. I have also today learned that recently Herr [Theodor] Blank [Adenauer's personal military adviser] told one of our C.I.A. men that he had three plans of organization, one for the present, one for EDC, if the treaties are ratified, and one for another alternative.

There can be no doubt that some American Army and Naval officers have been making statements to Blank and some German officers and politicians suggestive of something pretty close to a German-American military alliance while expressing disdain for the French. A little of this sort of talk will go a long way in the present mood in a country which today is feeling its oats. Indeed, I am distressed with the increasing tensions between France and Germany since I am convinced that there is no future for Western Europe unless these tensions can be diminished and European integration accomplished, however slowly.

I believe we must now face the possibility that the Chancellor has really changed his mind about a German national army and about the possibility of a solution of the Saar problem. Indeed, his realization of the difficulties he faces here with a solution of the Saar problem may have led him, step by step, to the conclusion that he must throw over EDC and temporarily, at least, EPC and the movement toward European integration. How he can hope to go down this road and yet be known in history as the great statesman that brought about European integration, I fail to see. . . .[107]

Whatever information had triggered his concerns—the precise nature remains unclear[108]—Conant spent part of the day pacing along the Rhine and had trouble getting to sleep that night. His diary entries over the next few days reflected his sense of a growing crisis.

Nov. 13: Very strange "goings on" reported. Trouble in the offing. Wrote another very personal letter to the Sec[retary]. It turns out my vague suspicions of a letter of Oct. 28 may have some foundation.

Nov. 14: The ups and downs of the Hallstein affair (which now seems down) and the failure of Berlin to form a coalition gov't, are minor compared with what seems to be in the wind. It may be the Chanc. is getting ready for an "alternative." Certainly he is having great trouble with his own people with the Saar and is blaming [French Prime Minister Georges P.] Bidault who for the moment seems anxious to put the EDC through. It is hard to tell what is reality and what is bluff but too many U.S. officers & politicians and allies are making noises like a national army in NATO to be laughed off. . . . So very privately I am making noise too to be certain if I can that Washington stays firm. The next few weeks (Bermuda [U.S.-U.K.-French summit] on Dec. 5) promise to be exciting!

Nov. 15: . . . All the signs indicate that the Chanc. is in great difficulty with members of his own party on the question of the Saar. . . . Believe an explosion in the offing.

On November 16, Conant and NATO commander Gruenther paid a joint visit to Adenauer and, without disclosing the reason for their concern, solemnly reminded him that there was no alternative to Franco-German cooperation to defend Western Europe.[109] Meanwhile, in Washington, where Conant's letter had, as intended, generated alarm, a German envoy (Heinz Krekeler) openly raised the lurking question of America's future military commitment to Europe, telling Under Secretary of State Walter Bedell Smith on November 18 that Adenauer was "seriously concerned" that the United States was contemplating "withdrawal of a large part of its forces and reliance instead on new weapons." Smith "emphatically" disavowed any such notion.[110]

Dulles agreed with Conant that a stronger and higher level message was necessary to put Adenauer in line. On November 20 he prepared with the State Department's counselor, Douglas MacArthur II, a strong letter reaffirming the American commitment to EDC and to West European integration and warning Adenauer against any thought of the Federal Republic's rearming on its own. If the EDC failed, Dulles warned, it would be a waste of resources for the United States to try to defend Western Europe militarily. "I am writing you this personal note at the suggestion of the President," the secretary of state began, "because of our very real concern over reports which have reached us from a number of sources indicating that certain elements within Germany are speculating on German participation in Western security arrangements by means other than the European Defense Community." U.S. policy was predicated, Dulles stressed, on the "imperative necessity" of Franco-German collaboration — and failure to achieve such unity would throw into doubt the entire U.S. commitment to defending the Continent. If the two former enemies could not be "woven together in a European fabric of mutual understanding and common endeavor," Dulles explained, "not only will there be no real strength in Europe, but the resources which the United States in its own enlightened self-interest has been pouring into Europe will be wasted and will not serve the long-term purpose for which they were appropriated." Turning to the Saar, Dulles warned Adenauer that it would be "an infinite tragedy for all the free world" if that issue blocked French ratification of the EDC and called on him to spare "no effort" to reach an agreement.[111]

To Conant, who was to deliver the letter to Adenauer, Dulles appended a covering letter (a portion of which still remains classified) urging him to be tough. "As a practical matter," Saar and EDC were linked, Dulles wrote, and it was "essential for Adenauer to go to the extreme limit to reach agreement" as "Germany is in a better position politically to make reasonable concessions than are the French." "I would hope," he added, "that in your talks with Adenauer you will . . . impress upon him that we have reached a decisive moment in history. The foundation of our present European policy is that real strength and stability and effective defense in Europe depend on the development of an organic unity which includes France and Germany. If the Chancellor harbors any idea that effective defense or real stability can be built on Germany alone, bypassing France, he is laboring under a disastrous illusion."[112]

Eisenhower approved the stern message to Adenauer, but in a manner that showed his detachment from day-to-day foreign-policy implementation. On the evening of November 20, when Dulles read the letter over the phone to him and mentioned that it was impossible to get Adenauer to talk to Conant—which had been an open secret within the State Department for months—Eisenhower was "shocked" to hear this, and remarked forlornly that he had "thought they [Adenauer and Conant] were getting along all right."[113]

"On the European front this is a day and night of suspense," Conant wrote in his diary on November 23, after receiving the missives from Dulles. The denouement was coming in the midst of yet another stormy debate in the French Assembly over EDC and a few days before an anticipated Franco-German showdown about the Saar at a planned Adenauer-Bidault meeting at The Hague. With Bidault's position shakier than ever, and EDC apparently hanging in the balance, Conant prepared to give Dulles's letter to Adenauer and to press him "to go to the limit" with Bidault.[114] He also compiled newspaper clippings on the explosive subject of potential German defection from EDC, so that if Adenauer questioned the basis for American concern he would not have to disclose information gathered through intelligence channels.

When Conant met Adenauer on November 25, to the former's surprise and relief, Adenauer did not challenge the accusatory first paragraph of Dulles's letter.[115] The issue was passed over in silence, but Conant believed the message had gotten through. He concluded that Dulles's letter and Gruenther's "plain talk" had scuttled any thoughts of advocating a national German army or any alternative to EDC for the time being.[116]

Yet the undercurrents of tension in Washington-Bonn relations continued to flow, and the Russians failed to exploit them at their last, best opportunity to do so: the long-anticipated four-power Foreign Ministers' conference in January–February 1954, the first such gathering since the outbreak of the Korean War.

Soviet agreement to such a parley had come with the arrival of a November 26 note essentially agreeing to Western terms for four-power talks and proposing Berlin as a venue. Apparently sensing a chance to disrupt the momentum toward EDC—a tool of "former Hitlerites and other German revanchists who in order to serve their aggressive purpose are striving to prepare unleashing of new war"—the USSR accepted the Western request for a conference on Germany prior to any larger talks (in which the Soviets wanted to include China) on reducing international tension, particularly to resolve the lingering confrontations in Korea and Indochina.[117]

Adenauer's response to this latest sally, which Washington regarded as an "important [tactical] shift," was crucial, even decisive—and he privately remained dead set against East-West talks.[118] He told Conant that it would be "dangerous in extreme," even "suicide," to hold a four-power conference anytime soon and preferred instead that the Western powers continue to stall

and to convene another preparatory tripartite foreign ministers' meeting.[119]
With the Bermuda conference less than a week off, these strong objections to
a four-power conference threatened a serious breach in Allied relations.
Typically, Adenauer relied on a more direct channel to Dulles to ascertain
American intentions. Foreign Secretary Hallstein met secretly with Dulles in
Washington on December 1, and heard an impassioned argument on the
"danger of delaying" a four-power conference and the need quickly to convene a "brief and conclusive" gathering whose purpose would be to "persuade
the French that they must proceed with ratification on EDC."[120]

Dulles's arguments appear to have worked. After hearing Hallstein's
report, Adenauer completely if grudgingly reversed his opposition when he
met with Conant on December 4—the same day the long-awaited U.S.-British-
French Summit opened in Bermuda. But this did not mean he was enthusiastic about talks with Moscow: far from it. Conant wrote in his diary:

> The Chanc. is in a worried depressed mood. He is afraid of what will happen
> at the 4 power meeting and I don't blame him. As I reminded Hallstein if my
> advice had been followed last July there would be [no] 4 foreign minister
> meeting. I was then all for sticking to the line deeds not words but at the last
> moment the Chanc. got cold feet and sent Blankenhorn with his famous
> letter. The "magic words" four power meeting have now come home to roost
> I'm afraid.[121]

Adenauer's fear was that Molotov would make a superficially appealing,
negotiable offer about German reunification, thereby further delaying West
German rearmament and just possibly enticing the Western powers into an
unpredictable poker game over Germany's future. In fact, Eisenhower also
clearly valued West German rearmament over German reunification; most
importantly, the two leaders shared such a basic distrust of Moscow that they
would have suspected a trick in any proposal that met their conditions.

Still, if at Berlin the Soviets proposed a mutual withdrawal of the Red
Army and the Western forces from Germany, leading to a democratically
elected, unified German government—even on condition that the country
remain demilitarized and neutral—this would appeal to many Germans and
other Europeans. It would be a huge headache for Eisenhower, Adenauer,
and other Western leaders who were trying to bring greater coherence and
strength to the anti-Soviet military and political alliance, and who feared the
Kremlin's dividing tactics more than they desired a lessening of hostilities.
Thus it was to their great relief—especially Adenauer's—when Molotov
offered only to permit German reunification with elections of the kind that
had taken place in East Germany. When at Conant's suggestion evidence was
introduced to demonstrate that the balloting had been a farce, Molotov, who
is said to have once remarked that he disliked openly contested votes because
"you never know how they are going to turn out," did not dispute it but

offered, to Conant's amazement, what Conant thought was "a bare-faced exposition of the Soviet philosophy of free elections." For Molotov to defend the East German leaders and their political system was "O.K. from our point of view," Conant observed in his diary, "because it assures all West German parties are behind us. His purpose seems to be to try and convince the voters in the Satellite states that their form of democracy is best suited to the modern day. He threatens them with monopolists, militants, and another Hitler! The chances of any progress on German unification is 'nil' at this conference."[122] Molotov's offer was easy to reject, and more importantly, it seemed to accomplish Washington's intended purpose of alienating German and European public opinion sufficiently to permit Western military arrangements to go forward—even if the preferred method of the moment, EDC, in fact was doomed. In his memoirs Conant candidly related that the Berlin conference "had been conceived by the Americans and the British as an instrument to convince the French that the rearming of the Germans was a necessity and therefore the treaties establishing a European Army must be ratified." This was "not the aim stated publicly, of course"—the declared objective was to solve the German problem, although Conant doubted if "few on the American side thought there was more than an off-chance that the public aim could be achieved." As for the ulterior motive, Conant judged, the French Assembly's rejection of EDC six months later meant that Berlin had been "a waste of time and energy."[123]

The conference had also been a "disaster," he later concluded privately, because it led directly to the follow-up foreign ministers conference in Geneva "that lost us Indochina (or seemed to)." To Conant, both were exercises in futility that he blamed in large measure on Churchill's May 1953 speech, which he saw as a naive and misguided attempt to lower Cold War tensions that had the result of encouraging Western public opinion to lower its guard. "It shows my fears of what will happen one fine day when the Russians get tough again, and the American public will be so afraid of a Third World War as to require the gov't to appease at every turn."[124]

But even before subsequent events hardened his negative verdict on Berlin, Conant also had a more personal reason to be disappointed. His dealings with the U.S. delegation confirmed his suspicion that Dulles and his senior State Department aides had no intention of fulfilling Ike's pledge to grant his envoys a serious role in policy making. Although he sat in on the working sessions, Conant had been locked out of the close circles around Dulles where strategy was determined, and had also received a blunt if indirect warning to watch his step on the treacherous terrain of bureaucratic warfare. Hearing one top Dulles aide vow that an official "would get his hands sawed off" if he challenged higher authority, Conant deduced that "the wheels within wheels of the State Department machinery may be buzz saws" and that the lesson of this "illuminatingly frank statement of power politics" at State was that "perhaps JBC . . . had better be *careful.*"[125]

After Berlin, Conant hoped for rapid action by both France and Germany to bridge the gap between them and bring final EDC ratification. Dulles had thrown more American troops into the pot to entice a final settlement, he recorded in early March, and "has put the heat" on British Foreign Minister Anthony Eden to guarantee the long-term presence of British troops on the Continent, on Adenauer to "solve the Saar," and on Bidault to put the treaties up for a vote in the French Assembly.[126]

But instead, more delays, recriminations, backpedaling, and jockeying for position pushed Conant's exasperation and disgust close to bursting. Discerning ominous signs of growing nationalism in *both* France and Germany, he muttered in his diary: "What growling dogs they both are. Can this European business be made to work by the present bunch of politicians unless the Russians scare them more? I am in my Robert A. Taft mood." Aggrieved by having to wait longer for sovereignty, the West Germans were also losing patience with the French and faith in EDC, and increasingly were "casting eyes at a German-American-British alliance. Things are going to blow up in a short time if we are not careful or lucky or both!"[127]

Sensing a need to palliate German sensitivities and to spur the French, Conant now ventured a rare personal diplomatic initiative. Speaking to a group of American lawyers in Frankfurt on March 27, he made what he privately called a "calculated indiscretion" by, after the requisite call to implement EDC, casually remarking that, even if EDC failed, the United States was intent on "going out of the occupation business" and he was confident that the three Western occupying powers would see to it that West Germany was restored to full sovereignty in short order. Since alternatives to EDC were still taboo and since France had made no such commitment, Conant expected his remarks to raise a ruckus, and they did; German officials and newspapers hailed the speech, the French and British grumbled, and the United States . . . Conant waited expectantly, and a bit fearfully, to see if disapproval would crash down from the seventh floor of the State Department for saying something new without explicit prior approval.[128] But Washington, he would soon discover, had other matters to worry about.

In the midst of the labyrinthine maneuvering over EDC, Conant suddenly found himself propelled into the middle of a different drama. In the spring of 1954, a brief but bitter postscript to the nuclear career that he thought he had left for good two years earlier occurred when the Atomic Energy Commission held secret hearings to decide whether to revoke the security clearance of J. Robert Oppenheimer—proceedings that centered on the General Advisory Committee's futile, controversial 1949 recommendation against the development of the hydrogen bomb.[129] Conant had been familiar with Oppenheimer's security problems before, of course: in 1947 he had given the Truman administration his word to smooth over the difficulties Oppenheimer was having with clearance and, after the H-bomb dispute, he had heard mounting reports of plots against Oppenheimer, culminating with, in November 1952, a long conversation with James Killian "on the 'split' among the scientists about national defense and the 'dirty ball' being played on Oppenheimer."[130]

A year later, after the Soviets had announced proudly in August 1953 the explosion of their own hydrogen device, William Borden, formerly on the staff of the congressional Joint Committee on Atomic Energy, had sent J. Edgar Hoover a long indictment of Oppenheimer, rehashing old charges of his leftist ties in the 1930s, questioning his cooperation with security officers during the Manhattan Project, and adding the explosive allegation that he had opposed and then undermined U.S. work on thermonuclear weapons. Borden's conclusion: America's most famous atomic physicist, the father of the atomic bomb, was "more probably than not" a Soviet "espionage agent" actively working to undermine U.S. national security.[131] Borden's message found a sympathetic audience with Hoover, in the air force, and at the AEC, whose chairman, Lewis Strauss, who had bitterly opposed the GAC's stand in 1949, had a personal animus toward Oppenheimer stemming from a series of perceived slights.

In early December 1953, Eisenhower secretly ordered the erection of a "blank wall" between Oppenheimer and all atomic secrets (an order that later inspired scorn from critics who noted that Oppenheimer himself had been responsible for some of those same secrets). Engrossed in his diplomatic chores in Germany, Conant learned of Eisenhower's secret action a month later from a visiting Vannevar Bush, who relayed the grim news to him during an automobile ride—perhaps to evade surveillance.[132] Conant was aghast. He had loyally refrained from public criticism of the decision to develop the hydrogen weapon, and had done his utmost to prevent his private position from leaking into print. At his confirmation hearings—eager to ingratiate himself, and conscious that transcripts of the hearing would be made public—he had answered a question on the subject with a masterpiece of obfuscation:

> SEN. HICKENLOOPER: Have you ever taken a positive position, Mr. Conant, on whether or not this country should explore the field of development of hydrogen weapons or thermonuclear weapons in the atomic development field?
>
> MR. CONANT. I have never take[n] a public stand on that, Senator. As a member of the General Advisory Committee for the Atomic Energy Commission, which I was for 5 years until last August, I may say on the record that I favored the exploration from a theoretical point of view and by laboratory experimentation of all phases of the development of all possible weapons.[133]

But now, a year later, Conant showed more gumption when he learned that Oppenheimer (who had been given the alternative of quietly resigning his consulting contracts with the government, thereby implicitly admitting his unfitness to handle secret data) was fighting to keep his clearance in a hearing that was his right under AEC statutes. "In retrospect," he wrote Bush in late March 1954, "I have no apologies whatsoever for the position which I took and to which all the other members [of the GAC] subscribed in general. Indeed, I think I was as much a leader of this point of view as any person."[134] Nor had his mind been changed by the Soviet Union's thermonuclear test the previous autumn, or by the most recent U.S. accomplishment earlier that month: the AEC exploded its first deliverable superbomb, with a yield of fifteen megatons, twice as strong as predicted, in the Pacific. (The test alerted the world for the first time to the vastly enlarged magnitude of thermonuclear weapons, for radioactive debris spread over a large area and irradiated a Japanese fishing trawler (*The Lucky Dragon*), killing one crewman and inducing radiation sickness among others; this incited panic in the nation that had suffered the first atomic attack nine years earlier, where thousands of fish were dumped and buried to avoid contamination.) To Conant, the rapid progress of both the United States and Soviet Union toward thermonuclear arsenals only intensified his belief that Truman's decision had been a disaster. "I think that the proposition which we put up to the Government, if it had been accepted, would have resulted in a better situation today than now exists," he told Bush. Masking his reference to the Oppenheimer case, then still secret, Conant noted that he had "even heard rumors that the patriotism of some or all of us involved in this recommendation has been impugned. The best answer to that, apart from the record of all of us, is the fact that the same group recommended such vigorous action in regard to the use of atomic weapons by ground forces as to bring about a revolution. . . . "[135]

Conant saw only trouble ahead when he received, on March 22, a lengthy appeal from Oppenheimer's eminent New York attorney, Lloyd Garrison (who in turn had been recommended to Oppenheimer by John Lord O'Brian), seeking a written testimonial to the physicist's character and loyalty and a promise to appear as a supporting witness at the upcoming hearing.[136] Conant's first reaction was to dash off a handwritten note to Bush, written cryptically since German air mail was "*not* secure," seeking more information. He had no compunctions about testifying for Oppenheimer, but wanted Bush's personal advice, access to relevant records, and—since he had no doubt that "everything will be out in the open eventually"—aid in obtaining the counsel of a "*first rate* lawyer," perhaps Elihu Root, Jr., before he composed a statement that would enter the permanent record.[137]

But what made Conant most apprehensive was his firm conviction that the three-man Personnel Security Board assembled by the AEC—the president of the University of North Carolina, Gordon Gray, as chair; Thomas Morgan, a retired corporate executive (chairman of Sperry Gyroscope, a Pentagon contractor); and the only scientist, Ward Evans, a retired professor of chemistry from Northwestern University—would be incompetent to assess fairly or comprehensively the complex technical decisions of the past, especially in an atmosphere of political poison. Though in this case he would not be the target (or only implicitly, as an Oppenheimer ally against the H-bomb), Conant may well have thought back to the days during the war when he had dreaded an endless congressional inquest if the Manhattan Project had failed; now, in a sense, the nightmare seemed to be coming true. "I do not believe," he wrote to Bush, "that the Board . . . can possibly undertake to pass judgment on the wisdom or lack of it of the G.A.C. recommendations in 1949."[138]

The strongest evidence of Conant's feelings about the proceedings against Oppenheimer is shown in his determination to testify on behalf of his former colleague, despite strong discouragement from Secretary Dulles. Conant blandly related in his memoirs that Dulles and Eisenhower approved his wish to appear,[139] but surviving documents tell a more dramatic story. On April 1, Conant made plans to return to Washington and sent a "personal and confidential" letter to inform Dulles. "If you do not think it improper to give what evidence I can in support of Mr. Oppenheimer's case, I shall proceed to do so," he wrote. "I have not the slightest doubt myself of his loyalty to the United States and his conscientious work for the United States Government in connection with all aspects of the atomic bomb development. I suppose that it is not incompatible with my position as United States High Commissioner for Germany to make my views known to this Personnel Security Board which is considering Mr. Oppenheimer's case."[140]

Dulles's response was frosty. He first dispatched an "eyes only" cable to Conant claiming that "factors unknown to you make [an appearance] undesirable," then elaborated in an "eyes only" letter from London:

> Before I left Washington I checked up at the White House with reference to the problem mentioned in your personal, confidential letter to me of April 1, 1954.
>   I have the impression there is more on the adverse side than is generally known, and there is the general feeling in White House circles that it would be a good deal better if you did not become publicly involved in the matter. I do not mean to indicate there is any evidence to throw doubt on the gentleman's loyalty, and I do not think that any effort will indeed be made to prove disloyalty, at least as far as the Executive is concerned—I cannot vouch for what might happen in Congress. However, there is considerable evidence of laxity and poor judgment and, in some cases, lack of veracity.
>   I thought you ought to know this.[141]

Conant had already told both Garrison and Bush that he intended to testify; he flew to Washington and met with Dulles on Monday, April 19—the day before his scheduled appearance before the Personnel Security Board. By then, the case had blown into the open with the front-page publication the previous week of the charges in the *New York Times,* and Conant already knew that there were "some misgivings on the White House side" about his plans to testify.[142] Only a brief diary note survives to describe the encounter:

> [Saw the] Sec. for a brief ½ hr. Covered Germany in 15 min. Told him I had no choice but to testify at Oppenheimer hearings. He said I should know this might destroy my usefulness to govt. I said I quite realized this and he only had to give the word and I was through![143]

Dulles's bluff was called, and he did not give Conant his walking papers, but their already strained relations became even chillier.

The next afternoon, Tuesday, April 20, after an hour-and-half prep session with Garrison, Conant made his way to room 2022 of AEC Building T-3. His testimony to the Gray board is a model of restrained anger, clipped sentences, and a refusal to play along with the tactics of the AEC's aggressive attorney, Roger Robb. (When Robb repeatedly suggested that "you gentlemen on the committee" had overstepped their mandate as technical advisers by giving "advice on military strategy," Conant refused to budge: The GAC gave opinions on a great many matters, and "Nobody has to take the advice if they don't want to.") On the other hand Conant's account is frustratingly sparse, constrained by the propriety that was his creed, a short appearance to accommodate his busy schedule, and an allegedly hazy memory of the events in question. But Conant did not pull any punches, and steadfastly defended Oppenheimer; he declared that if a man's opinion as an adviser could render him unfit for government service, as the AEC's charge seemed to imply, then "it would apply to me because I opposed [the H-bomb] strongly, as strongly as anybody else on the committee."[144]

On April 26, after testifying, Conant took his concerns directly to President Eisenhower.[145] "Saw the President for 30 minutes," he wrote in his diary on April 26. "He opened up at once on the Oppie case. Prayed it would come out O.K., but doubted it." Conant told Eisenhower he was "very worried" about the H-bomb's inclusion in the AEC's letter of charges against the physicist. Conant also related his showdown with Dulles, and received Eisenhower's assurance that "of course" it had been all right to testify.[146]

Later that day Eisenhower drafted a letter to his friend "Jim" assuring him that "no criticism was directed toward the Doctor because of his adverse opinion regarding production. That opinion was recited merely to give background to certain other allegations to the effect that, even after decision to produce had been made by the highest possible authority, the Doctor departed from his proper role as principal adviser and attempted to slow down development."[147] (As Stephen Ambrose has pointed out, this proposed letter contradicts Eisenhower's subsequent assertion, in his memoirs, that he gave "no weight" to Oppenheimer's opposition to the H-bomb.)[148] But, perhaps dissuaded by Strauss, Eisenhower decided not to send the note, which is just as well, since Conant would not have found the argument persuasive: he wrote to White House aide Robert Cutler a few days later that only a clear-cut public statement could remove the widespread impression that Oppenheimer was being punished for his opinions.[149]

While in the United States, Conant also transacted some business relating to Germany, making the rounds at the State Department and appearing on the Hill for annual budget appropriations hearings, but he heard "amazingly little 'table thumping' about the slowness of EDC," as he had expected to, and found most of Washington distressed, distracted, and fearful. Upcoming elections preoccupied Congress; Joseph McCarthy and the army squared off in gripping televised hearings over charges of lax security; and those in charge of foreign policy wondered whether besieged French troops at Dien Bien Phu could stave off Communist forces, whether the United States should militarily intervene to rescue them, and how to handle a French defeat in Indochina at the East-West foreign ministers' conference due to convene shortly in Geneva.

But among Conant's friends, anger over the Oppenheimer affair and other abuses of the security system dominated conversations, and what struck him afterward—as, back in Germany, he awaited the AEC board's final determination—was not only what they said but that they lowered their voices when they said it:

> At the Cosmos Club, in Cambridge and everywhere one wanted to talk about the Oppenheimer case in a whisper. Everyone is mad about it one way or another. R. Adams reported that the gossip at the Nat'l Academy meeting was that the Calif. chemists thought Oppie was a security risk. But Rabbi [*sic*], Bush, Dubridge (whom I saw in Bonn) Fred Osborn, Jack McCloy, Lamont etc. were furious about the matter. I had a run in with Bobby Cutler about the drafting of Nichols' letter.
>
> The atmosphere in the U.S.A. today is pretty close to a mild reign of terror. Apart from the Oppenheimer case 3 other security cases came to my attention all of which seemed to be character assassination by someone with a "peeve." But if the leading citizens get upset about this business as they are beginning to, I think the tide will turn. When? In about a year but much will depend on the report of Gray's committee on Oppie.[150]

On May 28, the Gray board voted two-to-one to strip Oppenheimer of his security clearance; on June 29, the AEC commissioners voted four-to-one to confirm the verdict; in both cases, the only scientist on the respective bodies was the single voice in favor of reinstating his clearance.[151] The next day, from the high commissioner's residence in Bonn, Conant vented his anger about this "first-class mess," so "badly handled in the White House," in a letter to his friend Bill Marbury.

> It was a great error to have ever introduced the H bomb into the indictment and, as the record shows, the "prosecution" tried to establish that all (or a

large number) of Opie's advisory opinions were wrong and motivated by pro-Soviet sympathies. . . . This part of the record is really shocking!!!

On the other hand, there never would have been an Oppenheimer case if the scientists in the other camp had not circulated the rumours which they did. The basic trouble started as a row between technical advisers to the government so to speak and became very bitter. The administration should have known this and been guided by this fact. . . .

That Opie was "vulnerable," i.e., had some things in his record which did not read well, many of us suspected. I still stick completely to my statement about his loyalty—his judgment and discretion are another matter, and almost all the negative evidence refers to period a long time ago. . . . [152]

Years later, Conant was far from convinced that history had in any way excused or condoned what he regarded as a gross miscarriage of justice. "It is the story," he suggested sadly, "of a man that too many people wanted to assassinate, and so they assassinated him."[153] When, in late 1963, President John Kennedy approved the Atomic Energy Commission's decision to award its second Fermi Prize for achievement to Oppenheimer (Teller got the first, a year earlier), he hoped it was a conciliatory honor that would close an embarrassing chapter in America's political and nuclear history. Conant was pleased for his friend, but his handwritten note of congratulation still brimmed with anger: "Heaven knows you have earned it as a scientist many times over and much more . . . no prizes from the U.S. govt can wipe out the disgrace to the nation of your trial and judgment. . . ."[154] Yet the Gray board, in its kangaroo-court proceedings, had only followed the stern advice that Conant and Oppenheimer themselves had suggested in 1949, when as members of the National Academy of Sciences review committee they urged that security investigations "must resolve doubt not in favor of the individual but in favor of security." If "a shadow of doubt exists," Conant had recommended, "the individual should be prevented from having access to confidential information."[155] At the height of McCarthyism, a shadow turned out to be more than enough.

By the time Conant returned to Bonn, NATO was in a crisis over the collapse of French Indochina, a crisis that came to a head when the nationalist forces of the Viet Minh overran the isolated garrison at Dien Bien Phu on May 7. Slipping into near paralysis, French governments writhed and fell as they desperately sought a means to escape the consequences of their colonial misadventure. Conant, who in March had confessed in his diary to being "very fed up" with the French, by July was comparing the traumatized country to "a man mentally incapable of attending to business." Though still backing EDC, Winston Churchill remained, to Conant's mind, "a pain in everyone's neck," still prone to exaggerate the slightest sign of Soviet moderation, and both Conant and Adenauer had by now concluded that his May 1953 speech had been "the turning point in the wrong direction."[156]

While the still unratified EDC treaty languished, Adenauer ("in one of his panicky moods") and the West Germans stewed, all too aware that their promised resumption of sovereignty depended on the completion of satisfactory Western rearmament arrangements; and the international spotlight shone on the international conference in Geneva, where foreign ministers from east and west struggled to come up with the compromises that partitioned Korea and Indochina.[157]

Against this depressing backdrop, U.S. officials correctly by the summer of 1954 viewed the prospects for EDC's passage in the French parliament as grim, and Conant's private estimates grew downright morbid: "All the doctors are around the patient but I'm afraid the undertaker will be required." "The patient is at death's door, the plans for the funeral and the division of property are being made." Nervously awaiting the "fatal day" of the French vote, Conant sadly surveyed the evidence of disarray—more French "excuses," a new Russian "monkey wrench," a defection by a senior West German security official—and concluded, "In general the free world seems to be coming apart at the seams and the European movement . . . is very sick indeed."[158] Partly in compensation for the disappointment of France's dawdling over EDC, by now Conant's judgment of West Germany, and more importantly Adenauer's motives, had grown more benign. "I never was more convinced of the sincerity of the Chanc. & his close friends as to their belief in EDC," he wrote in his diary on August 26. "I detect fear bordering on panic at the thought of a national army as an alternative."[159] Writing the same day to a State Department colleague, he admitted that he had previously suspected that the Adenauer government's backing for EDC represented "simply the acceptance of the conditions under which Germany would be rearmed, and that their secret preference was for a German National Army. I am now thoroughly persuaded that they not only do not wish a German National Army, but are rather terrified at the prospects that such an army might be forced upon them."[160] If EDC failed, Conant recorded Adenauer as worrying, "Christianity in Europe was doomed!"[161]

When frantic last-minute conferences prior to the French vote led nowhere, gossip intensified among British, West German, and U.S. officials over possible alternatives to the unified European army. Eisenhower and Churchill met and declared that the Federal Republic of Germany "should take its place as an equal partner" in the Western Alliance, making a "proper contribution to the defense of the free world," and instructed aides to meet in London to investigate ways to accomplish those objectives should France fail to act. Washington's official line, however, remained EDC or bust; and Conant, both publicly and privately, could foresee no practical alternative method of rearmament, despite his best efforts to devise an "end run" around the French veto.[162] Like many a disconsolate U.S. official, he could not imagine the French, if they rejected EDC, then turning around and accepting a West German national army in NATO, especially on the nondiscriminatory basis on which Adenauer insisted. Besides another try on EDC, he wrote a State Department colleague on August 26, the only other possibilities Conant foresaw were:

** "non-discriminatory German rearmament with all the wrong elements in Germany soon to become dominant"

** "a deal with Russia for German reunification and all the dangers of a reunified Germany ready to rearm and go one way or the other"

** "the U.S. packing up its equipment and going home"

"To say I am distressed about the present situation," he concluded, "would be an understatement."[163]

Four days later, still clinging to a "very slim but not absolutely null" hope of French ratification, Conant breakfasted in Frankfurt with CIA director Allen Dulles, then spent the afternoon escorting a pair of visiting congressmen around Heidelberg before a glum evening meal. "Heard of action of French assembly on EDC at dinner," he scribbled in his notebook that night. "**Bad news!**"[164] On this "D–Day" or "Defeat Day," as he called it—Monday, August 30, when the French Assembly voted 319–264, with 43 abstentions, to postpone debate on EDC, in effect killing the treaties—there was no evident path to follow to recoup what was universally recognized as a resounding defeat for U.S. policy and for Adenauer. To Dulles the vote constituted "a crisis of almost terrifying proportions," a "shattering blow" which imperiled the security of the West as well as dashing Jean Monnet's dream of a unified, integrated Europe.[165]

With the nightmare scenario that U.S. officials had long dreaded now a reality, the future of NATO and the Western alliance fell into doubt. The Dulles-Eisenhower policy of applying pressure and refusing to countenance any modification of EDC had apparently backfired. "What will happen?" Conant wondered in his diary on the night of August 31. "Anyone's guess." Though ready for "a second try for the Europeanization movement, even for EDC with amendments and a new name," he correctly suspected that neither Adenauer nor Washington had much interest in another go-round.[166]

In mid-September, Conant speculated grimly about the likely rise of an "Asia First" American foreign policy if, as he thought likely, NATO collapsed after a failure quickly to admit West Germany. After hearing U.S. ambassador to Italy Clare Boothe Luce (the wife of *Time*'s publisher, Henry Luce) speak glowingly of the "Pacific school"—which favored "giving up the defense of Europe on the ground" and supporting a "Chiang-Rhee offensive against China if need be"—Conant thought such an "Asialationist" policy might spark World War III. But, he confessed, if Franco-German cooperation proved impossible, then Washington might have to give up the defense of Europe on the ground, adopt the premises of the "Pacific School," and tilt back toward isolationism. In that case, he wrote in his diary, "What is likely to happen is a neutralized divided Germany and that is a much less attractive picture [than a neutralized unified Germany] from any standpoint. What a mess! . . . I am getting ready to wear a Robert A. Taft hat permanently!"[167]

But to Conant's surprise and delight, the next few weeks saw developments he would describe as "almost miraculous" and "one of the most unpredictable events in history"—the sudden cohesion and universal acceptance among the Western allies of a plan to permit West German entry into NATO, with its own national army—precisely the concept that had so horrified the French, not to mention Conant, Dulles, and Eisenhower, not so long before. After the basics were hammered out in London, all parties signed accords in Paris to seal the deal (pending ratification) in Paris on October 23, less than two months after EDC's seemingly catastrophic death.[168]

The forces impelling this rush, "with history breathing hot down the necks of those who were concerned," in Conant's phrase, are not hard to find. Most important was the West European allies' common fear of being militarily vulnerable to a menacing Soviet Union despite underlying suspicions, double-crossing, and espionage among them. Washington's threat to withdraw its troops from the Continent—implied by Dulles's famous statement in December 1953 about an "agonizing reappraisal" and replayed in his deliberately "cagey" reaction of "playing hard to get" after EDC's downfall—imparted special urgency to the rush to devise a replacement for EDC.[169] And, at the same time, Dulles's broad hints of unilateral action to arm West Germany (an option he discussed with Adenauer, and one which "scared" Conant) put on more pressure. But the tactical breakthroughs that led to this jury-rigged, lightning-fast solution to the quandary that had plagued the alliance for four years were two steps aimed at alleviating French fears of being stuck on the Continent alongside a remilitarized Germany: British foreign minister Eden's surprise pledge to retain British ground forces on the Continent for fifty years, and Adenauer's unilateral vow (at Churchill's suggestion) in the name of his country not to develop atomic or other weapons of mass destruction.[170]

Reflecting on the events two years later, Conant judged, in fact, that Dulles deserved more credit than he got for the result: "He threatened the French & British with a German-American alliance just enough to get *them* to take the necessary steps. But the whole EDC story is a great tragedy."[171]

U.S.-West German relations still had to surmount a residue of distrust remaining from World War II, and Adenauer made determined efforts to cultivate American support and patronage—efforts that showed the German understanding that the road to acceptance in the international community ran through the White House—while leading Americans, Conant among them, campaigned for popular acceptance of the "new Germany." Yet Conant's doubts about the wisdom of West German rearmament, which he suppressed in the euphoria of the new arrangements, exemplify the mutual suspicions of Americans and West Germans that went deeper than officials in either nation publicly acknowledged or than many historians have since supposed. "Bluntly put," one historian has written, the United States "did not completely trust the country on which so much of its security depended." Some historians have summed up Washington's strategy to prevent either the USSR or Germany from dominating the European continent in the phrase "double containment" or "dual containment": containing the Soviet threat with the help of (West) Germany, and exploiting the Soviet threat to keep the Federal Republic firmly ensconced in the Western military and political alliance.[172]

For Eisenhower, Dulles, Conant, and others, the memories of World War II were too fresh to be completely ignored in their calculations of how to integrate Germany into Western Europe and the anti-Soviet Cold War alliance.[173] Still, Conant, ever the pragmatist, saw little point in rehashing old, bitter memories—especially since he himself had "boxed the compass" so many times. When Bill Marbury visited him in Bonn, he offered a counsel that said much about how America viewed the compromises of morality and memory that it had made in order to win World War II and wage the Cold War, and about how Conant viewed history as a servant of political necessity. Marbury should converse freely with his German hosts, Conant advised, except for one question that should be avoided at all costs. The ultimate social *faux pas* in Germany, he explained, was to ask your dinner companion what he or she did during the war.[174]

CHAPTER 34

"I Want to Accentuate the Positive"

Ambassador to West Germany
1955–1957

What irony. First we were afraid the Germans would rearm, now we are
afraid they won't!

                   —Diary, July 23, 1955

General deterioration of German–American relations . . . plus repeated evidence of failure of communication between State Dept top & lower levels
and Bonn makes me very glad I am to get out of this business very soon. An
interesting experience but enough is enough.

                   —Diary, October 3, 1956

"Finis! Noon, May 5, 1955." Conant scrawled those words on a scrap of
HICOG stationery moments after he and the high commissioners of the
United Kingdom and France, following the requisite eleventh-hour mix-ups
and haggling, signed the documents officially reposing sovereignty in the
Federal Republic of Germany. With a few more strokes of the pen, Conant
and his allied colleagues formalized West Germany's entry into the North
Atlantic Treaty Alliance, and its right to establish a national army. Four days
later, in response, the Soviet Union formally established the Warsaw Pact, its
long campaign to prevent West German rearmament having failed. Together
with the U.S.-Soviet summit meeting held in Geneva a few months later, and
the normalization of Soviet–West German relations soon after, these developments ended the decade of perilous instability and uncertainty that had
followed the defeat of Hitler and the destruction of Hiroshima. Suspense and
fluidity gave way to a seemingly permanent order that was to endure for more
than a generation.

    With the end of the occupation of Germany, the high commissioner's
office lapsed into history, and Conant now became the first U.S. ambassador
to the new Federal Republic. But he had already seen the accomplishment of
his most critical objective, the transformation of America's former enemy into
a firm, healthy, armed, sovereign, "brisk and prosperous" ally of the "free

world."[1] And within a few weeks of the ceremony that ended the Occupation he was restlessly angling for yet another career: at a meeting on June 13 with the National Education Association's William Carr, who asked him to become his deputy, Conant raised the possibility of studying educational issues for the NEA with funds from the Carnegie Corporation, adding, "Perhaps in 1957."[2] He had maintained his warm ties with Carnegie, his and Harvard's benefactor for many years, and received assurances of its strong interest in "seeing that JBC's talents were used in the public interest whenever he was ready to return to home base."[3] He soon entered into correspondence with Carnegie's new president, John W. Gardner, tossing around ideas for a project to study American education after leaving Germany, whenever that might happen — and by the fall of 1955 he told Gardner that he would in all likelihood resign as ambassador following the 1956 presidential elections, prompting Gardner to offer Carnegie's "blank check" for any studies he might undertake.[4]

Conant's diplomatic career had not been entirely satisfying for him. While grateful for the chance to link the severed moral and intellectual connections he had with a nation that had alternately bewitched and horrified him since his youth, he had no desire to extend his tenure as an errand boy for John Foster Dulles. Though outwardly the two remained on good terms, Conant never considered him a friend as he did Dean Acheson, and chafed at being excluded from decision making and even from quality information about U.S. policies that he could use in his dealings with Adenauer. "I never met an Ambassador who worked for [Dulles] who was very favorably inclined towards him, and this includes myself," he said later. "I would not have served in another post under him."[5]

Conant's desire to leave Bonn was reciprocated by Adenauer's mounting desire to be rid of him. In April 1955, raising the possibility that Eisenhower might not wish to name Conant as ambassador after the high commissioner's office went out of existence, Dulles had conceded that "there has not developed the intimacy I would have desired" between the American envoy and the German leader but optimistically observed that the situation had "somewhat improved during recent weeks, and there is a greater disposition on the part of Adenauer to deal with Conant rather than to bypass him through personal emissaries to Washington or through CIA channels." "I prefer to appoint Conant," Eisenhower scribbled on the memo.[6]

But Adenauer's complaints intensified and were echoed by other State Department informants. A month after the signing ceremony, Dulles forwarded to Eisenhower the contents of a private report by a senior U.S. journalist stationed in Bonn claiming that Conant's "downright embarrassing" ignorance of political realities and "very mediocre, negative" performance had become a topic of cocktail party gossip and caused him to be routinely bypassed by government aides. (One despairing American observer wrote that Conant "seeks to cover an obvious inadequacy with rigid emphasis upon protocol," and had won the nickname "Bubble-head" among the local press corps.)[7] Despairing of Conant's not subscribing to the political legerdemain he specialized in, Adenauer, it was said, threw up his hands in disgust, muttering, "What can you tell a man like that; he doesn't even listen."[8]

In public, however, the two men kept up appearances as friends and partners, and in June 1955 Conant had the genuine pleasure of escorting Adenauer to Cambridge for Harvard Commencement ceremonies, where both dined with the Puseys at 17 Quincy Street (with Patty Conant translating) and the next day received honorary degrees, with the ambassador introducing the chancellor in German. "A wonderful day, enjoyed myself immensely," felt Conant, who considered the occasion a fine postscript to his Harvard career.[9] Yet the amity between Conant and Adenauer was superficial—only a few weeks later, Dulles reluctantly decided that "there was a lack of sympathy between the two which was not good in the light of the necessity for very close relations," although John McCloy refused the Secretary of State's conspiratorial request that he advise Conant to consider retirement.[10]

Conant seems to have gotten an inkling that he had fallen into disfavor with Dulles and Adenauer from their tepid response to his alarms about the latest troubles involving Allied access to West Berlin. Since May Conant had become the ranking U.S. envoy to Berlin, still under four-power rule, in addition to being ambassador in Bonn, and he visited Berlin at least once a month, sometimes more, taking the overnight trip from Bad Godesberg on a private train (a relic of the Third Reich, equipped with two sleeping cars and a diner) to demonstrate America's continued commitment to maintaining Western rights there. Often, he made a point of driving through East Berlin, in part to exercise his prerogative under the four-power agreements to travel throughout the city, in part to take the pulse of conditions there and assess the Communist sector's economic progress. Indulging his weakness for bookstores, he would invariably ask his chauffeur to stop so he could browse the shelves for the latest in literature from the Communist world, to get "a slant on which way the wind blows."[11]

After a period of relative calm, the situation in Berlin was heating up again, for the East German regime imposed exorbitant tolls for traffic and goods passing along the autobahn between West Germany and West Berlin. Conant protested to the Soviet high commissioner that the action violated Allied undertakings to maintain normal traffic along the designated access routes, but the Russian simply referred him to the East German leadership, saying that it was the "master of the roads" and that officials of the Federal Republic should contact GDR authorities to "settle these purely German matters."[12]

To Conant this stance was nothing less than a blatant attempt to "blackmail" the West (and West Germany) into direct dealings with and, in short order, recognition of, what Conant contemptuously referred to as "the so-called German Democratic Republic." And that, of course, was blasphemy, for it would implicitly endorse Germany's permanent division and violate the West's declared determination to insist on its reunification. Conant discerned not another full-blown crisis brewing, like the Berlin blockade of 1948–49, but a steady tightening of the screws, with the Soviets establishing new precedents favorable to the GDR and thereby weakening the West's ties to its Berlin outpost. He was "disturbed" by the State Department's willingness to treat the matter as an inter-German affair (*"cold feet!"*),[13] and, on May 21, he warned Dulles that failing to rise to the Soviet challenge would undermine pro-Western forces in the Federal Republic and encourage those who favored unification by means of a neutralization, disarmament, and political merger of the two Germanys (which would be similar to the solution the Soviets had just agreed upon with the Western powers to end the division of Austria). Including Communists in a coalition government, he added, risked repeating the disastrous scenario such as that which had led to the coup in Czechoslovakia in 1948, and was "perhaps the one way in which we might lose Germany."

Rather than accepting the steeper autobahn fees or pleading with East Berlin to reduce them, Conant recommended a stern alternative that, he admitted, might lead to war if Moscow resisted. This entailed, first, secretly telling the Soviets that unless the situation immediately improved, "all talk" of the East-West summit meeting the Russians wanted would halt, "and that instead of speaking of a climate of opinion which is relaxing, we shall be in a state of tension which is most serious indeed." If that didn't work, then the United States should announce the impasse publicly, impose punitive sanctions against East Germany ("the Soviet Zone"), and, most dramatically, ameliorate the West German transport industry's burden by itself going into the "trucking business"—transporting goods to and from Berlin in military vehicles (and paying the GDR the earlier, cheaper fees) or, if necessary, employing another airlift. Conant thought Moscow would back down, especially given the weak East German economy, but he stressed that he did not want to "dodge the implications" of what he was proposing: "If the Russians should shoot down our planes or stop our military vehicles (which they now say they will not interfere with), then the possibilities of a general war would be just over the horizon."[14]

Although an aide to Dulles agreed that "a fairly stiff line should be taken,"[15] the secretary of state and the West German chancellor viewed the situation (and the prospect of contacts between the two Germanys to resolve it) with rather less alarm, as Conant discovered when he raised the issue to them during Adenauer's visit to Washington in June. "These gentlemen had many other matters on their minds and rather brushed aside my arguments," he recalled in his memoirs.[16] He was, in fact, seriously out of step with both of them, for their thoughts were dominated by the summit meeting that was to take place in Geneva the following month between Eisenhower and the Kremlin troika of Communist Party First Secretary Nikita Khrushchev, Chairman of the Council of Ministers Nikolai Bulganin, and Defense Minister Marshal Georgi Zhukov. Both Washington and Moscow wanted a placid backdrop for their first leadership meeting since Potsdam—as evidenced by the signing of the State Treaty of Austria on May 15—and the controversy over the autobahn fees soon fizzled out after some informal contacts between representatives of the two German governments yielded a twenty percent reduction.[17] Conant's efforts inside the State Department to place the Berlin issue on the agenda for the July 18–23 summit received "the chilliest sort of answer — that is practically no answer,"[18] and he complained afterward that "Blackmail continues to be paid by Bonn."[19] But Conant's alert had one practical effect: it stimulated renewed Allied contingency planning for a possible use of "limited military force" in response to any future Soviet blockade.[20]

Conant was manifestly unimpressed by the "spirit of Geneva," a momentary improvement in at least the atmospherics of superpower relations. The summit conference (to which he was not invited) struck him as a fraud, a farcical propaganda exercise "conceived in sin and born in iniquity," as he put it — that is, it stemmed from Dulles's determination to undercut the charges made by West European leftist opposition parties that inadequate efforts were being made to relax Cold War tensions; "If you don't hold this conference," Conant believed the British had told Dulles, "you're going to get a Labor government."[21]

Pronouncing himself "completely skeptical" on the likelihood of any positive results from the meeting, Conant thought Dulles and Adenauer wrongly held that Moscow's internal troubles would force them to make significant concessions on Germany at the bargaining table, perhaps offering to ditch the GDR and accept an "Austrian solution." Conant himself reasoned that Kremlin leaders were "playing for a divided Germany with *both* sides on healthy terms with Moscow and each other. Then when Adenauer goes and the depression comes, a merger and Germany is theirs!"[22]

When the meeting broke up with friendly words but few concrete results, it was obvious that reunification was a dead letter and it was time for Adenauer (who needed to "pull some ideological rabbits out of his hat to replace EDC and take people's minds off reunification," in Conant's estimation) to make peace with the USSR. When Adenauer made his uneasy pilgrimage to Moscow in September to normalize relations and obtain the release of Soviet-held German prisoners and refugees — a visit immediately followed by a far friendlier meeting between the Soviets and their GDR allies — Conant grasped that it meant that "the de facto split of Germany is there," and he felt a visceral distaste at the prospect of a Soviet Embassy opening in Bonn.[23]

Continuing tension in Berlin helped keep strong his basic distrust of Soviet motives and intentions. On November 27, East German police briefly detained, at gunpoint, two visiting American congressmen who were being driven through East Berlin in a U.S. Army car, allegedly on the grounds that they had violated GDR law by having a radio telephone. When the local Soviet commander rejected a U.S. protest because, he said, East Berlin was part of the GDR, Conant decided personally to challenge this claim, which violated Western contentions that the city was still under four-power rule, and impulsively boarded his private train and went to Berlin, where he drove through the eastern sector in his diplomatic limousine, flying the American flag; no one stopped him to check his radio telephone. At a press conference immediately afterward he revealed the defiant gesture, which received wide coverage in the newspapers back home. His friends in the United States applauded this impromptu initiative, but not Dulles's aides, one of whom sent a cable admonishing him that decisions of this kind could be made only in Washington. Conant stewed at this patronizing slap, but "felt no reply was necessary."[24]

To Conant the brave people of West Berlin were the "real commandos of the Cold War"[25] — a phrase that obliquely hinted at his continuing skepticism about the secret agents and covert operators whom his government was sponsoring in Germany, a skepticism that did not endear him to administration officials who favored even more aggressive activities. "Conant was deliberately left out of the loop," recalled one senior CIA official, who remembered that he "had his doubts about the wisdom of those activities, concluded they were going to take place in any case, and preferred not to know about them."[26]

In theory, the CIA was supposed to inform the ambassador of sensitive operations that might have diplomatic repercussions, but, it appears, this rule was not always followed. The most famous covert project during this period was the joint CIA–British Operation Gold, launched in 1953, to build a tunnel beneath East Berlin in order to intercept underground Soviet communications cables. The 1,476-foot, air-conditioned passageway was finished in February 1955 and the wiretaps remained in operation until Soviet security forces (tipped off by the British double agent George Blake) discovered it, supposedly by accident, on April 21, 1956.[27] When newspapers reported on the tunnel's existence, CIA officers Robert Amory and Tracy Barnes dashed to Bonn to brief Conant, but he had already heard the news. "Well, fellows, looks like you got your hands caught in the cookie jar," he greeted them; "Tell me all about it."[28] When relating the tale of the tunnel to a visiting friend a couple of months later — MIT president Killian, then working on his own covert effort to develop the U-2 high-altitude reconnaissance plane — he noted wryly that the tunnel had been built under not only the Soviets' noses, but his own.[29]

Conant did, on occasion, express serious concerns about other U.S. intelligence projects and proposals, with mixed results. His protest failed to terminate the supersecret Project Paperclip, which since the war's end had been luring German scientists and engineers to the United States to work on classified military projects. Conant wrote to John Foster Dulles in July 1956 urging him to halt what he called a "continuing U.S. recruitment program which has no parallel in any other Allied country," but authorities simply renamed and reshuffled the project, ignoring his pragmatic argument that the United States should forestall a formal West German complaint about it; it is not known if anyone was struck by the irony of the United States' welcoming men who had labored for the Nazi war machine at the same time that American scientists (such as Oppenheimer) were losing their security clearances because of having allegedly associated with Communists in the 1930s.[30]

Conant had more success blocking the Volunteer Freedom Corps scheme when it came up again late in 1955. Despite renewed entreaties from its champion, Henry Cabot Lodge, he stuck to his view that the proposed corps would cause major political problems for Adenauer and should be rejected out of hand. In the following spring, Dulles, citing Conant, shelved the program indefinitely, on the grounds that this "psychological" step would be "misunderstood by Free World opinion and exploited by the Soviets as being inconsistent with the objectives of the [resumed] disarmament negotiations."[31]

These were minor issues, however, compared with Conant's principal assignment in the months following West Germany's entry into NATO – to press the Federal Republic to move forward on its plans to build a 500,000-man army, and to impose mandatory two-year conscription to that end. Relations between Washington and Bonn appeared at a high point after the successful resolution of the five-year struggle to win the right to rearm, yet to the Americans' great annoyance their new ally seemed lackadaisical about actually doing so. "I doubt if Chanc. is dragging his heels on purpose in this question of military buildup but no one seems to be in any great rush," Conant wrote in his diary in July 1955. "What irony. First we were afraid the Germans would rearm now we are afraid they won't!"[32] For the next year his instructions were to "keep needling" the West Germans to move as fast as possible both to rearm and to approve higher payments of "support costs" to defray the expenses of American troops deployed in the country. Conant dutifully "pushed [Adenauer] hard in the winter of 1955–56" to accelerate rearmament, and Dulles taunted Foreign Secretary Heinrich von Brentano that he had hoped West German membership would "strengthen" NATO's military effectiveness, not "weaken" it – a barb that did not sit well with Adenauer.[33] But U.S. officials (as well as Adenauer himself) faced an uphill battle in trying to get the West Germans to speed up military preparations, largely because, just as Conant feared, those messages conflicted with intimations of an imminent thaw in East-West relations – rumors fanned by the summitry in Geneva and the revelation of Khrushchev's speech denouncing Stalin to the CPSU 20th Party Congress in February 1956.[34] The rumors made Adenauer jittery, and he sent a note to Dulles in June inquiring whether the United States was plotting behind his back to invite Soviet leaders to Washington.[35]

Adenauer as well as other West Germans was also unsettled by signs that the United States wished to reduce its conventional forces in Europe in favor of tactical nuclear weapons: in mid-1955 it was disclosed that NATO's "Carte Blanche" exercises, simulating its response to a Soviet-bloc attack on West Germany, had ended in a ferocious mock nuclear battle, fought in large measure on and over German soil, which "killed" 1.7 million Germans and "wounded" 3.5 million more.[36]

Still, by the summer of 1956, faced with considerable reluctance in public opinion, in the opposition SDP and in his own CDU, Adenauer had under American pressure dutifully backed an eighteen-month military draft and was on the verge of getting final parliamentary approval for conscription legislation when the worst crisis in U.S.-German relations during Conant's tenure in Bonn erupted. On July 13, in the midst of the Bundestag's intense debate over the conscription legislation, the *New York Times* reported that Adm. Arthur Radford, chairman of the Joint Chiefs of Staff, was proposing to slash 800,000 personnel from U.S. armed forces over the next four years on the grounds that a war with the Soviet Union was increasingly unlikely.[37] Though State Department officials reassured a worried German ambassador that rumors that Dulles was behind the story were without foundation, when the secretary of state was asked about the report at a news conference a few days later, he refused to disavow the notion of cutting U.S. ground forces in Europe. A few days later, Adenauer learned that the British government was to submit a document to NATO implying plans to dramatically cut its ground forces on the Continent in light of "new weapons" and a new Soviet government.[38]

These reports completely pulled the rug out from under the CDU's advocacy of intensified military readiness, and it seemed to confirm the SPD's charge that the United States was going to rely on nuclear weapons, pull out its troops, and go home—and undercut Adenauer a year before he had to win reelection. Enhancing his sense of betrayal was the fact that no such reduction of forces had been mentioned during his meetings with Eisenhower and Dulles in Washington only a month before. To the chancellor's "suspicious nature," Conant later privately reflected, it now appeared "that the American & British [were] in a conspiracy to withdraw their troops (or reduce the numbers dramatically) leaving him to *fight an election* with evidence he had been let down by his friends."[39]

Adenauer on July 22 poured out his wrath and fears to Dulles in a bitter, anguished letter complaining of U.S. "undependability" and accusing the Eisenhower administration of giving up on disarmament and retreating into a policy of "atomic isolationism." America's evident tilt favoring atomic bombs over conventional ground forces, he warned, would increase the danger of nuclear war, tempt the Soviets to consider a nuclear first strike, and was "incompatible with the basic tenets of Christianity and humanity."[40]

Though unaware, for the moment, of Adenauer's letter, Conant discerned big trouble and grasped the importance of assuaging the chancellor's fury. What made the matter even more problematic, in his private view, was that Adenauer was justified in suspecting that Dulles had been lying to him. "I think that the so-called Radford plan break was due to the fact that somebody in Bonn really smelled what the real situation was," he later recalled. "And the Chancellor knew perfectly well we were, in a way, playing poker with each other. The Americans wanted the Germans to rearm as quickly as they could, having as long a draft as possible, promising they would never withdraw their troops, but thinking that honestly they would the first moment they could."[41] Obviously, however, Conant could not say as much to either Adenauer or Dulles, who were "sore" at each other, with him struck in the middle. Instead he warned Dulles that, unless the controversy was quickly

One year after the first atomic explosion took place in a desert of New Mexico in July 1945, Conant and Vannevar Bush come to a warehouse in Harvard Square to reenact their witnessing of the fateful event for a "March of Time" newsreel.

In Moscow with Secretary of State James F. Byrnes, for whom he served as an adviser on atomic matters at a December 1945 U.S.–Soviet–U.K. foreign ministers conference

(*Below*) With two principal collaborators in the development of the atomic bomb, J. Robert Oppenheimer (*left*) and Vannevar Bush (*right*), at a 1948 gathering in Boston

For their work on the
atomic bomb, Bush and
Conant (*above*) receive
Oak Leaf Cluster medals
from President Truman
at the White House,
May 1948.

The Harvard president
leaves Massachusetts
Hall for the last time
before becoming
Eisenhower's envoy to
Germany. Preceding
Conant is the provost,
Paul Buck.

The Conants shortly after
arriving in Germany

In West Berlin, Conant
visits a Red Cross refugee
camp for escapees
from the Communist
East Zone of Germany.

Edward R. Murrow interviews the U.S. High Commissioner in front of Berlin's Brandenburg Gate in September 1953.

(*Below*) Conant's work as U.S. envoy to Germany was complicated by strained personal relations with Secretary of State John Foster Dulles (*standing, right*) and West German Chancellor Konrad Adenauer (*seated, right*), gathered here with President Eisenhower during a Washington summit conference in October 1954.

Reviewing the troops on the Cold War frontier in Germany

Conant and his wife, appearing grim, back in the United States after he ended his short-lived diplomatic career and took up the study of American public education

Cuddling a family kitten in Randolph, New Hampshire, 1946

Three Harvard presidents (*from left to right*): Derek Bok, Nathan Pusey, and Conant

Conant (*far right*) receiving the Atomic Pioneer Award from President Nixon (*second from left*), together with (*from left to right*) Glenn T. Seaborg, Gen. Leslie R. Groves, and Vannevar Bush

The Conants, with grandchildren Jim and Jennet, touring "Steam Town," 1970

In his New York apartment during the writing of *My Several Lives*

dampened, "grave complications" in efforts to achieve timely West German rearmament would result, Adenauer's domestic standing would plummet, and Conant would have to revise his confident predictions for a CDU victory in 1957 elections.[42]

Dulles did his best to reassure Adenauer, writing him on August 11 that Radford's plan had been neither authorized nor approved and denying that Washington had lost interest in nuclear disarmament (it simply wasn't possible for the foreseeable future) or saw no purpose for conventional forces in Western Europe.[43] But CIA director Allen Dulles, after a lengthy session with Adenauer later that month, had the impression that he was still deeply worried about the direction of U.S. policy and, moreover, "is badly in need of having near him some high ranking American preferably the Ambassador in whom he has confidence and in whom he can confide."[44]

Obviously Conant was not fulfilling that need—and even before receiving his letter, the secretary of state had concluded that "Adenauer would like someone different in Bonn." On July 16 Dulles suggested to Eisenhower that Conant be transferred to Rome ("I don't know whether Conant could afford Italy," he told his aides, "but he probably would not have to operate on the extravagant style of Mrs. [Clare Boothe] Luce").[45] A week later, after checking with Sherman Adams, Ike's chief of staff, he shifted his thinking—and obtained Eisenhower's warm consent to offer Conant the ambassadorship to *India*.[46] The arrival of Adenauer's July 22 letter could only have strengthened his determination to push Conant out of Germany and replace him with an American envoy in whom Adenauer reposed confidence and who could more convincingly explain U.S. policy.[47]

Conant, meanwhile, at the end of July had departed Germany for his annual summer break, flying to Boston for a dentist's appointment, a weekend on Cape Cod with the Donald Davids (dean of the Harvard Business School and his wife), and a visit to Patty's ailing mother before settling in at the rustic, isolated family cottage in Randolph. On August 3 he was irritated to be awoken by the arrival of an FBI agent conducting a background check on an associate, but that disturbance paled in comparison to the interruption that happened the next day. After lunch with his son Jim, who had arrived that morning from Montreal with his wife and children, he was puzzled to be summoned to a telephone at a country inn in the nearby town of Gorham to receive an urgent telephone call from the secretary of state, and he gasped, "flabbergasted," when he heard his offer, made in the president's name. Despite "considerable 'double-talk,'" Dulles recorded after their conversation, he accurately gathered that Conant's immediate instinctive response was "strongly negative," although he agreed to think it over. For a few days, disturbed by the turn of events, he mulled over the idea with his wife while roaming the local mountain ledges and trails, but his decision remained the same—he had never taken much interest in India or other Third World countries (opposing, for example, U.S. economic aid beyond that necessary to counter Communist influence),[48] was loath to spend another term working under Dulles, and was more than ready to leave the diplomatic corps and take up his researches on education. "Examined India possibility thoroughly," he jotted after one long talk with Patty. "Pros & cons. cons. have it." Calling Dulles back to say no, he was told to think it over for a week; he was probably just tired. But, despite an administration leak to the *Washington Post* that his appointment was under consideration, the extra time only strengthened his determination to say no and tell Dulles he would leave the diplomatic corps after the election.[49] The decision now final, Conant resumed his regimen of mountain climbing, hiking, and relaxing with family and friends and started to turn his attention to life after Germany; a lunch with his protégé Frank Keppel, dean of the Harvard School of Education, encouraged him to concentrate in his plans for an intensive educational project on the problems facing American public high schools.[50]

First, however, Conant knew that several months of intensive diplomacy lay ahead, and, after a fishing trip with Jim Baxter and Charlie Coolidge, among others, he left on Labor Day for Boston to catch the "Federal Express" to Washington for a round of consultations prior to returning to Bonn. With some spare time before the train, he stopped at the Dana Palmer House, his old wartime residence (now moved across Quincy Street to make room for the Lamont Library), and penned some "Reflections at Leisure" on the German, American, and international scenes. More immediately, he wondered apprehensively whether Dulles and Eisenhower would be "miffed" that he had turned down India and might offer another ambassadorial slot, and how to handle reporters who would be waiting to question him about his plans.[51]

Conant reached Washington as a new international crisis boiled in the Middle East—over Eisenhower's firm objections Britain threatened to go to war to reclaim the Suez Canal, which Egypt's nationalist leader, Gamal Abdel Nasser, had defiantly nationalized two months earlier. With London emotionally adhering to imperial prerogatives and Eisenhower sharply warning against the precipitous use of force, the old Anglo-American alliance seemed on the verge of collapse, and Conant found his friend in a troubled mood (if in better health after his heart attack a year earlier) when he was ushered into the Oval Office for an unpublicized meeting on the afternoon of September 7. "How to cut Nasser down to size without war or uniting the Arabs??" the president wondered, in Conant's paraphrase. He also complained to Conant of demagoguery from another source, his Democratic rival Adlai E. Stevenson, accusing the Illinois senator of being a "small politician" for proposing an end to the draft and nuclear testing.[52]

To Conant's relief, neither Eisenhower nor Dulles pressed him too hard to reverse his decision (for which he again apologized) to decline their entreaties to go to New Delhi. His meeting with Dulles dwelt instead on the nasty turn U.S.–West German relations had taken over the summer, and Conant was "shocked" when Dulles for the first time showed him the July 22 letter from Adenauer condemning America's nuclear policies as wicked and un-Christian, a letter Conant found "strange" and "incredible." Despite the placatory tone of his reply, which he did not show Conant, Dulles now had harsh words for Adenauer, and Conant silently reflected that he was stuck in the middle between two powerful men who were "very sore" at each other. "[Dulles was d]isturbed about Chanc and not very sympathetic about his problems," Conant thought. "Seems like the end of a great friendship!"[53]

Flying to Bonn after taking the night train to New York, Conant assured reporters that he would remain as ambassador in Germany "at least" through the end of Eisenhower's current term, and steeled himself for the task of restoring Adenauer's confidence in American policy. It would not be an easy task, as Conant quickly discovered on September 10 during an intense hour-and-a-half meeting with the "physically fit" chancellor along with the visiting secretary of the air force, Donald A. Quarles. Conant began soothingly, relaying Eisenhower's personal greetings and declaring that his reelection was a foregone conclusion. But Adenauer, brushing this off, immediately presented a laundry list of grievances about U.S. leadership of the Western alliance: an alleged NATO decision to abandon the "forward strategy" of defending West Germany in case of Soviet attack, a report (which Conant had never heard of and found "silly" when he did) to a U.S. congressional subcommittee calling for American unilateral disarmament, and disarray on Suez among Washington, London, and Paris. All told, it was "not too much to say that it is all over with NATO"—and then he lowered the boom, in what Conant considered a "non sequitur!": in view of these circumstances, Adenauer was now abandoning his pledge of pushing an eighteen-month military draft, and could now get only a twelve-month conscription bill through the Bundestag. Quarles and Conant hastened to reassure Adenauer that his concerns about U.S. readiness and determination to confront the Soviets in Europe were misplaced, dismissing the Radford plan as an unapproved working paper and stressing the value of a new generation of tactical nuclear weapons. Hearing the chancellor's comment that reductions in ground forces would only be justified when such weapons were available to army infantry at the level of atomic cannon shells, Quarles informed him that the United States *already* possessed such weapons and was prepared to use them to beat back a Russian thrust in Europe. Shifting gears, Adenauer then exasperated the Americans by wondering, then, why did West Germany need forces at all if tactical nuclear weapons were so effective. They were needed, Quarles patiently explained, to fight off an East German "guerrilla" attack or to show the world the seriousness of a Soviet conventional assault so that a nuclear retaliation could then be justified.[54]

Conant thought the session helpful in "setting Chanc straight on a number of fronts," but thought the wily leader had used the Radford flap as a "very thin excuse" to renege on an eighteen-month draft and get himself out of a political hole.[55] And in the coming weeks, Adenauer continued to issue blistering private complaints about what he charged was a basic shift in U.S. security that might lead to a withdrawal of ground forces from Europe. Nor was Conant any happier than Adenauer about what seemed to be a sense of drift in American policy, exacerbated by Dulles's failure to keep his envoys informed on critical policy issues (like Suez), top-level exchanges, and even personnel shifts. "General deterioration of German-American relations . . . plus repeated evidence of failure of communication between State Dept top & lower levels and Bonn makes me very glad I am to get out of this business very soon," he confided to his diary on October 3. "An interesting experience but enough is enough."[56]

Ironically, even as Conant prepared to leave his post, U.S.-West German relations did improve palpably, although this was mostly the result of outside events. The sharp increase in tensions at the time of the Suez crisis and the Soviet Union's invasion of Hungary threw the United States and West Germany closer into their awkward embrace (as Conant put it, "events in Hungary brought home with increased force extent of German dependency on US").[57] On Monday, October 29, the night Israel attacked Egypt in the first act of a carefully plotted scenario leading to British and French intervention to seize the Suez Canal, Conant sat beside Adenauer at a white-tie dinner for the president of Costa Rica. Adenauer expressed understanding of the Israeli action, reminding Conant he had long predicted such an explosion. "I argued that preventive war was immoral," Conant noted in his diary, but Adenauer was "not so sure! Most general but intimate talk I ever had with him. He seemed relaxed but said world was *too* interesting!"[58]

The Anglo-French imperial last hurrah produced "general consternation on all sides," Conant recorded the next day, but the news from Budapest, where Moscow's supporters were momentarily on the run, seemed "unbelievably good!"[59] Yet by the following Sunday, he wrote darkly in his diary:

Weather bad. News terrible! Radio reports . . . Soviets moving in on Budapest. UN helpless. UN concerned with Egypt problem. Br. & F continue action and start landing forces. By night revolt in Budapest wiped out! Most depressing day since the Fall of France in 1940 . . . News arrives Sec. Dulles operated on for perforated intestine. . . . What a week end.[60]

With flags at the embassy at half-mast to honor the martyrs in Budapest — as with the failed East Berlin revolt three years earlier, Washington could offer only sympathy — an ominous Soviet warning arrived saying that London and Paris were susceptible to nuclear destruction if they continued down the path of aggression. "What sounded like a herald of World War III from the Kremlin came in late last night," a shaken Conant wrote. "We are quite uncertain about what the future has in store." (The one thing about which he was certain was that no one would be attending the reception the next evening at the Soviet Embassy to commemorate the anniversary of the Bolshevik Revolution.)[61]

What the future held in store, after Eisenhower's overwhelming reelection, was several months of gradually lessening tension between Washington and the furtive Anglo-French coalition, as well as renewed anger at and suspicion of Moscow — both of which naturally encouraged the further steadying of the shaky relations between the United States and West Germany, where anger about Hungary (and at Britain and France for distracting the world with their Suez escapade) was matched only by apprehension that a similar fate might one day be in store for East Germany.

Conant was increasingly hopeful about the prospects for the Federal Republic's continued close ties to the West and advancement along the path of parliamentary democracy, a free press, and a market economy, but his estimate was tempered by his intrinsic skepticism about human nature, as he had explained to a friend in the State Department in 1955:

> I am not basing my optimistic forecast of the future on any such premise as "the Germans have changed." If I live long enough to write anything about my experience here in the last three years, I shall devote a chapter to attacking such glib phrases as "the Germans have changed" or "the Germans haven't changed." Anyone who has been a college president in the United States for twenty years can not start from any other assumption than the premise that the vast majority of human beings are quite ready to double-cross their friends and partners if occasion arises! Therefore we can eliminate what I would call the sentimental argument from the discussion and get down to a prognosis of possibilities.[62]

Conant kept this cold-eyed calculation to himself and concentrated publicly on delivering optimistic homilies on "Our Common Future," "Strengthening Cultural Ties," and similarly positive topics.[63] By the fall of 1956, by one estimate, *Herr Doktor Conant* had delivered 150 major speeches and informal remarks on 500 occasions to German audiences (and mostly *in* German, albeit with a flat New England twang); barnstorming like an American presidential candidate, he (and Patty) attended assorted ceremonies, ribbon-cuttings, and theatrical performances, inspected refugee centers and orphanages, chatted up business, social, and educational groups in every major city and many minor ones in the country in addition to his morale-boosting visits to Berlin. (As a diplomat he might not have been so hot, one embassy colleague told a reporter after Conant left Germany, but the public relations job would be remembered when the rest was forgotten.)[64] He took special pleasure in dropping in on schools and universities, where he startled and delighted students by engaging in question-and-answer sessions after speeches, a most un-German practice for authority figures. "I want to accentuate the positive," he told Robert Shaplen of the *New Yorker* — he was referring at that moment to his desire to smooth over the occasional problems caused by the presence of U.S. troops in West Germany, but the comment with equal accuracy describes the whole of his public discourse on U.S.-West German relations.[65] In a November 1956 letter to Eisenhower, he even professed to discern in young West German students hopeful signs of idealism, anti-militarism, and pro-Americanism, refuting the dark prophecies he had voiced a decade earlier that it would be "not ten years or even twenty" but well over a generation before a nation "hardened by [Nazi] party discipline" could recover its moral bearings.[66]

And in private, Conant was perhaps most reassured, ironically, by the same footdragging on military measures by Bonn that so irritated Washington, for it strengthened his private analysis, as he looked back upon his time as high commissioner and ambassador, that *"the Germans did not rush to arms when the band began to play!"*[67]

Conant had not, however, completely banished his private fears about German intentions—particularly where atomic energy was concerned. Despite Adenauer's welcome pledge to have the Federal Republic abstain from constructing nuclear weapons, he viewed with suspicion the enthusiasm of some West German officials and industrialists to take part in Eisenhower's "Atoms for Peace" program, according to which the United States proposed to cooperate with friendly countries interested in civilian nuclear power. As discussions for a West European atomic agency ("Euratom") progressed,[68] Conant strongly urged Eisenhower and Dulles against advisers like Lewis Strauss who favored rushing ahead with a bilateral aid program for Bonn and a nuclear power plant for West Berlin. The West German Economics Ministry as well as "some German industrialists" were disingenuously "playing down" the danger that plutonium produced in atomic-power plants could be siphoned off to build explosives, he told the State Department in November 1955.[69] If a supranational nuclear science agency with tight safeguards against cheating were not established, he warned Ike soon afterward, such activities "could well go underground."[70] And he cautioned Washington about the danger "that Germans will develop on a nationalistic basis their own atomic development in competition with the French unless some degree of European cooperation is achieved."[71] Devoted as Adenauer was to the ideal of continent-wide collaboration, there remained "forces in Germany" working against Euratom.[72] In late October 1956, Conant presented arguments to Adenauer in favor of Euratom and government rather than private ownership of atomic plants with the intention of "forcing an open door" into West German facilities as a safeguard against prohibited activities being carried out clandestinely.[73]

The controversy over the Radford plan only deepened Conant's worries about West Germany's readiness to deal with the nuclear issue, and his conversations with the chancellor left him convinced that Adenauer was having difficulty coming to grips with the dilemmas of the nuclear age. By then, in fact, reading the nuclear handwriting on the wall so far as NATO strategy was concerned, Adenauer had already reversed gears and strongly (albeit secretly) supported arming the Bundeswehr with tactical nuclear weapons (the euphemistically designated "modern weapons" would be provided by NATO rather than built in the FRG so as to sidestep Bonn's promise to refrain from nuclear production); emblematic of this new effort to gain nuclear status, which was seen as essential to assuring West Germany a major role in determining the Alliance's political and military strategy, was Adenauer's selection in October of Bavarian nuclear enthusiast Franz Josef Strauss as defense minister.[74] In November, Adenauer and Conant traded sharp words on the subject of U.S. atomic policy near the end of a tense encounter in which Adenauer lambasted U.S. policy errors that he said had paved the way to the Suez debacle, which had caused disarray in NATO and gains for Moscow. Conant listened silently, his irritation mounting not only at Adenauer, but even more at Dulles for failing to keep him informed of the real rationales for U.S. policies on major issues outside Germany.[75]

But when Adenauer "spoke strongly" about what he said was the "basic error of U.S. foreign policy" — a shift from an interest in "controlled disarmament" to an unvarnished and "unrealistic" striving for permanent nuclear superiority — Conant could contain himself no longer and he interrupted the tirade.

Would you, he asked acidly, prefer that the U.S. was number two in "atomic superiority" rather than number one?

Of course not, Adenauer answered, but the U.S. was "no longer interested" in nuclear disarmament.

Conant started to point out the difficulties in pursuing negotiations to that end, to which Adenauer shot back that they were not sufficient to justify giving up the attempt. Conant denied that the United States had done so, prompting Adenauer to claim that "our new policy of giving up conventional weapons made it impossible for us to consider atomic disarmament." Conant challenged him again, but Adenauer stood firm, and the two men parted in considerable disagreement. Afterward, Conant reported to Dulles that it was "clear [that the] Chancellor is confused about our military policy and the whole atomic military picture and its relation to US foreign policy. If I may venture the comment, it is my belief that it is [the] Chancellor who is unrealistic and this is due to his fundamental lack of knowledge of realities of atomic age in which we live."[76]

In Conant's final annual review of events, dispatched in late January 1957, this assessment of West German nuclear immaturity and Adenauer's lack of realism struck a discordant note in what was largely an optimistic forecast of the Federal Republic's future economic prosperity and political stability. West Germans wanted U.S. ground forces to stay in their country, he cabled, as a result of their "[a]ll-pervading . . . desire to avoid World War III"; Adenauer was "particularly sensitive" to any hint of a withdrawal, and "almost pathologically fearful US might either reach agreement with Soviets on disarmament, before reunification problem solved, or become so reliant on 'strategic' atomic weapons as to withdraw into some form of isolation." Conant in fact perceived a sort of nuclear schizophrenia, not so different from the phenomenon he had himself witnessed when the United States struggled to adjust to atomic weapons a decade earlier. Simultaneously fearing nuclear war yet bewitched by the potential advantages of wielding "more power with fewer men (and less money) by use of nuclear weapons," Germans were

> only beginning to struggle with following questions: What is relationship in nuclear age of military power to national strategy, how far can one rely on a deterrent concept which is based on weapons whose use might mean destruction of civilization, and how can a gov[ernmen]t of democratic processes long maintain large (and expensive) military establishment without creating by-products dangerous to democratic structure of state itself?[77]

Though he didn't say so in his cable, Conant, too, was still struggling with those questions.

After declining to go to India in August 1956 Conant looked forward to embarking on the Carnegie-funded study of U.S. public high schools, and he soon found out that he could get an earlier start on the project than he had expected: due to the press of world events he had expressed to the State Department his willingness to stay on in Bonn through the spring, but on January 10 he opened a letter from Dulles informing him, to his shock, that his resignation had been accepted effective when he returned to the United States in February for some speaking engagements. Conant was "dumbfounded" by this sudden change, which he wasn't sure whether to attribute to an innocent misunderstanding, a promise of a slot to the Republican National Committee, the Radford letter, Dulles being "sore" at him for turning down India, or impatience on the part of the State Department's top echelon to be rid of him. "Or was the Chanc at the bottom of all this? Did the Chanc want to get me out of Germany before the election campaign was in full swing because of his (silly) opinion of my being too friendly with the SPD?"[78] (U.S. journalists had criticized Conant for not being *close enough* to the opposition.) Probably the alacrity with which the State Department replaced Conant stemmed from both Adenauer's impatience and Washington's belief that a genuine improvement in relations required a new man in Bad Godesberg—following his combative November 16 argument with Conant, Adenauer had yet again signaled to Eisenhower his urgent desire to achieve closer contact between Bonn and Washington, and Dulles decided to replace Conant with the respected career diplomat David K. E. Bruce, a man whom Adenauer knew and trusted.[79] (Bruce, Dulles later explained to Adenauer, "might be more politically minded than Ambassador Conant, who had been a very learned person but perhaps somewhat lacking in a political touch."

Adenauer replied, according to Dulles, that "the trouble with Conant was that he was too 'liberal.' "[80] On later reflection, in a lengthy "self-judgment" of his performance, Conant surmised that the "core" of Adenauer's dissatisfaction had been the rearmament problem—"perhaps he never forgave me.")[81]

Determined to leave with dignity and eager to begin the next phase of his life, Conant loyally saluted these new orders, packed his bags, said good-bye to his staff, attended a round of dinners and parties in his honor in Bonn and Berlin, and on February 18 paid a formal farewell call on Adenauer, who was "pleasant but not over cordial"; the next day he and Mrs. Conant boarded a train at Mehlem station and headed for home, and his four-year career as a diplomat was over.[82]

Conant did not allow the slightly sour nature of his departure, or his strained relations with Adenauer, to interfere with his earnest campaign in the United States to rehabilitate "Free Germany" as a loyal and reliable friend and partner. Eradicating the sordid legacy of World War II had been uppermost in Conant's mind ever since his very first meeting with Adenauer, in February 1953, when he had stressed the importance to U.S. and world public opinion of swift ratification by the West German parliament of the 1952 Luxembourg Treaty providing for reparation payments to Israel for Nazi crimes against the Jews.[83] Now, four years later, that was the message he spread, acknowledging that if anyone had then predicted he would one day return to Germany to assist in that country's "rapid rearmament" and urge listeners to embrace "Germany, our new ally," he would have judged the would-be prophet as suffering from "a case of permanent insanity!"[84]

But exactly that was his goal. Nazism in West Germany was "dead and buried," Conant assured Americans, anti-Semitism had been extirpated, and the reconstituted Federal Republic would, barring the collapse of NATO or a global economic upheaval, remain democratic, tolerant, moderate, free, capitalist, and a "powerful and reliable partner" in the global struggle against Communism. Of course, Conant reiterated horror at the abuses of Hitler's day, but he encouraged Americans to avoid dwelling on them—in other words, to observe the same etiquette lesson he had privately passed to Marbury—and to squelch dissenting voices about the propriety and wisdom of current policy.[85]

Conant did his best to stifle any attempt, by Soviets, Germans, or Americans, to consider West Germany's future outside the framework of the Western alliance. When George Kennan had the temerity in the fall of 1957 to urge publicly a variant of the plan he had advocated within the government in 1948–49—a demilitarized, neutral, and unified Germany as part of a general East-West settlement ending Europe's postwar division and permitting a mutual pullout of U.S., British, and Soviet troops—Conant helped to organize a counterattack sharply to rebuff this heresy from the "architect of containment" and to chorus the new gospel that made West Germany a full and irrevocable NATO partner. In January 1958, he headlined a group of seventeen American experts on Germany (organized by the American Council on Germany) who issued a manifesto denouncing Kennan's proposals, which they called a dangerous isolationist throwback that would reduce NATO "to a paper organization" and actually encourage Soviet aggression; before publication the group circulated a draft (co-authored by Conant) to Dean Acheson, who not only approved but wrote his own tart "Reply to Kennan." Opening an extended and at times acrimonious debate with his former State Department partner, he declared that Kennan had never "grasped the realities of power relationships but takes a rather mystical attitude toward them." Both the Eisenhower and Adenauer administrations warmly welcomed this campaign to prevent Kennan's proposals from stimulating public opinion in West Germany against NATO or in favor of recent Soviet proposals for a "nuclear-free zone" in central Europe and a mutual pull-back of NATO and Warsaw Pact forces from Germany (they were embodied in the Rapacki Plan advanced by Poland's foreign minister and endorsed by Soviet Foreign Minister Bulganin).[86]

Conant also used his January 1958 Godkin Lectures at Harvard (published as *Germany and Freedom: A Personal Appraisal*) to admonish those who raised doubts. "Anything that is said or done to stir up German suspicions about American intentions in Europe or American suspicions about Germany vis-à-vis the Soviets is a blow against the solidarity of NATO; conversely, anything that can be done to quiet such suspicions will strengthen the defenses of our freedom." Alluding to Kennan's plan (without naming him), Conant cautioned against impatience or advancing "risky" schemes to resolve the nagging problem of Germany's division. He may well have been remembering the bitterness of the Radford Affair when he stated that proposals for a mutual withdrawal of U.S. and Soviet forces from central Europe "have from time to time threatened to poison our good relations" with Bonn and still raised fears that the United States would leave the Federal Republic "in the lurch."[87]

Conversely, Conant also asked his listeners to ignore those who said that Nazi Germany's sins disqualified the Federal Republic from being considered a reliable ally. Retracing the path of German history during the twentieth century—and his own shifting reaction to them—he drew uniformly reassuring conclusions from the success of postwar political and economic developments in West Germany; among the encouraging events since his departure from Bonn a year earlier were Adenauer's reelection and the FRG's inclusion in two newly created institutions, the European Economic Community (EEC) and Euratom, which expressed the hope of a European unity that transcended nationalistic enmities. "The spirit of free Germany, today, is the spirit of a people who have turned their back on the Nazi past," he declared, and predicted that history would record that Adenauer and his associates had "restored the moral worth of Germany in the eyes of the free world." In present-day West Germany, he reported, "die-hard" ex-Nazis had only a "negligible" influence, and anti-Nazi West Germans had learned to distinguish "between former members of the party who, they consider, were never 'real Nazis' and others whom they regard as '*terrible* Nazis' and with whom they will have no traffic." In any case, foreigners were "demanding a great deal" if they expected German society to deal with the issue frankly. "Necessary reticence . . . has become a general reticence. In this sense, for all except writers and historians, modern German history does begin in 1945." Ever the pragmatist, and a believer in reticence himself, Conant made pronouncements that dovetailed with Washington's strategy of allowing Cold War imperatives to prevail over denazification, condoning the reemergence in West German society of military, industrial, scientific, social, academic, and other figures who had peopled the Nazi apparatus. And his rationale for shunning arguments about responsibilities for the monstrosities of the Hitler years, and for quashing any remaining doubts about the wisdom of rearming Germans, echoed the one he had employed in quelling the debate over the morality of using the atomic bomb on Hiroshima. "If we quarrel about the past," he quoted Churchill, "we cannot get ahead with the future."[88]

So, too, did his advice to Americans on the German issue resemble his advice on the bomb a decade earlier—they should sit tight, trust their leaders, stay strong, and patiently await better times. "The German problem," he counseled, "must be viewed as part of the larger problem created by the divided world in an age of fission and fusion bombs and rockets. It seems unlikely that it can be solved separately or in a hurry."[89]

CHAPTER 35

"The Inspector General"

Educational Statesman
1957–1965

Those now in college will before long be living in the age of intercontinental ballistic missiles. What will be then needed is not more engineers and scientists, but a people who will not panic and political leaders of wisdom, courage, and devotion, with a capacity for solving intricate human problems.
— Telegram to Eisenhower after Sputnik, October 1957

I am convinced we are allowing social dynamite to accumulate in our large cities.

— *Slums and Suburbs*

When he left West Germany in February 1957, Conant was nearing age sixty-five, for many the age of retirement. But for some months Conant had been gearing up to begin yet another career, as full-time author, commentator, and critic on American public education. By one estimate, over half his public addresses in Germany had dealt with educational issues, as Conant politely yet firmly tried to imbue listeners with an appreciation of the democratizing function of American public education in contrast to the traditional German model; and, even as ambassador, he found occasion to pen essays ventilating pet educational ideas and observations on such subjects as the ideological warping of learning and research in the GDR and the comparative pros and cons of American education from a European perspective. Already promised generous underwriting and staff support by the Carnegie Corporation, Conant in late December 1956 had dictated a memorandum to its president, John Gardner, sketching his proposed project. Its objective reflected his devotion to public education as the meritocratic "engine of democracy" and its methodology flowed from his rigorous empiricism—a study of "the education of the talented youth" in U.S. comprehensive public junior and senior high schools, to be based on data personally gathered from a packed itinerary of visits to schools.[1]

In late February the Conants came home to the United States, but not to Cambridge, where they had lived for more than five decades. The last thing Conant would have wanted was to be around Harvard, where he would be seen as looking over the new president's shoulder no matter what else he was doing. Instead, this pair of lifelong New Englanders moved to Manhattan, taking up temporary quarters at the Westbury Hotel on Madison Avenue. Assuredly not yet ready for restful retirement (although his New Hampshire cottage remained available for summer retreats), Conant still yearned to be among the power brokers and establishment leaders whose ranks he had joined as Harvard president; that implied, barring some special opportunity, living in Washington or New York.

The decisive factor in the Conants' move to New York City, though, was its proximity to his new bankroller. In March and April Conant spoke with Carnegie officials and gathered old associates from the educational world— the EPC's William Carr; the Harvard Education School dean Frank Keppel; the Baltimore school superintendent John Fischer, and Henry Chauncey, director of the Educational Testing Service (ETS)—to refine his project's objectives and strategy; the goal was to discover examples of the ideal "comprehensive high school," which provided a well-rounded, scholastically strong education to all students, with a beefed-up curriculum that would include more English composition, foreign languages, and math to prepare them for citizenship and vocations, while also offering appropriate special instruction for the most advanced, gifted, college-bound students.[2] Or, as he put it in a letter to a prospective staff member:

> Let me explain the objectives of my inquiry. I want to shape my ideas about the public high school by actual examination of certain types of schools and either fortifying my present prejudices or modifying them by what I find. I am committed to the general idea of a comprehensive high school, meaning by that a school which enrolls all the youth of a given area. I am a believer in theory of the use of various devices to break down social barriers between different types of students in such a school with the hope of engendering a spirit of democracy and a respect for all forms of honest labor. At the same time, I am aware of the difficulties of handling adequately the more talented youth in such a school; that is, talented from the point of view of a university. Therefore, I wish to identify the schools which are doing a good job in preparing for college the youth with I.Q. above 115, but at the same time are handling adequately the vocational courses and schools where the academic group is not more than 50 percent and the community is not a primarily white collar community or a suburban community.[3]

To seek out, explain, and extol those model schools capable of accomplishing both these divergent tasks, he proposed to visit only schools in middle-sized, middle-class communities, excluding rural or urban areas; and to enhance the relevance, applicability, and effect of his eventual recommendations he vastly expanded the project's geographic scope; now he envisioned touring schools nationwide, not just in the Northeast, though he still aimed to publish the results within two years.

Though now the laboratory would be the nation's schools, the process of assembling a team of Ph.D.-equipped assistants, devising a research agenda, refining hypotheses, and designing experiments to test them all recalled fondly remembered days as a chemist.[4] Except that now Conant was not hunting some objective truth, but seeking hard data to buttress and hone his already fairly well-formed philosophy. What this all amounted to, Conant told friends, was that he "intended to devote a year to sharpening my prejudices about secondary education and a subsequent year peddling said prejudices all around the United States." Now that he had filled in the "blank check" Gardner had given him, Carnegie appropriated a budget of $350,000 over two years for Conant's project; rented office space for him and his start-up staff of four educators—three high school administrators and a Berkeley assistant professor of history—on the sixth floor of 588 Fifth Avenue on Manhattan's Upper East Side; and contracted with ETS, in Princeton, New Jersey, to provide "logistic support." While his new staff began to plan for the travel and research ahead, including the detailed questionnaires to be dispatched to schools they planned to visit, Conant and his wife left on April 19 on a trans-Atlantic cruise that led to a two-month vacation in Switzerland followed by planning meetings with his staff in New York in late June and early July before the requisite summer sojourn in New Hampshire.[5]

At the end of the summer, however, they were jolted by two events. First came startling news from Korea: in Seoul, on August 26, their younger son, Theodore, now thirty-one, had married Ellen D. Psaty, a historian of East Asian art, in a civil ceremony at the Seoul mayor's office. Details of the whirlwind romance dribbled in via a cable and letter from Ted and from their friends at the U.S. embassy in Seoul, Ambassador Walter "Red" Dowling and his wife, Alice. Ted had gone to Korea after graduating from Swarthmore in 1951 to make radio, film, and television documentaries and newsreels for the United Nations (his privately produced *Children in Crisis,* an avant-garde portrayal of young victims of the fighting, won an award at the 1955 Berlin Film Festival). And now the lean, gangling, iconoclastic filmmaker had startled the local expat community by wedding the then assistant professor at the University of Georgia, less than three weeks after she had arrived for a visit to select modern Korean art for an upcoming exhibition in the United States. They met in a UN mess hall and, after a lightning-like courtship, flew off to Thailand, Angkor Wat, Hong Kong, and Bali, for a honeymoon that exploited Psaty's planned research trip to Southeast Asia.[6]

As was her custom upon learning exciting news, Patty Conant immediately informed her mother, Miriam Richards. Ted had cabled that he was to marry an "attractive, intelligent American girl," she wrote, and Alice Dowling had assured her that Psaty had "a great deal of social charm, and she thinks I will like her." Mrs. Dowling, who had attended the civil marriage ceremony and hosted a hastily arranged reception, reported that Ted looked " 'wonderfully groomed and brushed and tidy, and like the cat who swallowed the canary!' So we are very happy for him—and naturally *eager* to see the lady!" A few days later, she informed her mother that a letter from Ted had arrived stating, " 'I can well imagine your doubts and qualms. I can only say I am surer about this thing than anything I have ever done, and when you meet Ellen I think you will see why.' This sounds good!" Patty added.[7]

But within a month, the joy turned to gloom; almost three decades after being widowed by her renowned husband, Miriam Thayer Richards died in a Boston hospital after a long illness, removing one of the pillars of her daughter's existence and leaving her lonely and more dependent than ever on her husband for support.

In September, the Conants moved into a three-bedroom apartment on an upper floor at 200 East 66th Street; it would be their New York residence, with frequent interruptions, for the next two decades. It was a rental—Conant was suspicious of the real-estate market—that Patty appointed with New England colonial furniture (including an heirloom eighteenth-century grand-father clock) complemented by an assortment of artwork, ranging from paintings purchased in Germany to landscapes by William Trost Richards, and an abundance of bulging bookcases. Their view overlooked the midtown skyline, as yet unobscured by the skyscrapers that would be built later, and Conant could work in a small study that supplemented his Carnegie office.[8]

The family traumas had not disrupted Conant's plans for his fieldwork. He and his staff planned not only to swoop en masse into each targeted school, to observe classroom tactics, and to interview students, teachers, and administrators, but also to lay the groundwork for a massive publicity campaign, scheduling scores of press interviews, speeches, and television appearances. On October 3, he addressed a memorandum to his staff—"First Crystalliza-tion of J.B. Conant's Prejudices"—to elucidate his criteria for the survey.[9] And on October 4, the Russians orbited the world's first artificial satellite, and gave the country a new reason to pay close attention to his findings.

Even before the basketball-sized Sputnik was blasted into space, the national importance of Conant's endeavor was established by statistics show-ing the explosive growth in the number of Americans attending and finishing high school since World War II, a number that figured to rise even faster as the "baby boom" generation being raised in large measure in the mushrooming postwar suburbs passed puberty. Existing Cold War tensions assured, moreover, that any reassessment of U.S. education would be judged in a context set by the ideological conflict with the Soviet Union. But Moscow's latest triumph suddenly shot educational issues to the top of the national agenda. Coming a little more than a month after Nikita Khrushchev proudly announced that the Soviet Union had successfully test-fired an intercontinental-range missile—the Ameri-can tests had all been flops—Sputnik sparked a panic in the United States that exceeded that which the first Soviet atomic bomb had created eight years earlier, for it suggested that the USSR had edged ahead of the United States technologically, and might attain a superiority in ballistic missiles that would render the country vulnerable to a thermonuclear Pearl Harbor.[10]

There was a loud outcry that the United States should immediately plunge vast new resources into educating and training young Americans to become better scientists and engineers than their counterparts in Minsk and Kiev. Eisenhower favored a less dramatic response than some of his more unnerved advisers, and so did Conant. Though the Soviet scare might encourage support for improving public high schools, he told Eisenhower in a telegram to resist the pressure (from his successor as Harvard president, Nathan Pusey, among many others) for a "crash" science education program. "Those now in college will before long be living in the age of intercontinental ballistic missiles," he suggested Ike tell the nation. "What will be then needed is not more engineers and scientists, but a people who will not panic and political leaders of wisdom, courage, and devotion, with capacity for solving intricate human problems. Not more Einsteins, but more Washingtons and Madisons." The president read Conant's telegram carefully and said, "That represents my thinking exactly."[11]

The Eisenhower administration also solicited Conant's counsel on its new, fairly restrained proposals to "strengthen our educational system in its capacity to meet critical national needs"—he generally approved of them, especially their provision for increased foreign language instruction ("the greatest single weakness in our public high school curricula today"), but cautioned against special salary increases for science and math high-school teachers, which might hurt morale, and recommended instead greater expenditures for all teachers. "I only wish you were down here," wrote Robert Cutler, Eisenhower's national security adviser.[12]

But Conant was by now an itinerant educational investigator: traveling (with an aide lugging his bags) by bus, train, plane, and automobile, recording observations by Dictaphone in hotel rooms, drafting on the road on scrap paper or napkins in greasy spoons and saloons, downing orange juice in the morning to protect his throat and screwdrivers in the evening to salve his nerves, he visited fifty-five high schools in eighteen states during the 1957–58 academic year, speaking to thousands of teachers, administrators, and students.[13] And he had no desire to return to the realms of missiles, nuclear weapons, or national security which he had left behind. George Kistiakowsky discovered as much when he tried to interest his old friend in the activities of the President's Science Advisory Committee (PSAC), the souped-up version of the science advisory panel that Conant had served on under Truman, which, in the immediate aftermath of Sputnik, Eisenhower elevated from the Office of Defense Mobilization to the White House. In an effort to palliate popular demands for superior military hardware, Eisenhower had also named PSAC's chairman, MIT's president Killian, as his science adviser (a move Truman had resisted). Given the high regard in which he and Eisenhower held him, it was only natural for Kistiakowsky, PSAC's foremost missile expert, to see if Conant wanted to take an active part in PSAC's work, but, Kistiakowsky later recalled, he "told me he wasn't going to get involved, that we scientists, engineers, were doing harmful things to the country by pushing technology too much. He was really unsympathetic to what we were doing."[14]

Conant was reassured by a January 1958 lunch at the Harvard Faculty Club with Kistiakowsky, who, he recorded in his diary, had given him "an earful of confidential information about the real low down on rockets." Though Kistiakowsky was gloomy about the immediate situation, Conant saw no cause for panic: "By 1961 we should be O.K. (he says) and I didn't believe Soviets will outplay us politically in the meantime."[15] Though pleased that Sputnik had put educational reform on the front burner, he resisted alarmist assertions that Russian education was outpacing America's—queried by a Senate investigator whether such claims were valid, he replied that he had not supposed that one could get a better engineering education in the world than at MIT or a better scientific education than at the leading American universities.[16] In April 1958 he chided some commentators who had "spoken in desperate terms about training scientists and engineers"—an allusion that apparently included, among others, navy admiral Hyman G. Rickover, the developer of the nuclear-powered submarine, who argued that Russia's technological progress forced drastic changes in the nation's educational system and called for the establishment of separate academies to train youngsters of "superior intellect" who could lend their brainpower to the national defense.[17]

Conant's commitment to public education's democratizing function made him abhor and reject such a step, and he resolutely insisted on educating high school students of all social and intellectual backgrounds in the same comprehensive curriculum, under one roof and mixing them in the same homerooms, even if they were segregated for instruction on particular subjects. Yet the popular mood, as well as his own meritocratic sensibilities, influenced him to lavish more attention on the problems of identifying and educating the academically talented in subjects directly related to national security needs— "those boys and girls who have the ability to study effectively and rewardingly advanced mathematics, foreign language, and tough courses in chemistry and physics"[18]—than on what should be done for those who did not quickly display or embrace such skills.[19] The National Defense Education Act, enacted by Congress in 1958 and reluctantly signed by Eisenhower, took a step in this direction, appropriating new federal aid for high school educational programs in fields relevant to national security.[20]

Though Conant was glad that he had started his project for Carnegie early enough to avoid accusations that it had been undertaken in response to Sputnik,[21] his final report attempted to tap into the fears that the Soviet advance had provoked and channel them constructively. *The American High School Today,* published in February 1959, listed twenty-one steps to help the country's educational system reach the point where it could provide a positive answer to the study's central question: "Can a school at one and the same time provide a good general education for all the pupils as future citizens of a democracy, provide elective programs for the majority to develop useful skills, and educate adequately those with a talent for handling advanced academic subjects—particularly foreign languages and advanced mathematics?" Of the fifty-five high schools he visited, only eight came close to meeting his definition of a "comprehensive high school." Still, aside from a controversial idea to consolidate smaller public high schools (those with fewer than one hundred students) into larger "comprehensive" ones offering a broader range of advanced academic opportunities, Conant expressly disclaimed any need for "radical alteration in the basic pattern of American education" and urged only incremental, though specific, changes ranging from increased attention to guidance counseling and testing to additional advanced courses in foreign languages, math, and science to a compulsory twelfth-grade class for all students on "American problems" to enhance "the development of future citizens of our democracy who will be intelligent voters, stand firm under trying national conditions, and not be beguiled by the oratory of those who appeal to special interests."[22]

Conant's mixed platter was tasty enough for an American public ravenous for solutions to what was widely perceived as a dangerous crisis in the country's educational system. Helped by Conant's massive prepublication barnstorming publicity campaign, a retail price that was cheap even by 1959 standards ($1), high praise from reviewers and educators, and, most of all, a clear, accessible, yet well-documented and authoritative prose style, *The American High School Today* immediately gained oracular status, becoming the first number-one best-seller on educational issues since the far flashier *Why Johnny Can't Read* (Rudolf Flesch, 1955). It made front-page news in papers around the country, sold 170,000 copies in a year and a half, and inspired an adulatory *Time* magazine cover story—his third—on a man it hailed as "The Inspector General" of U.S. education.[23]

There were cogent objections expressed—alarmists thought he didn't go far enough to turn high schools into breeders of rocket scientists, some professors of education thought his ideas "were too conservative, if not plain reactionary,"[24] and some humanists wished he had devoted more attention to students who opted for "soft" subjects such as art and literature. Conant had urged extra guidance counseling for talented female students, but John Kenneth Galbraith, who praised his "extraordinarily informative and generally elegant report," couldn't help wishing that more could be done:

> Your reference to the soft courses chosen by the girls also brought up something which has been troubling me for years. I have been on the Board at Radcliffe and have also been watching the Radcliffe undergraduates in the classes. These people do good and sometimes superlative work and then promptly on graduation get married and disappear into what is called home life. This is assumed invariably to be superior to any form of organized intellectual activity. The women's colleges have endless rationalizations for this—most of them created by people whose own unmarried state has given

them a sense of inferiority. Frankly, I don't think it is something that can be rationalized or should be. You show that the same problem, in a much more serious form, is afflicting the high schools.

I wonder if part of the problem isn't biology but simply bad propaganda. Especially since World War II all sorts of people have been extolling the conservative values of motherhood, the home, and the avoidance of the intellectual and rebellious spirit. It is a kind of brood mare doctrine, and I have discovered that even some of the girls, when you talk with them about it, are decidedly uneasy. They are not wholly enamored of a life in New Rochelle. But they feel they must conform. . . . I am coming to favor a stern attack on home and motherhood.[25]

Conant admitted to Galbraith that he had treated the subject of girls' education "gingerly" to avoid arousing strong emotions (and, he added, "I certainly don't wish to complicate my educational recommendations by a 'stern attack on home and motherhood'").[26] In fact, aides had had repeatedly to remind him to "mention girls," with one later writing to him, "Only careful editing saved you at all from the clutches of the feminists!"[27]

To the president of Bennington College, Conant frankly acknowledged that his criteria for reforming the public high schools, tilted toward male-dominated "hard" subjects, had been determined by his perceptions of what America required to wage and win the Cold War:

My case for the recommendation for the academically talented was very largely based on national need. If we were not living in such a grim world, I doubt that I should advocate the high school program I recommend in my report. From the academically talented will come the future doctors, lawyers, engineers, scientists and scholars, as well as . . . business executives. . . . These professional people will be 97 percent men.[28]

Statistics confirmed these concerns that the Cold War's priorities were hampering women's educational opportunities—even as overall college enrollment leapt dramatically in the early postwar era, from 1.5 million in 1940 to 2.3 million in 1950 to 3.6 million in 1960, the proportion of women attending college and obtaining postgraduate degrees declined until the trend was reversed in the 1960s.[29]

The American High School Today did spur some changes, focused in a constructive way the furor over Sputnik, and stirred debates on educational reforms for years; viewed from the long term, however, its influence has been questioned. The most thorough study of Conant's report concludes that despite providing "some direction and a considerable boost in morale to America's aimless, dispirited high schools," and despite receiving widespread acceptance and praise from educators, schools lagged in implementing its specific recommendations (except for those concerning the academically talented), and its lasting impact "on the content or structure of American

secondary education" was nil.[30] And, although he had deliberately resisted
the temptation explicitly to link his suggested reforms to Sputnik, a Carnegie-
sponsored (and Gardner-endorsed) report on American high schools published a quarter-century later judged it to have been "symbolic of the time."[31]

Conant's new career as a "trenchant but friendly critic" of U.S. public
schools,[32] a continuation and capstone of his lifelong romance with Jeffersonian
democracy as applied to education, was clearly well launched. Throughout
1958 and into 1959 he kept up an intense pace of speeches, interviews, and
related appearances to promote his educational ideas—by his own estimate
he had addressed seventy thousand people in twenty-one states in one
year—and as *The American High School Today* appeared he was reshuffling
staff and making plans for a second study that would concentrate on two
areas neglected in the first: secondary education in the suburbs and in the
inner cities.

But his candid admission that the "grim world" had crucially influenced
his educational recommendations pointed to the fact that, despite his new
vocation, he still could not escape another side of his life—as supporter
and occasional maker of the U.S. government's Cold War policies. That he
still valued this service was clear in his many speeches on Germany, particularly his Godkin Lectures and his part in rebutting George Kennan's
controversial proposals, in his ongoing correspondence with John Foster Dulles
and other former State Department colleagues on German issues, and in the
alacrity with which he responded when, in late 1958, a string of menacing
developments drove Conant and other Cold War loyalists back to battle
stations.

The year (which Eisenhower later called the worst of his life) brought
increased tensions on several Cold War fronts—more clashes with Communist China over the Nationalist-occupied offshore islands of Quemoy and
Matsu, charges by Democrats and some Pentagon officers that the Soviets
were opening a "missile gap" as they raced ahead in ICBM production and
technology, unrest in Lebanon that prompted Eisenhower to send in the
Marines, a revolution in Cuba that propelled Fidel Castro to power. Illness
also cast a shadow on Eisenhower's foreign policy—John Foster Dulles was
operated on for colon cancer, the postsurgery diagnosis was not optimistic,
and his resignation if not death seemed imminent.[33]

But the most serious danger, the one that raised the threat of a superpower war, arose over a subject close to Conant's heart. On November 27, a
new Berlin crisis began when Khrushchev announced that he planned to sign
a peace treaty with East Germany within six months, giving the GDR control
over Western access routes to West Berlin, which he suggested vaguely should
be incorporated with East Berlin into a "free city." The Soviet ultimatum,
which validated Conant's forebodings of a few years earlier, immediately
raised fears of another blockade, and seemed clearly designed to pressure the

West into recognizing East Germany or else face expulsion from West Berlin, whether by economic strangulation or military force.[34]

The Western powers immediately announced that they would not sign an agreement that would have the effect of abandoning West Berlin, but fractures in the Alliance quickly emerged as French officials said that "low level" recognition of the GDR would be preferable to war. The ailing Dulles made plans to fly to Brussels to try to formulate a unified NATO response, but before leaving he solicited the views of the three previous American overseers in Germany: Lucius Clay, John McCloy, and Conant, all three of whom urged Dulles to stand firm and to warn the Russians that interference with Western access to Berlin would be a *casus belli.*[35] None recommended a more aggressive response than Conant:

> I am still firmly of the opinion that no negotiation of any sort should be opened with the German Democratic Republic. And I hope that first public statement of the Western position will make it plain that we will use force if necessary to insure that West Berlin remains under the control of the present freely elected government, and that likewise we will use force if necessary to insure that the city is supplied *as at present.* In private communication to the Soviets, I would suggest spelling out in detail what this statement means. I would favor stating that the day Kruschev [*sic*] carries out his threat and declares that his government has no further responsibility in the [East German] Zone or in Berlin, we would be prepared to occupy with our troops as much of his Zone as would be necessary to insure free passage of goods to Berlin by rail and autobahn. We would consider that his abdication of authority over the East Germans leaves us no choice but to exert our authority of [over?] as much of Germany as is necessary for us to fulfill our commitment to free Berlin.

If East Germany stopped at merely harassing traffic to West Berlin and did not sever it entirely, Conant suggested that the United States back a full West German economic embargo against the GDR. But if it came to a "showdown" and the GDR blocked the flow of supplies to civilians in West Berlin, he hoped that East German soldiers "would have to be the first to shoot" at American forces deploying to seize access routes and as a result "public opinion in the U.S. and in the free world would be on our side."[36] Conant did not expect it to come to that: as in 1955, Conant was ready to risk war on the calculation that the Soviets would back down.

Eisenhower also thought that Khrushchev was bluffing, but for the next few months the crisis kept fears of nuclear war running high. By early 1959, many alumni of the Committee on the Present Danger considered the situation grave enough to reconstitute themselves in a new edition to back the administration's policies. In February, Conant turned down a plea from the Council on Foreign Relations director, Frank Altschul, to head a new citizens' committee, arguing that it would look like a CPD clone and not wanting to add another job on top of his full-time education research, which also caused him to turn down invitations from Eisenhower to join or head governmental commissions on foreign economic aid and "national goals." Tracy Voorhees, citing "the Russian offensive," also sought out Conant to argue the case for a new citizens' group "to alert the country to the need to respond adequately to the truly all-out war which is being waged against us—and at present so successfully."[37]

Encouraging Voorhees to continue his efforts, Conant fully agreed on the need to encourage Eisenhower to stick to a firm line, seeing any concessions as opening the door to another Munich. Although Khrushchev's looming May 27 deadline for a Berlin settlement prompted more calls for four-power negotiations, he believed that

> as far as Berlin is concerned and access to that city, we should merely reject the Soviet proposals, and reject them with a bang! To do anything else would be to yield to threat and if we start doing this, there will be no end to our appeasement. Perhaps Mr. Khrushchev is trying to see how far he can go with us before we lose our nerve. Since I am convinced that a global war would be as disastrous to him as to us, I do not see why we should be the ones to be worried about his aggressive actions.[38]

In mid-March, Conant analyzed the motives behind Khrushchev's gambit in a speech to the Canadian Club of Montreal (he was in the city to visit his son, Jim, who had moved there three years earlier from St. Louis to take a job as a spokesman for the Canadian branch of the International Paper Company). Conant attributed the Soviet pressure tactics to concern about the abject economic conditions and stunted political status of the East German "puppet regime," which was a "very poor show indeed" alongside the thriving Federal Republic. This humiliating contrast was accentuated in Berlin, the only place where the Iron Curtain opened to permit residents of the Communist East to escape via subway to the West. "Why don't the Russians close the exit, the escape hatch?" Conant asked. Because it would be too embarrassing, it would deprive East Berlin of ten thousand skilled workers from West Berlin, and most of all, it would be a tacit admission that they had given up on absorbing West Berlin into the GDR's capital. Instead, Moscow was now acting out of desperation, taking the world to the brink of war because "things have gone so badly for them in their Zone over the years that they'll either have one day to give it up, which is, after all, the hope of all of us who want reunification of Germany and peace and freedom . . . or else succeed in bullying the Western powers into getting out of Berlin and giving their regime prestige and status."[39]

Conant told his audience that it was neither helpful nor appropriate for citizens to presume to advise the government on such sensitive questions as how to respond to a new Berlin blockade, though he naturally did not feel constrained from privately transmitting his own recommendations to senior policymakers. Two days later, with Dulles hospitalized again, he communicated his own evolving prescriptions for how to handle the situation to Assistant Secretary of State Livingston Merchant, one of the few senior State Department aides with whom he felt comfortable. Wanting to ensure that the United States won world opinion to its side in any military clash, he advised "Livie" that Washington should step up regular supply flights to West Berlin in advance of a possible blockade, because "the only way to insure that the GDR was the aggressor would be to have them interfere with the traffic in the air which would involve shooting. Road blocks are not the sort of interference which could be dramatized as military aggression, but forcing an airplane down certainly is."[40] This revised advice fit better with the president's own thinking, for Eisenhower had reacted skeptically to a provocative recommendation from the Joint Chiefs of Staff that the United States send a division of troops up the autobahn at the first sign that access routes to West Berlin were being blocked—an act that would force the Soviets to "put up or shut up" and possibly provoke an all-out war.[41]

Conant was invited, following a long conversation with Eisenhower, to serve as a consultant to the National Security Council Planning Board for its yearly "review of basic national security policy," a one-day survey of highly classified materials that was likely to focus on the continuing test of wills over Berlin.[42] He was making plans to visit Washington when in late March, just before his sixty-sixth birthday, a crisis of another sort suddenly arose: a "small nodule" was discovered in his thyroid gland, and emergency surgery was necessary to remove it. Fortunately, the tumor proved benign, and after a few days in the hospital Conant was able to return to work on a slightly reduced schedule, although he was forced to cancel his meeting with the NSC.[43]

Soon another family crisis hit. In mid-April Conant received a frantic telephone call from Norice Conant in Montreal; for the first time since the end of the war fourteen years earlier, James Richards Conant had suffered a nervous breakdown, a relapse of the condition brought on by his submarine experiences. Conant immediately canceled plans for a visit to England and made arrangements to see his daughter-in-law and hospitalized son. Doctors gave a guardedly optimistic prognosis, and discharged him in two months, but the improvement was temporary.[44] Over the next year and a half James R. Conant had two additional serious breakdowns, and left Montreal to enter a psychiatric clinic near Baltimore for prolonged treatment. To complicate an already nightmarish situation, Canadian immigration authorities repeatedly threatened to expel Norice Conant, who was having difficulty coping not only with her husband's condition but with raising three young children, forcing Conant to intercede to find legal help.[45]

The collapse of the Conants' elder son, in whom they had invested so many fond hopes, came as a shattering blow, both to his father and especially to Patty Conant: she had thrived on the elaborate social and intellectual adventures of the Bonn diplomatic scene, but her brittle psyche had already been bruised by the death of her mother and the suicide of her second brother. It also worsened relations between Conant and his other son, Ted, who dated his resentment on this subject to the day in 1945 when he visited his brother in a San Francisco hospital and had been, first, shocked to discover the severity of his condition, and, second, angry at his father for concealing it from him; from then on, he recalls, he assumed that he wasn't getting the full story from his father on sensitive family matters.[46] Though hidden from public view, over the next two decades the disintegration of James R. Conant—manic episodes, hospitalizations, treatments, broken marriages, troubled children—took a profound and constant mental toll on his extended family. And lurking beneath the crisis of the moment were questions that were painful to think about, let alone raise: What, or who, was to blame for this terrible turn of events—plain bad luck, the wartime submarine traumas? Defects in parenting? Or, most hauntingly and explosively, as the Conant sons started their own families, were genetic factors at work, spreading a predisposition to mental illness?

In the spring of 1959, some of the tension surrounding the Berlin crisis lifted as Eisenhower opened the door a crack to negotiations with Moscow, and hinted at concessions in talks taking place between Soviet and American scientists in Geneva on a nuclear test ban. Khrushchev stopped invoking his six-month deadline, and instead agreed to a "big four" foreign ministers' meeting in May to review the situation (they also ended up attending Dulles's funeral; he was replaced as secretary of state by Christian Herter). The talks dragged on for weeks, were recessed and resumed in August, and led to no noteworthy results on Germany or Berlin, but the relaxation of tensions was such that Eisenhower invited Khrushchev to tour the United States and meet with him at Camp David when he came to the UN General Assembly session in September.

The crisis temporarily went into remission, but the swerve toward negotiations only made Conant and others opposed to any serious compromises on Berlin or East German recognition even more apprehensive (Adenauer was particularly upset). "Once the Soviets are successful in creating a situation where we are forced to talk to Pankow [the GDR] about what goes on in Free Berlin," he cautioned Merchant, "then we have started down a slippery slope which would end by Berlin being almost worthless from our point of view even if we had free access . . . the Soviets would have won!"[47] Sensing a continuing need to buck up the public's nerve for inevitable future Cold War confrontations, Conant signed on in June as a founder of a venture called the Committee to Strengthen the Frontiers of Freedom—chaired by Vannevar Bush, vice-chaired by Henry Wriston, organized by Tracy Voorhees, and assembling a CPD-like cast of centrist internationalists from Lewis Douglas and Averell Harriman to Samuel Goldwyn and Dean Rusk. Like the earlier interventionist groups, this one accorded with Conant's philosophy of urging "the American people to have confidence in their elected officials and their technical advisers on matters which cannot be discussed openly . . . this may be contrary to the old fashioned teachings of popular democracy, but I have always been a believer in representative government rather than in town meetings!"[48] As one would expect, Voorhees regularly consulted with Conant, and had originally planned to resuscitate the "Committee on the Present Danger" until Conant suggested the new name.[49] And, like the CPD and CDAAA before it, the nominally private and independent CSFF received behind-the-scenes support from the executive branch; Secretary of Defense Neil McElroy unofficially but warmly welcomed Conant's efforts to build support for the administration's Mutual Security Program, and Eisenhower used it occasionally at sensitive moments to catalyze public support.[50]

Conant had one interesting disagreement with Voorhees and the committee; while fully in accord with their campaign to rouse public support for increased U.S. foreign military and economic aid, he disagreed that such assistance was worthwhile in the case of poor nations "irrespective of the Communist threat." Frankly, he told Voorhees, he did "not buy this line *at all*"—it was just "emotive language" designed to "appease the woolly headed international do-gooders!" Why not "get hardboiled and realistic about our Mutual Security Program" instead of worrying about a "land of make-believe" in which the Communist threat did not exist.[51] But he kept those qualms private, and concentrated in his public statements on rallying public support behind tough Cold War measures. "I am afraid the job of shaking the country out of its complacency is something that can't be done officially" because of the partisan preelection atmosphere, Conant wrote to Jim Killian in late 1959, but perhaps Voorhees's new venture could help.[52]

His own contribution to shaking the country out of "complacency" was his November 12 speech ("The Defense of Freedom"), upon receiving the Woodrow Wilson Award for Distinguished Service, an address he deliberately "slant[ed]" to aid the Voorhees committee's program.[53] Though the "missile gap" was later revealed by U-2 overflights to have been an illusory, mirrorlike reflection of the actual overwhelming *American* nuclear superiority at the time, Conant sternly intoned that "freedom in this year 1959 is as severely threatened as any time in our history" by the external threat of Communist aggression. The need for military spending was "obviously as pressing as though we were engaged in an actual armed conflict." And in the suspenseful Berlin standoff, he cautioned, Americans must not let themselves be wheedled into a "step-by-step surrender." They must bolster Washington's efforts to stay abreast of Soviet military advances during the imminent "age of rockets and thermonuclear bombs." An invulnerable U.S. thermonuclear retaliatory force, he declared, was the "one essential for our survival as a free nation" and the "number one priority in terms of national budget and the national effort."[54]

Foreshadowing the doctrine of "mutual assured destruction" (MAD) championed in the 1960s by defense secretary Robert S. McNamara, Conant stipulated that adequate "retaliatory power" meant a deterrent force capable of absorbing a Soviet thermonuclear first strike and still delivering enough H-bombs to ensure that "at least three-fourths of the industrial complexes of the Soviet Union would be utterly destroyed." Yet, while rejecting calls for a ban on nuclear testing, he continued to insist that his goal remained the same as it had since he had given up hope for international control of atomic weapons—not military victory, but a "thermonuclear stalemate" until the Cold War thawed.[55]

Conant's speech, widely covered in the press and reprinted by the CSFF, offered clues to a significant evolution of his private thinking about nuclear weapons, one that stemmed from the fast approach of the missile age, the frightening dilemmas of devising a usable strategy to defend West Berlin, and his growing disenchantment with Dulles's "massive retaliation" and "brinkmanship" doctrines—a dissatisfaction he shared with analysts such as William Kaufman, Bernard Brodie, and a young Harvard historian named Henry Kissinger (who had popularized the results of a Council on Foreign Relations study group on the subject in a best-selling 1957 book, *Nuclear Weapons and Foreign Policy*). At a time when U.S. war plans contemplated an immediate all-out nuclear strike on the Soviet Union and its allies at the outset of a conflict, Conant stressed that the choice facing an American president in a crisis "should *not* be between surrender and large-scale war." It was necessary, therefore, "to maintain for the foreseeable future a strong, modern, flexible military force which could respond to local aggression anywhere on the far-flung frontiers of freedom."[56]

Conant deliberately eschewed any specific indication of how the "horrifying nature of the new weapons" had influenced his view of the Berlin crisis. But the next day he sent a more explicit confidential "supplement" to "Red" Dowling, who had just been named the new U.S. ambassador to West Germany. After suggesting that he consult Tracy Voorhees and George Kistiakowsky (who had just replaced Killian as Eisenhower's science adviser), Conant offered his views on the subject "that will be foremost in your mind, namely, what is the military response to aggression in Berlin?"

Here I am frank to say my own thinking has undergone a change because of the change in the weapon situation which is just around the corner. In the age in which I am looking forward to when the airplane is no longer of significance, I do not think it possible for the United States to respond to local aggression by a thermonuclear attack. Our rockets will be aimed primarily at the heavily industrialized areas of Russia, because this is the point at which our retaliatory power must be made effective if retaliatory power is required. And I believe if the Russians know retaliatory power is possible from a truly invulnerable system, we shall never have to use it. But you will quickly see that this whole concept reverses completely Mr. Dulles' original idea of responding with massive retaliation to local aggression. Such ideas, to my mind, are dead as the dodo. I hope we shall have a larger, more effective, and flexible military force for the entire free world, particularly for NATO. This is the force which must be counted on in a Berlin crisis. I used to say that the Berlin garrison only had to be ready to fight long enough to insure an atomic war in order to keep the Russians from attacking. I now think this is not in accord with the situation as it will be in a few years. I should rather say that they have to be prepared to fight long enough to rouse world opinion as to the dangers of starting a global conflict, and it is world opinion rather than thermonuclear bombs which is the main deterrent to local situations such as might be created in Berlin.[57]

Conant assured Dowling that he remained just as committed to standing firm in West Berlin and refusing to kow-tow to Khrushchev or the GDR—just the previous month, he had visited West Germany, along with Acheson, McCloy, Kissinger, and other notables gathered by the American Council on Germany, to express the U.S. establishment's solidarity with Adenauer.[58] But he now shied away from risking all-out thermonuclear war over Berlin, preferring another airlift instead of a frontal military response to a new blockade ("though I know this idea is abhorrent to Jack McCloy, General Clay, and some in high authority in Washington"), and advocating new contingency planning to emphasize a local, limited nuclear response should the Communists then fire the first shot and hostilities break out. "Unless the Russians brought up reinforcements on the continent, a local 'old fashioned' war would result which, with very small yield nuclear weapons, could result in anything but a triumph for the Communists and the GDR forces," he reasoned. "It is true that Berlin itself could not be long defended, but the possibility of considerable ground warfare on the continent of Europe, even assuming no thermonuclear exchange takes place, would be a highly unpleasant aspect for the dwellers in the Kremlin who regard themselves and their successors as the rulers of a Communist world."[59]

In opting for a strategy to use nuclear weapons against attack military forces rather than Soviet cities should there be an assault on West Berlin or West Germany, Conant was in tune with shifting intellectual currents. In West Germany itself, suspecting American reluctance to go to war in Europe if it meant the destruction of U.S. cities, Adenauer's government was now trying to obtain tactical nuclear weapons for its own forces. And Conant's emphasis on "flexible" military forces for the United States—which harkened back to his earlier alliance with those, like Oppenheimer, who feared the H-bomb would worsen the "imbalance" in U.S. military plans and had wanted to "bring the battle back to the battlefield"—also presaged the Kennedy administration's embrace of "flexible response" in dealing with Berlin when the crisis flared up again in 1961 and planning for nuclear weapons use again became a live issue. By then, however, Conant was engrossed in trying to alert Americans that another kind of explosive material was nearing critical mass.

In the 1960s, the conflagrations that Conant feared were liable to consume America's cities were ignited not by Communist missiles but by simmering racial fury. In *The American High School Today,* Conant had not addressed the predicament of black students in the segregated schools of the South, consciously neglecting to mention, as he later acknowledged, "that certain schools I visited were comprehensive only in so far as white youth were concerned."[60] (He feared that he would be asked at a press conference or other public session about his failure to include southern schools or deal with the segregation issue, though the question never came.)[61] But in his second major Carnegie-funded study he set out to remedy that omission. This time, when he went on the road again, rather than the relatively placid, middle-sized communities that had previously been his focus he and his staff visited high schools in New York, Chicago, Detroit, St. Louis, and other large cities, most of which had seen large black migrations from the rural South since the onset of World War II.

In part, Conant's new willingness to tackle the controversial subject of race and education was inspired by revulsion at the conditions in black-only schools and the contrasts with comfortable white schools he had encountered while researching his first study for Carnegie. But there were other reasons for Conant to take a more visible and outspoken interest. The civil rights movement was transforming the country: the 1954 *Brown v. Board of Education of Topeka* Supreme Court decision had outlawed segregation in public schools; Rosa Parks's refusal to move to the back of a Montgomery, Alabama, public bus the next year sparked a tumultuous months-long boycott that catapulted the Reverend Martin Luther King, Jr., to national prominence and the presidency of the Southern Christian Leadership Conference. In 1957, just as Conant was launching his research, Congress created a Commission on Civil Rights and the issue seized headlines as racist Arkansas officials, including Governor Orval E. Faubus, tried to block the integration of Little Rock schools, as mandated by the Supreme Court; Eisenhower reluctantly had to call in National Guard paratroopers to protect black students from white mobs. And in the first months of 1960, as Conant researched the inner city's schools, a sit-in by young blacks at a lunch counter at a Woolworth's department store in Greensboro, North Carolina, set off a wildfire of activist protests in southern states against officially enforced public segregation; King himself was arrested in Atlanta in late October, causing a sensation in the final weeks of the presidential campaign when Democratic candidate John F. Kennedy phoned in an expression of sympathy while Vice President Nixon confined himself publicly to a "no comment."[62]

These and other events pricked at the nation's conscience, heated tempers, and raised citizens' awareness of the civil rights issue, turning it into an acceptable subject for national discourse. Equally significantly, for Conant, they drew international attention to the most egregious shortcoming of American society, vividly depicted in images of blacks being segregated, beaten, and lynched by racist southerners, just as the Soviet Union courted anticolonial movements in Africa and Asia and dazzled the world with Sputnik.

Conant finished work on his study in June 1961, and *Slums and Suburbs,* published in September, presciently and passionately underlined the appalling conditions of poverty, racial discrimination, endemic violence, social disintegration, and hopelessness that later in the decade would indeed fuel the fires of black rage blazing in Watts, Newark, Detroit, and other cities. "I am convinced we are allowing social dynamite to accumulate in our large cities," he warned; he likened the "mass of unemployed and frustrated Negro youth in congested areas" to the "piling up of inflammable material in an empty building in a city block."[63] For the first time in his public career, Conant embraced the racial issue as a central rather than a peripheral concern, depicting himself as a committed partisan of racial justice since childhood:

> Since I am going to be completely frank about Negro education in the largest cities, it may be well to take a few paragraphs to set forth my own interpretation of the distressing history of the Negro in the United States. At the outset I must make it plain that I approach the delicate and complex problem of interrace relations with the background of a one hundred per cent New Englander. My mother, who remembered the Civil War, used to say that as a child she was brought up to think Negroes were if anything better than white people. It is as difficult for me to imagine myself in the position of the well-educated Southerner who in the 1850s argued for Negro slavery as it is for me to understand how intelligent Germans in the 1930s ardently supported Hitler.[64]

The United States had been saddled from birth with "a congenital defect—Negro slavery"—a "curse from which we are not yet free,"[65] and now it faced an undermining of its position in the Cold War if it failed adequately to confront the racial issue. "I do not have to remind the reader that the fate of freedom in the world hangs very much in the balance," Conant told readers. "Our success against the spread of communism in no small measure depends upon the successful operation of our own free society." Especially disconcerting was the high rate of unemployment among black youths under twenty-one (then at seventeen percent), more than twice the rate among whites the same age. "These young people are my chief concern, especially when they are pocketed together in large numbers within the confines of the big city slum," he wrote. "What can words like 'freedom,' 'liberty,' and 'equality of opportunity' mean for these young people? With what kind of zeal and dedication can we expect them to withstand the relentless pressures of communism? How well prepared are they to face the struggle that shows no signs of abating?"[66]

Conant's urgent call for change extended beyond the classroom—it frankly recognized that the educational afflictions of black America could not be alleviated without creating new opportunities for economic and social justice. In the spirit of the "Great Society" programs that were to characterize Lyndon Johnson's presidency later in the decade, he called for major federal programs to create jobs and affordable, livable housing in the inner cities, and for massive and speedy federal aid to inner-city public high schools. These increased funds would be used not only to improve conditions for students, build and renovate buildings, buy textbooks, and lure and train more and better teachers, but to help high schools assume additional responsibilities in poor black communities by hiring more guidance counselors who would help youths aged sixteen to twenty-one to develop "marketable skills" and to locate employment even if they had already dropped out.[67]

Slums and Suburbs devoted far more space and ardor to the predicament of young urban blacks than to the far less troubling puzzles involved in educating college-bound suburbanites. After recounting tales of seeing inner city schools plagued by gang warfare, where teenagers slept through classes because they had been kept up all night by "incredibly violent family fights and horrors through the night," Conant asked comfortable readers to "ponder the contrast between the lives and education of the boys and girls in the neighborhoods I have been describing. It is after visits to schools like these that I grow impatient with both critics and defenders of public education who ignore the realities of school situations to engage in fruitless debate about educational philosophy, purposes, and the like. These situations call for action, not hair-splitting arguments."[68] In conclusion, Conant implored the American people "to take prompt action before it is too late."[69]

Attentive readers and reviewers could not but notice that Conant's latest book had an intensity and immediacy lacking from his earlier pronouncements on education. "For the first time," the *New York Times* education reporter observed, "the reserved, understating New England scientist and university administrator appeared moved by anger. He had seen the underprivileged slums and the prestige-obsessed overprivileged suburbs. The sight offended his sense of justice as much as his ideology."[70]

Conant incorporated his concerns about the racial problem in his recommendations to the Kennedy administration. As vice chairman of the President's Committee on Youth Employment, he repeatedly prodded Secretary of Labor Arthur J. Goldberg to make a study of youth unemployment in black ghettos in the country's five largest cities the group's top priority.[71] Conant's sympathetic view of the difficulties faced by African-Americans in exploiting America's vaunted social mobility was also apparent in a letter in late 1961 to the head of the Educational Policies Commission:

> I feel that there are great differences between the hillbillies from the South, the Puerto Ricans, and the Negroes in our large cities. . . . Although the

white slum dweller is temporarily disadvantaged, there will be many in such families who will find a place in society by climbing rapidly the conventional American ladder. I believe the same is true to a considerable degree for the Puerto Rican except in one city where they are congregated in large numbers, namely, New York. The Negro, on the other hand, runs up against racial discrimination at every turn. This racial discrimination in regard to employment is the main problem I believe.[72]

Slums and Suburbs made front-page news around the country, and was generally lauded for shining a bright yet cool light in a neglected corner of America that desperately needed attention, and recommending timely and well-considered measures. Tragically, however, it—and Conant personally—failed to attract support from the constituency most concerned and most in need of allies: black educational leaders, whose ambitions were growing and whose timetables for change and progress were shortening. The success of the Greensboro sit-in movement had thrust to the fore more militant, younger activists who favored a greater reliance on confrontational (but nonviolent) civil disobedience—a tactic Conant had always instinctively disdained even when he agreed with the objective, as in the teacher's oath disputes of the mid-thirties[73]—and put a premium on casting off the shackles of segregation, not pursuing gradual reforms through Congress or the courts.[74] They appreciated Conant's effort to tug at white America's conscience, and welcomed his advocacy of more federal money to improve urban schools and to raze discriminatory hiring barriers so as to accelerate a "drastic change in the employment prospects for urban Negro youth." They were less enthusiastic at Conant's criticism of them for compounding the problem by refusing to face hard realities about the situation, and for showing hypersensitivity on questions of terminology (e.g., resisting terms like "Negro slum").[75]

But, most galling of all, they and other civil rights leaders scented a whiff of an old-time "separate but equal" doctrine in Conant's dismissal of the concept of transporting students out of homogeneous racial districts in order to break up de facto segregation.[76] Conant had interpreted *Brown v. Board of Education* to mean that only de jure public school segregation was barred, and that therefore single-race schools resulting from "voluntary" neighborhood population patterns were neither illegal nor "morally wrong." Nor, he went on, despite the court's ruling that "Separate educational facilities are inherently unequal," need they necessarily be inferior, especially since there was no convincing evidence that race automatically determined intelligence or academic performance (a hypothesis Conant deemed a "fallacy" after extensive consideration). Therefore, "satisfactory education can be provided in an all-Negro school through the expenditure of more money for needed staff and facilities," and cities which were "yielding to pressure" to have "Negro children attend essentially white schools" were "on the wrong track." Aside from the "quite insoluble" transportation problems involved, to rely on busing to force integration meant taking an "extremely defeatist view of Negro education in the large cities"—and he urged those who were "agitating" for busing "to accept *de facto* segregated schools as a consequence of a present housing situation and to work for the improvement of slum schools whether Negro or white." Besides, it wasn't education's responsibility— approvingly quoting a school superintendent's comment that he was "in the education business" and not that of redressing "the consequences of voluntary segregated housing." The "real issue," he concluded, was "not racial integration but socio-economic integration."[77]

In the abstract, and for the long term, Conant made a plausible argument— some tenets of which, ironically, accorded with the views of black radicals like Malcolm X who scorned "token integration" and instead urged blacks to practice racial "separation" and concentrate on building up their own businesses, schools, and neighborhoods.[78] But it was disingenuous and unrealistic of Conant to ignore the obvious political and human reality that "de facto segregation" and racism were connected, and that integrating schools was one valid way, albeit a difficult one, to force affluent suburban white Americans to pay attention in a hurry to the need to improve the "de facto" situation in inner cities, and to educate those urban poor young blacks likely to grow old awaiting concrete changes in the nation's "socio-economic situation."

Conant counted on better-supported inner city schools ultimately to allow the meritocratic selection process to compensate for economic and social disadvantages for black youths, rather than trying directly to overcome structural segregation. But his critics, from civil rights groups like the National Association for the Advancement of Colored People to educational organizations like the Public Education Association, found unconvincing his distinction between de facto and de jure segregation and saw no reason why integration and measures to improve slum schools could not proceed simultaneously; some even seemed to question Conant's sincerity. "He is really arguing for a Northern urban version of separate but equal education," said Kenneth Clark, a professor of psychology at City College in New York. "I couldn't disagree with Mr. Conant more."[79]

As one study later concluded, *Slums and Suburbs*'s prescriptions amounted to "tinkering with, but not challenging, the racial separation" in American society. Peering "through the lens of an establishment leader," justifiably fearing a violent conflagration, he hoped to convert the urban school from a combustible tinderbox into "an institution of containment," steering slum youths into jobs while suburban schools concentrated on boosting talented individuals toward college.[80]

Trying to accommodate his critics, and undoubtedly influenced by both advances in the civil rights movement and the first tremors of inner city upheaval in the intervening three years, Conant thoroughly revised his section on "De Facto Segregation" when *Slums and Suburbs* was reprinted in paperback in 1964. "I was clearly wrong," he now admitted, "when I suggested several years ago that busing high school youngsters around a big city was impractical."[81] Conant no longer tried to justify opposition to busing on the basis of *Brown v. Board of Education,* mentioning simply that the Supreme Court had not yet resolved the question of whether segregated schools resulting from segregated housing patterns were illegal. And he still had grave doubts about busing, and opposed it for elementary school children. But in the reissue of *Slums and Suburbs* and in *Shaping Educational Policy,* published the same year, he now grudgingly endorsed transporting youths in grades 9–12 to "comprehensive high schools" as a last resort to achieve integration, pledging fealty to the principle that "the more schools we can integrate the better."[82]

But, having modified his view to accord with the moving mainstream, Conant beat a hasty escape from the race issue, and made no effort to come to terms with his critics. Five years later, in *My Several Lives,* Conant rued that failure—a successful reconciliation with the alienated black leaders, he thought in retrospect, might have created what should have been a natural alliance. Instead, he decided that he was now "persona non grata" among them, shelved work on the race issue, and shifted his energies to other topics. By the end of the 1960s, he had come full circle and endorsed "bussing wherever possible" to attain mixed-race classrooms in segregated cities, but, with the ghettoes already burning and Martin Luther King dead by a sniper's bullet, Conant sensed that his belated conversion hardly mattered. *Slums and Suburbs* had been a valiant, salutary, prescient show of concern and emotion, but it had been too little, too late, to cut the fuse of the "social dynamite" he had revealed.[83]

In the midst of Conant's own awkward encounter with racial sensitivities, he and other members of the East Coast establishment were reminded of the changing times and mores in an uncomfortably personal way. The dispute flared suddenly in the first weeks of 1962 at an unlikely setting: the Cosmos Club, the all-white, all-male Washington fraternity house for Washington's intellectual elite, founded in 1878 and now housed in a turn-of-the-century French Renaissance mansion on Massachusetts Avenue, and Conant's inevitable rendezvous point for meals and meetings in the capital since the war. During the first year of the Kennedy administration, Conant's Cosmos membership had already involved him in a quintessential rite of generational passage to mark the new era in Washington. Though he had voted for Nixon in 1960, Conant easily adjusted to the presence in the White House of John F. Kennedy, who, after all, as a Harvard undergraduate had broken with his father in 1940 when he publicly commended Conant's vigorous interventionism.[84] Kennedy had, moreover, vigorously revived the Washington-Harvard connection initiated by FDR at the outset of the New Deal: so-called action-intellectuals with Harvard ties, especially economists and military strategists, streamed down from Cambridge to stock the new administration, some, like

McGeorge Bundy and Arthur Schlesinger, Jr., taking senior positions on the White House staff, and they admired their pre-Pusey leader.[85]

Now, twenty years after presenting Kennedy with a diploma, the Harvard president emeritus helped arrange for the forty-two-year-old leader of the United States to receive the Washington establishment's equivalent stamp of approval: membership in the Cosmos. A month or two after Inauguration Day, Conant chatted with John Kenneth Galbraith, who had accepted the new president's invitation to go to India as his ambassador (the same job Conant had turned down), about informally asking whether JFK would accept nomination. Kennedy said yes "with pleasure" and with the proviso that his participation in Cosmos activities "would be at best episodic," and on May 8, 1961, Conant, seconded by Galbraith, formally nominated the new president for membership, citing his authorship of *Profiles of Courage* ("a best-seller which has won high praise from professional historians") and his "record of service to the country, first in the Navy, then as Congressman, now as President."[86]

As Conant moved to propose JFK's name to the admissions committee, he received a letter from the journalist Raymond Gram Swing seeking his support for another Cosmos Club application. Swing was raising the name of Carl T. Rowan, now serving in the State Department and "undoubtedly the ablest Negro journalist in this country," and he urged Conant to endorse Rowan's nomination, especially if he shared the view that it was "time the Club had a Negro member." Conant had never met Rowan and, as he wrote Swing, had "frankly never heard of him," but he also agreed that the Cosmos Club needed to break the color line; to the admissions committee he wrote admitting his ignorance of Rowan's credentials but expressing the hope that his application would be approved provided Swing's description was warranted. "I am frank to say that I think it would be a splendid thing if an outstanding Negro should be made a member," he added, and it was "unfortunate that there is no Negro member at the present time."[87]

Swing and the State Department official Rowan was replacing, Edwin Kretzmann, had urged Rowan to apply to the Cosmos (despite the $1500 entry fee) because they were confident that the Cosmos Club would transcend the behavior of certain other, ostensibly less erudite Washington establishments; the openly segregationist membership policy of the Metropolitan Club caused attorney general Robert F. Kennedy and several members to resign, and the president to comment at a news conference that he "personally approved of his brother's action."[88]

Their confidence in the Cosmos Club's enlightenment diminished that summer, however, after learning that one member of the admissions committee (who, naturally, insisted that "I count Negroes among some of my best friends") had decided to vote against Rowan in deference to the sensibilities of friends who professed to become "physically ill" in the presence of members of his race. And on January 8, 1962, after taking its customary good time, the admissions committee formally rejected Rowan. Not only were his sponsors enraged, but Galbraith immediately resigned, too—withdrawing the still pending application of President Kennedy, who personally telephoned Rowan to express support against "those bastards."[89]

On January 10, the *New York Times* broke the story. Suddenly, the segregation issue had intruded from the inner cities to the inner sanctum. In the next few days, members chose up sides, announcing that they might also resign (Edward R. Murrow, Harlan Cleveland, Howard K. Smith, Bruce Catton, J. P. Warburg, and Jerome Wiesner, Kennedy's science adviser) or stay and fight against segregation (New York governor Nelson A. Rockefeller, senators Ernest Gruening and John Sherman Cooper); others kept a silence that could be interpreted as a tacit assent to blackballing Rowan, who later wrote that one of the episode's "most fascinating aspects" had been "to watch prominent white Americans grapple with their consciences as they tried to determine how to respond to their club's action."[90]

Conant's name was conspicuously absent from the news reports. As soon as Rowan's application was rejected, Wiesner had called Conant's office, but he had already left that day for a vacation in the Virgin Islands. From New York, a secretary relayed news clippings and messages from friends, and, somewhat apologetically, informed him of the unfortunate coincidence that she had, just before reading the *Times* article, sent in his $55 membership fee for 1962, a payment she admitted "may be misinterpreted."[91] Grateful that his isolation gave him an excuse to sit on the fence for a few days, Conant tried to monitor the brouhaha at long distance, instructing his staff to sound out trusted friends in the club like Smithsonian Institution director Leonard Carmichael (who felt it was all a misunderstanding, that Rowan had been rejected on merit) and Carnegie Institution of Washington president Caryl Haskins (who felt racism was to blame, but was not yet ready to resign). "I must decide whether I agree with Gov. Rockefeller or Amb. Galbraith before I reach Washington on Jan. 23," Conant wrote an aide from the Buccaneer hotel in St. Croix. Though loath to take a public stand, he wrote that if the decision against Rowan were not reversed, he would have "no alternative to resigning."[92]

To his relief, the Cosmos Club membership voted on January 15 formally to bar racial or religious discrimination, quieting the controversy. The next day his secretary wrote to him: "You could not have picked a better time to leave the country!"[93]

After *Slums and Suburbs*, Conant spent the 1961–62 academic year preparing a study on the education of American teachers—a subject that he described as a " 'can of worms' and a hornet's nest combined," but one that was in truth far less incendiary than race relations[94]—and also a broader, more personal and autobiographical private document for the Carnegie Corporation that summed up his findings after four years of educational investigations. Sketching out the conclusions of a skeptical "cranky New Englander" who believed that "free men would do well to take their problems piecemeal, bit by bit, rather than hunt for unifying principles," Conant reaffirmed the findings of his earlier studies, again adhering to his educational credo of fostering "equality of opportunity" through public education. He again prescribed strong national leadership to alleviate the brewing racial crisis in the cities—"Unless there is a radical change in the attitude of management and labor, fair opportunities for employment of Negroes can be found only through the use of Federal funds"—but confessed uncertainty over two issues, the education of women and "aesthetic judgments" in scholastic curricula (he was mystified by the appeal of modern or abstract art or theater, or of avant-garde, nonlinear documentaries like the ones his son made).[95]

Conant's final report for Carnegie, completed in the spring of 1962, freed him to consider new challenges. Nearing the age of seventy, he had considerable cause for satisfaction, secure in his status as best-selling authority and public commentator, *éminence grise* of education and science, the target of an unceasing barrage of honors, awards, degrees, invitations to speak or sit on prestigious boards and commissions. The six books produced in rapid succession by "the Schools' Mr. Fixit" after returning from Germany had, the *New York Times* declared, an "unequalled impact," selling more than half a million copies and dominating debate on American educational policy.[96]

Yet, despite the accolades, on the personal plane these were difficult times for Conant. Age was beginning to catch up with him, causing him to curtail his speaking schedule; furrows deeply lined his brow and his neatly groomed hair turned from salt-and-pepper to a distinguished white; since 1958 he had needed to wear a hearing aid in his left ear. In the summer of 1961, while summering in New Hampshire, Conant had a sudden, shocking reminder of mortality when his old friend the physicist Percy Bridgman, dying of cancer, committed suicide by shooting himself in the head, an event made even more haunting by Conant's arrival on the scene soon afterward in response to a phone call from the scientist's family.[97] And the strain of dealing with the ongoing woes of James Richards Conant and his fragmenting family was even more painful, especially for Patty Conant, as the Conants found personal meetings with their mentally ill son difficult to cope with.[98] "At the end of [1961] we were in trouble," Conant later wrote in his diary. On Christmas morning, the Conants were in Cambridge at Ted and Ellen's, when a telephone call from Montreal brought word that Norice Conant, wife of James Richards, who had already been confined because of mental illness, had "gone all to bits," and the two children were in the care of neighbors. After going through the motions of enjoying the party, Conant canceled appointments and spent the next two weeks flying to Montreal and New

York, talking to lawyers and psychiatrists, and hastily arranging for Norice's hospitalization and for his law firm (the Fiduciary Trust Company of Boston) to set up a trust fund for his elder son's children, who were, for the moment at least, effectively orphaned. James, meanwhile, was in a "telephoning mood" from his hospital bed, as often happened during this period, and in the months that followed continued to suffer "ups and downs." Even though he was able to resume work at a Baltimore newspaper and pay occasional visits to the children, Conant feared he was still "on the manic side."[99]

This trying period in Conant's personal life coincided with professional worries about the reception likely to greet his report on teacher education, which he knew would be harshly critical and which was slated for publication in 1963—he anticipated bitter criticism and "could see trouble ahead"[100]— and with uncertainty about what to do for his next project. As a sign of respect Kennedy officials vainly cajoled him to accept the post of U.S. Commissioner of Education, but settled instead for his protégé Frank Keppel.[101] And when John Gardner suggested after reading his final report to Carnegie that he write an autobiography, his reaction was sharply negative—both because of his characteristic disdain for introspection, and because he felt strongly that a "change of scene was necessary."[102]

Much to his relief, a new venture that combined an escape from the United States, a meaningful personal tie, and service to both education and U.S. foreign policy goals serendipitously presented itself when Conant and his wife made a private visit to Berlin in May 1962.

Conant had firm views on the need for the West to stand fast in West Berlin, and he offered no complaints on the way the Kennedy administration had responded to renewed Soviet bluster in 1961. At a summit conference in Vienna in June, Khrushchev had told the new American president that he intended by the end of the year finally to sign his long-threatened peace treaty with the GDR, an act that would hand over control of Western access routes to West Berlin. Grimly, Kennedy announced new military mobilization and civil defense measures and issued statements making clear that the West would go to war rather than abandon West Berlin. A first-class war scare ensued, which only impelled skilled East Germans to escape to West Berlin at an even faster rate, rubbing salt in the wound that so irked Khrushchev and GDR leader Walter Ulbricht. On the night of August 13, 1961, the Communist leaders took drastic action, erecting temporary barriers around the western sectors of the city to cut off the embarrassing refugee exodus; soon the barriers were reinforced and the world saw the rise of the Cold War's companion symbol to the Bomb: the Wall. Actually, the effect of the erection of the Wall was to defuse the crisis. Severing Easterners' escape routes to West Berlin—which Washington had always seen as a possible step, and which it had no intention of resisting by force—had been a substitute for cutting off the West's access to the city, which raised a high risk of escalation.

But this was little consolation to furious West Germans, and especially to those in West Berlin, where rage was accompanied by disillusionment with the United States for failing to knock the Wall down, and by an intensified feeling of isolation.[103]

Eager to raise the morale of the surrounded West Berliners (and Washington's damaged standing), officials at the U.S. mission and the city government, headed by Lord Mayor Willy Brandt, conjured up a series of "viability projects" to develop West Berlin's cultural attractions and to demonstrate the West's long-term commitment; Washington would help with the funding. One such proposed project was a Pedagogical Center that would serve as a center for studies and training on elementary and secondary education, and when Conant and his wife visited in May 1962 as guests of their friends the Dowlings, a West Berlin education official solicited his "moral support" as honorary president of the project's planning committee.

Saddened and disturbed by his first sight of the Wall, as well as by a "wave of anti-German sentiment which is sweeping the [United States]" stemming from a spate of recent historical publications about the Nazi era,[104] Conant agreed to this request, and back in New York he approached the Ford Foundation to see about funding. The frightening U.S.-Soviet confrontation in October over Khrushchev's deployment of nuclear missiles in Cuba—an act some analysts interpreted as another chess move in the stalemated battle of wits and wills over Berlin—only strengthened the arguments he was hearing about the need to show steadfastness toward Russia, and when Conant and his wife visited Berlin the following month for a German-American conference, he answered yes when Brandt asked if he would take up residence in West Berlin for a year to take personal charge of planning the Pedagogical Center.[105] Besides allowing him to promote cherished educational and foreign policy ideas, Brandt's proposal also neatly fit his covert agenda of escaping the critics of his forthcoming teacher education study, and, more importantly, distancing his wife from the turmoil of grappling with her disturbed son and family—whose troubles and expenses were largely left in the hands of lawyers and trustees. Patty had kept up her interest in German affairs since leaving Bonn, having written a scathing magazine critique of Communist mind control tactics in the GDR and a generally favorable appraisal of West Germany's willingness to confront its Nazi past in textbooks,[106] and Berlin may well have beckoned as a welcome safe harbor that would put an ocean between her and the family's stresses. Shortly before leaving, Patty planned a seventieth birthday party for her husband in New York, inviting both sons and his sister Esther; but the day before, they learned that James Richards Conant had suffered another "setback" and was confined to a "S–P closed ward"; she canceled the party, and her husband spent the day "reading trash."[107]

In June 1963, their living expenses underwritten by the Ford Foundation,

Jim and Patty moved into a residence provided by the West Berlin government at Wachtelstrasse 7 in Dahlem, the same suburb where at the Kaiser Wilhelm institutes Conant almost forty years before had visited Fritz Haber and where during World War II German scientists had worked on weapons for the Nazis. As they unpacked, Berliners were marking the tenth anniversary of the June 17 anti-Communist uprising, and Conant had turned down an invitation from the *New York Herald Tribune* to reminiscence because, he noted privately, he would have been forced to note the disagreements over how to respond to the revolt that had flared at the time between the United States and its allies, who were "really afraid the new Eisenhower Administration wanted to risk an atomic war for the sake of making trouble in the Satellite states." Surveying the local political scene, Conant was struck by the transformations in the past decade—unemployment had almost vanished, the SPD and CDU had essentially identical foreign policies, and deaths had caused an almost total change in leading personalities. The next month, he was scheduled to give a speech in honor of the martyrs who had plotted to kill Hitler in July 1944, and who were instead executed in the *plotz* where the rite would take place. "The city is full of ghosts," Conant reflected.[108]

Ironically, the highlight of what would be Conant's two-year stay in Berlin, punctuated by frequent quick trips home to keep up his educational obligations and consult with his staff in the United States, occurred only a few weeks after he arrived. On June 26, 1963, a pleasant, sunny Wednesday, the Conants joined throngs of Berliners clogging the downtown area trying to catch a glimpse of John F. Kennedy as he made a triumphal visit to the city. In the midst of a waving, clapping mass at a corner of the Kurfürstendamm, the main commercial artery, the Conants stood too far back to see the president as his motorcade sped by. Though the size and anticipation of the crowd prompted one German standing near him to crack, *"Der Führer komment,"* Conant thought the cheering "much less than we expected."

They felt no such disappointment later in the day, however, recording a "tremendous ovation" from a mass of several hundred thousand listening to Kennedy's *"Ich bin ein Berliner"* speech outside City Hall. Conant found the speech inspiring and the reception "all we could expect," and in recounting the event in his diary could not resist pointing out that Kennedy's steadfast defense of Berlin as the front line of freedom had only echoed his own unyielding stance as envoy to Germany not so many years before:

> The President went very far in committing himself emotionally to the Berliners. "If one wants to understand the modern world let him come to Berlin." Excellent and moving sentiments with which I not only heartily agree but could claim to have anticipated him in their formulation (before the wall).

Flying to Ireland that night, Kennedy told his speechwriter he never expected to have another day like that as long as he lived, and as he wrote in his diary about that same moment, Conant, too, shared the excited afterglow common to many who had been present: "The President's Visit!" he began his account. "What a day!"109

The Conants had planned to stay in Berlin for fifteen months, until October 1964, but delays in getting the Pedagogical Center started, combined with pleas from city officials and the U.S. mission to extend their residency—as "visible proof that a former U.S. Ambassador and his wife are ready to throw their lots in with the Berliners for a considerable period of time"—caused the Conants to move their departure back to June 1965. Conant did not really mind the extra time in Berlin, for it offered a chance at leisure to resume his on-again, off-again romance with a country that had pulled at him since childhood. Still, after his customary intensive personal investigations through reading, visits, and interviews, he was depressed to find that despite all the efforts at reform since the war, German secondary schools and universities were still dominated by conservatism, tradition, and overly close relations with the state. In a stern private summation to a Berlin professor, he concluded that the "conservatism inherent in the tradition which was formed in the late 19th century has been reinforced by the events of the Nazi period and the immediate post war experiences with the occupying powers," leaving the educational system little changed in its essential structure from what it was before World War I and unresponsive to changing conditions. He quoted a colleague's saying that "a good past is positively dangerous if it makes one complacent about the present." "I hope you, Professor Becker," he added, "will not take it amiss if I say that this remark applies, it seems to me, to the present state of German educational and applies with particular force to the German universities."110

Conant found greater satisfaction in West Berlin's gradual recovery from the shock of the Wall, noting that "in erecting . . . and administering it brutally (and stupidly) the Communists have made this our propaganda attack against themselves. So Berlin as an element in the cold war still serves its purpose." And, like other frustrated and angered Westerners in the city, he gradually resigned himself to the new status quo, despite periodic outrages as East German border guards slaughtered people trying to flee. He recognized that the U.S. commitment to defend and supply West Berlin blocked a "rapprochement with the Kremlin" and could "understand why those who wish for disarmament so feverishly wish Berlin would dry up and blow away," but reasoned that the city "simply personifies" the problem of a divided Germany which would persist in any case.111 To his surprise, that problem remained dormant during his stay, and even disturbing international events like China's acquisition of nuclear weapons and Khrushchev's fall and replacement by a group of hardliners led by Leonid Brezhnev failed to disturb the seeming calm that had settled over the divided city. "From the time I arrived until very recently Berlin has been as relaxed as Atlantic City!" he wrote the American ambassador in Bonn on his departure in mid-1965, though from the latest reports of "cold blooded murder on the canal, the helicopters and the threats to Berlin traffic" he sensed a new "period of tension."[112] Perhaps the palpable Communist presence even added a welcome sense of purpose and menace, not only evoking his term as high commissioner but faintly echoing his heady trip to England during the Blitz. Only if you "have lived here," he wrote friends in the United States,

> and heard the Russian jet planes overhead breaking the sound barrier day after day and see[n] the sky often full of their vapor trails can you realize the meaning of the phrase "an island of freedom in a sea of tyranny." We came here a year ago May because we believed holding free Berlin was important and could only be accomplished if Berlin flourished culturally, was recognized as a culture center and attracted people from all over Europe. My belief is unchanged. I am convinced the Pedagogical Center will eventually serve a highly useful purpose for German education and be an attractive magnet for educators all over Europe. When it does, it will be serving the free world (and thus the U.S.) by strengthening Berlin as a cultural center.[113]

Though Conant lived outside the United States for two years, he was by no means forgotten. On July 4, 1963, John F. Kennedy recognized his singular status as educational and scientific statesman by announcing that he would present Conant the Presidential Medal of Freedom, the highest award given by the government to civilians. Conant was making plans to attend the ceremony in Washington, which was set for noon on December 6, when he participated in late November in a five-day conference for teachers from foreign countries. On Friday evening, Conant attended the closing banquet at the Hotel Kempinski. About eight-thirty, as the guests were finishing their meal, the manager walked over to Conant's table and whispered in his ear, in German, that President Kennedy had been attacked and "very, very badly wounded." Conant asked him to tell him if more news arrived and "with a feeling of horror, some disbelief and anxiety" turned back to his neighbor to resume chatting about education. Inside, he churned with fears: assuming the attacker was a "fanatic white supremacist," had political chaos broken out in the United States? Did another Cuban crisis loom? Were the gains of Kennedy's visit to Berlin canceled? A few minutes later the manager returned, made "a despairing gesture with his hands," and whispered: "*Er ist tot*" — He is dead. Conant's face showed the bad news, prompting an inquiry from a neighbor; he went to the hotel lobby to hear the RIAS radio report for himself, then returned and confirmed the news, urging that his table companions keep it to themselves "until the social evening would break up." But the host rapped his knife on his glass and announced what had happened. All stood in silence, then left. Conant was so shaken that to words of sympathy—he and Patty were the only Americans present—he could answer with only a broken word of thanks.

The next few days were a blur of memorial meetings, candle- and torchlight processions, renamings, signing of condolence books, and a new rush of horror and outrage at the shooting of Lee Harvey Oswald while in the custody of the Dallas police (who had been "less than thorough," thought Conant, though he was contemptuous of East German propaganda broadcasts blaming both murders on an ultra-right-wing conspiracy). On a bright, cool Saturday morning the day after the assassination, the Conants gathered with other Berlin and allied dignitaries for a service at a U.S. Army barracks, and although the military band had had no time to practice, the sound of taps played by two buglers "went right through our hearts." Never close to Kennedy or entranced by his family's mystique, Conant was surprised by his own intensely emotional reaction:

> I found myself asking myself why I, a cold reserved New Englander and not a personal friend, should have been so overcome last night and at the ceremony this morning. I felt and still feel the way I did the afternoon of Pearl Harbor. I don't know the answer myself but almost all of free Berlin feels the same way. Probably I was (and still am) responding to this Berlin situation. The meeting between Kennedy and the Berliners had been so hearty and so reassuring last summer that the Berliners' present stunned mood of grief has to be witnessed and felt to be understood.[114]

Conant guessed that in light of the circumstances the December 6 ceremony would be canceled, but he soon learned this was not the case and flew to Washington. Two weeks to the hour after Kennedy's death, Lyndon B. Johnson bestowed the Medals of Freedom as scheduled, except for an additional medal posthumously awarded to the slain president. Conant, who stopped by to say hello to Bundy, Schlesinger, and other acquaintances, found the atmosphere at the White House a "mixture of sadness and festivity."[115] Robert F. Kennedy, like his dead brother a Conant-era graduate of Harvard College, sent a poignant note of congratulations:

> I just want to add my congratulations to you on receiving the Presidential Medal of Freedom.
>
> As you know, President Kennedy was intensely interested in the awards and I couldn't help but reflect throughout the ceremony how pleased he would have been to have participated.
>
> I also know that he must be happy and very proud to be included as a recipient of the Medal of Freedom in such distinguished company.[116]

Johnson did not wait long before unveiling, in his first State of the Union address in January 1964, an ambitious program to combat America's domestic ailments. The "War on Poverty" envisioned a massive new commitment of government funds and energy to tackle the structural problems of American society, including the deplorable conditions of the inner cities. Combined with the 1964 Civil Rights Act that Johnson pushed through with the aid of Kennedy's memory, it was, at least in part, a belated apprehension of the "social dynamite" that Conant had so cogently and urgently warned of several years earlier in *Slums and Suburbs,* and so it was only natural that the man Johnson put in charge of organizing the antipoverty assault — Sargent Shriver, director of the Peace Corps and, now, of the Office of Economic Opportunity, created that August — should turn to Conant as he began to marshal his forces. Familiar with Conant's educational prowess from heading the Chicago board of education, Shriver later recalled that he desired the former Harvard president to lend his prestige, intellect, and experience, to be the administration's "strategic thinker on education," to "lead and direct the troops."[117] The logic of recruiting him was only reinforced by the first of the "long hot summers," when rioting broke out in Harlem, Rochester, and several New Jersey cities. That 1964 was an election year gave Johnson extra incentive to show that he was making serious and powerful efforts to tackle these problems (during the campaign he had pointedly labeled education his number-one priority) — and aside from Conant's unrivaled national stature he also had, as Bill Moyers recalled, "marquee value in the world Johnson admired."[118]

Thus it was that in September 1964 Conant received a telephone call from his old friend Frank Keppel, still serving as commissioner of education, sounding him out as to whether he would be interested in accepting what Conant later described to John Gardner as "a full-time administrative job directly responsible to Sargent Shriver in charge of the educational aspects of the campaign against poverty." But Conant answered negatively on four grounds — that he was "too old for an administrative job," that the "educational matters involved were only on the periphery of my main interests," and that he was committed to attending some conferences in the United States on teacher education and to staying in Berlin until the following June. Distinctly unimpressed, Keppel told Conant that his stated reasons didn't amount to much, and that Shriver himself would soon call to try to convince him to sign on. A few hours later the phone rang again, and, as Conant told Gardner afterward,

> Shriver gave an eloquent succinct statement as to the importance of the job and why I was the only man in the whole United States who could do it. He explained I would have all manner of administrative and other assistants so it would not be a difficult administrative task but rather a job of explaining to Congress and the public of what was involved. (Just what the program is to be is still a mystery to me.) He asked if I would come to Washington to talk with him and the President so that he could explain more and I could understand the significance of his request.[119]

Shriver's offer opened the possibility of yet another major challenge for Conant, one that, despite misgivings, he might have been tempted to accept. At age seventy-one, he was still a year younger than Henry Stimson had been when he accepted Franklin Roosevelt's offer to become secretary of war in 1940. But to Keppel and Shriver, Conant did not mention what were probably equally, if not more, serious considerations than the ones he cited—the turmoil in his family, in particular the pressures that Washington's fish-bowl atmosphere would put on his wife; his trying experiences serving as an administrator at Harvard and as an underling to Dulles; and, given the likely predominance of the civil-rights issue, his bitter experiences with black leaders over *Slums and Suburbs,* which were likely to resurface if he took such a high-visibility post despite his more positive recent statements on busing. Planning a visit to the United States earlier that year, Conant had told John S. Hollister not to bother arranging TV or radio interviews during his stay. "All one would get would be questions about the Negro problem, and whatever I said would make me more enemies than friends," he wrote. "So I would like to avoid publicity."[120]

So despite more entreaties from Shriver, Conant held his ground, and the most he would agree to was to be a part-time consultant. After meeting with Shriver during a visit to the United States in December, Conant was named to Shriver's fourteen-member National Advisory Council "to represent the public in the operations of the war on poverty," along with, among others, Galbraith, child specialist Benjamin Spock, National Urban League executive secretary Whitney Young, and Mrs. Robert S. McNamara.[121] His work on that panel supplemented the influence Conant already had in the White House educational policy-making machinery by virtue of his ties to Johnson's Task Force on Education, which was chaired by John Gardner (who had also led JFK's task force on the same subject), who collaborated closely with Frank Keppel, among others, and consulted regularly with Conant; the panel's report, not surprisingly, included key aspects of Conant's longstanding program—the urgency of increasing federal aid to public education, special support to poor areas, special programs for talented youths in foreign language, math, and science—and led to the Elementary and Secondary Education Act passed by Congress in early 1965.[122]

After returning to the United States in mid-1965 he was, indeed, consulted from time to time on educational matters, and his ideas continued to influence policy though his friends and protégés; Keppel remained as the education commissioner, and Carnegie's Gardner soon got the call to become Johnson's new Secretary of Health, Education, and Welfare.

But Conant's turndown of Shriver's offer signaled that the inevitable, so long forestalled, had arrived—his public career was drawing to a close. That winter, at the urging of educational associates, he began making arrangements to hire assistants for his next and last major project: his memoirs.[123]

EPILOGUE

"Winter for the Conant Family!"

Any doubts about Conant's decision not to take on a major new burden disappeared in the summer of 1965 during a farewell tour of France at the end of his two-year European stay. One night in Avignon, after feeling short of breath during a tiring day of sightseeing, he thought he was going to suffocate and tossed and turned until Patty gave him a sleeping pill. She guessed that he had asthma and a hotel doctor prescribed medicine for an allergy attack, but after taking a train to Paris he still felt too weak to walk more than a block and again feared suffocating during a sleepless night. Now a doctor diagnosed an abnormal heart rhythm, and on June 14, after a fit of vomiting, Conant was taken by ambulance to the American Hospital, where he spent the next two weeks undergoing intensive tests and receiving intravenous medication. At the end of June he flew to New York, and immediately checked into a hospital. An attempt to stem the auricular fibrillation using drugs failed, and Conant read a James Bond novel and Gar Alperovitz's *Atomic Diplomacy* as he waited nervously for several days to find whether doctors would try "electrical methods." Meanwhile, Patty, who had been visiting regularly, came down with a sore throat and went in for her own checkup. On July 5 Conant learned that the examination had revealed "something wrong in her lower intestine" and an immediate biopsy had been scheduled. "Visited Patty as a fellow patient. She is in 1302 I am in 1707."

Two days later doctors discharged him on a regimen of digitalis and rest, and with the assurance that aside from rigorous exertion he could otherwise soon resume a normal life, but then came word about Patty: a malignant tumor, immediate major surgery, a permanent colostomy. That evening he saw Patty "as a *visitor,*" and sat with her as she received the news, then called relatives, ate alone in a hospital restaurant, and slept in a room at the Union Club. "What a *terrible* day," he wrote in his diary. "I am now the visitor who worries not the patient. Sick at heart."

At the top of the page for July 7, 1965 he wrote in large letters: "First Day of Winter for the Conant family!"[1] The next page: "2d day of winter. Winter came on fast! . . ."

* * *

Patty's cancer operation, on July 12, went well and doctors gave her an "excellent" prognosis, but it was in this shaken and debilitated state that the couple tried to resume their life in the United States. Within a week Conant had returned to educational work, leading a panel at a major White House Conference on Education in Washington, chaired by Gardner, who anticipated (correctly) that he was about to be offered the post of secretary of health, education, and welfare (the idea made no sense to Conant, who thought Gardner could do more for education at Carnegie, but he suspected his friend had "Potomac fever" and would accept; he did). James Richards Conant came from Baltimore for dinner with his father at the Hotel Lafayette, but their conversation revolved around finances—Conant grudgingly offered five hundred dollars as "a Xmas present in advance," and was disturbed by James's seeming lack of interest in his son's welfare or education; neither he nor Norice was mentioned.[2] On a more positive note, he soon learned that Patty's mood had improved, then received a cautiously optimistic interpretation of his own latest ECG results (the fibrillations were only "intermittent"); and soon he was energetically charting his future plans. He laid out seven possible activities for the next two years at lunch on August 13 with an official of the Carnegie Corporation, which between 1957 and 1965 had given upwards of one million dollars to underwrite his educational studies: involvement in an effort, conceived by Conant in *Shaping Educational Policy* and headed by former North Carolina governor Terry Sanford, to create an interstate commission to reach a national educational policy; "peripheral involvement" in a five-college New York State project to reform teacher training; membership on Shriver's antipoverty council; a revision of *The American High School Today* and a new book "on basic issues in American education" to be called *A Layman's Guide to Education;* membership on a Carnegie panel on educational television; and, in what promised to be the most time-consuming and difficult undertaking, the writing of his memoirs: two doctoral candidates supported by Carnegie were already hard at work gathering research materials, and Conant already feared that it would require several books to tell the story![3]

After vacationing in Aspen and Randolph before returning to New York, it was not until October, when their belongings arrived from Berlin, that the couple moved into their Upper East Side apartment, and Conant began full-time work on his autobiography. He was still not entirely comfortable with the idea, despite having sought and received permission from the Harvard Corporation to open his papers to the project despite its normal fifty-year secrecy rule, and having deputized Merle Borrowman, a professor at the University of Wisconsin who had assisted his teacher education study, to make an initial survey of his Harvard papers and to recruit two research assistants. While in Berlin, Conant had repeatedly turned over in his mind the issues involved in reconstructing his life, and the mystery of self-knowledge daunted him. In a 1964 essay, he confessed the impossibility of delineating "the set of beliefs which have guided my actions during the fifty years since I was graduated from college." Unable confidently to capture the motives behind his *own* actions, he doubted any biographer could do better:

> It is true that all through these years, four themes were entangled — chemistry, Harvard, Germany, and education. But I am completely unable to answer such questions as the following: Why did I leave chemistry for educational administration? Why did I retire from the presidency of Harvard at the age of sixty in order to become High Commissioner in Germany? Or why, after four years in Germany, did I choose to make a study of the American comprehensive high schools? Frankly, I am skeptical of writers who attempt to answer such personal questions. The answers provided seem to be rationalizations after the event. They may or may not provide entertaining reading, but in the light of modern psychology they can only be regarded as a form of fiction. Evidence of this fact is my recollection of the changing ways I have viewed my decision to accept the presidency of Harvard in 1933. The explanation I then had in my mind was not the same as I would have offered, say, in 1953, and today I would describe my motives in still a different fashion.[4]

Swallowing his misgivings, Conant went forward with the project, and from 1965 through 1969 his work on *My Several Lives* consumed the majority of his time. Under doctor's orders, he worked only half days, at first at his apartment and then at an office at 730 Third Avenue. Outside obligations he confined to a bare minimum, though he did occasionally advise state and federal governments on education, telling one interviewer that were he twenty years younger he would move to Albany as a full-time lobbyist to support public schools and reform teacher education in the New York State Legislature.[5] In November 1966 he resigned from Shriver's advisory council, citing doctor's orders to cut his workload.[6] But at the same time, at the urging of his son Ted, he participated in a Carnegie Corporation Commission on Educational Television (along with such notables as Ralph Ellison, Lee DuBridge, Edwin Land, Leonard Woodcock, and chairman James Killian). The topic was close to both Conants' hearts and minds: since chairing the Carnegie Committee on Scientific Aids to Learning three decades earlier he had been an advocate of developing new technologies for education, and in the aftermath of World War II had enlisted Harvard along with other local universities to help establish Boston's noncommercial educational television station, WGBH–TV, one of the flagships of public television, which later employed his son as a consultant.[7] But by the late sixties Conant had grown distrustful of what he called the "gadget-hunting age," and Carnegie invited him to join their study despite his candid caution that he was "extremely skeptical of the claims made for television as an educational medium and would be a deliberately difficult Commission member." In 1967, the Carnegie group issued a report hailing TV's awesome power to inform and educate, and recommending the establishment of a government-funded corporation to run a national public broadcasting system—and Conant sat silently at the press conference unveiling, despite having almost issued a dissenting report because of his fear that the Commission, in its eagerness to gain federal funding, had not included safeguards to insulate the new public television agency from political manipulation, a concern that was later vindicated in the Nixon administration.[8]

The writing itself Conant found an exercise in frustration. His memory was failing, and as his research assistants, William M. Tuttle, Jr., and Charles D. Biebel, scavenged the archival crypt in Cambridge, Conant repeatedly found that he had completely forgotten important episodes. "It's a race between my approaching senility and my pen," he told an interviewer in April 1967, "to see whether I ever get this stuff put together." Reluctant to engage in self-analysis, careful to excise topics or information that he thought might cause offense—they tended to be the same ones that might interest readers—Conant at first attacked the stories of his life as he had so many vexing educational issues, trying to place them in an orderly, rational form. It soon became clear, however, that he was ill-equipped to relate a human drama—when his editors at Harper & Row saw some of his early efforts, they advised him to "forget about tables of contents and outlines, and start telling a more personal story." Repeatedly they prodded him to delve into subjects like the atomic bomb and the Walsh-Sweezy case that he would rather have left untouched, but the task of managing a collective writing effort on a gargantuan, complicated narrative concerning an instinctively reticent subject proved unwieldy; for a time, Conant imagined putting out three books: the memoirs, a volume called *A Self-Appointed Investigator of the Public Schools,* and a book on his experiences as a diplomat in Germany. The project was further complicated when one senior editor resigned and another died. Through it all, Conant couldn't help wonder if there were a better way to spend his time. Like his friend Vannevar Bush, who was also being dragooned into writing his memoirs, Conant was uneasy with the memoirist's implicit imperative for self-aggrandizement, introspection, and candor, and the futility of trying to recapture the past; the more he wrote, the more he became "convinced that autobiographical writing is essentially writing a fiction."[9]

Conant's heart condition deprived him of some of his few true pleasures in life, the rigorous hiking, mountain climbing, and fishing that he so often had used to escape from the fray, to reflect, and to test himself. Customarily, the Conants would spend their winters in New York City and the warmer months in Randolph, New Hampshire, taking in the fresh air and surrounding mountains. But, under orders not to exert himself, now he could only gaze longingly at the peaks over which he used to clamber. "Jim is determined not to go back to Randolph—not even for a few weeks, he says, at the moment," Patty Conant told a friend in October 1967. "I think he can't bear to look at those peaks, and be condemned to the one easy walk in our neighboring woods, which bored him to extinction last summer."[10] (The next year, at the urging of their friend John S. Dickey, the president of Dartmouth College, the family purchased a new summer cottage in Hanover, closer to medical facilities and surrounded by gentler hills.) While in Manhattan, the couple's recreation revolved around meals, seminars, or other occasions at elite "gentleman's" or social clubs or groups—the women's-only Cosmopolitan (where Patty was a member), the Century Association, the Harvard Club, the Metropolitan, the Council on Foreign Relations. They derived scant real satisfaction from these social rounds, however. Another letter from Patty fills in a plaintive picture of these years:

> Jim leads a life centered on his mornings of writing, and this takes all his energy, and I feel I should stick around most of the time and do little chores for him and be on hand when he wants company. As you know, we have changed identities so often (and gone really from one lone wolf existence to another!) that we have not many social ties. Also, his deafness, which is a real trial, and his need for rest, early bed, etc., mean that we don't do much in the evenings. So it would be dreary for him if I went off gallivanting much.[11]

Even more painful than the infirmities of age and the somber duties of attending to the ailments and funerals of contemporaries, the most acute disappointment continued to come from family troubles, worst of all those of his elder son. His condition, and his father's view of it, improved somewhat after 1963, when he became one of the first patients in the country to be experimentally treated with lithium as a prophylactic to lessen the severity of the predictable, cyclical outbursts, rather than with antidepressants, which were given only after the symptoms of his manic-depressive illness appeared. According to the psychiatrist who supervised the program (and who had to bootleg the lithium until it was officially approved), James B. Conant enjoyed discussing the chemical aspects of the lithium used in his son's treatment not only because lithium promised to control the sharpest side effects better than previous methods but because he seemed more at ease dealing with the painful subject as a fascinating scientific puzzle rather than as a consequence of difficult family relationships. Moreover, the psychiatrist sensed distinctly Conant's relief at a revised diagnosis attributing his son's illness to hereditary factors, not poor parenting. The lithium helped, but considerable damage had already been done, and the danger of a relapse remained ever-present. Until his death in 1981 from complications following surgery for a broken hip sustained in a fall, James Richards Conant put in years of productivity as a journalist—rising to senior editorial writer on the *Baltimore News-American*— but continued to suffer from periodic "blow ups," as Conant put it in his diary, of manic behavior and wild mood swings that led to hospitalization and institutionalization, job and family disruptions, and the disintegration of two marriages, in both cases leaving troubled children and spouses in the wreckage.

While the Conants were in Berlin his erratic behavior had continued, leading to one incident in Randolph over the summer of 1964 when Ted and Ellen Conant had felt compelled to call the police to convince him to seek help. Institutionalized for long stretches, permitted to see the children for only limited visits, he was, in his father's words, "not too realistic" about what had happened. From his hospital in Baltimore, James wrote his father to ask whether he had been adopted. In 1964 he and Norice divorced, and his remarriage in the summer of 1966, at a time when he was under psychiatric observation (alternately on an in-hospital and outpatient basis), only occasioned another, sadly typical illustration of the strained ties between father and son. Conant, after learning of the impending nuptials shortly beforehand in a brief if friendly note from his son, quietly contacted his doctor in Maryland to discover if the bride was real or imaginary or whether she knew "what she was in for," and—although Ted received an invitation to be the best man— noted in his diary that "we were not urged to attend." That marriage, too, ended in failure, and phlebitis and other physical and personal setbacks made his remaining years a struggle.[12]

Theodore Richards Conant fared far better, carving out a peripatetic, zigzagging, and rewarding existence as a filmmaker, teacher, and foundation consultant in motion picture and television technology. Based in Cambridge during the sixties (where he worked for an educational foundation affiliated with WGBH), then spending several years in Japan and finally settling in New York City, Ted and Ellen raised two children, Jim and Jennet, who went on to start careers as a philosopher and journalist, respectively, after a sometimes rocky childhood.

But the most serious problems continued to derive from the sad saga of Ted's brother, and they tore at the already tenuous fabric of the extended Conant family. Faced with the pressures, Ted recalls, his father reacted by using "triage"—withdrawing from his troubled son in order to insulate his wife. Reviewing the Richards family history of psychiatric problems, Patty wrote to a friend in 1968, "I have my much more realistic and earthy spouse to thank that I turned out fairly normal!"[13]

The convulsions in the family were as wrenching and convoluted as those in the O'Neill dramas Conant preferred to modern existentialist theater. Perhaps seeking evidence that James Richards's troubles were an aberration, Jim and Patty Conant assiduously kept up the rituals of a close extended family, regularly scheduling holiday gatherings with Ted and Ellen and the grandchildren, and sisters Marjorie and Esther in New York or Cambridge at Thanksgiving and Christmas and over the summer in New Hampshire. Yet undertones of sadness, tension, and even resentment sometimes permeated outwardly festive occasions; Conant frequently left the worst news and hardest decisions unspoken—and in the impersonal hands of a Boston law firm that oversaw a trust fund that handled such matters as disbursement of family finances (a touchy subject when the question was whether to pay for a disturbed relative's hospitalization or education). Despite the regular clan meetings, Conant's handling of James Richards's psychological instability, family breakups, children's affairs, and other difficulties lengthened the emotional chasm separating him from his other son and daughter-in-law, who were distressed by what they regarded as an inadequately sensitive and compassionate response. Many years later, Ted and Ellen Conant vividly recalled the assessment of a prominent psychiatrist who said, after conversing with Conant, that he had never encountered a man of such daunting intellectual prowess who had such a blind spot in comprehending psychological problems or irrationality.[14]

This was by no means a unanimous view, however. A Johns Hopkins University psychiatrist who treated James Richards Conant for several years during the 1960s recalled that James Richards apparently did not feel abandoned by his father, and that James B. Conant's reactions seemed appropriately sympathetic and concerned if not particularly emotional. The elder Conant, with whom he was in frequent contact, struck him as a "totally rational person, not without caring or feeling but [whose feelings were] subordinated to his logical side."[15] Nor did James Richards Conant's three children resent their grandparents' handling of the situation, according to his daughter Clark Conant, whose empathetic analysis is informed by her training as a psychologist. Although Theodore Conant's son Jim was left with the impression that his grandfather had an "incapacity for intimacy" and related awkwardly to children,[16] Clark Conant has fond, warm memories of James B. Conant. Recalling her childhood, she describes a playful, tender side to him that few others besides Patty were permitted to see, including hours spent reading and acting out fairy tales, picking blueberries, building a play-world together in the yard, and hamming it up at the dinner table to entertain the kids. From a distance of three decades, Clark Conant harkened back to one incident (in August 1957) to illustrate why she believed her allegedly aloof grandfather was actually sensitive to a child's concerns. At about age eight or nine, Clark and her family were about to leave Randolph at the end of a summer vacation when she suddenly noticed, to her horror, that the family cat, a black Persian named "Shoufie" (a nickname derived from *choufleur*, French for "cauliflower"), was missing. A frenzied search failed to locate the feline, and the little girl grew desperate as her parents impatiently insisted that they had to leave for the long drive back to Montreal. When Conant learned what had happened, he furrowed his brow, reflected seriously for a few moments, and then quietly pronounced judgment: "Well, if the cat's lost, you can't leave until we find the cat." That settled the matter. For the distraught girl, her new ally's help was like the sun parting the clouds—and, happily, Shoufie soon turned up.[17]

The crises of later years were not so simply resolved, however. Reflecting on the disparate reactions to her father's prolonged illness and repeated setbacks, which strained feelings not only between Conant and his sons but between the two brothers and their families, Clark Conant takes a tolerant view: "Everyone in the family has a different and intensely colored view of what went on . . . almost as if each were watching a different movie." Even the actions (or inaction) on the part of Jim and Patty Conant that so incensed Ted and Ellen—the seeming effort to detach themselves from James Richards's travails—looked to Clark Conant like an understandable psychological self-defense mechanism rather than callousness or indifference. As she acknowledged, "all of us would draw a line, and take distance in some way."[18]

Clearly, no amount of Roshomon-like analysis of Conant's most intimate family relationships can yield a definitive interpretation or allotment of blame. Nor would it be fair, on the basis of necessarily limited evidence, to judge Conant too harshly, to accuse him of lacking a father's, husband's, or human being's normal capacity for love, pain, or concern. But it would be wrong to ignore or gloss over this sad, bitter, and trying part of his life that shadowed his private existence even as he ascended the heights of public prominence and esteem. Even if genes rather than deficiencies in parenting were responsible for his elder son's medical condition, Conant cannot be absolved from some responsibility for his family's woes. His ingrained meritocratic sensibilities (the same ones that once caused him to advocate a confiscatory inheritance tax) appear to have restrained him from showering upon his sons every financial or other advantage available to him; he had difficulties conveying and demonstrating the love he may indeed have felt for them; and at important junctures of his life he consciously chose to chase challenges and ambitions—to enlarge his own power and advance his career, to promote the ideas and causes he valued, and to extend the boundaries of knowledge and understanding—in the full knowledge that in so doing he was sacrificing the time, energy, and privacy that others might have chosen to devote to family and personal life. During World War II, Patty Conant had copied into a notebook and then underlined this sentence from Thoreau's *Journals:* "At what expense any valuable work is performed! At the expense of a life!"[19]

In the late 1960s the war in Vietnam also deeply troubled Conant. Admittedly poorly informed of affairs in the world beyond North America, Europe, and the Soviet Union, like most Americans of the era he had initially accepted the need to prop up the faltering, fractious Saigon regime against a monolithic ideological enemy, "the Sino-Soviet Communist Bloc." Resigned to the necessity of waging small twilight struggles along the periphery of the East-West conflict, he had suggested in 1959 that Washington maintain "for the foreseeable future a strong, modern, flexible military force which could respond to local aggression anywhere on the far-flung frontiers of freedom."[20]

Conant's fealty to these ideas was not shared by Ted and Ellen Conant. Citing their lengthy firsthand experience in Asia—Ellen's studies, Ted's sympathetic witnessing of the revolt by South Korean activists against the pro-American military government headed by Syngman Rhee—the couple warned the old Cold Warrior that an unlimited U.S. military involvement in a bitter civil war that had brought the French such *maladies* was neither wise nor proper, especially on the side of forces who were open to the charge of colluding with foreigners against nationalist rivals.

But Conant, like President Kennedy's and Johnson's advisers who advocated escalation, hoped that a show of force—the tried-and-true formula of a few gunboats, overt and covert military and economic aid, juggling local potentates and generals—would safeguard the pro-West Diem regime in South Vietnam that emerged after the nation was divided following the 1954 Geneva Conference. Two years after that conference, Conant had seemed puzzled that "the disastrous consequences of this 'licking' in the Far East [had] not come off,"[21] yet he never seriously questioned the validity of the "domino theory" advanced by Eisenhower during the Indochina crisis, that the fall of one nation to Communism, no matter how insignificant in itself, could not be tolerated because it would inexorably lead to takeovers in neighboring states. And when the old methods did not quickly smother this latest "brushfire," and voices of discontent at the dispatch of U.S. ground troops began to be expressed around the country, especially among the young people expected to risk their lives to enforce their country's containment strategy in the jungles of Southeast Asia, Conant and other old-fashioned internationalists resorted to the same method they had refined ever since coalescing to prod FDR toward belligerency in the summer of 1940: they formed elite committees to reassure Americans that their leaders were doing the right, necessary thing, that their sons and dollars would not be wasted.

By late 1965, advertisements were appearing in the *New York Times* and other leading newspapers in support of Washington's Vietnam policy in the name of a group called the Committee for an Effective and Durable Peace in Asia. Dean Acheson, John McCloy, Conant, and other "former high government officials, financiers, educators and business executives" declared (in a statement organized by White House staff members) that they had created the nationwide committee so that "American people would have a better understanding on Vietnam."[22] After an early antiwar rally in Washington, another pro-administration statement signed by Conant, Acheson, Richard Nixon, Lucius Clay, Sidney Hook, John Dos Passos, Samuel Rosenman, Douglas Dillon, and more than a hundred other worthies made the rounds urging Americans to stand firm and dismissing the protesters as a fringe minority oblivious to the lessons of Munich. "The consensus, which is clear to all experienced observers, must not be obscured by the behavior of a small segment of our population," they asserted. "They have a right to be heard, but they impose on the rest of us the obligation to shout to make unmistakably clear the nation's firm commitment."[23]

Two years later, with Pentagon timetables for finishing the job slipping despite steady troop reinforcements and heavy B-52 bombing of North Vietnam, protests were spreading, and these same people nervously decided it was time to haul out the big guns to stiffen the national will. Headlined by former presidents Eisenhower and Truman, the Citizens Committee for Peace and Freedom in Vietnam, founded in October 1967, was a lineal descendant of the Committee to Defend America by Aiding the Allies and the Committee on the Present Danger in urging Americans to "stay the path" in support of their government's interventionist foreign policies. Like its predecessors, the new committee also derived behind-the-scenes impetus from a White House eager to exhibit private backing for a new and costly foreign policy commitment: the idea had come from a California businessman and was brought by John Gardner to the attention of LBJ staff members John P. Roche and Harry McPherson, who, assuring "no overt White House involvement," recruited recently defeated Senator Paul H. Douglas as chairman and Charles Tyroler II as director. They called on leading citizens to fill out the roster, and once again Conant's name stood near the top of the familiar cast of elite persuaders— Dean Acheson, Omar Bradley, Lucius Clay, Henry Cabot Lodge, Leverett Saltonstall—united in their proclaimed task of "educating the public and articulating the need for resolve."[24]

But around the edges, Conant's own confidence was beginning to fray. Hesitating before joining, he privately expressed misgivings that revealed both discomfiture (at least in terms of public relations) at the mass killings of civilians he had accepted as a desirable byproduct of strategic bombing during World War II, and the same misreading of public sensitivity to high casualties that had led to his fruitless advocacy of a mandatory draft in the early 1950s. The Committee needed to face up to the mounting "stop the bombing" cries, he urged, or risk consignment to irrelevance. Suggesting a doubling of U.S. ground troop levels as a viable alternative, Conant wanted the group to check with Pentagon experts to ascertain whether it was truly militarily essential to continue the politically "fatal" B-52 raids on North Vietnamese targets.

"Because of the nature of bombing," he contended, "civilian casualties are high and can be exploited by those who are against American policy in terms of the suffering of innocent people. . . . There can be no doubt that our policy of bombing the North has given the United States a very black eye throughout the world and is the one point on which the critics of our policy internally can concentrate."[25]

Eager to get Conant as a founding member, the committee's organizers checked with official sources, and chairman Douglas passed on reassurances that current tactics were working without any necessity for raising troop levels. Soon Conant signed on, and in mid-January 1968 he also joined Eisenhower, Bradley, the physicist Eugene Wigner, and four others in a special statement backing Johnson's proposal for a bombing pause only in exchange for concessions from Hanoi.[26]

But at the end of that month, the Tet Offensive shook Conant's faith, as it did that of many other staunch defenders of the war. For months, Gen. Westmoreland and the administration had promised imminent victory, the "light at the end of the tunnel." Now an enemy supposedly on its last legs had displayed an ability to coordinate assaults on major cities throughout South Vietnam, even shooting their way into the U.S. Embassy compound in Saigon. There was talk of sending additional forces to handle the offensive, and Conant felt burned by his earlier swallowing—and endorsement—of the Pentagon's Pollyanna projections, and even suspected an air force coverup. "I was assured," he wrote Douglas,

> that those who understood the military situation were absolutely certain that no further increase in American fighting men was needed. In view of the events of the last two weeks, I now question the accuracy of this reply. I am afraid that I am becoming more and more suspicious that the Air Force Generals are in control and, as I know from my World War II experience, they may be extremely dogmatic and even unscrupulous in respect to questions which challenge their premises. I don't see how the Committee on which you asked me to serve can ignore the disastrous events of recent days. I submit that if any such demonstration of the inadequacy of the plans and predictions of a top field commander in a normal war were uncovered, the commander would be relieved of his responsibility. At the very minimum, should not the Committee try to obtain from Cabot Lodge and the Generals some explanation of why they were so wrong both in making an answer to my proposal and in presenting such ridiculously optimistic statements to the general public?[27]

This time, the former senator had little to offer in the way of reassurance, confessing that he too was troubled by "the long and dismal record of overly optimistic statements" by government officials. Reflecting the soul-searching in progress in many establishment quarters, he added: "I am at the point where I don't know who or what to believe, so I am depending more and more on my own visceral reactions."[28]

By no means had Conant turned dovish, rigidly adhering to his opposition to negotiations for a coalition government in South Vietnam as a cowardly sell-out of loyal allies that would lead to a Communist bloodbath. "As I see it," he wrote Douglas, "the Communist World has not disintegrated; China and the Soviet Union undoubtedly have different objectives, but those in command still remain Marxists in that their whole conception of governmental process is conditioned by their ideology they absorbed as youths." The apparent willingness of once reliable liberals like John Kenneth Galbraith to consider a coalition government disturbed and mystified Conant, who sensed a gulf opening "between some of the President's critics and those who, like myself, are still cold warriors."[29]

But Conant, too, soon began to scale down his former unqualified support for expending "whatever resources are required" to keep the South

Vietnamese allies in power.[30] In early March 1968, as a Pentagon request for an additional 206,000 troops was leaked to the press and the anti-war candidate Eugene McCarthy staggered the incumbent president in the New Hampshire Democratic primary, support for the war wavered again. Though the Pentagon's request fit the spirit of Conant's own proposal to double ground forces so as to permit a bombing halt, he sensed that "a proposal to bring in another 200,000 men *now* is going to be difficult to sell the country." At the same time, he blanched at the idea of escalating the bombing—even if, as some Hawks argued, a massive hike in air raids on North Vietnam were the only alternative to permitting a Communist takeover in South Vietnam, either through a direct military takeover or via a Viet Cong coalition government. "If I should be persuaded that such a line of reasoning were correct, I think I might reverse myself completely," Conant confessed to committee director Charles Tyroler II on March 11. "If the choice were defeat, i.e. abandoning the South Vietnamese to the Viet Cong or massive bombing which might start *the* World War we have been hoping to avoid, I think I might be on the side of accepting defeat."[31]

With the storm of protest now spreading well beyond the core of campus radicals, even the mainstream media and "Wise Men" of the foreign policy establishment began to seriously consider a pullout from Vietnam even without guaranteed achievement of all of the goals dictated by two decades of Cold War assumptions and the anti-appeasement axioms of Munich. "I admit I am confused," Conant wrote a committee official on April 10, in the tumultuous aftermath of Lyndon Johnson's announcement that he would forgo a reelection campaign in favor of seeking a peace in Vietnam, and Martin Luther King's assassination. Though "more convinced than ever that the President is the victim of bad military advice," he still clung to the bedrock of opposing any coalition government. But now he doubted whether his fellows on the committee would, or "whether the temper of the people" was adequate for the U.S. government realistically to fight on rather than to accept a cease-fire "on the basis of some concessions to the Viet Cong . . . it is at this point that I have recently begun to falter."[32]

Typically, Conant kept his faltering and confusion to himself, and publicly projected firmness and resolve. In a proposed statement of basic principles for the committee to issue, Conant made the minor philosophical adjustment of conceding that the conflict was "a civil war among the inhabitants of Vietnam," with each faction supported by superpower patrons, rather than a classic case of international aggression, as often claimed by supporters of U.S. involvement. Yet, he insisted, the public should be told that there was "no place for compromise" in negotiations—talking to the enemy about a coalition government would be "the equivalent of betraying the lives of those South Vietnamese who have trusted us in the past."[33] In late May 1968, as moves toward peace talks in Paris did slowly get under way, Conant joined Douglas for a press conference to warn the American people against impatience, "our deadliest enemy" in the forthcoming talks. Claiming to represent a "silent center"—the same mute constituency that Johnson's successor, Richard Nixon, would claim as his own—Conant and Douglas tried to buck up the administration by condemning in advance any one-sided concessions as "the road to surrender."[34]

Though he voted for Hubert Humphrey over Richard Nixon in November 1968, Conant saw no reason to alter his philosophical predilection for urging Americans to trust authority. In late October 1969, a few days after huge "Moratorium Day" protests mobilized a vast outpouring of anti-war sentiment, Conant urged the Peace and Freedom group to launch a public "support the President program" and privately counsel Nixon "to stand firm" against any tendencies toward a cut-and-run settlement as opposed to a gradual withdrawal. "Whether you like him or not, or like his domestic policies, he is the only man who has the necessary information and the power to act," he reasoned.[35]

But America had changed from the days when the consolidated voice of the establishment could effectively shape mass opinion—and the "establishment" itself was fast fractionating over Vietnam and its implications for American foreign policy.[36] If Americans could no longer trust the military or government—and if men like Conant, at least in private, expressed their own doubts over the veracity of military estimates—why should the public trust the collective voices of those traditional authorities who had steadily counseled policies that had resulted in disaster?

Moreover, the very culture of trusting authority, of letting the experts with access to secret information handle the nation's critical decisions, had come under harsh attack. Conant had thrived in that culture, but now the democratic activism his rhetoric long implied was moving in directions that he never intended. The marchers in the streets felt no less qualified than the generals in the Pentagon or the politicians in Washington loudly to express their opinion, and act on it.

And, to put it mildly, the same went for the students at the universities— the anger and violence of the protests had even reached Harvard Yard, where in April 1969 radicals had occupied Conant's old headquarters, University Hall, only to be evicted by baton-swinging local policemen called in by President Pusey, an action that radicalized even moderates on the campus and triggered a general student strike. Conant, however, had little sympathy for those who incited acts of civil disobedience and who voiced a radical, comprehensive, sometimes shrill critique of the country's basic institutions, and he wired Pusey to express his full support. To his friend Bill Marbury, still a member of the Harvard Corporation, he wrote: "I am sure you people have made the right decisions and will continue to do so. As I see the situation, what has happened at Cambridge makes even clearer than before the nature of the disturbances in our colleges. A fanatical group of anarchists who are using social institutions of higher education to attack the whole social structure of our society have succeeded in winning the allegiance of some softheaded, well-meaning youths."[37]

While no radical, Conant was forced by the Vietnam failure to question assumptions that had shaped his worldview since World War II, at least in private. In 1972, he told his son, furious at Nixon's policies on public education and cover-up of the emerging Watergate scandal, he voted for George McGovern—the liberal Democratic presidential candidate who advocated a rapid exit from Vietnam, and a general retreat from Cold War interventionism in favor of devoting resources to domestic needs.[38]

Overshadowing all his other concerns, nuclear weapons never entirely escaped Conant's thoughts, and in his final years he began to express the mixed feelings that had always shadowed his involvement with them more frequently. "I have never been one of those who thought the use of atomic energy held such potential benefits for the human race that we should all rejoice at the discovery of atomic fission," he wrote in *My Several Lives*. "To my mind, the potentialities for destruction are so awesome as to outweigh by far all the imaginable gains that may accrue in the distant future when atomic power plants may exist all over the world."[39]

During the rush of postpublication publicity appearances, the television journalist Edwin Newman asked Conant whether he ever woke up in the morning "surprised that the world is still here"?

"Oh, very much," he replied. "And I think, of course I go back, jumping to another phase of what I record, to my work with the atomic bomb. Before that instrument was first used, some of us who knew about it and its potentialities, I think, I remember thinking, couldn't say it to anybody, not even my wife, that if we can't find some way of controlling this under international or some kind of control, within five years the whole world would disappear. It hasn't. So in that sense, perhaps I'm pleasantly surprised when I wake up alive, every morning."[40]

Jennet Conant, Ted Conant's daughter, as a teenager spent several summers in Hanover and recalls that her grandfather was "haunted" by the bomb, that he meticulously sifted each new account to ascertain whether it portrayed him in the correct light. "He was always mulling it over. As he grew older, he grew more fretful. He would read all the new books that came out."[41]

Conant never expressed regret for the use of the bomb on Hiroshima, however, even in long arguments with Ted and Ellen Conant on lazy summer afternoons in New Hampshire, although his grandson Jim recalls one day his grandfather conceding it had been a "mistake" to destroy Nagasaki, and Jennet Conant sensed that there was "a dose of guilt there"—but for taking part in the development of nuclear weapons generally, not their use on two Japanese cities in particular.[42] He certainly gave no apologies for either atomic bombing in *My Several Lives* or, in February 1970, when he, Bush, and Groves were handed Atomic Pioneer Awards by Richard Nixon at a White House ceremony.

But until his death in 1978, Conant remained an inveterate "unenthusiast" about the hydrogen bomb and nuclear power, doubtful that the U.S.-Soviet arms control talks that had finally come to pass would dispel the nuclear predicament he had helped create. Despite a 1970 interview in the *New York Times* in which he seemed to concede that his position on the H-bomb had been in error—an admission that prompted a gleeful letter of inquiry from Lewis Strauss (with a copy to Roger Robb) to confirm that he had not been misquoted[43]—Conant in his final, private pronouncement on that subject was more comfortable with the stand he had taken. "I'm not completely sure that we were wrong, as most people would now say," he told an interviewer in 1974. "I wasn't too happy it was built. It couldn't win any war; it could only destroy the world."[44]

Conant leapt at a chance to air his longstanding profound skepticism toward nuclear power in the mid-seventies when the Arab oil boycott triggered lines at the gas pumps and a political crisis over scarce energy resources. Terming the accumulation of radioactive waste generated by atomic plants the "systematic poisoning of our descendants," he made common cause with the liberal Union of Concerned Scientists and like-minded atomic veterans such as George Kistiakowsky and Victor Weisskopf (and even David Lilienthal) in urging the U.S. government to turn toward coal and other, less polluting energy sources such as solar power.[45]

"It was no mistake, following Hiroshima, to try to use nuclear power for peaceful purposes," stated one scientists' petition signed by Conant and delivered to the White House on the thirtieth anniversary of the first use of the bomb. "But it was a serious error in judgment in the following decades to devote resources to nuclear development to the virtual exclusion of other alternatives."[46]

Relieved to have *My Several Lives* behind him—the chief lesson he learned writing it, he reported to Carnegie, was that "anyone who contemplates writing an autobiography had better have a second thought"[47]—Conant started to draft chapters for his Germany book, recounting his experiences as high commissioner in greater detail and candor than in his autobiography. But he was fast running out of energy and time; his eyesight and hearing faded; his handwriting grew jagged, he had a prostate operation, then explorative surgery for what turned out to be a benign tumor, then phlebitis in his leg; soon he was virtually homebound. "Jim has been having a rather miserable time," Patty Conant wrote a friend as her husband passed his eightieth birthday. "He is very patient, and he does not complain at all, but I grieve to see the limitations (of all sorts) with which his dynamic personality is burdened."[48]

The last years were difficult ones. Jennet Conant observed a stilted, formal relationship between her grandparents—"They did not have personal conversations," she said, at least in her presence—and discerned that her grandmother "lorded" over her ill husband: "she bossed over him, humiliated him ... it was awful to see ... she enjoyed having power over him."[49] More problems arose over Patty Conant's flustered attempts to hire household help, a perennial problem exemplified by this 1977 letter to a friend: "I have not had really happy experiences in getting 'live-in' help (very few people want to live in)—we are now on our fourth incumbent this winter and I don't know whether she and I are going to be able to stand each other till summer!!"[50] Conant remained a meticulous and fastidious dresser, wearing a jacket and tie and keeping his hair precisely combed, but increasingly, according to relatives, his physical deterioration defeated his efforts to retain a dignified front, and humiliated him, even within the privacy of his immediate family.[51]

Though increasingly hampered, Conant followed the news and read widely for as long as possible; he missed the "buzz-buzz," the insider gossip he had reveled in for a half century. In the mid-seventies, the news gave him much to be pessimistic about. The defeat in Vietnam had driven apart the interventionist consensus he had helped forge at the outset of World War II; the nuclear arms race was surging, despite a couple of palliative superpower treaties, and nuclear power plants were going up; for all Conant's efforts, U.S. education was, if anything, heading away from the meritocratic ideal he had fought for; and in cities, "social dynamite" continued to accumulate. The writer Robert J. Donovan found him in a somewhat melancholy mood when he interviewed him for the first volume of his Truman biography about the decision to use the atomic bomb. As they arose from lunch, Conant said matter-of-factly, "Everything I've worked for has been rejected."[52]

Intensifying in the summer of 1977, a series of debilitating strokes corroded his faculties, confined him to a wheelchair, and drove him to paranoid delusions and nightmares, to reliving ancient experiences, to long stretches of "bedeviled" confusion punctuated by moments of terrifying clarity; "You know, Jamie," he told his grandson after one reverie, "I think I'm losing my mind,"[53] and another time he sat stroking his granddaughter Jennet's cat, looked up and said, "Well, Misty and I are about the same now."[54] Nevertheless the end came suddenly, with only Patty nearby, when Conant died in a Hanover, New Hampshire, nursing home on February 11, 1978, having expressed a strong, typically unsentimental wish for a private burial and no public ceremony. Within days, he was cremated and interred in the Thayer-Richards family plot in Mt. Auburn Cemetery in Cambridge. The university at which he had been student, professor, and president could not refrain from marking the event, however, and a modest secular service was held at which a few friends and colleagues—George Kistiakowsky, Frank Keppel, John Finley—said a few words, and Harvard's incumbent president, Derek C. Bok, paid a rather parochial tribute to Conant's emphasis on building a strong faculty.[55] (Patty Conant, who greeted mourners at 17 Quincy Street that day, was to die in a Pennsylvania nursing home seven years later.)

One can hardly doubt, however, Conant would have regarded the anti-

Communist revolutions that ended Germany's division, the Cold War in Europe, and the Soviet Union itself as the most fitting tribute to—and vindication of—his life and career. Every action he had taken or supported during World War II, the Cold War, and the nuclear arms race, every moral compromise, had been justified on the grounds that it would promote peace—or a tense stalemate that one day would give way to a fading away of global hostility. "I believe," he told students in 1947, "that given patience, intelligence, and courage on the part of this country we may within your lifetime, if not mine, work out a basis for a real peace with our former ally, the Soviet Union."[56]

Even the end of the Cold War, however, has not eased the social, class, and racial divisions he believed threatened American democracy, nor erased the existential dilemma the human race faces as a result of the advent of nuclear weapons. Congratulated on his return to Washington from Alamogordo the day after the Trinity test, Conant replied: "As to congratulations, I am far from sure—that remains for history to decide." In 1969, recounting the incident in *My Several Lives*, Conant frankly admitted that the "verdict of history has not yet been given."[57] Until the end of his life, I feel sure, he saw no reason to alter his own admission upon leaving the GAC in 1952 that he felt "no sense of accomplishment" for his work on the atomic bomb.[58]

And if the ghost of James Bryant Conant returned to Harvard Yard to attend the Class of 1914's seventy-fifth anniversary celebrations in June 1989, amid the debris of the once feared Communist monolith, there is every reason to believe that he would still have felt shadowed by the doomsday vision that he included in the after-dinner remarks he delivered to his class's fiftieth reunion in June 1964. On that warm Cambridge evening, he intended to express wonder at being able to address his classmates at a thriving university that he had long since expected to have been reduced to radioactive rubble, incinerated by a "superblitz" that had destroyed civilization, and to explain in sobering terms why he believed the chances were very high that a nuclear war might still occur. His wife pleaded with him not to put a damper on the festivities.[59]

And so he ended on a brighter note. After "scaring them all with the bomb and Berlin as a measurement of good and evil among men," as he noted in his diary, he raised his glass high—and offered a toast to the Class of 2014.[60]

Appendixes

1. *Some Thoughts on International Control of Atomic Energy*

May 4, 1944

Alternatives Race between nations and in the next war destruction of civilization, or a scheme to remove atomic energy from the field of conflict.

(1) Association of nations for this purpose
(2) International Commission on Atomic Energy
British, US, Russian (3 each)
other nations nominate 6
(3) Complete power of Commission over all work on atomic energy
(4) License research and development in all countries
(5) Finance research and development in all countries
(6) All results published
(7) Inspection by agents of all labs, factories (of any sort, etc.) Bound by oath to treat all information as confidential
(8) Full publicity as to raw materials, potential weapons, etc.
(9) Trustees and custodians of an arsenal to be located in Canada: minimum supply
(10) Commission to have own planes and force of 10,000 men (international) pledged to Commission and prevention of seizure of supply
(11) Right of entry of Commission men irrespective of state of war of a nation with any other nations
(12) Interference with the Commission by government of any nation to be considered an act of war
(13) Power to move any material connected with atomic energy from one country to another
(14) Arsenal to release supply only on unanimous vote of Commission, representatives of any nation refusing to obey edict disqualified from voting

Query: (1) What happens if a nation refuses entry to factories, etc., or disobeys edicts of Commission?

Answer: Other nations are pledged to declare war.

Whether atomic bombs are not to be released for the purposes of this war to be decided by Commission.

(2) What happens if the Commission finds a prohibited weapon being built in a country?

(a) So announces

(b) Can on majority vote remove weapons to arsenal

(3) What is to prevent Canada or U.S. or British seizing arsenal?

(a) Guards of arsenal

(b) Use of bombs by arsenal guards in Canada or U.S.

(4) If this works what next? Next step after a decade would be to enlarge scope of agreement and include all armament inspection and publication of figures.

If eventually, why not at start? Perhaps so might try International Commission on Military Science with powers as above on atomic energy but powers of inspection and publication of all armament problems and military secrets.

What would be the result: Everyone would know where each nation stood.

—J. B. Conant

Box 9, folder 97, S-1, Bush-Conant Correspondence, Office of Scientific Research and Development, Record Group 227, National Archives, Washington, D.C.

2. *Notes on the "Trinity" Test held at Alamogordo bombing range*

125 miles south east of Albuquerque New Mexico
5:30 a.m., Monday, July 16

V. Bush, Gen. Groves and J.B.C. arrived at the Base Camp located 10 miles from the bomb at about 8 p.m. Sunday evening. After dinner at the mess and some brief explanation by Oppenheimer, Tolman, Kistiakowsky and Rabbi [sic] in very informal conversation we went to bed. The atmosphere was a bit tense as might be expected but everyone felt confident that the bomb would explode. The pool on the size of the explosion ran from 0 (a few pessimists) to 18,000 (Rabbi [sic]) and perhaps someone at 50,000 [several words censored]. My own figure was 4400 [tons of T.N.T.] but I never signed up. It was a bad night though the weather forecast had been favorable for a clear early morning with light winds (the desired condition). From about 10:30 to 1 a.m., it blew very hard thus preventing sleep in our tent and promising a postponement of the Test. Then it poured for about an hour!

At 1 a.m. General Groves arose and went out to the forward barricade with the key personnel. There were two forward bases located 10,000 yds. N. & S. of the bomb. The [wiring?] from [this?] point to the test and to the camp was fantastic in the [extreme?]. The instrumentation of the test included a vast array of equipment. At 3:15 a.m., the rain having just ceased, Rabbi [sic] came into our tent (V. Bush and JBC) and said that there had been much talk of a postponement because of the weather but reports indicated a 75% chance of going through with it but at 5 a.m. instead of the scheduled 4 a.m.

We got up & dressed and drank some coffee about 4 a.m. and wandered around. The sky was still overcast. It had not rained however at the zero point (the bomb) and the [wires?lines?] were O.K. Word then came through about 4:30 that 5:10 would be the time. About 5 p.m. [sic — a.m.] or a little after, word came that the firing would occur at 5:30. Shortly after, General Groves came back from the forward area. We prepared to view the scene from a slight rise near the camp. Col. S[tafford]. Warren [was] in charge of health. Tolman, Rabbi [*sic*], Gen. Groves & J.B.C. were more or less together. It was agreed that because of the expected (or hoped!) bright flash and the ultra violet light (no ozone to absorb) it would be advisable to lie flat and look away at the start, then look through the heavy dark glass.

At 5:20 the sirens blew the 10 min signal then another at 5:25 and I think another 2 mins. before. We lay belly down facing 180 [degrees] away from the spot on a tarpaulin. I kept my eyes open looking at the horizon opposite the spot. It was beginning to be light, but the general sky was still dark particularly in the general direction I was looking. Through the loud speaker nearby I heard Allison counting the seconds minus 45, minus 40, minus 30, minus 20, minus 10. (The firing was done by some kind of timing device started at minus 45 sec.) These were long seconds! Then came a burst of white light that seemed to fill the sky and seemed to last for seconds. I had expected a relatively quick and bright flash. The enormity of the light and its length quite stunned me. My instantaneous reaction was that something had gone wrong and that the thermal nuclear transformation of the atmosphere, once discussed as a possibility and jokingly referred to a few minutes earlier, had actually occurred. Slightly blinded for a second, I turned on my back as quickly as possible and raising my head slightly, could see the "fire" through the dark glass. At that stage it looked like an enormous pyrotechnic display with great boiling of luminous vapors, some spots being brighter than others. A picture from memory is as seen through *heavy* dark glass.

Very shortly this view began to fade and without thinking the glass was lowered and the scene viewed with the naked eye. The ball of gas was enlarging rapidly and turning into a mushroom. It was reddish purple and against the early dawn very luminous, though I instantly thought of it as colored [somewhere?]. Then someone shouted watch out for the detonation wave (this was 40 sec after zero time). Still on my back I heard the detonation but was not in a position to notice any blast (there was relatively little felt here). The sound was less loud or startling than I expected, but the shock of the sensory impression was still dominant in my mind. Then I got up and watched the spread of the colored luminous gas. There were two secondary explosions, after the detonation wave reached us or just before. The cloud billowed upward when these occurred and very soon thereafter [billowed?] up as would an oil fire, the color became [word illegible] and the whole looked more like a [unintelligible] fire (though on an enormous scale). The column of smoke then began to spread and took on a Z form which persisted for some time. The spectacular part must have been confined to about 90 seconds. The phases observed by the eye were as follows from memory.

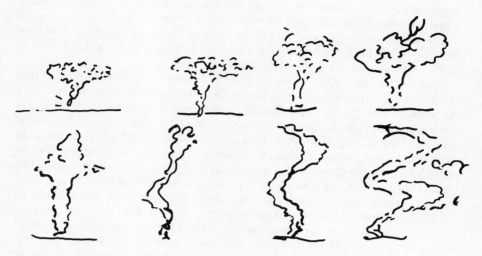

As soon as I had lowered my dark glass and before rising I shook Gen. Groves hand who said "Well, I guess there is something in nucleonics after all." Tolman as we rose said, that is something very different from the 100-ton TNT shot, "entirely different, there is no question but what they got a nuclear reaction." Then several people began saying, "Very much larger than expected. Rabbi [*sic*] said it was 15,000 Tons equivalent at least."

At about 60 sec. as the cloud billowed up, the assembled group including many MPs' gave out a spontaneous cheer.

Then the reports began to come in. Oppenheimer arrived in about 5 or 10 minutes and said the equivalent was 2100 Tons which was greeted with great skepticism. It afterwards turned out he had made an error in converting the first blast measurements and the figure showed 7,000 tons.

The most exciting news was that the steel tower over "Jumbo" 800 yards away had disappeared. This was reported by some one with a telescope and verified by all. This was unexpected and showed a very much more powerful effect than expected.

Before we left at noon, the best estimate seemed to be between 10,000–15,000 though Rabbi [*sic*] maintained 18,000 would yet prove right. Careful exploration of the crater showed 1200 yards again more than expected. The toxicity problem proved not serious. Those at 10,000 [yards] North evacuated in a hurry as their meter went off the scale almost at once and the cloud of smoke seemed to chase them they declared! All evacuation was by car, of course. One man at the Camp Site who looked at the explosion without dark glasses got a bad eye burn and was given morphine: the prognosis was that he would not lose his sight. G. Kistiakowsky, all [word illegible], came in to report that the shock wave had knocked him down as he stood outside the barricade at 10,000 S. There were reports of two others being knocked down at the same spot.

My first impression remains the most vivid, a cosmic phenomenon like an eclipse. The whole sky suddenly full of white light like the end of the world. Perhaps my impression was only premature on a time scale of years!

J. B. Conant, Washington, D.C.
July 17, 1945 4:30 p.m.

Box 5, folder 38, S-1, Bush-Conant Correspondence, Office of Scientific Research and Development, Record Group 227, National Archives, Washington, D.C.

3. *Conant to Harvey H. Bundy, September 23, 1946*

Dear Harvey:

I am enclosing a clipping from the September 14th issue of The Saturday Review of Literature. I am considerably disturbed about this type of comment which has been increasing in recent days. I wonder if you have seen Leland Stowe's "While Time Remains." In the first part of the book he gives a list of things the United States Government did which were wrong in regard to the atomic bomb. He starts off with what he considers the error of using it against the Japanese. And then recently, I believe, Halsey made an unfortunate statement blaming the scientists for insisting on using the atomic bomb, though a later dispatch indicates that he takes this back. Of course, it was to be expected that professional pacifists and perhaps certain religious leaders would take a strong stand against the use of this new weapon. I am disturbed, however, by nonreligious groups and people taking up the same theme.

You may be inclined to dismiss all this talk and representing only a small minority of the population, which I think it does. However, this type of sentimentalism, for I so regard it, is bound to have a great deal of influence on the next generation. The type of person who goes in to teaching, particularly school teaching, will be influenced a great deal by this type of argument. We are in danger of repeating the fallacy which occurred after World War I. You will recall that it became accepted doctrine among a group of socalled intellectuals who taught in our schools and colleges that the United States had made a great error in entering World War I, and that the error was brought about largely by the interests of the powerful groups. Of course, there is little relation between these two types of fallacies, but I mention the history after World War I only to emphasize that a small minority, if it represents the type of person who is both sentimental and verbally minded and in contact with our youth, may result in a distortion of history.

It seems to me of great importance to have a statement of fact issued by someone who can speak with authority. There is no one who could do this better than Mr. Stimson. I talked with Van Bush about this the other day and he said that I could quote him to you to the effect that he wishes Mr. Stimson would make a statement clarifying what actually happened with regard to the decision to use the bomb against the Japanese.

I wish you would think this over and perhaps talk over the phone with Mr. Harrison about it. Could you not, the two of you, suggest to Mr. Stimson that what was needed was a short article from him pointing out the conditions under which the decision was made and who made it? Furthermore, I think it is important to show that while there was a small group of scientists who protested, that the scientific leaders of the movement, including the members of that scientific panel who met with Mr. Stimson in May or June, raised no protest against the proposed plan. On the contrary, you will remember that in the presence of Oppenheimer, Lawrence, Compton and Fermi there was discussion of the actual target to be chosen. I think it unfair for the scientists by implication to try to dodge the responsibility for this decision, although of course they were not in a position to influence greatly whatever was done at Potsdam.

I am quite unrepentant as to my own views about the matter. In the committee, of which I was a member and Mr. Harrison was acting as chairman, I expressed my views that the bomb should be used. I did so on the grounds (1) that I believed it would shorten the war against Japan, and (2) that unless it was actually used in battle there was no chance of convincing the American public and the world that it should be controlled by international agreement. Nothing that has come to light since then has changed my opinion. I think it important to point out in a statement by Mr. Stimson that the proposal at the eleventh hour to hold the demonstration was not a realistic one. Furthermore, it should be pointed out how much Monday morning quarterbacking is now involved in the statements that Japan would have surrendered anyway.

At the same time the statement should be largely factual and not an attempt to argue too much as to the military necessity for the bomb.

I should be glad to talk this over with you at greater length on the phone, or preferably if we could both find a time when you could come out to lunch. I close by saying that I think it a matter of real importance and considerable urgency.

With all good wishes,

Sincerely,
JAMES B. CONANT

"Bu–By" correspondence folder, box 296, James B. Conant Presidential Papers, Harvard University Archives, Pusey Library, Harvard University, Cambridge, Massachusetts.

4. *Excerpts from "The President's Stand," the* Harvard Crimson June 9, 1949

It is hard to believe. If President Conant himself had not personally confirmed his complete agreement with the Commission's policy statement, it would be almost impossible to believe. The CRIMSON respects and admires the President both as an individual and as a national figure. President Conant and his administration have fought the enemies of academic freedom. They have helped make the University one of the stronger positive forces in this country protecting the privileges of an unhampered search for knowledge and truth. It is therefore with regret and disappointment that the CRIMSON finds itself opposed to President Conant on an issue that is so vital to academic freedom.

The CRIMSON believes that membership in the Communist Party does not automatically "render an individual unfit to discharge the duties of a teacher." First, there is proof that many Communist cardholders are not required to follow the party line. In order to keep many "big names" in the party, the Communists do not demand blind obedience to party policies. Second, even if all Communists surrendered their "intellectual integrity," there are large areas of learning where politics is completely irrelevant. An ardent party-liner in the field of government is one thing—his dogma could well make him incompetent to teach objectively—but a party-liner in Spanish or psychology or Old English is an entirely different case.

The CRIMSON believes that competence alone should be the standard for hiring or firing a teacher. A political standard is irrelevant; it is dangerous; it is a repudiation of the traditional American principle that an individual be judged for what he is, and not for what he belongs to. The Communist Party is still a legal organization.

Communism is also a point of view. It is a point of view many intelligent men have honestly reached. And it is a point of view that President Conant and his colleagues on the Educational Policies Commission want studied in American schools and colleges. But the Commission would prevent intelligent Communists from teaching that point of view—not because they might be incompetent teachers, not because they might propagandize or exclude unfavorable textbooks, but because they would as Communists automatically do those things. This is an attitude of fear. The Commission wants Communism studied, but evidently under unfavorable conditions.

The Commission's report is a policy statement. It does not discuss ways and means of preventing the employment of Communists as teachers. But such "implementation" is a logical second step. The Commission feels strongly that Communists should be kept out of education; the Commission also condemns the "unjust use of such words as 'Red' or 'Communist' to attack teachers and other persons who in point of fact are not Communists, but merely have views different from those of their accusers."

This statement in itself is commendable. There are innumerable cases where anti-Communist programs have ended up as assaults upon radicals and liberals. But how is the Commission's own program to be carried out, and who is to carry it out? They are questions of the utmost importance, and yet the Commission has disregarded them. Are the agents to be state legislatures? This country has seen how consistently these "little Dies Committees" have ignored the distinction between Communists and non-Communists. Are the agents to be college administrators or trustees or school superintendents? These people are often as sensitive to social pressure as legislators. And what man or group of men in America can be trusted to decide whether a teacher is a Communist or not, if he chooses to hide his party card?

The Commission cannot afford to remain silent on the ways and means of its policy. The Commission cannot dismiss these problems with a statement deploring indiscriminate smears. There is no questioning the sincerity and sober principle of President Conant and his fellow Commissioners. But on this issue they now stand with men of little principle and no discernment, men who are attempting to stifle ideas and change our constitutional guarantees of civil liberties to suit their purpose. So long as President Conant and his colleagues refuse to discuss implementation, these men will be able to say: we have on our side one of the most outstanding and respected scholars in America.

Every teacher and every student and every citizen in the country has the right to ask: what does the Commission's policy mean? Does the Commission want every faculty and school staff in America investigated—thoroughly and competently—for Communists? Does the Commission want every professor and instructor required to state his political affiliation? To be plain, how much of our civil liberties are we expected to surrender?

The CRIMSON is convinced that any answer will be unsatisfactory. Even the most intelligent men in the country could not devise just and fair methods of carrying out this policy: for it is a dangerous policy, it is a policy based on fear, it is a policy that is subversive of the American tradition.

Acknowledgments

In the course of this enterprise I have accumulated a daunting array of debts: to family, friends, and teachers; to archivists and librarians; to editors and employers; to other researchers, scholars, and students; and to the people—above all the Conant family—who graciously consented to my prying into their lives by granting me interviews and permission to see and use documents in their possession. I thank all, hope the results offer some compensation for burdens imposed, promise those who must listen to me on a regular basis that I will stop explaining every human or natural phenomenon through analogy to some aspect of the life or thought of James B. Conant, and apologize to any I have inadvertently forgotten to mention.

Though I never met Dr. Conant, his relatives were exceptionally cooperative, candid, and helpful in sharing memories and sources and suggesting new avenues of inquiry. As a biographer, I had the rare luck of happening upon a subject whose close family members were willing to discuss all sides, positive and negative, of the man and their relationship to him, rather than erecting a protective shield. Prior to her death in 1985, the late Grace Richards Conant granted me permission to examine and quote from her husband's personal papers while I was an undergraduate at Harvard, sat through an interview with me, and endorsed a Freedom of Information Act petition to the FBI. Over the past decade, Theodore Richards and Ellen Conant have submitted generously, cordially, and with informative results to countless inquiries on some of the most sensitive subjects. They even telephoned me on occasion to suggest new research possibilities, and kindly let me into their homes and records in Manhattan and Hanover. Their son and daughter, Jim and Jennet Conant, spoke to me at length about their grandfather, as did Clark Conant, a daughter of the late James Richards Conant. Reconstructing the personal life of a man who (in a friend's words) "never let his hair down" would have been utterly impossible without his family's cooperation.

Many colleagues and teachers helped me along the way. It has been my great pleasure and good fortune to have as thesis and dissertation adviser, colleague, mentor, and friend Martin J. Sherwin, a historian at Princeton, Tufts, and now Dartmouth, whose *A World Destroyed* first stimulated my interest in Conant and the atomic bomb. I and many others have gained from Marty's expertise, idealism, and concern for current and former students and teaching assistants. His invitation in 1986 to become a doctoral candidate and teaching assistant at Tufts and a research fellow at his Nuclear Age History and Humanities Center (NAHHC) allowed me to continue the study of Conant I had begun at Harvard. Over the next four years, he, his wife, Susan, son, Alex, and daughter, Andrea, provided a warm home away from home, and the NAHHC evolved into a collegial oasis that was a welcome respite from solitary research and writing; friends such as Philip Nash, Mark Feierstein, Gerry Gendlin,

Hans Fenstermacher, Eitan Levine, Yaacov Tygiel, and Meredith Mosier kept my existence from becoming too hermitlike. Quite unexpectedly, working with Marty, who had launched an innovative exchange program with Moscow State University, also led to unique opportunities to observe the changes in the Soviet Union and to participate in other exchanges and conferences that accelerated my initiation into academia and book publishing. For all this and more, I am immensely thankful.

I am also grateful to Daniel J. Kevles, Koepfli Professor of the Humanities at the California Institute of Technology, for the chance to spend six months in Pasadena in 1991 in the Program in Science, Ethics, and Public Policy, which is jointly supported by Caltech's Division of the Humanities and Social Sciences and the Mellon Foundation. Dan and Bettyann Kevles acclimated this East Coaster to Pasadena with their hospitality, along with the pleasant surroundings; friendly and erudite colleagues such as Diana Barkan, W. T. Jones, and Tim Moy, and exceptional staff assistance of Helga Galvan, Sheryl Cobb, and others helped me to research and write a significant chunk of the book in a relatively short time.

My study of Conant was enriched by a number of superb dissertations on various aspects of his multifaceted life. I was fortunate enough to meet William M. Tuttle, Jr., and Jeanne Amster, both of whom freely shared their ideas and sources on Conant; the works of Charles DeWayne Biebel and Barry James Teicher added further insight. Ellen W. Schrecker, who as my freshman expository writing teacher and later as author of *No Ivory Tower* encouraged my efforts, read several chapters in draft, and offered detailed and informed comments; my dissertation committee—Marty Sherwin, Gregg Herken, Paul Joseph, and Everett Mendelsohn—also gave useful counsel; Steve Connors translated materials relating to Conant from the German. In addition to citations mentioned in the footnotes, many historians and other scholars aided my research and understanding in various ways, in particular: Gar Alperovitz, Brian Balogh, Ron Bee, Bart Bernstein, Kai Bird, David Bradley, McGeorge Bundy, William Burr, Malcolm Byrne, Warren Cohen, Vera Dunham, Hunter DuPree, Daniel Ellsberg, John Lewis Gaddis, Lloyd Gardner, Ray Garthoff, Stanley Goldberg, Allen Greb, Hope Harrison, David Holloway, Warren Kimball, Mark Kramer, Bill Lanouette, Mel Leffler, Priscilla McMillan, Vojtech Mastny, Ernest May, Mikhail Narinsky, Allan Needell, Craig Nelson, Dan Pagis, Amos Perlmutter, Constantine Pleshakov, Nathan Reingold, Peter Roman, David Rood, David Alan Rosenberg, Thomas A. Schwartz, Chris Simpson, Bill Taubman, Marc Trachtenberg, Christian Tuschoff, Robert Wampler, Paul Watanabe, Kathryn Weathersby, George Abbott White, Mark White, Greg Zachary, Vlad Zubok, and David Zweig.

Many friends and associates of James B. Conant answered questions in person, by telephone, and in written form; my debt is acknowledged in the footnotes, but I would like to extend particular thanks to William T. Golden, Elaine Kistiakowsky, John Lansdale, and the late William Marbury for permitting me to use documents in their personal possession. The Harry S Truman Presidential Library supplied a travel grant that allowed me to visit it as well as the Eisenhower Library, and the family of Matt Bronfman sheltered me in Kansas City.

Working on this book showed me the extent to which historians in this country depend, first, on the aid, patience, encouragement, and expertise of professional archivists; and, second, on the traditions of openness and accountability in the United States—the right to appeal (through the Freedom of Information Act and other means) in the face of excessive official secrecy. (One may hope that the Cold War's end will hasten the relaxation of inordinate secrecy in government archives on both sides of the shredded Iron Curtain, and—who knows?—perhaps one day Harvard University will even ease its fifty-year rule and substitute a more reasonable restriction.) For handling my (usually breathless) requests for research assistance with courtesy, professionalism, and skill, I wish to express my gratitude to the staffs of the following archives and institutions: the Harvard University archives, Pusey Library; the National Archives, particularly the modern military, diplomatic, legislative, and scientific branches, and the reading room and duplication services personnel; Manuscript Division, Library of Congress; the Law School, Business School, and Houghton libraries, Harvard University; the Roosevelt, Truman, Eisenhower, Kennedy, and Johnson presidential libraries; Sterling Library, Yale University; Mudd Library, Princeton University; Dartmouth College Library; Rutgers University archives, Alexander Library; National Defense University; American Institute of Physics; the California Institute of Technology archives; the Department of Energy archives; the National Security Archive; the National Education Association archives; the National Academy of Sciences archives; the University of Chicago archives, Regenstein Library; the Columbia University archives, Butler Library; Public Records Office, Kew Gardens, England; American Philosophical Society; the Los Alamos National Laboratories archives; the Boston University archives; Carnegie Institution of Washington; State Historical Society of Wisconsin; the Rockefeller Institute archives; Roxbury Latin School; the Tufts University archives; the University of Arizona archives; the University of Minnesota archives; the University of California (Berkeley) and University of California (San Diego) archives; the University of Pennsylvania archives; the University of Washington archives.

A special word of thanks is due to Harley Holden, Harvard University archivist, who from the days of my undergraduate thesis research forward helped me gain the maximum access possible to the Conant papers, all the while keeping his sense of humor, and to Michael Raines and other staff at Pusey Library, who tolerated years of my pestering and desperate efforts to examine or transcribe material even as the clock struck the fatal time of 4:45 P.M.

During my work on this book, I was fortunate to have friends who provided encouragement, sustenance, companionship, conversation, and/or a place to crash. For all of the above I could always depend on my world trip traveling companions Mark Doctoroff and Steve Kantor (and his wife, Aileen), and on Tom Blanton, now director of the National Security Archive in Washington, D.C. Since being lured away from my dissertation to research the Iran–contra affair in the summer of 1987, I have found working with Tom and his NSA colleagues such as Malcolm Byrne, Peter Kornbluh, Sheryl Walter, and Bill Burr to be a pleasure and an education in the vicissitudes of government secrecy and of U.S. foreign policy. Special thanks also to Bill McKibben and Sue Halpern, Jeff Toobin and Amy McIntosh, Alexandra Korry, Scott Rosenberg, David and Jane DeMilo, Bob Boorstin, Nancy Bauer, Craig Keller, Alan Cooperman, David Edelstein, Larry and Rebecca Grafstein, Lizzie Leiman, Betsy and Jacques Gordon, Mike Abramowitz, Bob and Fran Elvin, Mark Feierstein, Robbie Hart and Mari-José Barnwell, Susan Chira and Michael Shapiro, P. J. Simmons, Liz and Bryan O'Leary, Seth Lloyd, Esme Murphy, Rich Daly, Sara Rimer, Bill Finnegan, Mary Ellen Fleck, Gary Girzon, Susan Brown, Bill and Anu Echikson, Naomi Pierce, Steve Latham, Tovia Smith, Ned Lafer, David and Naomi Solo, Pat Sorrento, Paul Wallfish, Adrienne Weiss, and Rabbi Bernice Weiss.

My agent, Doe Coover, boosted the confidence of a fledgling first-time author by agreeing to represent me, and then proved I was right to stop trying to do the job myself by shielding me from many depressing rejection letters and by finding a publisher and editor of hallowed distinction.

At Alfred A. Knopf, I was incredibly lucky to have as an editor Elisabeth Sifton, whose experience, confidence, enthusiasm, integrity, and line editing—and a few well-aimed jabs to push me to probe still deeper into the story—immeasurably strengthened the manuscript during the two years between submission and publication. With humor, patience, and skill, George Andreou finished the task of assembling and publishing a gargantuan book and extracting missing paraphernalia from its author. I would also like to thank my production editors Karen Leh and Dori Carlson, and Cassandra Pappas, who designed this book.

My employers at the Woodrow Wilson International Center for Scholars in Washington, D.C., in particular Robert S. Litwak and Samuel F. Wells, Jr., generously permitted me to take time from my post as coordinator of the Cold War International History Project to work on the editing and completion of the book.

The most important acknowledgments come last. I could never have written this book without a loving and supportive family who has tolerated my eccentric interests and at times erratic career path. My parents, David and Arline Hershberg; my sisters, Ann Hershberg and Susan Carlacci (and her husband, Cesare); my grandparents, Ethel and Bill Ackerman and Ben and Anne Hershberg; and other relatives, especially Phyllis and Lewis Morrison and Kenny and Karen Ackerman—all have always been there when I needed them, in every way, and this book in some inadequate way is an effort to repay the faith they have shown in me. I hope they feel the wait has been worth it.

Finally, words cannot express my gratitude and appreciation to my wife, Annie. I had long anticipated that the final stages of writing this book would be the most difficult and trying; instead, because of her, they were by far the easiest, most productive, and most joyous.

—JAMES G. HERSHBERG
Washington, D.C., July 1993

Abbreviations List

AEC   U.S. Atomic Energy Commission.

AEY   David E. Lilienthal, *The Journals of David E. Lilienthal, Volume II: The Atomic Energy Years,* 1945–1950 (New York: Harper & Row, 1964).

B–C   Bush-Conant correspondence, S-1 files, Office of Scientific Research and Development (OSRD), Record Group 227, National Archives, Washington, D.C.

BG   *Boston Globe.*

BMB   Bernard M. Baruch.

Buck
Interview   Paul H. Buck, interview by William Bentinck-Smith, summer 1974, Buck papers, HUG (B)—B857.50, Pusey Library, Harvard University.

CCP   Carnegie Corporation Papers, Butler Library, Columbia University.

CFP   Conant Family Papers, Hanover, N.H., in possession of Theodore R. Conant.

CPD   Committee on the Present Danger.

CPD
Papers   Committee on the Present Danger collection, Tracy S. Voorhees Papers, Rutgers University, New Brunswick, N.J.

DDE   Dwight D. Eisenhower.

DDEL   Dwight D. Eisenhower Library, Abilene, Kans.

DEL   David E. Lilienthal.

DoE   Department of Energy.

DoS   Department of State.

EPC   Educational Policies Commission of the National Education Association.

FDRL   Franklin D. Roosevelt Library, Hyde Park, N.Y.

FF   Felix Frankfurter.

FFP   Felix Frankfurter Papers, Harvard Law School Library, Cambridge, Mass.

FPF   "Fishing Party" file, John Foster Dulles Papers, Mudd Library, Princeton University, Princeton, N.J.

FRUS   *U.S. State Department, Foreign Relations of the United States* series (Washington, D.C.: Government Printing Office).

GAC   General Advisory Committee, U.S. Atomic Energy Commission.

GC	Grenville Clark.
GCP	Grenville Clark Papers, Baker Library, Dartmouth College, Hanover, N.H.
GRC	Grace ("Patty") Richards Conant, née Grace Thayer Richards, wife of James B. Conant.
HICOG	U.S. High Commissioner to Occupied Germany.
HICOG Papers	Papers of the U.S. High Commissioner to Germany, decimal 350, Record Group 84, National Archives, Suitland, Md.
HLS	Henry L. Stimson.
HSPS	*Historical Studies in the Physical and Biological Sciences.*
HST	Harry S Truman.
HSTL	Harry S Truman Library, Independence, Mo.
IMJRO	U.S. Atomic Energy Commission, *In the Matter of J. Robert Oppenheimer* (Washington, D.C.: Government Printing Office, 1954; MIT Press reprint ed., 1971).
JBC	James B. Conant.
JBC COHP	James B. Conant Columbia Oral History Project interview, Carnegie Corporation Project, April 5, 1967, Butler Library, Columbia University.
JBC diary	JBC diaries, daily reminders, scrapbooks, and journals kept in JBC PERP, UA I.15.898.13, box 8 (trips to England, 1941, and Moscow, 1945); boxes 11-13 (1911, 1935-71, some years missing, including 1942-1950); and box 22 (Germany, 1953-57).
JBC OH	JBC oral history interview by Gordon Craig, July 11, 1964, in JBC Personal Papers, Harvard University, and John F. Dulles Papers, Princeton University. Page citations from the Harvard transcript.
JBC PERP	James B. Conant Personal Papers, Harvard University Archives, Nathan M. Pusey Library, Cambridge, Mass.
JBC PREP	James B. Conant Presidential Papers, Harvard University Archives, Nathan M. Pusey Library, Cambridge, Mass.
JBC Speech File	UA I.5.168.48, JBC PREP.
JCAE Records	Joint Committee on Atomic Energy Records, Record Group 128, National Archives, Washington, D.C.
JFD	John Foster Dulles.
JRC	James Richards Conant, son of James B. Conant.
JRDB	Joint Research and Development Board.

JRO	J. Robert Oppenheimer.
JROP	J. Robert Oppenheimer Papers, Library of Congress, Washington, D.C.
KTC	Karl T. Compton.
Landers interview	JBC interview by John C. Landers, "The Manhattan Project, as Seen by Dr. Conant, And a Commentary on the Unprecedented and What It Has Left Us," March 8, 1974, JBC PERP.
LBJL	Lyndon B. Johnson Library, Austin, Tex.
LC	Library of Congress, Washington, D.C.
LRG	Leslie R. Groves.
MED	Manhattan Engineering District.
MSL	*James B. Conant, My Several Lives: Memoirs of a Social Inventor* (New York: Harper & Row, 1970).
NA	National Archives, Washington, D.C.
NAS	National Academy of Sciences.
NDRC	National Defense Research Committee.
NEA	National Education Association.
NSF	National Science Foundation.
NYT	*New York Times.*
OSRD	Office of Scientific Research and Development.
OF	(President's) Official Files.
PRO	Public Records Office, London (Kew Gardens), England.
PSF	President's Secretary's Files.
RDB	Research and Development Board.
RG	Record Group.
RRC	Russian Research Center, Harvard University, Cambridge, Mass.
S/AE	Records of the Special Assistant to the Secretary of State for Atomic Energy Matters (S/AE), 1944-1952, Series 1—General Records Relating to Atomic Energy Matters, 1944-1952, Lot 57 D 688, Record Group 59, National Archives, Washington, D.C.
THC	*The Harvard Crimson.*
TRC	Theodore Richards Conant, son of James B. Conant.
TSV	Tracy S. Voorhees.
TWR	Theodore William Richards.
UMS	Universal Military Service.
UMT	Universal Military Training.
VB	Vannevar Bush.
VBP	Vannevar Bush Papers, Library of Congress, Washington, D.C.
WLM	William L. Marbury.

Principal Sources

MANUSCRIPT COLLECTIONS

American Institute of Physics, New York, N.Y.

Niels Bohr papers (microfilm)
Bart J. Bok oral history interview
Theodore Dunham oral history interview

Willard Libby oral history interview
Harlow Shapley oral history interview

American Philosophical Society, Philadelphia, Penn.

Leonard Carmichael papers
Hans T. Clark papers

Simon Flexner papers
Henry D. Smyth papers

California Institute of Technology, Pasadena, Calif.

Lee A. DuBridge papers
William A. Fowler papers

Charles C. Lauritsen papers
Richard C. Tolman papers

University of California, Berkeley, Calif.
Bancroft Library

Ernest O. Lawrence papers

Robert Sproul papers

University of Chicago, Chicago, Ill.
Regenstein Library

Samuel K. Allison papers
Association of Cambridge Scientists papers
Committee to Frame a World Constitution
  papers
Federation of American Scientists papers

Federation of Atomic Scientists papers
Enrico Fermi papers
James Franck papers
Robert Hutchins papers

Columbia University, New York, N.Y.
Butler Library

Jacques Barzun papers
Carnegie Corporation papers
Carnegie Endowment for International
  Peace papers
Columbia Oral History Project interviews
  Paul H. Buck
  Harvey H. Bundy

James B. Conant
William L. Lawrence
Norman Ramsey
Henry L. Stimson
Dwight D. Eisenhower papers
Frederick P. Keppel papers
Warder W. Norton papers

Dartmouth College Library, Hanover, N.H.

Grenville Clark papers and diaries

John S. Dickey papers

Department of Energy, Germantown, Md.
Historian's Office/Archives

General Advisory Committee (U.S. Atomic Energy Commission) papers

Atomic Shield footnote file

Dwight D. Eisenhower Library, Abilene, Kans.

John Foster Dulles papers
Dwight D. Eisenhower prepresidential papers
Dwight D. Eisenhower presidential papers

Ann Whitman File
White House Central Files
Gordon Gray papers
Alfred M. Gruenther papers

Harvard University, Cambridge, Mass.

News Office files

Registrar's Office files

Pusey Library

Percy W. Bridgman papers
Paul H. Buck papers
James B. Conant personal papers
   presidential papers
   speech files
   diaries
Harvard Crimson papers

Jerome D. Greene papers
Edwin C. Kemble papers
Clyde Kluckhohn papers
A. Lawrence Lowell papers
Theodore W. Richards papers
Harlow Shapley papers
Samuel Stouffer papers

Houghton Library

John Marquand papers
George Sarton papers

Robert E. Sherwood papers

Baker Library, Harvard Business School

Chester I. Barnard papers

Thomas W. Lamont papers

Langdell Library, Harvard Law School

David F. Cavers papers
Zechariah Chafee, Jr., papers
Felix Frankfurter papers
Learned Hand papers

Mark DeWolfe Howe papers
W. Barton Leach papers
Charles E. Wyzanski papers

Federal Bureau of Investigation, Washington, D.C.
(Freedom of Information Act files)

James B. Conant
Harvard Crimson
J. Robert Oppenheimer

Russian Research Center, Harvard University

Lyndon B. Johnson Presidential Library, Austin, Texas

John W. Gardner oral history
Frank Keppel oral history
Frank Keppel Office of Education oral

history
John Macy Office Files
White House Central Files

John F. Kennedy Presidential Library, Boston, Mass.

John Kenneth Galbraith papers
Arthur M. Schlesinger, Jr., papers

James P. Warburg papers

Library of Congress, Washington, D.C.

Joseph Alsop papers
Vannevar Bush papers
Felix Frankfurter papers and diaries
Averell Harriman papers
Archibald MacLeish papers

Reinhold Niebuhr papers
J. Robert Oppenheimer papers
Robert P. Patterson papers
I. I. Rabi papers

Massachusetts Institute of Technology, Cambridge, Mass.

Vannevar Bush papers
Karl T. Compton—James R. Killian papers

Carroll L. Wilson papers and diaries

National Archives and Records Administration
National Archives, Washington, D.C.

Bureau of the Budget (RG 51)
Department of State (RG 59)
Leslie R. Groves (RG 200)
Manhattan Engineering District (RG 77)
National Defense Research Committee
  (RG 227)
National Science Foundation (RG 307)
Office of Scientific Research and Development (RG 227)

Research and Development Board
  (RG 330)
Secretary of Defense (RG 330)
Secretary of War (RG 107)
U.S. Atomic Energy Commission (RG 326)
U.S. Congress, Joint Committee on Atomic
  Energy (RG 128)
U.S. Congress, Special Committee on
  Atomic Energy (RG 46)

Washington National Records Center, Suitland, Md.

U.S. High Commissioner for Germany (RG 466)

Princeton University, Princeton, N.J.
Mudd Library

Bernard M. Baruch papers
Harold Dodds papers
John Foster Dulles papers
John Foster Dulles Oral History Collection
  James B. Conant interview

Allen W. Dulles papers
James Forrestal papers and diaries
David E. Lilienthal papers and diaries
Edward Earl Mead papers
Livingston Merchant papers

Franklin D. Roosevelt Library, Hyde Park, N.Y.

Oscar Cox papers
Harry Hopkins papers
Henry Morgenthau papers and diaries

Franklin D. Roosevelt presidential papers
  President's Secretary's Files
  President's Personal Files

Rutgers University, New Brunswick, N.J.

Committee on the Present Danger papers   Tracy S. Voorhees papers

Harry S Truman Library, Independence, Mo.

Dean G. Acheson papers
William L. Clayton papers
Clark Clifford papers
Lansing Lamont papers
Frederick Osborn diaries
Oral History Collection
    E. Allan Lightner, Jr.

H. Freeman Matthews
Psychological Strategy Board Papers
Harry S Truman—Official Files
    President's Personal Files
    President's Secretary's Files
    White House Central Files
    White House Confidential Files

Tufts University, Medford, Mass.

Vannevar Bush papers
Leonard Carmichael papers

Edward R. Murrow papers

State Historical Society of Wisconsin, Madison, Wis.

Marquis W. Childs papers
Alexander Meiklejohn papers

Arthur W. Page papers

Yale University, New Haven, Conn.
Sterling Library

Dean G. Acheson papers
A. Whitney Griswold papers
Walter Lippmann papers

Charles Whitney Seymour papers
Henry L. Stimson papers and diaries

Other Collections Consulted

Roger Adams papers, University of Illinois, Urbana, Ill.
Isaiah Bowman papers, Johns Hopkins University, Baltimore, Md.
James F. Byrnes papers, Robert Muldrow Cooper Library, Clemson University, Clemson, S.C.
Carnegie Institution of Washington archives, Washington, D.C.
Arthur H. Compton papers, Washington University, St. Louis, Mo.
Edmund E. Day papers, Cornell University, Ithaca, N.Y.
Lewis W. Douglas papers, University of Arizona, Tucson, Ariz.
Educational Policies Commission papers, National Education Association archives, Washington, D.C.
Herbert S. Gasser papers, Rockefeller Archive Center, Pocantico Hills, North Tarrytown, N.Y.
William T. Golden papers, courtesy of Mr. Golden.
Sidney Hook papers, Hoover Institution on War, Revolution, and Peace, Stanford, Calif.
George B. Kistiakowsky papers, courtesy of Elaine Kistiakowsky.
Douglas MacArthur papers, MacArthur Memorial, Norfolk, Va.
Deane Malott papers, University of Kansas, Lawrence, Kans.
William L. Marbury papers, courtesy of Mr. Marbury.
George C. Marshall papers, George C. Marshall Research Library, Lexington, Va.
F. O. Matthieson papers, Beinecke Library, Yale University, New Haven, Conn.
National Academy of Sciences archives, Washington, D.C.
National War College files, National Defense University, Fort McNair, Va.

Alfred N. Richards papers, University of Pennsylvania, Philadelphia, Penn.
Glenn T. Seaborg journals, 1946–1958, Lawrence Berkeley Laboratory, University of California
Lewis L. Strauss papers, Herbert Hoover Presidential Library, West Branch, Iowa.
Harold Urey papers, University of California, San Diego, La Jolla, Calif.
Henry Wriston papers, Brown University, Providence, R.I.

PERSONAL INTERVIEWS

Interviews indicated with an asterisk were conducted by telephone; all others were conducted in person.

Luis Alvarez, February 1985.*
Jeanne Amster, 1988–1990.
Kenneth T. Bainbridge, February 1982.
Paul D. Bartlett, December 1992.*
Hans Bethe, January 1985.*
Richard Bissell, September 1992.*
Edwin F. Black, February 1985.*
Robert W. Bowie, October 1988, June 1993.
David Bradley, February 1989.
McGeorge Bundy, November 1986, April 1991.*
I. B. Cohen, January 1987.
Clark Conant, February 1993.*
Grace Richards Conant, November 1983.
Jim Conant, August 1986, 1991–1993.
Jennet Conant, March 1992, January 1993.*
Theodore and Ellen Conant, 1982, 1986–93.
R. Ammi Cutter, April 1987.
John S. Dickey, 1982.*
Robert J. Donovan, June 1992.
Lee A. DuBridge, January 1982,* August 1986,* April 1991.
Daniel Ellsberg, 1988–1989.
John King Fairbank, March 1989.*
John H. Finley, September 1986.
John Kenneth Galbraith, January 1989, November 1990.*
John Gardner, November 1992.*
Owen Gingrich, November 1988.*
William T. Golden, January 1987.
Jesse L. Greenstein, May 1991.
Gerald Holton, April 1993.*
H. Stuart Hughes, April 1989.*
Rudolph Kass, 1989.
Francis Keppel, February 1989.

Elaine Kistiakowsky, October–November 1986.
George B. Kistiakowsky, January 1982.
Arnold Kramish, February 1993.*
Thomas S. Kuhn, June 1993.*
John Lansdale, December 1992.
John H. Manley, November 1986.*
William L. Marbury, August 1986.
Dr. Allan R. McClary, February 1993.*
Everett Mendelsohn, 1988–1989.
Philip Morrison, October 1988.
Bill Moyers, November 1992.*
Kenneth Pitzer, February 1985.*
Tom Polgar, November 1991.*
Don K. Price, January 1982.
I. I. Rabi, January 1982,* February 1985,* April 1985.
Norman K. Ramsey, January 1982.
David Riesman, January 1989.
Carl Rowan, March 1993.*
Dick Rowsen, October 1992.
Abram Sachar, May 1991.*
Glenn T. Seaborg, February 1985.*
Robert Serber, May 1992.*
Sargent Shriver, November 1992.*
William A. Shurcliff, December 1986.*
John G. Simon, February 1989.
Alice Kimball Smith, January 1987.
Alan Sweezey, June 1991.*
Harold Taylor, May 1991.*
Edward Teller, November 1986.*
Robert C. Tucker, September 1992.*
William M. Tuttle, Jr., 1982, 1989.
Adam Ulam, January 1989.
Victor Weisskopf, February 1988.*
Fred Whipple, November 1988.*
Carroll L. Wilson, March 1982.*
E. Bright Wilson, December 1986.

DISSERTATIONS AND THESES

Amster, Jeanne Ellen. "Meritocracy Ascendant: James Bryant Conant and Cultivation of Talent." Ph.D. diss., Graduate School of Education, Harvard University, 1990.

Balogh, Brian. "Trouble in Paradise: Institutionalized Expertise in the Development of Nuclear Power, 1945–1975." Ph.D. diss., Johns Hopkins University, 1987.

Biebel, Charles DeWayne. *Politics, Pedagogues and Statesmanship: James B. Conant and the Public Schools, 1933–1948.* Ph.D. diss., University of Wisconsin, 1971; Ann Arbor, Mich.: University Microfilms International, 1971.

Hershberg, James G. "Ends vs. Means: James B. Conant and American Atomic Policy, 1939–1947." B.A. thesis, History Department, Harvard University, 1982.

——. *James B. Conant, Nuclear Weapons, and the Cold War, 1945–1950.* Ph.D. diss., Tufts University, 1989; Ann Arbor, Mich.: University Microfilms International, 1989.

Jones, Daniel Patrick. *The Role of Chemists in Research on War Gases in the United States During World War I.* Ph.D. diss., University of Wisconsin, 1969; Ann Arbor, Mich.: University Microfilms International, 1970.

Jones, Kenneth MacDonald. *Science, Scientists, and Americans: Images of Science and the Formation of Federal Science Policy, 1945–1950.* Ph.D. diss., Cornell University, 1975; Ann Arbor, Mich.: University Microfilms International, 1975.

Marsden, David Lane. "The Cold War and American Education." Ph.D. diss., University of Kansas, 1976.

Miscamble, Wilson Douglas. *George F. Kennan, The Policy Planning Staff and American Foreign Policy, 1947–1950.* Ph.D. diss., University of Notre Dame, 1980; Ann Arbor, Mich.: University Microfilms International, 1980.

O'Connell, Charles. "The Political Context of the Period: The Cold War and its Influence upon University Scholars at the Harvard Russian Research Center." Draft chapter, Ph.D. diss., University of California at Los Angeles, 1990.

Saltzman, Kevin Michael. "Countdown to Sputnik: The Institutionalization of Scientific Expertise in the White House, 1945–1957." B.A. thesis, History Department, Harvard University, 1988.

Teicher, Barry James. *James Bryant Conant and the American High School Today.* Ph.D. diss., University of Wisconsin, 1977; Ann Arbor, Mich.: University Microfilms International, 1977.

Tuttle, William M. Jr. *James B. Conant, Pressure Groups, and the National Defense, 1933–1945.* Ph.D. diss., University of Wisconsin, 1967; Ann Arbor, Mich.: University Microfilms International, 1970.

FREQUENTLY CITED BOOKS

Acheson, Dean G. *Present at the Creation.* New York: Norton, 1969.

Alperovitz, Gar. *Atomic Diplomacy: Hiroshima and Potsdam.* New York: Simon and Schuster, 1965; rev. ed., Penguin Books, 1985.

Balogh, Brian. *Chain Reaction: Expert Debate and Public Participation in American Commercial Nuclear Power, 1945–1975.* Cambridge: Cambridge University Press, 1991.

Bernstein, Barton J., ed. *The Atomic Bomb: The Critical Issues.* Boston and Toronto: Little, Brown, 1976.

Bird, Kai. *The Chairman: John J. McCloy: The Making of the American Establishment.* New York: Simon & Schuster, 1992.

Boyer, Paul. *By the Bomb's Early Light.* New York: Pantheon, 1985.

Bundy, McGeorge. *Danger and Survival: Choices About the Bomb in the First Fifty Years.* New York: Random House, 1988.

Bush, Vannevar. *Pieces of the Action.* New York: William Morrow, 1970.

Caute, David. *The Great Fear: The Anti-Communist Purge Under Truman and Eisenhower.* New York: Simon and Schuster, 1978.

Compton, Arthur H. *Atomic Quest: A Personal Narrative.* New York: Oxford University Press, 1956.

Conant, James B. *On Understanding Science.* New Haven, Conn.: Yale University Press, 1947.

——. *Education in a Divided World.* Cambridge, Mass.: Harvard University Press, 1948.

——. *Science and Common Sense.* New Haven: Yale University Press, 1951.

——. *Anglo-American Relations in the Atomic Age.* Oxford: Oxford University Press, 1952.

——. *Modern Science and Modern Man.* New York: Columbia University Press, 1952.

——. *Education and Liberty: The Role of the Schools in a Modern Democracy.* Cambridge: Harvard University Press, 1953.

——. *Germany and Freedom: A Personal Appraisal.* Cambridge: Harvard University Press, 1958.

——. *Slums and Suburbs.* New York: McGraw-Hill, 1961; rev. ed., New American Library, 1964.

——. *My Several Lives: Memoirs of a Social Inventor.* New York: Harper & Row, 1970.

Diamond, Sigmund. *Compromised Campus: The Collaboration of Universities with the Intelligence Community.* New York: Oxford University Press, 1992.

Donovan, Robert J. *Conflict and Crisis: The Presidency of Harry S Truman, 1945–1948.* New York: W.W. Norton, 1977.

——. *Tumultuous Years: The Presidency of Harry S Truman, 1949–1953.* New York: W.W. Norton, 1982.

Educational Policies Commission. *American Education and International Tensions.* Washington, D.C.: National Education Association of the United States and the American Association of School Administrators, 1949.

English, J. Merton. *A Patron for Pure Science: The National Science Foundation's Formative Years, 1945–1957.* Washington, D.C.: National Science Foundation, 1983.

Etzold, Thomas H., and John Lewis Gaddis, eds. *Containment: Documents on American Policy and Strategy, 1945–1950.* New York: Columbia University Press, 1978.

Freeland, Richard M. *The Truman Doctrine and the Origins of McCarthyism: Foreign Policy, Domestic Politics, and International Security, 1946–48.* New York: Schocken Books, 1974.

Gaddis, John Lewis. *Strategies of Containment: A Critical Appraisal of Postwar American National Security Policy.* New York: Oxford University Press, 1982.

Galambos, Louis, ed. *The Papers of Dwight David Eisenhower.* Baltimore: Johns Hopkins University Press, 1945, 1970, 1984, 1989.

Gilpin, Robert. *American Scientists and Nuclear Weapons Policy.* Princeton: Princeton University Press, 1962.

Gowing, Margaret. *Britain and Atomic Energy, 1939–1945.* New York: St. Martin's Press, 1964.

Greenberg, Daniel S. *The Politics of Pure Science.* New York: New American Library, 1967; repr. ed. 1971.

Halle, Louis J. *The Cold War as History.* New York: Harper & Row, 1967.

Herken, Gregg. *The Winning Weapon: The Atomic Bomb in the Cold War, 1945–1950.* New York: Random House, 1981.

——. *Counsels of War,* 2d ed. New York: Oxford University Press, 1987.

——. *Cardinal Choices: Presidential Science Advising from the Atomic Bomb to SDI.* New York: Oxford University Press, 1992.

Hewlett, Richard G., and Oscar E. Anderson, Jr. *The New World, 1939 1946.* Vol. I, *A History of the United States Atomic Energy Commission.* University Park, Penn.: Pennsylvania State University Press, 1962.

Hewlett, Richard G., and Francis Duncan. *Atomic Shield, 1947/1952:* Vol. II, *A History of the United States Atomic Energy Commission.* University Park, Penn.: Pennsylvania State University Press, 1969.

Isaacson, Walter, and Evan Thomas. *The Wise Men: Six Friends and the World They Made.* New York: Simon and Schuster, 1986.

Kaplan, Fred. *The Wizards of Armageddon.* New York: Simon and Schuster, 1983.

Kennan, George F. *Memoirs, 1925-1950.* Boston: Atlantic—Little, Brown, 1967.
Kevles, Daniel J. *The Physicists: The History of a Scientific Community in Modern America.* New York: Alfred A. Knopf, 1978; Vintage ed., 1979.
Killian, James R., Jr. *The Education of a College President.* Cambridge, Mass.: MIT Press, 1985.
Lilienthal, David E. *The Journals of David E. Lilienthal.* Vol. II: *The Atomic Energy Years, 1945-1950.* New York: Harper & Row, 1964.
———. *The Journals of David E. Lilienthal.* Vol. III, *Venturesome Years, 1950-1955.* New York: Harper & Row, 1966.
Lipset, Seymour Martin, and David Riesman. *Education and Politics at Harvard.* New York: McGraw-Hill, 1975.
Marbury, William L. *In the Catbird Seat.* Baltimore: Maryland Historical Society, 1988.
Messer, Robert L. *The End of an Alliance: James F. Byrnes, Roosevelt, Truman, and the Origins of the Cold War.* Chapel Hill, N.C.: University of North Carolina Press, 1982.
Mills, C. Wright. *The Power Elite.* New York: Oxford University Press, 1956.
Morison, Samuel Eliot. *Three Centuries of Harvard.* Cambridge, Mass.: The Belknap Press, 1936.
Powers, Thomas. *Heisenberg's War: The Secret History of the German Bomb.* New York: Alfred A. Knopf, 1993.
Rhodes, Richard. *The Making of the Atomic Bomb.* New York: Simon and Schuster, 1986.
Sanders, Jerry W. *Peddlers of Crisis: The Committee on the Present Danger and the Politics of Containment.* Boston: South End Press, 1983.
Schlesinger, Arthur M., Jr. *The Vital Center: The Politics of Freedom.* Boston: Houghton Mifflin, 1949; repr. ed., New York: Da Capo Press, 1988.
Schrecker, Ellen W. *No Ivory Tower: McCarthyism and the Universities.* New York: Oxford University Press, 1986.
Schwartz, Thomas Alan. *America's Germany: John J. McCloy and the Federal Republic of Germany.* Cambridge, Mass.: Harvard University Press, 1991.
Servos, John W. *Physical Chemistry from Ostwald to Pauling: The Making of a Science in America.* Princeton, N.J.: Princeton University Press, 1990.
Sherwin, Martin J. *A World Destroyed: The Atomic Bomb and the Grand Alliance.* New York: Alfred A. Knopf, 1975; references are to the 1987 Vintage paperback edition, *A World Destroyed: Hiroshima and the Origins of the Arms Race.*
Smith, Alice Kimball. *A Peril and a Hope: The Scientists' Movement in America, 1945-47.* Cambridge, Mass.: MIT Press, 1965.
Smith, Richard Norton. *The Harvard Century: The Making of a University to a Nation.* New York: Simon and Schuster, 1986.
Stimson, Henry L., and McGeorge Bundy. *On Active Service in War and Peace.* New York: Harper & Brothers, 1947, 1948.
Synott, Marcia Graham. *The Half-Opened Door: Discrimination and Admissions at Harvard, Yale, and Princeton, 1900-1970.* Westport, Conn.: Greenwood Press, 1979.
Taubman, William. *Stalin's America Policy: From Entente to Detente to Cold War.* New York: W.W. Norton, 1982.
Theoharis, Athan G., ed. *Beyond the Hiss Case: The FBI, Congress, and the Cold War.* Philadelphia: Temple University Press, 1982.
Truman, Harry S *Memoirs.* Vol. 1, *Year of Decisions* (Garden City, N.Y.: Doubleday, 1955.
———. *Memoirs.* Vol. 2, *Years of Trial and Hope, 1946-1952.* Garden City, N.Y.: Doubleday, 1956.
U.S. Atomic Energy Commission. *In the Matter of J. Robert Oppenheimer: Transcript of Hearing Before the Personnel Security Board, Washington, D.C., April 12, 1954, through May 6, 1954.* Washington, D.C.: U.S. Government Printing Office, 1954; Cambridge, Mass.: MIT Press ed., 1971.
U.S. Congress. Senate Committee on Foreign Relations. *Nomination of James B. Conant.* 83d Cong., 1st sess., 1953.

U.S. Department of State. *Documents on Germany, 1944-1985.* Washington, D.C.: Department of State Publication 9446.

———. *Foreign Relations of the United States.* Washington, D.C.: U.S. Government Printing Office.

York, Herbert. *The Advisors: Oppenheimer, Teller and the Superbomb.* San Francisco: W. H. Freeman, 1976.

Notes

INTRODUCTION

1. JBC, *MSL*; *NYT*, Mar. 4, 1970, 45; *Time* (Mar. 16, 1970), 96–97.
2. JBC, "Notes on Writing an Autobiography," May 22, 1969, JBC PERP.
3. JBC, "The President's Farewell," *THC*, Jan. 22, 1953. "As far as I am concerned," he wrote one correspondent seven years later, tongue only half in cheek, "everything that happened at Harvard while I was President which is not on the record never happened!" JBC to Mrs. Jonathan Bingham, Jan. 28, 1960, JBC PERP.
4. Russell Maloney, "James B. Conant—Ambassador to the Cosmos," *Saturday Review of Literature* 30 (Dec. 6, 1947), 15.
5. TRC interview, Jan. 1987.
6. JBC, "Notes on Writing an Autobiography."
7. JBC to VB, Mar. 26, 1954, box 27, folder 614, VBP; on JBC, HLS, and Hiroshima, see chap. 16.
8. E. H. Carr, *What Is History?* (New York: Random House, 1961), esp. chap. 1.
9. FF to GC, Aug. 8, 1956, box 184, folder 2, FFP. The "red tape" and "gnostic priest" comments were recalled in interviews with, respectively, I. I. Rabi and Adam Ulam; "cold reserved New Englander": JBC to TSV, Nov. 29, 1963, JBC PERP, box 14 ("Daily Calendars, 1958–1970"); "cranky New Englander": JBC, unpublished ms., "A Guide to Public Education" (1962), 15–16, in Jeanne Ellen Amster, *Meritocracy Ascendant: James Bryant Conant and Cultivation of Talent* (Ph.D. diss., Graduate School of Education, Harvard University, 1990), 258.
10. Telephone interview with Robert C. Tucker, Sept. 21, 1992; John H. Finley, "Mr. Conant and Harvard College," in *James Bryant Conant: A Remembrance* (Cambridge, Mass.: Harvard University, 1978), 10; Clarence B. Randall, *Adventures in Friendship* (Boston: Atlantic Monthly Press, 1965), 33.
11. JBC, *MSL*, 35.
12. Merle Borrowman, "Conant, the Man," *Saturday Review of Literature* 46 (Sept. 21, 1960), 58–60.
13. Kermit Roosevelt, "Harvard's Prize Kibitzer," *Saturday Evening Post* 226 (Apr. 23, 1949), 75.
14. The author's previous published works on JBC include: "Ends vs. Means: James B. Conant and American Atomic Policy, 1939–1947" (Harvard College thesis, 1982); "Present at the Creation," *THC*, June 1982 Commencement Issue; "James B. Conant and the Atomic Bomb," *Journal of Strategic Studies* 8:1 (March 1985), 78–92; "Preserving 250 Million Pages of Knowledge," *Washington Post*, Aug. 31, 1986; "Harvard to Hiroshima: James B. Conant and the Birth of the Nuclear Age," *Harvard Review* 1:1 (Fall 1986), 31–51; "'Over My Dead Body': James B. Conant and the Hydrogen Bomb," in Everett Mendelsohn, et al., eds., *Science, Technology and the Military* (Dordrecht, the Netherlands: Klewer Academic Publishers, 1988), vol. 2, 379–430; *James B. Conant, Nuclear Weapons, and the Cold War, 1945–1950* (Ph.D. diss., Tufts University, 1989; Ann Arbor, Mich.: University Microfilms

International, 1989); "'Explosion in the Offing': German Rearmament and American Diplomacy, 1953-55," *Diplomatic History* 16:4 (Fall 1992), 511-49.

CHAPTER 1

1. Harvard Class of 1914, *Twenty-Fifth Anniversary Report* (Cambridge, Mass.: Cosmos Press, 1939), 164 (hereafter *Twenty-Fifth Anniversary Report*).
2. JBC, *MSL*, xvi.
3. Edward Weeks, *My Green Age: A Memoir* (Boston: Little, Brown & Co., 1973), 11.
4. TRC interview, 1987. In a 1937 speech, JBC called himself an "educational Calvinist" who believed in "predestination if not at birth at least at the college entrance age." JBC, "Liberal Education: The Selective Principle in American Colleges," *Vital Speeches* 3 (Feb. 1, 1937), 254, quoted in Barry James Teicher, *James Bryant Conant and "The American High School Today"* (Ph.D. diss., University of Wisconsin, 1977; Ann Arbor, Mich.: University Microfilms International, 1977), 167.
5. Eulogy of JBC, 1978, by John H. Finley, Jr., and George B. Kistiakowsky, courtesy of Finley.
6. Quoted, Robert R. Mullen, "Harvard's Conant: Defender of Freedom," *Christian Science Monitor* magazine, Mar. 1, 1941.
7. Ralph Waldo Emerson, "Swedenborg; Or, The Mystic," in R. E. Spiller, ed., *Selected Essays, Lectures, and Poems of Ralph Waldo Emerson* (New York: Simon & Schuster, 1965), 129-56.
8. JBC, *MSL*, 9-11; "cautious but optimistic theism": JBC, *Baccalaureate Sermon to the Harvard College Class of 1950* (Cambridge: Harvard University, 1950), 8, 9; see also William M. Tuttle, Jr., *James B. Conant, Pressure Groups, and the National Defense, 1933-1945*, (Ph.D. diss., University of Wisconsin, 1967; Ann Arbor, Mich.: University Microfilms International, 1970), 3-5; and for "perfection of man": Emerson, "Swedenborg: Or, The Mystic," 146.
9. JBC, *MSL*, 7-8, 11; see also Paul F. Douglass, *Six Upon the World: Toward an American Culture for an Industrial Age* (Boston: Little, Brown & Co., 1954), 331.
10. JBC, *MSL*, 11; see also Charles DeWayne Biebel, *Politics, Pedagogues, and Statesmanship: James B. Conant and the Public Schools, 1933-1948* (Ph.D. diss., University of Wisconsin, 1971; Ann Arbor, Mich.: University Microfilms International, 1971), 9-10.
11. JBC, *MSL*, 11-12; see also Tuttle, *James B. Conant*, 5.
12. Samuel Eliot Morison, *One Boy's Boston: 1887-1901* (Boston: Northeastern University Press, 1983), 81.
13. Sam Bass Warner, *Streetcar Suburbs* (Cambridge, Mass.: Harvard University Press, 1978), 35-37, cited in Amster, *Meritocracy Ascendant*, 23.
14. JBC, *MSL*, 4-7; Biebel, *Politics, Pedagogues, and Statesmanship*, 4-8; "rich equine flavor": Morison, *One Boy's Boston*, 23.
15. Tuttle, *James B. Conant*, 5-6; "Black, Formerly Instructor of Conant, Recalls Early Youth of New President," *THC*, May 9, 1933.
16. 1904 entrance examination results, Roxbury Latin School archives, West Roxbury, Mass. See also Henry F. Pringle, "Profiles: Mr. President," pt. 1, *New Yorker* (Sept. 12, 1936), 23; and Douglass, *Six Upon the World*, 331-32.
17. JBC to E. M. Purcell, Apr. 24, 1962, JBC PERP.
18. On JBC's relationship to Black: JBC, *MSL*, 15-19; JBC to E. M. Purcell, Apr. 24, 1962, and JBC to Susan Singer, Mar. 8, 1962, JBC PERP. See also Amster, *Meritocracy Ascendant*, 26-29; Douglass, *Six Upon the World*, 332-33; and John R. Tunis, "John Harvard's Biggest Boy," *American Magazine* (Oct. 1933), 20-21, 135-37, "towhead with a Dutch cut" is on 135.
19. JBC, *MSL*, 17.
20. Richards to N. Henry Black, Oct. 29, 1909; Black to Richards, Nov. 1, 1909; Richards

to Black, Nov. 5, 1909: JBC PERP, "Correspondence Re: Harvard Admission" folder; JBC, *MSL*, 17–19; see also Amster, *Meritocracy Ascendant*, 26–28.

21. Grade cards, JBC PERP, in Amster, *Meritocracy Ascendant*, 27–28.
22. Concentrating on his accelerated science classes, JBC slipped in the humanities on his college entrance exams, however, scoring D's and C's in English, history, Latin, German, and French, and A's and B's in physics, chemistry, and geometry. JBC transcript, Office of the Registrar, Harvard University; *Tripod* 22:9 (June 1910), 10, Roxbury Latin archives.
23. *Tripod* 22:9 (June 1910), 7.
24. *Tripod* 22:5 (Feb. 1910), 4–5. See also Pringle, "Profiles: Mr. President," I, 23; Tuttle, *James B. Conant*, 6–7; Amster, *Meritocracy Ascendant*, 24–25, 28; Douglass, *Six Upon the World*, 332; Biebel, *Politics, Pedagogues, and Statesmanship*, 10–17.
25. JBC, "Application for a Scholarship," May 12, 1910, JBC file, Office of the Registrar, Harvard University.
26. D. O. S. Lowell to J. G. Hart, May 4, 1910, JBC file, Office of the Registrar, Harvard University.
27. N. Henry Black to J. G. Hart, May 3, 1910, JBC file, Office of the Registrar, Harvard University.
28. *Tripod* 22:9 (June 1910), 15; see also Amster, *Meritocracy Ascendant*, 24–25.
29. The actual words, spoken by Isabella to Lord Deputy Angelo as she pleads with him to spare her brother's life, are: "O! it is excellent/To have a giant's strength; but it is tyrannous/To use it like a giant."

CHAPTER 2

1. Pringle, "Profiles: Mr. President," pt. 1, 23.
2. Marcia Graham Synott, *The Half-Opened Door: Discrimination and Admissions at Harvard, Yale, and Princeton, 1900–1970* (Westport, Conn.: Greenwood Press, 1979), 4. Sources for Eliot's presidency include Samuel Eliot Morison, *Three Centuries of Harvard* (Cambridge, Mass.: Belknap Press, 1936), 323–99; Richard Norton Smith, *The Harvard Century: The Making of a University to a Nation* (New York: Simon & Schuster, 1986), 27–61; Richard S. Kennedy, *Dreams in the Mirror: A Biography of E. E. Cummings* (New York: Liveright Publishing Corporation, 1980); Virginia Spencer Carr, *Dos Passos: A Life* (Garden City: Doubleday & Co., 1984).
3. Cited in Morison, *Three Centuries of Harvard*, 429.
4. George Santayana, *The Middle Span* (*Persons and Places*, vol. 2) (New York: Scribner's & Sons, 1945), 159.
5. John Reed, "Almost Thirty," *New Republic* 136 (Apr. 15, 29, 1936), 332–33.
6. See John Stuart, intro., *The Education of John Reed: Selected Writings* (New York: International Publishers, 1955), 10–12; Carr, *Dos Passos: A Life*, 67; Morison, *Three Centuries of Harvard*, 434–38; "moved out into the great world of hellroaring and confusion" is from Dos Passos's reminiscence, "P.S. to Dean Briggs," in Brooks Atkinson, ed., *College in a Yard: Minutes by Thirty-Nine Harvard Men* (Cambridge, Mass.: Harvard University Press, 1957), 63–68; John Mason Brown, *The Worlds of Robert E. Sherwood: Mirror to His Times, 1896–1939* (New York: Harper & Row, 1962, 1965); Ronald Steel, *Walter Lippmann and the American Century* (Boston: Little, Brown & Co., 1980), 12–32.
7. See Charles Norman, *The Magic-Maker: E. E. Cummings* (New York: Macmillan Co., 1958), 46.
8. Reed, "Almost Thirty," 333.
9. Morison, *Three Centuries of Harvard*, 419–28 (quotation on 422).
10. Morison, *One Boy's Boston*, 56.
11. Cited in Kennedy, *Dreams in the Mirror*, 53.

12. See Robert A. Rosenstone, *Romantic Revolutionary: A Biography of John Reed* (New York: Alfred A. Knopf, 1975), 38–41.

13. John P. Marquand, *The Late George Apley* (New York: Grosset & Dunlap, 1936, 1937), 73–74.

14. Marquand, *The Late George Apley*, 215–19.

15. Loyally reading his friend's novels, JBC in 1941 praised Marquand's "penetrating sociological analysis of a highly interesting and complex bit of society. Since it has fallen to my lot to be peculiarly enmeshed in the web of this society, I appreciated with particular relish some of your analyses." In 1949, Conant nostalgically complimented Marquand's "great knack for portraying a period which all our generation must remember somewhat bitterly." JBC to Marquand, Nov. 13, 1939, Jan. 3, 1941, and Mar. 14, 1949, in John P. Marquand Papers, Houghton Library, Harvard University.

16. JBC address, Sept. 23, 1933, as quoted in *BG* PM edition, Sept. 23, 1933; *NYT,* Sept. 24, 1933; [New York] *American,* Sept. 24, 1933; *THC,* Sept. 25, 1933; and H. I. Brock, "Conant States His Creed for Harvard," *NYT Magazine,* Mar. 18, 1934.

17. Morison, *Three Centuries of Harvard,* 446–47.

18. JBC, *MSL,* 24; on JBC's undergraduate experience, see esp. JBC, *MSL,* 20–26; Amster, *Meritocracy Ascendant,* 29–42; Biebel, *Politics, Pedagogues, and Statesmanship,* 17–20; and Tuttle, *James B. Conant,* 7–8.

19. JBC diary, 1911–12, JBC PERP, UA I.15.898.13, box 11.

20. Amster, *Meritocracy Ascendant,* 37.

21. John W. Servos, *Physical Chemistry from Ostwald to Pauling: The Making of a Science in America* (Princeton, N.J.: Princeton University Press, 1990), 78.

22. See Servos, *Physical Chemistry from Ostwald to Pauling,* 78–82; JBC, *MSL,* 27–30; JBC, "Theodore William Richards, January 31, 1868–April 2, 1928," in National Academy of Sciences, *Biographical Memoirs* 44 (Washington, D.C.: National Academy of Sciences, 1974), 251–86; Sheldon Jerome Kopperl, *The Scientific Work of Theodore William Richards* (Ph.D. diss., University of Wisconsin, 1970); Aaron J. Ihde, "Theodore William Richards and the Atomic Weight Problem," *Science* 164 (May 9, 1969), 647–51.

23. Servos, *Physical Chemistry from Ostwald to Pauling,* 80, 118–19; JBC, *MSL,* 31; on TWR's skeptical view of Bohr, Einstein, and their "modern" views on atomic structure, see esp. TWR to Svante Arrhenius, Jan. 18, 1923, and TWR to Robert N. Peace, Feb. 19, 1923, professional and personal correspondence, box 5, TWR Papers.

24. JBC, "Elmer P. Kohler, 1865–1938," in National Academy of Sciences, *Biographical Memoirs* 27 (Washington, D.C.: National Academy of Sciences, 1952), 264–91; JBC, *MSL,* 31–37.

25. JBC undergraduate transcripts, 1910–13, Office of the Registrar, Harvard University; on JBC's affinity for James: Perry Miller, "Dr. Conant Graduates: Harvard to Bonn," *Perspectives USA* 4 (Summer 1953), 78–85, 84.

26. JBC, "History in the Education of Scientists," *American Scientist* 48:4 (Dec. 1960), 528–43.

27. Reed, "After Thirty," 332; Steel, *Lippmann and the American Century,* 28.

28. Both reports can be found in the collection of *THC* papers in the Harvard University archives.

29. JBC, *MSL,* 24–25; Amster, *Meritocracy Ascendant,* 37–38.

30. Assignment List, *THC,* Tuesday, Dec. 19, 1911, pasted inside JBC's copy of the *THC* bound volume for 1912 (vol. 61) in his Hanover, N.H., summer house.

31. JBC diary, Jan. 17, 1912, JBC PERP, UA I.15.898.13, box 11.

32. Many decades later, JBC was rummaging through his old papers in Hanover with his son Theodore, and discovered a term paper he had written for Arthur Post's Renaissance art course. "I got an A, dammit," he announced proudly. His daughter-in-law, Ellen P. Conant, an art historian, gave it a critical reading and deemed it unworthy of such a high mark. "You don't understand," Conant responded, "I was on the *Crimson*"—the imputation being that such a mark of literary accomplishment

won respect from teachers. Interviews with Theodore and Ellen Conant, June 7, 1991.
33. JBC, *MSL,* 24.
34. Randall, *Adventures in Friendship,* 24-25.
35. Douglass, *Six Upon the World,* 333-35; Millicent Bell, *Marquand: An American Life* (Boston: Little, Brown & Co., 1979), 61; Stephen Birmingham, *The Late John Marquand: A Biography* (New York: J. B. Lippincott Co., 1972), 31-36; Amster, *Meritocracy Ascendant,* 34-36.
36. John P. Marquand, *H. M. Pulham, Esquire* (Boston: Little, Brown & Co., 1940, 1941; reprint, Bantam, 1963), 62.
37. Bell, *Marquand,* 58-60; tie incident: JBC to John P. Marquand, Nov. 13, 1939, Marquand Papers, Houghton Library, Harvard University.
38. JBC diary, July 5, 1912, quoted in Smith, *The Harvard Century,* 106-7.
39. Quoted in Carroll L. Wilson diary, Feb. 24, 1941, in Wilson Papers, 79-99, box 1, Massachusetts Institute of Technology archives, Cambridge.
40. Morison, *Three Centuries of Harvard,* 438.

CHAPTER 3

1. JBC, *MSL,* 629.
2. Robert van Gelder, "Dr. Conant's Triple Life," *NYT Magazine,* July 20, 1941, 23.
3. JBC, *MSL,* 25-26, 32-33, 38-40; Douglass, *Six Upon the World,* 335.
4. JBC, *MSL,* 41-42.
5. JBC, "When May a Man Dare to Be Alone," *Vital Speeches* 3 (July 15, 1937), 581, quoted in Tuttle, *James B. Conant,* 39-40; see also Morison, *Three Centuries of Harvard,* 450-56, and for TWR, correspondence in box 4, professional and personal correspondence, TWR Papers, Harvard University.
6. John Dos Passos, *The Best Times: An Informal Memoir* (New York: New American Library, 1966), 23; "outskirts of battle": Morison, *Three Centuries of Harvard,* 450. Sources for wartime Harvard include Morison, *Three Centuries of Harvard,* 450-60; John Mason Brown, *The Worlds of Robert E. Sherwood: Mirror to His Times, 1896-1939,* 92; Helen Howe, *The Gentle Americans, 1840-1960: The Biography of a Breed* (New York: Harper & Row, 1965), 236-40; Melvyn Landsberg, *Dos Passos' Path to U.S.A.: A Political Biography, 1912-1936* (Boulder: Colorado Associated University Press, 1972), 39.
7. Quoted in James P. O'Donnell, "Professor in a Hot Spot," *Saturday Evening Post* 226 (Dec. 5, 1953), 141.
8. JBC, *MSL,* 43.
9. Quoted in Robert Shaplen, "Sabbatical," *New Yorker* 32 (Oct. 13, 1956), 130ff.; Biebel, *Politics, Pedagogues, and Statesmanship,* 20-21.
10. JBC, *MSL,* 43-44; see also Shaplen, "Sabbatical."
11. *Twenty-Fifth Anniversary Report,* 164.
12. Servos, *Physical Chemistry from Ostwald to Pauling,* 202-213; JBC, *MSL,* 25-26, 38-40, 42.
13. "Three Men Die in Explosions," *Newark Evening News,* Nov. 27, 1916; "Blast in Benzoic Plant Is Probed," "Pennock Was Three Years on All-America Line-Up," *Newark Evening News,* Nov. 28, 1916; "Funerals Are Held Today for Two Explosion Victims," *Newark Evening News,* Nov. 29, 1916; in Newark, N.J., Public Library microfilm collection. Oddly, JBC only lists two persons as having been killed, Pennock and a plumber. JBC, *MSL,* 43-45.
14. JBC, *MSL,* 45.
15. JBC to Dr. George L. Kelley, Mar. 26, 1917, JBC PERP.
16. As noted in Amster, *Meritocracy Ascendant,* 43-44.

17. JBC, *MSL*, 47; see also *Twenty-Fifth Anniversary Report*, 165.
18. Quoted in Brown, *Worlds of Robert E. Sherwood*, 94.
19. Morison, *Three Centuries of Harvard*, 459–60.
20. JBC, *MSL*, 48.
21. The following account of the battle of Ypres, including the quotation from Byron, is from Daniel Patrick Jones, *The Role of Chemists in Research on War Gases in the United States during World War I* (Ph.D. diss., University of Wisconsin, 1969; Ann Arbor, Mich.: University Microfilms International, 1970), 52–55. Jones provides the most authoritative account of U.S. chemists' involvement in World War I poison gas work. See also the official Army history, Leo P. Brophy, Wyndham D. Miles, and Rexmond C. Cochrane, *The Chemical Warfare Service: From Laboratory to Field (United States Army in World War II: The Technical Services)* (Washington, D.C.: Office of the Chief of Military History, Department of the Army, 1959), chap. 1.
22. Report of Field Marshal Sir J. D. P. French, quoted in Victor Lefebure, *The Riddle of the Rhine: Chemical Strategy in Peace and War* (New York: Chemical Foundation, 1923), 31.
23. See L. F. Haber, *The Poisonous Cloud: Chemical Warfare in the First World War* (Oxford: Clarendon Press, 1986), 239–58; Jones, *The Role of Chemists*, 178–80.
24. On German scientists in World War I and the Kaiser Wilhelm Institute in particular, see Haber, *The Poisonous Cloud*, esp. 2, 127–28, 309; Jones, *The Role of Chemists*, 52–79; and Fritz Stern, *Dreams and Delusions: The Drama of German History* (New York: Alfred A. Knopf, 1987), esp. 34–37, 59–68.
25. Stern, *Dreams and Delusions*, 63; see also Richard Rhodes, *The Making of the Atomic Bomb* (New York: Simon & Schuster, 1986), 90–95.
26. Jones, *The Role of Chemists*, 54–68, 76.
27. JBC, "A Skeptical Chemist Looks into the Crystal Ball," Sept. 5, 1951, JBC Speech File, JBC PREP.
28. Daniel J. Kevles, *The Physicists: The History of a Scientific Community in Modern America* (New York: Alfred A. Knopf, 1978; Vintage ed., 1979), 111–18. On the impact of World War I on science-government relations in the United States, see also A. Hunter Dupree, *Science in the Federal Government: A History of Policies and Activities* (Cambridge, Mass.: Harvard University Press, 1957; Johns Hopkins University Press reprint ed., 1986), chap. 16; and Rexmond G. Cochrane, *The National Academy of Sciences: The First Hundred Years, 1863–1963* (Washington, D.C.: National Academy of Sciences, 1978), chap. 8.
29. Jones, *The Role of Chemists*, 89–109.
30. Jones, *The Role of Chemists*, 98–104.
31. JBC to George L. Kelley, Mar. 26, 1917, JBC PERP, Special Subject File.
32. Morison, *Three Centuries of Harvard*, 459.
33. JBC to H. D. Gibbs, May 31, 1917, JBC PERP; JBC, *MSL*, 48.
34. Jones, *The Role of Chemists*, 71.
35. See Jones, *The Role of Chemists*, 68–73, 75–76; Haber, *The Poisonous Cloud*, 188–95, 204–206, 211–19, 223–229, 256–57.
36. Pringle, "Profiles: Mr. President," pt. 1, 24.
37. JBC, *MSL*, 48.
38. JBC, *MSL*, 49; Jones, *The Role of Chemists*, 110.
39. Jones, *The Role of Chemists*, 122, 145; Brophy, Miles, and Cochrane, *The Chemical Warfare Service: From Laboratory to Field*, 5–8.
40. Jones, *The Role of Chemists*, 118, 133–35; Brophy, Miles, and Cochrane, *The Chemical Warfare Service: From Laboratory to Field*, 6.
41. Jones, *The Role of Chemists*, 136–39; Haber, *The Poisonous Cloud*, 111–13.
42. Pringle, "Profiles: Mr. President," pt. 1, 24; JBC, *MSL*, 48–49.
43. *Twenty-Fifth Anniversary Report*, 165. See also Amster, *Meritocracy Ascendant*, 46; Pringle, "Profiles: Mr. President," pt. 1, 24.
44. Tuttle, *James B. Conant*, 11. See also "Our Super-Poison Gas," *NYT Magazine*, Apr.

20, 1919; "Conant States His Creed for Harvard," *NYT Magazine,* Mar. 18, 1934; Jones, *The Role of Chemists,* 149-50; Tunis, "John Harvard's Biggest Boy," 21, 135; and Brophy, Miles, and Cochrane, *The Chemical Warfare Service: From Laboratory to Field,* 67.

45. Jones, *The Role of Chemists,* 150. Later studies raised questions about lewisite's military effectiveness, though it was routinely employed by the Imperial Japanese Army during its operations in China, though not against the Americans or British for fear of retaliation. See Haber, *The Poisonous Cloud,* 299, 344 n. 27; Jones, *The Role of Chemists,* 146, 191; and Meiron and Susie Harries, *Soldiers of the Sun: The Rise and Fall of the Imperial Japanese Army* (New York: Random House, 1991), 336-59. I thank TRC for informing me of lewisite's mention in *Soldiers of the Sun.* During World War II, the U.S. Chemical Warfare Service manufactured 20,000 tons of lewisite, then stopped production after concluding that the gas would be of only limited use should chemical warfare begin. See Brophy, Miles, and Cochrane, *The Chemical Warfare Service: From Laboratory to Field,* 67-69

46. Maj. Gen. William L. Sibert to Maj. James B. Conant, Feb. 4, 1919, "Subject: Commendation for Unusual Service," JBC PERP, Special Subject File, box 9.

47. JBC, *MSL,* 49-53; Pringle, "Profiles: Mr. President," pt. 1, 24; Douglass, *Six Upon the World,* 337; Tuttle, *James B. Conant,* 12; Biebel, *Politics, Pedagogues, and Statesmanship,* 22-26, 29-30.

48. Quoted in Pringle, "Profiles: Mr. President," pt. 1, 24.

49. Quoted in Tuttle, *James B. Conant,* 11-12.

50. JBC, *MSL,* 49-50.

CHAPTER 4

1. Servos, *Physical Chemistry from Ostwald to Pauling,* 215.

2. JBC, "Memorandum I: Teaching and Research in the 1920s," n.d. but dictated in mid-1960s, JBC PERP; see also Servos, *Physical Chemistry from Ostwald to Pauling,* 211-20.

3. JBC, *MSL,* 52.

4. See Tom Lutz, *American Nervousness, 1903: An Anecdotal History* (Ithaca, N.Y.: Cornell University Press, 1991); Michael Vincent Miller, "Anybody Who Was Anybody Was Neurasthenic," *NYT Book Review,* July 7, 1991.

5. On GRC's childhood: interviews with TRC (1987, 1991); interview with Jennet Conant, March 26, 1992; and various journals and documents in CFP, including GRC to Jean Demos, Feb. 22, 1968; GRC, "German influences on TWR and MTR," n.d. handwritten notes.

6. Tuttle, *James B. Conant,* 14-15.

7. GRC to JBC, Jan. 6, 1921, CFP; engagement: TWR diary, Aug. 22-29, Sept. 20, Oct. 22, 1920; ring: Clark Conant inteview, Feb. 1993. JBC had an unplanned chance to get on more intimate terms with his future in-laws when he spent Christmas week in 1920 at Follen Street recuperating from a spinal injury suffered when he was thrown from a horse. TWR diary, Dec. 20, 26, 1920, Jan. 1, 1921, TWR Papers.

8. GRC journal, Mar. 19, 25, 1921, CFP.

9. John H. Finley, draft eulogy for GRC, 1985, courtesy of Finley; TWR diary, Apr. 13-17, 1921.

10. JBC, *MSL,* 54; the editor's comment was recalled to the author by Ellen Conant, who recalls JBC feeling it a "terrible intrusion" of the editors to desire an account, in this autobiography, of how he came to be married.

11. Interviews with TRC and Ellen Conant, June 7, 1991; "matrimonial model": Biebel, *Politics, Pedagogues, and Statesmanship,* 27-28. JBC's son and daughter-in-law recall GRC's recollection of JBC's prior romance, although JBC never spoke of it to them. JBC's courtship of his wife: interviews with TRC and Ellen Conant (1987,

1991); JBC's grandson, Jim (1986); JBC's granddaughter, Jennet (1992); and with another JBC granddaughter, Clark Conant (1993).

12. JBC, *MSL,* 52.

13. TRC interview, June 7, 1991.

14. JBC, *MSL,* 55-58, 67; GRC diary, Summer 1921, CFP; "informal elite": JBC quoted in Biebel, *Politics, Pedagogues, and Statesmanship,* 29. On the postwar rift in international science, see Daniel J. Kevles, " 'Into Hostile Camps': The Reorganization of International Science in World War I," *ISIS* (Spring 1971).

15. GRC to "Precious Mother," Miriam T. Richards, Oct. 6, 1921, CFP. GRC's troubles with household help, which caused considerable distress throughout her life, fill page after page of anguished diary entries during the 1920s and 1930s. GRC's miscarriages: Jennet Conant interview, Mar. 26, 1992.

16. GRC to Miriam T. Richards, n.d. (1922) and Mar. 20, 1923, CFP.

17. Wendt to JBC, Feb. 21, 1919, JBC PERP.

18. Telephone interview with Paul D. Bartlett, Dec. 9, 1986.

19. Kermit Roosevelt, "Harvard's Prize Kibitzer," pt. 2, *Saturday Evening Post* 221 (Apr. 30, 1949), 142.

20. Colleagues' comments are cited in Pringle, "Profiles: Mr. President," pt. 2, *New Yorker* (Sept. 19, 1936), 23-24; see also John Finley and George Kistiakowsky, eulogy of JBC, 1978, courtesy of Finley.

21. G. B. Kistiakowsky and F. H. Westheimer, "James Bryant Conant, 1893-1978," *Biographical Memoirs of Fellows of the Royal Society* 25 (Nov. 1979), 209-232, 212; for assessments of JBC's scientific career see also Paul D. Bartlett, "James Bryant Conant," in National Academy of Sciences, *Biographical Memoirs* 34 (Washington, D.C.: National Academy, 1983), 91-124, and George B. Kistiakowsky, "J. B. Conant," *Nature* 273 (1978), 793-95.

22. Under the arrangement reached after hard bargaining to keep him from leaving Harvard for Caltech, JBC won an annual salary of $7,000, a requirement of one lecture course per year, plus a grant of $49,000 for research spread out over five years with a promise of additional funds "provided you have shown yourself to be so successful in your research as your work hitherto gives abundant reason to expect you will be." Clifford H. Moore to JBC, May 13, 1927, JBC PERP; see also Biebel, *Politics, Pedagogues, and Statesmanship,* 30-35, and folder 783, A. Lawrence Lowell papers, 1925-28 series, Pusey Library, Harvard University.

23. On JBC's relationship with Flexner and the Rockefeller Institute, which continued until June 1949, sixteen years into JBC's Harvard presidency, see esp. Biebel, *Politics, Pedagogues, and Statesmanship,* 35, 50 fn. 52, and correspondence in the Flexner papers, American Philosophical Society Library, Philadelphia, and Herbert S. Gasser papers, Rockefeller Institute archives.

24. David Hounshell and John K. Smith, *Science and Corporate Strategy: DuPont R&D, 1902-1980* (New York: Cambridge University Press, 1988), 299. In paraphrasing JBC's doubts about consulting for Du Pont, the authors cite his letters to Elmer K. Bolton of June 6 and 18, July 12 and 15, 1929, JBC PERP, box 3.

25. Quoted in *NYT,* Feb. 12, 1978; for JBC's consulting work, see Amster, *Meritocracy Ascendant,* 55-58 and JBC, *MSL,* 43, 61-63, 308.

26. JBC, *MSL,* 115.

27. Tuttle, *James B. Conant,* 23.

28. JBC, "Memorandum I, Teaching and Research in the 1920s," JBC PERP; JBC, *MSL,* 135-36.

29. Smith, *Harvard Century,* 85, citing interviews with Francis Burr and Charles Wyzanski.

30. Paul H. Buck, interview by William Bentinck-Smith, Summer 1974, p. 5, Buck Papers, HUG (B)—B857.50, Harvard University Archives, Nathan M. Pusey Library.

31. Leonard Baker, *Brandeis and Frankfurter: A Dual Biography* (New York: Harper & Row, 1984), 245-72.

32. The most detailed study of quotas at Harvard can be found in Synnott, *The*

Half-Opened Door, esp. xvii–xix, 3–124, 202–210; see also Stephan Thernstrom, "'Poor but Hopefull [*sic*] Scholars,'" in Bernard Bailyn et al., eds., *Glimpses of the Harvard Past* (Cambridge: Harvard University Press, 1986), 127–28.

33. Quoted in Synnott, *The Half-Opened Door,* 86.
34. Synnott, *The Half-Opened Door,* 60. For the perspectives of two prominent Jews associated with Harvard who held sharply differing views on the quota issue as well as their own Jewishness, Felix Frankfurter and Walter Lippmann, see Baker, *Brandeis and Frankfurter,* 220–244; and Steel, *Walter Lippmann and the American Century,* 193–95.
35. Synnott, *The Half-Opened Door,* 68–69, 89, 110, 252 fn. 33; Minutes of Harvard faculty meeting, June 2, 1922, Harvard University Archives; see also Sigmund Diamond, *Compromised Campus: The Collaboration of Universities with the Intelligence Community,* 1945–1955 (New York: Oxford University Press, 1992), 316 n. 5.
36. JBC, *MSL,* 135–36.
37. TRC interview, July 1991.
38. TRC and Ellen Conant interviews, 1991; Jennet Conant interview, Mar. 26, 1992.
39. JBC, *MSL,* 85–86; JBC, "History in the Education of Scientists," 541.
40. George Santayana, *The Middle Span,* 162.
41. Pringle, "Profiles: Mr. President," pt. 2, 27; Tuttle, *James B. Conant,* 17–18.
42. Arthur M. Schlesinger, *In Retrospect: The History of a Historian* (New York: Harcourt, Brace & World, 1963), 84.
43. JBC, *MSL,* 73–75; JBC, "Memorandum I, Teaching and Research in the 1920s," JBC PERP; correspondence in folder 783, Lowell Papers, 1925–28 series, Harvard University.
44. JBC, *MSL,* 58–59.
45. Quoted in James P. O'Donnell, "Professor in a Hot Spot," *Saturday Evening Post* 226 (Dec. 5, 1953), 141. For JBC's 1925 trip to Germany I have used JBC, diary of scientific encounters and ideas in Germany in 1925, JBC PERP; Tuttle, *James B. Conant,* 41–45; JBC, *MSL,* 67–73; Shaplen, "Sabbatical," 134; *Twenty-Fifth Anniversary Report,* 165; O'Donnell, "Professor in a Hot Spot," 141; JBC to TWR, Mar. 22, Apr. 22, May 15, June 1, 1925, TWR Papers.
46. JBC, diary of scientific encounters and ideas in Germany in 1925, JBC PERP; see also O'Donnell, "Professor in a Hot Spot."
47. JBC, *MSL,* 69–73.
48. JBC to Frank C. Whitmore, Jan. 7, 1927, JBC PERP.
49. For JBC's account of this meeting, see *MSL,* 629–30.
50. JBC, "Memorandum I, Teaching and Research in the 1920s," JBC PERP.
51. JBC, diary of scientific encounters and ideas in Germany in 1925, entry of June 16, 1925.
52. JBC, *MSL,* 59–61.
53. See *Twenty-Fifth Anniversary Report,* 165.
54. Shaplen, "Sabbatical," 134; *MSL,* 141.
55. Quoted in Tuttle, *James B. Conant,* 43–44.
56. JBC, *MSL,* 68; Tuttle, *James B. Conant,* 45, citing an interview with JBC, offers a slightly different account.
57. Shaplen, "Sabbatical," 138.

CHAPTER 5

1. Tunis, "John Harvard's Biggest Boy," 136.
2. Pringle, "Profiles: Mr. President," pt. 1, *New Yorker* (Sept. 12, 1936), 20.
3. Tuttle, *James B. Conant,* 21, and Biebel, *Politics, Pedagogues, and Statesmanship,* 39, both citing JBC, "An Account of the Year 1933," Apr. 1934, unpub. ms.
4. Pringle, "Profiles: Mr. President," pt. 2, *New Yorker* (Sept. 19, 1936), 24; Roosevelt,

"Harvard's Prize Kibitzer," *Saturday Evening Post* 226 (Apr. 23, 30, 1949), 38–39ff.; 34, 140–42.

5. I. B. Cohen, "James Bryant Conant," Massachusetts Historical Society *Proceedings* 90 (1978), 123–24.

6. JBC, *MSL*, 86, 98–99. GRC did join him a month later, leaving Ted in her mother's care, and over the course of the summer sent home to various relatives a series of chatty letters describing JBC's energetic networking at Oxford and Cambridge and his relaxing—stretching, reading, "vegetating," practicing French—in the French countryside. "This trip has been just the thing for us both," GRC wrote JBC's sister, Esther. "Bryant—both of us at times—finds the moving about in a vacuum, as it were, with an agitated past on one side and an agitating future on the other, a rather curious and unearthly sensation. . . . B. was terribly tired after we left England, and has gotten back much of his native springiness now." GRC to Esther Conant, July 16, 1933, CFP; also GRC letters of June 8, 19, 23, 25, and July 14, 22, all in CFP.

7. JBC to Marjorie (Mrs. Harold) Bush-Brown, May 17, 1933, JBC PERP.

8. *THC*, Jan. 12, 1953.

9. Interview with John Davey, Roxbury Latin historian, who quoted internal school records.

10. *BG, Boston Herald,* June 1, 1923, in Tuttle, *James B. Conant,* 2–3; TWR diary, June 1, 1923.

11. Pringle, "Profiles: Mr. President," pt. 2, *New Yorker* (Sept. 19, 1936), 23.

12. The account of JBC's succession is drawn from unpublished correspondence in GCP and FFP, magazine articles as noted, and *MSL*, 81–97; Smith, *Harvard Century,* 101–105; Tuttle, *James B. Conant,* 18–23; Amster, *Meritocracy Ascendant,* 59–65; Gerald T. Dunne, *Grenville Clark, Public Citizen* (New York: Farrar, Straus, Giroux, 1986), 75; and Biebel, *Politics, Pedagogues, and Statesmanship,* 35–40.

13. Shaplen, "Sabbatical," 138.

14. JBC, *MSL*, 81–83.

15. Robert Homans to GC, Jan. 25, 1933, GCP; Amster, *Meritocracy Ascendant,* 112.

16. Smith, *Harvard Century,* 102–3; John H. Finley interview; transcript of 1974 interview with Paul H. Buck conducted by William Bentinck-Smith, 9–10, in Buck Papers, Harvard University Archives, HUG (B)—B857.50 (hereafter Buck interview); GC to Thomas Nelson Perkins, Mar. 8, 1933, series IV, box 6, GCP.

17. Pringle, "Profiles: Mr. President," pt. 2, *New Yorker* (Sept. 19, 1936), 23; "dabbled in painting": Robert Homans to GC, Apr. 11, 1933, series IV, box 4, GCP.

18. Servos, *Physical Chemistry from Ostwald to Pauling,* 119–20.

19. Alfred North Whitehead, *Science and the Modern World* (New York: Macmillan, 1925), passim., esp. preface, chap. 1, 9, 12, 13.

20. Whitehead, *Science and the Modern World,* 282–83.

21. FF to GC, Mar. 31, 1933, box 217, folder 5, FFP; Robert Homans to GC, Apr. 5, 1933, series IV, box 4, GCP.

22. GC to Robert Homans, Mar. 8, 1933, series IV, box 4, GCP; in a similar letter the same day to Thomas Perkins, GC also expressed concerns about JBC's youth and because "he might take the thing too hard and get all fussed up about it." GCP, series IV, box 3, in Amster, *Meritocracy Ascendant,* 63.

23. GC to Robert Homans, Mar. 8 and Apr. 12, 1933, series IV, box 4, GCP; see also Dunne, *Grenville Clark,* 17, 23–24, 36–45, 75; Mary Clark Dimond, Norman Cousins and J. Garry Clifford, eds., *Memoirs of a Man: Grenville Clark* (New York: W. W. Norton & Co., 1975), 12–14, 42, 69–71, 92–94.

24. Robert Homans to GC, Apr. 11, 1933, series IV, box 4, GCP.

25. Henry James, *"FLEXNER RE CONANT THIS AFTERNOON,"* Mar. 20, 1933, w. Henry James to GC, Mar. 21, 1933, series IV, box 5, Harvard Corp., James H. 1933 folder, GCP; for examples of these exacting appraisals, see JBC to Flexner, Jan. 22 and June 8, 1931, Flexner papers, American Philosophical Society Library, Philadelphia.

26. GC to Robert Homans, Apr. 12, 1933, series IV, box 4, GCP.

27. JBC to Marjorie (Mrs. Harold) Bush-Brown, May 17, 1933, JBC PERP.
28. JBC, *MSL*, 87–88; JBC, "An Account of the Year 1933," in Biebel, *Politics, Pedagogues, and Statesmanship,* 37–39.
29. JBC to Marjorie (Mrs. Harold) Bush-Brown, May 17, 1933, JBC PERP.
30. Thomas N. Perkins to GC, Mar. 14, 1933, series IV, box 6, GCP, in Amster, *Meritocracy Ascendant,* 63.
31. GC to George Agassiz, May 20, 1933, GCP, series IV, box 1, in Amster, *Meritocracy Ascendant,* 65.
32. JBC, *MSL,* 89.
33. JBC to GC, May 6, 1933, GCP, series 4, box 2, Harvard Corporation, Conant, James B.—1933 folder.
34. Joseph P. Lash, ed. and intro., *From the Diaries of Felix Frankfurter* (New York: W. W. Norton & Co., 1975), 137.
35. Samuel Eliot Morison, "The Harvard Presidency," *New England Quarterly* 31:4 (Dec. 1958), 444.

CHAPTER 6

1. Tunis, "John Harvard's Biggest Boy," 136.
2. A. Lawrence Lowell to JBC, June 27, 1933, in Amster, *Meritocracy Ascendant,* 76–77.
3. Morison, *Three Centuries of Harvard,* 55–56. After JBC had pledged his "entire strength and devotion . . . that knowledge and understanding may increase, and be transmitted to the youth of our country," guests were served what Morison contemptuously described as "a wretched temperance punch." For details, see S. E. Morison, "The Installation of President Conant," JBC PERP.
4. Interview with Jesse L. Greenstein, May 16, 1991.
5. For JBC's cutting of ties from Roxbury Latin, see JBC to Leonard F. Holmes, Jan. 13, 1961, JBC PERP and JBC to Roger Ernst, Nov. 7, 1938, box 143, JBC PREP.
6. Pringle, "Profiles: Mr. President," pt. 1, 20; John H. Finley interview.
7. GC to Charles P. Curtis, Sept. 1, 1933, GCP; FF to GC, Sept. 27, 1933, GC to FF, Oct. 11, 1933, FF to GC, Oct. 26, 1933, box 217, folder 5, FFP. On GC's friendship with JBC, see GC to FF, June 11, 1938, box 217, folder 9, FFP.
8. FF to GC, Oct. 26, 1933, box 217, folder 5, FFP.
9. Quoted in Tunis, "John Harvard's Biggest Boy," 136; Pringle, "Profiles: Mr. President," pt. 2, 25, contains a pithier variant: "Bryant has a formula for everything, and he will be a success."
10. As David Riesman put it in a 1989 interview with the author: "Woodrow Wilson believed in Princeton in the nation's service; Conant believed in a Harvard in the world's service."
11. JBC, *President's Report, 1932–33* (Jan. 8, 1934) (Cambridge: Harvard University Press, 1934), 2. JBC's annual presidential report to Harvard's board of overseers, published each January, constitute an invaluable source for his evolving educational philosophy and activities.
12. Buck interview.
13. WLM interview, Aug. 1986.
14. For details, see JBC's annual reports during this period. For JBC's central part in the rise of educational instruction at Harvard, see Arthur G. Powell, *The Uncertain Profession: Harvard and the Search for Educational Authority* (Cambridge, Mass.: Harvard University Press, 1980), chap. 8–10, epilogue.
15. JBC to Kenneth Murdock, Dec. 6, 1933, quoted in Amster, *Meritocracy Ascendant,* 91–97; see also JBC, *MSL,* 157–161.
16. E. Digby Baltzell, *The Protestant Establishment: Aristocracy & Caste in America* (New York: Random House, 1964; Vintage reprint, 1966), 340; but see also Nelson

W. Aldrich, Jr., *Old Money: The Mythology of America's Upper Class* (New York: Alfred A. Knopf, 1988), esp. 34–44.

17. Henry Adams, *The Education of Henry Adams* (Boston: Houghton Mifflin, 1918), cited in Aldrich, *Old Money,* 39.

18. Theodore H. White, *In Search of History: A Personal Adventure* (New York: Harper & Row, 1978), 40–44.

19. See Biebel, *Politics, Pedagogues, and Statesmanship,* 58–62, 115–21 ("vanguard" quotation on p. 118; "ignorant" quotation is from JBC to Ben. D. Wood, Mar. 24, 1934, JBC PERP); Powell, *The Uncertain Profession,* 206-13; and JBC, *MSL,* 417–32 ("almost naive faith": p. 417).

20. See John Larew, "Why Are Droves of Unqualified, Unprepared Kids Getting into Our Top Colleges?" *Washington Monthly* 23:6 (June 1991), 10–14.

21. To track JBC's early fellowship efforts, large in ambition if small in scope, see JBC's *Annual Reports* for 1932–33 (pp. 4–5), 1933–34 (pp. 12–14), 1934–35 (pp. 5–6, 10–11, 21–22), 1935–36 (pp. 17–19), 1936–37 (pp. 9–12), and 1938–39 (pp. 23–24).

22. Amster, *Meritocracy Ascendant,* 86.

23. Baker, *Brandeis and Frankfurter,* 348–49.

24. Teicher, *James Bryant Conant and "The American High School Today",* 167.

25. See Sam Bass Warner, *Province of Reason* (Cambridge, Mass.: Belknap Press of Harvard University Press, 1984), 224.

26. JBC Speech File includes a folder ("Conant, JB: Material for Speeches, 38–39") containing such ice-breaking gems as: "Coloured gentleman buys a razor. 'Safety razor?' 'No sur, this am for social purposes.'" Another: "Coloured gentleman elected a deacon. Bad character. Why elected? 'There was a disreputable faction that just rise up and demanded recognition.'" Responding to GC's urgings in 1942 that he assume a senior government post to oversee the war effort, JBC wrote: "After reading your memorandum and other enclosures, I feel very much like the colored gentleman who, when asked to change a $10 bill, replied: 'I can't do it, but I certainly do appreciate the compliment!'" JBC to GC, Nov. 13, 1942, GCP, series 10, box 3.

27. "Young ladies": see Derek Bok, "The Conant Legacy," *James Bryant Conant: A Remembrance* (Cambridge: Harvard University, 1978), 28; "throw up my hands,": JBC to William T. Brewster, Feb. 8, 1939, "Barn-Baz" folder, box 127, JBC PREP. For the diminishing, yet still present, signs of anti-Semitism during his presidency, see Synott, *The Half-Opened Door,* 202–210; Stephen Thernstrom, "'Poor But Hopefull [sic] Scholars,'" in Bailyn, et al., *Glimpses of the Harvard Past,* 127–28; Committee of Eight report, 1939, quoted in Baker, *Brandeis and Frankfurter,* 349; "dynamite": JBC, quoted in Sheldon [Glueck] to FF, Jan. 26, 1937, reel 88, FF Papers, LC.

28. JBC, "The Future of Our Higher Education," *Harper's* 176 (May 1938), 563. For thorough accounts of JBC's actions to foster a more democratic student body and other reforms from 1933–39, see Biebel, *Politics, Pedagogues, and Statesmanship,* chaps. 2–3, and Amster, *Meritocracy Ascendant,* 69–70, 78–91; for a cogent overview of his philosophy, see Tuttle, *James B. Conant,* 24–34.

29. Cited in Frank Freidel, *Franklin D. Roosevelt: A Rendezvous with Destiny* (Boston: Little, Brown & Co., 1990), 92–93.

30. JBC, *MSL,* 447–48.

31. Tuttle, *James B. Conant,* 80, 37–81, and Tuttle, "American Higher Education and the Nazis: The Case of James B. Conant and Harvard University's 'Diplomatic Relations' with Germany," *American Studies* 20 (Spring 1979), 49–70.

32. Tuttle, "American Higher Education and the Nazis," 53–54; Tuttle, *James B. Conant,* 50–54; JBC, *MSL,* 143; see also Diamond, *Compromised Campus,* 114–116, 316 n. 5, and Bessie Zaban Jones, "To the Rescue of the Learned: The Asylum Fellowship Plan at Harvard, 1938–1940," *Harvard Library Bulletin* 32:3 (Summer 1984), 205–38, esp. 212.

33. Hanfstaengl affair: Tuttle, *James B. Conant,* 54–66; Tuttle, "American Higher Education and the Nazis," 54–59, 69; JBC, *MSL,* 140–45.

34. William L. Shirer, *The Rise and Fall of The Third Reich: A History of Nazi Germany*

(New York: Simon & Schuster, 1960), 113; John Toland, *Adolf Hitler* (New York: Random House, 1976), 173–76, 182–86, 331–32; Alan Bullock, *Hitler and Stalin: Parallel Lives* (New York: Alfred A. Knopf, 1992), 82, 84.

35. Tuttle, *James B. Conant,* 60.
36. "My Leader," *Collier's* 44 (Aug. 4, 1944), 9.
37. FF, "Memorandum of Conversation with Pound and President Conant regarding an invitation from Pound," Sept. 14, 1934, box 217, folder 6, FFP; see also Baker, *Brandeis and Frankfurter,* 346–47.
38. Quoted in *NYT,* Sept. 18, 1934, in Tuttle, *James B. Conant,* 63–64.
39. JBC to Hanfstaengl, Sept. 24, 1934, in JBC, *MSL,* 144.
40. Tuttle, *James B. Conant,* 65–66.
41. FF to JBC, Oct. 4, 1934, box 217, folder 6, FFP.
42. JBC to C. C. Burlingame, Oct. 8, 1934, copy in box 184, folder 9, FFP.
43. Petition of sixteen presidents of universities and colleges in Massachusetts, June 4, 1935, copy in GCP, series 6, box 1.
44. Pringle, "Profiles: Mr. President," pt. 2, 26.
45. JBC, "Free Inquiry or Dogma?" *Atlantic Monthly* (Apr. 1935), 436–42; "pestered": JBC to Dexter M. Keezer, Dec. 7, 1939, "Re" folder, box 142, JBC PREP.
46. JBC to Harvard faculty, Oct. 8, 1935.
47. JBC, *MSL,* 449–53.
48. JBC to GC, Dec. 14, 1935, GCP, series 6, box 1; see also JBC, *Report of the President of Harvard University to the Board of Overseers,* 1935–36 (Mar. 1, 1937) (Cambridge, Mass.: Harvard University Press, 1937), 11.
49. JBC, *MSL,* 147, 405, 446–49.
50. Lawrance Thompson and R. H. Winnick, and Edward Connery Lathem, ed., *Robert Frost: A Biography* (New York: Holt, Rinehart, & Winston, 1981), 360. On JBC's opposition to the court-packing plan: Paul F. Douglass, *Six Upon the World,* 370. A few months later, when JBC was considered for a membership on a public health advisory committee, FDR's oldest son, James, reacted coldly. "Why appoint somebody so bitterly opposed on everything? There ought to be an outstanding educational man they can appoint who is reasonably friendly." Stephen Early to James Roosevelt, Roosevelt to Early, Sept. 13, 1937, President's personal file 91, container 1, Franklin D. Roosevelt Papers, FDRL.
51. Reagan broke the string, skipping the 350th celebration in 1986.
52. A. Lawrence Lowell to JBC, Mar. 9, 1936, JBC PERP.
53. *Roosevelt and Frankfurter: Their Correspondence,* 1928–1945, annotated by Max Freedman (Boston: Little, Brown & Co., 1967), 322–31, 355–56; JBC, *MSL,* 153; FDR to JBC, Nov. 1934, in Nancy Bauer, "My Dear Mr. President," *Harvard Review* 1:1 (Fall 1986), 184.
54. Lowell to JBC, Mar. 9, 1936; JBC to Lowell, Mar. 12, 1936; Lowell to JBC, Mar. 21, 1936; JBC to Lowell, Mar. 26, 1936, JBC PREP, in Bauer, "My Dear Mr. President," 183–88; *Roosevelt and Frankfurter,* 326–27. Despite JBC's advice, Lowell could not resist one more jab, writing FDR on Apr. 14 that he assumed the president would "say something about what Harvard has meant to the nation," and observing that speakers might limit themselves to "ten, or at most fifteen minutes. Does this not strike you as appropriate?" Angry enough to consider staying away ("Damn," he wrote Frankfurter), Roosevelt rebuffed his foe in magisterial fashion:

The White House, April 29, 1936

Dear President Lowell: —
Thank you for your letter of April fourteenth. You are right in thinking that I will want to say something about the significance of Harvard in relation to our national history.

Very sincerely yours,
Franklin D. Roosevelt

55. This and subsequent quotations are taken from "Statement of Robert K. Lamb" (re conversation of Mar. 23, 1936), box 184, folder 9, FFP.

56. The characterization is from a June 1991 interview with Alan R. Sweezy, who hastened to add that his stereotype of scientists had been shattered by boisterous colleagues at the California Institute of Technology, where he taught after leaving Harvard.

57. Quoted in Louis Mertins, *Robert Frost: Life and Talk-Walking* (Norman, Okla.: University of Oklahoma Press, 1965), 240–42.

58. JBC to Walter Lippmann, Apr. 24, 1936, Lippmann Papers, Sterling Library, Yale University.

59. JBC to E. B. Wilson, Sept. 23, 1940, box 193, Sn-Sta correspondence folder, JBC PREP.

60. Roy Hoopes, *Ralph Ingersoll: A Biography* (New York: Atheneum, 1985), 101–102; see also Scott Donaldson with R. H. Winnick, *Archibald MacLeish: An American Life* (Boston: Houghton Mifflin, 1992), 253.

61. U.S. Senate, Committee on Foreign Relations, *Nomination of James B. Conant*, 83d Cong., 1st sess. (Washington, D.C.: Government Printing Office, 1953), 93.

62. For Heidelberg episode, see Tuttle, *James B. Conant*, 68–75, 80–81; Tuttle, "American Higher Education and the Nazis," 61–63; JBC, *MSL*, 145–47.

63. Baker, *Brandeis and Frankfurter*, 347–48; Pringle, "Profiles: Mr. President," pt. 2, 26.

64. JBC to Charles Singer, June 23, 1936, box 184, folder 4, FFP.

65. JBC to Harold Dodds, Mar. 23, 1937, in Tuttle, *James B. Conant*, 72.

66. Tuttle, *James B. Conant*, 73–75.

67. This account of the tercentenary is drawn primarily from "Cambridge Birthday," *Time* 28:13 (Sept. 28, 1936), 22–26; JBC, *MSL*, 146–56; Smith, *Harvard Century*, 122–31.

68. Not everyone answered Harvard's call; Einstein stayed away, disgusted at the invitations to Nazi-controlled universities that had collaborated in anti-Jewish purges, and George Bernard Shaw had responded to the offer of an honorary Doctor of Laws with the gracious acknowledgment that Harvard would give him "the liveliest satisfaction" if it celebrated its 300th anniversary "by burning itself to the ground and sowing its site with salt . . . as an example to all the other famous old corrupters of youth, including Yale, Oxford, Cambridge, the Sorbonne etc. etc. etc." For Einstein: Tuttle, "American Higher Education and the Nazis," 64; for Shaw, Bauer, "My Dear Mr. President," 188.

69. JBC, Oration at the Solemn Observance of the Tercentenary of Harvard College, Cambridge, Sept. 18, 1936, in JBC, *MSL*, 651–58.

70. FF to Marguerite (Missy) LeHand, Sept. 18, 1936, and FDR to FF, Sept. 22, 1936, *Roosevelt and Frankfurter*, 355–56.

71. The class-conscious Angell added: "So long as they are Harvard's rich, I don't care. But the endowed institutions of the U.S. cannot long survive under the threat of unjust taxation. . . ."

72. Eulogy for JBC, 1978, John K. Finley and George B. Kistiakowsky, courtesy of Finley; Finley, "Mr. Conant and Harvard College," *James Bryant Conant: A Remembrance*, 6.

73. Dixon Wecter, *The Age of the Great Depression, 1929–1941* (New York: Macmillan, 1948), 193.

74. Pringle, "Profiles: Mr. President," pt. 1, 21.

75. TRC interview, July 5, 1991.

76. TRC interview, July 8, 1991.

77. TRC interview, 1987; Pringle, "Profiles: Mr. President," pt. 2, 27.

78. Interviews with TRC, Jan. 1987, July 1991, and Jim Conant (grandson), Aug. 1986; Smith, *Harvard Century*, 105.

79. The quotations which follow are taken from handwritten journal entries by GRC

discovered at the Conant house in Hanover, N.H., in a folder marked: "G R Conant—very personal memorabilia—Diary pages and notes—kept for the *happy* passages—not for the self-lacerations." Also in the folder were some pages from another journal, entitled "Conduct of Life," written by Miriam Thayer Richards. In a handwritten note, GRC acknowledged destroying materials from both journals. I am deeply grateful to Theodore Conant and his family for permitting me to read and quote from these highly personal items.

80. GRC journal, Apr. 15, 1936, CFP.
81. GRC journal, May 19, 1934, CFP.
82. GRC journal, Feb. 27, 1934, Nov. 16, 1935, CFP.
83. Miriam Thayer Richards journal, "Conduct of Life," May 14 (possibly 1934), CFP.
84. GRC journal, n.d. note, 1935, CFP; also GRC to Marjorie Bush-Brown, 1933, CFP, in which GRC expressed concern over the "solemn" and "appalling" aspects of the official life ahead: "The hardest thing for me will be to see people continually that I shall enjoy talking to, and yet talk to them without saying anything indiscreet!"
85. GRC journal, July 19, 1938, CFP.
86. GRC journal, Sept. 10, 1938, CFP.
87. GRC journal, Nov. 24, 1938, CFP.
88. JBC diary, Jan. 18, June 21, 22, 1940, in Amster, *Meritocracy Ascendant*, 135, n. 32.
89. On JBC's family life and demands on his time: TRC interviews, Jan. 1987, July 1991; GRC diaries and correspondence, CFP; Douglass, *Six Upon the World*, 400–401; Pringle, "Profiles: Mr. President," pt. 2, 25–26; Maloney, "Ambassador to the Cosmos," 86; Roosevelt, "Harvard's Prize Kibitzer," pt. 2, 141 drawing in JBC PERP.
90. JBC to GC, June 6, 1938, series 4, box 2, Harvard Corp—Conant, James B. folder, GCP.
91. Pringle, "Profiles: Mr. President," pt. 1, 20, pt. 2, 24–25; Schlesinger, *In Retrospect*, 94–96.
92. Cambridge Union of University Teachers, "Harvard's Liberalism: Myth or Reality?" *American Teacher* (May–June 1937), 7–8; Irwin Ross, "The Tempest at Harvard," *Harper's* 181 (Oct. 1940), 544–52.
93. Buck interview, 19, 37.
94. Buck interview, 12.
95. DeVoto's own account of the spring 1936 incident, toned down somewhat for an official board of inquiry during the Walsh-Sweezy affair two years later, can be found in Wallace Stegner, *The Letters of Bernard DeVoto* (Garden City, N.Y.: Doubleday & Co., 1975), 217–24; see also Thompson and Winnick, ed. Lathem, *Robert Frost: A Biography*, 360; and Mertins, *Robert Frost: Life and Talk-Walking*, 240–42.
96. Accounts of the Walsh-Sweezy affair abound in histories of Harvard, but the recent opening of JBC's presidential papers for those years suggests that a new study by a historian of education might be worthwhile. I have used JBC, *MSL*, 157–71; Amster, *Meritocracy Ascendant*, 95–103; Smith, *The Harvard Century*, 133–38, 354–55; Seymour Martin Lipset and David Riesman, *Education and Politics at Harvard* (New York: McGraw-Hill, 1975), 163–70; Schlesinger, *In Retrospect: The History of a Historian*, 94–96; correspondence in the Lippmann, Frankfurter, and Clark papers; Buck interview; Finley interview; Ross, "The Tempest at Harvard," 544–52.
97. Schlesinger, *In Retrospect: The History of a Historian*, 94.
98. Charles A. Coolidge to JBC, July 5, 1938, JBC PREP, in Amster, *Meritocracy Ascendant*, 101.
99. Buck interview, 19.
100. Lewis S. Finer to JBC, Dec. 18, 1975, in Smith, *Harvard Century*, 135–37, 354–55; though Walsh is mentioned as one of the plotters, incidentally, Sweezy later commented mildly that he didn't think JBC's policy was unfair and thought the whole affair was a misunderstanding that was "blown out of proportion." Interview, June 18, 1991. Murdoch's warm congratulatory letter, n.d. but apparently May 1933, was found in CFP; Murdoch professed to be "genuinely delighted" at the outcome, though he

confessed that "if the election had gone to almost anyone but you I'm sure I should have felt a real pang at not getting the job myself."

101. Buck interview, 9–12, 23.
102. FF to GC, June 14, 1938, responding to GC to FF, June 11, 1938, box 217, folder 9, FFP.
103. Quoted in Edmund Wilson, *The Thirties* (paperback ed.; Washington Square Press, 1982), 698.
104. JBC, *MSL*, 171.

CHAPTER 7

1. *Twenty-Fifth Anniversary Report*, 164.
2. Tuttle, *James B. Conant*, 85; Tuttle, "American Higher Education and the Nazis," 60–61.
3. JBC, *MSL*, 146.
4. Tuttle, *James B. Conant*, 67–68.
5. Tuttle, *James B. Conant*, 77–79.
6. Archibald MacLeish, "Speech to the Scholars," *Saturday Review of Literature*, June 12, 1937, 12; see also Donaldson with Winnick, *Archibald MacLeish: An American Life*, 266–67.
7. JBC to MacLeish, June 18, 1937, Conant folder, box 5, Archibald MacLeish Papers, Library of Congress.
8. MacLeish to JBC, June 21, 1937, Conant folder, box 5, MacLeish Papers.
9. JBC to MacLeish, June 25, 1937, Conant folder, box 5, MacLeish Papers. JBC also insisted that the position of Russian and German scholars was not a "new phenomenon," but rather "the usual state of affairs during the last thousand years— the new thing was the freedom of the liberalism of 1860–1914. The loss of this I bemoan as much as you do."
10. Lippmann to MacLeish, June 29, 1937, Lippmann folder, box 14, MacLeish Papers.
11. MacLeish to Lippmann, July 2, 1937, Lippmann folder, box 14, MacLeish Papers.
12. JBC to FF, May 3, 1938, box 49, JBC folder, FF Papers, LC; Baker, *Brandeis and Frankfurter*, 350–51.
13. JBC, *MSL*, 213.
14. JBC to Walter Lippmann, Aug. 12, 1938, Lippmann Papers.
15. JBC, "Education and Peace," June 18, 1939, *Vital Speeches of the Day* 5 (July 1, 1939), 552–53; JBC, "The Demands of the Market Place," June 22, 1939, *Vital Speeches of the Day* 5 (Aug. 15, 1939), 647–48. "So irrational and emotional": JBC to J.F. Neyland, May 6, 1939, "Na–Ne" folder, box 139, JBC PREP. JBC and refugee scholars: Bessie Zaban Jones, "To the Rescue of the Learned: The Asylum Fellowship Plan at Harvard, 1938–1940," *Harvard Library Bulletin* 32:3 (Summer 1984), 205–38; Tuttle, "American Higher Education and the Nazis," 67–68 fn. 15. Correspondence in JBC PREP yields signs of JBC's lack of enthusiasm, including his faltering fund-raising efforts (JBC to F. K. Richtmyer, Aug. 31, 1939, box 127); his opposition to pressuring U.S. government officials to admit more refugee scholars (JBC to Marion Park, Feb. 29, 1939, box 128); and, most damningly, his rejection of a suggestion to send lists of U.S. universities to scholars still trapped in Nazi-threatened Europe to which they could apply on the grounds that this would result in a "bombardment" of paperwork for the institutions (G. H. Chase to Richtmyer, May 10, 1939; box 127).
16. JBC's interventionist activities in 1939–41 is Tuttle, *James B. Conant*, 82–286; JBC, *MSL*, 207–233, and Biebel, *Politics, Pedagogues, and Statesmanship*, 145–84.
17. JBC to Archibald MacLeish, Sept. 7, 1939, MacLeish folder, box 159, JBC PREP.
18. JBC, "Humanity's Experiment with Free Institutions," Sept. 26, 1939, *Vital Speeches of the Day* 6 (Oct. 15, 1939), 26.

19. JBC to VB, Sept. 27, 1939, "Carn-Ce" folder, box 151, JBC PREP.
20. Interview with George B. Kistiakowsky, Feb. 1982; JBC, "Comments on V. Bush's ms." n.d. (1968), Vannevar Bush Papers, 1931–1974, Massachusetts Institute of Technology, box 17, folder marked "J.B. Comments . . ."; Tuttle, *James B. Conant*, 86.
21. JBC to Frederick Middlebush, Sept. 26, 1939, and JBC to Harold Dodds, Aug. 28, Sept. 21, 1939, both in JBC PREP.
22. Stephen Early to FDR, Sept. 14, 1939, in Elliott Roosevelt, ed., *FDR: His Personal Letters*, 1928–1945, II (New York: Duell, Sloan & Pearce, 1950), 921.
23. JBC to Landon, Sept. 28, 1939, in JBC, *MSL*, 213-4.
24. JBC to Henry Cabot Lodge, Sept. 22, 1939, Lin-Loq Folder, box 159, JBC PREP.
25. "Armageddon": *THC*, Oct. 18, 1939; poll (*THC*, Nov. 9, 1939) and JFK editorial (*THC*, Oct. 9, 1939): Nigel Hamilton, *JFK: Reckless Youth* (New York: Random House, 1992), 290–94. Joseph P. Kennedy's isolationism: Michael R. Beschloss, *Kennedy and Roosevelt: The Uneasy Alliance* (New York: W. W. Norton, 1980).
26. JBC to Dodds, Sept. 28 and Oct. 3, 1939, Princeton University folder, box 165, JBC PREP; JBC to A.C. Smith, Smith folder, box 168, JBC PREP.
27. JBC to GC, w. enc., Nov. 16, 1939; JBC to GC, Nov. 23, 1939; GC to JBC, Nov. 24, 1939; all in GCP, series 4, box 2, Harvard Corporation, Conant, James B. — 1939.
28. Re Russell: JBC diary, Apr. 8, 22, 23, 25, 28, 1940; Henry James to JBC, Apr. 23, 26, 1940, GCP, series 4, box 5, Harvard Corp. James, H. 1940; *THC*, Apr. 8, 1940; GC to James M. Landis, Apr. 11, 1940, GCP, series 4, box 5, Harvard Corp. Landis, J.; Bertrand Russell, *The Autobiography of Bertrand Russell: The Middle Years*, 1914-44 (Boston: Little, Brown & Co., 1968), 322, 335–43; Gerald T. Dunne, *Grenville Clark*, 110–11; JBC to Harvard Corporation, Apr. 24, 1940, proposed statement on Russell case, Apr. 29, 1940, both in "Harvard Archives Research" folder, box 20, JBC PERP, UAI.15.898.13.
29. TRC interview, 1987; JBC diary, Jan. 30, Feb. 2, 1940; JBC to Robert Dort, Feb. 2, 1940, Conant personal folder, box 152, JBC PREP.
30. JBC, *MSL*, 227.
31. JBC diary, May 9, 1940.
32. JBC diary, July 6, 1940.
33. JBC diary, May 17, 1940.
34. Tuttle, *James B. Conant*, 107.
35. *NYT*, May 30, 1940; quoted, Tuttle, *James B. Conant*, 108; see also JBC diary, May 27, 28, 29, 30, June 1, 6, 1940; JBC to FDR, May 29, 1940, PPF 91, container 1, FDR Papers, FDRL.
36. See *MSL*, chap. 18, and Tuttle, *James B. Conant*, 107–286.
37. Tuttle, *James B. Conant*, 129–30, 203–204; Biebel, *Politics, Pedagogues, and Statesmanship*, 171–77, 185–231.
38. For GC's role in advancing Stimson's appointment: Geoffrey Hodgson, *The Colonel: The Life and Wars of Henry Stimson*, 1867–1950 (New York: Alfred A. Knopf, 1990), 221–23; Dunne, *Grenville Clark*, 125–28.
39. For JBC's role in the tangled story of pre–Pearl Harbor conscription legislation: JBC, *MSL*, 329–38; Tuttle, *James B. Conant*, 117–74; Biebel, *Politics, Pedagogues, and Statesmanship*, 167–71; 195–97; JBC, "A Memorandum of Historical Notes on the Fate of Section 7c of the Burke-Wadsworth Bill," Nov. 17, 1940, GCP, series 9, box 2; J. Garry Clifford and Samuel R. Spencer, Jr., *The First Peacetime Draft* (Lawrence, Kans.: University Press of Kansas, 1986).
40. See Mark Lincoln Chadwin, *The Warhawks: American Interventionists before Pearl Harbor* (New York: W. W. Norton, 1970), esp. 43–73.
41. FDR to JBC, June 8, 1940; JBC to FDR, June 15, 1940; President's Personal File 91, container 1, FDRL; Robert Hillyer to JBC, May 30, 1940, and Felix Frankfurter to JBC, June 3, 1940, in JBC PERP, WWII Papers, UAI.15.898, box 2. Like other folders

containing responses to JBC's May 29, 1940 speech, it is misfiled under "Radio Address: May 27, 1940."

42. Message from André Morize broadcast from "Paris-Mondial," May 30, 1940; Mrs. André Morize to JBC, June 15, 1940; JBC to Mrs. Morize, June 18, 1940; JBC PERP, WWII Papers, UAI.15.898, box 2.
43. Prof. A. Loewenbein to JBC, June 3, 1940; JBC to Loewenbein, July 1, 1940; JBC PERP, WWII Papers, UAI.15.898, box 2.
44. See "Unfavorable Comments" folder, JBC PERP, WWII Papers, UAI.15.898, box 2.
45. *THC*, June 9, 1940; Herbert S. Parmet, *Jack: The Struggles of John F. Kennedy* (New York: Dial Press, 1980), 66–68; Hamilton, *JFK: Reckless Youth,* 328.
46. JBC diary, June 19, 1940.
47. JBC to FF, June 11, 1940, JBC PERP, WWII Papers, box 1, UAI.15.898; JBC to Prof. Charles K. Webster, July 15, 1940, JBC PERP, UAI.15.898, WWII Papers, box 2; JBC to Archibald MacLeish, May 30, 1940, JBC PERP; JBC, speech to Jewish War Veterans, June 12, 1940, JBC Speech File; JBC, *MSL,* 216–17.
48. James R. Conant '40, Class Oration, *Phillips Exeter Bulletin* 36:5 (July 1940), 6–8.
49. JBC diary, June 23, 1940; also GRC to Miriam Thayer Richards, June 25, 1940, CFP.
50. JBC to GC, Jan. 10, 1940, GCP, series 21, box 8, "G.C. Writings—'A Memorandum with regard . . . 'Federation of Free Peoples . . . '—Replies from College Presidents" folder.
51. JBC diary, June 29, 1940. Dodds's Canadian wife replied to JBC by observing that "perhaps Canada would rather be run by U.S. than by Hitler but they would hate either!"
52. JBC diary, May 24, 1940; JBC, *MSL,* 234. Bethuel M. Webster, "Lunch at the Century" (June 1948), and minutes, Committee on Scientific Aids to Learning, 9th meeting, May 24, 1940, "National Academy of Sciences–National Research Council–Committee on Scientific Aids to Learning 1940" folder, CCP; Biebel, *Politics, Pedagogues, and Statesmanship,* 161–62.
53. See James Phinney Baxter III, *Scientists Against Time* (Boston: Little, Brown & Co., 1948), 15; Robert E. Sherwood, *Roosevelt and Hopkins: An Intimate History* (New York: Harper & Row, 1948), 153–56; Cochrane, *The National Academy of Sciences,* 387–95; JBC diary, June 14, 1940; JBC, *MSL,* 234–35.
54. On VB: G. Pascal Zachary, "To Dream in a Definite Way: The Life of Vannevar Bush," unpublished ms., 1991; Zachary, "America's First Engineer—The Career of Vannevar Bush," *Upside,* Apr. 1991, 92–101; and Zachary, "Vannevar Bush Backs the Bomb," *Bulletin of the Atomic Scientists* 48:10 (Dec. 1992), 24–31.
55. "My relation to Bush was as a man who had been recruited by him to do a job for the government which I was very anxious to have done . . . I suppose he turned to me because 'a', I knew him, and 'b', he wanted a college president, with what prestige he had to be in the picture. A couple of times later, as the thing went on, when I thought of resigning this position and going back to purely academics, both he and Groves were anxious that I shouldn't. They wanted the . . . President of Harvard in this picture." Quoted in John C. Landers, "The Manhattan Project, as Seen by Dr. Conant," Mar. 8, 1974, JBC PERP (hereafter Landers interview).
56. VB to KTC, June 18, 1934, "Confidential," Compton-Killian Papers, Massachusetts Institute of Technology.
57. VB, *Pieces of the Action* (New York: William Morrow & Co., 1970), 32.
58. On Sarton, see correspondence in Carn–Ce folder, box 129, and History of Science folder, box 157, JBC PREP.
59. Harvey H. Bundy Oral History interview, Butler Library, Columbia University, 171.
60. Dupree, *Science in the Federal Government,* 369–71.
61. JBC diary, June 18, 25, 1940; Baxter, *Scientists Against Time,* 17.
62. JBC diary, June 27, 1940.
63. Louis F. Fieser, *The Scientific Method: A Personal Account of Unusual Projects in War and in Peace* (New York: Reinhold Publishing Corp., 1964), 9.

64. GRC to Miriam T. Richards, July 1940, CFP.
65. Max Slater to TRC, Feb. 24, 1960, JBC PERP; Tuttle, *James B. Conant,* 113, 136–37.
66. JBC diary, July 9, 1940.
67. JBC diary, July 13, 14, 1940; JBC to Eichelberger, July 15, 1940, in JBC, *MSL,* 219–20.
68. JBC diary, Aug. 4, 1940; Winston S. Churchill, *Their Finest Hour* (Boston: Houghton Mifflin Co., 1949), esp. 280–416.
69. JBC diary, July 15, Aug. 5, 6, 7, 12, 25, 1940; JBC to GC, Aug. 16, 1940, GCP, series 4, box 2.
70. Tuttle, *James B. Conant,* 161–74.
71. JBC, *MSL,* 220–21; Tuttle, *James B. Conant,* 190.
72. JBC diary, Sept. 1, 5, Nov. 5, 1940.
73. JBC to William A. White, Nov. 13, 19, 1940, JBC to Clark M. Eichelberger, Nov. 19, 1940, "Committee to Defend America, General Correspondence, 1939–40" folder, UAI.15.898, WWII Papers, box 3, JBC PERP; JBC to GC, Nov. 13, 1940, GCP, series 4, box 2.
74. JBC, "Aid to the Allies," Nov. 20, 1940, in *Vital Speeches of the Day* 7 (Dec. 15, 1940), 148.
75. JBC, "Aid to the Allies," 149.
76. JBC to Eliot, Oct. 21, 1940, Eliot folder, box 179, JBC PREP.
77. See Eliot, "National Objectives," Oct. 24, 1940; Eliot to JBC, Oct. 26, 1940; JBC to Eliot, Nov. 13, 1940; all in Eliot folder, box 179, JBC PREP.
78. JBC to Francis P. Miller, Sept. 27, 1940, JBC PREP.
79. Clay Judson to JBC, Dec. 18, 1940; JBC to Judson, Dec. 27, 1940; "Committee to Defend America by Aiding the Allies 1939–40" folder, UAI.15.898, WWII Papers, box 3, JBC PERP.
80. JBC to FDR, Dec. 19, 1940, PPF 91, container 1, FDR Papers, FDRL.
81. FDR to JBC, Dec. 18, 1940; JBC to FDR, Dec. 23, 1940; PPF 91, container 1, FDR Papers, FDRL.
82. Chadwin, *The Warhawks,* 149–50.
83. JBC to GC, Dec. 31, 1940, GCP, series 4, box 2. In his memoirs, JBC politely snips out the reference to the possibility of splitting the CDAAA. *MSL,* 228–29.
84. JBC to Frank B. Jewett, Dec. 27, 1940, "Mission to England, 1941" folder, UA I.15.898.13, box 8, JBC PERP.
85. JBC, *MSL,* 43.
86. Frank B. Jewett to JBC, Jan. 1, 1941, "Mission to England, 1941" folder, UA I.15.898.13, box 8, JBC PERP.
87. JBC, *MSL,* 248.

CHAPTER 8

1. Numerous histories of the origins of the Manhattan Project are available; among those consulted were: Richard G. Hewlett and Oscar E. Anderson, Jr., *The New World, 1939 1946: Volume 1, A History of the United States Atomic Energy Commission* (University Park: Pennsylvania State University Press, 1962); Richard Rhodes, *The Making of the Atomic Bomb* (New York: Simon & Schuster, 1986); Martin J. Sherwin, *A World Destroyed: The Atomic Bomb and the Grand Alliance* (New York: Alfred A. Knopf, 1975; references are to the 1987 Vintage paperback edition, *A World Destroyed: Hiroshima and the Origins of the Arms Race,* which contains a new introduction and additional appendices); Ronald W. Clark, *The Greatest Power on Earth: The International Race for Nuclear Supremacy* (New York: Harper & Row, 1980); Lennard Bickel, *The Deadly Element: The Story of Uranium* (New York: Stein & Day, 1979); Kevles, *The Physicists;* McGeorge Bundy, *Danger and Survival: Choices About the Bomb in the First Fifty Years* (New York: Random House, 1988); Margaret Gowing, *Britain and Atomic Energy, 1939–1945* (New

York: St. Martin's Press, 1964); Peter Wyden, *Day One: Before Hiroshima and After* (New York: Simon & Schuster, 1984); Len Giovannitti and Fred Freed, *The Decision to Drop the Bomb* (New York: Coward-McCann, 1965); and John Newhouse, *War and Peace in the Nuclear Age* (New York: Alfred A. Knopf, 1988). The official 1945 U.S. government report on the development of the atomic bomb has recently been conveniently reprinted, with supplementary essays: Henry DeWolf Smyth, *Atomic Energy for Military Purposes* (Stanford, Calif.: Stanford University Press, 1989). For the official Army history see Vincent C. Jones, *Manhattan: The Army and the Atomic Bomb (United States Army in World War II: Special Studies)* (Washington, D.C.: Center of Military History, 1985). Two useful compilations of original documents and other primary source materials are: Philip L. Cantelon, Richard G. Hewlett, and Robert C. Williams, eds., *The American Atom: A Documentary History of Nuclear Policies from the Discovery of Fission to the Present* (2nd ed.) (Philadelphia: University of Pennsylvania Press, 1984, 1991); and Michael B. Stoff, Jonathan F. Fanton, and R. Hal Williams, eds., *The Manhattan Project: A Documentary Introduction to the Atomic Age* (Philadelphia: Temple University Press, 1991).

2. On early concern over the apparent German advantage, see Thomas Powers, *Heisenberg's War: The Secret History of the German Bomb* (New York: Alfred A. Knopf, 1993), esp. chap. 1, 2, 6, 7; and Mark Walker, *German National Socialism and the Quest for Nuclear Power, 1939–1949* (Cambridge, England: Cambridge University Press, 1989), esp. chap. 5.

3. Hewlett and Anderson, *New World*, 19–20; on Szilard's early efforts see William Lanouette with Bela Silard, *Genius in the Shadows: A Biography of Leo Szilard: The Man Behind the Bomb* (New York: Charles Scribner's Sons, 1992).

4. *William Theodore Richards, 1900–1940*, a set of college classmates' memoirs reprinted from the Vicennial Report of the Class of 1921, Harvard College, and provided to the author by TRC.

5. Luis W. Alvarez, "Alfred Lee Loomis," *Biographical Memoirs* 51 (Washington, D.C.: National Academy of Sciences, 1980), 309–41; TRC interviews, 1987, 1991.

6. *William Theodore Richards, 1900–1940*, 7.

7. *William Theodore Richards, 1900–1940*, 14.

8. JBC to Robert Dort, Feb. 2, 1940, box 152, "Conant, J. B.: Personal" folder, JBC PREP.

9. Willard Rich (William Richards), *Brain-Waves and Death* (New York: Charles Scribner's Sons, 1940); "scientific pleasures": *William Theodore Richards, 1900–1940*, 5.

10. Rich, *Brain Waves and Death*, 204ff.; TRC interview, July 5, 1991; Miriam T. Richards, n.d. letter [1940], "Important-Preserve-Letters Written after Bill's Death," CFP.

11. Willard Rich (William Richards), "The Uranium Bomb," ms. courtesy of TRC, CFP; on Szilard and Richards, see Lanouette with Silard, *Genius in the Shadows*, 187; and Szilard to Richards, July 9, 1939, Szilard Papers, University of California at San Diego (UCSD), courtesy of Lanouette.

12. Alfred L. Loomis to JBC, May 14, 1940, JBC to Loomis, May 16, 1940, box 159, Lin-Loq folder, JBC PREP; correspondence between JBC and VB, KTC, Arthur H. Compton, and Lawrence, et al., in Caa–Carm and Carn–Ce folders, box 129, University of Chicago folder, box 130, MIT folder, box 138, Physics: Cyclotron 1938–39 folder, box 141, and "Physics, 39–40" folder, box 165, JBC PREP; JBC diary, Mar. 30, May 4, 1940; JBC desk calendar, May 8, 1940; TRC interview, July 1991; Ernest O. Lawrence to JBC, Apr. 4, 1940, JBC to Lawrence, Apr. 10, 1940, Lawrence to JBC, May 21, 1940, JBC to Lawrence, May 30, 1940, all in carton 4, folder 13, Lawrence Papers, call no. 72/117C, Bancroft Library, University of California, Berkeley; Nuel Pharr Davis, *Lawrence and Oppenheimer* (New York: Simon & Schuster, 1968), 93.

13. Daniel S. Greenberg, *The Politics of Pure Science* (New York: New American Library, 1967; 1971 reprint ed.), 75–79, citing a May 9, 1940, confidential letter from KTC to VB, and the Carnegie Executive Committee's decision of May 23, 1940.

14. TRC interviews, 1987, 1991.
15. See William L. Laurence, *Men and Atoms* (New York: Simon & Schuster, 1946, 1959, 1962), 41–50.
16. JBC, *MSL*, 276–78. On the Conference on Applied Nuclear Physics held at MIT, Oct. 28–Nov. 2, 1940, see correspondence in MIT folder, box 186, JBC PREP, including JBC to Urey, June 15, 1940; and JBC diary, Oct. 31, 1940.
17. JBC, "Trip to England—1941" ms., 11, 11a, 15–20, "1941 Mission to England—Notes, etc." folder, JBC PREP, UAI.15.898.13, box 8.
18. JBC, "Trip to England—1941," 9–10; JBC, *MSL*, 229–31.
19. JBC, "Trip to England—1941," 12.
20. JBC, *MSL*, 231–33; Tuttle, *James B. Conant*, 248–54.
21. JBC, *MSL*, 224–25.
22. JBC to Lewis Douglas, Oct. 4, 1940, Douglas Papers, Special Collections, University of Arizona Library.
23. JBC diary, Oct. 2, 1940; James Phinney Baxter III, *Scientists Against Time*, 119–21.
24. "American might pausing on the brink": VB, *Pieces of the Action*, 42.
25. This account of JBC's trip to England is drawn from JBC, "Trip to England—1941" diary and letters to his wife in JBC PERP, UAI.15.898.13, box 8, "Mission to England—1941" folder; JBC, *MSL*, 248–71; Tuttle, *James B. Conant*, 254–59.
26. England diary, Mar. 8, 1941; JBC, *MSL*, 256–57.
27. JBC, *MSL*, 253–55, 262.
28. JBC, *MSL*, 270–71.
29. JBC, "Report by J. B. Conant on the Organization of Research on Instrumentalities of War in Great Britain in 1941," Apr. 29, 1941, B–C, box 4, folder 20.
30. Landers interview.
31. Hewlett and Anderson, *New World*, 258.
32. JBC to VB, "Notes on the history of the S-1 project by J. B. Conant," Apr. 23, 1942, B–C Correspondence, folder 86. However, Carroll L. Wilson, JBC's traveling partner, recalled in a 1982 interview with the author his impression that Conant was already aware of the possibility of a bomb by the time of the England trip.
33. Landers interview.
34. Hewlett and Anderson, *New World*, 35–6; Arthur H. Compton to VB, Mar. 17, 1941, AEC Historical Document 292.
35. VB to Frank Jewett, June 7, 1941, B–C Correspondence, folder 4, cited in Zachary, "Vannevar Bush Backs the Bomb," 30; Rhodes, *Making of the Atomic Bomb*, 360–62.
36. JBC, "A History of the Development of an Atomic Bomb," Spring 1943, B–C, folders 1 and 4. Classified until 1979, Conant's own account of the bomb is split into two parts running forty-seven typed pages. (Hereafter, "History.")
37. JBC, "History"; Hewlett and Anderson, *New World*, 37–8.
38. Hewlett and Anderson, *New World*, 37–38; JBC, "History."
39. JBC, *MSL*, 278.
40. JBC, "History."
41. Hewlett and Anderson, *New World*, 41; VB, *Pieces of the Action*, 44; JBC, *MSL*, 272–4.
42. For JBC's NDRC work see Baxter, *Scientists Against Time*, and Irvin Stewart, *Organizing Scientific Research for War* (Boston: Little, Brown & Co., 1948).
43. JBC to Harvard Corporation and Overseers, confidential memorandum, Aug. 25, 1945, box 1, Conant folder, Jerome D. Greene Papers, Harvard University Archives, HUG 4436.14; JBC to Frank C. Whitmore, Aug. 24, 1945. B–C, box 18, folder 234.
44. VB, *Pieces of the Action*, 59.
45. VB, *Pieces of the Action*, 60; JBC, *MSL*, 288.
46. Hewlett and Anderson, *New World*, 42.
47. Clark, *Greatest Power on Earth*, 108.
48. The MAUD report is reprinted in Gowing, *Britain and Atomic Energy*, 394–436; see

also JBC, "History"; Hewlett and Anderson, *New World,* 43; Bundy, *Danger and Survival,* 24–29, 42–44.

49. JBC, "History." On VB's conversion to belief in the bomb's feasibility, see Stanley Goldberg, "Inventing a Climate of Opinion: Vannevar Bush and the Decision to Build the Bomb," *Isis* 83:3 (Sept. 1992), 429–52, and Zachary, "Vannevar Bush Backs the Bomb," 25–29.

50. JBC, *MSL,* 279; Landers interview; on previous pre-1941 isotope separation research at Harvard: Kistiakowsky interview; E. Bright Wilson, Jr., interview; Kistiakowsky to Lyman Briggs, Sept. 9, 1940, B–C, box 5, folder 31; JBC diary, Aug. 31, Oct. 10, Nov. 11, 22, 1940; Kistiakowsky to JBC, June 3, 1941, box 175, "Chemistry" folder, JBC PREP.

51. Arthur H. Compton, *Atomic Quest: A Personal Narrative* (New York: Oxford University Press, 1956), 6–9, takes JBC's doubtful attitude at the meeting at face value; JBC explains in his declassified "History" that he was "quite well aware of the British conclusion [that a bomb could be built] but was not at liberty to reveal this knowledge nor the plans afoot in Washington to step up the program. . . . " The notion that Lawrence and Compton at this meeting "convinced Conant the bomb would work" is still frequently repeated, e.g., Powers, *Heisenberg's War,* 173.

52. JBC, "History."

53. Hewlett and Anderson, *New World,* 45.

54. VB, *Pieces of the Action,* 60.

55. JBC, "When Shall America Fight?" May 4, 1941, *Vital Speeches of the Day* 7 (June 15, 1941), 517–19.

56. See Tuttle, *James B. Conant,* 268–69.

57. R. M. Sedgwick to CDAAA executive committee, June 24, 1941, reporting on meeting of June 22, 1941, in UAI.15.898, WWII Papers, box 3, "Committee to Defend America, General Correspondence, 1939–49" folder, JBC PERP.

58. *NYT,* July 1, 1941; JBC, "Our Country and the World Situation," June 30, 1941 speech to the National Education Association, in Tuttle, *James B. Conant,* 271–73.

59. JBC to GC, July 2, 1941, GCP, series 4, box 2.

60. JBC, England diary, Mar. 7, JBC PERP; JBC diary, June 29, 1940.

61. Neither German physicists nor government officials had, in fact, advanced as far toward a bomb as JBC feared: see Powers, *Heisenberg's War,* chap. 1–13.

62. Tuttle, *James B. Conant,* 283–84.

63. VB to JBC, Oct. 9, 1941, AEC Historical Document 17, OSRD, B–C, box 1, folder 2.

64. JBC to GC, Oct. 22, 1941, GCP, series 4, box 2.

65. National Academy report, Nov. 6, 1941, in JBC, "History"; JBC, *MSL,* 281.

66. Compton, *Atomic Quest,* 70; JBC, *MSL,* 282; Kenneth S. Davis, *Experience of War: The United States in World War II* (Garden City, NY: Doubleday & Co., 1965), 78–87.

67. Tuttle, *James B. Conant,* 282–83; JBC to Roosevelt, Dec. 8, 1941, Roosevelt folder, box 215, JBC PREP.

68. This and other quotes from this speech are from JBC, "What Victory Requires," Dec. 22, 1941, *Vital Speeches of the Day* 8 (Jan. 3, 1942), 199–202.

69. When JBC cabled a version of this speech to London for publication, he politely altered this phrase from "must be ready to assume political and economic leadership of the world" to "must be ready to *play its part in the* political and economic leadership of the world." (Emphasis added.) See JBC, "America's War Aims: Full Victory—and After," *London Sunday Times,* Dec. 21, 1941.

CHAPTER 9

1. JBC to Arthur H. Compton, Dec. 1, 1942, B–C, folder 16; Compton, *Atomic Quest*, 68.
2. JBC, *MSL*, 280–81; Harvey H. Bundy, "Remembered Words," *Atlantic Monthly*, Mar. 1957, 57; Bundy Oral History interview, Columbia University, 176–77.
3. JBC, "History."
4. Tuttle, *James B. Conant*, 287–320, 336, 337–62; JBC, *MSL*, chap. 25; JBC, "Mobilizing American Youth," *Atlantic* (July 1942), 48–53.
5. Landers interview; Interview with George B. Kistiakowsky, Feb. 1982; JBC's request for a wartime pay cut: JBC to Corporation, Jan. 5, 1942, Corporation folder, box 203; JBC PREP; JBC to GC, Jan. 12, 1942, Clark folder, box 202, JBC PREP; GC to Walter Edmonds, Jan. 28, 1949, GCP.
6. TRC interviews, July 5–8, 1991.
7. JBC, *MSL*, 297; TRC interview, Feb. 10, 1993.
8. Interview with John Lansdale, Dec. 16, 1991, Washington, D.C.; Lansdale to Hershberg, Dec. 17, 1991. See also Peter Michelmore, *The Swift Years: The Robert Oppenheimer Story* (New York: Dodd, Mead, & Co., 1969), 69–71; *IMJRO*, 259; on JBC's worries: JBC to A. H. Compton, Jan. 30, 1942, B–C, box 1, folder 2.
9. Lansdale interview.
10. Vladimir Chikov, "How the Soviet Intelligence Service 'Split' the American Atom," *New Times* 16 (Apr. 23–29, 1991), 37–40, and *New Times* 17 (Apr. 30–May 6, 1991), 36–39.
11. FDR to VB, Mar. 11, 1942, B–C, box 1, folder 2.
12. JBC, "History"; JBC, *MSL*, 285; Anderson and Hewlett, *New World*, 67–71; JBC to VB, May 14, 1942, AEC Historical document 33, B–C, box 1, folder 2; JBC to VB, "Report on S-1 Conference Saturday, May 23," May 25, 1942, AEC historical document 108, B–C, box 1, folder 2.
13. JBC to VB, May 14, 1942.
14. Hewlett and Anderson ("lifted verbatim"), *New World*, 73–74; VB and JBC to Wallace, Stimson, and Marshall, June 13, 1942; VB to FDR, June 17, 1942; FDR to VB, June 23, 1942; VB to FDR, June 24, 1942; all in B–C, box 1, folder 4.
15. Hewlett and Anderson, *New World*, 75–6, 78–81.
16. Tuttle, *James B. Conant*, 321–37, and "The Birth of an Industry: The Synthetic Rubber 'Mess' in World War II," *Technology and Culture* 22:1 (Jan. 1981); 35–67; JBC, *MSL*, chap. 23; BMB, *Baruch: The Public Years* (New York: Holt, Rinehart and Winston, Inc., 1960; Pocket Books, 1962), 280–87.
17. Hewlett and Anderson, *New World*, 113–14.
18. Rhodes, *Making of the Atomic Bomb*, 424–28; Stanley Goldberg, "Groves Takes the Reins," *Bulletin of the Atomic Scientists* 48:10 (Dec. 1992), 32–36, 38–39; VB to JBC, Sept. 17, 21, 1942, box 6, JBC PERP; and also see William Lawren, *The General and the Bomb: A Biography of General Leslie R. Groves, Director of the Manhattan Project* (New York: Dodd, Mead, & Co., 1988).
19. JBC to LRG, Oct. 26, 1942, B–C, AEC Historical Document 295; on JBC's exasperation, see, for instance, JBC's handwritten notes to VB in Oct. 1943, describing centrifuge advocate E. V. Murphree as "the damndest 'professor' I ever met," ridiculing his assertion that by resuscitating the centrifuge project it would be available to be "quickly picked up" if the diffusion method should fail. It was already too late to be used in the war, JBC heatedly argued, and any additional money spent on the centrifuge would go down the drain. Murphree to VB, Oct. 7, 1943; JBC to VB, n.d. (approx. Oct. 11, 1943); JBC to VB, Oct. 22, 1943; in B–C, box 3, folder 16.
20. JBC, *MSL*, 282.
21. JBC, *MSL*, 289; Landers interview; JBC to S-1 Executive Committee, Nov. 20, 1942, Conant folder, box 3, Briggs Alphabetical File, OSRD, S-1, RG 227, NA.
22. Compton, *Atomic Quest*, 68. Compton may have been paraphrasing a Dec. 1, 1942,

letter from JBC: "I am anxious that the record will show that everyone concerned made the most careful critical analysis of the situation and stated the prognostication, not in terms of faith but in terms of scientific fact."

23. JBC to Arthur H. Compton, Dec. 1, 1942, B–C, box 3, folder 16. On JBC's concern over the impurities issue, also see his handwritten postscript on JBC to JRO, Nov. 20, 1942, Los Alamos National Laboratory Archives.

24. Hewlett and Anderson, *New World*, 108–110.

25. Compton, *Atomic Quest*, 144; JBC, *MSL*, 290.

26. JBC to LRG, Dec. 9, 1942, B–C, box 9, folder 86.

27. See correspondence in B–C, box 8, folder 75 ("Espionage DSM"), inc. Arthur H. Compton to VB, June 22, 1942, Harold C. Urey to JBC, June 26, 1942, Arthur H. Compton to JBC, July 15, 1942, and W.A. Akers to JBC, Aug. 18, 1942.

28. See Powers, *Heisenberg's War*, for an absorbing account of why Germany failed to build nuclear weapons during World War II. Powers argues essentially that because of political and moral distaste for Hitler's regime Heisenberg and other top German physicists deliberately downplayed to Nazi officials the chances for completing a weapon during the war, thus assuring that there was no crash program. Sharply disputing this view, Mark Walker debunks what he calls "The Myth of the German Atomic Bomb" in *German National Socialism and the Quest for Nuclear Power, 1939–1949*, chap. 7. See also Daniel J. Kevles, "Heisenberg's Uncertainties," *The New Yorker*, Mar. 8, 1993, 102ff.; Rudolf Peierls, "The Bomb That Never Was," *The New York Review of Books* 40:8 (Apr. 22, 1993), 6–9; and Jeremy Bernstein, "The Farm Hall Transcripts: The German Scientists and the Bomb," *The New York Review of Books* 39:14 (Aug. 13, 1992), 47–53; Stanley Goldberg and Thomas Powers, "Declassified Files Reopen 'Nazi Bomb' Debate," *Bulletin of the Atomic Scientists* 48:7 (Sept. 1992), 32–40; and William J. Broad, "Saboteur or Savant of Nazi Drive for A-Bomb?" *NYT*, Sept. 1, 1992.

29. Landers interview.

30. Hewlett and Anderson, *New World*, 114–115; JBC to VB, Dec. 15, 194; VB to FDR, Dec. 16, 1942, enc. "Report on Present Status and Future Program on Atomic Fission Bombs" (Dec. 15, 1942), B–C, box 1, folder 4.

31. Report of Army agent Robert M. Stepp, Sept. 20, 1942, box 1, file A, Oppenheimer Hearings Records, General Administrative Files, RG 326, NA.

32. Peter Goodchild, *J. Robert Oppenheimer: Shatterer of Worlds* (Boston: Houghton Mifflin, 1981), 49.

33. War Department notice of May 13, 1942, enc. with Frederick T. Hobbs to H. T. Wensel, June 10, 1942, B–C, box 11, folder 140; see also Irvin Stewart to Richard C. Tolman, May 15, 1942, box 1, file A, Oppenheimer Hearings Records, General Administrative Files, RG 326, NA.

34. "sc," memorandum, Aug. 18, 1942, box 1, file A, Oppenheimer Hearings Records, General Administrative Files, RG 326, NA.

35. Ernest O. Lawrence to JBC, Mar. 26, 1942, B–C, box 1, folder 2; Richard C. Tolman to Irvin Stewart, May 1, 1942, box 1, file A, Oppenheimer Hearings Records, General Administrative Files, RG 326, NA.

36. JBC to VB, "Security Measures in Connection with the S-1 Work," Oct. 2, 1942, box 5, folder 35; Irvin Stewart to VB, Oct. 2, 1942, B–C, box 10, folder 128.

37. VB to Harvey Bundy, Oct. 5, 1942, B–C, box 5, folder 35.

38. LRG, "Some Recollections of July 16, 1945," in Richard Lewis, Jane Wilson and Eugene Rabinowitch, eds., Alamogordo Plus Twenty-Five Years (New York: Viking Press, 1977), 48–51; Lawren, *The General and the Bomb*, 97–102; Stanley Goldberg, "Groves, Szilard, and Oppenheimer," *Bulletin of the Atomic Scientists* 48:10 (Dec. 1992), 37.

39. Russell E. Harris to H. T. Wensel, Nov. 3, 1942, B–C, box 11, folder 140.

40. JBC's offer, at the end of the war, involved one of Harvard's select University Professorships, entitling recipients to lavish funding and total freedom from aca-

demic responsibilities. JRO wavered before rejecting it, and four years later quoted JBC as telling him that "as long as he was president, and I had not totally lost my wits, the job would be open; and I have taken this as a real invitation." JRO to Clarence I. Lewis and Donald C. Williams, May 24, 1949, box 38, "Harvard University — Job offer to Robert Oppenheimer" folder, JROP. For the 1945 offer: JBC to JRO, Sept. 14, 1945, JRO to JBC, Sept. 29, 1945, copies in JBC PREP, box 286, "Ol-Oz," 1945–46 folder, and box 27, Conant folder, JROP.

41. Interview with John H. Manley, Nov. 1986.
42. "mentor in national policy matters": Richard G. Hewlett and Francis Duncan, *Atomic Shield, 1947/1952: Vol. II, A History of the United States Atomic Energy Commission* (University Park, Pa., and London, 1969), 378; Manley interview, Nov. 1986.
43. Interview with Hans Bethe, Jan. 1985.
44. *IMJRO*, 378; B–C correspondence.
45. Hewlett and Anderson, *New World*, 230–32.
46. JBC to JRO, Oct. 28, 1942, B–C, box 11, folder 140. JBC's efforts were unavailing in this case.
47. JRO to John H. Manley, Nov. 6, 1942, Alice Kimball Smith and Charles Weiner, eds., *Robert Oppenheimer: Letters and Recollections* (Cambridge: Harvard University Press, 1980), 236.
48. JBC to LRG, Dec. 21, 1942, B–C, box 3, folder 16; Lawren, *The General and the Bomb*, 105–106; on tensions over recruiting: JBC to JRO, Oct. 28, 1942; JBC to VB, "Transference of personnel from the Radiation Laboratory (MIT) to S-1 for the use of Mr. Oppenheimer's group," Nov. 20, 1942; VB to JBC, Nov. 23, 1942; JRO to JBC, Nov. 23, 30, 1942; all in B–C, box 11, folder 140; JRO to JBC, Oct. 21, Nov. 2, and Dec. 19, 1942, and JBC to JRO, Nov. 20, 1942, all in Los Alamos National Laboratory Archives; and JRO to JBC, Dec. 24, 1942, B–C, box 9, folder 86.
49. JBC to LRG, Jan. 7, 1943, B–C, box 11, folder 140.
50. JBC to VB, Jan. 20, 1943, B–C, box 11, folder 140.
51. Sherwin, *A World Destroyed*, 53.
52. JRO to JBC, Feb. 1, 1943, AEC Historical Document 296.
53. JRO and LRG to JRO, Feb. 25, 1943, B–C, AEC Historical Document 66; LRG, *Now It Can Be Told*, 151; Landers interview.
54. JBC, *MSL*, 288; LRG, *Now It Can Be Told*, 44–45.
55. LRG, *Now It Can Be Told*, 150–51.
56. JRO to I. I. Rabi, Feb. 26, 1943, B–C, box 11, folder 140; Rhodes, *Making of the Atomic Bomb*, 449–55.
57. JBC to JRO, Mar. 4, 26, 1943, B–C, box 11, folder 141.
58. JBC, "History."
59. JBC, "History."
60. Compton, *Atomic Quest*, 283–84.
61. "I would have been blamed if the bomb hadn't gone off"; quoted, "Dr. Conant: In Science Pure, in Education Controversial," *Newsweek* 40:12 (Sept. 22, 1952), 74.
62. Compton, *Atomic Quest*, 103–4.
63. JBC to VB, "Final Phase of S-1 Project," Mar. 4, 1943, B–C, folder 12.
64. Beneath that hopeful conclusion one finds, in JBC's hand, a sad addendum: "This possibility was eliminated as far as any one could short of an actual atomic explosion by experiments performed at 'Y' [Los Alamos] during the late summer of 1943. Note added Nov. 24, 1944."

CHAPTER 10

1. Buck interview, 46–54; Paul H. Buck, "The Trials and Tribulations of Ada Comstock," Paul H. Buck Papers, Pusey Library, Harvard University. It took a while for the implications of the merger to sink in. Distracted by his war work, JBC was startled a couple of years later one day while walking through Harvard Yard with Buck. "Paul," he asked, "what are all these girls doing in the Yard?" Buck interview, 73. Harvard's change of heart regarding women was neither total nor immediate, however. On June 21, 1943, the Corporation rejected an overwhelming faculty recommendation in favor of admitting women to Harvard Medical School; it went along, however, when the issue was raised again the following year. See memorandum regarding materials in box 230, PREP, in JBC Special Subject File, box 8, JBC PERP.
2. Leo P. Brophy and George J. B. Fisher, *The US Army in World War II: The Technical Services: The Chemical Warfare Service: Organizing for War* (Washington, D.C.: Office of the Chief of Military History, Department of the Army, 1960), 59–62.
3. VB to JBC, Dec. 22, 1942, B–C, box 2, folder 9.
4. For accounts of the interchange controversy, see Hewlett and Anderson, *New World*, chap. 12; Gowing, *Britain and Atomic Energy*, pt. 2; Sherwin, *A World Destroyed*, esp. 68–88; Bundy, *Danger and Survival*, 98–113; Bertrand Goldschmidt, *Atomic Rivals: A Candid Memoir of Rivalries Among the Allies Over the Bomb* (New Brunswick, N.J.: Rutgers University Press, 1990).
5. "Fight for Liberty," *Vital Speeches of the Day* 9 (Feb. 15, 1943), 281–83.
6. JBC, "Wanted: American Radicals," *Atlantic Monthly* 171 (May 1943), 41–45.
7. Henry James to GC, June 25, 1943, GC to James, July 12, 1943, in GCP, series 4, box 5, James folder; "hero-worship": Henry James to GC, Nov. 9, 1942, box 1, JBC folder, Jerome D. Greene Papers; JBC to GC, June 14, 1943, GCP, series 4, box 2; Laski to JBC, June 7, 1943, and other reactions in boxes 222–223, JBC PREP.
8. JBC, *MSL*, 404–407.
9. Thomas W. Lamont to JBC, draft, May 21, 1943, box 264, folder 13, Lamont Papers, Baker Library, Harvard Business School.
10. Lamont to George Whitney, June 7, 1943, box 264, folder 13, Lamont Papers.
11. Lamont to JBC, June 22, 1943, box 264, folder 14, Lamont Papers.
12. JBC to Lamont, July 26, 1943, box 264, folder 14, Lamont Papers.
13. Lamont to JBC, Oct. 21, 1943, and JBC to Lamont, Oct. 27, 1943, in box 264, folder 15, Lamont Papers.
14. JBC to Alf Landon, May 7, 1940, JBC PREP, box 149; JBC, "Education for a Classless Society," *Atlantic Monthly* 165 (May 1940), 593–602; JBC, "A Free Classless Society," *Vital Speeches of the Day* 6 (Nov. 15, 1939), 87–89; Tuttle, *James B. Conant*, 24–34; JBC, "What Are We Arming to Defend," Oct. 21, 1940, in JBC, *MSL*, 662–65.
15. Max Lerner, *PM*, May 31, 1943, quoted in Tuttle, *James B. Conant*, 33.
16. JBC speech at University of California at Berkeley, Mar. 28, 1940, JBC Speech File.
17. JBC diary, Oct. 25, 1940.
18. Buck interview, 69–70.
19. The use of the bomb on Hiroshima finally allowed JBC to explain his conduct to the Corporation. In a hastily prepared report, JBC detailed his secret atomic activities, adding: "On more than one occasion I debated with myself the advisability of insisting that the Governing Boards accept my resignation. The decision was difficult as for security reasons I could not even hint to my closest Harvard advisers what stakes were involved. Each time I decided in the negative. To the difficulties of making a change in the presidency in war time was added the undoubted fact that the prestige of Harvard's name contributed much to my value in the work. On those two counts it seemed I was warranted in continuing to serve in a dual capacity." JBC to Harvard Overseers and Corporation, confidential memorandum, Aug. 25, 1945, box 1, Conant folder, Jerome D. Greene Papers, HUG 4436.14, Harvard University Archives.

20. JBC, "Fight for Liberty," *Vital Speeches of the Day* 9 (Feb. 15, 1943), 281–83.
21. VB to JBC, Oct. 9, 1941, B–C, box 1, folder 2, AEC Historical Document 17; Hewlett and Anderson, *New World,* 259; FDR to Churchill, Oct. 11, 1941, in Francis L. Loewenheim et al., eds., *Roosevelt and Churchill: Their Secret Wartime Correspondence* (New York: Dutton, 1975), 161–62.
22. Gowing, *Britain and Atomic Energy,* 122–26; Hewlett and Anderson, *New World,* 259.
23. VB to Sir John Anderson, Apr. 20, 1942, B–C, AEC Historical Document 307.
24. FDR to VB, July 11, 1942, B–C, box 2, folder 9.
25. Sir John Anderson to prime minister, July 30, 1942, in Gowing, *Britain and Atomic Energy,* 437–38.
26. JBC to E. V. Murphree, May 15, 1942, B–C, AEC Historical Document 293.
27. JBC to VB, Oct. 1, 1942, B–C, box 5, folder 32; a month earlier, after VB had sent two equally evasive letters to Anderson, JBC praised his boss for producing "masterpieces! You should have been a lawyer or a diplomat!" JBC to VB, n.d. re VB to Anderson, Sept. 1, 1942, B–C, box 2, folder 9.
28. JBC to VB, "Some thoughts concerning the S-1 project," Oct. 26, 1942, B–C, AEC Historical Document 295.
29. JBC to VB, "U.S.-British Relations on S-1 Project," Dec. 14, 1942.
30. Hewlett and Anderson, *New World,* 264; HLS diary, Oct. 29, 1942.
31. VB to JBC, Nov. 2, 1942, B–C, box 2, folder 9.
32. W. A. Akers to Gordon Munro, Dec. 28, 1942, AB1/357 Directorate of Tube Alloys 1/12/1, Pt. 1, PRO; Akers to M. W. Perrin, Dec. 21, 1942, AB1/128.96155, PRO; Akers to R. Gordon Munro, Jan. 14, 1943, AB1/374.96620, PRO; Akers to C. J. Mackenzie, Jan. 30, 1943, AB1, H. 4-1-1 (1), PRO.
33. Akers to M. W. Perrin, Aug. 31, 1943, AB1/376.96220, PRO.
34. Akers to Hans von Halban, Jan. 1, 1943; Akers to M. W. Perrin, Jan. 2, 1943; both in AB1/128.96155, PRO.
35. JBC to VB, "Some thoughts concerning the correspondence between the President and the Prime Minister on S-1," March 25, 1943, B–C, box 1, folder 2 (hereafter, "Some thoughts . . ."); JBC to VB, "International complications of the S-1 project," Nov. 13, 1942, B–C, AEC Historical Document 310; Hewlett and Anderson, *New World,* 271.
36. JBC, "Science and Society in the Post-War World," speech to the Annual Dinner of the New York Academy of Public Education, Feb. 18, 1943, *Vital Speeches of the Day* 9 (Apr. 15, 1943), 396.
37. Bundy, *Danger and Survival,* 101; Hewlett and Anderson, *New World,* 271.
38. Gowing, *Britain and Atomic Energy,* 154.
39. W. A. Akers to M. W. Perrin, Aug. 19, 1943, Personal No. 7, AB1/376.96220, PRO.
40. JBC to George F. Elliot, Oct. 21, 1940, Elliot folder, box 179, JBC PREP.
41. JBC to William A. White, Nov. 13, 1940, JBC PERP.
42. Sherwin, *A World Destroyed,* 88–89; Robert Dallek, *Franklin D. Roosevelt and American Foreign Policy, 1932–1945* (New York: Oxford University Press, 1979, 1981), 342, 390.
43. JBC to VB, "U.S.-British Relations on S-1 Project," Dec. 14, 1942, B–C, AEC Historical Document 149.
44. JBC to VB, "U.S.-British Relations on S-1 Project," Dec. 14, 1942.
45. JBC to VB, "U.S.-British Relations on S-1 Project," Dec. 14, 1942.
46. VB to FDR, "Report on Present Status and Future Program on Atomic Fission Bombs," Dec. 15, 1942, pp. 22–27, 29, and VB to FDR, Dec. 16, 1942, B–C, box 1, folder 4; Hewlett and Anderson, *New World,* 267–68; Sherwin, *A World Destroyed,* 71–73; HLS diary, Dec. 27, 1942.
47. JBC, Memorandum on the interchange with the British and Canadians on S-1, Jan. 7, 1943, AEC Historical Document 152, B–C, box 5, folder 33A (and draft of Jan. 1, 1943, same folder); Gowing, *Britain and Atomic Energy,* 156.

48. Hewlett and Anderson, *New World*, 271; Gowing, *Britain and Atomic Energy*, 156–60.
49. JBC to VB, handwritten note, with JBC to Akers, Dec. 15, 1942, B–C, box 5, folder 32; JBC to Akers, Feb. 6, 1943, B–C, box 3, folder 16; Sherwin, *A World Destroyed*, 81–82 fn.
50. Dominions Office to Canada (H.C.) (Sir John Anderson to Malcolm MacDonald), March 4, 1943, AB1/374.96220, PRO.
51. "mutual admiration society": Akers to M. W. Perrin, Sept. 13, 1943, Letter No. 21, AB1/376.96220, PRO; JBC to Malcolm MacDonald, Mar. 10, 1943, B–C, box 10, folder 101.
52. Dominions Office to Canada (H. C.) (Anderson to Malcolm MacDonald), Mar. 26, 1943, AB1/374.96220, PRO; Gowing, *Britain and Atomic Energy*, 160–61.
53. JBC to VB, "Report on Meeting on March 9, 1943, held in Dr. Urey's Office on the Future of the Heavy Water Program," Mar. 10, 1943, B–C, box 2, folder 10.
54. Urey to JBC, June 21, 1943, climaxing a torrid correspondence arguing the history of the heavy-water program. See MED decimal file, box 29, "201 (Urey)" folder, MED collection, RG 77, NA, and box 3, Conant file, OSRD, S-1, Briggs Alphabetical File, RG 227, NA. For background on Halban, see Goldschmidt, *Atomic Rivals*, esp. chap. 11–15.
55. JBC had formally invited Halban to come to New York, but on the British side it was decided that Halban would not be able to make the trip until the interchange question was resolved. JBC to Dean C. J. Mackenzie, Mar. 13, 1943, B–C, folder 83a.
56. JBC to Urey, June 29, 1943; LRG to JBC, July 12, 1943; both in MED decimal file, box 29, "201 (Urey)" folder, RG 77, NA.
57. Urey to JBC, Jan. 14, 1944, JBC to Urey, Jan. 18, 1944, both in B–C, box 17, folder 230.
58. C. L. Sulzberger, *A Long Row of Candles: Memoirs and Diaries, 1934–1954* (New York: Macmillan, 1969), 882.
59. JBC to VB, "Complaints about the S-1 Project reaching the President," July 31, 1943, B–C, folder 13.
60. Sherwin, *A World Destroyed*, 81.
61. JBC to VB, Inter-Office Memorandum, Dec. 15, 1942, B–C, folder 9a ("Superbomb"). Alluding to the heavy-water plant at Trail, British Columbia, whose products were being considered for use in a pile to produce plutonium, JBC urged VB, when he saw FDR, to "point out that if the by-product of the power plant is a 'superexplosive,' the implications of that for the future of civilization are even graver than you predict in your report."
62. JBC to VB, "Some thoughts . . . ," Mar. 25, 1943.
63. JBC to VB, "Some thoughts . . . ," Mar. 25, 1943.
64. VB to Hopkins, Mar. 31, 1943, *FRUS*, 1943, II, 6–10.
65. Davis, *Lawrence and Oppenheimer*, 138–39, 202. After the Manhattan Project, the U.S. government dropped the electromagnetic separation program in favor of pluto- nium for weapons-grade cores for nuclear weapons. But the relative simplicity of Lawrence's calutron method, the aspect that had so impressed JBC, also appealed to Saddam Hussein, whose use of this seemingly obsolete technology for Iraq's secret nuclear weapons program shocked proliferation experts when it was discovered in mid- 1991. "Iraqi Atom Effort Exposes Weakness in World Controls," *NYT,* July 15, 1991.
66. JBC to LRG, Dec. 9, 1942, B–C, box 9, folder 86; see also JBC to VB, Oct. 26, 1942, box 3, folder 16; JBC to VB, Dec. 11, 1942, B–C, box 3, folder 16; and JBC to VB, Jan. 21, 1943, handwritten comments added Mar. 10, 1943, B–C, box 4, folder 21.
67. "Even if the electromagnetic plan only produces one bomb every six months, it would be a great comfort to have this production if the enemy started the use of such a weapon. It must be remembered that by the diffusion method it will require completion of the whole plant before material enough can be assembled to try out

the explosive technique. And as far as the production of 49 [plutonium] is concerned, one must always remember there is an additional uncertainty as to the explosive nature of this material as compared to 25 [Uranium-235], which is produced by the electro-magnetic method." JBC to LRG, Dec. 9, 1942.

68. Sherwin, *A World Destroyed*, 79; Bush, "Memorandum of Conference," Sept. 22, 1944, AEC Historical Document 185.

69. Winston S. Churchill, *The Hinge of Fate* (Boston: Houghton Mifflin, 1950), 809; Hewlett and Anderson, *New World*, 272–74.

70. Harvey Bundy, memorandum of meeting at 10 Downing Street on July 22, 1943, *FRUS, 1943*, II, 634–36. For another contemporary indication of British fears that the war would "leave Russia the diplomatic master of the world," see General J. C. Smuts to Churchill, Aug. 31, 1943, in Churchill, *The Hinge of Fate*, 126–27.

71. JBC to VB, "Exchange of Information on S-1 Project with the British," July 30, 1943, *FRUS, 1943*, II, 639.

72. JBC to VB, Aug. 3, 1943, B–C, box 1, folder 2.

73. JBC to VB, "Exchange of Information on S-1 Project with the British," Aug. 6, 1943, B–C, box 1, folder 2.

74. *FRUS, 1943*, II, Quebec, 1117–19; Sherwin, *A World Destroyed*, 85–8; Hewlett and Anderson, *New World*, 276–80; Gowing, *Britain and Atomic Energy*, 164–71, 439–40.

75. Churchill to Lord Cherwell, May 27, 1944, quoted in Clark, *Greatest Power on Earth*, 152.

76. VB to JBC, Sept. 26, 1944, B–C; VB, *Pieces of the Action*, 284.

77. VB to FDR, Aug. 7, 1943, *FRUS, 1943*, II, 652.

78. Harvey H. Bundy to HLS, Aug. 6, 1943, *FRUS, 1943*, II, 648.

79. Hewlett and Anderson, *New World*, 279.

80. Akers to Perrin, Sept. 13, 1943, AB1/376.96220, PRO.

81. Lord Moran, *Winston Churchill: The Struggle for Survival, 1940–1965* (London: Constable & Co., 1966), 116–17; see also Sherwood, *Roosevelt and Hopkins*, 749–50.

82. GRC, "A Hostess Remembers Mr. Churchill," *Harvard Magazine* (Sept.–Oct. 1983), 93–94, 98.

83. JBC, *MSL*, 262; Moran, *Winston Churchill*, 116; TRC interview, July 1991.

84. Churchill, *The Hinge of Fate*, 123–25; *Christian Science Monitor*, Sept. 7, 1943.

CHAPTER 11

1. JBC to Maj. Gen. W.D. Styer, May 19, 1943, enc. H. T. Wensel to Adm. W. R. Purnell, B–C, box 16, folder 216; VB to JBC, Jan. 20, 1943, B–C, box 4, folder 18; VB to JBC, June 17, 1943, JBC to VB, June 24, 1943, B–C, box 1, folder 3; VB, "Memorandum of Conversation with the President," June 24, 1943, B–C, box 2, folder 10; JBC, "Conversation with Dean Mackenzie on the evening of July 7," July 8, 1943, B–C, box 1, folder 2; Powers, *Heisenberg's War*, 209–11.

2. Powers, *Heisenberg's War*, 537–38 n 6.

3. Quoted in *NYT*, Dec. 4, 1943.

4. Quoted in Gertrude Weiss Szilard and Spender R. Weart, eds., *Leo Szilard: His Version of the Facts: Selected Recollections and Correspondence*, vol. 2 (Cambridge: MIT Press, 1978), 169.

5. Szilard to VB, Dec. 13, 1943, B–C, box 16, folder 217.

6. JBC to VB, Dec. 23, 1943, B–C, box 16, folder 217. JBC did offer to take Szilard off VB's hands, however, and meet with him.

7. JBC to VB, n.d., B–C, box 16, folder 217.

8. LRG memorandum, "Re: Szilard," Oct. 17, 1963, Groves Papers, RG 200, NA. On Szilard's activities on the bomb project, including his run-ins with JBC and LRG, see Lanouette with Silard, *Genius in the Shadows*.

9. JBC, "S-1 Diary", B–C, box 9, folder 86; JBC, *MSL*, 295; JBC to VB, "Complaints about the S-1 Project reaching the President," July 31, 1943. Other correspondence in the Lowen case can be found in the Franklin D. Roosevelt Papers, Atomic Bomb file, folder 2; see also Joseph P. Lash, *Eleanor and Franklin* (New York: W. W. Norton & Co., 1971), 907–11. For Met Lab–Du Pont frictions, see Hewlett and Anderson, *New World*, 185–226.
10. JBC to VB, "Complaints about the S-1 Project reaching the President," July 31, 1943, B–C, folder 13.
11. Sherwin, *A World Destroyed*, 46–53.
12. Szilard to VB, Jan. 14, 1944, B–C, box 1, folder 4, and in Szilard and Weart, eds., *Leo Szilard*, 169.
13. See Sherwin, *A World Destroyed*, 91–8; JRO, "Niels Bohr and Atomic Weapons," *New York Review of Books* 3 (Dec. 17, 1966), 6–8; Smith, *A Peril and a Hope*, 5–12; and Abraham Pais, *Niels Bohr's Times, In Physics, Philosophy, and Polity* (Oxford, Eng.: Oxford University Press, 1991), 490–508.
14. Bohr memorandum of Apr. 2, 1944, in Bohr-Frankfurter folder, box 34, JROP.
15. Gowing, *Britain and Atomic Energy*, 346–49; Sherwin, *A World Destroyed*, 98–99.
16. On Bohr's contacts with Frankfurter, see various documents in Bohr-Frankfurter folder, box 34, JROP, especially Frankfurter's memoranda of May 1945; Gowing, *Britain and Atomic Energy*, 349–62; Sherwin, *A World Destroyed*, 99–109; Bundy, *Danger and Survival*, 114, 116–18; Pais, *Niels Bohr's Times*, 499–503; Baker, *Brandeis and Frankfurter*, 388–89.
17. "Alas, imagination is not a gift with which Jim is especially endowed." FF to GC, Aug. 8, 1956, box 184, folder 2, FFP; for JBC–FF correspondence in early 1944, see exchanges in Frankfurter Papers, LC, box 49, Conant file, and FFP, box 184, folder 10.
18. These include both major secondary accounts and tertiary works citing them. See, for example, Smith, *A Peril and a Hope*, 7–8; Sherwin, *A World Destroyed*, 90–127, 257–58; Michael Mandelbaum, *The Nuclear Question: The United States and Nuclear Weapons*, 1946–1976 (Cambridge, Eng.: Cambridge University Press, 1979), 6–8; Wyden, *Day One*, 119–25; Gerard H. Clarfield and William M. Wiececk, *Nuclear America: Military and Civilian Nuclear Power in the United States*, 1940–1980, (New York: Harper & Row, 1984), 45–50.
19. Smith, *A Peril and a Hope*, 14.
20. JBC, "Some Thoughts on the International Control of Atomic Energy," May 4, 1944, B–C, box 9, folder 97. Hewlett and Anderson briefly cite this document in *New World* but, in my view, miss its significance, perhaps because the focus on Bohr's role emerged only subsequently to its publication. While noting that by late August 1944, VB, JBC, and Bohr "were moving in the same direction," they do not cite the well-developed nature of JBC's views several months earlier. See Hewlett and Anderson, *New World*, 325–31, 689 n. 9.
21. JBC, handwritten comments, VB to JBC, "Shurcliff's memo on Post-War Policies," Apr. 17, 1944, AEC Historical Document 180.
22. See Mandelbaum, *Nuclear Question*, 5–6, and Sherwin, *A World Destroyed*, 94–95, for discussions of the link between sovereignty and nuclear weapons in relation to Bohr's ideas.
23. Cited in JRO, "Niels Bohr and Atomic Weapons," 8.
24. JBC, speech to the Harvard Club of New York City, Jan. 13, 1944, in Tuttle, *James B. Conant*, 371.
25. JBC, "The Tough-Minded Idealist," address of Sept. 23, 1946, *Harvard Alumni Bulletin* 49:2 (Oct. 12, 1946), 71–72. "The tough-minded idealist operates from unconscious premises which permit no roseate view of human nature either in the present or in the immediate future. His mode of action is in terms of the calculated risk, and to calculate the risk he prefers to talk in terms of concrete and limited objectives. For him all phrases which describe noble sentiments are subject for

analysis. Some he may find largely poetical expressions to be defined only in terms of the emotions they evoke; many others, including the description of such American ideals as 'equality of opportunity' and 'social justice' on the other hand, he will find to have real content."

26. Sherwin, *A World Destroyed,* 105–109; Gowing, *Britain and Atomic Energy,* 353–58; JBC does not mention Bohr in *MSL.*
27. VB, "Memo of Conference," Sept. 22, 1944, B–C, AEC Historical Document 185, makes clear FDR's displeasure at Bohr's discussing the atomic program with Frankfurter.
28. FDR and Churchill, Hyde Park *aide-mémoire,* Sept. 18 ("actually 19th"), 1944, reprinted in Sherwin, *A World Destroyed,* 284, and Gowing, *Britain and Atomic Energy,* 447.
29. JBC, Urey, and Compton, "The Use of Radioactive Material as a Military Weapon," Sept. 4, 1943, MED decimal files, box 55, decimal 319.1 ("Literature"), and box 70, decimal 471.6, RG 77, NA.
30. JRO to Enrico Fermi, May 25, 1943, Fermi folder, box 33, JROP.
31. Concern over radiological warfare: various documents in MED decimal files, RG 77, box 70, decimal 471.6, and box 55, decimal 319.1; also LRG, *Now It Can Be Told,* 200.
32. JBC to James P. Baxter III, Oct. 4, 1945, NDRC folder, box 285, JBC PREP.
33. Thomas F. Troy, ed., *Wartime Washington: The Secret OSS Journal of James Grafton Rodgers* (Lanham, Md.: University Publications of America, 1987), 157.
34. JBC diary, Mar. 9, 1941; JBC to A. C. Smith, June 16, 1941, JBC to Donovan, July 2, 1941, both in "Do" correspondence folder, box 178, JBC PREP; JBC to Stanley King, Sept. 30, 1941, box 198, JBC PREP.
35. Troy, ed., *Wartime Washington,* 97 ("spry"), 157, 160 ("taboo").
36. Quoted in Tuttle, *James B. Conant,* 12.
37. JBC to Maj. Francis B. Stewart, Nov. 6, 1945, NDRC folder, box 285, JBC PREP.
38. VB to LRG, Nov. 15, 1943, box 55, "319.1 Literature" folder, MED Decimal Files, RG 77, NA.
39. JBC to VB, "S-1 Legislation," July 27, 1944, B–C, AEC Historical Document 297.
40. Hewlett and Anderson, *New World,* 302–303 for JBC's discovery that plutonium could not be used in a gun-type bomb; also JBC, "S-1 Historical Note," July 27, 1944, B–C.
41. "Russia's Position," quoted in Sherwood, *Roosevelt and Hopkins,* 748.
42. W. Averell Harriman and Elie Abel, *Special Envoy to Churchill and Stalin, 1941–1946* (New York: Random House, 1975), 256–83; Churchill, *Closing the Ring,* 405.
43. Winston S. Churchill, *Triumph and Tragedy* (Boston: Houghton Mifflin, 1953), 73.
44. Herbert Feis, *Churchill, Roosevelt, Stalin: The War They Waged and the Peace They Sought* (Princeton, N.J.: Princeton University Press, 1957, 1967), 327.
45. JBC, *MSL,* 300.
46. Smith, *Peril and a Hope,* 18–20; JBC found "imaginative" a July 1944 attempt by Jeffries to estimate the postwar course of nuclear energy, concentrating on its industrial uses, and it undoubtedly stimulated his thinking on postwar issues: see Jeffries to Arthur H. Compton, July 14, 1944, and JBC to VB, July 26, 1944, both in B–C, box 9, folder 91.
47. FDR and Churchill, Hyde Park *aide-mémoire,* Sept. 18 ("actually 19th"), 1944, in Sherwin, *A World Destroyed,* 284.
48. VB, *Pieces of the Action,* 143.
49. VB and JBC to HLS, "The need for: (1) Release of information to the public. (2) National legislation controlling the production of and experimentation with atomic power. (3) A treaty with Great Britain and Canada dealing with atomic power," Sept. 19, 1944, B–C, AEC Historical Document 279.
50. VB, "Memo of Conference," Sept. 22, 1944, B–C, AEC Historical Document 185.

51. VB to JBC, Sept. 25, 1944, B-C, AEC Historical Document 280; VB to JBC, Sept. 23, 1944, B-C, AEC Historical Document 186.
52. VB and JBC to HLS, Sept. 30, 1944. The package included, first, a one-page cover letter laying out the six main points; then two in-depth documents: "Some Salient Points Concerning Future International Handling of Subject of Atomic Bombs" —reprinted in Sherwin, *A World Destroyed*, 286-88—and "Supplementary memorandum giving further details concerning military potentialities and the need for international exchange of information," Harrison-Bundy files, box 154, MED records, RG 77, NA.
53. Sherwin, *A World Destroyed*, 91, 121-22, 257; for a revised view, see Sherwin, "How Well They Meant," *Bulletin of the Atomic Scientists* 41:7 (Aug. 1985) 9-15.
54. Sherwin, *A World Destroyed*, 127, 126 n.
55. Minutes of Interim Committee, June 21, 1945, MED records; Hewlett and Anderson, *New World*, 368; and JBC and VB to G. Harrison, June 22, 1945, B-C, folder 20B; Sherwin, *A World Destroyed*, 215-16.
56. Rhodes, *The Making of the Atomic Bomb*, 562, 832-33.
57. VB to JBC, "Memorandum for Dr. Conant," Oct. 11, 1944, B-C, box 5, folder 38. The date of this Bush-Bohr meeting is unclear in Ruth Moore, *Niels Bohr* (New York: Alfred A. Knopf, 1966; MIT Press reprint ed., 1985), 358-59, and Pais, *Niels Bohr's Times*, 503.
58. Ken Mansfield, memorandum for the files (classified "Secret") "Conversation with Dr. Conant," June 22, 1951, Classified Box 32, Records of the Joint Committee on Atomic Energy, RG 128, NA.
59. JBC's comments on pp. 98-99 of *A World Destroyed* appear in his copy of the book at the Conant family home in Hanover, N.H.

CHAPTER 12

1. For the *Halibut's* journeys, see Adm. I. J. Galantin, U.S.N. (Ret.), *Take Her Deep! A Submarine Against Japan in World War II* (Chapel Hill, N.C.: Algonquin Books, 1987); Eliot H. Bryant, Chief of Staff, Cmdr. Submarines, Seventh Fleet, to Lt. James R. Conant, "Award of Silver Star Medal," Apr. 20, 1945, CFP.
2. TRC interviews, July 5-8, 1991, Feb. 1993.
3. TRC interviews, 1987, July 1991.
4. TRC interviews, July 5-8, 1991.
5. GRC, "Daily Reminder 1942," May-Nov. 1944 entries, CFP; May Sarton, *Faithful Are the Wounds* (New York: W. W. Norton & Co., 1955).
6. VB, "Memorandum of Conference," Dec. 8, 1944, B-C, folder 20A; VB to JBC, Dec. 13, 1944, B-C, AEC Historical Document 284.
7. VB to JBC, Dec. 13, 1944.
8. VB to JBC, Oct. 24, 1944, B-C, AEC Historical Document 188.
9. George Kistiakowsky recalled: "I remember one time it was pretty much all over. He was saying how he agonized over the decision of which methods of industrial production of weapons-grade fissionable materials to approve. And he chose all three, because he wasn't sure. As it was, incredibly enough, every one of them worked. . . . " Interview, Feb. 1982.
10. Efforts to determine German progress are covered in Samuel A. Goudsmit, *Alsos* (New York: H. Schuman, 1947); LRG, *Now It Can Be Told*; Boris T. Push, *The Alsos Mission* (New York: Charter, 1980; Award House, 1969); Walker, *German National Socialism and the Quest for Nuclear Power*; and Powers, *Heisenberg's War*.
11. Ronald H. Spector, *Eagle Against the Sun: The American War with Japan* (New York: Macmillan, Inc., 1984), chap. 13-22.
12. Hewlett and Anderson, *New World*, 253; VB, "Memorandum of conference with the president," June 24, 1943, AEC Historical Document 133, B-C, box 2, folder 10.
13. Arnold Kramish interview, Feb. 17, 1993; Kramish, "They Were Heroes Too,"

Washington Post, Dec. 15, 1991, C7; Hewlett and Anderson, *New World*, 296–98, 299, 624.

14. JBC, "Summary of Trip to 'Y,'" Dec. 1944, B–C, box 1, folder 3.
15. JBC to VB, Dec. 15, 1942, B–C, box 2, folder 9a ("S-1 Superbomb").
16. Though he is cited in some accounts as having supported the Morgenthau Plan, JBC later denied discussing their respective plans with the treasury secretary or his aides and, at his nomination hearings before being sent to Germany as U.S. high commissioner in 1953, distanced himself from what he said was the Morgenthau Plan's "vindictive spirit." U.S. Senate, Committee on Foreign Relations, *Nomination of James B. Conant*, 83d Cong., 1st sess. (Washington, D.C.: Government Printing Office, 1953), 82–86, 100–101. Compare with John Morton Blum, *From the Morgenthau Diaries*, vol. 3, *Years of War 1941–1945* (Boston: Houghton Mifflin, 1967), 343, 377, and Henry Morgenthau III, *Mostly Morgenthaus: A Family History* (New York: Ticknor & Fields, 1991), 366. Morgenthau received an advance copy of JBC's speech from Oscar Cox of the Foreign Economic Administration, but no direct communication between JBC and the treasury secretary regarding their plans was located. See Cox to Morgenthau, Oct. 4, 1944, and Morgenthau to Cox, Oct. 5, 1944, Morgenthau diary, book 779, pp. 333–350, Morgenthau Papers, FDRL, and Oscar Cox diary, Oct. 9, 1944, Cox Papers, FDRL.
17. JBC, "The Effective Disarmament of Germany and Japan," Oct. 7, 1944, *Vital Speeches of the Day* 11 (Nov. 15, 1944), 75–78; reprinted in *Life* 18 (Apr. 2, 1945), 65–68, 70, 72.
18. VB and JBC to HLS, "Supplementary information concerning . . . ," Sept. 30, 1944, Harrison-Bundy files, box 54, MED records, RG 77, NA.
19. JBC to L. W. Douglas, Oct. 11, 1944, JBC PREP, box 258, and Douglas Papers, University of Arizona; FDR's comment is quoted in Frank A. Ninkovich, *Germany and the United States: The Transformation of the German Question since 1945* (Boston: Twayne Publishers, 1988), 21.
20. JBC to L. W. Douglas, Oct. 11, 1944.
21. JBC to VB, May 9, 1945, B–C, box 5, folder 38.
22. VB, "Memorandum of Conference," Sept. 22, 1944, B–C, AEC Historical Document 185; VB to JBC, Sept. 25, 1944, B–C, AEC Historical Document 280.
23. VB and JBC to HLS, "Supplementary memorandum . . . ," Sept. 30, 1944, Harrison-Bundy files, folder 77, RG 77, NA.
24. John Lewis Gaddis, *Strategies of Containment: A Critical Appraisal of Postwar American National Security Policy* (New York: Oxford University Press, 1982), 15–16; Sherwin, *A World Destroyed*, chap. 5.
25. FDR's espousal of the idea is mentioned in a March 25, 1945, draft memo from Churchill to Anthony Eden, in Sherwin, *A World Destroyed*, 290–91. Churchill wrote, in a passage deleted from the final draft: "I was shocked at Yalta too when the President in a casual manner spoke of revealing the secret to Stalin on the grounds that de Gaulle, if he heard of it, would certainly double-cross us with Russia."
26. FDR to Churchill, Apr. 11, 1945, *FRUS*, 1945, V, 210, in John Lewis Gaddis, *The United States and the Origins of the Cold War, 1941–1947* (New York: Columbia University Press, 1972), 172.
27. Smith, *A Peril and a Hope*, 19, 110.
28. Smith, *A Peril and a Hope*, 22, 554. Excerpts from the Jeffries Report are reprinted in *A Peril and a Hope*, 539–59, and Sherwin, *A World Destroyed* (rev. ed.), 315–22.
29. Hewlett and Anderson, *A World Destroyed*, 341.
30. Barton J. Bernstein, "The Quest for Security: American Foreign Policy and International Control of Atomic Energy, 1942–46," *Journal of American History* 60 (Mar. 1974), 1003–44, 1008.
31. JBC to Douglas, Oct. 11, 1944, JBC PREP, box 258.

32. JBC to Thomas W. Lamont, July 26, 1943, box 264, folder 15, Lamont Papers, Baker Library, Harvard Business School.
33. JBC to Walter L. Lippmann, Apr. 20, 1943, box 63, folder 491, Lippmann Papers.
34. JBC to Douglas, Oct. 11, 1944.
35. JBC, "The Effective Disarmament of Germany and Japan," 75.
36. Bohr memorandum, June 25, 1944, Bohr-Frankfurter file, JROP.
37. JBC to Eliot, Jan. 29, 1945, JBC PREP, box 259.
38. HLS diary, Dec. 31, 1944, HLS Papers, Yale; Sherwin, *A World Destroyed,* 103, 255 n 28.
39. JBC to Eliot, Jan. 29, 1945.
40. JBC to VB, May 9, 1945, B–C, box 5, folder 38.
41. The first major advancement of this thesis was contained in P. M. S. Blackett, *Fear, War and the Bomb: Military and Political Consequences of Atomic Energy* (New York: Whittlesey House, 1949), and the first significant attempt to document it was Gar Alperovitz's *Atomic Diplomacy: Hiroshima and Potsdam* (New York: Simon & Schuster, 1965; Penguin, 1985); more nuanced and better documented variations on this theme have appeared subsequently in the writings of such historians as Martin J. Sherwin, Barton J. Bernstein, Gregg Herken, Alperovitz in the revised edition of his book, and others. For more on the historiography of the bomb, see chap. 16.
42. JBC limits his conception of immediate U.S. objectives in his letter to Douglas, Oct. 11, 1944. Though HLS reversed his position that fall, he advised HST in mid-1945 to use the atomic bomb to press for a political liberalization of the Soviet Union; "more manageable" refers to the views expressed by James F. Byrnes, shortly before he became HST's secretary of state, to Leo Szilard and Harold Urey in Spartanberg, S.C., on Apr. 28, 1945. See HLS to HST, "Reflections of the Basic Problems Which Confront Us," July 26, 1945, in HLS and McGeorge Bundy, *On Active Service in Peace and War* (New York: Harper & Bros., 1947, 1948), 638–41; and for Byrnes, see Weart and Szilard, eds., *Leo Szilard: His Version of the Facts,* 183–85.
43. JBC to Eliot, Jan. 29, 1945.
44. VB and JBC to HLS, "Supplementary Memorandum," Sept. 30, 1944. As Sherwin notes (p. 127), the administrators followed the reasoning in Szilard's Jan. 14, 1944, note to Bush. Before reversing his position in early 1945, Szilard had written that "it will hardly be possible to get" international control "unless high efficiency atomic bombs have actually been used in this war and the fact of their destructive power has deeply penetrated the mind of the public."
45. VB to JBC, Oct. 24, 1944, B–C, AEC Historical Document 188.
46. "camouflage": JBC to VB, May 22, 1945, B–C, folder 20B.
47. VB and JBC to HLS, "Memorandum on the Future of Biological Warfare as an International Problem in the Postwar World," Oct. 27, 1944, B–C, folder 20A.
48. JBC, *MSL,* 271. "I feel that the essence of political action is sticking to what has been reached by negotiations for compromise between negotiators in whom you have confidence." JBC to Roger Adams, Apr. 22, 1946, box 2, Conant file, Adams Papers, University of Illinois (Urbana).
49. VB to JBC, Oct. 24, 1944, B–C, AEC Historical Document 188.
50. VB, "Memorandum of Conference," Dec. 8, 1944, B–C, folder 20A.
51. VB to JBC, Dec. 13, 1944, B–C, AEC Historical Document 284; HLS diary, Dec. 13, 1944.
52. HLS diary, Dec. 30, 31, 1944.
53. VB to Bundy, Jan. 30, 1945, Harrison-Bundy files, folder 69, RG 77, NA.
54. Bundy to HLS, Mar. 3, 1945, Harrison-Bundy files, folder 69, RG 77, NA.
55. HLS diary, Mar. 5, 1945.
56. HLS diary, Mar. 8, 1945.
57. HLS diary, Mar. 15, 1945, quoted in HLS, "The Decision to Use the Atomic Bomb," *Harper's,* 194:161 (Feb. 1947), 98.
58. HLS, "The Decision to Use the Atomic Bomb"; Byrnes to HLS, Mar. 3, 1945, Byrnes Papers, folder 596.

59. HLS, Memorandum Discussed with President Truman, Apr. 25, 1945, reprinted in Sherwin, *A World Destroyed,* 291–92; Hewlett and Anderson, *New World,* 342–43.
60. HST, *Memoirs,* vol. 1, *Year of Decisions* (Garden City, N.Y.: Doubleday, 1955), 104.
61. Gaddis, *The United States and the Origins of the Cold War,* 204–6; Sherwin, *A World Destroyed,* 151–60.
62. HST, *Year of Decisions,* 79–82.
63. For a thorough, impressively researched accounting of HST's national security policies and the outbreak of the Cold War, see Melvyn P. Leffler, *A Preponderance of Power* (Stanford, Calif.: Stanford University Press, 1992).
64. Harrison to Bundy, May 1, 1945; Hewlett and Anderson, *New World,* 344–45; Sherwin, *A World Destroyed,* 294–95; HLS to VB, May 4, 1945, B–C, AEC Historical Document 205.
65. JBC to HLS, May 5, 1945, B–C, AEC Historical Document 287.
66. Hewlett and Anderson, *New World,* 342; for accounts of discontent at the Met Lab regarding the decision to drop the bomb: David H. Frisch, "Scientists and the Decision to Drop the Bomb," *Bulletin of the Atomic Scientists* 26:6 (June 1970), 107–115; Arthur Steiner, "Baptism of the Atomic Scientists," *Bulletin of the Atomic Scientists* 31:2 (Feb. 1975), 21–28; Steiner, "Scientists, Statesmen, and Politicians: The Competing Influences on American Atomic Energy Policy, 1945–46," *Minerva* 12:4 (Oct. 1974), 469–509; Alice Kimball Smith, "Behind the Decision to Use the Atomic Bomb: Chicago 1944–45," *Bulletin of the Atomic Scientists* 14:7 (Sept. 1958), 288–312; Smith, *A Peril and a Hope,* pt. 1; Sherwin, *A World Destroyed,* 210–19; Lanouette with Silard, *Genius in the Shadows,* 259–80.
67. Arthur H. Compton to K. D. Nichols, "Tentative Explanation of the Interview with Justice Byrnes," June 4, 1945, MED decimal files, box 88, "201/Szilard" folder, MED records, RG 77, NA.
68. JBC to HLS, May 5, 1945.
69. JBC, *MSL,* 300; Hewlett and Anderson, *New World,* 691.
70. JBC to HLS, May 5, 1945.
71. Robert Gilpin, *American Scientists and Nuclear Weapons Policy* (Princeton, N.J.: Princeton University Press, 1962), 52.
72. HLS to JBC, May 9, 1945, B–C, box 4, folder 20B.
73. HLS to VB, May 4, 1945, B–C, AEC Historical Document 205.
74. JBC, *MSL,* 302.

CHAPTER 13

1. "Fight for Liberty," valedictory delivered to Harvard undergraduates on Jan. 10, 1943, *Vital Speeches of the Day* 9 (Feb. 15, 1943), 282.
2. JBC, *MSL,* 303.
3. Bard's dissent: Sherwin, *A World Destroyed,* 307–308.
4. The minutes are printed in Sherwin, *A World Destroyed,* 295–304. Italics in original.
5. Clark, *Greatest Power on Earth,* 194.
6. JBC, *MSL,* 302.
7. HLS, "The Decision to Use the Atomic Bomb," 98.
8. VB and JBC to HLS, "Salient Points Concerning the Future International Handling of Subject of Atomic Bombs," Sept. 30, 1944, Harrison-Bundy files, folder 69, RG 77, NA; reprinted in Sherwin, *A World Destroyed,* 286–88.
9. VB to JBC, Sept. 23, 1944, B–C, AEC Historical Document 186.
10. Reprinted in Sherwin, *A World Destroyed,* 284; HLS diary, June 25, 1945.
11. JBC to LRG, Dec. 9, 1942, B–C, box 9, folder 86.
12. HLS later wrote: "The entire purpose was the production of a military weapon; on no other ground could the wartime expenditure of so much time and money have been justified." ("The Decision to Use the Atomic Bomb," 98.)

13. Quoted by Szilard, in Szilard and Weart, eds., *Leo Szilard: His Version of the Facts,* 184.
14. VB to JBC, Oct. 9, 1941, B–C, box 1, folder 2.
15. JBC, *MSL,* 302–303; JBC to Herbert Feis, Apr. 13, 1960, JBC PERP; Compton, *Atomic Quest,* 226–27. For HLS's version of the military situation, see "The Decision to Use the Bomb," 101–104, 106.
16. HST, *Year of Decisions,* 415–26, esp. 417; HLS, "The Decision to Use the Atomic Bomb," 102, and HLS and Bundy, *On Active Service in War and Peace,* 612–33, esp. 631–32; and Churchill, *Triumph and Tragedy* (Boston: Houghton Mifflin, 1953), 638, who stated that conquering Japan might otherwise have claimed "a million American lives plus half that number of British—or more."
17. See chap. 16.
18. "All you know in wartime is what you are told by the military. As we were told, they were preparing an enormous expedition to invade these Japanese islands." Landers interview. JRO has recalled: "We didn't know beans about the military solution. We didn't know whether they could be caused to surrender by other means or whether the invasion was really inevitable. But in the back of our minds was the notion that the invasion was inevitable because we had been told that. . . ." Giovannitti and Freed, *The Decision to Drop the Bomb,* 123.
19. Minutes, Interim Committee, May 31, 1945, in Sherwin, *A World Destroyed,* 302.
20. Landers interview.
21. JBC to VB, May 9, 1945, B–C, box 5, folder 38.
22. JBC to Herbert Feis, Apr. 13, 1960, JBC PERP; Arthur Compton, *Atomic Quest,* 238–39; Ernest O. Lawrence to Karl K. Darrow, Aug. 17, 1945, carton 20, folder 20, Lawrence Papers, call number 72/117C, Bancroft Library, University of California (Berkeley); Sherwin, *A World Destroyed,* 207–208; Giovanitti and Freed, *The Decision to Drop the Bomb,* 101–104; James F. Byrnes, *Speaking Frankly* (New York: Harper & Bros., 1947), 261. Asked in 1974 by Landers why no warning was given, JBC replied: "That's a good question . . . the question was—what kind of warning?" He said a warning would have endangered the plane that would carry the bomb, and loss of a bomb would have left only one remaining. "We thought, I thought, because it would prevent the assurance that the bomb would be dropped."
23. JBC to McGeorge Bundy, Nov. 30, 1946, HLS Papers, box 154, folder 111.
24. JBC, *MSL,* 49.
25. Interview with TRC, New York City, Jan. 1982; Nagasaki a mistake: interview with Jim Conant (JBC's grandson), Hanover, N.H., July 1991.
26. JBC to Mrs. R. L. Popper, June 21, 1968, JBC PERP, in Amster, *Meritocracy Ascendant,* 150.
27. JBC to VB, "Some thoughts concerning the correspondence between the President and the Prime Minister on S-1," Mar. 25, 1943, B–C, box 1, folder 2.
28. JBC to VB, "Possibilities of a Super Bomb," Oct. 20, 1944, B–C, box 1, folder 3; Interim Committee minutes, May 31, 1945, in Sherwin, *A World Destroyed,* 297–98.
29. Compton, *Atomic Quest,* 127–28.
30. For JBC's distinctions between peacetime and wartime morality: "Humanity's Experiment with Free Institutions," *Vital Speeches of the Day* 6 (Oct. 15, 1939), 26; "Fight for Liberty," *Vital Speeches of the Day* 9 (Feb. 15, 1943), 281–83; "From War to Peace," *Harvard Alumni Bulletin* 48:2 (Oct. 6, 1945), 81–82; "Force and Freedom," *Atlantic Monthly* (Jan. 1949), 19–22.
31. JBC, "Atomic Energy," *Texas Reports on Biology and Medicine* 5 (Summer 1947), 191.
32. "part and parcel": JBC to Niebuhr, Mar. 6, 1946, Niebuhr Papers, LC.
33. The Franck Report is reprinted in Smith, *A Peril and a Hope,* 560–72, and Sherwin, *A World Destroyed,* 323–33.
34. Reprinted in Sherwin, *A World Destroyed,* 304–305; on the Franck Report's fate, see *A World Destroyed,* 210–13.

35. JBC to George Harrison, May 9, 1945, B–C, folder 20B.
36. Minutes, Interim Committee, June 21, 1945, quoted in Sherwin, *A World Destroyed,* 215; Hewlett and Anderson, *New World,* 367–68; JBC and VB to Harrison, June 22, 1945, B–C, folder 20B.
37. Szilard, "Reminiscences," ed. Gertrude Weiss Szilard and Katherine R. Winsor, in Donald Fleming and Bernard Bailyn, eds., *The Intellectual Migration: Europe and America, 1930–1960* (Cambridge, Mass.: Harvard University Press, 1969), 127–28; Weart and Szilard, eds., *Leo Szilard: His Version of the Facts,* 183–85. On Byrnes's attitude toward the bomb in the summer of 1945 and his influence on HST, see Robert L. Messer, *The End of an Alliance: James F. Byrnes, Roosevelt, Truman, and the Origins of the Cold War* (Chapel Hill, N.C.: University of North Carolina Press, 1982), 84–92, 93–95, 102–107, 111–18, 127–30.
38. HLS's repeated diary entries in early 1945 conflating the bomb and troubles with Moscow gave rise to revisionist historical claims that the Truman administration's desire to intimidate the Soviets strongly influenced its atomic policy decisions leading up to Hiroshima. See esp. HLS's entries of Feb. 13, 15, May 10, 13, 14, 15, 16, 31, and June 6, 1945, HLS Papers, Sterling Library, Yale University. Key works making this claim include Alperovitz, *Atomic Diplomacy,* and Sherwin, *A World Destroyed,* chap. 7, while Herbert Feis, who discounted atomic diplomacy in *Japan Subdued: The Atomic Bomb and the End of the War in the Pacific* (Princeton, N.J.: Princeton University Press, 1961), acknowledged the influence of HLS's diary in a revised edition, *The Atomic Bomb and the End of World War II* (Princeton, N.J.: Princeton University Press, 1961, 1966). However, Sherwin, Barton J. Bernstein, Robert Messer, and other historians ascribing various degrees of importance to the bomb in the Truman administration's deliberations in the summer of 1945 seem to have reached a loose consensus that diplomatic considerations were a supporting, confirming, reinforcing, or bonus motivation in the decision to use the bomb, as compared to the principal (though not *exclusive*) goal of winning the war as quickly as possible with minimum loss of Allied lives. See Bernstein, "Eclipsed by Hiroshima and Nagasaki," *International Security* 15:4 (Spring 1991), 149–73, esp. 168–70, and the subsequent exchange between Bernstein, on the one hand, and Alperovitz and Messer, on the other, in *International Security* 16:3 (Winter 1991/92), 204–21, esp. 219. On the historiographical debate over Hiroshima, see chap. 16.
39. HLS diary, June 6, 1945.
40. HLS diary, Apr. 3, 1945.
41. HLS diary, June 6, 1945; Sherwin, *A World Destroyed,* 191n.
42. JBC, "Notes on the 'Trinity' Test," July 17, 1945, B–C, folder 38, reprinted in James G. Hershberg, "Ends vs. Means: James B. Conant and American Atomic Policy, 1939–1947" (undergraduate thesis, Pusey Library, Harvard University), 191–94; see also Maloney, "James B. Conant—Ambassador to the Cosmos," 87; Roosevelt "Harvard's Prize Kibitzer," 76; Lester Velie, "Conant of Harvard," *Coronet* (Jan. 1946), 44–52; JBC speech in Berlin, Sept. 25, 1954, as reported in Associated Press and United Press International dispatches. The numerous accounts of the test include: Laurence, *Men and Atoms,* 115–33; LRG to HLS, "The Test," July 18, 1945, reprinted in LRG, *Now It Can Be Told* (New York: Harper & Row, 1962), 433–44; and Sherwin, *A World Destroyed,* 308–14; various articles in Lewis, Wilson, and Rabinowitch, eds., *Alamogordo Plus Twenty-Five Years;* Rhodes, *Making of the Atomic Bomb,* chap. 18; Wyden, *Day One,* chap. 18; Ferenc Morton Szasz, *The Day the Sun Rose Twice: The Story of the Trinity Site Nuclear Explosion, July 16, 1945* (Albuquerque: University of New Mexico Press, 1984); Lansing Lamont, *Day of Trinity* (New York: Atheneum, 1965); James W. Kunetka, *City of Fire: Los Alamos and the Birth of the Atomic Age, 1943–1945* (Englewood Cliffs, N.J.: Prentice-Hall, 1978), chap. 14; Kenneth T. Bainbridge, "'All in our Time'—A Foul and Awesome Display," *Bulletin of the Atomic Scientists* 22:2 (Feb. 1966), 35–37; William L.

Laurence, "Drama of the Atomic Bomb Found Climax in July 16 Test," *NYT,* Sept. 26, 1945; LRG, "Some Recollections of July 16, 1945," *Bulletin of the Atomic Scientists* 26:6 (June 1970), 21-27.

43. JBC, Sept. 25, 1954, speech.
44. O. R. Frisch, "Eye Witness Report of Nuclear Explosion, 16.7.45," in Gowing, *Britain and Atomic Energy,* 441-42.
45. Farrell's account is quoted in LRG to HLS, "The Test," July 18, 1945, reprinted in Sherwin, *A World Destroyed,* 310-12.
46. Farrell, in LRG to HLS, July 18, 1945, in Sherwin, *A World Destroyed,* 312.
47. JBC, "Notes on the 'Trinity' Test"; LRG, "The Test."
48. Churchill, *Triumph and Tragedy,* 637-41.
49. *NYT,* Sept. 26, 1945.
50. Roosevelt, "Harvard's Prize Kibitzer," 76.
51. Roosevelt, "Harvard's Prize Kibitzer," 76.
52. LRG, *Now It Can Be Told,* 303.
53. JBC, "Notes on the 'Trinity' Test."

CHAPTER 14

1. JBC, handwritten note, July 19, 1945. "Notebook of Quotations for Guidance and Future Plans Outlines, 1950-1957," JBC PERP, UA I.15.898.13, no. 15.
2. Report of a Harvard Committee, *General Education in a Free Society* (Cambridge, Mass.: Harvard University Press, 1945); Amster, *Meritocracy Ascendant,* 153-59; JBC, *MSL,* 363-73; Smith, *Harvard Century,* 160-65; Biebel, *Politics, Pedagogues, and Statesmanship,* 246-50; JBC, *President's Report* 1945 (Jan. 14, 1946) (Cambridge, Mass.: Harvard University, 1946), 7-11.
3. JBC, "From War to Peace," *Harvard Alumni Bulletin* 48:6 (Oct. 6, 1945), 81.
4. White House press release, in *NYT,* Aug. 7, 1945.
5. On the atomic bombings' influence on the Japanese surrender, the standard source in English remains Robert J. C. Butow, *Japan's Decision to Surrender* (Stanford, Calif.: Stanford University Press, 1954).
6. HST, *Year of Decisions,* 421.
7. JBC and VB to Interim Committee, July 18, 1945, B-C, AEC Historical Document 210.
8. HST diary, July 25, 1945, in Robert H. Ferrell, ed., *Off the Record: The Private Papers of Harry S. Truman* (New York: Harper & Row, 1980), 55-56.
9. HLS diary, July 21, 22, 1945. Numerous accounts of the bomb's role at the Potsdam Conference have been published, relying heavily on Stimson's diary and on the *FRUS* volumes devoted to the meeting. For an assessment incorporating HST's diary, see Robert L. Messer, "New Evidence on Truman's Decision," *Bulletin of the Atomic Scientists* 41:7 (Aug. 1985), 50-56.
10. HST, *Year of Decisions,* 416.
11. On the Soviet World War II atomic effort, see David Holloway, "Entering the Nuclear Arms Race: The Soviet Decision to Build the Atomic Bomb, 1939," *Social Studies of Science* 11 (1981), 159-97; Holloway, *The Soviet Union and the Arms Race* (2d. ed.) (New Haven: Yale University Press, 1983, 1984), 15-20; Holloway's forthcoming *Stalin and the Bomb*; Dimitri Volkogonov, *Stalin: Triumph & Tragedy* (New York: Grove Weidenfeld, 1991), 498 (Stalin cable to Beria), 531-33; and Arnold Kramish, *Atomic Energy in the Soviet Union* (Stanford, Calif.: Stanford University Press, 1959), 3-107. Stalin's quotation, as cited by Holloway, is from A. Lavrent'yeva in "Stroiteli novogo mira," *V mire knig* 9 (1970), 4. On Fuchs, see Norman Moss, *Klaus Fuchs: The Man Who Stole the Bomb* (London: Grafton Books, 1987), and Robert Chadwell Williams, *Klaus Fuchs, Atom Spy* (Cambridge, Mass.: Harvard University Press, 1987); Christopher Andrew and Oleg Gordievsky give an overview of wartime Soviet efforts to obtain atomic secrets in *KGB: The*

Inside Story (New York: HarperCollins, 1990), 311–18, 375–77; for recent evidence that the Soviet espionage penetration of the Manhattan Project was more widespread than previously believed, see Vladimir Chikov, "How the Soviet Intelligence Service 'Split' the American Atom," *New Times* 16 (Apr. 23–29, 1991), 37–40, and 17 (Apr. 30–May 6, 1991), 36–39; Michael Dobbs, "How Soviets Stole U.S. Atom Secrets," *Washington Post*, Oct. 4, 1992; Serge Schmemann, "1st Soviet A-Bomb Built from U.S. Data, Russian Says," *NYT*, Jan. 14, 1993; and several articles in the May 1993 *Bulletin of the Atomic Scientists*, including an account by Yuli B. Khariton, described by Holloway as "the Soviet equivalent of J. Robert Oppenheimer" by virtue of his position as scientific director of early Soviet atomic bomb laboratories. Khariton essentially confirmed that Soviets used espionage data to copy the U.S. fission bomb design.

12. HST felt "certain" that Stalin had not understood his allusion: HST to Cate, Dec. 31, 1952, Jan. 12, 1953, President's Secretary's Files, box 112, PSF–General File–Atomic Bomb, HST Papers, HSTL. So did Churchill: *Triumph and Tragedy*, 669–70. However, a senior Soviet military officer at Potsdam later wrote that Stalin had feigned ignorance to Truman but immediately afterward informed Molotov, who reportedly reacted by suggesting that they contact Igor Kurchatov, the head of the Soviet atomic effort, "and get him to speed things up." *The Memoirs of Marshal Zhukov* (New York: Delacorte Press, 1971), 674–75. This account may have been the source of the Volkogonov claim cited above.

13. GC to JBC, Aug. 13, 1945, GCP, series 15, box 1, Conant folder.

14. TRC interviews, 1987, 1991.

15. JBC to GC, Aug. 17, 1945, GCP, series 15, box 1, Conant folder; JBC to Philip Johnson, Sept. 20, 1945, "Conant: Personal, 1945–46" folder, box 296, JBC PREP; TRC interview; JBC thanked a navy captain for "passing on informally and unofficially information about our son." JBC to O. B. Jensen, Oct. 15, 1945, "Conant: Personal, 1945–46" folder, box 296, JBC PREP.

16. JBC to GC, Aug. 17, 1945, GCP, series 15, box 1.

17. JBC to GC, Aug. 20, 1945, GCP, series 4, box 2, "Harvard Corporation–Conant, James B.–1945" folder.

18. JBC to GC, Aug. 29, 1945, GCP, series 15, box 1.

19. Quoted in Paul Boyer, *By the Bomb's Early Light: American Thought and Culture at the Dawn of the Atomic Age* (New York: Pantheon, 1985), 36.

20. JBC to GC, Oct. 8, 1945, enc. in JBC to VB, Oct. 17, 1945, VBP, box 27, folder 14; also in JBC PREP, box 273, "Atomic Bomb, 1945–46" folder.

21. JBC to George L. Harrison, Aug. 24, 1945, B–C, box 9, folder 86. He also sent along suggestions for postwar military organization. JBC to Ferdinand Eberstadt, Aug. 24, 1945, JBC PREP, box 291, "U.S. Navy Department, 1945–46" folder.

22. JBC to GC, Oct. 8, 1945, JBC PREP, box 273, "Atomic Bomb, 1945–46" folder.

23. "From War to Peace," Sept. 25, 1945, *Harvard Alumni Bulletin* 48:2 (Oct. 6, 1945), 81.

24. Keyes DeWitt Metcalf, *My Harvard Library Years, 1937–1955* (Cambridge, Mass.: Harvard College Library, 1988), 117; James G. Hershberg, "Preserving 250 Million Pages of Knowledge," *Washington Post*, Aug. 31, 1986; TRC, Jim Conant (grandson) interviews. Some uncertainty remains about the dates of the JBC–Metcalf encounters; Metcalf says Sept. 1945, but JBC's desk calendar for late 1945 records only appointments for Oct. 16 and 29.

25. Nor, apparently, did JBC ever take steps to implement the idea through any other method. In 1986 interviews with the author, TRC said that Metcalf apparently talked JBC out of the proposal, for "if he had done it, he would have done it through Metcalf," and Lee A. DuBridge, who sat alongside JBC on the General Advisory Committee to the U.S. Atomic Energy Commission from 1947 to 1952, said JBC never raised the idea. According to TRC, after leaving Harvard, Metcalf as a consultant encouraged the extensive construction of libraries in far-flung places

around the world, partly to improve the chances of preserving basic knowledge in the event of a catastrophic nuclear war.

26. "Conant on the Bomb," speech to the Cleveland Chamber of Commerce, Nov. 20, 1945, *Harvard Alumni Bulletin* 48:6 (Dec. 8, 1945), 238 (hereafter, "Conant on the Bomb"). JBC also gave a similar speech on Dec. 3, 1945 to the Harvard Club of Boston: JBC, "National Defense in the Light of the Atomic Bomb," Harvard News Office release, Dec. 4, 1945.

27. JBC, *Education in a Divided World*, 232.

28. JBC–VB to Interim Committee, July 18, 1945, B–C, AEC Historical Document 210.

29. O. C. Carmichael, chairman, The Committee on the Relationships of Higher Education to the Federal Government, American Council on Education, et al., to HST, Sept. 25, 1945, "General File-Atomic Energy Commission, United Nations" folder, box 112, PSF, HSTL.

30. VB, "Notes toward an atom statement," enc. with VB to JBC, Aug. 29, 1945, Carnegie Institution archives, Washington, D.C.

31. JBC to VB, Sept. 27, 1945, VBP, box 27, folder 614.

32. JBC to GC, Oct. 8, 1945, VBP, box 27, folder 614; also copy in JBC PREP, box 273, "Atomic Bomb, 1945–46" folder. *Hearings on Science Legislation, S. 1297 and Related Bills, Subcommittee on War Mobilization, Committee on Military Affairs, U.S. Senate, 79th Congress, 1st Session* (Washington, D.C.: Government Printing Office, 1946), 988. Hearing of Nov. 2, 1945 (hereafter Nov. 2, 1945, transcript).

33. JBC to GC, Oct. 8, 1945, VBP, box 627, folder 14; also copy in JBC PREP, box 273, "Atomic Bomb, 1945–46" folder.

34. "Conant on the Bomb," 236–39; "Inspector Corps Urged for World," *BG*, Dec. 12, 1945.

35. Nov. 2, 1945, transcript, 986; "Conant on the Bomb," 236–39.

36. JBC to GC, Oct. 8, 1945, VBP, box 27, folder 614; also copy in JBC PREP, box 273, "Atomic Bomb, 1945–46" folder.

37. "Conant on the Bomb," 238.

38. JBC to VB, Sept. 27, 1945, VBP, box 27, folder 614.

39. J. Edgar Hoover to Matthew Connelly, Sept. 12, 18, 27, 29, 1945, PSF–Subject File, box 167, Subject File—FBI—Atomic Bomb, HST Papers, HSTL; Hoover to Harry Vaughan, Oct. 19, 1945, PSF–Subject File, box 167, Subject File—FBI—C, HST Papers, HSTL.

40. JBC to VB, Sept. 27, 1945, VBP, box 27, folder 614.

41. Ely Culbertson, pamphlet, "How to Control the Atomic Threat," Sept. 1945.

42. JBC to VB, Sept. 27, 1945, VBP, box 27, folder 614; JBC also advised Culbertson to send his plan to HST and Byrnes, receiving the reply that Culbertson had already had a "long and satisfactory talk" with HST on the subject. VB also appeared to be impressed with Culbertson's ideas. For JBC's correspondence with Culbertson, see JBC PREP, box 273, "Atomic Bomb, 1945–46" folder.

43. See esp. JBC to GC, Sept. 7, 1939, two letters, in GCP 4:2 and GCP 21:8, and JBC to GC, Oct. 24, 1944, and GC to JBC, Oct. 31, 1944, in GCP 21:9.

44. See Dunne, *Grenville Clark*, 140–43.

45. GC diary, Sept. 1945, GCP, series 1, box 4, "Bio-Notes, 1945–46" folder.

46. GC diary, Sept. 1945, GCP, series 1, box 4, "Bio-Notes, 1945–46" folder.

47. GC to HLS, Oct. 2, 1945, HLS Papers.

48. For JBC's memorandum see JBC to GC, Oct. 8, 1945, VBP, box 27, folder 614; also copy in JBC PREP, box 273, "Atomic Bomb, 1945–46" folder. For documentation on the First Dublin Conference, see GCP, series 15, box 2.

49. JBC to GC, Oct. 25, 1945, GCP, series 15, box 1, Conant file; GC to JBC, Oct. 18, 1945, GCP, series 15, box 1, Conant file.

50. JBC to VB, Oct. 17, 1945, VBP, box 27, folder 614.

51. "Conant on the Bomb," 239.

52. JBC to VB, May 18, 1945, B–C, folder 20B; Anderson and Hewlett, *New World,* 354.
53. JBC to GC, Oct. 8, 1945; JBC to VB, Oct. 17, 1945; "Conant on the Bomb," 237.
54. Gregg Herken, " 'A Most Deadly Illusion': The Atomic Secret and American Nuclear Weapons Policy, 1945–1950," *Pacific Historical Review* (Feb. 1980), 51–76; Herken, *The Winning Weapon: The Atomic Bomb in the Cold War,* 1945–1950 (New York: Alfred A. Knopf, 1981), esp. 97–113.
55. JBC to GC, Oct. 8, 1945, JBC PREP, box 273, "Atomic Bomb, 1945–46" folder.
56. JBC to VB, May 18, 1945, B–C.
57. Hewlett and Anderson, *New World,* 359–60; Interim Committee minutes, June 1, 1945, MED records, RG 77, NA.
58. JBC–VB to Interim Committee, July 18, 1945, B–C.
59. "Conant on the Bomb," 237.
60. Joseph E. Davies diary, July 29, 1945, in Messer, *The End of an Alliance,* 107.
61. HLS to HST, Sept. 11, 1945, HLS Papers, box 149, folder 47. A key influence on HLS's change in position after Potsdam, and on his memorandum to HST, was War Department adviser John J. McCloy, who in turn had been educated to the bomb's significance by VB and JBC; see Kai Bird, *The Chairman: John J. McCloy: The Making of the American Establishment* (New York: Simon & Schuster, 1992), 250–64; and Walter Isaacson and Evan Thomas, *The Wise Men: Six Friends and the World They Made* (New York: Simon & Schuster, 1986), 318–21.
62. VB to JBC, Sept. 24, 1945, VBP, box 27, folder 614.
63. VB to HST, Sept. 25, 1945, B–C, box 2, folder 6.
64. Quoted in Gaddis, *The United States and the Origins of the Cold War,* 249.
65. *Public Papers of the Presidents, 1945, I:* 381–88.
66. VB to JBC, Nov. 7, 1945, VBP, box 27, folder 614; see also VB to HLS, Nov. 13, 1945, HLS Papers, Sterling Library, Yale University.
67. Handwritten postscript, JBC to VB, Oct. 23, 1945, Carnegie Institution archives, Washington, D.C.
68. Nov. 2, 1945, transcript, 988.
69. JBC to Patterson, Nov. 2, 1945, B–C, folder 20B.
70. Herken, *Winning Weapon,* 64–66; Hewlett and Anderson, *New World,* 459–69; VB to JBC, Nov. 7, 8, 10, 1945, VBP, JBC PREP; VB to HLS, Nov. 13, 1945, HLS Papers.
71. JBC to HST, Nov. 15, 1945, HST Official File, box 1523, folder 692 (Misc. 1945), HSTL; "Conant on the Bomb," 238.
72. Herken, *Winning Weapon,* 61–66.
73. Novikov cable, Archive of the Foreign Policy of the USSR, Moscow, cited in Scott Parrish, "A Diplomat Reports" (review of Novikov's memoirs), *Cold War International History Project Bulletin* 1 (Spring 1992), 21.
74. Hewlett and Anderson, *New World,* 469; Herken, *Winning Weapon,* 67–68.
75. Unless otherwise indicated, the account which follows of JBC's activities at the Dec. 1945 Moscow Council of Foreign Ministers conference is based on a detailed seventeen-page handwritten diary (box 8, JBC PERP, UA I.15.898.13) kept by JBC during the trip and covering events from Dec. 10 to Dec. 29, which contains passages not printed in *MSL,* 475–89. Other firsthand accounts include: Charles Bohlen, *Witness to History,* 1929–1969 (New York: W. W. Norton, 1973); James F. Byrnes, *All in One Lifetime* (New York: Harper & Row, 1958) and *Speaking Frankly;* Harriman and Abel, *Special Envoy to Churchill and Stalin,* 1941–1946, 523–27; George F. Kennan, *Memoirs, 1925–1950* (Boston: Atlantic-Little, Brown & Co., 1967); secondary accounts include Hewlett and Anderson, *New World,* 469–77; Herkin, *Winning Weapon,* 66–94; Gaddis, *Origins of the Cold War,* 276–84; and Messer, *The End of An Alliance,* chap. 8. JBC's journal includes impressions of the trip, a wealth of gossipy tidbits about the negotiations, the personalities, the opinions of Americans in Moscow at the time, the appearance of the Russian capital, travel problems, and JBC's recurrent ailments.
76. Herken, *Winning Weapon,* 67–68.

77. Cable to State Department, Sept. 30, 1945, quoted in Kennan, *Memoirs 1925–1950*, 296–97.
78. *Public Opinion Quarterly* 10:1 (Spring 1946), 531.
79. *NYT,* Dec. 20, 1945; Anderson and Hewlett, *New World,* 473.
80. Acheson to Byrnes, Dec. 15, 1945, copies in State Department decimal file 740.00119 Council/12-1545, RG 59, NA, and "General File-Atomic Energy Control Commission, United Nations" folder, box 112, PSF, HSTL.
81. John H. Hancock, "Memorandum for Atomic Energy File," Apr. 19, 1946, BMB Papers, box 52, folder marked "U.S. Policy Toward the June 14 Proposal"; Herken, *Winning Weapon,* 354; JBC diary.
82. Harriman to Secretary of State, Dec. 17, 1945, and JBC to Secretary of State, Dec. 17, 1945, both in December 1945 folders, Averell Harriman papers, LC; Harriman and Abel, *Special Envoy,* 526; JBC diary.
83. JBC diary, Dec. 20, 1945.
84. British ambassador in the Soviet Union (Kerr) to British Secretary of State for Foreign Affairs (Bevin), Dec. 3, 1945, *FRUS,* 1945, II, 82–84.
85. Byrnes had placed the topic at the top of the agenda. The quote is from JBC's diary.
86. Byrnes, *Speaking Frankly,* 267.
87. JBC diary, Dec. 23, 1945; on JBC's meeting with the education minister, see "Conversation with Mr. V. P. Potemkin, People's Commissar of Education," Dec. 24, 1945, Harriman Papers, LC.
88. Telephone interview with Robert C. Tucker, Sept. 21, 1992.
89. Hewlett and Anderson, *New World,* 469; JBC diary.
90. Hewlett and Anderson, *New World,* 469.
91. Bohlen, *Witness to History,* 249; Byrnes, *Speaking Frankly,* 268. Robert L. Messer, in *The Making of a Cold Warrior: James F. Byrnes and American Soviet Relations* (Ph.D. diss., University of California; Ann Arbor, Mich.: University Microfilms, 1975), 384, and *The End of an Alliance,* 151, concludes that the Stalin-Molotov confrontation—"this little farce"—may have been staged. Herken concludes that Stalin's rebuff of Molotov, symbolizing recognition of importance of the atomic energy issue, "was not only of personal satisfaction for Byrnes, but the sign to him of a change in Soviet-American relations."
92. JBC diary, Dec. 25, 1945; Stalin's message was also written down for transmittal to the State Department and can be found in the Dec. 1945 folders, Harriman Papers, LC.
93. JBC to VB, Dec. 31, 1945, VBP, box 27, folder 614.
94. JBC diary, Dec. 20, 1945.
95. Telephone interview with Robert C. Tucker, Sept. 21, 1992.
96. JBC omitted this sentence when he reprinted the memorandum in his memoirs. Compare the version of the memo in JBC, *MSL,* 485–89, with JBC to Byrnes, "The Interchange of Scientists," Dec. 26, 1945, JBC PERP, UA I.15.898.13, box 8, Special Subject File, "Moscow Trip—1945." While in Moscow, JBC received through State Department channels a proposal by the University of Chicago's Chancellor, Robert Hutchins (who in turn had been prompted by Leo Szilard), a proposal to invite 5 or 10 Russian atomic physicists to U.S. universities for informal discussions. Benton to JBC, Dec. 22, 1945, in Lanouette and Szilard, *Genius in the Shadows,* 300–301.
97. Daniel Yergin, *Shattered Peace: The Origins of the Cold War and the National Security State* (Boston: Houghton Mifflin, 1977), 148.
98. VB to JBC, Jan. 2, 1946, VBP, box 27, folder 614.
99. JBC's view accorded with the assessments of Byrnes in Herken, "Stubborn, Obstinate, and They Don't Scare: The Russians, the Bomb, and James F. Byrnes," presented at Nov. 9, 1979, symposium, "James F. Byrnes and the Origins of the Cold War," sponsored by the Institute of International Studies, University of South Carolina, Columbia; Herkin, *Winning Weapon,* 57ff.; Kennan, *Memoirs,* 286–88.
100. JBC diary, Dec. 24, 1945. JBC naturally kept his doubts about Byrnes's sincerity

quiet, congratulating him "most heartily" for the conference's success and expressing thanks for a "most enjoyable trip" even though "it turned out I was not needed." Byrnes responded by insisting on the value of JBC's contribution, recalling that the educator had drafted the conference's atomic communiqué: "What I mean by all of this is that I like you." JBC to Byrnes, Dec. 31, 1945, Byrnes to JBC, Jan. 5, 1946, Byrnes Papers, folder 626.

101. JBC, *MSL*, 489.

CHAPTER 15

1. JBC to VB, "S-1 Legislation," July 27, 1944. AEC Historical Document 297; JBC to VB, "Summary of conversation between JBC, VB and [Irvin Stewart] on proposed legislation covering S-1," Sept. 15, 1944, AEC Historical Document 184.
2. Hewlett and Anderson, *New World*, chap. 2; WLM, *In the Catbird Seat* (Baltimore: Maryland Historical Society, 1988), 243–49.
3. "Notes of Interim Committee Meeting," July 19, 1945, Harrison-Bundy files, folder 100, MED Records, RG 77, NA; Hewlett and Anderson, *New World*, 413.
4. Interim Committee notes, July 19, 1945: "Dr. Bush favored a committee composed only of civilians, as did Dr. Conant." Hewlett and Anderson, *New World*, 413.
5. Interim Committee notes, July 19, 1945.
6. JBC to VB, May 9, 1945, B–C, box 5, folder 38; Arthur H. Compton to LRG, Mar. 1 and 5, 1945, and Compton to LRG for HLS, "Research in Nuclear Science as Essential to the Nation's Continual Safety," Mar. 5, 1945, all in Compton folder, box 1, formerly Classified Breit/Briggs Files, S-1, OSRD, RG 227, Na.
7. *NYT*, Oct. 10, 1945, 1.
8. *Hearings before the Committee on Military Affairs, House of Representatives, 79th Congress, 1st Session, on H.R. 4280, An Act for the Development and Control of Atomic Energy* (Washington, D.C.: Government Printing Office, 1945), 51–59. Testimony of Oct. 9, 1945.
9. Donald A. Strickland, *Scientists in Politics: The Atomic Scientists Movement, 1945-46* (Lafayette, Ind.: Purdue University Studies, 1968), 105.
10. In July, he had scrawled a sharply critical resignation letter ("Much of the action we have taken has been hasty and without most of us really knowing what we were doing") to Conant, grudgingly agreeing to stay on ("if for no other reason than the love I have for you, Van and the other horseman") only in response to a solicitous hand-holding reply imploring him to remain on the job and to hold his arguments until "we fight the Battle of Washington over our whiskey and soda as old men." Frank B. Jewett to JBC, July 9, 1945, JBC to Frank B. Jewett, July 24, 1945, both in JBC PREP, box 285, "National Defense Research Committee" folder.
11. Frank B. Jewett to JBC, Oct. 10, 1945, JBC PREP, box 273, "Atomic Bomb, 1945-46" folder.
12. Frank B. Jewett to JBC, Oct. 22, 1945, JBC PREP, box 284, "National Academy of Sciences, 1945-46" folder; JBC to Frank B. Jewett, Oct. 15, 1945, JBC PREP, box 273, "Atomic Bomb, 1945-46" folder; see also Cochrane, *The National Academy of Sciences*, 454-55. See also Jewett to E. U. Condon, Nov. 6, 1945, in NAS-NRC Central File: Congress 1945: Committees: Atomic Energy: Special, NAS archives, Washington, D.C.
13. "Nay, Johnson," *Washington Post*, Oct. 19, 1945, stated: "We think it about time for JB Conant and others drafting this clumsy and dangerous measure to recall it and then help Congress to get off to a better start." Irvin Stewart, erstwhile OSRD aide to JBC, sent along the clipping with a playful handwritten note: "Dear Jim—naughty naughty." JBC PREP, box 273, "Atomic Bomb, 1945-46" folder.
14. JBC to VB, Oct. 23, 1945, Carnegie Institution archives, Washington, D.C.
15. Strickland, *Scientists in Politics*, 121.

16. Herb Anderson to William Higinbotham, Oct. 11, 1945, Association of Los Alamos Scientists Papers, box 5, folder 11, Regenstein Library, University of Chicago. For the atomic scientists campaign against the May-Johnson bill: Hewlett and Anderson, *New World,* 421–3; Smith, *A Peril and a Hope,* 128–73.

17. JBC to JRO, Aug. 24, Sept. 14, 1945, box 27, Conant folder, JROP; JRO to JBC, Sept. 29, 1945, Smith and Weiner, eds., *Robert Oppenheimer: Letters and Recollections,* 162–3.

18. Quoted in Smith, *A Peril and a Hope,* 166.

19. Anderson to Higinbotham, Oct. 11, 1945.

20. JBC to VB, Oct. 4, 1945, VBP, box 27, folder 614.

21. Ernest Pollard to William M. Woodward, Oct. 16, 1945, Association of Los Alamos Scientists Papers, 4:1.

22. JBC to Robert Patterson, Dec. 10, 1945, B–C, box 4, folder 20B.

23. Smith, *A Peril and a Hope,* 14–19; Sherwin, *A World Destroyed,* 57–58; JBC to Stimson, May 5, 1945, B–C, AEC Historical Document 287.

24. Condon's remark was recounted by WLM, who witnessed the incident, in a letter to the author (Sept. 17, 1986); WLM, *In the Catbird Seat,* 246.

25. *THC,* Apr. 18, 1946, 2.

26. Minutes of meetings of secretaries of state, war, and navy, Oct. 16 and 23, 1945, *FRUS,* 1945, II, 59–62.

27. JBC to VB, July 27, 1944, B–C, AEC Historical Document 297.

28. Interview with Donald K. Price, Jan. 1982.

29. HST to secretaries of war and navy, Nov. 28, 1945, B–C, folder 20B; Hewlett and Anderson, *New World,* 441ff.

30. JBC, *MSL,* 491–2; for the Acheson-Lilienthal report: Hewlett and Anderson, *New World,* chap. 15; Bundy, *Danger and Survival,* chap. 4; Herken, *Winning Weapon,* 158–65; Dean G. Acheson, *Present at the Creation* (New York: W. W. Norton, 1969), chap. 17; DEL, *AEY,* 10–53; JBC, *MSL,* 491–94; Bird, *The Chairman,* 275–82; Daniel Lang, "Seven Men on a Problem," *New Yorker,* Aug. 17, 1946; and Lang, *From Hiroshima to the Moon: Chronicles of Life in the Atomic Age* (New York: Simon and Schuster, 1959), 66–81.

31. On the politics of the tests see Lloyd J. Graybar, "The 1946 Atomic Bomb Tests: Atomic Diplomacy or Bureaucratic Infighting?" *Journal of American History* 72:4 (Mar. 1986), 888–907.

32. Patterson and Forrestal to JBC, Jan. 25, 1946, JBC PREP, box 291, "U.S. Navy Department, 1945–46" folder.

33. JBC to Forrestal and Patterson, Feb. 4, 1946, JBC PREP, box 291, "U.S. Navy Department, 1945–46" folder.

34. Acheson memo, Sept. 25, 1945, *FRUS,* 1945, II, 48–50.

35. Draft minutes, meeting of Secretary of State's Committee, Jan. 14, 1946, B–C, folder 20B.

36. Hewlett and Anderson, *New World,* 534.

37. JRO, "Atomic Explosives", "restricted" talk, Apr. 6, 1946, box 52, "US Policy— Toward the June 14 Proposal" folder, BMB Papers, Princeton University.

38. U.S. Department of State, *A Report on the International Control of Atomic Energy* (Washington, D.C.: Government Printing Office, 1946); Hewlett and Anderson, *New World,* 533–54.

39. Hewlett and Anderson, *New World,* 545.

40. JBC to VB, Oct. 27, 1945.

41. JBC to GC, Oct. 8, 1945.

42. JBC, *MSL,* 492–93; Hewlett and Anderson, *New World,* 546–47.

43. Herken, *Winning Weapon,* 127–37; "Conant on the Bomb," *Harvard Alumni Bulletin* 48:6 (Dec. 8, 1945), 236–37; Hewlett and Anderson, *New World,* 501.

44. *Newsweek* 27 (Mar. 25, 1946), 24, in Gaddis, *United States and the Origins of the Cold War,* 310. Rumors claiming that HST privately threatened to use the atomic

bomb if Moscow refused to withdraw from Iran have repeatedly circulated, but no documentary corroboration has yet emerged. Considering the fact that the United States then had only a handful of bombs at its disposal, the story seems quite implausible.

45. On Churchill's influence on HST at this juncture, see Fraser J. Harbutt, *The Iron Curtain: Churchill, America, and the Origins of the Cold War* (New York: Oxford University Press, 1986).

46. Kennan to Byrnes, Feb. 22, 1946, *FRUS,* 1946, VI, 696–709; Kennan, *Memoirs, 1925–1950,* 292–95.

47. JBC, *MSL,* 506; Tuttle, *James B. Conant,* 386.

48. DEL, *AEY,* 29.

49. HST, *Year of Decisions,* 551–52.

50. JBC, "International Controls of Atomic Energy," Apr. 12, 1946 talk, introduced by Thomas W. Lamont. *Records of Meetings,* Vol. XII, July 1945–June 1947, Council on Foreign Relations Archives, New York City (hereafter CFR notes).

51. John M. Hancock, "Memorandum for Atomic Energy File," Apr. 19, 1946, "Toward the June 14 Proposals" folder, box 52, BMB Papers, reported that Secretary of State Byrnes had "briefly reviewed his impression that the Russians don't know much about atomic energy or its use in bombs. Dr. Conant got no facts regarding it while he was in Russia, and the assumption is that they know nothing."

52. On the question of whether the U.S. "should give Russia all our atomic secrets now in order to invite her confidence," JBC "disagreed with this view and stated that in any event, it is not politically feasible. We cannot keep our favorable position with respect to atomic energy indefinitely . . . and the way we can best use our temporary advantage is to trade it gradually for the type of plan we believe will work. Some say the Russians will never agree to such a gradual process; they have, however, agreed to the establishment of a United Nations Commission on Atomic Energy in spite of predictions that they would never do so." CFR notes.

53. Gaddis, *Strategies of Containment,* 18–24.

54. Proposed policy statement, Association of Los Alamos Scientists, Nov. 28, 1945, Association of Los Alamos Scientists Papers, 3:2.

55. W. A. Higinbotham to Irving Kaplan, Feb. 11, 1946, Federation of American Scientists Papers, 6:1, Regenstein Library, University of Chicago.

56. Herken, *Winning Weapon,* 159–63; Anderson and Hewlett, *New World,* 554–58; BMB to KTC, Apr. 8, 1946, Compton-Killian Papers, box 14, folder 29: "As you know I am the most ignorant man in the world regarding . . . the atomic matter." If the talks progressed well, BMB promised to call KTC, JBC, and VB ("You reactionaries") for consultation.

57. Smith, *A Peril and a Hope,* 454.

58. CFR notes; and Committee on Atomic Energy, Carnegie Endowment for International Peace, Report of Meeting, Apr. 13, 1946, New York City, BMB Papers, box 61, AEC folder "Special, A–F" (hereafter Carnegie notes). For Groves's dissatisfaction: *Now It Can Be Told,* 411–12.

59. CFR notes.

60. Carnegie notes.

61. CFR notes.

62. JBC, *MSL,* 493.

63. DEL, *AEY,* 30.

64. Strickland, *Scientists in Politics,* 121; Bundy, *Danger and Survival,* 162; see also DEL, *AEY,* 42–43, 54, 60, 69–71.

65. JBC to BMB, Mar. 19, 1946, BMB Papers, box 58, JBC folder.

66. JBC to BMB, May 23, 1946, BMB Papers, box 58, Conant folder; Carnegie notes; "argued very strenuously": W. A. Higinbotham to Richard L. Meier, May 4, 1946, box 13, folder 2, Federation of American Scientists Papers, Regenstein Library, Univer-

sity of Chicago; regarding JBC's opposition to publication of Shotwell's proposal, see Carroll L. Wilson to Herbert S. Marks, May 24, 1946, DEL Papers and Wilson Papers; Wilson to JBC, May 29, 1946, Wilson Papers, 79–99, box 1, "State Dept."; and Chester I. Barnard to DEL, May 27, 1946, quoting letter from JBC to Barnard.

67. Wilson to Marks, May 21, 1946, Wilson Papers, 79–99, box 1, "State Dept."
68. JBC to BMB, Mar. 19, 1946, and Nov. 13, 1959, BMB Papers, box 58, Conant folder; JBC, *MSL,* 493; JBC desk calendar, JBC PREP; JBC to James F. Byrnes, Apr. 18, 1946, S/AE, box 23, folder 15F Policy 30 State Department, a.AEC Policy, 1946–1949.
69. Hewlett and Anderson, *New World,* 560–72; see also BMB, *Baruch: The Public Years,* 336–51.
70. Transcripts of JRO's conversations can be found in the FBI Oppenheimer file; Herken, *Winning Weapon,* 162; on VB and BMB: J. Hancock, Memo for Files, May 1, 1946, S/AE, box 22, folder 15F Policy 19. Hancock Memoranda, 1946–47; on DEL and BMB: DEL, *AEY,* 42; on JRO and BMB: F. Osborn, Notes of Conversation with J. Robert Oppenheimer, Mar. 6, 1947, S/AE, box 64, folder 15D AEC Meetings 10. Advisers and Consultants Meetings, 1947 & 1948; and Acheson and BMB: *Present at the Creation,* 156; BMB to Acheson, Aug. 21, 1946, and Acheson to BMB, Aug. 23, 1946, both in S/AE, box 38, folder 20.11 Baruch, Bernard (2 of 4).
71. DEL, *AEY,* 42–44.
72. JBC described his May 6, 1946, conversation with JRO to Richard C. Tolman, who recorded the contents in his diary. Tolman diary, box 1, "U.S. Atomic Energy Commission" folder, OSRD, S-1, R. C. Tolman files, RG 227, NA.
73. Tolman diary.
74. JBC to BMB, May 23, 1946, BMB Papers, box 58, Conant folder.
75. JBC to BMB, May 23, 1946; JBC to Acheson, June 5, 1946, State Department decimal files, 811.646/6-546, RG 59, National Archives.
76. JBC to BMB, June 5, 1946, BMB Papers, box 58, Conant folder.
77. The negotiations are described in Hewlett and Anderson, *New World,* 576–79, 582–619. See also Joseph I. Lieberman, *The Scorpion and the Tarantula: The Struggle to Control Atomic Weapons, 1945-1949* (Boston: Houghton Mifflin, 1970); BMB, *Baruch: The Public Years,* 351–61; and Bundy, *Danger and Survival,* 166ff.
78. Hewlett and Anderson, *New World,* chap. 14.
79. JBC to BMB, May 24, 1946, BMB Papers, box 58, Conant folder.
80. BMB to JBC, Nov. 27, 1959, JBC PERP.
81. JBC, *MSL,* 493–94.
82. TRC interview, Jan. 2, 1982.
83. WLM, *In the Catbird Seat,* 165–66.
84. See DEL diary, Oct. 8, 1962, DEL papers, Mudd Library, Princeton, describing a dinner conversation with JBC at the Century Club in New York, comparing responses to Strauss's newly published memoirs (*Men and Decisions*). DEL recalled that Strauss had convinced him to "make it up" between him and JBC by arranging a luncheon at the Army-Navy Club, but ruefully added that he "wasn't too proud of my role in that conciliation, as I later found that Strauss did not have the best character of any man I had known." DEL omitted this passage from the published version of his diaries: DEL, *Journals,* vol. 5, *The Harvest Years, 1959-1963* (New York: Harper & Row, 1971), 406.
85. TRC interview; the timing of the 11:15 a.m. meeting is in "President's Appointments", Mon., July 29, 1946; President's Official File, HST Papers, HSTL. According to one account, Strauss by then had already accepted appointment by HST to the commission: see DEL, *AEY,* 81–82.
86. JBC to VB, Aug. 17, 1946, VBP, box 27, folder 614; JBC to HST, Aug. 1, 1946, "j.r." to HST, Aug. 2, 1946, HST to JBC, Aug. 7, 1946, all in PPF 91, box 174, HST Papers, HSTL. After turning down the post himself JBC "strongly backed" DEL's nomination to head the AEC. VB to HST, Aug. 16, 1946, OSRD, copy in JBC PERP, UA I. 15.898.13, box 5.

87. Bernard Brodie, *The Absolute Weapon: Atomic Power and World Order* (New York: Harcourt, Brace, 1946).

88. JBC to GC, May 25, 1946, GCP, series 4, box 2, "Harvard Corporation – Conant, James B." folder. JBC enclosed a copy of the "rough draft" with his letter, but I was unable to locate the document either in the Clark Papers at Dartmouth or in JBC's Harvard papers.

89. JBC to KTC, Jan. 16, 1947, Compton-Killian Papers, box 17, folder 22. JBC to VB, Oct. 14, 1946, VBP, box 27, folder 614.

90. Unless otherwise noted, subsequent quotations are from JBC's Sept. 16, 1946, speech to the National War College in Washington, entitled "The Atomic Age." Copies are in JBC PREP; "Atomic Energy Safe File 2," Patterson File, MED records, NA; and National Defense University archives, Washington, D.C.

91. JBC, *MSL*, 353–54; JBC, "Statement before the House Military Affairs Committee hearings scheduled for 10 a.m., Thursday, November 29, 1945," Harvard University News Office press release, copy in E. E. Day Papers, box 40, folder 25; also in *Universal Military Training: Hearings before the Committee on Military Affairs, House of Representatives, 79th Cong., 1st Session, H.R. 515,* Part I (Washington, D.C.: Government Printing Office, 1946), 359–74.

92. JBC to W. Barton Leach, Apr. 26, 1946, Leach Papers, box 52, folder 6, Harvard Law School Library.

93. Clifford's memorandum, "American Relations with the Soviet Union," Sept. 1946, is reprinted in Arthur Krock, *Memoirs: Sixty Years on the Firing Line* (New York: Funk & Wagnalls, 1968), 419–482; see also Clark Clifford with Richard Holbrooke, *Counsel to the President: A Memoir* (New York: Random House, 1991), 109–29.

94. Yergin, *Shattered Peace,* 245.

95. Herken, *Winning Weapon,* 233.

96. JBC to Frederick Osborn, May 3, 1947, JBC PREP, box 296, "Atomic Energy Com.: United Nations, 46–47" folder.

97. JBC, "Freedom House," Oct. 8, 1946, copies in BMB Papers, Princeton University; JBC Speech File 227, JBC PREP.

98. JBC to Richard C. Tolman, Oct. 17, 1946, JBC PREP, box 305, "National War College, 1946–47" folder.

99. Wilson to VB, Oct. 10, 1946, Wilson Papers, 82-15, box 1, "OSRD" folder.

100. VB to Carroll Wilson, Oct. 15, 1946, VBP, box 120, folder 2918.

101. VB to JBC, Oct. 21, 1946, VBP, box 27, folder 614. An early exploration of Soviet archives on this subject suggests some behind-the-scenes flexibility in the Soviet international control policy, but apparently only for devising a more attractive propaganda position: Vladimir Batyuk, "The Soviet Union and the Baruch Plan," paper presented at the Cold War International History Project Conference on New Evidence on Cold War History, Moscow, Jan. 12–15, 1993.

CHAPTER 16

1. Dwight Macdonald, editorial, *Politics,* Aug. 1945, 225, in Barton J. Bernstein, ed., *The Atomic Bomb: The Critical Issues* (Boston and Toronto: Little, Brown & Co., 1976), 144.

2. William Dyess, assistant secretary of state for public information, interviewed on "Newsmakers," NBC television, Feb. 3, 1980, in Daniel Ellsberg, "Introduction: Call to Mutiny," in E. P. Thompson and Dan Smith, eds., *Protest and Survive* (New York: Monthly Review Press, 1981), iv.

3. Transcript of "This Week with David Brinkley," ABC News, Feb. 3, 1991.

4. JBC to JRO, Mar. 14, 1947, box 27, Conant folder, JROP.

5. JBC to VB, Sept. 27, 1945, box 27, file 614, VBP.

6. JBC used this analogy on numerous occasions between Nov. 1945 (his first substantive post-Hiroshima statement on the bomb) and mid-1947. See, for example, JBC, "Conant on the Bomb," speech to the Cleveland Chamber of Commerce, Nov. 20, 1945, *Harvard Alumni Bulletin* 48:6 (Dec. 8, 1945), 236ff.; and JBC, "Atomic Energy," *Texas Reports on Biology and Medicine* 5:2 (Summer 1947), 188–89.

7. VB to JBC, Oct. 21, 1946, box 27, folder 614, VBP.

8. JBC to VB, Oct. 23, 1945 (handwritten postscript), Carnegie Institution archives, Washington, D.C.

9. JBC, "The Atomic Age: Discussion," secret remarks to the National War College, Sept. 16, 1946, National Defense University archives, Washington, D.C.

10. One example of this response occurred in Apr. 1982, when then Secretary of State Alexander Haig used press conferences and public speeches to rebut a *Foreign Affairs* article by four former government officials—Robert MacNamara, McGeorge Bundy, George Kennan, and Gerard Smith—who argued that the United States should adopt a "no first use" policy.

11. JBC to DEL, Sept. 19, 1946, "Leo-Lim" correspondence folder, box 303, JBC PREP.

12. In his writings on this question, Barton J. Bernstein has repeatedly neglected to distinguish between these quite different forms of guilt, and thus repeatedly attributed to JBC guilt "about Hiroshima and Nagasaki," "over the use of the bomb on Japan," or "over the atomic bombing," rather than a broader feeling of culpability over the advent of nuclear weapons and their potential for *future* destruction. See Bernstein, "The H-Bomb Decisions: Were They Inevitable?" in *National Security and International Stability*, ed. Bernard Brodie, M. Intriligator, and R. Kolkowicz (Cambridge, Mass., 1983), 332; Bernstein, "Truman and the H-Bomb," *Bulletin of the Atomic Scientists* 40 (Mar. 1984), 13; Peter Galison and Bernstein, "In Any Light: Scientists and the Decision to Build the Superbomb, 1942–1954," *Historical Studies in the Physical and Biological Sciences* 19 (1989), 292; and Bernstein, "Seizing the Contested Terrain of Early Nuclear History: Stimson, Conant, and Their Allies Explain the Decision to Use the Atomic Bomb," *Diplomatic History* 17:1 (Winter 1993), 42, n. 24, 71–72.

13. The "hysteria" warning appears in Harvey H. Bundy to HLS, March 3, 1945, Harrison-Bundy files, folder 69, MED records, RG 77, NA; for JBC's reasoning in promoting the Smyth Report, see Hewlett and Anderson, *The New World*, 400–401. See also H. D. Smyth, "The Smyth Report," *Princeton University Library Chronicles* 37 (Spring 1976), 173–89.

14. American Institute of Public Opinion (AIPO) poll, Aug. 26, 1945, *Public Opinion Quarterly* 9 (Fall 1945), 385, in Michael J. Yavenditti, "The American People and the Use of Atomic Bombs on Japan: The 1940s," *Historian* 36:2 (Feb. 1974), 225.

15. Richard P. Kraft to JBC, Feb. 20, 1946, "Atomic Bomb, 1945–46" folder, box 273, JBC PREP.

16. Bradford Young to JBC, Dec. 13, 1945, "Atomic Bomb, 1945–46" folder, box 273, JBC PREP; see also handwritten postscript to JBC to Reinhold Niebuhr, Mar. 6, 1946, box 3, Conant file, Niebuhr Papers, LC.

17. Richard Fox, *Reinhold Niebuhr: A Biography* (San Francisco: Harper & Row, 1985), xi.

18. JBC, *Baccalaureate Sermon to the Harvard College Class of 1950* (Cambridge: Harvard University, 1950), 8, 9; JBC, *MSL*, 9–11; "Conant liked Niebuhr's brand of religion: heavy on the preaching, topical, politically informed, intellectually vigorous, if not professionally polished." Fox, *Niebuhr*, 211. For an affectionate personal and political memoir of Niebuhr see that of his daughter Elisabeth Sifton, "Remembering Reinhold Niebuhr," *World Policy Journal* 10:1 (Spring 1993), 83–90.

19. 1942–43 correspondence in Niebuhr Papers, LC, box 3, Conant file; Fox, *Niebuhr*, 211–212; Joseph P. Lash, ed., *From the Diaries of Felix Frankfurter* (New York: W. W. Norton & Co., 1975), 184–85.

20. Reinhold Niebuhr, *The Children of Light and the Children of Darkness* (New York: Charles Scribner's Sons, 1944), esp. chap. 5.

21. TRC interview, 1987.
22. "Japan Atom Bombing Condemned in Federal Church Report" and "Report of Protestant Church Leaders on Atomic Warfare," *NYT,* Mar. 6, 1946, 1, 15; Federal Council of Churches of Christ in America, Commission on the Relation of the Church to the War in the light of the Christian Faith, *Atomic Warfare and the Christian Faith* (New York, 1946).
23. JBC to Harvey H. Bundy, Sept. 23, 1946, JBC PREP, "Bu-By" correspondence folder, 1946–47, box 296.
24. JBC to Niebuhr, Mar. 6, 1946, box 3, Conant file, Niebuhr Papers, LC.
25. Niebuhr to JBC, Mar. 12, 1946, box 3, Conant file, Niebuhr Papers. Niebuhr also made the point that the U.S. Strategic Bombing Survey had undercut arguments for effectiveness of strategic bombing.
26. When Niebuhr wrote Calhoun the next day, he noted, citing criticisms from unidentified correspondents, that the draft report's condemnation of the use of the atomic bomb against Japan was "subject to misunderstanding, at least the misunderstanding of those of us who are not pacifists. We objected to the use of the bomb without warning, but could not have said that it should in no case have been used. When the report is ultimately published I should think that it might be well to make this distinction sharper. It certainly existed in the minds of the Committee, as you will remember from the discussion." Niebuhr to Calhoun, Mar. 13, 1946, box 5, Niebuhr Papers, LC.
27. Niebuhr, *The Children of Light and the Children of Darkness,* 182–86.
28. Niebuhr to JBC, Mar. 12, 1946.
29. JBC to Niebuhr, Mar. 23, 1946, box 6, Niebuhr Papers, LC.
30. JBC to Niebuhr, Mar. 6, 1946, box 3, Conant file, Niebuhr Papers, LC.
31. JBC to BMB, Dec. 20, 1946, BMB Papers, box 58, Conant file.
32. D. Y. Bradshaw to Dean Little, June 13, 1946, Atomic Energy file, Carnegie Institution archives, Washington, D.C.
33. TRC interview, 1986; JBC to VB, June 18, 1946, Atomic Energy file Carnegie Institution archives; JBC to VB, June 25, 1946, box 27, file 614, VBP.
34. VB to JBC, dated July 18, 1946, but probably June 18, judging from content and a "received" stamp of June 20, JBC PREP, box 304, folder marked "Metro-Goldwyn-Mayer, 1945-46-47" (hereafter MGM folder).
35. Donald Higgins to Dean Little, undated telegram (June 1946), Carnegie Institution archives, Atomic Energy file.
36. John H. Teeter to JBC, July 30, 1946, "National Defense Research Committee, 1946–47" folder, box 309, JBC PREP.
37. John H. Teeter to JBC, July 30, 1946, "National Defense Research Committee, 1946–47" folder, box 309, JBC PREP.
38. In addition to documents in various archival collections, this account of the *Beginning or the End* saga draws on Michael J. Yavenditti, "Atomic Scientists and Hollywood: The Beginning or the End?" *Film and History* 8:4 (Dec. 1978), 73–88; Nathan Reingold, "MGM Meets the Atomic Bomb," *Wilson Quarterly* (Autumn 1984), 154–63, and Reingold, *Science, American Style* (New Brunswick, N.J.: Rutgers University Press, 1991), 334–50; Smith, *A Peril and a Hope,* 293–94; and Boyer, *By the Bomb's Early Light,* 194–95.
39. Charles E. Kurtzman to James M. [*sic*] Conant, Feb. 26, 1947, JBC PREP, MGM folder.
40. Kurtzman to JBC, Feb. 26, 1947, JBC PREP, MGM folder.
41. *Time,* Feb. 24, 1947, 106.
42. VB to JBC, March 6, 1946, JBC PREP, MGM folder.
43. Mayer to Einstein quoted from Reingold, "MGM Meets the Atomic Bomb," 158.
44. JBC to VB, May 24, 1946, box 27, file 614, VBP.
45. Draft screenplay excerpts dated Apr. 1946, enclosed with release form dated May 1, 1946, copy in JBC PREP, MGM folder.

46. James G. Hershberg, "Preserving 250 Million Pages of Knowledge," *Washington Post,* Aug. 31, 1986.
47. Draft screenplay excerpts dated Apr. 1946, enclosed with release form dated May 1, 1946, copy in JBC PREP, MGM folder.
48. VB to Charles G. Ross, May 20, 1946; Ross to VB, May 21, 1946; VB to Leslie R. Groves, May 22, 1946; all in JBC PREP, MGM folder.
49. H. T. Wensel to JBC, May 8, 1946; Samuel Marx to JBC, May 24, 1946, JBC PREP, MGM folder.
50. VB to JBC, dated July 18, 1946, but probably June 18, to judge from content and a June 20 stamped received date, JBC PREP, MGM folder.
51. VB to JBC, Dec. 6, 1946, JBC PREP, MGM folder; see also VB to JBC, Nov. 27, 1946, copy in BMB Papers.
52. See John M. Hancock to JBC, Dec. 4, 1946, enclosing Herbert H. Mass, Bohr's counsel, to MGM, Nov. 8, 1946, and Walter Lippmann to JBC, Nov. 4, 1946, JBC PREP, MGM folder; for JRO's views: Reingold, "MGM Meets the Atomic Bomb," 159–60. Bohr's action may have been motivated by his belief, as paraphrased by FF, that there was "a great deal of ignorant twaddle about the needlessness of discharging the bomb, because the Japs were almost defeated." See FF diary, Nov. 6, 1946, reel 1, FF papers, LC.
53. VB to JBC, Dec. 6, 1946, JBC PREP, MGM folder.
54. Reingold, "MGM Meets the Atomic Bomb," 159.
55. Reingold, "MGM Meets the Atomic Bomb," 162 n.; HST to HLS, Dec. 31, 1946, HLS Papers, Sterling Library, Yale University.
56. Lippmann to Frank Aydelotte, Oct. 28, 1946; Lippmann to John J. McCloy, Nov. 2, 1946; both enclosed in McCloy to Robert P. Patterson, Nov. 4, 1946, HLS Papers.
57. Isaacson and Thomas, *The Wise Men,* 335–36; Bird, *The Chairman,* 272–83.
58. John J. McCloy to Robert P. Patterson, Nov. 4, 1946, HLS Papers, Yale University.
59. James K. McGuiness to Lippmann, Nov. 11, 1946, JBC PREP, MGM folder.
60. Lippmann to JBC, Nov. 4, 1946, JBC PREP, MGM folder.
61. HST, *Year of Decisions,* 419.
62. Quoted in Herken, *Winning Weapon,* 20 fn.
63. Quoted in Alfred Steinberg, *The Man from Missouri* (New York: Putnam, 1962), 259, in Barton J. Bernstein, "A Postwar Myth: 500,000 U.S. Lives Saved," *Bulletin of the Atomic Scientists* (June/July 1986), 38.
64. Lippmann to JBC, Oct. 28, 1946, copy in VB Papers, LC, box 27, file 614.
65. JBC to Lippmann, Nov. 1, 1946, JBC PREP, MGM folder.
66. Reingold, "MGM Meets the Atomic Bomb," 160.
67. VB to JBC, Nov. 27, 1946, copy in Baruch papers; earlier in the month Bush was "not too disturbed" by Lippmann's criticisms: VB to JBC, Nov. 4, 1946, VBP, box 27, folder 614.
68. JBC to Hancock, Dec, 10, 1946, JBC PREP, MGM folder.
69. JBC to BMB, Dec. 20, 1946, BMB Papers, box 58, Conant file.
70. Lippmann to JBC, Jan. 8, 1947; JBC to Lippmann, Jan. 17, 1947, JBC PREP, MGM folder.
71. JBC to Loew's Inc., Jan. 22, 1947; see also JBC to S. D. Cohen, Jan. 13, 1947; S. D. Cohen to JBC, Jan. 15, 1947; all in JBC PREP, MGM folder.
72. *Time,* Feb. 24, 1947, 106.
73. Only one reviewer, writing in the *Bulletin of the Atomic Scientists,* challenged the film's historical accuracy, citing the "horrible falsification" of the advance warning to Hiroshima. Harrison Brown, "*The Beginning or the End:* A Review," *Bulletin of the Atomic Scientists,* Mar. 1947, 99.
74. Boyer, *By the Bomb's Early Light,* 195.
75. John Hersey, "Reporter at Large: Hiroshima," *New Yorker* (Aug. 31, 1946); Hersey, *Hiroshima* (New York: Alfred A. Knopf, 1946).
76. For analyses of the reactions to Hersey's article see Michael J. Yavenditti, "John

Hersey and the American Conscience: The Reception of 'Hiroshima,'" *Pacific Historical Review* 43 (Feb. 1974), 24-49; and Boyer, *By the Bomb's Early Light,* 205-10.

77. JBC's role in shaping public perceptions of Hiroshima was first detailed by the author in *James B. Conant, Nuclear Weapons, and the Cold War,* 1945-1950, chap. 3, and subsequently amplified by Barton J. Bernstein in "Seizing the Contested Terrain of Early Nuclear History: Stimson, Conant, and Their Allies Explain the Decision to Use the Atomic Bomb," *Diplomatic History* 17:1 (Winter 1993), 35-72.

78. U.S. Strategic Bombing Survey, *The Summary Report on the Pacific War* (Washington, D.C.: Government Printing Office, 1946), 26.

79. JBC to George Fort Milton, Sept. 18, 1946; see also Milton to JBC, Sept. 4, 1946, enclosing "Atomic Morality," *Buffalo Evening News,* Aug. 6, 1946; "Monday morning quarterbacking": JBC to Harvey H. Bundy, Sept. 23, 1946; all in "Bu-By" correspondence folder, 1946-47, box 296, JBC PREP.

80. Leland Stowe, *While Time Remains* (New York: Alfred A. Knopf, 1946); for Halsey's remark see AP dispatch, Sept. 9, 1946, quoted in "Stassen Rules Out Atom Control Veto," *NYT,* Sept. 11, 1946, 8, and BMB to James V. Forrestal, Sept. 10, 1946, S/AE, box 77, folder 20.51 Name File: Forrestal, James, 1951. JBC cited these two cases in JBC to Harvey H. Bundy, Sept. 23, 1946, JBC PREP, "Bu-By" correspondence folder, 1946-47, box 296.

81. Norman Cousins, "The Literacy of Survival," *Saturday Review of Literature* 29:37 (Sept. 14, 1946), 14.

82. Norman Cousins and Thomas K. Finletter, "A Beginning for Sanity," *Saturday Review of Literature* (June 15, 1946), 5-6; Finletter, like several other world federalists, later underwent a full-scale conversion to anti-Communism and became Truman's Secretary of the Air Force in 1950.

83. JBC to Harvey H. Bundy, Sept. 23, 1946, JBC PREP, "Bu-By" correspondence folder, 1946-47, box 296.

84. JBC to Harvey H. Bundy, Sept. 23, 1946.

85. JBC to Harvey H. Bundy, Sept. 23, 1946.

86. Harvey H. Bundy to JBC, Sept. 24, 1946; JBC to Harvey H. Bundy, Sept. 26, 1946, "Bu-By" correspondence folder, 1946-47, JBC PREP, box 296.

87. HLS to FF, Dec. 12, 1946, HLS Papers, box 154, folder 14.

88. HLS to JBC, Jan. 20, 1947; similar letters to George L. Harrison, Harvey H. Bundy, R. A. Winnacker, Felix Frankfurter, and Gordon Arneson. HLS Papers, box 154, folder 15. Bundy later said that the final article contained "basically all his [HLS's] arguments; the prose is mine." Interview with author, Nov. 16, 1986.

89. Harvey H. Bundy, "Notes on the Use by the United States of the Atomic Bomb," Sept. 25, 1945, Top Secret Documents Files of Interest to General Groves 20, MED records, RG 77, NA, in Bernstein, "Seizing the Contested Terrain of Nuclear History," 46-47.

90. Rudolph Winnacker, "The Debate About Hiroshima," *Military Affairs* 11 (Spring 1947), 25-30; see also Winnacker to HLS, w. enc., Nov. 12, 14, 1946, HLS Papers.

91. HST to HLS, Dec. 31, 1946, HLS Papers, box 154, folder 15. It must be said, however, that HST's detachment from the detailed deliberations of the Interim Committee is suggested by his remarkably fuzzy comment that he recalled appointing "a commission consisting of Mr. Byrnes, Vannevar Bush, and someone else whose name I have forgotten."

92. Farrell to BMB, Sept. 3, 1946, S/AE, box 39, folder 20.44 Farrell, Thomas.

93. John J. McCloy to Robert P. Patterson, Nov. 4, 1946, HLS Papers, Yale University.

94. BMB to James V. Forrestal, Sept. 10, 1946, S/AE, box 77, folder 20.51 Name File: Forrestal, James, 1951.

95. John M. Hancock to Adm. Chester A. Nimitz, Sept. 20, 1946, S/AE, box 77, folder 20.51 Name File: Forrestal, James, 1951.

96. JBC to George Fort Milton, Sept. 18, 1946, JBC PREP, "Bu-By" correspondence folder, 1946-47, box 296; KTC to JBC, Oct. 15, 1946, in which KTC encloses "a copy

of the brief article which I have written for Ted Weeks, following your suggestion," and JBC to KTC, Oct. 26, 1946, "Massachusetts Institute of Technology, 1946–47" folder, JBC PREP, box 303.

97. KTC, "If the Atomic Bomb Had Not Been Used," *Atlantic Monthly* (Dec. 1946), 54–56; HST to KTC, Dec. 16, 1946, *Atlantic Monthly* (Feb. 1947), 1.

98. JBC desk calendar, JBC PREP.

99. Unfortunately, researchers have been unable to locate a surviving copy of HLS's original ms., in either the HLS or the JBC papers, thus precluding a more detailed analysis of JBC's revisions.

100. JBC to McGeorge Bundy, Nov. 30, 1946, HLS Papers, box 154, folder 11. JBC's argument here stemmed from a strong sense that, as he had put it in a secret speech a couple of months earlier, the "atomic bomb" had "taken all the rap" for strategic bombing, whose "hideous" nature the American people had failed to grasp. JBC, "The Atomic Age: Discussion," Sept. 16, 1946, National Defense University archives, Washington, D.C.

101. McGeorge Bundy telegram to JBC, Dec. 7, 1946, "Bu-By" correspondence folder, 1946–47, JBC PREP, box 296.

102. JBC to HLS, Dec. 14, 1946, HLS Papers, box 154, folder 15.

103. JBC to Donald Tresidder, Jan. 22, 1947, JBC PREP, "Universal Military Training, 1946–47" folder, box 311. Italics in original.

104. JBC to HLS, Jan. 22, 1947, HLS Papers, box 154, folder 18. Italics in original.

105. HLS, "The Decision to Use the Atomic Bomb," *Harper's* 194:1161 (Feb. 1947), 97–107.

106. Yavenditti, "John Hersey and the American Conscience: The Reception of 'Hiroshima,'" 44. Shortly before HLS published his article, HST wrote, "Some time ago I think I suggested that you get out an article for the record on the facts regarding the atomic bomb and the procedure that was followed before it was dropped." HST to HLS, Dec. 31, 1946, HLS Papers. But no evidence has emerged to suggest that HST spurred rather than confirmed HLS's intention to write the *Harper's* piece.

107. "The 'Stimson Doctrine,'" *NYT*, Feb. 2, 1947.

108. HLS, "The Decision to Use the Atomic Bomb," 107.

109. For an indication of the importance of HLS's article to subsequent historiography of the atomic bomb decision, see Barton J. Bernstein, "The Atomic Bomb and American Foreign Policy, 1941–1945: An Historical Controversy," *Peace and Change* 2 (Spring 1974), 1–16; Bernstein's introduction to *The Atomic Bomb: The Critical Issues* (vii–xix), as well as his introduction to HLS's article in that volume; and Bernstein, "Seizing the Contested Terrain of Early Nuclear History," *passim*.

110. Interview with author, Nov. 16, 1986.

111. HLS to HST, Jan. 7, 1947, HLS Papers.

112. McGeorge Bundy to HLS, Feb. 18, 1947; LRG to HLS, Feb. 19, 1947; W. A. Higinbotham to HLS, Feb. 24, 1947; HST to HLS, Feb. 4, 1947; all in HLS papers, quoted in unpublished ms. by Martin J. Sherwin.

113. Joseph C. Grew to HLS, Feb. 12, 1947, Grew Papers, Houghton Library, Harvard University, quoted in Joseph C. Grew, *Turbulent Era: A Diplomatic Era of Forty Years, 1904–1945*, vol. II (Boston: Houghton Mifflin, 1952), 1425–28; for Grew's arguments and memoranda on retaining the Emperor, see *Turbulent Era*, chap. 36.

114. Stimson and Bundy, *On Active Service in War and Peace*, 626–29. To some extent Stimson's fear has proved justified, as Butow, author of the most used study on the issue, faulted Washington for not more explicitly indicating its willingness to tolerate the Emperor's continuance on the throne and concluded that this step would have given the pro-surrender faction in Tokyo a "tremendously powerful argument." Butow, *Japan's Decision to Surrender*, 133–35, 231.

115. Stimson and Bundy, *On Active Service in War and Peace*, 634–55. In a draft of their chapter "The Bomb and Peace with Russia," Bundy and Stimson had included even

stronger statements about the diplomatic relevance of the bomb to U.S. policy toward Russia just before and after Hiroshima. In the summer of 1945, they stated, State Department officials "developed a tendency to think of the bomb as a diplomatic weapon. Outraged by constant evidence of Russian perfidy, some of the men in charge of foreign policy were eager to carry the bomb for a while as their ace-in-the-hole." Moreover, they noted, HLS had presented his September 1945 memorandum at a time "when American statesmen were eager for their country to browbeat the Russians with the bomb 'held rather ostentatiously on our hip.'" These comments, clearly drawn from HLS's diary entries and alluding primarily to James F. Byrnes, were deleted from the final manuscript at the behest of the State Department's George Kennan, to whom Secretary of State George C. Marshall had forwarded the draft chapter after receiving it from McGeorge Bundy. Bundy excised the offending lines after Kennan denied their accuracy and, more convincingly, objected that they would be pounced upon by domestic critics of U.S. policy, producing a controversy that "would play squarely into the hands of the Communists who so frequently speak of our 'atomic diplomacy' and accuse us of trying to intimidate the world in general by our possession of the bomb." See Bundy to Marshall, Oct. 31 and Nov. 10, 1947; Marshall to Bundy, Nov. 7 and 19, 1947; Kennan to Bundy, Dec. 2 (including excerpts from the draft chapter, which itself has not been found, and Kennan's objections) and 19, 1947; Bundy to Kennan, Dec. 4, 8, and 22, 1947; Kennan to Marshall, Dec. 16, 1947; all in George C. Marshall Papers, Pentagon Office, Selected, box 86, George C. Marshall Library, Lexington, Va., in Bernstein, "Seizing the Contested Terrain of Early Nuclear History," 65–69, and Bird, *The Chairman*, 697 n. 113.

116. HST, *Year of Decisions*, 415–26; Barton J. Bernstein, "A Postwar Myth: 500,000 American Lives Saved," *Bulletin of the Atomic Scientists* 42 (June/July 1986), 38; responding to a historian's inquiry near the end of his presidency, HST drafted a reply that referred to a pre-Hiroshima estimate by Marshall that "¼ million casualties would be the minimum cost" in an invasion of Japan; with HST's OK, an aide added the phrase, "and might cost as much as a million, on the American side alone," in order to "avoid a conflict" with HLS's account. HST to James L. Cate, draft letter, Dec. 31, 1952; Kenneth W. Hechler to Lloyd, Jan. 2, 1953; David D. Lloyd to HST, Jan. 6, 1953; HST to James L. Cate; all in PSF–General File, box 112, Atomic Bomb folder, HST Papers, HSTL; see also Barton J. Bernstein, "Writing, Righting, or Wronging the Historical Record," *Diplomatic History* 16:1 (Winter 1992), 163–73.

117. Alperovitz's use of the HLS diaries prompted the most prominent mainstream historian of the end of World War II, Herbert Feis, to gingerly acknowledge the influence of postwar considerations in the atomic decision in *The Atomic Bomb and the End of World War II* (Princeton, N.J.: Princeton University Press, 1966), a revised version of his earlier *Japan Subdued: The Atomic Bomb and the End of World War Two in the Pacific* (Princeton, N.J.: Princeton University Press, 1961). Feis considered including in the earlier work, but ultimately omitted, restraining Soviet ambitions as one motivation for supporting the bomb's use. Barton J. Bernstein, "Ike and Hiroshima: Did He Oppose It?" *Journal of Strategic Studies* 10:3 (Sept. 1987), 386.

118. Rufus E. Miles, Jr., "Hiroshima: The Strange Myth of a Half a Million American Lives Saved," *International Security* 10:2 (Fall 1985), 121–40; Bernstein, "A Postwar Myth," 38; Sherwin, *A World Destroyed*, intro. to 1987 ed., xxii, Appendix U.

119. JBC, "Atomic Energy," *Texas Reports on Biology and Medicine* 5:2 (Summer 1947), 188–98.

120. JBC, "Atomic Energy."

121. Letter to JBC, Mar. 7, 1947, enclosed in JBC to JRO, Mar. 14, 1947, box 27, Conant folder, JROP.

122. JBC to JRO, Mar. 14, 1947, box 27, Conant folder, JROP.

123. Percy S. Straus, Jr., to Harold L. Oram, Mar. 13, 1947, call number 1982.1, box 2,

"Emergency Committee of Atomic Scientists" folder, Harold C. Urey Papers, University of California (San Diego) Library, La Jolla, Calif. Hanszen actually cited the press of affairs at Rice as his reason for not cooperating, but the ECAS officials deduced that Conant's objections were responsible. Harry C. Hanszen to Urey, Mar. 26, 1947, Urey Papers, "Emergency Committee of Atomic Scientists" folder.

124. Eileen A. Fry to Urey, Apr. 3, 1947, Urey Papers, "Emergency Committee of Atomic Scientists" folder; see also, in the same folder, Harold L. Oram, "Memorandum on Fund Raising Campaign, Emergency Committee of Atomic Scientists, Incorporated, October 1, 1946–April 30, 1947," Apr. 25, 1947, which noted the deleterious impact on ECAS activities of JBC's assertion that public involvement in atomic policy was inappropriate.

125. The telephone call was monitored by the FBI and described in a memorandum in JRO's FBI files, later released under the Freedom of Information Act. FBI Serial File 108-17829-148.

126. Weisskopf to JBC, Mar. 24, 1947, box 296, "Atomic Energy: Miscellaneous, 1946–47" folder, JBC PREP; Weisskopf telephone interview, May 5, 1988. In any event, Weisskopf added in his letter, he doubted the committee would be able to reach a unanimous position on the decision.

127. JBC to Weisskopf, Mar. 25, 1947, box 296, "Atomic Energy: Miscellaneous, 1946–47" folder, JBC PREP.

128. JRO to JBC, Apr. 14, 1947, JROP, box 172, "AEC: Correspondence Feb. 1947–June 1947" folder.

129. Yavenditti, "John Hersey and the American Conscience," 48–49; Boyer, *By the Bomb's Early Light,* 209–10.

130. Boyer, *By the Bomb's Early Light,* 209.

131. HLS to Raymond Gram Swing, Feb. 4, 1947, HLS Papers.

132. JBC, transcript of discussion following "The Atomic Age," secret address to the National War College, Oct. 2, 1947, National Defense University archives, Washington, D.C.

CHAPTER 17

1. Harvard Class of 1914, *Thirty-fifth Anniversary Report* (Cambridge: Harvard University, 1949), 60.

2. For details of the transfer of authority, see Hewlett and Anderson, *New World,* 651–55.

3. Robert F. Bacher to author, Jan. 14, 1982.

4. Daniel Ford, *Meltdown: The Secret Papers of the Atomic Energy Commission* (rev. ed. of *The Cult of the Atom*) (New York: Simon & Schuster, 1982, 1984, 1986), 33.

5. Kevles, *The Physicists,* 377.

6. DEL, *AEY,* 185.

7. Quoted in Richard T. Sylves, *The Nuclear Oracles: A Political History of the General Advisory Committee of the Atomic Energy Commission, 1947–1977* (Ames: Iowa State University Press, 1987), 16.

8. For an account of the rise of institutionalized expertise in the United States after World War II, as reflected in the U.S. atomic program, see Brian Balogh, *Chain Reaction: Expert Debate and Public Participation in American Commercial Nuclear Power, 1945–1975* (Cambridge, Eng.: Cambridge University Press, 1991).

9. Syvles, *The Nuclear Oracles;* on the GAC's "inordinate influence" in its early days see Balogh, *Chain Reaction,* 79.

10. JBC to Lee A. DuBridge, Dec. 20, 1946, JBC PREP, box 296, "Atomic Energy Advisory Committee, 1946–47" folder.

11. Steven L. Rearden, *History of the Office of the Secretary of Defense, Vol. I: The Formative Years, 1947–1950* (Washington, D.C.: Historical Office, Office of the

Secretary of Defense, 1984), 26, 33, 96–103; Herbert F. York and G. Allen Greb, "Military Research and Development: A Postwar History," *Bulletin of the Atomic Scientists* 33:1 (Jan. 1977), 14–16.

12. VB to JBC, Dec. 12, 1946, box 59, folder 1403, VBP.
13. JBC, *MSL,* 499–500.
14. FBI memorandum of Dec. 14, 1946, conversation between Robert and Kitty Oppenheimer. FBI Oppenheimer files, serial file 100-17828-120. *BG,* Dec. 13, 1946; White House press release, Dec. 12, 1946, HST Papers, official file, 692-B, General Advisory Committee, HSTL.
15. Lee A. DuBridge to JBC, Dec. 17, 1946, JBC PREP, box 296, "Atomic Energy Advisory Committee, 1946–47" folder; DuBridge had been urged to nominate Oppenheimer by I. I. Rabi: Rabi to DuBridge, Dec. 13, 1946, DuBridge Papers, California Institute of Technology; DuBridge to Rabi, Dec. 17, 1946, DuBridge folder, Rabi Papers, LC.
16. JBC to Lee A. DuBridge, Dec. 20, 1946, JBC PREP, box 296, "Atomic Energy Advisory Committee, 1946–47" folder.
17. JBC, *MSL,* 499–500.
18. JBC, *MSL,* 499–500.
19. DEL, *AEY,* 128; JBC, *MSL,* 500; Hewlett and Duncan, *Atomic Shield,* 16.
20. Strauss recalled bitterly that JBC had "jumped up at the start of the meeting nominating Oppie and more or less railroaded the deal through." William Borden to file, Aug. 13, 1951, in George F. Murphy to John T. Conway, July 14, 1966, Classified box 41, JCAE, General Subject files, Oppenheimer, J. R., Oct. 1953–June 1954, JCAE document 8796, JCAE Formerly Classified records, RG 128, NA.
21. Minutes, GAC 1, DoE archives.
22. Minutes GAC 1.
23. Hewlett and Duncan, *Atomic Shield,* 16.
24. Hewlett and Duncan, *Atomic Shield,* 8.
25. VB to Robert P. Patterson, Sept. 5, 1947, box 91, folder 2050, VBP. VB continued: "It had its tough moments, and its rather appalling responsibilities, and of course it had its very sad side in which you and I saw friends who lost their boys and the like. But there was one part of it that was on the other side of the ledger. The privilege of working with worthwhile men in the common cause and meeting and aiding those that one admired and respected was an experience that comes to very few men and one that I appreciated enormously."
26. The account of "Operation Pay-Off" is drawn from correspondence in the Bush Family Papers, folders marked "Correspondence—Misc. OSRD Party, Jan. 20, 1947," VBP, box 125; JBC PREP; VB, *Pieces of the Action,* 136; Harvey Bundy to JBC, Feb. 11, 1947, "National Defense Research Committee, 1946–47" folder, box 309, JBC PREP; JBC to VB, Nov. 13, 1946, VBP, Family Papers, box 125.
27. JBC, *MSL,* 500.
28. O. C. Carmichael, chairman, Committee on the Relationships of Higher Education to the Federal Government, American Council on Education, to Harry S. Truman, Sept. 25, 1945, HST PSF General File, box 112, "General File—Atomic Energy Control Commission, United Nations" folder, HSTL.
29. JBC, "National Defense in the Light of the Atomic Bomb," Dec. 3, 1945, Harvard News Office release, Dec. 4, 1945.
30. JBC, *MSL,* 354, 357–8. JBC and Tresidder were initially alarmed to learn that HST had blessed the group with a paean to military service's allegedly character-building effect on young men. Willing to support UMT if found desirable on military grounds— and pledged to do so if a qualified commission unanimously backed the idea—JBC hardly swallowed the idea of boot camp providing a substitute for college as the best route to adult maturity. Before promising to support their findings, JBC sought and received assurances from KTC and Dodds that they had been given free rein to consider all aspects of the military situation in making their recommendation, and

even to reject UMT altogether. Tresidder to JBC, Jan. 8, 1947; JBC to Tresidder, Jan. 15, 1947; JBC to Dodds, Jan. 16, 1947; Tresidder to JBC, Jan. 18, 1947; JBC to Tresidder, Jan. 22, 1947; all in "Universal Military Training, 1946–47" folder, box 311, JBC PREP.

31. JBC describes the views he planned to state to the Compton board in a letter to Tresidder, Feb. 25, 1947, "Universal Military Training, 1946–47" folder, box 311, JBC PREP; JBC desk calendar.

32. JBC to Owen J. Roberts, June 14, 1947, "Universal Military Training, 1946–47" folder, box 311, JBC PREP; by Oct. 1947, JBC had publicly begun to campaign for a universal military service act. "Fifty Groups Plan Drive for Training," *NYT,* Oct. 25, 1947.

33. Minutes, GAC 2. For an assessment of the problems hampering the U.S. nuclear program in 1945–47, see David Alan Rosenberg, "American Atomic Strategy and the Hydrogen Bomb Decision," *Journal of American History* 66 (June 1979), 62–87, esp. 65–66.

34. David Alan Rosenberg, "U.S. Nuclear Stockpile, 1945 to 1950," *Bulletin of the Atomic Scientists* 38 (May 1982), 25–30; Hewlett and Duncan, *Atomic Shield,* 47–48.

35. DEL, *AEY,* 137.

36. Rosenberg, "U.S. Nuclear Stockpile," 26–29. According to the figures released by the Department of Energy, the stockpile consisted of components for two weapons at the end of 1945, nine in July 1946, and thirteen in July 1947.

37. Minutes, GAC 2; "peek behind the curtains": JBC used this phrase in expressing frustration over the DEL nomination battle in a telephone conversation with JRO on Feb. 17, 1947, secretly monitored by the FBI. FBI JRO File Serial 100-17828-148. HST's shock: DEL, *AEY,* 165; and Hewlett and Duncan, *Atomic Shield,* 47–48.

38. JBC was also made a member of the subcommittee on research, chaired by DuBridge. The group also formed a panel on reactors, headed by Smith. JRO, as GAC chairman, served as an ex-officio member of all subcommittees.

39. Minutes, GAC 2, DoE archives.

40. Hewlett and Duncan, *Atomic Shield,* 7.

41. "Lilienthal Urges Wiser Atom Guard," Jan. 29, 1947. Baruch had taken up the theme, also criticizing the report's release: "Our Atom Secrets Tapped by Soviet, Baruch Believes; Value of Leaks Doubtful," *NYT,* Feb. 4, 1947.

42. "I shall always take a certain amount of satisfaction in having pushed for this volume," JBC wrote to Smyth in a congratulatory note following the Report's publication, "but even more in having suggested that you write it." JBC to Smyth, Oct. 1, 1945, Conant file, Henry D. Smyth Papers, American Philosophical Society Library, Philadelphia. Smyth later recalled that *he* had suggested the idea to Conant: H. D. Smyth, "The Smyth Report," *Princeton University Library Chronicles* 37 (Spring 1976), 173–89. See also Smyth to JBC, Feb. 4, 1947, and Smyth, "Memorandum on the History of the Preparation of My Report on Atomic Energy for Military Purposes," Jan. 10, 1947, Conant file, Smyth Papers, and "Atomic Energy: Miscellaneous, 1946–47" folder, box 296, JBC PREP.

43. DEL, *AEY,* 134–38; Hewlett and Duncan, *Atomic Shield,* 3–4.

44. JBC testimony, Feb. 4, 1947, U.S. Congress, Senate Section of the Joint Committee on Atomic Energy, *Hearings on the Confirmation of the Atomic Energy Commission and the General Manager,* 80th Cong., 1st sess., 1947, 111–19.

45. DEL, *AEY,* 139.

46. DEL, *AEY,* 135.

47. *NYT,* Feb. 5, 1947.

48. JBC to DEL, Feb. 5, 1947, Conant file, DEL Papers.

49. DEL, *AEY,* 139–151.

50. JBC described his efforts to lobby Vermont's Ralph Flanders, and Henry Cabot Lodge and Leverett Saltonstall of Massachusetts in a telephone conversation with JRO on Feb. 17, 1947, that was monitored and described by the FBI. FBI JRO File

Serial 100-17828-148. JBC's lobbying produced mixed results: Lodge and Saltonstall supported DEL, but Flanders voted no. *NYT,* Apr. 10, 1947; DEL, *AEY,* 147, 167; Ralph E. Flanders to JBC, Mar. 6, 1947, JBC PREP, box 296, "Atomic Energy: Miscellaneous, 1946–47" folder.

51. JRO to JBC telephone conversation, Feb. 17, 1947, FBI JRO File Serial 100-17828-148.
52. The case of the Clinton Laboratories at Oak Ridge, Tenn., illustrated the GAC's "almost overriding" weight in those early months. With its stock of weapons nearly bare, the AEC felt a need quickly to determine priorities for building new capabilities for producing fissionable materials. One candidate for reactor development was Clinton, a mainstay of the Manhattan Project. Though earmarked to receive nearly half the commission's initial $60 million research budget, Clinton had drifted since the war. The Monsanto Chemical Co. had replaced the University of Chicago in managing the lab the previous summer, but activities there were nearly paralyzed by low morale, uncertainty, and administrative confusion and tension among veteran scientists, newly arrived Monsanto engineers, and army officers. In late March and early April, the two top AEC officials responsible for planning, general manager Carroll Wilson and the new director of research, James B. Fisk, proposed building a high-flux reactor at Clinton as a first step toward a larger program, although the option of constructing a new, central laboratory at a different location remained open. Scientists at the lab, led by Farrington Daniels, also pushed for a major project to construct a gas-cooled reactor.
    The GAC effectively vetoed those plans. JBC and JRO argued against any expansion of activities at Clinton and questioned Monsanto's commitment to the lab as well as its ability to draw top-flight scientists. On Apr. 10, shelving the ideas of Fisk and Wilson, the commission opted for the course of action suggested by JBC and JRO: work at Clinton would be extended but not intensified, and the search for a home for the high-flux reactor and a central laboratory would go on. It was an unmistakable show of the GAC's power to sway its parent agency's direction. (Hewlett and Anderson, *New World,* 627; Hewlett and Duncan, *Atomic Shield,* 28–30, 33–35, 44–46, 66–68.) A few days later, JRO wrote JBC: "I expect you know from Carroll that the commission has had trouble taking all of our well meant advice. From his most recent call I learned that they are going to try to do so. I feel a measure of confidence that—in so far as we are responsible for this—we have had some use." (JRO to JBC, Apr. 14, 1947, "AEC: Correspondence February 1947–June 1947" folder, box 172, JROP.)
53. JBC desk calendar; JBC to Curtis E. LeMay, Mar. 4, 1947, "Le" folder, box 44, JROP.
54. This account of the handling of the Oppenheimer security issue in Mar. 1947 is drawn from the following sources: JRO FBI files; DEL, *AEY,* 157; testimony and documents in *IMJRO,* 179–80, 374–81, 387–91, 411–20, 422, 563–64; DEL, "Report of Telephone Conversation at 11:20 [a.m.] with Clark M. Clifford, Special Counsel to the President," Mar. 12, 1947, Clark M. Clifford Papers, HSTL.
55. JBC to DEL, Mar. 29, 1947, *IMJRO,* 378. The transcript incorrectly gives the date as Mar. 27. Kunetka incorrectly gives the dates of both VB's and JBC's letters as Mar. 11. Kunetka, *The Years of Risk,* 116. From Mar. 28 to 30, JBC was in Washington for the GAC's third meeting; on Mar. 29, JBC also attended a dinner meeting of the GAC's reactor subcommittee, and also joined JRO, Bacher, and Osborn for a late-afternoon meeting at the commission. It is uncertain, however, whether he discussed the security problem with JRO on any of these occasions.
56. "U.S. Atom Scientist's Brother Exposed As Communist Who Worked on A-Bomb," *Washington Times-Herald,* July 12, 1947. Until admitting party membership to HUAC in June 1949, Frank Oppenheimer denied the charge, ultimately bolstering JBC's belief that American Communists were inherently untrustworthy.
57. *IMJRO,* 424–25.
58. Acheson, *Present at the Creation,* 219.
59. JBC, *MSL,* 506.

60. JBC, "Education in an Armed Truce," *Atlantic Monthly* 182 (Oct. 1948), 49.
61. JBC diary, June 29, 1940, JBC PERP.
62. JBC to Lewis Douglas, Oct. 4, 1940, Lewis W. Douglas Papers, University of Arizona Library.
63. JBC to Marshall, Jan. 15, 1945; Marshall to JBC, Jan. 21, 1945; JBC to Marshall, Mar. 5, 18, 1946; Marshall to JBC, Mar. 20, 1946; all in George C. Marshall Papers, George C. Marshall Research Foundation, Lexington, Va., box 46, folder 34; JBC to Marshall, Jan. 28, 1947; Marshall to JBC, Feb. 3, 1947, Marshall Papers, box 143, folder 40; Marshall to JBC, May 9, 1947, Marshall Papers, box 130, folder 4. For Marshall's speech: Joseph M. Jones, *The Fifteen Weeks: An Inside Account of the Genesis of the Marshall Plan* (New York: Viking, 1955), 31–38; and Forrest C. Pogue, *George C. Marshall: Statesman, 1945–49* (New York: Viking Penguin, 1987), chap. 13.
64. Acheson, *Present at the Creation,* 232; Jones, *Fifteen Weeks,* 254–55.
65. Marshall to JBC, May 28, 1947, Marshall Papers, box 130, folder 4.
66. Acheson, *Present at the Creation,* 233–34; Jones, *Fifteen Weeks,* 255–56.
67. Enclosure to JBC to Robert E. Smith, Mar. 7, 1962, "S" folder, JBC Correspondence, 1957–64, JBC PERP, box 10, UA I.15.898.10; JBC, *MSL,* 506.
68. Louis J. Halle, *The Cold War as History* (New York: Harper & Row, 1967), 128–29.
69. JBC, "Remarks to the Graduating Class," Ohio University, June 9, 1947, JBC Speech File, 244.

CHAPTER 18

1. Tuttle, *James B. Conant,* 385.
2. "drop the pretense": Burton Y. Berry to George F. Kennan, July 31, 1947, in John Lewis Gaddis, *The Long Peace: Inquiries into the History of the Cold War* (New York, Oxford: Oxford University Press, 1987), 57.
3. McGeorge Bundy makes this error, and draws incorrect conclusions from it, in *Danger and Survival.* Bundy writes that it "did not occur to them [the creators of the Acheson-Lilienthal proposal]—any of them, as far as the records show—that the basic concept should be abandoned or even compromised" (p. 169) and that "No member of either body ever urged a retreat" (p. 194). From these assertions Bundy seems to infer that there was no responsible advocacy of a different course on international control in 1946–48 by those most intimately connected with formulating U.S. atomic policy. However, as I show in this chapter, JBC first urged substantial compromises on staging and then a full-scale revision of Acheson-Lilienthal's basic concept—if only the Russians would make concessions on inspection.
4. JBC, "Conant on the Bomb," speech to the Cleveland Chamber of Commerce, Nov. 20, 1945, *Harvard Alumni Bulletin* 48:6 (Dec. 8, 1945), 239.
5. JRO telegram to Tolman, Dec. 5, 1946, S/AE, box 77, folder 20.3, Name file: Oppenheimer, Robert.
6. Quoted in DEL, "Science and Man's Fate," *Nation,* July 13, 1946, 41, in Boyer, *By the Bomb's Early Light,* 126.
7. Minutes, GAC 2, DoE archives.
8. JBC, *MSL,* 278.
9. According to physicist Walter H. Zinn, as quoted in a confidential Oct. 1950 interview with a staff member of the congressional Joint Committee on Atomic Energy, JBC was the "only member of the scientific community of any stature who doubted that a chain reaction could be maintained." The staff member, seemingly eager to discredit JBC's pessimistic view of atomic energy, reported Zinn, one of the AEC's leading promoters of reactor development, as saying that his "faith" in JBC "will always be limited by what he regards as one of the most shocking incidents in his career." Walter Hamilton to William L. Borden, Apr. 17, 1952, JCAE records, Conant file, RG

128, NA. For JBC's last-minute doubts, see JBC to Arthur H. Compton, Dec. 1, 1942, B–C, box 3, folder 16.

10. JBC, "International Controls of Atomic Energy," Apr. 12, 1946, *Record of Meetings,* Vol. XII, July 1945–June 1947, Council on Foreign Relations Archives, New York City.

11. Committee on Atomic Energy, Carnegie Endowment for International Peace, report of meeting Apr. 13, 1946, BMB Papers, Princeton University Library.

12. JBC, "Atomic Energy," Feb. 21, 1947, speech, *Texas Reports on Biology and Medicine* 5:2 (Summer 1947), 194.

13. JBC, "Public Education and the Structure of American Society," speech to the Economic Club of Detroit, Nov. 11, 1946, JBC Speech File, 230; speeches to New England Council and Temple Ohabei Shalom (draft), Nov. 22, 26, 1946; JBC, "Atomic Energy," Feb. 21, 1947, speech, *Texas Reports on Biology and Medicine* 5:2 (Summer 1947), 188–98; "Atomic Energy," speech to Virginia Polytechnic Institute, Apr. 24, 1947, JBC Speech File, 239.

14. Ralph Waldo Emerson, "Fate," in *The Conduct of Life* (1860), reprinted in Robert E. Spiller, ed., *Five Essays on Man and Nature* (New York: Appleton-Century-Crofts, 1954), 111.

15. "The Atomic Age: Discussion," Oct. 2, 1947, transcript of question-and-answer session after secret speech to National War College, National Defense University archives, Washington, D.C.

16. JBC, *Education in a Divided World,* 52–54.

17. JBC to JRO, Nov. 1, 1947, JROP, box 27, Conant file.

18. Minutes, GAC 3, Mar. 28–30, 1947, 5, DoE archives.

19. Rhodes, *Making of the Atomic Bomb,* 223–24, 254, 279–81; Lanouette with Szilard, *Genius in the Shadows,* 145, 153, 156, 158, 160, 174ff.

20. Edward Teller was among those who had heard the comment attributed to Oppenheimer. *IMJRO,* 713.

21. Zay Jeffries et al., "The Impact of Nucleonics on International Relations and the Social Order," Nov. 18, 1944, excerpts reprinted in Sherwin, *A World Destroyed* (1987 ed.), 315–22, esp. 317–18.

22. Norman Cousins, "Modern Man Is Obsolete," *Saturday Review of Literature,* Aug. 18, 1945, 9.

23. Quincy Wright, "Draft for a Convention on Atomic Energy," *Bulletin of the Atomic Scientists* 1:8 (Apr. 1946), 11–13.

24. Whether JBC and Cavers were in personal contact on the power moratorium idea is unclear. Cavers sent an early version of his proposal to JBC in Dec. 1946, and JBC cited Cavers "and many others" as sources for his proposal when he wrote JRO in Nov. 1947. Cavers to JBC, Dec. 2, 1946, Atomic Energy Control box 1, Bulletin of Atomic Scientists folder, David F. Cavers Papers, Harvard Law School Library; JBC to JRO, Nov. 1, 1947, JROP, box 27, Conant file. However, no appointments with Cavers appear in JBC's desk calendar and no further communication between the two was located in the Cavers or JBC papers, nor did Cavers indicate in his correspondence any awareness of JBC's War College speech. Probably JBC, anxious that his views not become public, decided not to inform Cavers.

25. See Lincoln Gordon to JRO, Apr. 15, 1947, enclosing Cavers's proposal; JRO to Gordon, Apr. 21, 1947; and Gordon to JRO, Apr. 24, 1947, JROP, box 194, UN/AEC folder. While Harvard Business School professor Gordon viewed Cavers's proposal as "sufficiently persuasive" to have a significant influence on public opinion, he agreed with JRO's objections, "in the sense that the political conditions which would make his kind of agreement possible would also make possible the right kind of agreement." Gordon to Cavers, Apr. 24, 1947, AEC box 1, BAS folder, Cavers Papers. Voicing an objection similar to JRO's, Monsanto president and fellow Acheson-Lilienthal consultant Charles A. Thomas doubted that "any system that depends upon the thwarting

of progress will long be successful." Thomas to Gordon, May 6, 1947. AEC box 1, BAS folder, Cavers Papers.

26. J. K. Galbraith to Cavers, May 7, 1947, AEC box 1, BAS folder, Cavers Papers.
27. Cuthbert Daniels and Arthur M. Squires, "The International Control of Safe Atomic Energy," *Bulletin of the Atomic Scientists* 3:4–5 (Apr.–May 1947), 111–16, 135.
28. JRO commented on the Daniels-Squires proposal in the *New York Herald Tribune,* Apr. 30, 1947, 12, and in private correspondence with its authors: Daniels and Squires to JRO, May 9, 1947; JRO to Daniels and Squires, May 20, 1947, JROP, box 64, Sn-Sq folder.
29. JBC, *MSL,* 493.
30. One State Department adviser urged the appointment of "a man of national prominence such as, for example, President Conant," arguing that the naming of a prominent personage, even if available only on a part-time basis, would counter the "latent" and "mounting" skepticism surrounding the negotiations. Henry G. Ingraham to Charles Fahy, Jan. 27, 1947; Charles Fahy to Dean Acheson, Jan. 28, 1947; both in State Department decimal file, 501.BC Atomic, box 2212, RG 59, NA.
31. Letter, WLM to author, Oct. 10, 1986.
32. "Atomic Energy," speech to Virginia Polytechnic Institute, Apr. 24, 1947, JBC Speech File, 239; "Conant Believes Atom Control Plan Will Succeed," *BG* p.m. edition, Apr. 24, 1947. In that same speech, JBC also acknowledged the prevailing atmosphere of skepticism by emphasizing that a safe atomic pact would include a "transition period" during which "the United States does not run the risk of becoming unilaterally disarmed only to find that the international control scheme is in fact a myth."
33. JBC, speech to U.S. Chamber of Commerce, Washington, D.C., May 1, 1947, JBC Speech File, 241.
34. JBC to Osborn, May 3, 1947, JBC PREP, box 296, folder "Atomic Energy Com.: United Nations, 46–47."
35. Quoted in Richard C. Tolman to JBC, Nov. 26, 1947, Richard C. Tolman Papers, California Institute of Technology archives, Pasadena.
36. JBC to Osborn, May 3, 1947, JBC PREP, box 296, folder "Atomic Energy Com.: United Nations, 46–47." At the same time, however, JBC acknowledged to Osborn that if the U.S. *had* been more forthcoming, then "people like Senator [Robert A.] Taft might have immediately objected because we were suggesting how we were to give away government property!" A month before, the powerful isolationist Republican had given an inkling of his emotions on the subject by declaring that allowing an international agency to locate atomic plants in Russia would be "the limit of all asininity on our part." "Nomination of David E. Lilienthal," speech of Robert A. Taft, Apr. 2, 1947, Medford Evans, *The Secret War for the A-bomb* (Chicago: Henry Regnery Co., 1953), 210, 288, in Bundy, *Danger and Survival,* 191.
37. JBC seemed to recognize, however, that public opinion was running against flexibility in the talks. Any steps involving "the liquidation of American assets of a military nature," he acknowledged to Osborn, would require advance agreement by "military planners and others who could convince the Senate of their wisdom."
38. Osborn to JBC, May 7, 1947, JBC PREP, box 296, folder "Atomic Energy Com.: United Nations, 46–47."
39. "U.S. to Push Moves for U.N. Atom Plan," *NYT,* May 7, 1947.
40. Hewlett and Duncan, *Atomic Shield,* 270; JRO to Robert F. Bacher, Aug. 6, 1947, JROP, box 18, Bacher folder; *IMJRO,* 345.
41. Osborn testimony, *IMJRO,* 343–44; JRO, "The Failure of International Control," *Bulletin of the Atomic Scientists,* Feb. 1948. James W. Kunetka, *Oppenheimer: The Years of Risk,* 126–28.
42. Frederick Osborn diary, Mar. 29, 1947, "UNAEC Diary" folder, box 2, Osborn Papers, HSTL.
43. Herken, *Winning Weapon,* 189–90.
44. "I wish you could have heard the vehemence" with which Canadian, British, French,

and Belgian representatives responded when told of JRO's objection to continuing the talks, Osborn wrote State Department superiors. Osborn to Acheson (unsent draft; shown to Joseph Johnson), May 2, 1947, S/AE, box 23, folder 15F Policy 30 State Department, a. AEC Policy, 1946–1949.

45. Osborn testimony, *IMJRO*, 344–45.
46. Osborn diary, May 14, June 6, 1947, Osborn Papers, HSTL.
47. JBC apparently began urging this departure from the previous U.S. position around the time of his second conference with Osborn, on June 6, which he attended with JRO the day after both had witnessed Marshall's Commencement speech.
48. Paul Fine to Frederick Osborn, June 10, 1947, S/AE, box 22, folder "15 F—Policy 8. AEC Staff Conferences and Consultants, 1946–1949." At least one fellow consultant seemed to approve of the Conant-Oppenheimer scheme. Chester I. Barnard wrote Osborn that "the Conant-Oppenheimer scheme, on further reflection, seems to me to have real merit, assuming that the calculations quoted by Dr. Conant are correct and also assuming that plutonium cannot practicably be denatured. What disturbed me very much yesterday was that more than a year should have developed before the facts of the situation as now reported should have developed." The "calculations" to which Barnard referred are not specified, but may have been figures cited by JBC to show the impracticality of nuclear power for the foreseeable future or the ease of converting plant fuels to weapons. Barnard to Osborn, June 19, 1947, S/AE, box 12, "15A.3 UNAEC—General 3. Organization and Administration, 1947–1949" folder.
49. Johnson to Secretary of State, June 20, 1947, *FRUS*, 1947, I, 526–27.
50. DEL, *AEY*, 216.
51. Boyer, *By the Bomb's Early Light*, 96–97, 294–98; Balogh, *Chain Reaction*, 78–79.
52. DEL, *AEY*, 217.
53. Draft statement on atomic power, appended to minutes, GAC 5, July 28–29, 1947.
54. DEL, *AEY*, 229.
55. Arthur H. Compton to DEL, July 11, 1947, copy in JBC PREP, box 332, "Was-Wek," 1947–48 folder. Also see correspondence in Arthur H. Compton Papers, 1945–1953, series 1, box 1, folder: "Atomic Energy–Industrial," Washington University Libraries, St. Louis, Mo. Also expressing disappointment with Lilienthal's efforts to foster industrial development of atomic energy were Karl T. Compton, Frank B. Jewett, and Ernest O. Lawrence, all of whom expressed their views in July 1947 letters to Arthur Compton.
56. Minutes, GAC 5, July 28–29, 1947, DoE archives; see also Balogh, *Chain Reaction*, 80–84.
57. JRO to Robert F. Bacher, Aug. 6, 1947, JROP, box 18, Bacher folder.
58. JBC to Arthur H. Compton, July 30, 1947, Arthur H. Compton records, 1945–1953, series 1, box 1, folder: "Atomic Energy-Industrial," Washington University Libraries, St. Louis, Mo.
59. For JBC's caution toward new atomic-related ventures favored by the military, such as the nuclear-powered airplane and submarine, and his irritation with military pressure to proceed more quickly, see correspondence in JBC PREP, box 296, "Atomic Energy Commission: JRDB, 1946–47" folder, especially JBC, "Message telephoned by Dr. Langmuir's secretary in Washington," Mar. 4, 1947; JBC to David B. Langmuir, May 3, 1947; David B. Langmuir to JBC, May 14 and 16, 1947; and JBC to David B. Langmuir, May 19, 1947.
60. For the CAE's actions on NEPA and the nuclear submarine at this meeting, see Hewlett and Duncan, *Atomic Shield*, 106. For its decisions on radiological issues, see JBC, Committee on Atomic Energy, to JRDB, Appendices A–F, July 30, 1947. AEC Chairman's Files, Subject File, box 9, "Correspondence—Military Liaison Committee, 1948" folder, RG 326, NA. Though the CAE shunned the radiological warfare idea, it approved projects to develop protective equipment and decontamination devices against radioactivity for soldiers, and rather ominously directed the Armed Forces Special Weapons Project to investigate the limits of "wartime human tolerances for

exposure to radioactivity" given the probability that in an atomic war military operations would occur in heavily contaminated battlefields; precisely how such information would be obtained was not made clear, although the committee noted the AEC's urgent interest in the subject.

61. See William Taubman, *Stalin's American Policy: From Entente to Cold War* (New York: W. W. Norton & Co., 1982), 173-75; Yergin, *Shattered Peace*, 316-17, 324; "Stalin, Czechoslovakia, and the Marshall Plan: New Documentation from the Czecho-Slovak Archives," *Bohemia* 32:1 (1991), 133-44; Scott D. Parrish, "The Turn Towards Confrontation: Soviet Rejection of the Marshall Plan," and Mikhail Narinsky, "The Soviet Union and the Marshall Plan," papers presented to the Cold War International History Project Conference on New Evidence on Cold War History, Moscow, Jan. 12-15, 1993.

62. Osborn to Austin, Aug. 1, 1947, S/AE, box 38, folder 20.5: Austin, Warren.

63. Osborn to Bacher, Aug. 5, 1947, S/AE, box 22, "15F Policy 8. AEC Staff Conferences and Consultants, 1946-1949" folder.

64. JRO to Robert F. Bacher, Aug. 6, 1947, JROP, box 18, Bacher folder.

65. Meeting of Advisers and Consultants, July 31, 1947, S/AE, box 64, "15D AEC Meetings 10. Advisers and Consultants Meetings, 1947 and 1948" folder.

66. Osborn to Austin, Aug. 5, 1947, *FRUS*, 1947, I, 589-90.

67. Osborn to Austin, Aug. 1, 1947, *FRUS*, 1947, I, 586-88.

68. Osborn to Ridgway, Aug. 6, 1947, S/AE, box 22, folder 15F Policy 8. AEC Staff Conferences and Consultants, 1946-1949; Osborn diary, Aug. 4, 1947, HSTL.

69. Quoted in Osborn to Tolman, Aug. 5, 1947, S/AE, box 42, file 20.132 Tolman, Richard.

70. JRO's account of his meeting with Osborn can be found in JRO to Bacher, Aug. 6, 1947, JROP, box 18, Bacher folder.

71. Osborn to Austin, Aug. 5, 1947, *FRUS*, 1947, I, 589-90.

72. Osborn to Ridgway, Aug. 6, 1947, S/AE, box 22, "15F Policy 8. AEC Staff Conferences and Consultants, 1946-1949" folder; Osborn to JBC, Aug. 7, 1947, folder marked "Lawrence Scientific School Committee," JBC PREP, box 303.

73. JBC to Osborn, Aug. 4, 1947, enclosed in Osborn to JRO, Aug. 7, JROP, box 54, Osborn folder.

74. Osborn to Austin, Aug. 5, 1947, *FRUS*, 1947, I, 589-90. For his arguments for staying in the talks, also see Osborn to Tolman, Aug. 5, 1947, S/AE, box 42, file 20.132 Tolman, Richard.

75. JBC to Osborn, Sept. 25, 1947, JBC PREP, box 303, "Lawrence Scientific School Committee" folder. "I am very curious to know more about what happened at Lake Success. I am also curious as to whether Dr. Oppenheimer's or my opinion about the future has proved to be the accurate prognosis of what the American official position is going to be."

76. Charles W. Thayer, "special consultant for Russian broadcasts," to JRO, July 8, 1947, JROP, box 191, "State Department–Atomic Policy Broadcasts to Russia" folder.

77. "General United States Policy with respect to International Control of Atomic Energy (Through and after the Submission of the Second Report of the United Nations Atomic Energy Commission to the Security Council)," PPS 7, Aug. 21, 1947, *FRUS: 1947*, I, 604-608.

78. See, for instance, Halle, *The Cold War as History*, 137.

79. X (George F. Kennan), "The Sources of Soviet Conduct," *Foreign Affairs* 25:4 (July 1947), 566-82; Kennan later explained that he had meant to emphasize political, rather than military, containment, but acknowledged that this distinction was not readily apparent to readers at the time. George F. Kennan, *Memoirs: 1925-1950*, chap. 15.

80. Tuttle, *James B. Conant*, 386; see also Michael Wala, "Selling the Marshall Plan at Home: The Committee for the Marshall Plan to Aid European Recovery," *Diplomatic History* 10:3 (Summer 1986), 247-65.

81. Between Sept. 3 and 17, JBC spoke in, among other cities, Seattle, Portland, San

Francisco, Denver, and Omaha. Texts of these speeches can be found in Harvard University News Office releases of Sept. 8 and Sept. 17, 1947; JBC Speech File, 246, JBC PREP; "Conant Sees Peace Under Atom Pact," *NYT,* Sept. 9, 1947; and *Harvard Alumni Bulletin* 50:1 (Sept. 27, 1947), 14. The "rather strenuous" phrase is from JBC to GC, Sept. 4, 1947, GCP 4:2, "Harvard Corporation: Conant, James B. — 1947" folder.

As JBC voiced his frustration with Moscow, a similarly exasperated Frederick Osborn, who had to face Gromyko day after day at the UN AEC, in desperation suggested establishing a massive scholarly effort to probe Soviet behavior patterns — an idea that led directly to the creation in late 1947 of Harvard's Russian Research Center, the first academic institute for that purpose. See Paul H. Buck Columbia University Oral History interview (Mar. 21, 1967), 21.

82. JBC borrowed this quote, with attribution, from John Fischer's *Why They Behave Like Russians* (New York: Harper & Bros., 1946, 1947), 262.

83. JBC later narrowed his defense of free expression and free speech even in conditions of Cold War, when in June 1949 he publicly excluded Communists from such protections. See chaps. 21–23.

84. This and other quotes from the National War College address may be found in JBC, "The Atomic Age," Oct. 2, 1947, National Defense University archives. The NDU transcript differs in minor aspects from JBC's prepared text, copies of which can be found in the Dwight D. Eisenhower Pre-presidential Papers, 16-52 File, box 27, "James B. Conant (1)" folder, DDEL; the JBC PREP Speech File, the S/AE collection, and other collections. One State Department official noted that the speech contained "the best statement I know of Dr. Conant's own plan for international atomic energy control which substantially differs from the original U.S. proposals." Edmund A. Guillon to Robert Lovett, Oct. 21, 1947, S/AE, box 9, folder "8. Information — Speeches — Statements, General 1947."

85. Referring to Dr. Ralph E. Lapp, an AEC scientist and prominent nuclear power advocate through the 1970s.

86. JBC qualified this offer during the question-and-answer session following the speech, saying that "You have to save a little something to trade in to be sure they actually come through with the bargain. . . . We should still have a lot of secrets about the bomb left to trade." JBC, "The Atomic Age: Discussion," Oct. 2, 1947, National Defense University archives.

87. United Nations Atomic Energy Commission, *Official Records, Special Supplement, Report to the Security Council* (Lake Success, N.Y.: United Nations, 1946), Dec. 31, 1946, 27–28; United Nations Atomic Energy Commission, *Official Records, 2nd Year, Special Supplement, Second Report to the Security Council,* Sept. 11, 1947 (Lake Success, N.Y.: United Nations, 1947), 26.

88. UNAEC, Second Report, 16. In a secret address to the National War College five days after the report was issued, Osborn commented on this little-noticed provision: "The final provision [of the 2nd Report] is one which is entirely new and has had almost no publicity. People miss it. There is a lot of reading in this report and it is all in four or five lines. The provision is this: that the production of nuclear fuel will be at the minimum necessary to supply power plants actually under construction. That means the production of nuclear fuel would stop short all those great plants in the United States, the plants in Canada and England. They would all shut down because power is forty years away, and there won't be any power plants under construction for a long while to come. It means the world would stop making nuclear fuel, which is nothing but bombs. That is the most revolutionary thing, but nobody has noticed it yet." Frederick H. Osborn, "United Nations Atomic Energy Commission," secret speech to the National War College, Sept. 16, 1947, S/AE, box 9, "8. Information — Speeches — Statements, General 1947" folder. Osborn did not explicitly credit JBC for his views, but his comments are in line with what JBC had been advocating privately as a consultant since June.

89. State Department officials sharply disagreed, arguing that the lack of an intensive development role for the international agency would actually make inspection and policing more difficult. "Arguments Against Moratorium on Atomic Power," n.d., handwritten note reads, "Given to Arneson on 18 June 1948," S/AE, box 13, "15A UNAEC—General, 1948" folder; and "Moratorium on Atomic Power," Sept. 1, 1948, S/AE, box 23, "15F Policy 29. Squires-Daniel Power Moratorium Proposal (UNA Committee), 1948–1949" folder.

90. In response to a listener's query, JBC said his plan would permit small-scale atomic activities for scientific and medical research: "You could handle that. But one thing you couldn't do—and this part can only be said inside this room, I am verging on the line of military security—but under those conditions you couldn't look forward to making a lot of atomic power for peaceful purposes. The modification I am supporting would mean the world kissed goodbye to the large-scale use of atomic energy. It wouldn't mean you couldn't have atomic energy in restricted instances like heating the North Pole or whatever people suggest, or that you wouldn't have it for making isotopes and radiation. All that you would have. All that we are actually doing now you would have under this scheme. But you would kiss goodbye to running the mills of Lancaster and revolutionizing China's industry, all of which I think is a mirage anyway barring some unknown discovery." JBC, "The Atomic Age: Discussion," Oct. 2, 1947. JRO had earlier expressed strong disagreement with this idea, pointing out that "research and development, either in the field of tracers [used in medicine] or of the design and development of useful reactors cannot be fruitfully undertaken on so meager a budget of nuclear fuel." JRO to Lincoln Gordon, Apr. 21, 1947, JRO Papers, box 194, UN/AEC folder.

91. Other commentators would later make a similar case for the utility of nuclear disarmament. Almost forty years after JBC's talk, for example, Jonathan Schell echoed his argument that reducing nuclear weapons to zero, especially if all reactors had been dismantled, would offer at least a few weeks or months to head off a full-scale nuclear war, or launch a competing deterring program, if one side violated the agreement and commenced producing weapons. See Schell, *The Abolition* (New York: Alfred A. Knopf, 1984; Avon paperback ed., 1986), 151–52, 172–73, 181, 206–207.

92. JBC, "The Atomic Age: Discussion," Oct. 2, 1947.

93. JBC, *Education in a Divided World*, 232.

94. Forrestal to JBC, Oct. 8, 1947, "National War College, 1946–47" folder, box 305, JBC PREP. In his reply, JBC requested a meeting with Forrestal to "elaborat[e] on certain points which concern the international situation." JBC to Forrestal, Oct. 16, 1947. To JRO he confided that one reason for seeing Forrestal was to discover "whether or not he likes the suggestion of a re-examining of our policy with regard to secrecy." But JBC correctly suspected that Forrestal would not favor the drastic overhaul of secrecy restrictions he was advocating. JBC to JRO, Nov. 1, 1947, JROP, box 27, Conant folder.

95. Gruenther to JBC, Oct. 17, 1947, box 4, Gruenther Papers, DDEL.

96. VB to JBC, Oct. 21, 1947, VBP, box 27, folder 614. Forrestal to Capt. Buchanan and Capt. Berry, Oct. 9, 1947; VB's handwritten comment appears on Buchanan to Souers and VB, Oct. 16, 1947; both in Secretary of Defense Papers, box 43, CD8-1-4, RG 330, NA.

97. JBC to DDE, Oct. 16, 1947; DDE to JBC, Oct. 20, 1947; DDE to Col. Michaels, n.d. (Oct. 20, 1947); both in DDE Pre-Presidential Papers, box 27, James B. Conant (1) file, DDEL. JBC had asked DDE's judgment as to whether his "thinking is at all on the right track," but received only the general's bland assent that "study, patience, open-mindedness and at least a modicum of optimism are necessary to us in these conflicting times."

98. Hill to Tizard: Gruenther to JBC, Oct. 17, 1947, box 4, Gruenther Papers, DDEL; DEL: Carroll L. Wilson to JBC, Nov. 14, 1947, "A.E.C.—General Advisory Committee, 1947–48" folder, box 315, JBC PREP.

99. JBC to Osborn, Oct. 7, 1947; Osborn to JBC, Oct. 17, 1947; both in S/AE, box 22, "15F Policy 8. AEC Staff Conferences and Consultants, 1946–1949" folder.
100. JBC to JRO, Oct. 22, 1947, JROP, box 27, Conant folder.
101. The official history of the Joint Chiefs of Staff acknowledges that by mid-1947, "while lip service was being given to the need for changes in military forces and strategies as a result of the appearance of the atomic bomb, no really definitive recommendations or first principles had been agreed to by planners." James F. Schnabel, *The History of the Joint Chiefs of Staff: The Joint Chiefs of Staff and National Policy: Volume I, 1945–1947* (Wilmington, Del.: Michael Glazier, 1979), 298.
102. JBC to Gruenther, Oct. 7, 1947, and Gruenther to JBC, Oct. 17, 1947, both in box 4, Gruenther Papers, DDEL. It appears that the planning groups were, in fact, quickly established, and JBC and VB were invited to meet with them. See VB to JBC, Oct. 21, 1947, and JBC, "The Impending Atomic Age: 1948 Preview," address to National War College, Sept. 14, 1948, National Defense University archives, Washington, D.C. I was not able to ascertain what these groups ultimately produced, and whether they were involved in the process leading to a number of influential secret Defense Department studies on nuclear war—such as the Harmon Report—which were completed in 1948. In 1952, JBC recalled that the long-range planning group he recommended had been established, and he had met with it once in 1947, but he "had not heard what happened since." JBC, "The Problems of Evaluation of Scientific Research and Development for Military Planning," secret speech to the National War College, Feb. 1, 1952, National Defense University archives.
103. JBC wrote JRO that he was "curious to find out what sections of [the War College speech] seem to recommend themselves to Secretary Forrestal. I am hoping to see him the next time I am in Washington and discover whether or not he likes the suggestion of a reexamining of our policy with regard to secrecy. I am inclined to think this is not one of the suggestions of mine which appeal to him, but perhaps I am wrong." JBC to JRO, Nov. 1, 1947, JROP, box 27, Conant file. The two men scheduled a lunch for November 21, 1947, also attended by Lovett. KF to Forrestal, Nov. 3, 1947, Secretary of Defense papers, box 43, CD8-1-4, RG 330, NA; Forrestal calendar, James V. Forrestal Papers, Princeton University. I was unable to locate any specific record of what was discussed, however. On the subsequent secret study, see chap. 19.
104. VB to JBC, Oct. 21, 1947, VBP, box 27, Conant folder.
105. JRO to JBC, Oct. 29, 1947, JROP, box 27, Conant folder.
106. JBC to JRO, Nov. 1, 1947, JROP, box 27, Conant folder.
107. David F. Cavers, "Atomic Power Versus World Security," *Bulletin of the Atomic Scientists* 3:10 (Oct. 1947), 283–288, 302.
108. "Not That Easy," *New York Herald Tribune*, Oct. 7, 1947; "Atomic Power," *NYT*, Oct. 7, 1947; "Pandora and the Atom," *Providence Journal*, Oct. 5, 1947. Cavers admitted his discouragement at the reaction in a letter to Arthur M. Squires, Oct. 24, 1947. "I have been a little surprised by the attention the article has received and more than a little displeased by the caliber of most of the comment," Cavers wrote. "Very few of the editorial writers seem to have any appreciation of the nature of the proposal or the problem to which it was addressed." A sampling of editorials on the article can be found in the Cavers Papers at the Harvard Law School Library, Atomic Energy Control box 1, Bulletin of Atomic Scientists folder.
109. Gordon Arneson, "Current Aspects of the International Control of Atomic Energy," Dec. 4, 1947, S/AE, box 9, "8. Information—Speeches—Statements, General, 1947" folder.
110. DEL, *AEY,* 244, 259.
111. See rough notes taken the same day "Meeting of Staff Consultants on Friday, December 12, 1947," and a more formal version dated Dec. 17, 1947, both in S/AE,

box 64, "15D AEC Meetings 10. Advisers and Consultants Meetings, 1947 & 1948" folder. For the Feb. 18, 1948, meeting see Osborn diary, HSTL.

112. For the State Department's reasoning in rejecting the moratorium approach, see two secret internal papers: "Arguments Against Moratorium on Atomic Power," n.d., handwritten note reads, "Given to Arneson on 18 June 1948," S/AE, box 13, "15A UNAEC—General, 1948" folder; and "Moratorium on Atomic Power," Sept. 1, 1948, S/AE, box 23, "15F Policy 29. Squires-Daniel Power Moratorium Proposal (UNA Committee), 1948–1949" folder. Quotes in the text are from "Arguments Against Moratorium on Atomic Power."

113. That such an idea could even be raised, the Soviet commentator declared, proved that "modern capitalism" represented "the biggest obstacle" to scientific progress, while "true science" was on the side of the Communist camp. M. Rubinstein, "Ideology of Atomic Imperialism," *New Times* 41 (Oct. 6, 1948), 31, in Cavers Papers, Atomic Energy Control box 1, "Atomic Energy Control/Clippings 1947" folder.

CHAPTER 19

1. See Marc Trachtenberg, "A 'Wasting Asset': American Strategy and the Shifting Nuclear Balance, 1949–54," *International Security* 13:7 (Winter 1988/89), 5–49.
2. The subject of popular and cultural responses to the bomb's emergence has only recently received serious scholarly attention: examples include Boyer, *By the Bomb's Early Light*; Spencer Weart, *Nuclear Fear* (Cambridge: Harvard University Press, 1988); and Jeff Smith, *Unthinking the Unthinkable: Nuclear Weapons and Western Culture* (Bloomington, Ind.: Indiana University Press, 1989).
3. Minutes, GAC 6, Oct. 3–5, 1947, DoE archives; Hewlett and Duncan, *Atomic Shield*, 117; Balogh, *Chain Reaction*, 85–90; Steven L. Del Sesto, *Science, Politics, and Controversy: Civilian Nuclear Power in the United States, 1946–1974* (Boulder, Colo.: Westview, 1979), 39.
4. *New York Herald Tribune*, Oct. 9, 1947. At the same time, he tried to rouse industry's enthusiasm by creating an Industrial Advisory Committee to the AEC, modeled after the General Advisory Committee, to "speed up industrial opportunities" in the field of atomic energy. *NYT*, "Lilienthal Names Industry Advisers," Oct. 7, 1947.
5. Minutes, GAC 7, Nov. 21–23, 1947, DoE archives.
6. Minutes, GAC 6, Oct. 3–5, 1947.
7. Minutes, GAC 6, Oct. 3–5, 1947; GAC 7, Nov. 21–23, 1947. Interestingly, at this juncture the advisers apparently did not express any qualms, moral or otherwise, about developing the "Super," only a view that the weapon's perfection appeared so distant that lessening security restrictions could only promote progress.
8. GAC 7, Nov. 21–23, 1947.
9. As David Alan Rosenberg has commented, the "obsessive secrecy surrounding all atomic information during this period meant that even the highest policymakers did not have ready access to information about American nuclear capability. From the fall of 1945 to the spring of 1947, President Truman was not officially advised of the state of the American nuclear stockpile . . . High-level military decision-makers were no better informed. . . ." David Alan Rosenberg, "The Origins of Overkill: Nuclear Weapons and American Strategy, 1945–1960," in Steven E. Miller, ed., *Strategy and Nuclear Deterrence* (Princeton, N.J.: Princeton University Press, 1984), 121.
10. JBC, "The Atomic Age," Oct. 2, 1947, National Defense University archives.
11. JBC, "The Atomic Age: Discussion," Oct. 2, 1947, National Defense University archives.
12. Rosenberg, "U.S. Nuclear Stockpile, 1945 to 1950," *Bulletin of the Atomic Scientists* 38 (May 1982), 25–30.
13. GAC 7, Nov. 21–23, 1947.

14. JBC to JRO, Nov. 1, 1947, JROP, box 27, Conant folder; see also KF to Forrestal, Nov. 3, 1947, Secretary of Defense Papers, box 43, CD8-1-4, RG 330, NA; Forrestal calendar, James V. Forrestal Papers, Mudd Library, Princeton University.
15. GAC 7, Nov. 21–23, 1947.
16. GAC 7, Nov. 21–23, 1947.
17. Cited in Hewlett and Duncan, *Atomic Shield,* 116; see also Balogh, *Chain Reaction,* 83.
18. Hewlett and Duncan, *Atomic Shield,* 3–4.
19. JBC, "The Atomic Age: Discussion," Oct. 2, 1947, National Defense University archives.
20. DEL to JBC, Nov. 26, 1947, JBC PREP, box 315, "A.E.C.–General Advisory Committee, 1947–48" folder; DEL, "Democracy and the Atom," Nov. 28, 1947, AEC press release, Nov. 24, 1947, copy in S/AE, box 9, "Speeches–Statements: General, 1947" folder; JBC to DEL, Dec. 4, 1947, DEL Papers, Princeton University; and JBC PREP, box 315, "A.E.C.–General Advisory Committee, 1947–48" folder; DEL to JBC, Dec. 9, 1947, DEL Papers, Princeton University; "Lilienthal Urges Wide Atom Study," *NYT,* Nov. 29, 1947.
21. "Lilienthal Calls for Doubling Our Atomic Energy Outlays," *NYT,* Dec. 3, 1947.
22. "Democracy and the Atom," Nov. 28, 1947.
23. Robert M. Hutchins, "The Bomb Secret Is Out!" *American Magazine,* Dec. 1947.
24. JBC to H. D. Smyth, Dec. 5, 1947; H. D. Smyth to JBC, Dec. 3, 1947, w. enc.; both in Conant folder, Smyth Papers, American Philosophical Society.
25. JBC to DEL, Dec. 4, 1947, DEL Papers, Princeton University, and JBC PREP, box 315, "A.E.C.–General Advisory Committee, 1947–48" folder; see also Hewlett and Duncan, *Atomic Shield,* 122–23.
26. DEL to JBC, Dec. 9, 1947, DEL Papers, Princeton University; DEL, *AEY,* 261–63, 268, omits the candid assessments of JBC's letter and animus for Hutchins contained in the original diary entry in DEL diaries, Dec. 14, 1947, DEL Papers, Mudd Library, Princeton University.
27. JBC to DEL, Dec. 18, 1947, DEL Papers; "Big Farm Aid Seen in Atomic Energy," *NYT,* Dec. 18, 1947.
28. Carl Spaatz to VB, Jan. 7, 1948, VBP, box 107, folder 2502: Spaatz, Carl. At Spaatz's request, VB arranged a three-way meeting (VB, JBC, Spaatz) on Jan. 17, 1948, but the conference failed to shake JBC's skepticism. VB to JBC (telegram), Jan. 16, 1948, JBC PREP, box 315, "A.E.C.–General Advisory Committee, 1947–48" folder.
29. Minutes, GAC 8, Feb. 6–8, 1948. JBC's desk calendar records a lunch with Lawrence on Mar. 17, 1948; shortly afterward, George B. Kistiakowsky wrote an air force scientist based at the Rand Corporation that Lawrence's recent visit to Boston had been "occasioned by the skepticism of Conant about the practicability of the use of radioactive materials in warfare, and Lawrence's desire to convince him." George B. Kistiakowsky to David T. Griggs, Apr. 14, 1948, courtesy of Elaine Kistiakowsky; for Lawrence's interest in radiological warfare and impatience with JBC's skepticism also see Davis, *Lawrence and Oppenheimer,* 267–68, and testimony of Luis A. Alvarez, *IMJRO,* 805. Lawrence may also have raised the radiological warfare issue when he hosted JBC in Berkeley in Sept. 1947.
30. Minutes, GAC 10, June 4–6, 1948, DoE archives.
31. JRO et al., to HST, Dec. 31, 1947, PSF–Subject File, box 200, "NSC–Atomic–Atomic Energy Advisory Committee" folder, HSTL.
32. DEL, *AEY,* 248–52.
33. JBC to JRO, Jan. 5, 1948, Conant file, box 27, JROP.
34. JBC to JRO, Jan. 5, 1948, Conant file, box 27, JROP.
35. DEL, *AEY,* 287–88; Hewlett and Duncan, *Atomic Shield,* 151–52; James V. Forrestal diary, Princeton University; JBC appointment calendar, JBC PREP.
36. JBC, "The Atomic Age: Discussion," Oct. 2, 1947, National Defense University archives.
37. Osborn diary, Feb. 18, 1948, Osborn Papers, HSTL.

38. "Meeting of Advisers, A.E.C., February 25, 1948," n.d., and "Notes on Meeting of Delegation Consultants, Wednesday, 25 February, 1948," Feb. 27, 1948, both in S/AE, box 64, "15D AEC Meetings 10. Advisers and Consultants Meetings, 1947 & 1948" folder.

39. See Yergin, *Shattered Peace*, 343–60; Truman, *Memoirs*, vol. 2, *Years of Trial and Hope*, 1946–1952 (Garden City, N.Y.: Doubleday & Co., 1956), 240–44; Lucius D. Clay, *Decision in Germany* (Garden City, N.Y.: Doubleday, 1950), 353–57; Kennan, *Memoirs: 1945–1950*, 397–404; Lawrence S. Kaplan, *NATO and the United States: The Enduring Alliance* (Boston: Twayne Publishers, 1988), 16–24; Margaret Truman, *Harry S. Truman* (New York: William Morrow, 1973; Pocket Book ed., 1974), 391–93.

40. See Richard M. Freeland, *The Truman Doctrine and the Origins of McCarthyism: Foreign Policy, Domestic Politics, and Internal Security*, 1946–1948 (New York: Schocken reprint ed., 1974), 264–87; Yergin, *Shattered Peace*, 350.

41. Tuttle, *James B. Conant*, 387; JBC to Zechariah Chafee, June 20, 1949, Chafee Papers, box 34, folder 19.

42. See "Conant Withdraws Delegate to Prague," *THC*, Apr. 5, 1948.

43. JBC to Reinhold Niebuhr, Mar. 12, 1948, correspondence, box 6, "Harvard University, 1948–9" folder, Niebuhr Papers, LC.

44. JBC to Niebuhr, Mar. 12, 1948.

45. "Conant Predicts No Russian War in Eliot House Speech," *THC*, Mar. 20, 1948; JBC, "Some Problems of an Armed Truce," speech to Boston Rotary Club, Mar. 24, 1948, JBC Speech File, 260; "Conant Says: NO WAR, BUT ARMED TRUCE," *BG*, Mar. 24, 1948; "Conant Sees War Far Off," *Boston Herald*, Mar. 25, 1948; "Conant Urges Marshall Plan, UMT to Halt Soviet Advance," *THC*, Mar. 25, 1948.

46. JBC, "Some Problems of an Armed Truce," speech to Boston Rotary Club, Mar. 24, 1948, JBC Speech File, 260.

47. On the U.S. intervention in the 1948 Italian elections see James Edward Miller, *The United States and Italy*, 1940–1950: THE POLITICS AND DIPLOMACY OF STABILIZATION (Chapel Hill, N.C.: University of North Carolina Press, 1986), chap. 8; John Ranelagh, *The Agency: The Rise and Decline of the CIA* (Simon & Schuster, 1986; rev. reprint ed., Touchstone Books, 1987), 115, 176–78; Gregory F. Treverton, *The Limits of Intervention in the Postwar World* (New York: Basic, 1987), 20, 35–38, 73; Richard J. Barnet, *The Alliance* (New York: Simon & Schuster, 1983), 116, 139–40; Burton Hersh, *The Old Boys: The American Elite and the Origins of the CIA* (New York: Scribner's, 1992), 222–23, 231–32, 292–94. See also the recently published, but still partially classified, official CIA history for this period: Arthur B. Darling, *The Central Intelligence Agency: An Instrument of Government, to* 1950 (University Park: Pennsylvania State University Press, 1990), esp. 245–81.

48. See Melvyn P. Leffler, "The American Conception of National Security and the Beginnings of the Cold War, 1945–1948," *American Historical Review* 89:2 (Apr. 1984), 346–81, esp. 372–73, 379–80, and Leffler, *A Preponderance of Power*, passim.

49. The NSC approved that course on Mar. 11, though the precise form of intervention following a Communist victory was left open pending a subsequent decision. For a concise summary of U.S. responses to the prospect of an Italian Communist victory, see Steven L. Rearden, *History of the Office of the Secretary of Defense, vol. 1, The Formative Years: 1947–1950* (Washington: Historical Office, Office of the Secretary of Defense, 1984), 169–75. See also documents in *FRUS*, 1948, III.

50. Kennan to Marshall, Mar. 15, 1948, *FRUS*, 1948, III, 848–49, in Barnet, *The Alliance*, 139–40.

51. JBC, "Some Problems of an Armed Truce," speech to Boston Rotary Club, Mar. 24, 1948, JBC Speech File, 260.

52. JBC to VB, Mar. 19, 1948 "Bu-By" folder, box 317, JBC PREP.

53. Francis J. Brown to JBC, Mar. 25, 1948, JBC PREP, box 314, "American Council on Education, 1947–48" folder.

54. JBC to Raymond Walters, Mar. 29, 1948, JBC PREP, box 314, "American Council on Education, 1947–48" folder. JBC proposed that the educators seek only deferments for World War II veterans and students "over say 23 years of age who are engaged in industries essential to the military establishments or in preparation for careers in engineering, science, medicine, or dentistry." With characteristic unsentimentality, JBC grudgingly conceded that there would be a deferment for married men: "personally I have never seen the reason for this, but it appears to be one of the fixed American customs."

    In the event, the educators seemed to toss the ball into HST's court by deciding that deferments should be determined on the basis of "national needs" by the National Security Resources Board. "Minutes of Special Meeting of Committee on the Relationships of Higher Education to the Federal Government," Apr. 1, 1948, JBC PREP, box 314, "American Council on Education, 1947–48" folder.

55. NSC 7, "The Position of the United States with Respect to Soviet-Directed World Communism," Mar. 30, 1948, *FRUS,* 1948, I (part 2), 546–50, in Thomas H. Etzold and John Lewis Gaddis, eds., *Containment: Documents on American Policy and Strategy,* 1945–1950 (New York: Columbia University Press, 1978), 164–69.

56. JBC to VB, Mar. 29, 1948, "Bu-By" correspondence folder, box 317, JBC PREP.

57. JBC, "Some Problems of an Armed Truce," speech to Boston Rotary Club, Mar. 24, 1948, JBC Speech File, 260.

58. See JBC to Cord Meyer, Jr., Jan. 7, 1948; Meyer, Jr., to JBC, Dec. 26, 1947; Meyer to *Harvard Alumni Bulletin,* Dec. 26, 1947; all in GCP 8:6. Meyer had earlier strongly denied that the world government movement advocated force to achieve its aims, as opposed to those people "led by James Burnham who believes in the establishment of an American empire by threat and by force, if necessary." See also Bertrand Russell, "The Atomic Bomb and the Prevention of War," *Bulletin of the Atomic Scientists* 2:7–8 (Oct. 1, 1946), 19–21.

59. Brock Chisholm, "Human Relations and the World Scene," Apr. 28, 1948, copy in FPF.

60. See Leo P. Brophy, Wyndham D. Miles, and Rexmond C. Cochrane, *The Chemical Warfare Service: From Laboratory to Field (United States Army in World War II: The Technical Services)* (Washington, D.C.: Office of the Chief of Military History, Department of the Army, 1959), chap. 5; Jeanne McDermott, *The Killing Winds: The Menace of Biological Warfare* (New York: Arbor House, 1987), esp. 139–45, Barton J. Bernstein, "America's Biological Warfare Program in the Second World War," *Journal of Strategic Studies* 11 (Sept. 1988), 292–317, Bernstein, "Origins of the U.S. Biological Warfare Program," and Susan Wright, "Evolution of Biological Warfare Policy, 1945–1990," in Susan Wright, ed., *Preventing a Biological Arms Race* (Cambridge: MIT Press, 1990). Marquand worked as a special consultant for Merck on biological warfare during World War II, assembled a classified report when the war ended, and helped compose a limited public release that emphasized defensive rather than offensive preparations. See correspondence in the Marquand Papers at Houghton Library, Harvard University, and the account in Bell, *Marquand: An American Life.*

61. JBC to VB, Sept. 27, 1945, VBP, box 27, folder 614, responding to VB, "Notes toward an atom statement," enc. with VB to JBC, Aug. 29, 1945, VBP, Carnegie Institution archives, Washington, D.C.

62. JBC, "The Atomic Age," speech to the National War College, Sept. 16, 1946, National Defense University archives, Washington, D.C.

63. JBC to Roger Adams, Sept. 19, 1946, box 2, Conant file, Adams Papers, University of Illinois Library (Urbana).

64. Roger Adams to JBC, Sept. 21, 1946, JBC PREP, box 309, "National Defense Research Committee, 1946–47" folder.

65. McDermott, *Killing Winds,* 146–47.

66. JBC to VB, Apr. 29, 1948, "Bu-By" correspondence folder, box 317, JBC PREP.

67. VB to JBC, May 13, 1948, "Bu-By" correspondence folder, box 317, JBC PREP.

68. JBC, "The Impending Atomic Age: 1948 Preview," Sept. 14, 1948, National Defense University archives, Washington, D.C.

69. JBC to James V. Forrestal, Oct. 27, 1948, JBC PREP, box 354, "Secretary of Defense, 1948–49" folder.

70. *NYT,* Mar. 13, 1949, in McDermott, *Killing Winds,* 147. In secret, however, VB's recommendation had prompted statements of a different kind. Forrestal assembled a dozen military and scientific experts on a high-level Ad Hoc Committee on Biological Warfare which intensively studied the subject during 1949 and concluded that the weapons were "at present potent, but not decisive," and recommended urgent measures to develop offensive and defensive BW capabilities. Report of the Secretary of Defense's Ad Hoc Committee on Biological Warfare, July 11, 1949, DDE Pre-Presidential Papers, box 62, "Johnson, Louis (2)" folder, DDEL.

71. See Avi Shlaim, *The United States and the Berlin Blockade: A Study in Crisis Decision-Making* (Berkeley: University of California Press, 1983).

72. JBC, *Education in a Divided World,* 218–19.

73. JBC, *Education in a Divided World,* 219–20.

74. JBC, *Education in a Divided World,* 223.

75. JBC, "Discussion following Lecture [to National War College] on The Atomic Age," Sept. 14, 1948, National Defense University archives, Washington, D.C.

76. See Richard H. Pells, *The Liberal Mind in a Conservative Age: American Intellectuals in the 1940 and 1950s* (New York: Harper & Row, 1985), 126.

77. Robert Whitney, "When Will the Shooting Start?" *Harvard Alumni Bulletin* 51 (Sept. 1948), 68ff.

78. JBC, "The Atomic Age: Discussion," Sept. 16, 1946, National Defense University archives, Washington, D.C.

79. JBC, "The Atomic Age: Discussion," Oct. 2, 1947, National Defense University archives, Washington, D.C.

80. JBC, "The Impending Atomic Age: 1948 Preview," Sept. 14, 1948, National Defense University archives, Washington, D.C. Among the world federalists JBC may have had in mind were his least favorite educator, Robert Hutchins, and his politically estranged friend Grenville Clark, who the previous month had vainly sent JBC a petition calling for an ad hoc Berlin peace effort. For the latter, see JBC to GC, Aug. 31, 1948, in response to Aug. 2, 1948 draft petition, GCP 13:27.

81. JBC also elaborated at some length the importance of preserving the country's resources, freedoms, and emotional stability during the period of armed truce—for as long as necessary to convince the Moscow Marxists that the capitalist camp did not intend to fold on its own. Then, the Soviets might seek a "joint retreat" from nuclear weapons, although he acknowledged that "raising the iron curtain will be for the Soviets like pulling teeth." When the day came that the U.S.-Soviet atomic talks could resume, JBC still hoped that his "alternative" proposal—"destruction of all but a trace of nuclear fuels and a tight control of all raw materials"—would form the basis for an agreement, since atomic power remained to JBC as illusory as ever.

82. James V. Forrestal to JBC, Oct. 16, 1948, JBC PREP, box 354, "Secretary of Defense, 1948–49" folder.

83. Kennan, *Memoirs, 1925–1950,* 354–55; "instrument of our foreign policy": Forrestal to Secretary of State, Mar. 8, 1946, quoted in Freeland, *Truman Doctrine,* 138.

84. JBC to James V. Forrestal, Oct. 27, 1948 (there is also a carbon dated Oct. 26), JBC PREP, box 354, "Secretary of Defense, 1948–49" folder.

85. JBC to Edward A. Weeks, Oct. 26, 1948, JBC PREP, box 336, "Atlantic Monthly, 1948–49" folder.

86. This and subsequent quotes are from JBC, "Force and Freedom in the 17th and 20th Century," Oct. 27, 1948, JBC Speech File, 271; Harvard News Office press release, Oct. 28, 1948.

87. JBC, "Force and Freedom," *Atlantic Monthly* 183 (Jan. 1949), 19–22; Edward A.

Weeks to JBC, Dec. 14, 1948, JBC PREP, box 336, "Atlantic Monthly, 1948–49" folder.
88. *Washington Post,* Jan. 9, 1949.
89. James V. Forrestal to William R. Matthews, Mar. 3, 1949, quoted in Arnold A. Rogow, *James Forrestal: A Study of Personality, Politics and Policy* (New York: Macmillan, 1963), 207–209.
90. Randolph, Vt., *White River Herald,* Jan. 6, 1949.
91. JBC, *Education in a Divided World,* 50.
92. JBC, "The Atomic Age," Sept. 14, 1948, National Defense University archives.
93. Transcript of Educational Policies Commission meeting 32, Sept. 22–25, 1948, 98–99, National Education Association archives, Washington, D.C.
94. JBC to William G. Carr, Jan. 28, 1949, JBC PREP, box 340, "Educational Policies Commission, 1948–49" folder.
95. "Notes on the Meeting of the Subcommittee on AEC," Mar. 11, 1949, JBC PREP, box 340, "Educational Policies Commission, 1948–49" folder. The group's members were JBC, Carr, William Jansen, and Paul R. Mort.

CHAPTER 20

1. NSC-30, "United States Policy on Atomic Weapons," Sept. 10, 1948, appears in *FRUS,* 1948, I (part 2), 624–28, and is reprinted in Etzold and Gaddis, eds., *Containment,* 339–42.
2. Bradley Dewey, "High Policy and the Atomic Bomb," *Atlantic Monthly,* Dec. 1948, 38; William D. Leahy, chief of staff to the commander in chief of the armed forces, "Memorandum for the Secretary of Defense," Jan. 8, 1948, records of the Secretary of Defense, RG 330, CD 25-1-12, NA; KTC, "U.S. Policies Governing the Use of Certain New Weapons and Release of Information Regarding the Capabilities of, and Defense Against, the Use of these Weapons," n.d. but apparently written between Mar. 8 and 14, 1949, FPF, JFD Papers, Princeton University Library, Princeton, N.J.
3. *The Evaluation of the Atomic Bomb as a Military Weapon: The Final Report of the Joint Chiefs of Staff Evaluation Board for Operation Crossroads,* June 30, 1947, copy attached to Forrestal to HST, Apr. 6, 1948, PSF, General File, HSTL. I am grateful to David Alan Rosenberg for copies of this and several other documents on the Conant Committee. Also serving on the JCS Evaluation Board were, in addition to KTC and Dewey, former Maj. Gen. T. F. Farrell, the only other civilian member; Gen. J. W. Stilwell, who died and was succeeded by Lt. Gen. A. C. Wedemeyer; Lt. Gen. L. H. Brereton; Vice Adm. John H. Hoover; and Rear Adm. Ralph A. Ofstie.
4. Leahy to Forrestal, Jan. 8, 1948, records of the Secretary of Defense, CD 25-1-12, RG 330, NA.
5. See Yergin, *Shattered Peace,* 357.
6. Forrestal to HST, Apr. 6, 1948, Atomic Bomb file, PSF, General File, HSTL; also in PSF, Subject File, box 157, Secretary of Defense, Special Letters, J. Forrestal, HSTL.
7. The quotations following are from Bradley Dewey, "High Policy and the Atomic Bomb," *Atlantic Monthly,* Dec. 1948, 37–39.
8. Dewey's intention to go public with his views is referred to in VB to Leahy, Dec. 18, 1947, "Enclosure D," with James V. Forrestal to HST, Apr. 6, 1948, Atomic Bomb file, PSF, General File, HSTL; also in PSF, Subject File, box 157, Secretary of Defense, Special Letters, J. Forrestal, HSTL.
9. VB to Forrestal, Dec. 20, 1948, FPF.
10. See Hewlett and Duncan, *Atomic Shield,* 352–53.
11. KTC, "U.S. Policies Governing the Use of Certain New Weapons and Release of Information Regarding the Capabilities of, and Defense Against, the Use of these

Weapons," n.d. (Mar. 1949), FPF; KTC to JFD, Mar. 1949, FPF, and in KTC to Louis
   T. Johnson, Oct. 26, 1949, CD 3-1-31, TSRD entry 199A, RG 330, NA.
12. KTC, "U.S. Policies Governing . . . "
13. DEL to Commissioners, Mar. 30, 1949, box 4, "Commissioners—Miscellaneous"
   folder, Chairman's Files, Offices Files, David E. Lilienthal, Subject File, 1946–1950,
   AEC records, RG 326, NA.
14. KTC, "U.S. Policies Governing . . . "; Black recalls that VB and Forrestal were
   mainly responsible for stocking the committee; interview with author, Feb. 1985.
15. JBC to KTC, May 2, 1949, FPF.
16. At another point the paper stated: "It is by no means certain . . . that the Soviets will
   have 100 bombs by 1960 and experts differ widely as to the time-scale of their
   armament with this weapon." These and all other statements from the capabilities
   paper are found in "Capabilities of the Weapons Mentioned in the Directive from the
   Secretary of Defense," undated but written in Apr. 1949, CD 3-1-31 TSRD entry
   199A, RG 330, NA (hereafter, "Capabilities" paper). For more extensive excerpts,
   also see Hershberg, *James B. Conant, Nuclear Weapons, and the Cold War,* 1945–1950,
   609–15.
17. In the case of the Soviet nuclear stockpile, the projections were a full order of
   magnitude off the mark, and had to be radically revised upward following the U.S.
   detection, in Sept. 1949, of the first Soviet atomic explosion. By Feb. 10, 1950, less
   than a year after the experts placed a ceiling of 100 Soviet fission bombs by 1960, the
   CIA's Office of Reports and Estimates (ORE) was predicting a Soviet arsenal of 100
   bombs by 1953 and 200 by the end of 1955. In 1955 a CIA National Intelligence
   Estimate predicted a Soviet stockpile of between 1,540 and 1,760 weapons by
   mid-1959 and between 1,850 and 2,450 by mid-1960. John Prados, *The Soviet
   Estimate: U.S. Intelligence Analysis and Russian Military Strength* (New York: Dial
   Press, 1982), 21–23. Another source estimated that the Soviet stockpile held 340
   warheads in 1955 and 2,220 by 1960. "Military record of CBR/atomic happenings,"
   Aviation Studies Atlantic (London), Jan. 1982, in *Armaments or Disarmament,*
   Stockholm International Peace Research Institute, 1983. Though not mentioned, the
   Pentagon briefers of the Conant committee may also have underestimated the size of
   the American supply of nuclear weapons a decade hence: 18,000. Rosenberg,
   "Origins of Overkill," 133.
18. The Soviets tested a prototype ICBM by 1957, and deployed a number of "primitive,
   first generation" models over the next five years. Richard Smoke, "The Evolution of
   American Defense Policy," in John F. Reichart and Steven R. Sturm, eds., *American
   Defense Policy* (Baltimore: Johns Hopkins University Press, 1982), 115. The U.S.
   built an Atlas ICBM with a range of 2,500 miles by Aug. 1958 and began deploying
   Minutemen in 1962. Herbert York, *Race to Oblivion: A Participant's View of the
   Arms Race* (New York: Simon & Schuster, 1970), 94, 97. For Bush's predictions, see
   Modern Arms and Free Men (New York: Simon & Schuster, 1949), 116; Greenberg,
   The Politics of Pure Science, 139 n; Lawrence Freedman, *The Evolution of Nuclear
   Strategy* (New York: St. Martin's Press, 1981), 27–28.
19. Interview with author, Feb. 1985. At the time, in fact, JBC had good reason for
   doubting the technical basis for the hydrogen bomb—the designs then being bandied about ultimately proved fruitless, and it was not until the spring of 1951 that a
   workable concept for the superweapon emerged. See chap. 24 and 30.
20. JBC to KTC, with draft final report, n.d. but circulated to JFD on July 22, 1949, FPF.
   The names of the opposing factions do not appear on a committee document until
   Sept. 1949, but it seems plausible to extrapolate backward to July. Black confirmed
   that no dramatic shifts in position took place among committee members other than
   Eisenhower's reversal in October.
21. Draft final report, with JBC to KTC, July 22, 1949, FPF.
22. Remarks by the four interviewed figures appear in the following documents, all in
   FPF: Black to JBC, July 7, 1949, re Vandenberg; Black to JBC, July 8, 1949, re

Roberts; Black to JBC, July 12, 1949, re Acheson; Black to JBC, July 19, 1949, re Van Dusen. It should be noted that the quoted comments are as summarized by Black.
23. Draft final report of Conant committee (with "Majority Opinion" and "Minority Opinion"), n.d. but distributed to JFD on July 22, 1949, FPF.
24. The second draft account is based on JBC et al. to KTC (not transmitted), "Draft of the Committee's Final report," Aug. 1, 1949, FPF.
25. JBC to committee, Aug. 1, 1949, FPF.
26. JBC to committee, Sept. 23, 1949, Louis Johnson folder, box 56, 1916–52, DDEL.
27. JBC et al. to KTC, Sept. 28, 1949, Louis Johnson folder, box 56, 1916–52, DDEL.
28. JBC to committee, Sept. 23, 1949, attachment to JBC et al. to KTC, Sept. 28, 1949.
29. DDE to Edwin F. Black, Oct. 5, 1949, Louis Johnson folder, box 56, DDE Papers, 1916–1952, DDEL.
30. JBC et al. to KTC, "Conant Committee Report," Oct. 15, 1949, CD 3-1-31, RG 330, NA.
31. DEL, *AEY,* 581.
32. McGeorge Bundy, "The Missed Chance to Stop the H–Bomb," *New York Review of Books* (May 13, 1982), 13.
33. U.S. Department of Defense, *Semiannual Report of the Secretary of Defense et al. July 1 to December 31, 1949* (Washington: 1950), 63–72. The Conant committee also coincided with the preparation of a government-sponsored handbook on the effects of nuclear weapons, though it is not clear whether the panel had any role in its publication. *The Effects of Atomic Weapons* (Washington, D.C.: Government Printing Office, 1950).
34. KTC to JBC, Oct. 26, 1949; JBC to KTC, Nov. 3, 1949; both in JBC PREP, box 381, "Research and Development Board (National Military Establishment), 1949–50" folder. DDE also reacted ambivalently to a similar note of thanks sent by KTC, responding that it "made me squirm just a bit because I did not feel that the 'fishing party,' during its deliberations, was ever able to provide you with convincing arguments or advice." DDE to KTC, Oct. 27, 1949, in Louis Galambos, ed., *The Papers of Dwight David Eisenhower* (Baltimore: Johns Hopkins University Press, 1984), 10:799–800.
35. Louis Johnson to HST, Oct. 31, 1949, HST PSF—General File, box 112, Atomic Bomb folder, HSTL.

CHAPTER 21

1. Associated Press report, June 8, 1948; *THC,* June 9, 1949; *NYT,* June 9, 1949; "Anti-Party Line," *Time* 53:25 (June 20, 1949), 52.
2. "Truman Says Reds Should Not Teach," *NYT,* June 10, 1949.
3. "But that ray is still dim indeed," the paper quickly added, blasting JBC for his continued opposition to loyalty oaths for teachers and on-campus investigations to root out faculty subversives. "President Conant's Inconsistency," *Manchester Union,* June 24, 1949.
4. JBC used such rhetoric consistently in speeches and writings from 1946 through mid-1948, e.g., his speech to Ohio University's commencement on June 9, 1947, JBC Speech File, 244, and *President's Report,* 1947 (Jan. 12, 1948), *Official Register of Harvard University* 46:30 (Dec. 1, 1949) (Cambridge: Harvard University, 1949), 6–8.
5. *THC,* June 9, 1949.
6. *Pawtucket-Central Falls [R.I.] Times,* June 10, 1949.
7. JBC, "Remarks of President Conant to the Harvard Foundation for Advanced Study and Research," June 22, 1949, copies in JBC Speech File; *THC, BG,* June 23, 1949.
8. Sources consulted for the "Red scare" included: Peter H. Buckingham, *America Sees Red: Anticommunism in America, 1870s to 1980s* (Claremont, Calif.: Regina Books, 1988); David Caute, *The Great Fear: The Anti-Communist Purge Under Truman*

and Eisenhower (New York: Simon & Schuster, 1978); Freeland, *The Truman Doctrine and the Origins of McCarthyism;* M. J. Heale, *American Anticommunism: Combating the Enemy Within,* 1830–1970 (Baltimore: Johns Hopkins University Press, 1990); Murray B. Levin, *Political Hysteria in America: The Democratic Capacity for Repression* (New York: Basic Books, 1971); and Ellen W. Schrecker, *No Ivory Tower: McCarthyism and the Universities* (New York: Oxford University Press, 1986).

9. For "most deadly illusion" quote see Chester I. Barnard to JRO, Feb. 10, 1950, in Herken, *Winning Weapon,* 338.

10. J. Edgar Hoover to George E. Allen (to be passed to HST), May 29, 1946, PSF— Subject File, box 167, "Subject File—FBI—Atomic Bomb" folder, HSTL. The alleged leaders of the spy ring were as follows: State Department: Acheson, Marks, McCloy; War: Howard C. Peterson; Commerce: Henry Wallace; Bureau of the Budget: Paul H. Appleby, George Schwartzwalder; Bureau of Standards: Edward U. Condon; United Nations: Alger Hiss, Abe Feller, Paul Appleby (to be transferred from Budget); Office of War Mobilization and Reconversion: James R. Newman; Advisers to the JCAE: James R. Newman, Condon.

11. JBC to Zechariah Chafee, June 20, 1949, Chafee Papers, box 34, folder 19, Harvard Law School Library, Cambridge.

12. JBC, "The Atomic Age," secret speech to the National War College, National Defense University archives, Washington, D.C. In his draft, JBC had written, "All this and no way out but war," but softened the spoken version to, "All this and no way out if we go it alone."

13. JBC to Connor, Oct. 11, 1946, JBC PREP, Box 311, "U.S. Navy Department, 1946–47" folder.

14. Ralph Connor to JBC, Oct. 9, 1946; this letter, like other documentation of the Paul case, can be found in JBC PREP, Box 311, "U.S. Navy Department, 1946–47" folder.

15. One JBC protégé, Louis P. Hammett, a professor at Columbia and one of those vouching for Paul, warmly commended his former instructor's willingness "to lend your wisdom and influence in this manner." Louis P. Hammett to JBC, Oct. 25, 1946, JBC PREP, box 311, "U.S. Navy Department, 1946–47" folder. See also L. H. Farinholt to JBC, Oct. 22, 1946.

16. JBC to James V. Forrestal, Oct. 31, 1946, enc. Ralph Connor to Forrestal, Oct. 23, 1946; L. H. Farinholt to Forrestal, Oct. 22, 1946; and Louis Hammett to Forrestal, Oct. 25, 1946, JBC PREP, box 311, "U.S. Navy Department, 1946–47" folder.

17. John L. Sullivan to JBC, Dec. 9, 1946, JBC PREP, box 311, "U.S. Navy Department, 1946–47" folder.

18. Reaction of Paul's supporters can be found in Connor to JBC, Dec. 31, 1946; Farinholt to JBC, Jan. 3, 1947 ("completely un-American" and "blackening a man's reputation"); Hammett to JBC, Jan. 6, 1947 ("very little to reassure me"); all in JBC PREP, box 311, "U.S. Navy Department, 1946–47" folder.

The Paul case was not the last one that would cause headaches for Connor and JBC. Dr. Raymond Boyer, a Canadian scientist who had worked on explosives for Connor and on an NDRC committee appointed by JBC, was charged with giving information during the war to a Russian official. Connor informed JBC of developments in the case and of his own assistance in Boyer's defense. JBC, while faulting Boyer for poor judgment, privately wrote that he thought it "extremely important" to emphasize the "extenuating circumstance that all those who acted contrary to official governmental policy were giving information to an ally, not a potential enemy"—a point that would become increasingly blurred in subsequent spy scares, including the Rosenberg case. Ralph Connor to JBC, Aug. 21, 26, 1947; JBC to Connor, Sept. 20, 1947, all in JBC PREP, box 315, "Atomic Energy: Miscellaneous, 1947–48" folder.

19. JBC to Sullivan, Dec. 17, 1946; JBC to Hammett, Farinholt, and Connor, Dec. 17, 1946, JBC PREP, Box 311, "U.S. Navy Department, 1946–47" folder.

20. For a thorough study of the postwar science-government-military relationship see Walter Gelhorn, *Security, Loyalty, and Science* (Ithaca, N.Y.: Cornell University Press, 1950).
21. Baxter, *Scientists Against Time*, Appendix C, 456, in Greenberg, *Politics of Pure Science*, 98.
22. JBC, *The President's Report 1946* (dated Jan. 13, 1947) (Cambridge, Mass.: Harvard University, 1947), 10; JBC, *MSL*, 244–45; I. B. Cohen, "Statements on Secret or Classified Research at Harvard: A Report for the Brooks Committee" (confidential), Nov. 3, 1969, JBC PERP, UA I.15.898.13, box 3, "Ingoing and Outgoing Correspondence, 1969" folder.
23. On the struggle over the NSF's creation: J. Merton English, *A Patron for Pure Science: The National Science Foundation's Formative Years, 1945-1957* (Washington, D.C.: National Science Foundation, 1983); Cochrane, *The National Academy of Sciences*, 433–54, 457–59, 463–74, 480–83; Greenberg, *Politics of Pure Science*, chap. 6. For the Bush report, see the 1990 reissue of *Science: The Endless Frontier* (National Science Foundation: Washington, D.C., 1990), intro. by Daniel J. Kevles.
24. JBC to VB, Oct. 31, 1946, VBP, box 27, file 614. On ONR, see S. S. Schweber, "The Mutual Embrace of Science and the Military: ONR and the Growth of Physics in the United States after World War II," in Mendelsohn, Smith, and Weingart, eds., *Science, Technology, and the Military*, vol. 1, 3–45.
25. VB to JBC, Nov. 4, 1946, VBP, box 27, file 614.
26. JBC, "Education and the Federal Government," Crimson Network Speech, Dec. 12, 1946, JBC Speech File, 232; JBC, "Remarks by President James B. Conant at the Science Writers Award Luncheon," Dec. 27, 1946, JBC Speech File, 233; excerpted in *Science*, 105:6 (Jan. 3, 1947), 6; JBC, *The President's Report 1946*, 9–11; see also JBC, *MSL*, 244–45, and Gellhorn, *Security, Loyalty, and Science*, 175–202, esp. 182–83.
27. JBC, "Education and the Federal Government," Crimson Network Speech, Dec. 12, 1946, JBC Speech File, 232; JBC, *The President's Report*, 11.
28. JBC to Brien McMahon, May 18, 1949, JBC PREP, box 336, "Atomic Energy: General Advisory Committee, 1948–49" folder.
29. B. F. Skinner, *A Matter of Consequences: Part Three of an Autobiography* (New York: New York University Press, 1983), 10–12, 51–52.
30. JBC, "Education and the Prospects of World Peace," Sept. 8, 1947, JBC Speech File, 246.
31. "Report of the Provost on the Faculty of Arts and Sciences," 1948–49, *Official Register of Harvard University* 49:10 (Apr. 30, 1952), 44; quoted in I. B. Cohen, "Statements on Secret or Classified Research at Harvard: A Report for the Brooks Committee" (confidential), Nov. 3, 1969, JBC PERP, UA I.15.898.13, box 3, "Ingoing and Outgoing Correspondence, 1969" folder; Jerome Bruner, *In Search of Mind: Essays in Autobiography* (New York: Harper & Row, 1983), 245.
32. *Harvard University Catalogue, 1949-1950* (Cambridge: Harvard University, 1950), 552.
33. Trustees of the High Altitude Observatory of Harvard University and the University of Colorado to Robert L. Stearns and JBC, June 8, 1949, enc. with Robert L. Stearns to JBC, June 14, 1949, JBC PREP, box 338, "Col-Con," 1948–49 folder.
34. JBC to Robert L. Stearns, June 24, 1949, JBC PREP, box 338, "Col-Con," 1948–49 folder.
35. Bruner, *In Search of Mind*, 244–46.
36. Fischer, *Why They Behave Like Russians*, 262.
37. Arthur M. Schlesinger, Jr., *The Vital Center: The Politics of Freedom* (Boston: Houghton Mifflin, 1949; reprint ed. with new intro., New York: Da Capo Press, 1988). For a critical perspective on the "Cold War liberals," see Kenneth O'Reilly, "Liberal Values, the Cold War, and American Intellectuals," in Athan G. Theoharis, ed., *Beyond the Hiss Case: The FBI, Congress, and the Cold War* (Philadelphia: Temple University Press, 1982), 309–40.

38. Quoted in Alan D. Harper, *The Politics of Loyalty: The White House and the Communist Issue, 1946–1952* (Westport, Conn.: Greenwood Publishing Corp., 1969), 35.

39. See Taubman, *Stalin's American Policy*, 139, 177, 224–25, for evidence of this Soviet belief.

40. JBC expressed these arguments repeatedly during 1946–48; JBC Speech File, 230, "Public Education and the Structure of American Society," address to Detroit Economic Club, Nov. 11, 1946, and JBC Speech File, 231, speech to New England Council, Nov. 22, 1946; JBC, address to San Francisco Commonwealth club, Sept. 8, 1947, JBC Speech File, 246; JBC, "America's Capacity to Lead," speech to Economic Club of Chicago, Feb. 19, 1948, JBC Speech File, 258; JBC, *Education in a Divided World*, 230; see also Biebel, *Politics, Pedagogues, and Statesmanship*, 273–77.

41. Freeland, *Truman Doctrine*, 227–30, and Powell, *The Uncertain Profession*, 231–33.

42. Larry G. Gerber, "The Baruch Plan and the Origins of the Cold War," *Diplomatic History* 6:1 (Winter 1982), 69–95, quote on p. 81.

43. Henry A. Wallace to HST, July 23, 1946, in Gerber, "Baruch Plan," 81; Wallace, "The Path to Peace with Russia," *New Republic* 115 (Sept. 30, 1946), 401–406.

44. BMB to Herbert Marks, Sept. 22, 1946, quoted in Gerber, "Baruch Plan," 81.

45. Clark Clifford, "American Relations with the Soviet Union," Sept. 24, 1946; in Etzold and Gaddis, eds., *Containment*, 69–70.

46. JBC, "Public Education and the Structure of American Society," speech to Detroit Economic Club, Nov. 11, 1946, JBC Speech File, 230. "I sometimes think we underestimate our own strength, not only materially but spiritually, not only in terms of machines but in terms of men," he told a Boston audience in March 1948. "The seeming chaos which is the essence of a democracy with our traditions deceives those of us who live in it and see its inefficiency and faults." JBC, speech to Rotary Club of Boston, Mar. 24, 1948, Harvard News Office press release, JBC Speech File, 260.

47. JBC, "The University and the State," *Journal of Higher Education* 18:6 (June 1947), 281.

48. Subsequent quotations from JBC, "Remarks to the Graduating Class," Ohio University, June 9, 1947, JBC Speech File, 244.

49. For summaries of JBC's social philosophy, see Tuttle, *James B. Conant*, 24–34; Warner, *Province of Reason*, 225–26, 235–36, 239–44; and Douglass, *Six Upon the World*, esp. 359–62, 381–88, 407–409, 411–35.

50. Cited in Keith W. Olson, *The G.I. Bill, the Veterans, and the Colleges* (Lexington, Ky.: University Press of Kentucky, 1971), 249, in Amster, *Meritocracy Ascendant*, 162.

51. On JBC's attitude on postwar educational issues at Harvard: Amster, *Meritocracy Ascendant*, 160–70; Biebel, *Politics, Pedagogues, and Statesmanship*, chap. 6; Powell, *The Uncertain Profession*, chap. 9–10.

52. *NYT,* Apr. 10, 1947.

53. *NYT,* Feb. 19, 1948.

54. During one two-month span in early 1947 when an education bill was before Congress, JBC spoke out for increased federal education, in speeches and in testimony before congressional committees, often enough to be cited in *NYT* on four occasions: Apr. 10, 19, May 16, 30, 1947.

55. See Warner, *Province of Reason*, 240–41; Tuttle, *James B. Conant*, 27–34.

56. JBC, "Remarks to the Graduating Class," June 9, 1947.

57. JBC, *Education in a Divided World*, 66.

58. JBC, *Education in a Divided World*, 66–67.

59. Critiquing *Education in a Divided World*, Warner (*Province of Reason*, 240–41) incisively limns JBC's sanitized, bureaucratic style: "His book was freighted with the vocabulary of social ecology for the nasty words in the American vernacular. There are no slums in this book, but 'congested areas'; no poor, but 'low income groups'; no

working class, but 'neighborhoods where 90 percent of the families have union cards.' There are 'those concerned with running machines or distributing machine products,' and there are 'well-to-do residential suburbs.' "

60. Caute, *Great Fear*, 26.

61. Freeland, *Truman Doctrine*, 89. E.O. 9835 is reprinted in Bontecou, *The Federal Loyalty-Security Program*, 275–81, and Harper, *The Politics of Loyalty*, 255–63.

62. "The Reds, phonies and 'parlor pinks' seem to be banded together, and are becoming a national danger," HST wrote in his diary in the fall of 1946 in the heat of his anger at Henry Wallace's apostasy. "I am afraid they are a sabotage front for Uncle Joe Stalin." Buckingham, *America Sees Red*, 56–57; Freeland, *Truman Doctrine*, 140; Caute, *Great Fear*, 29.

63. See Belfrage, *American Inquisition*, 70–71; Buckingham, *America Sees Red*, 58–59; Caute, *Great Fear*, 112, 169–70, 268–72; Freeland, *Truman Doctrine*, chap. 3, 5; Gelhorn, *Security, Loyalty, and Science*, 167–68; Harper, *The Politics of Loyalty*, chap. 2; Schrecker, *No Ivory Tower*, 4–5, 86, 93; HST, *Memoirs: Years of Trial and Hope, 1946–1952* (Garden City, N.Y.: Doubleday & Co., 1956), 278–83; and Athan G. Theoharis, *Seeds of Repression: Harry S. Truman and the Origins of McCarthyism* (Chicago: Quadrangle Books, 1971); Clifford with Holbrooke, *Counsel to the President*, 175–80; Clifford, quoted in Carl Bernstein, *Loyalties: A Son's Memoir* (New York: Simon & Schuster, 1989), 197–200, in Garry Wills, "Keeper of the Seal," *New York Review of Books* 38:13 (July 18, 1991), 19–20. For a survey of Truman administration actions on the loyalty issue, see Barton J. Bernstein and Allen J. Matusow, eds., *The Truman Administration: A Documentary History* (New York: Harper & Row, 1966), 356–428.

64. Caute, *Great Fear*, 28. On the attorney general's list, see also Bontecou, *The Federal Loyalty-Security Program*, 157–204, 239–41; Freeland, *Truman Doctrine*, 208–16; Gelhorn, *Security, Loyalty, and Science*, 133–43.

65. The quotations in succeeding paragraphs are drawn from JBC's stock speeches between June 1947 and Jan. 1948, including "Remarks to the Graduating Class," Ohio University commencement address, June 9, 1947, JBC Speech File, 244; JBC, "Education and Prospects of World Peace," Sept. 8, 1947, and "Education in a Free Society," Sept. 17, 1947, both in JBC Speech File, 246; JBC, "American Education in a Divided World," Oct. 17, 1947, JBC Speech File, 250; JBC, *President's Report 1947* (Jan. 12, 1948) (Cambridge: Harvard University, 1948), 2–5.

66. The move brought much criticism and "legal harassment and adverse publicity"; on Oct. 8, also with an eye to appeasing Congress, the Department declared a preemptive crackdown on internal "security risks, even one-upping the administration's loyalty-security program by stating that it would consider as grounds for firing even associating with persons associated with organizations on the attorney general's list. Freeland, *Truman Doctrine*, 203–204, 236–37.

67. "Education and Prospects of World Peace," Sept. 8, 1947, JBC Speech File, 246; JBC, "American Education in a Divided World," Oct. 17, 1947, JBC Speech File, 250; *NYT*, Oct. 18, 1948.

68. Freeland, *Truman Doctrine*, 243–44.

69. JBC, "The University and the State," *Journal of Higher Education* 18:6 (June 1947), 281; C. Wright Mills, *The Power Elite* (Oxford University Press, 1956).

70. On JBC's attitude toward social sciences as an academic discipline, see his 1947 correspondence with the Harvard sociologist Samuel A. Stouffer in the Stouffer Papers, Harvard University archives, and especially JBC's outgoing address as president of the American Association for the Advancement of Sciences: "The Role of Science in Our Unique Society," Dec. 27, 1947, JBC Speech File, 254; *NYT*, "Oath is Proposed in Social Science," Dec. 28, 1947. In the latter he propounded a stillborn idea for a social scientists' "Hippocratic oath" to support the goals of "equality of opportunity, a minimum of class distinction, a maximum degree of individual freedom, and a wide distribution of centers of initiative"—a sign of his quest to

860 *Notes for Pages 407-10*

infuse education with "democratic" ideology. See also Powell, *The Uncertain Profession*, esp. 232–33, 237.

71. Robert K. Merton and Arnold Thackray, "On Discipline-Building: The Paradoxes of George Sarton," *ISIS* 63 (1972), 673–95; I. Bernard Cohen, "A Harvard Education," *ISIS* 75 (1984), 13–20.

72. JBC to George Sarton, June 20, 1952, Sarton Papers, Houghton Library, Harvard University.

73. JBC to George Sarton, May 4, 1927, Sarton Papers.

74. Cohen, "A Harvard Education," 16–17; Thackray and Merton, "Paradoxes of George Sarton," 489–90; Gerald Holton interview, Apr. 16, 1993; "real interest": JBC to Sarton, Jan. 7, 1935, Sarton papers. In 1939–40, the budget-conscious administrator shrewdly arranged to split Sarton's salary with the Carnegie Institution of Washington, reducing Harvard's share even while granting Sarton tenure. For Sarton's frustrations in obtaining JBC's support for history of science, also see other correspondence between them in the Sarton Papers, esp. between 1935 and 1943.

75. Sarton to JBC, July 21, 1940, Sarton Papers.

76. Sarton to JBC, Mar. 22, 1943, Sarton Papers.

77. JBC to Sarton, Apr. 12, 1943, Sarton Papers.

78. JBC, "A Proposal for a Commission on 'Science in General Education' or 'The Teaching of Science,'" Nov. 15, 1945, GCP, series 4, box 8.

79. See 1945–46 correspondence in "Conant, James B., 1934–55" folder, CCP, esp. JBC, "A Proposal for Promoting the Development of a New Type of Course at the College Level on 'The Strategy and Tactics of Science,'" Jan. 21, 1946.

80. JBC, *On Understanding Science: An Historical Approach* (New Haven, Conn.: Yale University Press, 1947).

81. JBC, *Overthrow of the Phlogiston Theory: The Chemical Revolution of 1775-1789* ("Harvard Case Histories in Experimental Science," Case 2: Cambridge, 1950); see also John W. Shirley, "The Harvard Case Histories in Experimental Science: The Evolution of an Idea," *American Journal of Physics* 19:7 (Oct. 1951), 419–23.

82. JBC, *MSL*, 371–73; Kuhn, Holton, Cohen interviews.

83. JRO, "Physics in the Contemporary World," Nov. 25, 1947, in JRO, *The Open Mind* (New York: Simon & Schuster, 1955), 97–99.

84. Thomas S. Kuhn, *The Structure of Scientific Revolutions* (Chicago: University of Chicago Press, 1962, 1970 2d ed.), passim., reference to JBC on xi.; "incremental and cumulative": I. B. Cohen, *Revolution in Science* (Cambridge: Belknap Press of Harvard University Press, 1985), 389. After seeing Kuhn's draft manuscript, JBC vigorously dissected his "use (and abuse)" of "paradigm" as a "magic verbal word to explain everything!" and "a word you seem to have fallen in love with!" Kuhn's investment of every scientific advance as a "new world view" struck JBC as "far too grandiose a characterization of most of the revolutions you cite as examples," and cordially accused him of "taking refuge in the word 'paradigm'" to circumvent the difficulties in his vague treatment of the scientific community as "a community with a single point of view." JBC to Kuhn, June 5, 1961; JBC to Kuhn, Dec. 19, 1962; both in JBC PERP. JBC's critique accurately presaged postpublication reaction to Kuhn's book, which like its "paradigm" theory remains a subject of intense debate. See John Horgan, "Profile: Reluctant Revolutionary: Thomas S. Kuhn Unleashed 'Paradigm' on the World," *Scientific American,* May 1991, 40, 49. Kuhn dated his transformation into a historian and philosopher of science (rather than a practitioner) to his first meeting with JBC upon being invited to be his graduate teaching assistant for Nat Sci 11 (a precursor to Nat Sci 4). Then a graduate student in physics taking time off from working on his dissertation, Kuhn recalls being startled when JBC turned to him and, acknowledging that his own expertise was limited to chemistry, matter-of-factly assigned him to prepare a series of case studies and lectures on the history of mechanics—a task that ultimately sent him on a new career. Kuhn interview, June 21, 1993.

85. Gerald Holton, "Ernst Mach and the Fortunes of Positivism in America," *ISIS* 83 (1992), 27–60; interview with Gerald Holton, Apr. 16, 1993; JBC's quotation is from JBC, "Greetings to the National Conference of the Institute for the Unity of Science, Boston, Massachusetts—April 1950," *Proceedings of the American Academy of Arts and Sciences* 80 (Boston: American Academy of Arts and Sciences, 1951–1954), 9.

86. JBC, "The University and the State," *Journal of Higher Education* 18:6 (June 1947), 285–86.

87. JBC, "The University and the State," 281.

88. On the creation of the Russian Research Center: Diamond, *Compromised Campus*, 52–55, 65–79; Lipset and Riesman, *Education and Politics at Harvard*, 184–85; Paul H. Buck 1967 Columbia University Oral History Interview (hereafter Buck COHI); Smith, *Harvard Century*, 171, 182; Adam Ulam interview, Jan. 1989; and documents in Harvard University–Russian Research Center (hereafter HU–RRC) folders, CCP. For in-depth examinations of political issues surrounding the Russian Research Center, see the 1990 dissertation of Charles O'Connell, a doctoral candidate at UCLA, who kindly provided a draft chapter ("The Political Context of the Period: The Cold War and Its Influence upon University Scholars at the Harvard Russian Research Center"), and Diamond, *Compromised Campus*, 47, 50–110.

89. Memorandum, "CD [Charles Dollard] and Frederick Osborn," Sept. 30, 1947, HU–RRC 1947 folder, CCP; "last hope": memorandum, Francis Keppel to Paul H. Buck, Oct. 7, 1947, quoted in Buck COHI, 21.

90. Diamond, *Compromised Campus*, 51.

91. Buck COHI, 31–32.

92. Buck COHI, 39. Buck denied there were any limitations on the freedom of Russian Research Center scholars to delve into any subjects they wished, but acknowledged, in the same interview (p. 36), that there "may have been certain aspects that were done under the grant of the Air Force that approached it. For example, they were interested in the structure of the Russian economy for war purposes. But I don't know that was ever really true that there were restrictions."

93. *Boston Traveler*, Dec. 5, 1947. The article did not cite any sources for this information.

94. Buck COHI, 4, 35.

95. Harvard University News Office press release, Dec. 5, 1947.

96. See Diamond, *Compromised Campus*, 57–60, 81–86, 100–103 ("poop sheets" and "maximize positive psychological reactions"), 108–10, and annual reports in HU–RRC folders, CCP. According to a 1951 FBI report, later declassified, one of Kluckhohn's "jobs" was to "obtain pertinent information requested by government departments and, within limits, shape the research program of the Center to the needs of the United States"—should, say, the State Department mention its interest in a particular subject, Kluckhohn is quoted as saying, he might then suggest the idea to a graduate student as a thesis topic, concealing the interest of the State Department, which would then be alerted to the eventual results. SAC Boston report, Aug. 17, 1951, in Diamond, *Compromised Campus*, 58–59.

97. JBC and FBI: SAC Boston to Hoover, Feb. 9, 1949, in Diamond, *Compromised Campus*, 47; JBC and CIA: Kluckhohn to Buck, June 13, 1949, in Diamond, *Compromised Campus*, 109–10.

98. Frederick Osborn to Clark Armstrong, Aug. 1, 1950, HU–RRC-1950 folder, CCP.

99. O'Connell, "Political Context. . . ."

100. SAC, Boston, to Director, FBI, Dec. 12, 1947, FBI Freedom of Information Act file, Russian Research Center, FOIPA No. 310,880. On the FBI–RRC relationship I have used O'Connell, "Political Context. . . ."; Diamond, *Compromised Campus*, and Diamond, "The Arrangement: The FBI and Harvard University During the McCarthy Period," in Theoharis, ed., *Beyond the Hiss Case*, 341–71; and my own set of FBI documents obtained through the Freedom of Information Act.

101. Caute, *Great Fear*, 404; for particular loyalty oath cases see Schrecker, *No Ivory Tower.*

102. In early Jan. 1948, Harvard and MIT officials agreed to "whack up the list of private educational institutions in Massachusetts" and divide them up for lobbying purposes to assure a broad array of protesting institutions. David W. Bailey to Phillips Ketchum, Jan. 2, 1948, JBC PREP, box 316, "Barnes Bill, 1947–48" folder. For correspondence on JBC's behind-the-scenes efforts to rally opposition to the loyalty oath measure, see JBC PREP, box 316, "Barnes Bill, 1947–48" folder.
103. Smith, *The Harvard Century,* 83–84.
104. Schrecker, *No Ivory Tower,* 184.
105. Z. Chafee, Jr., "Revised Memorandum on the Pending Barnes Bill," Dec. 31, 1947, JBC PREP, box 316, "Barnes Bill, 1947–48" folder. On Dec. 14, Chafee had sent an earlier version to JBC, which was also circulated to Corporation members and to a handful of Massachusetts university presidents. JBC to Compton, Baxter, Marsh, Cole, et al., Dec. 15, 1947.
106. Chafee to JBC, Dec. 14, 1947, JBC PREP, box 316, "Barnes Bill, 1947–48" folder.
107. David W. Bailey to JBC, Jan. 7, 1948, JBC PREP, box 316, "Barnes Bill, 1947–48" folder. For a complete list of recipients of the confidential Chafee memo, see R. C. Brown to files, Jan. 7, 1948, JBC PREP, box 316, "Barnes Bill, 1947–48" folder.
108. JBC, *President's Report,* 1947 (Jan. 12, 1948), (Cambridge: Harvard University, 1948), 2–5; see also Jan. 21, 1948, Harvard News Office press release, and *NYT,* "College Freedom Upheld by Conant," Jan. 21, 1948.
109. JBC, text of statement to the Joint Committee on Education considering Document No. H. 220 ("the Barnes bill"), Feb. 9, 1948, Harvard News Office press release, Feb. 10, 1948.
110. *BG,* Feb. 10, 1948.
111. Hutchins: Schrecker, *No Ivory Tower,* 113. Barnes bill's defeat: "Barnes and Sullivan Bills Fail on Local Scene: Harvard Administration Served as Focus for Opposition in State," *THC,* May 26, 1949; Schrecker, *No Ivory Tower,* 112.
112. Roger Baldwin to JBC, Feb. 14, 1948, JBC PREP, box 316, "Barnes Bill, 1947–48" folder; "Conant Scores Ban on Reds in Schools," *NYT,* Feb. 10, 1948, 25.
113. "Memorandum for Mr. Nichols Re: James B. Conant, Research," M. A. Jones to Louis B. Nichols, Mar. 12, 1948, JBC FBI FOIA file 94-38918-3. The first comment is signed "L," and Ladd is the only official receiving the memo whose last name begins with that letter; the second comment is signed "H," and the handwriting matches Hoover's on other documents. This exchange is also noted in Diamond, "The Arrangement," 357–58. For other indications of Hoover's animus toward JBC see various documents in his FBI file, described in an article by the author in *THC,* Nov. 1983.
114. John King Fairbank, *Chinabound: A Fifty-Year Memoir* (New York: Harper & Row, 1982), 315–51; Fairbank interview, Jan. 1989.
115. On the Hughes case: O'Connell, "Political Context. . . . "; H. Stuart Hughes, *Gentleman Rebel: The Memoirs of H. Stuart Hughes* (New York: Ticknor & Fields, 1990), 195–208; Buck COHI, 39–45; Lipset and Riesman, *Education and Politics at Harvard,* 184–85; Smith, *Harvard Century,* 182–83; Hughes telephone interviews with author, Jan. and Apr. 1989; Diamond, *Compromised Campus,* 74–76, 78, 299 n. 12.
116. Hughes, *Gentleman Rebel,* 208.
117. Interview with Hughes cited in O'Connell, "Political Context. . . . "
118. Buck COHI, 40–41.
119. Lipset and Riesman, *Education and Politics at Harvard,* 185.
120. That JBC sometimes took a personal interest in Russian Research Center personnel decisions is shown by an Apr. 1, 1951, diary entry: "Conference with Dean Buck . . . about a letter I wrote him about appointment in Russian Research Center. Not a good man." Unfortunately, JBC's diaries for the period 1942–50, if he kept them, have not been found.
121. Buck COHI, 37.
122. For the most thorough account of the Condon case, see Jessica Wang, "Science, Security, and the Cold War: The Case of E. U. Condon," *ISIS* 83 (1992), 238–69; for

Condon's part in the debate over postwar atomic control, see Smith, *A Peril and a Hope*.

123. A. N. Richards to JBC, Mar. 10, 1948, with draft statement, JBC PREP, box 326, "National Academy of Sciences, 1947–48" folder. On the 1947 NAS invitation to JBC, and his declination, see Roger Adams to members of the nominating committee, Mar. 31, 1947, and other correspondence in box 82, folder 1865: "N.A.S. Nominating Committee," VBP. On the NAS response to the Condon case, see materials in the NAS-NRC Central File: Congress: 1947–1948: Committees: Un-American Activities: Condon Case, NAS archives, Washington, D.C.

124. VB urged Richards to "make it clear that the scientists will serve the country through hell and high water but they don't enjoy the Thomas kind of treatment." A. N. Richards, notes of conversation with VB, Mar. 11, 1948, A. N. Richards Papers, University of Pennsylvania, box 27, "Condon, Edward U." folder.

125. JBC to A. N. Richards, Mar. 12, 1948, JBC PREP, box 326, "National Academy of Sciences, 1947–48" folder.

126. A. N. Richards to JBC, Mar. 16, 1948, A. N. Richards Papers, University of Pennsylvania, box 27, "Condon, Edward U." folder; JBC to A. N. Richards, Mar. 17, 1948, JBC PREP, box 326, "National Academy of Sciences, 1947–48" folder. "A Statement by Members of the National Academy of Scientists Concerning a National Danger," n.d. second draft, with Richards to Members of the Council of the National Academy of Sciences, Mar. 16, 1948.

127. National Academy of Sciences press release, May 3, 1948, A. N. Richards Papers, University of Pennsylvania, box 27, "Condon, Edward U." folder. See also Cochrane, *The National Academy of Sciences*, 478–79.

128. Alfred N. Richards to Frank B. Jewett, May 7, 1948, A. N. Richards Papers, University of Pennsylvania, box 26, "Frank B. Jewett" folder.

129. See, for example, JBC's speeches to the Boston Rotary Club, Mar. 24, 1948, JBC Speech File, 260; to the New York Community Service Society, Apr. 28, 1948, JBC Speech File, 262; and his baccalaureate address of June 6, 1948, JBC Speech File, 264, reprinted as "Challenge of the Times: A National Philosophy," *Vital Speeches of the Day* 14:21 (Aug. 15, 1948), 643–45.

130. It was also excerpted in a major magazine: "Education in an Armed Truce," *Atlantic Monthly* 182 (Oct. 1948), 48–52.

131. See, for example, "Conant Proposes Plan for Education," *NYT,* Oct. 14, 1948, and "Dr. Conant in Plea for U.S. Leadership," *NYT,* Oct. 20, 1948; and "Dr. Conant Discusses His Book," *BG,* Oct. 14, 1948.

132. JBC, *Education in a Divided World,* 172–73. In reiterating his view that "freedom of discussion, unmolested inquiry" were "essential" to scholarly analysis of pressing problems, JBC dropped the modifying "absolute" and "absolutely" present in earlier pronouncements containing similar passages dating back to 1936: "absolute freedom of speech" and "absolutely unmolested inquiry," appear in, among other places, JBC's Harvard tercentenary speech of Sept. 18, 1936 (JBC, *MSL,* 656) and "The University and the State," *Journal of Higher Education* 18:6 (June 1947), 286.

133. JBC, *Education in a Divided World,* 173.

134. *Book Review Digest,* 1948, 168.

135. William Barrett, *The Truants: Adventures Among the Intellectuals* (Garden City, N.Y.: Anchor/Doubleday, 1983), 83–85; see also Pells, *Liberal Mind in a Conservative Age,* 21–23, 124–25; Sidney Hook, *Out of Step: An Unquiet Life in the 20th Century* (New York: Harper & Row, 1987), passim.

136. Sidney Hook, "Conant on Politics and Education," *NYT Book Review,* Oct. 24, 1948, 5.

CHAPTER 22

1. Pells, *Liberal Mind in a Conservative Age,* 270.
2. Cited in *Time* 52:1 (July 5, 1948), 38.
3. Freeland, *Truman Doctrine,* 337–38; *Time* 52:5 (Aug. 2, 1948), 11.
4. On the Communist issue in the 1948 campaign, see Harper, *The Politics of Loyalty,* chap. 4; Robert J. Donovan, *Conflict and Crisis: The Presidency of Harry S Truman, 1945–1948* (New York: W. W. Norton & Co., 1977), 413–15; Freeland, *Truman Doctrine,* 307–18; Athan Theoharis, "The Rhetoric of Politics: Foreign Policy, Internal Security, and Domestic Politics in the Truman Era, 1945–1950," in Barton J. Bernstein, ed., *Politics & Policies of the Truman Administration* (Chicago: Quadrangle Books, 1970), 196–241.
5. HST press conference, Aug. 5, 1948, *Public Papers of the President, 1948,* 432–33.
6. Many commentators seem to have accepted the verdict of Allen Weinstein, whose *Perjury: The Hiss-Chambers Case* (New York: Alfred A. Knopf, 1978) concluded that Hiss was indeed guilty; others, especially on the left, have raised questions about Weinstein's evidence and conclusions, e.g., Victor Navasky, "Weinstein, Hiss, and the Transformation of Historical Ambiguity into Cold War Verity," and Athan G. Theoharis, "Unanswered Questions: Chambers, Nixon, the FBI, and the Hiss Case," in Theoharis, ed., *Beyond the Hiss Case,* 215–45, 246–308. A 1992 search of Soviet archives by Russian historian Dmitrii Volkogonov failed to locate evidence linking Hiss to espionage, but Volkogonov subsequently acknowledged that his search was not comprehensive: *NYT,* Oct. 29, Dec. 17, 1992.
7. Letter, Hiss to author, Jan. 21, 1989.
8. JBC, *MSL,* 561.
9. WLM interview, Aug. 1986.
10. For the struggle over WLM's election to the Corporation: correspondence in GCP; WLM, *In the Catbird Seat,* 256–58; WLM interview, Aug. 1986; John Finley interview; Smith, *Harvard Century,* 173–74; Dunne, *Grenville Clark,* 166–68; WLM, "Grenville Clark," in Cousins and Clifford, eds. (collected by Dimond), *Memoirs of a Man: Grenville Clark,* 163–64.
11. Buck interview, 18.
12. JBC to Harvard Board of Overseers, Jan. 6, 1948, GCP, in Dunne, *Grenville Clark,* 167.
13. FF to GC, Jan. 20, 1948, GCP.
14. WLM interview, Aug. 1986; WLM, *In the Catbird Seat,* 257.
15. This account of WLM's and JBC's initial responses to the Hiss case is based largely on an interview with WLM, Aug. 1986; WLM to author, Sept. 17, 1986; WLM, *In the Catbird Seat,* 261–85, esp. 272–73; correspondence in "Marbury, William L., 1948–49" folder, box 345, JBC PREP; Weinstein, *Perjury,* esp. chap. 5; Alger Hiss, *In the Court of Public Opinion* (New York: Alfred A. Knopf, 1957); John Chabot Smith, *Alger Hiss: The True Story* (New York: Penguin, 1976, 1977); and Dunne, *Grenville Clark,* 173–77. In *MSL* (p. 561), JBC notes his initial belief in Hiss's innocence but does not mention his involvement in urging WLM to file the libel suit against Chambers.
16. WLM, *In the Catbird Seat,* 273; WLM to author, Sept. 17, 1986.
17. Quoted in GC to WLM, Sept. 18, 1948, copy in JBC PREP, box 345, "Marbury, William L., 1948–49" folder; Weinstein, *Perjury,* 163.
18. WLM to JBC, Sept. 29, 1948, JBC PREP, box 345, "Marbury, William L., 1948–49" folder.
19. Schrecker, *No Ivory Tower,* esp. 5–11, chap. 4–6; Caute, *Great Fear,* chap. 22.
20. Caute, *Great Fear,* 408–10; Schrecker, *No Ivory Tower,* 94–102.
21. JBC, *Education in a Divided World,* 216. This assessment sharply contrasted with Harvard's *General Education in a Free Society* (1945), which barely touched on the urgency of teaching contemporary political affairs.

22. Buck COHI, 38; see also FBI documents and interviews cited in O'Connell, "Political Context. . . . "
23. Interview with Adam Ulam, Jan. 1989.
24. Correspondence with former Russian Research Center assistant director Alfred Meyer cited in O'Connell, "Political Context. . . . "
25. Buck COHI, 38–39. "The New York Public did the same thing. That's why in some ways our collections are fuller than the Library of Congress."
26. David Lane Marsden, *The Cold War and American Education* (Ph.D. diss., University of Kansas, 1976), 131, 137. Conversely, Sigmund Diamond claims in *Compromised Campus* (p. 116) that the "decisive" influence in JBC's shift was a 1947 *Foreign Affairs* article by Henry Stimson stating that "those who now choose to travel in company with American Communists are very clearly either knaves or fools . . . Are either to be tolerated in an academic community?" However, Diamond provides no supporting evidence for his assertion, which is belied by the fact that JBC adhered to his opposition to a ban on Communist teachers until late 1948, e.g., *Education in a Divided World,* 172–73.
27. JBC to DDE, Oct. 25, 1948, DDE Pre-Presidential Papers, 16–52 File, box 27, James B. Conant (1) folder, DDEL; on JBC's earlier EPC activities, see Biebel, *Politics, Pedagogues, and Statesmanship,* 171–77, 185–231 ("apprenticeship" quotation on p. 220).
28. Transcript of Educational Policies Commission, 32nd Meeting, Sept. 22–25, 1948 (hereafter EPC 32), National Education Association archives, Washington, D.C.
29. JBC, *MSL,* 453–59.
30. EPC 32, 200.
31. EPC 32, 200–202, 207.
32. EPC 32, 204.
33. "Report of Committee A," *AAUP Bulletin* 34:1 (Spring 1948), 126, in Schrecker, *No Ivory Tower,* 94.
34. EPC 32, 204–205.
35. EPC 32, 207.
36. EPC 32, 208. He stressed that view again a few minutes later after Spinning voiced indignation over the fact that teachers were being smeared by "people who think that anybody one step to the left of Calvin Coolidge is a communist." EPC 32, 210.
37. EPC 32, 208, 210–13.
38. EPC 32, 214. Stretching for ways to defend the studying and keeping in libraries of Communist books, JBC also urged the citing of a congressional report whose appendices were "chock-full" of original Communist documents. "Nobody can claim that this document issued by the United States Government is a subversive document," JBC said. "I am going to use that for all it is worth." His argument, with its unstated and probably unintentional implication that universities needed to justify by government standards the contents of its libraries, made its way into the published report. EPC 32, 216; Educational Policies Commission, *American Education and International Tensions* (Washington, D.C.: National Education Association of the United States and the American Association of School Administrators, 1949), 37.
39. EPC 32, 215.
40. EPC 32, 325–26.
41. EPC 32, 325.
42. EPC 32, 327.
43. Caute, *Great Fear,* 466.
44. *NYT,* Sept. 7, 1948, cited in Gellhorn, *Security, Loyalty, and Science,* 254–55.
45. Caute, chap. 25; Boyer, *By the Bomb's Early Light,* 101–106.
46. That morning, the congressmen had barraged Martin D. Kamen with questions about a 1944 meeting at a San Francisco seafood restaurant with a Soviet diplomat that had forced the physicist's resignation from the atomic project. Kamen denied that he had passed any information. "Spy Investigators Act to Cite Balky Witness for

Contempt," *NYT*, Sept. 15, 1948. Rumors and charges about this and other cases had been front-page news for weeks. A few days earlier, one HUAC member, Rep. Richard B. Vail (R.-Ill.), citing unspecified closed-door testimony but clearly referring to Condon and Kamen, said he was "certain" that Soviet spies stole atomic secrets during the war. "Russians Got Data on Bomb, Vail Says; Quotes an Officer," *NYT*, Sept. 12, 1948.

47. JBC, "Discussion following Lecture on the Atomic Age," Sept. 14, 1948, National Defense University archives, National Defense University, Washington, D.C.

48. JBC, "Discussion following Lecture on the Atomic Age," Sept. 14, 1948, National Defense University archives, National Defense University, Washington, D.C.

49. Minutes of NAS Council Meeting, June 10, 1948, in "Civil Liberties," enc. with Alfred N. Richards to JBC, Dec. 8, 1948, JROP, box 134, "NAS—Civil Liberties Committee" folder.

50. Alfred N. Richards to JRO, Nov. 2, 1948, JROP, box 134, "NAS—Civil Liberties Committee" folder; see also Cochrane, *The National Academy of Sciences*, 479 n. 8. On the activities of this committee, in addition to the sources cited below, see materials in NRC: Central File: ORG–NAS: Com on Civil Liberties: Ad hoc 1948, 1949, NAS archives, Washington, D.C.

51. For details of these developments, see accounts of the Hiss case previously noted, as well as Whittaker Chambers, *Witness* (New York, 1952; Washington, D.C.: Regnery Gateway, reprint ed., 1989), chap. 12–13.

52. On Cold War liberals' reactions, see Kenneth O'Reilly, "Liberal Values, the Cold War, and American Intellectuals," in Theoharis, ed., *Beyond the Hiss Case*, 309–40; and Pell, *Liberal Mind in a Conservative Age*, 270–76. Some Hiss friends and supporters, such as Zechariah Chafee, resolutely remained convinced of his innocence, but the revelation of Chambers's documents gave many stalwart Hiss backers their first sharp pang of doubt. For Chafee, see Donald L. Smith, *Zechariah Chafee, Jr.: Defender of Liberty and Law* (Cambridge, Mass.: Harvard University Press, 1986), 244–49.

53. Kurt Vonnegut, *Jailbird* (New York, 1979: Dell ed., 1980), 95–96.

54. Interview with David Riesman, Jan. 1989.

55. JBC, *MSL*, 561.

56. JBC to JRO, Dec. 22, 1948, JBC PREP, box 348, "National Academy of Sciences, 1948–49" folder, and JROP, box 134, "NAS—Civil Liberties Committee" folder.

57. Hewlett and Duncan, *Atomic Shield*, 340.

58. JBC to JRO, Dec. 22, 1948, JBC PREP, box 348, "National Academy of Sciences, 1948–49" folder, and JROP, box 134, "NAS—Civil Liberties Committee" folder.

59. "Findings and Recommendations of the Personnel Security Board in the Matter of J. Robert Oppenheimer," May 27, 1954, *IMJRO*, 1000; see also Chap. 33.

60. For references to the Dec. 29 meeting and subsequent consultations over the next week, see JBC desk calendar, correspondence in JBC PREP, box 348, "National Academy of Sciences, 1948–49" folder, and JROP, box 134, "NAS—Civil Liberties Committee" folder, including JBC to JRO, Dec. 22, 1948; JRO to JBC, Dec. 30, 1948 (JBC PREP), and O. E. Buckley to JBC, Jan. 3, 1949. From references in correspondence and in JBC's desk calendar, it appears that the subcommittee also discussed the proposed statement on Dec. 29 with Bethuel M. Webster, who was examining atomic energy and security-related issues for the New York City Bar Association. Enclosing a copy of the draft statement from their meeting on Dec. 29, JRO sent JBC a handwritten note which guiltily acknowledged that the problem required a greater concentration of effort than the busy academy threesome could give it: "Of our time with Webster, it seemed to me that the very disparity between what it seemed right to do, & what there was the least chance of actually getting done, did indicate the need for a bit more attention—perhaps not on our part, but surely on somebody's. Happy new year. Oppie. Dec. 30." JRO to JBC, Dec. 30, 1948, JBC PREP, box 348, "National Academy of Sciences, 1948–49" folder.

61. The practice of allowing persons on whom suspicion was cast to resign without prejudice or publicity hardly represented a "happy ending" in terms of "political significance," for it permitted people to be forced from their jobs by a government department "either unwilling or unable to offer any basis for the dismissals" or "motivated only by a desire to appease the appropriations committees." Freeland, *Truman Doctrine*, 204. But for JBC, this kind of "compromise" (which encouraged intimidatory tactics) became appealing—and he fell back on it repeatedly when involved, as high commissioner to Germany, in dealing with McCarthyite attacks on the State Department.

62. See draft statements, dated Jan. 3, 1949, with marginal notations dated Jan. 13, 1949, in "National Academy of Sciences, 1948–49" folder, box 348, JBC PREP, and "NAS–Civil Liberties Committee" folder, box 134, JROP; these drafts differ in only minor respects from the final statement mailed to HST and dated Feb. 3, 1949.

63. JBC to John Lord O'Brian, Jan. 10, 1948, JBC PREP, box 348, "National Academy of Sciences, 1948–49" folder; JBC spoke to O'Brian by telephone on Jan. 12, before sending the statement to Richards the next day. JBC desk calendar, JBC PREP. O'Brian's reaction is described in JBC to Alfred N. Richards, Jan. 13, 1948, JROP 134, "NAS–Civil Liberties Committee" folder; JBC PREP, "National Academy of Sciences, 1948–49" box 348.

64. JBC to Alfred N. Richards, Jan. 13, 1948, JROP 134, "NAS–Civil Liberties Committee" folder; JBC PREP, "National Academy of Sciences, 1948–49" box 348.

65. JRO to A. N. Richards, Feb. 10, 1949, JROP, box 134, "NAS–Civil Liberties Committee" folder. Perhaps the most damning criticism came from JRO's mentor and dissertation adviser, the Harvard physicist-philosopher Percy W. Bridgman, who was also JBC's friend and esteemed colleague. Bridgman found the statement in general "a defeatist abandonment" of the Academy's function as "the highest representative of science in this country" (as opposed to that of a government agency) and was particularly offended by its assertion that "Neither the secret investigations of the employee's record, nor the act of judgment itself, which must resolve doubt not in favor of the individual but in favor of security, can be subject to our traditional juridical safeguards." Appalled by this "abandonment of the tradition of democracy in this country, which regards the government as the servant of the individual," Bridgman concluded: "Perhaps the most ominous aspect of this apparent willingness to condone and accept the encroachment of a totalitarian philosophy is that it was perfectly gratuitous, for the entire sentence could have been omitted with no effect on the rest of the document." Richards, in response, vigorously defended the sentence as "the belief of three of the wisest members of the Academy, all having had long and intimate association with problems of loyalty and security," and suggested Bridgman "talk it over with Conant." See Bridgman to Richards, Feb. 23, 1949, and Richards to Bridgman, Feb. 25, 1949, in NRC: Central File: ORG: NAS: Com on Civil Liberties 1949, NAS archives.

66. Alfred N. Richards to HST, Feb. 11, 1949, HST OF, HSTL.

67. John R. Steelman to Alfred N. Richards, Mar. 2, 1949; Steelman's letter came in place of a draft reply lauding the statement's sentiments but disclaiming the need for executive action; see draft letter from HST to Alfred N. Richards, dated Feb. 23, 1949, and G. F. Schwarzwalder to Dave Stone, Feb. 24, 1949, all in HST OF, official file, HSTL.

68. JBC to Sen. Brien McMahon, May 18, 1949, JBC PREP, box 336, "Atomic Energy: General Advisory Committee, 1948–49" folder; General Advisory Committee, "Statement of the General Advisory Committee to the Atomic Energy Commission Regarding the Fellowship Program," June 6, 1949, box 4, "Miscellaneous GAC" folder, Chairman's Files, Office Files, David E. Lilienthal, Subject File, 1946–1950, AEC Papers, RG 326, NA; Hewlett and Duncan, *Atomic Shield*, 340–42, 450–51; Schrecker, *No Ivory Tower*, 289–90; Gellhorn, *Security, Loyalty, and Science*, 186–202.

69. JBC to Sen. Brien McMahon, May 18, 1949, JBC PREP, box 336, "Atomic Energy: General Advisory Committee, 1948–49" folder.
70. Hewlett and Duncan, *Atomic Shield,* 450–51.
71. Freeland, *Truman Doctrine,* 230–38.
72. JBC, "Education and the Prospects of World Peace," Sept. 8, 1947, JBC Speech File, 246.
73. JBC to John K. Norton, Jan. 3, 1949, "Educational Policies Commission, 1948–49" folder, box 340, JBC PREP.
74. See, e.g., JBC to Harry D. Gideonse, June 5, 1958, JBC PERP.
75. Paul H. Nitze to author, Jan. 21, 1987.
76. Transcript of Educational Policies Commission, 33rd Meeting, March 11–12, 1949 (hereafter EPC 33), National Education Association archives, Washington, D.C., 69.
77. JBC to John K. Norton, Jan. 3, 1949, "Educational Policies Commission, 1948–49" folder, box 340, JBC PREP.
78. JBC to DDE, Oct. 25, 1948; DDE to JBC, Nov. 11, 1948; JBC to DDE, Nov. 16, 1948; all in DDE Pre-Presidential Papers, 16–52 File, box 27, "James B. Conant (1)" folder, DDEL; copies also in "Educational Policies Commission, 1948–49" folder, box 340, JBC PREP.
79. EPC 33, 42–43.
80. DDE to JBC, Nov. 29, 1948; JBC to DDE, Dec. 1, 1948; both in DDE Pre-Presidential Papers, 16–52 File, box 27, "James B. Conant (1)" folder, DDEL.
81. EPC 33, 44–45.
82. EPC 33, 17.
83. EPC 33, 113.
84. EPC 33, 113–14.
85. EPC 33, 114. JBC admitted that by his "own definition," closet Communists would lie about their affiliations. "You will have to do a job inside out" to find hidden Communist faculty members, he said, as at the University of Washington. "I spoke to the president [Raymond B. Allen]. I asked, 'Would you start that investigation if you had to do it again?' He said, 'No.'" Allen had conducted the inquiry under pressure from the state legislature, and JBC feared sparking a similar drive to make him live up to his own words about the need to rid the profession of Communist teachers: "I would hate to have somebody throw this back at me: 'You signed this and, therefore, you are obligated to find out about them.'" EPC 33, 114–15.
86. EPC 33, 115.
87. Schrecker, *No Ivory Tower,* 42–44, 107.
88. JBC to Sen. Brien McMahon, May 18, 1949, JBC PREP, box 336, "Atomic Energy: General Advisory Committee, 1948–49" folder.
89. EPC 33, 115.
90. EPC 33, 116.
91. For the Waldorf conference: *THC,* Mar. 26, 28, 1949; Freda Kirchwey, "Battle of the Waldorf," *Nation,* Apr. 2, 1949, 377–78; Pells, *Liberal Mind in a Conservative Age,* 123–34; O'Neill, *A Better World,* 163–70.
92. *THC,* Mar. 26, 1949: Other Harvard professors backing the AIF picket were Crane Brinton, Seymour Harris, Michael Karpovich, and Perry Miller.
93. *THC,* Mar. 26, 28, 1949.
94. *THC,* Mar. 25, 28, 1949.
95. Frank Ober to JBC, Apr. 26, 1949, in *Harvard Alumni Bulletin,* 51 (June 25, 1949), 730.
96. JBC to GC, May 9, 1949, GCP, series 4, box 2, "Harvard Corporation, 1949–Conant, James B." folder.
97. Chafee to GC, May 11, 1949, Chafee Papers, box 34, folder 17.
98. Chafee to Williams, May 10, 1949, Chafee Papers, box 34, folder 17.
99. Williams to Chafee, June 9, 1949, Chafee Papers, box 34, folder 19. At JBC's behest, Chafee tried to placate Williams by sending him a copy of *Education in a Divided*

World and pointing out that JBC could not help it if the press did not publicize his views on "the American way of life" as widely as they did Shapley's activities. Chafee to JBC, June 14, 1949; Chafee to GC, June 14, 1949; JBC to Chafee, June 18, 1949; Chafee to Williams, June 22, 1949; JBC to Chafee, June 24, 1949; all in Chafee Papers, box 34, folder 19.
100. Chafee to GC, June 14, 1949, Chafee Papers, box 34, folder 19.
101. JBC to GC, May 9, 1949, GCP, series 4, box 2, "Harvard Corporation, 1949—Conant, James B." folder.
102. GC to JBC, May 17, 1949, GCP, series 4, box 2, "Harvard Corporation, 1949—Conant, James B." folder; Chafee to GC, May 20, 1949, Chafee Papers, Harvard Law School library, box 34, folder 19. For GC's letter and related correspondence, see *Harvard Alumni Bulletin* 51 (June 25, 1949); also JBC, *MSL*, 455-59; Diamond, *Compromised Campus*, 116-21; Dunne, *Grenville Clark*, 168-73; and correspondence in GCP and Chafee papers.
103. Chafee to GC, June 3, 1949, Chafee Papers, box 34, folder 18.
104. Shapley oral history interview, American Institute of Physics, 1966, unedited draft, p. 235, copy in "Interview typescript—most complete" folder, HUG 4773.84, Harlow Shapley Papers, Harvard University archives.
105. GC to Ober, May 27, 1949, *Harvard Alumni Bulletin*, 51 (June 25, 1949), 731-35.

CHAPTER 23

1. Sarton, *Faithful Are the Wounds*, 120.
2. William G. Carr to EPC, May 5, June 1, 1949, JBC PREP, box 340, "Educational Policies Commission" folder.
3. "Educators Insist on Ouster of Reds," *NYT,* May 30, 1949. JBC's carefully hedged contribution:

> Admittedly we are living in a world in which an ideological rivalry that goes as deep as the religious hatred of four centuries ago breeds similar poisonous incidents and inflames suspicions. But I am convinced that our American doctrines in which tolerance plays so large a role will prove to have unsuspected stamina and resilience. The disruptive forces, however, will be powerful at times, and near-panic may be threatened; strong points will be required by the friends of freedom. That is why our universities are of great importance.

4. James R. Killian, Jr., *The Education of a College President: A Memoir* (Cambridge: MIT Press, 1985), 150-54.
5. JBC to Sen. Brien McMahon, May 18, 1949, JBC PREP, box 336, "Atomic Energy: General Advisory Committee, 1948-49" folder. For background on the fellowship controversy, see Hewlett and Duncan, *Atomic Shield*, 340-42, 450-51; Schrecker, *No Ivory Tower*, 289-90; Gellhorn, *Security, Loyalty, and Science*, 186-202.
6. John S. Wood to JBC, June 1, 1949, copies in, among other places, GCP, series 4, box 2, "Harvard Corporation, Conant, James B." folder, and Chafee Papers, box 34, folder 19. See also numerous press reports after the letter became public knowledge on June 10. Accounts give varying numbers for recipients of Wood's letter: *Harvard Alumni Bulletin* gave 71 (June 25, 1949, 720); Caute, 81 (*Great Fear,* 404), *Time* magazine, 107 (June 27, 1949, 60).
7. Chafee to GC, June 22, 1949, Chafee Papers, box 34, folder 19.
8. See JBC's handwritten addendum to JBC to GC, June 9, 1949, GCP, series 4, box 2, "Harvard Corporation, Conant, James B." folder; and GC to Edmund E. Day, June 13, 1949, Chafee Papers, box 34, folder 19.
9. "House Committee Asks Book Lists," *THC,* June 11, 1949.
10. *NYT,* June 12, 1949; *Harvard Alumni Bulletin,* June 25, 1949, 720.
11. *Harvard Alumni Bulletin* 51 (June 25, 1949), 720.

12. Educational Policies Commission, *American Education and International Tensions.*
13. *American Education and International Tensions,* 15–19.
14. *American Education and International Tensions,* 38–39.
15. JBC to John K. Norton, Jan. 3, 1949, JBC PREP, box 340, "Educational Policies Commission, 1948–49" folder.
16. *American Education and International Tensions,* 46.
17. *American Education and International Tensions,* 39–40.
18. On distribution of the report, see William G. Carr to EPC members, June 1, 1949; on the "overwhelming reaction [which] has extended from favorable to enthusiastically commendatory," see John K. Norton to JBC, June 23, 1949; both in JBC PREP, box 340, "Educational Policies Commission" folder. See also Schrecker, *No Ivory Tower,* 111–12.
19. Excerpts from ABC radio interview with Willard E. Givens, NEA executive secretary, June 8, 1949, copy in JBC PREP, box 340, "Educational Policies Commission: *Comments on Report of,* 1948–49" folder.
20. "Anti-Party Line," *Time* 53:25 (June 20, 1949), 52; "The Role of Education," *NYT,* June 9, 1949, 30.
21. Ober to GC, June 8, 1949, in *Harvard Alumni Bulletin* 51 (June 25, 1949). Underlining in original. See also Diamond, *Compromised Campus,* 120–21, 316–17.
22. "The Role of Education," *NYT,* June 9, 1949, 30; the *Post* is quoted in "Anti-Party Line," *Time* 53:25 (June 20, 1949), 52; for a similar objection see "The Educators and the Communists," *Nation* 168:25 (June 18, 1949), 676–77.
23. Lipset and Riesman, *Education and Politics at Harvard,* 159, 179–81, 188–89.
24. *THC,* June 4, 21, 1949; interview with John G. Simon, Feb. 8, 1989; see also Diamond, *Compromised Campus,* 151–66, 326.
25. Simon interview, Feb. 7, 1989. I have also drawn from Paul H. Buck to JBC, June 11, 1949, JBC PREP, box 340, "Educational Policies Commission: *Comments on Report of,* 1948–49" folder; John G. Simon to JBC, June 20, 1949, and JBC to John G. Simon, June 24, 1949, both in JBC PREP, box 337, "Cr–Cz," 1948–49 folder.
26. "Conant, Eisenhower, 18 Educators Urge Ban on Communist Teachers," *THC,* June 9, 1949.
27. "The President's Stand," *THC,* June 9, 1949.
28. JBC's citation failed to convince Simon, who an hour after their meeting wrote a letter recalling that Laski, during a visit to Harvard in April, had said (in Simon's paraphrase): " 'So long as the Communist Party is legal in the United States, I see no reason why Communists should not teach.' I mention this because it seems relevant to our debate over whether or not a Communist *might be* intellectually free and honest in the *teaching profession.* We disagreed over whether a distinction could be made between Communists in teaching and Communists in a labor union, for instance. It would appear that Professor Laski does make that distinction between Communists in 'non-intellectual' walks of life (v. his 'Communist Manifesto') and Communists in teaching (v. his press conference)." JBC, in response, acknowledged that Laski would disagree with his stand and politely terminated the exchange by remarking that was "no need to prolong the discussion which we had the other day and which I enjoyed so much." John G. Simon to JBC, June 20, 1949, and JBC to John G. Simon, June 24, 1949, both in JBC PREP, box 337, "Cr–Cz," 1948–49 folder.
29. "The 20's Mistake," *THC,* June 11, 1949.
30. See "Mather, Beer, Schlesinger Criticize E.P.C. Report; Taylor Backs It," *THC,* June 9, 1949.
31. JBC to Carr, June 11, 1949, JBC PREP, box 340, 'Educational Policies Commission, 1948–49" folder. JBC told Carr that there was some merit to the *THC* view that the report could be used to justify "procedures [not] in the best interests of American society and academic life" to persecute teachers holding unpopular views. He added, "I am not in the habit of usually taking the advice of this undergraduate journal seriously, but I think they may have a point."

32. Wilbur F. Murra to JBC, June 14, 1949; Murra to John K. Norton, June 14, 1949, both in JBC PREP, box 340, "Educational Policies Commission: *Comments on Report of, 1948–49*" folder; Norton to JBC, June 23, 1949, JBC PREP, box 340, "Educational Policies Commission, 1948–49" folder. Unlike JBC, DDE had no second thoughts about *American Education and International Tensions.* Norton, without naming JBC as the source, informed DDE that the view had been expressed that the report might be used "to justify undesirable educational procedures," and that, therefore, the EPC should issue a statement disavowing practices which, "under the guise of excluding members of the Communist Party from teaching, attack liberal viewpoints and academic freedom." DDE replied that he "saw no such need" and that "it would be unwise to do so . . . my suggestion would be to stand on the report as it is." DDE to John Kelley Norton, June 27, 1949, responding to Norton to DDE, June 23, 1949, in Galambos, ed., *The Papers of Dwight David Eisenhower* 10:670–71.

33. *Harvard Alumni Bulletin,* June 25, 1949, 720. JBC's fishing trip with Baxter—as distinguished from the "Fishing Trip" Defense Department project—is noted in JBC desk calendar, JBC PREP, and JBC to VB, June 20, 1949, folder 1164, box 47, VBP.

34. JBC telephoned GC on June 18 to catch up on both issues. GC diary, GCP, series I, box 4, "Biography—Diary, April 3–Sept. 18, 1949" folder.

35. *THC,* June 11, 15, 1949.

36. It lies, unmarked, in JBC PREP, box 337, "Cr–Cz," 1948–49 folder.

37. Chafee to GC, June 14, 1949, and GC to Chafee, June 17, 1949, both in Chafee Papers, box 34, folder 19.

38. All quotations from Chafee's speech are from Zechariah Chafee, Jr., "Freedom and Fear," Phi Beta Kappa Oration, June 20, 1949, Box 85, folder 14, Chafee Papers, Harvard Law School Library. Description of the scene and "great surgeon" analogy are from "Chafee Assails Mundt-Johnson Bill," *THC,* June 21, 1949.

39. JBC to Chafee, June 20, 1949, Chafee Papers, box 34, folder 19.

40. See Kunetka, *Oppenheimer: The Year of Risk,* 137–39.

41. JBC, *MSL,* 457.

42. "Remarks of President Conant to the Harvard Foundation for Advanced Study and Research—June 22, 1949," JBC Speech File, 284; the full text is reproduced in *BG* and *THC,* June 23, 1949; for relevant excerpts see JBC, *MSL,* 457–58.

43. Telephone interview with Samuel Beer, Jan. 1989.

44. JBC, *MSL,* 449.

45. Sarton, *Faithful Are the Wounds,* 121.

46. Chafee to JBC, June 22, 1949, Chafee Papers, box 34, folder 19.

47. See Smith, *Harvard Century,* 174–75.

48. GC to Edward R. Burke, July 9, 1949, Chafee Papers, box 34, folder 20.

49. Among numerous examples, see JBC, *MSL,* 456–59; "Remarks of President Conant to the Harvard Foundation for Advanced Study and Research—June 22, 1949," JBC Speech File, 284; JBC to Chafee, June 20, 1949, Chafee Papers, box 34, folder 19.

50. JBC to unidentified correspondent, 1949, quoted in JBC, *MSL,* 458.

51. Lipset and Riesman, *Education and Politics at Harvard,* 185–88; Smith, *Harvard Century,* 182–83.

52. "An Exchange on 'Veritas at Harvard,'" *New York Review of Books* 24:9 (May 26, 1977), 45.

53. Diamond, "The Arrangement: The FBI and Harvard University in the McCarthy Period," in Theoharis, ed., *Beyond the Hiss Case,* 365.

54. TRC recalls that during this period his father carefully gathered and read primary Communist documents. One should be cautious, however, in evaluating the importance of a statement by one of his colleagues, quoted by both Diamond ("The Arrangement," 359) and Schrecker (*No Ivory Tower,* 111), that JBC's "opposition to Communism is almost violent in its strength." Harvard Business School dean Donald K. David made the statement to the FBI during a background check of JBC's loyalty in 1953, when his nomination to become high commissioner in Germany was under

fire from McCarthy and there was an obvious incentive for friends and colleagues to emphasize his hard-line credentials. A generally unemotional man, JBC was "violent" about very few things, and often discussed Communist philosophy in a detached manner.

55. JBC to VB, May 26, 1949, VBP, Speeches & Writings, 1932–1955: Book File, *Modern Arms and Free Men,* box 145, "Distribution and Correspondence on first and second editions of ms. of book" folder.
56. JBC to Harold Dodds, Mar. 23, 1937, in Tuttle, *James B. Conant,* 72.
57. Fairbank, *Chinabound,* 338.
58. JBC, "Force and Freedom," *Atlantic Monthly* 183 (Jan. 1949), 21.
59. *American Education and International Tensions,* 25.
60. JBC to Thomas J. Cunningham, Dec. 28, 1970; Cunningham to JBC, Dec. 22, 1970; JBC PERP. "I am still wondering if the phrase 'members of the Communist Party' still is adequate description of a group of people of whose pattern of behavior I once disapproved so heartily," JBC explained. "If I were in a position to have to consider the sort of problem to which my statement applied in 1949, I should have to make a study of a great many aspects of the behavior of those whom we roughly classify as being on the extreme left, and a study of the recent decisions—legal and otherwise— about teachers and professors who hold unorthodox views."

CHAPTER 24

1. The Conant family vacation is described in a series of letters from PRC to Miriam T. Richards, Aug. 11, 18, 29, Sept. 4, 1949, kept in an envelope marked "1949—Happy letters from Glacier Park," CFP.
2. Kenneth P. O'Donnell, "Professor in a Hot Spot," *Saturday Evening Post,* Sept. 5, 1953, 141. The voice on the telephone probably belonged to JRO or VB, both of whom had helped evaluate evidence of the Soviet atomic explosion, gathered from fallout by high-altitude reconnaissance planes. Hewlett and Duncan, *Atomic Shield,* 363–66.
3. JBC to LRG, Feb. 9, 1949, Groves Papers, RG 200, NA.
4. Teller testimony, *IMJRO,* 714.
5. "Statement by the Educational Policies Commission, Adopted at a meeting of the Commission held in Rye, New York, October 6–8, 1949," National Education Association archives, Washington, D.C.
6. O'Donnell, "Professor in a Hot Spot," 141; JBC to Niebuhr, Dec. 15, 1949, Conant folder, box 47, Niebuhr papers, LC.
7. Interview with I. I. Rabi, Jan. 1982.
8. Andrei Sakharov, a leader of the Soviet H-bomb program, stated in his memoirs that by the fall of 1949 the "Soviet government (or, more properly, those in power: Stalin, Beria, and company) already understood the potential of the new weapon, and nothing could have dissuaded them from going forward with its development. Any U.S. move toward abandoning or suspending work on a thermonuclear weapon would have been perceived either as a cunning, deceitful maneuver or as evidence of stupidity or weakness. In any case, the Soviet reaction would have been the same: to avoid a possible trap, and to exploit the adversary's folly at the earliest opportunity." See Andrei Sakharov, *Memoirs* (trans. Richard Lourie) (New York: Alfred A. Knopf, 1990), chap. 6, esp. 94, 98–101, and articles by several authors in the May 1993 issue of the *Bulletin of the Atomic Scientists.* According to David Holloway, the closest Western student of Moscow's nuclear program, Soviet work on thermonuclear weapons started as early as 1947–48, and was embarked on "as a matter of priority" around the beginning of November 1949—two months after the first Soviet fission test (Aug. 29, 1949) and two months before HST's Jan. 31, 1950, announcement of the U.S. program. See Holloway, "Research Note: Soviet Thermonuclear Develop-

ment," *International Security* 4 (Winter 1979/1980), 192–97, citing I. N. Golovin, *I. V. Kurchatov* (Moscow: Atomizdat, 1978, 3d ed.), 92, 43; and Holloway, *The Soviet Union and the Arms Race*, 23–27. Holloway concludes that the Soviet decision to build the H-bomb predated Truman's decision, but that "the overall effect of American actions"—especially early reports of U.S. thermonuclear studies and the Mike test of thermonuclear reactions in late 1952—"was to speed up the Soviet effort to develop thermonuclear weapons." Holloway's new history of the early Soviet nuclear program, *Stalin and the Bomb* (Yale University Press; forthcoming), will undoubtedly provide the most comprehensive, informed, and judicious assessment of these issues.

9. Some important accounts of the H-bomb decision include Herbert York, *The Advisors: Oppenheimer, Teller and the Superbomb* (San Francisco: W. H. Freeman & Co., 1976; reissue with new preface and epilogue: Stanford University Press, 1989; citations from 1976 edition); Hewlett and Duncan, *Atomic Shield*, chap. 12; Norman Moss, *Men Who Play God: The Story of the H-Bomb and How the World Came to Live with It* (New York: Harper & Row, 1968; Penguin, 1972); Herken, *Winning Weapon*, chap. 15, epilogue; Herken, *Cardinal Choices*, 34–48; Peter Galison and Barton Bernstein, "In Any Light: Scientists and the Decision to Build the Superbomb, 1952–54," *Historical Studies in the Physical and Biological Sciences* 19:2 (1989), 267–347; David Alan Rosenberg, "American Atomic Strategy and the Hydrogen Bomb Decision," *Journal of American History* (June 1979), 62–87; Hans Bethe, "Comments on the History of the H-Bomb," *Los Alamos Science*, Fall 1982, 43–53 (reprinted as "Observations on the Development of the H-Bomb" in 1989 ed. of *The Advisors*, 163–81); McGeorge Bundy, "The Missed Chance to Stop the H-Bomb," *New York Review of Books* (May 13, 1982), 13–22, and Bundy, *Danger and Survival*, chap. 5; Richard Rhodes, who covers the Super in the epilogue of his *The Making of the Atomic Bomb*, is reported to be working on a sequel devoted to the making of the hydrogen bomb; Barton J. Bernstein, "Truman and the H-Bomb," *Bulletin of the Atomic Scientists* 40 (Mar. 1984), 12–18; Acheson, *Present at the Creation*, 345–49; DEL, *AEY*, 580–634; Gaddis, *Strategies of Containment*, 79–82; Lewis L. Strauss, *Men and Decisions* (Garden City, N.Y.: Doubleday & Co., 1962), 208–30; Roger M. Anders, ed., *Forging the Atomic Shield: Excerpts from the Office Diary of Gordon E. Dean* (Chapel Hill, N.C.: University of North Carolina Press, 1987), 34–64; Powers, *Heisenberg's War*, 465–69; Edward Teller with Allen Brown, *The Legacy of Hiroshima* (Garden City, N.Y.: Doubleday & Co., 1962), 34–57; S. M. Ulam (and the preface to the 1991 edition by William G. Matthews and Daniel O. Hirsch), *Adventures of a Mathematician* (Berkeley, Calif.: University of California Press, 1991, 1976), esp. chap. 11; R. Gordon Arneson, "The H-Bomb Decision," *Foreign Service Journal*, May 1969, 27–29, and June 1969, 24–27, 43; and Warner R. Schilling, "The H-Bomb Decision: How to Decide without Actually Choosing," *Political Science Quarterly*, Mar. 1961, 24–46. Key official documents include the transcript of JRO's security hearing—*IMJRO*—and an incomplete but helpful ninety-one-page chronology secretly prepared by congressional staffers in 1953 and declassified in 1987, "Policy and Progress in the H-Bomb Program: A Chronology of Leading Events," Joint Committee on Atomic Energy, Jan. 1, 1953, JCAE declassified records, RG 128, NA. My thanks to Gregg Herken for providing this document.

10. Hewlett and Duncan, *Atomic Shield*, 362.

11. JRO to K. D. Nichols, Mar. 4, 1954, *IMJRO*, 11.

12. JBC, "Notes on the 'Trinity' Test," July 17, 1945, B–C, box 5, folder 38; "red herring": Bethe interview with author, Jan. 1985.

13. JBC and VB to HLS, Sept. 30, 1944, Harrison-Bundy Papers, folder 77, MED Records, RG 77, NA; JRO to Richard C. Tolman, Sept. 20, 1944, in *IMJRO*, 953–58.

14. JBC to VB, "Possibilities of a Super Bomb," Oct. 20, 1944, B–C, box 1, folder 3. JBC referred in the memo to "the leading theoretical man" there—identified by Bethe as Teller in an interview with author, Jan. 1985.

15. Interim Committee minutes, May 31, 1945, quoted in Sherwin, *A World Destroyed,* 297–98.
16. JBC, *MSL,* 278.
17. JBC to VB, "Possibilities of a Super Bomb," Oct. 20, 1944.
18. JBC to VB, May 9, 1945, B–C, box 5, folder 38. Emphasis in original.
19. Minutes, GAC 2, Feb. 2–3, 1947, DoE archives.
20. I. I. Rabi to S. Ulam, Dec. 18, 1945, Rabi Papers, LC.
21. "McCloy Predicts Super Atomic Bombs Within Decade," *Bulletin of the Atomic Scientists* 2:1 (Jan. 1947), 5.
22. A three-day, top-secret seminar at Los Alamos in Apr. 1946 reached a mixed verdict—an H-bomb could "likely" be built but doing so would require overcoming huge technical hurdles and expending a "considerable fraction" of the resources of the entire U.S. atomic program. See Herken, *Cardinal Choices,* 36–37, 233, and Rhodes, *Making of the Atomic Bomb,* 764–65.
23. DuBridge interview, Apr. 3, 1991.
24. York, *Advisors,* 25; Hewlett and Anderson, *Atomic Shield,* 32.
25. *IMJRO,* 236.
26. Minutes, GAC 9, April 23–25, 1948, DoE archives.
27. For instance, Bernstein, "Truman and the H–Bomb," 13.
28. The "Fishing Party"'s secretary, Lt. Col. Edwin F. Black, recalled that JBC had a "fixed opinion" as early as Mar. 1949 that the H-bomb "wasn't scientifically feasible and wanted to knock what he considered a crazy idea in the head once and for all." Black interview, Feb. 1985. That his skepticism was well founded is suggested by Hans Bethe and Herbert York, who notes that the doubts expressed in 1949 about the technical basis for developing the Super proved correct; it was not until early 1951 that the ideas that led to the weapon were developed. See Bethe, "Comments . . . ," and York, *Advisors,* 20–28, 106–107. Bethe's article, originally written in 1954, echoed his testimony before the Oppenheimer hearings: "When President Truman decided to go ahead with the hydrogen bomb in January 1950, there was really no clear technical program that could be followed. This became even more evident later on when new calculations were made at Los Alamos, and when these new calculations showed that the basis for technical optimism which had existed in the fall of 1949 was very shaky, indeed. The plan which then existed for the making of a hydrogen bomb turned out to be less and less promising as time went on." *IMJRO,* 330.
29. "Capabilities of the Weapons Mentioned in the Directive from the Secretary of Defense," undated but apparently Apr. 1949, CD-1-31 TSRD entry 199A, RG 330, NA.
30. Draft Fishing Party Committee Final report, circulated July 22, 1949, FPF. The committee ultimately backed this recommendation by a narrow 5–4 margin before submitting its conclusions in mid-Oct., but it seems doubtful the final report, despite its timeliness, significantly influenced the H-bomb debate. Conant Committee Final report, Oct. 15, 1949, CD-1-31 TSRD entry 199A, RG 330, NA.
31. Quoted in Frederick Osborn, "Memorandum of Conversation," Mar. 10, 1949, *FRUS,* 1949, I, 39–43.
32. DEL, *AEY,* 354.
33. Hewlett and Duncan, *Atomic Shield,* 337–38.
34. DEL, *The Journals of David E. Lilienthal,* vol. 7, *Unfinished Business,* 1968–1981 (New York: Harper & Row, 1983), 160.
35. JBC to JRO, Mar. 7, 1949, box 27, Conant file, JROP.
36. *IMJRO,* 805.
37. Robert Jungk, *Brighter Than a Thousand Suns: A Personal History of the Atomic Scientists* (New York: Harcourt Brace Jovanovich, 1958), 328–29.
38. Manley interview, Nov. 1986.
39. "Both [John] von Neumann and I remember that Dr. Conant was the first member of

the GAC who was strongly opposed to the hydrogen development," the physicist Hans Bethe later recounted. Hans Bethe to Samuel Silverman, Mar. 18, 1954, "Oppenheimer case" file, box 12, Bethe Papers, Cornell University, in Galison and Bernstein, "In any light," 295, n. 93. For an example of an account that has JRO leading the anti-H-bomb crusade, see Robert Chadwell Williams, *Klaus Fuchs, Atom Spy*, 111, wherein Williams writes that JRO "persuaded other scientists" on the GAC to recommend against the H-bomb. For the insinuation during the 1954 AEC hearing that JRO propagandized JBC against the weapon, see *IMJRO*, 243. Among the few accounts to note JBC's sharper stand are Michelmore, *The Swift Years: The Robert Oppenheimer Story*, 168, 176; John Major, *The Oppenheimer Hearing* (New York: Stein & Day, 1971), 144; Galison and Bernstein, "In any light," 294–95.

40. JRO to DEL, Sept. 26, 1949, box 46, "Lilienthal, David E.—From JRO" folder, JROP.
41. JRO to William M. Rand, Oct. 11, 1949, box 122, "Harvard University—Board of Overseers—Chemistry Department—Visiting Committee" folder, JROP. See also JRO desk calendar, JBC social notebooks, JBC PERP. The social notebooks also show that JBC and JRO enjoyed a Sunday dinner at JBC's on Nov. 20, 1949, but unfortunately recorded only the substance of their meal (roast lamb, apple pie, ice cream), not of their conversation.
42. *IMJRO*, 401–2; JRO to JBC, Oct. 12, 1949, box 27, Conant folder, JROP.
43. For a description of the "infinite containment" school into which the pro–H-bomb scientists have been placed, see Robert Gilpin, *American Scientists and Nuclear Weapons Policy* (Princeton: Princeton University Press, 1962), 102–107.
44. Testimony of Edward Teller, *IMJRO*, 715.
45. *IMJRO*, 328.
46. Interview with Bethe, Jan. 1985; see also Jeremy Bernstein, *Hans Bethe: Prophet of Energy* (New York: Basic Books, 1980), 93.
47. Interview with Bethe, Jan. 1985. Though not asked about the letter during the hearings, JRO in 1957 privately recalled receiving "some kind of communication from Conant" in which he used the "over my dead body" phrase. JRO told a researcher, however, that "they were never able to find the letter." Warner R. Schilling, "Interview with J. Robert Oppenheimer, 11 June 1957 (12 June)," 6, Case file, Box 65, Schilling file, JROP. The letter's fate remains a mystery. I was unable to locate it despite searching AEC, JRO, and JBC manuscript collections. It would not be surprising if JBC asked JRO to destroy the letter at the time.
48. Interview with Kenneth S. Pitzer, Feb. 1985; Pitzer testimony, *IMJRO*, 699, 702–703. Pitzer believes the encounter took place on October 14, but JRO's desk calendar puts Pitzer's visit a week later.
49. Author's telephone interview with Robert Serber, May 15, 1992; Serber was unsure whether JRO described JBC's viewpoint or showed him a document written by JBC, but had a "faint" memory that it was a typed letter or memorandum. My thanks to Gregg Herken for informing me of Serber's story.
50. *IMJRO*, 782. This was also the impression of the Harvard physicist Norman Ramsey, a Manhattan Project veteran who was an air force consultant during the H-bomb controversy, who recalled that JBC's opposition was "vigorous" and "stronger than Oppenheimer's." Ramsey interview, p. 315, Columbia University Oral History Project.
51. *IMJRO*, 231. At the Oppenheimer hearings, the AEC's attorney, Roger Robb, insinuated that JRO attempted to "propagandize" JBC prior to the GAC meeting. *IMJRO*, 243. JRO's attorney, Lloyd Garrison, rebutted this claim in his closing summation. *IMJRO*, 976.
52. JRO to JBC, Oct. 21, 1949, *IMJRO*, 242–43.
53. DEL, *AEY*, Oct. 10, 1949, 577.
54. *IMJRO*, 385, 387.
55. Gordon Dean, "Sequence of events leading to the decision on the 'super' bomb," [Jan. 27, 1950,] Department of Energy archives, Germantown, Md.; reprinted in Anders, ed., *Forging the Atomic Shield*, 57–64.

56. DEL diary, entry of Oct. 29, 1949, DEL diaries, Princeton University Archives, Princeton, NJ; compare with DEL, *AEY,* 580–81. DEL apparently decided to omit the phrase as a result of an October 1962 dinner conversation with JBC at the Century Club in New York City. The two men reminisced about the H-bomb controversy, about which, DEL recorded JBC as saying, "Some of us, you included, are in the dog house"—a passage that was itself excised when DEL's diaries from this period were published. See DEL diary entry of Oct. 8, 1962, DEL diaries, Princeton University Archives, and DEL, *Journals,* vol. 5, *The Harvest Years,* 1959–1963 (New York: Harper & Row, 1971), 406. The GAC's minutes of the Oct. 28–30 meeting—reprinted in Cantelon, Hewlett, and Williams, eds., *The American Atom,* 113–15—do not relate individual viewpoints.

57. Author's telephone interview with Serber, May 15, 1992.

58. Warner R. Schilling, "Interview with J. Robert Oppenheimer, 11 June 1957 (12 June)," 6–7, Case file, box 65, Schilling folder, JROP.

59. Interview with George Kistiakowsky, Jan. 1982; interview with E. Bright Wilson, Jr., Dec. 1986; interview with I. I. Rabi, Feb. 1982.

60. On the air force: JBC to W. Barton Leach, Apr. 26, 1946, Leach Papers, box 52, folder 6, Harvard Law School Library. On UMS and the bomb: JBC, "Statement . . . (and Comments)" to the House Military Affairs Committee, Nov. 29, 1945, *Hearing on H.R. 4280,* 51–9, U.S. House of Representatives (Washington, D.C., 1945).

61. DEL, *AEY,* Oct. 29, 1949 entry, 581. Manley believed JBC may also have been alluding to previous proposals he considered outlandish, such as the nuclear-powered airplane.

62. Fox, *Reinhold Niebuhr,* 240–41.

63. Borden interview with Federal Bureau of Investigation agents, Feb. 20, 1954. FBI J. Robert Oppenheimer Serial file (100-17828), released under the Freedom of Information Act. (Hereafter JRO FBI.)

64. JBC, *MSL,* 49–50.

65. The GAC report is reprinted in York, *The Advisors,* 150–59.

66. York, *The Advisors,* 49.

67. York, *The Advisors,* 154–55, 157. JBC's role in drafting the majority annex is noted by DuBridge in *IMJRO,* 519.

68. For suggestions that JBC's stand on the H-bomb was motivated by guilt about the atomic bomb's use on Japan, see Bernstein, "Truman and the H-bomb," 13, and Galison and Bernstein, "In any light," 292. On JBC's lack of guilt over the use of the bomb: JBC, *MSL,* 303; JBC to R. L. Popper, June 21, 1968, in Amster, *Meritocracy Ascendant,* 150; TRC interviews, Jan. 1982, 1987, 1991; Jim Conant (grandson) interviews, 1991, 1993. It is quite clear, in my view, that JBC's role in developing and endorsing the use of the atomic bomb gave him a special feeling of *responsibility* or *concern* that was reflected in his H-bomb stand—but guilt, in the sense of regretting his actions or wishing he had acted differently, no.

69. JBC, "Fight for Liberty," valedictory to Harvard undergraduates, Jan. 10, 1943, *Vital Speeches of the Day* 9 (Feb. 15, 1943), 282.

70. JBC, "Force and Freedom," *Atlantic Monthly,* Jan. 1949, 19–22.

71. See JBC's comments to State Defense Policy Review Group, Mar. 2, 1950, in *FRUS,* 1950, I, 178.

72. All quotations from the GAC report are in York, *The Advisors,* 151–59.

73. York, *The Advisors,* 156; DEL, *AEY,* 581.

74. York, *The Advisors,* 158–59; DEL, *AEY,* 582.

75. Interview with DuBridge, Jan. 1982; interview with Rabi, Feb. 1982. Both scientists also recounted JBC's leading role at the October meetings in 1976 interviews with William M. Tuttle, Jr., according to Galison and Bernstein, "In any light," 295, n. 93.

76. Hewlett and Duncan, *Atomic Shield,* 385; Office Diary, Oct. 31, 1949, box 1, DEL Office Files—Office Diaries, AEC Papers, RG 326, NA.

77. Strauss, *Men and Decisions,* 216–17; Bundy, *Danger and Survival,* 304, discloses the

influence on Strauss of a Sept. 25, 1949 letter from William T. Golden, a former staff aide.

78. JCS, "Comments on Military View of Members of General Advisory Committee," Jan. 13, 1950, in Etzold and Gaddis, eds., *Containment: Documents on American Policy and Strategy, 1945–1950,* 368–73.

79. Teller, *Legacy of Hiroshima,* 44.

80. McMahon to HST, Nov. 21, 1949, HST Papers, Naval Aide File, Box B, Atomic Energy folder, HSTL, copy in I. I. Rabi papers, LC; this copy contains materials deleted from the version printed in *FRUS,* 1949, I, 588–95.

81. Gordon Dean, "Sequence of events leading to the decision on the 'super' bomb," [Jan. 27, 1950,] Department of Energy archives, Germantown, Md.; Anders, ed., *Forging the Atomic Shield,* 50, 60.

82. The GAC members' arguments are paraphrased in J. H. Manley to Roy B. Snapp, "Meeting of Certain GAC Members with Commission, November 7, 1949," Nov. 9, 1949, Atomic Energy History Collection, Department of Energy archives, Germantown, Md.

83. Schilling, "Interview with J. Robert Oppenheimer, 11 June 1957 (12 June)," 17, Case file, box 65, Schilling folder, JROP. See also chap. 24, n. 68.

84. JRO to Uncle Nick (Niels Bohr), Nov. 2, 1949, box 21, Bohr folder, JROP.

85. Edwin F. Black to JBC, Nov. 29, 1949 [received Dec. 1, 1949], JBC PREP, box 382, "Secretary of Defense, 1949–50" folder, enclosing "Scientists and National Policy," Nov. 29, 1949.

86. JBC to Edwin C. [*sic*] Black, Dec. 14, 1949, JBC PREP, box 382, "Secretary of Defense, 1949–50" folder.

87. Interview with Glenn Seaborg, Feb. 1985; Hewlett and Duncan, *Atomic Shield,* 395–96.

88. Hewlett and Duncan, *Atomic Shield,* 394, 398. Although one presidential aide specifically recommended that the group appoint a working staff consisting of JBC, JRO, Kennan, air force general Lauris Norstad (the only H-bomb supporter of the four), "and others of similar caliber," HST and/or those around him preferred a "safer, more controllable process"—and, certainly, a far less critical (if less prestigious) staff. Robert Dennison, "Memorandum for the President," Nov. 18, 1949, HST PSF—Subject File, box 201, "Subject File—NSC Atomic—Atomic Energy—Superbomb data" folder, HSTL; Bundy, *Danger and Survival,* 215; HST to Souers, Nov. 19, 1949, *FRUS,* 1949, I, 587–88.

89. See Kennan, *Memoirs: 1925–1950,* 471–76; Gaddis, *Strategies of Containment,* 79–80; on the power moratorium idea, see JRO to George F. Kennan, Nov. 17, 1949, Kennan folder, box 43, JROP.

90. Minutes of Policy Planning Staff meeting, Nov. 3, 1949, *FRUS,* 1949, I, 576.

91. On the Kennan-Acheson divergence, see Isaacson and Thomas, *The Wise Men,* 486–90.

92. The lunch is noted in a chronology of Acheson meetings on the H-bomb in the Acheson Papers, HSTL, and in JBC's desk calendar, JBC PREP.

93. Arneson, "H-Bomb Decision," *Foreign Service Journal,* May 1969, 29; see also Acheson, *Present at the Creation,* 346.

94. Acheson, *Present at the Creation,* 346.

95. Memorandum of telephone conversation with Admiral Souers by the secretary of state, January 19, 1950, *FRUS,* 1950, I, 511–12.

96. JCAE, hearing of Jan. 9, 1950, "Development of a Super Weapon," 30–32, 40, JCAE formerly classified records, box 4, tab 3, RG 128, NA.

97. *IMJRO,* 897–98.

98. *IMJRO,* 86.

99. DEL, *AEY,* 581.

100. "Statement by the President on the Hydrogen Bomb," Jan. 31, 1950, in Cantelon, Hewlett, and Williams, eds., *American Atom,* 127.

101. DEL, *AEY,* 633.
102. JBC to WLM, June 30, 1954, courtesy of WLM.
103. Indeed, a leader of the Soviet project, Yuli B. Khariton, later confirmed that "Fuchs enabled us to detonate a [fission] bomb two years earlier." *NYT,* Jan. 14, 1993; see also Khariton and Smirnov, "The Khariton Version," *Bulletin of the Atomic Scientists* 49:4 (May 1993), 20–31; and Roald Sagdaev, "Russian Secrets," *Bulletin of the Atomic Scientists* 49:4 (May 1993), 34–35. Khariton insisted, however, that Fuchs's information played no part in the development of the Soviet H-bomb.
104. Whether or how much Fuchs's help advanced the Soviet H-bomb program remains uncertain, since the design he passed to Moscow turned out to be a cul-de-sac, and the breakthrough that was ultimately employed was not conceived until early 1951. See Herken, *Winning Weapon,* 322–23, 340 n.; Herken, *Cardinal Choices,* 52–53, 238–39; Bethe, "Observations on the Development of the H-Bomb"; Holloway, "Research Note," 193, and *Stalin and the Bomb;* Daniel Hirsch and William G. Mathews, "The H–Bomb: Who Really Gave Away the Secret?" *Bulletin of the Atomic Scientists* 46:1 (Jan./Feb. 1990), 22–30. Khariton minimized the significance of Fuchs's data in the Soviet H-bomb project (*NYT,* Jan. 14, 1993; Khariton and Smirnov, "The Khariton Version," 29–31; *Izvestia,* Dec. 8, 1992), but another Russian account credits a 1947 Soviet intelligence report on U.S. H-bomb plans with spurring the Kremlin to develop the weapon: Sergei Leskov, "Dividing the Glory of the Fathers," *Bulletin of the Atomic Scientists* 49:4 (May 1993), 39. Further research is clearly indicated. It is also unclear whether the revelation of Fuchs's espionage influenced HST's Jan. 31 decision; he was not officially informed until the next day, but DEL told the JCAE on Feb. 3 that British intelligence had notified the FBI and AEC the previous fall that Fuchs was under suspicion and investigation. DEL didn't "think" the Fuchs case affected HST's decision but said the president "may have had earlier information" on the case. See transcript of JCAE hearing of Feb. 3, 1950, JCAE doc. no. CXXXI, sanitized copy declassified to author on Oct. 22, 1991, JCAE records, RG 128, NA.
105. Interview with John G. Simon, Feb. 7, 1989.
106. Richard Rovere, *Senator Joe McCarthy* (Cleveland: World Publishing Co., 1959), 119–40.
107. JBC to JRO, Feb. 14, 1950, with Nat S. Finney to JBC, Feb. 14, 1950, box 27, Conant folder, JROP.
108. Rovere, *Senator Joe McCarthy,* 131.
109. JBC to BMB, Feb. 24, 1950, BMB Papers, Mudd Library, Princeton University.
110. Portions of NSC-68 quoted in Etzold and Gaddis, eds., *Documents on Containment,* 435–42.
111. Except as noted, this account of JBC's meeting with NSC-68's authors is drawn from the official memorandum of the conversation: "Record of the Meeting of the State-Defense Policy Review Group, Department of State, Thursday, March 2, 1950," *FRUS,* 1950, I, 176–82.
112. Paul H. Nitze to author, Jan. 21, 1987.
113. Joel H. Hildebrand, " 'Vendetta'?" letter to *Science* (June 5, 1967), 1177–78; National Academy of Sciences, "Conference of the Council of the Academy with the Committee on Nominations," Jan. 22, 1950, copy in box 138, "NAS—President—Selection of New" folder, JROP.
114. E. C. Stakman to JBC, Mar. 25 and Apr. 7, 1950; JBC to E. C. Stakman, Apr. 5, 1950; both in box 376, "National Academy of Sciences, 1949–50" folder, JBC PREP. On the 1947 offer: Roger Adams to members of the nominating committee, Mar. 31, 1947, and other correspondence in box 82, folder 1865: "N.A.S. Nominating Committee," VBP.
115. "Minutes of the Business Session, April 25, 1950," mailed on May 15, 1950. A second version of the minutes that omitted the names of Latimer and LaMer was mailed later at the suggestion of a member "anxious to suppress the names of the chemists

[because] it will not look well . . . to emphasize that the coup d'etat was engineered by chemists." Edwin B. Wilson to Zwemer, June 3, 1950. Both in NAS archives, Washington, D.C.

116. JBC, *MSL*, 498; D. S. Greenberg, "The National Academy of Sciences: Profile of an Institution (II)," *Science* 156 (Apr. 21, 1967), 361. Hereafter "Academy."

117. Greenberg, "Academy," 361; "authoritarian" behavior: Nathan Reingold, entry for Detlev Wulf Bronk, in *Dictionary of Scientific Biography*, vol. 17, supp. II (New York: Charles Scribner's Sons, 1991), 111–13; Reingold cites a diary entry made by one Academy member, D. A. MacInness, who recorded that the chemists "were in active revolt against [Conant's] selection, the trouble with Conant being the manner in which he behaved during the war." MacInness reported that opponents to Conant also included some geneticists and mathematicians. MacInness diary, Apr. 27, 1950, D. A. MacInness Papers, Rockefeller Archive Center, Pocantico Hills, North Tarrytown, New York.

118. Kistiakowsky interview, Jan. 1982.

119. Edwin B. Wilson to Zwemer, June 3, 1950, NAS archives.

120. 77–71 vote: MacInness diary, Apr. 27, 1950, D. A. MacInness Papers, Rockefeller Archive Center; "majority of votes": "Minutes of the Business Session, April 25, 1950," May 15, 1950, NAS archives; Lee A. DuBridge interview, Apr. 3, 1991.

121. JBC, *MSL*, 498–99; interview with WLM, Aug. 1986; Bronk to JBC, Apr. 10, 1950, 1949–50 correspondence, "J" folder, JBC PREP.

122. George B. Kistiakowsky to GRC, May 1, 1980, courtesy of Elaine Kistiakowsky; interview with George B. Kistiakowsky, Jan. 1982.

123. Kistiakowsky to GRC, Feb. 19, 1978, courtesy of Elaine Kistiakowsky.

124. "conspired": Kistiakowsky to GRC, May 1, 1980, courtesy of Elaine Kistiakowsky; "innocent beneficiary": Greenberg, "Academy," 364.

125. William T. Golden, memorandum for the record: Interview with Lawrence R. Hafstad, Jan. 4, 1951, courtesy of Mr. Golden; Cochrane, *The National Academy of Sciences*, 515–16.

126. E. B. Wilson to Zwemer, June 3, 1950, NAS archives. Italics in original.

127. Greenberg, "Academy," 360–64; see also Greenberg, *Politics of Pure Science*, 14, 126 n.

128. JBC, *MSL*, 499.

129. Hildebrand, " 'Vendetta'?"; for a contemporary record of Hildebrand's plea for a full-time president see National Academy of Sciences, "Conference of the Council of the Academy with the Committee on Nominations," Jan. 22, 1950, copy in box 138, "NAS—President—Selection of New" folder, JROP.

130. JBC, *MSL*, 498.

131. Pitzer interview, Feb. 1985.

132. Alvarez interview, Feb. 1985.

133. One liberal scientist who worked with LaMer during the war vividly recalled his reputation as a "genuine reactionary bastard" on the "far right" of his colleagues. Interview with Jesse L. Greenstein, May 16, 1991.

134. See Latimer's testimony in *IMJRO*, 656–71.

135. *IMJRO*, 660.

136. *IMJRO*, 663, 665.

137. *IMJRO*, 387.

138. Mar. 5, 1954, FBI interview with Latimer, in memorandum by C. A. Rolander, Jr., dated Mar. 15, 1954, JRO FBI serial file, 100-17828-947, 10. In this interview, Latimer contended that "DuBridge had supported Oppenheimer on the thermonuclear because of being naive and Conant had gone along with what he thought was the majority side."

139. Lawrence R. Hafstad, quoted in William T. Golden, memorandum for the record, Jan. 4, 1951, courtesy of Mr. Golden.

140. Edwin B. Wilson to Detlev W. Bronk, May 1, 1950, NAS archives.

141. Pitzer interview, Feb. 1985; Mar. 5, 1954, FBI interview with Pitzer, in memorandum by C. A. Rolander, Jr., dated Mar. 15, 1954, JRO FBI serial file, 100-17828-947, 8.
142. Joel H. Hildebrand, "Wendell Mitchell Latimer," in NAS *Biographical Memoirs* (Washington, D.C.: National Academy, 1958), 221–37, 227.
143. Mar. 5 and 8, 1954 FBI interviews with Alvarez, in memorandum by C. A. Rolander, Jr., dated Mar. 15, 1954, JRO FBI serial file, 100-17828-947, 18.
144. Pitzer and Alvarez interviews with author, Feb. 1985.
145. May 1952 FBI interview with Teller, in report by FBI Albuquerque bureau dated May 27, 1952, AQ 100-1224, JRO FBI serial file.
146. Hewlett and Duncan, *Atomic Shield*, 440. Borden's reply expressed doubt that either JBC or JRO would prove helpful to the program.
147. Chester Heslep to Lewis L. Strauss, May 3, 1954, in Peter Goodchild, *J. Robert Oppenheimer: Shatterer of Worlds*, 252–53; my thanks to Priscilla McMillan for a copy of this document.
148. JBC to VB, "Complaints about S-1 Project at Chicago Reaching the President," July 31, 1943, B–C, folder 13.
149. Before HST announced DEL's selection, Urey had privately offered his own suggestions to Senator McMahon. "Because of his [JBC's] intimate connection with the May-Johnson Bill I would not be particularly happy about his appointment," he wrote. Harold C. Urey to Brien McMahon, Oct. 8, 1946, JCAE records, box 7.
150. DEL diary, Jan. 28, 1950, Princeton University. DEL excised this reference to Urey from the published version of the diaries.
151. TRC interview, Jan. 1982.
152. MacInnes diary, Apr. 27, 1950, Rockefeller Archive Center. Pitzer recalled that Urey was "undoubtedly involved" in the anti-Conant plotting, including "corridor conversation" on the day of the revolt. Pitzer interview, Feb. 1985.
153. Hewlett and Anderson, *New World*, 134; on Libby's ties to Latimer, see Hildebrand, "Wendell Mitchell Latimer," 225–26.
154. *IMJRO*, 659; Hewlett and Duncan, *Atomic Shield*, 537; on Libby's friendship with LaMer: interview with Jesse L. Greenstein, May 16, 1991.
155. May 6, 1952, FBI interview with Libby, in report of Chicago bureau dated May 9, 1952, JRO FBI serial file; on Libby's politics: Greenstein interview, May 16, 1991.
156. For a positive appraisal of Bronk's term, see Cochrane, *The National Academy of Sciences*, chap. 16.
157. JBC, " 'If' Game," 1968, special subject file, box 7, JBC PERP, UA I.15.898.13; JBC, *MSL*, 499. In the handwritten " 'If' Game," JBC diagrammed a flowchart of his life and speculated:

> If I had been elected Pres. of National Academy in 1950 the impact of Korean War etc. would have wiped out [concentrating on public schools.] Furthermore President Eisenhower would never have asked me to give up Presidency of National Academy as well as of Harvard for a diplomatic job. In other words my career after 1950 would have been totally different.
> On the other hand, there was no *public* break with the Academy; after the incident I was appointed NSF and elected as first president of the NSF board. Was still a member of Gen. Advisory Council. If I had not accepted Eisenhower's invitation I might have left Harvard and *either* devoted energies to education or to science. The NAS decision did not close the door to science but *if* it had gone the other way I would have closed door to "education" by concentrating in 1950 *in science*.

158. Greenberg. "National Academy," 361.
159. E. C. Stakman to JBC, Apr. 27, 1950, and JBC to Stakman, Apr. 28, 1950, box 376, "National Academy of Sciences, 1949–50" folder, JBC PREP.
160. JBC, *MSL*, 499. JBC pleased the academy with his tactful handling of the affair in

his memoirs; in 1975 the academy's council, in changing JBC's membership status to emeritus, voted to convey the group's "great admiration and respect for the spirit in which Mr. Conant accepted and described in his autobiography the sequence of events preceding the election of Detlev W. Bronk as President of the Academy." NAS archives.

161. JBC hints at his own interpretation of the academy snub in an affectionate memoir of E. P. Kohler that he completed and sent to the academy in the fall of 1950 — after more than a decade of procrastination and false starts, and only a few months after the debacle over the presidency. JBC noted that Kohler's "pathological" nervousness about formal presentations outside of the classroom had led him to skip scientific meetings and unwittingly gain a reputation as a snob. A recent painful experience may have prodded JBC's insight that Kohler had "suffered thereby the fate of more than one shy person whose aloofness is attributed to pride." JBC to Detlev Bronk, enc. Kohler manuscript, Nov. 18, 1950, "National Academy of Sciences, 1950–51" folder, box 406, JBC PREP.

CHAPTER 25

1. The account of the Commencement ceremony is from " 'Live and Let Live,' Acheson Bids Reds," *NYT,* June 23, 1950, and "Dr. Conant Raps Red Repudiation of Scholarship," *BG,* June 23, 1950.
2. "Conant Has Operation," *NYT,* June 24, 1950; JBC to JFD, Nov. 5, 1956, box 1, Conant folder, JFD papers, Mudd Library, Princeton University.
3. HST, *Years of Trial and Hope,* 333, 339.
4. Acheson to JBC, June 28, 1950, Acheson Papers, HSTL.
5. JBC, *MSL,* 507.
6. Record of Meeting of State-Defense Policy Review Group, Mar. 2, 1950, *FRUS,* 1950, I, 179.
7. TSV, "Confidential notes of Talk with Dr. Conant at Sugar Hill, New Hampshire on August 4, 1959," TSV Papers, Rutgers, box 8, E–Conant correspondence folder; on JBC's indifference toward Nehru, see the papers of Grenville Clark, who was disappointed by his friend's attitude, esp. GC to Charles C. Burlingame, Oct. 19, 1949, series IV, box 1, Harvard College, Burlingame, and FF to GC, Aug. 8, 1956, box 184, folder 2, FFP.
8. JBC to JFD, Nov. 13, 1953, *FRUS,* 1952–54, VII, 553–55.
9. HST to JBC, June 24, 1950, and GRC to HST, June 26, 1950, HST OF, PPF 91, HSTL; HST to JBC, July 5, 1950 (in which HST thanked JBC for his telegram of July 1 expressing support for the decision to extend military support to South Korea), JBC PREP, box 394, "Conant: June Operation, M–Z, Misc. 1950–51" folder; JBC to Acheson, July 17, 1950, Acheson Papers, box 62, "Personal Correspondence, 1945–52, Co–Cz" folder, HSTL.
10. JBC to James R. Killian, Jr., July 17, 1950, Killian Papers, Massachusetts Institute of Technology.
11. George F. Kennan, "Reflections on the Walgreen Lectures," in *American Diplomacy* (paperback ed., Chicago: University of Chicago Press, 1984), 161.
12. Kathryn Weathersby, "Soviet Policy and the Outbreak of the Korean War, 1945–1950," paper and presentation to the Cold War International History Project Conference on New Evidence on Cold War History, Moscow, Jan. 12–15, 1993; Taubman, *Stalin's American Policy,* 202; Jerrold L. Schecter w. Vyacheslav V. Luchkov, trans. and ed., *Khrushchev Remembers: The Glasnost Tapes* (Boston: Little, Brown & Co., 1990), 144–47; Edward Crankshaw, intro., Strobe Talbott, trans. and ed., *Khrushchev Remembers* (Boston: Little, Brown & Co., 1970; citation from Bantam ed., 1971), 400–407.
13. HST, *Years of Trial and Hope,* 437.

14. "Mobilizing Urged as Reply to Russia," *NYT,* Dec. 13, 1950.
15. Taubman, *Stalin's America Policy,* 202.
16. JBC, "A Skeptical Chemist Looks in the Crystal Ball," Sept. 5, 1951, JBC Speech File.
17. See JBC, "The Soviet Challenge," Jan. 27, 1950, JBC Speech File; and JBC, "The Soviet Challenge to American Education," Feb. 11, 1950, JBC Speech File, 296.
18. *FRUS,* 1950, I, 177.
19. JBC, "Scholarly Inquiry and the American Tradition," May 5, 1950, JBC Speech File, 301.
20. JBC, "The Present Danger," Feb. 7, 1951, JBC Speech File.
21. JBC to James R. Killian, Jr., July 17, 1950, Killian Papers, Massachusetts Institute of Technology.
22. JBC, *MSL,* 508; interview with R. Ammi Cutter, Cambridge, Mass., Apr. 29, 1987. TSV's encounter with JBC may have been a setup, according to WLM, who says he and TSV had discussed the situation a few days earlier and conspired to convince JBC to head a citizens' committee if he could be talked into it. WLM, *In the Catbird Seat,* 296, and WLM to JBC, Apr. 30, 1970, JBC PERP. TSV vigorously disputed WLM's account, however, insisting that JBC came up with the idea first. TSV to JBC, July 28, 1970, JBC PERP; TSV, "Memorandum for record," Aug. 27, 1970, TSV Papers, Rutgers, Box 5.6, "CPD–Additional Material" folder.
23. JBC, *MSL,* 508–509.
24. Winston S. Churchill, *The Gathering Storm* (Boston: Houghton Mifflin, 1948).
25. Reaffirming NSC 30/4, NSC-68 concluded that to succeed the U.S. government must "Keep the U.S. public fully informed and cognizant of the threats to our national security so that it will be prepared to support the measures which we must accordingly adopt."
26. Acheson, *Present at the Creation,* 374.
27. Cited in Gaddis, *Strategies of Containment,* 107–109. Reaffirming another hard-line secret document, NSC 20/4, adopted in late 1948, NSC-68 had emphasized that attainment of its goals would require keeping "the U.S. public fully informed and cognizant of the threats to our national security so that it will be prepared to support the measures which we must accordingly adopt." NSC-68, in Gaddis and Etzold, eds., *Containment,* 440.
28. Press conference of May 4, 1950, *Public Papers of Harry S. Truman,* 1950 (Washington, D.C., 1965), 284–88, cited in Ernest R. May, "The American Commitment to Germany, 1949-1955," *Diplomatic History* 13:4 (Fall 1989), 439.
29. Cited in Thomas and Isaacson, *The Wise Men,* 504; another HST aide recalled: "We were sweating over it, and then—with regard to NSC-68—thank God Korea came along." Edward W. Barrett, cited in Thomas G. Paterson, *On Every Front: The Making of the Cold War* (New York: W. W. Norton & Co., 1979), 171.
30. Acheson, *Present at the Creation,* 374ff.
31. JBC, *MSL,* 509.
32. Sproul recounted the remark by Cornell president E. E. Day in a letter to TSV, June 6, 1951, Sproul Papers, Berkeley.
33. TSV, CPD history.
34. TSV, quoted in William M. Tuttle, "James B. Conant and the Committee on the Present Danger, 1950-52," p. 4, typescript in TSV Papers, box 5.6, "CPD—Additional Materials" folder.
35. Barnard named JBC, DDE, and Robert G. Sproul (presidents, respectively, of Harvard, Columbia, and the University of California at Berkeley)—all later to play crucial roles in CPD's formation.
36. Records of Meetings of the State–Defense Policy Review Group, Feb. 27, Mar. 10, 16, 1950, *FRUS,* 1950, I, 168–75, 190–200.
37. TSV, CPD history, 11.
38. In fact, according to Acheson, by the end of July he and HST had determined that

West German rearmament would be a necessary component of any feasible defense plan for Western Europe, but until September, as Korea dominated attention, neither took active steps to reverse the previous refusal to countenance it, or toward JBC's goal of a universal draft to stock a U.S. contribution to European ground defense. Acheson, *Present at the Creation*, 435–38.

39. TSV, "The Committee on the Present Danger, 1950–1953," TSV Papers, box 5.5, "CPD" folder.

40. JBC to Wriston, Sept. 8, 1950, quoted in JBC, *MSL*, 522–23.

41. JBC to Carr, Sept. 18, 1950, JBC PREP, box 397, "Educational Policies Commission, 1950–51" folder.

42. Marsden, *The Cold War and American Education*, 400.

43. See Stephen E. Ambrose, *Eisenhower, Volume One: Soldier, General of the Army, President-Elect*, 1890–1952 (New York: Simon & Schuster, 1983), 489, 494–99.

44. JBC to Carr, Sept. 18, 1950, JBC PREP, box 397, "Educational Policies Commission, 1950–51" folder.

45. Confidential notes by Harry Bullis, quoted in TSV, 2nd draft, "The Committee on the Present Danger, 1950–1953," TSV Papers, box 5.5, "CPD" folder, TSV Papers.

46. JBC to Marshall, Sept. 19, 1950, Marshall Papers, box 186, folder 44.

47. JBC, "Memorandum for the Conference to be Held in New York September 28 Called by Seven College Presidents," n.d., copy in DDE Pre-Presidential Papers, box 27, James B. Conant (2) folder, DDEL.

48. See Taubman, *Stalin's America Policy*, 202; and Marc Trachtenberg, "A 'Wasting Asset': American Strategy and the Shifting Nuclear Balance, 1949–1954," *International Security* 13:3 (Winter 1988/89), 16.

49. Wriston memo re Military Preparedness, "Eisenhower Study Group Letter to President Truman, Dec 12, 1950," CFR, Eisenhower Study Group File, DDEL, quoted in Marsden, *The Cold War and American Education*, 409.

50. TSV, CPD History, 23; Confidential notes by Harry Bullis, quoted in TSV, 2nd draft, "The Committee on the Present Danger, 1950–1953," TSV Papers, box 5.5, "CPD" folder, TSV Papers, Rutgers.

51. JBC to DDE, Sept. 22, 1950, quoted in JBC, *MSL*, 523.

52. HST later made the same argument. HST, *Years of Trial and Hope*, 55.

53. DDE to JBC, Sept. 26, 1950, DDE Pre-Presidential Papers, 16–52 File, box 27, James B. Conant file (2), DDEL and Louis Galambos, ed., *Papers of Dwight David Eisenhower*, 11:1341–42. JBC incorrectly wrote (in *MSL*, 523) that he only learned "much later" of DDE's "delighted" response to his plan.

54. JBC to DDE, Oct. 3, 1950, DDE Pre-Presidential Papers, 16–52 File, box 27, James B. Conant file (2), DDEL.

55. JBC, *MSL*, 523.

56. JBC to Carr, Sept. 18, Sept. 27, Oct. 3, 1950, Feb. 26, 1951, JBC PREP, "Educational Policies Commission, 1950–51" folder, box 397.

57. JBC to Marshall, Oct. 24, 1950, quoted in JBC, *MSL*, 511, and WLM, *In the Catbird Seat*, 297–98; Marshall to TSV, Nov. 3, 1950, quoted in JBC, *MSL*, 511. Despite this endorsement, doubts soon emerged about Marshall's support for a key element of the new group's program, universal military service. See chap. 27.

58. Memorandum, TSV to Executive Committee, Nov. 14, 1950, quoted in Tuttle, "James B. Conant and the Committee on the Present Danger, 1950–52," TSV Papers, box 5.6, "CPD—Additional Materials" folder.

59. JBC to TSV, Oct. 27, 1950, JBC PREP, box 413, "Universal Military Service, 1950–51" folder. The name, of course, invoked Oliver Wendell Holmes's 1919 Supreme Court ruling that free speech rights "ordinarily" protected by the First Amendment could be abridged in cases (such as shouting "fire!" in a crowded movie house) where "a clear and present danger" existed. It was an appropriate choice, and not only because JBC's friend John Lord O'Brian, who would act as the CPD's lawyer, had as a young Justice Department lawyer argued the Holmes case brief more than three

decades earlier. More importantly, as in *Schenck v. United States,* which had upheld the conviction of a New York socialist for distributing anti-conscription leaflets, the CPD would cite external threats to justify extreme mobilization measures "ordinarily" unheard of in peacetime. *Schenck v. United States,* 249 U.S. 47, 48 (1919).

60. On JBC's health in late 1950: JBC to James L. Morrill, July 14, 1950, JBC PREP, box 394, "Conant: June Operation, M–Z, Misc. 1950–51" folder; JBC to JRO, July 25, 1950, box 27, JROP; JBC to William Carr, Sept. 18, 1950, JBC PREP, box 397, "Educational Policies Commission, 1950–51" folder; JBC to DDE, Sept. 22, 1950, DDEL; JBC desk calendar, JBC PREP; "Conant Reported Gaining After Second Operation," *BG,* Oct. 17, 1950; "Conant's New Operation," *NYT,* Oct. 17, 1950; JBC to Arthur M. Schlesinger, Jr., Nov. 16, 1950, "Col-Con" folder, box 394, JBC PREP.

61. For new evidence on the Chinese intervention, see Chen Jian, "The Sino-Soviet Alliance and China's Entry into the Korean War," Cold War International History Project Working Paper No. 1 (Washington, D.C., 1992); Thomas J. Christensen, "Threats, Assurances, and the Last Chances for Peace," *International Security* 17:1 (Summer 1992), 122–54; and Michael Hunt, "Beijing and the Korean Crisis, June 1950–June 1951," *Political Science Quarterly* 107:3 (Fall 1992), 453–78.

62. Acheson, *Present at the Creation,* 475.

63. Robert H. Ferrell, ed., *Off the Record: The Private Papers of Harry S. Truman* (New York: Penguin, 1980), 204.

64. Erwin N. Griswold to Faculty, Dec. 27, 1950, enc. David F. Cavers to Griswold, "A Task for Law School Research in the Rearmament Period," Dec. 21, 1950, Cavers Papers, Harvard Law School Library, Atomic Energy Control box 1. Anticipating objections to his idea, Cavers reasoned that even if war did not occur, the investigation might well yield a "fresh approach" to new legal questions, and if the Russians did interrupt the project by launching a nuclear strike, "the persons trained by participation in the research, if not wiped out in the first attack, would be invaluable in helping the nation meet the many unsolved problems. . . ." Like JBC's comparable proposal in 1945 to microfilm the written record of Western civilization, Cavers's suggestion was apparently not undertaken. For an impassioned objection to the plan, see Z. Chafee to Erwin N. Griswold, Jan. 8, 1951, box 1, folder 19, Chafee Papers, Harvard Law School Library.

65. HST rejected the advice, which came from the chairman of the National Security Resources Board, Stuart Symington. NSC 100, Jan. 11, 1951, quoted in Richard J. Barnet, *The Alliance* (New York: Simon & Schuster, 1983), 134.

66. DDE diary entries of Nov. 6 and Dec. 5, 1950, quoted in *The Eisenhower Diaries* (New York: W. W. Norton & Co., 1981), ed. Robert H. Ferrell, 181–83.

67. Niebuhr to Schlesinger, Dec. 1, 1950, Schlesinger Papers, box P-20, "Niebuhr, Reinhold, 1948–1952, Folder 1" file, John F. Kennedy Library, Boston.

68. "Universal Service Urged at Pentagon," *NYT,* Dec. 14, 1950.

69. "Text of Group's Statement on Present Peril," *NYT,* Dec. 13, 1950.

70. C. Wright Mills, *The Power Elite* (New York: Oxford University Press, 1956), 184.

71. JBC to James P. Warburg, Dec. 26, 1950, Warburg Papers, Kennedy Library.

72. The "Paul Reveres" quotation is cited in TSV, CPD History, 20; "Military Manpower," WP, Dec. 13, 1950; "'The Present Danger,'" *NYT,* Dec. 14, 1950.

73. JBC, "A Stern Program for Survival," *Look* 14:26 (Dec. 19, 1950), 33–35; JBC, *MSL,* 523–25.

74. See Schulzinger, *The Wise Men of Foreign Affairs,* 136–40.

75. TSV, CPD history; DDE to HST, Dec. 11, 1950, Council on Foreign Relations archives, in Galambos, ed., *Papers of Dwight David Eisenhower,* 11:1464–67.

76. "Universal Service Urged at Pentagon," *NYT,* Dec. 14, 1950.

77. Sanders, *Peddlers of Crisis,* 54–55.

78. "The Present Danger," *NYT,* Dec. 22, 1952.

79. "Mobilizing Urged as Reply to Russia," *NYT,* Dec. 13, 1950.

80. JBC to JRO, Mar. 26, 1951; JRO to JBC, Mar. 30, 1951; JBC to JRO, Apr. 3, 1951, all in "CPD—General Correspondence" folder, box 118, JROP; Alexander Kendrick, *Prime Time: The Life of Edward R. Murrow* (Boston: Little, Brown & Co., 1969), 331–32; A. M. Sperber, *Murrow: Life and Times* (New York: Freundlich Books, 1986; Bantam, 1987), 358.

81. JBC testimony to House Armed Services Committee, Mar. 8, 1951.

82. Fred Warner Neal to Edward R. Murrow, May 16, 1951, Murrow Papers, Tufts University.

83. On the PSB's creation, see *FRUS*, 1951, I, 58–61, 178–80; Ludwell Lee Montague, *General Walter Bedell Smith as Director of Central Intelligence: October 1950–February 1953* (University Park: Pennsylvania State University Press, 1992), 203–6, 212–15; John Prados, *Keepers of the Keys: A History of the National Security Council from Truman to Bush* (New York: William Morrow & Co., 1991), 53–56, 64–65. A full account of this secretive Cold War body remains to be written.

84. James R. Killian, *The Education of a College President: A Memoir* (Cambridge: MIT Press, 1985), 65–68; Allan A. Needell, " 'Truth is Our Weapon': Project TROY, Political Warfare, and Government—Academic Relations in the National Security State," *Diplomatic History* 17:3 (Summer 1993), 399–420.

85. JBC diary, Jan. 13, 1951; VB to JBC ("Dear Jim"), Jan. 8, enclosing draft of VB to JBC ("Dear Dr. Conant"), Jan. 8, 1951; VB to JBC, Jan. 18, 1951; in VBP, box 27, file 614; VB to James R. Killian, Jr., Jan. 25, 1951, Killian Papers, MIT.

86. Mills, *The Power Elite*, 4, 11, 18.

87. Mills, *The Power Elite*, 24–25.

88. Interview with Dick Rowsen, Oct. 16, 1992. Rowsen then headed the FPA's Providence office and recalls close cooperation with the CPD and widespread use of its materials.

89. Mills, *The Power Elite*, 356.

90. Acheson, *Present at the Creation*, 375.

CHAPTER 26

1. Sanders, *Peddlers of Crisis*, 77–81; Frederick F. Siegel, *Troubled Journey: From Pearl Harbor to Ronald Reagan* (New York: Hill & Wang, 1984), 65–85; Selig Adler, *The Isolationist Impulse: Its Twentieth Century Reaction* (New York: Collier Books, 1957, 1961), 368–427; Robert J. Donovan, *Tumultuous Years: The Presidency of Harry S. Truman, 1949–1953* (New York: W. W. Norton & Co., 1982), 321–24; Richard H. Rovere and Arthur Schlesinger, Jr., *The MacArthur Controversy and American Foreign Policy* (originally published in 1951 as *The General and the President*) (New York: Noonday Press, 1965), 229–35.

2. Acheson, *Present at the Creation*, 488.

3. "The Enemy Within Our Gates: The Pious Pretenders," *Washington Times-Herald*, Jan. 10, 1951; "A Pledge Recalled," *Chicago Tribune*, Dec. 25, 1952; and *Chicago Tribune*, Apr. 12, 1951, quoted in *THC*, Apr. 14, 18, 1951.

4. DDE diary entry of Dec. 16, 1950, Ferrell, ed., *The Eisenhower Diaries*, 183.

5. JBC to TSV, Oct. 27, 1950, JBC PERP, box 413, "Universal Military Service, 1950–51" folder.

6. JBC to CPD members, July 7, 1951, Murrow Papers.

7. JBC, *MSL*, 524–25.

8. Acheson, *Present at the Creation*, 489.

9. TSV, Memorandum to members of the CPD, Jan. 2, 1951, Tab P, TSV Papers, in Sanders, *Peddlers of Crisis*, 58.

10. DDE diary entry of Nov. 6, 1950, Ferrell, ed., *The Eisenhower Diaries*, 181.

11. DDE to JBC, June 26, 1951, DDE Pre-Presidential Papers, 16-52 File, box 27, James B. Conant file (2), DDEL.

12. JBC to DDE, Dec. 21, 1950, DDE Pre-Presidential Papers, 16–52 File, box 27, James B. Conant file (2), DDEL.
13. DDE to JBC, Dec. 31, 1950, DDE Pre-Presidential Papers, 16–52 File, box 27, James B. Conant file (2), DDEL.
14. Report to Members of the CPD and Tentative Projection of Activities, May 17, 1951, tab Y, TSV Papers, in Sanders, *Peddlers of Crisis,* 89–90.
15. Acheson, *Present at the Creation,* 494.
16. "Civic Group Asks Aid to Eisenhower" and "Text of Committee's Statement," *NYT,* Jan. 8, 1951.
17. JBC, "The Present Danger," Feb. 7, 1951, JBC Speech File; JBC, *MSL,* 514–17.
18. DDE testimony on the Mutual Defense Assistance Program, Feb. 2, 1951, in U.S. House of Representatives, Committee on International Relations, *Selected Executive Session Hearings of the Committee, 1943-50,* vol. 6, *Military Assistance Program,* pt. 2 (Washington, D.C.: Government Printing Office, 1976), 273.
19. JBC to CPD members, July 7, 1951, Murrow Papers.
20. CPD statement of Jan. 7, 1951, in *NYT,* Jan. 8, 1951.
21. German chancellor Konrad Adenauer, among others, feared that "Stalin was planning the same procedure for Western Germany as had been used in Korea." Adenauer, *Memoirs, 1945-1964* (Chicago: Henry Regnery Co., 1965), 273, in Kaplan, *NATO and the United States,* 44. In fact, according to Khrushchev, Stalin was terrified of provoking Washington into a preemptive nuclear strike. *Khrushchev Remembers: The Glasnost Tapes,* 146.
22. Kaplan, *NATO and the United States,* 48.
23. NYT, Apr. 5, 1951; JBC, *MSL,* 526–27.
24. W. Barton Leach to JBC, Apr. 26, 1951, Leach Papers, box 52, folder 6.
25. Copies of all the CPD radio addresses can be found in the TSV and CPD Papers at Rutgers.
26. JBC, *MSL,* 517.
27. Sanders, *Peddlers of Crisis,* 16.
28. This account of the Truman-MacArthur controversy is drawn from Rovere and Schlesinger, *The MacArthur Controversy,* passim.; Acheson, *Present at the Creation,* chap. 46–51, 53–54; Donovan, *Tumultuous Years,* chap. 27–33; William Manchester, *American Caesar: Douglas MacArthur 1880-1964* (Boston: Little, Brown & Co., 1978; Dell paperback ed., 1982), chap. 9–10; Michael Schaller, *Douglas MacArthur: The Far Eastern General* (New York: Oxford University Press, 1989), chap. 12–14; HST, *Years of Trial and Hope,* chap. 22–28.
29. Merle Miller, *Plain Speaking: An Oral Biography of Harry S. Truman* (New York: Putnam, 1973), 314–18.
30. MacArthur to Joint Chiefs, Nov. 9, 1950, in Schnabel and Watson, *The History of the Joint Chiefs of Staff,* vol. III, *The Korean War,* pt. 1, 302, in Schaller, *Douglas MacArthur,* 210.
31. HST, *Years of Trial and Hope,* 416.
32. HST, *Years of Trial and Hope,* 438–42.
33. HST, *Years of Trial and Hope,* 440–45; Acheson, *Present at the Creation,* 519.
34. HST diary entry of Apr. 6, 1951, in Ferrell, ed., *Off the Record: The Private Papers of Harry S. Truman,* 210.
35. MacArthur's comments are quoted in HST, *Years of Trial and Hope,* 445–46; Schaller, *Douglas MacArthur,* 235; Rovere and Schlesinger, *The MacArthur Controversy,* 171–72; Acheson, *Present at the Creation,* 520.
36. CPD, "Objectives," Apr. 5, 1951, copy in TSV Papers, box 5.5, "CPD" folder.
37. JBC diary, Apr. 11, 1951.
38. *THC* reported that faculty "lined up solidly behind President Truman" while student reaction "ranged from active support to violent opposition." "Faculty Lauds Truman's Dismissal of MacArthur," *THC,* Apr. 12, 1951.
39. JBC diary, Apr. 11, 1951.

40. Rovere and Schlesinger, *The MacArthur Controversy*, 5.
41. See Donovan, *Tumultuous Years*, 358–61; Manchester, *American Caesar*, 775–81; Stephen E. Ambrose, *Rise to Globalism: American Foreign Policy Since 1938* (New York: Penguin, 5th rev. ed., 1988), 128–31; Schaller, *Douglas MacArthur*, 239–42.
42. Ambrose, *Rise to Globalism*, 129.
43. MacArthur's speech is reprinted in Barton J. Bernstein and Allen J. Matusow, eds., *The Truman Administration: A Documentary History* (New York: Harper & Row, 1966), 461–69.
44. Miller, *Plain Speaking*, 336–339.
45. [Bailey?] to JBC, c/o The Rector, Lincoln College, Oxford, Apr. 24, 1951, "Conant: Personal, 1950–51" folder, box 394, JBC PREP.
46. JBC diary, May 6, 7, 14, 15, 1951; *THC*, Apr. 18, 20, 24, May 25, 1951.
47. Cutler to Sam Goldwyn, Apr. 25, 1951, quoted in Sanders, *Peddlers of Crisis*, 99.
48. TSV, CPD history, 51.
49. Goldwyn to TSV, Apr. 21, 1951, enc. with Goldwyn to Murrow, Apr. 21, 1951, Murrow Papers.
50. Murrow to Goldwyn, Apr. 27, 1951, Murrow Papers.
51. See TSV, "Areas of Agreement in the MacArthur Controversy," Apr. 26, 1951, and TSV to CPD members, "Notes as to the present status of the MacArthur question and what the Committee on the Present Danger might do about it," May 14, 1951, both in TSV Papers.
52. See Sanders, *Peddlers of Crisis*, 104–105; Adler, report of talk with MacArthur, May 23, 1951, TSV Papers.
53. JBC, "The Defense of Europe in the Atomic Age," address to Chicago Association of Commerce and Council on Foreign Relations, May 17, 1951, JBC Speech File.
54. MacArthur's supposed enthusiasm for atomic retaliation against Chinese or Soviet targets (in Feb. 1951 he suggested spreading "a field of radioactive wastes" to "sever Korea from Manchuria" and interrupt enemy supply lines) so alarmed HST and his advisers that they kept secret from him orders transferring atomic weapons from the AEC to military custody, because, as Bradley later acknowledged, of the danger that MacArthur "might make a premature decision" to use them. Schaller, *MacArthur*, 193, 225, 236; Manchester, *American Caesar*, 748. See also Acheson, *Present at the Creation*, 514; Roger Dingman, "Atomic Diplomacy During the Korean War," *International Security* 13:3 (Winter 1988/89), 50–91, esp. 62, 67–68; Newhouse, *War and Peace in the Nuclear Age*, 83–84; Ambrose, *Eisenhower: The President*, 34–35.
55. Quoted in Manchester, *American Caesar*, 799.
56. TSV to CPD members, May 14, 1951, TSV Papers.
57. Quoted in Bernstein and Matusow, eds., *The Truman Administration*, 478.
58. See Trachtenberg, "A 'Wasting Asset,' " passim.
59. JBC to Walter Lippmann, Feb. 20, 1951, Lippmann Papers, Sterling Library, Yale University, box 63, folder 491.
60. Lippmann to JBC, Feb. 26, 1951, Lippmann Papers, box 63, folder 491.
61. JBC to Lippmann, Mar. 5, 1951, Lippmann Papers, box 63, folder 491.
62. JBC to Lippmann, Mar. 5, 1951, Lippmann Papers, box 63, folder 491.
63. MacArthur's statement: Manchester, *American Caesar*, 798.
64. Sanders, *Peddlers of Crisis*, 102.
65. JBC, "The Defense of Europe in the Atomic Age," May 17, 1951, and "The Defense of the Free World in the Atomic Age," June 3, 1951.
66. TSV to CPD Executive Committee, "Subject: Notes of proposal made to me orally by Dr. Conant as to how the Committee might approach the MacArthur matter," May 29, 1951, Robert G. Sproul Papers, Bancroft Library, University of California (Berkeley).
67. Lloyd C. Gardner, *A Covenant with Power: American and World Order from Wilson to Reagan* (New York: Oxford University Press, 1984), chap. 5–7; David L. Anderson, "J. Lawton Collins, John Foster Dulles, and the Eisenhower Administration's 'Point of No Return' in Vietnam," *Diplomatic History* 12 (Spring 1988), 127–47.

68. "protectorate": Gardner, *A Covenant with Power,* chap. 4; "empire by invitation": Geir Lundestad, *The American "Empire"* (London: Oxford University Press and Norwegian University Press, 1990), esp. 31–115.
69. JBC, "The Defense of Europe in the Atomic Age."
70. JBC to members of the CPD, July 7, 1951, TSV Papers, CPD collection, Office File (3), June–Nov. 1951.
71. JBC to CPD members, July 7, 1951, Murrow Papers.
72. Ambrose, *Rise to Globalism,* 130.
73. JBC to CPD members, July 7, 1951.
74. Minutes of CPD meeting, New York City, Oct. 24, 1951, TSV Papers, CPD collection.

CHAPTER 27

1. See chap. 33.
2. See projected manpower figures in Doris M. Condit, History of the Office of the Secretary of Defense, vol. 2, The Test of War, 1950–1953 (Washington, D.C., 1989), 240, 255, 278, 301, cited in Ernest R. May, "The American Commitment to Germany, 1949–55," *Diplomatic History* 13:4 (Fall 1989), 441.
3. JBC, *MSL,* chap. 24–25.
4. See Donovan, *Conflict and Crisis,* 136–37, 285, 357, 361; George Q. Flynn, *Lewis B. Hershey, Mr. Selective Service* (Chapel Hill: University of North Carolina Press, 1985), 154–76, 194–96; JBC, *President's Report* 1948 (Jan. 10, 1949) (Cambridge: Harvard University, 1949), 14–17.
5. JBC to CPD members, July 7, 1951.
6. JBC to Marshall, Feb. 7, 1951, George C. Marshall Papers, box 189, folder 20.
7. JBC to Marshall, Feb. 7, 1951, George C. Marshall Papers, box 189, folder 20.
8. JBC to Charles Cole, Feb. 14, 1951, "Col-Con," 1950–51, folder, JBC PREP, box 394.
9. EPC 37, Mar. 29–31, 1951, 52, 57.
10. EPC 37, Mar. 29–31, 1951, 67.
11. JBC testimony, Mar. 8, 1951, in U.S. House of Representatives, 82d Cong., 1st Sess., Committee on Armed Services, *Universal Military Training,* 820.
12. JBC, "The Defense of Europe in the Atomic Age," address to Chicago Association of Commerce and Council on Foreign Relations, May 17, 1951.
13. JBC to CPD members, July 7, 1951.
14. Robert Patterson, quoted in minutes of CPD meeting, Oct. 24, 1951, CPD Papers; also copy in Murrow Papers.
15. See Samuel P. Huntington, *The Common Defense: Strategic Programs in National Politics* (New York: Columbia University Press, 1961; paperback ed., 1966), 58–59.
16. "Memorandum of Conversation, by the Director of the State Department Policy Planning Staff (Nitze), Meeting, October 9, 1950," *FRUS,* 1950, III, 364–66.
17. DDE diary entry of Nov. 6, 1950, in Ferrell, ed., *The Eisenhower Diaries,* 181.
18. This account is drawn from a letter from WLM to JBC, approx. Nov. 23, 1950, in WLM, *In the Catbird Seat,* 298–301, and a fuller version provided to the author by WLM.
19. See WLM, *In the Catbird Seat,* 300–1.
20. Galbraith interview, Jan. 1989.
21. "The Prospect Before You," *THC,* Sept. 1950 registration issue.
22. *THC,* Oct. 16, 17, 18, 1950.
23. Tuttle, "James B. Conant and the Committee on the Present Danger," 12, TSV Papers, box 5.6, "CPD—Additional Materials" folder; *THC,* Oct. 30, 1950; Flynn, *Louis B. Hershey,* 197–98.
24. JBC, "A Stern Program for Survival," *Look* 14:26 (Dec. 19, 1950), 33–35.
25. JBC to Gray, Nov. 1, 1950, "Universal Military Service, 1950–51" folder, box 413,

JBC PREP; Tuttle, "James B. Conant and the Committee on the Present Danger, 1950-52," TSV Papers.

26. "Conant's Plan Hit by College Heads," *NYT,* Dec. 15, 1950.
27. Charles W. Cole, "A Reply to Harvard's Dr. Conant: Total Conscription Will *Hurt* America," *Look* 15:1 (Jan. 2, 1950), 54-55.
28. Letter to JBC, Dec. 18, 1950, JBC PREP, box 403, "LOOK MAGAZINE: Comments on, 1950-51" folder.
29. Iva Mae Cookreau to JBC, Dec. 1, 1950, JBC PREP, box 403, "LOOK MAGAZINE: Comments on, 1950-51" folder.
30. Pearl S. Buck to editors of *Look,* n.d., enc. with E. Raymond Wilson to Robert G. Sproul, Dec. 13, 1950, Sproul Papers, University of California (Berkeley).
31. "A Pledge Recalled," *Chicago Tribune,* Dec. 25, 1952.
32. Cole, "A Reply to Harvard's Dr. Conant," 54-55. Emphasis in original.
33. Edmund E. Day, "The Utilization of Human Resources in Peace and War," Dec. 7, 1950, Day Papers, Cornell University, box 53, folder 57.
34. William T. Golden, interview with JBC, Dec. 14, 1950, Golden Papers. See also his early 1951 exchange with Walter Lippmann, in which JBC elaborated the reasoning behind his fears of a Soviet attack, grappled with the implications of preventive war, and developed his understanding of the dynamics of nuclear deterrence. JBC to Lippmann, Feb. 20 and Mar. 5, 1951, and Lippmann to JBC, Feb. 26, 1951, all in Lippmann Papers, box 63, folder 491. By then JBC's estimate of the period of the "maximum danger" of a Soviet attack seemed to have slipped to 1954-56, rather than the 1952-54 period he had earlier mentioned, not unlike the sliding predictions in the late forties of when the Soviets would attain the atomic bomb.
35. JBC, *MSL,* 523.
36. JBC, *President's Report 1949-1950* (Jan. 8, 1951) (Cambridge: Harvard University, 1951), 1-3; JBC to Charles Dollard, Jan. 10, 1951, "Conant, James B. 1934-55" folder, CCP.
37. JBC to Dave [Bailey], Nov. 20, 1950, box 403, "LOOK MAGAZINE: Comments on, 1950-51" folder, box 403, JBC PREP.
38. JBC to Cole, Dec. 22, 1950, "LOOK MAGAZINE: Comments on, 1950-51" folder, box 403, JBC PREP; Cole to JBC, Dec. 29, 1950; Cole to JBC, Feb. 12, 1951; JBC to Charles Cole, Feb. 14, 1951; Charlie Cole to JBC, Feb. 19, 1951; all in "Col-Con" folder, box 394, JBC PREP.
39. JBC to Charles Cole, Feb. 14, 1951, "Col-Con" folder, box 394, JBC PREP.
40. JBC to VB, Dec. 26, 1950, "Bush, Vannevar, 1950-51" folder, box 392, JBC PREP.
41. VB to JBC, Dec. 18, 1950, and JBC to VB, Dec. 26, 1950, "Bush, Vannevar, 1950-51" folder, box 392, JBC PREP.
42. JBC, *President's Report 1949-1950,* 1-3; see also JBC, *President's Report, 1950-1951* (Jan. 14, 1952) (Cambridge: Harvard University, 1952), 1, 7, 20-21. Contemplating the inevitable dislocations and possible fifty percent drop in male enrollment facing U.S. colleges in even a partial mobilization, JBC felt comforted by Harvard's healthy, fluid fiscal reserves, and vindicated for having taken unpopular austerity measures to trim faculty departments and to assure a diversity of funding sources. "I can't help feeling," he wrote the Carnegie Corporation's president, Charles Dollard, "that some of those who are howling the loudest now are people who have run their budgets on an extremely short-sighted basis and allowed their commitments to equal their revenue even in the years of demobilization which clearly were years of great income. But far be it from me to criticize my colleagues." JBC proposed to Dollard that the Carnegie, Ford, and Rockefeller philanthropic foundations together create a loan company to finance money-strapped private colleges (but *not* Harvard, he promised) for the duration of the emergency, estimating the cost involved at $20 million a year for two or three years with at least half later to be repaid with interest. "You may say, 'But what if there is a global war[?],' in which case I would say, 'All bets are off and you have lost your money, but everyone else will have lost a great

deal more.'" JBC urged Dollard not to circulate this "wild idea" very freely "as I don't want to be committed to the insane asylum yet," and Dollard didn't—he politely deferred the proposal, which a Carnegie aide described as "bold" but "away off the beam!" See JBC to Dollard, Jan. 10, 1951; [?] to CD, n.d.; Dollard to JBC, Jan. 20, 1951; all in "Conant, James B. 1933–54" folder, CCP.

43. *THC*, Mar. 8, 1951.
44. *BG*, May 27, 1951.
45. *THC*, Jan. 16, 1951.
46. JBC, statement to American Council on Education, Jan. 19, 1951, JBC Speech File, 305, JBC PREP; see also JBC to VB, Dec. 26, 1950, "Bush, Vannevar, 1950–51" folder, JBC PREP, box 392, and JBC to Cole, Dec. 22, 1950, JBC to Cole, Dec. 22, 1950, "LOOK MAGAZINE: Comments on, 1950–51" folder, box 403, JBC PREP.
47. For JBC's emphasis on minimizing disruption and his opposition to "acceleration" proposals see JBC, *President's Report* 1949–1950, 1–3; "College Must Move Forward Despite War, Conant Warns," *THC*, Jan. 15, 1951; "College Plans No 3 Term Schedule" and "New Draft Law Cuts Withdrawals; Defer Men Now in School— Conant," *THC*, Jan. 23, 1951; JBC diary, Jan. 16, 17, 18, 24, 1951; and correspondence in "U.S. Govt: Department of Defense" folder, box 445, JBC PREP.
48. EPC 37, March 29–31, 1951, 297.
49. Rep. William G. Bray, Indiana, to JBC, Jan. 20, 1951, "LOOK MAGAZINE: Comments on, 1950–51" folder, box 403, JBC PREP.
50. JBC to Bray, Jan. 23, 1951, "LOOK MAGAZINE: Comments on, 1950–51" folder, box 403, JBC PREP.
51. WLM, "The Manpower Program of the Committee on the Present Danger," Sept. 8, 1970, TSV Papers, box 5.6, "CPD—Additional Material" folder; see also JBC diary, Jan. 20.
52. JBC to Marshall, Feb. 7, 1951, Marshall Papers, box 189, folder 20.
53. Marshall to JBC, Feb. 20, 1951, "U.S. Govt: Department of Defense" folder, box 445, JBC PREP.
54. JBC diary, Mar. 8, 1951; JBC's testimony: U.S. House of Representatives, 82d Cong., 1st Sess., Committee on Armed Services, *Universal Military Training*, 815–21.
55. JBC diary, Mar. 13, 1951.
56. JBC to LRG, May 19, 1951, Groves Papers, RG 200, NA.
57. Ironically, the outfit to which the Selective Service System turned to administer the nationwide tests (the Selective Service College Qualification Test, or SSCQT), which JBC abhorred on principle, was the Educational Testing Service (ETS)—an organization that owed its existence to JBC's efforts in the late 1930s to spread the use of educational testing in order to locate candidates for Harvard's national scholarships, and his postwar midwifing of negotiations to merge three separate testing businesses into ETS. The Selective Service contract was critical to ETS's rise to become the largest U.S. educational testing service. On JBC's part in ETS's creation: JBC, *MSL*, chap. 31, and Biebel, *Politics, Pegagogues, and Statesmanship*, 112–22, 257–66; on ETS and selective service: Flynn, *Lewis B. Hershey*, 198, 201–202, and the forthcoming study on meritocracy in America by Nicholas Lemann (New York: Alfred A. Knopf; anticipated publication date, 1996), who kindly shared some of his findings with me. JBC expressed his concern over ETS's involvement with selective service to Henry Chauncey in late December and urged him to remember the "limitations" of testing: "OCC and James B. Conant," Dec. 28, 1950, "Conant, James B. 1934–55" folder, CCP.
58. Patterson to WLM, Mar. 27, 1951, quoted in WLM, "The Manpower Program of the Committee on the Present Danger," and WLM ms. on UMS, n.d., TSV Papers, box 5, "5: CPD: Marbury material" folder.
59. Transcript of Educational Policies Commission meeting 37, March 29–31, 1951, pp. 42–43, 45–46, NEA archives, Washington, D.C.
60. "Your Son & Universal Service," CBS, Apr. 8, 1951, CPD Papers, tab AA.

61. JBC to William G. Carr, Oct. 3, 1950, Feb. 26, and Mar. 2, 1951; Carr to JBC, June 15, 1951; box 397, "Educational Policies Commission" folder, JBC PREP.
62. Transcript of Educational Policies Commission meeting 37, March 29–31, 1951, 36, NEA archives, Washington, D.C. For the draft that appalled JBC, see "Education and National Security," Feb. 1951 draft, NEA archives.
63. William M. Tuttle, Jr., "James B. Conant and the Committee on the Present Danger, 1950–52," Mar. 1967, 25, copy in TSV Papers, box 5.6, "CPD–Additional Materials" folder; JBC to Carr, Mar. 2, 1951, JBC PREP, box 397, "Educational Policies Commission" folder.
64. JBC to DDE, June 19, 1951, JBC PREP, box 397, "Educational Policies Commission" folder.
65. Carr to JBC, June 15, 1951, JBC PREP, box 397, "Educational Policies Commission" folder.
66. Carr, "Memorandum of a conversation with General Eisenhower, September 11, 1951," Oct. 3, 1951; and transcript of EPC 38, October 4–6, 1951, vol. 1, 17–19, 340–345, both in NEA archives.
67. See *Education and National Security* (Washington, D.C.: Educational Policies Commission and American Council on Education, Dec. 1951), 41–60.
68. JBC diary, Dec. 4, 1951.
69. WLM to *Baltimore Sun*, June 1, 1951, in WLM, *In the Catbird Seat*, 304.
70. For the dispute over the bill's import, see Rosenberg telegram to TSV, May 23, 1951; TSV to Rosenberg, June 22, 1951; Rosenberg to TSV, July 2, 1951; JBC to CPD, July 7, 1951; all in CPD Papers.
71. JBC, address to Harvard Alumni Association, Harvard Yard, June 21, 1951, Harvard News Office release, JBC Speech File; see also JBC, *President's Report*, 1950–1951, 3.
72. Huntington, *The Common Defense*, 58–59.
73. In fact, despite his earlier support for UMS, for a mix of fiscal, political, and strategic reasons DDE upon becoming president quickly moved even further away from the concept when he instituted his "New Look" military strategy, which emphasized a greater reliance on nuclear weapons.
74. JBC, *MSL*, 530–31.
75. JBC to WLM, Feb. 20, 1971, in TSV Papers, box 5, "5: CPD: Marbury Material" folder.
76. JBC to WLM, Feb. 20, 1971, in TSV Papers, box 5, "5: CPD: Marbury Material" folder.
77. WLM to TSV, Feb. 23, 1971, in TSV Papers, box 5, "5: CPD: Marbury Material" folder.
78. JBC to WLM, Feb. 20, 1971, in TSV Papers, box 5, "5: CPD: Marbury Material" folder.

CHAPTER 28

1. *THC*, "Harvard: Russian View," Nov. 30, 1951.
2. See Paul Forman, "Behind Quantum Electronics: National Security as Basis for Physical Research in the United States, 1940–1960," *Historical Studies in the Physical and Biological Sciences (HSPS)* 18:1 (1987), 149–229; and Daniel J. Kevles, "Cold War and Hot Physics: Science, Security, and the American State, 1945–1956," *HSPS* 20:2 (1990), 239–64; Kevles, *The Physicists*: chap. 12–13; and Gellhorn, *Security, Loyalty, and Science*, 175–77.
3. On the evolution of the presidential science advisory apparatus see Herken, *Cardinal Choices*, passim.; William T. Golden, ed., *Science Advice to the President* (New York: Pergamon, 1980); James R. Killian, Jr., *Sputnik, Scientists, and Eisenhower: A Memoir of the First Special Assistant to the President for Science and Technology* (Cambridge: MIT Press, 1977), 6off.

4. JBC, "The Problems of Evaluation of Scientific Research and Development for Military Planning," speech to the National War College, Feb. 1, 1950, National Defense University archives, Washington, D.C. For JBC's advocacy of this idea, see also "Science and Politics in the Twentieth Century," *Foreign Affairs* 28:2 (Jan. 1950), 201; JBC, "The Soviet Challenge," talks to Rochester Harvard Club and Rochester Chamber of Commerce, Jan. 27, 1950, text in Harvard News Office press release, JBC Speech File, 293, JBC PREP; *Science and Common Sense* (New Haven: Yale University Press, 1951), 335–39; minutes, SAC/ODM meeting 7, Jan. 11, 1952, Killian-Compton Papers, MIT, and DuBridge papers, Caltech.

5. JBC to Philip L. Graham, Mar. 6, 1950, "Was-Wek" folder, box 386, JBC PREP; see also JBC to Chester I. Dollard, June 5, 1950, "Harvard University Support of an Experiment in Teaching Science to Non-Scientists" folder, CCP.

6. JBC, *Science and Common Sense*, 4; C. P. Snow, *The Two Cultures and the Scientific Revolution* (New York: Cambridge University Press, 1959).

7. Snow, *The Two Cultures: And a Second Look* (Cambridge, 1963; Mentor Book ed.), 90; also Snow, *Science and Government* (Cambridge, Mass.: Harvard University Press, 1962; Mentor Book ed.), esp. 9–11, 116–119, and Max Tishler, "Shadows on Today: Reflections on Tomorrow," *The Chemist* (May 1977), copy in JBC PERP.

8. JBC, *Science and Common Sense*, 10, 13–14.

9. Philipp Frank, "Introductory Remarks," and JBC, "Greetings to the National Conference of the Institute for the Unity of Science, Boston, Massachusetts—April 1950," *Proceedings of the American Academy of Arts and Sciences* 80 (Boston: American Academy of Arts and Sciences, 1951–1954), 5–8, 9–13, esp. 13. I am grateful to Gerald Holton for referring me to this source and describing its context in an interview of Apr. 16, 1993. See also Holton, "Ernst Mach and the Fortunes of Positivism in America," *ISIS* 83 (1992), 27–60, esp. 55.

10. On popular post–World War II adulation of scientists and the "scientific method" idea, see Jones Kenneth MacDonald, *Science, Scientists, and Americans: Images of Science and the Formation of Federal Science Policy, 1945–1950* (Ph.D. diss., Cornell University; Ann Arbor: University Microfilms International, 1975), esp. 92–93, 108, 133–37, 173–74; "nonsense": JBC to Charles Dollard, Nov. 8, 1951, "Harvard University 1946–1955" folder, CCP.

11. JBC, *Science and Common Sense*, 25.

12. JBC, *Science and Common Sense*, 120–21, 304–305, 315–24, 339–40, 346–48.

13. JBC, *Science and Common Sense*, 320–23, 341.

14. Quoted in J.R. Killian, "Military research in the universities," *Journal of Engineering Education* 43 (1952), 13–17 in Forman, "Behind Quantum Electronics," 201.

15. JBC, *Science and Common Sense*, 346–53.

16. JBC, *Science and Common Sense*, 339–40.

17. See Reardon, *History of the Office of the Secretary of Defense*, vol. 1, 96–103, cited in Forman, "Behind Quantum Electronics," 157; Kevles, "Cold War and Hot Physics," 247.

18. Kevles, *The Physicists*, 364, citing a contemporary report, gives $29 million as the 1949 ONR figure; National Academy, *Federal Support of Basic Research in Institutions of Higher Learning* (Washington, D.C., 1964), quoted in Penick et al., *The Politics of American Science: 1939 to the Present* (Cambridge: MIT Press, 1965, 1972), 22–24, gives $20 million; Kevles, "Cold War and Hot Physics," 245.

19. Kevles, "Cold War and Hot Physics," 246–52; Thaddeus J. Trenn, *America's Golden Bough: The Science Advisory Intertwist* (Cambridge: Oelgeschlager, Gunn & Hain, 1983), 37; SAC/ODM meeting 2, June 23, 1951, attach. 1, "Notes on Report of the Committees on Plans for Mobilizing Science, RDB 148/14," box 17, "SAC of ODM—1951" folder, NSF records—Director's Office—Subject Files, RG 307, NA.

20. For VB's disappointment with NSF, see Nathan Reingold, "Vannevar Bush's new deal for research: or The triumph of the old order," *HSPS* 17:2 (1987), 299–344, esp. 299–301, 341–42. For the process leading to NSF's creation, see J. Merton English, *A*

Patron for Pure Science: The National Science Foundation's Formative Years, 1945-1957 (Washington: National Science Foundation, 1983); MacDonald, *Science, Scientists, and Americans,* chap. 2, 6, 7; Cochrane, *The National Academy of Sciences,* 457–68, 480–83.

21. William T. Golden, conversation with VB, Oct. 24, 1950; conversation with Dr. Irvin Stewart, Nov. 14, 1950; conversation with Carroll L. Wilson, Nov. 21, 1950, as of Nov. 15; conversation with Dr. Alfred Lee Loomis, Nov. 21, 1950, as of Nov. 16; conversation with Dr. I. I. Rabi, Nov. 21, 1950, as of Nov. 16, 1950; "left scars": conversation with Dr. Lawrence Hafstad, Jan. 4, 1951, as of Jan. 3, 1951; telephone conversation with Mr. Carroll L. Wilson, Jan. 30, 1951; all courtesy of Mr. Golden (hereafter Golden Papers).

22. Frederick C. Schuldt, Jr. to files, Dec. 18, 1950, "First Meeting of the National Science Board," "National Science Foundation—General Administration" folder, box 18, series 39.33, Bureau of Budget Papers, RG 51, NA.

23. JBC to George B. Kistiakowsky, Dec. 21, 1950, courtesy of Elaine Kistiakowsky.

24. Golden, conversation with Dr. James B. Conant, Dec. 14, 1950; telephone conversation with Dr. James B. Conant, Jan. 2, 1951, as of Dec. 29, 1950; see also conversation with Gen. Leslie R. Groves, Dec. 20, 1950, as of Dec. 16, 1950; all in Golden Papers.

25. JBC to VB, Dec. 26, 1950, "Bush, Vannevar, 1950–51" folder, box 392, JBC PREP.

26. Kistiakowsky to JBC, Dec. 14, 1950; JBC to Kistiakowsky, Dec. 21, 1950; courtesy of Elaine Kistiakowsky.

27. Golden to HST, Dec. 18, 1950, with attached memo, "Mobilizing Science for War: A Scientific Adviser to the President," Golden Papers.

28. William T. Golden, memorandum of conversation with DuBridge, Jan. 8, 1951, Golden Papers.

29. Minutes of National Science Board, National Science Foundation, Meeting 2, Jan. 3, 1951, HST OF, box 682, National Science Foundation, folder 192-E-Misc, HSTL.

30. Frederick C. Schuldt, Jr. to Files, "Recent Developments in the National Science Board," Jan. 9, 1951, Bureau of Budget Papers, RG 51, NA, series 39.33, box 18, "National Science Foundation—General Administration" folder.

31. William T. Golden, meeting with Conant, Stauffacher, Staats, Carey, and Levi at Bureau, Jan. 5, 1951, Golden Papers; English, *A Patron for Pure Science,* 125.

32. English, *A Patron for Pure Science,* 125; William T. Golden, memorandums of conversation with I. I. Rabi, Jan. 5, 1951, and with DuBridge, Jan. 8, 1951, Golden Papers. Bronk's reported advocacy of a strong military involvement for NSF in Jan. 1951 contradicted his subsequent claim that he supported a purely nonmilitary role for the foundation. Bronk, "Science Advice in the White House," *Science* 186 (Oct. 11, 1974), 116–121, in Golden, ed., *Science Advice to the President,* 245–56.

33. JBC diary, Jan. 3, 1951.

34. JBC diary, Jan. 5, 1951; see also Golden, conversation with Lee A. DuBridge, Jan. 8, 1951, Golden Papers.

35. English, *A Patron for Pure Science,* 124–26.

36. JBC diary, Jan. 15, 1951.

37. JBC diary, Mar. 8, 1951; JBC to HST, Feb. 13, 1951; Golden to Donald S. Dawson, Feb. 16, 1951; HST to Dawson, Feb. 20, 1951; Dawson to HST, Mar. 7, 1951; all in HST OF, box 682, National Science Foundation, folder 192-E-Misc, HSTL.

38. JBC, *MSL,* 562.

39. Waterman security memorandum, n.d. but apparently Mar. 1951, HST OF, box 682, National Science Foundation, folder 192-E-Misc, HSTL.

40. JBC diary, Mar. 9, 1951.

41. JBC diary, Mar. 9, 1951; English, *A Patron for Pure Science,* 127.

42. Frederick C. Schuldt, Jr. to Files, "Recent Developments in the National Science Board," Jan. 9, 1951, Bureau of Budget Papers, RG 51, NA, series 39.33, box 18, "National Science Foundation—General Administration" folder.

43. Golden, conversation with Dr. Vannevar Bush, Oct. 24, 1950, Golden Papers; Kevles, *The Physicists,* 355–59; Kevles, "Cold War and Hot Physics," 259.
44. Lee A. DuBridge, "Science and National Security," in the *Bulletin of the California Institute of Technology* 58:3 (Sept. 1949), 1–19, an expanded version of the article appearing in *Atlantic Monthly* (Oct. 1949), 26–29.
45. Forman, "Behind Quantum Electronics," 185. While protesting excessive security restrictions, DuBridge later pleaded with the Eisenhower administration not to transfer all basic research to NSF because, he wrote, it was "most important" that the Defense Department "energetically maintain the position that, for the security of the country, the various military establishments must engage in and support basic research on a broad front." It was vital to do this, DuBridge added defensively, "not for the objective of supporting universities, but with the objective of maintaining a strong base of science which will be of value to our security." DuBridge to Donald Quarles, Jan. 14, 1954, DuBridge Papers, folder 187.2. On Caltech's links to defense work, see Clayton R. Koppes, *JPL and the American Space Program: A History of the Jet Propulsion Laboratory* (New Haven: Yale University Press, 1982), esp. preface, chap. 2–5.
46. English, *A Patron for Pure Science,* 142–44; Schuldt to William D. Carey, "Recent Developments in the National Science Foundation," Mar. 8, 1951, Bureau of Budget Papers, RG 51, NA, series 39.33, box 18, "National Science Foundation—General Administration" folder.
47. Waterman diary note, Mar. 9, 1951, box 4, "Diary Notes—Alan T. Waterman—1951 NSF" folder, NSF records, RG 307, NA; English, *A Patron for Pure Science,* 143–44; Frederick C. Schuldt, Jr., to Elmer B. Staats, "Meeting with National Science Board," Mar. 9, 1951, Bureau of Budget Papers, RG 51, NA, series 39.33, box 18, "National Science Foundation—General Administration" folder; Schuldt to Carey, "Draft 1952 Budget of the National Science Foundation," Mar. 12, 1951, box 18, "National Science Foundation—Preliminary Planning" folder, Bureau of the Budget Papers, RG 51, NA, series 39.33.
48. Cited in Bronk, "Science Advice in the White House," 248.
49. Schuldt to Carey, "Draft 1952 Budget of the National Science Foundation," Mar. 12, 1951, box 18, "National Science Foundation—Preliminary Planning" folder, Bureau of the Budget Papers, series 39.33, RG 51, NA; Schuldt to Staats, "NSF Fellowship Program," Feb. 12, 1951, and Schuldt to Staats, "Bill Golden's Comments on NSF's Fellowship Plans," May 16, 1951, both in box 18, "Scholarships fellowship & research program" folder, Bureau of Budget records, RG 51, NA, series 39.33.
50. The committee's explanation was quoted in Clifford Grobstein, "National Science Foundation: Another Round," *Bulletin of the Atomic Scientists* 8 (Apr. 1952), 98, cited in MacDonald, *Science, Scientists, and Americans,* 370.
51. Waterman diary notes, Aug. 29, Sept. 3, 4, 17, 25, 1951, box 4, "Diary Notes—Alan T. Waterman—1951 NSF" folder, NSF records, RG 307, NA; "Conant Scores House Vote to Give Science Foundation Only $300,000," *NYT,* Sept. 13, 1951.
52. JBC testimony, Sept. 19, 1951, U.S. Senate, Committee on Appropriations, *Supplemental Appropriations for 1952,* Hearings on H.R. 5215, 82d Cong., 1st sess. (Washington, D.C.: Government Printing Office, 1951), 1104, 1143.
53. English, *A Patron for Pure Science,* 158–60.
54. Waterman diary note, Oct. 23, 1951, box 4, "Diary Notes—Alan T. Waterman—1951 NSF" folder, NSF records, RG 307, NA.
55. Daniel J. Kevles, "Principles and Politics in Federal R&D Policy, 1945–1990: An Appreciation of the Bush Report," intro. to 1990 reissue of *Science—The Endless Frontier* (Washington, D.C.: NSF, 1990), ix–xxxiii.
56. Kevles, "Cold War and Hot Physics," 259.
57. Quoted in Forman, "Behind Quantum Electronics," 228–29.
58. JBC, "An Old Man Looks Back: Science and the Federal Government: 1945–1950," *Bulletin of the N.Y. Academy of Medicine* 47 (11) Nov. 1971, 1248–51.

59. Killian, *Education of a College President*, 325; Killian, *Sputnik, Scientists, and Eisenhower*, 65; Kevles, "Cold War and Hot Physics," 254; Herken, *Cardinal Choices*, 56.

60. William T. Golden, memorandum of conversation with Lovett, Mar. 7, 1951, Golden Papers.

61. HST to Oliver E. Buckley, Apr. 19, 1951, Killian/Compton Papers, MIT.

62. On SAC/ODM's early years: Bruce L. R. Smith, *American Science Policy Since World War II* (Washington: Brookings Institution, 1990), 112–13; Kevles, "Cold War and Hot Physics," 255–56; Killian, *Education of a College President*, 325; Greenberg, *Politics of Pure Science*, 144–45; Herken, *Cardinal Choices*, 56–57; Killian, *Sputnik, Scientists, and Eisenhower*, 65–66. For JBC's proposal: minutes of SAC/ODM meeting 7, Jan. 11, 1952, box 17, SAC-1952 folder, NSF director's papers, RG 307, NA; DuBridge Papers; Compton/Killian Papers.

63. Quoted in Kevles, "Cold War and Hot Physics," 256.

64. *IMJRO*, 93–94; "Scientists and Mobilization, Some Views of the Science Advisory Committee on the Role of Academic Scientists," Sept. 11, 1951, box 17, SAC-1951 folder, NSF Director's Papers, RG 307.

65. As cited in Waterman diary note, June 25, 1951, box 4, "Diary Notes—Alan T. Waterman NSF 1951" folder, NSF Papers, RG 307, NA.

66. Buckley to HST, May 1, 1952, Compton/Killian Papers; on advising the American Association of Universities, also see minutes of SAC/ODM meeting 5, Nov. 8, 1951.

67. *IMJRO*, 93–94.

68. DuBridge's comment, in minutes of SAC/ODM meeting 11, June 15, 1952, "Secretary's Notes—For File Record," DuBridge Papers, file 186.8.

69. Herken, *Cardinal Choices*, 57.

70. Draft SAC/ODM statement, Nov. 1952, JROP, box 189; minutes, SAC 14, Nov. 7–9, 1952, and other documents in DuBridge Papers, folder 186.9.

71. JBC to JRO, Nov. 6, 1952, JROP, box 189.

72. JBC to DuBridge, Nov. 26, 1952; DuBridge to JBC, Dec. 1, 1952; DuBridge Papers, folder 186.9.

73. Herken, *Cardinal Choices*, chap. 5–7, Kevles, "Cold War and Hot Physics," 256–57; Smith, *American Science Policy Since World War II*, 111–19; William G. Wells, Jr., "Science Advice and the Presidency: An Overview from Roosevelt to Ford," in Golden, ed., *Science Advice to the President*, 200–202.

74. JBC to JRO, Nov. 6, 1952, JROP, box 189.

75. JBC diary, Nov. 25, 1952; Killian, *Education of a College President*, 325.

76. JBC, "The Problems of Evaluation of Scientific Research and Development for Military Planning," speech to the National War College, Feb. 1, 1952. National Defense University archives.

77. R. G. Arneston, "Notes on Informal Discussion on Atomic Energy Policy," Institute for Advanced Study, Princeton, Jan. 24–25, 1949 [draft], S/AE, box 57, folder 4.11.9 (Princeton Papers, 1948–1949).

78. Margaret Gowing, asst. Lorna Arnold, *Independence and Deterrence: Britain and Atomic Energy, 1945–1952*, vol. 1 (New York: St. Martin's Press, 1974), 273–321; Bundy, *Danger and Survival*, 463–72; Hewlett and Duncan, *Atomic Shield*, chap. 10; Newhouse, *War and Peace in the Nuclear Age*, 57–61.

79. See Verne W. Newton, *The Butcher's Embrace: The Philby Conspirators in Washington* (London: Macdonald & Co., 1991), esp. chap. 10–11.

80. JBC to JRO, Jan. 15, 1952, Conant folder, box 27, JROP.

81. JBC to Sir Charles K. Webster, Jan. 9, 1952, "England, 1951–52" folder, box 428, JBC PREP.

82. This and other quotes are from JBC, *Anglo-American Relations in the Atomic Age* (Oxford: Oxford University Press, 1952); "Conant Advocates Joint Atomic Body," *NYT*, Mar. 18, 1952.

83. JBC, *Anglo-American Relations in the Atomic Age*; see also JBC, *Modern Science and Modern Man* (New York: Columbia University Press, 1952), 14–16.

84. JBC's Bampton Lectures were collectively published in slightly revised form by Columbia University Press as *Modern Science and Modern Man.*
85. JBC diary, Apr. 23, 1952.
86. JBC, "Modern Science and Modern Man: Science and Technology in the Last Decade," Harvard News Office release, Apr. 18, 1952; for a different version, omitting the religious claim: JBC, *Modern Science and Modern Man,* 4–6.
87. For an analysis of the changing public image of the scientist in the aftermath of World War II, see MacDonald, *Science, Scientists, and Americans,* esp. chap. 4, 7.
88. JBC, *Anglo-American Relations in the Atomic Age,* 9.
89. Bart J. Bok, 1978 oral history interview, 39, 51, 98, 102, American Institute of Physics, New York City.
90. *THC,* June 19, 1951; JBC, *President's Report,* 1950–1951, 4, 22.
91. Greenberg, *Politics of Pure Science,* 127.
92. Norman Ramsey testimony, *IMJRO,* 442.
93. Arthur B. Darling, *The Central Intelligence Agency: An Instrument of Government, to 1950* (University Park: Pennsylvania State University Press, 1990 ed. of secret history written in 1952–53), 419–21.
94. JBC, *President's Report,* 1950–1951, 5.
95. In early 1951, JBC lobbied Ivy League presidents and the Association of American Universities to agree to a resolution opposing extra payments to scholars working as government consultants and stating that the practice of educational institutions conducting large, federally funded military research projects "should be kept to a minimum and only initiated when the need of the government is clearly of the utmost importance to the defense of the nation." JBC to Frederick A. Middlebrush, w. enc., Apr. 7, 1951; Killian to Middlebrush, Apr. 10, 1951; Middlebrush to Lee DuBridge, Apr. 11, 1951; DuBridge to Middlebrush, Apr. 13, 1951; all in box 98, J-Q correspondence folder, William A. Fowler Papers, California Institute of Technology, Pasadena; Alan T. Waterman diary note, conversation with Killian, Apr. 16, 1951, box 4, "Diary Notes—Alan T. Waterman NSF 1951" folder, NSF Papers, RG 307, NA. On scrutinizing contracts, see JBC to James R. Killian, tel., Jan. 10, 1952, Killian Papers, MIT; on outside funding, see *President's Report,* 1950–1951, 20–24.
96. JBC, Commencement address, June 19, 1952, Harvard News Office release.
97. *THC,* 1952 registration issue, in Amster, *Meritocracy Ascendant,* 180.
98. *Harvard Alumni Bulletin* 55 (Feb. 7, 1953), 376.
99. "Scientists and Mobilization: Some Views of the Science Advisory Committee on the role of Academic Scientists," Sept. 12, 1951, copy in DuBridge Papers, folder 186.7.
100. Buckley to HST, May 1, 1952, Killian/Compton Papers.
101. Forman, "Behind Quantum Electronics," 180.
102. Quoted in Kevles, *The Physicists,* 383.
103. Forman, "Behind Quantum Electronics," 180.
104. Quoted in Forman, "Behind Quantum Electronics," 224; TRC interview.
105. JBC, "An Old Man Looks Back: Science and the Federal Government: 1945–1950"— *Bulletin of the N.Y. Academy of Medicine* 47 (11) Nov. 1971, 1248–51; see also "Science Subsidies Traced by Conant," *NYT,* Jan. 9, 1971.
106. Kevles, *The Physicists,* 360–61.
107. James R. Killian, in "Science Subsidies Traced by Conant," *NYT,* Jan. 9, 1971; A. Roland, "Institutionalization in the military establishment," quoted in Forman, "Behind Quantum Electronics," 225–26.
108. Forman, "Behind Quantum Electronics," 228–29.
109. Kevles, "Cold War and Hot Physics," 264.
110. JBC, *MSL,* 244–45.
111. JBC, "An Old Man Looks Back," 1251.

CHAPTER 29

1. JBC to John L. Bower, "Philosophy 150 (A Philosophy of Science)," Sept. 12, 1952, JBC PERP; JBC, *Modern Science and Modern Man*, 109–11. On the Vienna Circle and logical empiricism, see Gerald Holton, "Ernst Mach and the Fortunes of Positivism in America," *ISIS*, 1992, 83:27–60.
2. Gerald L. Schroeder, *Genesis and the Big Bang: The Discovery of Harmony Between Modern Science and the Bible* (New York: Bantam, 1990), 116, in Daniel J. Kevles, "'The Final Secret of the Universe'?" *New York Review of Books* 38:9 (May 16, 1991), 30.
3. "Divinity School Undergoes Periodic Crisis," *THC*, Dec. 8, 1951; Douglas, *Six Upon the World*, 390–91.
4. JBC to Coolidge, Feb. 8, 1940, Coolidge folder, box 152, JBC PREP.
5. JBC, *President's Report* 1945, 13–14.
6. HLS to JBC, Dec. 27, 1949, series 12, box 1, GCP. HLS once wrote that at Harvard Law School, "the whole atmosphere was electric with the sparks of competitive argument," and the teaching "created a greater revolution in my power of thinking than any teaching that I got from Yale, while the faith in mankind that I learned on the campus at New Haven was greater and stronger than any such faith I achieved at Harvard." Quoted in Hodgson, *The Colonel*, 46–47.
7. The quote is from Jared Sparks, Harvard president from 1849–52; see JBC, *President's Report* 1949–1950, 18, and JBC, *President's Report, 1951–1952*, 12, in Amster, *Meritocracy Ascendant*, 178.
8. See Powell, *The Uncertain Profession*, 214.
9. Max Hall, *Harvard University Press: A History* (Cambridge: Harvard University Press, 1986), 4.
10. JBC to Henry James, Dec. 6, 1943, JBC PREP, in Hall, *Harvard University Press*, 109; see 105–111, 121–24 for JBC's efforts.
11. See Mark Silk, *Spiritual Politics: Religion and America Since World War II* (New York: Simon & Schuster, 1988), 74.
12. See William F. Buckley, *God and Man at Yale* (Washington: Regnery Gateway, 1986 reprint of 1951 ed., with new intro.), 38–40.
13. Cited in John B. Judis, *William F. Buckley, Jr.: Patron Saint of the Conservatives* (New York: Simon & Schuster, 1988), 11–12.
14. From transcript of Educational Policies Commission, Mar. 30–Apr. 1, 1950, vol. II, 328–30, National Education Association archives, Washington, D.C.
15. JBC, *Baccalaureate Sermon to the Harvard College Class of 1950* [June 18, 1950] (Cambridge: Harvard University, 1950).
16. JBC, *Baccalaureate Sermon to the Harvard College Class of 1950* [June 18, 1950].
17. O'Brian to Niebuhr, June 20, 1950, Niebuhr to O'Brian, June 22, 1950, both in box 6, Niebuhr Papers, LC. In a letter to O'Brian on June 6, JBC had stated that the Corporation had decided to "put everything over until the fall" and strongly hinted that he should drop the idea, at least for the time being. Series 12, box 1, GCP.
18. See Niebuhr to JBC, Sept. 20, 1950, and Niebuhr to O'Brian, Sept. 26, 1950, box 6, Niebuhr Papers; and JBC to Niebuhr, Sept. 27, 1950, box 47, Niebuhr papers.
19. Sources for this account of the Divinity School struggle include correspondence in the Niebuhr and Clark papers; JBC annual reports; George Hunston Williams, ed., *The Harvard Divinity School: Its Place in Harvard University and in American Culture* (Boston: Beacon Press, 1954), 221–24; Dunne, *Grenville Clark*, 182–83; and Smith, *Harvard Century*, 185.
20. JBC to William Carr, Sept. 27, 1950, JBC PREP, "Educational Policies Commission, 1950–51" folder, box 397.
21. The references are, respectively, to Mark 8.36/Matthew 16.26, and 2 Corinthians 4.18.
22. "Educators Plead for Moral Values," *NYT*, Feb. 19, 1951.

23. Douglas T. Miller and Marion Nowak, *The Fifties: The Way We Really Were* (Garden City, N.Y.: Doubleday & Co., 1977), 248–68.
24. JBC, "The Superintendent Was the Target," *NYT Book Review,* Apr. 29, 1951.
25. See "Dr. Conant: In Science Pure, In Education Controversial," *Newsweek* 15:12 (Sept. 22, 1952), 72–73.
26. See 1948 entry, JBC quote notebook, JBC PERP, in Amster, *Meritocracy Ascendant,* 170.
27. For extensive documentation of JBC's findings on these trips, see JBC PERP and JBC folders, CCP.
28. JBC, *Education and Liberty: The Role of the Schools in a Modern Democracy* (Cambridge: Harvard University Press, 1953); JBC, Page-Barbour Lectures, Feb. 12–14, 1952, JBC PREP.
29. JBC, "Unity and Diversity in Secondary Education," speech to American Association of School Administrators, Boston, Apr. 7, 1952, reprinted in *Vital Speeches of the Day* (1952), 463–65, and as "Education: Engine of Democracy," *Saturday Review* (May 3, 1952), 11–14.
30. "Good Friday Fills Churches of City," *NYT,* Apr. 12, 1952.
31. "Catholic Teachers Score Conant View," *NYT,* Apr. 16, 1952; "Educator Attacks Conant's View on Church Schools," *BG,* Apr. 16, 1952; James M. O'Neill, "Religious Education and American Democracy," Apr. 15, 1952, *Vital Speeches of the Day* (1952), 465; Archbishop Richard J. Cushing, "The Case for Religious Schools," *Saturday Review* (May 3, 1952), 14.
32. JBC diary, July 1, 1952.
33. JBC, *MSL,* 460–72.
34. JBC diary, Sept. 24, 29, 1952.
35. JBC to John L. Bower, "Philosophy 150 (A Philosophy of Science)," Sept. 12, 1952, JBC PERP. See also JBC, *Modern Science and Modern Man,* 109–11, and John Gribbin, *In Search of the Big Bang: Quantum Physics and Cosmology* (New York: Bantam, 1986), 151–58, 396. My thanks to Annie Brown (now Hershberg) for pointing out JBC's intellectual tie to Descartes; on the Cartesian compromise, see W. T. Jones, *Hobbes to Hume: A History of Western Philosophy* (vol. III) (New York: Harcourt Brace Jovanovich, 1952, 1969, 2nd ed.), 176–77.
36. JBC to William Carr, Sept. 27, 1950, "Educational Policies Commission, 1950–51" folder, box 397, JBC PREP.

CHAPTER 30

1. *IMJRO,* 897–98.
2. JBC to JRO, May 15, 1950, JROP, Box 27, Conant folder, and JBC PREP, box 378, "Ol–Oz," 1949–50 folder. In mid-1950, however, the GAC's membership changed with the departure of Fermi, Rowe, and Seaborg, and their replacement by Libby, Edgar V. Murphree, president of Standard Oil, and Walter G. Whitman, an MIT engineer.
3. Rabi telephone interview, Feb. 1982.
4. JRO to JBC, June 8, 1951, box 27, Conant folder, JROP; *IMJRO,* 81 ("technically sweet"), 84, 229.
5. JBC, "The Soviet Challenge to American Education," speech at Barnard College, Feb. 11, 1950, JBC Speech File, 296.
6. See *IMJRO,* 83.
7. See *Atomic Shield,* 530–31; JCAE, "Policy and Progress in the H-Bomb Program: A Chronology of Leading Events," Jan. 1, 1953, declassified 1987, JCAE records.
8. The Vista delegation paid its visit at just about the same time that SAC commander Curtis LeMay made his own call on Eisenhower to obtain his consent to an agreement ensuring SAC's prerogatives in NATO war planning in Europe. See Peter J.

Roman, "The Air Force and Atomic Air Support for NATO, 1950–1952," paper presented to American Political Science Association, Sept. 3, 1992.

9. David C. Elliot, "Project Vista and Nuclear Weapons in Europe," *International Security* 11:1 (Summer 1986), 163–83; Gregg Herken, *Counsels of War* (2nd ed., Oxford University Press, 1987), 64–73, 103; Fred Kaplan, *The Wizards of Armageddon* (New York: Simon & Schuster, 1983), 81, 84; Hewlett and Duncan, *Atomic Shield*, 580; for a highly critical air force account of JRO's influence on Vista, see Garrison North to Thomas K. Finletter, July 1, 1952, FBI Oppenheimer file, 100-17828, and testimony of air force witnesses in *IMJRO*.

10. JBC diary, Dec. 13, 1951.

11. JBC to JRO, Jan. 15, 1952, box 27, Conant file, JROP.

12. For JBC's 1951 emphasis on tactical nuclear weapons, see JBC, "The Present Danger," Feb. 7, 1951, JBC Speech File 304; JBC, "Worlds in Conflict," speech to *Philadelphia Bulletin* forum, Mar. 13, 1951, JBC Speech File; "Your Son and Universal Military Service," CBS Radio Broadcast, Apr. 8, 1951, JBC Speech File, also in CPD Papers, tab AA; JBC, "The Defense of Europe in the Atomic Age," address to Chicago Association of Commerce and Council on Foreign Relations, May 17, 1951, JBC Speech File; "Conant Says A-Bomb to Aid Ground Troops Is Not Far Off," *BG*, Aug. 3, 1951. For his belief that tactical nuclear weapons might make rearming Germany unnecessary, see JBC, "The Defense of Europe in the Atomic Age," May 17, 1951, and JBC diary, Oct. 11, 1951, JBC PERP.

13. "Conant Sees 'Exaggeration,'" *NYT*, July 14, 1951; JBC, "A Skeptical Chemist Looks into the Crystal Ball," Sept. 5, 1951, address to the American Chemical Society Diamond Jubilee Meeting, 71st Regiment Armory, New York City, draft in JBC Speech File and verbatim transcript in HO Bio Files, Conant, Dr. James B., AEC records, RG 326, NA; reprinted in Foreign Policy Association headline series (no. 90), "The Story of U.S. Foreign Policy," Nov.–Dec. 1951, and in *Chemical and Engineering News* 29:38 (Sept. 17, 1951).

14. Cited in Lawrance Thompson and R. H. Winnick, *Robert Frost: The Later Years, 1938–1963* (New York: Holt, Rinehart & Winston, 1976), 197–98. As one of myriad intellectual hobbies, JBC had monitored scientific studies on birth control issues since the early 1930s, when he had learned from Frederick Osborn of the advent of new "scientific" methods for analyzing and predicting population growth. When families started having larger families during the war JBC initially viewed it as a temporary aberration, but he was startled when the "baby boom" stretched into the postwar era and was curious as to what factors had caused this to occur, despite predictions to the contrary. JBC's persistent interest led Osborn and John D. Rockefeller III to invite him, in 1957, to join the board of directors of the Population Council, where he followed developments in the field, although his idea of adding birth control drugs to foods remains unimplemented. See JBC to Charles Dollard, May 24, 1954, Dollard to Osborn, June 2, 1954, and Dollard to JBC, June 21, 1954, w. enc., all in "Conant James B. 1934-55" folder, CCP; and JBC to Dr. Somers H. Sturgis, Aug. 9, 1967, JBC PERP.

15. JBC's view of GC: JBC diary, Sept. 29, 1951; "scareheads": JBC to JRO, Jan. 15, 1952, box 27, Conant folder, JROP.

16. Robert G. Hooker, Jr., to George F. Kennan, Sept. 19, 1951, box 43, "Kennan, George F.–Correspondence" folder, JROP.

17. Kennan to JRO, Sept. 23, 1951, box 43, "Kennan, George F.–Correspondence" folder, JROP.

18. JRO to Kennan, Sept. 29, 1951, box 43, "Kennan, George F.–Correspondence" folder, JROP.

19. Stefan T. Possony, "An Outline of American Atomic Strategy in the Non-Military Fields," Oct. 6, 1952; Byron L. Enyart, "Re-analysis of Dr. Possony's Paper on Psychological Use of Atomic Energy," Nov. 18, 1952, folder 471.6, records of the Psychological Strategy Board, HSTL.

20. "War Will Be Averted, Dr. Conant Predicts," *NYT,* Sept. 6, 1951; "Conant Assurance Called Confusing," *NYT,* Sept. 7, 1951.

21. John S. Walker to McMahon, "Address by Dr. James Bryant Conant," Sept. 10, 1951, Speeches, Conant, James Bryant folder, JCAE General Correspondence 1946–1977, box 678, JCAE records.

22. Borden to McMahon, Sept. 11, 1951, Speeches, Conant, James Bryant folder, box 678, JCAE records.

23. Walter Hamilton to William L. Borden, Apr. 17, 1952, Conant, James B. folder, box 260, JCAE records.

24. Borden to McMahon, Sept. 11, 1951, Speeches, Conant, James Bryant folder, box 678, JCAE records.

25. "Atomic Delay Laid to A.E.C. Advisers," *NYT,* Mar. 8, 1952; Pitzer, remarks to the Southern California Section of the American Chemical Society, Mar. 7, 1952, copies in "Pi-Po" correspondence folder, 1951–52, box 440, JBC PREP, box 58, and DuBridge Papers, folder 168.3. See Pitzer to Harold C. Urey, Feb. 26, 1952, for evidence of Pitzer's search for usable quotations from GAC members, and Urey's response to Pitzer of Mar. 10, both in box 81, "Misc P corresp." folder, Urey Papers, University of California (San Diego), La Jolla.

26. William T. Golden, memorandum of conversation with I. I. Rabi, Jan. 5, 1951, Golden Papers.

27. On Livermore and the second lab question, see *Atomic Shield,* 528, 541, 554, 558, 562, 568–71, 581–84; J. L. Heilbron, Robert W. Seidel, and Bruce R. Wheaton, *Lawrence and His Laboratory: Nuclear Science at Berkeley, 1931–1961* (Berkeley, 1981), 75; Seidel, "Accelerating Science: The Postwar Transformation of the Lawrence Radiation Laboratory," *HSPS* 13:2 (1983), 375–400, and Seidel, "A Home for Big Science: The Atomic Energy Commission's Laboratory System," *HSPS* 16:1 (1986), 135–176, esp. 151–56.

28. See minutes of GAC 30, Apr. 27–29, and JRO to Gordon Dean, Apr. 30, 1952, DOE archives; Heilbron et al., *Lawrence and His Laboratory,* 64–75.

29. Lee A. DuBridge to Kenneth S. Pitzer (draft), Mar. 10, 1952, box 31, DuBridge folder, JROP; DuBridge Papers, folder 168.3.

30. JRO to DuBridge, Mar. 18, 1952, box 31, DuBridge folder, JROP; DuBridge Papers, folder 168.3.

31. DuBridge to Pitzer, Mar. 18, 1952, DuBridge Papers, folder 168.3.

32. Pitzer to JBC, handwritten note on Mar. 7, 1952, speech "Pi-Po" correspondence folder, 1951–52, box 440, JBC PREP.

33. JBC to Pitzer, Apr. 10, 1952, "Pi-Po" correspondence folder, 1951–52, box 440, JBC PREP.

34. Pitzer to JBC, Apr. 15, 1952, "Pi-Po" correspondence folder, 1951–52, box 440, JBC PREP.

35. Borden to file, Mar. 22, 1952, classified box 41, JCAE 2704, JCAE formerly classified collection.

36. Pitzer to HST, Apr. 4, 1952, HST OF, box 1533, 692-B General Advisory Committee, HSTL; for Pitzer's statements to FBI agents made the same day, see declassified documents from the FBI's Oppenheimer file: SAC, San Francisco, to Director, FBI, Apr. 5, 1952, FBI 100-17828-275, and J. Edgar Hoover to Sidney Souers, Apr. 16, 1952, FBI 100-17828-291.

37. "Atomic Delay Laid to A.E.C. Advisers," *NYT,* Mar. 8, 1952.

38. Minutes, GAC 28, Dec. 12–14, 1951, DOE archives; JBC diary, Dec. 13, 1951, JBC PERP, and JBC to JRO, Jan. 15, 1952, box 27, Conant folder, JROP; and Urey to HST, June 2, 1952, HST OF, box 1533, folder 692-B, HSTL, and Urey Papers, box 93, "AEC" folder. Urey also falsely gossiped to Gordon Dean that JRO and his "slavishly" complaisant advisers had caused Teller to be expelled from H-bomb research for the AEC, a charge that Dean denied. Urey to Dean, Apr. 10, 1952; Dean to Urey, Apr. 17, 1952; Urey to Dean, Apr. 24, 1952; all in box 93, "AEC" folder, Urey Papers,

University of California at San Diego (UCSD). It should be noted that Urey did strongly oppose the removal of JRO's security clearance in 1954 despite his "mistake in judgment" on the H-bomb. Urey statement, Apr. 15, 1954, box 35, "Oppenheimer" folder, Urey papers, UCSD.

39. Daniels to HST, June 16, 1952; Latimer to HST, May 29, 1952; both in HST OF, box 1533, folder 692-B, HSTL.

40. See various documents in the FBI Oppenheimer file [FBI JRO 100-17828]. For Pitzer: SAC, San Francisco, to Director, FBI, Apr. 5, 1952; Hoover to Souers, Apr. 16, 1952; for Teller: SAC, Albuquerque, to Director, May 14, 1952; also a revised version, after Teller "emphatically" requested that his identity be concealed to prevent "embarrassment" among fellow scientists should the document leak, referring to Teller as "T-1," SAC, Albuquerque to Director, FBI, May 15, 1952, in which Teller specifically blasted JBC for downgrading atomic power in favor of solar energy; SAC, Albuquerque to Director, May 27, 1952; FBI report, Newark, May 27, 1952; W. A. Branigan to A. H. Belmont, June 10, 1952; Hoover to Attorney General, June 12, 1952; Hoover to Souers, June 12, 1952; for Libby, FBI report, Chicago, May 9, 1952; Alvarez, Lawrence, Latimer, Teller, and others gave evidence to the FBI and/or AEC in early 1954 before JRO's security hearings.

41. For Strauss, see Borden to McMahon, May 28, 1952, JCAE—Previously classified collection, NA; for Murray, see V. P. Keay to A. H. Belmont, Apr. 28, 1952, FBI Oppenheimer file, 100-17828; D. M. Ladd to Hoover, Jan. 23, 1952, FBI 17828-271, and A. H. Belmont to D. M. Ladd, March 11, 1952, FBI 100-17828-272.

42. Griggs to Finletter, June 21, 1952, describing conversation of May 23, 1952, FBI Oppenheimer file, 100-17828; *IMJRO*, 757-58.

43. Borden to McMahon, May 28, 1952, classified box 6, CD3831, JCAE formerly classified collection.

44. Chairman, JCAE, to President [draft], May 21, 1952, classified box 41, JCAE DCXXXVII, Oppenheimer, 1947–Aug 1953 folder; L. B. Nichols to Tolson, May 29, 1952, FBI Oppenheimer file, 100-17828, also notes McMahon's intention to urge HST against reappointment; the correspondence that did ensue is McMahon to HST, May 30, 1952, and Truman to McMahon, June 10, 1952, JCAE—Previously classified collection. HST's description of JRO as a "'cry baby' scientist" with blood on his hands is from HST to Dean Acheson, May 7, 1946, PSF, box 201, "Subject File—NSC Atomic—Atomic Test" folder, HSTL.

45. Minutes, GAC 30, Apr. 27-29, 1952, and JRO to Gordon Dean, Apr. 30, 1952, DOE archives. The GAC had heard an impassioned presentation in favor of a second lab from Edward Teller (GAC 28, Dec. 12-14, 1951), but instead recommended establishing an advanced development section at Los Alamos. A measure of the GAC's exasperation can be gleaned from the punctuation of an Apr. 1952 report advising that the Radiation Laboratory "be encouraged" in its work on thermonuclear weapons, "PROVIDED ONLY THAT THESE STEPS SHOULD NOT DEPRIVE THE LOS ALAMOS LABORATORY OF THE SERVICES OF ITS PRESENT PERSONNEL, CONSULTANTS, AND SUBCONTRACTORS."

46. JBC diary, May 9, 1952. News of the split among atomic advisers over the GAC reappointments first surfaced in "Atom Argument: One Group of Scientists Wants 'Daring' Boost in H-Bomb, Other Work," *Wall Street Journal*, July 15, 1952.

47. J. Edgar Hoover to Tolson, Ladd, Nichols, July 10, 1952, quoting Truman aide Adm. Sidney W. Souers, FBI JRO serial file, 100-17828-324.

48. See Hewlett and Duncan, *Atomic Shield*, 518.

49. JBC, "Possibilities for report to the President," June 1952, DoE archives; Hewlett and Duncan, *Atomic Shield*, note only JBC's desire that "the President should be made aware of the results of Project Gabriel on the number of nuclear weapons that could be detonated without causing a health hazard" (p. 518).

50. GAC to the President, June 14, 1952, declassified with deletions, DoE archives.

51. Minutes, GAC 31, June 13-14, 1952, DOE archives; JBC diary, June 14, 1952, JBC PERP.

52. See David Halberstam, *The Best and the Brightest* (New York: Simon & Schuster, 1969), 72. More than three decades later, Bundy vindicated JBC's skeptical stamp of approval on his academic promise by writing a thoughtful history of the nuclear arms race (*Danger and Survival*, published in 1988).

53. The State Department listed JBC as a member of the group in a May 13 announcement, according to a chronology compiled by air force official Garrison North to Thomas K. Finletter, July 1, 1952, FBI JRO file, FBI 100-17828; also see Joseph and Stewart Alsop, "Matter of Fact," *Washington Post*, May 21, 1952.

54. Borden to McMahon, May 28, 1952, JCAE—Formerly classified, classified box 6, CD3831; Garrison North to Thomas K. Finletter, July 1, 1952, FBI JRO file, FBI 100-17828; Barton J. Bernstein, "Crossing the Rubicon: A Missed Opportunity to Stop the H-Bomb?" *International Security* 14:2 (Fall 1989), 141.

55. JBC diary, May 9, 1952.

56. JBC, *Modern Science and Modern Man* 14–16; also JBC, *Anglo-American Relations in the Atomic Age* (London: Oxford University Press, 1952), 26–32.

57. McGeorge Bundy, "Panel of Consultants on Disarmament, Minutes of Meeting of June 19–21, 1952, at Cambridge, Massachusetts," Department of State records, RG 59, NA. Bundy's minutes, declassified in 1987 and kindly provided by Barton J. Bernstein, disguise JBC's identity, but his appearance can be deduced both by content and by coordination with JBC's diary entry of June 19, 1952. That evening, JBC wrote, he "went to Mac Bundy's to give evidence to Oppie, John Dickey, Johnson of Carnegie, about international control of atomic bomb." JBC found the session either "Not encouraging" or "Most encouraging," depending on one's interpretation of his handwriting. Bundy's minutes identify the first of two witnesses appearing that day as a Soviet expert, so JBC must have been the anonymous "second witness." Bundy has acknowledged the case for identifying JBC as "really conclusive" and discerned "important connections between Conant's remarks at this meeting and the eventual report." Bundy to Hershberg, Apr. 12, 1991.

58. McGeorge Bundy, "Early Thoughts on Controlling the Nuclear Arms Race: A Report to the Secretary of State, January 1953," *International Security* 7 (Fall 1982), 3–27, esp. 18–21; also Bundy to Hershberg, Apr. 12, 1991. At about the same time the Disarmament Panel transmitted its report, JBC hinted at the concerns he had expressed to the group in his last report as Harvard president, released in Jan. 1953, and in farewell remarks to Harvard audiences. Reviewing his university's endurance through many moments of stress, he noted: "Today once again we live in a period of peril, far greater peril to my mind than many of us appear to realize. The prospect of the physical annihilation of all of Harvard is for the first time in our history a possibility which we must admit." *President's Report*, 1951–52 (Cambridge: Harvard University, Jan. 1953), 39; JBC, speech to New York Harvard Club, Jan. 16, 1953, JBC PREP. For a National Security Council staff report on implementing the panel's recommendations for greater candor, see NSC Planning Board to NSC, NSC 151, "Armaments and American Policy," May 8, 1953, Office of the Special Assistant to the President for National Security Affairs Papers, NSC Series, Policy Papers Subseries, box 5, NSC 151-12 folder, DDEL.

59. For VB's proposal and the panel's history see Bundy, "Early Thoughts," 3–4; Bundy, *Danger and Survival*, 288–89; *IMRJO*, 95–96, 247–48, 562–65; VB to JBC, Mar. 29, 1954, box 27, folder 614, VBP; Bernstein, "Crossing the Rubicon," 132–160; and Herken, *Cardinal Choices*, 58–73. For JRO's article, see "Atomic Weapons and American Policy," *Foreign Affairs* 31:4 (July 1953), 525–35.

60. The quotation from JBC is from minutes, GAC 19, Jan. 31–Feb. 1, 1950; also *IMJRO*, 248, 563–65; Daniel Hirsch and William G. Mathews, "The H-Bomb: Who Really Gave Away the Secret?" *Bulletin of the Atomic Scientists* 46:1 (Jan./Feb. 1990), 22–30, and the fuller version available from the authors. However, it remains uncertain whether the Soviet scientists actually profited by analyzing the U.S. fallout. See Andrei Sakharov, *Memoirs*, 158; Gregg Herken, "Teller Retells," *Bulletin*

of the Atomic Scientists 46:8 (Oct. 1990), 40–41; and David Holloway, *Stalin and the Bomb* (forthcoming from Yale University Press). A senior scientific director of the Soviet nuclear weapons program, Yuli Khariton, stated in 1993 that no analysis of the U.S. test's fallout was made: Yuli Khariton and Yuri Smirnov, "The Khariton Version," *Bulletin of the Atomic Scientists* 49:4 (May 1993), 30–31.

61. For JBC: Norman Ramsey interview, Columbia Oral History Project, 315–16; for VB: *IMJRO,* 564–65.
62. Minutes of the Meeting of the Special NSC Committee, Oct. 9, 1952, *FRUS,* 1952–54, II, 1034–35.
63. HST to JBC, Sept. 27, 1952, "Atomic Energy: 1952–1953" folder, box 450, JBC PREP.
64. "Dr. Conant: In Science Pure, In Education Controversial," *Newsweek* 40:12 (Sept. 22, 1952), 74.

CHAPTER 31

1. JBC, report to Annual Meeting of the Harvard Alumni Association, Tercentenary Theatre, Harvard Yard, afternoon of Commencement Day, Thursday, June 21, 1951, Harvard News Office press release.
2. Mary McCarthy, *The Groves of Academe* (New York: Harcourt, Brace, & World, Inc., 1952; Signet paperback ed., 1963); DeVoto's comment is reprinted on the back cover.
3. Paul H. Buck to JBC, Nov. 20, 1952, Buck Papers, Pusey Library, Harvard University.
4. Samuel Eliot Morison, "The Harvard Presidency," *New England Quarterly* (Dec. 1958), 444.
5. "Conant Says Red Teachers Should Be Refused Post," *THC,* Nov. 5, 1951.
6. Sidney Hook, "What Shall We Do About Communist Teachers?" *Saturday Evening Post,* Sept. 10, 1949; Sidney Hook, "Academic Integrity and Academic Freedom," *Commentary* (Oct. 1949), 329–339, see p. 334 for the reference to JBC; Schrecker, *No Ivory Tower,* 105–9; Pell, *Liberal Mind in a Conservative Age,* 284–85, 290–94, 298–300.
7. *THC,* June 9, 1949.
8. "State laws requiring special oaths for teachers, or laying down detailed prescriptions for the school curriculum, or establishing uniform tests and criteria of loyalty impair the vigor of local school autonomy and thus do harm to an important safeguard of freedom in education." EPC statement adopted at meeting in Rye, New York, Oct. 6–8, 1949, NEA archives, Washington, D.C.
9. JBC to Robert G. Sproul, Apr. 16, 1950, CU-5, 666 2 — Loyalty Oath Corresp., 1950 A–C, Robert G. Sproul Papers, Bancroft Library, University of California (Berkeley).
10. This account of the California controversy is drawn from "Court Rules Against California Oath," *THC* academic freedom survey, June 1951 Commencement issue; David P. Gardern, *The California Oath Controversy* (Berkeley: University of California Press, 1967); and Schrecker, *No Ivory Tower,* 116–25.
11. JBC to Sproul, Aug. 4, 1950, Sproul Papers, CU-5, 666 2 — Loyalty Oath Corresp.
12. Corliss Lamont, *Freedom Is as Freedom Does: Civil Liberties in America* (New York: Continuum, 1956; 4th ed., 1990), 167–86; Schrecker, *No Ivory Tower,* 112–25.
13. *THC,* "Coolidge Statement Throws State Hearing into Uproar," Apr. 24, 1951.
14. John Kenneth Galbraith, *A Life in Our Times: Memoirs* (Boston: Houghton Mifflin Co., 1981), 274.
15. JBC, *MSL,* 434.
16. JBC, *MSL,* 440–41.
17. Galbraith, *A Life in Our Times,* 275.
18. For the most detailed study of the USSBS see David MacIsaac, *Strategic Bombing in World War Two: The Story of the United States Strategic Bombing Survey* (New York: Garland Publishing, 1976); MacIsaac also edited a ten-volume compilation of

the survey's reports, *The United States Strategic Bombing Survey,* published by Garland in 1976. Numerous economists, lawyers, administrators, and others affiliated with Harvard participated in the USSBS—Assistant War Secretary Robert A. Lovett "all but insisted" that the Harvard Business School be involved, according to MacIsaac—and in June 1944 JBC was the first choice of the army air force's commanding general, "Hap" Arnold, to serve as civilian chairman of the survey, but VB vetoed the idea, citing the press of his OSRD duties. JBC remained vitally interested in the issue of strategic bombing's effectiveness, however, and on at least one occasion informally advised the survey on personnel. See MacIsaac, *Strategic Bombing in World War Two,* 40, 44, 95, 188 n. 9.

19. Paul H. Buck to JBC, Apr. 15, 1949, GCP, Galbraith folder.
20. Galbraith, *A Life in Our Times,* 274–77; see also memorandum from: J. K. Galbraith, n.d. [Oct. 8, 1949], John Kenneth Galbraith Papers—Harvard University File: 1948–1965, box 70, "Correspondence Re: Appointment of JKG as Professor of Economics, 3/22/47–3/22/50" folder, John Kenneth Galbraith Papers, John F. Kennedy Library.
21. Buck to JBC, Apr. 15, 1949, w. enclosures.
22. JBC, "Memorandum to the members of the Harvard Corporation," June 24, 1949, JBC PERP.
23. JBC to Harvard Corporation, June 24, 1949.
24. GC diary, July 6–7, 1949, I/4/Bio-Diary Apr. 3–Sept. 18, 1949, GCP, series IV, box 6.
25. Edward S. Mason to GC, w. note by Paul H. Buck, Oct. 3, 1949, GCP, series IV, box 6; Buck, memorandum of conversation with Guido R. Perera, Apr. 7, 1949, and Mason interview with Nitze, Apr. 13, 1949, GCP.
26. See materials in Galbraith papers—Harvard University File: 1948–1965, box 70, "Correspondence Re: Appointment of JKG as Professor of Economics, 3/22/47–3/22/50" folder, Galbraith Papers, Kennedy Library.
27. Smith, *The Harvard Century,* 175.
28. JBC to Paul H. Douglas, Feb. 13, 1968, Committee on Peace and Freedom in Vietnam folder, JBC PERP.
29. Galbraith, *A Life in Our Times,* 275–76.
30. Galbraith interview, Jan. 1989, Cambridge, Mass.
31. Randall, *Adventures in Friendship,* 25–27.
32. JBC, *MSL,* 433–38; Galbraith, in *The Affluent Society* (2d ed.: New York: Mentor Books, 1958, 1969), xvii, acknowledges that Keynes's teachings came to America "primarily by way of apostles at Harvard. . . ."
33. The incident is described in Thomas D. Cabot to GC, June 21, 1949, GCP 4:1, Harvard Corporation–Cabot, Thomas folder.
34. DEL, *Journals,* vol. 3, *Venturesome Years,* 1950–1955 (New York: Harper & Row, 1966), 53–54.
35. DEL, *Venturesome Years,* 54.
36. JBC diary, Apr. 2, 9, 1951.
37. JBC diary, Nov. 5, 1951.
38. JBC believed strongly that each faculty must be responsible for paying its own way, and may have reacted strongly to avoid setting a precedent for shared appointments.
39. JBC, *MSL,* 443–44; JBC, "Confidential Report of the President of the University to the Two Governing Boards on the Department of Economics of the Faculty of Arts and Sciences," Jan. 3, 1952, Joseph Alsop Papers, LC.
40. JBC diary, Jan. 7, 14, 1952. Also see JBC to George Whitney, tentative draft ("Never sent!"), Jan. 21, 1952, JBC PERP; and GC to JBC, July 24, 1952, and JBC to GC, Aug. 1, 1952, both in GCP 4:2, "Harvard Corporation: James B. Conant" folder.
41. McGeorge Bundy, "Were Those the Days?" *Daedalus* (Summer 1970), 532–34.
42. Seymour Harris, *The Economics of Harvard* (New York: McGraw-Hill, 1970), 189, in Lipset and Riesman, *Education and Politics at Harvard,* 184.
43. David M. Oshinsky, *A Conspiracy So Immense: The World of Joe McCarthy* (New

York: Free Press, 1983), 109, 125-26; on the FBI and Shapley: Diamond, *Compromised Campus*, 35-37, 38, 293 n. 13, 320 n. 23.

44. FF to GC, Mar. 31, 1933, box 217, folder 5, FFP; interviews with Fred Whipple and Owen Gingrich, both June 2, 1988.
45. JBC diary, Oct. 1, 1951.
46. Interviews with Whipple and Gingrich, both June 2, 1988.
47. Thomas Powers, *The Man Who Kept the Secrets: Richard Helms and the CIA* (New York: Knopf, 1979; Pocket ed., 1981), 76.
48. Even Bok later acknowledged that the observatory's reputation declined as a result of Shapley's outside activities, and felt it "a pity that about 1946 he did not resign his post as Director of Harvard Observatory to assume an important administrative scientific post in the national or international realm." Bart J. Bok, "Harlow Shapley," in *Biographical Memoirs* 49 (Washington, D.C.: National Academy of Sciences, 1978), 254-56.
49. Bart J. Bok, oral history interview, American Institute of Physics, New York City, 36-39, 50-51, 98, 103, 125.
50. Bok oral history interview, 1978, 103, 125, American Institute of Physics, New York City.
51. JBC to JRO, July 28, 1952, box 128, "Harvard University/Observatory—Conant, J.B.—Memoranda. & Corresp." folder, JROP.
52. JBC to Corporation, "Astronomy at Harvard," Aug. 1, 1952; "Observatory Committee Report," June 18, 1952; Memorandum to Harvard Corporation, "Draft Report on Astronomy at Harvard," Nov. 11, 1952; and related correspondence in JROP, esp. box 128, "Harvard University/Observatory—Survey Com.—Reports and Memoranda, Recommendations of Committee" folder.
53. WLM, *In the Catbird Seat*, 287; Oshinsky, *A Conspiracy So Immense*, 108-10.
54. "Time Labels Fairbank 'Apologist' for Reds," *THC*, May 18, 1951; "3 Professors Deny Backing Chinese 'Reds'; McKay Deplores Accusations," *THC*, Sept. 27, 1951; Schrecker, *No Ivory Tower*, 162-67, 303-304, 390.
55. Quoted in Walter LaFeber, *America, Russia, and the Cold War, 1945-1990* (New York: McGraw-Hill, 1991), 137.
56. "College Freedoms Being Stifled by Students' Fear of Red Label" and "Colleges Fighting Repressive Forces," *NYT*, May 10, 11, 1951, in Lionel S. Lewis, *Cold War on Campus: A Study of the Politics of Organizational Control* (New Brunswick, N.J.: Transaction Books, 1988), 22-23.
57. JBC, "The Superintendent Was the Target," *NYT Book Review*, Apr. 29, 1951; Chafee cited in Alan Barth, "The Loyalty of Free Men," University of Chicago *Round Table*, Oct. 18, 1951.
58. JBC, Baccalaureate Sermon, Harvard News Office release, June 18, 1951.
59. JBC, Baccalaureate Sermon, Harvard News Office release, June 16, 1952; "Conant Predicts Reformer Return," *NYT*, June 16, 1952.
60. JBC to John H. Manley, Oct. 5, 1949, responding to Manley to JBC, Sept. 9, Oct. 3, 1949, in "California: University of, 1949-50" folder, box 363, JBC PREP. Manley, a technical associate director at Los Alamos, wanted to hire a Harvard professor, Garrett Birkhoff, as a consultant.
61. JBC to Alan Barth, Sept. 19, 1949, quoted in "Part IV—Postwar Years at Harvard," JBC PERP, box 14, "Supporting documents for JBC memoirs" folder. Publicly, however, he stuck to his more general assertion that Communists should not be employed (or appointed) as teachers.
62. WLM to Frederick W. Brune, Dec. 21, 1949, quoted in Greene to JBC, Apr. 7, 1950, series 4, box 2, "Harvard Corporation, Conant, James B." folder, GCP.
63. Jerome D. Greene to FBI, Boston, Sept. 10, 17, Oct. 8, 23, 1940, "Fe-Fj" folder, box 179, JBC PREP.
64. "Liberals Safe from Spying, Watson States," *THC*, May 17, 1951; "FBI Claims It Does Not Seek Student Clubs," *THC*, May 21, 1951.

65. Keppel interview, 1989, Cambridge, Mass.
66. See various documents—especially FBI Boston field office memos to Hoover dated June 16 and 29, 1950, and Hoover's reply of July 31, 1950—quoted in Diamond, "The Arrangement," in Theoharis, ed., *Beyond the Hiss Case*, 351-55, and in Diamond, *Compromised Campus*, 40-47.
67. SAC Boston to FBI Director, Feb. 9, 1949, in Diamond, *Compromised Campus*, 47.
68. Hoover to Francis Walter, Feb. 16, 1959, FBI 61-7582-4053; quoted in Athan G. Theoharis and John Stuart Cox, *The Boss: J. Edgar Hoover and the Great American Inquisition* (Philadelphia: Temple University Press, 1988), 321; Diamond, "The Arrangement," 356-61.
69. JBC, *MSL*, 538.
70. Schrecker, *No Ivory Tower*, 194; 180-83, 393 n. 40.
71. Griswold to JBC, Dec. 19, 1952, and Buck to JBC, Dec. 22, 1952, both in "Congressional Investigation, 1952-53" folder, box 453, JBC PREP. Buck specified that the "excitement and emotion" among Harvard faculty members were localized in three groups: those in the Law School, Government Department, and elsewhere with a "professional interest in the defense of civil rights"; individuals who were potential targets of investigation; and Democrats who feared "that the Republicans will use their power for the next four years in a series of investigations to discredit the professors who supported Roosevelt, Truman, and Stevenson."
72. See Victor S. Navasky, *Naming Names* (New York: Viking Press, 1980), for the issues involved in informing in the entertainment industry.
73. Quoted in Schrecker, *No Ivory Tower*, 176.
74. For accounts of the Rutgers controversy, see Schrecker, *No Ivory Tower*, 171-79, and Lewis, *Cold War on Campus*, 157-62, 171.
75. Resolution of the Rutgers University Board of Trustees Adopted at its Meeting— Dec. 12, 1952, Rutgers University archives.
76. Schrecker, *No Ivory Tower*, 175-76; JBC read the Oct. 14, 1952, statement of Rutgers University President Lewis Webster Jones containing the Voorhees Committee's report, and forwarded it to Corporation attorney Oscar Shaw: see copy with JBC notation in "Congressional Investigation, 1952-53" folder, box 453, JBC PREP.
77. WLM to JBC, Dec. 8, 1952, and O. M. Shaw to JBC, Dec. 12, 1952, both in "Congressional Investigation, 1952-53" folder, box 453, JBC PREP; see also Schrecker, *No Ivory Tower*, 183, 394n. 46, Yale President A. Whitney Griswold notes quoted in Diamond, *Compromised Campus*, 223.
78. Statement of Corporation member Charles A. Coolidge, quoted in FBI report of Apr. 3, 1953, FBI Conant file (77-55208), FBI Freedom of Information Act documents; see also Diamond, "The Arrangement," 359-60.
79. Zechariah Chafee, Jr., "Thirty-Five Years with Freedom of Speech," *University of Kansas Law Review* 1:1 (Nov. 1952), 1-36, quotations on 29; JBC, handwritten notations on WLM to JBC, Dec. 8, 1952, and WLM to JBC, Dec. 29, 1952, both in "Congressional Investigation, 1952-53" folder, box 453, JBC PREP; JBC diary ("Argued with Z. Chaffee [*sic*] on whether a person could in honesty plead the 5th amendment"), Dec. 16, 1952; Chafee to JBC, Dec. 16, 1952, Chafee Papers, box 1, folder 6; WLM to Chafee, Dec. 29, 1952, Chafee Papers, box 35, folder 19. See also WLM, *In the Catbird Seat*, 287-88; JBC to WLM, Feb. 4, 1953 (in which JBC agrees with WLM's position on the Fifth Amendment), courtesy of WLM; WLM interview.
80. *THC*, Jan. 8, 1953; see Schrecker, *No Ivory Tower*, 183-4, and Diamond, *Compromised Campus*, 123-33, 317-19.
81. JBC diary, Jan. 6, 1953.
82. This and other quotations describing the Jan. 6 meeting are from JBC to Corporation, "The Report on the Meeting of the President with the Faculty of Law to Discuss the Attitude of the University Toward Forthcoming Congressional Investigations," Jan. 7, 1953, JBC PREP, "Congressional Investigation, 1952-53" folder, box 453.

83. Chafee to JBC, Dec. 16, 1952, Chafee Papers, box 1, folder 6.
84. Mark DeWolfe Howe to JBC, Jan. 7, 1953, Howe Papers, box 1, folder 3, Harvard Law School library; for another exchange on this issue, see Arthur M. Schlesinger, Jr., to JBC, Jan. 2, 1953, and JBC to Schlesinger, Jan. 12, 1953, in JBC PREP, "Congressional Investigation, 1952–53" folder, box 453.
85. JBC to Mark DeWolfe Howe, Jan. 12, 1953, "Congressional Investigation, 1952–53" folder, box 453, JBC PREP.
86. Seymour E. Harris to Buck, Jan. 16, 1953, Buck Papers. Similar expressions of regret, in some cases accusation, about JBC's leaving at a time of peril for U.S. education are contained in many of the scores of personal letters JBC received from friends. "I am unhappy and troubled by your decision," wrote George Kistiakowsky. "What you are giving up is not just private responsibility. You have succeeded in setting up Harvard as an example of what an American University can be in these troubled times. Will it continue on this path after you leave? And if it does not, there will be more excuse for others to compromise with 'realities.' "
87. *President's Report,* 1951–52 (Cambridge: Harvard University, Jan. 12, 1953), esp. 5–7, 19–22.
88. *President's Report,* 1951–52, 21.
89. JBC testimony at Germany confirmation hearings, Feb. 2–3, 1953: U.S. Senate, Committee on Foreign Relations, *Nomination of James B. Conant,* 83d Cong., 1st sess. (Washington, D.C.: Government Printing Office, 1953), 96–97 (hereafter *Nomination of James B. Conant*).
90. *Nomination of James B. Conant,* 80, 95–96.
91. *Nomination of James B. Conant,* 86–87, 96–97.
92. JBC to WLM, Feb. 4, 1953, courtesy of WLM.
93. Sigmund Diamond, in *Compromised Campus* (p. 225), transcribes Griswold's notes of his conversation with JBC as reading, "N.B.: Disregard Chafee in Harvard Law Review. N.B.: Very bad advice. Way out of perspective." But this is almost certainly a garbled reference to Chafee's article in the Nov. 1952 *University of Kansas Law Review* advocating use of the Fifth Amendment, for his only *Harvard Law Review* article around this time, a book review, does not contain any specific "advice" on the Fifth (see *Harvard Law Review* 66:3 [Jan. 1953], 547–59).
94. See Diamond, *Compromised Campus,* 220–26.
95. Schrecker, *No Ivory Tower,* 198.
96. George Packer Berry to Faculty of Medicine, Apr. 9, 1953, Chafee Papers, box 35, folder 18; William Bentinck-Smith, " 'He Carried the Load,' " *Harvard Magazine* (July–Aug. 1974), 60.
97. JBC to WLM, Jan. 21, 1954; see also JBC to WLM, July 26, 1953, both courtesy of WLM.
98. For Harvard's actions in the 1953–54 confrontation with McCarthy, see Schrecker, *No Ivory Tower,* 194–218; Lewis, *Cold War on Campus,* 69–75; WLM, *In the Catbird Seat,* 286–96; Smith, *The Harvard Century,* 194–97, 205–10.
99. Quoted in Edmund Wilson, *The Thirties* (paperback ed., New York: Washington Square Press, 1982), 698.
100. Schrecker, *No Ivory Tower,* 339.
101. Buckingham, *America Sees Red,* 88.

CHAPTER 32

1. "Gallup Says Conant Fifth Behind 'Ike' in GOP Race," *THC,* Sept. 1951 registration issue. For other examples of speculation concerning JBC's presidential possibilities, see "Chemist of Ideas," *Time* 48:13 (Sept. 23, 1946), 60; " 'Another Yale Joke,' Says Pres. Conant of Politics Rumor," *BG,* Sept. 8, 1947; Russell Maloney, "James B. Conant — Ambassador to the Cosmos," *Saturday Review of Literature* 30 (Dec. 6,

1947), 15; and Kermit Roosevelt, "Harvard's Prize Kibitzer" (pt. 2), *Saturday Evening Post* (Apr. 30, 1949), 142.

2. WLM interview, Aug. 1986.
3. "Conant Set College History Through 20 Years of Reign," *THC*, Jan. 12, 1953.
4. JBC diary, Jan. 18, 1952.
5. JBC diary, Feb. 15, 1951.
6. JBC, *MSL*, 113.
7. Quoted in William Bentinck-Smith, " 'He Carried the Load,' " *Harvard Magazine* (July–Aug. 1974), 44.
8. DEL, *Venturesome Years, 1950–1955*, 54: Jan. 9, 1951, entry; Bruner, *In Search of Mind*, 244–46; interview with David Riesman, Jan. 1989; interview with John H. Finley, Jr., Sept. 1986.
9. Paul H. Buck, interview by William Bentinck-Smith, Summer 1974, Buck Papers, HUG (B) – B857.50, Harvard University Archives, 1–4, 23, 46, 68–75, 90.
10. See Joe Bertagna, *Crimson in Triumph: A Pictorial History of Harvard Athletics, 1852–1985* (Lexington, Mass.: Stephen Greene Press, 1986), 5–6.
11. JBC diary, Jan. 22, 23, Feb. 8, 9, 10, 15, 19, 24, 1951.
12. Lamenting the fact that "the public entertainment business in which almost all of us are engaged has become so competitive as to generate public scandals," he blamed the failure of colleges "to demonstrate the nature of their primary task" for fostering a general popular distrust toward institutions of higher education. JBC, *Report of the President, 1951–52*, 20.
13. WLM, *In the Catbird Seat*, 307–11; WLM interview; Cousins and Clifford, eds., *Memoirs of a Man*, 13 ("dirty pool"), 26, 150–51; Dunne, *Grenville Clark*, 177–82; TRC interviews, 1987.
14. WLM interview.
15. JBC diary, Oct. 20, 1952; also see entries of Apr. 7, 1951, and Dec. 31, 1952.
16. JBC diary, July 17, Aug. 2, 5, 28–31, Sept. 23, 30, Oct. 1, 9, 10, 1952.
17. JBC diary, Sept. 8, 10, 1951. Smith then asked KTC, who "agreed to make the desired survey of the entire field of scientific intelligence, but later he excused himself," according to the CIA's official historian, who mistakenly wrote that Smith's reference to a planned meeting with JBC "must have been a slip of the tongue." Montague, *General Walter Bedell Smith as Director of Central Intelligence*, 176–78. JBC's refusal to take on the assignment may have been one reason that Smith not long afterward angrily complained about "scientists like Vannevar Bush and James Conant, who shirked their military duty in laboratories and testing facilities." Hersh, *The Old Boys*, 301.
18. JBC diary, Jan. 11, 1952; on Roosevelt's CIA mission in Egypt: William Stadien, *Too Rich: The High Life and Tragic Death of King Farouk* (New York: Carroll & Graf, 1991), 13–16.
19. On McCloy's work in Germany see Thomas Alan Schwartz, *America's Germany: John J. McCloy and the Federal Republic of Germany* (Cambridge: Harvard University Press, 1991), and Bird, *The Chairman*, chap. 15–19.
20. JBC diary, Oct. 6, 1951; Dean G. Acheson to John J. McCloy, Oct. 15, 1951, Acheson Papers, box 66, Memoranda of Conversation series, Oct. 1951 folder, HSTL. See also McCloy to Acheson, Oct. 22, 1951, and Henry A. Byroade to Acheson, Oct. 24, 1951, in same folder.
21. JBC diary, Oct. 7, 8, 1951.
22. Acheson to McCloy, Oct. 15, 1951.
23. JBC diary, Oct. 11, 1951.
24. JBC, *MSL*, 469, 534.
25. JBC, *MSL*, 534.
26. JBC to DDE, Mar. 19, 1952, DDE Pre-Presidential Papers, DDEL.
27. TSV, "Notes of discussion with Dr. Conant in Cambridge on December 1, 1951," and TSV to Samuel Goldwyn, Dec. 7, 1951, in Sproul Papers, CU-5, 750.CPD 1951.
28. Sanders, *Peddlers of Crisis*, 111–14.

29. DDE to TSV, Feb. 27, 1952, in Galambos, ed., *The Papers of Dwight David Eisenhower*, 13:1016–17.
30. JBC diary, Jan. 19, Feb. 4, 24, 1952.
31. JBC diary, Mar. 22, 1952.
32. Wyzanski to JRO, July 8, 1954, box 79, Wyzanski folder, JROP, LC.
33. JBC diary, July 25, 1952.
34. JBC diary, Nov. 23, 26, 1952. After being offered the position a month later, JBC went back to these diary predictions and wrote, "Oh yeah? That's what you thought *then!*" and *"wrong!"*
35. JBC, *MSL*, 534–35; JBC OH, 51.
36. See Schwartz, *America's Germany*, 279–81, 386–87; Bird, *The Chairman*, 391–92; DDE calendar (Dec. 15) in Galambos, ed., *The Papers of Dwight David Eisenhower*, 13:1633.
37. See Charles F. Willis, Jr., to Sherman Adams, Apr. 26, 1955, President's Official Files 8-F, Conant, DDE Papers, DDEL.
38. JBC diary, Dec. 22, 23, 1952.
39. JBC, *MSL*, 535–36.
40. JBC diary, Dec. 26, 27, 28, 1952.
41. JBC diary, Jan. 1, 1953; *Time* 61:7 (Feb. 16, 1953), 52; Bundy, quoted in Smith, *Harvard Century*, 186.
42. JBC to George B. Kistiakowsky, Jan. 6, 1953, courtesy of Elaine Kistiakowsky.
43. JBC to Bridgman, Jan. 21, 1953, CFP.
44. I. B. Cohen interview, Jan. 1987; I. B. Cohen, "James Bryant Conant," Massachusetts Historical Society *Proceedings* 90 (1978), 122–30, quote on 128.
45. Finley interview, Sept. 1986.
46. See photograph and accompanying note by Buck dated Nov. 1, 1953, in photograph files, Pusey Library, Harvard University, HUP Conant, James B., A.B. 1914 (94).

CHAPTER 33

1. JBC diary, Jan. 29, 1953. During his years in Germany (1953–57), JBC simultaneously recorded his activities and observations in both a "daily reminder" and a series of scrapbooks or journals, often interspersed with news clippings. Both can be found in JBC PERP, UAI.15.898.13, the diaries in box 12 and the scrapbooks in box 22. Since the events and information described therein often overlap, I have simply referred in footnotes to entries from JBC diary, but researchers should consult both sources.
2. See Wilton B. Persons to Thomas Stephens, Feb. 4, 1953, Ann Whitman File, Name Series, box 22, "McCarthy," DDEL; Stephen E. Ambrose, *Eisenhower: The President*, vol. 2 (New York: Simon & Schuster, 1984), 59; DDE, *The White House Years: Mandate for Change, 1953–1956* (Garden City, N.Y.: Doubleday & Co., 1963), 319; Roy Cohn, *McCarthy* (New York: Lancer Books, 1968), 51–52; Richard M. Nixon, *RN: The Memoirs of Richard Nixon*, vol. 1 (New York: Warner Books ed., 1979), 171.
3. U.S. Senate, Committee on Foreign Relations, *Nomination of James B. Conant*, 83d Cong., 1st sess. (Washington, D.C.: Government Printing Office, 1953), passim.; JBC, *MSL*, 538–46; JFK's view is in *BG*, Jan. 30, 1953.
4. McCarthy to DDE, Feb. 3, 1953, Ann Whitman File, Name Series, box 22, "McCarthy," DDEL; Cohn, *McCarthy*, 51–52.
5. JBC's FBI file, released to the author in response to a Freedom of Information Act request, contains numerous testimonials to JBC's hard-line Cold War credentials.
6. JBC diary, May 31, June 21 (Furry case, diagram), 1953; JBC, *MSL*, 551; JBC to Paul Buck, June 27, 1953, Conant folder, Buck Papers, Harvard University archives.
7. John Le Carré, *A Small Town in Germany* (New York: Putnam's Sons, 1968), 16–17.
8. Alistair Horne, *Return to Power: A Report on the New Germany* (Praeger, 1956), 402.
9. 100,000 refugees in Mar. 1953: see JBC statement, Apr. 28, 1954, *Executive Sessions*

of the Senate Foreign Relations Committee (Historical Series), vol. 6, 83d Cong., 2d sess., 1954 (Washington, D.C.: Government Printing Office, 1977), 223. On the flow of refugees from East Berlin in early 1953 see *FRUS, 1952–54*, VII, 1307-9, 1316-17, 1322; JBC diary, Mar. 6, 21, 1953.

10. JBC diary, Mar. 6, 1953.
11. U.S. Senate, 94th Cong., 2d sess., *Final Report of the Select Committee to Study Governmental Operations with Respect to Intelligence Activities,* book IV (Washington, D.C.: Government Printing Office, 1976), 49; see also David C. Martin, *Wilderness of Mirrors* (New York: Ballantine Books, 1980, 1981), 49.
12. See Christopher Simpson, *Blowback: America's Recruitment of Nazis and Its Effects on the Cold War* (New York: Weidenfeld & Nicolson, 1988), 146-48.
13. Telephone interview with Thomas Polgar, Nov. 26, 1991.
14. Draft SAC/ODM statement, Nov. 1952, JRO Papers, box 189; folder 186.9, Lee A. DuBridge Papers, Caltech.
15. Secondary accounts used for U.S.–West German relations during this period include Rolf Steininger, "John Foster Dulles, the European Defense Community, and the German Question," and Hans-Jurgen Grabbe, "Konrad Adenauer, John Foster Dulles, and West German-American Relations," in Richard H. Immerman, ed., *John Foster Dulles and the Diplomacy of the Cold War* (Princeton, N.J.: Princeton University Press, 1990), 79-108, 109-32; Anne-Marie Burley, "Restoration and Reunification: Eisenhower's German Policy," in Richard A. Melanson and David Mayers, eds., *Reevaluating Eisenhower: American Foreign Policy in the Fifties* (Urbana and Chicago: University of Illinois Press, 1987), 220-40; Mark Cioc, *Pax Atomica: The Nuclear Defense Debate in West Germany During the Adenauer Era* (New York: Columbia University Press, 1988); Robert McGeehan, *The German Rearmament Question: American Diplomacy and European Defense after World War II* (Urbana, Ill.: University of Illinois Press, 1971); Frank Ninkovich, *Germany and the United States: The Transformation of the German Question Since 1945* (Boston: Twayne Publishers, 1988); Wolfram F. Hanreider, *Germany, America, Europe: Forty Years of German Foreign Policy* (New Haven, Conn.: Yale University Press, 1989); Brian R. Dulchin, "The 'Agonizing Reappraisal': Eisenhower, Dulles, and the EDC," *Diplomatic History* 16:2 (Spring 1992), 201-21; Marc Trachtenberg, "The Berlin Crisis," *History and Strategy* (Princeton: Princeton University Press, 1991), 169-234; Ernest R. May, "The American Commitment to Germany, 1949–1955," *Diplomatic History* 13 (Fall 1989), 431-60; Hershberg, " 'Explosion in the Offing': German Rearmament and American Diplomacy," *Diplomatic History* 16:4 (Fall 1992), 511-49; and Catherine Kelleher, *Germany and the Politics of Nuclear Weapons* (New York: Columbia University Press, 1975). Assessing the early 1950s, historians have also contrasted France's resilient suspicion of Germany with the "readiness of the United States to welcome Germany back into the international family almost without restriction." Most accounts emphasize that the United States was exasperated—and Eisenhower corroborates this impression in his presidential memoirs—with procrastination on EDC by successive French governments while displaying a "pro-German bias" reflecting full confidence in this new enemy-turned-ally. McGeehan, *The German Rearmament Question,* 231, 244; DDE, *Mandate for Change,* 396-409. On Adenauer's reported closeness with JFD, see Geir Lundestad, *The American "Empire"* (Oxford: Oxford University Press, 1990), 61, and Kelleher, *Germany and the Politics of Nuclear Weapons,* 30.
16. Acheson, memorandum of conversation, Dec. 24, 1952, *FRUS, 1952–54*, I, 33.
17. JBC OH, 51-52.
18. Townshend Hoopes, *The Devil and John Foster Dulles* (Boston: Little, Brown & Co., 1973), 160.
19. Hoopes, *Devil and John Foster Dulles,* 5.
20. JBC diary, July 4, 1953.
21. JBC, *MSL,* 563, 576.

22. Quoted in JBC, *MSL*, 577.

23. JBC diary, May 31, 1953.

24. C. L. Sulzberger, *A Long Row of Candles*, 882.

25. Marquis Child's report and JBC's reaction can be found in JBC statement, Apr. 28, 1954, *Executive Sessions of the Senate Foreign Relations Committee (Historical Series)*, vol. 6, 83d Congress, 2d session, 1954 (Washington, D.C.: Government Printing Office, 1977), 225–227.

26. JBC diary, July 4, 1953, describing lunch of June 9, 1953.

27. See Bird, *The Chairman*, 405–409.

28. To his credit, JBC prints extensive excerpts from the hearing in *MSL*, chap. 41; see also JBC diary, July 4, 1953. For the full transcript of the June 15, 1953, hearing, see U.S. Senate, *The Supplemental Appropriation Bill, 1954: Hearings Before the Committee on Appropriations*, 83d Cong., 1st sess., on H.R. 6200 (Washington, D.C.: Government Printing Office, 1953), 1–91.

29. JFD telephone conversation with McCloy, June 23, 1953, JFD telephone conversation series, box 1, folder "May–June 1953 (1)," JFD Papers, DDEL; JBC diary, June 27, 1953; JBC, *MSL*, 576–77; and JFD–JBC, Sept. 3, 1953, Dulles-Subject Series, Box 8, folder "Germany 1953 1954 (2)," JFD papers, DDEL.

30. JBC OH, 42, 44.

31. Quoted in Hoopes, *Devil and John Foster Dulles*, 131.

32. See M. Steven Fish, "After Stalin's Death: The Anglo-American Debate Over a New Cold War," *Diplomatic History* 10 (Fall 1986), 333–55, and John J. Yurechko, "The Day Stalin Died: American Plans for Exploiting the Soviet Succession Crisis of 1953," *Journal of Strategic Studies* 3 (May 1990), 43–73.

33. JBC, "My Six Years in Germany," unfinished and unpublished ms. written in late 1960s and early 1970s (first three chapters completed), III-15, JBC PERP, UA I.15.898.13, box 7, JBC PERP; JBC, "Summary of Highlights of First Eleven Months in Office as United States High Commissioner for Germany," Jan. 22, 1954, p. 14, box 7, UA I.15.898.13, JBC PERP (hereafter "Highlights").

34. See *FRUS*, 1952–54, VII, 434, 442, 454. For JBC's private reflections on complications regarding German ratification of EDC, see JBC, "The Rearmament of Germany," Aug. 1957, in JBC scrapbooks, JBC PERP (hereafter "Rearmament").

35. JFD, telephone conversation with McCloy, Mar. 27, 1953, JFD telephone call series, box 1, folder marked "telephone memoranda (excepting to and from White House), Jan. 53–April 53 (2)," JFD Papers, DDEL; McCloy, "Memorandum of Blankenhorn Visit to McCloy, Sunday, March 15, 1953," Mar. 16, 1953, *FRUS*, 1952–54, VII, 405–8; Riddleburger to JFD, Mar. 29, 1953, *FRUS*, 1952–54, VII, 416–9.

36. Ironically, the only important Soviet leader who appears to have favored permitting East Germany's disappearance as a socialist state was Interior Minister Lavrenti Beria, Stalin's secret police chief, whose consideration of this possibility was cited as a reason for his arrest and subsequent execution. The transcripts of the July 1953 CPSU Central Committee plenums at which these charges were leveled have now been published and translated: D. M. Stickle, ed., *The Beria Affair* (Commack, N.Y.: Nova Science Publishers, 1992); see also James Richter, "Reexamining Soviet Policy Towards Germany during the Beria Interregnum," Cold War International History Project Working Paper no. 3, 1992, Woodrow Wilson International Center for Scholars, Washington, D.C.; Vladislav Zubok, "Soviet Intelligence and the Cold War: The 'Small' Committee of Information, 1952–53," Cold War International History Project Working Paper no. 4, 1992, Wilson Center; and a forthcoming biography of Beria by Amy Knight.

37. JBC, "Highlights," 3.

38. Powers, *The Man Who Kept the Secrets*, 55–56. Much material related to U.S. policy toward the 1953 revolt and other anticommunist uprisings in East-Central Europe during this period remains classified, particularly related to covert operations, but

for a well-documented account see James F. Marchio, *Rhetoric and Reality: The Eisenhower Administration and Eastern Europe,* 1953–1959 (Ph.D. diss., American University, 1990).

39. JBC OH, 21.
40. JBC, *MSL,* 600–601.
41. Rudolph Kass interview, Cambridge, Mass., 1989; JBC to Paul Buck, June 27, 1953, and Buck to JBC, July 16, 1953, Conant folder, Buck Papers.
42. JBC to DoS, Feb. 13, 1953, HICOG Papers.
43. NSC 160/1, *FRUS,* 1952–54, VII, 510–20. A more explicit guidance prepared by the Joint Chiefs of Staff outlined further military and CIA measures to "stiffen [the East Germans'] spirit of resistance" and "sustain their hope of eventual liberation," to encourage "disaffection towards the regime and defection from the Soviet and East German military or para-military forces," and to undermine the "Soviet and communist administrative and control apparatus by conducting in a nonattributable manner psychological, political and economic harassment activities in the Soviet Zone, and to prepare, under controlled conditions, for such more active forms of resistance as may later be authorized." [JCS, "Guidance for the Peacetime Conduct of Military Activities in Support of U.S. National Strategy with Respect to Germany," n.d. but apparently late Aug. 1953, *FRUS,* 1952–54, VII, 521–31.] During the summer of 1953, JFD is reported to have told a cabinet meeting, in a gush of rollback rhetorical excess: "We ought to be *doubling* our bets, not reducing them—as all the Western parliaments want to do. This is the time to *crowd* the enemy—and maybe *finish* him, once and for all." Hoopes, *Devil and John Foster Dulles,* 179–80.
44. JBC to JFD, Aug. 8, 1953, *FRUS,* 1952–54, VII, 1639–40.
45. JBC to DoS, Aug. 8, 1953, HICOG Papers. See also JBC to Theodore C. Streibert, Sept. 10, 1953, HICOG Papers.
46. As in, "the P.W. boys are in the aggressive harsh phase." JBC diary, Sept. 27, Oct. 1, 1953.
47. Cook, *Declassified Eisenhower,* 177–78.
48. Minutes of NSC meeting 150, June 18, 1953, *FRUS,* 1952–54, VII, 1587, 1590.
49. JBC, "Reflections at Leisure Sept. 1956," Sept. 3, 1956, in JBC scrapbooks, JBC PERP (hereafter "Reflections").
50. JBC, "Reflections."
51. For documentation on VFC: *FRUS,* 1952–54, VIII, 159–238, and *FRUS,* 1955–57, XXV, 23–24, 47–48, 53–64, 79–80, 160–61.
52. DDE to Lay, Feb. 14, 1953, *FRUS,* 1952–54, VIII, 180–82.
53. JBC to DoS, July 11, 1953, *FRUS,* 1952–54, VIII, 224.
54. Memorandum Prepared in the Department of State, "Concepts and Ideas for Psychological Warfare in Europe Developed by the Chief of Mission Meeting at Luxembourg on September 18–19, 1953," *FRUS,* 1952–54, VI, 678–81. Conferring a few days later in Vienna, U.S. ambassadors posted to Eastern Europe generally endorsed the Luxembourg meeting's conclusions, prophetically declaring that the Communist system's intrinsic shortcomings "will contribute to the disintegration of the Soviet Empire more inexorably than we can through psychological warfare activities which are essentially uncontrollable and whose results may too often prove the opposite to those intended." Memorandum prepared in the Department of State, "Principal Conclusions [of] Chief of Mission Meeting in Vienna, Sept. 22–24, 1953," *FRUS,* 1952–54, VI, 681–3.
55. See the minutes of NSC meeting 150, June 18, 1953, *FRUS,* 1952–54, VII, 1587.
56. Perhaps one incident more than any other demonstrated to JBC how reluctant the West European allies were to confront Moscow. A few days after the June 17 revolt, he was astonished to receive a "lecture" from the British high commissioner to Germany, Sir Ivone A. Kirkpatrick, on "the danger of siding with those who had 'risen up' in East Berlin." "Do you want the Germans in your Zone to do the same thing?" Kirkpatrick asked. JBC expressed incredulity that the British envoy could

imply that Germans under U.S. occupation might revolt as had those in the Soviet Zone, but Kirkpatrick insisted that the principle was the same. JBC diary, June 11, 1963. For more on JBC's complaints about British reticence in the aftermath of the revolt, see JBC to DDE, Oct. 19, 1953, and DDE to JBC, Oct. 26, 1953, FRUS, 1952–54, VII, 1660–62, 1664.

57. Memorandum prepared in the Department of State, "Concepts and Ideas for Psychological Warfare in Europe Developed by the Chief of Mission Meeting at Luxembourg on September 18–19, 1953," *FRUS, 1952–54,* VI, 678–81.

58. JBC to JFD, July 27, 1953, *FRUS, 1952–54,* VII, 496.

59. Jackson to Minnich, Oct. 12, 1953, *FRUS, 1952–54,* VIII, 102–3.

60. DDE to Montgomery, July 14, 1953, DDE Papers, Ann Whitman files, DDE diary series, box 3, folder marked "DDE Diary, Dec. 52–July 53 (1)," DDEL.

61. DDE to JFD, Oct. 24, 1953, *FRUS, 1952–54,* VI, 684.

62. The diplomats' conclusions paralleled those of a secret foreign policy review (Operation Solarium) conducted by the administration in mid-1953, which also endorsed a policy that essentially continued the hold-the-line formula of containment. See also JBC's analysis in "Reflections."

63. JBC, "My Six Years in Germany," II-2, 17, JBC PERP, UA I.15.898.13, box 7.

64. NSC 160/1, United States Position with Respect to Germany, Aug. 17, 1953, *FRUS, 1952–54,* VII, 515.

65. See Ninkovich, *Germany and the United States,* 95.

66. For an argument that the West may have missed an opportunity to negotiate with Moscow to reunify Germany on mutually acceptable terms, see Rolf Steininger, *The German Question: The Stalin Note of 1952 and the Problem of Reunification* (New York: Columbia University Press, 1985).

67. Adenauer to JFD, July 21, 1953, *FRUS, 1952–54,* VII, 1591.

68. CIA National Intelligence Estimate (NIE) 53/1, "Review of Probable Soviet Courses of Action with Respect to Germany during 1952, in the light of recent Soviet Moves," Apr. 24, 1952, HST Papers, PSF, Box 254, Central Intelligence Reports, folder NIE 53–62, HSTL.

69. "Review of Probable Soviet Courses of Action."

70. Acheson to U.S. Embassies, Oct. 3, 1952, *FRUS, 1952–54,* VII, 368–70. In a similar vein, a British diplomat privately advised: "Best we c[ou]ld hope to accomplish w[ou]ld be a reply which w[ou]ld satisfy Ger[man] public opinion but be rejected out of hand by Sov[iet]s. . . . " Gifford to DoS, Mar. 11, 1952, *FRUS, 1952–54,* VII, 172.

71. JBC to JFD, June 25, 1953, *FRUS, 1952–54,* VII, 478–81.

72. JBC to DoS, July 2, 1953, *FRUS, 1952–54,* V, 1587–90.

73. JBC to DoS, July 6, 1953, *FRUS, 1952–54,* V, 1591–93.

74. David K. Bruce diary, July 9, 1953, *FRUS, 1952–54,* VII, 484–85; JBC to JFD, July 17, 1953, *FRUS, 1952–54,* VII, 488–89.

75. Communiqué by Western Foreign Ministers, July 14, 1953, U.S. Department of State, *Documents on Germany, 1944–1985* (Washington, D.C.: Dept. of State Publication 9446), 401.

76. See Hoopes, *Devil and John Foster Dulles,* 175. An NSC policy report of Aug. 17, 1953 — NSC 160/1 — stated: "Although the possibility of holding four-power talks on Germany will tend further to postpone action on these agreements [EDC and Bonn conventions], French ratification of EDC appears unlikely until four-power talks have been held or blocked by the Soviets." *FRUS, 1952–54,* VII, 515.

77. *FRUS, 1952–54,* VII, 601–602.

78. JBC diary, July 19, 1953.

79. JBC to JFD, July 17, 1953, *FRUS, 1952–54,* VII, 487–90.

80. Cioc, *Pax Atomica,* intro., chap. 1. These peaked in the summer of 1956 in the flap over the "Radford Plan" to reduce U.S. troop contributions to NATO drastically and increase reliance on nuclear weapons. See next chap.

81. JBC OH, 28–29. Declassified U.S. documents confirm JBC's (and Adenauer's) suspi-

cions that the Eisenhower administration secretly hankered for the eventual withdrawal of ground forces from Europe. The administration's policy was thus, as Marc Trachtenberg has said, "based on deceit: if the Europeans knew that the Americans intended to pull out, they would not agree to measures, relating especially to the rearmament of West Germany, that would make an American 'redeployment' a real possibility. So the real American goal had to be concealed from them, and they had to be given false assurances about America's intention to stay in Europe." Trachtenberg, *History and Strategy,* 163–68.

82. "dispelled his fears": Hans W. Gatzke, *Germany and the United States: "A Special Relationship?"* (Cambridge: Harvard University Press, 1980), 184; Potsdam nightmare: Grabbe, "Konrad Adenauer, John Foster Dulles, and West German-American Relations," 113.

83. JBC to DoS, Oct. 12, 1953, *FRUS,* 1952–54, VII, 652–53.

84. "Minutes of the Chiefs of Mission Meeting at Luxembourg, Sept. 18–19, 1953," *FRUS,* 1952–54, VI, 672; JFD to U.S. Embassy in U.K., Oct. 13, 1953, *FRUS,* 1952–54, VII, 655.

85. JFD to DDE, Sept. 6, 1953, in Gaddis, *Strategies of Containment,* 190.

86. DDE to JFD, Sept. 8, 1953, DDE Papers, Ann Whitman files, DDE diary series, box 3, folder marked "DDE Diary, Aug.–Sept. 1953 (2)," DDEL.

87. JFD to JBC, Sept. 8, 1953, HICOG Papers.

88. JFD to U.S. Embassy in U.K., Oct. 13, 1953, *FRUS,* 1952–54, VII, 655.

89. Sulzberger, *Long Row of Candles,* 905.

90. JBC, "Highlights," 17, 20, JBC PERP.

91. C. Douglas Dillon to DoS, Oct. 2, 1953, *FRUS,* 1952–54, VII, 1461.

92. JBC to DoS, Sept. 7, 11, 1953, *FRUS,* 1952–54, VII, 533–34, 1454–55.

93. See Coburn Kidd to MacArthur, July 23, 1953, *FRUS,* 1952–54, VII, 1449.

94. JFD to HICOG, Oct. 3, 1953, *FRUS,* 1952–54, VII, 1463; Dillon to DoS, Oct. 2, 1953, *FRUS,* 1952–54, VII, 1461–62.

95. JBC to DoS, Oct. 10, 1953, HICOG Papers.

96. JBC to JFD, Oct. 8, 1953, *FRUS,* 1952–54, V, 819–20.

97. See MacArthur (Dillon) to DoS, Oct. 24, 1953, *FRUS,* 1952–54, VII, 1467–69.

98. Sulzberger, *Long Row of Candles,* 900.

99. Hans-Peter Schwartz, *Adenauer. Der Staatsman:* 1952–1967 (Stuttgart: Deutsche Verlags-Anstalt, 1991), 23.

100. JBC to Theodore Streibert, Sept. 2, 1953, JBC PERP, UA I.15.898.13, box 22. Streibert, director of the U.S. Information Agency, had suggested that JBC visit Washington after the West German elections. JBC's distress was evident in his reply: "To be quite frank, I am not too anxious to come back to Washington unless I am requested to do so personally by the Secretary of State himself or the President (and I mean personally, not by a cable bearing the Secretary's signature)! Only under those conditions would I have an opportunity of talking at some length to both of these gentlemen, and I feel that it is important for me to keep my contacts at that level."

101. JBC diary, Sept. 8, 1953.

102. What a long way Adenauer had come, JBC mused, since the days four years earlier when the Allied high commissioners had kept him waiting when he arrived for meetings. JBC diary, Sept. 17, 20, 1953.

103. JBC to JFD, Oct. 28, 1953, *FRUS,* 1952–54, VII, 550–51.

104. Lewis to JBC, Oct. 28, 1953, *FRUS,* 1952–54, 549–50.

105. Douglas R. MacArthur II (Dillon) to DoS, Oct. 24, 1953, *FRUS,* 1952–54, VII, 1467–68.

106. JFD to JBC, Nov. 9, 1953, *FRUS,* 1952–54, VII, 552–53.

107. JBC to JFD, Nov. 13, 1953, JFD Papers, Subject Series, box 8, folder marked "Germany 1953 1954 (2)," DDEL. The reference to the CIA is deleted from the version of the letter printed in *FRUS,* 1952–54, VII, 553–55.

108. JBC's diary entries imply that he had learned that Eugen Gerstenmaier, the CDU chairman of the Bundestag Foreign Affairs Committee, was circulating ideas contradicting Adenauer's public stance, perhaps involving the strengthening the police force to handle "internal" Communist threats. See JBC diary, Nov. 15, 1953, and JBC, "Rearmament." He may also have had concerns about Blank's military office, where a "clique of officers, conservative in outlook," old school guardians of German military power opposed to reforms and led by a flamboyant Prussian ex-colonel, Bogislav von Bonin, had been opposed by other officers who were veterans of the July 20, 1944, assassination attempt against Hitler. See Horne, *Return to Power*, 82–91. The high commissioner's investigators concluded in early December that Blank and his immediate circle were "thoroughly anti-Nazi" and that the "unpleasant indications which have come to our attention thus far stem from remnants of conservative military thinking (e.g., Bonin) but not pro-Nazi sentiment." [JBC to DoS, Dec. 3, 1953, HICOG Papers. The date of the cable suggests it may have been timed for the opening of the Bermuda summit the following day, perhaps as evidence to allay French fears of German rearmament.] It is also possible that information was gained through wiretaps thought to have been maintained by the Allies on Adenauer and other German officials during this period. [Barnet, *The Alliance*, 55, alludes to British tapping of Adenauer's phones; JBC wrote cryptically to a State Department official of "special sources, the existence of which you are well aware, and which I believe to be thoroughly reliable," and proceeds to paraphrase the views of an Adenauer aide. JBC to Cecil B. Lyon, Aug. 26, 1954, HICOG Papers.]
109. JBC to DoS, Nov. 16, 1953, *FRUS*, 1952–54, VII, 840–41.
110. Memorandum of conversation, Nov. 18, 1953, *FRUS*, 1952–54, VII, 555; see also *NYT*, Nov. 19, 1953.
111. JFD to Adenauer, Nov. 20, 1953, *FRUS*, 1952–54, VII, 1477–78.
112. JFD to JBC, Nov. 20, 1953, *FRUS*, 1952–54, VII, 1474–77. Most of the first paragraph is deleted both from this version and the copy of this letter in the JFD Papers. It apparently deals with the concerns JBC expressed in his letter of Nov. 13, 1953, about Adenauer planning to defect from EDC.
113. JFD memorandum of conversation with the president, 6:14 p.m., Nov. 20, 1953, JFD telephone series, box 10, folder marked "White House Telephone Conversations — May–Dec. 31, 1953 (1)," JFD papers, DDEL. Previous accounts have noted Adenauer's coolness toward JBC, but not DDE's ignorance of the basic facts of their relationship. Burley, "Restoration and Reunification," 239.
114. JBC diary, Nov. 23, 1953.
115. JBC to JFD, Nov. 25, 1953, *FRUS*, 1952–54, VII, 1480.
116. JBC diary, Dec. 5, 1953; JBC to JFD, Dec. 5, 1953, *FRUS*, 1952–54, VII, 684–86.
117. The Soviet note of Nov. 26 appears in *FRUS*, 1952–54, VII, 675–77.
118. Charles Bohlen to DoS, Nov. 27, 1953, *FRUS*, 1952–54, VII, 677–79; JFD to U.S. Embassies Nov. 28, 1953, *FRUS*, 1952–54, VII, 680–81.
119. JBC to JFD, two cables, Nov. 30, 1953, *FRUS*, 1952–54, VII, 681–84. In arguing against a conference, Adenauer evidenced insecurity about every major Western ally. It was "foolish and [perhaps] disastrous," he told JBC, to hold a conference while an internal power struggle roiled the French government. Moreover, he had heard that Churchill was in a "very precarious state of health" — the implication being that the British statesman, thus enfeebled, might be more willing to sacrifice German interests for East-West peace. And Adenauer still sought reassurance as to America's commitment to a ground presence in Europe, urging Washington to make a firm declaration on the matter. Europe was "imprisoned in its past" and needed America's military presence and "guiding hand" to overcome that legacy; besides, Germany "did not want to be left alone on [the] continent with hysterical France."
120. JBC diary, Dec. 5, 1953; JBC to JFD, Dec. 5, 1953, *FRUS*, 1952–54, VII, 684–86; see also *FRUS*, 1952–54, VII, 682 n.

121. JBC diary, Dec. 5, 1953.
122. JBC diary, Feb. 4, 6, 1954; see also JBC, "Highlights," 25–26. For the Western counterproposal (introduced by Anthony Eden) detailing safeguards for free all-German elections: *Documents on Germany, 1944–1985*, 408–11. For Molotov's quote see Anthony Nutting, *Europe Will Not Wait* (London, 1960), 61, cited in Fish, "After Stalin's Death," 354.
123. JBC, *MSL,* 603.
124. JBC, "Reflections."
125. JBC diary, Feb. 22, 1954. Referring to State Department counselor Douglas R. MacArthur II and Assistant Secretary of State Livingston T. Merchant, JBC added: "I can clearly see that Messrs. McArthur [*sic*] & Merchant have no idea of letting the Ambassadors in the field have any leeway. The idea of the President that [Ambassador to France C. Douglas] Dillon & I & [Ambassador to England Winthrop W.] Aldrich would meet frequently and settle things is not in the picture."
126. The transcript of the Oppenheimer hearings, originally declassified by the government in 1954, is most conveniently available in a 1971 MIT Press reprint edition which includes valuable indices as well as an introductory essay; unfortunately, passages deleted in the original transcript apparently remain classified. JBC added little of interest beyond reprinting excerpts from his own testimony in *MSL,* 500–504; the author previously examined JBC's actions in " 'Over My Dead Body,' " 418–21, and *James B. Conant, Nuclear Weapons, and the Cold War,* 714–21. Important analyses of the hearings include Major, *The Oppenheimer Case;* Philip M. Stern with Harold P. Green, *The Oppenheimer Case: Security on Trial* (New York: Harper & Row, 1969); Barton J. Bernstein, "The Oppenheimer Conspiracy," *Discover* 6:3 (Mar. 1985), 22–32; Bernstein, "In the Matter of J. Robert Oppenheimer," *Historical Studies in the Physical Sciences* 12:2 (1982), 195–252; and, in his most detailed study, Bernstein, "The Oppenheimer Loyalty-Security Case Reconsidered," *Stanford Law Review* 42:6 (July 1990), 1383–1484.
127. JBC diary, Mar. 2, 1954.
128. JBC diary entries, Mar. 1954.
129. JBC diary, Mar. 27, 28, Apr. 1, 3, 1954.
130. JBC diary, Nov. 25, 1952; Killian, *Education of a College President,* 325.
131. William L. Borden to J. Edgar Hoover, Nov. 7, 1953, *IMJRO,* 835–38.
132. JBC to VB, Mar. 23, 1954, box 27, folder 614, VBP. VB visited JBC in Bonn on Jan 8, 1954, driving with him to inspect a coal mine near Cologne.
133. *Nomination of James B. Conant,* 91.
134. JBC to VB, Mar. 26, 1954, box 27, folder 614, VBP, and JBC Special Subject File, box 8, JBC PERP.
135. JBC to VB, Mar. 26, 1954; VB fully agreed with these views: see VB to JBC, Mar. 29, 1954, box 27, folder 614, VBP.
136. Lloyd K. Garrison to JBC, Mar. 12, 1954, JBC Special Subject File, box 8, JBC PERP.
137. JBC to VB, Mar. 23, 1954, box 27, folder 614, VBP.
138. JBC to VB, Apr. 1, 1954, box 27, folder 614, VBP.
139. JBC, *MSL,* 501.
140. JBC to JFD, Apr. 1, 1954, JFD Papers, General Correspondence and Memoranda Series, box 3, Strictly Confidential N–P (2), DDEL.
141. JFD to JBC, Apr. 12, 1954, and JFD to JBC, n.d. cable (Apr. 1954), both in JFD Papers, General Correspondence and Memoranda Series, box 3, Strictly Confidential N–P (2), DDEL.
142. JBC diary, April 16, 1954; *NYT,* Apr. 13, 1954.
143. JBC diary, Apr. 19, 1954; see also JBC to VB, April 8, 1954, box 27, folder 614; and JBC diary, Apr. 16, 1954, for indications that JBC evidently considered as "approval" JFD's failure to order him explicitly not to appear.
144. For JBC's testimony see *IMJRO,* 383–94.
145. This encounter has apparently not previously been discovered by historians. McGeorge

Bundy, for instance, writes in *Danger and Survival* that "there is no evidence" that DDE read JBC's testimony (or that of two other JRO supporters whom the president greatly respected, McCloy and Rabi), and that none of the three "appears to have mentioned the case to him." In explaining the "tragedy" of the president's allowing himself "to be a party to a miscarriage of justice," Bundy lays considerable weight on his supposed failure to be exposed to credible witnesses who could provide the other side of the Oppenheimer story. *Danger and Survival,* 316–18.

146. JBC diary, Apr. 26, 1954.
147. DDE to JBC, unmailed draft, Apr. 26, 1954, DDE Presidential Papers (Ann Whitman file), Conant folder, DDEL.
148. Ambrose, *Eisenhower: The President,* 167; DDE, *Mandate for Change,* 312. Ambrose incorrectly writes that DDE's letter was in response to a "strong defense" of JRO written by JBC from Bonn.
149. JBC to "Bobby" [Robert Cutler], Apr. 30, 1954, copy in Lewis Strauss Papers, Conant file, Herbert Hoover Presidential Library.
150. JBC diary, May 23, 1954. After JBC lunched on April 26 with Roger Adams, the foreign secretary of the National Academy of Sciences, he noted in his diary that Adams "said Nat. Acad. members divided on Oppie! The Calif. gang of chemists said he was a security risk. . . . "
151. The dissenting scientists were, respectively, Gray board member Ward V. Evans and AEC commissioner Henry D. Smyth. For the opinions, see *IMJRO,* 999–1021, 1049–1065.
152. JBC to WLM, June 30, 1954, courtesy of WLM.
153. Quoted in DEL diary entry, Dec. 9, 1969, in Helen M. Lilienthal, ed., *The Journals of David E. Lilienthal,* vol. 7, *Unfinished Business: 1968–1981* (New York: Harper & Row, 1983), 161. JBC also blamed Garrison for a poor job defending JRO, though he later softened his criticism after reading (in Stern's *The Oppenheimer Case*) that he had unsuccessfully sought a replacement: JBC to TSV, Dec. 4, 1969, .12 Miscellaneous Correspondence Folder, box 15, TSV Papers.
154. JBC to JRO, Dec. 7, 1963, box 27, Conant file, JROP.
155. JBC to JRO, Dec. 22, 1948, JBC PREP, box 348, "National Academy of Sciences, 1948–49" folder, and JROP, box 134, "NAS—Civil Liberties Committee" folder; draft statements by JBC, JRO, and Oliver E. Buckley, dated Jan. 3, 1949, with marginal notations dated Jan. 13, 1949, in "National Academy of Sciences, 1948–49" folder, box 348, JBC PREP, and "NAS—Civil Liberties Committee" folder, box 134, JROP.
156. JBC diary, May 23, 1954.
157. JBC to Livingston T. Merchant, July 12, 1954, *FRUS,* 1952–54, VII, 585; JBC diary, Mar. 24 ("panicky moods"), May 5, 1954.
158. "undertaker": JBC diary, June 27, 1954; "death's door," "coming apart": JBC diary, July 10, 1954; "fatal day": July 29, 1954.
159. JBC diary, Aug. 26, 1954.
160. JBC to Lyon, Aug. 26, 1954, HICOG Papers.
161. JBC, "Rearmament."
162. JBC, "Current Conditions in Western Europe," digest of off-the-record talk at the Council on Foreign Relations, Apr. 29, 1954, *Records of Meetings,* vol. XIX, July 1953–June 1954 (A–P), Council on Foreign Relations archives, New York City; "end run": JBC, "Rearmament."
163. JBC to Lyon, Aug. 26, 1954, HICOG Papers.
164. JBC diary, Aug. 30, 1954. These last two words were underlined twice.
165. See Hoopes, *Devil and John Foster Dulles,* 246.
166. JBC diary, Aug. 31, 1954.
167. JBC diary, Sept. 11, 1954.
168. For JBC's analysis of the events leading up to the signing of the Oct. 1954 Paris accords: JBC, address to National War College, Oct. 29, 1954, National Defense University archives; JBC, "The Future of Germany: The Significance of the New

Agreements," delivered to General Assembly of the States, Dec. 2, 1954, *Vital Speeches of the Day* (1954), 932-37; JBC statement, Feb. 18, 1955, U.S. House of Representatives, Committee on Foreign Affairs, *Selected Executive Session Hearings of the Committee,* 1951-56, Vol. XV, European Problems (Washington, D.C.: Government Printing Office, 1980), 481-95; and JBC, "Reflections at Leisure September 1956," in JBC diaries, JBC PERP.

169. "history . . . concerned": JBC, address to National War College, Oct. 29, 1954; "hard to get": JBC diary, Sept. 12, 1954; play it "cagey": Minutes of NSC meeting 216, Oct. 6, 1954, *FRUS,* 1952-54, V, 1382.

170. JBC, "Rearmament."

171. JBC, "Reflections."

172. Hanrieder, *Germany, America, Europe,* 6-11, 30-31, 142-44; Schwartz, *America's Germany,* 299; Thomas A. Schwartz, " 'Dual Containment:' John J. McCloy and the Federal Republic of Germany" (Paper presented at the Society for Historians of American Foreign Relations, Washington, D.C., June 20, 1991); Ninkovich, *Germany and the United States,* 82-106.

173. Steininger, "The EDC and the German Question," 93-94.

174. WLM, *In the Catbird Seat,* 398.

CHAPTER 34

1. JBC, cited in Ninkovich, *Germany and the United States,* 108.

2. JBC diary, June 13, 1955. Regarding JBC diary entries in 1953-57, see footnote 1 in previous chapter.

3. CD [Charles Dollard], "CD and JBC," Apr. 30, 1954, "Conant, James B. 1934-55" folder, CCP. Carnegie president Dollard had extended that invitation even before JBC reached Germany: Dollard to JBC, Jan. 13, 1953, CFP.

4. JBC, *MSL,* 614-15; Amster, *Meritocracy Ascendant,* 192-98; JBC diary, Jan. 9, 1956.

5. JBC OH, 20, 34-40.

6. DDE's comment is noted in Ann Whitman to Phyllis Bernau, Apr. 4, 1955, responding to JFD to DDE, Apr. 2, 1955, both in JFD White House Memoranda, box 3, "WH Correspondence—General 1955 (3)," JFD Papers, DDEL.

7. Frank Littell to Reinhold Niebuhr, May 5, 1955, box 8, Niebuhr Papers, LC.

8. See report of unidentified U.S. foreign magazine correspondent attached to note to "Herb," May 16, 1955, JFD Papers, White House Memoranda collection, box 3, folder marked "Meetings with President 1955 (4)," DDEL. A notation indicates that JFD brought two copies of the sharply critical report to a June 10, 1955, meeting with DDE shortly before a meeting with Adenauer. JBC's journals for 1953-57 are also replete with references to press criticisms, which he monitored carefully.

9. JBC diary, June 15, 16, 1955.

10. JFD, "Memorandum of Conversation with Mr. McCloy on Saturday, July 9, 1955," July 11, 1955, "Memoranda of Conversation—General L-M (3)" folder, box 1, General Correspondence and Memoranda Series, JFD Papers, DDEL.

11. See Robert Shaplen, "Sabbatical," *New Yorker* (Oct. 13, 1956), 128-49 (quotation on 145).

12. See JBC to JFD, May 21, 1955, *FRUS,* 1955-57, XXVI, 376-81; JBC, *MSL,* 603-605.

13. JBC to DoS, Apr. 26, 1955, *FRUS,* 1955-57, XXVI, 365-66; *"cold feet!":* JBC diary, Apr. 29, 1955.

14. JBC to JFD, May 21, 1955.

15. Herbert Hoover, Jr., to JFD, June 1, 1955, appended to JBC to JFD, May 21, 1955, in DoS Decimal File 762.00/5-2155, RG 59, NA.

16. JBC, *MSL,* 605; see also memorandum of conversation, June 14, 1955, *FRUS,* 1955-57, XXVI, 386-87.

17. See *FRUS,* 1955–57, XXVI, 387 n. 3, and JBC, *MSL,* 605.
18. JBC, "Reflections."
19. JBC diary, July 31, 1955.
20. See *FRUS,* 1955–57, XXVI, 381–83, 384–85, 393–95.
21. JBC OH, 53–54; JBC, "Reflections."
22. JBC diary, July 3, 1955.
23. JBC diary, Sept. 15 (Soviet embassy), 27 ("de facto split"), 1955.
24. JBC, *MSL,* 605–8; *FRUS,* 1955–57, XXVI, 546–49.
25. Quoted in Shaplen, "Sabbatical," 130.
26. Telephone interview with Richard Bissell, Sept. 22, 1992.
27. See Ranelagh, *The Agency,* 288–96; Andrew and Gordievsky, *KGB: The Inside Story,* 437; Allen Dulles, *The Craft of Intelligence* (New York: Signet, 1963, 1965), 193; and for an imaginative reconstruction, Norman Mailer, *Harlot's Ghost* (New York: Random House, 1991).
28. Amory interview cited in Hersh, *The Old Boys,* 379.
29. See Killian, *Education of a College President,* 331, and JBC diary, July 2, 3, 1956.
30. JBC to JFD, July 13, 1956, State Department "Operation Paperclip" microfiche, Civil Reference Branch, RG 59, NA, in Linda Hunt, *Secret Agenda: The United States Government, Nazi Scientists, and Project Paperclip, 1945 to 1990* (New York: St. Martin's Press, 1991), 3, 193–94; see also John Gimbel, "Project Paperclip: German Scientists, American Policy, and the Cold War," *Diplomatic History* 14 (Summer 1990), 343–65.
31. JFD to Lodge, Apr. 30, 1956, *FRUS,* 1955–57, XXV, 160–61, and minutes of National Security Council meeting, Sept. 8, 1955, *FRUS,* 1955–57, XXV, 79–80, n. 3.
32. JBC diary, July 3, 1955.
33. JFD to DoS, May 4, 1956, *FRUS,* 1955–57, XXVI, 93–95; JBC diary, Aug. 17, 1957.
34. JBC OH, 26–27.
35. See JFD to Adenauer, June 29, 1956, responding to Adenauer to JFD, June 22, 1956, in *FRUS,* 1955–57, XXVI, 129–30.
36. See Cioc, *Pax Atomica,* 21–32; Alfred Grosser, *The Western Alliance* (New York: Continuum, 1980), 167; Jeffrey Boutwell, *The German Nuclear Dilemma* (Ithaca, N.Y.: Cornell University Press, 1990), 17–18.
37. "Radford Seeking an 800,000 Man Cut," *NYT,* July 13, 1956.
38. JBC diary, July 21, 23, 24, 1956; Memorandum of conversation, July 17, 1956, *FRUS,* 1955–57, XXVI, 131–33. For a detailed account of these events, using recently declassified records, see Robert A. Wampler, *Ambiguous Legacy: The United States, Great Britain, and the Foundations of NATO Strategy, 1948–1957* (Ph.D. diss., Harvard University, 1991; Ann Arbor, Mich: University Microfilms, 1991), chap. 12.
39. JBC diary, Aug. 17, 1957; see also Boutwell, *The German Nuclear Dilemma,* 18–20.
40. See Schwartz, *Adenauer. Der Staatsman: 1952–1967,* 292–95; and Cioc, *Pax Atomica,* 33. Despite its publication in Germany, the letter was treated as still classified in the relevant volume of the State Department's diplomatic series; see *FRUS,* 1955–57, XXVI, 139 fn. 1.
41. JBC OH, 28–29; see also Trachtenberg, *History and Strategy,* 160–68, 185–86.
42. JBC to JFD, July 24, 1956, *FRUS,* 1955–57, XXVI, 133–38.
43. JFD to Adenauer, Aug. 11, 1956, *FRUS,* 1955–57, XXVI, 139–43.
44. Cabell (Allen Dulles) to JFD, Aug. 28, 1956, *FRUS,* 1955–57, XXVI, 144–49.
45. JFD to Hoover and Henderson, July 16, 1956, general correspondence, strictly confidential, box 2, "C-D (1)" folder, JFD Papers, DDEL; JFD, "Memorandum of Conversation with the President, the White House," July 16, 1956, JFD White House Memoranda series, box 4, "Meetings with President Jan.–July 1956 (1)" folder, JFD Papers, DDEL.
46. JFD, "Memorandum of Conversation with the President," July 23, 1956, memorandum of conversation series, A–D(3), box 1, JFD Papers, DDEL; memoranda of JFD

conversations with Adams, July 20, 1956, in JFD telephone call series, box 11, "Memoranda of Tel. Conv. *WH* Jan. 3, 1956–Aug. 31, 1956" folder, JFD Papers, DDEL.

47. Schwartz, *Adenauer. Der Staatsman:* 1952–1967, 295, incorrectly writes that Adenauer's letter prompted JFD to remove JBC; actually, it probably reinforced a decision that had already been made.

48. See TSV, "Confidential notes of talk with Dr. Conant at Sugar Hill, New Hampshire, on August 4, 1959," Conant correspondence file, box 8, TSV Papers.

49. JBC, *MSL*, 615–16; JBC OH, 49; JFD, memorandum of conversation with Amb. Conant, Aug. 4, 1956, and telephone call from Amb. Conant in New Hampshire, Aug. 6, 1956, in General Correspondence series, memoranda of conversations, A–D(3), box 1, JFD Papers, DDEL; JBC diary, Aug. 4, 5, 6, 8, 1956.

50. JBC diary, Aug. 16, 1956; JBC, *MSL*, 616–17.

51. JBC, "Reflections."

52. JBC diary, Sept. 7, 1956.

53. JBC diary, Sept. 6, 1956; "shocked": Memorandum of conversation between JBC and JFD, Sept. 6, 1956, *FRUS*, 1955–57, XXVI, 153–54; "strange": JBC, "Rearmament"; "incredible": JBC diary, Sept. 11, 1956; "very sore . . . in the middle": JBC diary, Aug. 17, 1957.

54. The account of this meeting is drawn from memorandum of conversation, Sept. 10, 1956, *FRUS*, 1955–57, XXVI, 155–61, and JBC diary, Sept. 10, 11, 1956.

55. JBC diary, Sept. 10, 1956; JBC, "Rearmament."

56. JBC diary, Oct. 3, 1956; on Adenauer's dissatisfaction: JBC to DoS, Sept. 28, 1956, DoS memorandum of conversation, Sept. 29, 1956, JBC to DoS (JFD), Oct. 16, 1956, and JBC to DoS, Nov. 16, 1956, in *FRUS*, 1955–57, XXVI, 161–63, 164–65, 167–68, 172–74.

57. JBC to DoS, Jan. 25, 1957, *FRUS*, 1955–57, XXVI, 193.

58. JBC diary, Oct. 29, 1956.

59. JBC diary, Oct. 30, 1956.

60. JBC diary, Nov. 4, 1956.

61. JBC diary, Nov. 5, 6, 7, 1956.

62. JBC to Merchant, Dec. 5, 1955, *FRUS*, 1955–57, XXVI, 401–7, quotation on 402.

63. JBC, "Our Common Future," *Department of State Bulletin* 32 (June 27, 1955), 1034–39; JBC, "Strengthening Cultural Ties with Germany," *Department of State Bulletin* 35 (Nov. 12, 1956), 766–67.

64. Quoted in JBC diary, Aug. 17, 1957.

65. See Shaplen, "Sabbatical," *passim.*, esp. 141 (number of speeches), 142 ("accentuate the positive").

66. JBC to DDE, Nov. 21, 1956, DoS decimal file 762.00/11-2156, RG 59, NA; JBC, "The Effective Disarmament of Germany and Japan," Oct. 7, 1944, *Vital Speeches of the Day* 11 (Nov. 15, 1944), 75–78. JBC struck a nerve with Adenauer when he described German students' reactions to the Suez and Hungary events. The students he had conversed with, in Hamburg, Marburg, and Aachen, angrily opposed the actions of England, France, and the Soviets, and strongly favored Eisenhower's policy, JBC told Adenauer. "A few spoke of England & France's attack on Egypt as being worse than Hitler's attack on Norway. One said why didn't U.S. & Germany alone work together as they were the only nations with moral right on their side! When I repeated this to the Chancellor the other day he went off with a violent denunciation of Hitler and dwelled on his starving 3 million Russians! He said no German had the right to speak of moral right considering what the Germans had done under Hitler!" JBC diary, Dec. 6, 1956.

67. JBC, "Rearmament."

68. On Euratom's creation, see Jonathan E. Helmreich, "The United States and the Formation of EURATOM," *Diplomatic History* 15 (Summer 1991), 387–410.

69. JBC to DoS, Nov. 4, 1955, *FRUS*, 1955–57, IV, 344–46.

70. DDE diary entry of Jan. 19, 1956, in Robert H. Ferrell, ed., *The Eisenhower Diaries* (New York: Norton & Co., 1981), 309.

71. JBC to DoS, Feb. 9, 1956, *FRUS,* 1955–57, IV, 413–15; also JFD to JBC, Sept. 30, 1956, *FRUS,* 1955, IV, 467–68.
72. Quoted in Butterworth to DoS, Oct. 25, 1956, *FRUS,* 1955–57, IV, 477.
73. JBC diary, Oct. 29, 1956; JBC to DoS, Oct. 30, 1956, *FRUS,* 1955–57, IV, 480–81.
74. On Adenauer's shift: Boutwell, *The German Nuclear Dilemma,* 19; Wampler, *Ambiguous Legacy,* chap. 12; Cioc, *Pax Atomica,* 34–35; and Hanns Jürgen Küsters, "Adenauer and Berlin," presentation to Nuclear History Program conference on New Perspectives on the Berlin Conference, Woodrow Wilson Center, Washington, D.C., May 19–21, 1993.
75. JBC made a point of noting in his cable to the State Department reporting the conversation that he had lacked information on which to base a counterargument. "I intended this to get under their skin which it did," he noted in his diary (Dec. 2, 1956), but the response that he should rely on summaries of JFD press conferences hardly satisfied him. He later said that JFD "never understood the untenable position of an ambassador who obviously didn't have the day to day confidence of the man he was working for. Not that he had lack of it, but he wasn't kept informed." JBC OH, 34–40.
76. JBC to DoS, Nov. 16, 1956, *FRUS,* 1955–57, XXVI, 172–74.
77. Telegram from the Embassy in Germany to DoS, Jan. 25, 1957, *FRUS,* 1955–57, XXVI, 192–98.
78. JBC diary, Jan. 10, 26, 1957; JBC, *MSL,* 617–18.
79. Adenauer's signal was conveyed in an oral message for DDE delivered by ambassador to NATO Herbert A. H. Blankenhorn to Gruenther: Gruenther to Goodpaster, Nov. 19, 1956, *FRUS,* 1955–57, XXVI, 174–76; Adenauer's confidence in Bruce: Schwartz, *Adenauer. Der Staatsman:* 1952–1967, 23, 85.
80. JFD, memorandum of conversation with Adenauer, May 28, 1957, *FRUS,* 1955–57, XXVI, 280.
81. JBC diary, Aug. 17, 1957.
82. JBC diary, Mar. 8, 1957.
83. Adenauer to Fritz Schaeffer, Feb. 12, 1953, in Hans Peter Mensing, ed., *Konrad Adenauer, Briefe* 1951–1953 (Berlin: Siedler Verlag, 1987), 342; on the reparations issue see Schwartz, *America's Germany,* 175–84, and Lily Gardner Feldman, *The Special Relationship between West Germany and Israel* (Boston: Allen & Unwin, 1984).
84. JBC, *The Federal Republic of Germany: Our New Ally,* Feb. 24, 1957 (Minneapolis: University of Minnesota Press, 1957), 3.
85. See JBC, *Germany and Freedom: A Personal Appraisal* (Cambridge: Harvard University Press, 1958).
86. See "Experts Oppose German Neutralization," American Council on Germany press release, Jan. 22, 1958, and Christopher Emmet to Charles Merz, Jan. 20, 1958, both in JBC PERP; and Douglas Brinkley, *Dean Acheson: The Cold War Years,* 1953–1971 (New Haven: Yale University Press, 1992), 76–93. For Kennan's proposal, see *Russia, the Atom, and the West* (New York: Harper & Bros. 1957, 1958) esp. chap. 3–4; and *Memoirs:* 1950–63 (Boston: Little, Brown and Co., 1972), 229–66.
87. JBC, *Germany and Freedom,* 102–10.
88. JBC, *Germany and Freedom,* 10–19.
89. JBC, *Germany and Freedom,* 110.

CHAPTER 35

1. JBC to Gardner, Dec. 21, 1956, JBC PERP, in Amster, *Meritocracy Ascendant,* 193–97. The most detailed account of JBC's study of American public high schools is Barry James Teicher, *James Bryant Conant and "The American High School Today"* (Ph.D. diss., University of Wisconsin, 1977; Ann Arbor, Mich.: University Microfilms, 1977); see also Amster, *Meritocracy Ascendant,* 187–242; and JBC, *MSL,* chap. 45.

On JBC and education while in Germany: Charles D. Biebel, "Education and Cultural Policy at the End of Occupation: James B. Conant in Germany, 1953–1957," copy in CFP; JBC, *Citadel of Learning* (New Haven: Yale University Press, 1956).

2. Amster, *Meritocracy Ascendant*, 207–15; JBC, *MSL*, 618–19; Teicher, *James Bryant Conant and "The American High School Today,"* 193–200, 204–206.

3. JBC to Eugene Youngert, Mar. 21, 1957, JBC PERP, in Amster, *Meritocracy Ascendant*, 214.

4. JBC to Merle Borrowman, Sept. 30, 1963, JBC PERP.

5. JBC, *MSL*, 619–20; Teicher, *James Bryant Conant and "The American High School Today,"* 204–206.

6. Interviews with TRC and Ellen Conant, July 5–9, 1991, correspondence, newspaper articles, and TRC résumé in CFP; biography of TRC w. JBC to Dana M. Cotton, Jan. 20, 1960, JBC PERP; JBC diary, Aug. 24, 1957, JBC PERP.

7. PRC to Miriam Thayer Richards, Aug. 27, 30, 1957, CFP.

8. TRC interview, Nov. 12, 1992. MTR's death: TRC interviews, JBC diary, Sept. 15, 23, 24, 1957.

9. See Teicher, *James Bryant Conant and "The American High School Today,"* 200–204.

10. For an influential example of this sort of thinking, see Albert Wohlstetter, "The Delicate Balance of Terror," *Foreign Affairs* 37 (Jan. 1959), 827–47. On the reaction to Sputnik see Walter A. McDougall, . . . *the Heavens and the Earth: A Political History of the Space Age* (New York: Basic Books, 1985), 142–76; Killian, *Sputnik, Scientists, and Eisenhower;* Herken, *Counsels of War,* 113–21; Herken, *Cardinal Choices,* 98–105; Kaplan, *Wizards of Armageddon,* 134–54; Sanders, *Peddlers of Crisis,* 125–30.

11. JBC to Sherman Adams for DDE, Nov. 10, 1957, Adams to JBC (quoting DDE), Nov. 12, 1957, JBC PERP; see also DDE, *Waging Peace: The White House Years, 1956–1961* (Garden City, N.Y.: Doubleday & Co., 1965), 241–42, and McDougall, *Heavens and the Earth,* 161.

12. Robert Cutler to JBC, Nov. 1, 1957, JBC to Sherman Adams, Dec. 2, 1957, and Adams to JBC, Dec. 10, 1957, all in JBC PERP.

13. "The Inspector General," *Time* 74:11 (Sept. 14, 1959), 74; Alden Dunham to JBC, Mar. 13, 1968, JBC PERP.

14. Kistiakowsky interview, Jan. 1982. In 1959, Kistiakowsky replaced Killian as Eisenhower's science adviser. JBC's public references to nuclear power, and technology in general, had become increasingly skeptical and critical during his time in Germany. He repeated his advocacy of solar-power research in preference to atomic-energy development, which he described as risky. Biebel, "Education and Cultural Policy at the End of Occupation," citing various JBC speeches in 1955–56.

15. JBC diary, Jan. 8, 1958.

16. JBC to Edwin L. Weisl, Special Counsel, Senate Preparedness Investigating Subcommittee, Dec. 31, 1957, JBC PERP.

17. H. G. Rickover, *Education and Freedom* (New York: E. P. Dutton & Co., 1959), quoted in Amster, *Meritocracy Ascendant*, 205–206.

18. JBC, *The Identification and Education of the Academically Talented Student* (Washington, D.C.: National Education Association, 1958), 16, in Amster, *Meritocracy Ascendant*, 221.

19. JBC's interim report, *Some Problems of the American High School: A Preliminary Report of a Study* (Miami: Lindsey Hopkins Educational Center, 1958), devoted twenty-two pages to the academically talented, compared to six for the regular curriculum, vocational instruction, and average students; see Amster, *Meritocracy Ascendant*, 228.

20. Ambrose, *Eisenhower,* vol. 2, *The President,* 459–60.

21. JBC, *MSL,* 618.

22. JBC, *The American High School Today* (New York: McGraw-Hill, 1959); Amster, *Meritocracy Ascendant*, 230–42; on the philosophy, methodology, and preparation of

the study, see Teicher, *James Bryant Conant and "The American High School Today,"* 186–244.

23. "The Inspector General," *Time* 74:11 (Sept. 14, 1959), 70–72, 74, 76, 79.

24. JBC, *MSL,* 622.

25. J. K. Galbraith to JBC, Jan. 2, 1959, JBC PERP.

26. JBC to Galbraith, Mar. 2, 1959, JBC PERP.

27. Alden Dunham to JBC, Mar. 13, 1968, JBC PERP.

28. JBC to William Feis, Feb. 5, 1959, JBC PERP, in Amster, *Meritocracy Ascendant,* 240.

29. Mary Beth Norton, et al., *A People & A Nation: A History of the United States,* vol. 2 (Boston: Houghton Mifflin Co., 1990), 897.

30. Teicher, *James B. Conant and "The American High School Today,"* 245–76.

31. Ernest L. Boyer, *High School: A Report on Secondary Education in America: The Carnegie Foundation for the Advancement of Teaching* (New York: Harper & Row, 1983), 54, 56.

32. JBC to DDE, Feb. 23, 1959, JBC PERP.

33. See Ambrose, *Eisenhower,* vol. 2, *The President,* chap. 19–21.

34. For extracts of the Soviet note, see U.S. State Department, *Documents on Germany, 1944–1985,* 552–59. Recent important analyses of the crisis include: Norman Gelb, *The Berlin Wall: Kennedy, Khrushchev, and a Showdown in the Heart of Europe* (New York: Times Books, 1987); Trachtenberg, "The Berlin Crisis," in *History and Strategy,* 169–234; and Bundy, *Danger and Survival,* 358–90; for a large collection of recently declassified U.S. documents, see William Burr, ed., *The Berlin Crisis* (Washington, D.C.: National Security Archive, 1992). The opening of archives in Moscow and East Berlin following the anti-Communist revolutions of 1989 to 1991 now permits an informed reconstruction and analysis of the Soviet and East German actions and strategy during the crisis. Two early accounts drawing on these new sources were presented to the Cold War International History Project's Conference on New Evidence on Cold War History, Jan. 12 to 15, 1993, Moscow, and published in expanded form as working papers: Hope M. Harrison, "Ulbricht and the Concrete 'Rose': New Archival Evidence on the Dynamics of Soviet–East German Relations and the Berlin Crisis, 1958–1961," Cold War International History Project Working Paper No. 5 (Washington, D.C.: Woodrow Wilson International Center for Scholars, May 1993); and Vladislav M. Zubok, "Khrushchev and the Berlin Crisis (1958–1962)," Cold War International History Project Working Paper No. 6 (Washington, D.C.: Woodrow Wilson International Center for Scholars, May 1993).

35. Livingston T. Merchant to JBC, Dec. 8, 1958; JBC to Merchant, Dec. 10, 1958; JBC to JFD, Dec. 10, 1958; John J. McCloy to Merchant, Dec. 10, 1958; all in JBC PERP.

36. JBC to JFD, Dec. 10, 1958. JBC also halfheartedly proposed a diplomatic "counterproposal with propaganda value," in deference to the sensitivities of West Europeans nervous about the situation (he noted in particular that the British Labour Party was demanding a "new look" at alternative solutions to the German question, having debated its leader, Hugh Gaitskell, the previous spring about Kennan's proposals). JBC suggested (and McCloy endorsed) daring the Soviets to permit free elections in East Germany to select representatives who would participate with elected FRG delegates in an all-German council to explore reunification issues. If the Russians accepted the offer, which JBC did not expect, the result would be a "delaying action" which would defuse the immediate crisis; if they rejected it, the West would score propaganda points.

37. TSV to JBC, Feb. 12, 1959, JBC to TSV, Feb. 26, 1959, and JBC to DDE, Feb. 23, 1959, all in JBC PERP.

38. JBC to Fritz E. Oppenheimer, Mar. 2, 1959, JBC PERP.

39. JBC, "Germany and Communism," speech to Canadian Club of Montreal, Mar. 16, 1959, copy in box 8, E-Conant Correspondence file, TSV Papers. Documents in newly opened Russian and East German archives have borne out JBC's analysis of

Soviet motives, suggesting that Moscow acted in large measure due to concern about the dire state of the GDR's economy and fear that East German socialism might collapse. See Harrison, "Ulbricht and the Concrete 'Rose,'" and Zubok, "Khrushchev and the Berlin Crisis."

40. JBC to Merchant, Mar. 18, 1959, JBC PERP. JBC expressed his admiration for Merchant in JBC OH, 19–20.
41. Ambrose, *Eisenhower,* vol. 2, *The President,* 503–504, 515–16.
42. Gordon Gray to JBC, Mar. 3, 1959, JBC PERP.
43. JBC to Gordon Gray, Apr. 1, 1959; DDE to JBC, Mar. 24; JBC to DDE, Mar. 31, 1959; JBC to John Dickey, Apr. 17, 1959; all in JBC PERP.
44. JBC to Sir Hector Hetherington, Apr. 21, 1959, JBC to John Dickey, June 13, 1959, both in JBC PERP; TRC interviews; JBC diary, Apr. 17–22, 25, May 2, June 3, 12, 1959.
45. JBC to S. G. Dixon, Nov. 15, 1960, JBC PERP; JBC diary, Oct. 18–21, Nov. 6–8, 1959.
46. TRC interview, Feb. 10, 1993.
47. JBC to Merchant, Apr. 3, 1959, JBC PERP.
48. JBC to Harry D. Gideonse, June 5, 1958, JBC PERP. JBC's preference for a "top-down" rather than "bottom-up" philosophy for the making of U.S. foreign policy once led to a clash with the staff of the New York–based Foreign Policy Association, a non-partisan educational group. One staff member recalled a rather tart exchange of views on this point when JBC, who was chairing a review panel for the group in the late 1950s, firmly rejected the notion that the public could play an activist role at the grass roots level in formulating foreign policy ideas and transmitting them to their elected leaders, as opposed to simply assimilating the wisdom handed down to them from government and elite experts. Interview with Dick Rowsen, Oct. 16, 1992, Washington, D.C.
49. TSV to JBC, Apr. 12, 1961, Conant folder, box 8, TSV Papers.
50. On the Committee to Strengthen the Frontiers of Freedom: JBC to Neil McElroy, June 19, 1959, and McElroy to JBC, July 9, 1959, JBC PERP; Herbert S. Parmet, *Eisenhower and the American Crusades* (New York: Macmillan Co., 1972), 287; JBC interview, "College News Conference," July 5, 1959, Conant folder, box 8, TSV papers.
51. JBC to TSV, Aug. 9, 1959, Conant folder, box 8, TSV Papers.
52. JBC to James R. Killian, Nov. 13, 1959, JBC PERP.
53. JBC to TSV, Aug. 9, 11, 1959, Conant folder, box 8, TSV Papers.
54. JBC, *The Defense of Freedom,* address on receiving the Woodrow Wilson Award for Distinguished Service from the Woodrow Wilson Foundation, Nov. 12, 1959 (Stamford, Conn.: Overbrook Press, 1960).
55. JBC, *The Defense of Freedom.* Trusting in nuclear deterrence as the only way to stop the Soviets, JBC shunned attempts by dovish scientists to promote a total halt to nuclear testing as the first step to general disarmament and ultimate abolition of nuclear weapons. One such petition, a post-Sputnik plea from the famed scientist Linus Pauling, had elicited this cordial reply on November 19, 1957:

> Dear Linus.
> In reference to your letter of November 6, and the enclosed petition, as you probably imagine I couldn't disagree with you more heartily. I, therefore, have high hopes that you will fail completely in your undertaking.
> Best wishes,
>
> As ever,
> James B. Conant

56. JBC, *The Defense of Freedom.* On U.S. war plans during the Eisenhower era, see David Alan Rosenberg's seminal "The Origins of Overkill: Nuclear Weapons and American Strategy, 1945–1960," *International Security* 7 (Spring 1983), 3–71. On the particular influence of the Berlin crisis on U.S. and NATO nuclear strategy, based on newly declassified Western sources, see essays by William Burr, David Alan Rosenberg,

Gregory Pedlow, Kori Schake, et al., in Wolfgang Krieger and David Alan Rosenberg, eds., *New Perspectives on the Berlin Crisis* (forthcoming); and William Burr, "Avoiding the Slippery Slope: The Eisenhower Administration and the Berlin Crisis, November 1958–January 1959," scheduled for publication in the spring 1994 issue of *Diplomacy History*.

57. JBC to Dowling, Nov. 13, 1959, JBC PERP.
58. Bird, *The Chairman,* 478; JBC diary.
59. JBC to Dowling, Nov. 13, 1959, JBC PERP.
60. JBC, *Shaping Educational Policy* (New York: McGraw-Hill, 1964), 39–40.
61. Interview with Nathaniel Ober, May 24, 1976, cited in Teicher, *James Bryant Conant and "The American High School Today,"* 210 n. 34.
62. On civil rights developments, see Taylor Branch, *Parting the Waters: America in the King Years, 1954–63* (New York: Simon & Schuster, 1988), and Juan Williams, *Eyes on the Prize: America's Civil Rights Years, 1954–1965* (New York: Viking Penguin, 1987).
63. JBC, *Slums and Suburbs: A Commentary on Schools in Metropolitan Areas* (New York: McGraw-Hill, 1961), 2, 18; see also JBC to James E. Russell, Oct. 27, 1961, JBC PERP; and Fred M. Hechinger, "Conant Says Slum Schools Pile Up 'Dynamite in Cities'" and "Educator in Action," *NYT,* Oct. 17, 1961.
64. JBC, *Slums and Suburbs,* 8.
65. JBC, *Slums and Suburbs,* 8.
66. JBC, *Slums and Suburbs,* 34.
67. JBC, *Slums and Suburbs,* chap. 1–2, 145–47.
68. JBC, *Slums and Suburbs,* 20–21.
69. JBC, *Slums and Suburbs,* 145–47.
70. Fred M. Hechinger, "Conant: A New Report by the Schools' Mr. Fixit," *NYT,* Mar. 5, 1967.
71. JBC to Goldberg, Nov. 20, 1961, and Mar. 5, 1962, both in JBC PERP; "Hard to Keep," *Rocky Mountain News,* Nov. 26, 1962; JBC to Keppel, Dec. 11, 1962, JBC PERP.
72. JBC to James E. Russell, Oct. 27, 1961, JBC PERP.
73. JBC, *MSL,* 451.
74. Williams, *Eyes on the Prize,* 135–36, 141–42.
75. JBC, *Slums and Suburbs,* 37.
76. JBC, *Slums and Suburbs,* 27–32.
77. JBC, *Slums and Suburbs,* 30.
78. See, e.g., Malcolm X with Alex Haley, *The Autobiography of Malcolm X* (New York: Random House, 1964, 1965; citation from Ballantine Books reprint, 1992), esp. 245–46, 271–76.
79. Clark's and other objections are noted in Robert H. Terte, "Conant Scored by School Groups," *NYT,* Oct. 17, 1961.
80. Amster, *Meritocracy Ascendant,* 245–56.
81. *BG,* Feb. 11, 1964.
82. JBC, *Slums and Suburbs* (New York: New American Library edition, 1964), 31–32; JBC, *Shaping Educational Policy,* 44–46.
83. JBC, *MSL,* 622–23, 646.
84. See chap. 7.
85. See Theodore H. White, "The Action-Intellectuals," *Life,* June 9, 16, 23, 1967, reprinted in Edward T. Thompson, ed., *Theodore H. White at Large: The Best of His Magazine Writing, 1939–1986* (New York: Pantheon Books, 1992), 389–431.
86. JBC to Admissions Committee, Cosmos Club, May 8, 1961; Galbraith to JBC, Apr. 3, 1961; John F. Kennedy to Galbraith, Mar. 22, 1961; all in JBC PERP.
87. Raymond Swing to JBC, Apr. 14, 1961; JBC to Admissions Committee, Cosmos Club, May 17, 1961; JBC to Swing, May 17, 1961; all in JBC PERP.
88. Carl T. Rowan, *Breaking Barriers: A Memoir* (New York: Little, Brown & Co.,

1991), 202; Arthur M. Schlesinger, Jr., *A Thousand Days: John F. Kennedy in the White House* (Boston: Houghton Mifflin, 1965), 932.

89. Rowan, *Breaking Barriers*, 202–206; John Kenneth Galbraith, *Ambassador's Journal: A Personal Account of the Kennedy Years* (New York: Signet, 1969, 1970), 269–70.

90. *NYT,* Jan. 10, 11, 13, 1962; Rowan, *Breaking Barriers*, 206.

91. Mrs. Polakoff to JBC, Jan. 10, 1962, JBC PERP.

92. JBC to Mrs. Polakoff, Jan. 12, 1962, JBC PERP.

93. *NYT,* Jan. 16, 1962; Mrs. Polakoff to JBC, Jan. 16, 1962, JBC PERP.

94. JBC, *The Education of American Teachers* (New York: McGraw-Hill, 1963); JBC to James E. Russell ("can of worms"), Oct. 27, 1961, JBC PERP. According to an aide who worked on the study, JBC in *The Education of American Teachers* decided "after long and careful deliberation" to omit "the grave and complex question of Negro education." Jeremiah S. Finch to Harold Taylor, Oct. 8, 1963, JBC PERP.

95. JBC, *A Guide to Public Education for the Conscientious Citizen* (June 1962), cited in Amster, *Meritocracy Ascendant*, 257–61; mystified: TRC interviews, 1991–92.

96. Fred M. Hechinger, "Conant: A New Report by the Schools' Mr. Fixit," *NYT,* Mar. 5, 1967.

97. TRC interviews, Nov. 12, 1992, Feb. 10, 1993.

98. TRC interviews, 1991.

99. JBC diary, Jan. 1–4, 1962 (though written "long after the event"), Jan. 30, April 19, May 6, 19, 21, 1962.

100. JBC, *MSL,* 624.

101. *Rocky Mountain News,* Nov. 26, 1962.

102. JBC, "Notes on Writing an Autobiography," May 22, 1969, JBC PERP.

103. For JBC's view, see JBC to Dean Rusk, Feb. 23, 1962, enc. JBC, "Issues in the Berlin-German Crisis," remarks to Hammarskjold Forum, New York City, Jan. 29, 1962. On the atmosphere surrounding these events, see Michael R. Beschloss, *The Crisis Years: Kennedy and Khrushchev, 1960–1963* (New York: HarperCollins, 1991), and Gelb, *The Berlin Wall.*

104. JBC to George N. Shuster, May 14, 1962, JBC PERP.

105. This account of JBC's activities in Berlin draws on JBC to Frank Keppel, Sept. 21, 1964, "Conant, James B. 1956–1978" folder, CCP; JBC, "Memorandum to Members of the Staff Concerned with the Education of American Teachers," Oct. 1, 1964, JBC PERP; JBC diaries and scrapbooks, JBC PERP; and JBC, *MSL,* chap. 46.

106. GRC, "The Cold War of the Mind: Regimentation in East Germany," *Modern Age* 5:2 (Spring 1961), 117–24, and GRC, "German Textbooks and the Nazi Past," *Saturday Review* 46:29 (July 20, 1963), 52–53.

107. JBC diary, Apr. 6–7, 1963.

108. JBC diary (Berlin journal), July 11, 1963.

109. JBC diary, June 26, 1963.

110. This is taken from JBC to Prof. Hellmut Becker, Max-Planck-Gesellschaft, Berlin, Aug. 4, 1965, CFP, a thirty-one-page report on the state of German education summing up his impressions after his stay in Berlin.

111. JBC diary, June 26, 1963.

112. JBC to George C. McGhee, June 29, 1965, JBC PERP.

113. JBC to Frank Keppel, Sept. 21, 1964, "Conant, James B. 1956–1978" folder, CCP; JBC, "Memorandum to Members of the Staff Concerned with the Education of American Teachers," Oct. 1, 1964, JBC PERP.

114. JBC to TSV, Nov. 29, 1963 (quoted section written on Nov. 23), box 14, UAI.15.898.13, JBC PERP; see also JBC diary, Nov. 1963.

115. JBC diary, Dec. 6, 1963.

116. Robert F. Kennedy to JBC, Dec. 11, 1963, JBC PERP.

117. Telephone interview with Sargent Shriver, Nov. 17, 1992.

118. Telephone interview with Bill Moyers, Nov. 12, 1992.

119. JBC to John Gardner, Sept. 21, 1964, "Conant, James B. 1956–1978" folder, CCP.

120. JBC to John S. Hollister, Apr. 22, 1964, JBC PREP.
121. White House press release, Jan. 28, 1965, Conant folder, box 113, Office Files of John Macy, LBJL.
122. On the task force: LBJ, *The Vantage Point: Perspectives of the Presidency* 1963–1969 (New York: Popular Library, 1971), 206–12; John W. Gardner Oral History (Ac 74–109), Dec. 20, 1971, 4–10, LBJL; Frank Keppel Oral History (Ac 72–22), Apr. 21, 1969, 8–10, LBJL; Frank Keppel Office of Education Administrative History Oral History (Ac 66–1), July 18, 1968, esp. 9–14, LBJL; on JBC's influence: John W. Gardner telephone interview, Nov. 24, 1964; JBC diaries, 1964–65.
123. JBC, "Notes on Writing an Autobiography," May 22, 1969, JBC PERP.

EPILOGUE

1. Sources for illness: JBC diary, June 10–July 12, 1965; JBC to Walter Dowling, July 9, 1965; JBC to J. F. Gross, July 9, 1965; JBC to C. Grove Haines, Aug. 3, 1965; all in JBC PERP; TRC interview, Nov. 12, 1992.
2. JBC diary, July 20–22, 1965.
3. "AP and James B. Conant," Aug. 13, 1965, "Conant, James B. 1956–1978" folder, CCP; on the interstate educational project, see also *MSL*, 647–49. Carnegie's support for JBC's educational work, which required considerable staff support, is reviewed in MK to EAD, Apr. 5, 1967, "Conant, James B. 1956–1978" folder, CCP: May 16, 1957: $350,000 for a Study of the American Comprehensive High School; Nov. 18, 1958: $85,000 for Further Study of American Public Education; May 19, 1960: $135,000 for Studies on American Public Education; Nov. 15, 1960: $300,000 for a Study of Teacher Education; June 22, 1961: $25,000 for Studies on American Public Education; and Mar. 18, 1965: $185,750 for Studies of American Education and Other Matters; JBC subsequently refunded $78,354.62.
4. JBC, *Two Modes of Thought: My Encounters with Science and Education* (New York: Pocket Books, 1964, 1965), xxv–xxvi.
5. Quoted in Terry Ferber, "Conant Revisited," *Saturday Review*, Mar. 18, 1967, 73.
6. JBC to Sargent Shriver, Nov. 25, 1966, Conant folder, box 113, Office Files of John Macy, LBJL.
7. TRC interviews; JBC, *President's Report 1946*, 19, and *President's Report 1950–1951*, 10–11.
8. *Public Television, A Program for Action: The Report and Recommendations of the Carnegie Commission on Educational Television* (New York: Harper & Row, 1967); Killian, *Education of a College President*, 343–55; TRC interview, Nov. 12, 1992; "gadget-hunting age": JBC Columbia Oral History Project interview, Carnegie Corporation Project, Apr. 5, 1967, 39, Butler Library, Columbia University (hereafter JBC COHP); "extremely skeptical": "AP and James B. Conant," Aug. 13, 1965, "Conant, James B. 1956–1978" folder, CCP.
9. JBC, "Notes on Writing an Autobiography," May 22, 1969, JBC PERP; JBC to Alden Dunham, Apr. 1, 1968 ("essentially writing fiction"), and JBC to Alan Pifer, Apr. 19, 1968, JBC PERP; JBC COHP, 52–53 ("approaching senility"); on VB: presentation by Larry Owens, History of Science Society annual meeting, Seattle, Oct. 1990.
10. GRC to Jean Demos, Oct. 16, 1967, CFP.
11. GRC to Jean Demos, Jan. 25, 1968, CFP.
12. JRC to JBC, Jan. 9, 1965; JRC to JBC, July 19, 1966; Wilfrid W. Ward to JBC, Aug. 2, 1966; Allan R. McClary to JBC, Aug. 6, 1966; JBC notes; all in JBC correspondence files, Aug. 1966 folder, box 5, JBC PERP. The account of JRC's troubles and JBC's response is based on interviews with TRC and Ellen Conant, 1987, 1991, 1992, 1993; with Jim Conant (grandson), 1986, 1991, 1993; with Jennet Conant (granddaughter), Mar. 26, 1992, and Clark Conant (granddaughter), Feb. 1993; remarks at a memo-

rial service in Aug. 1981 for JRC by Dan Fenn and Gregory Henderson, copies in CFP; and on diary entries and correspondence in JBC PERP, JBC PREP, and CFP.

13. GRC to Jean Demos, Feb. 22, 1968, CFP; "triage": TRC and Ellen Conant interviews, July 1991.

14. TRC and Ellen Conant interview, July 5, 1991.

15. Interview with Dr. Allan R. McClary, May 17, 1993.

16. Interview with Jim Conant (grandson), Jan. 23, 1993.

17. Interviews with Clark Conant, Feb. 23, 24, 1993; JBC diary, Aug. 24, 1957.

18. Interviews with Clark Conant, Feb. 23, 24, 1993.

19. GRC, "Quotation Notebook," Sept. 1941 (citing *The Heart of Thoreau's Journals,* 126), CFP.

20. JBC, *The Defense of Freedom,* 9.

21. JBC, "Reflections at Leisure Sept. 1956," Sept. 3, 1956, JBC PERP.

22. "U.S. Leaders Back Johnson in Vietnam," *NYT,* Sept. 9, 1965; see also Bird, *The Chairman,* 581, and Brinkley, *Dean Acheson,* 248-49.

23. "Vietnam Backers Urged to 'Shout,' " *NYT,* Nov. 29, 1965.

24. Harry McPherson, *A Political Education* (Boston: Little, Brown & Co., 1972), 402-404; Brinkley, *Dean Acheson,* 250-51, 378.

25. JBC to Paul H. Douglas, Oct. 4, 1967 (2 letters), resp. to Douglas to JBC, Sept. 19, 1967, Committee on Peace and Freedom in Vietnam folder, JBC PERP.

26. "Citizens' Panel Backs Johnson on Bombing Pause," *NYT,* Jan. 16, 1968.

27. JBC to Paul H. Douglas, Feb. 13, 1968, Committee on Peace and Freedom in Vietnam folder, JBC PERP.

28. Douglas to JBC, Feb. 16, 1968, Committee on Peace and Freedom in Vietnam folder, JBC PERP. See also Paul H. Douglas, *In the Fullness of Time: The Memoirs of Paul H. Douglas* (New York: Harcourt Brace Jovanovich, 1971, 1972), 608-11.

29. JBC to Douglas, Feb. 13, 1968.

30. "whatever resources" is from a statement signed by JBC quoted in "Vietnam Backers Urged to 'Shout,' " *NYT,* Nov. 29, 1965.

31. JBC to Charles Tyroler II, Mar. 11, 1968, Committee on Peace and Freedom in Vietnam folder, JBC PERP.

32. JBC to Tyroler, Apr. 10, 1968, Committee on Peace and Freedom in Vietnam folder, JBC PERP; "more convinced than ever": JBC to Tyroler, Mar. 11, 1968.

33. JBC, "Basic Principles of the Committee," Apr. 18, 1968, Committee on Peace and Freedom in Vietnam folder, JBC PERP.

34. "Public Figures Warn on Impatience in Peace Talks," *NYT,* May 24, 1968.

35. JBC to Charles Tyroler II, Oct. 21, 1969, Committee on Peace and Freedom in Vietnam folder, JBC PERP; JBC votes: JBC diary, Nov. 8, 1960, Nov. 5, 1968.

36. See Geoffrey Hodgson, "The Establishment," *Foreign Policy* 10 (Spring 1973), 3-40; Isaacson and Thomas, *Wise Men,* chap. 22-24; and John B. Judis, "Twilight of the Gods," *Wilson Quarterly* 15:4 (Autumn 1991), 43-55.

37. JBC to WLM, Apr. 15, 1969 (in which he also notes his telegram to Pusey), JBC PERP and courtesy of WLM; see also JBC diary, April 11, 12, 13, 1969; JBC, *MSL,* 640-42; "Conant Discusses Student Activism," Mar. 8, 1970.

38. Vote for McGovern: TRC interviews, 1982, 1987, 1991.

39. JBC, *MSL,* 304.

40. WNBC-TV, "Speaking Freely" transcript, 1970, JBC PERP.

41. Jennet Conant interview, Mar. 26, 1992.

42. Jim Conant (grandson) interview, July 1991; TRC interview, 1982; Jennet Conant interview, Mar. 26, 1992.

43. *NYT,* Mar. 9, 1970, Strauss to JBC, Mar. 10, 1970, JBC to Strauss, Mar. 30, 1970, Strauss papers.

44. "I think that before the H-bomb was made there was a chance of controlling this thing, but the military wouldn't consider it. I think it was the wrong decision in that it couldn't possibly accomplish what we set out to do." JBC interview in John C.

Landers, "The Manhattan Project, as Seen by Dr. Conant, and a Commentary on the Unprecedented and What It Has Left Us," Mar. 1974 (unpublished ms), JBC PERP.

45. See JBC, "On the Systematic Poisoning of Our Descendants," n.d. [June 1975], and DEL to JBC, n.d., both in Special Subject File, Box 6, The Atom Bomb (1975), JBC PERP.
46. "2,300 Scientists Petition U.S. to Reduce Construction of Nuclear Power Plants," *NYT,* Aug. 7, 1975.
47. JBC, "Notes on Writing an Autobiography," May 22, 1969, JBC PERP.
48. GRC to Jean Demos, Nov. 5, 1973, CFP.
49. Jennet Conant interview, Mar. 26, 1992; Clark Conant, by contrast, although she acknowledges she spent much less time with her grandparents than did Jennet Conant, remembers sensing a warm and romantic bond between JBC and GRC— "There was definitely something cooking between them."—as well as GRC's pain and weeping when her husband sank into a "cognitive muddle" in his final months. Interview with Clark Conant, Feb. 23, 1993.
50. GRC to Jean Demos, Mar. 3, 1977.
51. Jim Conant (grandson) interview, Jan. 23, 1993; Jennet Conant interviews, Mar. 26, 1992, Jan. 26, 1993.
52. Robert J. Donovan interview, June 30, 1992.
53. Jim Conant (grandson) interview, Jan. 23, 1992; Clark Conant interview, Feb. 23, 1993 ("bedeviled").
54. TRC interview, Feb. 10, 1993.
55. *James Bryant Conant: A Remembrance* (Cambridge: Harvard University Press, 1978).
56. JBC, "Remarks to the Graduating Class," Ohio University, June 9, 1947, JBC Speech File.
57. JBC, *MSL,* 304.
58. "Dr. Conant: In Science Pure, In Education Controversial," *Newsweek* 40:12 (Sept. 22, 1952), 74.
59. TRC interviews, 1982, 1993.
60. JBC diary, June 10, 1964. JBC's pessimism is hinted at in a diary that October, after learning that England had elected a Labour government, China had exploded an atomic bomb, and Soviet hardline Communists had overthrown Khrushchev. "What kind of a world will emerge? I think the chances of avoiding *the* catastrophe have decreased considerably. (My speech at the 50th reunion.)" JBC diary, Oct. 16, 1964.

Index

Absolute Weapon, The (Brodie), 273
Acheson, Dean, 3, 263–7, 271, 275–7, 331, 384–5, 394, 427, 491, 501, 502, 511, 513–14, 519, 590, 602, 642–6, 655, 663, 664, 668, 688, 704, 721
  and H-bomb, 480, 481
  as interventionist, 121, 128
  and Korean War, 492–3, 496–8, 505, 516
  and MacArthur firing, 525, 527, 528
  and Marshall Plan, 319–21
  and universal military service, 518, 540
  and Vietnam War, 747, 748
Acheson-Lilienthal plan, 198, 268–70, 275–7, 286, 323, 328, 329, 336, 339–42, 345, 358, 375, 469, 482
Adams, Henry, 80
Adams, Roger, 38, 56, 128, 366, 563
Adams, Sherman, 695
Adenauer, Konrad, 3, 642, 646, 652, 654–6, 658–9, 662–74, 682–5, 688–11, 693–5, 697–8, 700–701, 703, 718, 721
Adler, Julius Ochs, 507, 509, 529
Advisory Committee on Uranium, 135, 137
Akers, Wallace T., 173, 180–3, 185, 189
Al Azhar University, 97
Alamogordo Proving Grounds, 228, 231–4, 236, 239, 240, 288, 291, 300, 467, 589
Allen, Raymond B., 509, 512
Allison, Samuel K., 215
Alperovitz, Gar, 301
Alsop, Joseph, 121
Altschul, Frank, 509, 715–16
Alvarez, Luis W., 470–3, 475, 487, 488, 596
Ambrose, Stephen, 680
America First Committee, 141
American Academy of Arts and Sciences, 55, 411, 557
American Association for the Advancement of Science (AAAS), 397
American Association of School Administrators, 586
American Association of University Professors, 432
American Chemical Society, 44, 592, 596, 599
  Nichols Medal, 55
American Civil Liberties Union, 414, 416
American Council on Education (ACE), 120, 451, 500, 542, 550
  Committee on the Relationships of Higher Education to the Federal Government, 311, 363
American Council on Germany, 704, 721
American Education Fellowship, 354
American Education and International Tensions (EPC), 451–3
American Friends Service Committee, 544
American High School Today, The (Conant), 711–14, 722, 740
American Intellectuals for Freedom, 446
American Petroleum Institute, 56
American Physical Society, 136
Americans for Democratic Action, 399, 611
American Society of Mechanical Engineers, 354
American University, 45, 46
Amherst College, 88, 543
Amory, Cleveland, 12
Amory, Robert, 692
Amster, Jeanne, 17, 27
Anderson, Herbert, 261
Anderson, John, 179, 181, 184, 186, 189, 197
Angell, James R., 97, 99
Armed Forces Special Weapons Project (AFSWP), 356–7
Armstrong, Hamilton Fish, 508
Arneson, Gordon, 295
Aromatic Chemical, 38
Associated Harvard Alumni, 616
Association of American Colleges, 120, 311, 543
Association of American Universities (AAU), 500, 503, 543, 545, 547, 552, 575, 635
Association of Los Alamos Scientists, 268
Atlantic (magazine), 76, 89, 156, 176, 177, 296, 301, 370, 372, 376
Atlantic Conference, 183
atomic bomb, 3, 5, 400, 497, 501, 520, 573, 594, 635, 677, 731
  biological warfare compared to, 365, 366, 382
  Britain and, 172–93, 570, 571
  Committee on the Present Danger on, 512, 522
  development of, 135–60 (*see also* Manhattan Project)
  and Korean War, 505
  postwar policy on, 238–78, 322–48
  production rate for, 312–13
  public attitude toward, 279–304, 355, 572, 582

atomic bomb (*cont.*)
  and "Red scare," 393, 395
  Soviet, 381, 388, 464-7, 483-4, 496, 501, 506, 526, 545, 591, 677
  testing of, 230-4, 237, 286, 755
  used on Japan, 205, 211, 212, 219, 225-8, 230, 231, 234, 236, 282, 284, 292, 295, 303, 467, 479 (*see also* Hiroshima; Nagasaki)
  see also hydrogen bomb
Atomic Development Agency (ADA), 323, 334
Atomic Development Authority, 265
Atomic Diplomacy (Alperovitz), 301, 739
Atomic Energy Act (1946), 306-7
Atomic Energy Commission (AEC), 5, 271, 282, 290, 305, 307-9, 313-19, 330, 333, 340, 344, 350, 373, 375, 378, 398, 438, 450, 560, 561, 564, 570, 596, 681-2
  General Advisory Committee (GAC), 305-9, 312, 313, 316, 326, 329, 332, 341, 347, 350, 351, 353-4, 356-7, 416, 434, 438, 450, 463, 466, 468-84, 487-9, 555, 566, 568, 590, 591, 596-602, 605, 676-80, 755
  Personnel Security Review Board, 384, 678, 680
Atomic Pioneer Awards, 752
Atomic Power (film), 286
Atomic Shield (Hewlett and Anderson), 305
Attlee, Clement, 250, 255, 505
Attorney General's list, 405
Austin, Warren R., 328, 336, 338
Australia, 586, 592, 618
Austria, 690
  in World War I, 35

Bacher, Robert, 168, 306, 312, 313, 316, 329, 331, 333, 334, 347
bacteriological warfare, *see* biological warfare
Bailey, David, 414, 447, 504, 526, 528
Bainbridge, Kenneth T., 139, 141, 233
Baker, Newton D., 43
Balderston, John, 121
Baldwin, Roger, 416
Ball, George, 292, 611
Ballantine, Arthur, 428
Baltimore News-American, 743
Bard, Ralph A., 222, 225, 300
Barnard, Chester I., 264, 329, 334, 335, 358, 499
Barnes, Clarence, 414-16
Barnes, Tracy, 692
Barton, Ralph, 580
Baruch, Bernard, 160, 161, 195, 198, 268-71, 275-7, 290, 291, 295, 296, 313, 401, 463, 483, 517
Baruch Plan, 278, 297, 326, 328-30, 337, 339
Baxter, James Phinney, III, 73, 456, 503, 509, 548, 696
Beer Hall putsch, 63, 85
Beginning of the End, The (film), 287-91, 295
Belgian Congo, 434
Belgium, 216
  in World War I, 36, 42
  in World War II, 124
Bell Telephone, 126, 264

Laboratories, 260, 434, 474, 566
Benchley, Bob, 31
Bender, William, 81
Benelux nations, 359
Benes, Eduard, 359
Bennington College, 713
Bentley, Elizabeth, 425, 426
Beria, Lavrenti Pavlovich, 159, 237
Berlin, Isaiah, 9, 257
Berlin, University of, 37, 87
Berlin blockade, 301, 320, 346, 367-8, 424, 516, 538, 660, 689
Berlin Wall, 731-2, 734
Bermuda summit, 671, 674
Bethe, Hans, 466, 469, 471-3
Bevin, Ernest, 321
Bidault, Georges P., 671, 673, 676
Biebel, Charles DeWayne, 81, 742
Big Bang, 587
Bikini bomb tests, 263, 267, 312, 375-7, 385, 389
Bingham, Bill, 638-9
biological warfare (BW), 220, 244, 365-7, 382, 386, 387, 390
Bissell, Richard, 509
Black, Colonel Edwin F., 379, 382, 384, 388, 479-80
Black, Newton Henry, 16-18, 26, 27, 54, 407
blacks, education of, 722-7
  at Harvard, 58, 81, 82
Blake, George, 692
Blanck, Theodor, 671
Blankenhorn, 674
Bohlen, Charles "Chip," 255, 256, 651, 655
Bohr, Niels, 7, 28, 61, 136, 148-50, 165, 196-200, 205-7, 217, 222, 289-91, 342, 479
Bok, Bart J., 573-4, 620
Bok, Derek C., 754
Borden, William Liscumb, 475, 489, 596, 600, 677
Born, Max, 165
Borrowman, Merle, 740
Boston Globe, 526
Boston Rotary Club, 360
Boston Traveler, 660
Boston Trust Company, 509
Bowie, Robert R., 499, 670
Bowman, Isaiah, 379, 383
Boyden Station observatory, 620
Boyer, Paul, 304
Boyle, Robert, 592-3
Bradley, General Omar, 482, 531, 748
Brain-Waves and Death (Rich), 138, 140
Brandeis, Louis, 108
Brandt, Willy, 732
Bray, William B., 547-8
Brentano, Heinrich von, 693
Brezhnev, Leonid, 734
Bridgman, Percy W., 398, 410, 411, 575, 638, 648, 730
Briggs, Lyman J., 137, 140, 141, 147, 149, 150, 153
brinksmanship, 720
Brinton, Crane, 107
Brodie, Bernard, 273, 720

Bronk, Detlev W., 485-8, 490, 560, 562, 563, 565, 566
Browder, Earl, 118
Brown University, 500
Brown v. Board of Education of Topeka (1954), 722, 725, 726
Bruce, David K. E., 702
Bruner, Jerome, 399, 511, 639
Brussels Pact, 359
Bryan, William Jennings, 14
Bryant, Jane Breed, 13
Bryant, Seth, 13, 14
Buck, Paul H., 106, 107, 172-3, 177-8, 236, 412, 417-18, 430, 454, 504, 511, 607, 613-16, 630, 635, 639-40, 648-9
Buck, Pearl, 544
Buckley, Oliver, 434, 436, 437, 473, 474, 476, 565-7
Buckley, William F., Jr., 581, 651
Bulganin, Nikolai, 690, 704
Bulgaria, 202
Bulletin of the Atomic Scientists, 302, 327, 346, 468
Bullis, Harry, 509
Bundy, Harvey H., 127-28, 155, 156, 166, 174, 189, 191, 205, 281, 223, 293-5, 310
Bundy, McGeorge, 228, 294-7, 299, 300, 388-9, 460, 601-3, 617, 635, 647, 728, 736
Bureau of the Budget, 262
Bureau of Standards, 419
Burgess, Guy, 570
Burke-Wadsworth conscription bill, 130, 131
Burnham, James, 368
Bush, George, 280
Bush, Vannevar, 3, 5-7, 116, 126-30, 133, 140, 144, 146-50, 152, 153, 159, 241, 243-50, 256, 281, 293, 307, 310, 314, 316, 317, 343-6, 356, 357, 361-7, 377-9, 381, 419, 426, 461, 467, 496, 600, 602, 605, 752
    on Committee on the Present Danger, 503, 506, 509, 511, 513, 516, 522, 540, 541, 546
    on Committee to Strengthen the Frontiers of Freedom, 718
    and Manhattan Project, 139, 160-4, 166-8, 170, 172, 173, 179-83, 187, 189-91, 194-8, 202-8, 210-11, 213, 214, 218-21, 223, 224, 226, 227, 230, 232-6, 238, 286, 305, 309, 314
    memoirs of, 742
    and MGM film, 287-8, 290
    and National Science Foundation, 396, 397, 359-63, 576
    and Oppenheimer as security risk, 318, 319, 677-9
    and postwar control of nuclear power, 259-64, 266-70, 272, 277-8
Butler, Nicholas Murray, 97, 585
Byrnes, James F., 219, 221-3, 226, 230-1, 245, 248-57, 259, 262, 263, 266, 267, 269

Cabot, Charles Codman, 612
Cadbury, Henry J., 90
Caldwell, Millard, 595
Calhoun, Robert L., 285
California, University of, 608-10

    at Berkeley, 55, 137, 139, 157-8, 161, 164, 165, 168, 171, 188, 191, 209-10, 317, 398, 462, 466, 471, 485, 487, 488, 498, 596, 597, 609
California Institute of Technology (Caltech), 55, 56, 59-60, 93, 128, 166, 396, 509, 561, 564, 575, 591-2
Cambridge University, 96, 185
Canada, 198-9, 204
    Soviet spy ring in, 265, 394
Canham, Erwin D., 379, 383, 388, 550
Canwell, Albert, 429
Carmichael, Leonard, 729
Carnap, Rudolf, 411
Carnegie Committee on Scientific Aids to Learning, 126, 741
Carnegie Corporation, 3, 126, 409, 412, 417, 418, 509, 586, 688-9, 730, 731, 740, 753
Carnegie Corporation Commission on Educational Television, 741-42
Carnegie Endowment for International Peace, 269, 324, 425, 428, 602
Carnegie Foundation for the Advancement of Teaching, 81, 431, 702, 706-8, 711, 714
Carnegie Institution, 116, 126-8, 139, 153, 377, 509, 729
Carr, E. H., 10
Carr, William G., 373, 444, 445, 456, 500, 503, 550, 583, 687, 707
Casablanca summit, 152
Castro, Fidel, 714
Catholic Church, 584, 586-7, 646, 647, 651
Catton, Bruce, 729
Caute, David, 405
Cavers, David F., 327, 346
Central Intelligence Agency (CIA), 361, 365, 412, 413, 430, 502, 509, 511, 523, 534, 574, 602, 641-2, 650, 653, 664, 670, 688, 692
Century Association, 743
Century Group, 121, 131, 132
Chadwick, James, 185
Chafee, Zechariah, Jr., 57, 414, 447-8, 451, 456-8, 460, 580, 621, 628, 629, 631, 635
chain reaction, 183
Chamberlain, Neville, 98, 115
Chambers, Whittaker, 426-30, 435
Chauncey, Henry, 81, 707
Chemical Warfare Service, 45, 47, 48, 50, 56, 173, 201
chemical weapons, 382, 386, 387
    see also poison gas
Cheney, Richard, 280
Chevalier, Haakon, 317
Chiang Kai-shek, 417, 525, 527, 533, 620
Chicago, University of, 54, 93, 139, 150, 327, 355, 416, 435, 489, 585, 596, 597
    Metallurgical Laboratory, 162, 163, 168, 184, 185, 187, 194-6, 203, 206, 215, 217, 223, 230, 245, 259-61, 326
Chicago Association of Commerce, 530
Chicago Tribune, 516, 544
Children in Crisis (film), 708
Children of Light and the Children of Darkness (Niebuhr), 283-5

China, 211, 246, 393, 513, 527, 533, 619–20, 673, 714, 749
  Communist victory in, 417, 465, 482, 491, 492, 496, 516
  in Korean War, 504–5, 524, 525, 545, 560–1
  nuclear weapons of, 734
Chisholm, Brock, 365
Choate, Hall & Stewart, 295
Christian Science Monitor, 379, 550
Churchill, Winston, 3, 82, 130, 145, 146, 150, 151, 159, 203, 231, 234, 237, 238, 474, 501, 658, 675, 682, 705
  at Atlantic Conference, 183
  and atomic bombing of Japan, 226, 227, 301
  and atomic bomb research, 178–9, 181, 184, 188–91
  and fall of France, 125
  at Harvard, 191–2
  "iron curtain" speech of, 266
  memoirs of, 497
  and postwar atomic policy, 197, 198, 200, 207
  at Teheran Conference, 202
  and West Germany, 683, 685
  at Yalta Conference, 215–16
Ciardi, John, 446, 448
Citizens Committee for Peace and Freedom in Vietnam, 748, 751
Citizens' Conference, 543, 545
City College of New York, 118, 395
Civil Rights Act (1964), 737
civil rights movement, 722–7
Civil War, 14, 27, 134
Claflin, William, 119, 129–30, 142, 173, 177, 427
Clark, Grenville, 69, 71–6, 78, 120, 126, 133, 142, 152, 175, 238–41, 246–7, 273, 427, 428, 447–51, 456, 458, 481, 493, 593, 610, 640
Clark, Kenneth, 726
Clay, General Lucius D., 359, 567, 654, 661, 715, 747, 748
Clayton, William L., 121, 222, 503, 509, 516, 522
Cleveland, Grover, 99
Cleveland, Harlan, 729
Clifford, Clark, 276, 318, 401
Clinton Laboratories, 333, 355
Clucas, Lowell, 657
Coffin, Henry Sloane, 121
Cohen, Benjamin, 143, 146, 252
Cohen, I. B., 409
Cohn, Edwin J., 640–1
Cohn, Roy, 656
Cold War, 3, 5–8, 304, 310, 322, 338, 349, 350, 364, 371, 398, 401, 415, 430, 538, 573, 539, 581, 584, 592, 594, 622, 675, 686, 714
  and academic freedom, 421–2, 439, 443, 450, 458, 460, 610, 611, 634–7
  Asia during, 534
  and Central Intelligence Agency, 412–13, 523
  and Committee on the Present Danger, 493, 494, 512, 641

and Committee to Strengthen the Frontiers of Freedom, 718–20
education during, 709, 713
end of, 755
Germany during, 642, 643, 650, 651, 653, 660, 661, 663, 691, 692, 705, 731
and hydrogen bomb, 479, 484
as ideological struggle, 402
and Marshall Plan, 319–21, 339
militarization of scientific research during, 555, 565, 575, 577, 585
psychological warfare during, 604
and racial issue, 714
"Red scare" during, 404, 405, 425 (*see also* McCarthyism)
and Universal Military Service, 544–6
and Vietnam, 750, 752
Cole, Charles W., 543, 544
Colorado, University of, 398–9
Columbia University, 97, 137, 139, 140, 184, 185, 196, 379, 396, 443, 485, 489, 500, 585, 641, 646
  Bampton Lectures, 571
  Chandler Medal, 55
  Teachers College, 433
Combined Policy Committee, 190
Commager, Henry Steele, 608
Commission on Civil Rights, 722
Committee on Atomic Energy (CAE), 316, 356, 357
Committee to Defend America by Aiding the Allies (CDAAA), 119, 130–33, 141, 142, 151, 283, 510, 719, 748
Committee for Economic Development, 616
Committee for an Effective and Durable Peace in Asia, 747
Committee of Eight, 107–10
Committee for the Marshall Plan, 338, 510
Committee on Medical Research, 147
Committee on the Present Danger (CPD), 493–4, 498, 500–23, 525–7, 529–30, 535–8, 540–5, 547–52, 561, 587, 592, 627, 641, 643–6, 715, 719, 748
Committee to Save Harvard Education, 109
Committee to Strengthen the Frontiers of Freedom (CSFF), 718–20
Commonwealth Club, 391, 413
Communist Party, American, 245, 317, 319, 395, 405, 414, 425, 431–3, 438, 444–5, 450, 453, 457, 458, 460, 461, 608, 609, 621, 623, 624, 626, 627–35
Compton, Arthur H., 97, 139, 147, 149, 150, 153, 155, 156, 162 4, 166, 168, 170, 200, 201, 223, 230, 259, 261, 310, 332, 333, 560, 580, 599
Compton, Karl T., 116, 127, 128, 139, 147, 160, 222, 227, 296, 301, 303, 311, 376, 378, 382–3, 390, 414, 496, 642
Conant, Clark (grandchild), 745, 746
Conant, Ellen Psaty (daughter-in-law), 708, 730, 744–6, 752
Conant, Esther (sister), 13, 732, 744
Conant, Grace ("Patty") Thayer Richards (wife), 50–3, 61, 63, 68, 71, 74, 92, 100–4, 119, 129, 137, 138, 140, 143, 153, 157,

191-2, 212, 235, 321, 463-4, 486, 493, 638, 645, 688, 696, 699, 703, 706-9, 717-18, 730, 732-4, 736, 738-10, 742, 743-6, 753-5
Conant, James B.
and academic freedom issues, 391-462
at Alamogordo, 231-4
as Atomic Energy Commission adviser, 306-9, 313-19, 350-8, 373, 597-601
autobiography of, 3-6, 740-42, 752, 753
becomes president of Harvard, 65-83
and Berlin blockade, 367-8
and biological warfare, 365-7
birth of, 11
birth of children of, 53
as chemistry professor, 50, 53-60
childhood of, 12-16
civilian nuclear power opposed by, 592-5, 753
and Cold War, 319-23, 349-50
on Committee on the Present Danger, 491-537
death of, 754-5
democratic education philosophy of, 402-4
and development of atomic bomb, 134-207
diplomatic career of, 642-705
education of, 16-34
as educator, 372, 707-38
in "Fishing Party," 374-90
and government funding of university research, 397-9
H-bomb opposed by, 463-90, 590-2, 596, 753
and Hiroshima, 225-8, 235-40, 279-304, 349, 752
illnesses of, 739, 742-3, 754
interventionism of, 118-34
marriage of, 50-3
and McCarthyism, 606-35
and militarization of science, 554-77
moves to New York, 706-7
and National Science Foundation, 396-7
and Nazi rise to power, 84-9, 96-7, 112-15
and outbreak of World War II, 115-18
and postwar arms control, 208-24, 240-78, 323-48
religious views of, 578-89
retirement from Harvard presidency of, 638-41
and social sciences, 93-5
sons' relationships with, 100-4, 743-6
and Soviet aggression, 358-64, 369-72
and tercentenary of Harvard, 90-2, 97-9
Universal Military Service advocated by, 310-12, 361-3, 538-53
during Vietnam War, 746-52
and Walsh-Sweezy controversy, 104-10
in Weimar Germany, 63-5
during World War I, 35-50
Conant, James Richards (son), 53, 76, 100, 102-4, 123, 157, 208-9, 239, 464, 641, 695, 716-18, 730-2, 740, 743-5
Conant, James Scott (father), 12-16
Conant, Jennet (grandchild), 744, 752-4
Conant, Jennett Orr Bryant (mother), 12-14, 16, 78
Conant, Jim (grandchild), 744, 745, 752, 754
Conant, Marjorie (sister), 11, 13, 16, 67-8, 744
Conant, Norice (daughter-in-law), 641, 717, 730-1, 740, 744
Conant, Roger (ancestor), 12
Conant, Theodore Richards (son), 4, 11-12, 53, 58, 68, 76, 100-4, 123, 137, 138, 140, 157, 208-10, 239, 284, 464, 641, 708, 718, 730, 741, 744-6, 752
Condon, Edward U., 141, 258, 262, 394, 418-20, 434
Conference on Applied Nuclear Physics, 140
Congress, U.S., 130, 131, 252, 319-20, 345, 359, 375, 378, 386, 404, 419-20, 483, 491, 523, 527, 537, 539, 540, 551, 559, 560, 565, 570, 576, 577, 585, 597, 617, 629, 648, 652, 655, 669, 670, 680, 722, 725, 737, 738
Joint Committee on Atomic Energy (JCAE), 251, 307, 313, 378, 473, 481, 483, 489, 595-6, 600, 602, 677
see also House of Representatives; Senate
Connally, Tom, 374, 378
Connor, Ralph, 394-5
Considine, Robert, 288
Coolidge, Charles A., 108, 177, 427, 554, 579, 696
Cooper, John Sherman, 729
Cornell University, 84, 451, 544
Council of Foreign Ministers, 250, 253
Council on Foreign Relations, 121, 267-9, 324, 508, 509, 519, 530, 715, 720, 743
Cousins, Norman, 292-3, 326-7
Cowles, Gardner, 509, 542-3
Cowley, Malcolm, 22, 37
Cox, James, 57
Crombie, Charlie, 18, 32
Cromwell, Oliver, 59
Cuba, 714, 732
Culbertson, Ely, 246
cummings, e. e., 22, 24, 37
Curie, Marie, 57
Curtis, Charles P., Jr., 69
Cushing, Cardinal, 586
Cutler, Robert, 427, 509, 510, 529, 681, 710
Cutter, R. Ammi, 496, 498, 499, 509
cyclotron, 137, 139
Czechoslovakia, 122, 300-301, 320, 334, 661
Communist coup in, 358, 457, 458, 538

Daniel, Cuthbert, 327
Daniels, Farrington, 599
Dante, 242
Dartmouth College, 242, 450, 587, 602, 645
David, Donald K., 501, 616, 695
Davies, John Paton, 655
Davis, Elmer, 121
Davis, John W., 428
Day, Edmund E., 451, 544-5
Dean, Gordon, 474, 478-9, 599, 605
Defense Department, U.S., 376, 379, 480, 525, 541, 546, 554, 555, 558, 560, 561, 568, 569, 574, 576, 597, 599, 604
Democratic Party, 14, 57, 131, 417, 424, 451, 510, 535, 643-5, 714, 750, 752
Denmark, in World War II, 124, 196

Index

Depression, 3, 56, 66, 67, 83, 95, 105, 165, 176, 580
de Severesky, General Alexander, 365-6
Desert Storm, 551
Des Moines Register, 306
DeVoto, Bernard, 106, 607
Dewey, Bradley, 376-7
Dewey, Thomas E., 372, 426
Diamond, Sigmund, 412, 460-1, 624-5
Dickey, John S., 602, 743
Diem, Ngo Dinh, 534, 747
Dien Bien Phu, battle of, 681, 682
Dillon, Douglas, 747
Dirksen, Everett, 516, 522
Dodd, E. Merrick, Jr., 107
Dodds, Harold, 97, 117, 126, 311, 503, 509, 541
Dollard, Charles, 509
domino theory, 747
Donnelly, Walter, 655-6
Donovan, Colonel William J., 201, 509, 516, 523, 646
Donovan, Robert J., 754
Dos Passos, John, 20, 22, 37, 747
Douglas, L. W., 208, 216
Douglas, Lewis, 120, 121, 133, 142, 143, 718
Douglas, Paul H., 748-51
Dowling, Alice, 708, 732
Dowling, Walter "Red," 708, 720-1, 732
Dryden, Hugh, 566
Du Pont Chemical Company, 38, 56, 168, 185-7, 195-6, 306, 307, 379, 572-3
Dubinsky, David, 509, 516
DuBridge, Lee A., 141, 306-8, 332, 351, 353, 468, 474, 476, 478, 490, 561-4, 566-8, 590, 592, 596-600, 605, 731
Dulles, Allen, 121, 508, 602, 684, 695
Dulles, John Foster, 3, 379, 383, 388, 484, 534, 646-7, 650, 654-60, 663, 665-70, 672-6, 679, 684-6, 688-94, 696-8, 700-703, 714, 715, 717, 718, 720, 738
Dumbarton Oaks conference, 220
Duncan, Bob, 31

East Germany, 653, 660, 664, 665, 674, 689, 699, 714-16
Eberstadt, Ferdinand, 517
Eddington, Arthur, 97
Eden, Anthony, 676, 685
Edgewood Arsenal, 46
Educational Policies Commission, 724
Educational Testing Service (ETS), 81, 707, 708
Education and Liberty (Conant), 586, 587, 645
Education in a Divided World (Conant), 367-8, 370, 273, 421-3, 439-42, 585
Education and Politics at Harvard (Lipset and Riesman), 418, 460
Edwards, Al, 593
Egypt, 642, 696, 698
Eichelberger, Clark, 120
Einstein, Albert, 28, 42, 88, 136, 137, 240, 286, 288, 302, 303, 410, 589
Eisenhower, Dwight D., 3, 4, 77, 344, 357, 366, 383, 388, 505, 509, 568, 584
  candidacy of, 510, 549, 638, 644-5
  at Columbia, 379, 443, 498, 500, 572, 646

at Council on Foreign Relations, 508
on Educational Policy Commission, 443-5
election of, 567
farewell address of, 576
and MacArthur firing, 529, 530
as NATO commander, 515, 518-22, 526, 527, 537, 540, 549, 592
presidency of, 490, 511, 523, 534, 591, 604, 606, 625, 647, 650-2, 654-9, 661, 662-7, 670, 673-5, 677, 679, 680, 683-6, 688, 690, 694-7, 700, 702, 709-11, 714, 716-20, 722, 733
reelection of, 699
Universal Military Service supported by, 502, 503, 540, 550, 551
and Vietnam, 747, 748
Elementary and Secondary Education Act (1965), 738
Eliot, Charles William, 21, 26, 69, 70, 75, 78, 100, 105, 448
Eliot, Major George Fielding, 121, 132, 217, 218
Eliot, T. S., 22
Ellison, Ralph, 741
Elsey, George, 276
Elugelab, 605
Emergency Committee in Aid of Displaced German Scholars, 84
Emergency Committee of Atomic Scientists (ECAS), 302-3
Emerson, Ralph Waldo, 13, 175, 324-5
Emerson, Rupert, 107
Engels, Friedrich, 175, 431, 442
Enola Gay, 236
Ethiopia, Italian invasion of, 83
Euratom, 700, 704
European Economic Community (EEC), 704
European Defense Community (EDC), 537, 642, 644, 646, 648, 650, 654, 655, 664-76, 681-84, 691
European Recovery Program, 338, 361
Evans, Ward, 678

Fainsod, Merle, 107
Fairbank, John King, 70, 80, 107, 461-2, 620, 623
Faithful Are the Wounds (Sarton), 210, 424, 450, 459
Farouk, King of Egypt, 642
Farrell, Gen. Thomas F., 233, 295, 329, 334
Fascism, 89
"Fat Man," 232, 291, 312
Faubus, Orval E., 722
Federal Bureau of Investigation (FBI), 245, 270, 309, 316-19, 329-30, 392, 394, 398, 404, 413, 416, 425, 426, 430, 438, 450, 453, 454, 475, 566, 581, 599, 606, 608, 623-5, 627, 634, 651
Federal Council of Churches, 284, 285
Federal Employee Loyalty Program, 404
Federation of Atomic Scientists, 266, 268, 300
Federative Alliance, 246
Ferguson, Frank, 288
Ferguson, William S., 107, 110
Fermi, Enrico, 136, 141, 162, 183, 185, 186, 230, 232, 261, 306, 313, 324, 326, 351, 353, 471, 474, 478, 488, 596

Fiduciary Trust Company of Boston, 731
Fifth Column, 404
Fight for Freedom, 510
Fine, Paul, 330
Finland, 493
Finletter, Thomas K., 293, 600
Finley, John, 648, 754
Fischer, John, 339, 399, 707
"Fishing Party," 378–90, 469, 479, 550, 604
Fisk, Jim, 600
fission, 136, 139
Flesch, Rudolf, 712
flexible response, 721
Flexner, Simon, 56, 73–4
Ford Foundation, 509, 732
Foreign Affairs, 338, 370, 555, 604
Foreign Policy Association, 212, 214, 513
Forman, Paul, 577
Forrestal, James V., 3, 249, 263, 296, 310, 343, 344, 353, 357, 363, 367, 370, 372, 373, 376–9, 385, 387, 388, 395, 559
Fortune magazine, 94
France, 64, 83, 221, 521, 531
    and Asian Communism, 524, 533–5
    and Berlin crisis, 367, 368
    and European Defense Community, 644, 658, 659, 667–9, 671, 672–3, 675, 676, 683–4
    postwar, 216, 246, 359
    and Suez crisis, 698, 699
    universities in, 113
    and Vietnam, 681
    and West Germany, 652, 687
    in World War I, 35, 36, 42
    in World War II, 115–17, 119–20, 122, 124, 125, 144, 496
Franck, James, 42
Franck Report, 230
Frank, Philipp, 411, 557
Frankfurter, Felix, 9, 57, 72–3, 75, 76, 78, 84, 87–8, 90, 91, 96, 99, 107, 108, 114, 121, 123, 195, 197, 198, 200, 206, 295, 427, 618
Franz Ferdinand, Archduke of Austria, 35
Freedom House, 77, 638
Freeland, Richard, 406, 439
Freidel, Frank, 83
Freud, Sigmund, 410, 589
Frisch, Otto, 149
Frost, Robert, 8–9, 91–3, 106, 593
Fuchs, Klaus, 237, 482–3, 491, 570, 619, 622, 632
Fulbright, J. William, 633–4
Fuller, Buckminster, 574
Furry, Wendell, 635, 652

G.I. Bill, 81, 403, 539, 581
Gaddis, John Lewis, 268
Galbraith, John Kenneth, 107, 292, 327, 416, 450, 456, 460, 541, 610–17, 623, 636, 712–13, 728, 729, 738, 749
Gardner, John W., 688, 706, 708, 714, 731, 737, 738, 740, 748
Garrison, Lloyd, 678, 680, 681
Gathering Storm, The (Churchill), 497

General Education in a Free Society (Conant), 581
General Electric, 36, 38, 127, 264, 356
General Mills, 509
Geneva summit, 690
George VI, King, 145
Georgia, University of, 708
Germany, 8, 112, 177, 490
    atomic bomb research in, 136, 139, 152, 154–6, 158–60, 163, 164, 170, 174, 187, 194, 200, 211, 212, 215
    defeat of, 188, 211–14, 218, 227, 253
    division of, 359, 367 (*see also* East Germany; West Germany)
    educational system in, 403
    and Harvard, 84–9, 96–7
    Hitler's rise to power in, 63, 64, 66, 70, 83, 447
    occupation of, 311, 369
    persecution of Jews in, 66, 86, 87, 96, 115, 122
    postwar, 3, 4, 6, 7, 216, 237
    reunification of, 755
    scientific scholarship in, 16, 28, 37, 51, 165
    universities in, 113
    Weimar, 61–4
    in World War I, 35, 36, 40–6, 201
    in World War II, 114–15, 117, 119–20, 122–6, 129–32, 134, 137, 143, 151, 153, 173, 202, 292, 338, 411
Gestapo, 122, 153
Gilkey, J. Gordon, 31
God and Man at Yale (Buckley), 581
Goebbels, Joseph, 97
Goethe, Johann Wolfgang von, 242
Goldberg, Arthur J., 724
Golden, William T., 545, 560–2, 564
Goldwyn, Samuel, 509, 529, 718
Gorbachev, Mikhail, 479
Goslin, Willard E., 584–5
Göttingen, University of, 165
Graham, Philip L., 556
Gray, Gordon, 512, 542, 678, 680, 682
Great Debate, 513, 516, 521, 522
Great Society programs, 724
Greece, 203, 317, 319–20, 364, 393, 404, 405
Greenbaum, Edward S., 509
Greene, Jerome, 579
Greenewalt, Crawford H., 307, 333, 379, 383, 388
Grew, Joseph C., 300
Griggs, David T., 600
Griswold, A. Whitney, 635
Griswold, Erwin N., 505, 626, 628, 629
Gromyko, Andrei, 271, 305
Grosz, George, 41
Groves, General Leslie R., 9, 157, 161, 163, 164, 166–70, 179–81, 184, 186, 188, 195, 197, 200, 201, 211, 215, 223, 231–4, 238, 248, 259, 260, 264, 266–8, 271, 287, 288, 290, 295, 300, 306, 314, 315, 317–19, 329, 334–6, 356–8, 419, 465, 752
Groves of Academe, The (McCarthy), 606, 607
Gruening, Ernest, 729

Gruenther, General Alfred M., 343, 344, 496, 499, 646, 672, 673
Gulf War, 280, 551, 553

H. M. Pulham, Esquire (Marquand), 32
Haber, Fritz, 42, 43, 45, 64–5, 733
Hafstad, Lawrence, 488
Hague Conventions, 41
Hahn, Otto, 42, 136, 194
Halban, Hans von, 146, 185, 186
Halberstam, David, 454
Halberstam, Michael, 454
Haldane, J. B. S., 461
Hale, George Ellery, 43
Halifax, Lord, 197
Hallstein, Walter, 668, 670, 671, 674
Halsey, Admiral William F., Jr., 292, 296
Hanfstaengl, Ernest F. S. "Putzi," 85–8, 96, 110, 112
Hansen, Harry, 303
Harper & Row, 3, 742
Harper's magazine, 106, 296–8, 300, 301
Harriman, Averell, 203, 214, 222, 252, 540, 718
Harrison, George L., 222, 227, 251, 294, 295, 426, 427
Harvard Alumni Bulletin, 368, 449–51, 456
Harvard Century, The (Smith), 460
Harvard Crimson, 29–34, 37, 40, 69, 85, 90, 117, 123, 391, 392, 453–6, 542, 575, 581, 629, 660
Harvard Law Review, 437, 633
Harvard University, 3–9, 12, 16–18, 20–40, 43, 48, 50–110, 112–20, 122, 127, 131, 134, 137–42, 144, 165, 167, 172, 173, 181, 201, 208, 224, 233, 236, 241, 283, 288, 290, 328, 356, 359, 402, 422, 426, 542, 573, 578–89, 687–9, 706, 720, 738, 741, 754–5
  academic freedom issues at, 393, 394, 396, 413–14, 416–18, 430, 445–51, 453–60, 610–19, 623–37
  Board of Overseers, 114, 150, 471, 510, 574, 610–14, 616, 617, 619, 639–40, 645
  Business School, 134, 327, 501, 616, 617, 695
  Churchill at, 191–2
  classified scientific research at, 396, 398, 438, 511, 576
  and Committee on the Present Danger, 512, 529
  Corporation, 65, 68, 70, 71, 74, 75, 87, 88, 142, 156, 175, 177–8, 226, 247, 258, 272, 426, 428, 448, 459, 499, 510, 526, 528, 554, 580, 610, 612, 613, 616–19, 624, 628, 635, 639–41, 647, 740
  Divinity School, 579–81, 583
  Foundation for Advanced Study and Research, 458
  and G.I. Bill, 403
  Godkin Lectures, 704
  Graduate School of Arts and Sciences, 624
  and Kennedy administration, 727–8
  Law School, 73, 157, 327, 425, 427, 446, 447, 456, 505, 626, 634
  Marshall at, 320–1, 361
  Medical School, 634
  Observatory, 399, 617
  Press, 113, 423, 580
  retirement from, 638–41, 647
  Russian Research Center at, 412–13
  School of Education, 403, 580, 624, 696, 707
  School of Public Administration, 613, 617
  science education at, 407–11
  Society of Fellows, 602
  Vietnam War protests at, 751
  Walsh-Sweezy controversy at, 105–8, 117, 118, 197, 393, 640, 641, 652
Hashem, Saleh, 97
Haskins, Caryl, 729
Haskins, Cheryl, 141
Haussermann, Oscar, 31
heavy-water research, 184–6
Heidelberg University, 96–7, 112
Heisenberg, Werner, 164, 194
Henderson, L. J., 58, 74, 407
Hersey, John, 291, 292, 295, 299, 304
Hershey, General Lewis B., 542, 549, 551, 562
Herter, Christian, 441, 718
Hickenlooper, Bourke, 313, 438, 677
Hicks, Grenville, 109
Higinbotham, W. A., 268, 300
Hildebrand, Joel, 487, 488, 489
Hill, Admiral Harry, 344
Hillyer, Robert, 22, 121
Hindenburg, General Paul von, 63, 64, 70
Hiroshima, 5–7, 10, 138, 140, 225, 228, 230, 235, 236, 238–40, 243, 253, 261, 279–80, 282, 284, 285, 289–97, 299, 301, 302, 304, 305, 309, 326, 349, 376, 409, 466, 467, 468, 475–7, 506, 589, 687, 705, 752
Hiss, Alger, 425–30, 435, 482, 491, 624
Hiss, Priscilla, 429
Hitler, Adolf, 3, 9, 83–6, 88, 117–20, 123–6, 143, 151, 152, 159, 189, 202, 214, 216, 283, 359, 368, 423, 497, 531, 643, 647, 703, 705, 723
  appeasement policy toward, 115, 117, 393, 494
  assassination plot against, 733
  and atomic bomb research, 136, 164, 9211
  defeat of, 687
  interventionist views on, 131–3, 142
  and Lebensraum, 112
  McCarthy compared to, 662
  parallel drawn between Stalin and, 367
  refugees from, 98, 165, 410
  rise to power of, 63, 64, 66, 70, 83, 447
  and Spanish Civil War, 113
Ho Chi Minh, 534
Hoffman, Paul, 509
Hollister, John S., 738
Holmes, Oliver Wendell, 21, 96
Holton, Gerald, 409
Homans, Robert, 69–71, 73
Hönigschmid, Otto, 61, 63
Hook, Sidney, 422–3, 446, 608, 609, 747
Hoover, Herbert, 68, 83, 121, 516–18, 520

Hoover, J. Edgar, 245, 317, 319, 392, 394, 404, 416, 425, 426, 430, 454, 599, 624-5, 677
Hopkins, Ernest M., 121
Hopkins, Harry, 126-7, 185, 187, 189
House of Representatives, U.S., 151, 397, 525, 551, 565
  Armed Services Committee, 521, 548, 552
  Appropriations Committee, 565
  Foreign Affairs Committee, 521
  Military Affairs Committee, 259, 260
  Naval Affairs Committee, 272
  Un-American Activities Committee (HUAC), 418-20, 425-9, 432, 434, 435, 451, 456, 457, 585, 609, 625, 628, 629, 633, 634
Hovde, Frederick L., 141, 146
Howe, Mark DeWolfe, 630-2
Hughes, Charles Evans, 37, 39
Hughes, H. Stuart, 417-18
Hulburd, David, 585
Humphrey, George M., 666
Humphrey, Hubert, 751
Hungary, 202, 231
  Soviet invasion of, 698, 699
Hussein, Saddam, 280
Hutchins, Robert, 355, 416, 585, 608, 626
Hyde Park pact, 203
hydrogen bomb (H-bomb), 3, 5, 6, 9, 380-2, 388, 389, 463-91, 539, 556, 568, 569, 590-2, 595-602, 604-5, 614, 676, 679-81, 720, 721, 753

Illinois, University of, 366
Imperial Chemical Industries, 181, 182
India, 493, 696, 702, 728
Indochina, 493, 534, 673, 675, 681-83, 747
Ingersoll, Ralph, 94
Institute of Pacific Relations (IPR), 621, 628
Institute for the Unity of Science, 411, 557
Inter-Allied Gas Conference, 46
Intercontinental ballistic missiles (ICBM), 381, 714
Interdepartmental Committee on Scientific Research and Development, 566
Interim Committee, 5, 223-5, 227, 228, 230, 236, 237, 243, 248, 249, 259, 280, 293-5, 297, 299, 300, 426, 467, 479, 512
Introduction to the History of Science (Sarton), 407
Iowa State College, 242
Iran, 280, 393, 523, 532, 534, 667
Iraq, 280
isolationism, 516-18, 523, 644
Israel, 698, 703
Italy, 203, 695
  fascist, 83, 96, 136
  postwar, 361, 364

Jackson, Andrew, 99, 175
Jackson, C. D., 661, 662
James, Henry, 73, 74, 426, 580
James, William, 21, 29, 30, 372, 410, 578
Japan, 183, 531
  atomic bombing of, 205, 211, 212, 219, 225-8, 230, 231, 234, 236, 282, 284, 292, 295, 303, 467, 479 (*see also* Hiroshima; Nagasaki)
  defeat of, 188, 203, 218, 257, 259, 434
  occupation of, 311, 523
  in World War II, 120, 153, 155, 211, 239, 338
Jefferson, Thomas, 33, 83, 175
Jeffries, Zay, 203, 215, 326
Jewett, Frank B., 126, 128, 133, 134, 139, 260, 310, 419, 485
Jewish War Veterans, 121, 129
Jews
  at Harvard, 58, 59, 81, 82, 454
  Nazi persecution of, 66, 86, 87, 96, 115, 122, 703
Johns Hopkins University, 379, 485, 619
  School of Advanced International Studies, 441
Johnson, Joseph, 602
Johnson, Louis, 374, 388, 390, 480, 482, 496, 500, 501, 602
Johnson, Lyndon B., 724, 736-8, 747, 748, 750, 751
Joint Chiefs of Staff, 343, 344, 375, 376, 478, 524, 533, 694, 717
  Evaluation Board, 263, 375, 376, 385
Joint Research and Development Board (JRDB), 307-8, 333, 352, 355-6, 366, 376, 377
Joliot-Curie, Frederic and Irene, 461
Jung, Carl C., 97, 98
Jungk, Robert, 470
Justice Department, U.S., 58, 425, 635

Kaghan, Theodore, 656, 657
Kaiser Wilhelm Institute, 42, 43, 62, 136, 139, 164, 194, 733
Kamin, Leon, 635
Kansas, University of, 311
Kaufman, William, 720
Kennan, George F., 251, 266, 338, 359, 361, 370, 401, 406, 473, 480-1, 483, 595, 703-4, 714
Kennedy, John F., 31, 77, 117, 123, 568, 651, 682, 721, 722, 724, 727-9, 731, 733-6, 747
Kennedy, Joseph P., 31, 117, 516, 520
Kennedy, Robert F., 728, 736
Keppel, Frank, 624, 696, 707, 731, 737, 754
Kevles, Daniel J., 566, 577
Keynes, John Maynard, 611, 615
Khrushchev, Nikita, 494, 690, 693, 709, 714, 716, 718, 721, 731, 732, 734
Killian, James R., Jr., 450, 493, 511, 566, 568, 569, 677, 692, 710, 719, 720, 741
Kim Il Sung, 494
King, Martin Luther, Jr., 722, 726, 750
Kissinger, Henry, 720, 721
Kistiakowsky, George B., 139, 140, 149, 233, 234, 398, 475, 485-6, 561, 568, 647, 710, 711, 720, 753, 754
Kittredge, George Lyman, 21
Kluckhohn, Clyde, 412, 413, 511
Knowland, William, 516, 527
Kohler, Elmer P., 28-9, 33, 35, 36, 45, 54, 55, 73, 109
Korean War, 310, 413, 473, 490, 492-8, 501-5,

Korean War (*cont.*)
516–17, 521, 523–5, 530, 531, 535, 527, 538, 540–3, 545, 551, 555, 559–61, 564, 566, 574, 577, 591, 609, 642, 650, 661, 667, 673, 683
Krekeler, Heinz, 672
Krokodil, 554
Krupp, Alfred, 642
Kuhn, Thomas S., 409, 410
Kuwait, 280

Ladd, Milton, 416
La Follette, Robert M., 57
La Guardia, Fiorello, 142
Lamb, Arthur B., 45, 92, 94–6
LaMer, Victor K., 485, 487, 489
Lamont, Thomas W., 175–7, 216, 611, 614
Land, Edwin, 741
Landon, Alf, 117, 177
Langer, William L., 574
Lansdale, John, 157–8
Larken, Felix, 541
Laski, Harold, 57, 175, 408, 448, 455, 457
Late George Apley, The (Marquand), 24–5, 65
Latimer, Wendell Mitchell, 485, 487–90, 596, 599
Lattimore, Owen, 619–20
Lauritsen, Charles, 592, 602
Lawrence, Ernest O., 137, 139–41, 146–7, 149, 150, 153, 156, 158, 166, 188, 209–10, 230, 234, 261, 332, 333, 350, 356, 470, 471, 473, 487–9, 596
Lawrence Livermore Laboratory, 597
Layman's Guide to Education, A (Conant), 740
Leach, Walter Barton, 574
League of Nations, 83
Lebanon, 714
le Carré, John, 652
Lee, Roger I., 69, 647
Lemann, Monte, 509
Lend-Lease Act (1940), 145
Lenin, V. I., 175, 431, 442, 462
Leonard, John, 3
Leva, Marx, 541
Leverett, John, 77
Lewis, Anthony, 454
Lewis, Geoffrey W., 670
Lewis, Gilbert N., 56
Lewis, John L., 113
Lewis, Winford Lee, 46–7, 201
Libby, Willard F., 489, 596, 597, 599
Library of Congress, 21, 430
Life magazine, 214
Lilienthal, David E., 264–7, 272, 282, 306–9, 312–19, 331–3, 344, 347, 349, 350, 354, 355–7, 374, 378–9, 438, 469–71, 473, 474, 477, 478, 480–2, 489, 615, 639, 753
see also Acheson-Lilienthal plan
Lilienthal, David E., Jr., 454
Lindbergh, Charles, 527
Lindemann, Frederick (later Lord Cherwell), 145, 146, 148, 149, 189, 204, 206
Lippmann, Walter, 3, 22, 29, 107, 114, 115, 156, 216, 287, 289–91, 295, 338, 362, 363, 513, 531–2, 613

Lipset, Seymour Martin, 418, 460
"Little Boy," 232, 291
Lodge, Henry Cabot, 117, 661, 692, 748, 749
Loeb, Robert F., 566
Loeb, William, 392
Loewenbein, A., 122
London, University of, 94, 448
London conference, 248
London School of Economics, 570
Look magazine, 491, 543, 545, 546
Loomis, Alfred Lee, 137–40, 147
Loomis, Chauncey C., 38–9
Los Alamos, 164, 166–9, 171, 185, 191, 197, 203, 212, 217, 221, 227, 233, 237, 306, 313, 317, 319, 326, 419, 471, 482, 570, 597, 623
Lovett, Robert, 343, 344, 498, 499, 501, 503, 540, 541, 567, 600, 605
Lowell, Abbot Lawrence, 21, 26, 37, 54, 57–60, 66, 68–71, 74, 77, 81, 84, 91, 92, 97–101, 105, 108, 118, 393, 448, 458, 616
Lowell, Ralph, 417
Lowen, Irving S., 195–6
Luce, Clare Boothe, 684, 695
Luce, Henry, 121, 661, 684
Lusitania, sinking of, 36, 40
Luther, Hans, 87–8
Luxembourg Treaty (1952), 703

MacArthur, Douglas R., II, 670, 672
MacArthur, General Douglas, 501, 504–5, 507, 515–17, 523–30, 533, 535, 540, 552, 644, 645
Maccoby, Michael, 454
Mach, Ernst, 410
Mackenzie, C. J., 186
Maclean, Donald D., 570
MacLeish, Archibald, 94, 111–14, 116, 123, 128, 406
Maginot line, 119, 124
Making of the Atomic Bomb, The (Rhodes), 205
Malott, Deane, 311
Manchester Union, 392
Manhattan Project, 4, 6, 9, 139, 149, 160–235, 300, 312, 357, 407, 408, 419, 457, 466, 487, 489, 580, 595, 655, 679
Britain and, 172–93, 571
and civilian atomic power, 323, 324, 326
and Emergency Committee of Atomic Scientists, 302
espionage during, 434
films about, 285–91
and May-Johnson bill, 261, 262
and postwar arms race, 194–207
security regulations of, 351, 623, 677
Smyth Report on, 238, 282, 314
start-up of, 160–71, 309
Manley, John H., 167, 470
Mao Tse-tung, 417
Marbury, William L., 259, 272, 328, 426–30, 435, 447, 485, 499, 503, 509, 510, 527, 540, 541, 548, 550, 552, 610, 619, 624, 627–9, 635, 636, 639, 641, 681, 686, 703, 751
"March of Time" newsreels, 286, 303
Marianas, 211

Maritime Service, U.S., 209
Markham, Helen Deane, 635
Marks, Herbert S., 264, 269, 394
Marquand, John P., 12, 24–5, 32, 33, 41, 365
Marshall, General George C., 3, 150, 160, 173, 268, 320–1, 343, 361, 418, 501, 503, 504, 516, 539–41, 547–9, 552
Marshall Plan, 319, 322, 334, 337–9, 359, 364, 368, 402, 424, 492
Martin, Joseph W., 525, 529
Marx, Karl, 175, 360, 431, 442, 462
Marx, Sam, 287–8
Maryland Bar Association, 446
Masaryk, Jan, 359
Mason, Edward S., 613, 615
Massachusetts Institute of Technology (MIT), 88, 116, 127, 139, 140, 210, 296, 311, 396, 398, 414, 450, 493, 511, 574, 575, 592, 692, 711
    Radiation Laboratory, 137–8, 167, 168, 306
massive retaliation, 720
Mather, Kirtley, 414, 630
Matsu, 714
Matthiessen, F. O., 70, 108, 359, 416, 430, 446, 459, 623
MAUD Committee, 148, 178, 331
May, Alan Nunn, 245
Mayer, Louis B., 288
May-Johnson Bill, 259–63, 266, 272
McCarran, Pat, 619
McCarran-Walter Immigration and Nationality Act, 620
McCarthy, Eugene, 750
McCarthy, Joseph, 454, 483, 491–2, 527, 529, 581, 585, 607, 608, 617–20, 625, 626, 629, 634, 644, 645, 648, 650–2, 655–7, 660, 662, 681
McCarthy, Mary, 606
McCarthyism, 3, 6, 8, 90, 405, 406, 460, 490, 511–12, 517, 563, 606–37, 640, 656, 658, 682
McCloy, John J., 3, 156, 221, 263, 266, 289, 295–6, 394, 424, 468, 499, 642, 643, 646, 654, 657, 659, 668, 689, 715, 721, 747
McCormack, General James, 353, 357
McCormick, Colonel Robert R., 516
McElroy, Neil, 719
McGovern, George, 752
McGrath, Earl J., 391
McKellar, Kenneth D., 315
McLean, Edward, 428
McLeod, Scott, 655, 656
McMahon, Brien, 263, 271, 272, 306, 314, 378, 438, 478, 481, 595–6, 599, 600
McNamara, Robert, 720
McPherson, Harry, 748
Meiklejohn, Alexander, 608
Meitner, Lise, 136, 291
Melbourne, Lord, 30
Menninger, William C., 509, 523
Menzel, Donald, 573, 618
Merchant, Livingston, 717, 718
Merck, George, 365
Metcalf, Keyes DeWitt, 235, 241–2
Metro-Goldwyn-Mayer, 287–91, 303

Meyer, Cord, Jr., 365
Michigan, University of, 157, 208–9
Middlebrush, Frederick A., 509
Midvale Steel Company, 36, 38
Military Liaison Committee (MLC), 357
Military Policy Committee, 161, 164–6, 170, 211, 252
Miller, Francis P., 121
Miller, Perry, 70
Millikan, Robert A., 56, 509
Mills, C. Wright, 507, 512, 513
Minnesota, University of, 379, 458
Modern Arms and Free Men (Bush), 381, 461
Molotov, Vyacheslav, 222, 245, 253–5, 334, 674–5
Monnet, Jean, 684
Monsanto Chemical Company, 379, 566
Mooney, Mary E., 31, 32
Moral and Spiritual Inquiry (EPC), 584
Morgan, Edmund M., 107
Morgan, J. P., 175
Morgan, Thomas, 678
Morgenthau, Henry, 212
Morison, Samuel Eliot, 23, 34, 36, 542, 607
Morize, André, 121
Morrill, James L., 370, 383, 388
Moscow Conference, 251–7, 268
Mossadegh, Mohammed, 523
Mundt, Karl, 457
Munich Conference, 115, 393
Munsterberg, Hugo, 448
Murdock, Kenneth B., 70, 74, 79, 105, 107–9
Murphree, Edgar V., 596
Murray, Thomas, 599
Murrow, Edward R., 130, 331, 509, 529, 549, 729
Mussolini, Benito, 83, 95, 96, 113
mustard gas, 44, 46, 173
mutual assured destruction (MAD), 719–20
Mutual Broadcasting System, 522
Mutual Security Program, 719
My Several Lives (Conant), 3, 5, 11, 14, 35, 39, 48, 49, 51, 58, 60, 81, 84, 110, 112, 135, 196, 257, 611, 625, 657, 727, 741, 753

Nagasaki, 228, 236, 238, 284, 285, 291, 292, 294, 296, 299, 304, 312, 380, 368, 469, 476, 752, 753
Nash, Leonard K., 409
Nasser, Gamal Abdel, 696
Nathan, Robert, 22
Nation, The, 424
National Academy of Sciences, 43, 55, 126, 146, 150, 152, 153, 169, 178, 260, 397, 419, 434, 484–90, 560, 585, 590, 596, 682
National Advisory Committee on Aeronautics, 127
National Advisory Council, 738
National Catholic Educational Association, 587
National Defense Education Act (1958), 711
National Defense Research Committee (NDRC), 127–9, 131, 133–5, 138, 140–3, 145–7, 149, 153, 156, 158, 166, 167, 178, 201, 228, 243, 260, 264, 286, 306, 309,

NDRC (*cont.*)
　310, 365, 366, 394-5, 397, 485, 559,
　　623
National Education Association (NEA), 120,
　624, 687
　Educational Policies Commission (EPC),
　　372-3, 392, 430-3, 439-45, 450-6, 458,
　　459, 461, 462, 465, 500, 503, 537, 539,
　　549-50, 581, 583-4, 609, 707
National Institutes of Health, 559
National Military Establishment, 307, 343, 376,
　399
National Organization for the Advancement
　of Colored People (NAACP), 726
National Research Council, 43, 126, 485
National Science Board, 560, 563-5
National Science Foundation (NSF), 396-7, 555,
　559-66, 573-4, 576, 577, 585
National Security Act (1947), 307
National Security Council (NSC), 361, 363,
　374-6, 384, 385, 480, 483, 512, 567, 605,
　660, 661, 663
　Planning Board, 717
National Urban League, 738
National War College, 258, 272-3, 277, 279,
　304, 322, 339-44, 346-7, 349, 350, 352-4,
　365-6, 369-72, 394, 434, 554, 569
Navy Department, U.S., 296, 395-6
Nazis, 64, 66, 84-8, 96, 112, 115, 116, 119, 120,
　122, 129, 131-33, 135, 136, 151, 158, 164,
　194, 202, 231, 280, 360, 367, 401, 402,
　404, 477, 497, 585, 642, 648, 653, 658,
　661, 700 703-5, 732-4
NBC Radio, 519
Nehru, Jawaharlal, 493, 593
Nernst, Walther, 28, 42
Neutrality Act, 117
New Committee on Nuclear Physics, 139,
　09149
New Deal, 9, 72, 84, 90, 99, 420, 425, 426, 428,
　611, 615, 727
New Guinea, 211
Newman, Edwin, 752
New Republic, 57
Newsweek, 9, 508, 590, 605, 638
New Yorker, The, 69, 71, 99, 100, 105, 295,
　299
New York Herald Tribune, 346, 422, 733
New York State Association of Colleges and
　Universities, 543
New York Times, The, 3, 75, 140, 284, 298,
　339, 346, 355, 367, 392, 422, 450, 453,
　456, 494, 507, 508, 510, 519, 565, 595,
　597, 620, 656, 694, 729, 730, 747
New York University, 422
New Zealand, education in, 586, 616
Niebuhr, Reinhold, 3, 283-5, 360, 475, 505, 572,
　578, 579, 583, 588
Nieman fellowships, 79
Nimitz, Admiral Chester, 310
Nitze, Paul, 292, 441, 483-4, 502, 540, 611
Nixon, Richard M., 426, 428, 435, 527, 528, 651,
　722, 727, 742, 747, 751, 752
Nobel Prize, 27, 50, 52, 54, 62, 65, 136, 137,
　306, 489

Normandy invasion, 202
Norris, James F., 45
North Atlantic Treaty (1949), 379, 515, 516
North Atlantic Treaty Organization (NATO),
　246, 494, 501, 515, 517-19, 521, 522,
　525, 533, 535-7, 540, 549, 551, 571, 592,
　642, 644-6, 662, 666, 669-72, 682-5,
　687, 693, 694, 697, 701, 703-4, 715,
　721
North Carolina, University of, 438, 543, 678
Northwestern University, 678
Norton, Charles Eliot, 21
Norton, John K., 433, 440, 443, 445, 452
Norway, 119, 124
Notre Dame University, 543
Novikov, Nikolai V., 250
Noyes, A. A., 56
Nuclear Energy for the Propulsion of Aircraft
　(NEPA), 333, 356
Nuclear Weapons and Foreign Policy
　(Kissinger), 720

Ober, Frank, 446-9, 453, 458, 461
Ober Law, 610
Oberlin College, 242
O'Brian, John Lord, 437, 451, 503, 509, 541,
　579, 583, 678
Office of Defense Mobilization (ODM), 567,
　710
Office of Economic Opportunity, 737
Office of Education, 431, 439
Office of National Estimates, 574
Office of Naval Intelligence, 395
Office of Naval Research (ONR), 397, 559, 561,
　563, 564, 566, 574
Office of Price Administration, 613
Office of Scientific Research and Development
　(OSRD), 135, 147-50, 152, 155, 156,
　159-61, 164-7, 169, 173, 178-80, 182,
　184-7, 189, 190, 194-7, 201, 203, 205, 207,
　210, 211, 231, 243, 261, 270, 272, 286,
　287, 306, 309, 310, 396, 409, 456, 466,
　559, 562, 563, 565
Office of Scientific and Technical Development,
　220
Office of Strategic Services (OSS), 201, 337,
　412, 509, 511, 574, 612
Ohio University, 401
Ollenhauer, Erich, 669
O'Malley, Clark, 641
On Active Service in War and Peace (Stimson),
　300
On Understanding Science (Conant), 556
Operation Barbarossa, 151
Operation Candor, 389, 604
Operation Crossroads, 375
Operation Gold, 692
Operation Pay-Off, 310
Operation Peppermint, 200-1
Operations Coordinating Board (OCB), 661
Oppenheimer, Frank, 317, 319, 457-8
Oppenheimer, Kitty, 308, 317
Oppenheimer, J. Robert, 3, 5, 280, 306, 322,
　327, 426, 434, 436, 483, 499, 509, 510,
　565-71, 574, 592, 604, 638, 648, 692

as Atomic Energy Commission adviser, 264, 308–9, 313, 351, 356–8, 590–1, 596–602, 605
and civilian nuclear power, 323–4
on Committee on the Present Danger, 509, 510
on Emergency Committee of Atomic Scientists, 302, 303
films on, 286, 287, 289
on Harvard Board of Overseers, 619, 645
and hydrogen bomb, 465–79, 481, 487–90
on Joint Research and Development Board committee, 307–8
in Manhattan Project, 165–9, 171, 201, 212, 227, 230, 231, 233, 326
and postwar atomic bomb control, 261, 262, 269, 270, 329–37, 344–6
on Science Advisory Committee, 566–9
and science education, 410
security risk accusations against, 316–19, 416, 437, 457–8, 489, 596, 676–82, 692
Organic Syntheses, 53
Osborn, General Frederick H., 328–31, 333–7, 358, 413
Ostwald, Wilhelm, 28, 61
Oswald, Lee Harvey, 736
Oxford University, 96, 97

Pace, Frank, 504
Page, Arthur W., 379, 383, 388
Pahlavi, Shah Muhammad Reza, 534
Palmer, George Herbert, 29
Pankow, 718
Parsons, Talcott, 107
Patterson, Robert P., 249, 259, 262, 263, 289, 295, 310, 318, 426–8, 503, 506, 509, 522, 540, 541, 549
Paul, Martin A., 394–6
Pearl Harbor, 8, 9, 115, 120, 153–7, 161, 174, 177, 179, 236, 309–11, 393, 517
Peddlers of Crisis (Sanders), 510
Peierls, Rudolf, 149, 185
Pennock, Stanley B., 38–9, 48
Pennsylvania, University of, Law School, 384
People's Commissariat for Internal Affairs, (NKVD), 158–9
Perera, Colonel Guido R., 613
Perkins, Thomas N., 68, 74
Perry, Bliss, 21
Perry, Ralph Barton, 107
Philadelphia Bulletin, 548
Philippines, 209, 211, 492
Pike, James A., 586
Pike, Sumner T., 306, 478
Pitzer, Kenneth S., 472, 487, 488, 596–9
Pius XII, Pope, 578
Planck, Max, 165
plutonium, 184
poison gas, 3, 41–7, 244, 572–3
Poland, 202, 222, 231, 704
Nazi invasion of, 115, 126, 411
postwar, 334
Pontifical Academy of Science, 578
Portugal, 143, 144

Potsdam Conference, 205, 230, 231, 233, 236, 248, 259, 300, 367, 658, 690
Pound, Roscoe, 87–8
Powers, Thomas, 194
Practical Chemistry (Black and Conant), 54
Pravda, 430
Presidential Medal of Freedom, 735, 736
Presidential Medal for Merit, 638
President's Committee on Youth Employment, 724
President's Science Advisory Committee (PSAC), 568, 710
Princeton University, 84, 117, 137, 139, 167, 311
Institute for Advanced Study, 471, 568, 570, 595
Princip, Gavrilo, 35
Profiles in Courage (Kennedy), 728
Progressive Party, 57, 399, 425
Project Alsos, 211
Project Charles, 592
Project Metcalf, 574
Project Paperclip, 692
Project Troy, 511
Project Vista, 591–2
Providence Journal, 346
Psychological Strategy Board (PSB), 511, 512, 595, 661
psychological warfare, 661–3
Public Education Association, 726
public television, 741–2
Puerto Ricans, 724–5
"Pumpkin Papers," 435
Purcell, Edward, 511
Pusey, Nathan M., 583, 635, 688, 710, 751

Quakers, 544
Quarles, Donald A., 697
Quebec Conference, 190, 191, 202
Quemoy, 714
Quine, Willard V., 107, 410, 411

Rabi, I. I., 3, 168, 169, 231, 233, 286, 306, 308, 332, 351, 466, 468, 473, 475, 478, 560, 590, 602, 605
Radcliffe College, 88, 173
Radford, Admiral Arthur, 694, 695, 697, 700, 702, 704
radiological warfare (RW), 200, 342, 356, 367, 382, 386, 387, 390, 470
Ramsey, Norman, 574
Randall, Clarence B., 31, 611, 614–17
Rand Corporation, 599
Rapacki Plan, 704
Rathenau, Walther, 64
Reagan, Ronald, 7, 267, 422, 509
Reber, Sam, 656
"Red scare," 58, 391–461
    see also McCarthyism
Reed, John, 21–4, 29
Reischauer, Edwin O., 620
Republican Party, 14, 57, 117, 131, 142, 177, 417, 424–6, 429, 510, 516, 517, 525, 611, 619, 627, 638, 644, 645, 702
Research and Development Board (RDB), 559, 561, 566

Resor, Stanley, 503, 509
Rhee, Syngman, 747
Rhodes, Richard, 205-6
Richards, Alfred N., 419-20, 434, 436, 437, 485
Richards, Miriam Thayer, 50, 102, 708-9
Richards, Theodore William, 17, 27-9, 33, 36, 50-2, 55, 61, 62, 137, 407
Richards, William, 119, 137-40
Rickover, Admiral Hyman, 711
Ridgway, General Matthew B., 335, 525
Riesman, David, 419, 435
Robb, Roger, 67, 488, 753
Roberts, Owen J., 384, 385
Robeson, Paul, 101, 563
Roche, John P., 748
Rockefeller, David, Jr., 616
Rockefeller, Nelson A., 729
Rockefeller Foundation, 139
Rockefeller Institute for Medical Research, 56, 73
Rodgers, James Grafton, 201
Romania, 202, 231
Romulo, Carlos P., 492
Roosevelt, Eleanor, 195
Roosevelt, Franklin D., 3, 5, 9, 57, 64, 66, 68, 75, 94-5, 137, 156, 191-2, 213, 237, 396, 497, 509, 560, 619, 647, 738, 747
  and atomic bombing of Japan, 226
  and atomic bomb research, 137, 140-1, 152, 153, 159, 172-5, 178-85, 188-91, 194, 195, 197, 198, 200-7, 210, 238, 287, 288, 570
  and conscription, 130, 131
  death of, 222
  as Harvard undergraduate, 29
  "Hundred Days" of, 77
  inaugural address of, 83
  and interventionism, 115, 116, 120-1, 130, 132-3, 145
  and National Defense Research Committee, 126-9, 141-3, 146
  New Deal of, 72, 90-1, 420, 611, 727
  and Office of Scientific Research and Development, 147, 150, 152, 160-1
  and peacetime draft, 274
  and Soviet Union, 159, 217, 221
  at tercentenary, 91-2, 97-9
  at Yalta Conference, 215, 425
Roosevelt, James, 30
Roosevelt, Kermit, 642
Roosevelt, Theodore, 14, 37
Root, Elihu, Jr., 73, 74, 678
Ropes, Gray, Best, Coolidge, & Rugg, 628
Rosenberg, Anna, 541, 548
Rosenberg, Julius and Ethel, 619
Rosenman, Samuel I., 509, 747
Ross, Charles, 288, 289
Rostow, Walt, 611
ROTC, 36, 542, 545
Rovere, Richard, 483, 527
Rowan, Carl T., 718-19
Rowe, Hartley, 306, 474, 476, 596
Roxbury Latin School, 16-19, 27, 32, 54, 69, 129
Royal Institute of International Affairs, 570
Royall, Kenneth C., 259, 356, 358

Royall-Marbury Bill, 259
Rubáiyát of Omar Khayyám, The, 27
Rusk, Dean, 718
Russell, Bertrand, 118-19, 365
Russian Research Center (RRC), 412-13, 417-18, 430, 511, 574
Russian Revolution, 22
Rutgers University, 628-10, 636
Rutherford, Ernest, 28, 136

Sacco, Nicola, 98
Sachs, Alexander, 137, 287
Saltonstall, Leverett, 647, 651, 748
Sanders, Jerry W., 510, 523
San Francisco Chronicle, 422
San Francisco Conference, 222
Sanford, Terry, 740
Sanitary Corps, 46
Santayana, George, 21, 29, 59
Sarton, George, 127, 407-9
Sarton, May, 210, 426, 459
Saturday Evening Post, 642
Saturday Review of Literature, 106, 292, 293, 326-7, 422
Schine, G. David, 656
Schlesinger, Arthur M., Jr., 399, 406, 414, 446, 505, 527, 728, 736
Schlesinger, Arthur M., Sr., 59, 107
Scholastic Aptitude Test (SAT), 81
Schrecker, Ellen, 445
Science Advisory Committee (SAC), 555, 566-9, 575-6, 654
Science and Common Sense (Conant), 556-9, 569
Science: The Endless Frontier (Bush), 396, 576
Science magazine, 486
Science and the Modern World (Whitehead), 71, 73
Screen Actors Guild, 509
Seaborg, Glenn T., 32, 185, 306, 474, 480, 596
segregation, 722-9
Seitz, Frederick, 141
Selective Training and Service Act (1940), 120
Selective Service System, 151, 311, 362, 539, 542, 543, 549, 551
Selke, George A., 432
Senate, U.S., 249, 250, 302, 315-16, 483, 522, 525, 650
  Appropriations Committee, 657
  Armed Services Committee, 363, 552
  Foreign Relations Committee, 142, 384, 631, 651
  Internal Security Subcommittee (SISS), 619, 625, 628, 633
  Military Affairs Committee, 130
  Nye Committee, 123, 419
Serber, Robert, 472, 473, 475
Seymour, Charles, 581
Shaping Educational Policy (Conant), 727, 740
Shaplen, Robert, 699
Shapley, Harlow, 72, 416, 430, 434, 446-8, 617-19, 623, 630, 636
Shattuck, Henry L., 69, 177-8, 447
Shaw, Oscar, 627
Sherwin, Martin J., 7, 187, 205

Sherwood, Robert E., 22, 121, 506, 509, 516, 523
Short, Dewey, 528
Shotwell, James T., 269
Shriver, Sargent, 737–8, 740, 741
Simon, John G., 454–5
Skinner, B. F., 398
Slater, Max, 129
Slums and Suburbs (Conant), 723–7, 729, 737, 738
Small Town in Germany, A (le Carré), 652
Smith, A. Calvert, 120, 129, 141, 142, 172–3, 201, 236
Smith, Al, 57
Smith, Cyril S., 306, 351
Smith, Howard K., 729
Smith, Richard Norton, 460, 474, 476
Smith, Walter Bedell, 641–2, 672
Smith Act, 425
Smithsonian Institution, 729
Smyth, Henry DeWolfe, 355, 478, 499, 603
Smyth Report, 238, 239, 256, 266, 282, 314, 354
Snow, C. P., 556
Socialists, 360
solar energy, 595
South Korea, 641, 708
  see also Korean War
Soviet Academy of Sciences, 254
Soviet Union, 8, 177, 183, 193, 222, 311, 352, 492, 535, 561, 605, 611, 643, 746, 749
  atomic bomb development in, 388, 464–7, 483–4, 496, 501, 506, 591, 677
  and atomic bomb research during World War II, 189, 197–200, 205, 214–17, 230, 231, 262
  and biological warfare, 220
  Cold War with, *see* Cold War
  collapse of, 755
  and Committee on the Present Danger, 508, 509, 511, 513, 520, 521
  de-Stalinization of, 693
  deterrence policy toward, 720
  and divided Germany, 648, 652, 654, 658–67, 673–4, 685–7, 690–2, 694, 697, 701, 716, 718
  "Fishing Party" analysis of, 379–84, 386
  Harvard study of, 412–13
  and H-bomb, 478–9, 483, 484
  Hungary invaded by, 698, 699
  Iran and, 280
  and Korean War, 492, 494–5, 502, 503, 517, 538, 545
  missile gap with, 714
  and moratorium on nuclear testing, 604
  nonaggression pact with Germany, 115, 117
  postwar, 216, 219, 243, 246–57, 263, 266–9, 271, 275–8, 281–2, 297, 300–301, 326, 330, 334–41, 346–8, 393–4, 399, 404, 415, 424, 425, 439, 462, 471, 621–2, 632
  purges in, 83
  space program of, *see* Sputnik
  spying by, 158–9, 265, 570–1
  and Superblitz, 274–5, 605
  and Universal Military Service, 544–5, 592
  use of nuclear weapons against, 531, 532

  in World War II, 151, 189, 202–3, 236, 259, 292, 300
Spaatz, Carl, 355–6
Spain, 143
Spanish-American War, 14
Spanish Civil War, 83, 101, 113, 317
Speaking as a Private Citizen (Conant), 142
Speer, Albert, 164
Sperry Gyroscope, 678
Spinning, James M., 431–2
Sproul, Robert, 498, 509, 608–9
Sputnik, 490, 558, 568, 576, 709–11, 713, 714, 723
Squires, Arthur M., 327
Stalin, Josef, 3, 83, 98, 158–9, 189, 200, 202–3, 205, 215, 216, 230, 231, 237, 238, 243, 254–6, 262, 273, 281, 283, 338, 340, 367, 394, 401, 419, 423, 425, 462, 479, 494, 498, 522, 605, 647, 648, 658, 664, 693
Stalin: Triumph & Tragedy (Volkogonov), 237
Stanford University, 84, 242, 310
Stassen, Harold, 646
State Department, U.S., 5, 206, 221, 263, 331, 338, 417, 428, 525, 570, 595, 652, 670, 673, 675, 676, 681, 698, 700, 702
  and Berlin crisis, 659, 689, 690
  and Bikini report, 376
  and civilian atomic power, 323, 324
  disarmament panel of, 602–4
  and Hiss case, 435
  and Marshall Plan, 319
  and McCarthyism, 406, 483, 619, 655–7
  Policy Planning Staff, 337, 480–1, 484
  and postwar atomic policy, 252, 263, 264, 268, 290, 306, 337, 348
  psychological warfare by, 510–11, 661
  and Russian Research Center, 412, 413, 430
Stein, Max, 39
Stern, Fritz, 42
Stern Program for Survival, 544
Stevenson, Adlai E., 645, 695
Stevenson Memorial Lecture, 570
Stewart, Irvin, 126, 559, 560
Stimson, Henry L., 3, 6, 120, 127, 150, 160, 173, 180, 184, 189, 191, 195, 201, 203–7, 210–11, 213, 214, 217, 219, 221–7, 231, 233–4, 238, 247, 248–50, 259, 260, 263, 268, 289, 291, 294–301, 303, 304, 338, 467, 579, 580, 589, 602, 738
Stouffer, Samuel, 511
Stowe, Leland, 292
Strassman, Fritz, 136
Strategic Air Command (SAC), 591, 602
Strategic Bombing Survey, U.S., 292, 296, 299, 611, 614
Strauss, Franz Josef, 701
Strauss, Lewis L., 258, 272, 272, 306, 308, 332, 474, 478, 489, 560, 599, 605, 677, 680, 700, 753
Structure of Scientific Revolutions (Kuhn), 410
Struve, Otto, 618
Studebaker, John, 439
Styer, Gen. Wilhelm D., 161
Suez crisis, 696–9, 701
Sullivan, John L., 395–6

Sulzberger, C. L., 656
Superblitz, 273-5, 312, 340, 344, 345, 369, 465, 605
Supreme Court, U.S., 91, 121, 722, 726
Sutherland, Arthur, 629, 633
Swarthmore College, 641, 708
Swedenborg, Emanuel, 13
Sweezy, Alan R., 105-8, 117, 118, 177, 197, 393, 580, 610, 640-1, 648, 652, 742
Swing, Raymond Gram, 718
Szilard, Leo, 136-9, 163, 195, 196, 219, 223, 231, 260-2, 286, 302, 303, 314, 326

Taft, Robert A., 516, 518, 520, 644, 645, 651, 676
Taft, William Howard, 121
Taiwan, 517, 518, 525
Task Force on Education, 738
Tatlock, Jean, 317
Taussig, Frank, 21, 29
Teeter, John H., 286
Teheran Conference, 202
television, educational, 741-2
Teller, Edward, 137, 138, 232, 313, 465-8, 471-3, 478, 487, 488, 591, 596, 599, 682
Tet Offensive, 748
Thayer, Charles W., 337, 656
thermonuclear weapons, 380
    see also hydrogen bomb
Third World, 402, 493, 534
Thomas, J. Parnell, 418-20, 429-30, 434
Thomas, Charles A., 264, 270, 379, 383, 388, 566
Thomson, George P., 330-1
Thoreau, Henry David, 89, 175
Three Centuries of Harvard (Morison), 23
Time Inc., 286
Time magazine, 3, 9, 97, 99, 292, 507, 661, 684
Tizard, Henry, 144, 344
Tolman, Richard C., 128, 166, 198, 223, 234, 270, 271, 276, 277, 329, 331, 334
Tresidder, Donald, 298, 311
Trident summit, 189
Trinity test, 230-4, 237, 286, 755
Trotsky, Leon, 507
Truman, Harry S, 3, 5, 266, 310, 313, 338, 343, 374, 388, 390, 417, 438, 465, 471, 497, 499, 642, 645, 655
    and atomic bombing of Japan, 227, 230, 234, 237, 280, 290, 295, 296, 298-301, 303
    and Atomic Energy Commission, 271, 272, 282, 305-7, 309, 315, 318, 320, 356, 357, 378, 596, 599-601
    becomes president, 222
    and Bikini report, 376-7, 389
    and Cold War, 267, 401, 663
    and Committee on the Present Danger, 508, 510-12, 516, 521
    and Greece and Turkey crisis, 319, 320
    and hydrogen bomb, 466, 472, 473, 478, 480-2, 597, 599, 605, 676, 678
    during Korean War, 492-4, 496, 498, 504-5, 517-19, 535
    MacArthur fired by, 507, 523-8
    and Marshall Plan, 360-2

    and MGM film, 287, 289, 290
    and National Science Foundation, 397, 559-65, 577
    and NATO, 515, 519, 522, 540
    and peacetime draft, 274, 311, 500, 501, 538, 547, 549, 552
    postwar atomic policy of, 219, 223, 243, 248-51, 255, 261-4, 268, 281, 330, 469
    at Potsdam Conference, 205, 231, 238, 248, 259
    and Quebec pact, 190
    and "Red scare," 291-2, 394, 404, 405, 424-6, 432, 439, 453, 457
    and Science Advisory Committee, 567, 568, 576, 710
    in Senate, 151
    Smyth Report released by, 314
    and Soviet spies, 245
    and Trinity bomb test, 237
    and Vietnam War, 748
Truman Doctrine, 319, 322, 327, 424, 439, 497
Truscott, General Lucian K., Jr., 653
Trytten Plan, 542, 543, 546, 549
Tube Alloys, 179, 185, 190, 203
Tucker, Robert C., 9, 254, 256
Tufts University, 127
Turkey, 319-20, 364, 404
Turner, Frederick Jackson, 29
Tuttle, William M., Jr., 85-6, 742
Tyroler, Charles, 748, 750

Ulam, Adam B., 430
Ulam, Stanislaus, 468, 591
Ulbricht, Walter, 731
"Unified Science," 410
Union of Concerned Scientists, 753
Union Theological Seminary, 283, 384
United Kingdom, 83, 177, 517, 531
    and Asian Communism, 524, 533-5
    atomic bomb research in, 148-50, 173, 178-93, 196-200, 203
    and Berlin crisis, 367, 368
    and biological warfare, 220
    during Cold War, 319, 484, 493, 506
    education in, 586
    and Marshall Plan, 321
    and nuclear arms control, 239
    postwar, 216, 217, 246, 256, 263, 330-1, 359, 360
    Soviet spy ring in, 570-1
    and Suez crisis, 696, 698, 699
    and Superblitz, 274-5
    universities in, 113, 616
    West Germany and, 652, 676, 687, 692
    in World War I, 35, 42
    in World War II, 115-17, 119-20, 123-5, 129, 133-7, 141, 143-7, 151-3, 292, 570
United Nations, 156, 199, 220, 230, 236, 239, 246, 250, 253, 255-7, 268, 276, 281, 286, 289, 291, 294, 297, 302, 327, 328, 330, 333, 334, 336, 338, 373, 412, 439, 441, 469, 506, 520, 526, 620, 661, 667, 698, 708
    Atomic Energy Commission, 263-5, 269-71, 273, 278, 328, 341
    General Assembly, 718

in Korean War, 505, 517, 521, 525
Security Council, 264, 270, 341, 492
U.S.-British Combined Policy Committee, 243
U.S. Chamber of Commerce, 328
U.S. Information Agency (USIA), 656-7
United World Federalists, 365
Universal Military Service (UMS), 310, 500, 502, 503, 506, 507, 516, 518-20, 529, 538-52, 592, 644, 646
Universal Military Training (UMT), 310-12, 362, 474, 496, 500, 503, 548, 549, 552
Urey, Harold C., 140, 141, 156, 185-7, 196, 200, 201, 223, 260-2, 302, 303, 489, 597, 599
U-2 program, 568

Vandenberg, Arthur H., 142, 251, 384, 385, 404
Van Dusen, Henry P., 121, 384, 385
Van Vleck, John H., 167, 466
Vanzetti, Bartolomeo, 98
Varieties of Religious Experience, The (James), 30
Versailles Treaty, 63, 112
Vienna Circle, 410-11, 578
Vietnam War, 8, 310, 462, 534, 551, 553, 577, 681-3, 746-52, 754
Vincent, John Carter, 655
Vinson, Carl, 272
Virginia, University of, 586
Virginia Polytechnic Institute, 328
Volkogonov, Dmitri, 237
Volunteer Freedom Corps (VFC), 661-2, 692-3
Voorhees, Tracy S., 491, 496, 498, 499, 503, 504, 509, 512, 517-19, 529, 530, 534, 540, 541, 627, 644, 646, 718-20

Wallace, Henry, 90, 150, 152, 160, 223, 276, 329, 366, 394, 399, 401, 416-18, 425, 430, 432
Walsh, Raymond J., 105-8, 117, 118, 177, 197, 393, 580, 610, 640-1, 648, 652, 742
Warburg, James, 121
Warburg, J. P., 729
War Council, 376, 378
War Department, U.S., 37, 43-5, 156, 159, 165, 166, 173, 194, 240, 247, 259, 272, 289-91, 294, 344, 412, 426
War on Poverty, 737
Warren, Earl, 609
Warren, Shields, 139
Warsaw Pact, 687, 704
Washington, University of, 429, 445
Washington Post, 260, 372, 507, 556, 565, 656, 696
Washington Times-Herald, 516
Waterman, Alan T., 563, 565, 566, 585
Watt, James, 94
Waymack, William W., 306
Weak, Frank, 288
Webster, Bethuel M., 126
Webster, William, 566
Wedemeyer, General "Al," 621
Weeks, Edward, 296, 370, 372
Weeks, Sinclair, 611, 614, 615, 617
Weinberger, Caspar W., 422
Weisskopf, Victor F., 303, 753

Wells, H. G., 41, 136, 339
Welte, Samuel, 39
Wendell, Barrett, 21
West Germany, 493, 501, 507, 537, 592, 625, 630, 642-3, 646-8, 650-77, 681-706, 714, 718, 720-1, 731-5, 742
Westmoreland, General William, 749
Wherry, Kenneth S., 516, 529
Whipple, Fred, 573, 574
White, Theodore H., 80
White, William Allen, 119-20, 131, 142
Whitehead, Alfred North, 71-2, 75, 93
Whitman, Walt, 175
Whitman, Walter G., 566, 596
Whitney, George, 640
Why England Slept (Kennedy), 123
Why Johnny Can't Read (Flesch), 712
Wiesner, Jerome, 568, 729
Wigner, Eugene, 137, 138, 195, 748
Will, George, 280
Williams, Robert W., 447
Williams College, 84, 456, 503
Willkie, Wendell, 121, 131, 133, 142
Willstätter, Richard, 42
Wilson, Carroll L., 141, 264, 269, 277, 308, 313-16, 560
Wilson, Charles E., 576
Wilson, E. Bright, Jr., 107, 139, 398, 475
Wilson, Woodrow, 37, 39-40, 44, 73, 118
Winant, John G., 143
Winnacker, Rudolph, 295
Wolfe, Glenn, 657
Wood, John S., 451
Wood, John T., 522
Woodcock, Leonard, 741
World Destroyed, A (Sherwin), 7, 205, 207
World Federative Body, 246
World Peace Force, 246
World Set Free, The (Wells), 136
World War I, 3, 35-49, 53, 63, 66, 73, 96, 112, 116, 117, 120, 123, 128, 129, 153, 168, 173, 201, 228, 294, 410, 448, 572-3, 636
World War II, 3, 5, 7, 8, 48, 49, 81, 84, 106, 115-59, 274, 320, 393, 411, 476, 486, 533, 542, 621, 624, 636, 685, 686, 703, 733, 746, 749, 755
Anglo-American Joint Chiefs of Staff during, 533
atomic bomb research during, 135-41, 146-50, 154-60 (*see also* Manhattan Project)
baby boom after, 586
black migration to northern cities during, 722
Churchill's memoirs of, 497
conscription during, 130, 131, 363, 475
England during, 143-6
interventionist position on, 116-26, 132-3, 150-4, 283, 538, 544, 754
mass killing of civilians in, 748
military research spending during, 576
National Defense Research Committee in, 127-9, 131, 133-5, 141-2
outbreak of, 115, 326
psychological warfare in, 661

Worthington, Hood, 306, 473
Wriston, Henry, 500, 502, 503, 508, 509, 516, 543, 635, 718
Wyzanski, Charles, 428, 460, 612, 645

Yale Daily News, 581
Yale University, 82, 97, 99, 108, 201, 285, 290, 581, 633
 Law School, 454
 Press, 556
Yalta Conference, 98, 215, 221, 425

Year of Decisions (Truman), 301
Yeshiva University, 456
York, Herbert, 476
Young, Bradford, 282-4
Young, Whitney, 738
Yugoslavia, 203, 231, 532

Zhukov, Georgi, 690
Zimmerman telegram, 40
Zook, George F., 451